Was the warrant EITHER:

A. actually valid because it:
1. was supported by **probable cause**;
2. was stated with **particularity**, both:
   (a) the places and/or people to be searched; and
   (b) the items to be seized; and
3. was issued by a **neutral, detached judicial officer**?

OR

B. facially valid such that law enforcement officers acted reasonably in **good faith reliance** on what appeared to be a valid warrant?

YES

Was the warrant executed:

A. in a **timely manner** (i.e., without unnecessary delay);

B. after being **announced** (if required); and

C. within the authorized **scope**?

YES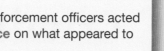

NO

YES **NO**

Was the behavior of law enforcement during the search and seizure **reasonable** (e.g., free from excessive force)?

YES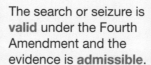

The search or seizure is **valid** under the Fourth Amendment and the evidence is **admissible**.

DISCARD

NO

The search or seizure is **invalid** under the Fourth Amendment.

Evidence is **inadmissible**.

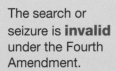

If the constitutional violation led police to the discovery of secondary/derivative evidence, the "**fruit of the poisonous tree**" doctrine must be applied to determine the admissibility of evidence that is "tainted fruit."

Can either the independent source, inevitable discovery, or attenuation doctrines (which applies to "knock-and-announce" violations) be applied to the fruit/derivative evidence?

YES

Derivative evidence/"fruit" may be **admissible** in spite of initial Fourth Amendment violation.

NO

Derivative evidence/"fruit" is also **inadmissible**.

Online Resources for Criminal Justice

Wadsworth Cengage Learning Criminal Justice Resource Center
academic.cengage.com/criminaljustice

Designed with both instructors and students in mind, this website features information about Wadsworth Cengage Learning's technology and teaching solutions, as well as several features created specifically for today's criminal justice student. Supreme Court updates, timelines, and hot-topic polling can all be used to supplement in-class assignments and discussions. You'll also find a wealth of links to careers and news in criminal justice, book-specific sites, and much more.

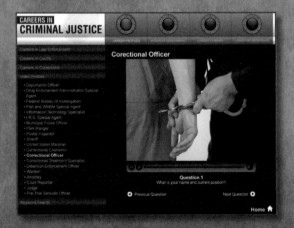

Careers in Criminal Justice Website
Accessible at academic.cengage.com/criminaljustice/careers

Helping students investigate and focus on criminal justice career choices that are right for them, the site includes:

▶ Career Profiles: video testimonials from a variety of practicing professionals
▶ Interest Assessment: helping students decide which CJ careers are suited for them
▶ Career Planner: resumé writing tips and successful job search strategies
▶ Links for Reference to federal, state, and local agencies (where students can get contact information)

Students: A card with a code allowing access to this site may have come with your text. If not, you may purchase

Criminal Procedure for the
Criminal Justice Professional

10e

John N. Ferdico
Member of the Maine Bar, Former Assistant Attorney General and
Director of Law Enforcement Education for the State of Maine

Henry F. Fradella, J.D., Ph.D.
California State University, Long Beach, Member of the State Bar
of Arizona

Christopher D. Totten, J.D., LL.M.
The College of New Jersey

WADSWORTH
CENGAGE Learning

Australia • Brazil • Japan • Korea • Mexico
Singapore • Spain • United Kingdom • United States

WADSWORTH
CENGAGE Learning™

Criminal Procedure for the
Criminal Justice Professional,
Tenth Edition

John N. Ferdico
Henry F. Fradella
Christopher D. Totten

Senior Acquisitions Editor, Criminal Justice:
  Carolyn Henderson Meier

Development Editor: Kirk Bomont

Assistant Editor: Beth Rodio

Technology Project Manager: Lauren Keyes

Marketing Manager: Terra Schultz

Marketing Assistant: Illeana Shevlin

Marketing Communications Manager: Tami Strang

Project Manager, Editorial Production: Jennie Redwitz

Creative Director: Rob Hugel

Art Director: Vernon Boes

Print Buyer: Judy Inouye

Permissions Editor: Tim Sisler

Production Service: Tom Dorsaneo

Text Designer: Lisa Delgado

Photo Researcher: Sue Howard

Copy Editor: Naomi Lucks

Illustrator: Newgen

Cover Designer: Bill Stanton

Cover Images: Clockwise from top left: Sarah Leen/
  National Geographic Image Collection; ThinkStock/
  Superstock; © Salvatore di Nolfi/epa/Corbis; and
  Corbis/Superstock

Compositor: Newgen

Photo Credits: 3: © Joseph Sohm/Visions of America/
CORBIS. 53: © Tim Pannell/CORBIS. 117: AP Images/
Ed Bailey. 183: © Tony Freeman/PhotoEdit. 247: AP
Images/David Maung. 305: Getty Images/Mandel
Ngan. 361: © Bob Daemmrich/The Image Works.
441: © 2008 Jupiterimages Corporation. 483:
© Park Street/PhotoEdit. 531: Dave Tatley/Mai/Time
& Life Pictures/Getty Images. 579: © Sonda Dawes/
The Image Works. 629: AP Images/Jerry Rife. 675:
© Michael Newman/PhotoEdit. 747: © Fat Chance
Productions/CORBIS.

For product information and technology assistance, contact us at
Cengage Learning Academic Resource Center, 1-800-423-0563
For permission to use material from this text or product,
submit all requests online at **cengage.com/permissions**.
Further permissions questions can be e-mailed to
permissionrequest@cengage.com.

Library of Congress Control Number: 2007939876

Student Edition:
ISBN-13: 978-0-495-09547-7
ISBN-10: 0-495-09547-8

Loose-leaf Edition:
ISBN-13: 978-0-495-50720-8
ISBN-10: 0-495-50720-2

Wadsworth
10 Davis Drive
Belmont, CA 94002-3098
USA

Cengage Learning is a leading provider of customized learning solutions
with office locations around the globe, including Singapore, the United
Kingdom, Australia, Mexico, Brazil, and Japan. Locate your local office at
international.cengage.com/region.

Cengage Learning products are represented in Canada by Nelson
Education, Ltd.

For your course and learning solutions, visit **academic.cengage.com**.
Purchase any of our products at your local college store or at our
preferred online store **www.ichapters.com**.

Printed in Canada
1 2 3 4 5 6 7 12 11 10 09 08

DATE DUE

MAY 1 7 2009	
APR 1 7 2012	
NOV 0 8 2016	
Dec. 6, 2016	

fo. his guidance, mentor-he, and men-ip H BR

To my p ... and Re ...mond ... instilling in me the
importanc ... of educat ... to my wife, by ... to, sho... me what
it means t ... for putting ... o ... the ... ed away

About the Authors

John N. Ferdico holds a J.D. from Northwestern University School of Law and a B.A. in Sociology from Dartmouth College. He is a former Assistant Attorney General and Director of Law Enforcement Education for the State of Maine. Other books he has published are *Ferdico's Criminal Law* and *Justice Dictionary the Maine Law Enforcement Officer's Manual*. Ferdico currently writes and runs a legal publishing company in Bowdoinham, Maine.

Henry F. Fradella is a Professor of Law and Criminal Justice Studies at California State University, Long Beach, where he also chairs the Department of Criminal Justice and serves as a pre-law advisor. He earned a bachelor of arts in psychology from Clark University, both a master's in forensic science and a law degree (juris doctorate) from The George Washington University, and a Ph.D. in interdisciplinary justice studies from Arizona State University.

Dr. Fradella's area of specialization is the social scientific study of courts and law. This includes research and teaching on the historical development of substantive, procedural, and evidentiary law (including courtroom acceptability and juror understanding of forensic and social scientific evidence, especially forensic psychological/psychiatric testimony); evaluation of law's effects on human behavior (including compliance and deterrence); the dynamics of legal decision making (including the roles of politics, discretion, morality, and popular culture); and the nature, sources, and consequences of variations and changes in legal institutions or processes (including law and social change). He teaches a variety of courses, including forensic psychology, criminal law, criminal procedure, courts and judicial processes, evidence, and several specialized forensic science courses.

In addition to having published several dozen articles, Dr. Fradella is also the author of three other books, including two published by Wadsworth Cengage Learning: *Key Cases, Comments, and Questions on Substantive Criminal Law,* and *Forensic Psychology: The Use of Behavioral Science in Civil and Criminal Justice.* Dr. Fradella is a past guest editor of the *Journal of Contemporary Criminal Justice,* and is currently the Legal Literature editor for West's *Criminal Law Bulletin.*

Christopher D. Totten has an A.B. from Princeton University, and a J.D. and LL.M. (Masters in Law) from Georgetown University Law Center. He is a member of the State Bar of Maryland, and has worked as an attorney and client advocate at a number of law firms. He is an assistant professor of Criminology at The College of New Jersey (TCNJ), where he acts as the faculty advisor for the Law and Society concentration and teaches numerous law courses. Prior to arriving at TCNJ, Professor Totten was a lecturer of law at West Virginia University College of Law. He has published in key journals such as the *Journal of Criminal Law and Criminology* and the *Berkeley Journal of International Law.*

Brief Contents

Contents

Preface

Criminal Procedure for the Criminal Justice Professional was originally published in 1975 as *Criminal Procedure for the Law Enforcement Officer.* Its primary emphasis was on providing practical guidelines for law enforcement officers with respect to the legal aspects of their daily duties. While the primary emphasis in the 10th edition remains on the policing aspects of criminal procedure, additional materials have been added that are relevant to professionals who work in other areas of the justice system.

Because we believe that criminal justice professionals should not have to read and interpret lengthy and complicated court opinions in order to determine the powers, duties, limitations, and liabilities associated with the performance of their jobs, this book is written in a clear, concise, and coherent narrative to make it accessible and understandable. Sufficient detail is provided to enable the reader to operate competently and effectively within the criminal justice system. Actual case excerpts are used to provide authoritative statements of legal principles, explanations of the "reasons behind the rules," and examples of the application of the law to real-life scenarios.

As appellate courts continue to deal with significant numbers of complex criminal procedure cases, the design and approach of this book provide an enduring vehicle for imparting the knowledge necessary to properly comply with this ever-changing area of the law.

▶MARKET

Criminal Procedure for the Criminal Justice Professional is intended for courses in criminal procedure or administration at both two- and four-year colleges for students preparing for careers in criminal justice, especially in law enforcement and corrections. Titles of courses that have used this book include: "Criminal Procedure," "Constitutional Law in Criminal Justice," "Law of Arrest, Search, and Seizure," "Legal Aspects of Law Enforcement," "Constitutional Criminal Procedure," and "Court Systems and Practices." Because it is written in plain English, rather than technical legal jargon, this book is also suitable as a criminal procedure textbook at law enforcement training academies and for high school courses dealing with constitutional law or law enforcement.

▶MAIN FEATURES OF THE TEXT

Over the years, in response to suggestions and comments from professors and students who have used it, many changes have been made to enhance the book's suitability for use as a classroom text.

Revised Content

- All chapters in the book have been updated with citations to (and often discussions of) the latest case law on each and every topic in the book.
- The chapter dealing with individual rights under the United States Constitution has been expanded to cover additional constitutional concerns in the areas of symbolic and offensive speech; the curtailment of free speech and expression in the military and correctional settings; the right to just compensation after *Kelo v. City of New London*; the Confrontation Clause in light of *Crawford v. Washington* and *Davis v. Washington*; the foundations of Sixth Amendment right to counsel; and recent Eighth Amendment developments concerning both the death penalty and the doctrine of proportionality's applicability to non-capital cases. Coverage of the Fourteenth Amendment's Due Process and Equal Protection Clause also has been expanded to include a discussion of "standards of review," "fundamental rights," and both suspect and quasi-suspect classifications.
- The chapter on criminal courts and criminal trials has been expanded so this book is appropriate for use in courses that combine the study of courts and criminal procedure, or for criminal

procedure courses that do not have a courts class as a prerequisite.

- The chapter on the foundational concepts of the exclusionary rule, privacy, probable cause, and reasonableness has been updated with the latest developments concerning the exclusionary rule in light of *Hudson v. Michigan*. The chapter now further develops the concept of "standing" with both better pedagogy and more case law examples.
- The order of former chapters four and five has been switched so that the chapter on warrants now comes *before* the chapter on arrest.
- The warrants chapter has been expanded to include a discussion of how the particularity requirement has been applied in high-tech searches, such as those involving forensic computing searches of e-mail, servers, and computer hard drives.
- A new chapter on administrative and special needs searches was added with significant coverage of Fourth Amendment concerns in the age of terror. Special sections were added on searches in schools, airports, public transportation systems, and DNA searches. A section on electronic monitoring of communications by law enforcement has been added, including statutory provisions of the USA PATRIOT Act as recently revised by Congress as well as a new section on FISA warrants.
- The chapter on stops and frisks has a new section on detentions of suspected terrorists. Special attention is devoted to the detentions of enemy combatants under the USA PATRIOT Act, the Detainee Treatment Act of 2005, and the Military Commissions Act in 2006.
- The chapters on warrant exceptions have been reorganized, updated, and streamlined to present material in better-organized manner.
- The chapter on interrogations and confessions has been reorganized into three parts: a section on the voluntariness approach; a section on *Miranda*'s Fifth Amendment self-incrimination approach; and a section on the Sixth Amendment right to counsel approach. New case law examples applying each of these approaches have been added in a topical outline format. New material on the custodial interrogations of enemy combatants that involve torture or coercive tactics has also been added.

- The chapter on pretrial identifications has been rewritten to include interdisciplinary coverage of the many factors that lead to misidentifications and wrongful convictions. Moreover, the chapter now contains the "state of the art" protocols for conducting lineups and photo arrays to minimize mistaken identifications.

Learning Tools and Pedagogical Devices

In recent years, several learning tools and pedagogical devices have been added to the book to enhance understanding of the law of criminal procedure.

Chapter Objectives—Student learning goals appear at the beginning of each chapter and are designed to provide purpose and context.

Key Points—Concise, clear statements of the essential principles of criminal procedure appear at the end of major sections of chapters and serve as mini-summaries of those sections. Their purpose is to aid the student in "separating the wheat from the chaff" and to expedite review by boiling down complexities into simple statements of fundamentals.

"Supreme Court Nuggets"—Essential quotations from U.S. Supreme Court opinions appear in boldface throughout the text. Their purpose is to familiarize students with judicial language as well as to highlight authoritative definitions of terms, clear statements of important legal principles, and the rationales behind those principles.

Discussion Points—Fact patterns and holdings from recent controversial opinions are summarized in a concise manner in these boxed features so that students can see how the "black letter law" was applied in a case related to the main points in a chapter. These summaries are then followed by discussion questions that instructors can use to stimulate class discussion on the law and related public policy issues.

Review and Discussion Questions—New review and discussion questions have been included to stimulate discussion and to expand students' understanding beyond the principles and examples used in the text.

Applications of the Law in Real Cases—(formerly Legal Scenarios) Statements of fact situations from actual reported court cases. These appear at the ends of chapters and are designed to supplement the more theoretical Review and Discussion Questions by challenging students to apply their knowledge to practical, everyday circumstances.

Glossary—Definitions of major terms used in criminal procedure law have been streamlined for easier use by students.

References—Citations to statutes and case law appear in the actual text. This Tenth Edition also adds a formal bibliography to reflect the many new interdisciplinary sources that have been integrated into the textual pedagogy.

▶SUPPLEMENTS

A number of pedagogic supplements are provided by Wadsworth to help instructors use *Criminal Procedure for the Criminal Justice Professional* in their courses and to aid students in preparing for exams. Supplements are available to qualified adopters. Please consult your local sales representative for details.

For the Instructor

Instructor's Resource Manual with Test Bank—Fully updated and revised by Rodney Brewer of the University of Louisville, the *Instructor's Resource Manual with Test Bank* includes learning objectives, detailed chapter outlines, key terms and figures, class discussion exercises, lecture suggestions, and a complete test bank. Each chapter's test bank contains approximately 80 multiple-choice, true-false, fill-in-the-blank, and essay questions, which include a full answer key. Our *Instructor Approved* seal, which appears on the front cover, is our assurance that you are working with an assessment and grading resource of the highest caliber. All *Test Bank* questions are included on the ExamView testing software program.

Lesson Plans—New to this edition, the instructor-created Lesson Plans bring accessible, masterful suggestions to every lesson. The Lesson Plans, prepared by Rodney Brewer of the University of Louisville, include a sample syllabus, learning objectives, lecture notes, discussion topics, in-class activities, tips for classroom presentation of chapter material, a detailed lecture outline, and assignments.

Classroom Activities for Criminal Justice—This valuable booklet, available to adopters of any Wadsworth criminal justice text, offers instructors the best of the best in criminal justice classroom activities. Containing both tried-and-true favorites and exciting new projects, its activities are drawn from across the spectrum of criminal justice subjects, including introduction to criminal justice, criminology, corrections, criminal law, policing, and juvenile justice, and can be customized to fit any course. Novice and seasoned instructors alike will find it a powerful tool to stimulate classroom engagement.

ExamView® (Window/Macintosh CD-ROM)—The comprehensive *Instructor's Resource Manual* is backed up by ExamView, an easy-to-use assessment and tutorial system with which you can create, deliver, and customize tests and study guides (both print and online) in minutes. You can easily edit and import your own questions and graphics, change test layouts, and reorganize questions. And using ExamView's complete word processing capabilities, you can enter an unlimited number of new questions or edit existing questions.

CNN® Today Video: America's New War: CNN Looks at Terrorism, Volume I—Sixteen 2- to 5-minute segments featuring CNN news footage, commentator remarks, and speeches dealing with terrorist attacks on U.S. targets throughout the world. Topics include: anthrax and biological warfare, new security measures, Osama bin Laden, Al Qaeda, asset freezing, homeland defense, renewed patriotism, new weapons of terrorism, the bombing of U.S. embassies in Kenya and Tanzania, the American psyche, and the Arab-American response to recent events.

PowerLecture—This one-stop lecture tool makes it easy for you to assemble, edit, publish, and present custom lectures for your course, using Microsoft® PowerPoint®. PowerLecture lets you bring together text-specific lecture outlines and art from Wadsworth texts with video and animations from the Web or your own materials—culminating in a powerful, personalized, media-enhanced presentation. For your convenience, the PowerLecture CD also features our JoinIn™ and ExamView tools.

WebTutor™ ToolBox—WebTutor ToolBox provides access to all the content of this text's rich Book Companion Website from within a professor's course management system. ToolBox is ready to use as soon as you log on and offers a wide array of web quizzes, activities, exercises, and web links. Robust communication tools such as a course calendar, asynchronous discussion, real-time chat, a whiteboard, and an integrated e-mail system make it easy to stay connected to the course.

For the Student

Study Guide—Fully updated and revised by Rodney Brunson of the University of Alabama at Birmingham, the *Study Guide* includes the following elements to help students get the most out of their classroom experience: learning objectives, a chapter outline and summary, key terms, and a self-test. The self-test consists of multiple choice, fill-in-the-blank, true/false, and essay questions.

Website for Criminal Procedure for the Criminal Justice Professional—*Includes Study Guide* This comprehensive student resource will help students succeed in this course! The updated Companion Website includes chapter quizzes, web links, and additional study aids.

eAudio—Audio Study Tools provides audio reinforcement of key concepts that students can listen to from their personal computer or MP3 player. Providing approximately ten minutes of audio content for each chapter, it gives students a quick and convenient way to master key concepts. Audio content allows students to test their knowledge with quiz questions, listen to a brief overview reflecting the major themes of each chapter, and review key terminology. Students can order Audio Study Tools directly at www.ichapters.com or contact your local sales representative for details about bundling with the text.

Careers in Criminal Justice Website—The Careers in Criminal Justice Website provides students with extensive career profiling information and self-assessment testing, and is designed to help them

investigate and focus on the criminal justice career choices that are right for them. With links and tools to assist students in finding a professional position, this new version includes ten new Career Profiles and four new Video Interviews, bringing the total number of careers covered to 64.

InfoTrac® College Edition—*Not Sold Separately* Now available, free four-month access to InfoTrac College Edition's online database of more than 18 million reliable, full-length articles from 5000 academic journals and periodicals (including *The New York Times, Science, Forbes*, and *USA Today*) includes access to InfoMarks stable URLs that can be linked to articles, journals, and searches. InfoMarks allow you to use a simple copy and paste technique to create instant and continually updated online readers, content services, bibliographies, electronic "reserve" readings, and current topic sites. And to help students use the research they gather, their free four-month subscription includes access to InfoWrite, a complete set of online critical thinking and paper writing tools. (*Journals subject to change. Certain restrictions may apply. For additional information, please consult your local Wadsworth representative.*)

Current Perspectives: Readings from InfoTrac® College Edition—These readers, designed to give students a deeper look at special topics in criminal justice, include free access to InfoTrac College Edition. The timely articles are selected by experts in each topic from within InfoTrac College Edition. They are available free when bundled with the text.

Terrorism and Homeland Security 0-495-12994-1

Cyber Crime 0-495-00722-6

Juvenile Justice 0-495-12995-X

Crisis Management and National Emergency Response 0-495-12996-8

Racial Profiling 0-495-10383-7

New Technologies and Criminal Justice 0-495-10384-5

White-Collar Crime 0-495-10385-3

Handbook of Selected Supreme Court Cases for Criminal Justice   This supplementary handbook covers almost 40 landmark cases, each of which includes a full case citation, an introduction, a summary from WestLaw, excerpts from the case, and the decision. The updated edition includes *Hamdi v. Rumsfeld, Roper v. Simmons, Ring v. Arizona, Atkins v. Virginia, Illinois v. Caballes,* and much more.

Internet Activities for Criminal Justice—In addition to providing a wide range of activities for any criminal justice class, this useful booklet helps familiarize students with the Internet resources they will use both as students of criminal justice and in their criminal justice careers. *Internet Activities for Criminal Justice* allows instructors to integrate Internet resources and addresses important topics such as criminal and police law, policing organizations, policing challenges, corrections systems, juvenile justice, criminal trials, and current issues in criminal justice. Available to adopters of any Wadsworth criminal justice text, this booklet will bring current tools and resources to the criminal justice classroom.

Terrorism: An Interdisciplinary Perspective, Third Edition—This provocative booklet includes a background to terrorism, the history of Middle Eastern terrorism, the intersection of religion and terrorism, the role of globalization, and domestic responses and repercussions. Also available online.

Careers in Criminal Justice 3.0 Interactive CD-ROM—Students can find the criminal justice career that is right for them with the Careers in Criminal Justice CD-ROM. Fifty-eight job descriptions, self-assessments, career worksheets, and web links help students find careers of interest. Includes video interviews with CJ professionals.

Guide to Careers in Criminal Justice—This handy guide gives students information on a wide variety of career paths, including requirements, salaries, training, contact information for key agencies, and employment outlooks.

Writing and Communicating for Criminal Justice—This book contains articles on writing skills, along with basic grammar review and a survey of verbal communication on the job, that will give students an introduction to academic, professional, and research writing in criminal justice. The voices of professionals who have used these techniques on the job will help students see the relevance of these skills to their future careers.

Internet Guide for Criminal Justice—This guide provides students with the background and vocabulary necessary to navigate and understand the Web, then provides them with a wealth of criminal justice websites and Internet project ideas.

Crime and Evidence in Action CD-ROM—The tools to practice investigation techniques are all here! This CD-ROM, with its accompanying website, places students in the center of the action as they make decisions as a patrol officer, detective, prosecutor, defense attorney, judge, corrections officer, and parole officer. As students interact with one of the three realistic in-depth simulations, they are guided through each stage of the case—from crime scene investigation to arrest, trial, incarceration, and parole or probation. Can be packaged with this text at a substantial discount—contact your Wadsworth representative for ordering information.

▶ACKNOWLEDGMENTS

We are grateful to the following criminal justice instructors for their time and effort in reviewing this edition of the book and their helpful comments and suggestions for its improvement: Philip Reichel of the University of Northern Colorado, Kenneth Novak of the University of Missouri–Kansas City, and Michael J. McCrystle of California State University, Sacramento. We also wish to thank again the following professors for their reviews of previous editions of this text: Kenneth Agran, Jack E. Call, Joseph Robert Caton, Alan W. Clarke, Nigel Cohen, Nancy Dempsey, Charles Dreveskracht, Jack Elrod, David V. Guccione, James Hague, Judy Hails, Craig Hemmens, G. G. Hunt, William Hyatt, Susan Jacobs, Richard Janikowski, David Kramer, Elizabeth Lewis, Milo Miller, Eric Moore, Thomas O'Connor, Ray Reynolds, Joseph G. Sandoval, Caryl Lynn Segal, Kurt Siedschlaw, Mark Stelter, Gene Straughan, Susette M. Talarico, John Worrall, John Wyant, and Alvin J. T. Zumbrun.

Our appreciation also extends to the staff at Wadsworth Cengage Learning and those who worked with them at all stages of the production of the Tenth Edition. We are particularly grateful to Naomi Lucks at YouCanWrite.com for her exceptional skill and care as copy editor for the Tenth Edition. Special thanks to our lead editorial and creative design team for all of their help and patience throughout the publication process: Tom Dorsaneo, Jennie Redwitz, Kirk Bomont, Marcus Boggs, and Carolyn Henderson Meier.

We owe a special debt to John Ferdico, who first created this book in the mid-1970s and then shepherded its evolution over eight more editions spanning thirty years. We hope that we have made you proud of the legacy that continues on in the Tenth Edition. We also are particularly grateful to Carolyn Henderson Meier for having entrusted this book to our care.

Finally, we thank our families—most especially our spouses—for their support and understanding while we went "MIA" from daily life during the preparation of this Tenth Edition.

Henry F. Fradella

Christopher D. Totten

Criminal Procedure for the
Criminal Justice Professional

10e

1

Individual Rights Under the United States Constitution

Learning Objectives

▶ Explain how criminal law and criminal procedure are often in conflict as courts try to balance the need for crime control with constitutional guarantees of due process.

▶ Understand the historical context that gave birth to the concern for the *individual* rights embodied in the United States Constitution.

▶ Explain how the legislative, judicial, and executive branches of government are involved in the protection of the constitutional rights of citizens.

▶ Understand the individual rights protected by the original Constitution of 1788, and the terms *habeas corpus*, bill of attainder, *ex post facto* law, and treason.

▶ Explain the general nature and limits of the rights embodied in the Bill of Rights, especially: the First Amendment freedoms of religion, speech, press, assembly, and petition; the Fourth Amendment prohibition against unreasonable searches and seizures; the Fifth Amendment protections against double jeopardy and self-incrimination and the right to due process of law; the Sixth Amendment rights to a speedy and public trial, notice of charges, confrontation with adverse witnesses, compulsory process for favorable witnesses, and assistance of counsel; and the Eighth Amendment rights against excessive bail and fines and against cruel and unusual punishment.

▶ Understand the concepts of due process and equal protection as guaranteed by the Fourteenth Amendment.

►CRIMINAL PROCEDURE AS THE BALANCE BETWEEN DUE PROCESS AND CRIME CONTROL

The law of criminal procedure can be described as rules designed to balance the important governmental functions of maintaining law and order and protecting the rights of citizens. These functions are common to every government that is not totally authoritarian or anarchistic, yet they conflict because an increased emphasis on maintaining law and order will necessarily involve greater intrusions on individual rights. Conversely, an increased emphasis on protecting individual rights will impede the efficient maintenance of law and order. The justice system in the United States, like those in most constitutional democracies continually experiences a tension between the need to respect individual rights on one hand, and the need to maintain public order on the other. Herbert L. Packer summarized this tension in his classic text *The Limits of the Criminal Sanction* (1968). As Table 1.1 illustrates, Packer viewed this tension as being embodied in two competing value systems: the **Crime Control Model** and the **Due Process Model**.

The Need for Balance

One of the biggest challenges for the criminal justice system is to keep its competing notions of due process and crime control in balance. A heavy focus on either model would have detrimental effects on American society.

For example, a policy overprotective of individual rights is likely to result in an atmosphere conducive to increased violation of and disrespect for the law. People with a propensity toward crime will perceive that restrictions on police authority to arrest, detain, search, and question will decrease their likelihood of getting caught—and complex and technical procedural safeguards designed to ensure the fairness of court proceedings will enable them to avoid punishment if they do get caught. The result is a society in which people do not feel secure in their homes or communities, and in which illegal activity abounds in government, business, and other aspects of daily life.

On the other hand, enforcement of criminal laws would be much easier if criminal suspects were presumed guilty; if they had no privilege against self-incrimination; if their bodies, vehicles, and homes could be searched at will; and if they could be detained for long periods of time without a hearing. Life in many totalitarian countries today is characterized by such governmental abuses. The citizens of these countries live in daily fear of official intrusion into the home, the disappearance of a loved one, or tight restrictions on movement, speech, and association.

Shifting the Balance Over Time

In practice, we do not choose between one model and the other. Rather, we strive to control crime while simultaneously honoring the constitutional rights of the accused. At different stages in our nation's history, we have clearly focused more on the underlying values of one model over the other—put simply, the criminal justice system has had different emphases at different times. Consider the following examples of how the pendulum can swing from a societal emphasis on crime control to due process and then back to crime control.

TABLE 1.1	HERBERT PACKER'S CRIME CONTROL VS. DUE PROCESS MODELS	
	Due Process Model	**Crime Control Model**
	Primary Goal: Protection of the innocent; limiting governmental power	Primary Goal: Apprehension, conviction, and punishment of offenders
	Focus: Due process; respect for individual rights	Focus: Crime control; repression of criminal conduct
	Mood: Skepticism	Mood: Certainty
	"Obstacle-Court Justice": Presents numerous obstacles to prevent errors and wrongful convictions	"Assembly-Line Justice": Processes cases quickly and efficiently to promote finality of convictions
	Concerned with legal guilt: The assumption that someone is innocent until proven guilty beyond a reasonable doubt. Relies on formal, adjudicative, adversary fact-finding processes.	Concerned with factual guilt: Assumes that someone arrested and charged is probably guilty. Relies on informal, non-adjudicative fact-finding—primarily by police and prosecutors.
	Dignity and autonomy of both the accused and the system are to be preserved.	Expedition processing of offenders to achieve justice for victims and society as a whole.

In the first half of the twentieth century, increased urbanization, immigration, and industrialization "transformed America from a rural agrarian, Anglo-Protestant society" into a more racially, ethnically, and religiously diverse one (Feld 2003: 1453). These changes produced great uncertainly in the minds of those whose more traditional ways of life were being challenged by the changes that accompanied this more diverse and industrial society. One of the byproducts of these changes was an increase in criminal activity, probably due, in part, to an ever-increasing population density. The increase in crime combined with fears of people from different races and cultures led to great increases in police power (Walker 1980) with a focus on "law and order" crime control (Monkkonen 1981).

In the civil rights era, social consciousness began to focus on social equality and equal justice under law. Part of this new consciousness brought to light abuses of police power, which disproportionately affected poor and uneducated minorities (Neeley 1996; Kamisar 1965). Led by Chief Justice Earl Warren, a former public defender, the Supreme Court began to "constitutionalize" criminal procedure with a focus on the individual rights and liberties. "Tired of the steady stream of abuses that continued to filter up from the states, the Supreme Court of the 1960s made policing the police, as well as state courts, a distinctly federal concern" (Barrett-Lain 2004: 1372). Today, we refer to this shift in policy as the **due process revolution** of the 1960s.

Many critics felt as if the due process revolution went too far, allowing criminals to escape punishment due to the technicalities of constitutional criminal procedures (*e.g.*, Bradley 1993; Friendly 1968). During the Nixon administration, such feelings led to a renewed focus on "law and order." As part of his "tough on crime" agenda, Nixon appointed conservative jurist Warren Burger as Chief Justice Earl Warren's successor on the U.S. Supreme Court. In the last twenty-five years of the twentieth century, the "war on drugs" led to an even greater shift away from many of the Warren Court's due process protections toward a renewed emphasis on crime control. At the dawn of the 21st century, as the United States fights the "War on Terror," the nation once again finds itself seeking to balance the need for social order and security with due process rights.

In the wake of the terrorist attacks on the World Trade Center and the Pentagon on September 11, 2001, Congress passed the Uniting and Strengthening America by Providing Appropriate Tools Required to Intercept and Obstruct Terrorism Act of 2001, commonly referred to as the **USA PATRIOT Act**. This legislation dramatically shifted our national focus even further away from the due process model in our attempts to control crimes by terrorists. These are some of the more controversial provisions of the Act:

▶ Financial, library, travel, video rental, phone, medical, and religious records can now be searched without a person's knowledge or consent, and without a warrant, so long as the government alleges such searches are being conducted to protect against terrorism.

▶ The Foreign Intelligence Surveillance Act (FISA) was amended to authorize secret searches (without public knowledge or Department of Justice accountability), so long as the government alleges a foreign intelligence basis for such a search.

▶ "Sneek and Peek" warrants are now expressly authorized by Congress. Prior to the Act, someone whose property was searched normally had to be notified of the execution of a search warrant. Today, sneak and peek warrants permit officers "to enter a home or dwelling without notice, look around, take pictures, examine electronic files, and leave without contemporaneous notification to the target that a search has taken place" (Ashdown 2006: 785-86).

▶ Upon the request of a federal law enforcement officer investigating international or domestic terrorism (very broadly defined to include "activities that involve acts dangerous to human life that are a violation of the criminal laws of the U.S. or of any state"), a judge or magistrate may now issue a nationwide search warrant, rather than only having the authority to authorize a search within the geographic jurisdictional boundaries of the court.

▶ "Pen registers"—devices that record the phone numbers dialed from a telephone—and "trap and trace" devices, which monitor the source of all incoming calls, are now available to law enforcement without a warrant so long as the government certifies that the information likely to be obtained is relevant to an ongoing investigation against international terrorism.

▶ The pen-register/trap-and-trace authority now applies to Internet surveillance to monitor any information "relevant to an ongoing criminal investigation."

▶ "Roving wiretaps" are now allowed. These permit taps to be placed on every phone or computer that the target of an investigation may use.

▶ "National Security Letters" may now be issued to obtain business records, rather than having to obtain a judicially issued warrant to obtain such information.

▶ The U.S. Attorney General now has authority to order the detention of aliens without any prior showing or court ruling that the person is dangerous.

Public concern that some of the provisions of the USA PATRIOT Act usurped too many constitutional due process protections led Congress to reauthorize the Act in a somewhat scaled-down version in 2006. Certainly, as the country moves forward in the age of terrorism, finding the right balance between due process and public order and security will continue to be a matter of great debate.

▶A BRIEF HISTORY OF THE U.S. CONSTITUTION

The Law of England

Early procedural protections for the criminally accused can be traced back in the English **common law** tradition to the thirteenth century. In 1215, the Magna Carta was formally adopted in England. Clause 30 of the original text (later numbered Chapter 29 of the statutory version of the Magna Carta) provided:

> No free man shall be taken, imprisoned, or disseised of his free hold, or liberties or free customs, or outlawed, exiled or in any way destroyed, nor will we proceed against him, save by the lawful judgment of his peers or by the law of the land. We shall not sell, deny or delay to any man right or justice.

For centuries, these provisions were interpreted as guaranteeing certain pillars of criminal procedure, including the right to have adequate notice of what is prohibited by law before being punished for violating law; the right to a fair trial; and the protection of property or possessions (Baker 2004). Yet, these guarantees were not always honored. For example, a number of procedural safeguards were commonly disregarded by the Star Chamber, a royal court whose abuses became so infamous that the very term is still synonymous with injustices perpetuated by a court (Riebli 2002). Although the Star Chamber was abolished by the Long Parliament in 1641, the English crown still wielded considerable influence over courts. This influence often led courts to issue decisions favorable to the crown as well as to those of the British aristocracy (Berman 2000).

Ultimately, dissatisfaction with a life that favored a select few in England was partially responsible for both the founding of the American colonies and the Glorious Revolution in Great Britain (Berman 2000). The latter event forever changed English Common Law, granting a new level of judicial independent to judges and focusing trials on proof, the independent decisions of juries, and rules of evidence.

Drafting a New Constitution

In light of their experience with governmental tyranny, when the United States was born as a nation, the Founding Fathers had a strong commitment to the protection of individual rights from governmental abuse. This commitment was embodied in the original Constitution of 1788 and in the Bill of Rights, adopted shortly thereafter.

On September 17, 1787, a convention of delegates representing all the original thirteen states except Rhode Island proposed a new Constitution to the Continental Congress and the states for ratification. The rights expressed and protected by this Constitution, and by the amendments adopted four years later, were not new. Some had roots in the societies of ancient Rome and Greece, and all were nurtured during the almost six hundred years of English history since the signing of the Magna Carta.

As colonists under English rule, Americans before the Revolution were familiar with the ideas that government should be limited in power and that the law was superior to any government, even the king. As the Declaration of Independence shows, the colonists rebelled because the English king and Parliament refused to allow them their historic rights as free English citizens. In September 1774, delegates from twelve colonies met in the First Continental Congress to petition England for their rights "to life, liberty, and property" and to trial by jury; "for a right peaceably to assemble, consideration of their grievances, and petition the King"; and for other rights they had been denied. The petition was ignored, and soon afterward fighting broke out at Lexington and Concord, Massachusetts.

Meanwhile, citizens in Mecklenburg County, North Carolina, declared the laws of Parliament to be null and void and instituted their own form of local government with the adoption of the Mecklenburg Resolves in May 1775. In June 1776, a resolution was introduced in the Continental Congress. Just one month later, on July 4, 1776, the Thirteen United Colonies declared themselves free and independent. Their announcement was truly revolutionary. They listed a large number of abuses they had suffered, and justified their independence in these historic words: "We hold these truths to be self-evident, that all men are created equal, that they are endowed by their Creator with certain Inalienable Rights, that among these are Life, Liberty and the pursuit of Happiness."

Two years later, in July 1778, the newly independent states joined in a united government under the Articles of Confederation, which was our nation's first Constitution. It soon became evident, however, that the Articles of Confederation did not adequately provide for a workable, efficient government. Among other weaknesses, the articles gave Congress no authority to levy taxes or to regulate foreign or interstate commerce. In May 1787, a convention of delegates, meeting in Philadelphia with Congress's approval, began to consider amendments to the Articles. Soon, however, they realized that a new system of government was necessary. After much debate, and several heated arguments, a compromise Constitution was negotiated.

Although we now honor their wisdom, the delegates had a different opinion of their work. Many were dissatisfied, and a few even thought a new Constitution should be written. No delegate from Rhode Island attended the convention or signed the document on September 17, 1787, when the proposed Constitution was announced. Delaware was the first state to accept the Constitution, ratifying it on December 7, 1787, by a unanimous vote. Not all states were as enthusiastic as Delaware, and in some states the vote was extremely close. For a while it was uncertain whether a sufficient number of states would ratify. A major argument against ratification was the absence of a Bill of Rights. Many feared that a failure to limit the federal government's power would diminish individual rights. Only after a general agreement that the first order of business of the new government would be to propose amendments for a Bill of Rights did a sufficient number of states accept the Constitution. On June 21, 1788, New Hampshire became the ninth state to sign on, and ratification of the new Constitution was completed. By the end of July 1788, the important states of Virginia and New York had also ratified the Constitution.

On September 25, 1789, Congress proposed the first ten amendments to the new Constitution—the Bill of Rights. With this proposal, North Carolina and Rhode Island, the last of the thirteen original colonies, ratified the Constitution. Ratification of the Bill of Rights was completed on December 15, 1791. Since that date, the Bill of Rights has served as our nation's testimony to its belief in the basic and inalienable rights of the people and in limitations on the power of government. Together with provisions of the original Constitution, it protects the great body of liberties that belongs to every citizen.

For ease of discussion, the remainder of this chapter treats the original Constitution separately from the Bill of Rights and later amendments.

The Original Constitution

The Constitution of 1789 has served as the fundamental instrument of our government for almost all of our country's history as an independent nation. Drawn at a time when there were only thirteen states, each dotted with small towns, small farms, and small industry, the Constitution has provided a durable and viable instrument of government—despite enormous changes in technology and in the political, social, and economic environments.

The Constitution was originally designed to serve a weak country on the Atlantic seaboard. Today, it serves a continental nation of fifty states, a federal district, and numerous territorial possessions, with over 290 million people producing goods and services at a rate thousands of times faster than in 1789. Nevertheless, the framework for democratic government set out in the Constitution has remained workable and progressive. Similarly, the rights of individuals listed in the Constitution and its twenty-seven amendments have retained an extraordinary vitality despite being tested in situations that could not have been envisioned by the Framers. Freedom of the press, for example, was originally understood only in the context of the small, primitive printing presses of the late eighteenth century. Today, that freedom applies not only to modern presses but also to radio, television, motion pictures, and computers—all products of the twentieth century.

Structure of the Original Constitution The original Constitution of the United States is divided into seven parts: a preamble and six articles. Although the preamble is technically not a part of the Constitution, it sets forth important principles. The articles that follow it each address a different topic relevant to the structure and operations of government.

▶ **Preamble** states both the purpose of the Constitution and specifies that it is the people who are the source of the document's authority:

We the People of the United States, in Order to form a more perfect Union, establish Justice, insure domestic Tranquility, provide for the common defence, promote the general Welfare, and secure the Blessings of Liberty to ourselves and our Posterity, do ordain and establish this Constitution for the United States of America.

▶ **Article I** establishes the U.S. Congress as the legislative branch of the United States and sets forth both the structure of congress and its major powers.

▶ **Article II** establishes the president as the head of the executive branch of government and sets forth some of the major powers of the presidency.

▶ **Article III** establishes the U.S. Supreme Court as the highest judicial body in the United States and specifies the Court's original and appellate jurisdiction.

▶ **Article IV** defines the relationship between the states.

▶ **Article V** prescribes the method for amending the Constitution.

▶ **Article VI** declares that the Constitution and treaties made by the U.S. government under its authority are "the supreme Law of the Land." Given the supremacy of the Constitution, this article requires that all state and federal judges and elected officials must swear an oath to support, uphold, and defend the Constitution.

The Constitution governs the government. This means that constitutional law establishes the structure of government and limits the power of government. Although the Constitution does not govern the day-to-day lives of the people, as statutory and administrative law does, people within the jurisdictional boundaries of the country possess rights that the Constitution grants to them. It is important to understand that these rights exist because the drafters of the Constitution wanted to limit the power of the government in ways that would maximize liberty for the citizens of the country.

The Impact of Article VI on the Courts: The Power of Judicial Review Article VI, Section 2 of the U.S. Constitution is known as the **Supremacy Clause**. As stated above, it declares that the Constitution is the "supreme law of the land." As the highest form of law in the nation, the **constitutional law** trumps all other forms of law including **statutory law** (laws enacted by a legislative body), **common law** (the law as set forth by judges in published judicial decisions), and **administrative law** (rules and regulations promulgated by a governmental agency that is empowered through statutory law to make such rules).

Each branch of the government—legislative, judicial, and executive—is charged by the Constitution with the protection of individual liberties. Within this framework, the judicial branch has assumed perhaps the largest and arguably most important role. Chief Justice John Marshall, speaking for the Supreme Court in the early case of *Marbury v. Madison*, 5 U.S. (1 Cranch) 137 (1803), declared that it was the duty of the judiciary to say what the law is, and that this duty included expounding and interpreting the law. Marshall stated that the law contained in the Constitution was paramount and that other laws that were repugnant to its provisions must fall. It was the province of the courts, he concluded, to decide when other laws were in violation of the basic law of the Constitution and, where this was found to occur, to declare those laws null and void, and thus unconstitutional. This doctrine, known as **judicial review**, became the basis for the application of constitutional guarantees by courts in cases brought before them:

Judicial review is the exercise by courts of their responsibility to determine whether acts of the other two branches are illegal and void because those acts violate the constitution. The doctrine authorizes courts to determine whether a law is constitutional, not whether it is necessary or useful. In other words, judicial review is the power to say what the constitution means and not whether such a law reflects a wise policy. Adherence to the doctrine of judicial review is essential to achieving balance in our government. . . . Judicial review, coupled with the specified constitutional provisions which keep the judicial branch separate and independent of the other branches of government and with those articles of the constitution that protect the impartiality of the judiciary from public and political pressure, enables the courts to ensure that the constitutional rights of each citizen will not be encroached upon by either the legislative or the executive branch of the government. *State v. LaFrance,* 471 A.2d 340, 343-44 (N.H. 1983) (italics added).

The judicial branch is not the only protector of constitutional rights. Congress has played an important role in the protection of constitutional rights by enacting legislation designed to guarantee and apply those rights in specific contexts. Laws that guarantee the rights of Native Americans, afford due process to military service personnel, and give effective right to counsel to poor defendants are examples of this legislative role.

Finally, the executive branch, which is charged with implementing the laws Congress enacts, contributes to the protection of individual rights by devising its own regulations and procedures for administering the law without intruding on constitutional guarantees.

To properly understand the scope of constitutional rights, one must recognize that our government is a federal republic, which means that an American lives under two governments: the federal government and the government of the state in which the person lives. The Constitution limits the authority of the federal government to the powers specified in the Constitution; all remaining governmental power is reserved to the states. The federal government is authorized, for example, to settle disputes among states, to conduct relations with foreign governments, and to act in certain matters of common national concern. The states hold the remainder of governmental power, to be exercised within their respective boundaries.

The Bill of Rights

Only a few individual rights were specified in the Constitution when it was adopted in 1788. The principal design of the original Constitution was not to specify individual rights, but to state the division of power between the new central federal government and the states. Shortly after its adoption, however, ten amendments—the **Bill of Rights**—were added to the Constitution to guarantee basic individual liberties, including freedom of speech, freedom of the press, freedom of religion, and freedom to assemble and petition the government.

The guarantees of the Bill of Rights originally applied only to acts of the federal government and did not prevent state and local governments from taking action that might threaten civil liberty. States had their own constitutions, some containing their own bills of rights that guaranteed the same or similar rights as those guaranteed by the Bill of Rights against federal intrusion. Not all states guaranteed these rights, however; the rights that did exist were subject to varying interpretations. In short, citizens were protected only to the extent that the states themselves recognized their basic rights.

In 1868, the Fourteenth Amendment, which provides in part that no state shall "deprive any person of life, liberty, or property without due process of law," was added to the Constitution. Not until 1925, in *Gitlow v. New York*, 268 U.S. 652, did the Supreme Court interpret the phrase "due process of law" to mean, in effect, **"without abridgement of certain of the rights guaranteed by the Bill of Rights."** Since *Gitlow*, the Supreme Court has ruled that a denial by a state of certain rights contained in the Bill of Rights represents a denial of due process of law. The members of the Court, however, have long argued about which provisions of the Bill of Rights are applicable to the states and to what extent. Three major due process approaches, with many variations, have evolved over the years:

1. The **"total incorporation"** approach held that the Due Process Clause of the Fourteenth Amendment made the entire federal Bill of Rights applicable to the states. This view never commanded a majority of the court and was rejected repeatedly in *Twining v. New Jersey*, 211 U.S. 78 (1908); *Palko v. Connecticut*, 302 U.S. 319 (1937); and *Adamson v. California*, 332 U.S. 46 (1947). In *Twining*, the Court noted that **"it is possible that some of the personal rights safeguarded by the first eight Amendments against National action may also be safeguarded against state action, because a denial of them would be a denial of due process of law. . . . If this is so, it is not because those rights are enumerated in the first eight amendments, but because they are of such a nature that they are included in the conception of due process of law."** 211 U.S. at 99.

2. The possibility mentioned in *Twining* became known as the "fundamental rights" or "ordered liberty" approach to due process, which was adopted by the Court in *Palko, Adamson*, and other cases and prevailed until the early 1960s. Under this approach, the Court found no necessary relationship between the Due Process Clause of the Fourteenth Amendment and the Bill of Rights. Instead, the Due Process Clause was said to have an "independent potency" that existed apart from the Bill of Rights. Due process was viewed as prohibiting state action that violated those rights that are "implicit in the concept of ordered liberty," that are "so rooted in the traditions and conscience of our people as to be ranked fundamental," that represent "fundamental fairness essential to the very concept of justice," or some similar phrase suggesting fundamental rights. Under the fundamental rights–ordered liberty approach, the Court looked to the "totality of the circumstances" of the particular case to determine what right, or what aspect or phase of a right, is "fundamental."

3. The **"selective incorporation"** approach combines aspects of the other two approaches and has prevailed since the early 1960s. This approach accepts the basic tenet of the fundamental rights–ordered liberty approach (that Fourteenth Amendment due process protects only rights that are "fundamental"). Also, under selective incorporation, every right in the Bill of Rights is not necessarily considered fundamental, and some rights outside the Bill of Rights might be considered fundamental. But the selective incorporation approach rejected the examination of the "totality of the circumstances" to determine whether particular aspects or phases of rights in the

Bill of Rights were fundamental. Instead, if a right was determined to be fundamental, it was incorporated into the Fourteenth Amendment through the Due Process Clause and thereby deemed applicable to the states to the same extent as to the federal government. As the Court said in *Duncan v. Louisiana*, "**Because we believe that trial by jury in criminal cases is fundamental to the American scheme of justice, we hold that the Fourteenth Amendment guarantees a right of jury trial in all criminal cases which—*were they to be tried in a federal court*—would come within the Sixth Amendment's guarantee**" (emphasis added). 391 U.S. 145, 149 (1968). The reference here to the American scheme of justice is significant, as is pointed out in footnote 14 of the *Duncan* opinion:

> **In one sense recent cases applying provisions of the first eight amendments to the States represent a new approach to the "incorporation" debate. Earlier the Court can be seen as having asked, when inquiring into whether some particular procedural safeguard was required of a State, if a civilized system could be imagined that would not accord the particular protection. . . . The recent cases, on the other hand, have proceeded upon the valid assumption that state criminal processes are not imaginary and theoretical schemes but actual systems bearing virtually every characteristic of the common-law system that has been developing contemporaneously in England and in this country. The question thus is whether given this kind of system a particular procedure is fundamental—whether, that is, a procedure is necessary to an Anglo-American regime of ordered liberty. . . . Of immediate relevance for this case are the Court's holdings that the States must comply with certain provisions of the Sixth Amendment, specifically that the States may not refuse a speedy trial, confrontation of witnesses, and the assistance, at state expense if necessary, of counsel. . . . Of each of these determinations that a constitutional provision originally written to bind the Federal Government should bind the States as well it might be said that the limitation in question is not necessarily fundamental to fairness in every criminal system that might be imagined but is fundamental in the context of the criminal processes maintained by the American States.**

What rights are fundamental to the concept of ordered liberty? Table 1.2 shows which rights set forth in the Bill of Rights have been deemed "fundamental" to our American sense of justice, and therefore have been selectively incorporated by the Fourteenth Amendment. Most of these are incorporated by the Fourteenth Amendment Due Process Clause. The only guarantees in the Bill of Right specifically concerning criminal procedure that do not apply to the states are: (1) the right to indictment by grand jury in the Fifth Amendment; (2) the prohibition against excessive bail in the Eighth Amendment; and (3) any guarantee that convictions be obtained only from unanimous twelve-member juries that may be implicit in the Sixth Amendment's right to a jury trial. However, in *Burch v. Louisiana*, 441 U.S. 130 (1979), the Supreme Court held that when as few as six jurors are impaneled, their verdict must be unanimous. And finally, while not relevant to criminal procedure, it should be noted that the Seventh Amendment's guarantee to the right to a jury trial in civil cases has not been incorporated by the Fourteenth Amendment. *See Curtis v. Loether*, 415 U.S. 189 (1974).

TABLE 1.2

PROVISIONS OF THE BILL OF RIGHTS INCORPORATED BY THE FOURTEENTH AMENDMENT RELEVANT TO CRIMINAL LAW AND CONSTITUTIONAL CRIMINAL PROCEDURE

Amendment	Right	Landmark Cases and Year
First	Freedom of Speech	*Gitlow v. New York*, 268 U.S. 652 (1925).
	Freedom of Peaceable Assembly	*DeJonge v. Oregon*, 299 U.S. 353 (1937).
	Freedom of the Press	*Near v. Minnesota*, 283 U.S. 697 (1931).
	Free Exercise of Religion	*Cantwell v. Connecticut*, 310 U.S. 296 (1940).
	Freedom from Governmental Establishment of Religion	*Everson v. Board of Education*, 330 U.S. 1 (1947).
Fourth	Unreasonable Search and Seizure	*Wolf v. Colorado*, 338 U.S. 25 (1949).
	Warrant Requirement	*Ker v. California*, 374 U.S. 23 (1963). *Aguilar v. Texas*, 378 U.S. 108 (1964).
	Exclusionary Rule	*Mapp v. Ohio*, 367 U.S. 643 (1961).
Fifth	Double Jeopardy	*Benton v. Maryland*, 395 U.S. 784 (1969).
	Self-Incrimination	*Malloy v. Hogan*, 367 U.S. 643 (1964).
	Taking of Private Property	*Chicago, Burlington & Quincy Railway Co. v. Chicago*, 166 U.S. 226 (1897).
Sixth	Right to Counsel (Capital Cases)	*Powell v. Alabama*, 287 U.S. 45 (1932).
	Right to Counsel (Felony Cases)	*Gideon v. Wainright*, 372 U.S. 335 (1963).
	Right to Counsel (Misdemeanors)	*Argersinger v. Hamlin*, 407 U.S. 25 (1972).
	Confrontation of Adverse Witnesses	*Pointer v. Texas*, 380 U.S. 400 (1965).
	Compulsory Process to Obtain Witness Testimony	*Washington v. Texas*, 388 U.S. 14 (1967).
	Notice of Accusation	*Rabe v. Washington*, 405 U.S. 313 (1972).
	Public Trial	*In re Oliver*, 333 U.S. 257 (1948).
	Trial by Impartial Jury in "Non-Petty" Criminal Cases	*Parker v. Gladden*, 385 U.S. 363 (1966). *Duncan v. Louisiana*, 391 U.S. 145 (1968).
	Speedy Trial	*Klopfer v. North Carolina*, 386 U.S. 213 (1967).
Eighth	Cruel and Unusual Punishment	*Robinson v. California*, 370 U.S. 66 (1962).
	Excessive Fines	*Cooper Industries v. Leatherman Tool Group, Inc.*, 532 U.S. 424 (2001).

To place these rights in a broader perspective, note that they make up only the core of what are considered to be **civil rights**—the privileges and freedoms that are accorded all Americans by virtue of their citizenship. Many other civil rights are not specifically mentioned in the Constitution, but nonetheless are recognized by the courts, have often been guaranteed by statute and are embedded in our democratic traditions. The right to buy, sell, own, and bequeath property; the right to enter into contracts; the right to marry and have children;

the right to live and work where one desires; and the right to participate in the political, social, and cultural processes of our society are a few of the rights that must be considered as fundamental to a democratic society as those specified by the Constitution.

Despite the premise that the rights of American citizenship are incontrovertible, the rights guaranteed by the Constitution or otherwise are not absolute rights in the sense that they entitle citizens to act in any way they please. Rather, to be protected by the law, people must exercise their rights so that the rights of others are not denied. As Justice Oliver Wendell Holmes observed, "Protection of free speech would not protect a man falsely shouting 'Fire' in a theater and causing a panic." Nor does freedom of speech and press sanction the publication of libel and obscenity. Similarly, the rights of free speech and free assembly prohibit knowingly engaging in conspiracies to overthrow by force the government of the United States. Civil liberties demand of all Americans an obligation to exercise their rights within a framework of law and mutual respect for the rights of others.

This obligation implies not only a restraint on the part of those exercising these rights but a tolerance on the part of those who are affected by that exercise. Citizens may on occasion be subjected to annoying political tirades, disagreeable entertainment, or noisy protest demonstrations. They may feel aggravated when a defendant refuses to testify or when they see a seemingly guilty defendant go free because certain evidence was ruled inadmissible in court. But these frustrations or inconveniences are a small price to pay for the freedom American citizens enjoy. If one person's rights are suppressed, everyone's freedom is jeopardized. Ultimately, a free society is a dynamic society, in which thoughts and ideas are forever challenging and being challenged. In such a society, people may listen to the wrong voice or follow the wrong plan. But a free society is one that learns by its mistakes and freely pursues the happiness of its citizens.

▶ INDIVIDUAL RIGHTS IN THE ORIGINAL CONSTITUTION

Habeas Corpus

Article I, Section 9, Clause 2

The Privilege of the Writ of Habeas Corpus shall not be suspended, unless when in Cases of Rebellion or Invasion the public Safety may require it.

This guarantee enables a person whose freedom has been restrained in some way to petition a federal court for a writ of *habeas corpus* to test whether the restraint violates the Constitution or laws of the United States. A petition for a writ of *habeas corpus* asks a federal court to examine an alleged illegal detention and order authorities to release an illegally confined petitioner. *Habeas corpus* can be suspended only when the president, with congressional authorization, declares that a national emergency requires its suspension and probably only when the courts are physically unable to function because of war, invasion, or rebellion. *Habeas corpus* is an important safeguard to prevent unlawful imprisonment and is discussed in further detail in Chapter 2.

Bills of Attainder

Article I, Section 9, Clause 3

No Bill of Attainder . . . shall be passed [by the federal government].

Article I, Section 10, Clause 1

No State shall . . . pass any Bill of Attainder. . . .

Historically, a **bill of attainder** is a special act of a legislature declaring that a person or group of persons has committed a crime and imposing punishment without a court trial. Under our system of separation of powers, only courts may try a person for a crime or impose punishment for violation of the law. Section 9 restrains Congress from passing bills of attainder, and Section 10 restrains the states.

Ex Post Facto Laws

Article I, Section 9, Clause 3

No . . . ex post facto Law shall be passed [by the federal government].

Article I, Section 10, Clause 1

No state shall . . . pass any . . . ex post facto Law. . . .

These two clauses prohibit the states and the federal government from enacting any *ex post facto* law—literally, a law passed "after the fact." **"[A]ny statute which punishes as a crime an act previously committed, which was innocent when done, which makes more burdensome the punishment for a crime, after its commission, or which deprives one charged with crime of any defense available according to law at the time when the act was committed, is prohibited as ex post facto."** *Beazell v. Ohio*, 269 U.S. 167, 169-70 (1925).

However, laws that retroactively determine how a person is to be tried for a crime may be changed so long as substantial rights of the accused are not curtailed. Laws that make punishment less severe than it was when the crime was committed are not *ex post facto*. An example of a statutory change that is not prohibited as *ex post facto* is the elimination of statutes of limitations—the time period in which a state must commence a criminal action. State legislatures are increasingly removing such limitations on sexual crimes that involve young victims.

Trial Rights

Article III, Sections 1 and 2

Article III, Sections 1 and 2, of the Constitution deal with the judicial system of the United States and are too long to be reproduced here.

Article III, Section 1, of the Constitution outlines the structure and power of our federal court system and establishes a federal judiciary that helps maintain the rights of American citizens. Article III, Section 2, also contains a guarantee that the trial of all federal crimes, except impeachment, shall be by jury. The Supreme Court carved out exceptions to this guarantee for "trials of petty offenses," trials before a court martial or other military tribunal, and some trials in which the defendant has voluntarily waived the right to a jury. The right to a jury trial is discussed further in Chapter 2.

Section 2 also requires that federal criminal trials be held in a federal court sitting in the state in which the crime was committed. This protects a person from being tried in a part of the United States far distant from the place where the alleged violation of federal law occurred.

Conviction for Treason

Article III, Section 3

Treason against the United States, shall consist only in levying War against them, or in adhering to their Enemies, giving them Aid and Comfort. No Person shall be convicted of Treason unless on the Testimony of two Witnesses to the same overt Act, or on Confession in open Court. The Congress shall have power to declare the Punishment of Treason, but no Attainder of Treason shall work Corruption of Blood, or Forfeiture except during the Life of the Person attainted.

Treason is the only crime defined by the Constitution. The precise description of this offense reflects an awareness by the Framers of the Constitution of the danger that unpopular views might be branded as traitorous. Recent experience in other countries with politically based prosecutions for conduct loosely labeled treason confirms the wisdom of the Constitution's authors in expressly stating what constitutes this crime and how it shall be proved.

▶INDIVIDUAL RIGHTS IN THE BILL OF RIGHTS

Amendment I

Congress shall make no law respecting an establishment of religion, or prohibiting the free exercise thereof; or abridging the freedom of speech, or of the press; or the right of the people peaceably to assemble, and to petition the Government for a redress of grievances.

Freedom of Speech, Expression, and Peaceable Assembly As a general rule, citizens may speak out freely on any subject they choose. They may do so alone or in concert with others. Thus, whether meeting for political activity, religious services, or other purposes, the First Amendment guarantees not only the right to speak one's mind but also the right to assemble peaceably to share one's thoughts with others. Like other constitutional rights, however, the First Amendment rights to free speech and assembly are not absolute. Public authorities may impose limitations reasonably designed to prevent fire, health hazards, obstruction and occupation of public buildings, or traffic obstruction.

Symbolic Speech A long string of judicial decisions have made it clear that "speech" goes beyond oral communication. "Free speech" includes nonverbal communication that includes both artistic expression and **symbolic speech**— conduct that expresses an idea or opinion. Wearing buttons or clothing with political slogans, displaying a sign or a flag, or burning a flag as a mode of expression are examples of symbolic speech. Table 1.3 summarizes some key symbolic speech cases. As these cases make evident, when conduct is the functional equivalent of speech, it gets significant First Amendment protection.

TABLE 1.3 SYMBOLIC SPEECH CASES

Symbolic Speech at Issue	Result and Case	Key Quote Expressing Rationale
Students were suspended from school for wearing armbands to school in protest of the Vietnam War.	Activity upheld by *Tinker v. Des Moines Independent Community School District*, 393 U.S. 503 (1969).	"School officials banned . . . a silent, passive expression of opinion, unaccompanied by any disorder or disturbance. . . . Accordingly, this case does not concern speech or action that intrudes upon the work of the schools or the rights of other students."
Members of the Communist Youth Brigade burned the American flag at a protest outside the 1984 Republican National Convention in Dallas while chanting "Red, White, and Blue—we spit on you."	Activity upheld (i.e., convictions invalidated) in *Texas v. Johnson*, 491 U.S. 397 (1989).	"If there is a bedrock principle underlying the FA, it is that the government may not prohibit the expression of an idea because society finds the idea offensive. We can imagine no more appropriate response to burning a flag than waving one's own."
The defendant, a union leader, joined a picket line that was protesting against his former employer. A state law made it an offense to picket. He was arrested and fined.	Activity upheld (i.e., conviction invalidated) by *Thornhill v. Alabama*, 310 U.S. 88 (1940).	Picketing allows "those interested—including the employees directly affected—[to] enlighten the public on the nature and causes of a labor dispute. The safeguarding of these means is essential to the securing of an informed and educated public opinion with respect to a matter which is of public concern."
A nineteen-year-old wore a jacket to a county courthouse that said: "Fuck the draft. Stop the War." He was convicted for "disturbing the peace" and sentenced to thirty days in jail.	Activity upheld (i.e., conviction invalidated) by *Cohen v. California*, 403 U.S. 15 (1971).	"For, while the particular four-letter word being litigated here is perhaps more distasteful than most others of its genre, it is nevertheless often true that one man's vulgarity is another's lyric. Indeed, we think it is largely because governmental officials cannot make principled distinctions in this area that the Constitution leaves matters of taste and style so largely to the individual."
A New Hampshire law required all noncommercial vehicles to bear license plates containing the state motto "Live Free or Die." A Jehovah's Witness covered the "or Die" part of his license plate since it offended his religious beliefs. He was convicted, fined, and sentenced to jail.	Activity upheld (i.e., conviction invalidated) by *Wooley v. Maynard*, 430 U.S. 705 (1977).	"New Hampshire's statute in effect requires that appellees use their private property as a 'mobile billboard' for the State's ideological message—or suffer a penalty." But, "the right of freedom of thought protected by the First Amendment against state action includes both the right to speak freely and the right to refrain from speaking at all."

Time, Place, and Manner Restrictions on the First Amendment While neither state, local, nor federal government may constitutionally ban the content of speech it may find objectionable, governmental entities are entitled to regulate the time, place, and manner of speech—including picketing and symbolic speech—in a content-neutral way for the good of society. In *United States v. O'Brien*, 391 U.S.

367 (1968), the Supreme Court established a four-part test to determine if a law is a valid governmental **time, place, and manner regulation of speech**. The case held that a governmental regulation on the time, place, and manner of speech is permissible if:

1. the regulation furthers an important or substantial governmental interest;
2. the governmental interest served by the regulation is unrelated to the suppression of free expression;
3. the regulation is narrowly tailored to serve the government's interest such that the restriction on free speech is not greater than is necessary to achieve the governmental interest; and
4. the regulation still leaves open ample, alternative means for people to communicate their message.

The *O'Brien* case is a good example of a valid "manner" restriction on free speech. Applying the four-part test above, the Court upheld a federal law that criminalized the destruction of Selective Service Certificates (commonly known as "draft cards"). The defendant in the case clearly was trying to communicate his dissatisfaction with the Vietnam War by burning his draft card; thus, his conduct was symbolic speech. However, he had other ways of expressing his opinions that did not involve the destruction of a piece of property issued by the government that was a necessary part of the government's ability to regulate the operation of the Selective Service System. Accordingly, the manner in which the defendant's "speech" occurred could be constitutionally regulated. Similarly, though people are free to make speeches on public streets, they may be prevented from doing so in a manner that disturbs the peace, such as using an amplifier or a bullhorn in a hospital zone or a residential neighborhood.

An example of a valid restriction on the time of speech would be restrictions on political protesters. Organizers of a protest may want to hold a demonstration in a large city to gain national media attention to their cause. Clearly, such protestors have a First Amendment right to hold their demonstration, but not whenever they choose. For example, no one has the right to **"insist upon a street meeting in the middle of Times Square at the rush hour as a form of freedom of speech."** *Cox v. Louisiana*, 379 U.S. 536, 1965). Thus, the time of the demonstration can be prescribed, but the content of it may not. Even groups espousing distasteful, unpopular, or offensive messages still have the right to speak their minds. A group of neo-Nazis, for example, had the right to parade down the streets in a predominantly Jewish neighborhood. *National Socialist Party of America v. Village of Skokie*, 432 U.S. 43 (1977). However, they had to obtain valid permits and conduct their demonstration at a time when authorities could maintain order.

Speech That Lies Beyond the Realm of First Amendment Protection The protections afforded by the First Amendment do not extend to all forms of expression. The Supreme Court has specifically identified a number of categories of speech as being of such little value to the core principles underlying the First Amendment that they receive no constitutional protection.

▶ **Defamation**: **Defamation** is false, public statement of fact (not opinion) that injures or damages a person's reputation. Defamation may be in writing, in which case it is called libel; or it may be spoken, in which case it is called slander. Although anyone can be defamed, public figures (such as celebrities and politicians) must prove a higher standard in court to collect civil damages for injury to their reputations from an act of libel or slander. *See New York Times Co. v. Sullivan*, 376 U.S. 254 (1964).

▶ **Words That Incite Immanent Lawlessness**: The First Amendment does not protect highly inflammatory remarks that are directed to inciting and likely to incite imminent lawless action. *Brandenburg v. Ohio*, 395 U.S. 444 (1969). **Fighting words** are an example of such speech that may be constitutionally proscribed. The fighting words doctrine was first announced by the Supreme Court in *Chaplinsky v. New Hampshire*, 315 U.S. 568 (1942). Chaplinsky was a Jehovah's Witness. He was arrested for calling a town marshal "a God-damned racketeer" and "a damned Fascist" in response to the marshal's attempts to stop Chaplinsky from preaching on a public sidewalk. The Court upheld the conviction because Chaplinsky used "fighting words"—words that by their very utterance are "likely to provoke the average person to retaliation, and thereby cause a breach of the peace."

▶ **Obscenity**: In evaluating the free speech rights of adults, the Supreme Court has held that sexually explicit expression that is indecent or profane but not "obscene" is protected by the First Amendment. *Reno v. American Civil Liberties Union*, 521 U.S. 844 (1997). But just because indecent speech is constitutionally protected, that does not mean it cannot be regulated under valid time, place, and manner restrictions like other protected forms of free speech. For example, the Federal Communications Commission is empowered to keep indecent speech off free, public airwaves, primarily to protect children. *FCC v. Pacifica Foundation*, 438 U.S. 726 (1978). However, the FCC has little to no power to regulate indecent materials transmitted on pay-cable television or satellite radio.

In contrast to materials that are merely indecent or profane, materials that are obscene receive no First Amendment protection. *Miller v. California*, 413 U.S. 15 (1973). But where is the line between material that is indecent, and therefore constitutionally protected, or material that is obscene, and may therefore be criminalized? Pornographic material presents special challenges in this context. Pornography is generally taken to mean sexually explicit material (verbal, written, or pictorial) that is primarily designed to produce sexual arousal in viewers. Justice Potter Stewart famously wrote, **"I can't define pornography, but I know it when I see it."** *Jacobellis v. Ohio*, 378 U.S. 184 (1964). Soft-core pornography is constitutionally protected free expression, while child pornography is always considered to be outside the realm of First Amendment protection. *New York v. Ferber*, 458 U.S. 747 (1982). But what about hard-core pornography involving adults? Such material receives constitutional protection under the First Amendment so long as it is not **obscene**. Under *Miller*, material is obscene if three criteria are met:

1. The work, taken as a whole by an average person applying contemporary community standards, appeals to the prurient interest (a shameful or morbid interest, in nudity, sex, or excretion);

Discussion

↑POINT

Are KKK Marches Protected Expression?

Brandenburg v. Ohio, 395 U.S. 444(1969)

Brandenburg was a leader of the Ku Klux Klan in rural Ohio. He invited a television reporter to come to a KKK rally. The reporter attended and filmed the rally, capturing images of men in hoods, some with firearms, burning a cross and making speeches advocating "revengeance" against "niggers" and "Jews" and their supporters. Brandenburg was subsequently charged and convicted of violating Ohio's Criminal Syndicalism Statute for "advocat[ing] . . . the duty, necessity, or propriety of crime, sabotage, violence, or unlawful methods of terrorism as a means of accomplishing industrial or political reform" and for "voluntarily assembl[ing] with any society, group, or assemblage of persons formed to teach or advocate the doctrines of criminal syndicalism." The Supreme Court reversed his conviction because the statute did not distinguish "mere advocacy" from "incitement to imminent lawless action."

Regarding speech that may incite lawlessness, do you think Brandenburg's imminent lawlessness test is a viable approach to dealing with hate speech? Why or why not? What, if any, alternative approach would you use instead to regulate hate speech within the confines of the First Amendment? How would your approach be used against a musician whose lyrics advocated rape or the killing of police officers?

2. The work depicts sexual conduct in a patently offensive way (meaning the work goes substantially beyond customary limits of candor in describing or representing such matters); and
3. The work, when taken as a whole, lacks serious literary, artistic, political, or scientific value.

The *Miller* test for obscenity contains a number of ambiguities that make it difficult to know where to "draw the line" between indecency and obscenity. First, by resorting to community standards, the Court may have created a serious question of the fairness of the *Miller* test because what may be deemed obscene in the rural Midwest or deep South may not be deemed obscene in a major metropolitan area like Los Angeles, Chicago, Atlanta, or New York. Second, when something has "serious" literary or artistic value is open to great debate. Consider the case of *Luke Records, Inc. v. Navarro*, 960 F.2d 134 (11th Cir.), *cert. denied* 506 U.S. 1022 (1992). The rap group 2 Live Crew released a recording entitled *As Nasty as They Want to Be.* The recording contained both profane and sexually graphic lyrics. It was declared obscene by a Florida judge. The group appealed and won.

The record is insufficient, however, for this Court to assume the fact finder's artistic or literary knowledge or skills to satisfy the last prong of the *Miller* analysis . . . We reject the argument that simply by listening to his musical work, the judge could determine that it had no serious artistic value. 960 F.2d at 138-39.

Freedom of the Press Freedom of the press is a further guarantee of the right to express oneself, in this case by writing or publishing one's views on a particular subject. The Framers recognized the importance of a free interplay of ideas in a democratic society and sought to secure the right of all citizens to speak or publish their views, even if those views were contrary to those of the government or society as a whole. Accordingly, the First Amendment generally forbids censorship or other restraints on speech or the printed word. Thus, a school board's dismissal of a teacher who had protested school board activities in a letter to the editor of the local newspaper was held to infringe on the teacher's First Amendment rights in the absence of evidence that the teacher's activity caused significant disruption or interference with the delivery of educational services. A state court order issued in anticipation of the trial of an accused mass murderer, restraining the press and broadcast media from reporting any confessions or incriminating statements made by the defendant or from reporting other facts "strongly implicative" of the defendant, was similarly struck down.

As with speech, however, freedom to write or publish is not absolute. The First Amendment does not protect the sale of obscene materials. Nor does it protect printed materials that are libelous. The Supreme Court has ruled, however, that public figures cannot sue for defamation unless the alleged libelous remarks were printed with knowledge of their falsity or with a reckless disregard for the truth. The Court has also ruled that the First Amendment prohibited the government from preventing the publication of a secret study into the origins of the United States' involvement in the Vietnam War. The Court indicated, however, that freedom of the press might not extend to similar matters that could be shown to have a more direct and substantial bearing on national security.

Finally, broadcasting—including radio, television, and motion pictures—receives the protections of the free press guarantee but is also subject to its limitations. The burgeoning development of computers and the Internet are providing unique First Amendment challenges to the courts. For example, in *United States v. American Library Association, Inc.*, 539 U.S. 19 (2003), the U.S. Supreme Court ruled that libraries can be required to use software filters intended to prevent children from accessing pornography on all computers or be denied federal financial assistance for Internet access. The Court found that the filters did not violate the First Amendment rights of library users, because the filters can be shut off on request.

Freedom of Religion The First Amendment contains two different types of freedoms having to do with religion. The first of these restricts the establishment of any government-sponsored religion. The second preserves people's rights to practice their religious beliefs without undue interference from the government.

The Establishment Clause The First Amendment provides two express guarantees with respect to religious freedom. First, the **Establishment Clause** provides that neither Congress nor a state legislature (by virtue of the Fourteenth Amendment) may "make any law respecting an establishment of religion." This means that no legislature may enact a law that establishes an official church that all Americans must accept and support, or to whose tenets all must subscribe, or that favors one church over another. The Supreme Court described the Establishment Clause as providing a **"wall of separation between church and state."** *Everson v. Board of Education*, 330 U.S. 1, 16 (1947):

> The "establishment of religion" clause of the First Amendment means at least this: Neither a state nor the Federal Government can set up a church. Neither can pass laws that aid one religion, aid all religions, or prefer one religion to another. Neither can force nor influence a person to go to or remain away from church against his will or force him to profess a belief or disbelief in any religion. No person can be punished for entertaining or professing religious beliefs or disbeliefs, for church attendance or non-attendance. No tax in any amount, large or small, can be levied to support any religious activities or institutions, whatever they may be called, or whatever form they may adopt to teach or practice religion. Neither a state nor the Federal Government can, openly or secretly, participate in the affairs of any religious organizations or groups and vice versa. 330 U.S. at 15-16.

In *Lemon v. Kurtzman*, 403 U.S. 602, 612-13 (1971), the Court refined these principles by establishing three tests to determine whether a statute or governmental practice is permissible under the establishment clause: (1) it must have a secular purpose; (2) its principal or primary purpose must be one that neither advances nor inhibits religion; and (3) it must not foster an excessive government entanglement with religion. Applying these tests, the Court has held that a state may not require prayer in the public schools, nor may a state supplement or reimburse parochial schools for teachers' salaries and textbooks. To permit or authorize such activities would constitute governmental support of the religious organization affected. On the other hand, the Court held that public schools may release students, at the students' own request, from an hour of class work so that those students may attend their own churches for religious instruction. Also, states may provide free bus transportation to children attending church or parochial schools if transportation is also furnished to children in the public schools. Furthermore, the Court upheld the tax-exempt status of church property used exclusively for worship purposes, sanctioned federal aid programs for new construction at church-related universities, and permitted states to designate Sunday as a day of rest.

The Free Exercise Clause Second, the **Free Exercise Clause** provides that no law is constitutional if it "prohibits the free exercise" of religion. The right to believe or not to believe is absolute under the Free Exercise Clause, but the freedom to act on those beliefs is not: people are free to practice their religion so long as those practices do not conflict with otherwise valid laws. Thus, the Supreme Court upheld a law criminalizing polygamy in *Reynolds v. United States*, 98 U.S. 145 (1878). The Court reasoned that a man cannot escape conviction for having multiple wives by attributing his conduct to his religious beliefs. Nor could a person commit an indecent act or engage in immoral conduct and then validate the actions on grounds of religious freedom. Thus, if one's religion sanctioned human sacrifice, homicide laws could still be used to punish such killings because laws prohibiting murder do not target the free exercise of religion; rather, they would merely have an **"incidental effect [on] a generally applicable and otherwise valid provision."** *Employment Division v. Smith*, 494 U.S. 872, 878 (1990).

While the freedom to practice one's religion is one of our nation's most valued liberties, this right may be constitutionally limited under certain circumstances, such as in the military or correctional settings. In *Goldman v. Weinberger*, 475 U.S. 503 (1986), for example, an officer in the Air Force who was an ordained Orthodox Jewish rabbi was not permitted to wear his yarmulke while on duty or in uniform because a military regulation banned indoor headgear unless worn "by armed security police in the performance of their duties." 475 U.S. at 505. The Supreme Court upheld the restriction, reasoning that allowing nonstandard dress **"would detract from the uniformity sought by dress regulations,"** 475 U.S. at 510, thereby interfering with fostering **"instinctive obedience, unity, commitment, and esprit de corps."** 475 U.S. at 507.

The free exercise of religion may be limited by a correctional institution under certain circumstances. For many years, correctional restrictions on the free exercise of religion were governed by the Supreme Court's decision in *O'Lone v. Estate of Shabazz*, 482 U.S. 342 (1987). *O'Lone* adapted the "reasonable penological interest test" set forth in *Turner v. Safley* to the question of religious free exercise. In *O'Lone*, Muslim inmates who worked in a maximum security setting challenged a prison regulation that required them to stay at their work assignment throughout the work shift. This rule prevented them from attending a Jumu'ah, a weekly prayer service held on Friday afternoons in the minimum security area of the prison. In spite of the fact that the regulation clearly burdened the free exercise of the inmates' religion, the Supreme Court upheld the prison regulation, finding it to be a "reasonable" restriction that helped to maintain institutional order and security. 482 U.S. at 350. The fact that the rule was not targeted at suppressing religion, but rather was a neutral safety regulation to which no easy alternatives existed, was key to the Court's rationale. 482 U.S. at 347. The fact that the inmates were free to practice the other tenets of their religion was also central to the Court's reasoning. 482 U.S. at 351-52.

Under the *O'Lone* standard, correctional officials were able to justify many restrictions on the free exercise of religious practices. For example, in *Hamilton v. Schriro*, 74 F.3d 1545 (8th Cir. 1996), the court upheld a ban on Native Americans holding a religious ceremony known as a "sweat lodge"—a ceremonial, spiritual cleansing ritual that takes place in an enclosed make-shift structure. During this ritual, rocks are heated in a fire. Participants, who are nude, then pour water on the rocks, creating steam. (Palmer & Palmer 1999: 95-96). An axe, a shovel, and deer antlers are all traditionally used during the ceremony. The court upheld the ban, citing concerns for the risks of assaults and fires. Similar safety concerns routinely led courts to uphold grooming codes that banned long hair or beards, since contraband could be easily concealed, *e.g., Scott v. Miss. Dep't of Corr.*, 961 F.2d 77 (5th Cir. 1992); and to uphold dress codes that banned certain religious attire, such as headgear that could be used to hide contraband or prayer beads that could be used to strangle someone. *E.g., Benjamin v. Coughlin*, 905 F.2d 571 (2d Cir. 1990).

In addition to safety concerns, the deferential *O'Lone* standard also upheld restrictions based on economic conditions. Circuit Courts of Appeal differed on whether prisons had to provide Kosher diets to Jewish inmates because, in some areas, preparing Kosher meals for a handful of Jewish inmates would have effectuated a significant economic hardship on the correctional institution. *Compare, e.g., Beerheide v. Suthers*, 286 F.3d 1179 (10th Cir. 2002) (mandating

Kosher diet) with *Kahey v. Jones*, 836 F.2d 948 (5th Cir. 1988) (holding depriva-
tion of Kosher diet did not violate *O'Lone*).

Congress attempted to give inmates, among others, more freedom to practice
their religions when it enacted the Religious Freedom Restoration Act (RFRA),
42 U.S.C. §§2000bb *et seq.* (2000). RFRA provided that the "government may
substantially burden a person's exercise of religion only if it demonstrates that
application of the burden to the person—(1) is in furtherance of a compelling
governmental interest; and (2) is the least restrictive means of furthering that
compelling governmental interest." The Supreme Court invalidated RFRA in
City of Borne v. Flores, 521 U.S. 507 (1997). In *Borne*, local zoning authorities
denied a Catholic archdiocese permission to expand a church under a local historic preservation ordinance. That decision was challenged under RFRA. The
Court sided with the municipality, that Congress had exceeded the scope of its
authority under Section 5 of the Fourteenth Amendment (see *infra* in the section
Amendment XIV). Congress responded to the invalidation of RFRA by enacting the Religious Land Use and Institutionalized Persons Act (RLUIPA) in 2000.
It used the same test adopted in RFRA by providing:

> No government shall impose a substantial burden on the religious exercise of
> a person residing in or confined to an institution, as defined in section 2 of the
> Civil Rights of Institutionalized Persons Act (42 U.S.C. 1997), even if the bur-
> den results from a rule of general applicability, unless the government dem-
> onstrates that imposition of the burden on that person—(1) is in furtherance
> of a compelling governmental interest; and (2) is the least restrictive means of
> furthering that compelling governmental interest. 42 U.S.C. § 2000cc(a).

The Supreme Court unanimously upheld the constitutionality of RLUIPA
in *Cutter v. Wilkinson*, 544 U.S. 709 (2005). Key to the Court's decision was
that RLUIPA was enacted under Congress' spending and commerce powers and,
therefore is limited to programs or activities "that receive[] Federal financial
assistance" or that affect "commerce with foreign nations, among the several
States, or with Indian tribes."

For an inmate to be able to challenge a correctional regulation that burdens
the free exercise of religion under RLUIPA, "a plaintiff must demonstrate that
the government action in question has burdened a 'religious belief,' and not a
'way of life . . . based on purely secular considerations' or a 'philosophical and
personal' choice" (Gaubatz 2006: 519). The plaintiff must also demonstrate "that
the religious belief is sincerely held" (521). Under the now defunct *O'Lone* test,
the burden was on a plaintiff to prove that the restriction on the free exercise
of religion was unreasonable. Under RLUIPA, correctional officials must now
prove both a compelling governmental interest for burdening the free exercise
of religion, and that there is no less burdensome way to achieve that goal than
the regulation at issue. Under this standard of strict scrutiny, inmates have been
winning cases that they used to lose under *O'Lone*. For example, denials of access to a religiously mandated diet, such as a Kosher one, have uniformly been
invalided under RLUIPA (Gaubatz 558-59). Similarly, blanket prohibitions on religious dress and hair styles are being scrutinized to such a degree that some
states have changed their prison regulations to allow exemptions to grooming
policies for religious reasons (Gaubatz 561-62). But bans on religious ceremonies
like the Native American sweat lodge are likely to be upheld in light of the compelling governmental security interests at stake (Gaubatz 565).

Amendment II

A well regulated Militia, being necessary to the security of a free State, the right of the people to keep and bear Arms, shall not be infringed.

The Second Amendment's "right of the people to keep and bear arms" has engendered some of the most spirited public debate since the adoption of the Bill of Rights. Two distinct interpretations have emerged. One theory holds that the amendment was primarily meant to convey individual rights, like other parts of the Bill of Rights. A contrasting theory contends that the Second Amendment was spelling out the right of the states, independent of a central federal government, to establish and maintain state militias like state police forces and the national guard.

During the era of the Framers, the right of citizens to protect themselves against both disorder in the community and attack from foreign enemies was deemed paramount. Some believe that this right to bear arms has become much less important in recent decades because the ongoing presence of well-trained military and police forces makes it unnecessary for people to have their own weapons available. Thus, the Supreme Court has held that the state and federal governments may pass laws prohibiting the carrying of concealed weapons, requiring the registration of firearms, and limiting the sale of firearms for other than military uses.

In spite of the ongoing controversy, Congress continues to enact statutes that directly affect a citizen's legal ability to purchase, receive, possess, or transport firearms. Indeed, since 1939, when *United States v. Miller*, 307 U.S. 174 (1939) upheld a federal statute barring the possession of sawed-off shotguns, the Supreme Court has upheld many statutes affecting the private ownership of firearms against Second Amendment challenges. Those who believe that the Second Amendment "right to bear arms" clause was meant to be an expression of the rights of the states to maintain a militia often point to the *Miller* case and its progeny. In *Miller*, the Court declared, "**[W]e cannot say that the Second Amendment guarantees the right to keep and bear such an instrument [sawed-off shotgun]. Certainly it is not within judicial notice that this weapon is any part of the ordinary military equipment or that its use could contribute to the common defense.**" 307 U.S. at 178. More recently, Congress has enacted legislation that bars possession of a firearm by any citizen previously convicted of a misdemeanor crime of domestic violence, supplementing an existing law stating that felons could not possess firearms. And the Supreme Court has refused to invalidate either the prohibition itself or the retroactive effect of these laws, under which persons convicted many years ago of "qualifying" misdemeanors cannot today possess firearms because of the intervening federal prohibition.

What seems clearly defined with respect to the "right to bear arms" clause of the Second Amendment, however, is that the restraint applies only to the federal government, and not to the states or to private interests. As far back as 1886, in *Presser v. Illinois*, 116 U.S. 252, 265 (1886), the Supreme Court said that "**a conclusive answer to the contention that this amendment prohibits the legislation in question lies in the fact that the amendment is a limitation only upon the power of Congress and the National Government, and not upon that of the state.**" As a result of this and other similar judicial determinations, the states are essentially free to establish their own schemes of regulations or state constitutional provisions respecting the purchase, possession, or transportation of firearms.

Just exactly what the Framers intended to protect by the Second Amendment will continue to cause public debate and consume legal and political resources until the U.S. Supreme Court offers a definitive resolution.

Amendment III

> *No Soldier shall, in time of peace be quartered in any house, without the consent of the Owner, nor in time of war, but in a manner to be prescribed by law.*

Before the American Revolution, colonists were frequently required, against their will, to provide lodging and food for British soldiers. The Third Amendment prohibited the continuation of this onerous practice.

Amendment IV

> *The right of the people to be secure in their persons, houses, papers, and effects, against unreasonable searches and seizures, shall not be violated, and no Warrants shall issue, but upon probable cause, supported by Oath or affirmation and particularly describing the place to be searched, and the persons or things to be seized.*

In some countries, police officers may, at their whim or the whim of political leaders, invade citizens' homes, seize citizens' property, or arrest or detain citizens without fear of punishment or reprisal. In the United States, the Fourth Amendment protects people and their property from unreasonable searches and seizures by governmental officers. In general, although there are exceptions to the rule, a police officer may not search the home of a private citizen, seize any of the citizen's property, or arrest the citizen without first obtaining a court order called a **warrant**. Before a warrant is issued, the police officer must convince an impartial judicial officer that there is **probable cause**—defined by the U.S. Supreme Court as a fair probability—either that the person involved has committed a crime or that contraband or evidence, fruits, or implements of a crime are in a particularly described place.

Because most of this book deals with the topics of arrest, search and seizure, and probable cause, further discussion of the Fourth Amendment appears in the chapters dealing with those topics.

Amendment V

> *No person shall be held to answer for a capital, or otherwise infamous crime, unless on a presentment or indictment of a Grand Jury, except in cases arising in the land or naval forces, or in the Militia, when in actual service in time of War or public danger; nor shall any person be subject for the same offense to be twice put in jeopardy of life or limb; nor shall be compelled in any criminal case to be a witness against himself, nor be deprived of life, liberty, or property, without due process of law; nor shall private property be taken for public use, without just compensation.*

Indictment by Grand Jury The Fifth Amendment requires that before a person is tried in federal court for an infamous crime, he or she must first be indicted by a grand jury. The grand jury's duty is to make sure that there is probable cause to believe that the accused person is guilty. This provision prevents a person from being subjected to a trial when there is not sufficient proof that he or she has committed a crime.

Generally, an infamous crime is a **felony** (a crime for which a sentence of more than one year's imprisonment may be imposed) or a lesser offense that is punishable by confinement in a penitentiary or at hard labor. An indictment is not required for a trial by court martial. Furthermore, the constitutional requirement of grand jury indictment does not apply to trials in state courts because the Supreme Court's decision in *Hurtado v. California*, 110 U.S. 516 (1884) refused to incorporate the Fifth Amendment's guarantee of a grand jury indictment through the Fourteenth Amendment's Due Process Clause. However, the Supreme Court has ruled that when states do use grand juries in their criminal proceedings, they must be free of racial bias. The grand jury is discussed in further detail in Chapter 2.

Freedom from Double Jeopardy The clause "nor shall any person be subject for the same offense to be twice put in jeopardy of life or limb" is often referred to as the **Double Jeopardy** Clause. The U.S. Supreme Court has recognized three separate guarantees embodied in the Double Jeopardy Clause: "**It protects against a second prosecution for the same offense after acquittal, against a second prosecution for the same offense after conviction, and against multiple punishments for the same offense.**" *Justices of Boston Municipal Court v. Lydon*, 466 U.S. 294, 306-07 (1984). Note that the Double Jeopardy Clause "**protects only against the imposition of multiple criminal punishments for the same offense.**" *Hudson v. United States*, 522 U.S. 93, 99 (1997). It does not protect against criminal prosecution of a person after the person has been penalized in a civil proceeding. The double jeopardy protections were explained in *Ohio v. Johnson*, 467 U.S. 493, 498-99 (1984):

> **[T]he bar to retrial following acquittal or conviction ensures that the State does not make repeated attempts to convict an individual, thereby exposing him to continued embarrassment, anxiety, and expense, while increasing the risk of an erroneous conviction or an impermissibly enhanced sentence. . . . [P]rotection against cumulative punishments is designed to ensure that the sentencing discretion of courts is confined to the limits established by the legislature.**

Jeopardy attaches in a jury trial when the jury is impaneled and sworn and in a nonjury trial when the judge begins to hear evidence. Jeopardy attaches to all criminal proceedings, whether felony or misdemeanor, and to juvenile adjudicatory proceedings, even though they are civil in nature.

There are exceptions to the general rules protecting a person from double jeopardy. First, a second trial for the same offense may occur when the first trial results in a mistrial (for example, a deadlocked jury), if there is a "manifest necessity" for the mistrial declaration, or "the ends of public justice would otherwise be defeated." *Richardson v. United States*, 468 U.S.317, 324 (1984). Generally, the Double Jeopardy Clause does not bar reprosecution of a defendant whose conviction is overturned on appeal. "**It would be a high price indeed for society to pay were every accused granted immunity from punish-**

ment because of any defect sufficient to constitute reversible error in the proceedings leading to conviction." *United States v. Tateo*, 377 U.S. 463, 466 (1964). If, however, the reason for the reversal of the conviction was insufficiency of the evidence to support the conviction, the government may not reprosecute the defendant. *Burks v. United States*, 437 U.S. 1 (1978).

Double jeopardy does not arise when a single act violates both federal and state laws and the defendant is exposed to prosecution in both federal and state courts. This is called the **dual sovereignty doctrine,** and it also applies to prosecutions by two different states. In *Heath v. Alabama*, 474 U.S. 82 (1985), the U.S. Supreme Court held that the key question under this doctrine was whether the two entities seeking to prosecute the defendant for the same criminal act are separate sovereigns that derive their power to prosecute from independent sources. Because local governments are not sovereigns for double jeopardy purposes, the Double Jeopardy Clause prohibits successive prosecutions by a state and a municipality in that state or by two municipalities in the same state. A criminal prosecution in either a state court or a federal court does not exempt the defendant from being sued for damages by anyone who is harmed by his or her criminal act. Finally, a defendant may be prosecuted more than once for the same conduct if that conduct involves the commission of more than one crime. For instance, a person who kills three victims at the same time and place can be tried separately for each killing.

The Double Jeopardy Clause also embodies the **collateral estoppel doctrine.** The U.S. Supreme Court explained that collateral estoppel **"means simply that when an issue of ultimate fact has once been determined by a valid and final judgment, that issue cannot again be litigated between the same parties in any future lawsuit."** *Ashe v. Swenson*, 397 U.S. 436 (1970). The collateral estoppel doctrine is often applied in civil suits brought by a citizen against a police officer where (1) the citizen has been previously convicted of a crime associated with the same event providing the basis for the lawsuit; and (2) as part of the conviction, the court determined that the citizen had acted with a particular state of mind. To the extent that the plaintiff's state of mind becomes significant in the civil litigation, the plaintiff is estopped (precluded) from litigating that issue because of the collateral estoppel doctrine. In other words, because the issue of state of mind has previously been determined "by a valid and final judgment" (the criminal conviction), it cannot be relitigated.

Privilege Against Self-Incrimination The Fifth Amendment protects a person against being incriminated by his or her own *compelled* **testimonial communications.** This protection is applicable to the states through the Due Process Clause of the Fourteenth Amendment. *Malloy v. Hogan*, 378 U.S. 1 (1964). To be testimonial, a **"communication must itself, explicitly or implicitly, relate a factual assertion or disclose information"** that is **"the expression of the contents of an individual's mind."** *Doe v. United States*, 487 U.S. 201, 210 n.9 (1988). Therefore, the privilege against self-incrimination is not violated by compelling a person to appear in a lineup, produce voice exemplars, furnish handwriting samples, be fingerprinted, shave a beard or mustache, or take a blood-alcohol or breathalyzer test. With respect to the requirement that the communication be incriminating, the U.S. Supreme Court said:

> The privilege afforded not only extends to answers that would in themselves support a conviction under a . . . criminal statute but likewise embraces those which would furnish a link in the chain of evidence needed to prosecute the claimant for a . . . crime. . . . But this protection must be confined to instances where the witness has reasonable cause to apprehend danger from a direct answer. . . . To sustain the privilege, it need only be evident from the implications of the question, in the setting in which it is asked, that a responsive answer to the question or an explanation of why it cannot be answered might be dangerous because injurious disclosure could result. The trial judge in appraising the claim must be governed as much by his personal perception of the peculiarities of the case as by the facts actually in evidence. *Hoffman v. United States*, 341 U.S. 479, 486-87 (1951).

In other words, the Fifth Amendment protects not only the compelled confession to the commission of a crime, but also incriminating admissions that, while not sufficient in and of themselves to support a conviction, would provide "a link in the chain of evidence needed to prosecute" the person. An example of the latter is a suspect's statements that he or she was at or near the scene of a crime.

The protection against self-incrimination enables a person to refuse to testify against himself or herself at a criminal trial in which the person is a defendant and also **"privileges him not to answer official questions put to him in any other proceeding, civil or criminal, formal or informal, where the answers might incriminate him in future criminal proceedings."** *Minnesota v. Murphy*, 465 U.S. 420, 426 (1984). The privilege also applies to the compelled preparation or offering of incriminating documents. *United States v. Doe*, 465 U.S. 605 (1984). When a defendant chooses not to testify at trial, neither the prosecutor nor the trial judge may make any adverse comment about the defendant's failure to testify. *Griffin v. California*, 380 U.S. 609 (1965). Moreover, the defendant is entitled to have the jury instructed that no inference of guilt may be drawn from his or her failure to testify. The *Miranda* safeguards to secure the privilege against self-incrimination when a defendant is subjected to custodial interrogation are discussed in detail in Chapter 13.

The Fifth Amendment privilege protects a witness at a civil or criminal proceeding from answering questions when the answers might be incriminating in some future criminal prosecution. If authorized by statute, however, the prosecution may compel the witness to testify by granting **immunity** from prosecution. The type of immunity usually granted is use immunity, which prevents the prosecution from using the compelled testimony and any evidence derived from it in a subsequent prosecution. A witness who has been granted immunity and still refuses to testify may be held in contempt of court.

The Right to Due Process The words **due process of law** express the fundamental ideals of American justice. Due process is violated if a practice or rule **"offends some principle of justice so rooted in the traditions and conscience of our people as to be ranked as fundamental."** *Snyder v. Massachusetts*, 291 U.S. 97, 105 (1934). A Due Process Clause is found in both the Fifth and Fourteenth Amendments. While originally construed as a restraint only on the federal government, later interpretations by the U.S. Supreme Court have established that the restraint is similarly applicable to the states. "The Due Process Clause of the Constitution prohibits deprivations of life, liberty, or property without 'fundamental fairness' through governmental conduct that offends the community's sense of justice, decency and fair play." *Roberts v. Maine*, 48 F.3d 1287, 1291 (1st Cir. 1995).

The following rights are recognized as within the protection of the Due Process Clause: the right to timely notice of a hearing or trial that adequately informs the accused of the charges against him or her; the right to present evidence in one's own behalf before an impartial judge or jury; the right to be presumed innocent until proven guilty by legally obtained evidence; and the right to have the verdict supported by the evidence presented at trial. These types of rights are sometimes referred to as **procedural due process.** Note that "due process of law" also applies to noncriminal matters and does not necessarily require a proceeding in a court or a trial by jury in every case involving personal or property rights. **"In all cases, that kind of procedure is due process of law which is suitable and proper to the nature of the case, and sanctioned by the established customs and usages of the courts."** *Ex parte Wall*, 107 U.S. 265, 289 (1883).

The Due Process Clauses of the Fifth and Fourteenth Amendments also provide other basic protections against the enactment by states or the federal government of arbitrary and unreasonable legislation or other measures that would violate peoples' rights. This is sometimes referred to as **substantive due process:**

> **It is manifest that it was not left to the legislative power to enact any process which might be devised. The article is a restraint on the legislative as well as on the executive and judicial powers of the government, and cannot be so construed as to leave congress free to make any process "due process of law" by its mere will.** *Murray's Lessee v. Hoboken Land and Improvement Co.* 59 U.S. (18 How.) 272, 276 (1856).

Due process imposes limits on governmental interference with important individual liberties—such as the freedom to enter into contracts, engage in a lawful occupation, marry, move without unnecessary restraints, and make intimately private decisions about sexual activity between consenting adults, including decisions regarding procreation. To be valid, governmental restrictions placed on these liberties must be reasonable and consistent with justice and fair play. Courts have applied this type of due process analysis to subjects as varied as regulation of railroads and public utilities, collective bargaining, interstate commerce, taxation, and bankruptcy.

The Due Process Clause of the Fifth Amendment has been interpreted as also guaranteeing the **equal protection of law**—the notion that similarly situated people should be treated in a similar manner. *Plyler v. Doe*, 457 U.S. 202, 216 (1982) (**"all persons similarly circumstanced shall be treated alike."**). The Fifth Amendment does not mention equal protection per se; it is specified in the Equal Protection Clause of the Fourteenth Amendment. These two concepts are associated with each other and sometimes overlap. **"[Due process] tends to secure equality of law in the sense that it makes a required minimum of protection for every one's right of life, liberty and property, which the Congress or the legislature may not withhold. Our whole system of law is predicated on the general, fundamental principle of equality of application of the law."** *Truax v. Corrigan*, 257 U.S. 312, 331 (1921). For example, in *Bolling v. Sharpe*, 347 U.S. 497, 499 (1954), the Court held that segregation of pupils in the public schools of the District of Columbia violated the Due Process Clause:

> **The Fifth Amendment, which is applicable in the District of Columbia, does not contain an equal protection clause as does the Fourteenth Amendment which applies only to the states. But the concepts of equal protection and due process, both stemming from our American ideal of fairness, are not mutually exclusive. The "equal protection of the laws" is a more explicit safeguard of prohibited unfairness than "due process of law," and, therefore, we do not imply that the two are always interchangeable phrases. But, as this Court has recognized, discrimination may be so unjustifiable as to be violative of due process.**

The Right to Just Compensation The power of the government to acquire private property is called **eminent domain**. The Fifth Amendment limits the government to taking a person's property for "public use" and requires that the full value of the property be paid to the owner. Thus, governmental entities cannot simply take property from one person and give it to another. However, what constitutes "public use" is a matter of some debate. In *Kelo v. City of New London*, 545 U.S. 469 (2005), the Supreme Court upheld the use of eminent domain to transfer land from one private owner to another to further economic development under a comprehensive redevelopment plan for an economically depressed city. The Court reasoned that the economic benefits that such redevelopment would bring to the community as a whole qualified the taking as a permissible "public use."

To qualify for just compensation, property need not be physically taken from the owner. If governmental action results in a lower value of private property, that action may constitute a "taking" and require payment of compensation. Thus, the Supreme Court held that disturbing the egg-laying habits of chickens on a man's poultry farm by the noise of low-level flights by military aircraft from a nearby air base lessened the value of that farm and that, as a result, the landowner was entitled to receive compensation equal to his loss. *United States v. Causby*, 328 U.S. 256 (1946).

Amendment VI

> *In all criminal prosecutions, the accused shall enjoy the right to a speedy and public trial, by an impartial jury of the State and district wherein the crime shall have been committed, which district shall have been previously ascertained by law, and to be informed of the nature and cause of the accusation; to be confronted with the witnesses against him; to have compulsory process for obtaining witnesses in his favor, and to have the Assistance of Counsel for his defence.*

The Right to a Speedy and Public Trial The right to a speedy and public trial requires that, after arrest or indictment, the accused be brought to trial without unnecessary delay and that the trial be open to the public. In *Barker v. Wingo*, 407 U.S. 514 (1972), the U.S. Supreme Court held that intentional or negligent delay by the prosecution that prejudices a defendant's right to defend himself or herself is grounds for dismissal of the charges. In *Barker*, the Court identified four factors that courts should assess in determining whether a particular defendant has been deprived of the right to a speedy trial: **"Length of delay, the reason for the delay, the defendant's assertion of his right, and prejudice to the defendant."** 407 U.S. at 530. The Court said that the length of the delay was to some extent a "triggering mechanism." If there is no delay that is prejudicial on its face, judicial inquiry into the other three factors is not necessary. The Court also said that prejudice should be assessed in the light of defendants' interests that the speedy trial right was designed to protect: (1) preventing oppressive pretrial incarceration; (2) minimizing anxiety and concern of the accused; and, most important, (3) limiting the possibility that the defense will be impaired.

Although the Sixth Amendment guarantees a criminal defendant the right to a public trial, the First Amendment implicitly gives the press and the general public the right to attend criminal trials. Therefore, the "right to an open public trial is a shared right of the accused and the public, the common concern being the assurance of fairness." *Press-Enterprise Co. v. Superior Court*, 478 U.S. 1, 7 (1986). In addition to ensuring fairness, the constitutional commitment to public trials helps to maintain confidence in the criminal justice system, promote informed discussion of governmental affairs, ensure that judges and prosecutors perform their duties responsibly, encourage witnesses to come forward, and discourage perjury. *Waller v. Georgia*, 467 U.S. 39 (1984). Although a defendant may waive the Sixth Amendment right to a public trial and request a closed proceeding, such a request must be balanced against the First Amendment rights of the press and the public to have access to criminal trials.

Trial by an Impartial Jury The guarantee of trial by an impartial jury supplements the earlier jury trial guarantee contained in Article III of the Constitution. Jury trials are discussed further in Chapter 2.

The Right to Notice of Charges The Sixth Amendment requires that a person "be informed of the nature and cause of the accusation." This means that an accused person must be given notice regarding exactly how he or she has allegedly broken the law, in order to provide the accused with an opportunity to prepare a defense. For this reason, the indictment or information must be sufficiently specific in setting forth the charges to enable the defendant to plead and prepare a defense. (The indictment and information are discussed in detail in Chapter 2.)

The crime charged must also be established by statute beforehand so that all persons are aware of what is illegal before they act. (See the earlier discussion of *ex post facto* laws under "Individual Rights in the Original Constitution.") Finally, the statute must not be so vague or ambiguous that it does not make clear the exact nature of the crime.

The Right to Confrontation of Witnesses The **Confrontation Clause** guarantees accused persons the right to confront hostile witnesses at their criminal trial. This right is designed to promote the truth-finding function of a trial by **"ensur[ing] the reliability of the evidence against a criminal defendant by subjecting it to rigorous testing in the context of an adversary proceeding before the trier of fact."** *Maryland v. Craig*, 497 U.S. 836 (1990). This rigorous testing is accomplished both through the defendant's face-to-face confrontation during the witness's testimony and through the opportunity for **cross-examination**. To accomplish the former goal, the defendant is entitled to be present at all important stages of the criminal trial, unless the right to be present is waived (1) by voluntarily being absent from the courtroom, *Taylor v. United States*, 414 U.S. 17 (1973), or (2) by continually disrupting the proceedings after being warned by the court.

> **It is essential to the proper administration of criminal justice that dignity, order, and decorum be the hallmarks of all court proceedings in our country. The flagrant disregard in the courtroom of elementary standards of proper conduct should not and cannot be tolerated. We believe trial judges confronted with disruptive, contumacious, stubbornly defiant defendants must be given sufficient discretion to meet the circumstances of each case. No one formula for maintaining the appropriate courtroom atmosphere will be best in all situations. We think there are at least three constitutionally permissible ways for a trial judge to handle an obstreperous defendant like Allen: (1) bind and gag him, thereby keeping him present; (2) cite him for contempt; (3) take him out of the courtroom until he promises to conduct himself properly.** *Illinois v. Allen*, 397 U.S. 337, 343-44 (1970).

The defendant's right to the opportunity for cross-examination permits the defendant to test both the witness's credibility and the witness's knowledge of relevant facts of the case:

> **The opportunity for cross-examination . . . is critical for ensuring the integrity of the fact-finding process. Cross-examination is "the principal means by which the believability of a witness and the truth of his testimony are tested." Indeed the Court has recognized that cross-examination is the "greatest legal engine ever invented for the discovery of the truth."** *Kentucky v. Stincer*, 482 U.S. 730, 736 (1987).

Cross-examination is discussed further in Chapter 2.

Like most constitutional rights, the Confrontation Clause has never been interpreted as an absolute bar to the admission of out-of-court testimony. Rather, the Supreme Court interpreted the Confrontation Clause within the context of the centuries-old rules on the admissibility of **hearsay evidence**. Hearsay evidence is defined by Rule 801(c) of the Federal Rules of Evidence as "a statement, other than one made by the declarant while testifying at the trial or hearing, offered in evidence to prove the truth of the matter asserted." This is a fancy way of saying that people may not testify in a judicial proceeding about what they heard someone else say out-of-court if the substance of the other person's out-of-court statement is concerned with what the parties are trying to prove or disprove in court. In general, the Confrontation Clause prohibits the admission of hearsay evidence because the defendant cannot confront an absent declarant.

In *Ohio v. Roberts* , 448 U.S. 56, 66 (1980), the Supreme Court specifically ruled that hearsay evidence posed no Confrontation Clause problem so long as (1) the out-of-court declarant was "unavailable" to testify at trial; and (2) the statement bore some "indicia of reliability." The case went on to explain that hearsay statements that were covered by any of the more than twenty "firmly rooted" exceptions to the hearsay rule were presumptively admissible. Moreover, even those hearsay statements not covered by an applicable hearsay exception could still be admitted into evidence without running afoul of the Confrontation Clause if the statement were somehow demonstrated to have "particularized guarantees of trustworthiness." 448 U.S. at 66. In 2004, however, the Supreme Court reversed itself when *Crawford v. Washington*, 541 U.S. 36 (2004) overruled *Ohio v. Roberts*. The *Crawford* decision interpreted the Confrontation Clause more literally, and more in line with what history suggests the Framers had in mind when they wrote the Sixth Amendment. *Crawford* held any out-of-court statement that was "testimonial" in nature—no matter how reliable it might be—was inadmissible unless the defendant had the opportunity to cross-examine the declarant. 448 U.S. at 68. *Crawford*, therefore, did not implicate nontestimonial out-of-court statements, the admissibility of which continues to be governed by the law of evidence and its rules on hearsay.

> **[The Confrontation Clause] applies to "witnesses" against the accused— in other words, those who "bear testimony." "Testimony," in turn, is typically "[a] solemn declaration or affirmation made for the purpose of establishing or proving some fact." An accuser who makes a formal statement to government officers bears testimony in a sense that a person who makes a casual remark to an acquaintance does not. The constitutional text, like the history underlying the common-law right of confrontation, thus reflects an especially acute concern with a specific type of out-of-court statement.**

Although the *Crawford* Court made it clear that regardless of what the rules of evidence might say about a particular hearsay statement, the Confrontation Clause bars the admission of those statements that are testimonial in nature. The Court, however, did not fully define what it meant by "testimonial." Instead, the Court recognized there were competing notions of what might be considered testimonial, and left the precise meaning of the term open for future consideration. It did specify that "prior testimony at a preliminary hearing, before a grand jury, or at a former trial" were clearly "testimonial" statements, as were statements made during police interrogations. 44 U.S. at 68.

This language created an ambiguity in the law. While prior testimony under oath before a court in a preliminary hearing, a grand jury, or a trial seemed to clearly fit into a common understanding of what is meant by "testimony," which statements made during police interrogations qualify as testimonial was much less clear. The Court clarified this ambiguity in *Davis v. Washington*, 126 S. Ct. 2266 (2006), when it provided the following definition of **testimonial evidence** for Confrontation Clause purposes:

> **Statements are nontestimonial when made in the course of police interrogation under circumstances objectively indicating that the primary purpose of the interrogation is to enable police assistance to meet an ongoing emergency. They are testimonial when the circumstances objectively indicate that [the] primary purpose of the interrogation is to establish or prove past events potentially relevant to later criminal prosecution.** 126 S. Ct. 2273-75.

Thus, under *Crawford* and *Davis*, "initial inquiries" by police at a crime scene are not likely to produce responses that are "testimonial" since police "need to know whom they are dealing with in order to assess the situation, the threat to their own safety, and possible danger to the potential victim." 126 S. Ct. at 2279. Since such statements are not likely to be testimonial, the Confrontation Clause will not bar their admission so long as the requirements of a valid hearsay exception applies. On the other hand, when police question people to investigate a potential crime with the intent of gathering evidence to be used during a criminal prosecution, responses to such police questions will be deemed "testimonial." As such, the Confrontation Clause will bar the admissibility of such statements at trial.

Guarantee of Compulsory Process The Compulsory Process Clause guarantees the defendant's right to compel the attendance of favorable witnesses at trial, usually by means of a court-issued **subpoena.** To obtain **compulsory process,** the defendant must show that a witness's testimony would be relevant, material, favorable to the defendant, and not cumulative. *United States v. Valenzuela-Bernal*, 458 U.S. 858 (1982). Cumulative evidence is evidence tending to prove the same point as evidence already offered, and is generally disallowed because it does little more than contribute to inefficiency. Cumulative evidence should not be confused with corroborating evidence, which supplements or strengthens evidence already presented as proof of a factual matter.

The Right to Representation by Counsel Finally, the Sixth Amendment provides a right to be represented by counsel in all criminal prosecutions that may result in imprisonment. "**[A]bsent a knowing and intelligent waiver, no person may be imprisoned for any offense, whether classified as petty, misdemeanor, or felony unless he was represented by counsel at his trial.**" *Argersinger v. Hamlin*, 407 U.S. 25, 37 (1972). As the quotation implies, by knowingly and intelligently waiving the right to counsel, defendants have the right to conduct their own defense in a criminal case. This is known as a *pro se* defense. "**[I]t is one thing to hold that every defendant, rich or poor, has the right to the assistance of counsel, and quite another to say that a state may compel a defendant to accept a lawyer he does not want.**" *Faretta v. California*, 422 U.S. 806, 832–33 (1975).

The right to counsel attaches at the initiation of adversary judicial criminal proceedings "**whether by way of formal charge, preliminary hearing, indictment, information or arraignment.**" *Kirby v. Illinois*, 406 U.S. 682, 689 (1972). A person is entitled to the assistance of counsel, however, only at a "critical stage" of the prosecution "**where substantial rights of a criminal accused may be affected.**" *Mempa v. Rhay*, 389 U.S. 128, 134 (1967). The U.S. Supreme Court has accorded this right at the following:

▶ Preindictment preliminary hearings and bail hearings, *Coleman v. Alabama*, 399 U.S. 1 (1970).

▶ Postindictment pretrial lineups, *United States v. Wade*, 388 U.S. 218 (1967).

▶ Postindictment interrogations, *Massiah v. United States*, 377 U.S. 201 (1964).

▶ Arraignments, *Hamilton v. Alabama*, 368 U.S. 52 (1961).

▶ Interrogations after arraignment, *Brewer v. Williams*, 430 U.S. 387 (1977).

▶ Felony trials, *Gideon v. Wainwright*, 372 U.S. 335 (1963).

▶ Misdemeanor trials involving a potential jail sentence, *Argersinger v. Hamlin*, 407 U.S. 25 (1972).

▶ First appeals as a matter of right, *Douglas v. California*, 372 U.S. 353 (1963).

▶ Juvenile delinquency proceedings involving potential confinement, *In re Gault*, 387 U.S. 1 (1967).

▶ Sentencing hearings, *Mempa v. Rhay*, 389 U.S. 128 (1967).

▶ Hearings regarding psychiatric examinations, *Estelle v. Smith*, 451 U.S. 454 (1981).

Separate and apart from the Sixth Amendment right to counsel, prior to the initiation of adversary judicial criminal proceedings, a person has a Fifth Amendment right to counsel during custodial interrogation under *Miranda v. Arizona*, 384 U.S. 436 (1966) (see Chapter 13).

For many years, courts interpreted the guarantee of representation by counsel to mean only that defendants had a right to be represented by a lawyer if they could afford to hire one. In the 1930s, however, the U.S. Supreme Court began to vastly expand the class of persons entitled to the right to counsel in preparing and presenting a defense. *Powell v. Alabama*, 287 U.S. 45 (1932) held that the right to counsel was so fundamental that the Due Process Clause of the Fourteenth Amendment required states to provide all defendants charged with capital crimes with the effective aid of counsel. Six years later, *Johnson v. Zerbst*, 304 U.S. 458 (1938) held that the Sixth Amendment required all federal defendants to be provided legal counsel for their defense, unless the right to counsel was properly waived. That decision raised the question of whether the constraint on the federal courts expressed a rule so fundamental and essential to a fair trial—and thus to due process of law—that it was made obligatory on the states by the Fourteenth Amendment. The Supreme Court said no in *Betts v. Brady*, 316 U.S. 455 (1942), holding that **"while want of counsel in a particular case may result in a conviction lacking in such fundamental fairness, we cannot say that the amendment embodies an inexorable command that no trial for any offense, or in any court, can be fairly conducted and justice accorded a defendant who is not represented by counsel."** 316 U.S. at 473.

Twenty-one years after deciding *Betts* the Court changed its mind, recognizing that **"lawyers in criminal courts are necessities, not luxuries."** In *Gideon v. Wainwright*, 372 U.S. 335 (1963), the Supreme Court overruled *Betts*. The Court now held that the Sixth Amendment imposed an affirmative obligation on the part of the federal and state governments to provide at public expense legal counsel for those who could not afford it, in order to have all defendants' cases adequately presented in courts of law. In addition, indigent persons were given the right to a free copy of their trial transcripts for purposes of appealing their convictions. *Griffin v. Illinois*, 351 U.S. 12 (1956).

The Sixth Amendment right to counsel is a right to the *effective assistance of counsel*. **"The very premise of our adversary system of criminal justice is that partisan advocacy on both sides of a case will promote the ultimate objective that the guilty be convicted and the innocent go free."** *Herring v. New York*, 422 U.S. 853, 862 (1975). The absence of effective counsel undermines faith in the proper functioning of the adversarial process. In *Strickland v. Washington*, 466 U.S. 668 (1984), the Court held that to establish a claim of ineffective assistance of counsel, a defendant must show (1) that counsel's representation fell below an objective standard of reasonableness; and (2) that there is a reasonable probability that, but for counsel's unprofessional errors, the result of the proceeding would have been different. A reasonable probability is one sufficient to undermine confidence in the trial's outcome. In *Lockhart v. Fretwell*, 506 U.S. 364 (1993), the Court refined the *Strickland* test to require that not only would a different trial result be probable because of attorney performance but that the actual trial result was fundamentally unfair or unreliable.

Amendment VII

> *In suits at common law, where the value in controversy shall exceed twenty dollars, the right of trial by jury shall be preserved, and no fact tried by a jury, shall be otherwise re-examined in any Court of the United States, than according to the rules of the common law.*

The Seventh Amendment applies only to federal civil trials and not to civil suits in state courts. Except as provided by local federal court rules, if a case is brought in a federal court and a money judgment is sought that exceeds twenty dollars, the party bringing the suit and the defendant are entitled to have the controversy decided by the unanimous verdict of a jury of twelve people.

Amendment VIII

> *Excessive bail shall not be required, nor excessive fines imposed, nor cruel and unusual punishments inflicted.*

The Right to Bail Bail has traditionally meant the money or property pledged to the court or actually deposited for the release from custody of an arrested or imprisoned person as a guarantee of that person's appearance in court at a specified date and time. Accused persons who are released from custody and subsequently fail to appear for trial forfeit their bail to the court.

The Eighth Amendment does not specifically provide that all citizens have a right to bail but only that bail may not be excessive. A right to bail has, however, been recognized in common law and in statute since 1789. Excessive bail was defined in *Stack v. Boyle*, 342 U.S. 1, 4-5 (1951):

> **From the passage of the Judiciary Act of 1789 . . . to the present . . . federal law has unequivocally provided that a person arrested for a noncapital offense shall be admitted to bail. This traditional right to freedom before conviction permits the unhampered preparation of a defense, and serves to prevent the infliction of punishment prior to conviction. . . . Unless this right to bail before trial is preserved, the presumption of innocence, secured only after centuries of struggle, would lose its meaning.**
>
> **The right to release before trial is conditioned upon the accused's giving adequate assurance that he will stand trial and submit to sentence if found guilty. . . . Like the ancient practice of securing the oaths of responsible persons to stand as sureties for the accused, the modern practice of requiring a bail bond or the deposit of a sum of money subject to forfeiture serves as additional assurance of the presence of an accused. *Bail set at a figure higher than an amount reasonably calculated to fulfill this purpose is "excessive" under the Eighth Amendment* (emphasis added).**

The excessive bail clause "has been assumed" to be applicable to the states through the Fourteenth Amendment. *Schilb v. Kuebel*, 404 U.S. 357 (1971).

Under many state constitutions, when a capital offense such as murder is charged, bail may be denied altogether if **"the proof is evident or the presumption great."**

In 1966, Congress enacted the Bail Reform Act to provide for pretrial release of persons accused of noncapital federal crimes. Congress sought to end pretrial imprisonment of indigent defendants who could not afford to post money bail and who were, in effect, confined only because of their poverty. The act also discouraged the traditional use of money bail by requiring the judge to seek other means as likely to ensure that the defendant would appear when the trial was held.

The Bail Reform Act of 1984 substantially changed the 1966 act to allow an authorized judicial officer to impose conditions of release to ensure community safety. This change marked a significant departure from the basic philosophy of the 1966 act: namely, that the only purpose of bail laws was to ensure the defendant's appearance at judicial proceedings. The 1984 act also expanded appellate review and eliminated the presumption in favor of bail pending appeal. Most significantly, however, the 1984 act allowed an authorized judicial officer to detain an arrested person pending trial if the government could demonstrate by clear and convincing evidence after an adversary hearing that no release conditions **"will reasonably assure . . . the safety of any other person and the community."** In *United States v. Salerno*, 481 U.S. 739 (1987), the U.S. Supreme Court held that pretrial detention under the act, based solely on risk of danger to the community, did not violate due process or the Eighth Amendment.

Freedom from Cruel and Unusual Punishment The prohibition against the infliction of **cruel and unusual punishment** is concerned with punishments imposed after a formal adjudication of guilt. The prohibition is applicable to the states through the Due Process Clause of the Fourteenth Amendment. *Robinson v. California*, 370 U.S. 660 (1962). The Cruel and Unusual Punishment Clause of the Eighth Amendment limits the punishment that may be imposed on conviction of a crime in two ways.

First, the clause **"imposes substantive limits on what can be made criminal and punished as such."** *Ingraham v. Wright*, 430 U.S. 651, 667 (1977). For example, a statute making the condition or status of narcotics addiction a crime was held unconstitutional because it imposed punishment of personal characteristics rather than illegal acts. *Robinson v. California*, 370 U.S. 660 (1962). Similarly, a person may not be punished in retaliation for exercising a constitutional right. *United States v. Heubel*, 864 F.2d 1104 (3d Cir. 1988).

Second, the Cruel and Unusual Punishment Clause proscribes certain kinds of punishment, such as torture and divestiture of citizenship. It does not, however, prohibit capital punishment in and of itself. *Gregg v. Georgia*, 428 U.S. 153 (1976). However, particular modes of capital punishment may be unconstitutional if they violate **"evolving standards of decency that mark the progress of a maturing society."** *Trop v. Dulles*, 356 U.S. 86, 101 (1958). Under such a standard, the Court has invalidated the death penalty under following circumstances:

▶ Statutes that give the juries complete sentencing discretion that may result in the arbitrary or capricious imposition of death sentences are cruel and unusual. *Furman v. Georgia*, 408 U.S. 238 (1972).

▶ Mandatory death statutes that leave the jury or trial judge no discretion to consider individual defendants and their crime are cruel and unusual. *Woodson v. North Carolina*, 428 U.S. 280 (1976).

▶ Execution of someone who is incompetent or insane at the time of his execution is cruel and unusual. *Ford v. Wainwright*, 477 U.S. 399 (1986).

▶ The execution of the mentally retarded is cruel and unusual punishment. *Atkins v. Virginia*, 536 U.S. 304 (2002).

▶ The execution of offenders who were under the age of eighteen when their crimes were committed is cruel and unusual. *Roper v. Simmons*, 543 U.S. 551 (2005).

Under certain circumstances, the Cruel and Unusual Punishment Clause limits the criminal sanction by prohibiting punishment that is excessive in relation to the crime committed. This limitation is referred to as the principle of **proportionality**. In short, this is the embodiment of the notion that the punishment should "fit the crime."[1]

In *Weems v. United States*, 217 U.S. 349 (1910), the U.S. Supreme Court first signaled that the principle of proportionality was a part of Eighth Amendment jurisprudence. In this case, the defendant was convicted of falsifying a cash book for a small amount of money. He was sentenced to a fine and fifteen years of punishment called a "cadena temporal"—imprisonment in shackles at the ankles and hands while being forced to perform hard labor. The Supreme Court sided with Mr. Weems, finding his sentence was disproportionately lengthy in light of the offense he committed—and, further, that it was **"cruel and unusual because of its harsh and oppressive nature."** Decades later, however, in *Rummel v. Estelle*, 445 U.S. 263 (1980), the Court explained that it was not the length of Weems's incarceration that rendered his sentence violative of the Eighth Amendment, but rather it was the "unique nature" of the cadena punishment that was cruel and unusual.

In *Gregg v. Georgia*, 428 U.S. 153 (1976), the Supreme Court made it clear "that excessiveness alone, without regard to the barbaric nature of the punishment, was sufficient to invalidate a sentence" (Grossman 1995: 113). In the year after the *Gregg* decision, the Court decided *Coker v. Georgia*. It held that the death penalty for the crime of rape was unconstitutionally cruel and unusual punishment in light of the disproportionate nature of the offense to the punishment, again signaling that the excessiveness of a sentence was in and of itself a sufficient basis to render a criminal sanction unconstitutional. The *Rummel* Court, however, dismissed both of these decisions as being "'of limited assistance' in deciding the constitutionality of terms of imprisonment" because they involved sentences of death, not imprisonment (Grossman 1995: 113).

The dismissive approach the Supreme Court took in *Rummel* toward the principle of proportionality was further solidified in *Hutto v. Davis*. In Virginia, the defendant was sentenced to forty years in prison and a fine of $20,000 for possession with intent to distribute nine ounces of marijuana. In upholding the sentence, the Supreme Court reiterated its pronouncement in *Rummel* that the

---

[1] The material on the doctrine of proportionality is taken from the following source: Fradella, Henry F. 2006. "Mixed Signals and Muddied Waters: Making Sense of the Proportionality Principle and the Eighth Amendment." *Criminal Law Bulletin, 42(4)*: 498–503. Used by the gracious permission of Thomson/West and the *Criminal Law Bulletin*.

cases requiring an Eighth Amendment proportionality analysis were limited to death penalty cases; any "assessment of the excessiveness of a prison term was inherently subjective and therefore 'purely a matter of legislative prerogative.'" (Grossman 1995: 122, citing *Hutto*, 454 U.S. at 373 and quoting *Rummel*, 445 U.S. at 274).

Surprisingly, the Supreme Court breathed new life into the principle of proportionality just six years after deciding *Hutto* when it rendered its decision in *Solem v. Helm*, 463 U.S. 277 (1983). The defendant had been convicted of offering a forged check, a felony under applicable state law that carried a maximum penalty of five years incarceration and a $5,000 fine. But the defendant already had three prior felony convictions, so he was sentenced under a recidivist statute ("three strikes") to life in prison without the possibility of parole. The Court vacated the defendant's sentence as being excessive and, therefore, unconstitutional under the Eighth Amendment's Cruel and Unusual Punishment Clause. In doing so, it set forth three factors to guide courts when wrestling with questions of proportionality: (1) the proportionality between the severity of the crime and the severity of the sentence; (2) the proportionality of sentence imposed in other jurisdictions for the crime at issue in a case; and (3) the proportionality of the sentence imposed in the jurisdiction at issue in the given case on other criminals who commit similar or more serious crimes. 463 U.S. at 291-92. When weighing these factors, the *Solem* Court noted that "there are generally accepted criteria for comparing the severity of different crimes." 463 U.S. at 294. These criteria reflect back to utilitarian ideals such as the "harm caused or threatened to the victim or society" and the relative culpability of the defendant in terms of his or her level of mens rea. 463 U.S. at 292-94. Decisions of the Supreme Court after *Solem*, however, have cast serious doubt on the validity of these factors in proportionality challenges, even though *Solem* has not yet been expressly overruled.

The decisions of the Supreme Court discussed above sent "a mixed and confusing message with respect to . . . the requirement of proportional sentencing" (Grossman, 1995: 141). This confusion led the Court to issue another pronouncement on the role of the proportionality principle in Eighth Amendment jurisprudence in *Harmelin v. Michigan*, 501 U.S. 957 (1991). The defendant in *Harmelin* was convicted of possession of 672 grams of cocaine. Under Michigan law, anyone possessing more than 650 grams of cocaine received a mandatory sentence of life in prison without the possibility of parole. The highly fractured Court appeared to agree on very little. A majority of five justices agreed the sentence was not disproportionate to the offense, so they affirmed his sentence. But two justices—Chief Justice Rehnquist and Justice Scalia—wrote a concurring opinion to emphasize their view that the Cruel and Unusual Punishment Clause contains no guarantee of proportional punishment. Justice Thomas later echoed their views when he wrote in *Ewing v. California*, 539 U.S. 11, 32 (2003) "that the proportionality test announced in *Solem v. Helm* . . . is incapable of judicial application," and that "the Cruel and Unusual Punishments Clause of the Eighth Amendment contains no proportionality principle."

Since the Court's decision in *Harmelin*, most proportionality-based appeals have failed. It appears the lower courts have embraced Justice Kennedy's conclusion regarding the proportionality principle in his concurring opinion in *Harmelin*: **"The Eighth Amendment does not require strict proportionality between crime and sentence. Rather, it forbids only extreme sentences that are 'grossly disproportionate' to the crime."** 501 U.S. at 1001. The Supreme

Discussion

POINT

What Is the Appropriate Punishment?

In *Coker v. Georgia*, 433 U.S. 584, 585 (1977), the Supreme Court held that the death penalty was a disproportionate penalty for the crime of rape of an adult woman. "Although rape deserves serious punishment, the death penalty, which is unique in its severity and irrevocability, is an excessive penalty for the rapist who, as such and as opposed to the murderer, does not take human life." In *State v. Bethley*, 685 So. 2d. 1063 (La. 1996), *cert. denied*, 520 U.S. 1259 (1997), an HIV-positive defendant raped his daughter and two of her friends. All three girls were under the age of ten at the time of the rapes. Louisiana sought the death penalty against Bethley. The trial court quashed the indictment on the grounds that such a sentence would be unconstitutional under *Coker.* The prosecution appealed and the state supreme court upheld the constitutionality of the Louisiana law that made the rape of a child under the age of twelve a capital offense. The court distinguished the crime from the one at issue in *Coker* on the basis that the aggravated rape of child was a more severe offense than the rape of an adult. The court reasoned that "given the appalling nature of the crime, the severity of the harm inflicted upon the victim, and the harm imposed on society, the death penalty is not an excessive penalty for the crime of rape when the victim is a child under the age of twelve years old." 685 So. 2d at 1070.

Do you agree with the holding in the case? Why or why not?

Court cited Justice Kennedy's concurrence in *Harmelin* favorably in its two most recent pronouncements on proportionality. In *Ewing v. California*, 539 U.S. 11, 32 (2003), the Court upheld California's "three strikes and you're out" sentencing scheme. The defendant in that case had been sentenced to life in prison for having shoplifted three golf clubs valued at approximately $1,200. He had several prior misdemeanor and felony convictions, including one for robbery and three for residential burglary, which served as the triggering crimes for application of the three strikes rule. In affirming his sentence, the Court found Ewing's life sentence was not unconstitutionally disproportionate to the theft, but rather that it reflected "a rational legislative judgment, entitled to deference, that offenders who have committed serious or violent felonies and who continue to commit felonies must be incapacitated." Using the same logic, the Court reached an identical result in *Lockyer v. Andrade*, 538 U.S. 63, 72 (2003), in which it upheld two consecutive life sentences under California's three-strikes law for a defendant who had stolen approximately $150 worth of videotapes. Thus, it appears that the principle of proportionality has little relevance today to Eighth Amendment jurisprudence other than in death penalty cases.

Amendment IX

> *The enumeration in the Constitution, of certain rights, shall not be construed to deny or disparage others retained by the people.*

The Ninth Amendment emphasizes the Framers' view that powers of government are limited by the rights of the people. The Constitution did not intend, by expressly guaranteeing certain rights of the people, to grant the government unlimited power to invade other rights of the people.

The Supreme Court has on at least one occasion suggested that this amendment is a justification for recognizing certain rights not specifically mentioned in the Constitution or for broadly interpreting those that are. The case involving the Ninth Amendment was *Griswold v. Connecticut*, 381 U.S. 479 (1965), in which a statute prohibiting the use of contraceptives was voided as an infringement of the right of marital privacy. At issue was whether the right to privacy was a constitutional right and, if so, whether the right was one reserved to the people under the Ninth Amendment or only derived from other rights specifically mentioned in the Constitution.

Courts have long recognized particular rights to privacy that are part of the First and Fourth Amendments. As the Court in *Griswold* said, the **"specific guarantees in the Bill of Rights have penumbras, formed by emanations from those guarantees that help give them life and substance."** 381 U.S. at 484. Thus, freedom of expression guarantees freedom of association and the related right to be silent and free from official inquiry into such associations. It also includes the right not to be intimidated by government for the expression of one's views. The Fourth Amendment's guarantee against unreasonable search and seizure confers a right to privacy because its safeguards prohibit unauthorized entry onto one's property and tampering with one's person, property, or possessions.

The Court in *Griswold* ruled that the Third and Fifth Amendments, in addition to the First and Fourth, created "zones of privacy" safe from governmental intrusion and, without resting its decision on any one of these or on the Ninth Amendment itself, simply held that the right of privacy was guaranteed by the Constitution.

Amendment X

> *The powers not delegated to the United States by the Constitution, nor prohibited by it to the States, are reserved to the States respectively, or to the people.*

The Tenth Amendment embodies the principle of federalism, which reserves for the states the remainder of powers not granted to the federal government or expressly withheld from the states.

►LATER AMENDMENTS DEALING WITH INDIVIDUAL RIGHTS AND LIBERTIES

Amendment XIII

> *Section 1. Neither slavery nor involuntary servitude, except as a punishment for crime whereof the party shall have been duly convicted, shall exist within the United States, or any place subject to their jurisdiction.*

> *Section 2. Congress shall have power to enforce this article by appropriate legislation.*

The Thirteenth Amendment prohibits slavery in the United States. It has also been interpreted to prohibit certain state laws that had the effect of jailing debtors who did not perform their financial obligations. The Supreme Court has ruled that the Thirteenth Amendment does not prohibit selective service laws, which authorize the draft for military duty.

Courts have also justified certain civil rights legislation that condemned purely private acts of discrimination but that did not constitute "state action" on the basis of the authority granted in Section 2 of this amendment and Section 5 of the Fourteenth Amendment, which is similar. An example is the civil rights legislation of 1866 and 1964 designed to end discrimination in the sale or rental of real or personal property. These discriminatory practices were seen as "badges of servitude," which the Thirteenth Amendment was intended to abolish.

Amendment XIV

> *Section 1. All persons born or naturalized in the United States, and subject to the jurisdiction thereof, are citizens of the United States and of the State wherein they reside. No State shall make or enforce any law which shall abridge the privileges or immunities of citizens of the United States; nor shall any State deprive any person of life, liberty, or property, without due process of law; nor deny to any person within its jurisdiction the equal protection of the laws. . . .*
>
> *Section 5. The Congress shall have power to enforce, by appropriate legislation, the provisions of this article.*

The Right to Due Process As discussed above, the Fifth Amendment contains a Due Process Clause that applies to actions of the federal government. The Fourteenth Amendment's Due Process Clause limits the states from infringing on the rights of individuals. Through judicial interpretation of the phrase "due process of law" in the Fourteenth Amendment, many of the Bill of Rights guarantees have been made applicable to actions by state governments and their subdivisions, such as counties, municipalities, and cities. Under this principle, certain rights and freedoms are deemed so basic to the people in a free and democratic society that state governments may not violate them, even though states are not specifically barred from doing so by the Constitution. (See the discussion of incorporation of guarantees in the Bill of Rights, through the Due Process Clause of the Fourteenth Amendment, in this chapter under "The Bill of Rights.") In determining whether state action violates the Due Process Clause, a court considers:

> **First, the private interest that will be affected by the official action; second, the risk of an erroneous deprivation of such interest through the procedures used, and the probable value, if any, of additional or substitute procedural safeguards; and finally, the Government's interest, including the function involved and the fiscal and administrative burdens that the additional or substitute procedural requirement would entail.** *Mathews v. Eldridge,* 424 U.S. 319, 335 (1976).

The concept of due process under law is explored in greater detail throughout this book.

The Right to Equal Protection of the Laws In addition to guaranteeing due process, the Fourteenth Amendment also prohibits the denial of the **equal protection of the laws**. This requirement prevents any state from making unreasonable, arbitrary distinctions between different persons as to their rights and privileges. If a law does not discriminate in any way, but rather applies evenly to all people, the mandates of equal protection are satisfied. However, if a law treats different classifications of people differently even though the people are similarly situated (*e.g.*, they are in similar circumstances under similar conditions), then the law might run afoul of the Constitution's guarantee of equal protection. Because so many laws have historically denied women and minorities the same rights and privileges that were guaranteed or extended to others, Section 5 of the Fourteenth Amendment provided the authority for Congress to address this history of inequality by enacting much of the civil rights legislation passed by Congress in the 1960s. Section 5 remains the source of constitutional authority for anti-discrimination legislation enacted today.

Analyzing a classification in the law that treats different classes of people differently is a multi-step process. First, a court must examine the type of distinction that the law makes in order to determine the **standard of review** to be applied in the case. Figure 1.1 summarizes the three standards of review used in equal protection litigation, and the next section of the text explains these standards of review in detail. Then the court must determine if the distinctions made in the law are "similarly situated" with respect to their circumstances and conditions under the law. If the groups are not similarly situated, then the constitutional line of inquiry ends, since groups that are not similarly situated do not have be treated in a similar manner. Only if the groups are found to be similarly situated do courts have to analyze the classifications at issue in the law under the relevant standard of review.

Strict Scrutiny for Laws Making Suspect Classifications and/or Burdening Fundamental Rights **Strict scrutiny** is the most exacting level of judicial review. The formal test for strict scrutiny is whether a law is narrowly tailored to achieve a compelling governmental interest. If the government does not have a "compelling" reason for justifying a law's failure to treat similarly situated people in a similar manner, then the law will be declared unconstitutional under this test. Even if the government has such a "compelling" governmental interest, if there were other ways of achieving its goals without burdening the right to equal protection, then the law will also fail strict scrutiny review.

Strict scrutiny under the Equal Protection Clause applies only to laws that make classifications based on suspect classifications or those that burden fundamental rights. Race, religion, and national origin have all been held to be **suspect classifications.** Courts will presume that laws that treat suspect classes differently than the way other people are treated are unconstitutional unless the government can prove that the differential treatment under the law is narrowly tailored to achieve a compelling governmental interest. Using such strict scrutiny, courts have struck down racial segregation in public schools and other public places, *Brown v. Bd. of Educ.*, 347 U.S. 483 (1954), and laws that prohibit the sale or use of property to certain races or minority groups, *e.g., Reitman v. Mulkey*, 387 U.S. 369 (1967). Furthermore, the Supreme Court has held that purely private acts of discrimination can be in violation of the equal protection clause if they are customarily enforced throughout the state, whether or

Standard of Review	When Used	Test	Usual Outcome
Strict Scrutiny	• Fundamental Rights (speech, privacy, voting, religion, running for office, access to courts, interstate travel) • Suspect Classifications (race, religion, national origin)	• Compelling Governmental Interest 2. Narrowly tailored means the law must be used to achieve the ends identified as the compelling governmental interest.	Law is presumed unconstitutional unless government can prove it has a compelling governmental interest that cannot be achieved in a less restrictive way.
Intermediate Scrutiny	Quasi-Suspect Classifications (gender and illegitimacy)	• Important Governmental Interest 2. Substantially related means to achieving ends	No presumption.
Rational Basis Test	For everything else	• Legitimate Governmental Interest • Rational connection between means (the law) and ends (the identified legitimate governmental interest)	Law is presumed constitutional unless the challenger to the law can show no legitimate governmental interest, or show irrational basis for how the law achieves the stated ends.

▶**Figure 1.1** **STANDARDS OF JUDICIAL REVIEW FOR EQUAL PROTECTION CLAUSE LITIGATION**

not there is a specific law or other explicit manifestation of action by the state. *Shelley v. Kraemer*, 334 U.S. 1 (1948).

Strict scrutiny is also used when a law makes distinctions among people with regard to a fundamental right. **Fundamental rights** are those rights that are "implicit in the concept of ordered liberty," *Palko v. Connecticut*, 302 U.S. 319, 325 (1937)—that is, fundamental to American notions of liberty and justice. These include the freedom of speech, the freedom of religion, the freedom to travel, the right to access the courts, and the right to vote. In fact, courts have interpreted the Equal Protection Clause to mean that a citizen may not arbitrarily be deprived of the right to vote and that every citizen's vote must be given equal weight to the extent possible. Thus, the Supreme Court held that state legislatures and local governments must be strictly apportioned in terms of their populations in such a way as to accord one person one vote. *E.g., Reynolds v. Sims*, 377 U.S. 533 (1964). There are also a select group of fundamental rights that are not explicitly provided for in the text of the Constitution, but are strongly implied therein, and thus are considered "fundamental." These include the right to marry, *Loving v. Virginia*, 388 U.S. 1 (1967), and the right to privacy, *Griswold v. Connecticut*, 381 U.S. 479 (1965).

Intermediate Scrutiny for Quasi-Suspect Classifications **Intermediate scrutiny** asks if the governmental classifications at issue in a case are substantially related to achieving an important governmental interest. This intermediate level of judicial scrutiny is used only when a law makes a distinction using what the Supreme Court has held to be **quasi-suspect classifications.** Gender and illegitimacy are the only classifications that the Supreme Court has determined to be quasi-suspect classifications. For an example of a case applying intermediate scrutiny, see the Discussion Point on statutory rape laws, on page 48.

Rational Basis Test for Everything Else   The **rational basis test** asks if the governmental classification at issue is rationally related to a legitimate governmental interest. It is a highly deferential standard of review that presumes the constitutional validity of all types of distinctions made in laws that do not involve suspect or quasi-suspect classifications, and/or laws that do not burden any fundamental rights. The person challenging a legislative classification that does not burden a fundamental right or a protected class bears a difficult burden: proving that there is no rational basis for the distinction in the law; or alternatively, that the law bears no reasonable relationship to any legitimate governmental interest.

For example, in 1982, Alaska experimented with legalizing marijuana by allowing adults over the age of nineteen to possess less than four ounces of the drug. Possession of marijuana remained illegal for minors who could be charged through the juvenile justice system for violating the law. The law, however, criminalized possession of marijuana by eighteen-year-olds, even though they were no longer minors. In *Allam v. State*, 830 P.2d 435 (Alaska App. 1992), the validity of a state's possession law was challenged by an eighteen-year-old who was caught in possession of a small amount of the substance. He argued that the law illegally discriminated on the basis of age because all adults in the state could possess small quantities of the drug except for those who were eighteen years of age. Because age is neither a suspect classification nor a quasi-suspect classification, and because possession of marijuana is not a fundamental right, the court applied the rational basis test to review the constitutionality of the law. Applying that test, the court upheld the age-based classification, finding that the state had two rational bases to discriminate against eighteen-year-olds. First, many eighteen-year-olds are in high school, where they would be able to share marijuana with underage minors. Second, eighteen-year-olds are still relatively inexperienced drivers; giving them an extra year to mature before allowing them access to a drug was a "rational" legislative judgment.

Amendments Protecting Voting Rights

Amendment XV

Section 1. The right of citizens of the United States to vote shall not be denied or abridged by the United States or by any State on account of race, color, or previous condition of servitude.

Section 2. The Congress shall have power to enforce this article by appropriate legislation.

Amendment XIX

Section 1. The right of citizens of the United States to vote shall not be denied or abridged by the United States or by any State on account of sex.

Section 2. Congress shall have power to enforce this article by appropriate legislation.

Discussion POINT

Do Gender-Specific Statutory Rape Laws Violate the Equal Protection Clause?

Michael M. v. Superior Ct. of Sonoma County, Cal., 450 U.S. 464 (1981)

In the early 1980s, California's statutory rape law mirrored the centuries-old Common Law definition of the crime, defining statutory rape as "an act of sexual intercourse accomplished with a female not the wife of the perpetrator, where the female is under the age of 18 years." 450 U.S. at 466. Thus, the statute only criminalized the statutory rape of an underage female by a male; it did not criminalize the statutory rape of an underage male by a female.

Michael M. was seventeen and a half years old when he had sexual intercourse with a sixteen-and-a-half-year-old girl. He was charged with statutory rape, and sought to have the case dismissed on equal protection grounds. Specifically, Michael M. claimed that the law unconstitutionally discriminated on the basis of sex because only males were punished under the statutory rape law. The Supreme Court disagreed, determining that the sexes were not similarly situated with respect to the underlying purpose of the law: to prevent illegitimate teenage pregnancies. The Court accepted this purpose as being an important governmental interest. It reasoned that is "hardly unreasonable for a legislature acting to protect minor females to exclude them from punishment" because "young men and young women are not similarly situated with respect to the problems and the risks of sexual intercourse. Only women may become pregnant, and they suffer disproportionately the profound physical, emotional, and psychological consequences of sexual activity." 450 U.S. at 471. Since no "similar natural sanctions deter males," the Court concluded that a "criminal sanction imposed solely on males thus serves to roughly 'equalize' the deterrents on the sexes." 450 U.S. at 473.

Do you agree with the outcome of the *Michael M.* case? Why or why not? What do you think most feminists would say about the Supreme Court's reasoning? Why?

Today, many states have abandoned this gender-specific approach to statutory rape. They impose criminal liability to males and females alike. Indeed, several notable cases have highlighted situations in which female high school teachers have taken sexual advantage of their underage male students (Levine 2006). When these women are convicted of statutory rape, however, they tend to receive significantly more lenient sentences than when a male statutorily rapes a female. Many researchers in psychology have documented what these light sentences seem to intuitively tell us—namely, that we appear to have a double standard for what is acceptable intergenerationally (Dollar et al. 2004; Quas et al. 2002; Broussard et al. 1991). One of these researchers concluded that people see "sexual interaction between a fifteen-year-old male and a thirty-five-year-old female [as] an acceptable means of providing sex education for boys" (Broussard 275). What do you make of these findings? What, if anything, does this say about societal notions regarding statutory rape and sex between teenagers and people who are significantly older than they are?

Amendment XXVI

Section 1. The right of citizens of the United States, who are eighteen years or older, to vote shall not be denied or abridged by the United States or any State on account of age.

Section 2. The Congress shall have power to enforce this article by appropriate legislation.

Together, these three amendments ensure the right to vote. This is the keystone of our democratic society, and may not be denied any citizen over the age of eighteen because of race, color, previous condition of servitude, or gender. The Twenty-sixth Amendment, which lowered the voting age for all elections from twenty-one to eighteen years of age, became law on July 1, 1971. These amendments, together with the Fifth and Fourteenth, prohibit any arbitrary attempt to disenfranchise any American citizen.

Amendment XXIV

Section 1. The right of citizens of the United States to vote in any primary or other election for President or Vice President, for electors for President or Vice President, or for Senator or Representative in Congress, shall not be denied or abridged by the United States or any State by reason of failure to pay any poll tax or other tax.

Section 2. The Congress shall have power to enforce this article by appropriate legislation.

The Twenty-fourth Amendment prohibits denial of the right to vote for federal officials because a person has not paid a tax. This amendment was designed to abolish the requirement of a poll tax, which, at the time of its ratification, five states imposed as a condition to voting. The Supreme Court subsequently held that poll taxes were unconstitutional under the Equal Protection Clause of the Fourteenth Amendment on the basis that the right to vote should not be conditioned on one's ability to pay a tax. Accordingly, poll taxes in any election, state or federal, are prohibited.

▶CONCLUSION

In addition to the specific constitutional rights outlined in this chapter, certain safeguards for the individual are inherent in the structure of American government. The separation of powers among legislative, executive, and judicial branches of government is the basis for a system of checks and balances—which prevents excessive concentration of power, with its inevitable threat to individual liberties. With respect to legislative power itself, the existence of two houses of Congress—each chosen by a different process—is itself a protection against ill-advised laws that might threaten constitutional rights. Similarly, our federal system, which divides authority between the national government and the various state governments, has provided a fertile soil for the nourishment of constitutional rights.

No matter how well a constitution may be written, the rights it guarantees have little meaning unless there is popular support for those rights and that constitution. Fortunately, that support has historically existed in the United States. Indeed, in this country the most fundamental protection of personal liberty rests in the well-established American traditions of constitutional government, obedience to the rule of law, and respect for the individual. These traditions provide the groundwork for the entire body of law dealing with criminal procedure and should be foremost in the minds of students of and participants in the American criminal justice system. The remainder of this book shows how the criminal justice system operates to achieve a balance between the protection of individual rights guaranteed by the Constitution and the maintenance of the rule of law and public order in our society.

Key Terms

administrative law, 10
bail, 38
bill of attainder, 16
Bill of Rights, 11
civil rights, 14
collateral estoppel doctrine, 29
common law, 7, 10
compulsory process, 36
Confrontation Clause, 33
constitutional law, 10
Crime Control Model, 4
cross-examination, 34
cruel and unusual punishment, 39
defamation, 19
double jeopardy, 28

dual sovereignty doctrine, 29
Due Process Model, 4
due process of law, 30
due process revolution, 5
effective assistance of counsel, 37
eminent domain, 32
equal protection of law, 31, 45
Establishment Clause, 22
ex post facto, 16
felony, 28
fighting words, 20
Free Exercise Clause, 23
fundamental rights, 46
habeas corpus, 15

hearsay evidence, 34
immunity, 30
intermediate scrutiny, 46
judicial review, 10
obscene, 20
probable cause, 27
procedural due process, 31
proportionality, 40
quasi-suspect classifications, 47
rational basis test, 47
selective incorporation, 12
standard of review, 45
statutory law, 10
strict scrutiny, 45

subpoena, 36
substantive due process, 31
Supremacy Clause, 10
suspect classifications, 45
symbolic speech, 17
testimonial communications, 29
testimonial evidence, 35
time, place, and manner regulation of speech, 19
total incorporation, 12
treason, 17
USA PATRIOT Act, 6
warrant, 27

Review and Discussion Questions

1. How has the Constitution been able to remain a durable and viable instrument of government despite the enormous changes that have occurred in our society since its adoption? Discuss this issue in terms of specific changes.

2. Discuss generally the most important roles and functions under the Constitution of each of the following: the three branches of the federal government; the state governments; the average citizen; and the law enforcement officer. Explain the interrelationships among some of those roles and functions.

3. The Constitution speaks predominantly in terms of the protection of individual rights from governmental abuse or abridgment. What corresponding obligations and burdens must each citizen undertake or bear to ensure that everyone remains free to exercise these rights to their full extent?

4. Discuss the nature of First Amendment liberties and the restraints on them that are constitutionally permissible to the public at large. What additional restraints on First Amendment liberties may be placed on students, military personnel, or correctional inmates?

5. Name three constitutional sources for the protection of the right to privacy, and explain how they differ.

6. A state legislature passes a law requiring all bookstores that have, in the last six months, sold or advertised for sale pictures of the Pope to be closed down and their owners immediately arrested and jailed. What provisions of the Constitution might be violated by this law?

7. Because of religious beliefs, a terminally ill cancer patient wishes to refuse medical treatment and die a "natural" death. Can that person be required under state law to undergo treatment? What if the wish to die is not based on a religious belief, but the person is a minor or is mentally incompetent? What if the cancer was caused by exposure to radiation and the person wishes his or her death to be a political statement on the dangers of nuclear power and nuclear war?

8. A journalist is being compelled to reveal a confidential source of information, but the source would be useful to the government in a criminal investigation, or helpful to a criminal defendant at trial. What constitutional issues are involved? Should the government be able to obtain a search warrant to look into files, audit tapes, or view films that are in the possession of the news media to find evidence of crime?

9. Should members of the news media have greater access than the general public to court proceedings and court records? What about greater access to prisons to interview prisoners? What about greater access to police investigative files?

10. Would the Fifth Amendment privilege against self-incrimination prohibit the government from any of the following: requiring all participants in a lineup to speak certain words; requiring a person to produce income tax records; threatening a person with a reduction in pay in his government job if he does not make incriminating testimonial admissions about a matter not related to his job?

11. What are the similarities and differences between due process of law and equal protection of the laws?

12. What are the three standards of review in equal protection litigation? When are they used?

13. Are the Fifth and Sixth Amendments violated by the provisions of the USA PATRIOT Act that permit the government to detain suspected terrorists for an indefinite period without access to an attorney or the filing of charges?

2

Criminal Courts, Pretrial Processes, and Trials

Learning Objectives

▶ Explain the structure of the court system of the United States and of the state.

▶ Trace the progress of a criminal case through its various stages from initial complaint through appeal and post-conviction remedies.

▶ Understand the characteristics and functions of a complaint, an affidavit, a summons, a warrant, an indictment, an information, a motion, a subpoena, and a deposition.

▶ Explain the differences between preliminary hearings, grand jury proceedings, and arraignments.

▶ Understand the meaning of prosecutorial discretion and explain the difference between selective and vindictive prosecution.

▶ Understand why plea bargaining and discovery are essential to the administration of criminal justice.

▶ Understand the difference between venue and jurisdiction.

▶ Understand the rights, duties, and functions of the judge, the jury, the prosecuting attorney, and the defendant in a criminal trial.

▶ Explain the different types of evidence and the different evidentiary burdens of proof.

▶ Understand the powers of and limitations on judges in determining the sentence.

▶ Explain the major differences between appeal and *habeas corpus*.

The law enforcement officer's daily duties include enforcing the laws, investigating and preventing crime, keeping the public peace, and community caretaking. To perform these duties properly, officers must be sensitive to the constitutional rights of all persons (discussed in Chapter 1) and be familiar with the criminal laws of their jurisdictions. Just as important, officers must understand the laws dealing with arrest, search and seizure, confessions, and pretrial identifications. Most of the remainder of this book is concerned with these legal topics.

Most law enforcement officers are not as familiar with the rules and procedures that govern the course of a prosecution beyond the investigatory or arrest stage; nevertheless, officers play an important role in this process, often as chief witnesses for the prosecution. After they have testified, officers play a lesser role as their cases move through pleadings, motions, jury selection, trial, and appeal. To many officers, the entire process may look like a complex legal jumble involving the prosecuting attorney, the defense attorney, the judge, and the jurors. Law enforcement officers are an integral part of the criminal justice system, and their early actions in a case vitally affect its outcome at nearly all stages of the prosecution. For these reasons, they should have a basic understanding of what happens to the case, and why, when it reaches the prosecutor and the courts. Other criminal justice professionals, even those who are less involved in a criminal case, can also function more effectively within the criminal justice system if they have a general knowledge of that system's structure and operation.

Criminal court procedure is governed primarily by court rules and statutes designed to ensure the just and efficient processing of criminal offenders. Many of these rules and statutes are complex and of little interest to law enforcement officers or other criminal justice professionals. This chapter highlights pertinent court procedures and legal terms to provide a comprehensive, chronological view of a criminal trial from arrest through post-conviction remedies, without concerning itself with details of little direct concern to the criminal justice professional.

Court procedures for serious offenses only are discussed here; this chapter does not cover procedures for traffic violations and other less serious misdemeanors. When another chapter covers certain aspects of criminal court procedure, reference is made to that chapter. Because the information in this chapter is general, and because criminal court procedure differs by state, readers should consult their own state's pertinent statutes and rules for authoritative information.

►STRUCTURE OF THE U.S. COURT SYSTEM

To properly understand the preliminary proceedings in a criminal case, it is important to understand the basic structure of the federal court system and a typical state court system, and the criminal trial jurisdiction of the different courts. As used here, the term jurisdiction simply means the authority of a court to deal with a particular type of case.

Federalism and Dual Court System

At the time of the Constitutional Convention in 1787, there was great debate as to how to divide power between the state and federal governments. The resulting Constitution of the United States set forth the unique compromises of the Framers. In sum, the states formed a union and granted power to the federal government over national matters, while maintaining their separate existence and power over local matters. This unique interrelationship between the states and the federal government is known as *federalism*. As a result of federalism, each state, as well as the District of Columbia and the federal government, has its own separate court system, each with its own limited jurisdictional authority. Figure 2.1 illustrates the interrelated structure of the dual U.S court systems.

Jurisdiction

Jurisdiction is defined as "the authority given by law to a court to try cases and rule on legal matters within a particular geographic area and/or over certain types of legal cases" (Law.Com Dictionary 2007). More simply, jurisdiction refers to the power of a court to hear and decide a case.

Geographical Jurisdiction and Venue Courts do not have the power to adjudicate any and all disputes. The cases courts are empowered to adjudicate are limited to disputes that occur within specified territorial boundaries. The lands within these territorial boundaries are referred to as being within a court's *geographical jurisdiction*. For example, if a violation of Wyoming state criminal law were committed in Wyoming, then the Wyoming courts would have proper geographical jurisdiction over that criminal case. Courts in other states would lack geographical jurisdiction. But which courts within the state of Wyoming would hear the case? That is a matter of venue.

"**Venue** is defined as the particular county or geographical area in which a court with jurisdiction may hear and determine a case" (Norwood 1995: 270). Proper venue is based on geographic subdivisions within a given geographical jurisdiction. These subdivisions are often determined by city or county boundaries, but other geographical boundaries can be set that are unrelated to county lines. Divisions in the federal system are a good example of this. The state of Washington is a large and populous state. Instead of having one federal district coterminous with the boundaries of the state, there are two federal districts in Washington, the eastern district and the western district. Larger states are subdivided even further; California, for example, has a northern, eastern, central, and southern district. A federal case that arises from an act in Sacramento is properly tried in the northern district of California; the other districts in California would lack proper venue.

The federal constitution guarantees (in both Article III, Section 2, and the Sixth Amendment) that a criminal trial will be held in the state in which the crime was committed. A typical state statute or rule requires that the trial of certain types of cases be held in the geographic division of the court in which the offense was committed. Most jurisdictions also have special rules relating to the proper venue for an offense that is committed on a boundary of two counties, or for an offense partly committed in one county and partly in another. (These technicalities are not discussed here.) But due to the Fourteenth Amendment's

United States Supreme Court

The High Court of Last Resort in the United States

Discretionary appellate jurisdiction over decisions of the U.S. Courts of Appeals and the decisions of the highest courts in the state systems if a question of federal law (including federal constitutional law) is presented.

The Federal Courts

United States Courts of Appeals

Mandatory appellate jurisdiction over the decisions of the U.S. District Courts, 12 Regional Circuits, and one Federal Circuit. Hears appeals from specialized trial courts like the U.S. Court of International Trade, the U.S. Claims Court, and the U.S. Court of Veterans' Appeals.

United States District Courts

Trial courts of original jurisdiction over federal cases. Ninety-four federal districts (including territorial ones in the District of Columbia, Puerto Rico, Guam, the U.S. Virgin Islands, and the Northern Mariana Islands). Mandatory appellate jurisdiction over decisions by non-Article III courts.

Non-Article III Courts

U.S. Bankruptcy Courts, U.S. Tax Court, decisions of U.S. Magistrate Judges, and Administrative Law Judges (ALJ) in various federal agencies like the FCC, Social Security Administration, EEOC, NLRB, FTC, etc.

The State Courts

State High Courts of Last Resort

Mandatory and discretionary appellate jurisdiction over decisions rendered by lower state courts.

State Intermediate Appellate Courts
(40 out of 50 states)

Mandatory appellate jurisdiction over decisions by the state's major trial courts.

State Major Trial Courts

Superior Courts/Courts of Common Pleas/District Courts. Trial courts of general jurisdiction (felonies and major civil cases.) Sometimes there is appellate jurisdiction over state's minor trial courts.

State Minor Trial Courts

Municipal Courts/Justice of the Peace Courts/Magisterial District Courts. Limited original jurisdiction to hear misdemeanor cases, traffic violations, local ordinance violations, and small claims of a civil nature.

▶**Figure 2.1** **STRUCTURE OF THE U.S. COURT SYSTEMS**

guarantee of due process, both the federal government and all states have provisions that allow a criminal defendant to waive these rights and have venue transferred to another forum so that a case can be tried in a different place than the one authorized by statute.

To accomplish this, the defendant may make a motion for a change of venue. The motion is usually required to be made before the jury is impaneled or, in non-jury trials, before any evidence is received. The defendant must give adequate reasons in support of the motion. Typical grounds for granting a motion for change of venue are:

▶ such prejudice prevails in the county where the case is to be tried that the defendant cannot obtain a fair and impartial trial there; or

▶ another location is much more convenient for the parties and witnesses than the intended place of trial, and the interests of justice require a transfer of location.

For example, Timothy McVeigh, the defendant in the Oklahoma City bombing case, was tried for his crimes outside of Oklahoma, even though that is where he committed the offenses. The extensive pretrial publicity and the intense personal connection the potential jurors in Oklahoma City made it very likely that the defendant could not get a fair and impartial trial in Oklahoma. The case was therefore transferred to Denver, Colorado, where the jury pool was less personally involved and more likely to meet the constitutional due process guarantees of a fair and impartial jury. This was only possible, however, because it was a federal case. Federal courts throughout the country had jurisdiction to hear the case, but venue was technically only proper in Oklahoma. Given the pretrial publicity, venue was transferred to another court of competent jurisdiction in Colorado. The same was not true, however, for the state trial of McVeigh's accomplice, Terry Nichols. He was charged with over 160 counts of murder under Oklahoma state homicide law. Geographic jurisdiction was proper anywhere in the state of Oklahoma. Venue, however, would have been proper only in Oklahoma County, the county in which Oklahoma City is located. Venue, however, was transferred to McAlester County for Nichols' trial.

Hierarchical Jurisdiction and Court Structure Although the states and the federal government have separate court systems, established by their own constitutions and statutes, there are some basic similarities in American court systems. Most court systems follow a hierarchal structure beginning at the lowest level with **courts of limited jurisdiction**, followed by major trial **courts of general jurisdiction**, intermediate courts of appeal, and courts of last resort. The following general characteristics of the trial and appellate systems are applicable to both the state and federal courts.

Trial Courts and Original Jurisdiction **Original jurisdiction** means that a court has the power to hear a case for the first time. In other words, the court will act as a trial court. In popular culture, most of our exposure to the court system is to trial level courts. It is in the trial level of courts that witnesses testify and evidence is presented. The **litigants** at the trial court are the parties involved in the specific case. In criminal cases, the **prosecution** files the case. The prosecution may be called by several names depending on the jurisdiction, including, but not limited to, "the State," "the People," and "the Commonwealth." Finally, the party against whom the criminal case is filed is called the **defendant**.

Trial courts are presided over by one judge, sitting with or without a jury. A trial court hears evidence, applies the law, and decides which side should prevail. To arrive at a final determination, there are usually two types of decisions that need to be made during the course of a trial: legal decisions and factual decisions. The judge makes all of the legal decisions, ruling on all matters of law. Factual decisions, however, are made by the **trier-of-fact**. In a **jury trial**, the jury is the trier-of-fact responsible for making factual findings such as whether the defendant is guilty of a crime. In a **bench trial**, a trial is conducted without a jury. The judge acts as the trier-of-fact in addition to ruling on matters of law.

Both the state and federal trial courts of the United States are empowered to hear certain types of cases. *Subject matter jurisdiction* is concerned with the type of case a court hears. It is an absolute prerequisite to a court hearing a case. Courts are either courts of limited subject matter jurisdiction or courts of general subject matter jurisdiction. In courts of *special or limited subject matter jurisdiction*, the court will hear only specialized cases. Small claims courts are not the proper forum to adjudicate multimillion dollar disputes, as their subject matter jurisdiction is limited to a specific, small amount. Similarly, traffic courts do not adjudicate murder cases, as their subject matter jurisdiction is limited to determining if quasi-criminal violations of motor vehicle laws have occurred. Tax cases are adjudicated in tax court; bankruptcy cases are heard in bankruptcy court; violations of ordinances are determined in municipal courts. Collectively, the trials courts of limited subject matter jurisdiction in the state system are typically referred to as *minor trial courts.* These minor trial courts have jurisdiction over misdemeanor or traffic cases; over the initial setting of bail; over preliminary hearings in felony cases; and, occasionally, over felony trials in which the penalty prescribed for the offense is below a statutorily specified limit.

Courts of *general subject matter jurisdiction* are the courts of original jurisdiction having the power to adjudicate all types of disputes not specifically delegated to a court of limited jurisdiction. These courts are typically referred to as *major trial courts.* States' major trial courts are typically arranged by county and are empowered to hear all types of criminal and civil cases. The federal system, in contrast, has no such courts of general jurisdiction because the federal courts of the United States are all courts of limited subject matter jurisdiction. As such, federal courts only adjudicate criminal cases that involve violations of federal laws.

Appellate Courts and Appellate Jurisdiction **Appellate jurisdiction** refers to the power to review decisions originally made by a court that exercised original jurisdiction over a given case. In appellate cases, the party bringing the appeal is known as the **petitioner** or the **appellant**, depending on the jurisdiction. The party responding to the appeal is called the **respondent** or **appellee.**

The petitioner or appellant is arguing that an error was made by the court below. Not every error, however, is grounds for appeal. For an appeal to be successful, there must have been some kind of **prejudicial error.** In other words, the error must have been such that it could have affected the outcome of the case. Errors that were not prejudicial (i.e., mistakes that were not likely to have had an effect on the outcome of the case) are called **harmless errors.** In order to prevail on an appeal, the appellant is usually required to show harmful or prejudicial error. Harmless errors are rarely, if ever, grounds for a successful appeal.

Although parties to an appeal often get the opportunity to argue their cases before a panel of appellate judges at **oral arguments,** appeals are primarily argued in writing. This is accomplished when parties submit **briefs**—formal legal memoranda that summarize the facts of the case, their views on the applicable law, and their respective arguments on why they should prevail on appeal.

Briefs are written by lawyers. However, behavioral scientists may play an important role in the preparation of briefs in two ways. First, they may provide important facts through their opinions and their research that lawyers rely upon in their briefs. Secondly, behavioral scientists may offer their own briefs as *amicus curie*, a "friend of the court," even though they are not parties to a particular dispute. For example, the American Psychological Association, the American Psychiatric Association, the American Medical Association, just to name a few, regularly submit amicus briefs on important cases concerning the intersection of law and the behavioral sciences.

In forty states, appellate jurisdiction is first exercised by **intermediate courts of appeals**. In terms of the hierarchical structure of the courts, the intermediate courts of appeals rank higher than trial courts of original jurisdiction, and below the court of last resort. They are typically comprised of an uneven number of judges who hear and decide an appeal as a panel. These judges review the record of the lower court and the merits of the case, as set forth in both written and oral arguments of the attorneys. If the appellate court agrees with the decision of the lower court, it affirms the lower court decision; if it disagrees, it reverses. The appellate court may also modify the decision of the lower court, or remand (send back) the case, so that the lower court may retry all or part of the case in accordance with the rulings of the appellate court.

Ten states—Delaware, Maine, Montana, Nevada, New Hampshire, Rhode Island, South Dakota, Vermont, West Virginia, and Wyoming—do not have intermediate courts of appeal. Instead, appellate jurisdiction in these states is exercised by the **state court of last resort**. Courts of last resort are the highest courts in a court system's hierarchical structure, and every state and the federal system has one. These courts are referred to as the "Supreme Court" by forty-six states. The court of last resort in New York and Maryland is called the "Court of Appeals." In Maine and Massachusetts, the court of last resort is called the "Supreme Judicial Court." Courts of last resort exercise appellate jurisdiction as a second level of review in the federal court system and in the forty states that have intermediate courts of appeals; they are the first and only courts exercising appellate jurisdiction in the ten states without intermediate courts of appeals. As with the intermediate court of appeals, a panel of judges or justices on courts of last resort hears and decides cases based on a review of the record from the lower courts, as well as the arguments of attorneys.

In addition to exercising appellate jurisdiction, courts of last resort have original jurisdiction over a limited range of cases. This is quite rare, however; original jurisdiction usually lies in the major trial courts, and courts of last resort almost always exercise their appellate jurisdiction.

Nature of Mandatory and Discretionary Appellate Jurisdiction If an appellate court is required by law to hear an appeal of a certain type of case, it is called **an appeal of right**. When such a right exists, the appellate court is said to have **mandatory appellate jurisdiction**. Appeals of right exist to the courts of last resort in the ten states without intermediate courts of appeals. In the forty jurisdictions that have intermediate courts of appeals, though, the appeal of right from a decision made by a court of original jurisdiction generally exists only to the intermediate court of appeals. (The one major exception to this rule is in death penalty cases; capital crimes are always reviewed by a state's highest court.) Any appeal of right must be exercised by the appealing party within a statutorily prescribed period of time, typically ten or thirty days, depending on the laws of the particular state.

There are also appeals of right that exist to courts of last resort even when an intermediate court of appeals has heard a case, although they are uncommon.

For example, if a federal court of appeals invalidates a state statute, a party relying on that statute has a right to appeal the decision to the United States Supreme Court, which has mandatory appellate jurisdiction over the case under 28 U.S.C. § 1253. Barring one of these rare appeals of right to a court of last resort, courts of last resort exercise *discretionary appellate jurisdiction*. The party seeking review of a lower court's decision asks the appellate court to exercise its discretionary appellate jurisdiction by filing a **petition for a writ of certiorari** along with a formal brief that sets forth the reasons why the court should accept jurisdiction. If the high court decides to accept discretionary appellate jurisdiction and thereby review a decision of a lower court, it grants the petition and issues a **writ of certiorari.** This writ is an order compelling the lower court to produce the record from the proceedings below. If the court decides not to hear the case, certiorari is denied, and the decision of the lower court stands. Denial of a petition for certiorari is not, however, an approval of the lower court decision; it is merely the conclusion of the high court that its limited resources should not be discretionarily used to review the lower court decision.

Standards of Appellate Review Appellate courts, at both the intermediate and highest levels, generally do not disturb the factual findings of the lower courts. This is due to the **standard of review.** When reviewing factual determinations, the standard of review is generally referred to as the **clearly erroneous** standard. Under this standard, the factual determinations of the trial level court are left undisturbed unless it is patently clear from a review of the record that a factual error was made. Evidence is presented and witnesses testify at trial level, so the trial court alone has the opportunity to observe a witness's facial expressions, body language, and vocal intonations Accordingly, appellate courts are highly deferential to the factual findings of trial courts, and appellate reversals under the clearly erroneous standard are quite rare.

Most appellate inquiries concern review of questions of law. Since appellate judges are just as qualified to review questions of law as trial court judges, their review is *de novo* or plenary. That is to say, they review the law without any deference to the legal decisions of the trial court.

The other primary standard of review that appellate courts apply is called the **abuse of discretion** standard. This highly deferential standard is applied by appellate courts reviewing the discretionary decision-making of a trial court judge. Many rulings are left to the discretion of a trial court, such as whether to allow expert testimony; what the scope of permissible examination will be; and whether to sanction a party. If one wishes to challenge such a ruling on appeal, it must be shown that the trial court made decisions in an arbitrary, capricious, or unreasonable manner.

Concurrent and Exclusive Jurisdiction **Concurrent jurisdiction** exists when both the state and federal courts have jurisdiction over a particular case (Concurrent jurisdiction can also exist when two courts within the same court system have original jurisdiction over the same matter). In most general federal questions and civil rights cases, federal jurisdiction is concurrent with the state courts. In these cases, parties bringing the action must decide whether they should file suit in state or federal court. In some cases, such as bankruptcy, patent, or copyright actions, the federal courts have **exclusive jurisdiction**, meaning that these actions must be brought in federal court.

Federal Courts

Article III, Section 1 of the United States Constitution provides:

The judicial power of the United States shall be vested in one supreme Court, and in such inferior Courts as the Congress may from time to time ordain and establish. The Judges, both of the supreme and inferior Courts, shall hold their Offices during good Behaviour, and shall, at stated Times, receive for their Services, a Compensation, which shall not be diminished during their Continuance in Office.

With the Judiciary Act of 1789, Congress established the lower federal courts. Although the Judiciary Act of 1789 has been amended several times since its inception, the basic structure of the federal courts remains the same, with specialized courts, trial level courts, intermediate courts of appeal, and the court of last resort remaining the United States Supreme Court. See 28 U.S.C. § 1 et seq.

Federal District Courts The trial level court for the federal court system is the United States District Court (see Figure 2.1). Each state has at least one district court, while some of the larger states have as many as four. As Figure 2.2 illustrates, there are a total of ninety-four district courts in the fifty states, the District of Columbia, the Commonwealth of Puerto Rico, and the territories of Guam, the U.S. Virgin Islands, and the Northern Mariana Islands. District courts may have divisions (for example, Eastern and Western Divisions of North Dakota), usually in districts covering a large geographic area, and may have several locations where the court hears cases.

With the exception of the territorial courts, all district court judges are appointed for life by the president, with the advice and consent of the Senate. Congress authorizes judgeships for each district based in large part on its caseload. At this writing, there are over 678 district court judges. Usually, only one judge is required to hear and decide a case in a district court. The district courts have original jurisdiction over criminal cases, and the great majority of federal criminal cases begin in the district courts. Cases from the district courts are reviewable on appeal by the applicable court of appeals. Each district court has one or more bankruptcy judges, a clerk, a U.S. attorney, a U.S. marshal, probation officers, court reporters, and a support staff.

Each district court also has one or more U.S. magistrate judges. Magistrate judges are appointed for eight-year terms by district court judges and are required to be members of the bar. A magistrate judge, at the designation of the district court judge, may issue search warrants, hear and determine certain kinds of pretrial matters, conduct preliminary and other hearings, and submit proposed findings and recommendations on motions for the court's approval. Perhaps the most important power magistrate judges possess is the authority to conduct misdemeanor trials with the defendant's consent and to conduct trials in civil cases with the consent of the parties involved. Since the enactment of the Federal Magistrates Act in 1968, Congress has expanded the services magistrate judges may perform. As a result, magistrate judges are playing an increasingly significant role in the administration of justice in the federal system.

Federal Circuit Courts of Appeals The United States Circuit Courts of Appeals are intermediate appellate courts created by Congress to relieve the U.S. Supreme Court from considering all appeals in cases originally decided by the

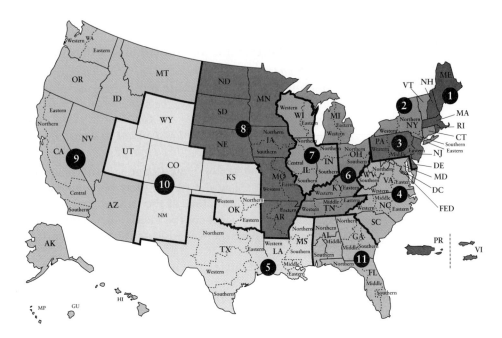

▶**Figure 2.2** GEOGRAPHICAL BOUNDARIES OF FEDERAL DISTRICT AND CIRCUIT COURTS

federal trial courts. The courts of appeal are empowered to review all final decisions and certain interlocutory decisions of district courts. They also have the power to review and enforce orders of many federal administrative bodies. The decisions of the courts of appeals are final, except that they are subject to discretionary review or appeal in the U.S. Supreme Court. The Circuit Courts of Appeals are divided into circuits, each circuit hearing appeals from specific district courts. Presently, there are thirteen circuits in the United States Courts of Appeals; eleven numbered circuits (each containing at least three states); a Circuit Court of Appeals for the District of Columbia; and the Court of Appeals for the Federal Circuit, which was created by act of Congress in 1982 to have nationwide jurisdiction to hear specialized appeals in patent and copyright cases. The geographical locations of the thirteen federal judicial circuits and the ninety-four federal districts are presented in Figure 2.2.

Appeals court judges are appointed for life by the president of the United States, with the advice and consent of the Senate. Each court of appeals has from six to twenty-eight permanent circuit judgeships, depending on the amount of judicial work in the circuit. At this writing, there are 179 judges in the thirteen judicial circuits. One of the justices of the U.S. Supreme Court is assigned as a circuit justice for each of the thirteen judicial circuits. Each court of appeals normally hears cases in panels consisting of three judges but may sit *en banc*. En banc refers to a session of a court in which all the judges of the court participate, as opposed to a session presided over by a single judge or a mere quorum of judges. The judge who has served on the court the longest and who is under sixty-five years of age is designated as the chief judge and performs administrative duties in addition to hearing cases. The chief judge serves for a maximum term of seven years.

U.S. Supreme Court The United States Supreme Court is the court of last resort in the federal court system, meaning that it is a court from which no appeal is possible. The Supreme Court has one chief justice and such number of associate justices as may be fixed by Congress. By act of Congress in 1948, the number of associate justices is eight. Power to nominate the justices is vested in the president of the United States, and appointments are made with the advice and consent of the Senate. Once confirmed to the Supreme Court, there is no mandatory retirement age for Supreme Court justices; so as long as they maintain "good behavior," the justices may remain on the court until their death or until they voluntarily choose to retire. Article III, Section 1, of the Constitution further provides that "[t]he Judges, both of the supreme and inferior Courts, shall hold their Offices during good Behaviour, and shall, at stated Times, receive for their Services, a Compensation, which shall not be diminished during their Continuance in Office." The term of the United States Supreme Court commences on the first Monday in October and usually ends nine months later.

The Constitution grants the Supreme Court original jurisdiction in a limited number of cases. In other words, the Supreme Court acts as a trial court in certain types of cases, such as controversies between the United States and a state, between two states, or those involving foreign ministers or ambassadors. Such cases are quite rare; so in the overwhelming majority of cases, the Supreme Court exercises its appellate jurisdiction, reviewing the decisions of the lower federal courts and the highest state courts.

The Supreme Court exercises its appellate jurisdiction through the granting of a *writ of certiorari*, which means that the Court, upon petition of a party, agrees to review a case decided by one of the circuit courts of appeals or the highest court of a state. A vote of four Supreme Court justices is required to grant certiorari to review a case (sometimes referred to as the rule of four). Certiorari is granted at the Court's discretion when a case presents questions the resolution of which will have some general "importance beyond the facts and parties involved." *Boag v. MacDougall*, 454 U.S. 364, 368 (1982) (Rehnquist, J., dissenting). For example, the Court may grant certiorari in cases involving important and unsettled questions of federal law; or in situations involving a conflict among state high courts or the federal circuits concerning the interpretation of federal law, most especially one ruling on a question of interpretation of the U.S. Constitution. Note that failure to grant certiorari is not an affirmation in disguise of the lower court's decision. It simply means that the petitioner failed to persuade four of the nine justices to hear the appeal.

Non-Article III Federal Courts In addition to the courts described above, the federal court system also includes a number of specialized courts of limited subject matter jurisdiction established to hear particular classes of cases. Examples are the U.S. Court of International Trade, the U.S. Court of Federal Claims, and the U.S. Tax Court. Courts outside the judicial branch of government include the U.S. Court of Military Appeals and the U.S. Tax Court. There are also quasi-judicial boards or commissions that have special and limited jurisdiction under specific federal statutes.

State Courts

The constitution and statutes of each state dictate the structure of their individual court systems. A typical state court system has the same basic structure as the federal system. Courts of original jurisdiction are usually divided into (1) courts of limited jurisdiction whose trial jurisdiction either includes no felonies or is limited to less than all felonies; and (2) higher courts of general jurisdiction with trial jurisdiction over all criminal offenses, including all felonies. The courts of limited jurisdiction are usually established on a local level and may be called municipal courts, police courts, magistrate courts, district courts, or something similar. These courts have jurisdiction over misdemeanor cases, traffic cases, initial setting of bail and preliminary hearings in felony cases, and, occasionally, felony trials in which the penalty prescribed for the offense is below a statutorily specified limit. The courts of general jurisdiction have original jurisdiction over all criminal offenses and are usually established on a county or regional level. They may be called circuit courts, district courts, superior courts, or something similar. Generally, the most serious criminal cases are tried in these courts.

In some states, courts of general jurisdiction may also exercise a limited appellate jurisdiction over certain cases appealed from courts of limited jurisdiction. Such appeals result in a **trial *de novo*** in the court of general jurisdiction. A trial de novo is a new trial or retrial in which the whole case is examined again as if no trial had ever been held in the court of limited jurisdiction. In a trial de novo, matters of fact as well as law may be considered, witnesses may be heard, and new evidence may be presented, regardless of what happened at the first trial. Some states also have lower-level specialized courts, such as juvenile courts, traffic courts, or family courts, that may have criminal jurisdiction or partial criminal jurisdiction.

From a court of general jurisdiction, a case may usually be appealed as a right to an intermediate appellate court. Some of the less populous states, however, do not have an intermediate court of appeals; therefore, in those states, appeals from the trial courts go straight to the courts of last resort as a matter of right. In the majority of states that have intermediate appellate courts, however, most appeals are resolved at that level. Few cases, other than death penalty cases, are heard by the highest court of a state. These state courts of last resort, usually called a state supreme court, typically exercise discretionary appellate jurisdiction over cases from the intermediate appellate courts using a process much like the U.S. Supreme Court's certiorari process.

If a case decided by a state high court involves important federal constitutional issues or questions of federal law, it may finally reach the U.S. Supreme Court for review. Generally, the state high court of last resort also has the power to prescribe rules of pleading, practice, and procedure for itself and the other lower courts of the state.

▶PRELIMINARY PRETRIAL CRIMINAL PROCEEDINGS

The remainder of this chapter focuses on the progress of a **felony** case through the criminal court system. A brief note about misdemeanor cases is useful at the outset to emphasize the differences between the two types of cases. Generally, **misdemeanors** are crimes for which the maximum possible sentence is less than one year's imprisonment. Misdemeanors are tried in courts of limited jurisdiction. Although misdemeanor proceedings are similar to felony proceedings, they are usually less formal and more abbreviated. For example, jury trials are available but unusual in misdemeanor cases, and six-person juries are common. Also, in some jurisdictions, if the defendant pleads guilty, misdemeanor charges may be disposed of at the initial appearance before the magistrate. Because misdemeanor proceedings differ greatly from jurisdiction to jurisdiction, and because they are similar in many ways to felony proceedings, the remainder of this chapter focuses primarily on felony proceedings. Figure 2.3 gives a general view of the progress of a case through the criminal justice system.

Charging

Prosecutorial Discretion Police investigate crimes, but they do not officially charge people with criminal defendants; prosecutors do. Prosecutors have great *discretion* with regard to their charging function, both in terms of "the initial screening determination as to whether or not to charge (the 'screening function'); and, if the answer is yes, the subsequent decisions as to choice and number of charges (the 'selection function')" (Krug 2002: 645).

> [S]o long as the prosecutor has probable cause to believe that the accused committed an offense defined by statute, the decision whether or not to prosecute, and what charge to file or bring before a grand jury, generally rests entirely in his discretion. *Wayte v. United States*, 470 U.S. 598, 607 (1985).

A prosecutor also has broad discretion in determining when to bring charges, whether to investigate, whether to grant immunity, whether to plea bargain, and, if so, the type of plea which will ultimately be acceptable.

Why might a prosecutor decline to file charges against someone? The most common reason for releasing someone without prosecution is insufficient evidence. "Witness availability, credibility, and memory also influence the results of prosecutions, as well as the existence of alternative remedies, such as restitution to the victim. *McCleskey v. Kemp*, 481 U.S. 279, 307 n. 28 (1987). The American Bar Association's Standards for Criminal Justice set forth the main factors prosecutors are supposed to consider when exercising their charging discretion in Standard 3-3.9 (b) (2d ed. 1980):

> The prosecutor is not obliged to present all charges which the evidence might support. The prosecutor may in some circumstances and for good cause consistent with the public interest decline to prosecute, notwithstanding that sufficient evidence may exist which would support a conviction. Illustrative of the factors which the prosecutor may properly consider in exercising his or her discretion are:
>
>   (i) the prosecutor's reasonable doubt that the accused is in fact guilty;
> (ii) the extent of the harm caused by the offense;
> (iii) the disproportion of the authorized punishment in relation to the particular offense or the offender;
> (iv) possible improper motives of a complainant;
>   (v) reluctance of the victim to testify;
> (vi) cooperation of the accused in the apprehension or conviction of others; and
> (vii) availability and likelihood of prosecution by another jurisdiction.

The discretion exercised by prosecutors in both the screening and selection is great, but not absolute; it is constrained by the Constitution. Accordingly,

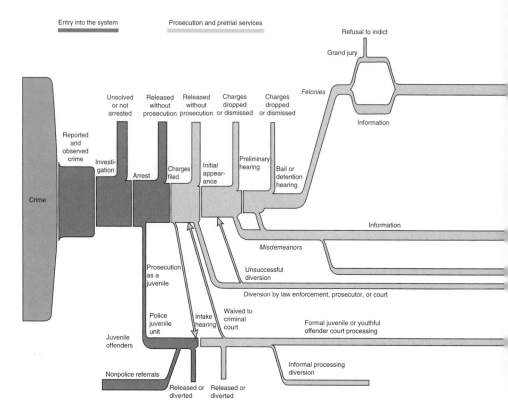

▶**Figure 2.3** **THE SEQUENCE OF EVENTS IN THE CRIMINAL JUSTICE SYSTEM**

Source: Bureau of Justice Statistics: The Criminal Justice System Flowchart (1997), available online at http://www.ojp.usdoj.gov/bjs/flowchart.htm.

prosecutorial discretion is subject to limited judicial review in cases in which selective prosecution or vindictive prosecution is alleged.

Selective prosecution is a violation of the Constitution's guarantee of equal protection of the law. To establish selective prosecution, a defendant bears a heavy burden to show that others similarly situated were not prosecuted and that the defendant's prosecution was "**deliberately based upon an unjustifiable standard such as race, religion, or other arbitrary classification.**" *Bordenkircher v. Hayes,* 434 U.S. 357, 364 (1978).

Vindictive prosecution violates due process. Vindictive prosecution occurs when a prosecutor increases the number or severity of charges to penalize a defendant who exercises constitutional or statutory rights. In *Blackledge v. Perry,* 417 U.S. 21 (1974), a case involving a felony charge brought against a defendant who exercised a statutory right to appeal from a misdemeanor conviction for the same offense, the Court said the real basis of the vindictiveness rule is that "**the fear of such vindictiveness may unconstitutionally deter a defendant's**

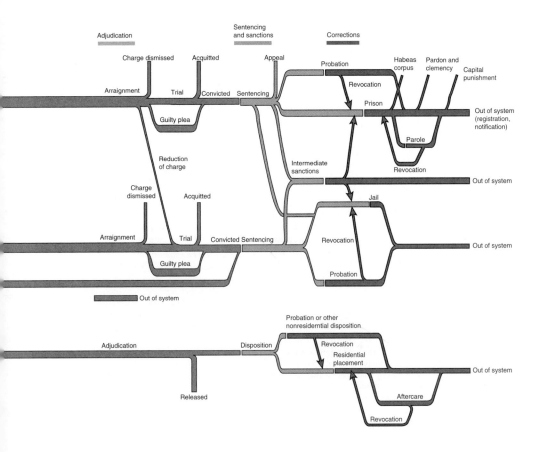

exercise of the right to appeal or collaterally attack his first conviction. . . ."
417 U.S. at 28.

Once a prosecutor has decided move forward with a criminal prosecution, criminal charges may be filed against someone in one of three ways: by a complaint, an information, or an indictment. Figure 2.4 illustrates the different ways in which a defendant may be criminally charged by a prosecutor.

The Complaint A criminal process against a felony defendant formally begins with a **complaint**. The word formally is used here because a person can be arrested for an offense before a complaint is filed or a warrant is issued. However, because an arrest without a warrant is considered an exception to the basic warrant requirement, the complaint is still considered the formal beginning of proceedings. Also, a person may be arrested based on a report of, or a law enforcement officer's observation of, the commission of a crime, but for various reasons the prosecutor may decide not to charge the defendant.

According to Federal Rule of Criminal Procedure 3, a complaint is "a written statement of the essential facts constituting the offense charged." The complaint serves a dual purpose in a criminal proceeding. If the defendant has been arrested without a warrant, the complaint serves as the charging document at the defendant's initial appearance before a **magistrate, justice of the peace,** or municipal court judge. The reading of the complaint at this initial appearance

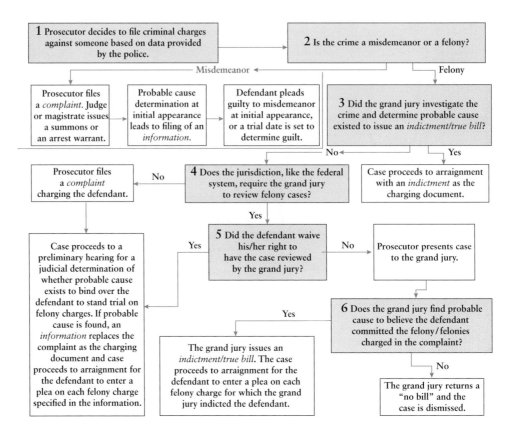

▶**Figure 2.4** CHARGING DOCUMENTS FLOWCHART

is what converts someone from being a mere suspect to a formal criminal defendant. If the defendant has not been arrested and is not before the court, the complaint serves as the basis for determining whether an arrest warrant should be issued.

The complaint must be made on oath or affirmation, must state the essential facts of the offense being charged, must be in writing, and must be made before a judicial officer authorized to issue process in criminal cases. This officer is usually a magistrate or a justice of the peace, although a judge may also authorize a complaint. The information in the complaint may come from a law enforcement officer's personal observation or experience, or it may come from victims, witnesses, or informants. Nevertheless, the evidence put forth in the complaint must be strong enough to convince the magistrate that there is **probable cause** that an offense has been committed and that the defendant committed it. Probable cause is explored in much greater detail in Chapter 3. For now, think of probable cause as being a fair probability, under all of the reliable facts and circumstances known at the time, to believe that a crime has been or is being committed. *Draper v. United States*, 358 U.S. 307 (1959). A typical complaint appears in Figure 2.5.

Affidavits Information not contained in the body of the complaint, or that comes from witnesses other than the complainant, may be brought to the court's attention in the form of an **affidavit**. An affidavit is a sworn written statement

AO91 (Rev. 12/03) Criminal Complaint

UNITED STATES DISTRICT COURT

_____ DISTRICT OF _____

UNITED STATES OF AMERICA
V.

CRIMINAL COMPLAINT

Case Number:

(Name and Address of Defendant)

I, the undersigned complainant, state that the following is true and correct to the best of my

knowledge and belief. On or about _____ in _____ County, in

the _____ District of _____ defendant(s) did,
                          (Date)

(Track Statutory Language of Offense)

in violation of Title _____ United States Code, Section(s) _____ .

I further state that I am a(n) _____ and that this complaint is based on the
                              Official Title

following facts:

Continued on the attached sheet and made a part of this complaint: ☐ Yes   ☐ No

_____
Signature of Complainant

_____
Printed Name of Complainant

Sworn to before me and signed in my presence,

_____   at   _____
Date   City   State

_____   _____
Name of Judge   Title of Judge   Signature of Judge

▶**Figure 2.5** **A SAMPLE CRIMINAL COMPLAINT**

of the facts relied on in seeking the issuance of a warrant. An affidavit need not be prepared with any particular formality. It is filed with the complaint, and together the complaint and affidavit provide a written record for a reviewing court to examine in determining whether probable cause existed for the issuance of a warrant.

Warrant or Summons Issued on the Complaint Once the magistrate has determined from the complaint and accompanying affidavits that there is probable cause to believe that an offense has been committed and that the defendant committed it, the magistrate issues either a summons or an arrest warrant for the defendant's appearance in court. A **summons**, pictured in Figure 2.6, is a court order that commands someone to appear before a court to respond to charges filed against them. An **arrest warrant** authorizes police to take someone into custody and bring them before the court to respond to the charges against them. As you can see in Figure 2.6, an arrest warrant looks very much like a summons, but it is directed at law enforcement personnel rather than the defendant. If the defendant is already before the court, then neither a summons nor an arrest warrant is necessary.

Once a summons or warrant is issued, a law enforcement officer to whom it is directed must serve the summons or execute the warrant by arresting the defendant and bringing the defendant before a judicial officer as commanded in the warrant. A detailed discussion of summons and arrest warrant procedures appears in Chapter 6.

Initial Appearance Before a Magistrate A person who has been arrested without a warrant is required by statute to be brought before a magistrate "without unnecessary delay," or "forthwith," or some similar statutory language for an **initial appearance.** The initial appearance is also called a *Gerstein* hearing, so-called after the case *Gerstein v. Pugh*, 420 U.S. 103 (1975), that held a prompt judicial determination of probable cause is required when someone is arrested without an arrest warrant. As a general rule, the Supreme Court expects an initial appearance to occur within forty-eight hours of a warrantless arrest. *County of Riverside v. McLaughlin*, 500 U.S. 44 (1991). Note that in indictment jurisdictions, if a grand jury has already returned an indictment, an initial appearance is not mandated under *Gerstein v. Pugh*, although some states require an initial appearance upon all arrests. The details of this procedure are discussed in Chapter 6.

Preliminary Hearing The initial appearance before the magistrate may or may not include a preliminary hearing. At the **preliminary hearing** (also called the preliminary examination), the magistrate must determine whether there is probable cause to believe that a felony was committed and that the defendant committed it. The purpose of the preliminary hearing is to provide another judicial determination of probable cause and to protect the defendant from a totally baseless felony prosecution. Rule 5 of the Federal Rules of Criminal Procedure provides that, when the preliminary hearing is required, "[t]he magistrate judge must hold the preliminary hearing within a reasonable time, but no later than 10 days after the initial appearance if the defendant is in custody and no later than 20 days if not in custody." A preliminary hearing is not required if the defendant is charged with a petty offense or misdemeanor or if the defendant waives the hearing. Moreover, a defendant is not entitled to a preliminary hearing if the defendant has been indicted by a grand jury since that body has already established probable cause exists for the defendant to stand felony trial.

The preliminary hearing is a formal adversarial proceeding conducted in open court with a transcript made of the proceedings. The U.S. Supreme Court held that the preliminary hearing is a "critical stage" of a criminal prosecution, entitling the defendant to have an attorney present at the hearing. *Coleman v. Alabama*, 399 U.S. 1 (1970). Indigent defendants who cannot afford an attorney must be provided one at the government's expense. The preliminary hearing

Summons Form (AO83 Rev. 10/03)

%AO83 (Rev. 10/03) Summons in a Criminal Case

UNITED STATES DISTRICT COURT
_____ DISTRICT OF _____

UNITED STATES OF AMERICA
V.

SUMMONS IN A CRIMINAL CASE

Case Number: _____

(Name and Address of Defendant)

YOU ARE HEREBY SUMMONED to appear before the United States District Court at the place, date and time set forth below.

Place	Room
Before:	Date and Time

To answer a(n)
☐ Indictment ☐ Information ☐ Complaint ☐ Probation Violation Petition ☐ Supervised Release Violation Petition ☐ Violation Notice

Charging you with a violation of Title _____ United States Code, Section(s) _____

Brief description of offense:

Signature of Issuing Officer _____ Date _____

Name and Title of Issuing Officer _____

Return of Service Form

AO83 (Rev. 10/03) Summons in a Criminal Case

RETURN OF SERVICE

Date

Service was made by me on:

Check one box below to indicate appropriate method of service

☐ Served personally upon the defendant at:

☐ Left summons at the defendant's dwelling house or usual place of abode with a person of suitable age and discretion then residing therein and mailed a copy of the summons to the defendant's last known address. Name of person with whom the summons was left:

☐ Returned unexecuted:

I declare under penalty of perjury under the laws of the United States of America that the foregoing information contained in the Return of Service is true and correct.

Returned on _____ _____
Date   Name of United States Marshal

_____
(by) Deputy United States Marshal

Remarks:

As to who may serve a summons, see Rule 4 of the Federal Rules of Criminal Procedure.

Warrant for Arrest Form (AO 442 Rev. 10/03)

%AO 442   (Rev. 10/03) Warrant for Arrest

UNITED STATES DISTRICT COURT
_____ District of _____

UNITED STATES OF AMERICA
V.

WARRANT FOR ARREST

Case Number: _____

To: The United States Marshal
and any Authorized United States Officer

YOU ARE HEREBY COMMANDED to arrest _____
Name

and bring him or her forthwith to the nearest magistrate judge to answer a(n)

☐ Indictment ☐ Information ☐ Complaint ☐ Order of court ☐ Probation Violation Petition ☐ Supervised Release Violation Petition ☐ Violation Notice

charging him or her with   (brief description of offense)

in violation of Title _____ United States Code, Section(s) _____

Name of Issuing Officer _____ Signature of Issuing Officer _____

Title of Issuing Officer _____ Date and Location _____

RETURN		
This warrant was received and executed with the arrest of the above-named defendant at		
DATE RECEIVED	NAME AND TITLE OF ARRESTING OFFICER	SIGNATURE OF ARRESTING OFFICER
DATE OF ARREST		

Warrant Information Form

AO 442   (Rev. 10/03) Warrant for Arrest

THE FOLLOWING IS FURNISHED FOR INFORMATION ONLY:

DEFENDANT'S NAME: _____
ALIAS: _____
LAST KNOWN RESIDENCE: _____
LAST KNOWN EMPLOYMENT: _____
PLACE OF BIRTH: _____
DATE OF BIRTH: _____
SOCIAL SECURITY NUMBER: _____
HEIGHT: _____ WEIGHT: _____
SEX: _____ RACE: _____
HAIR: _____ EYES: _____
SCARS, TATTOOS, OTHER DISTINGUISHING MARKS: _____

FBI NUMBER: _____
COMPLETE DESCRIPTION OF AUTO: _____

INVESTIGATIVE AGENCY AND ADDRESS: _____

▶**Figure 2.6** **SAMPLES OF A TYPICAL SUMMONS AND AN ARREST WARRANT** consists mainly of the presentation of evidence against the defendant by the prosecuting attorney. The Court in *Coleman v. Alabama* described the defense attorney's function:

> First, the lawyer's skilled examination and cross-examination of witnesses may expose fatal weaknesses in the State's case that may lead the magistrate to refuse to bind the accused over. Second, in any event, the skilled interrogation of witnesses by an experienced lawyer can fashion a vital impeachment tool for use in cross-examination of the State's witnesses at the trial, or preserve testimony favorable to the accused of a witness who does not appear at the trial. Third, retained counsel can more effectively discover the case the State has against his client and make possible the preparation of a proper defense to meet that case at the trial. Fourth, counsel can also be influential at the preliminary hearing in making effective arguments for the accused on such matters as the necessity for early psychiatric examination or bail. 399 U.S. at 9.

If the magistrate finds probable cause to believe that the defendant committed the offense, the magistrate **binds over** the defendant to the trial court for adjudication of the felony charges. The magistrate may admit the defendant to **bail** at the preliminary hearing or may continue, increase, or decrease the original bail. (Bail is discussed in further detail in Chapter 1.) If the magistrate does not find probable cause, the magistrate dismisses the complaint and releases the defendant. A dismissal at this stage does not invoke the constitutional safeguard against double jeopardy. This means that the prosecution may recharge the defendant and submit new evidence at a later preliminary hearing. Nor does a dismissal prevent the prosecution from going to the grand jury and obtaining an indictment in states that have both grand jury and preliminary hearing procedures. Table 2.1 compares the preliminary hearing with grand jury proceedings.

Indictments and Informations

In felony cases in jurisdictions that have a grand jury system, an **indictment** replaces the complaint as the document that charges the defendant with an offense and on which the defendant is brought to trial. Under Rule 7 of the Federal Rules of Criminal Procedure, an indictment "must be a plain, concise, and definite written statement of the essential facts constituting the offense charged and must be signed by an attorney for the government" as well as by the foreperson of the grand jury.

In some jurisdictions, grand jury indictments are not required to move forward with felony trials. Instead, felony trials may proceed using an **information**—a charging document that is signed and sworn to only by the prosecuting attorney, without the approval or intervention of the grand jury. Laws governing when the indictment or the information is used vary from state to state.

An example of a typical indictment appears in Figure 2.7. Note the language "a true bill" in the example. This means that the grand jury found probable cause to justify the prosecution of the defendant. If the grand jury had rejected the prosecutor's evidence and found no grounds for prosecution (which is rare), it would have endorsed on the indictment form "no true bill," "not a true bill," "no bill," or some similar language. A variety of technical statutes and rules deal with drafting, amending, and dismissing indictments and informations. These provisions are of direct concern only to judges and attorneys and are not discussed here.

TABLE 2.1 **DIFFERENCES IN PRETRIAL PROCEDURES TO DETERMINE IF PROBABLE CAUSE EXISTS TO MAKE A DEFENDANT STAND TRIAL IN FELONY CASES**

Grand Jury Proceedings	Preliminary Hearing
Primary function is to determine whether there is probable cause to believe that the defendant committed the crime or crimes charged.	Primary function is to determine whether there is probable cause to believe that the defendant committed the crime or crimes charged.
If probable cause is found, the grand jury returns an indictment/"true bill" against the defendant that is signed both by the prosecutor and by the foreperson of the grand jury.	If probable cause is found, the judge binds over the defendant for the trial court for adjudication by signing an information.
Held in the grand jury room in a closed session (i.e., secret proceedings not open to the public).	Held in open court (i.e., open to the public).
Informal proceeding in which no judicial officer presides.	Formal judicial proceeding presided over by a judge or magistrate.
Non-adversarial proceeding in which the grand jury only hears evidence presented by the prosecution.	Adversarial proceeding in which both the prosecution and the defense may present evidence to the presiding judicial officer.
Defendant has no right to be present or to offer evidence.	Defendant has the right to be present, to offer evidence, and to cross-examine adverse witnesses.
Defendant has no Sixth Amendment right to counsel.	Defendant has a right to the effective assistance of counsel under the Sixth Amendment.
Grand jury has the power to investigate crimes on its own initiative.	No power to investigate crime.
Grand jury has the power to subpoena witnesses and evidence.	No subpoena power.
Grand jury has the power to grant immunity.	No power to grant immunity.

Grand Jury The Fifth Amendment provides that "[n]o person shall be held to answer for a capital, or otherwise infamous crime, unless on a presentment or indictment of a Grand Jury." As explained in Chapter 1, this requirement applies only to the federal government, although states have developed their own laws and rules regarding the use of the grand jury. The primary duty of the **grand jury** is to receive complaints in criminal cases, hear the evidence put forth by the state, and return an indictment when the jury is satisfied that there is probable cause that the defendant has committed an offense. The concurrence of a specified number of grand jurors is required to return an indictment.
The grand jury is unique in that:

> The whole theory of its function is that it belongs to no branch of the institutional Government, serving as a kind of buffer or referee between the Government and the people. . . . Although the grand jury normally operates, of course, in the courthouse and under judicial auspices, its institutional relationship with the Judicial Branch has traditionally been,

UNITED STATES DISTRICT COURT
DISTRICT OF MAINE

UNITED STATES OF AMERICA   )

)   Criminal Case Number: CR-2007-0142
                                                    v.   )   For Violations of: 21 U.S.C §§ 841(a)(1),
)   841(b)(1)(B), 853(a); and 18 U.S.C § 2.
ROY L. PAINE   )

_____   )

INDICTMENT

The Grand Jury Charges:

Count One

On or about February 15, 2007, in the District of Maine, ROY L. PAINE, defendant herein, did unlawfully, knowingly and intentionally manufacture and aid and abet in the manufacture of in excess of one hundred (100) marijuana plants, a Schedule I controlled substance listed in Title 21, United States Code, Section 812, in violation of Title 21, United States Code, Sections 841(a)(1), 841(b)(1)(B), and Title 18, United States Code Section 2.

Count Two

On or about February 15, 2007, in the District of Maine, ROY L. PAINE, defendant herein, did unlawfully, knowingly and intentionally possess with intent to distribute and aid and abet the possession with intent to distribute in excess of one hundred (100) marijuana plants, a Schedule I controlled substance listed in Title 21, United States Code, Section 812, in violation of Title 21, United States Code, Sections 841(a)(1) and 841(b)(1)(B) and Title 18, United States Code, Section 2.

Count Three

In committing violations of Title 21, United States Code, Section 841(a)(1) which are punishable by imprisonment for more than one year, to wit: the offenses charged by Counts One and Two of this indictment, ROY L. PAINE, defendant herein, used and intended to use real property located off the John Tarr Road in the Town of Bowdoin, County of Sagadahoc and State of Maine which is better described in a deed from Guy Dwyer to the said ROY L. PAINE, defendant herein, dated November 9, 2000 and recorded in the Sagadahoc County Registry of Deeds at Book 733 and Page 231, including any buildings and structures located thereon, to commit and facilitate the commission of said offenses, and by virtue of the commission of said felony offenses, ROY L. PAINE, defendant herein, is forfeit of any and all interest in the said real property and such interest is vested in the United States of America and is forfeitable thereto pursuant to Title 21, United States Code, Section 853.

A TRUE BILL.

_____

Grand Jury Foreperson

_____

Assistant U.S. Attorney   A TRUE COPY

Dated: _____   ATTEST: Ray Van Rant, Clerk

                                                                       By: _____

▶**Figure 2.7** A SAMPLE INDICTMENT–A "TRUE BILL"

> so to speak, at arm's length. Judges' direct involvement in the functioning of the grand jury has generally been confined to the constitutive one of calling the grand jurors together and administering their oaths of office. *United States v. Williams*, 504 U.S. 36, 47 (1992).

The grand jury usually consists of sixteen to twenty-three jurors, selected from their communities according to law to serve during the criminal term of the appropriate court. Either the prosecution or the defendant, on the grounds of improper selection or legal disqualification, may challenge the composition of a grand jury. Bias in grand jury selection results in dismissal of the indictment. In *Rose v. Mitchell*, the U.S. Supreme Court said:

> **Selection of members of a grand jury because they are of one race and not another destroys the appearance of justice and thereby casts doubt**

> on the integrity of the judicial process. The exclusion from grand jury service of Negroes, or any group otherwise qualified to serve, impairs the confidence of the public in the administration of justice. As this Court repeatedly has emphasized, such discrimination "not only violates our Constitution and the laws enacted under it but is at war with our basic concepts of a democratic society and a representative government." 443 U.S. 545, 555–56 (1979).

Grand jury proceedings are non-adversarial and are traditionally conducted in secrecy. During deliberations or voting, no one other than the jurors is allowed to be present. When the grand jury is taking evidence, however, the attorneys for the state, the witnesses under examination, and, when ordered by the court, an interpreter and an official court reporter may be present. Matters occurring before the grand jury, other than the deliberations or the votes of any juror, may be disclosed to the prosecuting attorney for use in performing his or her duties. Otherwise, these matters are to be kept secret, unless the court orders that they be disclosed.

The reasons for keeping grand jury proceedings secret were summarized in *United States v. Procter & Gamble Co.*, 356 U.S. 677, 681 n.6 (1958):

> (1) to prevent the escape of those whose indictment may be contemplated; (2) to insure the utmost freedom to the grand jury in its deliberations, and to prevent persons subject to indictment or their friends from importuning the grand jurors; (3) to prevent subornation of perjury or tampering with the witnesses who may testify before grand jury and later appear at the trial of those indicted by it; (4) to encourage free and untrammeled disclosures by persons who have information with respect to the commission of crimes; (5) to protect innocent accused who is exonerated from disclosure of the fact that he has been under investigation, and from the expense of standing trial where there was no probability of guilt.

The grand jury also has broad investigative powers, including the power to subpoena people or documents as illustrated by the grand jury subpoena contained in Figure 2.8.

Traditionally the grand jury has been accorded wide latitude to inquire into violations of criminal law. No judge presides to monitor its proceedings. It deliberates in secret and may alone determine the course of its inquiry. The grand jury may compel the production of evidence or the testimony of witnesses as it considers appropriate, and its operation generally is unrestrained by the technical procedural and evidentiary rules governing the conduct of criminal trials. *United States v. Calandra*, 414 U.S. 338, 343 (1974).

The Fourth Amendment prohibits unreasonably vague or overbroad subpoenas for documents, and some courts hold that the evidence sought must be relevant to the investigation. Failure to obey a subpoena is punishable as contempt of court. A grand jury may also grant **immunity** to compel testimony from witnesses who exercise their Fifth Amendment privilege against self-incrimination and refuse to testify. There are two different types of immunity: use immunity and transactional immunity. *Transactional immunity* is the broader type of protection because it immunizes the witness from prosecution for the offense(s) concerning the witness' testimony, as well as from future prosecutions for crimes uncovered as a result of evidence derived from the immunized testimony. *Use immunity* proves much less protection; it prohibits the government from using the immunized testimony in any subsequent prosecution of the witness (except in a subsequent prosecution for perjury or giving a false statement).

AO110 (Rev. 12/89) Subpoena to Testify Before Grand Jury

UNITED STATES DISTRICT COURT

DISTRICT OF _____

TO:

**SUBPOENA TO TESTIFY
BEFORE GRAND JURY**

SUBPOENA FOR:
☐ PERSON   ☐ DOCUMENT(S) OR OBJECT(S)

YOU ARE HEREBY COMMANDED to appear and testify before the Grand Jury of the United States District Court at the place, date, and time specified below.

PLACE	COURTROOM
	DATE AND TIME

YOU ARE ALSO COMMANDED to bring with you the following document(s) or object(s):*

☐   *Please see additional information on reverse.*

This subpoena shall remain in effect until you are granted leave to depart by the court or by an officer acting on behalf of the court.

CLERK	DATE
(By) Deputy Clerk	

This subpoena is issued on application of the United States of America	NAME, ADDRESS AND PHONE NUMBER OF ASSISTANT U.S. ATTORNEY

* If not applicable, enter "none".

▶**Figure 2.8** SUBPOENA TO TESTIFY BEFORE THE GRAND JURY

Waiver of Right to Grand Jury Indictment In some jurisdictions, a defendant who does not wish to be prosecuted by indictment may waive the indictment and be prosecuted by information. The waiver of indictment procedure is of great advantage to a defendant who wishes to plead guilty or *nolo contendere*. (These pleas are discussed in further detail later in this chapter.) In effect, the waiver of indictment procedure enables a defendant to begin serving a sentence sooner instead of having to wait for a grand jury, which sits only during the criminal term of court. The defendant can thereby secure release from custody at an earlier date than by going through the indictment procedure.

Warrant or Summons Issued on the Indictment An indictment may sometimes be handed down against a defendant by a grand jury before the defendant has been taken into custody and brought before the court. In these cases, at the request of the prosecuting attorney or by direction of the court, a summons or arrest warrant is issued for each defendant named in the indictment. This process indicates no change of procedure for law enforcement officers, who are required to execute the warrant or serve the summons in the same way as they would any other warrant or summons. Procedures for executing an arrest warrant or serving a summons appear in Chapter 6.

Arraignment and Pleas

After the issuance of a true bill on the indictment or a bind over order in the preliminary hearing, the next step is the **arraignment.** A defendant who has been arrested often confuses the meaning of the term *arraignment* with the term *initial appearance* before a magistrate. Part of the reason for this confusion is that, in misdemeanor proceedings in courts of limited jurisdiction, the two procedures are combined. The essence of the arraignment is that the defendant is called on to plead formally to the charge after the magistrate reads the substance of the charge. In misdemeanor proceedings, if there is no requirement of prosecution by indictment or information, the complaint is read to the defendant and the plea is made to the complaint. However, in courts that require prosecution by grand jury indictment or a bind over at a preliminary hearing, either the indictment or the information must be read to the defendant at an arraignment and the defendant must then enter a formal plea on each charge.

Pleas Although the pleas available to defendants vary by jurisdiction, a defendant may always plead guilty or not guilty. In some jurisdictions, a defendant may also plead *nolo contendere* (no contest), although these pleas are rare. And, in most jurisdictions, a fourth plea of not guilty by reason of insanity is also available. A plea of *not guilty* puts in issue all the material facts alleged in the indictment, information, or complaint. Unless a not guilty plea is subsequently changed to a plea of guilty as part of the plea bargaining process (more on plea bargaining below), then the factual question of the defendant's guilt will be resolved at trial. A defendant may refuse to plead at all, in which case the court must enter a plea of not guilty on the defendant's behalf. Refusing to plead (sometimes called standing mute) may occur for various reasons, such as obstinacy, dumbness, insanity, mental illness or retardation, or ignorance of the language used in the proceedings.

Requirements of Guilty Pleas and *Nolo Contendere* Pleas To plead guilty or *nolo contendere*, the defendant must obtain the court's consent. Both these pleas simply mean that the defendant does not wish to contest the charge and will submit to the judgment of the court. A *guilty plea* may constitute an admission of guilt by the defendant and may be used against him or her in a civil action based on the same facts. A plea of *nolo contendere,* however, is not an admission of guilt and cannot be used against the defendant in a civil action. Therefore, the court may not accept a plea of guilty or *nolo contendere* in a felony proceeding unless the court is satisfied, after inquiry: (1) that the defendant committed the crime charged; (2) that the plea is made knowingly, intelligently, and voluntarily; and (3) that the defendant is mentally competent to enter the plea and thereby waive several important constitutional rights. This inquiry by the court is often referred to as a "Rule 11 proceeding" because Rule 11 of the Federal Rules of Criminal Procedure and similar state provisions establish guidelines for courts in making these and other determinations.

Rule 11 requires that the judge "address the defendant personally in open court and determine that the plea is voluntary and did not result from force, threats, or promises (other than promises [contained] in the plea agreement)." In addition to finding that a plea is voluntary, the court must also be sure that a plea is a knowing and intelligent waiver of the defendant's constitutional rights. By pleading guilty or *nolo contendere*, a defendant waives many constitutional rights, including:

▶ the right to a trial by jury;

▶ the right to confront and cross-examine adverse witnesses;

▶ the right to compel the attendance and testimony of witnesses;

▶ the right to testify on one's own behalf;

▶ the right to be free from being forced to incriminate oneself;

▶ the right to be presumed innocent until proven guilty beyond a reasonable doubt; and

▶ the right to appeal one's conviction.

To satisfy Rule 11's requirement that the court be satisfied that the defendant actually committed the crime charged in order for the court to accept a plea, the defendant must **allocute** to each charge. (In some jurisdictions, the Rule 11 hearing is therefore called an "**allocution hearing**.") To allocute, a defendant must provide a "factual basis" for the plea; in other words, the defendant, in open court, must admit to the conduct central to the criminality of crimes charged.

Rule 11 does not specifically state that a court must ensure a criminal defendant is competent to waive any constitutional rights. But the Supreme Court has held that because pleading guilty involves waiving the numerous rights discussed below, a court may not accept a guilty or *nolo contendere* plea from a defendant who is not mentally competent. *Godinez v. Moran*, 509 U.S. 389 (1993). This determination involves the same considerations as the determination of competency to stand trial, discussed later in this chapter. Normally, a defendant's lawyer plays a key role in negotiating a plea. But what if a defendant wishes to waive the right to counsel and serve as his/her own attorney? *Godinez* made clear that the Constitution does not require states to use a heightened level of competency for waiving counsel than for waiving any other constitutional right. The Court's decision in *Godinez* received much criticism from scholars of the law and behavioral science (Winick 1995; Felthous 1994). In fact, some mental health scholars, urged "psychologists to employ a functional approach to competency determinations, argu[ing] that following the unitary

Godinez standard would 'represent a substantial deviation from the accepted standard of care in conducting such evaluations'" (Corinis 2000, citing Shapiro 1997). Unfortunately, the *Godinez* opinion has left the approach to various criminal competencies in a state of disarray, with each state opting for one of three approaches.

> Some states . . . do not require a heightened competency standard, or even a separate competency hearing, before determining whether a defendant is competent to waive counsel. Rather, they construe *Godinez* as requiring only a voluntary and knowing waiver of Sixth Amendment rights, without regard to a defendant's mental capacity. Other courts, after *Godinez,* assert that the constitutional right to waive counsel mandates using only the *Dusky* test to determine competence to choose self-representation, in spite of [the Court's] express invitation to adopt enhanced standards. Other states . . . have followed [the] suggestion, employing a standard for determining a defendant's competency to waive counsel that is higher than the standard for determining competency to stand trial.

Regardless of the shortcomings of *Godinez*, it is clear that if someone is found competent to waive counsel, the court need not inform the defendant that waiving counsel's assistance in deciding whether to plead guilty risks overlooking a viable defense and foregoes the opportunity to obtain an independent opinion on the wisdom of pleading guilty. *Iowa v. Tovar*, 541 U.S. 77 (2004). In other words, the defendant who acts as his own counsel proceeds at his own peril and is stuck with the consequences of that decision.

Judicial Approval of Guilty Pleas and *Nolo Contendere* Pleas While there are minor variations by jurisdiction, most states follow the same procedures used in the federal system concerning judicial approval of plea agreements. Rule 11(c) gives the trial court judge the discretion to accept or reject a plea agreement. Thus, even though the prosecutor, defense counsel, and the defendant may all agree on a plea, ultimately the court must approve the agreement. If the court finds that the plea agreement is not in the interest of justice, the court may reject it.

Pleading Insane In most, but not all U.S. jurisdictions, another plea that a defendant may enter at an arraignment is a plea of **not guilty by reason of insanity** or some variation on it like "guilty except insane." Such a plea is required if the defendant intends to raise the defense of insanity at trial. A defendant may plead not guilty and not guilty by reason of insanity to the same charge. When a plea of not guilty by reason of insanity is entered, a court usually orders the defendant committed to an appropriate institution for the mentally ill for a comprehensive examination, the results of which are critical to the issue of legal insanity at trial. The insanity plea is rarely raised. It is almost never pled in a misdemeanor proceeding, and it is only raised in approximately 1 percent of all felony cases. Moreover, when invoked in this small percentage of cases, the insanity defense is successful less than 25 percent of the time (Perlin 1997). Defendants found not guilty by reason of insanity usually face a lengthy post-acquittal period of confinement in a secure mental institution. In fact, most states automatically commit someone found not guilty by reason of insanity to a mental hospital for at least a sixty-day period and then place the burden on the person committed to show when they are no longer mentally ill and dangerous. This typically results in insanity acquittees spending many more years incarcerated in a mental institution than what they would have served in prison had they been criminally convicted (Morris 1997).

Plea Bargaining

> The disposition of criminal charges by agreement between the prosecutor and the accused, sometimes loosely called "plea bargaining," is an essential component of the administration of justice. Properly administered, it is to be encouraged. If every criminal charge were subjected to a full-scale trial, the States and the Federal Government would need to multiply by many times the number of judges and court facilities.
>
> Disposition of charges after plea discussions is an essential part of the process and a highly desirable part for many reasons. It leads to prompt and largely final disposition of most criminal cases; it avoids much of the corrosive impact of enforced idleness during pretrial confinement for those who are denied release pending trial; it protects the public from those accused persons who are prone to continue criminal conduct even while on pretrial release, and, by shortening the time between charge and disposition, it enhances whatever may be the rehabilitative prospects of the guilty when they are ultimately imprisoned.
>
> This phase of the process of criminal justice, and the adjudicative element inherent in accepting a plea of guilty, must be attended by safeguards to insure the defendant what is reasonably due in the circumstances. Those circumstances will vary, but a constant factor is that when a plea rests in any significant degree on a promise or agreement of the prosecutor, so that it can be said to be part of the inducement or consideration, such promise must be fulfilled. *Santobello v. New York*, 404 U.S. 257, 260-62 (1971).

Most states have developed statutes or rules governing the **plea bargaining** process, just as the federal government has done in Rule 11(c) of the Federal Rules of Criminal Procedure.

In general, plea agreements are treated as contracts. If the defendant breaches the agreement, the prosecution may not only reprosecute the defendant, but also may bring more serious charges. For example, in *Bordenkircher v. Hayes*, 434 U.S. 357 (1978), the U.S. Supreme Court found no due process violation when the prosecutor carried out a threat made during plea negotiations to reindict the defendant on more serious charges if the defendant did not plead guilty to the original charge. If the defendant alleges that the prosecution breached a plea agreement and the allegations are not "palpably incredible" or "patently frivolous or false," the defendant is entitled to an evidentiary hearing. *Blackledge v. Allison*, 431 U.S. 63 (1977). If the defendant establishes such a breach, the court may allow the defendant to withdraw the plea, alter the sentence, or require the prosecution to honor the agreement.

Preparing for Trial

Motions A **motion** is an oral or written request asking a court to make a specified finding, decision, or order. Many standard motions are available, but an attorney may also fashion unique motions in response to particular circumstances requiring court action. Some of the most common standard pretrial motions are: motion to be admitted to bail, motion to quash a grand jury indictment, motion to inspect grand jury minutes, motion to challenge the sufficiency of the indictment, motion for a competency hearing, motion for discovery, motion for a continuance, motion for change of venue, motion to dismiss an indictment, and motion to withdraw a guilty plea. Most of these motions are discussed elsewhere in this chapter or are primarily of concern to judges and attorneys and, therefore, beyond the scope of this book.

Two pretrial motions, however, are central to criminal procedure law: (1) the motion to suppress evidence and (2) the motion to suppress a confession. These motions are made by defendants who believe they are aggrieved by either an unlawful search and seizure or an unlawfully obtained admission or confession. The purpose of a motion to suppress is twofold:

▶ To enable the defendant to invoke the exclusionary rule and prevent the use of illegally obtained evidence at trial.

▶ To enable the court to resolve the issue of the legality of a search and seizure or confession without interrupting the trial

The hearing on a motion to suppress is often the point in the proceedings at which the court carefully scrutinizes a law enforcement officer's performance in a case. If a defendant is able to prove that an officer illegally obtained evidence, and if the evidence is essential to the prosecution's case, suppression of the evidence is likely to result in a dismissal of charges or the granting of a motion for judgment of acquittal. Therefore, law enforcement officers must know the law not only when they conduct a search and seizure or obtain a confession, but also when they are called on to justify their actions at a hearing on a motion to suppress.

Depositions A court may order the **deposition** of a witness who is unable to attend a criminal trial and whose testimony is material to a just determination of the case to be taken at any time after the filing of an indictment or information. A deposition involves taking the out-of-court testimony of a witness and preserving that testimony in writing for later use in court. A deposition is used only in exceptional circumstances and not for the mere convenience of a witness or party. Either the prosecution or the defendant may request a deposition, and the opposing party may attend the taking of the deposition. A deposition, or a part of a deposition, may be used at a trial or hearing if it appears that:

▶ The witness who gave the deposition is dead;

▶ The witness is out of the jurisdiction (unless the party offering the deposition caused the witness's absence);

▶ The witness is unable to attend or testify because of sickness or infirmity; or

▶ The party offering the deposition is unable to procure the attendance of the witness by subpoena.

Furthermore, depositions may be used even if the witness does testify at the trial, but only for the purposes of contradicting the witness's testimony. This is known as **impeaching** the witness.

Discovery **Discovery** is a procedure whereby the defendant and/or the prosecution is allowed to inspect, examine, copy, or photograph items in the possession of the other party. The general purpose of discovery is to make the criminal trial **"less a game of blindman's bluff and more a fair contest with the basic issues and facts disclosed to the fullest practical extent."** *United States v. Procter & Gamble Co.,* 356 U.S. 677, 682 (1958).

While there is **"no general constitutional right to discovery in a criminal case,"** *Weatherford v. Bursey,* 429 U.S. 545, 559 (1977), there are a series of court decisions, statutes, and court rules that provide the framework for the criminal discovery process. Discovery in federal cases is governed primarily by sections of Rules 12, 16, and 26 of the Federal Rules of Criminal Procedure; many states have similar counterparts to these rules. Collectively, these rules provide a defendant, upon motion, rights to discovery concerning tangible objects; tape recordings; books, papers and documents (including written or recorded statements made by the defendants or witnesses) that are relevant to the case; the defendant's prior criminal record, if any; the results or reports of physical examinations, scientific tests, experiments, and forensic comparisons; and summaries of any expert testimony that the government intends to offer in its case-in-chief. The rules often afford the government similar reciprocal discovery upon its compliance with the request of the defendant.

Ordinarily, to obtain discoverable information, a party must make a timely motion before the court and must show that the specific items sought are material to the preparation of its case and that its request is reasonable. Nevertheless, jurisdictions differ considerably with respect to both the conditions under which discovery is allowed and the items subject to discovery. A recent development is automatic informal discovery for certain types of evidence, without the necessity for motions and court orders. The state of the law governing discovery is constantly changing, but the trend appears to be in favor of broadening the right of discovery for both the defense and the prosecution.

There is no general constitutional right to discovery in criminal cases. Nonetheless, in order to protect defendants' due process rights, courts have created rules requiring disclosure of evidence in certain situations.

Exculpatory Evidence **Exculpatory evidence** is any evidence that may be favorable to the defendant at trial either by tending to cast doubt on the defendant's guilt or by tending to mitigate the defendant's culpability, thereby potentially reducing the defendant's sentence. In *Brady v. Maryland,* 373 U.S. 83, 87 (1963), the U.S. Supreme Court held that **"the suppression by the prosecution of evidence favorable to an accused upon request violates due process where the evidence is material either to guilt or punishment, *irrespective of the good faith or bad faith of the prosecution"*** (italics added). This is commonly referred to as the *Brady* rule. Exculpatory evidence is material **"only if there is a 'reasonable probability' that, had the evidence been disclosed to the defense, the result of the proceeding would have been different. A 'reasonable probability' is a probability sufficient to undermine confidence in the outcome."** *United States v. Bagley,* 473 U.S. 667, 682 (1985).

As the Court explained in *Kyles v. Whitley,* 514 U.S. 419, 434 (1995), **"[t]he question is not whether the defendant would more likely than not have received a different verdict with the evidence, but whether in its absence he received a fair trial, understood as a trial resulting in a verdict worthy of confidence."** *Kyles v. Whitley* required disclosure of exculpatory evidence to the defense even if the police had not revealed the evidence to the prosecutor.

According to the Court, prosecutors are responsible for ensuring that police communicate relevant evidence to the prosecutor's office.

The *Brady* rule is limited to admissible evidence. Thus, the prosecution has no obligation to provide the defense potentially exculpatory information that would not be admissible in court. For example, in *Wood v. Bartholomew*, 516 U.S. 1 (1995), the U.S. Supreme Court held that there is no requirement to turn over the results of a polygraph examination of a witness because polygraph results are inadmissible.

Brady does not require the prosecution to make its files available to the defendant for an open-ended "fishing expedition." Nor does *Brady* require the disclosure of inculpatory, neutral, or speculative evidence. However, prosecutors' obligations under *Brady* are not limited to situations in which the defendant specifically requests the evidence. As the "attorney for the sovereign," the prosecutor **"must always be faithful to his client's overriding interest that 'justice shall be done.'"** *United States v. Agurs*, 427 U.S. 97, 110-11 (1976).

Impeachment Material In *Jencks v. United States*, 353 U.S. 657 (1957), the Supreme Court ruled that the government must disclose any prior inconsistent statements of prosecutorial witnesses so that the defense could conduct a meaningful cross-examination of such witnesses. Congress both expanded and limited the holding in *Jencks* when it enacted The Jencks Act, 18 U.S.C. § 3500. That Act requires the prosecutor to disclose, after direct examination of a government witness and on the defendant's motion, any statement of a witness in the government's possession that relates to the subject matter of the witness' testimony. Thus, the Jencks Act requires disclosure of all prior statements of witnesses, even if the prior statements are not inconsistent with any subsequent statement by the witnesses, expanding the holding of *Jencks*. Yet, Congress placed the burden on defense counsel to ask for the information (unlike *Brady* material that the prosecutor has an ethical obligation to disclose even if not asked). Congress also limited the time frame for such disclosure such that it need not take place until after the direct examination of a governmental witness by the prosecution.

In *Giglio v. United States*, 405 U.S. 150 (1972), the Supreme Court clarified that all impeachment evidence, even if not a prior statement by a witness, also falls within the *Brady* rule. Thus, *Giglio* mandated that the prosecution disclose any and all information that may be used to impeach the credibility of prosecution witnesses, including law enforcement officers. Impeachment information under *Giglio* includes information such as the prior criminal records or other acts of misconduct of prosecution witnesses, or such information as promises of leniency or immunity offered to prosecution witnesses. *United States v. Henthorn*, 931 F.2d 29 (9th Cir. 1991), held that the government has a duty to examine the personnel files of testifying law enforcement officers for *Brady* or *Giglio* material; for example, information that could compromise the officers' credibility, including past accusations of misconduct.

As with *Brady* material, the mandates of *Jencks* and *Giglio* do not require the prosecution to make its files available to the defendant for an open-ended "fishing expedition."

Subpoena The term **subpoena** describes a court order used to secure the attendance of witnesses at a criminal proceeding. A **subpoena** *duces tecum* production of books, papers, documents, or other objects is the primary vehicle by

AO89 (Rev. 7/95) Subpoena in a Criminal Case

UNITED STATES DISTRICT COURT

DISTRICT OF

V.

SUBPOENA IN A CRIMINAL CASE

Case Number:

TO:

☐ YOU ARE COMMANDED to appear in the United States District Court at the place, date, and time specified below, or any subsequent place, date and time set by the court, to testify in the above referenced case. This subpoena shall remain in effect until you are granted leave to depart by the court or by an officer acting on behalf of the court.

PLACE	COURTROOM
	DATE AND TIME

☐ YOU ARE ALSO COMMANDED to bring with you the following document(s) or object(s):

U.S. MAGISTRATE JUDGE OR CLERK OF COURT	DATE
(By) Deputy Clerk	

ATTORNEY'S NAME, ADDRESS AND PHONE NUMBER:

AO89 (Rev. 7/95) Subpoena in a Criminal Case (Reverse)

PROOF OF SERVICE		
RECEIVED BY SERVER	DATE	PLACE
SERVED	DATE	PLACE
SERVED ON (PRINT NAME)		FEES AND MILEAGE TENDERED TO WITNESS ☐ YES ☐ NO AMOUNT $
SERVED BY (PRINT NAME)		TITLE

DECLARATION OF SERVER

I declare under penalty of perjury under the laws of the United States of America that the foregoing information contained in the Proof of Service is true and correct.

Executed on ______________ DATE

SIGNATURE OF SERVER

ADDRESS OF SERVER

ADDITIONAL INFORMATION

Figure 2.9 A SAMPLE SUBPOENA

which a defendant exercises the Sixth Amendment right to "compulsory process for obtaining witnesses in his favor" (see Chapter 1). The subpoena is usually issued by a judicial officer, and it commands the person to whom it is directed to attend a trial, hearing, or deposition for the purpose of testifying at the proceeding or bringing a named document or object. As discussed earlier, the grand jury also has broad subpoena powers. A law enforcement officer or any other adult person who is not a party to the proceedings may serve a subpoena. A typical form for a subpoena in a criminal case appears in Figure 2.9.

Competency to Stand Trial The U.S. system of criminal justice requires that one be competent or "fit" to stand trial before one's guilt or innocence is assessed at a criminal trial. The Constitution's guarantee of due process prohibits trying an incompetent defendant for several reasons. The legal bar against trying incompetent defendants dates back to common law England.

> Blackstone wrote that a defendant who becomes "mad" after the commission of an offense should not be arraigned "because he is not able to plead . . . with the advice and caution that he ought," and should not be tried, for "how can he make his defense?" The ban on trial of an incompetent defendant stems from the common law prohibition on trials in absentia, and from the difficulties the English courts encountered when defendants frustrated the ritual of the common law trial by remaining mute instead of pleading to charges. Without a plea, the trial could not go forward (Winick 1995: 574, citing Blackstone 1783).

At this point in the history of English common law, a person rarely had the right to counsel; in fact, counsel was prohibited in many cases. A defendant, therefore, usually had to represent himself or herself. As a result, "the defendant stood alone before the court, and trial was merely 'a long argument between the prisoner and the counsel for the Crown.' Thus, it was imperative that defendants be competent because they were required to conduct their own defense" (Winick 1995: 575).

Unlike with English common law, the right to counsel is guaranteed to nearly all criminal defendants today by the Sixth Amendment (see Chapter 1). As a result, the common law rationale underlying the doctrine of incompetence to stand trial is no longer applicable. But there are important justifications for the doctrine in modern times.

> First, it increases the accuracy and reliability of the trial since an incompetent defendant cannot, for example, adequately testify on his behalf. The requirement also enhances fairness, since an incompetent defendant cannot make decisions regarding the course and nature of his defense. In addition, it maintains the "dignity" of the trial, in that an incompetent defendant may behave in an offensive or inappropriate manner. Finally, a competent defendant's comprehension of why he is being punished makes the punishment more just (Meyers 1997: 1017).

Accordingly, when the fitness of a particular criminal defendant to stand trial becomes an issue in a case, his or her **competency to stand trial** must be determined before a trial can proceed. Competency to stand trial, however, may be raised at any time in the criminal process, even after conviction. While the issue of competency to stand trial is usually raised by the defense, the prosecution can raise the issue, as can the court on its own.

Due process requires a court to hold a competency hearing if there is bona-fide doubt regarding a defendant's competency. "**[E]vidence of a defendant's irrational behavior, his demeanor at trial, and any prior medical opinion on competence to stand trial are all relevant in determining whether further inquiry is required. . . .**" *Drope v. Missouri*, 420 U.S. 162, 180 (1975). Most requests for a clinical determination of competency go unopposed by opposing counsel and are routinely granted by judges. Once granted the opportunity to have such a determination made, the process of determining competency to stand trial involves forensic psychological evaluations followed by an evidentiary hearing on the issue of competency. At the competency hearing, the prosecution must usually prove, by a preponderance of the evidence, that the defendant is competent to proceed with the criminal trial. E.g., 18 U.S.C. § 4241(d). However, some states have shifted the burden of persuasion to the defense, who must show the incompetency of the defendant by a preponderance of the evidence. The Supreme Court specifically approved of this allocation of the burden of persuasion over a due process challenge in *Medina v. California*, 505 U.S. 437 (1992). The Court, however, struck down Oklahoma's attempt to require the defendant to show his or her competence by clear and convincing evidence, finding it to violate the guarantee of due process. *Cooper v. Oklahoma*, 517 U.S. 348, 369 (1996). In doing so, it invalidated the laws of the four states—Connecticut, Oklahoma, Pennsylvania, and Rhode Island—that had set the burden unconstitutionally high.

The test for determining competency to stand trial was set forth by the Supreme Court in *Dusky v. United States*, 362 U.S. 402, 402 (1960). *Dusky* held that to be competent to stand trial, a defendant must have (1) "**a rational as well as factual understanding of the proceedings against him**" and (2) "**sufficient**

present ability to consult with his lawyer with a reasonable degree of rational understanding." The first question—can the defendant understand the proceedings against him or her—is not directed at whether the defendant understands the intricacies of the criminal process. Rather, it is concerned with whether the defendant has a basic understanding of the circumstances in which he or she finds himself or herself. More simply, does the defendant understand that he or she has been charged with a crime and faces government-imposed punishment if convicted? The second criterion is whether the defendant is capable of assisting in his or her own defense. If the defendant cannot communicate with his or her attorney in a manner that permits the defense lawyer the ability to formulate a defense, there is little likelihood that the defendant will be found competent.

Although the determination of competency to stand trial is purely a legal determination—not a clinical one—the importance of the role of the evaluating clinician(s) cannot be overstated. First and foremost, the overwhelming number of competency determinations are based on the clinical assessment of a single clinician. Second, although courts are supposed to hold competency hearings, defendants are frequently determined to be incompetent by a court without an actual hearing. In this case, the prosecution and the defense stipulate that the defendant is not competent if the evaluating clinician's psychological report finds that the defendant is not competent. Even when a hearing is held, judges almost always defer to the findings of mental health professionals. Thus, if a psychologist or psychiatrist determines that a defendant is incompetent, the court is likely to agree.

When a court finds that a defendant is incompetent to stand trial, criminal proceedings against the defendant are suspended until the defendant is found competent. If future competency is highly probable, the defendant may be committed to a mental institution for a reasonable period of time to determine future competency. During this period, the court may order periodic examinations of the defendant to determine whether competency has been regained. After a reasonable period of time, the government must either institute civil commitment proceedings or release the defendant. *Jackson v. Indiana*, 406 U.S. 715 (1972).

A claim that a defendant is incompetent to stand trial is different from a claim that a defendant is not guilty by reason of insanity. The former concerns only the defendant's mental fitness at the time of trial and is unrelated to any determination of guilt. The latter is a defense to prosecution on the ground that the defendant was mentally impaired at the time that an alleged crime was committed.

TRIAL

Trial by Jury

The Sixth Amendment to the U.S. Constitution guarantees a defendant in a criminal prosecution the right to a speedy, public, and impartial trial by jury. The right to a **trial by jury** was made applicable to the states through the due process clause of the Fourteenth Amendment in *Duncan v. Louisiana*:

> Because we believe that trial by jury in criminal cases is fundamental to the American scheme of justice, we hold that the Fourteenth Amendment guarantees a right of jury trial in all criminal cases which—were they to be tried in federal court—would come within the Sixth Amendment guarantee. 391 U.S. 145, 149 (1968).

There is, however, no right to a jury trial in juvenile court proceedings because, technically, they are not criminal proceedings. *McKeiver v. Pennsylvania*, 403 U.S. 528 (1971).

The right to a trial by jury means that the government must provide a defendant with a jury trial in all criminal prosecutions except those for petty offenses. *Baldwin v. New York*, 399 U.S. 66, 69 (1970), held that **"no offense can be deemed 'petty' for purposes of the right to trial by jury where imprisonment for more than six months is authorized."** A defendant who is prosecuted in a single proceeding for multiple counts of a petty offense, however, does not have a constitutional right to a jury trial, even if the aggregate of sentences authorized for the offense exceeds six months. *Lewis v. United States*, 518 U.S. 322 (1996). For an offense punishable by a sentence of six months or less, a defendant has a constitutional right to a jury trial only if the additional statutory penalties **"are so severe that they clearly reflect a legislative determination that the offense in question is a 'serious' one."** *Blanton v. City of North Las Vegas*, 489 U.S. 538, 543 (1989). In *Blanton*, the Supreme Court upheld the denial of a jury trial to a drunk-driving defendant who faced up to six months incarceration, finding that the other statutory penalties—which included community service, a fine of up to $1,000, special conditions of probation including an educational course on alcohol abuse, and loss of a driver's license for ninety days—were not severe enough to reflect that the state legislature believed the offense to be a "serious one." Note, however, that a number of states provide a statutory right to a trial by jury for driving under the influence cases and other misdemeanor crimes for which a period of incarceration may be imposed, even if less than six months.

Bench Trials

Defendants who do not wish to be tried by a jury may, with the approval of the court, waive their right to a jury trial and, instead, opt for a *non-jury trial* known as a **bench trial.** While a defendant has no absolute constitutional right to a bench trial, a criminal defendant may want such a trial in lieu of a jury trial for a number of reasons, most frequently because the defendant believes that a jury might be biased or prejudiced against him and therefore would not provide a fair and impartial trial.

> The inability of a jury to provide a fair trial may occur for various reasons. For example, a jury can be affected by adverse pretrial publicity. . . . The defendant's right to a fair trial may also be threatened by forcing a jury upon him if the correct resolution of a case requires command of a difficult subject matter beyond the knowledge of the average layman. Even with the guidance of experts, the jury may be incapable of rendering a fair and reasoned verdict. Furthermore, if the defendant is charged with a particularly heinous crime, a jury may not be able to decide the case without bringing preconceived notions into consideration. (DeCicco 1983: 1094-96).

When a defendant seeks to waive the constitutional right to a trial by jury, such a waiver, like those of other constitutional rights, must be voluntary, knowing, and intelligent.

When a case is tried without a jury, the judge must perform the jury's functions, detailed in the next paragraph. Outside these jury functions, the judge's other regular duties are essentially the same in either a jury or non-jury trial. Therefore, the remainder of this chapter focuses on jury trials.

Jury Selection

Once it has been determined that the trial will be by jury, the next step in the criminal proceeding is the selection of the jurors. Jurors perform the crucial tasks of weighing the evidence, determining the credibility of witnesses, finding the facts, and ultimately rendering a verdict of guilty or not guilty. Because of the importance of the jury's functions, detailed rules govern the selection of jurors to protect the prosecution or the defendant from having a person prejudiced against its cause sitting as a member of the jury during the trial.

Summoning the Venire In order to assemble a jury, potential jurors receive a **summons** in the mail ordering them to appear in court at a specified time and date. The people who are so summoned comprise the *venire*—the prospective jurors for cases. The summons is usually accompanied by a juror questionnaire (like the one in Figure 2.10) that is used to make sure the recipient is qualified to serve as a member of the venire panel. In a run-of-the mill case, forty or fifty people might be summoned in order to select a twelve-person jury. In a high-profile case, hundreds might be called for jury service.

Of course, just because a person is summoned to jury service does not mean he or she will respond to the summons. Any number of factors might prevent someone summoned from responding. Some people simply never receive a summons because they are transient. This most affects disenfranchised minority populations, and has the secondary effect of limiting the representativeness of the venire. But even when people do receive a summons, between 20 percent and 45 percent of people simply disregard them, leaving as little as 55 percent of people summoned for jury service who actually appear for service (Saunders 1997). Disregarding a summons for jury duty is dangerous business, however, since a warrant can be issued for the arrest of anyone who disregards a court order like a jury summons.

The venire is supposed to be representative of society as a whole. Federal law and the law of most states require that no citizen be excluded from service as a juror on account of race, color, religion, gender, national origin, or economic status. But this does not mean that the venire must be **"a perfect mirror of the community or accurately [reflect] the proportionate strength of every identifiable group."** *Swain v. Alabama*, 380 U.S. 202, 208 (1965). It does mean that the venire is supposed to be drawn from a fair cross-section of the community. *Taylor v. Louisiana*, 419 U.S. 522 (1975). Unfortunately, this foundation of constitutional law has proven to be more aspirational than effective in reality. Historically, venire panels were not representative of a community. Middle-aged to older white men were over-represented for decades, mainly because the venire used to be drawn exclusively from the voter-registration rolls. As we began to recognize that homogeneity in the venire led to both blatant

JUROR QUALIFICATION QUESTIONNAIRE

AO178
(Rev. 8/97)

PLEASE READ LETTER ON THE NEXT PAGE ■ PRINT OR TYPE YOUR ANSWERS

1. IF YOUR NAME AND PERMANENT ADDRESS ARE NOT CORRECT, PLEASE CHECK ☐ AND SHOW CORRECTIONS ON NEXT PAGE.

2. RETURN THIS FORM IN THE ENCLOSED ENVELOPE TO:
UNITED STATES DISTRICT COURT
ATTENTION: JURY CLERK

3. COUNTY YOU NOW LIVE IN →

4. HAS YOUR PRIMARY RESIDENCE FOR THE PAST YEAR BEEN IN → IF "NO" GIVE NAMES OF OTHER COUNTIES OR STATES OF PRIMARY RESIDENCE DURING THE PAST YEAR, AND SHOW DATES (USE REVERSE IF NECESSARY.)
- THIS STATE ☐ YES ☐ NO
- THE SAME COUNTY ☐ YES ☐ NO

5. PHONE { HOME / WORK

A. IDENTIFICATION

6. BIRTH DATE { month / day / year
7. AGE
8. U.S. CITIZEN ☐ YES ☐ NO

9. Mr. Mrs. Miss Ms. 10. ☐ Single ☐ Married ☐ Divorced/Separated ☐ Widowed
☐ MALE SEX: ☐ FEMALE

11. PLEASE INDICATE YOUR RACE ON THE FOLLOWING LIST

FEDERAL LAW REQUIRES YOU AS A PROSPECTIVE JUROR TO INDICATE YOUR RACE. THIS ANSWER IS REQUIRED SOLELY TO AVOID DISCRIMINATION IN JUROR SELECTION AND HAS ABSOLUTELY NO BEARING ON QUALIFICATIONS FOR JURY SERVICE. BY ANSWERING THIS QUESTION YOU HELP THE FEDERAL COURT CHECK AND OBSERVE THE JUROR SELECTION PROCESS SO THAT DISCRIMINATION CANNOT OCCUR. IN THIS WAY THE FEDERAL COURTS CAN FULFILL THE POLICY OF THE UNITED STATES WHICH IS TO PROVIDE JURORS WHO ARE RANDOMLY SELECTED FROM A FAIR CROSS SECTION OF THE COMMUNITY

☐ BLACK
☐ WHITE
☐ ASIAN
☐ NATIVE AMERICAN
☐ OTHER (Spcfy.)
ARE YOU HISPANIC? ☐ YES ☐ NO

B. OCCUPATION

FEDERAL LAW REQUIRES THAT YOU ANSWER NO. 12, 13, 14 & 15 SO THAT THE FEDERAL COURTS MAY DETERMINE PROMPTLY WHETHER YOU FALL WITHIN AN EXCUSE OR EXEMPTION CATEGORY (See "E" & "F").

12. ARE YOU NOW EMPLOYED? ☐ YES ☐ NO
ARE YOU NOW A SALARIED EMPLOYEE OF THE U.S. GOVERNMENT? ☐ YES ☐ NO

13. YOUR EMPLOYER'S NAME

14. YOUR USUAL OCCUPATION, TRADE OR BUSINESS

15. BUSINESS ADDRESS OR EMPLOYER'S ADDRESS
Street
City   State

C. EDUCATION AND HEALTH

16. DO YOU READ, WRITE, SPEAK AND UNDERSTAND THE ENGLISH LANGUAGE? ☐ YES ☐ NO

17. SHOW THE EXTENT OF YOUR EDUCATION BY GIVING THE NUMBER
OF FULL YEARS COMPLETED { ☐ In High School ☐ Trade/Vocational School ☐ Above High School

18. DO YOU HAVE ANY PHYSICAL OR MENTAL DISABILITY THAT WOULD INTERFERE WITH OR PREVENT YOU FROM SERVING AS A JUROR?
IF "YES," SEE NOTES ON NEXT PAGE. ☐ YES ☐ NO

D. CRIMINAL RECORD

19. HAVE YOU EVER BEEN CONVICTED, EITHER BY YOUR GUILTY OR NOLO CONTENDERE PLEA OR BY A COURT OR JURY TRIAL OF A STATE OR FEDERAL CRIME FOR WHICH PUNISHMENT COULD HAVE BEEN ONE YEAR OR MORE IN PRISON? ☐ YES ☐ NO

20. (IF "YES") WERE YOUR CIVIL RIGHTS RESTRICTED? ☐ YES ☐ NO
(IF "YES," EXPLAIN ON NEXT PAGE.)

21. ARE ANY CHARGES NOW PENDING AGAINST YOU FOR A VIOLATION OF STATE OR FEDERAL LAW PUNISHABLE BY IMPRISONMENT FOR MORE THAN ONE YEAR? ☐ YES ☐ NO

If your answer to either question 19 or 21 is YES, please state on the next page of this form,
a) date of the offense.
b) date of the conviction (or date of pending charge),
c) nature of the offense,
d) the sentence imposed (if a conviction), and
e.) the name of the court.
One is disqualified from jury service only for criminal offenses punishable by imprisonment for more than one year, but it is the maximum penalty, and not the actual sentence, which controls.

E. EXEMPTIONS

22. CHECK IF YOU ARE EMPLOYED ON A FULL-TIME BASIS AS ONE OF THESE. {
☐ PUBLIC OFFICIAL OF THE UNITED STATES, STATE, OR LOCAL GOVERNMENT WHO IS EITHER ELECTED TO PUBLIC OFFICE OR DIRECTLY APPOINTED BY ONE ELECTED TO OFFICE.
☐ MEMBER OF ANY GOVERNMENTAL POLICE OR REGULAR FIRE DEPT. (NOT INCLUDING VOLUNTEER OR COMMERCIAL DEPTS.)
☐ MEMBER IN ACTIVE SERVICE OF THE ARMED FORCES OF THE UNITED STATES.

F. GROUNDS FOR REQUESTING EXCUSE

You MAY be excused by the court from service as a juror if you are within a category shown below. If you request to be excused for that reason, mark the category which applies to you. HOWEVER, IF YOU WISH TO SERVE, DO NOT MARK YOUR CATEGORY.

☐ A person who serves without compensation as a volunteer firefighter or a member of a rescue squad or ambulance crew for federal, state, (including the District of Columbia and territories of the United States), or local government agency (describe your service and identify the agency for which you work under "Remarks," section).

REMEMBER, ALL CITIZENS HAVE AN OBLIGATION TO SERVE AS JURORS WHEN CALLED UPON

I SWEAR AND AFFIRM THAT ALL ANSWERS ARE TRUE TO THE BEST OF MY KNOWLEDGE AND BELIEF.

SIGN HERE →

DATE SIGNED   SOCIAL SECURITY NUMBER

▶ **Figure 2.10 SAMPLE JUROR QUALIFICATION QUESTIONNAIRE**

and subtle forms of discrimination, jury administrators began to use telephone lists, motor vehicle or driver's license rolls, and welfare and unemployment lists in assembling the venire, thereby increasing the cross-section of the community from which venire panels are drawn.

The jury questionnaire used to screen the venire is another factor contributing to the exclusion of people from jury service who might comprise a more diverse venire, thereby increasing the representativeness of the jury pool. For example, the visually or hearing impaired were prohibited from serving on juries, as were those who did not speak English, those convicted of felonies, and those who were not U.S. citizens. While those who are deaf or do not speak English have begun to serve on juries, their ability to do so depends on the services of translators who may or may not be available in any given jurisdiction. Felons are permanently excluded from jury service in more than half the states and in the federal justice system; the remaining states place various restrictions on jury service for convicts, including restrictions for those people on probation or parole. Given the fact that one out of every three African-American males between the ages of twenty and twenty-nine is currently under some form of correctional supervision, this bar against jury service for those who have been convicted of a crime further serves to exclude people who might contribute to the diversity of the jury (Olivares, Burton & Cullen 1996).

Another impediment to a representative jury is the way in which jurors are compensated for their time. Jurors are often paid only a nominal amount for their service. Since minorities are over-represented in low-paying jobs, they are disproportionately excluded from jury service on the grounds that serving would cause them an economic hardship.

Finally, the remaining exclusions or exemptions from jury service also work to prevent a truly diverse jury from being assembled. Public officials, including police and fire department employees, are excluded by federal law 28 U.S.C. § 1863(b)(5). Full-time students, teachers, clergy members, and lawyers have also traditionally been exempted from service or, alternatively, have been given the opportunity to exempt themselves from jury service. The same holds true today for full-time students because they cannot make up lost time in school. Nonetheless, teachers, lawyers, and physicians are no longer exempted from jury service in many jurisdictions, but police, fire-fighters, and emergency medical personnel (i.e., paramedics) continue to be in light of the essential roles they perform each day.

The *Voir Dire* Process The process of summoning venire members and excluding those whose juror questionnaires reveal information disqualifying them from jury service is only the first step in the jury selection process. Once otherwise qualified venire persons are then assembled in a courtroom, the actual process of selecting a jury from the venire panel begins. That process is known as ***voir dire***, a Latin term meaning "to speak the truth."

Selecting the right people from the venire to sit on the petit jury is one of the most important parts of the trial process. Given this fact, is it not surprising that behavioral scientists from a variety of disciplines (e.g., sociology, psychology, marketing, communications, etc.) are hired as jury consultants to assist in jury selection. These social scientists attempt to engage in a process commonly referred to as **scientific jury selection**—an attempt "to compile and implement the 'ideal' juror profile" (Barber 1994: 1234). The factors most frequently considered in assembling the ideal jury include juror sex, race/ethnicity, religion, occupation, age, educational level, military service, marital status, demeanor, appearance, and socio-economic class/status. The merit of scientific jury selection, however, is contested in both scholarly research and by legal practitioners.

The main purpose of *voir dire* is to weed out those members of the venire who would not be fair and impartial jurors. Typical questions relate to whether prospective jurors know the defendant, the attorneys, or any of the witnesses; whether they have read about the case in the newspapers; whether they have racial, nationality, or gender biases; and whether they have formed any opinions on the case. If either attorney wishes to have a prospective juror dismissed on the basis of these questions or for any other reason, the attorney may issue a challenge to that juror.

In addition, *voir dire* should establish rapport with the members of the venire, and begin to "sell" the side's respective theories regarding the case to the members of the venire by highlighting case strengths and neutralizing case weaknesses. But how that process is conducted varies greatly from courtroom to courtroom. The judge controls the entirety of *voir dire* process, ranging from who questions the venire, what questions will be asked, and how they are worded to whether questions will be asked individually or to the whole venire panel simultaneously and how long the whole process will be permitted to go on. In most federal courts, and increasingly in state courts, judges conduct *voir dire* even though most lawyers would prefer to conduct *voir dire* themselves. Regardless of who does the questioning, a venire person may be struck from the jury pool either for demonstrable cause or for impalpable reasons based on both verbal and nonverbal responses to the questions asked.

Strikes for Cause Every state and the federal court system all recognize the right of exercising **strikes for cause** by both sides in the case. Modern strikes for cause generally fall into one of two categories: principal challenges and fact-partial challenges. **Principal challenges** involve strikes of potential jurors because they have some relationship to one of the "principals" or participants in the case. They are presumed to be partial on account of this relationship. **Fact-partial challenges** involve strikes of potential jurors because the subject matter of the dispute presents issues on which the potential juror is biased, prejudiced, or predisposed to a particular outcome because of their belief system, experiences, or media exposure to the case. For example, someone who had a family member killed in a drunk-driving accident would not be a fair and impartial juror in a criminal driving under the influence case, even if the venire person knew no one involved in the case. The person's background would predispose him or her to be biased against the defendant, rendering the venire person fact-partial. Both sides to a case have an unlimited number of strikes for cause to ensure the most fair and impartial jury possible.

Peremptory Challenges **Peremptory challenges** occur when a party seeks to strike a venire person when there is not good cause to do so. Peremptory strikes first appeared in English common law in the latter part of the thirteenth century, but they could only be exercised by prosecutors and only in capital, criminal cases. As common law evolved, a finite number of peremptory strikes were granted to criminal defendants, first in capital cases, and later in all felony cases. As of the writing of this text, Federal Rule of Criminal Procedure 24(b) gives both sides twenty peremptory strikes in capital cases; the prosecution gets six and the defendant ten in non-capital felony cases; and each side gets three in misdemeanor cases. Most states have similar rules.

Regardless of the number of peremptory strikes each side has, the purpose of these strikes is usually the same. Originally, they were designed and used for a curative purpose: to correct the mistake of a judge for failing to strike a juror for cause. And they are still used in that manner today. But they are also used by lawyers to exclude from the jury those people whom they believe to be hostile to their side of the case, even if not so hostile that the venire person in question would be struck for cause. In other words, attorneys use peremptory strikes to eliminate the jurors they feel might not vote for their side during the jury deliberations process. Counsel must be careful, however, not to run afoul of the federal Constitution when they are exercising their peremptory challenges.

In 1986, the U.S. Supreme Court decided *Batson v. Kentucky*, 476 U.S. 79 (1986). The case involved an African American male who was convicted of burglary by a jury comprised of all Caucasians. The prosecution used four of its six peremptory challenges to strike African Americans from the venire. The Supreme Court held that the prosecution's actions violated the equal protection guarantee of the Constitution when it used its peremptory strikes to eliminate people on the basis of race.

> [T]he State's privilege to strike individual jurors through peremptory challenges is subject to the command of the Equal Protection Clause. Although a prosecutor ordinarily is entitled to exercise peremptory challenges "for any reason at all, as long as that reason is related to his view concerning the outcome" of the case to be tried . . . the Equal Protection Clause forbids the prosecutor to challenge potential jurors solely on account of their race or on the assumption that black jurors as a group will be unable impartially to consider the State's case against a black defendant. *Batson v. Kentucky*, 476 U.S. 79, 89 (1986).

The Supreme Court extended its holding in *Batson* to cover strikes based on gender in *J.E.B. v. Alabama ex rel. T.B.*, 511 U.S. 127 (1994).

A *Batson* challenge to a peremptory strike occurs in three phases. First, the party suspecting a peremptory strike has been exercised by opposing counsel in violation of *Batson* must object and make a showing that the juror in question is "a member of a racial group capable of being singled out for differential treatment." 476 U.S. at 94. The objecting party bears the burden of persuasion in establishing a *prima facie* case of impermissible discrimination. Once that is done, the side seeking to exercise the peremptory strike must respond to the objection by offering a non-discriminatory reason for wanting to strike the particular juror. "The reason need not rise to the justification of a challenge for cause, but cannot be a mere denial of discriminatory purpose . . . [;] the . . . explanation need not be persuasive, . . . but need only have a 'facial validity'" (Johnstone 1998: 446).

The principle of nondiscrimination at the core of *Batson* and *J.E.B.* has not yet been extended by the Supreme Court to other categories, such as ethnicity, religion, or sexual orientation. But some lower federal courts have done so on their own. For example, a federal court in New York upheld the application of *Batson* to strikes against Italian-Americans. *United States v. Biaggi*, 853 F.2d 89, 96 (2d Cir. 1988). But the Supreme Court refused to do so in a case involving Spanish-speaking Latinos. *Hernandez v. New York*, 500 U.S. 352 (1991). And although California law prohibits striking jurors on the basis of sexual orientation, the courts that have examined this issue have generally declined to apply *Batson* to that characteristic on the basis that doing so might pry too intimately into the private lives of the venire, potentially threatening to "out" gay, lesbian, or bisexual jurors during the voir dire process. *Johnson v. Campbell*, 92 F.3d 951, 953 (9th Cir 1996). The reasoning proffered for not extending *Batson* on religious grounds was explained in *State v. Davis*, 504 N.W.2d 767 (Minn. 1993), nicely summarized by Johnstone (1998: 451) as follows:

> The *Davis* court found that, although **"a juror's religious beliefs are inviolate . . . they are the basis for a person's moral values,"** and therefore a peremptory strike based on religion does not manifest a **"pernicious religious bias."** In other words, concerns about reinforcing impermissible stereotypes do not weigh as heavily with religion as with race, because a juror's religion may determine his views in a way that the law, the other jurors, and the juror himself can recognize as legitimate. This legitimacy mitigates cynicism among jurors, while striking jurors on the basis that religion correlates to moral values promotes impartiality.

Impaneling the Petit Jury   Once all the challenges available to both the prosecution and the defense are exercised, the judge selects the members of the venire who will be the **petit jury** in the case. The petit jury is normally comprised of twelve people who will serve as the trier-of-fact at trial. In some cases, additional jurors are selected as alternates; they hear the evidence just as the other jurors do, but they do not enter deliberations unless one of the regular twelve jurors becomes ill, dies, or is unable to serve for some other reason. After administering an oath to the jurors, the judge admonishes the jurors not to discuss the case with anyone until they go into deliberations to decide the case after hearing all the evidence. Once the jury is impaneled, the constitutional safeguard of double jeopardy attaches. (See the discussion of the Fifth Amendment in Chapter 1.)

Historically, juries have been composed of twelve members. In *Williams v. Florida*, 399 U.S. 78, 100-02 (1970), however, the U.S. Supreme Court held that a six-member jury satisfied the Sixth Amendment:

> **The purpose of the jury trial . . . is to prevent oppression by the Government. . . . Given this purpose, the essential feature of a jury obviously lies in the interposition between the accused and his accuser of the common-sense judgment of a group of laymen, and in the community participation and shared responsibility which results from this group's determination of guilt or innocence. The performance of this role is not a function of the particular number of the body which makes up the jury. To be sure, the number should probably be large enough to promote group deliberation, free from outside attempts at intimidation, and to provide a fair possibility for obtaining a representative cross-section of the community. But we find little reason to think that these goals are in any meaningful sense less likely to be achieved when the jury numbers six, than when it numbers 12—particularly if the requirement of unanimity is retained. And, certainly the reliability of the jury as a fact-finder hardly seems likely to be a function of its size. . . .**
>
> **Similarly, while in theory the number of viewpoints represented on a randomly selected jury ought to increase as the size of the jury increases, in practice the difference between the 12-man and the six-man jury in terms of the cross-section of the community represented seems likely to be negligible.**

Juries of less than six people, however, have been held to violate the Sixth Amendment. *Ballew v. Georgia*, 435 U.S. 223 (1978).

Starting Presumptions

All trials are governed by both rules of procedure and rules of evidence. One of the foundations of evidence law is that the trier-of-fact must have an evidentiary starting place at the outset of a trial. In a criminal trial, that starting place usually involves two presumptions. A **presumption** is a conclusion or deduction which the law *requires* the trier-of-fact to make in the absence of evidence to the contrary. In contrast, **inferences** are permissive; they are conclusions or deductions the trier-of-fact may reasonably make based on the facts which have been established by the evidence, but the trier-of-fact is not required to do so. Criminal trials start with two presumptions: the presumption of sanity and the presumption of innocence. The **presumption of sanity** requires that all defendants be presumed sane unless sufficient evidence of their insanity is proven, usually by clear and convincing evidence. The **presumption of innocence** requires the trier-of-fact to accept that the defendant is innocent unless the prosecution meets its burden to prove that the defendant is guilty beyond a reasonable doubt.

Evidence and Burdens of Proof

Evidence consists of physical objects, testimony, or other things offered to prove or disprove the existence of a fact. The law recognizes two major types of evidence: direct evidence and circumstantial evidence.

Direct evidence is first-hand evidence that does not require presumptions or inferences in order to establish a proposition of fact. The best example of direct evidence is eyewitness testimony. One need not draw any inference from a witness' testimony that she saw something. She either saw it or she did not. Thus, direct evidence does not necessarily establish truth; witnesses can be mistaken or misleading. In fact, some commentators consider faulty eyewitness testimony to be the leading cause of wrongful convictions in the United States (see Chapter 14 for a more in-depth discussion about eyewitness testimony).

Circumstantial evidence is indirect evidence. To reach a conclusion, the trier-of-fact would have to reason through [the circumstantial evidence] and infer the existence of some fact in dispute. If circumstantial evidence is believed, it requires additional inferences or presumptions, and may require the fact finder to examine a chain of evidence in order to accept the fact at issue.

Types of Evidence Evidence can be classified as testimonial evidence, real or physical evidence, scientific evidence, and demonstrative evidence. **Testimonial evidence** is oral testimony given under oath. Recall from Chapter 1 that anyone called to give testimony is subject to the requirements of the Sixth Amendment's Confrontation Clause. **Real evidence** (also referred to as **physical evidence**) consists of tangible objects such as contracts, bank statements, or other documentary evidence; firearms; drug paraphernalia; clothing; and traces of objects that may be found at a crime or accident scene, such as fingerprints or trace amounts of drugs. The scientific examination of real evidence, in a laboratory, for example, yields **scientific evidence**—the formal results of forensic investigatory techniques (often in documentary form), such as autopsy reports, firearm matches, and DNA analyses. **Demonstrative evidence** has no evidential value by itself. Rather, it serves as a visual or auditory aid to assist the fact finder in understanding the evidence. Charts, maps, videos, and courtroom demonstrations are forms of demonstrative evidence.

Finally, there is a fifth type of evidence called **judicial notice.** Judicial notice does not involve evidence per se, but rather is a process that excuses a party from having to introduce evidence in order to prove something. In other words, judicial notice is the process whereby the trier-of-fact accepts certain facts as true without the necessity of formal proof. It is a "short cut" that excuses a party from the burden of having to prove certain facts through testimonial, physical, or other means when the matter is commonly known in the community by judges and jurors without further proof. For example, a court would take judicial notice of the fact that Halloween falls on October 31 or that Christmas falls on December 25 without the requirement of having a calendar introduced into evidence. This would be appropriate because the dates of these holidays are within the common knowledge of the jury and the community at large. The meaning of certain words and phrases might be another example of something which a court might take judicial notice, such as "turning a trick" or "getting a fix."

Burdens of Proof The concept of burden of proof actually encompasses two separate burdens, the burden of production and the burden of persuasion. If a party has the **burden of production** (often referred to as the burden of going forward), they must produce *prima facie* evidence to put facts in issue. The **burden of persuasion,** more commonly called the burden of proof, is the obligation of a party to prove a fact to a certain level, either beyond a reasonable doubt, by a preponderance of the evidence, or by clear and convincing evidence. The various levels of proof used in evaluating if the burden of persuasion has been met are depicted in Table 2.2. The burden of persuasion comes into play after all the evidence is produced, when it is time for the judge to decide the

TABLE 2.2	LEVELS OF PROOF						
0%---50%---100%							
No Proof	**Mere Suspicion**	**Articulable Reasonable Suspicion**	**Probable Cause**	**Preponderance of the Evidence**	**Clear and Convincing Evidence**	**Beyond a Reasonable Doubt**	**Beyond All Doubt**
	A "hunch" serves law enforcement officers well, but is insufficient proof in any stage in the judicial process.	Standard established in *Terry v. Ohio* for a "stop and frisk"—a limited investigative detention.	Necessary to arrest a person, conduct a search, or seize evidence.	Plaintiff's burden in most civil cases; burden for establishing "knowing, intelligent, and voluntary" waivers of most constitutional rights; burden for establishing exceptions to exclusionary rule.	Plaintiff's burden in some civil cases; defendant's burden for proving insanity; government's burden to civilly commit a dangerous person.	Prosecution's burden to prove each element of a criminal offense.	Proof to an absolute certainty is not required in any phase of the judicial process in the United States.

ultimate issue in a bench trial, or time to instruct the jury. The prosecution always bears the burden in persuading the trier-of-fact that the defendant committed each and every element of all crime charged. In some circumstances, however, the defendant in a criminal trial bears the burden of persuasion to prove certain defense, such as insanity. When the defendant bears the burden of persuasion to prove a defense, it is called an **affirmative defense**.

At the low end of the scale, there is no proof. Just above that, there is what the law calls **mere suspicion**—a hunch or the feeling of intuition. While intuitively knowing something is undoubtedly a skill that serves law enforcement officers well, mere suspicion is insufficient proof of any fact in a court of law.

The next level up from mere suspicion is **reasonable, articulable suspicion**. It differs from mere suspicion only slightly, but in an important way. Instead of just having a hunch or an intuitive feeling, a person can articulate the reasons *why* he or she is suspicious. Moreover, the explanations offered as the bases for the suspicion are objectively reasonable—clearly understandable to another person who hears the explanations. This level of proof is necessary for law enforcement personnel to conduct a "stop and frisk." These brief, limited, investigative detentions are also known as "*Terry* stops" as a result of the U.S. Supreme Court's landmark decision in *Terry v. Ohio*, 392 U.S. 1 (1968). Details of these types of brief detentions are covered in Chapter 7.

The next highest level of proof is called **probable cause**. Defining probable cause is no easy task. It is differentiated from reasonable, articulable suspicion by the existence of *facts*—independently verifiable factual information that supports the conclusion that there is a "fair probability" that a crime occurred or that a particular person was involved in a crime. Probable cause is covered in greater detail in Chapter 3 and revisited in particular criminal procedural contexts throughout the text.

In most civil cases, the standard of proof is a **preponderance of the evidence**. It is commonly understood as proof that something is more likely than not. Thus, if the plaintiff is able to show the probability is more than 50 percent that the defendant did what is claimed, the judgment will be for the plaintiff. It is also the standard of proof used to establish the validity of waivers of constitutional rights, as well as the burden for proving that exceptions to the Exclusionary Rule apply (see Chapter 3).

Clear and convincing evidence is a higher level of proof than the preponderance of the evidence standard, yet it falls short of proof beyond a reasonable doubt. It is the standard of proof in some civil cases. It is also the level of proof to which a defendant in some criminal cases must establish an affirmative defense. If there is clear and convincing evidence, the trier-of-fact should be reasonably satisfied as to the existence of the fact, yet they may have some doubts.

Because the accused is presumed innocent, the prosecution has the burden to prove all the elements of the crime(s) charged its case **beyond a reasonable doubt**. If the prosecution fails to meet this burden of proof on any element, the defendant must be acquitted. *In re Winship*, 397 U.S. 358 (1970). Reasonable doubt is a term requiring little interpretation, although various courts have attempted to formulate somewhat involved definitions that add little beyond its plain meaning. A specific definition for the "beyond a reasonable doubt" standard has not been adopted by the U.S. Supreme Court, leading to some confusion amongst jurists and jurors alike. In fact, jury instructions explaining reasonable doubt are often the basis for appeal. It is sufficient to say that proof beyond a reasonable doubt requires that the guilt of the defendant be established to a reasonable, but not absolute or mathematical, certainty. Probability of guilt is not enough. In other words, to satisfy the "beyond a reasonable doubt" standard, the jury must be satisfied that the charges against the defendant are almost certainly true. A challenged definition of beyond a reasonable doubt that was upheld by the U.S. Supreme Court reads as follows: "**A reasonable doubt is an actual and substantial doubt arising from the evidence, from the facts or circumstances shown by the evidence, or from the lack of evidence.**" *Victor v. Nebraska*, 511 U.S. 1 (1994). Keep in mind that reasonable doubt is an inherently qualitative concept; it cannot be quantified, and any attempt to do so for a jury is likely to result in reversible error. *McCullough v. State*, 657 P.2d 1157 (Nev. 1983).

Order of Evidence Presentation at Trial

Opening Statements Once the jury has been impaneled and instructed regarding the presumptions of innocence (and sanity, if relevant to a particular case), the trial begins with **opening statements.** Because the government bears the burden of proof at trial, the prosecuting attorney gets to make the first opening statement. The prosecutor usually outlines what the government intends to prove by the evidence it will present. When the prosecution has completed its opening statement, the defense then has its chance to make an opening statement. The defendant is not, however, required to make an opening statement at that time. Defense counsel might elect to wait until the prosecutor has presented the government's evidence before giving an opening statement, thereby concealing the defense strategy until the government has disclosed its case.

Contrary to popular belief, opening statements are not allowed to be argumentative. Instead, opening statements serve to outline the parties' respective cases and to clarify main points for the judge or jurors. The importance of opening statements cannot be overstated. A properly crafted opening statement can be very influential in determining the outcome of the case.

Prosecution's Case-in-Chief After the opening statement or statements are given, the prosecutor begins introducing the government's proof in its **case-in-chief.** As with the opening statement, the prosecution is also entitled to present its evidence first in a criminal case because it bears the burden of persuasion.

The prosecution's case-in-chief begins with the **direct examination** of the prosecution's first witness, a person expected to give evidence favorable to the government's position. The examination of the witness is designed to produce evidence that will prove the prosecution's case against the defendant. In direct examination, attorneys are generally not allowed to ask leading questions. A leading question gives the witness hints at the answer the attorney is seeking. For example: "Mr. Brown, isn't it true that on October 4, you were home from eight to ten in the morning?" In direct examination, this question would be properly phrased, "Mr. Brown, where were you on October 4, between the hours of eight and ten in the morning?" Using the latter phrasing, Mr. Brown would be able to answer the question using his own recollection or knowledge, without any coaching or leading from the attorney. In criminal cases, a law enforcement officer is almost always involved as a witness for the prosecution; sometimes, a police officer is the prosecution's only witness.

When the prosecutor is through questioning the prosecution's witness, the defense counsel has a right to question the same witness. This is known as **cross-examination.** In cross-examination, the questions are usually limited to the subject matter of direct examination and the credibility of the witness. In some jurisdictions, the attorneys may cross-examine witnesses on any matter that is relevant to a matter at issue in the case. The purpose of cross-examination is to find and expose inconsistencies, inaccuracies, and anything that will make the trier-of-fact question the witnesses' credibility by showing inadequacy of observation, confusion, inconsistency, bias, contradiction, and the like. The judge determines what questions are relevant and may limit cross-examination if questions are prejudicial, cumulative, confusing, or lacking sufficient factual basis. (See the discussion of the Sixth Amendment in Chapter 1 for additional information on cross-examination.) Leading questions are appropriate during cross-examination; in fact, they are the tool through which one can most appropriately control an adverse witness.

Following cross-examination, the prosecutor is permitted to clarify questions raised in cross-examination and to attempt to rehabilitate the witness in the eyes of the jury. This second round of questioning is called **redirect examination.** It is usually strictly limited to matters raised on cross-examination. On rare occasions, a judge may permit *recross-examination* as well.

Motion for Acquittal After the prosecutor has presented the government's evidence, the defense counsel may move for a judgment of acquittal. A judge will grant a **motion for judgment of acquittal**—even in jury trials—when the evidence is insufficient to sustain a conviction on the offense or offenses charged. This usually means the judge decided that no reasonable juror could possibly conclude that guilt was proven beyond a reasonable doubt. If the judge does not grant the motion at the close of the prosecution's evidence, the defense may then offer its evidence by presenting its case-in-chief.

Defense Case-in-Chief Assuming that the court does not grant a motion for judgment of acquittal at the close of the prosecution's evidence, the defense counsel then has an opportunity to present evidence. The defense may put forth one or more of several possible defenses to refute the proof offered by the prosecution. Among the defenses available to the defendant are alibi, insanity, duress, self-defense, and entrapment. In presenting any of these defenses, the defense counsel may call witnesses on direct examination, who are then subject to cross-examination by the prosecution.

Defendants may choose to testify in their own behalf, or to exercise their constitutional privilege against self-incrimination and not testify. A defendant who chooses to testify is treated much like any other witness. If a defendant chooses not to testify, the prosecuting attorney may not comment to the jury about the failure to testify. *Griffin v. California*, 380 U.S. 609 (1965).

When the defense completes its case-in-chief, the defense rests. At that time, the defense may make a renewed motion for a judgment of acquittal. If the evidence presented by the defense in its case-in-chief is such that the judge believes no reasonable juror could possibly believe that the prosecution proved its case beyond a reasonable doubt, then the judge will grant the motion. But this is quite rare; such motions for acquittal are usually denied and the trial proceeds to its final stages. The judge, however, does have the discretion to hold off on ruling on a motion for a judgment of acquittal until after the jury returns a verdict or is discharged without having returned a verdict.

Rebuttal Case by the Prosecution If the judge does not grant a motion for judgment of acquittal at the close of defendant's evidence, the prosecution may present **rebuttal** proof at this time. Rebuttal proof is designed to controvert evidence presented by the defense and to rebut any special defenses raised. Rebuttal proof is limited to new material brought out in the defendant's presentation of evidence. Law enforcement officers may again be called as witnesses at this stage of the prosecution to correct errors or misleading impressions left after the defendant's presentation of evidence. After rebuttal, the defense may present additional evidence.

Closing Arguments After all the evidence has been presented, both the prosecutor and the defense attorney are allotted certain amounts of time, usually specified by statute or rule, for **closing arguments.** In this final argument, attorneys for each side attempt to convince the jury (or the judge in bench trials) of the correctness of their positions. The prosecutor presents the government's argument first, followed by the defense attorney. The prosecutor may then present a short rebuttal. Attorneys for both sides may use their wit, imagination, and persuasion to win the jury over to their respective positions. However, the attorneys are confined to a discussion of the evidence presented and reasonable inferences to be drawn from that evidence.

Jury Instructions After the closing arguments and before the jury retires for deliberations, the judge must give **jury instructions** to the jury regarding the law of the case. Attorneys for both sides have an opportunity to submit written requests to the judge for particular instructions. In a typical case, the instructions cover the respective responsibilities of the court and the jury, the presumption of innocence and the burden of proof, various evidentiary problems, a definition of the offense or offenses charged, additional clarification of the critical elements of those offenses, any defenses that are available in the case, and the procedures to be followed in the jury room. The exact content of the instructions is a matter for the judge's discretion, but the attorneys may object to any portion of the instructions or any omissions from them.

The judge may summarize the evidence for the jury members, help them recall details, and attempt to reduce complicated evidence into its simplest elements. However, the judge may not express an opinion on any issue of fact in the case or favor either side in summarizing the evidence. Furthermore, when a jury has no sentencing function, it should be instructed to "reach its verdict without regard to what sentence might be imposed." *Rogers v. United States*, 422 U.S. 35, 40 (1975):

> **The principle that juries are not to consider the consequences of their verdicts is a reflection of the basic division of labor in our legal system between judge and jury. The jury's function is to find the facts and to decide whether, on those facts, the defendant is guilty of the crime charged. The judge, by contrast, imposes sentence on the defendant after the jury has arrived at a guilty verdict. Information regarding the consequences of a verdict is therefore irrelevant to the jury's task. Moreover, providing jurors sentencing information invites them to ponder matters that are**

> **not within their province, distracts them from their factfinding responsibilities, and creates a strong possibility of confusion.** *Shannon v. United States*, 512 U.S. 573, 579 (1994).

Verdict After receiving instructions, the jury retires to the jury room to begin **deliberations** on a verdict. The verdict is the decision of the jury as to the defendant's guilt or innocence. In federal cases, court decisions and Rule 31(a) of the Federal Rules of Criminal Procedure require a unanimous verdict for conviction. In state jury trials, however, a verdict of fewer than twelve members of a twelve-member jury satisfies the Sixth Amendment. *Apodaca v. Oregon*, 406 U.S. 404 (1972), for example, upheld a conviction by ten votes of a twelve-member jury. And *Johnson v. Louisiana*, 406 U.S. 356 (1972), held that conviction by nine votes of a twelve-member jury in a state court did not violate the due process guarantee of the Fourteenth Amendment. If, however, a state uses six-member juries, the verdict must be unanimous. *Burch v. Louisiana*, 441 U.S. 130 (1979).

If jurors are so irreconcilably divided in opinion that they are unable to agree on a verdict, a **hung jury** results. The jurors are then dismissed, and the case must either be retried or dismissed. If, however, they reach agreement on a verdict, the jurors return to the courtroom and the jury foreperson reads the **verdict** in open court. Any party, or the court itself, may then request a poll of the jury, which involves *asking* each juror whether he or she concurs in the verdict. The purpose of polling the jury is to make sure that the verdict was not the result of coercion or domination of one juror by others or a juror's mental or physical exhaustion. If the poll reveals that any juror did not concur in the verdict, the whole jury may be directed to retire for further deliberations or may be discharged by the judge.

Jury nullification is the power of a jury to acquit regardless of the strength of the evidence against a defendant. Given the Double Jeopardy Clause of the Fifth Amendment, an acquittal is final and cannot be appealed by the prosecution. Nor can the prosecution bring charges based on the same offense against the defendant again. Nullification usually occurs when the defendant is particularly sympathetic or when the defendant is prosecuted for violating an unpopular law. In a decision rejecting the appellants' request to have the jury informed of its power of nullification, the court said:

> The way the jury operates may be radically altered if there is alteration in the way it is told to operate. The jury knows well enough that its prerogative is not limited to the choices articulated in the formal instructions of the court. The jury gets its understanding as to the arrangements in the legal system from more than one voice. There is the formal communication from the judge. There is the informal communication from the total culture—literature (novel, drama, film, and television); current comment (newspapers, magazines and television); conversation; and, of course, history and tradition. The totality of input generally conveys adequately enough the idea of prerogative, of freedom in an occasional case to depart from what the judge says. *United States v. Dougherty*, 473 F.2d 1113, 1135 (D.C. Cir. 1972).

Some states require courts to instruct juries on the power of nullification, and the issue continues to be debated.

Sentencing

Shared Responsibility **Sentencing** is technically a part of the judicial process. As a rule, the imposition of a criminal sentence is the responsibility of a trial court judge, although a handful of jurisdictions allow a jury to fix a defendant's sentence. A judge's determination of the sentence is perhaps the most sensitive and difficult decision a judge has to make due to its effect on the defendant's life. The responsibility for sentencing, however, is shared by the judiciary with both the legislative and executive branches of government. Legislatures set the parameters for criminal sentences when they designate crimes at a particular level of offense, and designate the permissible punishments for those offenses. The executive branch controls the imposition of sentence through two mechanisms, parole and executive clemency. The most important and frequently used of the two is the parole system (discussed below). The chief executive (i.e., the governor of a state or the president of the United States) may instead choose to grant executive clemency—a **pardon**—in which an inmate is "forgiven" for his or her crime and the sentence commuted accordingly.

Sentencing Schemes

Indeterminate Sentences The level of judicial sentencing discretion today is quite different than it was some years ago. From the 1940s through the 1950s, the rehabilitative model was the dominant philosophical justification behind criminal sentencing (Allen 1981). Accordingly, judges were supposed to tailor sentences to each offender, with the goal of changing the offender's behavior of offenders for the better. This approach involved what is called **indeterminate sentencing.** Legislatures prescribed a range of permissible sentences, usually setting a minimum but leaving the maximum up to the discretion of the judge. In other jurisdictions, legislatures set a minimum and maximum range but left the judge free to impose sentence as he or she saw fit using any criteria. Corrections officials—usually parole boards—were free to release inmates at any time if they believed them to be rehabilitated.

This system sometimes led to great disparities in sentences for similar or even identical crimes. Some of the differences in sentences were due to the philosophy of the sentencing judge; some were due to strategic lawyering; and some were due to discrimination on the basis of race, ethnicity, class, gender, and sexual orientation (Wang 1999; Reiman 1995).

Determinate Sentencing In response to the concerns over disparate sentencing, Congress passed the Sentencing Reform Act of 1984. Under the provisions of the Act, Congress created the United States Sentencing Commission and empowered it to create a uniform set of federal sentencing guidelines. These guidelines were intended to reduce sentencing disparities and to realistically project the needs of the federal correctional system. The Sentencing Commission promulgated the Federal Sentencing Guidelines, which went into effect on November 1, 1987. This officially moved the federal sentencing schema to a **determinate sentencing** structure: the sentence is fixed or predetermined for a given offense, with only minor adjustments, if any, being permissible based on the specific facts of a case.

The Federal Sentencing Guidelines consist of a grid of forty-three offense levels and six criminal history categories. They established a sentencing scheme primarily on two factors: the offense level and the defendant's criminal history.

> The Criminal History Category of the Guidelines measures the defendant's prior convictions of felonies and misdemeanors, while the Offense Level measures the seriousness of the instant crime through the (1) base offense level; (2) specific offense characteristics; and (3) additional adjustments. A judge applies the Guidelines by finding the intersection on the Sentencing Table Grid of the appropriate Criminal History Category on the horizontal axis and the Offense Level on the vertical axis. The intersection designates the number of months in the defendant's sentencing range within the statutory penalty range for the crime. The judge retains only minimal discretion because he is limited to imposing a sentence within that narrow sentencing range (Fuchs 2001: 1417-18).

The Sentencing Reform Act of 1984 also created a sentencing method in which the sentence imposed by a judge generally determined the actual time that a convicted person would serve in prison. The Act also made restitution a mandatory sentence for conviction of certain crimes.

State prosecutors often use these federal sentencing principles or similar guidelines in fashioning sentencing recommendations for judges.

One of the more controversial aspects of determinate sentencing is the notion of minimum **mandatory sentences.** Such sentences are set by legislatures and require a defendant to serve a statutorily set minimum period of incarceration if convicted of a particular offense. Judges dislike these sentences because they do not have the ability to fashion a sentence appropriate to the facts of a particular case; all offenders are sentenced the same way, without regard to individual circumstances. These types of sentences have been adopted in many states and in the federal system for drug offenses; the commission of crimes using a firearm; and for repeat felony offenders (e.g., "Three Strikes and You're Out" laws). Some states have even designed minimum mandatory sentences for first-time misdemeanor offenders of drunk driving laws.

Although the federal sentencing guidelines greatly curtailed discretionary sentencing, they did not completely eliminate discretion. In practice, the guidelines really just shifted power from the judge to the prosecutor. "[A]lmost without exception, the United States Department of Justice predetermined the outcome by the way in which it charged a defendant" (Jordan 2006: 624). That being said, judges did retain some power to affect the sentence imposed on a particular defendant through the use of **sentencing departures**. Unless the defendant was convicted of a crime carrying a mandatory minimum sentence, judges were permitted to make limited adjustments to the sentencing range called **upward departures** or **downward departures**, depending on whether the range is being increased or decreased. Judges were authorized to grant downward departures from the sentencing guidelines when a defendant provided substantial assistance in the investigation or prosecution of another person, and when the judge felt it necessary to correct unjust effects of the guidelines in extraordinary cases. Mustard (2001: 311) found that judicial use of sentencing departures perpetuated "differences in the length of sentence . . . on the basis of race, gender, education, income, and citizenship. These disparities occur in spite of explicit statements in the guidelines that these characteristics should not affect the sentence length." In fact, these impermissible factors accounted for more than half of the sentencing disparities found in Mustard's comprehensive study.

At the time the guidelines went into effect though 2005, the Federal Sentencing Guidelines were mandatory.

> Judges resented the fact that the Guidelines removed most of the judicial discretion and many concerned observers held the view that the Guidelines system failed to achieve the original goals: "Efforts to eliminate disparity in sentencing have resulted in an incursion on the independence of the federal judiciary, a transfer of power from the judiciary to prosecutors and a proliferation of unjustifiably harsh individual sentences." The most obvious result of the Guidelines has been harsher sentences, many with an adverse racial impact. Long prison sentences have become the norm in the federal system with little diversion to alternative punishment options. Essentially, judges simply did not have the flexibility to adjust sentences to alternative punishments, and instead were directed through the Guidelines structure to send offenders to prison (Jordan 2006: 626).

Some states, like California, adopted mandatory guidelines similar to the Federal Sentencing Guidelines. But most of the nearly twenty states that adopted sentencing guidelines opted for a voluntary guideline system wherein judges may sentence a defendant outside the guideline range as the facts of a case may warrant in their discretion. Federal judges gained the same prerogative in January of 2005 when the U.S. Supreme Court invalidated the Federal Sentencing Guidelines in the companion cases of *United States v. Booker* and *United States v. Fanfan*, 543 U.S. 220 (2005). *Booker* declared that the Federal Sentencing Guidelines were unconstitutional **"because they permitted a sentencing judge to impose a sentence based on facts found by a judge, not a jury,"** and therefore violated the Sixth Amendment's guarantee to have a jury decide factual issues under the proof beyond a reasonable doubt standard (Jordan 2006: 628). The Court, however, did not invalidate the Guidelines in their entirety. Rather, the Court's remedy was to excise the portions of federal law mandating the use of the Guidelines, thereby rendering them advisory. Federal courts now use the Sentencing Guidelines to help establish presumptively reasonable sentences from which sentencing judges and appellate courts can vary if they are unreasonable in light of the facts of a particular case (Jordan 2006: 633).

Presentence Investigation and Report In order to tailor a sentence that is appropriate for a particular offender, a judge needs information about the defendant that would not be garnered during the course of trial or during a Rule 11 allocution hearing. The gathering of this information is referred to as a **presentence investigation** ("PSI"). Probation officers generally conduct PSIs, investigating the convicted defendant's prior criminal background; financial condition; educational, military, employment, and social history; relationships with family and friends; use of alcohol and/or controlled substances; and circumstances affecting the defendant's behavior, such as their mental status, that may assist the court in imposing sentence. The PSIR may also include information on the effects of the offense on the victims, as well as available alternatives to imprisonment. After a PSI is completed, the investigating probation officer prepares a **presentence investigation report** ("PSIR") for the sentencing judge containing all of the relevant information gathered during the PSI. The report usually concludes with a sentencing recommendation, including any "special conditions of probation" that are designed to rehabilitate the offender, like alcohol or drug rehabilitation, anger management, psychotherapy, etc.

Statutes or rules usually require a court to consider a PSIR before imposing sentence. And judges live up to this obligation, rarely acting without due deference to the PSIR. Therefore, PSIRs are quite important. Judges overwhelmingly tend to impose sentences in accordance with the recommendations contained in a PSIR even though they are not bound to do so (Rush & Robertson 1987; Campbell et al. 1990).

Sentencing Options When we speak of the **correctional system,** we are actually referring to a variety of agencies, institutions, and programs that seek to punish and/or rehabilitate someone convicted of a crime. In addition to court-ordered fines and the revocation or suspension of state-granted licenses, the most typical sentences involve probation, intermediate sanctions, and incarceration.

Probation The court also has the power to place a defendant on probation for certain offenses. **Probation** is a sentence that allows a defendant to avoid incarceration, yet still places him or her under the jurisdiction of the correctional system in such a way that allows for the monitoring of the defendant's compliance with special restrictions placed upon him or her as a part of sentencing (e.g., abstaining from using drugs and/or alcohol; obeying all laws; participating in educational, psychological, or addiction counseling; supporting dependents; physically staying within a restricted geographical area).

A defendant's probation is usually effected in one of two ways: (1) The court may sentence the defendant, suspend the execution of the sentence, and place the defendant on probation on the condition that a violation of the terms of the probation may result in the defendant's being remanded to serve the underlying suspended sentence; or (2) the court may continue the matter for sentencing for no more than two years, and during that period place the defendant on probation on the condition that a violation of the terms of probation may result in the court then passing sentence on the underlying verdict. A defendant placed on probation is usually under the control and supervision of a probation and parole board or similar agency, although still under the jurisdiction of the court.

In federal cases, probation is governed by the Sentencing Reform Act of 1984, which treats probation as a sentence in its own right and not as a suspension of sentence. The act specifically limits the offenses for which probation may be granted and imposes mandatory conditions that the person on probation not commit another crime and not possess illegal controlled substances. For felony convictions, the act requires that one or more of the following be imposed as conditions of probation: a fine, an order of restitution, or community service. The U.S. Sentencing Commission Guidelines Manual recommends that the following conditions be imposed on all probationers:

1. restricted travel without prior permission;
2. regular reporting to a probation officer;
3. answering all inquiries of the probation officer;
4. supporting all dependents and meeting other family responsibilities;
5. working at a regular occupation;
6. notifying the probation officer of any change in residence or employment;

7. refraining from possession, use, or distribution of drugs and drug paraphernalia and excessive use of alcohol;
8. avoiding places where illegal drugs are sold;
9. not associating with people known to engage in criminal activity;
10. permitting a probation officer to visit at any time;
11. notifying the probation officer of any arrest;
12. not becoming a government informant without court permission; and
13. notifying any applicable third party of the probationer's criminal record.

The Guidelines Manual suggests that the following special conditions be imposed if appropriate: prohibition on ownership of weapons, restitution, fines, credit limitations, financial disclosure, community confinement, home detention, community service, occupational restrictions, participation in a mental health or substance abuse program, intermittent confinement, and curfew.

Probation can be as lax as requiring a probationer to check in with a supervising probation officer once per month at a designated time. At the other extreme, probation can be as intensive as maintaining both scheduled and random daily contacts between the probationer and a supervision probation officer, or electronically monitoring a probationer twenty-four hours per day. If the offender does not comply with any of the special terms of probation, a court can revoke the sentence of probation and resentence the defendant to a term of incarceration.

Probation revocation and modification are governed by the Sentencing Reform Act of 1984 and Rule 32.1 of the Federal Rules of Criminal Procedure. In general, probation can be revoked at any time before the end of the probationary period for any violation of probation conditions that occurs during the probation period. The burden of proof that the government must satisfy for probation violations is typically preponderance of the evidence (the standard typically applicable to civil lawsuits), a standard substantially less than proof beyond a reasonable doubt. Since probation revocation proceedings are not technically part of the criminal prosecution process, a probationer facing revocation has no constitutional right to be represented by court-appointed counsel at a revocation proceeding. *Hagnon v. Scarpelli*, 411 U.S. 778 (1973). State law, however, may grant such a right.

Intermediate Sanctions Between the sanctions of incarceration and probation are a wide range of criminal sentences referred to as **intermediate sanctions**. These include house-arrest, or required living in a community based correctional facility such as a halfway house, a boot camp, a work furlough camp, etc. These facilities are designed to hold people for part of each day, allowing them to maintain employment or attend school during applicable hours, while keeping them under correctional supervision at other times. These sanctions may be coupled with forms of intensive supervision by a probation officer or via electronic monitoring while a defendant is out of one's home or community based facility for work or school reasons.

Incarceration Rates of imprisonment were relatively stable through the 1970s—enough so that some commentators wrote of the "end of imprisonment" (Sommer 1976). But as "tough on crime" attitudes grew in the 1980s, so did attitudes toward more punitive criminal sentences (Clear 1994). As a result, the number of people under correctional supervision in the United States skyrocketed from

1.84 million people in 1980 to 4.35 million in 1990 and over 7.1 million by 2006 (Bureau of Justice Statistics 1980–2006), representing a 45.3 percent increase in just the 1990s alone. These numbers include the people on probation, in jails and prisons, and on parole.

Jails are local correctional facilities usually run by municipalities or counties. They are designed to hold two types of people: (1) those convicted of misdemeanors (crimes for which the period of incarceration is generally less than one year), and (2) those who have been denied bail while awaiting disposition of criminal charges. In contrast, **prisons** are run either by state governments or the federal government. They are designed to incarcerate people who have been convicted of felonies (crimes for which the period of imprisonment is greater than one year). These dichotomies are not always clear in practice, however. For example, some states incarcerate low-level felons for eighteen to twenty-four months in county jails, while others use a combined jail–prison system.

Parole After a Period of Incarceration **Parole** is a lot like probation, except it is granted to a prisoner after he or she has served some time incarcerated in a jail or prison. It is a conditional release prior to the expiration of the full length of the sentence term that requires the parolee to be supervised by a parole officer upon release from an institution. Parole is most frequently granted to prisoners as a reward for good conduct while incarcerated. As with probation, special conditions of release can be imposed on a parolee, requiring the convict to do certain things and refrain from doing other things. The violation of any of these special terms of release can result in the revocation of parole, thereby requiring the parolee to return to prison to serve out the balance of his or her original sentence.

The Sentencing Hearing Rule 32 of the Federal Rules of Criminal Procedure and similar state provisions require judges to impose sentence without unnecessary delay. This protects the defendant from a prolonged period of uncertainty about the future. Thus, sentencing usually occurs within a few weeks of conviction.

Sentence is imposed at a **sentencing hearing**. The sentencing hearing is quick compared to the other phases in the criminal process. It generally takes less than thirty minutes, and often lasts only ten or fifteen minutes.

At the sentencing hearing and before any sentence is imposed, Rule 32 of the Federal Rules of Criminal Procedure requires that the judge "(i) provide the defendant's attorney an opportunity to speak on the defendant's behalf;" and "(ii) address the defendant personally in order to permit the defendant to speak or present any information to mitigate the sentence. . . ." These provisions enable the defendant and defense counsel to present any information that may assist the court in determining punishment. The prosecution has an equivalent opportunity to speak to the court. In addition, in most jurisdictions, the victim of the crime (or their next-of-kin if the victim is dead or unable to speak on his or her own behalf) may participate at sentencing either by making an oral statement in open court or by submitting a written statement to the court. This is called a **victim impact statement**. The court, in its discretion, may allow others, such as the victim's family and friends and members of the victim's community, to participate at sentencing.

The Constitution places several substantive limitations on the information that a judge may consider when determining a criminal sentence at or before the actual sentencing hearing. Due process prohibits a judge from relying on materially untrue assumptions. *Townsend v. Burke*, 334 U.S. 736 (1948). Due process also prohibits a judge from vindictively imposing a harsher punishment on a defendant for exercising constitutional rights. *North Carolina v. Pearce*, 395 U.S. 711 (1969). And, as made clear when the Supreme Court invalidated the once-mandatory nature of the Federal Sentencing Guidelines, the Sixth Amendment restricts a judge to impose a sentence that is based solely on the **"facts reflected in the jury verdict or admitted by the defendant,"** not other facts that have not been proven beyond a reasonable doubt. *Booker*, 543 U.S. at 228.

The First Amendment prohibits a judge from considering the defendant's religious or political beliefs. *United States v. Lemon*, 723 F.2d 922 (D.C. Cir. 1983). *Wisconsin v. Mitchell*, 508 U.S. 476 (1993), however, held that, although the First Amendment protects the defendant's "abstract beliefs" from being considered at sentencing, a sentence may be enhanced because the defendant intentionally selected the victim on account of the victim's race. The court explained that the **"Constitution does not erect a per se barrier to the admission of evidence concerning one's beliefs and associations at sentencing simply because those beliefs and associations are protected by the First Amendment."** 508 U.S. at 486.

Finally, the Eighth Amendment prohibits the imposition of excessive fines and the infliction of cruel and unusual punishments on persons convicted of a crime. (See Chapter 1 for a discussion of the Eighth Amendment.)

After imposing sentence, but before adjourning the sentencing hearing, the court must notify the defendant of the defendant's right to appeal, including any right to appeal the sentence.

Judgment

A **judgment** is the written evidence of the final disposition of the case. It is signed by a judge or the clerk of a court. A judgment of conviction sets forth the plea, the verdict or findings, and the adjudication and sentence. If the defendant is found not guilty or is entitled to be discharged for some other reason, judgment is entered accordingly, and the defendant is guaranteed by the Double Jeopardy Clause to be free forever from any further prosecution for the crime charged. (See Chapter 1 for a discussion of double jeopardy.) If the defendant is found guilty, the judge must pass sentence on the defendant before entering judgment.

The formal entry of judgment is important for the appeals process (discussed below) because appeals may be taken only from cases that have come to a final judgment. This means that an appellate court will not decide any legal issues, nor will it review the denial of any motions, until the trial court has finally disposed of the case. The reason for this rule is to prevent unnecessary delays in the conduct of trials that would result if parties could appeal issues during the course of a trial. (There are minor exceptions to this final judgment rule, such as for interlocutory appeals, but these exceptions are beyond the scope of this text.)

Post-trial Motions

Motion for Judgment of Acquittal After judgment has been entered, the defendant still has several motions available to challenge the court's decision. One of these is the motion for judgment of acquittal, sometimes mistakenly called by its civil law counterpart as a motion for "judgment notwithstanding the verdict." This is the same motion that the defense can make at the close of the prosecution's case-in-chief during trial, and again at the close of the defense case-in-chief during trial. Statutes and rules usually provide that this motion can be renewed even after the jury has been discharged, if it is made within a specified time after the discharge. Courts do not usually grant these motions unless: (1) the prosecution's evidence was insufficient or nonexistent on a vital element of the offense charged; or (2) the indictment or information did not state a criminal offense under the law of the jurisdiction.

Motion for New Trial Another motion available to a defendant is a motion for a new trial. This motion may be made in addition to a motion for acquittal. When made alone, a motion for a new trial is sometimes deemed to include a motion for acquittal. In the latter case, if the defendant moves for a new trial, the court granting it may either enter a final judgment of acquittal or grant a new trial. The court may grant a new trial if it is required in the interest of justice. The usual ground for granting a new trial is insufficient evidence to support the verdict. Some courts also consider errors of law and improper conduct of trial participants during the trial under the motion.

Another ground for granting a motion for a new trial is the discovery of new evidence, which carries with it an extended time period for making the motion. The time period varies among jurisdictions, but is usually longer than the period for other motions to allow a reasonable time to discover new evidence. To justify granting a motion for a new trial on the ground of newly discovered evidence, the defendant must show several things: that the new evidence was discovered after the trial, that it will probably change the result of the trial, that it could not have been discovered before the trial by the exercise of due diligence, that it is material to the issues involved, and that it is not merely cumulative or impeaching.

Motion for Revision or Correction of Sentence In some jurisdictions, by motion of either the defendant or the court, the defendant may obtain a revision or correction of sentence. The power to revise a sentence enables a trial court to change a sentence that is inappropriate in a particular case, even though the sentence may be legal and was imposed in a legal manner. The power to revise a sentence includes a limited power to increase as well as to reduce the sentence. In contrast to the power to revise, the power to correct a sentence enables a court to change a sentence because the sentence was either illegal or imposed in an illegal manner. An example of an illegal sentence is one that was in excess of the statutory maximum. An example of an illegally imposed sentence is one in which the judge did not personally address the defendant and give the defendant an opportunity to be heard before sentencing, when required by statute. The power to revise or correct a sentence must be exercised within specific time periods, or the power is lost.

Remedies after Conviction

A defendant has two major avenues of relief after being convicted of a crime: appeal and *habeas corpus*. Both of these post-conviction remedies will be addressed in turn.

Appeal A defendant has a right to **appeal** after being convicted of a crime and after the trial judge has decided all post-trial motions and entered final judgment in the case. The appeal procedure varies among different jurisdictions and is not described in detail in this book. It involves, among other things, the filing of a notice of appeal, the designation of the parts of the trial record to be considered on appeal, the filing of a statement of points on appeal, the filing of briefs, and the arguing of the briefs before an appellate court. If a defendant is unable to afford a lawyer to handle an appeal, statutes and court rules provide for court appointment of a lawyer free of charge.

In some jurisdictions, the prosecution may also appeal adverse trial court decisions, but the right is usually more limited than the defendant's right. Typical statutes allow appeal by the prosecution of adverse rulings made before the jury hears the case or in cases in which the defendant has appealed. The procedure for appeal by the prosecution is essentially the same as appeal by the defendant.

The appeal procedure is not a retrial of the case, nor is it ordinarily a reexamination of factual issues. The determination of factual issues is the function of the jury or, in a non-jury case, the lower court judge. The appellate court's function in an appeal is primarily to review the legal issues involved in the case. The following example illustrates this point:

> Suppose a law enforcement officer obtained a confession from a defendant but failed to give *Miranda* warnings before a custodial interrogation. During the trial, the judge erroneously permitted the officer who obtained the confession to read it to the jury over the objection of the defense. The jury convicted the defendant. On appeal, the defendant argues that the trial judge committed an error of law in allowing the jury to hear the confession.
>
> The appellate court would very likely reverse the conviction because of the trial judge's error. Along with reversal, the usual procedure is to remand the case (send it back to the trial court for a new trial) with instructions to exclude the confession from the jury in the new trial. A different jury would then hear the evidence, without the illegally obtained confession, and render another verdict. Therefore, even though a conviction is reversed on appeal, the defendant is not necessarily acquitted and freed. The defendant has simply won the right to be tried again.

Generally, to obtain appellate court review of an issue, the appealing party (appellant) must preserve its claim by making a specific timely objection at or before trial. This is called the contemporaneous objection rule. If the appellant fails to make a timely objection, an appellate court will consider the claim only if it constitutes **"plain error."** Plain errors are defects seriously affecting substantial rights that are so prejudicial to a jury's deliberations "as to undermine the fundamental fairness of the trial and bring about a miscarriage of justice." *United States v. Polowichak,* 783 F.2d 410, 416 (4th Cir. 1986).

On the other hand, even when an appellant preserves a claim by timely objection and the appellate court finds that the trial court erred, the appellate court may still affirm the conviction if it finds that the error was "harmless." This so-called **harmless error** rule avoids **"setting aside of convictions for small errors or defects that have little, if any, likelihood of having changed the result of the trial."** *Chapman v. California,* 386 U.S. 18, 22 (1967). If the error was of constitutional dimensions, the appellate court must determine **"beyond a reasonable doubt that the error complained of did not contribute to the** verdict obtained." 386 U.S. at 23. If the error was not of constitutional dimensions, the appellate court must determine with **"fair assurance after pondering all that happened without stripping the erroneous action from the whole that the judgment was not substantially swayed by the error. . . ."** *Kotteakos v. United States*, 328 U.S. 750, 765 (1946).

Most types of error are subject to harmless error analysis, including classic trial errors involving the erroneous admission of evidence. *Arizona v. Fulminante*, 499 U.S. 279 (1991). Some types of error, however, involve rights so basic to a fair trial that they can never be considered harmless. Examples are:

▶ Conflict of interest in representation throughout the entire proceeding. *Holloway v. Arkansas*, 435 U.S. 475 (1978).

▶ Denial of the right to an impartial judge. *Chapman v. California*, 386 U.S. 18 (1967).

▶ Racial, ethnic or sex discrimination in grand jury or petit jury selection. *Vasquez v. Hillery*, 474 U.S. 254 (1986); *Batson v. Kentucky*, 476 U.S. 79 (1986); *J.E.B. v. Alabama ex rel. T.B.*, 511 U.S. 127 (1994).

▶ Failure to inquire whether a defendant's guilty plea is voluntary. *United States v. Gonzalez*, 820 F.2d 575 (2d Cir. 1987).

If an appellate court finds that a trial court committed no errors of law or only harmless errors, it affirms the defendant's conviction. If the appeal was heard in an intermediate appellate court, however, the defendant may still have an additional, discretionary appeal to the highest appellate court in the jurisdiction. And even if the appeal was heard in the highest appellate court in a state, the defendant may still file a petition for a writ of certiorari with the U.S. Supreme Court.

When an appellate court decides a case, it delivers a written opinion to explain and justify its decision. In this way the higher court explains the trial judge's errors and also informs the losing party that it has lost and why. The decisions of appellate courts are compiled and published in books of reported court decisions, which can be found in law libraries. Attorneys and judges use these reported decisions as authorities for arguing and deciding future cases that raise issues similar to those already decided.

Habeas Corpus

Federal *Habeas Corpus* for State Prisoners State prisoners who challenge the fact or duration of their confinement on constitutional grounds and seek immediate or speedier release may petition for a **writ of *habeas corpus*** (also known as the "Great Writ") in federal district court. The federal statute governing the *habeas corpus* remedy is 28 U.S.C.A. § 2254. Note that a state prisoner who challenges the conditions of confinement or attempts to obtain damages for violations of constitutional rights should seek relief by means of a civil action under 42 U.S.C.A. § 198, not by filing a petition for a writ of *habeas corpus*.

Since the Judiciary Act of 1867, *habeas corpus* has been available to state prisoners "in all cases where any person may be restrained of his or her liberty in violation of the Constitution or of any treaty or law of the United States." Initially, the constitutional grounds for which *habeas corpus* relief could be granted were limited to those relating to the jurisdiction of the state court, but the U.S. Supreme Court extended the scope of the writ to all constitutional challenges by its decision in *Fay v. Noia*, 372 U.S. 391 (1963):

> **Although in form the Great Writ is simply a mode of procedure, its history is inextricably intertwined with the growth of fundamental rights of personal liberty. For its function has been to provide a prompt and efficacious remedy for whatever society deems to be intolerable restraints. Its root principle is that in a civilized society, government must always be accountable to the judiciary for a man's imprisonment: if the imprisonment cannot be shown to conform with the fundamental requirements of law, the individual is entitled to his immediate release. Thus there is nothing novel in the fact that today *habeas corpus* in the federal courts provides a mode for the redress of denials of due process of law. Vindication of due process is precisely its historic office.** 372 U.S. at 401-02.

Brecht v. Abrahamson, 507 U.S. 619, 623 (1993), held that the standard for determining whether *habeas corpus* relief must be granted for a constitutional trial error is whether the error "had substantial and injurious effect or influence in determining the jury's verdict."

In 1976, the U.S. Supreme Court limited federal *habeas corpus* review of state prisoners' claims of violations of federal constitutional rights, holding that **"where the State has provided an opportunity for full and fair litigation of a Fourth Amendment claim, a state prisoner may not be granted federal *habeas corpus* relief on the ground that evidence obtained in an unconstitutional search or seizure was introduced at his trial."** *Stone v. Powell*, 428 U.S. 465, 494 (1976). With that limitation, however, other constitutional claims of state prisoners may be heard in a federal *habeas corpus* proceeding even though a state court has fully adjudicated the claims. *Townsend v. Sain*, 372 U.S. 293 (1963). Furthermore, **"Stone's restriction on the exercise of federal *habeas* jurisdiction does not extend to a state prisoner's claim that his conviction rests on statements obtained in violation of the safeguards mandated by *Miranda v. Arizona*. . . ."** *Withrow v. Williams*, 507 U.S. 680, 681 (1993).

Prisoners must exhaust available state remedies before a federal court will consider their constitutional claim on *habeas corpus*. This rule means that, if an appeal or other procedure to hear a claim is still available by right in the state court system, the prisoner must pursue that procedure before a federal *habeas corpus* application will be considered. Federal *habeas corpus* review may likewise be barred if a defendant is unable to show cause for noncompliance with a state procedural rule and to show some actual prejudice resulting from the alleged constitutional violation. *Wainwright v. Sykes*, 433 U.S. 72 (1977).

In 1996, Congress, in response to the bombing of the federal building in Oklahoma City, passed the Antiterrorism and Effective Death Penalty Act. The *habeas corpus* provisions of that Act establish a one-year limitation on filing *habeas corpus* petitions and provide new procedures governing the disposition of second or successive petitions. Before a federal district court will hear a second or successive petition, the petitioner must obtain an authorization order from a three-judge panel in the appropriate court of appeals. The grant or denial of an authorization order cannot be appealed to the U.S. Supreme Court and is not subject to rehearing. In *Felker v. Turpin*, 518 U.S. 651 (1996), the Supreme Court held that the "gatekeeping" requirements were constitutional but found nothing in the law to limit or remove its authority to hear original petitions for *habeas corpus*, thereby preserving its own power to review.

The remedies available to courts deciding *habeas corpus* petitions include reclassifying a petitioner's conviction or ordering the state to retry or resentence a petitioner. Release of a prisoner is granted only if the state fails to comply with the court's order of relief. *Burkett v. Cunningham*, 826 F.2d 1208 (3rd Cir. 1987).

Habeas Corpus Relief for Federal Prisoners In 1948, Congress enacted a statute that was designed to serve as a substitute for *habeas corpus* for federal prisoners. The primary purpose of the statute was to shift the jurisdictions of the courts hearing *habeas corpus* applications. The statute did not change the basic scope of the remedy that had been available to federal prisoners by *habeas corpus*. That statute, 28 U.S.C.A. § 2255, provides, in relevant part:

> *Federal custody; remedies on motion attacking sentence.* A prisoner in custody under sentence of a court established by Act of Congress claiming the right to be released upon the ground that the sentence was imposed in violation of the Constitution or laws of the United States, or that the court was without jurisdiction to impose such sentence, or that the sentence was in excess of the maximum authorized by law, or is otherwise subject to collateral attack, may move the court which imposed the sentence to vacate, set aside, or correct the sentence.

> * * *

> An application for a writ of *habeas corpus* in behalf of a prisoner who is authorized to apply for relief by motion pursuant to this section, shall not be entertained if it appears that the applicant has failed to apply for relief, by motion, to the court which sentenced him, or that such court has denied him relief, unless it also appears that the remedy by motion is inadequate or ineffective to test the legality of his detention.

Hill v. United States, 368 U.S. 424, 428 (1962), held that a petitioner is not entitled to *habeas corpus* relief under Section 2255 unless the violation of federal law was a **"fundamental defect which inherently results in a complete miscarriage of justice [or] an omission inconsistent with the rudimentary demands of fair procedure."** The Section 2255 remedy is similar to the *habeas corpus* remedy for state prisoners, discussed earlier. (Although there are some significant distinctions between the two remedies, they are beyond the scope of this text and are not discussed here.)

State Post-Conviction Relief Almost all states have post-conviction procedures permitting prisoners to challenge constitutional violations. These procedures may derive from statutes, court rules, or the common law. Many of these state remedies are as extensive in scope as federal *habeas corpus* for state prisoners. Other states provide much narrower remedies. (The differences in post-conviction remedies among the states are beyond the scope of this text and are not discussed here.)

Summary

This chapter is designed to help criminal justice students and professionals understand the dual structure of the court system in the United States, the pretrial processes used by the criminal courts that lead up to a trial, the criminal trial process, and the primary events that occur after someone is convicted at trial, including sentencing, appeal, and post-conviction relief. It includes information on the structural organization of both federal and state courts, various sub-types of court jurisdiction, and an overview of all of the pretrial criminal proceedings used to process criminal defendants through the courts from initial appearance through the eve of trial. Although a review of the chapter should make clear that each jurisdiction's court system has its own unique characteristics, the criminal pretrial process presented in this chapter should serve as a framework for the further study of one or more of these systems. When researching a specific court system, one should seek guidance from the applicable constitution, statutes, rules of court, and rules of evidence for that jurisdiction. The information contained in this chapter can enhance the justice professional's perception of his or her role in the entire criminal justice system and the importance of properly performing that role to the effective and just operation of the system.

Key Terms

abuse of discretion, 60
affidavit, 68
affirmative defense, 96
allocate/allocution hearing, 78
amicus curie, 59
an appeal of right, 59
appeal, 109
appellant, 58
appellate jurisdiction, 58
appellee, 58
arraignment, 77
arrest warrant, 70
bail, 72
bench trial, 87
bench trial/non-jury trial, 58
beyond a reasonable doubt, 96
bind over, 72
briefs, 58
burden of persuasion, 95
burden of production, 95
case-in-chief, 97
circumstantial evidence, 94
clear and convincing evidence, 96
clearly erroneous, 60
closing arguments, 99

competency to stand trial, 85
complaint, 67
concurrent jurisdiction, 60
correctional system, 104
courts of general jurisdiction, 57
courts of limited jurisdiction, 57
cross-examination, 98
de novo, 60
defendant, 57
deliberations, 100
demonstrative evidence, 94
deposition, 81
determinate sentencing, 101
direct evidence, 94
direct examination, 97
discovery, 81
en banc, 62
evidence, 94
exclusive jurisdiction, 60
exculpatory evidence, 82
fact-partial challenges, 91
felony, 64
grand jury, 73

harmless errors, 58
hung jury, 100
immunity, 75
impeaching, 81
indictment, 72
information, 72
initial appearance, 70
intermediate courts of appeals, 59
intermediate sanctions, 105
indeterminate sentencing, 101
jail, 106
judgment, 107
judicial notice, 95
jurisdiction, 55
jury instructions, 99
jury nullification, 100
jury trial, 57
litigants, 57
magistrate/justice of the peace, 67
mandatory appellate jurisdiction, 59
mandatory sentencing, 102
mere suspicion, 96
misdemeanor, 64

motion, 80
motion for judgment of acquittal, 98
nolo contendere, 77
not guilty by reason of insanity, 79
opening statements, 97
oral arguments, 58
original jurisdiction, 57
pardon, 101
parole, 106
peremptory challenges, 91
petit jury, 93
petition for a writ of certiorari, 60
petitioner, 58
plain error, 109
plea bargaining, 80
prejudicial error, 58
preliminary hearing, 70
preponderance of the evidence, 96
presentence investigation, 103
presentence investigation report, 103
presumption, 94
presumption of innocence, 94

Review and Discussion Questions

1. Draw a diagram of the hierarchy of federal and state courts with criminal jurisdiction in your state. Indicate whether each court has original or appellate criminal jurisdiction. Further explain the specifics of each court's subject matter jurisdiction (for example, if it hears only misdemeanors or whether it has a limited appellate jurisdiction).
2. What is the difference between jurisdiction and venue?
3. What is a writ of certiorari? Under what circumstances might a court of last resort, like the U.S. Supreme Court, grant certiorari?
4. Discuss the similarities and differences among the three types of charging documents (i.e., a complaint, an indictment, and an information).
5. Explain the purposes of an initial appearance and how it differs from an arraignment.
6. What is an affidavit? What documents in the pretrial criminal justice process are usually supported by affidavits?
7. What is a grand jury and what are its functions? Compare and contrast the similarities and the differences between preliminary hearings and grand jury proceedings.
8. What are the four types of pleas that defendants in most U.S. jurisdictions might enter at an arraignment?
9. Describe the things that are supposed to happen at a Rule 11 or similar state law proceeding at which a defendant enters a plea of guilty or *nolo contendere*. Be sure to include a discussion of the rights that a defendant waives when entering one of these pleas.
10. Describe the types of information that must be disclosed by a prosecutor to the defense as part of the mandatory criminal discovery process.
11. What is a motion to suppress evidence? Why is it particularly important to constitutional criminal procedure and, therefore, criminal justice professionals—especially law enforcement officers?
12. Before a court is permitted to allow a criminal defendant to stand trial, plead guilty, or waive constitutional rights, the court must be satisfied that the defendant is competent to engage in any of these activities. What is meant by competency? Describe the legal standard for determining competency to stand trial and waive rights in a criminal case.
13. What is the difference between a jury trial and a bench trial? When does a criminal defendant have the right to jury trial? Why might a defendant waive that right and opt for a bench trial?
14. Explain the process of assembling a venire panel and how it gets narrowed into a petit jury through the *voir dire* process.
15. What is the difference between a challenge for cause and a peremptory challenge? Describe the limitations the Equal Protection Clause places on the use of peremptory challenges.

16. What is the difference between a presumption and an inference? What two presumptions set the evidentiary starting points in all criminal trials?
17. What is the difference between direct evidence and circumstantial evidence? Give an example of each.
18. Describe the order of presentation of evidence during a criminal trial.
19. What are the different burdens of proof? Identify with particularity the levels of proof that play an important role in various criminal procedures.
20. Why is it important to differentiate a verdict from a judgment?
21. What are the primary differences between indeterminate sentencing schemes and determinate ones?
22. What is a presentence investigation report? What information is usually contained in one? Why are these reports important to the criminal sentencing process?
23. Name and briefly describe three ways in which a defendant can obtain relief from the courts after a verdict of guilty.

3

Basic Underlying Concepts: The Exclusionary Rule, Privacy, Probable Cause, and Reasonableness

Learning Objectives

▶ Understand the history of and reasons for the exclusionary rule, the exceptions to the rule, and the rule's significance in the law of criminal procedure.

▶ Understand generally the nature of the right of privacy in the law of criminal procedure and how it has affected court resolutions of Fourth Amendment issues.

▶ Define probable cause to search and to arrest.

▶ Know the indications of criminal activity that support probable cause.

▶ Understand the two-pronged test of the *Aguilar* case for establishing probable cause through the use of an informant's information.

▶ Understand how an informant's information can be bolstered by corroboration in order to establish probable cause.

▶ Explain the *Gates* "totality-of-the-circumstances" test for determining probable cause.

▶ Define reasonableness and understand generally its importance in the law of criminal procedure, especially with respect to arrests, searches, and seizures.

efore discussing in detail the law of criminal procedure—arrest, search and seizure, admissions and confessions, and pretrial identification—it's important to understand four concepts fundamental to criminal procedure: the exclusionary rule, privacy, probable cause, and reasonableness. They are developed in greater detail throughout the book and clarified by examples. Because these concepts are so pervasive and so essential to an understanding of criminal procedure, discussing them at the outset should make the following chapters more meaningful and easier to understand.

▶ THE EXCLUSIONARY RULE

The **exclusionary rule** requires that any evidence obtained by police using methods that violate a person's *constitutional* rights must be excluded from use in a criminal prosecution against that person. This rule is judicially imposed and arose relatively recently in the development of the U.S. legal system. Under the common law, the seizure of evidence by illegal means did not affect its admissibility in court. Any evidence, however obtained, was admitted as long as it satisfied other evidentiary criteria for admissibility, such as relevance and trustworthiness. The exclusionary rule was first developed in 1914 in the case of *Weeks v. United States*, 232 U.S. 383, and was limited to a prohibition on the use of evidence illegally obtained by *federal* law enforcement officers. Not until 1949, in the case of *Wolf v. Colorado*, 38 U.S. 25, 27-28, did the U.S. Supreme Court take the first step toward applying the exclusionary rule to the states by ruling that the Fourth Amendment was applicable to the states through the Due Process Clause of the Fourteenth Amendment:

> **The security of one's privacy against arbitrary intrusion by the police— which is at the core of the Fourth Amendment—is basic to a free society. It is therefore implicit in the "concept of ordered liberty" and as such enforceable against the States through the Due Process Clause.**

Wolf, however, left enforcement of Fourth Amendment rights to the discretion of the individual states and did not specifically require application of the exclusionary rule. That mandate did not come until 1961, in the landmark decision of *Mapp v. Ohio*, 367 U.S. 643, 655, in which the Court said:

> **Since the Fourth Amendment's right of privacy has been declared enforceable against the States through the Due Process Clause of the Fourteenth, it is enforceable against them by the same sanction of exclusion as is used against the Federal Government. Were it otherwise, . . . the assurance against unreasonable federal searches and seizures would be "a form of words," valueless and undeserving of mention in a perpetual charter of inestimable human liberties . . .**

Thus, with *Mapp*, the exclusionary rule became the principle, or traditional method to deter Fourth Amendment violations. (Other methods do exist, however. See Alternatives to the Exclusionary Rule later in this chapter.)

As discussed in Chapter 1, the Supreme Court has selectively incorporated other constitutional guarantees in the Bill of Rights through the Due Process

Clause of the Fourteenth Amendment, so these rights apply to the states. For example, the Fifth Amendment privilege against self-incrimination was made applicable to the states in *Malloy v. Hogan*, 378 U.S. 1 (1964); the Sixth Amendment right to appointed counsel was made applicable to the states in *Gideon v. Wainwright*, 372 U.S. 335 (1963); and the Eighth Amendment ban against cruel and unusual punishment was made applicable to the states in *Robinson v. California*, 370 U.S. 660 (1962). Later chapters discuss the manner in which the exclusionary rule is used to enforce the rights guaranteed in these amendments and others.

The U.S. Supreme Court has also invoked the exclusionary rule to protect certain "due process of law" rights that are not specifically contained in the Constitution or its amendments. For example, a confession that has been coerced and is therefore involuntary is excluded from evidence because it is a violation of due process of law. *Brown v. Mississippi*, 297 U.S. 278 (1936). Similarly, pretrial identification procedures that are not administered fairly may be violations of due process of law and therefore excludable from evidence at trial. For example, an unnecessarily suggestive police lineup, if also deemed unreliable, may be inadmissible at trial. *Neil v. Biggers*, 409 U.S. 188 (1972).

The exclusionary rule was designed to deter police misconduct. Generally speaking, it does not apply to evidence obtained by private citizens because it would usually have no deterrent effect. Most private citizens are unfamiliar with constitutional rules such as those governing search and seizure, have no reason to learn them, and would not be disciplined for violating them. In *Burdeau v. McDowell*, 256 U.S. 465 (1921), private citizens illegally seized certain papers from another private citizen, and turned them over to a government official who intended to use the papers as evidence in a criminal prosecution. The Court said:

> **The papers having come into the possession of the government without a violation of petitioner's right by governmental authority, we see no reason why the fact that individuals, unconnected with the government, may have wrongfully taken them, should prevent them from being held for use in prosecuting an offense where the documents are of an incriminatory character.** 256 U.S. at 476.

If, however, police encourage, order, or join in an illegal search by a private citizen, the private citizen is considered an agent of the government and any evidence obtained by the citizen would be subject to exclusion. *Corngold v. United States*, 367 F.2d 1 (9th Cir. 1966); *Machlan v. State*, 225 N.E.2d 762 (1967). Evidence gathered by a private citizen acting in conjunction with or upon the orders of a government official is subject to the exclusionary rule, just as if it had been gathered by a governmental official. In such a case, the private citizen is considered to be an agent or instrument of the government. *Coolidge v. New Hampshire*, 403 U.S. 443 (1971); *United States v. Lambert*, 771 F.2d 83, 89 (6th Cir. 1985). Also, evidence gathered by governmental actors who are not police officers, which includes many types of government inspectors and even public school teachers, is also subject to the exclusionary rule. *See, e.g., New Jersey v. T.L.O.*, 469 U.S. 325 (1985).

Federal-State Conflict

Individual states do not need to follow all interpretations of the U.S. Supreme Court in the area of criminal procedure. Rather, the states must only abide by what the Supreme Court sets as minimum thresholds for constitutional guarantees.

> **The States are not . . . precluded from developing workable rules governing arrests, searches and seizures to meet "the practical demands of effective criminal investigation and law enforcement" in the States,** *provided that those rules do not violate the [federal] constitutional proscription of unreasonable searches and seizures and the concomitant command that evidence so seized is inadmissible against one who has standing to complain.* Ker v. California, 374 U.S. 23, 34 (1963) (italics supplied).

Thus, when a state court is faced with a decision of whether or not a particular search or seizure is constitutional, it must apply standards *at least equal* to those on the federal level in determining whether the search or seizure is constitutional. However, if the state's own constitutional or statutory standards are more demanding than those in the federal system, then the state may apply its own standards as illustrated by the Discussion Point on garbage below.

State courts may afford the accused greater protection under state law through more demanding standards than those required by the U.S. Constitution. This practice is sometimes referred to as the "new federalism." It is derived from the well-established rule that state court decisions based on "adequate and independent state grounds" are immune from federal review. *Murdock v. Memphis*, 87 U.S. (20 Wall.) 590 (1874); *Herb v. Pitcairn*, 324 U.S. 117 (1945). Under this rule, state courts are free (as a matter of state constitutional, statutory, or case law) to expand individual rights by imposing greater restrictions on police than those imposed under federal constitutional law. State courts may not, however, decrease individual rights below the level established by the U.S. Constitution. Nor may state courts impose greater restrictions on police activity as a matter of federal constitutional law when the U.S. Supreme Court specifically refrains from imposing such restrictions. *Oregon v. Hass,* 420 U.S. 714 (1975).

A state court may respond in various ways to a U.S. Supreme Court decision that raises issues of federal constitutional law. For example, it may choose to:

▶ Apply the ruling as it thinks the Supreme Court would. This might include adopting the ruling, or holding of the Court, as a matter of state law.

▶ Avoid applying the holding of the Supreme Court by factually distinguishing the case before it from the Supreme Court case. Such a decision, however, may be subject to reversal by the Supreme Court.

▶ Reject the Supreme Court ruling on adequate and independent state grounds by interpreting the state constitution or state statutes to provide additional rights unavailable under the U.S. Constitution as interpreted by the Supreme Court. This approach clearly expresses disapproval of the Supreme Court ruling and insulates the state court decision from Supreme Court review. When a state court opinion is ambiguous as to whether it is based on an adequate and independent ground, the Supreme Court applies the so-called plain statement rule:

> [W]hen . . . a state court decision fairly appears to rest primarily on federal law, or to be interwoven with the federal law, and when the adequacy and independence of any possible state law ground is not clear from the face of the opinion, we will accept as the most reasonable explanation that the state court decided the case the way it did because it believed that federal law required it to do so. If a state court chooses merely to rely on federal

Is Garbage Private?

In *California v. Greenwood*, 486 U.S. 35 (1988), a police officer kept the defendant's home under surveillance for approximately two months. One day, after a garbage truck collected the trash from in front of the defendant's home, the officer asked the trash collector to allow the officer to search the defendant's garbage.

The officer found narcotics-related materials in the defendant's trash, leading to his arrest and prosecution on drug charges. The defendant sought to use the exclusionary rule to suppress the search of the trash under the Fourth Amendment. But the Supreme Court upheld the officer's actions, reasoning that people should not expect to enjoy any privacy with respect to their trash because they place their garbage outside their homes on a curb where animals, children, scavengers, snoops, and others could easily rummage through it. Thus, as a matter of federal constitutional law, the Fourth Amendment does not protect people's garbage. However, several states disagree with the U.S. Supreme Court's refusal to protect under the Fourth Amendment a person's garbage left curbside. These states require a search warrant to be issued before law enforcement may search someone's garbage deposited for collection on a street curb. See, *e.g., State v. Hempele,* 576 A.2d 793, 814 (N.J. 1990): "In summary, [the New Jersey Constitution] applies to the search but not to the seizure of a garbage bag left on the curb for collection. Law-enforcement officials need no cause to seize the bag, but they must have a warrant based on probable cause to search it [absent an emergency]."

States like New Jersey are free to disregard *Greenwood* because they provide more protection of privacy as a matter of state law than the Fourth Amendment does as a matter of federal constitutional law.

With which approach to the privacy of garbage do you agree: the one taken by the *Greenwood* Court, or the one taken by a minority of the states? Why? Assume for the moment that *Greenwood* had been decided differently, and the Court had ruled that a search warrant was necessary before police are permitted to search someone's trash. Would the states be free to disregard such a command? Why or why not?

precedents as it would on the precedents of all other jurisdictions, then it need only make clear by a plain statement in its judgment or opinion that the federal cases are being used only for the purpose of guidance, and do not themselves compel the result that the court has reached. If the state court decision indicates clearly and expressly that it is alternatively based on bona fide separate, adequate, and independent grounds, we, of course, will not undertake to review the decision. *Michigan v. Long,* 463 U.S. 1032, 1040-41 (1983).

In recent years, many state courts, reacting against the Burger and Rehnquist Courts' reluctant and sparing approach to protecting the rights of the accused, have resorted to this option to keep alive the Warren Court's active commitment to the protection and expansion of individual rights.

One example of this trend in the Fourth Amendment context is *South Dakota v. Opperman*, 428 U.S. 364 (1976). In that case, the South Dakota Supreme Court ruled that an automobile inventory conducted by South Dakota law enforcement officers violated the Fourth Amendment. But the U.S. Supreme Court reversed the decision, holding that the police conduct was reasonable on regulatory grounds. On remand, the South Dakota Supreme Court, in *State v. Opperman*, 247 N.W.2d 673 (S.D.1976), decided that the police inventory procedure violated the South Dakota Constitution and held that the evidence seized was inadmissible. This South Dakota court's decision is noteworthy because the search and seizure provision of the South Dakota Constitution is essentially similar to the Fourth Amendment of the U.S. Constitution and because neither the prosecution nor the defense in the case had raised the issue of the state constitution. Likewise, in the Fifth Amendment context, some state courts have declined to follow the Supreme Court's holding in *Harris v. New York*, 401 U.S. 222 (1971): that confessions obtained in violation of *Miranda* may be used to impeach a defendant's credibility at trial. By excluding these confessions even for impeachment purposes, these states have chosen to give defendants more protection than is available under the Fifth Amendment to the U.S. Constitution. See, *e.g.*, *State v. Santiago*, 492 P.2d 657 (1971). (Other examples of this "new federalism" are presented in later chapters dealing with particular areas of conflict.)

Alternatives to the Exclusionary Rule

Numerous attempts have been made to abolish the exclusionary rule in the United States Congress, but none as of yet have succeeded. Theoretically, though, there are several alternatives to the exclusionary rule. For example, conducting an illegal **search** and **seizure** could be designated as a crime. Under such an approach, an officer performing an illegal search or seizure could be criminally prosecuted. However, examples of officers being prosecuted in state courts for overzealous law enforcement are extremely rare due to strict state requirements regarding legal proof and broad legal defenses. An officer may also be liable criminally under 18 U.S.C. § 242, a federal statute making an officer who, under color of state law, willfully deprives a person of his federal constitutional rights, subject to fines and imprisonment. This statute, however, has not often been applied against officers by state prosecutors. In addition, on the federal level, though a law enforcement officer may also be sued criminally under various statutes, few prosecutions against officers have actually occurred.

In addition, an officer who makes an illegal search and seizure may also be subject to internal departmental disciplinary procedures resulting from a formal complaint brought by a citizen. Examples of meaningful and effective disciplinary actions against officers stemming from citizen complaints, however, are exceedingly rare. Internal police disciplinary procedures are sometimes reinforced through the findings of independent police review boards, which consist of citizens who hear complaints against officers and who can recommend disciplinary action against them. Unfortunately, findings of police misconduct by these review boards have not generally led to the successful discipline of police officers (Whitebread & Slobogin 2000: 64-65).

Victims of unconstitutional actions by police officers may also bring civil lawsuits against offending officers for monetary damages. For example, persons who have been illegally arrested or have had their privacy invaded in an illegal search by a state or local law enforcement officer (e.g., officers employed by a municipality or county) may sue the offending officer in a tort action available under state statute or common law. Moreover, state or local law enforcement officers acting under color of state law who violate Fourth Amendment or other federal constitutional rights are subject to a suit for damages and other remedies in federal courts under a federal civil rights statute: 42 U.S.C. § 1983. Officers sued under Section 1983, however, may claim qualified immunity if they acted reasonably under existing law. This immunity may prevent a Section 1983 action against many local law enforcement officers. Also, under § 1983, individuals deprived of their federal constitutional rights by local officers may, in certain circumstances, sue the corresponding local government entity (e.g., the municipality or county). See *Monell v. Dept. of Soc. Servs. of N.Y.*, 436 US 658 (1978).

Lawsuits under Section 1983 are much more prevalent in recent times, because the Supreme Court has clarified provisions of that section and provided a mechanism by which plaintiffs can recover significant legal costs if they prevail. Moreover, there are no limits on money damages in Section 1983 suits, making these actions more popular than tort actions under state laws, which usually place limits on liability and can also be subject to claims of immunity.

Federal officers and others acting under color of federal law are not subject to §1983, though they may be liable for constitutional violations in other types of civil actions known as "Bivens" actions. *Bivens v. Six Unknown Named Agents of the Federal Bureau of Narcotics*, 403 U.S. 388, 397 (1971), held that a plaintiff who sued federal narcotics agents "is entitled to recover money damages for any injuries he has suffered as a result of the agents' violation of the [Fourth] Amendment." In a *Bivens* action, which is essentially a civil action for monetary damages against federal officers for constitutional violations, absolute or qualified immunity may apply. For example, federal law enforcement officers are entitled to qualified immunity if, measured objectively, they acted reasonably, or in "good faith," under existing law. In the Fourth Amendment context, officers may be entitled to qualified immunity if they can establish that a reasonable officer could have believed that his or her conduct comported with the Fourth Amendment, even though it actually did not. As stated in *Anderson v. Creighton*, 483 U.S. 635, 639 (1987), "whether an official protected by qualified immunity may be held personally liable for an allegedly unlawful official action generally turns on the 'objective legal reasonableness' of the action assessed in light of the legal rules that were 'clearly established' at the time it was taken." Besides the legal problem of immunity, other practical problems stand in the way of a truly effective civil damage remedy. For example, potential plaintiffs are often disreputable people toward whom juries are unsympathetic, or they are indigent or imprisoned and cannot afford to bring suit.

Individuals who suffer a Fourth Amendment or other constitutional violation at the hands of federal law enforcement officers may also be able to sue the U.S. government in a Federal Torts Claim Act (FTCA) action under 28 U.S.C. § 1346(b) and 28 U.S.C. § 2680(h). This avenue can be especially helpful to plaintiffs given the vast financial resources (or "deep pockets") of the federal government.

Though civil lawsuits and other remedies for constitutional violations may provide some relief to potential plaintiffs, many scholars believe the exclusionary rule should still remain the principal deterrent against police misconduct. This

Should Police Pay Money for Their Misconduct or Mistakes?

In *Albright v. Oliver*, 510 U.S. 266 (1994), law enforcement authorities obtained an arrest warrant for defendant Albright on the basis of testimony by Detective Oliver that Albright sold a substance that resembled a drug. Albright was later arrested and released on bond. At a later hearing before his trial, the warrant was found invalid because it failed to state a charge against defendant. Defendant Albright then instituted a civil action under § 1983 against Detective Oliver, claiming that Oliver deprived him of his due process "liberty" interests "to be free from criminal prosecution except upon probable cause." 510 U.S. at 269. Though a majority of the members of the Supreme Court seemed to agree that Albright could bring a civil suit against Oliver under the Fourth Amendment for his illegal arrest, the Court dismissed Albright's action because he brought it on due process grounds.

More generally, do you think civil suits resulting in money damages, like the one instituted in *Albright*, are the best method to punish misbehaving officers for illegal arrests and searches under the Fourth Amendment (or for other constitutional violations)? What about using criminal lawsuits against officers which may result in possible jail time? Alternatively, do you think these sorts of constitutional violations are better addressed through internal police discipline? Or should concerned citizens sitting on independent review boards have the power to punish misbehaving officers? Finally, should officers be punished at all through lawsuits and police or community discipline, or should the exclusionary rule be the sole remedy for constitutional violations? (In this regard, see below for a discussion of current criticism of the exclusionary rule.)

is because successful civil lawsuits against officers as well as meaningful internal police discipline are both rare occurrences. In particular, officers may be immune from civil suits or damages associated with these suits may be too small for a suit to be brought by an attorney in the first place. In the case of police discipline, police officers will obviously be reluctant to impose punishment on a fellow officer. Even when they do, the punishment may not be significant enough to have an effect on the misbehaving officer.

Criticism of the Exclusionary Rule

The exclusionary rule has, throughout its existence, been the target of criticism and attempted reform. One such criticism is that individual police officers are not personally impacted by the exclusion of evidence they obtained unconstitutionally. In fact, Warren Burger, the former chief justice of the U.S. Supreme Court, offered this criticism in his dissent opinion in the case of *Bivens v. Six Unknown Named Agents of the Federal Bureau of Narcotics*, 403 U.S. 388 (1971). Burger commented:

> The rule does not apply any direct sanction to the individual official whose illegal conduct results in the exclusion of evidence in a criminal trial. With rare exceptions law enforcement agencies do not impose direct sanctions on the individual officer responsible for a particular judicial application of the suppression doctrine. . . . Thus there is virtually nothing done to bring about a change in his practices. The immediate sanction triggered by application of the rule is visited upon the prosecutor whose case against a criminal is either weakened or destroyed. The doctrine deprives the police in no real sense. . . . 403 U.S. at 416.

Burger went on to explain that prosecutors, though most directly affected by the exclusionary rule, cannot themselves exact any punishment upon individual police officers whose behavior directly leads to the exclusion of evidence. Specifically, Burger argued that:

> The suppression doctrine vaguely assumes that law enforcement is a monolithic governmental enterprise. . . . But the prosecutor who loses his case because of police misconduct is not an official in the police department; he can rarely set in motion any corrective action or administrative penalties. Moreover, he does not have control or direction over police procedures or police actions that lead to the exclusion of evidence. 403 U.S. at 416-17.

In addition, Burger argued that any educational effect the exclusionary rule might offer for police officers is substantially lessened by both the everyday practicalities of police work and the passage of time between a particular police action and a legal case:

> Whatever educational effect the rule conceivably might have in theory is greatly diminished in fact by the realities of law enforcement work. Policemen do not have the time, inclination, or training to read and grasp the nuances of the appellate opinions that ultimately define the standards of conduct they are to follow. The issues that these decisions resolve often admit of neither easy nor obvious answers, as sharply divided courts on what is or is not "reasonable" demonstrate. Nor can judges, in all candor, forget that opinions sometimes lack helpful clarity. The presumed educational effect of judicial opinions is also reduced by the long time lapse— often several years—between the original police action and its final judicial evaluation. Given a policeman's pressing responsibilities, it would be surprising if he ever becomes aware of the final result after such a delay. 403 U.S. at 417.

Finally, on a related note, Burger questioned the overall ability of the exclusionary rule to deter police misconduct, given the fact that criminal prosecutions do not necessarily arise after a particular instance of misconduct. In particular, Burger pointed out that "there are large areas of police activity that do not result in criminal prosecutions—hence the rule has virtually no applicability and no effect in such situations." 403 U.S. at 418.

Another significant criticism of the exclusionary rule is that it allows factually guilty individuals to be set free. Note, however, that the exclusionary rule does not necessarily bar or stop a prosecution. At most, it renders inadmissible evidence obtained as the result of a constitutional violation. If that evidence is essential to the prosecution's case against a defendant, however, the prosecution may decide that it is futile to continue the prosecution. On the other hand, if the prosecution has sufficient other legally obtained evidence, the prosecution may go forward despite the illegal police conduct.

Criticism and attempts at reform of the exclusionary rule have resulted in numerous limitations on the application of the rule and refusals to further extend the rule beyond the criminal trial context. Consider the following examples:

▶ *United States v. Calandra*, 414 U.S. 338 (1974), held that the Fourth Amendment did not prevent the use of illegally obtained evidence by a grand jury. In other words, illegally obtained evidence may serve as the basis for a grand jury's determination that probable cause exists to make someone stand trial for a felony offense even if that evidence cannot be introduced at the trial.

▶ *United States v. Janis*, 428 U.S. 433 (1976), held that illegally obtained evidence need not be excluded at certain civil trials brought by the United States. The Court reasoned that excluding evidence in the particular civil trial at issue in *Janis*—a federal tax proceeding—would not advance the deterrence purpose of the exclusionary rule. According to the Court, police officers would not be deterred from conducting an illegal search or seizure by applying the exclusionary rule to federal tax proceedings, as these proceedings do not fall within the primary interest or focus of a typical police officer's work.

▶ *Immigration and Naturalization Service v. Lopez-Mendoza*, 468 U.S. 1032 (1984), refused to apply the exclusionary rule in a civil deportation hearing after immigration officers had obtained incriminating statements following an apparently illegal arrest.

▶ *Pennsylvania Board of Probation and Parole v. Scott*, 524 U.S. 357, 364 (1998), held that: "the federal exclusionary rule does not bar the introduction at parole revocation hearings of evidence seized in violation of parolees' Fourth Amendment rights."

▶ *Harris v. New York*, 401 U.S. 222 (1971), allowed the use of evidence obtained in violation of the *Miranda* warnings to impeach the defendant's testimony at trial. Thus, after Harris, confessions and other incriminating statements obtained in violation of Miranda will not be excluded at trial if the prosecutor uses those statements to impeach the defendant's credibility or trustworthiness. Those statements, however, will still be excluded if the prosecutor attempts to use them to prove the defendant's guilt.

▶ *Stone v. Powell*, 428 U.S. 465 (1976), held that the exclusionary rule did not apply to a *habeas corpus* proceeding in which the prisoner attempts to prove the illegality of his or her detention. *Stone v. Powell* essentially eliminated federal review through *habeas corpus* claims of state court decisions concerning the Fourth Amendment. In particular, the Court held that "where the State has provided an opportunity for full and fair litigation of a Fourth Amendment claim, a state prisoner may not be granted federal *habeas corpus* relief on the ground that evidence obtained in an unconstitutional search or seizure was introduced at his trial." 428 U.S. at 494. *Stone v. Powell* is noteworthy not only because it limited the application of the exclusionary rule but also because it strengthened the authority of state courts in interpreting the Fourth Amendment.

▶ *Hudson v. Michigan*, 126 S. Ct. 2159 (2006), held that the exclusionary rule does not apply to evidence seized in a home after police officers fail to knock on the owner's door and announce their presence as required under the Fourth Amendment. Furthermore, the *Hudson* case is significant because Justice Scalia's majority opinion casts doubt more generally on the overall efficacy of the exclusionary rule. Scalia explains that due to certain changes since the Court's decision in *Mapp v. Ohio*, other remedies for Fourth Amendment violations by police may be able to replace the exclusionary rule. Scalia mentions civil rights lawsuits and internal police discipline as examples of other potential remedies. (*See* Discussion Point "Are 'knock-and-announce' violations sufficiently attenuated?" in this chapter for a detailed discussion of this recent and important case).

Despite the limitations on the application of the exclusionary rule by Supreme Court decisions, the Court's basic holding in *Mapp v. Ohio* remains good law, and the basic tenets of the exclusionary rule remain valid legal doctrine. Further limitations or expansions on the exclusionary rule will depend largely on the makeup of the Supreme Court and the opportunities presented to the Court in the cases brought before it.

Fruit of the Poisonous Tree Doctrine

The exclusionary rule is not limited to evidence that is the direct product of illegal police behavior, such as a coerced confession or items seized during an illegal search. The rule also requires exclusion of evidence *indirectly* obtained as a result of a constitutional violation. This type of evidence is sometimes called **derivative evidence** or secondary evidence. In *Silverthorne Lumber Co. v. United States*, 251 U.S. 385 (1920), the U.S. Supreme Court invalidated a subpoena issued on the basis of information obtained through an illegal search and, in the process, overturned the contempt conviction for failure to obey this subpoena. The Court reasoned as follows:

> **The essence of a provision forbidding the acquisition of evidence in a certain way is that not merely evidence so acquired shall not be used before the Court but that it shall not be used at all [e.g., to support a subpoena]. Of course this does not mean that the facts thus obtained [through an illegality] become sacred and inaccessible. If knowledge of them is gained from an independent source they may be proved like any others, but the knowledge gained by the Government's own wrong cannot be used by it in the way proposed.** 251 U.S. at 392.

Thus, the prosecution may not use in court evidence obtained directly *or indirectly* from a constitutional violation, such as the illegal search in *Silverthorne*. The prohibition against using this derivative, or secondary, evidence is often called the **fruit of the poisonous tree doctrine**, the tree being the initial constitutional violation and the fruit being the evidence obtained as a direct or indirect result of that violation.

Although the fruit of the poisonous tree doctrine was originally developed in applying the exclusionary rule to unconstitutional searches, it has been applied equally to evidence obtained as the indirect result of other constitutional violations. Thus, evidence is inadmissible if it is acquired directly or indirectly as a result of an illegal stop, an illegal arrest, an illegal identification procedure, or an involuntary confession. In this way, fruit of the poisonous tree doctrine may lead to the exclusion of additional evidence beyond the evidence obtained during the initial constitutional violation.

The fruit of the poisonous tree doctrine applies only when a person's *constitutional* rights have been violated. Nevertheless, the doctrine may apply in different ways depending on the type and severity of the underlying constitutional violation. As the U.S. Supreme Court stated, "unreasonable searches under the Fourth Amendment are different from unwarned interrogation under the Fifth Amendment." *Dickerson v. United States*, 530 U.S. 428 (2000). Indeed, a failure to give *Miranda* warnings before a suspect's confession may not trigger fruit of the poisonous tree analysis as to future incriminating statements by that same suspect. (See the discussion of *Oregon v. Elstad* in Chapter 13.)

Exceptions to the Fruit of the Poisonous Tree Doctrine

Courts loathe excluding derivative evidence under the Fruit of the Poisonous Tree Doctrine. Accordingly, the courts have developed several doctrines that mitigate the harsh effects of preventing the use of both illegally obtained evidence and the fruits derived from the illegality.

Independent Source The **independent source doctrine** allows the admission of tainted evidence if that evidence was also obtained through a source wholly independent of the primary constitutional violation (for example, when evidence was obtained by a source other than the police). The independent source exception is compatible with the underlying rationale of the exclusionary rule— the deterrence of police misconduct:

> **The independent source doctrine teaches us that the interest of society in deterring unlawful police conduct and the public interest in having juries receive all probative evidence of a crime are properly balanced by putting the police in the same, not a worse, position than they would have been in if no police error or misconduct had occurred.** *Nix v. Williams*, 467 U.S. 431, 443 (1984).

Thus, according to the Court, when there is a legal, independent source for the evidence the prosecutor seeks to use at trial, there is little or no deterrent value gained by applying the exclusionary rule to that evidence, even in the face of police misconduct.

In *Segura v. United States*, 468 U.S. 796 (1984), law enforcement officers illegally entered an apartment, secured it, and remained for about nineteen hours until a search warrant arrived. Despite the initial illegal entry, the U.S. Supreme Court admitted the evidence found during the subsequent execution of the warrant (but not during the initial entry). The Court found an independent source for the evidence discovered under the search warrant because the information on which the warrant was based came from sources entirely separate from the illegal entry and was known to the officers well before that entry. The Court held that **"[w]hether the initial entry was legal or not is irrelevant to the admissibility of the challenged evidence because there was an independent source for the warrant under which that evidence was seized."** 468 U.S. at 813-14 (1984).

In *Murray v. United States*, 487 U.S. 533 (1988), federal agents made an unlawful search of a warehouse they suspected contained marijuana, and discovered the drug. They then obtained a warrant to search the warehouse without revealing the unlawful search to the issuing magistrate. In executing this warrant, the police again (and unsurprisingly) found the marijuana. The Supreme Court found that if the police and prosecutor could prove that there was an independent source for the warrant apart from the initial unlawful search, then the same marijuana discovered during the second search would be admissible at trial. The Court reasoned that:

> [k]nowledge that the marijuana was in the warehouse was assuredly acquired at the time of the unlawful entry. But it was also acquired at the time of entry pursuant to the warrant, and if that later acquisition was not the result of the earlier entry there is no reason why the independent source doctrine should not apply. Invoking the exclusionary rule would put the police (and society) not in the same position they would have occupied if no violation occurred, but in a worse one. 487 U.S. at 541.

As a result of the Court's decision, evidence initially found during an illegal, warrantless entry by police may now be admissible if the prosecutor can show that the officers' subsequent discovery with a warrant of this very same evidence is based on a source independent of the illegal entry.

Attenuation Another exception to the fruit of the poisonous tree doctrine, first established in *Nardone v. United States*, 308 U.S. 338 (1939), is the **attenuation doctrine.** Under this doctrine, evidence obtained as the result of a constitutional violation is admissible if the means of obtaining the evidence is sufficiently remote from and distinguishable from the primary illegality. The key question is **"whether granting establishment of the primary illegality, the evidence to which instant objection is made has been come at by exploitation of that illegality or instead by means sufficiently distinguishable to be purged of the primary taint."** *Wong Sun v. United States*, 371 U.S. 471, 488 (1963). If evidence is obtained in a way that is not sufficiently connected to the primary illegality, the causal connection between the primary illegality and the evidence is said to be attenuated (or weakened), and the evidence is admissible. The rationale behind this exception to the exclusionary rule is this: the deterrent purpose of the rule is not served when officers could not have been aware of the possible benefit to be derived from their illegal actions at the time they took those actions.

In *Wong Sun,* narcotics agents illegally broke into Toy's laundry and followed Toy into his living quarters where they arrested and handcuffed him. Almost immediately after that, Toy told the agents that Yee had been selling narcotics and that he (Toy) used the drug at Yee's home. The agents then seized heroin from Yee, who told them that it had been brought to him by Toy and Wong Sun. Wong Sun was illegally arrested, arraigned, and released on his own recognizance. Several days later, Wong Sun returned voluntarily and confessed to a narcotics agent. Toy claimed that his statement and the heroin later seized from Yee were fruit of the illegal entry into his dwelling and his illegal arrest. The Court agreed and held both inadmissible against Toy. In particular, as to the statement, the Court said that it was not **"sufficiently an act of free will to purge the**

primary taint of the unlawful invasion." 371 U.S. at 416, 417. Wong Sun claimed that his statement was the fruit of his illegal arrest. The Court disagreed:

> We have no occasion to disagree with the finding of the Court of Appeals that his arrest, also, was without probable cause or reasonable grounds. At all events no evidentiary consequences turn upon that question. For Wong Sun's unsigned confession was not the fruit of that arrest, and was therefore properly admitted at trial. On the evidence that Wong Sun had been released on his own recognizance after a lawful arraignment, and had returned voluntarily several days later to make the statement, we hold that the connection between the arrest and the statement has "become so attenuated as to dissipate the taint." 371 U.S. at 491.

Thus, the Court in *Wong Sun* reasoned that though the police illegally arrested Wong Sun, the causal connection between this illegality and Wong Sun's subsequent confession was sufficiently weakened due to both the passage of time and the voluntary nature of the confession. Thus, it may be said that Wong Son's confession was "sufficiently an act of free will" which "purged the primary taint" of the unlawful arrest.

The U.S. Supreme Court set out three factors to consider in determining whether the connection between the primary illegality and the resulting evidence derived from it has been sufficiently weakened: (1) the time elapsed between the illegality and the acquisition of the evidence; (2) the presence of intervening circumstances; and (3) the purpose and flagrancy of the official misconduct. In the particular case of confessions as the resulting evidence (or fruit) derived from an illegality, another "attenuation" factor is whether *Miranda* warnings were given before the confession. *Brown v. Illinois*, 422 U.S. 590 (1975). (See the discussion of *Brown* in Chapter 6 under Effect on Evidence Gathered as a Result of Illegal Arrest.) Since *Brown*, Supreme Court cases analyzing the fruit of poisonous tree doctrine and possible attenuation have placed special emphasis on intervening circumstances and the flagrancy of police behavior (factors 2 and 3 above). In the process, the Court has tended to place less importance on the time factor, as well as whether or not *Miranda* warnings were given before a confession.

For example, when police behavior is especially flagrant (e.g., police arrest defendant involuntarily, without probable cause and on the basis of an uncorroborated tip), the fact that police give *Miranda* warnings to the defendant and let six hours pass between his illegal arrest and confession will not dissipate the taint of the illegal arrest. *Taylor v. Alabama*, 457 U.S. 687 (1982). However, even though only forty-five minutes separate the beginning of defendant's illegal detention and confession, the taint will likely dissipate when police do not act flagrantly and the confession is voluntary. See *Rawlings v. Kentucky*, 448 U.S. 98 (1980). In particular, the Court in *Rawlings* determined that the police acted courteously toward the defendant during his forty-five minute detention, and that this temporary detention did not constitute "flagrant" behavior.

Courts applying the attenuation doctrine may make a distinction between physical evidence (such as live witnesses and lineup identifications) and verbal evidence (like a suspect's confession). *United States v. Ceccolini*, 435 U.S. 268 (1978), held that, because of the cost to the truth-finding process of disqualifying knowledgeable witnesses, the exclusionary rule should be invoked with much greater reluctance when the fruit of the poisonous tree is a live witness rather than a confession. Therefore, courts do not exclude the testimony of a

Discussion
↑POINT

Are "Knock-and-Announce" Violations Sufficiently Attenuated?

In *Hudson v. Michigan*, 126 S. Ct. 2159 (2006), police entered a home with a warrant authorizing a search for drugs and guns. They discovered both items of contraband. Even though the police announced their presence and authority prior to entering the home, they failed to wait a reasonable time before "breaking" into the home and thereby violated the "knock-and-announce" rule of the Fourth Amendment. The Court, in an opinion by Justice Scalia, determined that even though the knock-and-announce rule had been violated, the contraband should not be excluded. Scalia attacked the use of the exclusionary rule for knock-and-announce violations by arguing that insufficient causation exists between an illegal, "no-knock" entry and subsequently discovered evidence. The required causal link is absent, according to Scalia, because "whether that preliminary misstep [of violating the knock-and-announce rule] had occurred or not, the police would have executed the warrant they had obtained and would have discovered the [the evidence] inside the house." 126 S. Ct. at 2164.

In addition, Scalia identified a different reason why the causal connection in *Hudson* was too weakened or attenuated: the interests protected by applying the knock-and-announce rule—preventing harm to police and others, while protecting property from unnecessary damage and occupants from unnecessary privacy intrusions—would not be served by excluding the evidence of the guns and drugs found in this case pursuant to the warrant. 126 S. Ct. at 2165.

Finally, Scalia argued that the social costs associated with applying the exclusionary rule to knock-and-announce violations outweigh any benefits the rule may have in this context. For example, Scalia mentioned that criminals will go free and needless litigation will occur as a result of applying the exclusionary rule. Any deterrence benefits gained by applying the rule would be minimal because officers do not have any significant incentive not to knock-and-announce. 126 S. Ct. at 2166.

Do you agree with Justice Scalia's two principal arguments for not applying the exclusionary rule to the knock-and-announce violations ("attenuation" of causal connection argument and costs-exceed-benefits argument)? Why or why not?

witness discovered as the result of a constitutional violation unless the court finds a more direct link between the discovery and the violation than is required to exclude physical evidence. In *Ceccolini* itself, the witness was discovered as a result of an illegal search; however, the Court found factors such as the passage of time between the search and the testimony of the witness as well as the voluntary nature of the testimony, relevant to its conclusion that the causal link had become attenuated. Furthermore, the court must find that the constitutional violation is the kind that will be deterred by application of the exclusionary rule. For example, in *Commonwealth v. Lahti*, 501 N.E.2d 511 (Mass. 1986), police obtained an involuntary statement from the defendant for the very purpose of discovering the defendant's crimes and witnesses to testify to those crimes.

The court held that legitimate concerns for the deterrence of police misconduct compelled the exclusion of the testimony of sexually abused children who were revealed through the defendant's coerced statement.

Inevitable Discovery The **inevitable discovery doctrine** allows admission of tainted evidence if the evidence would ultimately or inevitably have been discovered by lawful means—for example, as the result of the predictable and routine behavior of a law enforcement agency, some other agency, or a private person. Thus, it is really an extension of the independent source doctrine. *Murray v. United States*, 487 U.S. 533, 539 (1988).

The U.S. Supreme Court specifically adopted the inevitable discovery doctrine in *Nix v. Williams*, 467 U.S. 431 (1984), in which police initiated a search for a ten-year-old girl who had disappeared. While the search was going on, the defendant was arrested and arraigned. In response to illegal questioning without his attorney present, Williams led police to the girl's body. The search had been called off, but the girl's body was found in a place that was essentially within the area to be searched. Although the defendant's illegally obtained statements led directly to the discovery of the body, the Court found the evidence of the girl's body admissible under the inevitable discovery doctrine. The Court reasoned that volunteer search parties were approaching the actual location of the body, these parties would have resumed the search had the defendant not led the police to the body, and the body would inevitably have been found.

The Court justified its adoption of the inevitable discovery doctrine with the rationale for the independent source exception:

> [I]f the government can prove that the evidence would have been obtained inevitably and, therefore, would have been admitted regardless of any overreaching by the police, there is no rational basis to keep that evidence from the jury in order to ensure the fairness of the trial proceedings. In that situation, the State has gained no advantage at trial and the defendant has suffered no prejudice. Indeed, suppression of the evidence would operate to undermine the adversary system by putting the State in a worse position than it would have occupied without any police misconduct. 467 U.S. at 447.

The Court dismissed arguments that the inevitable discovery doctrine would promote police misconduct. A police officer faced with an opportunity to obtain evidence illegally will rarely, if ever, be able to determine whether that evidence would inevitably be discovered by other lawful means, and hence be found admissible by a court despite the illegality. Departmental discipline and potential civil liability are other disincentives to obtaining evidence illegally.

The timing of conduct is highly relevant to any claim of inevitable discovery. Courts carefully scrutinize claims of inevitable discovery to make sure that law enforcement personnel were actively seeking lawful means to get at the evidence *before* they engaged in any illegal conduct. The case of *United States v. Satterfield*, 743 F.2d 827 (11th Cir. 1984), illustrates this point. In *Satterfield*, police entered a private home without an arrest or search warrant to look for a man a neighbor claimed to have witnessed committing a murder using a shotgun. After arresting the suspect and putting him in custody, police reentered the house to search for the shotgun, which they eventually found. The defense moved to suppress the shotgun, on the grounds that neither the initial entry into the defendant's home nor the subsequent search for the shotgun had been supported by a valid warrant. The trial court ruled that the inevitable discovery doctrine applied because (1) the police, based on the neighbor's statement, would have been granted a valid warrant to search the house; and (2) during such an authorized search, they would have inevitably discovered the shotgun. An appellate court disagreed, stating:

> To qualify for admissibility, there must be a reasonable probability that the evidence in question would have been discovered by lawful means, and the prosecution must demonstrate that the lawful means which made discovery inevitable were possessed by the police and were being actively pursued *prior* to the occurrence of the illegal conduct. 743 F.2d 846 (*emphasis in original*).

Thus, because the police had not sought a warrant before they entered and searched the defendant's home, the inevitable discovery doctrine was deemed inapplicable.

United States v. Rullo, 748 F. Supp. 36 (D. Mass. 1990), is another good example of how the timing of police conduct is critical to claims of inevitable discovery. The defendant in *Rullo* was arrested and was forced to make incriminating statements by police. They used physical force to beat a confession out of him that included the location of a gun that he had disposed of shortly before his encounter with the police. As a result of his coerced statements, the police located the gun. The trial court ruled that the statements were illegally obtained, and therefore were subject to suppression under the exclusionary rule. The trial court also suppressed the gun as fruit of the poisonous tree. The prosecution contended, however, that the gun should have been admitted under the inevitable discovery doctrine. They posited that the police would have conducted a thorough search of the area in which they found the suspect and that search, in turn, would have led to the inevitable discovery of the weapon. The court agreed that such a search would have taken place, and that the gun would have been found during such a search. But they found the fact that a lawful search of the area had not been previously undertaken by law enforcement officers who did not participate in any police misconduct to be critical:

> [F]or a legal search to have been "truly independent" of the coerced admissions, it would have had to be conducted by officers who were unaware and uninformed of the content of defendant's statements. The participation or intervention in the lawful search of officers who were not involved in the police misconduct is a constant theme in decisions upholding the application of the inevitable discovery rule. . . . Yet in this case, the agents who would have participated in and directed the "inevitable" search of the area include the same officers who participated in the beating of the defendant and who heard him disclose the location of the weapon, or were told of his statements. It was apparently with precisely such situations in mind that [courts have required] active pursuit of the legal means *at the time* of the misconduct. . . . 748 F. Supp. 44 (emphasis added).

Occasionally, courts find inevitable discovery based on the behavior not of law enforcement officers but of ordinary civilians. In *State v. Miller*, 680 P.2d 676 (Or. 1984), a law enforcement officer violated the *Miranda* requirements in obtaining the defendant's statement that he had "hurt someone" in his hotel room. The officer conducted a warrantless search of the hotel room and discovered a dead body. The court held that evidence of the discovery of the body was admissible despite the *Miranda* violation, because the maid would have inevitably discovered the body and then would have cooperated with the police.

The Good-Faith Exception to the Exclusionary Rule

In *United States v. Leon*, 468 U.S. 897 (1984), the U.S. Supreme Court adopted the **good-faith exception** to the exclusionary rule. Unlike the fruit of the poisonous tree doctrine (which can lead to the exclusion of additional evidence), the good-faith exception, if applicable, will work to admit evidence otherwise excludable. Under this exception, if a law enforcement officer acting with objective good faith obtains a warrant from a neutral and detached magistrate and acts within the scope of the warrant, evidence seized pursuant to the warrant will be admissible even if the warrant is later determined to be invalid. The Court reasoned that excluding such evidence would not further the purposes of the exclusionary rule—deterrence of police misconduct—because officers who act in reliance on a warrant they believe in good faith to be valid are doing exactly what they should be doing under such circumstances. In determining what good faith is, the Court said:

> [O]ur good-faith inquiry is confined to the objectively ascertainable question whether a reasonably well-trained officer would have known that the search was illegal despite the magistrate's authorization. In making this determination, all of the circumstances—including whether the warrant application has previously been rejected by a different magistrate—may be considered. 468 U.S. at 922-23 n.23.

The Court described several circumstances under which an officer would not have reasonable grounds to believe that a warrant was properly issued (and hence the good-faith exception would not be found to apply):

▶ The issuing magistrate was misled by information in an affidavit that the affiant knew was false or would have known was false except for a reckless disregard of the truth (see Chapter 4).

▶ The issuing magistrate wholly abandoned a neutral and detached judicial role and acted as an arm of the prosecution (See Chapter 4 for further discussion of this topic).

▶ The warrant was based on an affidavit so lacking in indicia of probable cause as to render official belief in its existence entirely unreasonable. This type of warrant, issued by a "rubber stamp" magistrate, cannot be relied upon in good faith by a police officer. (See section on Probable Cause later in this chapter).

▶ The warrant was so facially deficient—failing to particularize the place to be searched or the things to be seized—that the executing officers could not reasonably presume it to be valid (see Chapter 4).

Under such circumstances, the warrant would be declared invalid and any evidence seized under the warrant would be ruled inadmissible.

Massachusetts v. Sheppard, 468 U.S. 981 (1984), gives an example of reasonable, good-faith behavior in the context of a facially defective warrant which failed to mention, or "particularize," all of the items eventually seized. The U.S. Supreme Court explained:

> The officers in this case took every step that could reasonably be expected of them. Detective O'Malley prepared an affidavit which was reviewed and approved by the District Attorney. He presented that affidavit to a neutral judge. The judge concluded that the affidavit established probable cause to search Sheppard's residence . . . and informed O'Malley that he would authorize the search as requested. O'Malley then produced the warrant form and informed the judge that it might need to be changed. He was told by the judge that the necessary changes would be made. He then observed the judge make some changes and received the warrant and the affidavit. At this point, a reasonable police officer would have concluded, as O'Malley did, that the warrant authorized a search for the materials outlined in the affidavit. 468 U.S. at 989.

Thus, even though the warrant in *Sheppard* failed to mention relevant evidentiary items outlined in the attached affidavit, the Court found these items admissible at trial because Detective O'Malley had an objective, good faith belief that the warrant authorized a search for these items. This belief stemmed from the fact that the Detective had included these items in the affidavit he prepared, and the judge informed him that the warrant would contain these items.

Arizona v. Evans, 514 U.S. 1 (1995), provides another example of good faith behavior by police officers, this time in the context of a computer record maintained by the government. The defendant in Evans was stopped by a police officer for a minor traffic violation. When the officer checked the computer system in his cruiser, he found that there was an outstanding warrant for the driver's arrest on unrelated misdemeanor charges. Based on this information, the officer arrested the defendant, searched his car, and found marijuana. The defendant sought to suppress the drug evidence because it was discovered incident to an unlawful arrest. It turned out that the arrest warrant had been quashed (annulled) seventeen days before the traffic stop during which he was arrested. But court personnel had failed to properly notify the police that the arrest warrant had been voided, so it still appeared in the system the arresting officer accessed when he pulled the defendant over for the traffic violation. Because the officer acted in good faith in arresting someone under the authority of an arrest warrant that the officer reasonably believed to be valid, the Supreme Court upheld the admissibility of the marijuana despite the clerical error by court personnel. The Court reasoned as follows:

> First . . . the exclusionary rule was historically designed as a means of deterring police misconduct, not mistakes by court employees. . . . Second, [there is] no evidence that court employees are inclined to ignore or subvert the Fourth Amendment or that lawlessness among these actors requires application of the extreme sanction of exclusion. . . . Finally, and most important, there is no basis for believing that application of the exclusionary rule in these circumstances will have a significant effect on court employees responsible for informing the police that a warrant has been quashed. Because court clerks are not adjuncts to the law enforcement team engaged in the often competitive enterprise of ferreting out crime, . . . they have no stake in the outcome of particular criminal prosecutions. 514 U.S. at 14-15.

Some courts now proceed directly to the good-faith issue when reviewing suppression rulings and bypass fundamental Fourth Amendment questions such as whether probable cause supported the warrant or whether the warrant was sufficiently particularized. For example, in *United States v. McLaughlin*, 851 F.2d 283, 284-85 (9th Cir. 1988), the court said:

> We need not decide whether the warrant was based on probable cause, because we find that even if the warrant lacked probable cause, the evidence was properly admitted under the exception to the exclusionary rule announced in *United States v. Leon*. . . . The officers in this case [reasonably] relied on the determination of a neutral magistrate that they had probable cause to search.

Likewise, in *Sheppard* (discussed above), the Court chose to directly address the good-faith exception instead of confronting the Fourth Amendment question of whether the warrant, in light of the accompanying affidavit, satisfied the particularity requirement.

Illinois v. Krull, 480 U.S. 340 (1987), extended the good-faith exception to the exclusionary rule to evidence obtained by police acting in objectively reasonable reliance on a *statute* that had authorized warrantless administrative searches but was later held to violate the Fourth Amendment. Following the approach used in *Leon*, the Court explained that applying the exclusionary rule to an officer's objectively reasonable reliance on a statute would have little deterrent effect:

> **Unless a statute is clearly unconstitutional, an officer cannot be expected to question the judgment of the legislature that passed the law. If the statute is subsequently declared unconstitutional, excluding evidence obtained pursuant to it prior to such judicial declaration will not deter future Fourth Amendment violations by an officer who has simply fulfilled his responsibility to enforce the statute as written.** 480 U.S. at 349-50.

Thus, after *Krull*, unless an officer unreasonably relies on a clearly unconstitutional statute, evidence discovered during a search by an officer pursuant to a statute will not be excluded at trial, *even if* the statute is later found unconstitutional by a court.

Interestingly, several states do not recognize the good-faith exception. For example, the Georgia Supreme Court "declined to adopt the 'good faith' exception to the exclusionary rule . . . holding that because the Georgia legislature has statutorily protected the right to be free from unreasonable search and seizure . . . 'the State of Georgia has chosen to impose greater requirements upon its law enforcement officers than that required by the U.S. Supreme Court.'" *Davis v. State*, 422 S.E.2d 546, 549 n.1 (Ga. 1992) (citing *Gary v. State*, 422 S.E.2d 426 (Ga. 1992)).

Standing to Assert an Exclusionary Rule Claim

"Standing," in the legal context, may be thought of as the ability to raise a legal claim. To challenge the admissibility of evidence and potentially have evidence excluded at trial, a defendant must first have **standing**. A defendant has standing when his or her own constitutional rights have been allegedly violated. For example, under the Fourth Amendment, a defendant has standing to challenge the constitutionality of a search or seizure and argue for the exclusion of evidence only when his or her legitimate expectations of privacy have been violated. In *Rakas v. Illinois*, 439 U.S. 128 (1978), a police search of a car yielded a box of rifle shells in the glove compartment and a sawed-off rifle under the passenger seat. The U.S. Supreme Court held that the defendants—passengers in

Discussion
⬆ POINT

Should General/Open-Ended Warrants Qualify for the Good-Faith Exception?

Should the good-faith exception apply when a judge issues a general, open-ended warrant allowing him to accompany officers to the "search" location and order certain items seized under that warrant after he finds probable cause to do so?

In *LoJi Sales Inc. v. New York*, 442 U.S. 319 (1979), the judge initially issued a warrant authorizing a search for and seizure of any copies of two obscene films at an adult bookstore. The warrant also included a clause allowing the seizure of other, unspecified items of evidence that the judge would later deem obscene while on location at the bookstore. The Court found that even though there may have been probable cause at the time the warrant was issued to search for and seize copies of the two obscene films, all evidence found at the store should be excluded because the judge, in issuing the warrant, exceeded his powers and was neither "neutral" nor "detached." In fact, the Court found that the judge, by authorizing himself to participate in the search and seizure of obscene material at the bookstore, was essentially behaving like an "adjunct law enforcement officer." 442 U.S. at 327. The Court also said that the warrant itself was facially defective by failing to specify in advance the other "obscene" items to be seized at the store. 442 U.S. at 326. Under these facts, the Court was unwilling to contemplate the application of a good-faith exception for any of the evidence seized pursuant to the warrant.

Do you agree with the Court's finding here? What would be the advantages and disadvantages of a judge accompanying law enforcement officers to a crime scene? Why do you think the Court was so concerned about what the judge could do under this warrant? In addition, what is the concern with open-ended, general warrants like the one issued by the judge in *LoJi Sales*? For example, why should warrants have to specify, or particularize, in advance all of the evidence for which there is probable cause to seize?

the car who had no ownership interest in the car, the rifle shells, or the sawed-off rifle—had no legitimate expectation of privacy in the areas searched. Therefore, according to the Court, the passengers suffered no invasion of their Fourth Amendment rights and, therefore, had no standing to object to the intrusion:

> "Fourth Amendment rights are personal rights which, like some other constitutional rights, may not be vicariously asserted." . . . A person who is aggrieved by an illegal search and seizure only through the introduction of damaging evidence secured by a search of a third person's premises or property has not had any of his Fourth Amendment rights infringed. . . . And since the exclusionary rule is an attempt to effectuate the guarantees of the Fourth Amendment, . . . it is proper to permit only defendants whose Fourth Amendment rights have been violated to benefit from the rule's protections. 439 U.S. at 133-34 (1978).

Rakas went on to say that "capacity to claim the protection of the Fourth Amendment depends not upon a property right in the invaded place but upon whether the person who claims the protection of the Amendment has a legitimate expectation of privacy in the invaded place." 439 U.S. at 143. A subjective expectation of privacy is legitimate if it is "one that society is prepared to recognize as 'reasonable.'" *Katz v. United States*, 389 U.S. 347, 361 (1967). For example, the Supreme Court held that a person's status as an overnight guest in a home is alone enough to show that the person had an expectation of privacy that society is prepared to recognize as reasonable. The Court said:

> To hold that an overnight guest has a legitimate expectation of privacy in his host's home merely recognizes the everyday expectations of privacy that we all share. Staying overnight in another's home is a longstanding social custom that serves functions recognized as valuable by society. We will all be hosts and we will all be guests many times in our lives. From either perspective, we think that society recognizes that a houseguest has a legitimate expectation of privacy in his host's home. *Minnesota v. Olson*, 495 U.S. 91, 98 (1990).

It is important to note that the *Olson* Court found that the defendant had standing even though he stayed only one night, possessed no key to the apartment and was never left alone there. 495 U.S. at 98.

Similarly, in *Jones v. United States*, 362 U.S. 257 (1960), where the houseguest was provided a key and given consent to stay in the home by the owner and friend who was away, the Court found that the houseguest had standing to challenge the admissibility of contraband found on him in the home. Notably, standing may also be found to challenge evidence found within a hotel room even when other individuals who are not the defendant live there, provided the defendant has been provided a key and consent to stay. *United States v. Jeffers*, 342 U.S. 48 (1951). Also, in *Jeffers*, standing was still found under the Fourth Amendment even though defendant and the occupants of the apartment were not present at the time of the search.

In contrast to the cases of both the overnight guest (*Olson*) and more traditional houseguest (*Jones*), the U.S. Supreme Court has held that a temporary, commercial visitor has no reasonable expectation of privacy in a home he or she is visiting. In *Minnesota v. Carter*, 525 U.S. 83 (1998), while the defendants bagged cocaine in the apartment, a law enforcement officer investigating a tip observed them by looking through a drawn window blind. The defendants did not live in the apartment, they had never visited that apartment before, their visit only lasted a matter of hours, and they did not possess a key to the apartment. Their only purpose there was to package cocaine. After they were arrested, they moved to suppress evidence obtained from the apartment and their car, arguing that the officer's initial observation was an unreasonable search in violation of the Fourth Amendment. The U.S. Supreme Court ruled they could not invoke the Fourth Amendment because they were in the apartment for such a short time for what amounted to no more than an illegal business transaction. Thus, it appears that by comparing the houseguest cases mentioned above (*Olson*, *Jones*, *Jeffers*) with the case of the temporary business visitor (*Carter*), we may state that "[a]n expectation of privacy in commercial premises . . . is different from, and indeed less than, a similar expectation in an individual's home." *New York v. Burger*, 482 U.S. 691 (1987). Importantly,

Discussion

⬆ POINT

Is What You Do in a Hotel Room Private?

On December 24, 1998, defendants Nerber and Betancourt-Rodriguez went to a Seattle La Quinta Inn to conduct a narcotics transaction with confidential informants. The informants brought the defendants to Room 303. The FBI and the King County Police had rented the room for the operation and installed a hidden video camera without first obtaining a warrant. The parties entered the room at 9:54 A.M., the informants gave the defendants one kilogram of sample cocaine, and the defendants briefly "flashed" money in a briefcase. The informants left the room at 10:00 A.M., telling the defendants they would return to deliver 24 more kilograms of cocaine. They did not return, however, because they believed the defendants intended to rob them. For three hours thereafter, law enforcement agents used the surveillance equipment to monitor the defendants' activities in the hotel room. They observed the other two defendants—Betancourt and Alvarez—enter the room, and watched as the defendants brandished weapons and sampled cocaine. All four defendants left the hotel at approximately 1:00 P.M. and were arrested shortly thereafter.

A grand jury returned an indictment charging all four defendants with narcotics offenses and two with possessing a firearm during the commission of a narcotics offense. The defendants moved to suppress the evidence derived from the video surveillance. In light of *Minnesota v. Carter*, do you think the motion to suppress should have been granted? The trial court granted the motion, finding that *Minnesota v. Carter* "was not controlling because the governmental intrusion in this case (the use of a hidden surveillance camera) was far more egregious than the intrusion in *Carter* (visual observation through a ground-floor apartment window)." *United States v. Nerber*, 222 F.3d 597, 600 (9th Cir. 2000). The appeals court affirmed this decision, holding that the Fourth Amendment protects people from secret video surveillance in another person's hotel room without a warrant or the consent of a participant in the monitored activity.

Do you agree with the courts' decisions? Why or why not?

however, an individual will generally be found to have a legitimate expectation of privacy in his or her own commercial office space, even if that space is shared with others. *Mancusi v. DeForte*, 392 U.S. 364 (1968). This means that an individual will be found to have standing to challenge a search of his or her business office, and consequently to have excluded any evidence illegally seized there by police.

In addition to the temporary business visitor, other individuals may be found to lack standing. For instance, a codefendant in a crime (like a co-conspirator or an accessory) has no standing to object to a search, unless he or she has a reasonable expectation of privacy in the place to be searched. *United States v. Padilla*, 508 U.S. 77 (1993). Likewise, one who carelessly places contraband belonging to him into another's purse may not have standing to object to a search of the purse. *Rawlings v. Kentucky*, 448 U.S. 98 (1980). Also, if an individual voluntarily hands over records to a bank and the government later subpoenas these records, that individual will not have standing under the Fourth Amendment to challenge the government's action. *United States v. Miller*, 425 U.S. 435 (1976).

Standing also applies in the context of the privilege against self-incrimination under the Fifth Amendment. For example, only the person who is forced by the government to speak incriminating information may raise a Fifth Amendment claim. This means that if the government forces (through threats or otherwise) *another* person to speak incriminating information about you, the concept of "standing" will prevent you from challenging and excluding that information under the Fifth Amendment. In this example, since another person's Fifth Amendment rights were violated and not yours, standing will not be found to exist.

key points

- To deter police misconduct, the exclusionary rule requires that any evidence obtained by police using methods that violate a person's constitutional rights must be excluded from use in a criminal prosecution against that person.
- The exclusionary rule does not apply to evidence obtained illegally by a private citizen, unless the private citizen acts as an agent of the police. This may happen if police order the private citizen to conduct a search or seizure.
- The exclusionary rule does not apply to evidence used in certain civil trials, deportation hearings, grand jury proceedings, parole revocation hearings, *habeas corpus* proceedings, or to evidence used to impeach a defendant's testimony at trial. It also does not apply to violations of the knock-and-announce rule.
- Under the fruit of the poisonous tree doctrine, evidence is inadmissible in court if it was directly or indirectly obtained by exploitation of some prior unconstitutional police activity (such as an illegal arrest or search). Evidence directly or indirectly obtained in this manner is called tainted evidence.
- The fruit of the poisonous tree doctrine does not require suppression of the tainted evidence if (1) the evidence was also obtained through a source wholly independent of the primary constitutional violation; (2) the evidence inevitably would have been discovered by some other lawful means already in process; or (3) the means of obtaining the tainted evidence were sufficiently remote from and distinguishable from the primary illegality.
- Under the good-faith exception to the exclusionary rule, evidence obtained by police who acted in good faith in objectively reasonable reliance on a warrant or statute is admissible, even if the warrant or statute is subsequently determined to be invalid.
- To have standing to invoke the exclusionary rule challenging the admissibility of evidence, a defendant's own constitutional rights must have been allegedly violated in obtaining the evidence.

▶PRIVACY

In a criminal case, for the Fourth Amendment to be applicable to a particular fact situation, there must be a search or seizure accompanied by an attempt by the prosecution to introduce what was searched or seized as evidence in court. Whether there was a search or seizure within the meaning of the Fourth Amendment—and, if so, whether the search or seizure violated someone's constitutional rights—depends on the nature of the interest that the Fourth Amendment protects.

The Old Property Rights Approach

Under the common law, it was clear that the security of one's property was a sacred right and that protection of that right was a primary purpose of government. In an early English case, the court said:

> The great end for which men entered into society was to secure their property. That right is preserved sacred and incommunicable in all instances where it has not been taken away or abridged by some public law for the good of the whole. . . . By the laws of England, every invasion of private property, be it ever so minute, is a trespass. No man can set foot upon my ground without my license but he is liable to an action though the damage be nothing. . . . *Entick v. Carrington*, 19 Howell's State Trials 1029, 1035, 95 Eng. Rep. 807, 817-18 (1765).

The U.S. Supreme Court initially adopted this common law of protection of property interests as the basis for the interests protected by the Fourth Amendment. Until relatively recently, analysis of Fourth Amendment issues centered on whether a physical intrusion into a "constitutionally protected area" had occurred. Four cases involving electronic surveillance illustrate this approach.

In *Olmstead v. United States*, 277 U.S. 438 (1928), one reason for the Court's holding that wiretapping was not covered by the Fourth Amendment was that there had been no physical invasion of the defendant's premises—the wiretap had not been installed *on* the defendant's property. Because the wiretap did not physically intrude into the defendant's home, the Court rejected the Fourth Amendment as a basis for any alleged invasion of privacy. Similarly in *Goldman v. United States*, 316 U.S. 129 (1942), the Court found no search or seizure under the Fourth Amendment because police placed a listening device against a wall in an office that adjoined the defendant's office. Thus, yet again, the lack of a physical intrusion into the area in which a defendant expected privacy was key to the Court's reasoning.

In contrast to *Olmstead* and *Goldman*, in *Silverman v. United States*, 365 U.S. 505 (1961), a "spike mike" was pushed through a common wall until it hit a heating duct in defendant Silverman's home. The Court held that the electronic surveillance was an illegal search and seizure. And in *Clinton v. Virginia*, 377 U.S. 158 (1964), the Court ruled inadmissible evidence obtained by means of a mechanical listening device stuck into the wall of an apartment adjoining the defendant's. The rationale for the *Silverman* and *Clinton* cases was that the listening devices had actually physically invaded the target premises, even though the invasion was slight.

The emphasis on property concepts in interpreting the Fourth Amendment began to lose favor in the 1960s. Justice Douglas, concurring in the *Silverman* case, said that **"our sole concern should be with whether the privacy of the home was invaded."** 365 U.S. at 513. By 1967, the Supreme Court made it clear that physical invasion of property rights would no longer govern the law of search and seizure. In its place, the Court made the concept of privacy central to Fourth Amendment analysis.

The Reasonable Expectation of Privacy Approach

In *Katz v. United States*, 389 U.S. 347 (1967), FBI agents had attached an electronic listening and recording device to the *outside* of a public telephone booth to overhear telephone conversations. They used this device to record the defendant Katz obtaining gambling-related information and placing illegal bets These conversations were then transcribed and used against Katz at trial. In a major reversal of its prior physical invasion of property rights line of analysis, the *Katz* Court held that the FBI's actions violated the Forth Amendment. The Court said:

> [T]his effort to decide whether or not a given "area," viewed in the abstract, is "constitutionally protected" deflects attention from the problem presented by this case. For the Fourth Amendment protects people, not places. What a person knowingly exposes to the public, even in his own home or office, is not a subject of Fourth Amendment protection. . . . But what he seeks to preserve as private, even in an area accessible to the public, may be constitutionally protected. 389 U.S. at 351-52.

The Court held that the government's electronically listening to and recording the defendant's words violated the privacy on which the defendant justifiably relied when using the telephone booth. Thus, it constituted a search and seizure within the meaning of the Fourth Amendment. The Court added, "**The fact that the electronic device employed to achieve that end did not happen to penetrate the wall of the booth can have no constitutional significance.**" 389 U.S. at 353.

The *Katz* case signaled a major shift in the interpretation of the Fourth Amendment away from a property approach toward a ***privacy*** approach. Court decisions since the *Katz* case no longer focus on physical intrusions into constitutionally protected areas. Now the formula for analysis of Fourth Amendment problems is that "**wherever an individual may harbor a reasonable 'expectation of privacy,' . . . he is entitled to be free from unreasonable governmental intrusion.**" *Terry v. Ohio*, 392 U.S. 1, 9 (1968). One would think that such a sweeping change in the interpretation of the Fourth Amendment would result in large-scale reversals of earlier decisions. Yet, as Justice Harlan noted in his concurring opinion in the *Katz* case, the determination of what protection the Fourth Amendment affords to people requires reference to a "place." Therefore, many of the pre-*Katz* decisions are not necessarily changed or overruled by the *Katz* decision.

For example, the pre-*Katz* decision of *On Lee v. United States*, 343 U.S. 747 (1952), remains good law and has not been overruled by the Supreme Court even though it was decided under the old and now defunct property concept. The Court in *On Lee* found no invasion onto defendant's property—and hence no search for Fourth Amendment purposes—when defendant freely allowed an undercover agent, secretly bugged with a recording device, onto his property and began speaking with him. In this sense, *On Lee* is typical of pre-*Katz* cases finding no search when the defendant consents to the intrusion onto his or her property. Pre-*Katz* cases like *On Lee* should, however, be evaluated not only in terms of their property-focused reasoning but also in terms of the new privacy-focused standard announced in *Katz* (see, in this regard, the Discussion Point "Are Your Conversations with 'Friends' Private?").

In later chapters dealing with the Fourth Amendment, this book discusses both pre- and post-*Katz* cases to help the reader gain a broader understanding of the Fourth Amendment "search" issue, an area of the law that is continually developing. For example, Chapter 12 deals with whether intrusions onto

Discussion
⬆ POINT

Are Your Conversations with "Friends" Private?

In *On Lee v. United States*, mentioned above, undercover agent Chin Poy entered defendant On Lee's laundry business and began conversing with him. On Lee divulged incriminating information during the course of this conversation. On Lee did not know that Chin Poy was wired with a device transmitting sound to another officer stationed outside. Significantly, Chin Poy was an old acquaintance and former employee of *On Lee.* The Court went as far as saying that On Lee "trusted" Chin Poy. 343 U.S. at 753.

Under the old property doctrine, the Court found that no search occurred under the Fourth Amendment because Chin Poy entered the laundry with On Lee's consent and therefore there was no trespass.

Should this case be decided differently under the new legal test for whether there is a Fourth Amendment "search"? In particular, in light of the fact that Chin Poy was a trusted acquaintance and employee, did On Lee have any reasonable expectation of privacy in the conversation he had with Chin Poy? Interestingly, the Court in *On Lee* mentioned in this regard that the radio transmitter and receiver used by Chin Poy and the other agent "had the same effect on privacy as if agent Lee had been eavesdropping outside an open window."

Do you agree with this assessment by the Court of the privacy interests at stake here?

open fields by police officers are searches under the Fourth Amendment, and whether police examination of abandoned property constitutes a search or seizure. Chapter 11 also addresses the "search" question, and one's reasonable expectations of privacy in the context of vehicles, containers, electronic devices, and even drug-sniffing dogs.

In analyzing the Fourth Amendment "search" issue, most courts borrow from the approach to privacy suggested by Justice Harlan in his concurring opinion in the *Katz* case. He said that "there is a twofold requirement, first that a person has exhibited an actual (subjective) expectation of privacy and, second, that the expectation be one that society is prepared to recognize as [objectively] 'reasonable.'" 389 U.S. at 361. If these requirements are satisfied, any governmental intrusion on the expectation of privacy is a search for purposes of the Fourth Amendment. Reflecting Justice Harlan's approach, the U.S. Supreme Court defined the terms *search* and *seizure* as follows:

> A "search" occurs when an expectation of privacy that society is prepared to consider reasonable is infringed. A "seizure" of property occurs when there is some meaningful interference with an individual's possessory interests in that property. *United States v. Jacobsen*, 466 U.S. 109, 113 (1984).

Maryland v. Macon, 472 U.S. 463 (1985), illustrates the application of these definitions. A plainclothes county police detective entered an adult bookstore. After browsing for several minutes, he purchased two magazines from a salesclerk and paid for them with a marked fifty-dollar bill. He then left the store and showed the magazines to his fellow officers, who were waiting nearby. The officers concluded that the magazines were obscene, reentered the store, and arrested the salesclerk. In determining that there had been no Fourth Amendment search under these facts, the Court said:

> [R]espondent did not have any reasonable expectation of privacy in areas of the store where the public was invited to enter and to transact business. . . . The mere expectation that the possibly illegal nature of a product will not come to the attention of the authorities, whether because a customer will not complain or because undercover officers will not transact business with the store, is not one that society is prepared to recognize as reasonable. The officer's action in entering the bookstore and examining the wares that were intentionally exposed to all who frequent the place of business did not infringe a legitimate expectation of privacy and hence did not constitute a search within the meaning of the Fourth Amendment. 472 U.S. at 469.

In determining whether there had been a seizure, the Court said:

> [R]espondent voluntarily transferred any possessory interest he may have had in the magazines to the purchaser upon the receipt of the funds. . . . Thereafter, whatever possessory interest the seller had was in the funds, not the magazines. At the time of the sale the officer did not "interfere" with any interest of the seller; he took only that which was intended as a necessary part of the exchange. 472 U.S. at 469.

Therefore, no seizure occurred for the purposes of the Fourth Amendment. However, if government officials search an adult bookstore and seize material there by removing its packaging without paying for it, a search and seizure will be found. *Lo-Ji Sales, Inc. v. New York*, 442 US 319 (1979). Here, the officials are going beyond what a member of the public could see and do. 442 US at 329. One might say that the owner of the bookstore in *Lo-Ji Sales* did not knowingly expose his material to the public in the way the officers chose to access the material. Therefore, a search and seizure occurred.

Using this same rationale originally developed from *Katz* that what one knowingly exposes to the public is not protected by the Fourth Amendment, the Court has also held that physical characteristics such as one's facial profile, the sound of one's voice, or the characteristics of one's handwriting do not implicate the Fourth Amendment. See *United States v. Dionisio*, 410 U.S. 1 (1973). This is because these characteristics are frequently exposed to members of the public. 410 U.S. at 14. Therefore, no seizure occurs for Fourth Amendment purposes when the police obtain an example of a person's handwriting or a recording of one's voice, provided these items will be used for identification purposes only and have been requested by a grand jury (as in *Dionisio*).

In *Warden v. Hayden*, 387 U.S. 294, 304 (1967), the U.S. Supreme Court observed that the "principal" object of the [Fourth] Amendment is the protection of privacy rather than property and that **"this shift in emphasis from property to privacy has come about through a subtle interplay of substantive and procedural reform."** Nevertheless, the Court did not suggest that this shift in emphasis had eliminated the previously recognized protection for property under the Fourth Amendment. For example, *Soldal v. Cook County, Ill.*, 506 U.S. 56 (1992), held that the Fourth Amendment protects against unreasonable seizures of property, even though neither privacy nor liberty is necessarily implicated and even though no search within the meaning of the amendment has taken place. *Soldal* involved the forcible repossession of a mobile home by deputy sheriffs and the owner of a mobile home park. In holding that the repossession of the mobile home constituted a seizure under the Fourth Amendment, the Court said that its past cases **"unmistakably hold that the [Fourth] Amendment protects property as well as privacy."** 506 U.S. at 62.

In this book, the primary concern is with governmental actions that are sufficiently intrusive as to be considered searches and seizures, as well as the legality of those actions. Generally, to be legal, a search or seizure must be reasonable. This means that most searches and seizures must be conducted under the authority of a valid warrant or must fall within a recognized exception to the warrant requirement. Parts Two and Three of this book deal with the warrant requirement and its exceptions.

Privacy is one of the basic rights guaranteed to individuals in our society. It encompasses much more than the protections offered by the Fourth Amendment, even as interpreted under the *Katz* formula. This point is perhaps best stated in the *Katz* decision itself:

> [T]he Fourth Amendment cannot be translated into a general constitutional "right to privacy." That Amendment protects individual privacy against certain kinds of governmental intrusion, but its protections go further, and often have nothing to do with privacy at all. Other provisions of the Constitution protect personal privacy from other forms of governmental invasion. But the protection of a person's general right to privacy—his right to be let alone by other people—is, like the protection of his property and of his very life, left largely to the law of individual States. 389 U.S. at 350-51.

key points

- The principal object of the Fourth Amendment is the protection of privacy rather than property.
- Wherever an individual may harbor a reasonable expectation of privacy, he or she is entitled to be free from unreasonable governmental intrusion.
- In determining whether a person has a reasonable expectation of privacy, there is a twofold requirement: (1) that a person has exhibited an actual expectation of privacy; and (2) that the expectation is one that society is prepared to recognize as objectively reasonable.
- A search occurs when an expectation of privacy that society is prepared to consider reasonable is infringed. A seizure of property occurs when there is some meaningful interference with an individual's possessory interests in that property.

▶ PROBABLE CAUSE

The actual text of the Fourth Amendment introduces the concept of **probable cause**:

> The right of the people to be secure in their persons, houses, papers, and effects, against unreasonable searches and seizures, shall not be violated, and no Warrants shall issue, but upon probable cause, supported by Oath or affirma-

tion, and particularly describing the place to be searched, and the persons or things to be seized.

From this language, it is apparent that probable cause is necessary for the issuance of an arrest or search warrant. It is not so apparent that the other clause of the Fourth Amendment declaring the right of the people to be secure against "unreasonable searches and seizures" is also founded on probable cause. In general, that clause governs the various situations in which police are permitted to make warrantless arrests, searches, and seizures. These warrantless police actions are usually held to be unreasonable if not based on probable cause. As the U.S. Supreme Court explained, if the requirements for warrantless arrests, searches, and seizures were less stringent than those for warrants, **"a principal incentive now existing for the procurement of . . . warrants would be destroyed."** *Wong Sun v. United States,* 371 U.S. 471, 479-80 (1963).

Defining Probable Cause

Two different but similar definitions of probable cause are presented here—one for search and one for arrest—because different types of information are required to establish probable cause in each instance. In *Carroll v. United States,* 267 U.S. 132, 162 (1925), the Court said that probable cause to search exists when **"the facts and circumstances within their [the officers'] knowledge and of which they had reasonably trustworthy information [are] sufficient in themselves to warrant a man of reasonable caution in the belief that [seizable property would be found in a particular place or on a particular person]."** 267 U.S. at 162. Paraphrasing *Carroll, Brinegar v. United States,* 338 U.S. 160, 175-76 (1949), defined probable cause to arrest:

> Probable cause exists where the "facts and circumstances within [the officers'] knowledge and of which they had reasonably trustworthy information [are] sufficient in themselves to warrant a man of reasonable caution in the belief that" an offense has been or is being committed [by the person to be arrested].

These definitions differ only in that the facts and circumstances that would justify an arrest may be different from those that would justify a search. This chapter is primarily concerned with the part of the definition of probable cause that is common to both arrests and searches—namely, the nature, quality, and amount of information (e.g., "facts and circumstances") necessary to establish probable cause. The definition of probable cause in *Illinois v. Gates,* 462 U.S. 213, 235 (1983), is helpful in this regard:

> "[T]he term 'probable cause,' according to its usual acceptation, means less than evidence which would justify condemnation. . . ." Finely tuned standards such as proof beyond a reasonable doubt or by a preponderance of the evidence, useful in formal trials, have no place in the magistrate's decision. While an effort to fix some general, numerically precise degree of certainty corresponding to "probable cause" may not be helpful, it is clear that "only the probability, and not a prima facie showing, of criminal activity is the standard of probable cause."

The *Gates* opinion also said:

> **Perhaps the central teaching of our decisions bearing on the probable cause standard is that it is a "practical, non-technical conception."** . . . **"In dealing with probable cause, . . . as the very name implies, we deal with probabilities. These are not technical; they are the factual and practical considerations of everyday life on which reasonable and prudent men, not legal technicians, act."** 462 U.S. at 231 (1983); *see also United States v. Ventresca,* 380 U.S. 102 (1965).

Stated simply, probable cause to search is **"a fair probability that contraband or evidence of a crime will be found in a particular place."** *Illinois v. Gates,* 462 U.S. 213, 238 (1983). Probable cause to arrest is a fair probability that a particular person has committed or is committing a crime. The probable cause standard generally requires the same level of proof for all searches and arrests, though some regulatory searches appear to proceed on less than probable cause. (See Chapter 5 for a discussion of regulatory searches.)

Police officers and magistrates may at times interpret the legal standard of probable cause differently. This chapter is designed to clarify this standard by giving specific examples of information that law enforcement officers must have before they may arrest or search, with or without a warrant. Such an understanding is critical to the operation of the justice system. Effective criminal investigation and prosecution depend on the quality and quantity of the facts and circumstances gathered by law enforcement officers, as well as their ability to communicate this information clearly in reports, affidavits, and testimony.

Preference for Warrants

As later chapters will show, many arrests and searches are conducted without a warrant. The amount of evidence required to establish probable cause for a warrantless arrest or search is somewhat greater than that required if a warrant is sought. The reason for the more stringent requirement in the warrantless situation is that the Supreme Court has a strong preference for arrest warrants, *Beck v. Ohio,* 379 U.S. 89 (1964), and for search warrants, *United States v. Ventresca,* 380 U.S. 102 (1965). This preference is so strong that less persuasive evidence will justify the issuance of a warrant than would justify a warrantless search or arrest. In *Aguilar v. Texas,* the Supreme Court said that **"when a search is based upon a magistrate's, rather than a police officer's, determination of probable cause, the reviewing courts will accept evidence of a less 'judicially competent or persuasive character than would have justified an officer in acting on his own without a warrant,' . . . and will sustain the judicial determination so long as 'there was a substantial basis for [the magistrate] to conclude that [seizable evidence was] probably present. . . . '"** 378 U.S. 108, 111 (1964).

The warrant procedure is preferred because it places responsibility for deciding the delicate question of probable cause with a neutral and detached judicial officer, who usually has more formal legal training than a police officer has. Warrants enable law enforcement officers to search certain places and to seize certain persons or things when they can show a fair probability that those persons, places, or things are significantly connected with criminal activity. Warrants also protect the Fourth Amendment rights of citizens because the decision to allow a search and seizure is removed from the sometimes hurried and overzealous judgment of law enforcement officers engaged in the competitive enterprise of investigating crime.

Methods of Establishing Probable Cause

Collective Knowledge of Police Probable cause is evaluated by examining the collective information in the possession of the police at the time of the arrest or search, not merely the personal knowledge of the arresting or searching officer. Therefore, if the police knowledge is sufficient in its totality to establish probable cause, an individual officer's actions in making a warrantless arrest or search on orders to do so is justified—even though that officer does not personally have all the information on which probable cause is based. *United States v. Nafzger* explained:

> [L]aw enforcement officers in diverse jurisdictions must be allowed to rely on information relayed from officers and/or law enforcement agencies in different localities in order that they might coordinate their investigations, pool information, and apprehend fleeing suspects in today's mobile society. In an era when criminal suspects are increasingly mobile and increasingly likely to flee across jurisdictional boundaries, this rule is a matter of common sense: it minimizes the volume of information concerning suspects that must be transmitted to other jurisdictions and enables police in one jurisdiction to act promptly in reliance on information from another jurisdiction. *United States v. Nafzger*, 974 F.2d 906, 910-11 (7th Cir. 1992).

Like information from fellow officers, "information received from the NCIC (National Crime Information Center) computer bank has been routinely accepted in establishing probable cause for a valid arrest." *United States v. Hines*, 564 F.2d 925 (10th Cir. 1977). Of course, if the collective knowledge of the police is later determined insufficient to establish probable cause, the actual arrest would be constitutionally invalid due to the absence of probable cause. *Whiteley v. Warden*, 401 U.S. 560 (1971). However, even though such an arrest would be invalid because it was not supported by probable cause, so long as an officer making such an arrest acts in good faith on the basis of information from other officers, the arresting officer would be protected from civil and criminal liability. *Henry v. United States*, 361 U.S. 98 (1959). If, on the other hand, an officer who makes an arrest without a good faith basis for the arrest's legality may be liable in a civil lawsuit for violation of the Fourth Amendment rights of the arrestee. *Albright v. Oliver*, 510 U.S. 266 (1994).

Law enforcement officers applying for an arrest or search warrant are usually required to state *in writing* in the complaint or affidavit the underlying facts on which probable cause for the issuance of the warrant is based (see Chapters 4, 5, and 6). All warrantless arrests and most warrantless searches must also be based on probable cause. Although no written document is required, officers must be prepared to justify a warrantless arrest or search with underlying facts if its validity is later challenged. Therefore, whether or not a warrant is sought, officers must have sufficient information supporting probable cause *before* conducting a search, arrest, or other seizure. Information on which probable cause may be based may come to the attention of a law enforcement officer in two ways: (1) the officer may personally perceive or gather the information; or (2) other persons (such as victims, witnesses, reporters, informants, or other police agencies) may perceive or gather the information and provide it to the officer. These information sources are treated differently by the courts and are discussed separately here.

key points

- Probable cause exists where the facts and circumstances within a law enforcement officer's knowledge, and of which the officer has reasonably trustworthy information, are (1) sufficient in themselves to warrant a person of reasonable caution in the belief that a crime has been or is being committed by a particular person; or (2) that seizable property will be found in a particular place or on a particular person.
- The fair probability of criminal activity is the standard for probable cause. The civil standards of pre-ponderance of the evidence or clear and convincing evidence, and the criminal standard of beyond a reasonable doubt, do not apply.
- Probable cause is evaluated by examining the collective information in the possession of the police at the time of the arrest or search, not merely the personal knowledge of the arresting or searching officer.

Information Obtained Through the Officer's Own Senses One type of information used to support probable cause is information from the officer's own senses: sight, hearing, smell, touch, and taste. Furthermore, an officer's experience or expertise in a particular area gives his or her perceptions additional credence:

> [I]n some situations a police officer may have particular training or experience that would enable him to infer criminal activity in circumstances where an ordinary observer would not. . . . In such situations, when an officer's experience and expertise is relevant to the probable cause determination, the officer must be able to explain sufficiently the basis of that opinion so that it "can be understood by the average reasonably prudent person." *State v. Demeter*, 590 A.2d 1179, 1183-84 (N.J. 1991).

A law enforcement officer's perceptions that a crime is being committed in his or her presence clearly provide probable cause to arrest the person committing the crime. Crimes are seldom committed in an officer's presence, however. Usually, an officer must develop probable cause over time from perceptions of a variety of facts and circumstances. The following discussion focuses on specific facts and circumstances that indicate criminal activity, together with court cases explaining their relative importance in the probable cause equation. It is important to remember that in all cases, the facts and circumstances establishing probable cause to arrest must come to the attention of the officer before the actual arrest and a search incident to that arrest.

Flight "[D]eliberately furtive actions and flight at the approach of strangers or law officers are strong indicia of mens rea [guilty mind], and when coupled with specific knowledge on the part of the officer relating the suspect to the evidence of crime, they are proper factors to be considered in the decision to make an arrest." *Sibron v. New York*, 392 U.S. 40, 66-67 (1968). Accordingly, flight should be thought of as a factor in the overall probable cause determination, but not as an action that automatically justifies arrest. *United States v. Bell*, 892 F.2d 959 (10th Cir. 1989), which first held that the following facts gave a narcotics officer reasonable suspicion to detain a suspect for investigation of transporting illegal drugs, illustrates this principle: The suspect disembarked from a flight originating in Hawaii and repeatedly went to a group of phones but did not appear to be talking; he had no luggage except his shoulder bag and appeared visibly nervous; he met another person, who was carrying a package, and walked with him around the airport. After citing the additional fact that when the officer detained and questioned the suspect, he dropped his bag and ran down the concourse, the court then held that this flight *plus* the other indications of criminal activity provided probable cause to arrest.

By itself, however, flight does not support a finding of probable cause. In *Wong Sun v. United States*, 371 U.S. 471 (1963), federal officers arrested a man named Hom Way at two o'clock in the morning and found narcotics in his possession. Hom Way told the officers that he had purchased an ounce of heroin from a person named Blackie Toy. At six o'clock that same morning, the officers went to a laundry operated by James Wah Toy. When Toy answered the door and an officer identified himself, Toy slammed the door and ran to his living quarters at the rear of the building. The officers broke in and followed Toy to his bedroom, where they arrested him. The U.S. Supreme Court held that the officers did not have probable cause to arrest Toy. First, the officers had no basis for confidence in the reliability of Hom Way's information. (The reliability of informants is discussed later.) Second, the Court explained that the mere fact of Toy's flight did not provide a probable cause justification for a warrantless arrest, at least without any further information. The Court said:

> **Toy's refusal to admit the officers and his flight down the hallway thus signified a guilty knowledge no more clearly than it did a natural desire to repel an apparently unauthorized intrusion. . . . A contrary holding here would mean that a vague suspicion could be transformed into probable cause for arrest by reason of ambiguous conduct [e.g., flight] which the arresting officers themselves have provoked.** 371 U.S. at 483-84.

However, when flight is combined with other factors, such as furtive conduct (discussed more fully below), lower courts are more willing to find the probable cause standard met as illustrated by the following quotation from *United States v. Hayes*, 236 F.3d 891, 894 (7th Cir. 2001).

> At the time that Hayes was arrested, the officers had been presented with facts sufficient to indicate that Hayes was committing the offense of carrying a concealed weapon. At that time, the officers had already heard from Webb who told them that he observed Hayes with the gun, and that Hayes attempted to place the gun in the couch cushions but then ran off with it. That eyewitness account was consistent with the officer's own observation of Hayes attempting to place something in the couch. Moreover, the officers had recovered a magazine for a nine-millimeter firearm that another witness identified as having been dropped by Hayes. In conjunction with Hayes' flight upon seeing the officers approaching him, the facts certainly warranted a person of reasonable caution to believe that Hayes had committed the offense of carrying a concealed weapon. [The] evidence established probable cause for the arrest.

Furtive Conduct Law enforcement officers frequently observe persons acting secretively or furtively. Such conduct usually at least justifies an officer's further investigation to determine whether a crime is being or is about to be committed. (See Chapter 7 on stops and frisks.) By itself, however, furtive conduct is insufficient to establish probable cause to arrest.

The person may be making a totally innocent gesture, exhibiting a physical or mental problem, or reacting in fear to an officer's presence. A person's nervousness in the presence of a law enforcement officer does not alone amount to probable cause. As the Supreme Court of Colorado stated, "It is normal for law-abiding persons, as well as persons guilty of criminal activity, to be nervous when stopped by a policeman for a traffic offense." *People v. Goessl*, 526 P.2d 664, 665 (Colo. 1974). A person should not be subject to arrest or search on the basis of a mistaken interpretation of an innocent action.

United States v. McCarty, 862 F.2d 143 (7th Cir. 1988), highlights well the idea that furtive conduct should be accompanied by other facts and circumstances before probable cause will be found to exist. Officers in *McCarty* had corroborated information from informants that the defendant was a convicted felon, that he was driving a tan compact car with Michigan license plates bearing the number 278, and that he was likely to be carrying a gun. Officers on routine patrol saw the described car and followed it. The car attempted to evade the officers, and, when stopped, the driver was observed leaning to the right as if to hide something under the passenger seat. The officers arrested the defendant and seized a handgun found in his car. The court found probable cause to arrest the defendant for possession of a firearm by a convicted felon. "The fact that McCarty tried to evade [the officers] while they were following him, and his furtive gesture when he was stopped, reinforced the reasonableness of the officers' belief that McCarty had committed or was committing a crime." 862 F.2d at 147. Furtive conduct, therefore, is relevant to probable cause but must be evaluated in light of all the facts and circumstances, including time of day, setting, weather conditions, persons present, and nature of the crime.

United States v. Burhoe, 409 F.3d 5, 10 (1st Cir. 2005), found probable cause to arrest a suspect named Burhoe based on a combination of facts observed by the officer, one of which was furtive conduct (number 6 in the list created by the court):

> There was ample evidence of probable cause for [the suspect's arrest]. When Detective Fahey saw Burhoe on St. James Road, he knew: (1) a bank robbery had just taken place minutes earlier by two white males; (2) the suspects' getaway car had been abandoned on Fourth Street, the next street north of St. James Road; (3) the suspects were escaping on foot in the immediate vicinity; (4) Burhoe, a white male, emerged from a private yard, consistent with the route of a fugitive escaping from the abandoned car on Fourth Street one block to the north; (5) Burhoe did not look like he belonged there—at 10:30 on a workday morning, Burhoe was disheveled, dirty, and possibly intoxicated, not the usual sight in a residential neighborhood; (6) Burhoe behaved strangely: his furtive, "hide-and-seek" movements, quick dash across the road, and his attempt to remain hidden; (7) Fahey noticed an abnormal bulge in Burhoe's waist; and (8) to boot, Burhoe attempted to run away from Fahey. A "reasonably prudent person" would believe [Burhoe] had committed or was committing a crime."

People v. Howell, 231 N.W.2d 650 (1975), is another example of a case ruling that furtive conduct, when combined with other facts, may be enough to justify a probable cause determination. In *Howell*, a police officer stopped a car for a traffic violation and observed a bag full of jewelry in the front seat passenger compartment. As he was heading back to his patrol car, the officer observed this same bag being passed from the front seat compartment area to the back seat. When the officer returned and asked about the bag, the response was, "What bag?" The officer then searched the car, and found and seized the bag. The court said:

> On these facts, this Court is of the opinion that the officers had probable cause [to search the car and seize the bag]. The following facts were in evidence:

(1) the bag was bulging and the jewelry was in plain view. An officer saw a variety and quantity of jewelry more akin to the results of a theft than to property likely to be the personal belongings of an occupant of the automobile; (2) the bag was not the kind a jewelry salesman would normally use; (3) the furtive behavior observed by the police officers; (4) the response, "What bag?" While furtive behavior by itself does not justify a search, furtive behavior may be considered a factor, and, as in this case, in combination with other factors, may help establish probable cause.

Real or Physical Evidence Officers may establish probable cause by the observation and evaluation of real or physical evidence. In *State v. Heald*, 314 A.2d 820 (Me. 1973), officers were summoned at 2:00 A.M. to a store that had recently been burglarized. The officers discovered two sets of footprints in fresh-fallen snow, leading from the store to the tire tracks of an automobile. Since the tire tracks were identifiable by a distinctive tread, the officers followed them. After a short distance, the officers met another officer. He had found a checkbook belonging to the storeowner in the road. Farther down the road the officers found a bag containing electrical parts. Then the officers came upon a car parked in the middle of the road with its lights off—the only other vehicle the officers had seen since leaving the scene of the crime. As the patrol car approached the parked car, its lights came on and the car was driven away. The officers stopped the car and arrested its two occupants for breaking and entering. The court held that the items of real evidence found and the reasonable inferences drawn from the evidence, together with the highly suspicious circumstances, provided probable cause to arrest the defendants. The court added that "although the possibility of mistake existed, as it invariably does in a probable cause situation, they would have been remiss in their duty if they had not arrested the defendants promptly." 314 A.2d at 825.

In *United States v. Harrell*, 268 F.3d 141 (2d Cir. 2001), the observation by the officer of tinted car windows in violation of a local traffic law, provided the probable cause to stop the vehicle:

> But we must assess whether there was "probable cause" to believe that a traffic violation occurred "from the standpoint of an *objectively* reasonable police officer" based on "historical facts." It is undisputed that Officer Briganti observed that the car's windows were tinted as he drove by it. It is also evident from the record that his testimony in this regard was not based on a casual glance. Rather, he and Officer Hill purposefully looked into the car as they passed it to determine how many people were in the car and whether any of them had guns. Thus, despite Officer Briganti's testimony that he did not "observe" a violation, the historical facts of this case persuade us that an "objectively reasonable" police officer would have suspected the windows were tinted in violation of § 375(12-a)(b) of the Vehicle & Traffic Law. Accordingly, we conclude that probable cause existed to stop the car.

Admissions A person's **admission** of criminal conduct to a law enforcement officer provides probable cause to arrest. In *Rawlings v. Kentucky*, 448 U.S. 98 (1980), a law enforcement officer with a search warrant ordered the defendant's female companion (Cox) to empty the contents of her purse. When she poured out a large quantity and variety of controlled substances, she told the defendant to take what was his. The defendant immediately claimed ownership of some of the controlled substances. The Court held that "[o]nce petitioner admitted ownership of the sizable quantity of drugs found in Cox's purse, the police clearly had probable cause to place the petitioner under arrest." 448 U.S. at 111.

Some "admissions," however, may not give rise to probable cause to arrest. For example, in *Kent v. Katz*, 312 F.3d 568 (2d Cir. 2002), the court found that redness of the eyes and the arrestee's statement "not too much" in response to an officer's question regarding whether the arrestee had been drinking, did not provide probable cause to arrest for driving while intoxicated:

> [T]he existence of probable cause is to be determined on the basis of the totality of the circumstances, and we cannot conclude that it would have been objectively reasonable as a matter of law for [the officer] to infer intoxication solely from the redness of [the arrestee's] eyes, while ignoring as a possible cause of discoloration the fact that [the arrestee] had been burning brush for the past 18 days, and from [the arrestee's] statement that he had not been drinking very much, while ignoring all other comportment that might reflect on the state of [the arrestee's] sobriety. 312 F.3d at 576.

The court explained that the officer's interpretation of the arrestee's "admission" of intoxication was misguided:

> And while [the officer] contends that [the arrestee's] "[n]ot very much" statement, regardless of the intention that lay behind those words, constituted an admission of alcohol consumption, even taken at face value the words "[n]ot very much" would not ordinarily seem to imply "enough to be intoxicated." 312 F.3d at 576.

False or Implausible Answers False or implausible answers to routine questions may be considered in determining probable cause; but, standing alone, they do not provide probable cause. For example, *United States v. Velasquez*, 885 F.2d 1076 (3d Cir. 1989), held that the following facts provided probable cause to arrest the defendant for interstate smuggling of contraband: (1) the defendant and her companion were on a long-distance trip from Miami, a major drug importation point, to the New York area; (2) they had given a law enforcement officer conflicting stories about the purpose of their trip and their relationship; (3) they appeared nervous when answering the officer's questions; (4) the defendant told the officer that the automobile she was driving belonged to her "cousin," but could not give her cousin's name; and (5) the automobile had a false floor in its trunk and appeared specially modified to carry contraband in a secret compartment. Facts two and four above appear to contain a falsity or implausibility. It is important to note, however, that the Court only found probable cause to arrest in light of other existing, "suspicious" facts, including ones related to physical evidence.

Similarly, *United States v. Anderson*, 676 F. Supp. 604 (E.D. Pa. 1987), held that police had probable cause to seize money found in a legally stopped car, based partially on the defendant's implausible statements. The court explained:

> The officers knew that defendants were driving towards New York on a known drug route in a car owned by someone else, a procedure used by drug dealers to avoid forfeiture. The officers had found a large sum of money in small denominations, wrapped with rubber bands in small bundles. These bundles were in three bags. At the time of the stop, defendant Anderson stated that they won the money in Atlantic City and were on their way to Chester, however,

the location where they were stopped and the way the money was packaged were not consistent with this story. Finally, a Chester police officer relayed that defendants were known drug pushers. Based on these facts, the police had probable cause to believe defendants were engaged in drug activity and that the money was drug-related. The money, therefore, was properly confiscated. 676 F. Supp. at 608.

Presence at a Crime Scene or in a High-Crime Area Mere presence at a crime scene or in a high-crime area does not by itself constitute probable cause to arrest. For instance, in *Johnson v. United States*, 333 US 10 (1948), the Court found an absence of probable cause to arrest when police placed a woman under arrest for suspicion of drug activity while she was inside of a hotel room. They then searched the hotel room. The officers' suspicions regarding the room stemmed from a tip they had received that unknown persons were smoking in a hotel as well as the smell of drugs emanating from the room. The Court acknowledged that the room was essentially a crime scene (drugs and drug paraphernalia were found there during a subsequent search). But the officers, *before* entering without a warrant, lacked evidence that established probable cause to *arrest* a *specific* individual for drug use within the room (e.g., perhaps not everyone or perhaps no one was engaging in drug use within the room). The Court did acknowledge that had the police sought a *search* warrant before entering the room, probable cause may have existed to issue such a warrant. Of course, had the police had a search warrant for the room and then discovered drugs upon entering the room, probable cause may have also existed to arrest the sole female occupant.

On more specific and numerous facts linking particular individuals to a crime, another case found probable cause to arrest the defendant at an automobile crime scene. *Maryland v. Pringle*, 540 U.S. 366 (2003), held that an officer who found drugs in the backseat of a car had probable cause to arrest the driver and the front and backseat passengers. The officer had stopped the car for speeding and, when the driver opened the glove compartment to obtain his registration, the officer observed "a large amount of rolled-up money." After obtaining consent to search the car, the officer found five baggies containing cocaine placed between the back armrest and the backseat of the car. Although the Court did not announce a bright-line rule that the discovery of drugs or contraband in the passenger compartment of a vehicle provides probable cause to arrest all the occupants, the Court found probable cause to arrest the defendant in the totality of the circumstances of this case:

▶ The defendant was one of three men riding in a car at 3:16 A.M.

▶ The glove compartment in front of the defendant contained $763 of rolled-up cash.

▶ Five baggies of cocaine were found behind the backseat armrest.

▶ The cocaine was accessible to all three occupants.

▶ All three occupants denied any knowledge about the money and cocaine.

▶ The amount of drugs and money found indicated that one or more of the occupants was selling drugs.

▶ It was reasonable for the officer to believe that all the occupants knew about the cocaine because drug dealing is "an enterprise to which a

> **dealer would be unlikely to admit an innocent person with the poten-
> tial to furnish evidence against him." 540 U.S. at 373.**

Because these circumstances made it reasonable for the officer to believe "that
any or all three of the occupants had knowledge of, and exercised dominion
and control over, the cocaine," the arrest of the defendant was lawful.

Even when no crime has been reported, suspicious activity in a high crime
area may contribute to probable cause. Simply being present in a high crime
area, however, is not enough for probable cause. *United States v. Green*, 670
F.2d 1148 (D.C. Cir. 1981), identified four factors to be evaluated in determining
whether the "totality of the circumstances" provides probable cause to arrest
for drug trafficking: (1) the suspect's presence in a neighborhood notorious for
drug trafficking or other crimes; (2) the suspect's engaging with others in a sequence of events typical of a drug transaction; (3) a suspect's flight after being
confronted by police; and (4) a suspect's attempt to conceal the subject of his
business.

Association with Other Known Criminals A suspect's association with other known
criminals does not by itself provide probable cause to arrest, but may be considered in the probable cause equation. *United States v. Di Re*, 332 U.S. 581 (1948),
held that a defendant's presence in a car with others who illegally possessed
counterfeit ration coupons did not provide probable cause to arrest, because no
other information linked him to the crime.

> **The argument that one who "accompanies a criminal to a crime rendez-
> vous" cannot be assumed to be a bystander, forceful enough in some
> circumstances, is farfetched when the meeting is not secretive or in a
> suspicious hide-out but in broad daylight, in plain sight of passersby, in
> a public street of a large city, and where the alleged substantive crime
> is one which does not necessarily involve any act visibly criminal. If Di
> Re had witnessed the passing of papers from hand to hand, it would not
> follow that he knew they were ration coupons, and if he saw that they
> were ration coupons, it would not follow that he would know them to be
> counterfeit. . . . Presumptions of guilt are not lightly to be indulged from
> mere meetings.** 332 U.S. at 593.

In contrast to *Di Re,* the Court in *Ker v. California,* 374 U.S. 23 (1963), found
probable cause to arrest the wife of a drug suspect based on her presence in an
apartment she shared with her husband that police knew was being used as the
base for his narcotics operation. Besides this particular knowledge, police also
found the wife in a room of the apartment where drugs were located, yet another distinction from the earlier, *Di Re* case (where the suspect was found near
less obvious illegal evidence). The Court explained:

> **Probable cause for the arrest of petitioner Diane Ker, while not present
> at the time the officers entered the apartment to arrest her husband, was
> nevertheless present at the time of her arrest. Upon their entry and an-
> nouncement of their identity, the officers were met not only by George
> Ker but also by Diane Ker, who was emerging from the kitchen. Officer
> Berman immediately walked to the doorway from which she emerged
> and, without entering, observed the brickshaped package of marijuana
> in plain view. Even assuming that her presence in a small room with the
> contraband in a prominent position on the kitchen sink would not alone**

> establish a reasonable ground for the officers' belief that she was in joint possession with her husband, that fact was accompanied by the officers' information that Ker had been using his apartment as a base of operations for his narcotics activities. Therefore, we cannot say that at the time of her arrest there were not sufficient grounds for a reasonable belief that Diane Ker, as well as her husband, was committing the offense of possession of marijuana in the presence of the officers. 374 U.S. at 36-37.

In *United States v. Lima*, 819 F.2d 687 (7th Cir. 1987), the Court also found probable cause to arrest a suspect clearly associated with other criminal actors. Here, the suspect arrived at the scene of a drug transaction shortly after the other participants, parked directly behind another participant's car, and conversed with another participant who walked over to the suspect's car while the transaction was taking place. The court added that "any innocent interpretation is further undermined by the fact that neither [of the other principals] called off or postponed the delivery of the drugs despite [the defendant's] presence." 819 F.2d at 690.

Officers may use their experience, training, and knowledge in determining probable cause to connect a defendant with criminal activity. *See Texas v. Brown*, 460 U.S. 730 (1983); *see also Terry v. Ohio*, 392 U.S. 1 (1968) (officers may rely on their experience to determine suspicious behavior). It should be pointed out, however, that officers must be ready and able to explain to others how their experience, training, and knowledge led them to develop probable cause. *United States v. Munoz*, 738 F. Supp. 800 (S.D.N.Y. 1990), held that an FBI agents' observations, knowledge, and assumptions that a kidnapper would take several people along for security when he went to pick up ransom money were enough to establish probable cause to arrest an accomplice who was "observed doing nothing but sitting as a passenger in the Jeep." 738 F. Supp. at 802. But *Ybarra v. Illinois*, 444 U.S. 85 (1979), a Supreme Court case, held that the search of a patron in a bar violated the Fourth Amendment because the patron was not named in the warrant and the searching officer, though possessing a warrant to search the bar premises and bartender, did not have probable cause connecting the patron to the criminal activity under investigation.

Past Criminal Conduct A suspect's criminal record does not by itself give an officer probable cause to arrest the suspect:

> We do not hold that the officer's knowledge of the petitioner's physical appearance and previous record was either inadmissible or entirely irrelevant upon the issue of probable cause. . . . But to hold that knowledge of either or both of these facts constituted probable cause would be to hold that anyone with a previous criminal record could be arrested at will. *Beck v. Ohio*, 379 U.S. 89, 97 (1964).

A suspect's prior criminal activity may, however, be considered with other indications of criminal activity in establishing probable cause. In *United States v. Harris*, 403 U.S. 573 (1971), an affidavit for a search warrant stated that the defendant had a reputation for four years as a trafficker in illegal whiskey, that during this period a large cache of illegal whiskey had been found in an abandoned house under the defendant's control, and that an informant said that he had purchased illicit whiskey within the house for two years and within the past two weeks. The Court found that this information provided probable cause for issuance of the search warrant.

Discussion

POINT

Can Matching a Criminal Profile Establish Probable Cause?

If a suspect's actions, demeanor, and/or appearance match the components of a predetermined criminal profile, can this fact alone give rise to probable cause to arrest? The Supreme Court has generally answered "no" to this question, as illustrated by *Florida v. Royer*, 460 U.S. 491 (1983). In that case, the police detained an individual at an airport because he fit the following components of the drug profile: (1) he carried a certain brand of luggage which appeared heavy in weight; (2) he was young and dressed casually; (3) he appeared nervous; (4) he bought his ticket with cash; (5) he failed to identify himself fully on his luggage tags; (6) he traveled from a drug import city (Miami); and (7) he possessed a different name from the one appearing on his airline ticket (i.e., it appeared that he used an alias while traveling). On these facts, the Supreme Court determined there was no probable cause to arrest the suspect, but that there was reasonable suspicion to briefly detain and question him. 460 U.S. at 506. (See Chapter 8 for a detailed description of two other cases—*Reid v. Georgia* and *United States v. Sokolow*—where the Court analyzed whether reasonable suspicion existed in "drug profile" cases).

In your mind, what is the concern with police using profiles to establish probable cause for an arrest? Should profiles be allowed as a legitimate law enforcement technique? What if the police were required to create and make known the profile before being allowed to detain individuals based on it? Does this change your thinking in any way?

key points

- Information perceived by a law enforcement officer through any of the five senses may support probable cause.
- An officer's perceptions may be given additional credence because of the officer's personal experience or expertise in a particular area. Officers should be prepared to explain how this experience or expertise, along with other factors, led them to develop probable cause.

- The following facts and circumstances may be considered in determining probable cause: flight; furtive conduct; physical evidence connecting a person with criminal activity; admission of criminal conduct; false or implausible answers to routine questions; presence at a crime scene or in a high-crime area; association with other known criminals; and past criminal conduct.

Information Obtained by the Officer through Informants Few crimes are committed in the presence of law enforcement officers. Therefore, officers must usually rely on information from sources other than their own perceptions to establish probable cause to arrest or search. This information may come from ordinary citizen informants or criminal informants who have themselves personally perceived indications of criminal activity. (The term **informant** means any person from whom a law enforcement officer obtains information on criminal activity.) The method of establishing probable cause through the use of an informant's information is sometimes referred to as the *hearsay method,* as opposed to the direct observation method discussed earlier. The problem with using information from informants is ensuring that the information is trustworthy and credible enough to be acted on. Courts have developed elaborate rules and procedures to ensure the trustworthiness of information from informants used to support probable cause.

The Dual-Prong Approach of *Aguilar–Spinelli* In *Illinois v. Gates,* 462 U.S. 213 (1983), the U.S. Supreme Court abandoned a particular approach to determining probable cause through the use of informants established by two previous decisions, *Aguilar v. Texas,* 378 U.S. 108 (1964), and *Spinelli v. United States,* 393 U.S. 410 (1969). *Aguilar* and *Spinelli* had established a two-pronged test for law enforcement officers to follow in determining probable cause using information from informants. The *Gates* decision abandoned rigid adherence to this test in favor of a "totality of the circumstances" approach to determining probable cause.

Despite *Gates,* there are good reasons for discussing *Aguilar* and *Spinelli* in detail. First, the underlying rationales of these decisions retain their vitality in analyzing the totality of the circumstances under *Gates.* Second, several states have rejected *Gates* on the basis of state constitutions or statutes. They still require affidavits based on informant testimony to be prepared according to the *Aguilar* and *Spinelli* requirements. For example, *People v. Griminger,* 524 N.E.2d 409 (N.Y. 1988), held that, as a matter of New York law, the *Aguilar–Spinelli* two-pronged test should be employed in determining the sufficiency of an affidavit submitted in support of a search warrant application. The court specifically found that the *Gates* test did not offer a suitable alternative to the *Aguilar–Spinelli* approach of determining credibility and reliability in the informant context.

Our discussion of the hearsay method of determining probable cause, therefore, begins with a detailed analysis of the *Aguilar–Spinelli* line of cases. We will then evaluate the effect of the *Gates* totality-of-the-circumstances approach to the hearsay method of determining probable cause. The discussion focuses on a law enforcement officer applying for a search warrant based on information from informants. This approach helps to emphasize that an officer should *write down* in the affidavit or complaint all the information on which probable cause is based. The same probable cause considerations are involved in arrest warrants and warrantless arrests and searches, except that the information is not written down in the warrantless situation. Officers should, however, keep careful written records of the circumstances surrounding warrantless arrests and searches.

Before *Gates, Aguilar v. Texas,* 378 U.S. 108 (1964), was the leading case on establishing probable cause either partially or entirely from informant testimony. *Aguilar* set out a *two-pronged test,* both of which prongs had to be satisfied to establish probable cause:

1. The affidavit must describe underlying circumstances from which a neutral and detached magistrate may determine that the informant had a *sufficient basis* for his or her knowledge and that the information was not the result of mere rumor or suspicion.

2. The affidavit must describe underlying circumstances from which the magistrate may determine that the informant was *credible* or that the informant's information was *reliable*.

PRONG 1: INFORMANT'S BASIS OF KNOWLEDGE

A law enforcement officer must demonstrate underlying circumstances to enable a magistrate to independently evaluate the accuracy of an informant's conclusion. The affidavit must show how the informant knows his or her information (e.g., the basis of the informant's information) by demonstrating that:

▶ the informant personally perceived the information given to the officer; or

▶ the informant's information came from another source, but there is good reason to believe it.

Informant's Information Is Firsthand: If the informant obtained the information by personal perception, the officer merely has to state in the affidavit *how, when,* and *where* the informant obtained the information furnished to the officer. In *State v. Daniels*, 200 N.W.2d 403 (Minn. 1972), the affidavit stated:

> For approximately the past two months I have received information from an informant whose information has recently resulted in narcotic arrests and convictions that a Gregory Daniels who resides at 929 Logan N (down) has been selling marijuana, hashish and heroin. My informant further states that he has seen Daniels sell drugs, namely: heroin and further that he has seen Daniels with heroin on his person. The informant has seen heroin on the premises of 929 Logan N (down) within the past 48 hours. 200 N.W.2d at 404.

The court said, "There seems to be no dispute that such personal observation satisfies that part of the *Aguilar* test which requires that the affidavit contain facts to enable the magistrate to judge whether the informant obtained his knowledge in a reliable manner." 200 N.W.2d at 406. Similarly, in *Jones v. United States*, 362 U.S. 257, 271 (1960), the U.S. Supreme Court found a sufficient basis of knowledge when the informant explained that he personally purchased drugs from the suspects at their apartment.

Stating the *time* when the informant obtained the information is very important, especially in applications for search warrants, because probable cause to search can become stale with time. In *United States v. Huggins*, 733 F. Supp. 445 (D.D.C. 1990), the court said, "[T]here is nothing in the affidavit from which the date of the controlled purchase can be determined and accordingly there was no way for the judicial officer to determine whether the information was stale. The controlled purchase could have occurred 'a day, a week, or months before the affidavit.'" 733 F. Supp. at 447.

Informant's Information Is Secondhand (Hearsay): If the informant's information comes from a third person, the third person and his or her information must also satisfy both prongs of the *Aguilar* test. The affidavit must show how the third person knows the information furnished to the informant. For example, if the third person saw criminal activity taking place at a particular time, a statement to that effect would be sufficient to satisfy *Aguilar*'s first prong. The officer must, however, also satisfy *Aguilar*'s second prong with respect to both the informant *and* the third person. (*Aguilar*'s second prong, dealing with whether the informant is trustworthy or credible, will be discussed later in this chapter.)

Detailing Informant's Information: Courts recognize another method of satisfying *Aguilar's* first prong besides stating how, when, and where the informant obtained his or her information. In *Spinelli v. United States*, 393 U.S. 410 (1969), the Court said:

> **In the absence of a statement detailing the manner in which the information was gathered, it is especially important that the tip describe the accused's criminal activity in sufficient detail that the magistrate may know that he is relying on something more substantial than a casual rumor circulating in the underworld or an accusation based merely on an individual's general reputation.** 393 U.S. at 416.

In *Spinelli* itself, the Court concluded that sufficient detail was not provided by the informant to satisfy *Aguilar's* first prong because the informant only mentioned that defendant was using two particular telephones for his illegal gambling operations. *Spinelli* cited *Draper v. United States*, 358 U.S. 307 (1959), as an example of sufficient use of detail to satisfy *Aguilar's* first prong. Although the informant in *Draper* did not state the manner in which he obtained his information, he did report that the defendant had gone to Chicago the day before by train and that he would return to Denver by train with three ounces of heroin on one of two specified mornings. The informant went on to describe, with minute particularity, the clothes the defendant would be wearing and the bag he would be carrying on his arrival in Denver. The Supreme Court said that **"[a] magistrate, when confronted with such detail, could reasonably infer that the informant had gained his information in a reliable way."** 393 U.S. at 417.

In summary, if a law enforcement officer does not know how, when, or where an informant obtained information, the officer can still satisfy *Aguilar's* first prong by obtaining as much detail as possible from the informant and stating all of it in the affidavit.

PRONG 2: INFORMANT'S VERACITY/TRUTHFULNESS

Aguilar's second prong requires the officer to demonstrate in the affidavit underlying circumstances to convince the magistrate of the informant's veracity—that is, that the informant is trustworthy or credible. The vast majority of cases have dealt with the credibility aspect of the informant's veracity rather than with the reliability of the informant's actual information. The amount and type of information required to establish credibility depends on whether the informant is an ordinary citizen informant or a criminal informant.

Ordinary Citizen Informants: Ordinary citizen informants, such as victims and eyewitnesses, are usually presumed credible and no further evidence of credibility need be stated in the affidavit beyond their name and address and their status as a victim of, or witness to, a crime.

> [A]n ordinary citizen who reports a crime which has been committed in his presence, or that a crime is being or will be committed, stands on much different ground than a police informer. He is a witness to criminal activity who acts with an intent to aid the police in law enforcement because of his concern for society or for his own safety. He does not expect any gain or concession for his

information. An informer of this type usually would not have more than one opportunity to supply information to the police, thereby precluding proof of his reliability by pointing to previous accurate information which he has supplied. *State v. Paszek*, 184 N.W.2d 836, 843 (Wis. 1971).

Another reason for accepting the credibility of an ordinary citizen is the average person's fear of potential criminal or civil action for deliberately or negligently providing false information. *People v. Hicks*, 341 N.E.2d 227 (N.Y. 1975). Indeed, the U.S. Supreme Court, in *Chambers v. Maroney*, 399 U.S. 42 (1970), did not require a special credibility showing for ordinary teenage citizens who were eyewitnesses to a robbery.

Nevertheless, some courts require additional information to establish the credibility of an ordinary citizen informant if the citizen merely provides an anonymous tip. For example, in *State v. White*, 396 S.E.2d 601, 603 (Ga. App. 1990), the court said:

> This court has always given the concerned citizen informer a preferred status insofar as testing the credibility of his information. . . . However, before an anonymous tipster can be elevated to the status of "concerned citizen," thereby gaining entitlement to the preferred status regarding credibility concomitant with that title, there must be placed before the magistrate facts from which it can be concluded that the anonymous tipster is, in fact, a "concerned citizen." . . . The affidavit in the case at bar contained no information from which it could be gleaned that the tipster was, in fact, a "concerned citizen." The magistrate was given nothing other than the affiant's conclusory statement that the tipster was a concerned citizen. That will not suffice.

Brown v. Commonwealth, 187 S.E.2d 160 (Va. 1972), found an ordinary citizen informant credible when the affidavit stated that, although the informant had not previously furnished information to the police concerning violations of the narcotics laws, he was steadily employed, was a registered voter, enjoyed a good reputation in his neighborhood, and had expressed concern for young people involved with narcotics.

In general, the cases discussed in this area show that regardless of whether the ordinary citizen informant is an anonymous or known informant, the more information provided in the affidavit about an ordinary citizen informant, the more likely this type of informant will be found to be credible. If, however, the informant appears in person before the magistrate and testifies under oath, subject to a charge of perjury if the information provided is false, no further evidence of credibility is needed. Personally testifying "provides powerful indicia of veracity and reliability." *United States v. Elliott*, 893 F.2d 220, 223 (9th Cir. 1990).

Also, as explained above in the context of probable cause and the collective knowledge of police, there is generally no special credibility showing needed when a police officer provides probable cause information to another officer. In this sense, police officers are treated similarly to "ordinary citizen informants."

For certain crimes, the law enforcement officer must show not only that the informant is credible but also that the informant has some expertise in recognizing that a crime has been committed. In *United States v. Hernandez*, 825 F.2d 846 (5th Cir. 1987), the informant (Marone) told the police that the defendant (Hernandez) had attempted to pass a counterfeit twenty-dollar note. The Court determined that Marone had sufficient expertise and experience with recognizing counterfeit bills because he dealt frequently with currency in his profession and was able to confidently ascertain the counterfeit nature of the bill Hernandez gave him. 825 F.2d at 849-50.

Criminal Informants: Unlike an ordinary citizen's credibility or truthfulness, which may sometimes be presumed, the criminal informant's credibility must always be established by a statement of underlying facts and circumstances. Criminal informants may be professional police informants, persons with a criminal record, accomplices in a crime, or persons seeking immunity for themselves. Usually, criminal informants do not want their identities disclosed in an affidavit. The U.S. Supreme Court held that an informant's identity need not be disclosed if his or her credibility is otherwise satisfactorily established. *McCray v. Illinois*, 386 U.S. 300, 306-07 (1967), stated the reasons for this rule:

> **If a defendant may insist upon disclosure of the informant in order to test the truth of the officer's statement . . . , we can be sure that every defendant will demand disclosure. He has nothing to lose and the prize may be the suppression of damaging evidence if the State cannot afford to reveal its source, as is so often the case. . . . The result would be that the State could use the informant's information only as a lead and could search only if it could gather adequate evidence of probable cause apart from the informant's data. . . . [W]e doubt that there would be enough talent and time to cope with crime upon that basis. Rather we accept the premise that the informer is a vital part of society's defensive arsenal. The basic rule protecting his identity rests upon that belief.**

Furthermore, while statements made by the police officer in the affidavit can be challenged by a defendant, statements by informants are much more difficult to challenge. See *Franks v. Delaware*, 438 U.S. 154, 171 (1978). (*Franks* is discussed in more detail in Chapter 4.) Whether or not the criminal informant's identity is disclosed, the affidavit must contain a statement of underlying facts and circumstances supporting credibility. The following facts and circumstances are relevant:

1. **Informant has given accurate information in the past.** The usual method of establishing the credibility of a criminal informant is by showing that the informant has in the past given accurate information that has led to arrests, convictions, recovery of stolen property, or the like. The affidavit may not state simply that an informant is credible because of proven credibility. Stating facts demonstrating that the informant has given accurate information in the past is sometimes referred to as establishing the informant's "track record." Magistrates are required to evaluate affidavits attempting to establish the credibility of informants in a commonsense manner and not with undue technicality. *United States v. Ventresca*, 380 U.S. 102 (1965). The main concern of the magistrate is the *accuracy* of the information supplied by the informant in the past.

   For example, *People v. Lawrence*, 273 N.E.2d 637 (Ill. App. 1971), found an informant credible even though none of his prior tips had resulted in convictions. The Court stated that "[c]onvictions, while corroborative of an informer's reliability, are not essential in establishing his reliability. Arrests, standing alone, do not establish reliability. . . . The true test of his reliability is the accuracy of his information." 273 N.E.2d at 639. Another case, *United States v. Dunnings*, 425 F.2d 836, 839 (2d Cir. 1969), found sufficient a statement that the informant had "furnished reliable and accurate information on approximately 20 occasions over the past four years." *State v. Daniels*, 200 N.W.2d 403, 406-07 (Minn. 1972), held that the credibility of the informant was sufficiently shown when the affidavit stated that the informant's information "has recently resulted in narcotic arrests and convictions." And in *McCray v. Illinois*, 386 U.S. 300 (1967), informant credibility was found when the informant gave police accurate information at least fifteen different times, many of these instances leading to arrest and conviction.

Generally, the more information provided about an informant's track record, the more likely the magistrate will find the informant credible. Types of information considered relevant in determining informant credibility are:

▶ The time when the informant furnished previous information

▶ Specific examples of verification of the accuracy of the informant's information

▶ A description of how the informant's information helped in bringing about an arrest, conviction, or other result

▶ Documentation of the informant's consistency in providing accurate information

▶ Details of the informant's **"general background, employment, personal attributes that enable him to observe and relate accurately, position in the community, reputation with others, personal connection with the suspect, any circumstances which suggest the probable absence of any motivation to falsify, the apparent motivation for supplying the information, the presence or absence of a criminal record or association with known criminals, and the like."** *United States v. Harris*, 403 U.S. 573 (1971) (dissenting opinion).

If an officer has no *personal* knowledge of an informant's credibility, the officer may state in the affidavit information about the informant's credibility received from other law enforcement officers. *State v. Lambert*, 363 A.2d 707 (Me. 1976). The officer should state the names of other law enforcement officers and describe in detail how those officers acquired personal knowledge of the informant's credibility.

A dog trained to react to controlled substances may also be considered an informant. The dog's credibility can also be established by demonstrating the track record of the dog and its handler. In *United States v. Race*, 529 F.2d 12 (1st Cir. 1976), a dog reacted positively to two wooden crates in an airline warehouse containing some three hundred crates. The dog's reaction provided the basis for probable cause to arrest the defendant. The court said:

> We do not, of course, suggest that any dog's excited behavior could, by itself, be adequate proof that a controlled substance was present, but here the government laid a strong foundation of canine reliability and handler expertise. Murphy [the dog's handler] testified that the dog had undergone intensive training in detecting drugs in 1971, that he had at least four hours a week of follow-up training since then, as well as work experience, and that the strong reaction he had to the crates was one that in the past had invariably indicated the presence of marijuana, hashish, heroin or cocaine. 529 F.2d at 14.

2. **Informant made a criminal admission or turned over evidence against the informant's own penal interest.** *United States v. Harris*, 403 U.S. 573 (1971), held that an admission made by an informant against the informant's own penal interest is sufficient to establish the credibility of the informant. The Court reasoned:

> People do not lightly admit a crime and place critical evidence in the hands of the police in the form of their own admissions. Admissions of crime, like admissions against proprietary interests, carry their own indicia of credibility—sufficient at least to support a finding of probable cause to search. That the informant may be paid or promised a "break" does not eliminate the residual risk and opprobrium of having admitted criminal conduct. 403 U.S. at 583-84.

State v. Appleton, 297 A.2d 363 (Me. 1972), held that an informant's turning over to police recently purchased drugs against his own penal interest was also strongly convincing evidence of credibility. "An informant is not likely to turn over to the police such criminal evidence unless he is certain in his own mind that his story implicating the persons occupying the premises where the sale took place will withstand police scrutiny." 297 A.2d at 369.

key points

- Probable cause may be based on information supplied to a law enforcement officer by ordinary citizen informants or criminal informants who have themselves personally perceived indications of criminal activity.
- Under the *Aguilar* two-pronged test for determining probable cause when the information in an affidavit was either entirely or partially obtained from an informant, (1) the affidavit must describe underlying circumstances from which a neutral and detached magistrate may determine that the informant had a sufficient basis for his or her knowledge and that the information was not the result of mere rumor or suspicion; and (2) the affidavit must describe underlying circumstances from which the magistrate may determine that the informant was credible or that the informant's information was reliable.
- To meet the first prong of *Aguilar*, the affidavit can explain how the informant obtained the information firsthand or can explain that the informant information was obtained through a secondhand source. In this case, the affidavit must also explain how the secondhand source acquired the informa-

tion. Finally, the officer can also satisfy this prong by providing intricate detail of the informant's tip (if available).
- Concerning the second *Aguilar* prong, an ordinary citizen informant is usually presumed credible. No further evidence of credibility need be stated in the affidavit beyond the informant's name and address and his or her status as a victim of or witness to crime.
- A criminal informant's credibility is never presumed but must be established. Usually, this is done by demonstrating the informant's "track record" of having given accurate information in the past. In the case of a secondhand source providing information to the informant, the affidavit must also demonstrate the track record of this source.
- A criminal informant's identity need not be disclosed if his or her credibility is otherwise satisfactorily established.
- A dog trained to react to controlled substances may be considered an informant. Its credibility can be established by demonstrating the "track record" of the dog and its handler.

Corroboration An officer may use **corroboration** to bolster information that is insufficient to satisfy either or both *Aguilar* prongs. Corroboration means strengthening or confirming the information supplied by the informant with supporting information obtained by law enforcement officers. For example, assume an officer receives a tip from a reliable informant about criminal activity. Through surveillance or independent investigation, the officer personally perceives further indications of that criminal activity. By including this corroborating information in the affidavit with the informant's information, the officer enables a magistrate to consider all facts that support probable cause, no matter what the source of the information.

The corroborative information provided by the law enforcement officer in the affidavit may work in three possible ways:

1. The information obtained by the officer may *in itself* provide probable cause independent of the informant's information. (See section entitled "Information Obtained Through the Officer's Own Senses" earlier in this chapter.) Corroborating information of this degree provides probable cause to search even if neither *Aguilar* prong is satisfied.

2. The officer's information may confirm or verify the information provided by the informant. In this case, the corroborating information may largely be of an innocent nature and not itself provide probable cause. For example, if significant yet innocent details of the informant's information are shown to be true by the independent observation of a law enforcement officer, the magistrate is more likely to be convinced of the trustworthiness of all the information provided by the informant. This occurred in the *Draper* case mentioned above when officers, through observation, were able to corroborate the intricate yet innocent details provided by the tip.

3. The officer's information may be added to an informant's information that meets *Aguilar* standards. Although neither standing alone is sufficient to establish probable cause, a combination of all the information may be sufficient.

Therefore, to ensure that a magistrate is presented with sufficient information on which to base a determination of probable cause, the affidavit should include:

▶   all information directed toward satisfying *Aguilar*'s two-pronged test for informant information;

▶   all information perceived by law enforcement officers that corroborates the informant's information; and

▶   all additional corroborating information perceived by officers relating to the criminal activity for which a search warrant is being sought.

To illustrate how courts deal with corroboration, let's look in detail at *Spinelli* and *Dawson*, two cases with similar fact situations but different results.

Spinelli v. United States, 393 U.S. 410 (1969). *Spinelli* is the leading case on corroboration. The defendant (Spinelli) was convicted of traveling to St. Louis, Missouri, from a nearby Illinois suburb with the intention of conducting gambling activities prohibited by Missouri law. On appeal, he challenged the validity of a search warrant used to obtain incriminating evidence against him. The affidavit in support of the search warrant contained the following allegations:

1. The FBI had tracked the defendant's movements during five days in August 1965. On four of those days, the defendant was seen crossing a bridge from

Illinois to St. Louis between 11 A.M. and 12:15 P.M. and parking his car in a lot used by residents of a certain apartment house between 3:30 P.M. and 4:45 P.M. On one day, the defendant was followed and was observed entering a particular apartment.

2. An FBI check with the telephone company revealed that this apartment contained two telephones with different numbers listed in the name Grace Hagen.

3. The defendant was known to the officer preparing the affidavit (the affiant) and to federal and local law enforcement agents as a "bookmaker, an associate of bookmakers, a gambler, and an associate of gamblers." 393 U.S. at 414.

4. The FBI had been informed by a confidential reliable informant that the defendant was operating a handbook, accepting wagers, and disseminating wagering information using Grace Hagen's telephone numbers.

The Court first discussed in detail allegation 4, the information obtained from the informant. The Court said:

> The informer's report must first be measured against *Aguilar*'s standards so that its probative value can be assessed. If the tip is found inadequate under *Aguilar*, the other allegations which corroborate the information contained in the [informant's] report should then be considered. 393 U.S. at 415.

The Court found that *Aguilar*'s second prong, addressing informant veracity, was not satisfied because the affiant merely stated that he had been informed by a "confidential reliable informant." This was insufficient, because no *underlying circumstances* were stated to show the magistrate that the informant was credible, such as examples from the informant's past "track record."

Nor was *Aguilar*'s first prong satisfied. The officer's affidavit failed to state sufficient underlying circumstances (e.g., a "basis") for the informant's conclusion that the defendant was running a bookmaking operation. It said nothing about how, when, or where the informant received his information—whether he personally observed the defendant "at work" or whether he ever placed a bet with him. If the informant obtained his information from third persons, the affidavit did not explain why these sources were credible or how they obtained their information.

Finally, as mentioned above, the informant's information did not describe the defendant's alleged criminal activity in sufficient detail to convince a magistrate that the information was more than mere rumor or suspicion.

The Court then considered allegations 1 and 2 of the affidavit tracking defendant's movements to the apartment to see if they provided sufficient corroboration of the informant's information or probable cause in and of themselves. The Court found no suggestion of criminal conduct. The defendant's travels to and from an apartment building and his entering a particular apartment did not necessarily indicate gambling activity. And certainly nothing was unusual about an apartment containing two separate telephones. The Court concluded:

> At most, these allegations indicated that Spinelli could have used the telephones specified by the informant for some purpose. This [corroborating information] cannot by itself be said to support both the inference that the informer was generally trustworthy and that he had made his charge against Spinelli on the basis of information obtained in a reliable way. 393 U.S. at 417.

Lastly, the Court considered allegation 3—that the defendant was "known" to the FBI and others as a gambler. The Court called this a bald and unilluminating assertion of police suspicion because it contained no facts indicating the defendant's past gambling activities to support it. Although criminal reputation may be considered in determining probable cause, without factual statements in support, such an allegation would not be useful in evaluating the affidavit.

The *Spinelli* case is instructive because it evaluates the *Aguilar* tests for establishing probable cause based on informant information and gives reasons why the affidavit failed those tests. It then evaluates other information in the affidavit in corroboration of the informant's information, and shows why the corroborative information was inadequate to credit the informant's information or itself support a probable cause finding.

Dawson v. State, 276 A.2d 680 (Md. Spec. App. 1971). Dawson is similar to *Spinelli* except that the search warrant in *Dawson* was found to be valid. This discussion focuses on the differences between the two cases that caused the court in *Dawson* to reach a different conclusion.

The defendant (Dawson) was convicted of unlawfully maintaining premises for the purpose of selling lottery tickets and unlawfully betting, wagering, or gambling on the results of horse races. He appealed, claiming among other things that the search warrant of his home was illegal because probable cause was lacking.

The affidavit for the warrant contained nine paragraphs. The first paragraph listed the investigative experience of the affiant and ended with his conclusion that gambling activities were at that time being conducted at the defendant's premises. The third through ninth paragraphs contained the direct observations of the affiant officer. (These paragraphs are considered later.) The second paragraph dealt with an informant's information and is quoted here:

> That on Thursday April 17, 1969 your affiant interviewed a confidential source of information who has given reliable information in the past relating to illegal gambling activities which has resulted in the arrest and conviction of persons arrested for illegal gambling activities and that the source is personally known to your affiant. That this source related that there was illegal gambling activities taking place at 8103 Legation Road, Hyattsville Prince George's County, Maryland by one Donald Lee Dawson. That the source further related that the source would call [telephone number] and place horse and number bets with Donald Lee Dawson. 276 A.2d at 685.

The court analyzed this paragraph under *Aguilar*'s two-pronged test. By stating that the informant personally called the phone number and placed horse and number bets with the defendant, the affidavit established the informant's basis of knowledge. In contrast, in *Spinelli,* nothing was said about how the informant obtained his information. The information supplied about the credibility of the informant was found barely sufficient, however. Since the affidavit stated that both arrests and convictions had resulted from the informant's information in the past, it was more than a mere conclusion or opinion of the affiant. It also went further than the affidavit in *Spinelli,* in which the informant was merely described as a "confidential reliable informant." Although more specific information on credibility would have been desirable, the court said:

> It may well be that the facts here recited are enough to establish the credibility of the informant. In view of the strong independent verification hereinafter

to be discussed, however, it is unnecessary for the State to rely exclusively on such recitation. 276 A.2d at 686.

The court assumed that the credibility of the informant had *not* been adequately established and proceeded to discuss corroboration, carefully comparing the affidavit with that in *Spinelli*.

Paragraphs 3 through 9 of the *Dawson* affidavit stated that surveillance by the officer of the defendant's activities conducted during a six-day period in April 1969 revealed the following information:

▶ The defendant was observed to be engaged in no apparent legitimate employment during the period.

▶ The defendant had two telephones in his residence with two separate lines, both of which had silent listings. One of the defendant's silent listings had been picked up in the course of a raid on a lottery operation three years earlier in another town. In *Spinelli*, neither Spinelli's nor Grace Hagen's phone number had been previously picked up in a raided gambling headquarters.

▶ On each day of observation, the defendant was observed purchasing an *Armstrong Scratch Sheet*, which gives information about horses running at various tracks that day. In *Spinelli*, there was no daily purchase of an *Armstrong* Scratch Sheet or the like to evidence some daily interest in horse races.

▶ On each morning of observation, the defendant was observed to leave his house between 9:02 and 10:20 A.M., to return to his house between 11:20 A.M., and 12:06 P.M., and to remain in his house until after 6:00 P.M. The affiant, an expert, experienced gambling investigator, stated that during the hours between noon and 6:00 P.M., horse and number bets can be placed and betting results become available.

▶ On each day of observation, the defendant was observed during his morning rounds stopping at a number of places, including liquor stores and restaurants, for very short periods. He never purchased anything from any of the stores, nor did he eat or drink at the restaurants. The affiant stated that such brief regular stops are classic characteristics of the pickup-man phase of a gambling operation: "He picks up the 'action' (money and/or list of bets) from the previous day or evening from prearranged locations— 'drops.' At the same time, he delivers cash to the appropriate locations for the payoff of yesterday's successful players." 276 A.2d at 689. In *Spinelli*, there were no observations of the pickup-man type of activity.

▶ On one of the days, the defendant was observed in close association all day with a person who had been arrested for alleged gambling violations three years earlier. In *Spinelli*, there was no observed association with a previously arrested gambler.

▶ Finally, the defendant had been arrested and convicted of gambling violations about three years earlier. In *Spinelli*, Spinelli was not a convicted gambler.

The court evaluated these allegations in their totality:

[P]robable cause emerges not from any single constituent activity but, rather, from the overall pattern of activities. Each fragment of conduct may communicate nothing of significance, but the broad mosaic portrays a great deal. The whole may, indeed, be greater than the sum of its parts. 276 A.2d at 687.

Thus, any doubt as to the credibility of the informant in *Dawson* was effectively removed by the officer's investigative efforts in corroborating the informant's information. Indeed, the court gave great weight to the officer's experience in investigating gambling activities and his interpretations of the defendant's conduct. The court concluded by noting how the direct observations of the officer and the informant information reinforced each other, and that the entire pattern of activity observed by the officer "weaves[s] a strong web of guilt." 276 A.2d at 689, 690. The court's emphasis on analyzing the overall pattern of activities and the totality of facts and circumstances in *Dawson* was an early harbinger of the approach to probable cause taken in the landmark decision of the U.S. Supreme Court in *Illinois v. Gates.*

key points

- Corroboration means strengthening the information supplied by the informant in the affidavit by stating supporting or confirming information obtained by the independent investigation of law enforcement officers.

- Corroboration is a two-way street. Direct observation of law enforcement officers may reinforce the hearsay information provided by the informant, and vice versa.

Totality-of-the-Circumstances Test under *Illinois v. Gates* As discussed earlier, *Illinois v. Gates,* 462 U.S. 213 (1983) abandoned rigid adherence to the *Aguilar–Spinelli* two-pronged test for determining probable cause through the use of informants for a totality-of-the-circumstances test. Nevertheless, the elements of the *Aguilar–Spinelli* test remain important considerations under the *Gates* test.

▶ The *Gates* Case

On May 3, 1978, the Bloomingdale, Illinois, Police Department received an anonymous letter that included statements that the defendants, Mr. and Mrs. Gates, made their living selling drugs; that the wife would drive their car to Florida on May 3rd and leave it to be loaded up with drugs; that the husband would fly down in a few days to drive the car back loaded with over $100,000 worth of drugs; and that the defendants had over $100,000 worth of drugs in the basement of their home. Acting on the tip, a police officer obtained the defendants' address and learned that the husband had made a reservation for a May 5th flight to Florida. The officer then made arrangements with a Drug Enforcement Administration (DEA) agent for surveillance of the May 5th flight. The surveillance revealed that the husband took the flight, and stayed overnight in a motel room registered to his wife. The next morning he headed north with an unidentified woman toward Bloomingdale, in a car bearing Illinois license plates issued to the husband. A search warrant for the defendants' residence and automobile was obtained, based on these facts observed by police and the anonymous informant letter. When the defendants arrived home, the police searched the car and the residence and found marijuana.

At the state level, the Illinois Supreme Court found that the *Aguilar–Spinelli* two-pronged test had not been satisfied. First, the veracity prong was not satisfied because there was no basis for concluding that the anonymous person who wrote the letter to the police department was credible. Second, the basis of knowledge prong was not satisfied because the letter gave no information about how its writer knew of the defendants' activities. The Court therefore concluded that no showing of probable cause had been made.

In reversing the Illinois Supreme Court's decision, the U.S. Supreme Court first said:

> **We agree with the Illinois Supreme Court that an informant's "veracity," "reliability" and "basis of knowledge" are all highly relevant in determining the value of his report. We do not agree, however, that these elements should be understood as entirely separate and independent requirements to be rigidly exacted in every case, which the opinion of the Supreme Court of Illinois would imply. Rather . . . they should be understood simply as closely intertwined issues that may usefully illuminate the commonsense, practical question whether there is "probable cause" to believe that contraband or evidence is located in a particular place.** *Illinois v. Gates,* 462 U.S. at 230.

In effect, the Court said that the elements of the *Aguilar–Spinelli* two-pronged test are important considerations in determining the existence of probable cause, but they should be evaluated only as part of the ultimate commonsense determination and not as independent, inflexible requirements or mechanistic rules. The Court believed that this totality-of-the-circumstances approach was more in keeping with the nature of probable cause as a fluid concept. According to the Court, the two prongs of *Aguilar–Spinelli* should be understood as "**relevant considerations in the totality of circumstances that traditionally has guided probable cause determinations: a deficiency in one may be compensated for, in determining the overall reliability of a tip, by a strong showing as to the other, or by some other indicia of reliability.**" *Illinois v. Gates,* 462 U.S. at 233. For example, if an informant has a very long and successful "track record" of providing accurate information leading to arrests and convictions, this fact may compensate for a relatively weak showing on how the informant obtained his information in a particular case (e.g., his or her "basis of knowledge"). The entire process of determining probable cause can be stated simply as follows:

> **The task of the issuing magistrate is simply to make a practical, commonsense decision whether, given all the circumstances set forth in the affidavit before him, including the "veracity" and "basis of knowledge" of persons supplying hearsay information, there is a fair probability that contraband or evidence of a crime will be found in a particular place.** 462 U.S. at 238-39.

With respect to the anonymous letter in *Gates,* the Supreme Court said that the corroboration of predictions that the defendants' car would be in Florida, that the husband would fly to Florida in a few days, and that the husband would drive the car back to Illinois indicated that the informant's other assertions regarding illegal activity were also true. In particular, the letter's accurate predictions of the defendants' future *innocent* actions made it more likely that the informant also had access to reliable information of the defendants' alleged illegal activities. Although the tip was corroborated only as to the defendants' seemingly innocent behavior, and although it by no means indicated with certainty that illegal drugs would be found in defendants' home, the Court believed that it provided details only "insiders" could know, and sufficed **"for the practical, common-sense judgment called for in making a probable cause determination to search. It is enough, for purposes of assessing probable cause, that 'corroboration through other sources of information reduced the chances of a reckless or prevaricating tale,' thus providing 'a substantial basis for crediting the hearsay.'"** 462 U.S. at 244.

The *Gates* totality-of-the-circumstances test does not radically change the procedure for law enforcement officers applying for search warrants. Affidavits prepared to satisfy the *Aguilar–Spinelli* test will very likely satisfy the *Gates* test. The *Gates* emphasis on the value of law enforcement officials corroborating detailed but facially innocent information from an informant should also make it easier to obtain a search warrant based on information from an anonymous informant. As the *Gates* opinion indicated, overly rigid application of the two-pronged test tended to reject anonymous tips, because ordinary citizens generally do not provide extensive recitations of the basis of their everyday observations, and because the veracity of anonymous informants is largely unknown and unknowable. The Court said:

> **[A]nonymous tips seldom could survive a rigorous application of either of the . . . prongs. Yet, such tips, particularly when supplemented by independent police investigation, frequently contribute to the solution of otherwise "perfect crimes." While a conscientious assessment of the basis for crediting such tips is required by the Fourth Amendment, a standard that leaves virtually no place for anonymous citizen informants is not.** 462 U.S. at 237-38.

▶ Application of the Totality-of-the-Circumstances Test under *Gates*

As a result of the Supreme Court's decision in *Gates*, some lower courts construct a list of factors that they will consider in ascertaining the overall reliability of informant information. For example, *United States v. Morales,* 171 F.3d 978, 981-82 (5th Cir. 1999), held that the totality-of-the-circumstances test includes four factors, one of which includes the *Aguilar* two-pronged test: (1) the nature of the information; (2) whether there has been an opportunity for the police to see or hear the matter reported; (3) the veracity and the basis of the knowledge of the informant; and (4) whether there has been any independent verification of the matters through police investigation."

In *United States v. De Los* Santos, 810 F.2d 1326 (5th Cir. 1987), the Supreme Court essentially applied these four factors, and determined that the informant's testimony could serve as a reliable basis for probable cause:

> [O]fficers had probable cause to believe that contraband would be found, and therefore they properly stopped and arrested De Los Santos. First, [DEA Special Agent] Castro knew that De Los Santos had dealt in heroin on previous occasions. He then received a tip from an informant who Castro knew and who had provided reliable information in the past. The informant told Castro that De Los Santos would travel to a certain area to store drugs and would pick them up the next day at a certain time. As predicted by the informant, the next morning De Los Santos arrived in the neighborhood in the same vehicle he had been in before. The agents observed him go to a residence and stay there for only two to four minutes. This surveillance, therefore, corroborated information provided by the informant.

> Moreover, Castro testified in [the judge's chambers] as to other information that the informant supplied. This information also is supportive of probable cause. As in *McCray*:
>
> > The officer[s] in this case described with specificity "what the informer actually said, and why the officer thought the information was credible." . . . The testimony of each of the officers informed the court of the "underlying circumstances from which the informant concluded that the narcotics were where he claimed they were, and some of the underlying circumstances from which the officer concluded that the informant . . . was 'credible' or his information 'reliable.'" *McCray*, 386 U.S. at 304 (citations omitted).
>
> Thus, under the totality of the circumstances test, "[t]here can be no doubt upon the basis of the circumstances related by [Castro], that there was probable cause to sustain the arrest. . . ." 810 F.2d at 1336.

The *De Los Santos* case illustrates the continuing validity of the *Aguilar–Spinelli* two-pronged test in determining probable cause using information supplied by an informant.

In contrast to *De Los Santos*, the *Gates* test was not satisfied in *United States v. Campbell*, 920 F.2d 793 (11th Cir. 1990), because law enforcement officials did not sufficiently corroborate information provided by the informant:

> The totality of the circumstances do not suggest that the Montgomery police had probable cause to arrest the defendants, much less search the vehicle when they first encountered it at the truck stop. The district court found that the confidential informant was not reliable, but still found that the officers had probable cause to arrest the occupants of the pickup based on reliability of the information provided by the informant. The key to the district court's conclusion was that the informant provided the police with the approximate time of the vehicle's arrival and the location where it would stop. In [another Supreme Court case], the police kept the suspect under surveillance in order to corroborate the information. [Here], there was not the type of corroboration of criminal activity . . . to elevate it to the level of probable cause. 920 F.2d at 796-97.

United States v. Brown, 744 F. Supp. 558 (S.D.N.Y. 1990), held that, under the *Gates* standard, probable cause for the issuance of a search warrant could be based almost entirely on information received from a single confidential informant. In *Brown*, the informant had provided highly reliable information in the past, had been providing information on the defendant for over a month, and had personal knowledge about the premises to be searched. The court said:

> The clear implication from the affidavit is that the informant had had a long relationship with law enforcement officials which had proved very reliable in the past. This information alone goes a long way to satisfying the totality of the circumstances test outlined in *Gates*. 744 F. Supp. at 567.

Thus, *Brown* is consistent with the suggestion in *Gates* itself that a strong showing on one *Aguilar* prong (e.g., veracity/ reliability prong) could compensate for a weak showing on the other prong (e.g., basis of information prong).

In *United States v. Danhauer*, 229 F.3d 1002 (10th Cir. 2000), though the officer/affiant already conducted a search pursuant to a warrant uncovering drug-related evidence, the Court found a confidential informant's information insufficient to establish probable cause for the original issuance of the warrant:

> The affidavit in this case failed to allege facts sufficient to establish probable cause. The affidavit contains repetitive statements regarding the physical

description of the Danhauer residence and the identity of the occupants. Further, the affidavit contains statements about the criminal histories of both Dennis and Robbi Danhauer. The affidavit does not reveal, however, the informant's basis of knowledge [for this information] or adequately verify the informant's most serious allegation, that the Danhauers were manufacturing methamphetamine. An affidavit replete with repetitive and tenuous facts does not provide a magistrate with a sufficient basis for drawing a reasonable inference that a search would uncover evidence of criminal activity.

When there is sufficient independent corroboration of an informant's information, there is no need to establish the veracity of the informant. . . . In this case, however, the affiant neither established the veracity of the informant, nor obtained sufficient independent corroboration of the informant's information. The only police corroboration of the informant's information was the affiant's verification of the Danhauer residence's physical description, a records check to confirm that the Danhauers resided at the premises in question, an observation of Robbi Danhauer coming and going from the house to the garage, and a search of the Danhauers' criminal histories, which brought to light Robbi Danhauer's latest urinalysis revealing the presence of methamphetamine. The detective made little attempt to link methamphetamine to the Danhauer residence. . . . The only possible nexus between Danhauer's residence and the alleged criminal activity [of manufacturing methamphetamine] was his wife's urinalysis result. This is not the type of [corroborating] evidence that enables the state magistrate to draw a reasonable inference that the items subject to the search warrant would be located at Danhauer's residence. Such a nebulous connection does not give a magistrate a substantial basis for concluding that probable cause existed. *Danhauer*, 229 F.3d at 1006.

The *Danhauer* case is notable, however, because even though the court found an absence of probable cause to search for evidence related to drug manufacturing, the court held that the good-faith exception to the exclusionary rule applied to admit this evidence because the officer's reliance on the search warrant was not unreasonable, or "wholly unwarranted":

Although the affidavit in support of the warrant did not establish probable cause, it was not so lacking in indicia of probable cause that the executing officer should have known the search was illegal despite the state magistrate's authorization. . . . Further, the absence of information establishing the informant's reliability or basis of knowledge does not necessarily preclude an officer from manifesting a reasonable belief that the warrant was properly issued . . . particularly when the officer takes steps to investigate the informant's allegation. Detective McCarthy, who both obtained and executed the search warrant, reasonably believed the fruits of his investigation into the informant's allegation sufficiently linked the manufacture of methamphetamine and Danhauer's residence. His affidavit contains more than conclusory statements based on the informant's allegation about the alleged criminal activity at Danhauer's residence.

This court concludes the search warrant failed to establish probable cause because the nexus between the alleged criminal activity and Danhauer's residence was insufficient. Nonetheless, the district court did not err in refusing to suppress the evidence seized because the officer acted in objectively reasonable, good-faith reliance on the warrant. 229 F.3d at 1007-08.

Danhauer also shows that once a judge has issued a search warrant, any evidence seized pursuant to it will likely be found admissible by a reviewing court, even if this court finds that probable cause had been lacking. More generally, the case illustrates the power and reach of the good-faith exception to the exclusionary rule.

▶REASONABLENESS

Reasonableness is an important basic underlying concept, and the last one we will discuss. Once it has been determined that the individual pursuing a Fourth Amendment claim has "standing" and that there has been a "search or seizure" for Fourth Amendment purposes, the final inquiry under this Amendment is whether the search or seizure is "reasonable." One way a search or seizure will be found reasonable is if there exists a valid warrant supported by probable cause. Without such a warrant, a search or seizure may still be found reasonable if a valid exception to the normal warrant requirement has been met. The figure shown inside the front cover of your book, illustrates the overall Fourth Amendment inquiry. (Note that future chapters will comprehensively address the warrant requirement and exceptions to that requirement, such as plain view and consent searches.)

Generally, the Fourth Amendment does not prohibit all searches and seizures, only those that are unreasonable. Reasonableness has therefore, at times, been called the "touchstone" of the Fourth Amendment.

> The fundamental command of the Fourth Amendment is that searches and seizures be reasonable, and although "both the concept of probable cause and the requirement of a warrant bear on the reasonableness of a search, . . . in certain limited circumstances neither is required." . . . Thus, we have in a number of cases recognized the legality of searches and seizures based on suspicions that, although "reasonable," do not rise to the level of probable cause. . . . Determining the reasonableness of any search involves a twofold inquiry: first, one must consider "whether the . . . action was justified at its inception," . . . second, one must determine whether the search as actually conducted "was reasonably related in scope to the circumstances which justified the interference in the first place." *New Jersey v. T.L.O.*, 469 U.S. 325, 340-41 (1985).

Other Fourth Amendment considerations, such as warrants, probable cause, exigency, and good faith, while necessary depending on the particular circum-

key points

- Under the *Gates* totality-of-the-circumstances test, the task of the issuing magistrate is to make a practical, commonsense decision whether, given all the circumstances set forth in the affidavit, there is a fair probability that contraband or evidence of crime will be found in a particular place.
- The elements of the *Aguilar–Spinelli* two-pronged test are important considerations in determining the existence of probable cause. Nonetheless, they

should be evaluated only as part of the ultimate commonsense determination—not as rigid rules to be applied mechanically.
- Corroboration of the details of an informant's tip by independent police investigation reduces the chances of a reckless or prevaricating tale. It is a valuable means of satisfying the *Gates* totality-of-the-circumstances test for determining probable cause.

Discussion

⬆POINT

How Much Corroboration Is Needed to Support the Information of a Cooperating Criminal?

In *United States v. Button,* 1999 WL 2463 (10th Cir. 1999), a federal magistrate judge issued a search warrant for the defendant's residence based on an affidavit submitted by a DEA agent. The affidavit described an ongoing drug trafficking conspiracy dating from 1989, with three drug seizures linked to Stephen Michael Pollack and those working with him. In a drug raid related to Mr. Pollock's alleged conspiracy, the police found defendant Button's phone number next to Mr. Pollock's in a confiscated notebook. The affidavit also indicated that a cooperating source had told agents that Button was a drug courier for Pollack. Among other details, the source stated that Pollack's conspiracy involved drug trafficking in Alamogordo, New Mexico, and Durango, Colorado.

The affidavit showed that the police had corroborated the information provided by the cooperating source by: (1) telephone records showing calls between Pollock and Button; (2) agent surveillance of Button's car in Pollack's driveway; (3) information showing that Button lived in Alamogordo, New Mexico, and that Pollack lived in Durango, Colorado; and (4) information provided by New Mexico state police that they had an informant who also said Button was a courier for Pollack. When agents executed the search warrant at Button's residence, they seized a semi-automatic pistol and a rifle. Button filed a motion to suppress the weapons, asserting the underlying affidavit to the warrant was defective.

Applying the totality-of-the-circumstances test of *Illinois v. Gates,* do you think the motion to suppress should have been granted or denied? The trial court denied the motion and Button was convicted of being a convicted felon in possession of a firearm. The appellate court affirmed, saying "the affidavit provided a range of sensibly connected evidence beyond bare conclusions and that the totality of the evidence supports a 'substantial basis' for a search warrant."

Do you agree that the *Gates* test was satisfied? Why or why not?

---

stances, are factors subservient to reasonableness. In *Terry v. Ohio*, 392 U.S. 1, 19 (1968), the Supreme Court said that **"the central inquiry under the Fourth Amendment [is] the reasonableness in all the circumstances of the particular governmental invasion of a citizen's personal security."** Also, the Court pointed out that reasonableness does not necessarily mean correctness.

> It is apparent that in order to satisfy the "reasonableness" requirement of the Fourth Amendment, what is generally demanded of the many factual determinations that must regularly be made by agents of the government—whether the magistrate issuing a warrant, the police officer executing a warrant, or the police officer conducting a search or seizure under one of the exceptions to the warrant requirement—is not that they always be correct, but that they always be reasonable. *Illinois v. Rodriguez*, 497 U.S. 177, 185-86 (1990).

Finally, the Court has said that "[t]here is no formula for the determination of reasonableness. Each case is to be decided on its own facts and circumstances." *Go-Bart Importing Co. v. United States*, 282 U.S. 344, 357 (1931).

The outcomes of cases in which the U.S. Supreme Court has applied a reasonableness balancing test have varied with the particularities of the cases and the philosophies of individual Supreme Court justices. Examples can be found in the discussions of administrative searches in Chapter 5, stops and frisks in Chapter 7, and elsewhere in this book. For example, unlike traditional warrants aimed at uncovering evidence of criminal activity, administrative search warrants seeking evidence of possible fire, health, and safety violations, remain subject to a more relaxed probable cause evaluation:

> [T]he probable cause requirement for administrative warrants is less stringent than that required in criminal investigations because the privacy interests at stake are deemed less critical. Specific evidence of an existing statutory or regulatory violation, or a reasonable plan supported by a valid public interest, will justify the issuance of an administrative search warrant (Georgetown Annual Review of Criminal Procedure, 2006: 115-116).

Essential to an understanding of the concept of reasonableness is an appreciation that it is a flexible standard to be liberally construed for the protection of individual freedom.

> **Implicit in the Fourth Amendment's protection from unreasonable searches and seizures is its recognition of individual freedom. That safeguard has been declared to be "as of the very essence of constitutional liberty," the guaranty of which "is as important and as imperative as are the guaranties of the other fundamental rights of the individual citizen. . . . While the language of the Amendment is "general," it "forbids every search that is unreasonable; it protects all, those suspected or known as to be offenders as well as the innocent, and unquestionably extends to the premises where the search was made. . . ."** *Go-Bart Importing Co. v. United States*, 282 U.S. 344, 357 (1931).
>
> **This Court's long-established recognition [is] that standards of reasonableness under the Fourth Amendment are not susceptible of Procrustean application. . . .** *Ker v. California*, 374 U.S. 23, 32-34 (1963).

It is fitting in these times to conclude this chapter with a quotation from Justice Brennan that succinctly summarizes the essence of the Fourth Amendment and neatly ties together the concepts of privacy, probable cause, and reasonableness:

> **The Fourth Amendment was designed not merely to protect against official intrusions whose social utility was less as measured by some "balancing test" than its intrusion on individual privacy; it was designed in addition to grant the individual a zone of privacy whose protections could be breached only where the "reasonableness" requirements of the probable cause standard were met. Moved by whatever momentary evil has aroused their fears, officials—perhaps even supported by a majority of citizens— may be tempted to conduct searches that sacrifice the liberty of each citizen to assuage the perceived evil. But the Fourth Amendment rests on the principle that a true balance between the individual and society depends on the recognition of "the right to be let alone—the most comprehensive of rights and the right most valued by civilized men."** *New Jersey v. T.L.O.*, 469 U.S. 325, 361-62 (1985).

key points

- The fundamental command of the Fourth Amendment is that searches and seizures be reasonable. This generally means that a valid warrant exists supported by probable cause, or in the absence of such a warrant, a valid exception to the warrant requirement applies.
- Probable cause and the warrant requirement as primary indicators of reasonableness under the Fourth Amendment are very important. Nonetheless, searches and seizures based on suspicions that are "reasonable"—but do not rise to the level of probable cause—are nevertheless legal, where a careful balancing of governmental and private interests suggests that the public interest is best served by a Fourth Amendment standard of reasonableness that stops short of probable cause. For

example, "stops and frisks" and certain administrative searches may be found reasonable under the Fourth Amendment in the absence of both probable cause and a warrant.
- Determining the reasonableness of any search involves a twofold inquiry: first, one must consider whether the action was justified at its inception; second, one must determine whether the search as actually conducted was reasonably related in scope to the circumstances that justified the interference in the first place.
- In order to satisfy the reasonableness requirement of the Fourth Amendment, government agents need not always be correct, but they must always be reasonable.

Summary

This chapter rounds out preparation for the detailed study of the law of criminal procedure. Chapter 1 introduced the Constitution, the wellspring from which flow all the rules and principles to follow. Emphasis was placed on the constitutional sources of individual rights and the inevitable conflict between the protection of individual rights and the maintenance of law and order. Future chapters deal with specific examples of this conflict, and show how the delicate balance among these competing interests is maintained.

Chapter 2 presented an overview of the criminal courts and the trial process. These are the arenas in which the balancing takes place, and in which the reasonableness, appropriateness, and thoroughness of the law enforcement officer's activities are ultimately tested. Chapter 2 gave an overall picture of the criminal justice system, as a backdrop for a more integrated understanding of the law of criminal procedure.

Finally, this chapter introduced the basic concepts of the exclusionary rule, privacy, probable cause, and reasonableness, all of which will resurface throughout this book. The law enforcement officer or other criminal justice professional who knows both the effect and scope of the exclusionary rule; who is sensitive to the constitutional rights of all citizens, especially to their reasonable expectation of privacy; who understands the meaning and importance of probable cause; and who embraces the concept of reasonableness as a guide is well on the way to appreciating the fundamental constitutional standards and restraints that characterize the operation of our criminal justice system. Succeeding chapters will provide the details of criminal procedure, the knowledge of which enables a criminal justice professional to function effectively within that system.

Key Terms

admission, 152
attenuation doctrine, 129
corroboration, 164
derivative evidence, 127
exclusionary rule, 118

fruit of the poisonous tree doctrine, 127
good-faith exception, 134
independent source doctrine, 128

inevitable discovery doctrine, 132
informant, 157
privacy, 140
probable cause, 145

reasonableness, 174
search, 122
seizure, 122
standing, 136

Review and Discussion Questions

1. Explain why the application of the exclusionary rule does not necessarily mean that the prosecution is ended and that the defendant goes free.

2. Discuss the probable effectiveness in deterring illegal police conduct of the following suggested alternatives to the exclusionary rule: criminal prosecution of law enforcement officers, administrative discipline of officers, and bringing civil actions for damages against officers.

3. Explain why a state court may refuse to follow certain holdings of the U.S. Supreme Court.

4. Give three reasons in support of the exclusionary rule and three reasons in support of its abolishment.

5. Discuss three theories under which evidence may be admissible in court even though it is fruit of the poisonous tree.

6. What did Justice Harlan mean when he said, in his concurring opinion in *Katz v. United States*, that the answer to the question of what protection the Fourth Amendment affords to people requires reference to a place?

7. Should a person in a telephone booth be given the same degree of Fourth Amendment protection as a person in his or her bedroom? As a person in his or her garage? As a person in his or her automobile?

8. Although *Katz v. United States* dispensed with the requirement of an actual physical trespass to trigger the Fourth Amendment, is a physical trespass always an intrusion on a person's reasonable expectation of privacy? See *On Lee v. United States*, 343 US 747 (1952).

9. Compare the standard of probable cause against the following statements of degree of certainty: absolutely positive; pretty sure; good possibility; beyond a reasonable doubt; reasonable suspicion; preponderance of the evidence; reasonable probability; strong belief; convinced.

10. Why is it important for a law enforcement officer to write down in a complaint or affidavit the facts and circumstances on which probable cause is based?

11. Give an example of a strong indication of probable cause to arrest that is arrived at through each of the five senses: sight, hearing, smell, taste, and touch.

12. List three possible strong indications of probable cause to arrest for each of the following crimes:

(a) theft, (b) assault, (c) arson, (d) breaking and entering, (e) rape, and (f) driving to endanger.

13. Discuss the significance in the probable cause context of the phrase "conduct innocent in the eyes of the untrained may carry entirely different 'messages' to the experienced or trained . . . observer." *Davis v. United States*, 409 F.2d 458, 460 (D.C. Cir. 1969). Discuss this specifically in terms of drug offenses and gambling offenses.

14. Must law enforcement officers know exactly the elements and name of the specific crime for which they are arresting or searching to have probable cause? See *People v. Georgev*, 230 N.E.2d 851 (Ill. 1967).

15. What does corroboration mean, and why is it important to a law enforcement officer in establishing probable cause through the use of informants?

16. How did the U.S. Supreme Court case of *Illinois v. Gates* change the requirements for establishing probable cause through the use of informants? Does the *Gates* decision make the law enforcement officer's task easier or harder?

17. Mr. A walks into a police station, drops three wristwatches on a table, and tells an officer that Mr. B robbed a local jewelry store two weeks ago. Mr. A will not say anything else in response to police questioning. A quick investigation reveals that the three watches were among a number of items stolen in the jewelry store robbery. Do the police have probable cause to do any or all of the following?

a. Arrest Mr. A.
b. Arrest Mr. B.
c. Search Mr. A's home.
d. Search Mr. B's home.

18. If you answered no to any of the items in question 18, explain why in detail. If you answered yes to any of them, draft the complaint or affidavit for a warrant, or explain why a warrant is not needed.

19. Why do reviewing courts accept evidence of a "less judicially competent or persuasive character" to justify the issuance of a warrant than they would to justify officers acting on their own without a warrant?

20. In what contexts has the Supreme Court refused to apply the exclusionary rule? In the particular context of knock-and-announce violations, why has the Court decided to forego application of the rule?

Applications of the Law in Real Cases

1 On March 20, 2005, Officer Don Pearman was on patrol and discovered defendant Frank S. in a high-crime area known specifically for its drug crime and where defendant had a number of friends. As Pearman drove past Frank S., the defendant attempted to hide behind one of these friends. Pearman knew that defendant was on parole and was probably hiding because he was prohibited under the conditions of his parole from being in this area of town. Pearman called for backup since he also knew that defendant had a history of fleeing from police. In his rear view mirror, Pearman saw defendant walk down a driveway towards a home. Pearman then parked his car, met two other officers, and walked toward the house. The officers approached a sliding glass door and remained there for ten to fifteen seconds. Pearman heard noises coming from the home that led him to believe there were multiple individuals there. He then reached through an opening in the door, and moved a curtain in order to see inside. He immediately saw defendant on a couch about three feet away. At that point, Officer Pearman entered the home, arrested the defendant, and patted him down for weapons. Defendant's friends were becoming aggressive, so Pearman waited to fully search defendant until he had arrived at the stationhouse. At the stationhouse, Pearman discovered in defendant's inner jacket pocket multiple bags containing marijuana.

Defendant Frank S. argued, and the court agreed, that Officer Don Pearman failed to knock and announce his presence and authority before arresting Frank S. at his friend's home. After the recent Supreme Court opinion in *Hudson v. Michigan* (explained in this chapter), should the drugs found on Frank S. be excluded? See *In re Frank S.*, 47 Cal. Rptr.3d 320 (2006).

2 Leslie Boles was driving a truck eastbound when a Nebraska state trooper stopped him for bypassing a weighing station. After being pulled over, Mr. Boles informed the trooper that his driver's license had expired and that he was transporting his girlfriend's furniture from Texas to Chicago. He also claimed that his girlfriend had the truck's lease agreement, that her name was Sandra Caballero, and that she was driving ahead of him in a white Ford Bronco with New Mexico plates.

A consensual search of the truck uncovered more than 1,000 pounds of marijuana. Mr. Boles was taken to the Nebraska State Patrol office, where an investigator informed him of his *Miranda* rights before interviewing him. The investigator testified at the suppression hearing that Mr. Boles "decided that he would come clean and tell the truth." Mr. Boles admitted to knowing that his truck contained marijuana, told the investigator that Mr. Gonzales and Sandra Carrion were his accomplices,

and provided a detailed description of the vehicle in which they were traveling.

Trooper William Leader testified at the suppression hearing that he and a colleague received information (ultimately derived from the investigator) that they were to look for a "red GM type pickup with New Mexico plates" headed eastbound on Interstate 80, that the vehicle had New Mexico license plate number 514 HMT, that there would be a male and a female in the vehicle, that the male was named Gonzales, and that there was a cell phone in the vehicle.

Trooper Leader also received information that the pickup was "escorting" another vehicle that had been stopped with a large quantity of marijuana. Trooper Leader thereafter identified and then stopped a vehicle headed eastbound on Interstate 80 that matched exactly the description that he had been given.

Sandra Carrion was driving, and Mr. Gonzales was the passenger. Trooper Leader asked for Ms. Carrion's driver's license and looked inside the vehicle, where he saw what he believed to be one marijuana cigarette on the passenger-side armrest. After asking Mr. Gonzales to exit the vehicle, Trooper Leader then saw what he believed to be two more marijuana cigarettes on the passenger-side armrest. Trooper Leader also saw a cell phone in the vehicle. Trooper Leader concluded that he had probable cause to arrest Mr. Gonzales and Ms. Carrion for their involvement in the distribution of controlled substances and therefore took them into custody.

Mr. Gonzales argues that Trooper Leader lacked reasonable suspicion for the initial stop, and that he had no probable cause justifying the arrest. Was there probable cause to arrest Gonzales? *See United States v. Gonzales*, 220 F.3d 922 (8th Cir. 2000).

3 On Saturday, April 10, 1999, Officer William Fuentes of the Union Township Police Department was in uniform, working off duty as a security guard at a local methadone clinic. He had performed this job on approximately fifty prior occasions and knew that the illegal sale of methadone was a constant problem, particularly on Saturdays when clinic patients received a bottle to take with them so that they would have a Sunday dosage. Fuentes had observed approximately thirty instances of illegal sales of methadone, although he did not specify over what period of time.

On the day in question, three of the clinic's patients told Fuentes there was a white male outside attempting to buy bottles of methadone. The officer knew each of these women from his work at the clinic, although he did not know their names. The third patient who approached him described the man attempting to purchase the drugs as a white male wearing a brown jacket, a plaid or "lumberjack" shirt, and blue jeans. She further said he had a "scruffy" appearance. This woman "continued on line, got medicated," and then accompanied Fuentes outside. She pointed out defendant, who was standing across the street. Defendant's appearance was consistent with the patient's description.

Fuentes approached defendant, who first tried to ignore the officer. As Fuentes got closer, defendant "was visibly nervous, shaking." In response to the officer's question, defendant denied attempting to purchase methadone. Fuentes informed defendant he was going to pat him down for his own safety. When he did so, he felt the distinctive shape of two methadone bottles in defendant's pocket. Defendant then admitted possessing the drugs. Defendant was not a clinic patient. The woman who had pointed out defendant left the area without Fuentes ever asking her name.

On these facts, the motion judge granted defendant's motion to suppress. The judge believed the officer was obligated to observe defendant in an effort to verify the information he received before approaching defendant, making inquiry of him and then patting him down. Was the motion judge correct? See *State v. Sibilia*, 750 A.2d 149 (N.J. Super. A.D. 2000).

4 On October 22, 1998, Secord took his car to a Firestone garage for servicing. While the car was being inspected and repaired, a Firestone mechanic, Gary Voit, noticed that one of the taillights was not working. Voit called Secord for permission to fix the light, and Secord agreed. To fix the taillight, Voit opened the car's hatchback and saw what he thought was a box of child pornography videotapes, as well as some soft-cover child pornography books. Voit showed his manager, Randy Petersen, and another employee, Timothy Hanlin, what he had found. They did not remove any of the materials from the car. Secord picked up his car later that afternoon.

On October 28, 1998, Sergeant Bernie Martinson of the Sex Crimes Unit of the Minneapolis Police Department received a phone call from a Hennepin County probation officer. The probation officer told Martinson that a friend who worked at the Firestone garage had told him about suspected child pornography in Secord's car. That same day, Martinson called the garage and talked to Peterson, who told him that while servicing Secord's car, several employees saw what they thought was child pornography in the car. Martinson also spoke with Hanlin, who gave a description of Secord and his clothes.

Based on this information, Martinson applied for and received a search warrant to search Secord's car and residence. Martinson executed the search warrant on October 29, 1998. He seized the box of videotapes and the soft-cover books from Secord's car.

Although some of the videotape titles suggested that they might be child pornography, none of them contained child pornography or photographic representations of sexual conduct involving minors within the meaning of the relevant statutes. The soft-cover books were not pornographic.

Martinson and another investigator also searched Secord's residence, where they seized pornographic tapes and magazines that did not contain child pornography or photographic representations of sexual conduct involving minors within the meaning of the relevant statutes. But Secord told the officers that he had used his computer to download "pictures of juveniles posing in sexual positions and having sex with adults." The officers seized the pictures.

Secord moved to suppress the materials seized from his residence on the grounds that the warrant was not supported by probable cause, did not establish a sufficient nexus to his residence to support a search of the residence, and contained misrepresentations. Should the motion to suppress be granted? See *State v. Secord*, 614 N.W.2d 227 (Minn. App. 2000).

5 On October 11, 1995, Detective Gary Lomenick of the Chattanooga Police Department received a tip from a CI (confidential informant) that a man called Red Dog, residing at 910 North Market Street, was in possession of cocaine. Red Dog was familiar to other officers, though not to Lomenick, as a person named Kenneth Allen— someone known to be involved with drugs. Based on the CI's information, Lomenick sought and obtained a search warrant that same day. The affidavit read in full as follows: I, Gary Lomenick, a duly sworn Chattanooga Police Officer, hereby apply for a search warrant and make oath as follows:

1. I am a sworn Chattanooga Police Officer with the Narcotics Division, where I have been assigned for over 15 years, and a commissioned Special Deputy Sheriff for Hamilton County, Tennessee.

2. On the 11th day of October 1995 I, Gary Lomenick, received information from an informant, a responsible and credible citizen of the county and state, who I know to be a responsible and credible citizen because, I have known said informant for 5 years and said informant has given me information about individuals involved in criminal activity in the past that has proven to be reliable. Said informant's name whom I have this day disclosed to the Judge to whom this application is made, that [sic] John Doe (Alias) Red Dog who resides in or occupies and is in possession of the following described premises 910 North Market Street, apartment directly underneath car-

port located in Chattanooga, Hamilton County Tennessee, unlawfully has in his possession on said premises legend and/or narcotic drugs including Cocaine in violation of law made and provided in such cases.

3. On the 11th day of October 1995 said informant advised me that said informant was on the premises of the said John Doe (Alias) Red Dog located at 910 North Market Street, apartment directly underneath carport within seventy-two hours prior to our conversation on October 11th, 1995 and while there saw Cocaine in possession of the said John Doe (Alias) Red Dog[.] WHEREFORE, as such officer acting in performance of my duty in the premises I pray that the Court issue a warrant authorizing the search of the said John Doe (Alias) Red Dog and the premises located at 910 North Market Street, apartment directly underneath the carport, for said legend and/or narcotic drugs including Cocaine and that such search be made either by day or by night.

Lomenick executed the warrant that day, with a team of other officers. When they approached the building, Allen, who was on a porch, saw them and fled inside. The officers gave chase. As Allen ran past a closet, the police heard a loud thump, and shortly thereafter found a 9-mm pistol on the floor of the closet. Allen left a trail of crack cocaine rocks behind him as he fled. When he was apprehended, more rocks of crack were found in his pockets, totaling 9.3 grams in all.

Allen was indicted on March 12, 1996. He was charged with (1) possession of cocaine base with intent to distribute, in violation of 21 U.S.C. § 841; (2) possession of a firearm in connection with a drug offense, in violation of 18 U.S.C. § 924(c); and (3) possession of a firearm by a convicted felon, in violation of 18 U.S.C. § 922(g). In a motion filed on April 18, 1996, he moved to suppress the evidence as illegally seized, alleging that the indictment was based on an insufficient affidavit, one that did not provide probable cause, because it did not claim or detail any expertise or previous reliability in narcotics contexts on the part of the CI. Should the motion to suppress be granted? See *United States v. Allen*, 211 F.3d 970 (6th Cir. 2000).

6 At the hearing on Cook's motion to suppress, Minneapolis Police Officer Michael Doran testified that on the morning of June 22, 1999, he received a telephone call from a CRI (confidential reliable informant). Doran had worked with this particular CRI in the past and had met him in person. The CRI had previously provided Doran and other officers known to Doran with information that had led to at least 12 other convictions. The CRI was paid for his information. To Doran's knowledge, the CRI had never given any false information.

In the two weeks prior to June 22, the CRI told Doran that a man named Shilow Cook was dealing crack cocaine in the Minneapolis area. In the June 22 phone call, the CRI told Doran that Cook was selling crack cocaine at the YMCA located at 34th and Blaisdell in Minneapolis, and that he had the crack cocaine in the waistband of his pants. The CRI further described Cook as a black male in his mid-forties, 5'6" tall, and weighing approximately 150 pounds. The CRI told Doran that Cook was wearing a red shirt, black pants, and a baseball cap. Finally, the CRI stated that Cook was driving a blue Lincoln with Minnesota license plate number 134PXH.

Within one hour, at approximately 11:30 A.M., Doran and other officers arrived at the YMCA. They saw a blue Lincoln with Minnesota license plate 134PXH parked in the lot. At approximately noon, the officers saw a man leave the YMCA. The man matched Cook's description as given by the CRI. The officers observed the man get into the driver's side of the blue Lincoln.

The officers approached the vehicle and placed the man under arrest. During a search, the officers found 7.2 grams of crack cocaine in the waistband of the man's pants and $1,186 in cash in his pockets. Cook was charged with a controlled substance crime in the second degree in violation of Minn. Stat. § 152.022, subd. 2(1) (1998) ("unlawfully possesses one or more mixtures of a total weight of six grams or more containing cocaine").

At the suppression hearing, Doran claimed that he did not obtain a search warrant prior to arresting Cook because there was insufficient time. Doran acknowledged that the CRI never indicated that he saw Cook selling drugs. Nor is there any evidence that the CRI ever claimed he had personally purchased drugs from Cook. Should the evidence be suppressed? See *State v. Cook*, 610 N.W.2d 664 (Minn. App. 2000).

4 Criminal Investigatory Search Warrants

Learning Objectives

▶ Know the general history of the development of the Fourth Amendment.

▶ Know how to obtain a search warrant, including the following: who issues search warrants; grounds for issuance; what may be seized; and how to describe the person or place to be searched and the things to be seized.

▶ Understand how triggering conditions affect the validity and execution of an anticipatory search warrant.

▶ Know how to execute a search warrant, including the following: who may execute a search warrant; when a search warrant may be executed, allowable delays, and how long the search may last; gaining entry to premises; authority to search persons not named in the warrant; allowable scope of the search and seizure; and duties after the search is completed.

▶ Understand the obligation of truthfulness in applying for search warrants and the consequences of having acted with reckless disregard for the truth.

▶ Explain the Rule 41 notice and inventory requirements and how those requirements might be altered by the rules covering covert entry and delayed notification.

▶ Understand the constitutional limits on the seizure of items found in a search.

▶ Understand the permissible scope of searching third parties and their belongings during the execution of a valid search.

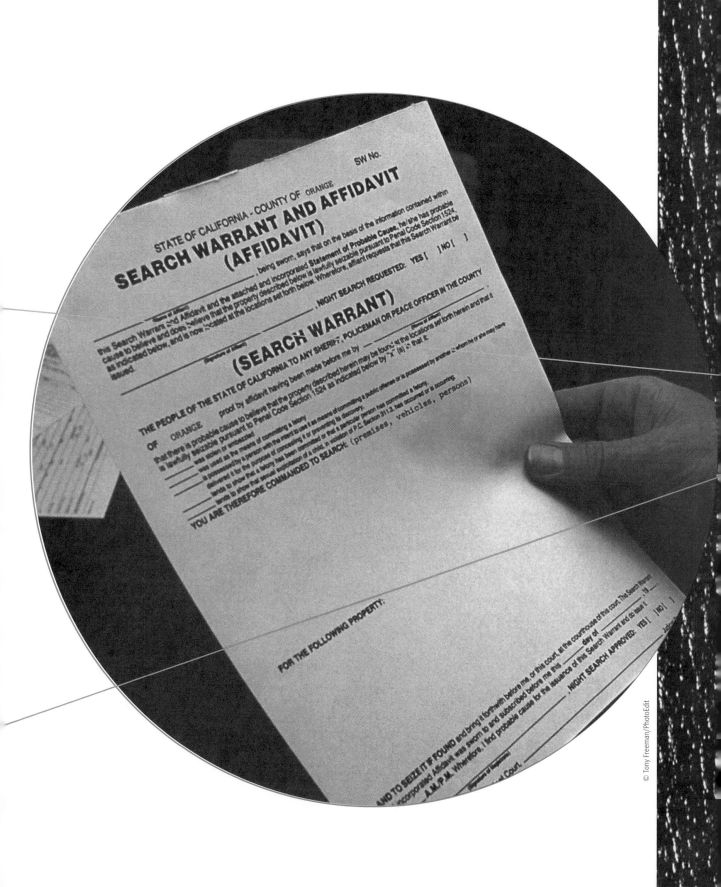

The law governing search warrants is based on guarantees in the Fourth Amendment to the U.S. Constitution:

> The right of the people to be secure in their persons, houses, papers and effects, against unreasonable searches and seizures, shall not be violated, and no Warrants shall issue, but upon probable cause, supported by Oath or affirmation, and particularly describing the place to be searched and the persons or things to be seized. U.S. Const., Amend. 4.

The Fourth Amendment to the Constitution was adopted in response to abuses of governmental search and seizure authority originating in England in the seventeenth and eighteenth centuries. The early development of legally authorized searches and seizures under English common law is somewhat obscure. It appears that search warrants were first used in cases involving stolen property. The use of warrants to recapture stolen goods became widespread and increasingly violated citizens' privacy.

Eventually, the use of warrants was extended to the enforcement of other laws. For example, in the eighteenth century, the government issued general warrants to enforce strict libel laws. A **general warrant** is one that fails to specify the person or place to be searched or the person or item to be seized, and that leaves the time and manner of the search to the discretion of the searching officer. Law enforcement officers abused these general warrants, and soon no person or property was free from unlimited search conducted at the whim of an officer on the mere suspicion that the person possessed literature critical of the king or others in high places. Despite their unpopularity with the citizenry, these abusive practices were transplanted to the American colonies. In the mid-eighteenth century, Parliament enacted legislation authorizing general searches, called *writs of assistance*, to be conducted against the colonists to enforce the Trade Acts. Writs of assistance authorized royal customs officers to search houses and ships at will to discover and seize smuggled goods or goods on which the required duties had not been paid. The colonists' strong reaction against the writs of assistance was one of the major causes of the American Revolution.

The experiences of the Founding Fathers with general warrants and writs of assistance caused them to insist on including in the basic charters of the states and nation suitable guarantees against unreasonable searches and seizures. A prohibition against searches conducted at the whim of a law enforcement officer without any restrictions on the person or place to be searched or the person or item to be seized was first embodied in the Virginia Bill of Rights, adopted in 1776. By the close of the Revolutionary War, most of the states had adopted similar provisions. The present Fourth Amendment to the Constitution, with its emphasis on the protection of warrants issued upon probable cause, was included in the Bill of Rights in 1791. Today, every state's constitution contains a similar provision.

Pursuant to the mandates of the plain text of the Fourth Amendment, the Supreme Court held in *Katz v. United States*, 389 U.S. 347, 357 (1967) that warrantless searches "are per se unreasonable under the Fourth Amendment subject only to a few specifically established and well-delineated exceptions." Accordingly, warrants play a very important role in criminal procedure. This chapter examines a broad array of matters concerning warrants for conducting searches of persons and places, as well as warrants authorizing the seizure of evidence. A **search** is generally defined as an examination or inspection of a location, vehicle, or person by a law enforcement officer for the purpose of locating objects or substances relating to or believed to relate to criminal activity. A **seizure** of property occurs when there is some meaningful interference with an individual's possessory interests in that property. *United States v. Jacobsen*, 466 U.S. 109, 113 (1984).

Courts analyze search and seizure issues in terms of violation of the right of privacy. They have expanded the definition of search to include any official intrusion into matters and activities about which a person has exhibited a reasonable expectation of privacy. As the text of the Fourth Amendment specifically states, searches and seizures by law enforcement officials require **probable cause**—a concept explored in great detail in Chapter 3.

APPLYING FOR SEARCH WARRANTS

> The point of the Fourth Amendment, which often is not grasped by zealous officers, is not that it denies law enforcement the support of the usual inferences which reasonable men draw from evidence. Its protection consists in requiring that those inferences be drawn by a neutral and detached magistrate instead of being judged by the officer engaged in the often competitive enterprise of ferreting out crime. Any assumption that evidence sufficient to support a magistrate's disinterested determination to issue a search warrant will justify the officers in making a search without a warrant would reduce the Amendment to a nullity and leave the people's homes secure only in the discretion of police officers. . . . When the right of privacy must reasonably yield to the right of search is, as a rule, to be decided by a judicial officer, not by a policeman or Government enforcement agent. *Johnson v. United States*, 333 U.S. 10, 13-14 (1948).

As the quotation above should make clear, search warrants issued by a neutral judicial officer are the preferred mechanism for authorizing and conducting searches and seizures, although several exceptions to the warrant requirement have been carved out over the years (see Part 3 of this book). A **search warrant** is (1) an order in writing, (2) issued by a proper judicial authority, (3) in the name of the people, (4) directed to a law enforcement officer, (5) commanding the officer to search for certain personal property, and (6) commanding the officer to bring that property before the judicial authority named in the warrant. A search warrant is similar to an arrest warrant, which is an order to take a person into custody and to bring the person before a proper judicial authority.

Law enforcement officers applying for search warrants must follow established laws and procedures. Otherwise, a magistrate will deny the application or a court will invalidate an illegally issued warrant. In either instance, valuable evidence may be lost to the prosecution. Search warrant procedures are set out in statutes, rules, and court decisions, and vary among different jurisdictions. This chapter summarizes and discusses the procedures common to most jurisdictions.

Who May Issue Search Warrants

Only judicial officers who have been specifically authorized to do so may issue search warrants. Most jurisdictions give this authority to judicial officers, such as clerks of court, magistrates, complaint justices, justices of the peace, and judges. The vesting of warrant-issuing power in a neutral and detached judicial officer stems from the Supreme Court's mandate that warrants can only be issued by people who are not involved in the "activities of law enforcement." *Shadwick v. City of Tampa*, 407 U.S. 345, 350 (1972).

Law enforcement officers need to know which judicial officers are authorized to issue search warrants in their jurisdictions. They may be different from the judicial officers authorized to issue arrest warrants. A search warrant issued by a person without authority has no legal effect, and a search made under such a warrant is illegal. For convenience, the term **magistrate** is used in this chapter to designate an official authorized to issue search warrants.

In *Shadwick v. City of Tampa*, 407 U.S. 345 (1972), the U.S. Supreme Court rejected the notion that all warrant authority must reside exclusively in a lawyer or judge, and upheld a city charter provision authorizing municipal court clerks to issue arrest warrants for municipal ordinance violations. The Court held that **"an issuing magistrate must meet two tests. He must be neutral and detached, and he must be capable of determining whether probable cause exists for the requested arrest or search."** 407 U.S. at 350. The clerk in *Shadwick* met these two tests because the clerk worked in the judicial branch of government as an employee assigned to a municipal court judge, and the process of determining probable cause for municipal violations was not very complicated. In contrast, *Coolidge v. New Hampshire*, 403 U.S. 443 (1971), held that a state attorney general—who, by his office, was also the state's chief investigator, and was later to be the chief prosecutor at trial—was not a neutral and detached judicial officer. The same holding would apply to any law enforcement officer or any other officials of the executive branch of government. *See United States v. U.S. Dist.Court*, 407 U.S. 297 (1972).

Shadwick, however, should not be read as permitting nonjudicial officers from authorizing the issuance of search warrants. For example, *United States v. Scott*, 260 F.3d 512, 515 (6th Cir. 2001), invalidated the issuance of a search warrant by a retired judge because he no longer held a judicial office and an active judge was available. But mere employment as a judicial official does not necessarily mean that a person is "neutral and detached." Consider that the U.S Supreme Court and a federal appellate court have held that the following persons were not sufficiently "neutral and detached" to issue warrants in spite of the fact that they held magistrate positions:

▶ An unsalaried magistrate who received a fee each time he issued a search warrant, but received nothing for denying a warrant application. *Connally v. Georgia*, 429 U.S. 245 (1977).

▶ A magistrate who participated in a search, helping officers determine what should be seized. *Lo-Ji Sales, Inc. v. New York*, 442 U.S. 319 (1979).

> ▶ A magistrate who also worked as a deputy jailer at a county jail who "stood to gain financially" when bookings and arrests were processed through her jail. *United States v. Parker*, 373 F.3d 770, 773-74 (6th Cir. 2004).

Grounds for Issuing Search Warrants

Before issuing a search warrant, a magistrate must have probable cause to believe that items subject to seizure are in a particular place or on a particular person at the time the warrant is issued. *See Warden v. Hayden*, 387 U.S. 294 (1967).

Establishing Probable Cause A law enforcement officer applying for a search warrant must supply the magistrate with the grounds for issuance of the warrant. This is usually accomplished by means of an **affidavit**, a written declaration or statement of facts sworn to before the magistrate. *See* FED. R. CRIM. P. 41(d). The person swearing-out an affidavit is referred to as the **affiant**. Figure 4.1 is a typical form for an affidavit for a search warrant. Several jurisdictions permit issuance of search warrants over the telephone or by e-mail or facsimile (FAX), but still require that the information provided by the affiant to the magistrate be taken under oath and recorded. For example, Rule 41(d)(3)(A) of the Federal Rules of Criminal Procedure authorizes the issuance of warrants "based on information communicated by telephone or other appropriate means, including facsimile transmission." Given, however, the strong preference for affidavits—and, indeed, the requirement of them in many jurisdictions—this chapter examines the probable cause inquiry as if a written affidavit were the exclusive vehicle for applying for a search warrant. Figures 4.2 and 4.3 illustrate the typical forms for search warrants, the first based on a traditional application supported by an affidavit, and the second based upon oral testimony.

Completeness of Affidavits All the information on which probable cause is based should be written in the affidavit. In *Whitely v. Warden*, 401 U.S. 560 (1971), *overruled on other grounds by Arizona v. Evans*, 514 U.S. 1 (1995), the Supreme Court made it clear that **"an otherwise insufficient affidavit cannot be rehabilitated by testimony concerning information possessed by the affiant when he sought the warrant but not disclosed to the issuing magistrate."** Nearly thirty U.S. jurisdictions are in accord with *Whitely*, insofar as they require that an affidavit contain *all* the information on which a magistrate is to base a finding of probable cause to issue a search warrant. *E.g., People v. Miller*, 75 P.3d 1108 (Colo. 2003), *cert. denied*, 541 U.S. 1082 (2004); *Valdez v. State*, 476 A.2d 1162 (Md. 1984). This forces law enforcement officers to think carefully about cases before applying for a warrant, and provides a complete record for reviewing courts to evaluate the magistrate's decision if the warrant is challenged. A minority of U.S. jurisdictions allow supplementation of a defective or incomplete affidavit by sworn oral testimony given before the magistrate. *E.g., State v. Hendricks*, 328 N.E.2d 822 (Ohio 1974).

Contents of Affidavits An affidavit for a search warrant should inform a magistrate (1) that a criminal offense has been or is being committed; and (2) that seizable evidence relating to that offense is in a particular place at a particular time.

▶Figure 4.1 **A TYPICAL AFFIDAVIT FOR A SEARCH WARRANT**

Number of Affidavits Only one sworn affidavit is necessary to obtain a search warrant. However, if multiple affidavits are submitted from several law enforcement officers, the judicial officer may review all of them and make a determination of probable cause based on the aggregate information contained in all affidavits submitted. *See United States v. Smith*, 499 F.2d 251 (7th Cir. 1974); *Blankenship v. State*, 527 S.W.2d 636 (Ark. 1975). If multiple affidavits are to be submitted, it is essential that they all be satisfactorily incorporated into the application for a

UNITED STATES DISTRICT COURT

District of _____

In the Matter of the Search of
(Name, address or brief description of person or property to be searched)

SEARCH WARRANT

Case Number: _____

TO: _____ and any Authorized Officer of the United States

Affidavit(s) having been made before me by _____ who has reason to believe

Affiant

that ☐ on the person of, or ☐ on the premises known as (name, description and/or location)

in the _____ District of _____ there is now
concealed a certain person or property, namely (describe the person or property)

I am satisfied that the affidavit(s) and any record testimony establish probable cause to believe that the person or property so described is now concealed on the person or premises above-described and establish grounds for the issuance of this warrant.

YOU ARE HEREBY COMMANDED to search on or before _____

Date

(not to exceed 10 days) the person or place named above for the person or property specified, serving this warrant and making the search ☐ in the daytime — 6:00 AM to 10:00 P.M. ☐ at anytime in the day or night as I find reasonable cause has been established and if the person or property be found there to seize same, leaving a copy of this warrant and receipt for the person or property taken, and prepare a written inventory of the person or property seized and promptly return this warrant to _____ as required by law.

U.S. Judge or Magistrate

at

_____ | _____
Date and Time Issued | City and State

_____ | _____
Name and Title of Judicial Officer | Signature of Judicial Officer

▶**Figure 4.2a** PAGE 1 OF A TYPICAL SEARCH WARRANT FORM

warrant in a sequential manner. The following procedure should ensure proper incorporation:

▶ Entitle the first or primary affidavit "Affidavit and Request for Search Warrant."

▶ Entitle all additional affidavits "Supplemental Affidavit 1," "Supplemental Affidavit 2," and so forth.

RETURN	Case Number:	
DATE WARRANT RECEIVED	DATE AND TIME WARRANT EXECUTED	COPY OF WARRANT AND RECEIPT FOR ITEMS LEFT WITH
INVENTORY MADE IN THE PRESENCE OF		
INVENTORY OF PERSON OR PROPERTY TAKEN PURSUANT TO THE WARRANT		

CERTIFICATION

I swear that this inventory is a true and detailed account of the person or property taken by me on the warrant.

_____

Subscribed, sworn to, and returned before me this date.

_____   _____
U.S. Judge or Magistrate   Date

▶ **Figure 4.2b PAGE 2 OF A TYPICAL SEARCH WARRANT FORM**

▶ Include the following statement in the first or primary affidavit: "This request is also based on the information in the sworn statements in Supplemental Affidavit 1, Supplemental Affidavit 2, . . . which are attached." (The law requires that clear reference be made to all supplemental affidavits.)

▶ Securely attach all supplemental affidavits to the primary affidavit. Use a stapler or other semi-permanent method of binding. A paper clip is unsatisfactory because it can easily slip off.

UNITED STATES DISTRICT COURT

District of _____

In the Matter of the Search of
(Name, address or brief description of person or property to be searched)

SEARCH WARRANT UPON ORAL TESTIMONY

Case Number:

TO: _____ and any Authorized Officer of the United States

Sworn oral testimony has been communicated to me by _____
Affiant

that ☐ on the person of, or ☐ on the premises known as (name, description and/or location)

in the _____ District of _____ there is now concealed a certain person or property, namely (describe the person or property)

I am satisfied that the circumstances are such as to make it reasonable to dispense with a written affidavit and that there is probable cause to believe that the property or person so described is concealed on the person or premises above described and that grounds for application for issuance of the search warrant exist as communicated orally to me in a sworn statement which has been recorded electronically, stenographically, or in long-hand and upon the return of the warrant, will be transcribed, certified as accurate and attached hereto.

YOU ARE HEREBY COMMANDED to search on or before _____
Date

the person or place named above for the person or property specified, serving this warrant and making the search ☐ in the day-time — 6:00 AM to 10:00 PM ☐ at anytime in the day or night as I find reasonable cause has been established and if the person or property be found there to seize same, leaving a copy of this warrant and receipt for the person or property taken, and prepare a written inventory of the person or property seized and promptly return this warrant to _____
U.S. Judge or Magistrate Judge
as required by law.

_____ at _____
Date and Time Issued   City and State

_____   _____
Name and Title of Judicial Officer   Signature of Judicial Officer

I certify that on _____ at _____
Date   Time

_____ orally authorized the
U.S. Judge or Magistrate Judge

issuance and execution of a search warrant conforming to all the foregoing terms.

_____   _____   _____
Name of affiant   Signature of affiant   Exact time warrant

▶**Figure 4.3 PAGE 1 OF A TYPICAL SEARCH WARRANT FORM BASED ON ORAL TESTIMONY**

By following these simple steps, the officer ensures that the magistrate will be simultaneously presented with all the information on which probable cause is to be based and that the appellate court will be able to effectively review the magistrate's decision.

Affidavits Must Be Sworn by Oath or Affirmation An affiant must swear or affirm that the information contained in the affidavit is true. Although no particular ceremony or form of swearing is mandated, it normally takes place face-to-face, between the affiant and the judicial officer. But face-to-face contact is not necessarily required (especially, for example, for telephonic warrants in which the affiant swears to tell the truth under penalty of perjury over the phone). However the swearing takes place, the procedures followed must be sufficient to allow criminal perjury charges to be filed against the affiant if any material allegation in the affidavit turns out to be false. *E.g., Simon v. State*, 515 P.2d 1161 (Okla. Crim. App.1973).

Sufficiency of Factual Allegations in Affidavits to Establish Probable Cause The factual allegations in an affidavit must persuade the magistrate that there is probable cause to issue the search warrant. The affiant must state the underlying facts and circumstances that, under the totality of the facts and circumstances, demonstrate **"a fair probability that contraband or evidence of a crime will be found in a particular place."** *Illinois v. Gates*, 462 U.S. 213, 238 (1983).

Recall from the discussion in Chapter 3 that there are many ways in which the facts and circumstances known to a law enforcement officer can establish probable cause. The knowledge of these facts and circumstances can come both from the affiant-officer's own senses as well as from what the affiant-officer learned from other police officers, informants, and witnesses who had personal knowledge based on what they perceived using their own senses. This knowledge typically includes one or more of the following:

▶ What officers viewed as a crime took place;

▶ What officers viewed as they examined a crime scene after-the-fact;

▶ What officers learned from interviewing victims and witnesses;

▶ What officers learned from credible and/or reliable informants (re-read the part of Chapter 3 devoted to the *Aguilar–Spinelli–Gates* line of cases);

▶ What officers learned from the observation and evaluation of real or physical evidence, including the results of scientific/forensic tests performed on such evidence; and

▶ What officers learned from observing or talking with a suspect, including:

  ▶ a suspect's flight;

  ▶ a suspect's furtive conduct;

  ▶ admissions made by a suspect;

  ▶ statements made by a suspect that contain false or implausible information;

  ▶ a suspect's presence at a crime scene;

  ▶ a suspect's presence in a high-crime area;

  ▶ a suspect's association with other known criminals; and

  ▶ a suspect's past criminal record.

Staleness Concerns Time is a very important factor in determining probable cause to search. The passage of time can render a search warrant void on the grounds of **staleness**. If the information on which probable cause was initially based becomes stale, there may no longer be good reason to believe that property is still at the same location:

> Staleness is not measured merely on the basis of the maturity of the information[, but also] in relation to (1) the nature of the suspected criminal activity (discrete crime or "regenerating conspiracy"), (2) the habits of the suspected criminal ("nomadic" or "entrenched"), (3) the character of the items to be seized ("perishable" or "of enduring utility"), and (4) the nature and function of the premises to be searched ("mere criminal forum" or "secure operational base"). *United States v. Bucuvalas*, 970 F.2d 937 (1st Cir. 1992).

The length of time that an item of property is likely to remain at a given location depends on the nature of the property, the nature of the criminal activity, the duration of the criminal activity, the criminal suspects, and many other factors. *United States v. Laury*, 985 F.2d 1293 (5th Cir. 1993), found probable cause to search a suspected bank robber's home for instrumentalities and evidence of the crime was not stale, even though nearly two months had passed since the date of the robbery. The affiant, an expert in bank robbery investigation, stated that bank robbers tend to keep evidence of the crime in their homes for as long as several years.

In contrast, in *United States v. Wagner*, 989 F.2d 69 (2d Cir. 1993), the information supporting probable cause to search the suspect's home was (1) a single small purchase of marijuana from the suspect in her home more than six weeks before the search; (2) a recorded statement of the suspect identifying her source for the marijuana; and (3) an unsubstantiated assertion that the suspect's home was owned by the source. These facts were insufficient for the court to find that the suspect engaged in continuing criminal activity in her home as a member of the source's drug distribution network. Because marijuana is the type of property that is likely to disappear or be moved, probable cause was found to be stale at the time the warrant was issued and the search was conducted. A similar finding of staleness occurred in *United States v. Helton*, 314 F.3d 812, 822 (6th Cir. 2003), in which allegations in an affidavit for a search warrant seeking stored drug money were based on a two-month-old report. The staleness finding resulted because "stacks of money" were unlikely to still be present after the passage of that much time.

Evidence of continuing crimes, especially white-collar crimes like fraud, is also likely to stay in one place for a long time. The U.S. Supreme Court found that business records of a fraudulent real estate scheme would probably remain at their location for an extended period of time after the business transactions had taken place:

> **The business records sought were prepared in the ordinary course of petitioner's business in his law office or that of his real estate corporation. It is eminently reasonable to expect that such records would be maintained in those offices for a period of time and surely as long as the three months required for the investigation of a complex real estate scheme.** *Andresen v. Maryland*, 427 U.S. 463, 479 n.9 (1976).

Other examples of continuing crimes are the cultivation and distribution of illegal drugs, *e.g.*, *United States v. Leasure*, 319 F.3d 1092 (9th Cir. 2003); gun control violations, *e.g.*, *United States v. Maxim*, 55 F.3d 394 (8th Cir. 1995); counterfeiting, *e.g.*, *United States v. Farmer*, 370 F.3d 435 (4th Cir. 2004); and the downloading of child pornography, *United States v. Chrobak*, 289 F.3d 1043, 1046 (8th Cir. 2002).

Truthfulness of Affidavit The information that a law enforcement officer swears to in an affidavit (or in live testimony) to establish probable cause for a warrant must be *"**truthful** in the sense that the information put forth is believed or appropriately accepted by the affiant as true."* *Franks v. Delaware*, 438 U.S. 154, 165 (1978). A law enforcement officer who intentionally or knowingly makes false statements in an application for a warrant clearly violates this requirement. But the rule on truthfulness is also violated if an officer swears to information with reckless disregard for the truth (i.e., disregarding a known risk that information may not be true even if the officer does not actually know the truth or falsity of the information). This rule is also violated if a law enforcement officer knowingly or recklessly omits material information from a warrant application. *United States v. Pace*, 898 F.2d 1218 (7th Cir. 1990). Any such violation of the truthfulness requirement due to a knowing or reckless misrepresentation or omission can serve as grounds for invalidating the warrant and for the evidence being deemed inadmissible under the Exclusionary Rule (see the section "Constitutionally Defective Warrants" later in this chapter).

Items Subject to Seizure Rule 41(c) of the Federal Rules of Criminal Procedure illustrates the types of property (and people) authorized to be seized under a search warrant:

(c) Persons or Property Subject to Search or Seizure—A warrant may be issued for any of the following:

(1) evidence of a crime;
(2) contraband, fruits of crime, or other items illegally possessed;
(3) property designed for use, intended for use, or used in committing a crime; or
(4) a person to be arrested or a person who is unlawfully restrained.

An affidavit for a search warrant should indicate, for each item of property sought in the warrant, the type of seizable property under which the item is classified according to the law of the jurisdiction. This informs the magistrate that the items sought are connected with criminal activity. The remainder of this chapter refers to items of property allowed to be seized under state or federal law as "items subject to seizure" or "seizable items" under Rule 41(c)(1)-(3); Chapter 6 deals with the search for and seizure of persons under Rule 41(c)(4).

Seizure Limited to Non-Testimonial Evidence Examples of items that may be seized under Rule 41(c) include clothing, blood, hair, fingerprints, money, weapons, drugs, computers, personal papers, and business records. Note that all of these examples are tangible items, not "testimonial evidence." Testimonial evidence may not be seized because the Fifth Amendment prevents witnesses from being compelled to testify against themselves. Non-testimonial evidence may be lawfully seized. Some physical items are clearly non-testimonial, but the legal status of some written items requires further explanation.

▶ **Personal Papers and Business Records** At one time, private personal papers and business records were assumed not subject to seizure under this limitation because of their supposed testimonial nature. *Andresen v. Maryland*,

427 U.S. 463 (1976), however, held that a seizure of personal papers or business records from persons under a search warrant does not necessarily compel those persons to be witnesses against themselves. The Court said that **"a party is privileged from producing the evidence, but not from its production."** 427 U.S. at 473. The defendant in *Andresen* was not compelled to be a witness against himself because he was not required to say or to do anything during the search. If, however, law enforcement authorities had attempted to subpoena the records, the defendant could have refused to give up the records by exercising his Fifth Amendment rights. The Court said:

> **[A]lthough the Fifth Amendment may protect an individual from complying with a subpoena for the production of his personal records in his possession because the very act of production may constitute a compulsory authentication of incriminating information, . . . a seizure of the same materials by law enforcement officers differs in a crucial respect—the individual against whom the search is directed is not required to aid in the discovery, production, or authentication of incriminating evidence.** 427 U.S. at 473-74.

▶ Bank Records Bank records have even less protection. *United States v. Miller*, 425 U.S. 435 (1976), held that a person's bank records are not private papers of the kind protected against compulsory production by the Fifth Amendment. By choosing to deal with a bank, people lose their expectation of Fourth Amendment protection against government investigation. **"The checks are not confidential communications but negotiable instruments to be used in commercial transactions. All of the documents obtained, including financial statements and deposit slips, contain only information voluntarily conveyed to the banks and exposed to their employees in the ordinary course of business."** 425 U.S. at 442. The *Miller* case concerned a subpoena; but either a search warrant or subpoena could be used to obtain a person's bank records without violating the Fifth Amendment right against compulsory self-incrimination. Note, however, that *Miller* does not automatically grant unrestricted access to bank records. Access may be restricted by state or federal statute.

Both *Andresen* and *Miller* highlight a basic principle regarding searches and seizures of papers: **"There is no special sanctity in papers, as istinguished from other forms of property, to render them immune from search and seizure, if only they fall within the scope of the principles of the cases in which other property may be seized, and if they be dequately described in the affidavit and warrant."** *Gouled v. United States*, 255 U.S. 298, 309 (1921). *How* the items are seized, however, is key to the legality of any seizure of personal papers or business records. Officers may *request* a suspect's assistance in seizing personal papers or business rcords, but may not *compel* the suspect's assistance in any way. Any compulsion would violate the defendant's Fifth Amendment rights and render the evidence inadmissible.

Seizure Must Aid in Particular Apprehension or Conviction Another limitation on the seizure of "evidence of a crime" is that it must aid in a particular apprehension or conviction. *Warden v. Hayden*, 387 U.S. 294, 306-07 (1967), stated the reason for this requirement:

> The requirements of the Fourth Amendment can secure the same protection of privacy whether the search is for "mere evidence" or for fruits, instrumentalities, or contraband. There must, of course, be a nexus—automatically provided in the case of fruits, instrumentalities, or contraband—between the item to be seized and criminal behavior. Thus, in the case of "mere evidence," probable cause must be examined in terms of cause to believe that the evidence sought will aid in a particular apprehension or conviction. In doing so, consideration of police purposes will be required.

Applying this logic, *Warden v. Hayden* upheld the seizure of clothing from a washing machine because the clothes matched the description of what a robber had been wearing. The police seizing the clothes reasonably believed that the clothes could help them identify the robber.

Particularity Requirement As the text of the Fourth Amendment makes clear, warrants must describe with **particularity** "the place to be searched and the persons or things to be seized."

Particular Description of the Place to Be Searched The affidavit supporting a request for a search warrant for a place must contain a description that points directly to a definitely ascertainable place to the exclusion of all others. *Steele v. United States*, 267 U.S. 498, 503 (1925), stated that "[i]t is enough if the description is such that the officer with a search warrant can with reasonable effort ascertain and identify the place intended."

The place to be searched need not be owned, occupied, or used by a particular suspect. A warrant may be issued for the search of the premises of a party who is not suspected of any crime. In *Zurcher v. The Stanford Daily*, 436 U.S. 547, 556 (1978), involving the search of newspaper offices, the U.S. Supreme Court said: "The critical element in a reasonable search is not that the owner of the property is suspected of crime but that there is reasonable cause to believe that the specific 'things' to be searched for and seized are located on the property to which entry is sought." *Zurcher* involved a warrant to search for photographs of demonstrators who had injured several police officers. (Note that the Privacy Protection Act (1980), 42 U.S.C. § 2000aa, provides extensive protection against searches and seizures of the communications media, unless there is probable cause to believe that the party in possession of the items is involved in the crime being investigated.)

▶ **Specific Addresses** A *correct* street address, especially in urban and suburban areas, is sufficient to identify the place to be searched because it allows the officers who will be executing the warrant to "locate the premises with reasonable effort, and (2) to be sure that the wrong premises are not mistakenly searched." *United States v. Dancy*, 947 F.2d 1232, 1234 (5th Cir. 1991); *United States v. Johnson*, 944 F.2d 396 (8th Cir.1991). But because mistakes can be made with regard to street address numbers (e.g., numbers may be inadvertently omitted or transposed), affidavits should include detailed descriptions of the place to be searched to help ensure that the particularity requirement is satisfied. *See, e.g., United States v. Lora-Solano*, 330 F.3d 1288 (10th Cir. 2003). For example, in *United States v. Turner*, 770

F.2d 1508, 1509-10 (9th Cir. 1985), the affidavit for search warrant and the search warrant itself described the house as follows:

> 2762 Mountain View, Escondido, California, and further described as a beige two-story stucco and adobe house with an attached two-car garage. The garage has entry doors on either side of a large garage door. The entry door located on the south side of the garage door has a brass-plated deadbolt lock installed. On the south side of this door are two windows covered by tinfoil. The doors and trim of the house are painted brown. The entry to the residence is located on the south side of the residence and the garage entry faces west. The driveway to the residence off of Mountain View Drive leads north from Mountain View Drive and is marked by three mailboxes numbered 2800, 2810 and 2756. This driveway leads past these three residences, the last identified by a residence marker of 2756, D.A. Mieir. The driveway then turns to concrete and dead ends at the 2762 Mountain View Drive residence. There is a farm road leading past 2762 Mountain View Drive and into an avocado grove. The driveway leads north from Mountain View Drive. Entry to the 2762 Mountain View Drive residence is located on the south side.

The description of the house was correct except for the street number. The house that the agents had under surveillance, intended to search, and actually did search was 2800 Mountain View Drive. Number 2762 Mountain View Drive was located approximately two-tenths of a mile away in a location that the agents did not know existed, and it did not resemble the description of the suspect house. The court held that the description in the search warrant was sufficiently particular despite the wrong street address:

> The verbal description contained in the warrant described the house to be searched with great particularity; no nearby house met the warrant's detailed description; the address in the warrant was reasonable for the location intended; the house had been under surveillance before the warrant was sought; the warrant was executed by an officer who had participated in applying for the warrant and who personally knew which premises were intended to be searched; and the premises that were intended to be searched were those actually searched. Under these circumstances, there was virtually no chance that the executing officer would have any trouble locating and identifying the premises to be searched, or that he would mistakenly search another house. 770 F.2d at 1511.

When additional, particularized information like that provided in *Lora-Solano* is not included in an affidavit, then a mistaken address can serve as the basis for invalidating a warrant. *See United States v. Thomas*, 263 F.3d 805 (8th Cir. 2001).

▶ **Descriptions without Addresses** When a specific address is unknown, affidavits must be particularly detailed in describing the location of premises to be searched. Merely using some general description of the location of property may not be sufficient to meet the particularly requirement of the Fourth Amendment. For example, in *United States v. Ellis*, 971 F.2d 701 (11th Cir. 1992), the warrant described the place to be searched as the "third mobile home on the north side" without any further description of its physical characteristics or mention of its occupant's name. The court found the description insufficiently particular.

The location of rural property is sometimes more difficult to describe, but may be easier to locate. Therefore, a description of a farm or other rural property by the owner's name, the dwelling's color and style, and general directions will usually suffice. *Gatlin v. State*, 559 S.W.2d 12 (Ark. 1977).

▶ **Descriptions of Multiple-Occupancy Dwellings** When the place to be searched is a multiple-occupancy dwelling, such as an apartment house, hotel, or rooming house, the affidavit must go beyond merely stating the location of the premises. In *Manley v. Commonwealth*, 176 S.E.2d 309 (Va. 1970), the affidavit on which the warrant was based described the place to be searched as "313 West 27th Street, a dwelling. The apartment of Melvin Lloyd Manley." The court held that the defendant's apartment was sufficiently described for the searching officers to locate it with very little effort:

> It has been generally held that a search warrant directed against a multiple-occupancy structure is invalid if it fails to describe the particular sub-unit to be searched with sufficient definiteness to preclude search of other units located in the larger structure and occupied by innocent persons. But there are exceptions to the general rule. Even though a search warrant against a multiple-occupancy structure fails to describe the particular sub-unit to be searched, it will ordinarily not be held invalid where it adequately specifies the name of the occupant of the sub-unit against which it is directed and provides the searching officers with sufficient information to identify, without confusion or excessive effort, such apartment unit. 176 S.E.2d at 314.

Similarly, *United States v. Strother*, 318 F.3d 64, 69-70 (1st Cir. 2003), held that a warrant was sufficiently particular even though it did not specify an apartment number because a reliable informant had identified the suspect's residence as the apartment on the first floor and the U.S. Postal Service confirmed that the suspect lived in the building described.

In contrast to *Manley* and *Strother,* when affidavits contain errors without additional supporting information that helps particularize the place to be searched, courts may invalidate a search warrant. *Jacobs v. City of Chicago*, 215 F.3d 758, 767-77 (7th Cir. 2000), for example, invalidated a warrant as insufficiently particular because the affidavit incorrectly described an apartment building as being a single family residence. Therefore, *whenever possible, an affidavit in support of a warrant to search premises located in multiple-occupancy dwellings should always include information such as room number, apartment number, building, and floor.* If necessary, a diagram showing the location should be attached to the affidavit. Doing so should allow a reviewing court to come to the same conclusion that was reached in *United States v. Darensbourg*, 520 F.2d 985, 987 (5th Cir. 1975), another case involving a multiple-occupancy dwelling. In *Darensbourg,* the description in the warrant of the place to be searched (a four-building apartment complex) gave an incorrect street address, but correctly stated the apartment number. Because there was only one apartment with that number in the entire complex, the court held that the description was sufficient:

> [T]he determining factor as to whether a search warrant describes the premises to be searched with sufficient particularity is not whether the description is technically accurate in every detail but rather whether the description is sufficient to enable the executing officer to locate and identify the premises with

reasonable effort, and whether there is any reasonable probability that another premises might be mistakenly searched which is not the one intended to be searched under the search warrant. 520 F.2d at 987.

Of course, if another apartment had the same number in one of the different buildings in the complex at issue in *Darensbourg,* then the warrant would have been invalidated. This fact should emphasize the need for police-affiants to be as particular as possible. To obtain sufficiently descriptive information, officers may need to view the premises, examine floor plans, or make inquiries of landlords, tenants, or others to determine the correct limits of the place to be searched. *Maryland v. Garrison,* 480 U.S. 79, 85 (1987), held that "[t]he validity of the warrant must be assessed on the basis of the information that the officers disclosed, or had a duty to discover and to disclose, to the issuing magistrate." If an officer is diligent in gathering the descriptive information of the place to be searched, the warrant will be valid even though hindsight reveals that honest mistakes were made.

▶ **Descriptions of Motor Vehicles** Unless one or more of the established warrant exceptions for the search of a motor vehicle apply (see Chapter 11), a warrant is required to search a motor vehicle. Because vehicles are considered "places," for search and seizure purposes, an affidavit must describe the vehicle to be searched with sufficient particularity that it can be located with reasonable certainty. Some courts hold that only the license plate number is necessary to sufficiently describe a motor vehicle for purposes of issuance of a warrant. "A vehicle search warrant ordinarily should include the license plate number on its face, but when this is not practicable a detailed description of the vehicle or a narrow geographical limit to the search may provide the requisite check on police discretion." *United States v. Vaughn,* 830 F.2d 1185 (D.C. Cir. 1987). To avoid any problems with the particularity requirement, a detailed description of a motor vehicle to be searched should include information such as the make, body style, color, year, location, and owner or operator of the vehicle.

▶ **Descriptions of Domestic Mail** In *United States v. Ramsey,* 431 U.S. 606 (1977), the U.S. Supreme Court held that international mail can be searched without a warrant under the border exception to the Fourth Amendment (see border searches in Chapter 5). Domestic mail, on the other hand, is considered a "place" for search and seizure purposes. Domestic mail is considered to be any letter or package traveling wholly within the United States. For more than a century, courts have ruled that first-class domestic mail may not be lawfully opened without a warrant. *See Ex Parte Jackson,* 96 U.S. 727 (1878). The affidavit for a warrant to search first-class domestic mail must describe the mail with particularity, just as for places, persons, and vehicles.

▶ **Descriptions of E-mail** E-mail has become a common form of communication. E-mail, like first-class domestic mail, is protected by the Fourth Amendment because senders of electronic communications have a reasonable expectation that their messages will remain private "until the transmissions are received." *United States v. Maxwell,* 45 M.J. 406, 418 (C.A.A.F. 1996). Thus, Internet service providers, although conduits for e-mail transmissions, may not disclose e-mails to law enforcement personnel without a warrant that describes, with particularity, the specific e-mails that are the targets of the criminal investigation. When an affidavit does so, and therefore complies with the particularity requirement, federal law allows for nationwide searches of both opened and unopened e-mail that may be stored on the servers of Internet service providers. *See* 18 U.S.C. § 2703. Under the provisions of the USA PATRIOT Act, such a warrant may be issued:

> [B]y any court that is a court of competent jurisdiction [so long as the affidavit] offers specific and articulable facts showing that there are reasonable grounds to believe that the contents of a wire or electronic communication, or the records or other information sought, are relevant and material to an ongoing criminal investigation. 18 U.S.C. § 2703(d).

Particular Description of a Person to Be Searched A magistrate may issue a search warrant to search a particular person for particular items of evidence, although such warrants are much rarer than warrants authorizing the search of particular places because the more common procedure is to arrest a person and conduct a search incident to arrest (see Chapter 8). If, however, a warrant to search a person is desired, the affidavit in support of that warrant must describe the person to be searched with sufficient particularity to enable identification with reasonable certainty. *Williams v. Comm.*, 261 S.W.2d 416 (Ky. 1953). Even though a person's name is unknown or incorrectly stated, a warrant may be valid if it includes the person's weight, height, age, race, clothing, address, and any aliases. *United States v. Ferrone*, 438 F.2d 381 (3d Cir. 1971); *State v. Tramantano*, 260 A.2d 128 (Conn. Super. 1969). The question is whether the description enables the searching officer to locate and identify the person with reasonable effort.

The U.S. Constitution places substantive limits to how far a search of a person can go before the search becomes "unreasonable" for Fourth Amendment purposes or violates due process under the Fifth or Fourteenth Amendments. Some searches and seizures on a person are clearly permissible in light of their minimal invasiveness so long as they are supported by probable cause, like seizing a hair sample by plucking it; swabbing someone's mouth for a DNA sample; and scraping under someone's fingernail for biological evidence. *See, e.g., In re Will County Grand Jury*, 604 N.E.2d 929, 936 (Ill. 1992) (plucking hair); *Rise v. Oregon*, 59 F.3d 1556 (9th Cir. 1995) (DNA sample); *Cupp v. Murphy*, 412 U.S. 291 (1973) (fingernail scrapings). Other searches and seizures that are more invasive of the human body have also been upheld as permissible intrusions. The leading case in this area is *Schmerber v. California*, 384 U.S. 757 (1966), which held that an intrusive search and seizure to obtain a sample of a drunk-driving suspect's blood was constitutionally permissible because (1) the process was a reasonable one performed in a reasonable manner (in *Schmerber*, blood was taken from a person arrested for drunk driving by a physician in a hospital environment according to accepted medical practices); and (2) there was a clear indication in advance that the evidence sought would be found (in *Schmerber*, the arrestee had glassy, bloodshot eyes and the smell of alcohol emanated from his breath). Although searches in *Schmerber* and *Cupp* were not authorized by warrants because the relevant evidence (alcohol in the blood, fingernail scrapings) may have disappeared by the time a warrant was obtained, when there is sufficient time, officers should secure a warrant before conducting an intrusive search on or into a suspect's body. This is especially the case when the suspect has not been arrested. (See Chapter on 8 for further discussion of this topic.)

Some searches, however, can go too far. *Rochin v. California*, 342 U.S. 165 (1952), held that the forcible pumping of a suspect's stomach for the purpose of seizing and analyzing the stomach contents was constitutionally impermissible. However, *Rochin* was decided on due process grounds before *Schmerber*. Even so, the spirit of *Rochin* was evident in *Winston v. Lee*, 470 U.S. 753 (1985), a case that examined the question of surgical intervention under the Fourth Amendment reasonableness inquiry adopted in *Schmerber*.

> **The reasonableness of surgical intrusions beneath the skin depends on a case-by-case approach, in which the individual's interests in privacy and security are weighed against society's interests in conducting the procedure. In a given case, the question whether the community's need for evidence outweighs the substantial privacy interests at stake is a delicate one admitting of few categorical answers.** 470 U.S. at 760.

Applying this balancing test, the Supreme Court unanimously determined that a surgical operation to remove a bullet from a suspect's chest, even though authorized by a search warrant, was too intrusive to be reasonable under the Fourth Amendment in light of the dangers of surgery under general anesthesia. The same result was reached in *United States v. Garcia-Ortiz*, 261 F. Supp. 2d 56 (D.P.R. 2003), in which a court refused to order the removal of a bullet from a defendant. In contrast, however, the administration of a laxative to cause a suspect to pass what law enforcement officers had probable cause to believe was a bag of heroin was upheld in *State v. Payano-Roman*, 714 N.W.2d 548 (Wis. 2006), because the nature of the invasion into the body was less intrusive than surgery and posed much less risk to the suspect.

Particular Description of Items to Be Seized The affidavit supporting a request for a search warrant must contain a particular description of the items to be seized:

> **The requirement that warrants shall particularly describe the things to be seized makes general searches under them impossible and prevents the seizure of one thing under a warrant describing another. As to what is to be taken, nothing is left to the discretion of the officer executing the warrant.** *Marron v. United States*, 275 U.S. 192, 196 (1927).

In general, the items to be seized must be described with sufficient particularity so that the officer executing the warrant (1) can identify the items with reasonable certainty, and (2) is left with no discretion as to which property is to be taken. The primary concern of courts evaluating descriptions of things to be seized in search warrants is to ensure that a person will not be deprived of lawfully possessed property by a seizure made under an imprecise warrant.

A description of items merely as "stolen goods," "obscene materials," or "other articles of merchandise too numerous to mention" is inadequate because it is imprecise. *Marcus v. Search Warrant*, 367 U.S. 717 (1961).

When an item can be described in detail, all available information about it should be included in the affidavit. For example, number, size, color, weight, condition, brand name, serial number, and other distinguishing features of an item to be seized should be a part of the description where applicable. The affidavit should also indicate how the item is connected with criminal activity by stating the category of items subject to seizure within which the item falls.

▶ **When Specificity Cannot Be Achieved** A more general description is allowed when specificity is impossible or very difficult. For example, in a case involving the robbery of a post office, the court found sufficiently specific a warrant directing the seizure of "a variety of items, including 'currency' and 'United States postage stock (stamps; envelopes; checks).'" The court said:

> At the time of the application and issuance of the warrant in the instant case, a more precise description of the stamps and currency taken during the robbery was unascertainable. Although the postal inspectors knew that stamps and currency had been stolen, no further information was available to more particularly describe the items in the warrant. We find that the description of the stamps and currency by generic classes was reasonably specific under the circumstances of this case. *United States v. Porter*, 831 F.2d 760, 764 (8th Cir. 1987).

▶ **Large Numbers of Indistinguishable Comman Items** A more general description may also be allowed when a large number of items to be seized are of a common nature and not readily distinguishable. In a case involving a stolen shipment of women's clothing, a search warrant authorized the seizure of "[c]artons of women's clothing, the contents of those cartons, lists identifying the contents of the cartons, and control slips identifying the stores intended to receive these cartons, such items being contraband and evidence of a violation of Title 18, United States Code, Section 659, Possession of Goods Stolen from Interstate Shipments." The court said:

> We recognize . . . that the overriding principle of the Fourth Amendment is one of reasonableness and on occasion have accepted general descriptions in warrants, holding that such descriptions are not always constitutionally infirm. . . . Such general descriptions are permissible only in "special contexts in which there [is] substantial evidence to support the belief that the class of contraband [is] on the premises and in practical terms the goods to be described [can] not be precisely described." In *United States v. Klein*, 565 F.2d 183 (1st Cir. 1977), we set forth two tests which in particular circumstances may help to illuminate whether this principle is satisfied: first, the degree to which the evidence presented to the magistrate establishes reason to believe that a large collection of similar contraband is present on the premises to be searched, and, second, the extent to which, in view of the possibilities, the warrant distinguishes, or provides the executing agents with criteria for distinguishing, the contraband from the rest of an individual's possessions. *United States v. Fuccillo*, 808 F.2d 173, 176 (1st Cir. 1987) (internal citations omitted).

The court in *Fuccillo* found that government agents could have but did not obtain specific information that would have enabled the agents executing the search to differentiate contraband cartons of women's clothing from legitimate ones. The warrants were invalidated for failure to specify as nearly as possible the distinguishing characteristics of the goods to be seized.

▶ **Fradulent Business Records** Courts also allow a relaxation of the particularity requirement for search warrants seeking business records of businesses "permeated with fraud":

[W]here there is probable cause to believe that a business is "permeated with fraud," either explicitly stated in the supporting affidavit or implicit from the evidence therein set forth, a warrant may authorize the seizure of all documents relating to the suspected criminal area but may not authorize the seizure of any severable portion of such documents relating to legitimate activities. *United States v. Oloyede*, 982 F.2d 133, 141 (4th Cir. 1991).

▶ **Contraband** Courts generally allow greater leeway in descriptions of contraband material. For example, in *United States v. Spears*, 965 F.2d 262 (7th Cir. 1992), the warrant authorized a search for and seizure of "controlled substances and other drug-related paraphernalia, and materials for packaging controlled substances." The court held:

> The terms "controlled substances" and "materials for packaging controlled substances" are sufficiently specific on their face. The catch-all term "other drug-related paraphernalia" also passes constitutional muster in that such items are easily identifiable and quickly found by drug law enforcement officers. A search warrant delineating those items generally, in combination with named contraband, sufficiently limits an officer's discretion to execute the warrant. 965 F.2d at 277.

United States v. Appoloney, 761 F.2d 520, 524 (9th Cir. 1985), similarly upheld a warrant that used the following description: "'wagering paraphernalia' such as betting slips, bottom sheets and owe sheets, and journals and schedules of sporting events." *Andresen v. Maryland*, 427 U.S. 463 (1976), similarly permitted the use of the "catch-all" phrase: "together with other fruits, instrumentalities and evidence of crime at this [time] unknown." The warrant's validity was upheld because the underlying crime, a complex fraud case, depended on evidence that police had diligently described in the warrant that they thought they would find on the premises, as well as other evidence about which they could not know until the search was completed.

In contrast, however, a general description is usually not allowed if a more specific description is possible. In *United States v. Townsend*, 394 F. Supp. 736 (E.D. Mich. 1975), a search warrant commanded the seizure of "Stolen firearms, app. ten (10), which are stored in the basement of the above location, and in bedrooms, and any and all other stolen items, contraband." The court held that the phrase "any and all other stolen items" was impermissibly vague. The court also found the phrase "10 firearms" to be constitutionally deficient.

> Firearms may be easily characterized by color, length, type, and other defining attributes. Therefore, further description in the instant case is far from a "virtual impossibility," and the generic description in combination with the other defects in particularity, constitutes a violation of defendant's Fourth Amendment Guarantee. 394 F. Supp. at 747.

General descriptions are also not allowed if the contraband to be searched for and seized are books, films, recordings, or other materials that have not yet been adjudged obscene. Because these materials are presumed protected by the First Amendment, a very high degree of particularity is required in both the affidavit and the warrant:

> [T]he constitutional requirement that warrants must particularly describe the 'things to be seized' is to be accorded the most scrupulous exactitude when

the 'things' are books, and the basis for their seizure is the ideas which they contain. . . . No less a standard could be faithful to First Amendment freedoms." *Stanford v. Texas*, 379 U.S. 476, 485-86 (1965).

In *Lo-Ji Sales, Inc. v. New York*, 442 U.S. 319, 325 (1979), a magistrate viewed two films from the defendant's adult bookstore, concluded they were obscene, and issued a warrant authorizing the seizure of all other obscene materials. The Court held that the warrant was a prohibited general warrant.

> [T]he warrant left it entirely to the discretion of the officials conducting the search to decide what items were likely obscene and to accomplish their seizure. The Fourth Amendment does not permit such action. . . . Nor does the Fourth Amendment countenance open-ended warrants, to be completed while a seizure is being conducted and items seized or after the seizure has been carried out." 442 U.S. at 325.

On the other hand, *United States v. Koelling*, 992 F.2d 817 (8th Cir. 1993), found a warrant authorizing a search for child pornography materials sufficiently particular in a case in which the warrant quoted the statute that particularly described the sexually explicit conduct depicted in the materials that was prohibited. Key to what differentiated this case from *Stanford v. Texas* and *Lo-Ji Sales* and cases in their progeny was the fact that the First Amendment does not protect materials depicting child pornography. *See Osborne v. Ohio*, 495 U.S. 103 (1990).

▶ **Electronically Stored Data** The law concerning the particularity of warrants authorizing searches of computer hard drives and the seizure of files contained on them is in a constant state of evolution as computer forensic techniques similarly evolve. For a while, some courts, perhaps due to a lack of technological savvy, seemed to minimize the importance of the particularity requirement when upholding general searches of computers; some courts still use this approach. Consider the following two cases, both decided by courts in the same year, yet reaching different results.

In *United States v. Upham*, 168 F.3d 532 (1st Cir. 1999) a search warrant was issued for "any and all computer software and hardware, computer disks, disk drives . . . [and] any and all visual depictions, in any format or media, of minors engaging in sexually explicit conduct." The Court held that the description of the items to be seized was not constitutionally overly broad:

> As a practical matter, the seizure and subsequent off-premises search of the computer and all available disks was about the narrowest definable search and seizure reasonably likely to obtain the images. A sufficient chance of finding some needles in the computer haystack was established by the probable-cause showing in the warrant application; and a search of a computer and co-located disks is not inherently more intrusive than the physical search of an entire house for a weapon or drugs. We conclude . . . that the first paragraph was not unconstitutionally overbroad.
>
> Of course, if the images themselves could have been easily obtained through an onsite inspection, there might have been no justification for allowing the seizure of all computer equipment, a category potentially including equipment that contained no images and had no connection to

> the crime. But it is no easy task to search a well-laden hard drive by going through all of the information it contains, let alone to search through it and the disks for information that may have been "deleted." The record shows that the mechanics of the search for images later performed off site could not readily have been done on the spot. 168 F3d at 535.

In contrast, *United States v. Carey*, 172 F.3d 1268, 1270 (10th Cir. 1999), concerned a warrant authorizing a search of files on a computer "for names, telephone numbers, ledger receipts, addresses, and other documentary evidence pertaining to the sale and distribution of controlled substances." When no evidence was found by searching the computer's hard drive using certain keywords such as "money, accounts, [and] people," the investigating officer began looking through the file directories on the computer when he came across a graphical image file in ".jpg" format, which he then opened and saw an image of child pornography. 172 F.3rd at 1271. The officer then searched over 200 more images for evidence of child pornography before returning to his initial task of searching for evidence of involvement in the illicit drug business. When facing child pornography charges, the defendant moved to suppress the evidence because "the search constituted general rummaging in 'flagrant disregard' for the terms of the warrant and in violation of the Fourth Amendment." 172 F.3d 1272. The court sided with the defendant and invalidated the search because it went beyond the scope of what the search warrant authorized. The warrant authorized a search of the computer for "names, telephone numbers, ledgers, receipts, addresses, and other documentary evidence pertaining to the sale and distribution of controlled substances," not graphics files. Moreover, the court rejected the application of the plain view doctrine to the search (see Chapter 10) to all but the very first picture that was inadvertently opened by the investigating officer because each time the officer opened a .jpg graphics file after the first one, he expected to find child pornography and not material related to drugs.

In the years since *Upham* and *Carey* were decided, the U.S. Department of Justice has recommended a new set of practices to ensure compliance with the particularity requirement of the Fourth Amendment. The federal government recommends that an affidavit should not only list "the specific hardware to be seized and searched," but also to explain "the techniques that will be used to search only for the specific files related to the investigation, and not every file on the computer" (Jekot, 2007: ¶ 2, citing U.S. Department of Justice, 2002: Part II.C.3). Thus, an affidavit to search a computer should specify the crimes for which evidence is being sought; the reasons why there is probable cause to believe the computer will contain such evidence; the dates and/or time frames that are relevant to the investigation; and a relevant search strategy in practical, nontechnical terms to ensure that the search does not become a general rummaging expedition as opposed to one with particularly defined parameters. (U.S. Dep't Justice, 2002: Part II.C.1.b). As of this writing, courts have not *required* that affidavits in support of search warrants comply with the Department of Justice's recommendation to include specific search strategies. However, as the law of computer forensics continues to evolve, a requirement of search strategies may well become commonplace. It is therefore highly advisable that search strategies be included in affidavits in support of warrants to search computers and seize the digitally stored data they contain (see Jekot, 2007).

Anticipatory Search Warrants

An **anticipatory search warrant**, also called a prospective search warrant, is a "search warrant based on an affidavit showing probable cause that evidence of a certain crime (such as illegal drugs) will be located at a specific place in the future" (Black's Law Dictionary, 2004: 1379). In *United States v. Grubbs*, 547 U.S. 90 (2006), the U.S. Supreme Court upheld the constitutionality of anticipatory search warrants under the Fourth Amendment. The Court found that anticipatory warrants are, at least in principle, no different from regular search warrants. The only real difference between anticipatory search warrants and regular warrants is that anticipatory warrants are dependent upon some triggering condition. So long as there is reliable evidence that the triggering event will take place, and assuming that the other requirements of valid warrants are met (i.e., the warrant is particularized and not otherwise defective), then the fact that "contraband has not yet reached the premises to be searched at the time the warrant issues is not, in constitutional terms, an insuperable obstacle." *United States v. Ricciardelli*, 998 F.2d 8, 11 (1st Cir. 1993).

Triggering Conditions A **triggering condition** is a condition precedent, other than the passage of time, which will establish probable cause to conduct a search and/or seizure. The Supreme Court explained in *Grubbs* how a triggering condition operates to establish probable cause.

> Anticipatory warrants . . . require the magistrate to determine (1) that it is *now probable* that (2) contraband, evidence of a crime, or a fugitive *will be* on the described premises (3) when the warrant is executed. It should be noted, however, that where the anticipatory warrant places a condition (other than the mere passage of time) upon its execution, the first of these determinations goes not merely to what will probably be found *if* the condition is met. (If that were the extent of the probability determination, an anticipatory warrant could be issued for every house in the country, authorizing search and seizure *if* contraband should be delivered—though for any single location there is no likelihood that contraband will be delivered.) Rather, the probability determination for a conditioned anticipatory warrant looks also to the likelihood that the condition will occur, and thus that a proper object of seizure will be on the described premises. In other words, for a conditioned anticipatory warrant to comply with the Fourth Amendment's requirement of probable cause, two prerequisites of probability must be satisfied. It must be true not only that *if* the triggering condition occurs "there is a fair probability that contraband or evidence of a crime will be found in a particular place," but also that there is probable cause to believe the triggering condition *will occur*. The supporting affidavit must provide the magistrate with sufficient information to evaluate both aspects of the probable-cause determination. 547 U.S. at 96-97 (italics in original) (internal citations omitted).

To summarize: (1) there must be a fair probability that specific contraband will be found if the triggering event occurs; and (2) there must be a fair probability to believe that the triggering condition will, in fact, occur.

The facts of the *Grubbs* case illustrate how a triggering condition operates to establish probable cause. The defendant in *Grubbs* had ordered a videotape containing child pornography from the Internet. Unbeknownst to him, the web site from which he ordered the video was run by an undercover U.S. postal inspector. Investigators arranged for a "controlled delivery" of the videotape so that the timing of its arrival at the defendant's home would be coordinated with law enforcement authorities. In an affidavit applying for an anticipatory search warrant, a postal inspector included the following triggering condition language:

> Execution of this search warrant will not occur unless and until the parcel has been received by a person(s) and has been physically taken into the residence. . . . At that time, and not before, this search warrant will be executed by me and other United States Postal inspectors, with appropriate assistance from other law enforcement officers in accordance with this warrant's command. 547 U.S. at 92.

The warrant was issued by a federal magistrate judge. When the package was delivered and taken into the defendant's home, the postal inspector executed the warrant. In upholding the validity of the anticipatory search warrant, the Court wrote:

> **In this case, the occurrence of the triggering condition—successful delivery of the videotape to Grubbs' residence—would plainly establish probable cause for the search. In addition, the affidavit established probable cause to believe the triggering condition would be satisfied. Although it is possible that Grubbs could have refused delivery of the videotape he had ordered, that was unlikely. The Magistrate therefore "had a 'substantial basis for . . . conclud[ing]' that probable cause existed." 547 U.S. at 97** (internal citations omitted).

Interestingly, however, while the warrant in *Grubbs* should have contained the triggering condition, it failed to do so. The Court held, however, that this omission did render the warrant invalid. The affidavit in support of the warrant and its supporting documentation not only clearly specified the triggering condition as described above, but also met the Fourth Amendment's particularity requirement by clearly describing both "the place to be searched" and "the persons or things to be seized." 547 U.S. at 97. The concurring justices warned, however, that the issuing magistrate's failure to have included the triggering condition in the text of the warrant itself could "lead to several untoward consequences with constitutional significance," including the potential invalidation of the search if it was not properly executed upon the occurrence of the correct triggering condition. 547 U.S. at 100 (Souter, J., concurring). Therefore, to be sure that an anticipatory warrant will withstand judicial scrutiny, law enforcement officers should make sure that their affidavits in support of an anticipatory search warrant and the warrant itself both contain language that particularly specifies the triggering condition that allows the warrant to be lawfully executed. Consider the advice of the First Circuit:

> There are two particular dimensions in which anticipatory warrants must limit the discretion of government agents. First, the magistrate must ensure that the triggering event is both ascertainable and preordained. The warrant should restrict the officers' discretion in detecting the occurrence of the event to almost ministerial proportions, similar to a search party's discretion in locating the

place to be searched. Only then, in the prototypical case, are the ends of explicitness and clarity served. Second, the contraband must be on a sure and irreversible course to its destination, and a future search of the destination must be made expressly contingent upon the contraband's arrival there. Under such circumstances, a number of courts have found anticipatory search warrants to be valid. *United States v. Ricciardelli*, 998 F.2d 8, 12 (1st Cir. 1993).

To ensure that a magistrate is provided with sufficient information to justify the issuance of an anticipatory search warrant, the affidavit should present strong evidence that the continuation of a process already initiated will result in seizable items arriving at a particular place at a particular time. To guard against premature execution of the warrant, the affidavit should carefully specify the time when the item to be seized will arrive at the place to be searched and the time when the execution of the warrant is planned. This information should satisfy the magistrate that the warrant will not be executed prematurely.

Content of Search Warrants

Although search warrants vary among jurisdictions, most search warrants contain the following information:

- ▶ the caption of the court or division of the court from which the warrant issues;
- ▶ a particular description of the place or person to be searched;
- ▶ a particular description of the property to be seized;
- ▶ the names of persons whose affidavits have been taken in support of the warrant;
- ▶ a statement of grounds for issuance of the warrant;
- ▶ the name of the officer or class of officers to whom the warrant is directed, together with a command to search the person or place named for the property specified;
- ▶ a specification of the time during the day when the search may be conducted;
- ▶ the name of the judicial officer to whom the warrant is to be returned;
- ▶ the date of issuance; and
- ▶ the signature of the issuing magistrate, together with a statement of the magistrate's official title.

Recall that Figures 4.2 and Figure 4.3 are typical search warrant forms, the former based exclusively upon an affidavit, the latter based on oral testimony (including testimony given telephonically).

key points

- An issuing magistrate for a search warrant must be neutral, detached, and capable of determining whether probable cause exists for the requested search.
- Before issuing a search warrant, the magistrate must have probable cause to believe that items

subject to seizure are in a particular place or on a particular person at the time of the issuance of the warrant.

- Time is a very important factor in determining probable cause to search. If the information on

(Continued)

key points

which probable cause was initially based becomes stale, there may no longer be good reason to believe that property is still at the same location.

- Generally, the types of property allowed to be seized under a search warrant are evidence of a crime, contraband, fruits of crime, other items illegally possessed, and instrumentalities of crime. A search warrant may also be issued to search for a person to be arrested or a person who is unlawfully restrained.

- The affidavit supporting a request for a search warrant for a place must contain a description of the premises to be searched that points directly to a definitely ascertainable place to the exclusion of all others.

- The affidavit supporting a request for a search warrant must contain a particular description of the items to be seized.

- An anticipatory or prospective search warrant is a "search warrant based on an affidavit showing probable cause that evidence of a certain crime (such as illegal drugs) will be located at a specific place in the future." Anticipatory search warrants are valid only if there is probable cause to believe that contraband will be found if a specific triggering event occurs, and if there is probable cause to believe that the triggering condition will, in fact, occur.

▶ CONSTITUTIONALLY DEFECTIVE WARRANTS

Some warrants may be constitutionally defective. These include warrants with misrepresentations and omissions; and warrants in which, perhaps due to human error, some information may be suppressible. In this case, severability may apply.

Material Misrepresentations and Omissions

As stated above, if a law enforcement officer knowingly and intentionally, or with reckless disregard for the truth, makes false statements or material omissions in an affidavit supporting a request for a search warrant, the warrant may not be lawfully issued. If the warrant does issue, evidence seized under the warrant may be suppressed by application of the Exclusionary Rule in a procedure known as a *Franks* **hearing**. *Franks* hearings are named after the case *Franks v. Delaware*, 438 U.S. 154 (1978), in which the U.S. Supreme Court held that a defendant may challenge the veracity of an affidavit used by the police to obtain a search warrant.

Necessary Preliminary Showing to Obtain a Franks Hearing A mere allegation of falsity and/or material omission is insufficient to trigger a *Franks* hearing. "A mere allegation standing alone, without an offer of proof in a sworn affidavit of a witness or some other reliable corroboration, is insufficient. . . . When no proof is offered that an affiant deliberately lied or recklessly disregarded the truth, a *Franks* hearing is not required." *United States v. Mathison*, 157 F.3d 541, 548 (8th Cir. 1998). Thus, for a defendant to qualify for a *Franks* hearing, he or she must first make a *prima facie* showing that the affiant's statement was deliberately false or demonstrated reckless disregard for the truth by coming forward with some evidence that makes a "substantial preliminary showing" to support an allegation of police misconduct in establishing probable cause for the issuance of a warrant. *Franks*, 438 U.S. at 155. If the defendant does so, then the trial court is obliged to hold a *Franks* hearing. If, however, the defendant cannot demonstrate a *prima facie* case of deliberate or reckless falsity or material omission in the establishment of probable cause, then the defendant is not entitled to a *Franks* hearing.

United States v. Johns, 851 F.2d 1131 (9th Cir. 1988), found that a *Franks* hearing was required when the defendants made a substantial preliminary showing that they never engaged in any activities at a storage unit that could have produced the odors the officers allegedly smelled. Two expert witnesses swore the officer's affidavit was necessarily false because it was scientifically impossible to smell what the officers claimed to have smelled given the contents of the storage space searched under the warrant. Without the alleged falsities, the probable cause support for the search warrant collapsed because the remainder of the affidavit merely described the location and ownership of the storage unit. The following are other examples of the types of showings that have been held to sufficiently establish a right to a *Franks* hearing:

▶ In *United States v. Hammond*, 351 F.3d 765 (6th Cir. 2003), an officer admitted that he made false statements in his affidavit regarding the steps he had allegedly taken to verify the reliability of an informant's tip, when, in fact, he had not taken such steps. Not only did this warrant a *Franks* hearing, but the court ultimately concluded that the violation warranted application of the Exclusionary Rule.

▶ In *United States v. Avery*, 295 F.3d 1158 (10th Cir. 2002), an officer failed to disclose in his affidavit that his confidential informant had a lengthy criminal history that cast doubt on his credibility as a source of information. While this omission was sufficient to warrant a *Franks* hearing, the court ultimately concluded at the subsequent *Franks* hearing that the omission did not warrant suppression of evidence.

▶ In *United States v. Reinholz*, 245 F.3d 765, 774 (8th Cir. 2001), an officer implied in his affidavit that his "confidential and reliable" informant had personal knowledge of the defendant's alleged drug use and dealings. However, the informant had no such knowledge and came forward to acknowledge his lack of personal knowledge. The court ruled that the defendant was entitled to a *Franks* hearing on the basis of the officer's reckless disregard for the truth.

Burden of Proof at a Franks Hearing A *Franks* hearing involves a two-step process. Initially, the defendant bears the burden of proving, by a preponderance of the evidence, that an application for a warrant contained false statements that were knowingly or recklessly made, or alternatively that material information was knowingly or recklessly omitted from the warrant application. If the defendant fails to meet this burden of proof:

> [T]he inquiry is at an end and the fruits of the search should not be suppressed. However, should the defendant meet his burden . . . , the court must expand its inquiry and determine whether the affidavit, when stricken of its falsity, is nonetheless sufficient to establish probable cause for issuance of the search warrant. *United States v. Whitley*, 249 F.3d 614, 620 (7th Cir. 2001).

If after the offending material is stricken from the application the remaining information still establishes probable cause, the warrant will be upheld. If, however, the remaining information contained in the affidavit after the offending data is set aside fails to establish probable cause, then **"the search warrant must be voided and the fruits of the search excluded to the same extent as if probable cause was lacking on the face of the affidavit."** *Franks*, 438 U.S. at 155-56. Moreover, the officer may be subject to criminal prosecution for perjury or a related offense, as well as to damages liability in a civil lawsuit. *See Malley v. Briggs*, 475 U.S. 335 (1986).

Recall that in *United States v. Reinholz*, an officer mislead a magistrate into believing that a reliable informant had personal knowledge of a suspect's drug usage and dealing. The court excised all of the information in the affidavit concerning the informant after concluding the statements were made with reckless disregard for the truth. Yet, the search and subsequent seizure were both upheld because the court determined that the remaining information in the affidavit was sufficient to establish probable cause based on the defendant's drug conviction record and drug paraphernalia that had been collected lawfully from the defendant's trash. In contrast, the officer's misrepresentations about the steps he had taken to verify the accuracy of an informant's tip was fatal to the prosecution's case in *United States v. Hammond*. Probable cause could not be established in that case on the basis of an unverified tip by an informant whose reliability was otherwise not known or demonstrated. Since there was insufficient information in the affidavit to establish probable cause once the tip was excised, the search was invalidated by the court.

Severability of Search Warrants

Search warrants may inadvertently contain some clauses that are constitutionally sufficient and other clauses that are not, due to human error—either a lack of probable cause, or a lack of particularity, also referred to as generality. Should courts suppress all evidence under these warrants, or only the evidence seized under the constitutionally insufficient clauses? To avoid the severe remedy of total suppression of all evidence seized under these warrants, courts have adopted the theory of **redaction** or **severability**, also called *partial suppression*.

The Doctrine of Severability Severability invalidates clauses in a warrant that are constitutionally insufficient for lack of probable cause or particularity and preserves clauses that satisfy the Fourth Amendment. *See United States v. Ninety-Two Thousand Four Hundred Twenty-Two Dollars and Fifty-Seven Cents*, 307 F.3d 137 (3rd Cir. 2002).

> By redaction, we mean striking from a warrant those severable phrases and clauses that are invalid for lack of probable cause or generality and preserving those severable phrases and clauses that satisfy the Fourth Amendment. Each part of the search authorized by the warrant is examined separately to determine whether it is impermissibly general or unsupported by probable cause. Materials seized under the authority of those parts of the warrant struck for invalidity must be suppressed, but the court need not suppress materials seized pursuant to the valid portions of the warrant. *United States v. Yusuf*, 461 F.3d 374, 389 (3d Cir. 2006).

Step 1: The warrant must be divided "in a commonsense, practical manner into individual clauses, portions, paragraphs, or categories." 463 F.3d at 1151.

Step 2: The constitutionality of each individual part must be examined "to determine whether some portion of the warrant satisfies the probable cause and particularity requirements of the Fourth Amendment." 463 F.3d at 1151.
   A. "If no part of the warrant particularly describes items to be seized for which there is probable cause, then severance does not apply, and all items seized by such a warrant should be suppressed." 463 F.3d at 1151. This ends the inquiry.
   B. "If, however, at least a part of the warrant is sufficiently particularized and supported by probable cause," courts then proceed to step 3. 463 F.3d at 1151.

Step 3: Courts must then "determine whether the valid portions are distinguishable from the invalid portions." 463 F.3d at 1151.
   A. If the parts are not distinguishable, then severance is inapplicable and the items seized must be suppressed.
   B. "If, however, parts of the warrant may be meaningfully severed," then courts proceed to step 4. 463 F.3d at 1151.

Step 4: The warrant as a whole must be examined both quantitatively and qualitatively, "to determine whether the valid portions make up 'the greater part of the warrant,'" in comparison to the invalid portion(s). "This analysis ensures that severance does not render the Fourth Amendment's warrant requirement meaningless." 463 F.3d at 1151.
   A. If the valid portions fail to comprise "the greater part of the warrant" (i.e., there are more invalid parts than there are valid sections), then severance is inapplicable and all of the evidence seized will be suppressed. 463 F.3d at 1151; *see also United States v. Naugle*, 997 F.2d 819, 822 (10th Cir.1993).
   B. If, however, the valid portions make up "the greater part of the warrant" then those portions may be severed and evidence seized pursuant to these valid, severed portions is admissible. The evidence seized pursuant to the invalid portions will be suppressed.

▶**Figure 4.4** STEPS IN SEVERABILITY DECISION PROCESS

United States v. Christine, 687 F.2d 749, 758 (3d Cir. 1982), is one of the leading federal cases on severability. *Christine* upheld the practice, finding that redaction is consistent with all five purposes of the warrant requirement:

First, with respect to the search and seizure conducted pursuant to the valid portion of the redacted warrant, the intrusion into personal privacy has been justified by probable cause to believe that the search and seizure will serve society's need for law enforcement. Second, because it is a duly issued warrant that is being redacted, the objective of interposing a magistrate between law enforcement officials and the citizen has been attained. Third, even though it may not be coterminous with the underlying probable cause showing, the scope of a search pursuant to a particularized, overbroad warrant is nevertheless limited by the terms of its authorization. In the case of a warrant containing some invalid general clauses, redaction neither exacerbates nor ratifies the unwarranted intrusions conducted pursuant to the general clauses, but merely preserves the evidence seized pursuant to those clauses particularly describing items to be seized. Fourth, as to the valid portions of the warrant salvaged by redaction, the individual whose property is to be searched has received notification of the lawful authority of the executing officer, his need to search, and the limits of his power to search. Fifth, redaction does not affect the generation of a record susceptible to subsequent judicial review.

Although the Supreme Court had never ruled specifically on severing constitutionally defective parts of warrants, the Court implied that doing so was permissible in *Andresen v. Maryland*, 427 U.S. 463, 480 (1976). Accordingly, all of the federal circuit courts of appeals and the courts of most states are in agreement with *Christine*'s conclusion that constitutionally defective parts of warrants can be severed. *State v. Roark*, 12 P.3d 225 (Ariz. App. 2000) (citing cases from all federal judicial circuits).

Determining Severability The severance of the unparticular descriptions is not allowed if the entire warrant "is facially general in nature" since that would render the entire warrant constitutionally deficient. *United States v. Giresi*, 488 F. Supp. 445, 459 (D.N.J. 1980). Similarly, the severance doctrine does not apply if the entire warrant is unsupported by probable cause. But, assuming that at least some portions of a warrant are sufficiently particular and supported by probable cause, then courts subscribing to the doctrine of severability engage in a complicated process to determine (1) whether the doctrine of severability is applicable to a particular warrant; and (2) if so, to which parts of the warrant. This process was described in detail by the Tenth Circuit Court of Appeals in *United States v. Sells*, 463 F.3d 1148 (10th Cir. 2006). The process described by the court is presented in Figure 4.4. While all courts do not rigidly adhere to particulars of the four-step process set forth in *Sells,* they all apply a test that is qualitatively similar.

key points

- If a law enforcement officer knowingly and intentionally, or with reckless disregard for the truth, makes false statements or material omissions in an affidavit supporting a request for a search warrant, the warrant may not be lawfully issued. If, however, a warrant based on an affidavit containing false statements or material omissions was issued, and a defendant can make a strong preliminary showing of this fact, the defendant is entitled to challenge the legality of the warrant and the ensuing search at a *Franks* hearing.
- At a *Franks* hearing, the defendant bears the burden of proving, by a preponderance of the evidence, either that an application for a warrant contained false statements that were knowingly or recklessly made or, alternatively, that material information was knowingly or recklessly omitted from the warrant application. If the defendant fails to meet this burden of proof, the warrant will be

upheld and the evidence gathered as a result of the search will be admissible. If, however, the defendant meets his or her burden, the court must then determine whether the affidavit, when stricken of its false or misleading statement, is nonetheless sufficient to establish probable cause for issuance of the search warrant. If the remaining information establishes probable cause, the warrant will be upheld. If, however, the remaining information contained in the affidavit after the offending data is set aside fails to establish probable cause, then "the search warrant must be voided and the fruits of the search excluded to the same extent as if probable cause was lacking on the face of the affidavit."

- Severance of search warrants invalidates portions of a warrant that are constitutionally insufficient for lack of probable cause or particularity, and preserves the portions that satisfy the Fourth Amendment.

▶EXECUTING SEARCH WARRANTS

The execution (also called service) of a search warrant is essentially the carrying out of the commands in the warrant. **"The Fourth Amendment confines an officer executing a search warrant strictly within the bounds set by the warrant. . . ."** *Bivens v. Six Unknown Named Agents*, 403 U.S. 388, 394 n.7 (1971). Furthermore, **"a search which is reasonable at its inception may violate the Fourth Amendment by virtue of its intolerable intensity and scope. . . . The scope of the search must be 'strictly tied to and justified by' the circumstances which rendered its initiation permissible."** *Terry v. Ohio*, 392 U.S. 1, 18 (1968). Although officers can determine many of their duties from simply reading the warrant, several aspects of the execution of search warrants need further explanation.

Who May Execute a Search Warrant

A search warrant is directed to a particular officer or class of officers. Usually, only the named officer or a member of the named class of officers may execute or serve the warrant. Normally, the officer to whom the warrant is directed must be personally present at the search. But if a warrant is directed to a sheriff, a deputy may execute the warrant and the sheriff need not be present. However, there can exist a narrow set of circumstances in which a search warrant may be executed by a civilian even outside the presence of a police officer. *United States v. Bach*, 310 F.3d 1063 (8th Cir. 2002), upheld the execution of a search warrant that allowed for the retrieval of certain e-mails from an Internet service provider. The court ruled that is was permissible for the warrant to have included a provision allowing for it to be faxed to an Internet service provider and executed by technicians there. Key to the court's rationale was that the actual physical presence of an officer would not have aided the search.

Police behavior during the execution of a search warrant must be related to the objectives specified in the warrant. Therefore, officers are limited with regard to whom they may bring with them during the execution of a search warrant. Officers may enlist private persons to help in the execution of a warrant so long as they serve a purpose within the authorized scope of the intrusion. Thus, for example, it would be permissible for police to bring civilian evidence technicians or forensic experts to the execution of a search warrant, but it would not be constitutional for them to bring members of the media or other third-party observers with them who are of no aid or assistance to actually executing the warrant. *See Wilson v. Layne*, 526 U.S. 603, 604 (1999); *Hanlon v. Berger*, 526 U.S. 808, 809 (1999).

Time Considerations

Three different aspects of time affect law enforcement officers in the execution of search warrants: how long after the issuance of a search warrant it is executed; the time of day the warrant is executed; and how long it takes to fully execute the search.

Delay and Staleness Concerns How much time may pass between the issuance of a warrant and its execution? Courts are concerned with delays in the execution of warrants because probable cause might become stale if not acted upon promptly. But there are many valid reasons for delaying the execution of a search warrant. Weather conditions, long travel distances, traffic problems, and similar obstacles may prevent the prompt execution of the warrant. Delays may be necessary to gather sufficient human resources for the search, to protect the safety of the searching officers, to prevent the destruction of evidence, and to prevent the flight of a suspect. When the warrant is for the search of both a person and premises, the search may be delayed until the person is present on the premises. *People v. Stansberry*, 268 N.E.2d 431 (Ill. 1971). Regardless of the justification for a delay, however, warrants must be executed before probable cause dissipates, a process commonly referred to as going "stale."

Fixed Time Limits To combat staleness problems, most U.S. jurisdictions set such a time limit by statute, court rule, or judicial decision. If a warrant is not executed within the prescribed time limit, the warrant is usually deemed void and any subsequent execution of the warrant will be invalid. *E.g., Spera v. State*, 467 So. 2d 329 (Fla. App. 1985). A minority of jurisdictions, however, merely consider the expiration of the prescribed time for warrant execution to give rise to grounds for applying the Exclusionary Rule upon a showing of prejudice to the defendant. *E.g., State v. Weaver*, 602 S.E.2d 786 (S.C. App. 2004).

"Forthwith" Requirements Other U.S. jurisdictions do not have any fixed time limits for the execution of search warrants, and simply require that warrants be executed "forthwith." But even in such states, warrants must still be executed within a reasonable time after issuance. Reasonableness, of course, depends on the facts and circumstances of each case. *See, e.g., Turner v. Comm.*, 420 S.E.2d 235 (Va. 1992) (upholding delay of eleven days because there were good reasons for the delay and probable cause had not gone stale).

Combination Requirements Just because a warrant is executed within the prescribed time limit does not necessarily mean that the search was constitutionally valid; a warrant can still go stale within the prescribed time period. Thus, many jurisdictions have dual requirements that warrants not only be executed within the relevant, prescribed time period, but also that warrants be executed "forthwith" or "without unnecessary delay" that would cause legal prejudice to the defendant. For example, Texas law provides:

> A peace officer to whom a search warrant is delivered shall execute it without delay and forthwith return it to the proper magistrate. It must be executed within three days from the time of its issuance, and shall be executed within a shorter period if so directed in the warrant by the magistrate. VERNON'S ANN. TEXAS C.C.P. ART. 18.06(a).

In the federal system, Federal Rule of Criminal Procedure 41 specifies that search warrants must be executed within ten days if the issuing authority has not specified a shorter limit, *so long as probable cause continues to exist*. Unnecessary delay is determined by evaluating all the facts and circumstances surrounding the execution of the warrant. In states with dual rules, a search can be invalidated because it occurred too long after the issuance of the warrant (i.e., not "forthwith") even though the warrant was executed within the relevant time frame. For example, in *Huffines v. State*, 739 N.E.2d 1093 (Ind. Ct. App.

2000), *cert. denied*, 753 N.E.2d 9 (Ind. 2001), a court invalidated a search that occurred eight days after a warrant had been issued even though state statute required warrants to be executed within ten days. The court reasoned that probable cause had gone stale in the case since the warrant had been issued based on the defendant's purchase of a small amount of cocaine. Since there was no evidence of any additional drug purchases, the court concluded that the evidence was no longer likely to have been found so many days later.

Time-of-Day Concerns In general, search warrants should be executed in the daytime. Courts have always frowned on nighttime searches. In *Jones v. United States*, 357 U.S. 493, 498 (1958), the U.S. Supreme Court said that **"it is difficult to imagine a more severe invasion of privacy than the nighttime intrusion into a private home. . . ."** *See also State v. Richardson*, 904 P.2d 886 (Haw. 1995); *United States v. Young*, 877 F.2d 1099, 1104 (1st Cir. 1989). Furthermore, nighttime searches are more likely to be met with armed resistance. *State v. Brock*, 633 P.2d 805 (Or. App. 1981); Therefore, most states have either statutes or court-mandated rules akin to Rule 41 of the Federal Rules of Criminal Procedure which require that warrants be executed during the daytime. FED. R. CRIM. P. 41(e)(2)(B); *see also*, *e.g.*, CAL. PENAL CODE § 1533.

Defining Daytime Daytime is expansively defined as the hours between 6:00 A.M. and 10:00 P.M. FED. R. CRIM. P. 41(h). But the terms *daytime* and *nighttime* are defined differently in different jurisdictions by statute, court rule, or court decision. If these terms are not defined in a particular jurisdiction, a good rule of thumb is that it is daytime when there is sufficient natural light to recognize a person's features; otherwise, it is nighttime.

Nighttime Searches In spite of the normal rules that require warrants to be executed during the daytime, courts may authorize a nighttime search if the affidavit in support of the warrant sets forth specific facts showing some need to execute the warrant at night. For example, Delaware's statute permits the issuance of warrants that authorize a nighttime search when "necessary in order to prevent the escape or removal of the person or thing to be searched." DEL. CODE ANN. tit. 11, § 2308 (2000). Justification for a nighttime search has been found when a nighttime delivery of contraband was expected, when the property to be seized was likely to be removed promptly, and when part of a criminal transaction was to take place at night. *United States v. Curry*, 530 F.2d 636 (5th Cir. 1976). Such circumstances most frequently exist when there is probable cause to suspect that a nighttime drug transaction will take place. *E.g.*, *United States v. Diehl*, 276 F.3d 32, 44 (1st Cir. 2002). In fact, Congress enacted a law specifically providing for nighttime searches in drug cases:

> A search warrant relating to offenses involving controlled substances may be served at any time of the day or night if the judge or United States magistrate judge issuing the warrant is satisfied that there is probable cause to believe that grounds exist for the warrant and for its service at such time. 21 U.S.C. § 879.

In interpreting this statutory provision, the Supreme Court ruled in *Gooding v. United States*, 416 U.S. 430 (1970), that the probable cause showing it requires is targeted at the existence of illicit drugs on premises only. Accordingly, there is no special showing that needs to be made to justify a nighttime search other than that there is probable cause to believe that controlled substances are likely to be on the property or person to be searched at the time the warrant is executed. Thus, Congress created what has become known as the "narcotics exception" to the rule that a special showing must be made to justify the nighttime execution of a search warrant.

Even if a nighttime search is not authorized, the execution of a search warrant that was begun in the daytime may be continued into the nighttime if it is a reasonable continuation of the daytime search. An officer is not required to cut short the reasonable execution of a daytime search warrant just because it becomes dark outside. *United States v. Squillacote*, 221 F.3d 542, 557 (4th Cir. 2000) (citing *United States v. Young*, 877 F.2d 1099, 1104-05 (1st Cir. 1989)).

Duration of Search In light of the Fourth Amendment's command of reasonableness, courts are also concerned with the amount of time it takes law enforcement personnel to perform a search once it is initiated pursuant to a valid warrant. *Segura v. United States*, 468 U.S. 796 (1984). *State v. Chaisson*, 486 A.2d 297, 303 (N.H. 1984), stated the general rule: "The police, in executing a search warrant for a dwelling, may remain on the premises only so long as it is reasonably necessary to conduct the search." Therefore, after all the objects described in a warrant have been found and seized, "the authority under the warrant expires and further governmental intrusion must cease." *United States v. Gagnon*, 635 F.2d 766, 769 (10th Cir. 1980). If, however, only some of the described items have been found, the search may lawfully continue.

Simply examining how long a search lasted is insufficient to determine the reasonableness of the duration of a search since the number of hours is only one factor in the totality of the circumstances. For example, *State v. Swain*, 269 N.W.2d 707 (Minn. 1978), upheld a search of a home that lasted for three days because chemical tests needed to be run in order to analyze bloodstains that were discovered on the first and second days of the search. And *United States v. Squillacote*, 221 F.3d 542 (4th Cir. 2000), upheld a search that lasted six days, during which time FBI agents stayed in the defendant's house overnight for five nights to guard against the possible destruction of evidence. Even though the "extensive and exhaustive" search lasted so long, the court determined the search was reasonable in light of the following circumstances which, when examined together, established the reasonableness of the search:

> A search for evidence of espionage requires extreme thoroughness in order to discover the covert instruments, communications, and records of the illegal activity. In addition, the search was complicated by the condition of the home. . . . The house was extremely cluttered, and the [appellants'] personal possessions and documents were of such quantity and in such a state of disarray as to create a great obstacle to the execution of the warrant. The search was further complicated because the house was undergoing renovations, which increased the clutter and made it difficult to search certain areas of the house. . . . The agents were unable to search the basement, where many items were located, for long stretches of time due to the irritation caused by an immense amount of dust and the odor of cat urine. Therefore, notwithstanding the large number of agents involved in the search, it is apparent that the search could not have been completed in a single day. 221 F.3d at 557 (*internal quotations and citations omitted*).

Securing People and Places while a Search Warrant Is Being Sought

When officers have probable cause to believe that evidence of criminal activity is in a dwelling, temporarily securing the dwelling to prevent removal or destruction of evidence while a search warrant is being sought is not an unreasonable seizure of either the dwelling or its contents:

> [T]he home is sacred in Fourth Amendment terms not primarily because of the occupants' possessory interests in the premises, but because of their privacy interests in the activities that take place within. . . . [A] seizure affects only possessory interests, not privacy interests. Therefore, the heightened protection we accord privacy interests is simply not implicated where a seizure of premises, not a search, is at issue. *Segura v. United States*, 468 U.S. 796, 810 (1984).

Segura held that insofar as the seizure of the premises is concerned, it made no difference whether the premises were secured by stationing officers within the premises or by establishing a perimeter stakeout after a security check of the premises revealed that no one was inside. Under either method, officers control the premises pending arrival of the warrant. Both an internal securing and a perimeter stakeout interfere to the same extent with the possessory interests of the owners.

In *Illinois v. McArthur*, 531 U.S. 326 (2001), police officers, with probable cause to believe that the defendant had hidden marijuana in his home, prevented him from entering the home for about two hours while they obtained a warrant. The U.S. Supreme Court balanced the privacy-related and law enforcement–related concerns and found the warrantless intrusion reasonable. First, the police had probable cause to believe that the defendant's home contained evidence of a crime and contraband: namely, unlawful drugs. Second, the police had good reason to fear that, unless restrained, the defendant would destroy the drugs before they could return with a warrant. Third, the police neither searched the home nor arrested the defendant, but imposed the significantly less restrictive restraint of preventing him from entering the home unaccompanied. Finally, the police imposed the restraint for a limited period of time: namely, two hours—the time reasonably necessary to obtain a warrant. "Given the nature of the intrusion and the law enforcement interest at stake, this brief seizure of the premises was permissible." 531 U.S. at 333.

key points

- Only the named officer or a member of the named class of officers may execute or serve a search warrant. Normally, the officer to whom the warrant is directed must be personally present at the search. Officers may enlist private persons to help in the execution of a warrant so long as they serve a purpose within the authorized scope of the intrusion.
- In general, a search warrant should be executed in the daytime within a reasonable time after its issuance, unless a warrant specifically provides for nighttime execution or nighttime execution is specifically statutorily authorized.

- Officers should remain on the searched premises only so long as is reasonably necessary to conduct the search.
- When officers have probable cause to believe that evidence of criminal activity is in a dwelling, temporarily securing the dwelling to prevent removal or destruction of evidence while a search warrant is being sought is not an unreasonable seizure of either the dwelling or its contents.

Notice Requirements

Notice requirements include the knock-and-announce requirement; notice when the premises are searched without the owner present; and covert entry "sneak-and-peek" warrants. This section discusses issues relevant to each.

The Knock-and-Announce Requirement As discussed in Chapter 3, law enforcement officers are generally required to **knock-and-announce** their presence, authority, and purpose before entering premises to execute a search warrant. In *Wilson v. Arkansas*, 514 U.S. 927 (1995), the U.S. Supreme Court held that the knock-and-announce principle was part of the Fourth Amendment's reasonableness requirement. The purposes of the so-called knock-and-announce requirements are:

▶ to prevent violence to the police or other persons on the premises;

▶ to protect the privacy of the occupants of the premises from unexpected intrusions;

▶ to prevent property damage; and

▶ to give the occupant an opportunity to examine the warrant and point out a possible mistaken address or other errors.

An announcement of identity as a law enforcement officer accompanied by a statement that the officer has a search warrant is usually sufficient. But failure to comply with this requirement, absent some exigent circumstance, can render a search constitutionally unreasonable. For example, in *State v. Maldonado*, 121 P.3d 901 (Haw. 2005), police opened a closed screen door and entered a home before they announced their presence and purpose. The court ruled that the knock-and-announce requirement had been violated.

Under 18 U.S.C. § 3109 (2000), a person who refuses entry to an officer executing a warrant risks forcible entry:

> The officer may break open any outer or inner door or window of a house, or any part of a house, or anything therein, to execute a search warrant, if, after notice of his authority and purpose, he is refused admittance or when necessary to liberate himself or a person aiding him in the execution of the warrant.

To comply with the requirements of § 3109, courts usually require police officers to wait at least ten to twenty, if not thirty seconds, after the knock-and-announce. *United States v. Valdez*, 302 F.3d 320 (5th Cir. 2002). But if officers knock and announce their authority and purpose and are refused entry, then they may forcibly enter the premises. Refusal does not have to be explicit; but, most commonly, is implied by an occupant's failure to admit officers within a reasonable time after they have knocked and announced. *United States v. Banks*, 540 U.S. 31 (2003), addressed the issue of what is a reasonable time for an occupant to respond. In *Banks*, officers arrived at Banks' two-bedroom apartment at 2:00 P.M. on a weekday afternoon to execute a warrant to search for cocaine and evidence of cocaine sales. An officer knocked loudly on the front door and shouted "Police, search warrant." Receiving no response from inside, the officers waited fifteen to twenty seconds and then broke open the door and entered. The search produced weapons, crack cocaine, and evidence of drug sales.

Banks testified that he was in the shower when the officers entered and did not hear the knock or announcement.

The Court held that the totality of the circumstances known to the officers at the time of entry is what counts in judging reasonable waiting time. Absent emergency circumstances, relevant factors include the size and nature of the structure, the time of day, valid reasons for delay known to the officers, and other reasons affecting the speed with which the occupant could reach the door. In this case, however, the crucial fact in examining their actions was not the time to reach the door, but the nature of the exigent circumstances claimed by the police:

> [W]hat matters is the opportunity to get rid of cocaine, which a prudent dealer will keep near a commode or kitchen sink. The significant circumstances include the arrival of the police during the day, when anyone inside would probably have been up and around, and the sufficiency of 15 to 20 seconds for getting to the bathroom or the kitchen to start flushing cocaine down the drain. That is, when circumstances are exigent because a pusher may be near the point of putting his drugs beyond reach, it is imminent disposal, not travel time to the entrance, that governs when the police may reasonably enter; since the bathroom and kitchen are usually in the interior of a dwelling, not the front hall, there is no reason generally to peg the travel time to the location of the door, and no reliable basis for giving the proprietor of a mansion a longer wait than the resident of a bungalow, or an apartment like Banks's. And 15 to 20 seconds does not seem an unrealistic guess about the time someone would need to get in a position to rid his quarters of cocaine. 540 U.S. at 40.

The Court therefore ruled the entry lawful. Applying similar logic, *United States v. Gay*, 240 F.3d 1222 (10th Cir. 2001) upheld police entry into the home of a drug dealer whom they believed to be armed and dangerous after only two to three seconds.

It should be noted that if police must use force to gain entry, the means they use to do so must be reasonable and necessary. In *Dalia v. United States* 441 U.S. 238 (1979), the U.S. Supreme Court said that it is generally left to the discretion of the executing officers to determine the details of conducting the search under the warrant:

> Often in executing a warrant the police may find it necessary to interfere with privacy rights not explicitly considered by the judge who issued the warrant. For example, police executing an arrest warrant commonly find it necessary to enter the suspect's home in order to take him into custody, and they thereby impinge on both privacy and freedom of movement. . . . Similarly, officers executing search warrants on occasion must damage property in order to perform their duty. 441 U.S. at 257-58.

Therefore, officers executing a search warrant may use whatever method is reasonably necessary to gain access to premises to be searched, even to the extent of damaging property, if no reasonable alternative is available.

Exceptions to the Knock-and-Announce Requirement
Exigent Circumstances The Supreme Court has made it clear that it is not necessary for police to knock-and-announce their presence and purpose if exigent circumstances exist for dispensing with the rule:

> It is not necessary when circumstances present a threat of physical violence, or if there is reason to believe that evidence would likely be destroyed if advance notice were given, or if knocking and announcing would be futile. We require only that police have a reasonable suspicion under the particular circumstances that one of these grounds for failing to knock and announce exists, and we have acknowledged that this showing is not high. *Hudson v. Michigan*, 126 S. Ct. 2159, 2162-63 (2006).

What types of circumstances justify reasonable suspicion to ignore the knock-and-announce rule? There is no blanket exception to the knock-and-announce requirement in drug cases—see *Richards v. Wisconsin*, 520 U.S. 385 (1997). Yet the destruction of evidence, especially drug evidence, as in *Banks* and *Hudson,* is clearly the common reason for dispensing with the knock-and-announce requirement under a totality of the circumstances approach. *See, e.g., United States v. Johnson*, 267 F.3d 498 (6th Cir. 2001). But courts have also upheld entries without a prior knock-and-announce under such exigent circumstances. These include:

▶ The sound of footsteps, whispers, or flushing toilets, indicating possible escape or destruction of evidence, may create exigent circumstances justifying an immediate forcible entry. *United States v. Stiver*, 9 F.3d 298 (3d Cir. 1993); *United States v. Mitchell*, 783 F.2d 971 (10th Cir. 1986).

▶ The suspect had a criminal record of violence, was armed; and police suspected that he was aware of the fact that police were investigating him. *United States v. Hawkins*, 139 F.3d 29, 32 (1st Cir. 1998).

▶ Police saw smoke and smelled what they believed to be explosives. *United States v. Combs*, 394 F.3d 739 (9th Cir. 2005).

▶ Police anticipated that the suspect had a rocket launcher inside premises to be searched. *United States v. Crippen*, 371 F.3d 842, 846 (D.C. Cir. 2004).

▶ Police observed the suspect exiting his apartment through a back door. *United States v. McGee*, 280 F.3d 803 (7th Cir. 2002).

Entry by Ruse or Deception Some courts also allow an exception to the knock-and-announce requirement for entries accomplished by ruse or deception. For example, in *United States v. Contreras-Ceballos*, 999 F.2d 432 (9th Cir. 1993), an officer executing a search warrant for drugs knocked on the defendant's door and replied "Federal Express" when asked who was there. When the door was opened, the officer pushed his way in and announced his authority and purpose. The court held that the use of force to keep the door open and to enter did not violate the knock-and-announce requirement because there was no "breaking." "To rule otherwise would dictate a nonsensical procedure in which the officers, after having employed a permissible ruse to cause the door to be opened, must permit it to be shut by the occupants so that the officers could then knock, re-announce, and open the door forcibly if refused admittance." 999 F.2d at 435.

If Police Presence and Purpose Is Already Known Finally, knocking and announcing "is excused when the officers are justifiably and virtually certain that the occupants already know their purpose." *United States v. Eddy*, 660 F.2d 381, 385 (8th Cir. 1981); *see also United States v. Dunnock*, 295 F.3d 431 (4th Cir. 2002).

No-Knock Warrants Some states have enacted **no-knock warrant** laws that permit magistrates to issue search warrants specifically authorizing officers to enter premises without knocking and announcing their authority and purpose. An officer applying for such a warrant need only articulate reasonable suspicion for believing that compliance with the knock-and-announce rule would result in the destruction of evidence or in some harm to the executing officer or others. If such grounds exist, it is wise for an officer to seek a no-knock warrant for two reasons. First, it would insulate the officer from potential civil liability for having misjudged exigent circumstances for himself or herself at the time of the execution of the warrant. Second, if the warrant issues and is later determined to have been invalid (i.e., if the reviewing judge were to determine that a no-knock entry was not appropriate after-the-fact), the good-faith exception under *Leon* would clearly apply.

Remedy for Knock-and-Announce Violations

Prior to the U.S. Supreme Court's decision in *Hudson v. Michigan,* the exclusionary rule was used as a remedy for knock-and-announce violations. Thus, if police failed to comply with the requirement of the knock-and-announce rule, the evidence seized as a result of the ensuing search would be suppressed. *See, e.g., United States v. Valdez,* 302 F.3d 320 (5th Cir. 2002). However, recall from Chapter 3 that in *Hudson v. Michigan,* 126 S. Ct. 2159 (2006), the U.S. Supreme Court reversed this long-standing application of the exclusionary rule by holding that the exclusionary rule was not an appropriate remedy for knock-and-announce violations. (See the Discussion Point "Are 'knock-and-announce violations sufficiently attenuated?" in Chapter 3 for more details about the *Hudson* case.) Since *Hudson* was decided, its logic has been squarely applied by lower courts not only to generalized (i.e., common law) knock-and-announce violations, but also to those that applied the knock-and-announce command of § 3109. *See United States v. Bruno,* 487 F.3d 304 (5th Cir. 2007); *United States v. Southerland,* 466 F.3d 1083 (D.C. Cir. 2006), *cert. denied,* 127 S. Ct. 1361 (2007); *United States v. Ramirez,* 196 Fed. Appx. 538, 539 (9th Cir. 2006). And, *Hudson* has also been extended to the execution of arrest warrants. *United States v. Pelletier,* 469 F.3d 194 (1st Cir. 2006). So what, then, is the status of the knock-and-announce rule?

The Supreme Court's decision in *Hudson* did not abandon the knock-and-announce rule in its entirety. Rather, it changed the remedy for a knock-and-announce violation from the application of the exclusionary rule to a civil enforcement mechanism. Thus, police may be held civilly liable for damages for violating the knock-and-announce in a Section 1983 or *Bivens* action. *See Hudson,* 126 S. Ct. at 2167-68. However, given issues of proof, litigation costs, and a variety of defenses to civil rights actions, some commentators, like Supreme Court Justice Breyer, view the decision in *Hudson* as having destroyed "much of the practical value of the Constitution's knock-and-announce protection." *Hudson,* 126 S. Ct. at 2171 (Breyer, J., dissenting).

Even if that is the case, compliance with the knock-and-announce requirement is simple and effortless. Recall that one of the main reasons for the knock-and-announce rule is to prevent violence to the police or other persons on the premises. A failure to knock-and-announce is likely to lead to the unnecessary destruction of property and increased violence stemming from the surprise and fright of an unexpected entry. Thus, unless circumstances give police reasonable suspicion that knocking and announcing would put them in more danger than they would face by announcing their presence and purpose, it is in law enforcement officers' own best interest to comply with the knock-and-announce rule both for their own safety, and to avoid the possibility of civil liability. Also, law enforcement officers should keep abreast of case law developments in their own jurisdictions. Although no state has done so as of the writing of this text, it is clear that any state is free to disregard *Hudson* and apply the exclusionary rule to knock-and-announce violations on state constitutional law grounds.

Notice When Premises Are Searched without Owner/Occupant Present **Rule 41(f)** of the Federal Rules of Criminal Procedure provides:

> The officer executing the warrant must give a copy of the warrant and a receipt for the property taken to the person from whom, or from whose premises, the property was taken or leave a copy of the warrant and receipt at the place where the officer took the property.

The mandate of this rule is that people are entitled to have notice that their premises have been searched and, if items were seized during a search, that those items have been taken. This is not a problem when the person whose premises have been searched was present during the execution of a search warrant, even if authorities did not knock-and-announce their presence and purpose. But if a search warrant is executed when premises are unoccupied, Rule 41 requires that timely notice be given to the lawful occupant of the searched property not only that a search warrant was executed, but also of what was taken. It should be noted, however, that states differ on their approaches to warrant notice. Several states have much more strict notice requirements than those imposed under Rule 41(f). For example, North Carolina law states:

> Before undertaking any search or seizure pursuant to the warrant, the officer must read the warrant and give a copy of the warrant application and affidavit to the person to be searched, or the person in apparent control of the premises or vehicle to be searched. If no one in apparent and responsible control is occupying the premises or vehicle, the officer must leave a copy of the warrant affixed to the premises or vehicle. N.C. GEN. STAT. § 15A-252.

Other states have similar laws. *See.*, *e.g.*, ORE. REV. STAT. § 133.575; S.C. CODE § 17-13-150; VERNON'S ANN. TEXAS C.C.P. ART. 18.06(a). But federal law and the laws of many states have created a major exception to the usual notice requirements: covert entry warrants, also referred to as "sneak-and-peek warrants."

Covert Entry under "Sneak-and-Peek" Warrants In some circumstances, law enforcement officers may need to execute a search warrant in complete secrecy. Complete secrecy means that officers enter the target premises when the occupants are absent, conduct the search, and leave, seizing nothing and leaving no indication that a search has been conducted. Complete secrecy may be necessary if (1) officers need to determine whether certain evidence is on the target premises; and (2) officers reasonably believe that suspects would disrupt the investigation by destroying evidence, threatening or killing witnesses, or fleeing, if they knew that a search had occurred.

A **covert entry warrant**, also known as a **sneak-and-peek warrant**, is a search warrant that specifically authorizes officers to enter unoccupied premises, search for specified evidence, and then leave—without seizing the evidence they find and without leaving a trace that an entry has been made. In conducting such a search, officers usually photograph or videotape the evidence or otherwise document exactly what they saw and its exact location.

Sneak-and-Peek Warrants before the USA PATRIOT Act Contrary to popular misconception, sneak-and-peek warrants were in use prior to the enactment of the USA PATRIOT Act in 2001. Their use can be traced back to the early 1980s when "the FBI and the DEA . . . embarked upon a widespread series of [court-authorized] covert entries in a variety of criminal investigations" (Duncan, 2004: 9-10). Although the U.S. Supreme Court never specifically ruled on the constitutionality of covert entry warrants during the eighties and nineties, the Court had upheld a covert entry to place wiretapping equipment in a suspect's home in *Dalia v. United States*, 441 U.S. 238 (1979). Relying on *Dalia,* early cases examining covert entry pursuant to sneak-and-peek warrants upheld the covert entry; but they ruled nonetheless that searches conducted pursuant to these warrants were invalid if they did not subsequently provide the notice that the version of Rule 41 required at the time. *See, e.g., United States v. Freitas*, 800 F.2d 1451 (9th Cir. 1986), *modified on subsequent app.*, 856 F.2d 1425 (9th Cir. 1988). The notice requirement enables the person whose property is to be searched to assert Fourth Amendment rights, such as pointing out errors, irregularities, and limitations in the warrant.

As stated by one of the early courts reviewing the constitutionality of covert entry warrants: "[W]hen the authorized entry is to be covert and no tangible property is to be seized, there must be some safeguard to minimize the possibility that the officers will exceed the bounds of propriety without detection." *United States v. Villegas*, 899 F.2d 1324, 1336-67 (2d Cir. 1990). In effect, these early cases carved out their own exceptions to the notice requirements of Rule 41, holding that a sneak-and-peek warrant could validly issue upon a showing of necessity for a covert entry *so long as notice was given within a reasonable period of time after the search.* The court in *Freitas* held that such notice had to be given within seven days of the execution of a sneak-and-peek warrant. 800 F.2d at 1456. *Villegas* followed suit, adopting the rule set forth in *Freitas* about requiring notice within seven days of the search. But *Villegas* also provided for later notice if the government could show "good cause" for a delay in notification beyond seven days. 899 F.2d at 1337. "Such extensions should not be granted solely on the basis of the grounds presented for the first delay; rather, the applicant should be required to make a fresh showing of the need for further delay." 899 F.2d at 1337. Few courts, however, applied the exclusionary rule to violations of the notice requirements set forth in these early cases unless the defendant could show how he or she was prejudiced by the delay. Their reasoning was basically that notice is a requirement of Rule 41, not of the Fourth Amendment itself. *E.g., United States v. Simons*, 206 F.3d 392, 403 (4th Cir. 2000).

Sneak-and-Peek Warrants after the USA PATRIOT Act The USA PATRIOT Act was enacted less than two months after the terrorist attacks of September 11, 2001. Section 213 of the Act, codified at 18 U.S.C. § 3103a(b), contained "the first express statutory authorization for the issuance of sneak-and-peek search warrants in American history" (Duncan, 2004: 24). This section provided:

(b) Delay—With respect to the issuance of any warrant or court order under this section, or any other rule of law, to search for and seize any property or material that constitutes evidence of a criminal offense in violation of the laws of the United States, any notice required, or that may be required, to be given may be delayed if—

(1) the court finds reasonable cause to believe that providing immediate notification of the execution of the warrant may have an adverse result [defined in Section 2705 as "endangering the life or physical safety of an individual, flight from prosecution, destruction or tampering with evidence, intimidation of potential witness, or otherwise seriously jeopardizing an investigation or unduly delaying a trial."];

(2) the warrant prohibits the seizure of any tangible property . . . except where the court finds reasonable necessity for the seizure; and

(3) the warrant provides for the giving of such notice within a reasonable period of its execution, which period may thereafter be extended by the court for good cause shown. [Note: this sub-section has been replaced by a newer version, reproduced below.]

The USA PATRIOT Act, however, did not define what constitutes "reasonable cause" to authorize delayed notification, or what constitutes a "reasonable period" for notification after execution of a covert entry warrant. This changed when several provisions of the original USA PATRIOT Act came up for renewal in the wake of automatic sunset provisions contained in the initial legislation (that means provisions in the original Act would automatically expire unless renewed by Congress by the end of 2005). Congress amended Section 213(b)(3) of the PATRIOT Act, and the previous requirement of notice "within a reasonable period" was changed. Section 213(b)(3) now states:

(3) the warrant provides for the giving of such notice within a reasonable period not to exceed 30 days after the date of its execution, or on a later date certain if the facts of the case justify a longer period of delay.

See USA PATRIOT Act Improvement and Reauthorization Act of 2005, Pub. L. No. 109-177, § 114(a)(1), 120 Stat. 191, 210 (2006). However, Section 114(a)(2) of the USA PATRIOT Act Improvement and Reauthorization Act allows for extensions beyond thirty days:

(c) Extensions of delay—Any period of delay authorized by this section may be extended by the court for good cause shown, subject to the condition that extensions should only be granted upon an updated showing of the need for further delay and that each additional delay should be limited to periods of 90 days or less, unless the facts of the case justify a longer period of delay.

Finally, Section § 114(c) of the USA PATRIOT Act Improvement and Reauthorization Act enacted reporting requirements. Judges must now report the following information to the Administrative Office of the United States Courts: whenever a warrant is applied for; the fact that the warrant or any extension thereof was granted as applied for, was modified, or was denied; the period of delay in the giving of notice authorized by the warrant, and the number and duration of any extensions; and the offense specified in the warrant or application.

In turn, the director of the Administrative Office must compile all of the reports submitted by judges into an annual report to Congress. Thus, every time a law enforcement official applies for a sneak-and-peek warrant and/or any subsequent order allowing for an extension of the notice requirement—regardless of the outcome of the application—Congress will be informed of the application and its disposition.

Sneak-and-Steal Warrants under the USA PATRIOT Act *Freitas, Villegas,* and the other cases examining the constitutionality of covert entry warrants never authorized the covert seizure of any items during the execution of a sneak-and-peek warrant. The holdings of these cases were premised upon a search taking place without any corresponding seizure of items. If law enforcement officers discovered contraband or other evidence of criminal activity during a surreptitious search, they were supposed to go back to court and seek a regular search warrant that specifically detailed the items to be seized. But the USA PATRIOT Act changed that requirement. It specifically authorized the seizure of items discovered during the execution of a covert entry warrant if there is a "reasonable necessity for the seizure." The practice has come to be known as a **sneak-and-steal** search.

The passage of the USA PATRIOT Act Improvement and Reauthorization Act of 2005 did not alter the statutory grant of authority in the original USA PATRIOT Act with respect to sneak-and-steal warrants. As of the time of the writing of this text, no court has explicitly ruled on the constitutionality of these searches. However, at least one court has recognized that Section 213 of the USA PATRIOT Act specifically authorized these new types of searches and that this statutory provision trumps the notice requirements of Rule 41 of the Federal Rules of Criminal Procedure. *See ACLU v. U.S. Dep't of Justice,* 265 F. Supp. 2d 20, 24 (D.C. Cir. 2003). The court, however, commented in a footnote that although a sneak-and-steal warrant must specifically authorize the seizure of evidence on the basis of "reasonable necessity," there is some doubt as to whether such a warrant would comply with the requirements of due process. 265 F. Supp. 2d at 24 n.5 (citing *City of West Covina v. Perkins,* 525 U.S. 234, 240 (1999) ("[W]hen law enforcement agents seize property pursuant to warrant, due process requires them to take reasonable steps to give notice that the property has been taken so the owner can pursue available remedies for its return."). Only time will tell whether such warrants will remain a part of the U.S. criminal procedure process.

Search and Seizure of Third Parties and Their Property

When a search warrant is issued for the search of a named person or a named person and premises, officers executing the warrant clearly may simultaneously detain and search the person named. May officers detain and search a person on the premises who is not named in the warrant? What rules apply?

Searches of Third Parties during Warrant Executions The general rule is that a search warrant for premises gives a law enforcement officer no authority to search a person not named in the warrant who merely happens to be on the premises. In *Ybarra v. Illinois,* 444 U.S. 85 (1979), police had a warrant to search a bar and a bartender who worked there. The defendant in the case was a patron in the bar who was not named in the warrant. The U.S. Supreme Court held that a search of the defendant was illegal because the police did not have probable cause particularized with respect to the defendant:

> [A] person's mere propinquity to others independently suspected of criminal activity does not, without more, give rise to probable cause to search that person. . . . Where the standard is probable cause, a search or seizure of a person must be supported by probable cause particularized with respect to that person. This requirement cannot be undercut or avoided by simply pointing to the fact that coincidentally there exists probable cause to search or seize another or to search the premises where the person may happen to be. The Fourth and Fourteenth Amendments protect the "legitimate expectations of privacy" of persons, not places. 444 U.S. at 91.

The Court said that a warrant to search a place cannot normally be construed to authorize a search of each person in that place. Therefore, if an officer wishes to search a place and also specific persons expected to be at that place, the officer should obtain a search warrant to search the place and each specific person. To obtain such a warrant, the officer must establish in the affidavit probable cause to search the place and each specific individual.

Detentions and Pat-downs of Third Parties during Warrant Executions A search warrant may authorize detention of persons present on premises to be searched in certain circumstances, however. *Michigan v. Summers*, 452 U.S. 692 (1981), held that officers executing a valid search warrant for contraband may detain the occupants of the premises while the search is being conducted. The Court said that "[i]f the evidence that a citizen's residence is harboring contraband is sufficient to persuade a judicial officer that an invasion of the citizen's privacy is justified, it is constitutionally reasonable to require that citizen to remain while officers of the law execute a valid warrant to search his home." 452 U.S. at 704-05. In explaining the justification for the detention, the Court emphasized the limited additional intrusion represented by the detention once a search of the home had been authorized by a warrant:

> In assessing the justification for the detention of an occupant of premises being searched for contraband pursuant to a valid warrant, both the law enforcement interest and the nature of the "articulable facts" supporting the detention are relevant. Most obvious is the legitimate law enforcement interest in preventing flight in the event that incriminating evidence is found. Less obvious, but sometimes of greater importance, is the interest in minimizing the risk of harm to the officers. Although no special danger to the police is suggested by the evidence in this record, the execution of a warrant to search for narcotics is the kind of transaction that may give rise to sudden violence or frantic efforts to conceal or destroy evidence. The risk of harm to both the police and the occupants is minimized if the officers routinely exercise unquestioned command of the situation. . . . Finally, the orderly completion of the search may be facilitated if the occupants of the premises are present. Their self-interest may induce them to open locked doors or locked containers to avoid the use of force that is not only damaging to property but may also delay the completion of the task at hand. 452 U.S. at 702-03.

Courts have interpreted *Summers* as holding that: "police have limited authority to detain the occupant of a house without probable cause while the premises are searched, when the detention is neither prolonged nor unduly intrusive, and

Discussion
POINT

How Far Is Too Far Before a Detention Becomes Unduly Intrusive?

Muehler v. Mena, 544 U.S. 93 (2005).

Based on information gleaned from the investigation of a gang-related, drive-by shooting, petitioners Muehler and Brill had reason to believe at least one member of a gang—the West Side Locos—lived at 1363 Patricia Avenue. They also suspected that the individual was armed and dangerous, since he had recently been involved in the drive-by shooting. As a result, Muehler obtained a search warrant for 1363 Patricia Avenue that authorized a broad search of the house and premises for, among other things, deadly weapons and evidence of gang membership. In light of the high degree of risk involved in searching a house suspected of housing at least one, and perhaps multiple, armed gang members, a Special Weapons and Tactics (SWAT) team was used to secure the residence and grounds before the search.

At 7 A.M. on February 3, 1998, petitioners, along with the SWAT team and other officers, executed the warrant. Mena was asleep in her bed when the SWAT team, clad in helmets and black vests adorned with badges and the word "POLICE," entered her bedroom and placed her in handcuffs at gunpoint. The SWAT team also handcuffed three other individuals found on the property. The SWAT team then took those individuals and Mena into a converted garage, which contained several beds and some other bedroom furniture. While the search proceeded, one or two officers guarded the four detainees, who were allowed to move around the garage but remained in handcuffs during the two to three hours that it took to execute the search warrant.

Aware that the West Side Locos gang was composed primarily of illegal immigrants, the officers had notified the Immigration and Naturalization Service (INS) that they would be conducting the search, and an INS officer accompanied the officers executing the warrant. During their detention in the garage, an officer asked for each detainee's name, date of birth, place of birth, and immigration status. The INS officer later asked the detainees for their immigration documentation. Mena's status as a permanent resident was confirmed by her papers.

when police are executing a validly executed search warrant for contraband." *Heitschmidt v. City of Houston*, 161 F.3d 834, 838 (5th Cir. 1998); *Leveto v. Lapina*, 258 F.3d 156, 170 n.6 (3d Cir. 2001). Thus, in *Heitschmidt*, the court ruled that the defendant had been illegally detained in light of *Summers* because he was handcuffed on the street, pushed into the trunk of a car, and then detained for over four hours without a bathroom break. Moreover, the search warrant in that case was targeted at finding evidence that the defendant's roommate was running a prostitution ring, not any type of contraband.

In *Williams v. Kaufman County*, 352 F.3d 994 (5th Cir. 2003), a group of people filed a civil suit under Section 1983 for various civil rights deprivations that occurred during the execution of a search warrant at a nightclub connected to a crack cocaine distribution ring. During the three-hour search, approximately

How Far Is Too Far Before a Detention Becomes Unduly Intrusive? *(Continued)*

The search of the premises yielded a .22 caliber handgun with .22 caliber ammunition, a box of .25 caliber ammunition, several baseball bats with gang writing, various additional gang paraphernalia, and a bag of marijuana. Before the officers left the area, Mena was released.

In her § 1983 suit against the officers, she alleged that she was detained "for an unreasonable time and in an unreasonable manner" in violation of the Fourth Amendment. In addition, she claimed that the warrant and its execution were overbroad, and that the officers failed to comply with the knock-and-announce rule.

After a trial, a jury, pursuant to a special verdict form, found that Officers Muehler and Brill violated Mena's Fourth Amendment right to be free from unreasonable seizures by detaining her both with force greater than that which was reasonable and for a longer period than that which was reasonable. A court of appeals affirmed, finding that it was objectively unreasonable to confine her in the converted garage and keep her in handcuffs during the search. The appeals court thought the officers should have released Mena as soon as it became clear that she posed no immediate threat. On appeal, the Supreme Court reversed, holding that the officers' actions were reasonable under the Fourth Amendment and within the scope of the behaviors authorized in *Michigan v. Summers.*

Do you agree with the Supreme Court that the conduct of law enforcement in this case was "reasonable," or do you believe that the decision of the court of appeals makes more sense? Explain your reasoning. With regard to the warrant at issue in this case, do you think it was sufficiently particular, or was it overbroad? Why? Finally, what do you make of the officers' failure to comply with the knock-and-announce rule? Explain what you think the consequences of this failure should be.

one hundred people were detained. During that time, the occupants of the club were strip-searched and some were handcuffed. Even though the warrant authorized a search for contraband, the court still held that the search was unreasonable. First and foremost, the strip-searches were invalid because the police had no reasonable, articulable suspicion that any one of the club's patrons, other than the few people specifically named in the warrant, would be carrying contraband. But the issue of the strip-searches aside, the court still held the mass detention of club patrons unreasonable in light of the length of the detention and because the club "was a public establishment and not a private residence"; therefore, the detainees "had no reason to remain at the club during the search." 352 F.3d at 1010.

In contrast to the detentions and searches at issue in *Heitschmidt* and *Williams*, officers are permitted to conduct a limited pat-down search or frisk for weapons of any person at the search scene whom the officer reasonably suspects is armed and dangerous. The officer must be able to justify the frisk with specific facts and circumstances to support the belief that a particular person is armed and dangerous; a mere suspicion or hunch or an unsupported assertion of "officer safety" do not justify a protective frisk. (See Chapter 7 for details on conducting protective frisks.)

Of course, if an officer at a search scene obtains information constituting probable cause to make a felony arrest, or if a crime is being committed in the officer's presence, the officer may arrest the offender and search him or her incident to the arrest. (See Chapter 8 for details on search incident to arrest.)

Searches and Seizures of Third Parties' Property during Warrant Execution

Similar rules apply to the search and seizure of the property of third persons on the premises described in a warrant. For purposes of this discussion, a third person is a person who is not the target of the warrant and is not a resident of the target premises. Courts are split on which of two tests to apply to such searches and seizures.

The Actual or Constructive Knowledge Test Under this approach, when a law enforcement officer executing a search warrant knows or reasonably should know that personal property located within the described premises belongs to a third person, the officer may not search or seize the property under authority of the warrant. However, when officers have no reason to believe that property belongs to a third person, they may search or seize the property. *See, e.g., Waters v. State*, 924 P.2d 437, 439 (Alaska App.1996). A comparison of the following two cases nicely illustrates the difference.

In *State v. Lambert*, 710 P.2d 693 (Kan. 1985), a police officer executing a warrant for an apartment and its male occupant discovered three women in the kitchen of the apartment. The officers searched a purse lying on the kitchen table and found drugs. The court invalidated the search, finding that the officer had no reason to believe that the purse either belonged to the occupant of the premises or was part of the premises described in the search warrant. In contrast, *Carman v. State*, 602 P.2d 1255 (Alaska 1979), upheld the search of a purse because the court found that the police neither knew nor did they have any objective reason to know, whether the purse belonged to a permanent resident of the apartment or a visitor. *See also State v. Thomas*, 818 S.W.2d 350, 360 (Tenn. Crim. App. 1991) (holding a search of a purse unlawful after finding that officers "knew or should have known" that it belonged to a nonresident).

The Physical Possession Test "Under the 'physical possession' test, officers executing a warrant may search all items that could contain articles identified in the warrant except those that are in the actual physical possession of a person not subject to the warrant." *State v. Reid*, 77 P.3d 1134, 1140 (Or .App. 2003). This test allows police to search any container that could conceal an item listed in the warrant "unless the container is being worn by, or is in the actual possession of, a person not named in the warrant." *State v. Leiper*, 761 A.2d 458, 461 (N.H. 2000). In *Leiper*, police executed a search warrant in an apartment looking for "marijuana and/or hallucinogenic mushrooms" during a time when they knew that the apartment's tenant would be hosting a party. The defendant was one of approximately a dozen people at the party when the police arrived. He was seated on the couch and his knapsack was "near him on the couch." When he was removed from the premises during the search "because he was acting in a disruptive manner," the police searched his knapsack and found hallucinogenic mushrooms in it. 761 A.2d at 460. Because the knapsack was on the premises being searched, was capable of containing the items named in the warrant, and was not in the defendant's physical possession at the time it was searched, the court upheld the search of the knapsack and the seizure of the contraband found in it.

The Automobile Exception As the material in Chapter 11 makes clear, different rules apply to searches of automobiles and containers found in them than apply for other types of searches. Given their inherently movable nature, *Wyoming v. Houghton*, 526 U.S. 295 (1999), ruled that neither the actual or constructive knowledge test nor the physical possession test was applicable to the execution of searches concerning motor vehicles. Instead, the U.S. Supreme Court ruled that police officers with probable cause to search a car may inspect passengers' belongings found in the car that are capable of concealing the object of the search.

key points

- Before law enforcement officers may lawfully force their way into a dwelling to execute a search warrant, they must knock on the door; announce their authority and purpose; demand admittance; and have their demand for admittance either be refused or go unacknowledged for a reasonable period of time, usually at least twenty to thirty seconds. To justify an exception to this requirement, officers must either have a previously authorized no-knock warrant, or have a reasonable suspicion that knocking and announcing, under the particular circumstances, would be dangerous or futile or that it would inhibit the investigation of the crime by risking the destruction of evidence or the escape of a suspect.
- Unless specifically authorized to do otherwise by a valid covert entry warrant, officers executing a search warrant must give a copy of the warrant and a receipt for the property taken to the person from whom, or from whose premises, the property was taken or leave a copy of the warrant and receipt at the place where the officer took the property.
- A covert entry, or sneak-and-peek warrant, may authorize a search without contemporaneous notice of the search upon a showing of reasonable cause

to believe that providing immediate notification of the execution of the warrant may endanger the life or physical safety of an individual, prompt flight from prosecution, destruction or tampering with evidence, intimidation of potential witness, or otherwise seriously jeopardize an investigation or unduly delay a trial. If such a covert entry warrant is issued, notice must be given to the person whose premises were searched within a reasonable period not to exceed thirty days after the date of the execution of the warrant unless the facts of the case justify a longer period of delay.
- A search warrant for premises gives a law enforcement officer no authority to search a person not named in the warrant who merely happens to be on the premises. Officers are permitted, however, to conduct a limited pat-down for weapons of any person at the search scene who the officer reasonably suspects is armed and dangerous.
- Police have limited authority to detain the occupants of premises being searched without probable cause so long as the detention is neither prolonged nor unduly intrusive, and when police are executing a validly executed search warrant for contraband.

Scope of the Search

The scope of law enforcement activities during the execution of the warrant must be strictly limited to achieving the objectives that are set forth with particularity in the warrant. If officers exceed the scope of the authorized invasion under the terms of the warrant, the evidence seized will usually be deemed inadmissible. *See, e.g., United States v. Fuccillo*, 808 F.2d 173, 177-78 (1st Cir. 1987).

The Physical Boundaries to Be Searched A search may not extend beyond the items or premises particularly identified in the warrant. For example, in *State v. Matsunaga*, 920 P.2d 376 (Haw. Ct. App. 1996), *cert. denied*, 922 P.2d 973 (Haw. 1996), a search warrant authorized police to search the office of a particular business located in an office building. When the police extended their search of the building to an office of an adjacent business, the court held that they had exceeded the scope of the warrant even though the other office was in the same building. The same rule holds true for smaller places to be searched. *People v. McPhee*, 628 N.E.2d 523 (Ill. App. 1993), for example, invalidated the search of a residence where a Federal Express parcel had been delivered because the warrant only authorized the search of the parcel itself, not the home to which it was being delivered.

Expansive Scope of Searches of Specific Premises *United States v. Ross*, 456 U.S. 798, 820-21 (1982), stated the general rule: **"A lawful search of fixed premises generally extends to the entire area in which the object of the search may be found and is not limited by the possibility that separate acts of entry or opening may be required to complete the search."** The Court provided examples of the application of the rule:

> **[A] warrant that authorizes an officer to search a home for illegal weapons also provides authority to open closets, chests, drawers, and containers in which the weapon might be found. A warrant to open a footlocker to search for marijuana would also authorize the opening of packages found inside. A warrant to search a vehicle would support a search of every part of the vehicle that might contain the object of the search. When a legitimate search is under way, and when its purpose and its limits have been precisely defined, nice distinctions between closets, drawers, and containers, in the case of a home, or between glove compartments, upholstered seats, trunks and wrapped packages, in the case of a vehicle, must give way to the interest in the prompt and efficient completion of the task at hand.** 456 U.S. at 821-22.

Curtilage and Areas "Appurtenant" to Specified Premises A search warrant authorizing the search of particularly described premises justifies a search not only of the described premises, but also the areas within the curtilage of the premises. **Curtilage** was defined by the U.S. Supreme Court in *Oliver v. United States*, 466 U.S. 170, 180 (1984), as the **"land immediately surrounding and associated with the home"** in which the owner or resident has taken steps to protect from observation by people passing by, such as a screened-in porch, a gated courtyard, or fenced-in backyard. *See Murphy v. Gardner*, 413 F. Supp. 2d 1156 (D. Colo. 2006). (For more details on curtilage, see Chapter 12.)

A search warrant authorizing the search of particularly described premises also justifies a search of all things **appurtenant**—incident to, belonging to, or going with—the principal property, such as buildings on the land (e.g., sheds) and other things attached to or annexed to the land. For example, a detached garage, even if not named in a warrant, can be searched as an appurtenant building to a house. *See United States v. Bonner*, 808 F.2d 864 (1st Cir. 1986).

United States v. Ferreras, 192 F.3d 5, 10 (1st Cir. 1999), upheld the search of an attic that was not named in a search warrant as being appurtenant to a second-floor apartment that has exclusive access to the attic.

The rule on the searchability of appurtenant areas extends to structures that are not single-family dwellings. For example, in *United States v. Principe*, 499 F.2d 1135 (1st Cir. 1974), a search of a cabinet in a hallway several feet away from the apartment described in the search warrant was justified when the owner testified that the cabinet "went with the apartment." The same result occurred in *State v. Llamas-Villa*, 836 P.2d 239 (Wash. App. 1992), with regard to a padlocked locker located in a storage room next to defendant's apartment.

Of course, officers executing a search warrant may look only where the items described in the warrant might be concealed. Thus, searches of an appurtenant area that could not contain specific items to be seized would not be authorized under this doctrine.

Motor Vehicles on Property Because a warrant generally authorizes the search of all items on the premises in which the objects of a search might be found—*see United States v. Ross*, 456 U.S. 798, 820-21 (1982)—"the scope of a warrant authorizing the search of a particularly described residence includes any automobiles, owned or controlled by the owner of such residence, which are located within the curtilage of the premises at the time the warrant is executed." *Com. v. McCarthy*, 705 N.E.2d 1110 (Mass. 1999). *State v. Brown*, 820 P.2d 878 (1991), *rev. denied*, 830 P.2d 596 (1992), upheld a search of the defendant's trailer even though it was not located within the legal boundary of the street address specified in warrant. The court reasoned:

> Although the trailer was not within the property line . . . , it was located only 40 to 50 feet from the residence at the address and reasonably appeared associated with the premises and is specifically and accurately described in the warrant. No fence or other obvious demarcation separated the two properties, and the officers executing the warrant had no reason to believe that the trailer was not within the boundary specified in the warrant. The warrant authorized the invasion of defendant's privacy and, [therefore,] his protected property interest in the trailer. Under the circumstances, we hold that the legal boundary or property line did not circumscribe the officers' authority under the warrant to search the trailer. The search of the trailer was within the . . . Oregon Constitution or the Fourth Amendment. 820 P.2d at 883.

If, however, a motor vehicle is not on the property or seemingly within its reasonable curtilage, then most courts hold that a warrant to search the premises will not justify a search of such a vehicle unless the vehicle was specifically named in the warrant. Thus, for example, a car not named in the warrant, and which was parked in the street along the curb, could not be lawfully searched pursuant to a warrant to search premises. *See, e.g., Henderson v. State*, 685 So. 2d 970, 971 (Fla. App. 1996).

Neighboring or Adjacent Property Searches of areas neighboring or adjacent to the particularly described premises are usually not allowed. *See, e.g., United States v. Schroeder*, 129 F.3d 439 (8th Cir. 1997). If neighboring or adjacent areas are only nominally separate, however, and are actually used as a single living or commercial area, courts may allow the search of the entire area despite a limited warrant description. *United States v. Elliott*, 893 F.2d 220 (9th Cir. 1990), held that the search of a storeroom behind an apartment did not exceed the scope of the warrant authorizing the search of the apartment. The storeroom was accessible through a hole cut in the wall of the suspect's bathroom and was covered by a burlap bag. The court found that the unconventional means of access did not sever the room from the rest of the apartment.

Common Areas on Shared Property As noted by the court in *United States v. King*, 227 F.3d 732 (6th Cir. 2000), courts appear to draw a "distinction between a dwelling occupied by a limited number of tenants, such as a small two-family house, and a large multi-unit apartment building for purposes of [the] Fourth Amendment." Courts usually hold that searches of common areas in the latter type of property do not give rise to Fourth Amendment concerns because people do not have a reasonable expectation of privacy in foyers, garages, backyards, lounges, and other common areas of large multi-unit apartment buildings. *See, e.g., United States v. McGrane*, 746 F.2d 632 (8th Cir. 1984).

In contrast, courts are divided as to whether occupants of smaller, shared dwellings have a reasonable expectation of privacy in the common areas. In *United States v. McGrane*, 746 F.2d at the Eighth Circuit held that tenants of a two-story building which contained four apartment units (two on each floor) and a basement did not enjoy a reasonable expectation of privacy in the basement area. Fifteen years after *McGrane*, the Eighth Circuit extended its holding when it ruled that a defendant did not have a reasonable expectation of privacy in a hallway closet that was located in the common area of a duplex. *United States v. McCaster*, 193 F.3d 930, 933 (8th Cir. 1999). The court reasoned that the defendant had not taken any steps to evidence any subjective expectation of privacy in the contents of the closet since the landlord and two other tenants had access to the closet.

Other courts disagree with the Eighth Circuit's approach and hold that the residents of smaller shared dwellings, like duplexes, have a reasonable expectation of privacy in the common areas of those buildings. *United States v. Fluker*, 543 F.2d 709 (9th Cir. 1976), ruled that a corridor separating the door of the defendant's apartment from the outer doorway of the apartment building was protected by the Fourth Amendment. Critical to the court's ruling was the fact that there were only two other tenants in the building and no one else could enter that hallway. The same conclusion was reached with regard to a backyard shared by the tenants of a four-unit apartment building in *Fixel v. Wainwright*, 492 F.2d 480 (5th Cir. 1974); and a common hallway shared by only two apartment units in *People v. Killebrew*, 256 N.W.2d 581 (1977).

More recently, some courts have recognized a legitimate expectation of privacy in the common basement shared by the dwellers of a two-family home. *See Connecticut v. Reddick*, 541 A.2d 1209 (Conn. 1988). In *United States v. King*, 227 F.3d 732, 753 (6th Cir. 2000), the warrant authorized the search of "the premises, curtilage, containers, and persons therein" at a location described as "1437 East 116th Street, Cleveland, Cuyahoga County, Ohio, and being more fully described as the downstairs unit in a two-family, two and one half story, white wood-sided dwelling with green trim." 227 F.3d at 737. Because this warrant only authorized the unit on the first floor of the duplex, the court ruled that police had exceeded the scope of a search warrant when they searched the basement and seized evidence in it.

Inaccurate Descriptions of Property An inaccurate description of premises to be searched may cause officers to exceed the scope of a warrant, especially with respect to multiple-occupancy dwellings. In *Maryland v. Garrison*, 480 U.S. 79 (1987), officers obtained and executed a warrant to search the person of Lawrence McWebb and "the premises known as 2036 Park Avenue third floor apartment." The officers reasonably believed, on the basis of the information available, that only one apartment was located on the third floor. In fact, the third floor was divided into two apartments, one occupied by McWebb and one by the defendant. Before the officers discovered that they were in the wrong person's apartment, they had discovered contraband that led to the defendant's conviction.

The Court held that the officers had made a reasonable effort to ascertain and identify the place intended to be searched, and that their failure to realize the overbreadth of the warrant was objectively understandable and reasonable. Nevertheless, the Court said:

> If the officers had known, or should have known, that the third floor contained two apartments before they entered the living quarters on the third floor, and thus had been aware of the error in the warrant, they would have been obligated to limit their search to McWebb's apartment. Moreover . . . they were required to discontinue the search of respondent's apartment as soon as they discovered that there were two separate units on the third floor and therefore were put on notice of the risk that they might be in a unit erroneously included within the terms of the warrant. 480 U.S. at 86-87.

Therefore, although some latitude is allowed for honest mistakes in executing search warrants, officers may not rely blindly on the descriptions in a warrant but must make a reasonable effort to determine that the place they are searching is the place intended to be searched. *See also United States v. Lora-Solano*, 330 F.3d 1288, 1294-95 (10th Cir. 2003) (evidence admissible even though a warrant misstated the address by a single digit because officers did not deliberately misstate the address, and a controlled delivery to the proper premises had been precisely described in the warrant).

Seizure of Unauthorized Items In *Coolidge v. New Hampshire*, 403 U.S. 443, 465 (1971), the Court said that "[a]n example of the applicability of the 'plain view' doctrine is the situation in which the police have a warrant to search a given area for specific objects, and in the course of the search come across some other article of incriminating character." In *Cady v. Dombrowski*, 413 U.S. 433 (1973), police investigating a possible homicide were told by the defendant that he believed there was a body lying near his brother's farm. The police found the body and the defendant's car at the farm. Police observed through the car window a pillowcase, a backseat, and a briefcase covered with blood, and obtained a warrant to search the car for those items. While executing the warrant, they discovered in "plain view" a blood-covered sock and floor mat, which they seized. The defendant claimed that the sock and the floor mat taken from his car were seized illegally because they were not specifically listed in the warrant. The Court held that the seizure of the items was constitutional. The warrant was validly issued, and the car was the item designated to be searched; therefore, the police were authorized to search the car. Although the sock and floor mat were not listed in the warrant, the officers discovered these items in plain view in the car while executing the warrant and therefore could constitutionally seize them without a warrant. Decisions of many courts since the *Dombrowski* decision have established the rule that a law enforcement officer lawfully executing a valid search warrant may seize items of evidence not particularly described in the warrant that are found at the searched premises, if the seizure satisfies all the requirements of the plain view doctrine. (See Chapter 10 for a complete discussion of the plain view doctrine.)

If, however, the plain view doctrine does not apply, unless one of the other warrant exceptions discussed in Part III of this text applies such as open fields (see Chapter 12), or some exigent circumstance justifies the warrantless seizure of an item that is beyond the scope authorized for seizure in the warrant, items beyond the scope of a search may not be seized. Rather, police must apply for a separate warrant that authorizes the seizure of the suspect material. *See, e.g., United States v. Robinson*, 275 F.3d 371, 382 (4th Cir. 2001) (holding seized evidence admissible because officers suspended search and obtained second warrant before seizing items not described with particularity within the original warrant). If officers fail to do so, then the items seized that were not authorized for seizure by the warrant will be inadmissible in court. Moreover, if officers act in flagrant disregard of the terms of a search warrant and treat a search as a general one, they risk the suppression of all evidence seized during the search—even the evidence that would have otherwise been lawfully seizable under the warrant. Which of these outcomes will occur depends not only on the degree of impropriety of the officer's conduct, but also on the law of the governing jurisdiction.

The Flagrant Disregard/Total Suppression Approach Some courts hold that when "law enforcement officers grossly exceed the scope of a search warrant in seizing property, the particularity requirement is undermined and a valid warrant is transformed into a general warrant thereby requiring suppression of all evidence seized under that warrant." *United States v. Medlin*, 842 F.2d 1194, 1199 (10th Cir. 1988). *Medlin* involved a search warrant that had authorized the entry into the defendant's home to search for and seize firearms illegally possessed by the defendant. While the search was being conducted, a deputy sheriff searched the premise for stolen property that he believed may have been on the defendant's property based on a tip he had received from an informant. The deputy seized over 660 items. The court ruled that the deputy sheriff's actions transformed the search from one that was particularized and authorized by the warrant into an unconstitutional, "general search." The Tenth Circuit reaffirmed this approach more recently in *United States v. Foster*, 100 F.3d 846 (10th Cir. 1996), and several other circuits have also adopted the flagrant disregard approach. *See United States v. Shi Yan Liu*, 239 F.3d 138 (2d Cir. 2000); *United States v. Squillacote*, 221 F.3d 542 (4th Cir. 2000), *cert. denied*, 532 U.S. 971 (2001); *United States v. Rettig*, 589 F.2d 418 (9th Cir. 1978).

The Partial Suppression Approach Not all jurisdictions follow the "flagrant disregard" approach of suppressing all evidence seized during an overbroad search. Some jurisdictions exclude from evidence only those items that the warrant did not authorize and were not otherwise seizable under the plain view doctrine (see Chapter 10), while admitting all items for which there was probable cause to support their seizure under the particular terms of the warrant. *See, e.g., United States v. Photogrammetric Data Services, Inc.*, 259 F.3d 229 (4th Cir. 2001), *cert. denied*, 535 U.S. 926 (2002). *Klingenstein v. State*, 624 A.2d 532 (Md. 1993); *State v. Johnson*, 605 So.2d 545 (Fla. App. 1992). And although the U.S. Supreme Court has not ruled squarely on the issue, their language in *Waller v. Georgia*, 467 U.S. 39, 43-44, n. 3 (1984), strongly suggests that the Court would reject the "flagrant disregard" approach.

> **Petitioners' second Fourth Amendment challenge is that police so "flagrant[ly] disregard[ed]" the scope of the warrants in conducting the seizures at issue here that they turned the warrants into impermissible general warrants. Petitioners rely on lower court cases . . . for the proposition that in such circumstances the entire fruits of the search, and not just those items as to which there was no probable cause to support seizure, must be suppressed. Petitioners do not assert that the officers exceeded the scope of the warrant in the places searched. Rather, they say only that the police unlawfully seized and took away items unconnected to the prosecution. The Georgia Supreme Court found that all items that were unlawfully seized were suppressed. In these circumstances, there is certainly no requirement that lawfully seized evidence be suppressed as well.**

Use of Force Officers executing a search warrant may use reasonable force in conducting the search. An otherwise reasonable search may be invalidated if excessive force is used. A search warrant gives officers authority to break into a house or other objects of the search and to damage property if reasonably necessary to properly execute the warrant. *United States v. Becker*, 929 F.2d 442 (9th Cir. 1991), held that the jack-hammering of a concrete slab to execute a search warrant for drugs was reasonable, based on an examination of all the facts and circumstances: (1) officers had found evidence of the manufacture of methamphetamine in the shop next to the slab, (2) the concrete slab had been poured within the preceding forty-five days, and (3) the shop appeared to have been recently and hastily repainted and repaired. In *United States v. Ross*, 456 U.S. 798, 823 (1982), involving a search of a vehicle for contraband, the Court said: "**An individual undoubtedly has a significant interest that the upholstery of his automobile will not be ripped or a hidden compartment within it opened. These interests must yield to the authority of a search, however. . . .**"

Nevertheless, officers must exercise great care to avoid unnecessary damage to premises or objects. They must conduct a search in a manner designed to do the least damage possible, while still making a thorough examination of the premises. They should carefully replace objects that were necessarily moved or rearranged during the search. Generally, "[i]n executing a search warrant, to the extent possible, due respect should be given to the property of the occupants of the premises searched." *State v. Sierra*, 338 So.2d 609, 616 (La. 1976). Finally, common decency and fair play mandate that officers executing a search warrant avoid any unnecessary injury to the feelings of persons present at the premises searched.

After a Search Warrant Is Executed

Once the items specified in a warrant have been found during a search and seized, the legal justification for law enforcement officers' intrusion onto premises comes to an end. They must therefore leave the premises in a timely

Discussion

⬆ POINT

What About Excessive Force When Executing a Warrant?

Turner v. Fallen, 1993 WL 15647 (N.D. Ill. 1993).

The present action arises out of the police officers' execution of a search warrant in Ms. Turner's establishment, a consignment clothing store known as Dynasty II located at 5222-24 West North Avenue in Chicago, Illinois. A search warrant set forth the following articles to be seized: three pairs of silk pants "Index" brand, two silk jackets "Index" brand, two silk shirts "Index" brand, one beige jacket "Index" brand, and one double breasted jacket "Index" brand. The warrant states that the above listed items to be seized constitute evidence of the offense of possession of stolen property and that there is probable cause to believe that these items are located upon the person and premises of Dynasty II.

Ms. Turner alleges that the actions of the police officers, in executing this search warrant of her consignment shop, were unreasonable. She claims that the officers were not searching for drugs, which could be concealed in crevices and small places. Despite this fact, Ms. Turner alleges that the police officers took the following unreasonable actions in executing their search for the clothing items identified in the warrant: broke the front door, broke several ceiling tiles, broke open the cash register without asking for the key despite the key's ready availability, broke open the file cabinet, and smashed the glass display cases.

Ms. Turner further alleges that the police officers confiscated a number of items, totally unrelated to the search warrant, including the following: all licenses from the consignment shop and the hair salon; approximately 300 skirts, blouses, dresses, slacks, and other clothing items; all business records and consignment receipts for clothing, which were in a six-drawer file cabinet; dress racks; checks payable to Ms. Turner; diamond earrings; several hundred dollars of U.S. currency; and numerous other clothing items. Allegedly, Ms. Turner's establishments were emptied

manner. *See, e.g., Taylor v. State*, 7 P.3d 15 (Wyo. 2000); *United States v. Menon*, 24 F.3d 550 (3d Cir. 1994). However, before departing, Federal Rule of Criminal Procedure 41 and its state counterparts say that proper execution of a search warrant entails several duties after the actual search is completed. Unless a sneak-and-peak and/or sneak-and-steal warrant provides otherwise, searching officers must inventory all the property seized and leave a copy of the warrant and inventory with the occupants or on the premises if no occupant is present.

After leaving the searched premises—regardless of whether the warrant is a traditional search warrant or one of the covert entry-type warrants—the warrant itself, together with a copy of the inventory, must be returned to the judicial officer designated in the warrant. A typical form for the return and inventory

What About Excessive Force When Executing a Warrant? (*Continued*)

in truckloads despite the police officers' having no evidence that this merchandise was stolen. Ms. Turner claims that the actions of the police officers put her out of business.

Ms. Turner's complaint also states that she had another establishment, the Dynasty II Hair Salon, located next door to the Dynasty II consignment shop. She alleges that, despite the fact that the hair salon did not sell clothes and, thus, had nothing to do with the search warrant, the police officers searched throughout the hair salon, committing damage, disrupting business, and harassing salon customers.

In reviewing and upholding Ms. Turner's complaint for damages, the court wrote:

> In the present case, the damage alleged by Ms. Turner surpasses the mere breaking down of her shop's door. Rather, Ms. Turner alleges specific facts to support her claim that the police officers' search was unreasonable. For example, she alleges that the police officers intentionally smashed the glass display cases in her shop in order to confiscate certain items found within the cases. Yet, the officers did not first notify her of their need to enter the cases, nor did they try to find another way into the display cases that could have avoided the unnecessary property damage. Likewise, Ms. Turner alleges that the police officers broke her cash register and file cabinet, when they could have avoided this property damage merely by asking her to unlock these items. As such, Ms. Turner alleges that the police officers destroyed and damaged property not reasonably necessary to effectively execute their search warrant. 1993 WL 15647 at *4.

Do you think excessive force was used during the execution of the search warrant? Explain your answer.

What do you make of the seizure of the items not named in the warrant? Do you think these seizures violate the Fourth Amendment? Why or why not?

(which is usually on the back of the search warrant) appears in Figure 4.2b (on page 190).

Courts generally hold that these post-search duties are ministerial acts, and that failure to perform them will not result in suppression unless the defendant demonstrates legal prejudice or shows that the failure was intentional or in bad faith. *United States v. Simons*, 206 F.3d 392 (4th Cir. 2000).

key points

- A search warrant authorizing the search of particularly described premises justifies a search of the described land, all of the buildings on the land, and other things attached or annexed to the land.
- A warrant authorizing a search for a particular object allows a search of the entire area in which the object may be found and allows the opening of closets, chests, drawers, and containers in which the object might be found.
- A law enforcement officer lawfully executing a valid search warrant may seize items not particularly described in the warrant that are found at the searched premises, if the seizure satisfies all the requirements of the plain view doctrine (see Chapter 10) or some other valid exception for warrantless seizures (see Part III). If the plain view doctrine does not apply, then items beyond the scope of what a warrant authorized to be seized may not be taken. Rather, police must apply for a separate warrant that authorizes the seizure of the suspect material. A violation of this rule may result in the suppression of evidence.

- Officers executing a search warrant may use reasonable force in conducting the search. An otherwise reasonable search may be invalidated if excessive force is used.
- Once the items specified in a warrant have been found during a search and seized, the legal justification for law enforcement officers' intrusion onto premises comes to an end. They must therefore leave the premises in a timely manner. However, before departing, unless a sneak-and-peak and/or sneak-and-steal warrant provides otherwise, searching officers must inventory all the property seized and leave a copy of the warrant and inventory with the occupants or on the premises if no occupant is present.
- After leaving the searched premises (regardless of whether the warrant is a traditional search warrant or one of the covert entry-type warrants), officers must return the warrant itself, together with a copy of the inventory, to the judicial officer designated in the warrant.

Summary

The general rule is that all searches and seizures conducted without a warrant are unreasonable and violate the Fourth Amendment to the U.S. Constitution. Although there are many well-defined exceptions to this rule, searches made under the authority of a warrant not only are greatly preferred by the courts, but also give law enforcement officers greater protection from liability.

A search warrant is a written order issued by a proper neu tral judicial officer commanding a law enforcement officer to search for certain personal property and bring it before the judicial authority named in the warrant. An officer may obtain a search warrant by submitting to a magistrate a written application in the form of a sworn affidavit. The affidavit must state underlying facts and circumstances supporting probable cause to believe that particularly described items are located in a particularly described place or on

a particularly described person. A search warrant may authorize seizure only of items connected with criminal activity, such as contraband, fruits, and instrumentalities of crime; items illegally possessed; and evidence of crime.

A magistrate who finds probable cause to search issues a search warrant directing an officer or class of officers to execute the warrant. Officers must conduct the search within a reasonable time after the warrant's issuance and within any time period specified by law or court rule. Before entering premises by force to execute the warrant, officers must knock and announce their authority and purpose and be refused admittance after waiting about thirty seconds, unless the officer reasonably suspects that this notice will result in the loss or destruction of evidence, the escape of a suspect, or danger to an officer or others. Persons on the premises may not be searched, unless the search warrant authorizes the search of a particular person. Property of persons who are not the target of the warrant and not residents of the target premises may not be seized. If officers are executing a warrant to search for contraband, persons on the premises may be detained during the course of the search. Any person on the premises whom officers reasonably believe to be armed and dangerous may be frisked for weapons.

A search under authority of a search warrant may extend to the entire premises described in the warrant, but only to those parts of the prem-

ises where the items to be seized might be concealed. The search must be conducted in a manner to avoid unnecessary damage to the premises or objects. Items not named in the warrant may be seized if all elements of the plain view doctrine are satisfied. After the search is completed, the officer must leave at the searched premises a copy of the warrant and an inventory of and receipt for property taken. The officer must return the warrant, along with a written inventory of property seized, to the judicial officer designated in the warrant.

Key Terms

affiant, 187
affidavit, 187
anticipatory search warrants, 206
appurtenant, 232
covert entry/sneak-and-peak warrants, 223

curtilage, 232
Franks hearing, 209
general warrant, 184
knock-and-announce, 219
magistrate, 186
no-knock warrant, 222

particularity, 196
probable cause, 185
redaction/severability, 211
Rule 41, 225
search, 185

search warrant, 185
seizure, 185
staleness, 192
triggering condition, 206
sneak-and-steal warrants, 226

Review and Discussion Questions

1. Why is time a more important factor in determining probable cause to search than it is in determining probable cause to arrest?

2. Formulate a set of circumstances in which there is probable cause to search but not probable cause to arrest; in which there is probable cause to arrest but not probable cause to search; in which there is probable cause both to arrest and to search.

3. Name three kinds of property that are unlikely to remain in a particular place for longer than a week. Name three kinds of property that are likely to remain in a particular place for longer than a week.

4. Why should law enforcement officers executing a search warrant refrain from asking the person against whom the search is directed to assist them in any way?

5. Assume that you are a law enforcement officer attempting to obtain a search warrant for urban premises, rural premises, a multiple-unit dwell-

ing, and a motor vehicle. Describe, as you would in the affidavit, one of each of these places that is familiar to you. (For example, describe for purposes of a search warrant application a friend's farm in the country.)

6. Law enforcement officers have a search warrant to search a house for heroin and to search the person of the house owners' 18-year-old daughter. When the officers arrive at the house to execute the warrant, the following persons are present:

   a. the owners;
   b. their 18-year-old daughter;
   c. their 15-year-old son, who appears extremely nervous;
   d. the daughter's boyfriend, whom the officers recognize as a local gang member who is known to carry a knife; and
   e. an unidentified elderly couple.

   To what extent may the officers search or detain each person present?

7. A law enforcement officer has a search warrant to search the defendant's house for cameras stolen from a particular department store. May the officer:

   a. look in desk drawers?
   b. search the defendant's body?
   c. seize a brown paper bag containing a white powder resembling heroin, found in a desk drawer?
   d. search the defendant's garage?
   e. look in the defendant's wife's jewelry box?
   f. break open a locked wall safe?
   g. seize a portable radio found on a table with a tag from the department store attached to it?

8. Is each of the following descriptions in a search warrant of items to be seized sufficiently particular?

   a. An unknown-make .38-caliber, blue steel, with wood grips, revolver. *See United States v. Wolfenbarger*, 696 F.2d 750 (10th Cir. 1982).
   b. Videotape and equipment used in a copyright infringement. *See United States v. Smith*, 686 F.2d 234 (5th Cir. 1982).
   c. All doctor's files concerning an accident patient. *See United States v. Hershenow*, 680 F.2d 847 (1st Cir. 1982).
   d. Plaques, mirrors, and other items. *See United States v. Apker*, 705 F.2d 293 (8th Cir. 1983).
   e. Items related to the smuggling, packing, distribution, and use of controlled substances. *See United States v. Ladd*, 704 F.2d 134 (4th Cir. 1983).
   f. Business papers that are evidence and instrumentalities of a violation of a general tax fraud statute. *See United States v. Cardwell*, 680 F.2d 75 (9th Cir. 1982).

9. Does a warrant to search a house authorize a search of a tent set up on the premises near the house? Does a warrant authorizing the seizure of stolen computers authorize the seizure of non-stolen computers commingled with them? Is the seizure of an entire book of accounts permissible when only two or three pages of the book are relevant to the specifications of the search warrant?

Applications of the Law in Real Cases

1 Before the police searched the defendants' home, Lake County agent David Walsh filed an application for a search warrant. In the application, Walsh named Bryan Burmeister and "2812 N. Elmwood, Waukegan" as the targets of the proposed search. Walsh did not allege that Bryan had any connection to the residence. Furthermore, Walsh mistakenly noted that the home is on the east side of the street when, in fact, it sits on the west side. A residence on the east side of the street, 2821 N. Elmwood, closely resembles the Burmeister residence.

Walsh stated that he had probable cause to believe that evidence of cocaine trafficking could be found in the defendants' home. Walsh's suspicions were supported by tips from "anonymous sources" and an investigation by unnamed police officers. Garbage in the defendants' neighborhood is collected weekly. On three consecutive trash days, the officers collected several black plastic garbage bags from the curb in front of the residence. The first search disclosed one 41.2-inch straw and "plastic baggies" containing a white powdery substance that field-tested positive for cocaine. The second search disclosed "two clear plastic bags with the corners missing that had a white powdery residue which field-tested for the presence of cocaine and indices." The third search disclosed one rolled-up tissue with residue that field-tested positive for cocaine. Agent Walsh did not allege that he had any personal knowledge of the trash searches. Walsh applied for a warrant two days after the third search. After reviewing the application, Judge John Radosevich issued a search warrant for the defendants' home. No evidence suggests that Walsh participated in the search of the residence.

The State offered no evidence at the hearing on the defendants' motion to quash the arrests and suppress evidence. However, each defendant submitted an affidavit stating that he never used black trash bags to deposit garbage because the use of the bags was prohibited by the trash collection rules; the defendants used only a large blue bin to deposit trash. The defendants introduced photographs of their home, adjacent homes, and the trash bin they used. The trial court granted their motion, concluding that there was no probable cause to search the defendants' home because the warrant application failed to establish a nexus between the curbside contraband and the residence. Should the defendant's motion to quash the arrests and suppress evidence be granted? *See People v. Burmeister*, 728 N.E.2d 1260 (Ill. App. 2000).

2 Appellant was staying for an indefinite period of time at the home of James Meixner in rural Cass County. This particular house had been the object of a search pursuant to warrant in June 1997, three months previous to the October 1997 search at issue herein. In the June search numerous weapons and drugs were found on the premises.

A confidential reliable informant (CRI) visited Meixner on September 25, 1997. The CRI had previously purchased marijuana and methamphetamines from Meixner, and on this visit observed drug paraphernalia present. The informant told police that Meixner said someone named "Smiley" might have methamphetamines and possibly would stop by on September 27, 1997.

On September 26, 1997, a sheriff's deputy applied for a search warrant for Meixner's property, cars, and Meixner himself. The application was based on the information from the CRI. The deputy also stated in the affidavit that he had personal knowledge that Meixner had two previous convictions for possession of controlled substances, including a conviction earlier that year. The deputy specifically requested a "no-knock, nighttime entry." The affidavit stated that the nighttime search was sought because: "Your Affiant believes that entering onto the described property could be [sic] affected by law enforcement officers, if done under the cover of darkness, and therefore allowing for the security of property without endangering law enforcement officers or subjects who may be located within the residence or outbuildings. A prior search warrant was executed on the 27th of June 1997 and numerous weapons were removed [from] the residence."

The affidavit disclosed the unannounced entry was sought because: "Your Affiant knows that, through experience and training that often persons involved in narcotics trafficking and transactions carry firearms and/ or other weapons to protect themselves and to protect their controlled substances. Your Affiant further knows through experience that those involved with controlled substance[s] often attempt to destroy those substances if they should [fear] substances are in [jeopardy] of being confiscated by law enforcement officers."

The deputy testified that most of this language was taken from other search warrant affidavits, and was commonly used in drug-related search warrant applications. A district court judge signed the warrant application September 26 and it was executed at 9:30 P.M. on October 3, 1997. When executing the warrant the officers parked about a quarter of a mile from Meixner's house. Before entering, they observed Meixner and appellant, whom they did not recognize, sitting across from each other at a coffee table, playing what appeared to be a word game. One of the officers tried the front door, and found it unlocked. The officers, in camouflage, helmets, and masks, entered with guns drawn, shouting, "police."

Meixner did not move other than raising his arms above his head. Appellant was startled by the entry, and tossed the dictionary he was holding into the air. He attempted to run out of the room, and did not obey officers' commands to keep his hands where they could be seen and to stand still. Appellant held his fist clenched, and then appeared to shove the contents of his fist down the front of his pants. Officers testified they thought appellant might be hiding a weapon. The officers eventually subdued him. Officers removed a buck knife from appellant's belt and two items containing methamphetamines—an inhaler and a plastic baggie. Appellant was arrested and charged with a fifth-degree controlled substance crime. He moved to suppress all the evidence obtained during the execution of the warrant, claiming there was no basis for the unannounced search. Should the evidence be suppressed? *See State v. Wasson*, 615 N.W.2d 316 (Minn. 2000).

3 Fish and Wildlife Trooper Danny Sides submitted the affidavit in support of the search warrant. The following facts are taken from the affidavit. Trooper Sides was investigating the illegal killing of a moose in the Point McKenzie area. On December 10, 1996, at 4:30 P.M., Trooper Sides interviewed Kenneth Webeck, who told Trooper Sides that he saw a man illegally shoot and kill a bull moose in the Point McKenzie area. Webeck stated that the suspect had fired six to eight shots from an "assault" style rifle. The suspect was driving an older model Yamaha snow machine with a single headlight. He was accompanied by another rider who also had a snow machine with a single headlight. Neither man made any attempt to salvage the meat or antlers from the dead animal. Webeck stated he had picked up a spent cartridge from the scene which he gave Trooper Sides. Trooper Sides described the casing as a "point 30 cal. military, 7.62 NATO ([c]ivilian version is .308 cal.) round with 'CAVIM 92' stamped on the bottom of the brass."

Twenty minutes later, Trooper Sides contacted two suspects about one mile from the illegal moose kill. Trooper Sides examined the men's hunting licenses and tags. One of the men was Sherman R. Lewis Jr. and the other man was Robert L. Lemoine. Trooper Sides saw Lewis place an assault style rifle in a rifle case. When he was talking with Lewis, Trooper Sides saw Lewis drop a cartridge on the ground. Trooper Sides picked up the cartridge and saw that it had "CAVIM 92" stamped on the bottom. Sides stated that Lewis was riding on an older model Yamaha snow machine with a single headlight and that Lemoine also had a snow machine with a single headlight. Sides also obtained the license number of the blue Ford Bronco that the men were driving and using to pull a trailer with the snow machines.

Trooper Sides then visited the site where the bull moose had been killed that morning. Sides described the moose as an illegal bull which had been killed by several rounds from a small caliber rifle.

The next day, Sides learned from computer records that Lewis had "a [f]elony conviction involving weapons." The records directed any law enforcement officer who had contact with Lewis to contact his probation officer. Trooper Sides contacted John Baiamonte, Lewis' probation officer. Baiamonte told Sides that Lewis was not allowed to be in possession of a firearm. He gave Sides Lewis' address. Fish and Wildlife Aide Larson went to the address and found the blue Ford Bronco and two snow machines.

Trooper Sides presented his affidavit to the magistrate to obtain a search warrant for evidence of the crimes of illegally taking a bull moose and wanton waste of the game. The magistrate issued a warrant authorizing the police to search Lewis' residence for evidence of these crimes. The warrant authorized the police to search for evidence of the game violations, including the assault style rifle and 7.62 caliber NATO military style ammunition with "CAVIM 92" stamped on the base of the bullet.

Based on comments made by Lewis' probation officer, Trooper Sides had reason to believe that Lewis was a heroin dealer. The warrants were executed on December 13, 1996 by Trooper Sides and six to eight other law enforcement officers. Probation Officer Baiamonte participated in the search. Trooper Sides knocked on Lewis' door and announced himself three times. He received no response, but heard scrambling noises inside. The officers then kicked the door in. The time between the first knock and the forced entry was about one minute. Upon entry, State Trooper Nashalook heard the toilet flush on the second level of the house. He ran upstairs and found Lewis sitting on the toilet with his shorts pulled up. Trooper Nashalook looked into the toilet bowl and saw a white substance dissolving rapidly. The trooper got a cup and scooped the white substance out of the toilet. He conducted a field test on the substance, which tested positive for cocaine. Troopers then obtained an additional warrant to search for evidence of a drug violation. Should the defendant's motion to suppress the evidence obtained as a result of the search be granted? *See Lewis v. State*, 9 P.3d 1028 (Alaska App. 2000).

4 On October 31, 1995, members of the Federal Bureau of Investigation's Caribbean Gang Task Force obtained a warrant to search 1437 East 116th Street, Cleveland, Ohio, for drug paraphernalia, and weapons.

The warrant authorized a search of the "premises, curtilage, containers, and persons therein" at a location described as "1437 East 116th Street, Cleveland, Cuyahoga County, Ohio, and being more fully described as the downstairs unit in a two-family, two and one half story, white wood[-]sided dwelling with green trim."

Although the record is sparse, it appears that the "downstairs unit" is a five-room apartment consisting of a front room, two bedrooms, a kitchen, and a bathroom. One bedroom and the kitchen are located in the rear of the apartment. There is a door in the kitchen that leads to a common hallway. The hallway contains a door that leads into the building's basement. A person cannot directly access the basement from the downstairs unit. Defendants Kenneth and Kewin King lived in the downstairs unit.

On November 1, members of the Task Force executed the warrant. As the agents entered the downstairs unit, they observed the defendants standing near the kitchen. Kenneth ran to the second floor but was apprehended by one of the agents. Both defendants were subsequently secured in the downstairs unit. The officers searched the downstairs unit and found 60.6 grams of cocaine base in one bedroom and 16.65 grams in the other bedroom. One of the agents exited the downstairs unit and searched the building's basement, where he discovered 443 grams of cocaine base. Should the defendants' motion to suppress the evidence seized from the basement be granted? *See United States. v. King*, 227 F.3d 732 (6th Cir. 1997).

5 Appellant was an eighth-grade science teacher at Fork Union Military Academy (the Academy) in Fluvanna County. He resided in an apartment located in the middle school student barracks and served as a barracks supervisor. In 1997, Academy officials advised local and state police that appellant may have abused one or more of the Academy's students. One official told police that he had entered appellant's apartment to check a water leak. On two different occasions, he observed in appellant's apartment nude photographs depicting two named cadets, J. L. and H. L. Some of the photographs had been taken in appellant's apartment. He observed several journals containing "information about 'boys needing discipline and spanking.'" He also saw a "delinquency report completed on . . . 11th grader, [J. L.] with the consequences listed as '3 whacks on the bare behind'" and had information that J. L. had been seen leaving appellant's barracks at 10:00 P.M. in violation of school rules. The Academy had a written corporal punishment policy, which provided that only the middle school commandant or headmaster could paddle middle school students. The policy also provided that such paddling could occur only while a student was fully clothed and required the parents' written permission.

The Academy official opined that, because appellant taught middle school, appellant's relationship with 11th grader J. L. was "strange"; and he opined that appellant's contact with an eight-grade student, which involved his constantly escorting the student to off-campus activities, exceeded the "normal student/teacher relationship" and was "unhealthy." Using this information, police obtained a warrant to search appellant's barracks apartment. The warrant specifically listed as subject to seizure, inter alia, "photographs . . . depicting nudity and/or sexual activities involving children," "[w]ritten materials (letters, diaries) . . . related to sexual conduct between juveniles and adults," and "books . . . and photographs depicting nudity and/or sexual activities of juveniles." While executing the warrant, Deputy Hogsten scanned appellant's numerous handwritten journals looking for photographs and other materials specified in the warrant. If Hogsten observed an "explicit" photograph in a journal, he marked the journal and handed it to Trooper Watson, who assisted with the search. If no explicit photograph was immediately apparent in a journal, Hogsten scanned it "[to] see if [he] could find anything that was in the warrant [they] were looking for." After reviewing all appellant's journals in this fashion, Hogsten and Watson seized fourteen volumes and left behind two or three. Subsequently, Deputy Craig reviewed the seized journals in greater detail and decided which portions would be used as evidence.

A grand jury indicted appellant on sixteen counts of taking indecent liberties with two minors, J. L. and H. L. Appellant moved to suppress the excerpts taken from his diaries, arguing that the seizure of the diaries violated the Fourth Amendment's prohibition against general warrants. He also argued that admission of the excerpts into evidence would violate his Fourth and Fifth Amendment privilege against self-incrimination. Should the appellant's motion to suppress be granted? *Moyer v. Commonwealth*, 531 S.E.2d 580 (Va. App. 2000).

5

Administrative Searches, Special Needs Searches, and Electronic Surveillance

Learning Objectives

▶ Know the differences between an administrative search warrant and a criminal search warrant.

▶ Know the meaning of and rationale justifying "special needs" searches.

▶ Understand which special needs searches allow for warrantless searches and seizures based on reasonable, articulable suspicion, and which special needs searches allow for warrantless searches and seizures without any particularized suspicion whatsoever.

▶ Understand the scope and applicability of Title III of the Omnibus Crime Control and Safe Streets Act of 1968 to wire, oral, and electronic communications for both private persons and state actors, including law enforcement personnel.

▶ Understand the following concerns of electronic surveillance under Title III: the conflicting demands for more effective law enforcement and individual privacy rights; the several ways in which Title III provides for judicial supervision of electronic surveillance; the similarities and differences between an interception order under Title III and an ordinary search warrant; the specific ways in which Title III protects individual rights, especially privacy rights; and the specific types of interceptions of wire, oral, or electronic communications that are not covered by Title III.

▶ Explain the statutory limitations on the use of pen registers, trap-and-trace devices, tracking beepers, and real-time, cell site data searching under the Communications Privacy Act of 1986.

▶ Understand the procedures for accessing e-mail and voice mail under the Stored Wire and Electronic Communications and Transactional Records Access Act.

▶ Explain the scope of counterintelligence and counterterrorism surveillance authorized under the Foreign Intelligence Surveillance Act (FISA) through the use of FISA warrants, including the different levels of proof needed for the issuance of such warrants in comparison to traditional criminal investigatory search warrants.

▶ Explain the jurisdiction and procedures of the Foreign Intelligence Surveillance Court (FISC), as well as when compliance with FISC is exempted under executive-approval exceptions to the usual FISA warrant procedures.

Protecting public safety is among the highest of governmental priorities. Certain governmental activities aimed at protecting the public health, safety, and welfare have a long history of regulatory enforcement that is—both in practice and intent—quite different from criminal investigation. As a result, the usual strictures of the Fourth Amendment have been modified to allow for more flexible enforcement of laws that keep us safer.

Enforcement of administrative or regulatory law is therefore governed not by normal criminal investigatory search warrants, but instead by administrative search warrants. Similarly, other searches are seizures that serve a special public safety need other than the enforcement of criminal law has given rise to the *special needs doctrine*: a theoretical framework for examining governmental searches and seizures that need not comply with the usual Fourth Amendment requirements of a warrant based on probable cause.

Finally, a series of special statutory provisions govern electronic surveillance, designed to balance privacy concerns against the needs of law enforcement and public safety. This task is especially complicated in the United States in the early part of the twenty-first century as the nation tries to fight a "war on terrorism" during an era of digital information. This chapter explores how the law attempts to deal with each of these three unique situations in light of the competing interests of privacy under the Fourth Amendment and those posed by the need to protect public safety.

▶ ADMINISTRATIVE SEARCH WARRANTS

An **administrative search** is a routine inspection of a home or business by governmental authorities responsible for determining compliance with various statutes and regulations. An administrative search seeks to enforce fire, health, safety, and housing codes, licensing provisions, and the like. Whereas a criminal search is directed toward gathering evidence to convict a person of a crime, an administrative search ordinarily does not result in a criminal prosecution.

Special Warrant Requirements for Administrative Searches

Before 1967, courts consistently held that administrative searches were not subject to the restrictions of the Fourth Amendment and that a search warrant was not needed to inspect residential or commercial premises for violations of regulatory and licensing provisions. However, in 1967, in *Camara v. Municipal Court*, 387 U.S. 523 (involving the safety inspection of a dwelling) and *See v. City of Seattle*, 387 U.S. 541 (involving inspection of business premises for fire safety reasons), the U.S. Supreme Court reversed earlier decisions and held that administrative inspections were subject to the warrant requirement of the Fourth Amendment. The basis for both decisions was the Court's belief that a person's right of privacy should not be determined by the nature of the search. In *Camara*, the Court said, **"It is surely anomalous to say that the individual and his private property are fully protected by the Fourth Amendment only when the individual is suspected of criminal behavior."** 387 U.S. at 530. In *See*, the Court said that **"a businessman, like the occupant of a residence, has a constitutional right to go about his business free from unreasonable official entries upon his private commercial property. . . ."** 387 U.S. at 543. Nevertheless, because administrative searches differ in nature and purpose from criminal searches, the Court held that the probable cause standard for administrative searches differs in nature and is less stringent than the standard for criminal searches:

> **The warrant procedure is designed to guarantee that a decision to search private property is justified by a reasonable governmental interest. But reasonableness is still the ultimate standard. If a valid public interest justifies the intrusion contemplated, then there is probable cause to issue a suitably restricted search warrant.** 387 U.S. at 539.

Marshall v. Barlow's, Inc., 436 U.S. 307, 320-21 (1978), involving a search of a business for occupational safety reasons, explained the less stringent probable cause standard:

> **Probable cause in the criminal law sense is not required. For purposes of an administrative search such as this, probable cause justifying the issuance of a warrant may be based not only on specific evidence of an existing violation but also on a showing that "reasonable legislative or administrative standards for conducting an . . . inspection are satisfied with respect to a particular [establishment]" [citing *Camara*]. A warrant showing that a specific business has been chosen for an [Occupational Safety and Health Agency] search on the basis of a general administrative plan for the enforcement of the Act derived from neutral sources such as, for example, dispersion of employees in various types of industries across a given area, and the desired frequency of searches in any of the lesser divisions of the area, would protect an employer's Fourth Amendment rights.**

Exceptions to Administrative Warrant Requirements

In spite of the commands of *Camara* and *See* and their less stringent probable cause standard, the Supreme Court began to reshape the landscape for administrative searches in *Collonade Catering Corp. v. United States*, 397 U.S. 72 (1970). In that case, the Court refused to apply *See* to inspections performed under the federal liquor law. Finding that there was a long history of pervasive regulation in the liquor industry, the Court upheld a provision of federal law that allowed for a warrantless inspection of places in which liquor was sold. In doing so, the

Court began to pave the way for a warrant exception for certain types of administrative searches.

Two years after deciding *Collonade Catering*, in *United States v. Biswell*, 406 U.S. 311 (1972), the Supreme Court recognized another exception allowing warrantless inspection of certain licensed and closely regulated enterprises. *Biswell* upheld a warrantless search of a gun dealer's storeroom licensed under the Gun Control Act of 1968. The Court said:

> [I]f inspection is to be effective and serve as a credible deterrent, unannounced, even frequent, inspections are essential. In this context, the prerequisite of a warrant could easily frustrate inspection; and if the necessary flexibility as to time, scope, and frequency is to be preserved, the protections afforded by a warrant would be negligible. It is also plain that inspections for compliance with the Gun Control Act pose only limited threats to the dealer's justifiable expectations of privacy. When a dealer chooses to engage in this pervasively regulated business and to accept a federal license, he does so with the knowledge that his business records, firearms, and ammunition will be subject to effective inspection. 406 U.S. at 316.

A few years later, in *Donovan v. Dewey*, 452 U.S. 594 (1981), the Court upheld warrantless inspections of mines, again finding the mining industry to be so comprehensively regulated that the statutory and regulatory scheme provided adequate notice to the owners of businesses that they could be inspected at any time without additional, prior notice. And a few years after that, the Supreme Court clarified its administrative search jurisprudence by holding in *New York v. Burger*, 482 U.S. 691 (1987), that warrantless inspections of licensed and closely regulated enterprises are reasonable if they satisfy three criteria:

1. a "substantial" government interest must support the regulatory scheme under which the inspection is made;
2. warrantless inspections must be necessary to further the regulatory scheme; and
3. the regulatory statute must provide a constitutionally adequate substitute for a warrant by advising the owner of commercial premises that the search is being made pursuant to the law, has a properly defined scope, and limits the discretion of the inspecting officers.

In *Burger*, the Court found that a New York statute allowing warrantless inspection of automobile junkyards satisfied these criteria. The state had a substantial interest in regulating the automobile junkyard industry because motor vehicle theft had increased in the state and was associated with this industry. Warrantless inspections were necessary because frequent and unannounced inspections provide an element of surprise crucial to regulating the market in stolen cars and parts. Finally, the statute gave adequate notice to automobile junkyard operators and authorized inspections only during business hours and within a narrowly defined scope.

Distinguishing Between Administrative and Criminal Searches

The line between an administrative and a criminal search sometimes blurs. In distinguishing between them, it is important to look at the search's purpose and competing privacy expectations.

Depends on Investigative Purpose and Privacy Expectations When an administrative search begins to take on the characteristics of a criminal search, the stricter standards applicable to criminal searches apply. If these standards are not satisfied, any evidence obtained is inadmissible in a criminal prosecution. Fire investigations often require both administrative and criminal searches because they serve several different purposes and present varying degrees of emergency. In addition, reasonable privacy expectations may remain in fire-damaged premises, necessitating compliance with the Fourth Amendment:

> **Privacy expectations will vary with the type of property, the amount of fire damage, the prior and continued use of the premises, and in some cases the owner's efforts to secure it against intruders. Some fires may be so devastating that no reasonable privacy interests remain in the ash and ruins, regardless of the owner's subjective expectations. The test essentially is an objective one: whether "the expectation [is] one that society is prepared to recognize as 'reasonable.'" . . . If reasonable privacy interests remain in the fire-damaged property, the warrant requirement applies, and any official entry must be made pursuant to a warrant in the absence of consent or exigent circumstances.** *Michigan v. Clifford*, 464 U.S. 287, 292-93 (1984).

If a warrant is necessary because a reasonable expectation of privacy remains in the premise and no exception to the warrant requirement applies, the purpose of the search determines the type of warrant required. If the primary purpose is to determine the cause and origin of a recent fire, only an administrative warrant is needed. To obtain an administrative warrant, **"fire officials need show only that a fire of undetermined origin has occurred on the premises, that the scope of the proposed search is reasonable and will not intrude unnecessarily on the fire victim's privacy, and that the search will be executed at a reasonable and convenient time."** *Michigan v. Clifford*, 464 U.S. 287, 294 (1984). If the primary purpose of the search is to gather evidence of criminal activity, a criminal search warrant may be obtained only on a showing of probable cause to believe that particularly described seizable property will be found in the place to be searched.

Criminal Evidence Discovered in Administrative Search Evidence of criminal activity discovered during the course of a valid administrative search may be seized under the plain view doctrine and used to establish probable cause to obtain a criminal search warrant. Fire officials may not, however, rely on such evidence to expand the scope of their administrative search without first satisfying an independent judicial officer that probable cause exists for a criminal search. The purpose of the search is important even if exigent circumstances exist:

> **Circumstances that justify a warrantless search for the cause of a fire may not justify a search to gather evidence of criminal activity once that cause has been determined. If, for example, the administrative search is justified by the immediate need to ensure against rekindling, the scope of the search may be no broader than reasonably necessary to achieve its end. A search to gather evidence of criminal activity not in plain view must be made pursuant to a criminal warrant upon a traditional showing of probable cause.** *Michigan v. Clifford*, 464 U.S. 287, 294-95 (1984).

An administrative search took on the characteristics of a criminal search in *Michigan v. Tyler*, 436 U.S. 499 (1978), involving a late-night fire in a furniture store leased by the defendant. When the fire was reduced to smoldering embers, the fire chief, while investigating the cause of the fire, discovered two plastic containers of flammable liquid. He summoned a police detective who took several pictures, but because visibility was hindered by darkness, steam, and smoke, departed the scene at 4:00 A.M. and returned shortly after daybreak to continue the investigation. More evidence of arson was found and seized at that time. About a month later, a state police arson investigator made several visits to the fire scene and obtained evidence that was used at trial in convicting the defendant. At no time was any warrant or consent to search obtained.

The Court held that the investigative activity on the date of the fire was legal but that the evidence-gathering activity a month after the fire was an illegal search and seizure:

> [W]e hold that an entry to fight a fire requires no warrant, and that once in the building, officials may remain there for a reasonable time to investigate the cause of the blaze. Thereafter, additional entries to investigate the cause of the fire must be made pursuant to the warrant procedures governing administrative searches. . . . Evidence of arson discovered in the course of such investigations is admissible at trial, but if the investigating officials find probable cause to believe that arson has occurred and require further access to gather evidence for a possible prosecution, they may obtain a warrant only upon a traditional showing of probable cause applicable to searches for evidence of crime. 436 U.S. at 511-12.

To summarize, once an administrative search focuses on gathering evidence for a criminal prosecution, a criminal search warrant must be obtained or the search must satisfy an exception to the warrant requirement.

key points

- An administrative search is a routine inspection of a home or business to determine compliance with various statutes and regulations, not to gather evidence for a criminal prosecution. Administrative searches are subject to the warrant requirement of the Fourth Amendment. However, because administrative searches differ in nature and purpose from criminal searches, the probable cause standard for administrative searches differs in nature and is less stringent than the standard for criminal searches.
- Exceptions to the administrative warrant requirement based on emergency, consent, plain view, and open fields have less stringent standards than corresponding exceptions for criminal searches. Warrantless searches are also allowed for certain licensed and closely regulated enterprises.
- Once an administrative search focuses on gathering evidence for a criminal prosecution, a criminal search warrant must be obtained or the search must satisfy an exception to the warrant requirement. However, evidence of criminal activity discovered during the course of a valid administrative search may be seized under the plain view doctrine and may also be used to establish probable cause to obtain a criminal search warrant.

▶ SPECIAL NEEDS SEARCHES

The U.S. Supreme Court has consistently recognized the so-called **special needs doctrine** as an exception to the warrant and probable cause requirements of the Fourth Amendment where special needs of the government **"beyond the normal need for law enforcement make the warrant and probable-cause requirement impracticable."** *Griffin v. Wisconsin,* 483 U.S. 868, 873 (1987). Under this exception, searches are evaluated under the "reasonableness" standard of the Fourth Amendment:

> **To be reasonable under the Fourth Amendment, a search ordinarily must be based on individualized suspicion of wrongdoing. . . . But particularized exceptions to the main rule are sometimes warranted based on "special needs, beyond the normal need for law enforcement. . . ." When such "special needs"—concerns other than crime detection—are alleged in justification of a Fourth Amendment intrusion, courts must undertake a context-specific inquiry, examining closely the competing private and public interests advanced by the parties.** *Chandler v. Miller,* 520 U.S. 305, 313-14 (1997).

This requires balancing the nature and quality of the intrusion on the individual's Fourth Amendment interests against the importance of the governmental interests alleged to justify the intrusion.

Searches of Governmental Employees

In *O'Connor v. Ortega,* 480 U.S. 709 (1987), a psychiatrist who worked at a state hospital had his desk and files searched by a hospital administrator for evidence of misconduct that was eventually used against him at an administrative hearing that resulted in the termination of his employment. The physician subsequently sued his employer for this invasion of privacy. While the Supreme Court found that the search did implicate the Fourth Amendment, it nonetheless sided with the employer, holding that "special needs" may justify a warrantless search of a public employee's office by the employee's supervisor. For searches conducted by a public employer, the invasion of the employee's legitimate expectations of privacy must be balanced against the government's need for supervision, control, and the efficient operation of the workplace.

> **[R]equiring an employer to obtain a warrant whenever the employer wished to enter an employee's office, desk, or file cabinets for a work-related purpose would seriously disrupt the routine conduct of business and would be unduly burdensome. Imposing unwieldy warrant procedures in such cases upon supervisors, who would otherwise have no reason to be familiar with such procedures, is simply unreasonable.** 480 U.S. at 722.

The Court applied a reasonableness standard rather than a probable cause standard.

> **[T]he "special needs, beyond the normal need for law enforcement make the . . . probable-cause requirement impracticable," . . . for legitimate work-related, non-investigatory intrusions as well as investigations of work-related misconduct. A standard of reasonableness will neither unduly burden the efforts of government employers to ensure the efficient and proper operation of the workplace, nor authorize arbitrary intrusions upon the privacy of public employees. We hold, therefore, that public employer intrusions on the constitutionally protected privacy interests of government employees for non-investigatory, work-related purposes, as**

> well as for investigations of work-related misconduct, should be judged
> by the standard of reasonableness under all the circumstances. Under
> this reasonableness standard, both the inception and the scope of the
> intrusion must be reasonable. . . . 480 U.S. at 725-26.

The Court said that, given the great variety of work environments in the public sector, the question of whether an employee has a reasonable expectation of privacy as well as the reasonableness of the overall search must be determined on a case-by-case basis. Some of the factors that courts use when applying this balancing test include:

> (1) whether the work area in question was given over to an employee's
> exclusive use, (2) the extent to which others had access to the work space,
> (3) the nature of the employment, and (4) whether office regulations
> placed the employee on notice that certain areas were subject to employer
> intrusions. *Rossi v. Town of Pelham*, 35 F. Supp. 2d 58 (D.N.H. 1997).

For example, the court in *Sabin v. Miller*, 423 F. Supp. 2d 943 (S.D. Iowa 2006), refused to extend *Ortega* to a situation in which state investigators entered the home of a state correctional worker to seize her computer and search for evidence that she had violated a number of the conditions of her employment in various interactions with inmates. Key to the court's decision was that the investigators entered her home to search her computer, where she had intermingled both personal and work-related files. Because the investigators intruded into Sabin's home rather than her office space at the correctional institution, any state employer "interest in 'the efficient and proper operation of the workplace' was not as great as was the interest of the government employers under the circumstances considered in *O'Connor*." 423 F. Supp. 2d at 950. In contrast, *Gossmeyer v. McDonald*, 128 F.3d 481 (7th Cir. 1997), upheld the search of a public employee's desk and file cabinet at work. The employee in *Gossmeyer* was a child protective services investigator. A coworker "made serious and specific allegations of misconduct—that [she] had pornographic pictures of children; and stated where those pictures could be found—in [her] file cabinets and desk." 128 F.3d at 491. Given her state-sanctioned access to and authority over children, the court found the search satisfied *Ortega's* mandates insofar as it was reasonable at the inception of the search and reasonable in terms of the scope of execution.

In *Ortega*, *Sabin*, and *Gossmeyer*, the courts all concluded that the public employee had a reasonable expectation of privacy in the area that was searched. But, if a public employee does not have a reasonable expectation of privacy in the area searched, then *Ortega's* balancing test is inapplicable since the Fourth Amendment is not implicated. For example, *Shaul v. Cherry Valley-Springfield Cent. School Dist.*, 363 F.3d 177 (2d Cir. 2004), upheld the search of a teacher's classroom, including his private desk, after the teacher had been suspended. The court reasoned:

> Whatever reasonable expectation of privacy [the teacher] may have had in
> his classroom while he was a teacher in good standing, . . . he had no such
> expectation on January 30, 1999, by which date [he] had (1) been suspended
> from teaching and barred from his classroom, (2) surrendered the key to the
> classroom's locked file cabinet at the same time that he declined to retrieve his
> personal property from the classroom, and (3) been afforded a second oppor-

tunity to spend an hour and a half removing personal items from the classroom. 363 F.3d at 182-83.

Similarly, in *Nelson v. Salem State College*, 845 N.E.2d 338, 341 (Mass. 2006), the court concluded that a public employee had no reasonable expectation of privacy while she was "videotaped by a hidden camera . . . as she changed clothes and applied sunburn medication to her upper chest area and neck" because she did so "in an open area of her workplace."

Law enforcement personnel must understand the limited nature of *Ortega's* holding as applying to searches conducted by public employers looking for evidence of job malfeasance. "Warrantless work-related searches conducted by police should not be upheld under the *Ortega* exception because a less-intrusive warrantless search by the employee's supervisor will fully realize the concern for workplace efficiency." *Rossi*, 35 F. Supp. 2d at 67.

Governmental Drug Testing

To protect public safety, governmental entities have sometimes required their employees to submit to drug testing. The Supreme Court has allowed these practices under circumstances that satisfy the requirements of the "special needs" doctrine.

Public Safety as Special Need In *Skinner v. Railway Labor Executives' Ass'n.*, 489 U.S. 602 (1989), the U.S. Supreme Court upheld governmental regulations requiring railroad companies to test the blood and urine of employees involved in major train accidents and employees who violate particular safety rules. The Court found that the tests were not significant intrusions and that railroad workers have a diminished expectation of privacy because they work in a heavily regulated industry. The searches were held to be reasonable, despite the absence of individualized suspicion, because the government's significant special need to ensure public safety outweighed the employee's diminished privacy interest.

National Treasury Employees Union v. Von Raab, 489 U.S. 656 (1989), upheld Customs Service regulations requiring employees seeking transfers or promotions to certain sensitive positions within the Service to submit to urinalysis. The Court found that the government's special need to deter drug use outweighed the diminished privacy interests of the employees. Specifically, the Court emphasized the public interest in "**ensuring that front-line interdiction personnel are physically fit, and have unimpeachable integrity and judgment**" [and in] "**prevent[ing] the promotion of drug users to positions that require the incumbent to carry a firearm, even if the incumbent is not engaged directly in the interdiction of drugs.**" 489 U.S. at 670.

In *Mich. Dep't of State Police v. Sitz*, 496 U.S. 444 (1990), the Supreme Court upheld a Michigan program that established roadside sobriety checkpoints without a warrant or particularized suspicion:

> **All vehicles passing through a checkpoint would be stopped and their drivers breifly examined for signs of intoxication. In cases where a checkpoint officer detected signs of intoxication, the motorist would be directed to a location out of the traffic flow where an officer would check the motorist's driver's license and car registration and, if warranted,**

> **conduct further sobriety tests. Should the field tests and the officer's observations suggest that the driver was intoxicated, an arrest would be made. All other drivers would be permitted to resume their journey immediately.** 496 U.S. at 447.

Although the stops were determined to be "seizures" within the meaning of the Fourth Amendment, the Court upheld them even though they occurred without a warrant or individual suspicion. Key to the Court's reasoning was the fact that a significant public safety need met by these motor vehicle stops outweighed the minimal intrusions such stops caused to driver's privacy rights.

Relying on *Von Raab, National Treasury Employees Union v. Yeutter*, 918 F.2d 968 (D.C. Cir. 1990), upheld random urinalysis drug testing of state motor vehicle operators, but invalidated the mandatory drug testing of employees who did not hold safety or security-sensitive jobs without reasonable suspicion of on-duty drug use or drug-impaired work performance.

The decision in *Yeutter* illustrates how a random, suspicionless search must be justified by some special need that goes beyond general law enforcement. Not all cases, however, prevent strong enough justifications to qualify as a bona fide special need. For example, *Chandler v. Miller*, 520 U.S. 305 (1997), struck down as unconstitutional a Georgia statute requiring candidates for designated state offices to certify that they have taken a drug test within thirty days prior to qualifying for nomination or election and that the test result was negative. The Court found that the alleged incompatibility of unlawful drug use with holding high state office was not sufficiently important to qualify as a special need for drug testing of candidates for state office: **"[T]he proffered special need for drug testing must be substantial—important enough to override the individual's acknowledged privacy interest, sufficiently vital to suppress the Fourth Amendment's normal requirement of individualized suspicion."** 520 U.S. at 318. The need to deter unlawful drug users from attaining high state office was not considered a concrete danger giving rise to a special need to depart from the Fourth Amendment's usual requirements, especially because there was no evidence of a drug problem among the state's elected officials; those officials did not perform high-risk, safety-sensitive tasks; and the required certification of non-drug use did not immediately aid any drug interdiction effort.

The court in *Robinson v. City of Seattle*, 10 P.3d 452 (Wash. App. 2000), similarly refused to uphold a policy requiring a drug test for a broad array of government employment applicants. The court ruled that such a policy would only be permissible with regard to "applicants whose duties will genuinely implicate public safety . . . [such as] sworn police officers and firefighters, and positions requiring an employee to carry a firearm." 10 P.3d at 470.

Distinguishing Special Needs Drug Testing from Law Enforcement Goals In *City of Indianapolis v. Edmond*, 531 U.S. 32 (2000), the Supreme Court invalidated a program in which a warrantless highway checkpoint had been established to discover and interdict illegal drugs. Unlike a special needs search designed for public safety reasons, like a highway sobriety checkpoint—*see ich. Dep't of State Police v. Sitz*, 496 U.S. 444 (1990)—the primary purpose of the program at issue in *Edmund* was crime-control-related; thus the Court refused to allow warrantless, suspicionless searches. (See the section entitled "Traffic Stops and Roadblocks" in Chapter 7 for more information on highway checkpoints.)

Ferguson v. Charleston, 532 U.S. 67 (2001), held unconstitutional a state hospital's policy involving warrantless, suspicionless, and nonconsensual testing of pregnant women for cocaine to obtain evidence for criminal prosecution. The policy, in which law enforcement authorities were extensively involved, used the threat of prosecution to coerce the patients into substance abuse treatment. The Court compared this case to *Skinner*, *Von Raab*, and *Chandler*, and found the invasion of privacy here far more substantial than in the previous cases. In the previous cases, there was no misunderstanding about the purpose of the test or the potential use of the test results, and there were protections against the dissemination of the results to third parties.

Moreover, those cases involved disqualification from eligibility for particular benefits—a much less serious intrusion on privacy than the unauthorized dissemination of results to third parties, such as police officers and prosecutors. The critical difference, however, lies in the nature of the "special need" asserted as justification for the warrantless searches. In each of the previous cases, the special need was divorced from the State's general interest in law enforcement. In *Ferguson*, however, "**the central and indispensable feature of the policy from its inception was the use of law enforcement to coerce the patients into substance abuse treatment.**" 532 U.S. at 80. The Court discussed the special needs doctrine further:

> While the ultimate goal of the program may well have been to get the women in question into substance abuse treatment and off of drugs, the immediate objective of the searches was to generate evidence for law enforcement purposes in order to reach that goal. The threat of law enforcement may ultimately have been intended as a means to an end, but the direct and primary purpose of MUSC's policy was to ensure the use of those means. In our opinion, this distinction is critical. Because law enforcement involvement always serves some broader social purpose or objective, under respondents' view, virtually any nonconsensual suspicionless search could be immunized under the special needs doctrine by defining the search solely in terms of its ultimate, rather than immediate, purpose. Such an approach is inconsistent with the Fourth Amendment. Given the primary purpose of the Charleston program, which was to use the threat of arrest and prosecution in order to force women into treatment, and given the extensive involvement of law enforcement officials at every stage of the policy, this case simply does not fit within the closely guarded category of "special needs."
>
> The fact that positive test results were turned over to the police does not merely provide a basis for distinguishing our prior cases applying the "special needs" balancing approach to the determination of drug use. It also provides an affirmative reason for enforcing the strictures of the Fourth Amendment. While state hospital employees, like other citizens, may have a duty to provide the police with evidence of criminal conduct that they inadvertently acquire in the course of routine treatment, when they undertake to obtain such evidence from their patients for the specific purpose of incriminating those patients, they have a special obligation to make sure that the patients are fully informed about their constitutional rights, as standards of knowing waiver require. 532 U.S. at 82-85.

Searches of Probationers and Parolees

Griffin v. Wisconsin, 483 U.S. 868 (1987), upheld a warrantless search of a probationer's home by probation officers under the authority of Wisconsin's probation regulation, which permitted such searches on "reasonable grounds" to believe that contraband was present. When two probation officers searched Griffin's

Discussion
POINT

Should the State Review Patient Prescriptions?

Murphy v. State, 62 P.3d 533 (Wash. 2003).

A Washington state statute provides:

> Every proprietor or manager of a pharmacy shall keep readily available a suitable record of prescriptions which shall preserve for a period of not less than two years the record of every prescription dispensed at such pharmacy which shall be numbered, dated, and filed, and shall produce the same in court or before any grand jury whenever lawfully required to do so. The record shall be maintained either separately from all other records of the pharmacy or in such form that the information required is readily retrievable from ordinary business records of the pharmacy. All record-keeping requirements for controlled substances must be complied with. Such record of prescriptions shall be for confidential use in the pharmacy, only. *The record of prescriptions shall be open for inspection by the board of pharmacy or any officer of the law, who is authorized to enforce* [relevant drug and pharmacy laws].

A review by the state pharmacy board of the defendant's prescription resulted in his being prosecuted for having obtained prescription narcotic drugs by deceit. He argued that the purpose of the pharmacy statute was to require recordkeeping and allow inspection for the purpose of regulating pharmacies, but not to allow a warrantless examination of a patient's prescription records to gather criminal evidence against the patient. The court rejected this contention and ruled that by indicating pharmacy records shall be "open for inspection . . . by any officer of the law," the legislature clearly contemplated unrestricted access by the appropriate law enforcement personnel.

In upholding the constitutionality of the statute and a search performed pursuant to it, the court found that the regulation of the warrantless review of patients' prescription information

home due to suspected gun possession in violation of his probation conditions, officers indeed found such a weapon. In upholding the admissibility of the weapons seized, the Supreme Court found that the probation system's necessity for non-adversarial supervision of probationers is a "special need" justifying lessened Fourth Amendment protection for the probationer. This special need makes the warrant requirement impracticable and justifies replacement of the probable cause standard by a "reasonable grounds" standard. The Court said:

> A warrant requirement would interfere to an appreciable degree with the probation system, setting up a magistrate rather than the probation officer as the judge of how close a [level of] supervision the probationer requires. Moreover, the delay inherent in obtaining a warrant would make it more difficult for probation officials to respond quickly to evidence of misconduct . . . and would reduce the deterrent effect that the possibility of expeditious searches would otherwise create. . . . 483 U.S. at 876.

Should the State Review Patient Prescriptions? *(Continued)*

was a part of a valid special needs search. The court focused on the fact that the governmental interest in monitoring the flow of drugs from pharmacies to patients outweighed a patient's limited expectation of privacy. The court wrote:

> When a patient brings a prescription to a pharmacist, the patient has a right to expect that his or her use of a particular drug will not be disclosed arbitrarily or randomly. But a reasonable patient buying narcotic prescription drugs knows or should know that the State, which outlaws the distribution and use of such drugs without a prescription, will keep careful watch over the flow of such drugs from pharmacies to patients. 62 P.3d at 541.

See also State v. Russo, 790 A.2d 1132, *cert. denied*, 537 U.S. 879 (2002); *State v. Welch*, 624 A.2d 1105 (Vt.1992).

After concluding that the warrantless search of the defendant's prescription records by the state pharmacy board was a lawful special needs search, the court upheld the board's disclosure of the improprieties it discovered to law enforcement personnel.

Do you agree with the court that such a law and the actions taken pursuant to it (i.e., the review of a patient's prescription information) fall within the realm of a "special needs" search? Why or why not?

Of what consequence, if any, is the statutory inclusion of permission for law enforcement officers to review pharmacy records? Does this not transform the nature of the warrantless searches authorized under the statute into ones that have a criminal investigatory purpose, rather than ones primarily aimed at generalized public safety? Explain your position.

A probation or parole search, however, should not serve as a subterfuge or ruse for a criminal investigation. Probation and parole officers may work together with police, provided that the correctional personnel are pursuing probation or parole-related objectives and are not acting as "a stalking horse for the police." *United States v. McFarland*, 116 F.3d 316, 318 (8th Cir. 1997).

United States v. Knights, 534 U.S. 112 (2001), reaffirmed the reasonable suspicion approach to searches of probationer and parolees. In *Knights*, a warrantless search was conducted based on a document that the defendant had signed as a condition of probation. The agreement provided for police access to his **"person, property, place of residence, vehicle, personal effects, to search at anytime, with or without a search warrant, warrant of arrest or reasonable cause by any probation officer or law enforcement officer."** 534 U.S. at 114. The defendant challenged the constitutionality of the document because there was no special need beyond normal law enforcement to support a warrantless search. The Supreme Court did not address the issue of defendant's consent for the search, evidenced by him signing the document, because it found that the search was "reasonable" under the Fourth Amendment, regardless of consent as a result of the police having reasonable suspicion to conduct the search. Thus, *Knights* stands for the proposition that law enforcement authorities need only reasonable suspicion to conduct a warrantless search of probationers or parolees, their homes, and their belongings. Key to the Court's rationale was that probationers and parolees have a diminished expectation of privacy that is outweighed when balanced against the government's concern that the defendant **"will be more likely to engage in criminal conduct than an ordinary member of the community."** 534 U.S. at 121.

The Court did not consider the question, however, if a condition of release could "so diminish or eliminate a released prisoner's reasonable expectation of privacy" such that a suspicionless search by a law enforcement officer would be permissible under the Fourth Amendment. *Samson v. California*, 126 S. Ct. 2193, 2196 (2006). But the Court answered that question in the affirmative in *Samson*, when it upheld the suspicionless search of a parolee. Under California law, all parolees are required to sign an agreement as a condition of their release that consents to warrantless, suspicionless searches for the duration of their parole. The Supreme Court did not apply a special needs analysis, but rather upheld the law under the "general Fourth Amendment principle" of reasonableness. 126 S. Ct. 2199.

Thus, warrantless searches of probationers and parolees will depend on the law of the particular jurisdiction. If state law permits warrantless, suspicionless searches as a condition of release, then such searches would be valid under *Samson*. If, however, state law does not authorize warrantless, suspicionless searches as a condition of release, then a warrantless search would be constitutionally permissible only if there were reasonable suspicion that the probationer or parolee were involved in criminal activity.

Searches of Elementary and High School Students

Our school systems are another example of places that require special measures to be taken in order to protect the health, safety, and well-being of the students. To help achieve this goal, the courts have established a specialized set of criteria governing searches of elementary and high school students.[1]

The Fourth Amendment Applies, but the Warrant Requirement Does Not *New Jersey v. T.L.O.*, 469 U.S. 325 (1985), created an exception to the warrant requirement, based on "special needs" for searches of students conducted by school officials. In that case, a fourteen-year-old girl was suspected of smoking cigarettes in a high school lavatory in violation of school policy. The girl was questioned about her smoking by the school's vice principal. When she denied smoking, the vice principal demanded to see the girl's purse. Upon looking in the girl's

---

[1] This section of the book on searches of elementary and high school students is derived from the following article: Fradella, Henry F., and John Connelly. 2007. The "Incredible Shrinking Amendment" Redux: Continued Erosion of the Fourth Amendment Rights of Students. *Criminal Law Bulletin*, *42(2)*: 246–251. Reprinted with the gracious permission of Thomson/West and the *Criminal Law Bulletin*.

purse, the vice principal not only saw a pack of cigarettes, but also some rolling papers typically used for smoking marijuana. This prompted the vice principal to search the purse more thoroughly. That search yielded a "small amount of marijuana, a pipe, a number of empty plastic bags, a substantial quantity of money in one dollar bills, an index card that appeared to be a list of students who owed T.L.O. money, and two letters that implicated T.L.O. in marijuana dealing." 469 U.S. at 328. The school turned over the evidence to the police who, in turn, used the evidence in juvenile delinquency proceedings against the girl. The Supreme Court ultimately upheld the actions of the vice principal over the girl's Fourth Amendment objections.

First, the *T.L.O.* Court affirmed that the Fourth Amendment was clearly applicable to the search in question because **"public school officials do not merely exercise authority voluntarily conferred on them by individual parents; rather, they act in furtherance of publicly mandated educational and disciplinary policies."** 469 U.S. at 336. The Court then went on to reject the state's argument that children in public schools have no reasonable expectation of privacy in their personal effects while at school. However, given the substantial state interest in maintaining security, order, and an appropriate educational environment in public schools, the Court concluded that the full protection of the Fourth Amendment was not applicable in the public school setting.

> **It is evident that the school setting requires some easing of the restrictions to which searches by public authorities are ordinarily subject. The warrant requirement, in particular, is unsuited to the school environment: requiring a teacher to obtain a warrant before searching a child suspected of an infraction of school rules (or of the criminal law) would unduly interfere with the maintenance of the swift and informal disciplinary procedures needed in the schools. Just as we have in other cases dispensed with the warrant requirement when "the burden of obtaining a warrant is likely to frustrate the governmental purpose behind the search," . . . we hold today that school officials need not obtain a warrant before searching a student who is under their authority. The school setting also requires some modification of the level of suspicion of illicit activity needed to justify a search. Ordinarily, a search, even one that may permissibly be carried out without a warrant, must be based upon "probable cause" to believe that a violation of the law has occurred. However, "probable cause" is not an irreducible requirement of a valid search. . . . [W]e have in a number of cases recognized the legality of searches and seizures based on suspicions that, although "reasonable," do not rise to the level of probable cause. . . .** 469 U.S. at 340-41 (internal citations omitted).

Applying these principles to the vice principal's actions in *T.L.O.,* the Court determined his initial search of the girl's purse was reasonable because a teacher had reported that the girl had been smoking in a lavatory. Given the teacher's report of her smoking, coupled with her denial, the Court concluded it was reasonable for the vice principal to check the girl's purse because **"if she did have cigarettes, her purse was the obvious place in which to find them."** 469 U.S. at 346. And, once the vice principal saw the rolling papers, the Court determined he had reason to suspect the purse contained further contraband, making his continued search of the purse reasonable.

The Diminution of Suspicion for Drug and Alcohol Testing

From Individualized Suspicion to Generalized, Non-Particularized Suspicion Determining the reasonableness of any search involves an inquiry into (1) whether the action was justified at its inception; and (2) whether the search as actually conducted was reasonably related in scope to the circumstances that justified the interference in the first place. The Court in *T.L.O.* said:

> Under ordinary circumstances, a search of a student by a teacher or other school official will be "justified at its inception" when there are *reasonable grounds for suspecting* that the search will turn up evidence that the student has violated or is violating either the law or the rules of the school. Such a search will be permissible in its scope when the measures adopted are reasonably related to the objectives of the search and not excessively intrusive in light of the age and sex of the student and the nature of the infraction. 469 U.S. at 341-42 (emphasis added).

With the knowledge that warrantless searches of students were constitutionally permissible with less suspicion than probable cause, a number of school districts around the country developed policies for conducting searches of students suspected of using drugs and alcohol. But some districts adopted policies that went beyond the ostensible prescriptions of the *T.L.O.* case by adopting policies that permitted random, suspicionless searches of students. At first blush, such policies appeared to violate the constitutional requirements of the Fourth Amendment as interpreted in *T.L.O.* because they permitted students to be searched without the type of individual, particularized suspicion that had existed against the girl suspected of smoking in *T.L.O.* Such policies, however, were upheld by the Supreme Court in *Vernonia School District 47J v. Acton*, 515 U.S. 646 (1995), at least as they applied to a drug testing program for student athletes.

The Court began its analysis of the issue by recognizing that high school student drug use is a matter of great concern, as it has **"deleterious effects . . . on motivation, memory, judgment, reaction, coordination, and performance."** 515 U.S. at 649. The Court then reiterated its line of Fourth Amendment inquiry in the student setting as set forth in *T.L.O.*, focusing on the requirement of reasonableness. Although the Court acknowledged the search at issue in *T.L.O.* was based on reasonable, articulable suspicion, it emphasized that **"the Fourth Amendment imposes no irreducible requirement of such suspicion."** 515 U.S. at 653. **"We have upheld suspicionless searches and seizures to conduct drug testing of railroad personnel involved in train accidents; to conduct random drug testing of federal customs officers who carry arms or are involved in drug interdiction; to maintain automobile checkpoints looking for illegal immigrants and contraband; and drunk drivers."** 515 U.S. at 653-54. The Court then extended this line of reasoning to cover random, suspicionless searches of student athletes for drug and alcohol violations.

Key to the reasoning in *Vernonia* was that the already diminished expectation of privacy in the school setting was even lower for student athletes. **"School sports are not for the bashful. They require 'suiting up' before each practice or event, and showering and changing afterwards. Public school locker rooms, the usual sites for these activities, are not notable for the privacy they afford."** 515 U.S. at 657. Moreover, the Court reasoned that by the very nature of voluntarily **"go[ing] out for the team,"** students **"subject** themselves to a degree of regulation even higher than that imposed on students generally." 515 U.S. at 657.

> **In Vernonia's public schools, they must submit to a preseason physical exam . . . includ[ing] the giving of a urine sample . . . , they must acquire adequate insurance coverage or sign an insurance waiver, maintain a minimum grade point average, and comply with any "rules of conduct, dress, training hours and related matters as may be established for each sport by the head coach and athletic director with the principal's approval."** 515 U.S. at 657.

Accordingly, the Court reasoned that much like adults who enter into a closely regulated industry, students who participate in school athletic programs should expect to have less privacy rights than might otherwise exist. Moreover, according to the majority opinion in *Vernonia,* this diminished level of privacy is what needed to be balanced against the state interest at issue in the case; namely, reducing and preventing teenage drug and alcohol use. The Court called such a need "important enough"—"perhaps even 'compelling'" to justify the intrusion into student athlete's diminished privacy rights. 515 U.S. at 661. However, the Court cautioned against the assumption that suspicionless drug testing would readily pass constitutional muster in other contexts.

From Generalized Suspicion to Suspicionless Drug Testing The Supreme Court expanded *Vernonia* when it upheld the random, suspicionless drug testing of students participating in extracurricular activities in *Board of Education of Ind. School District 92 of Pottawatomie County v. Earls,* 536 U.S. 822 (2002). As it did in *Vernonia,* the Court started with the premises that public school students have a diminished expectation of privacy while at school, and that drug testing via urinalysis posed only a minimal or "negligible" intrusion into students' privacy rights. But over a strong dissent that focused on the unique diminished expectation of privacy for student athletes in light of the factors elaborated upon in *Vernonia,* the *Earls* majority similarly asserted that **"students who participate in competitive extracurricular activities voluntarily subject themselves to many of the same intrusions on their privacy as do athletes."** 536 U.S. at 831. To support this dubious proposition, the Court wrote:

> **Some of these clubs and activities require occasional off-campus travel and communal undress. All of them have their own rules and requirements for participating students that do not apply to the student body as a whole. For example, each of the competitive extracurricular activities governed by the Policy must abide by the rules of the Oklahoma Secondary Schools Activities Association, and a faculty sponsor monitors the students for compliance with the various rules dictated by the clubs and activities. This regulation of extracurricular activities further diminishes the expectation of privacy among schoolchildren.** 536 U.S. at 832.

Yet, as Justice Ginsburg's dissent pointed out, although athletics "require close safety and health regulation, a school's choir, band, and academic team do not." 536 U.S. at 846. The rationale offered in *Vernonia* relied on medical literature that addressed the particular dangers of drug use and physical exertion that, when combined, "pose substantial physical risks to athletes." *Vernonia,* 515 U.S. at 662. Moreover, the record in *Vernonia* demonstrated a severe drug problem in the district in which student athletes "were the leaders of the drug culture."

515 U.S. at 649. In contrast, there was no evidence that students engaging in extracurricular activities were involved with drugs. Quite the contrary, as Justice Ginsburg's dissent in *Earls* stated: "nationwide, students who participate in extracurricular activities are significantly less likely to develop substance abuse problems than are their less involved peers." 536 U.S. at 853. Thus, the policy upheld by the *Earls* Court had the ironic effect of testing students who needed drug deterrence least while risking "steering students at greatest risk for substance abuse away from extracurricular involvement that potentially may palliate drug problems." 536 U.S. at 853.

A year after *Earls* was decided, the New Jersey Supreme Court upheld an extension of a random, suspicionless drug testing program to all students who drive to school. *Joye v. Hunterdon Central Bd. of Educ.*, 826 A.2d 624 (N.J. 2003). A similar policy was also upheld by the Indiana Supreme Court. *Linke v. Northwestern School Corp.*, 763 N.E.2d 972 (Ind. 2002).

In light of these cases, the following propositions summarize the status of the law concerning school-initiated searches of elementary and high school students:

▶ physical searches of students and their possessions may be conducted by school officials without a warrant based merely on reasonable suspicion;

▶ warrantless, random, suspicionless testing of students by school officials for controlled substances based on any seemingly logical reason appear to be constitutionally valid tools to combat teenage drug and alcohol use.

Searches of College Students

The law of search and seizure in the college and university setting is downright inconsistent. A comprehensive review of the case law in this area is beyond the scope of this text. Moreover, it would be unnecessarily confusing to the reader because there are a multitude of contradictions in cases across time and across jurisdictional lines. That being said, however, a few generalizations can be made.

Police-Initiated Investigations If law enforcement officials initiate an investigation that involves a college or university campus (whether private or public), and they gain entry to a student's room without a warrant through cooperation with school officials, such a search would be invalid and all evidence seized would be inadmissible under the Fourth Amendment. *E.g., Piazzola v. Watkins*, 316 F. Supp. 624 (M.D. Ala. 1970), *aff'd* 442 F.2d 284 (5th Cir. 1971). Similarly, if police enlist school officials to participate in a criminal investigation and get them to act on their behalf, then the school officials will be deemed state actors for Fourth Amendment purposes. Thus, police are well advised that there are no "college student exceptions" to the normal requirements of the Fourth Amendment. The materials in this subsection are concerned with searches and seizures that take place as a result of actions initially taken by college or university officials.

Actions by Private College or University Officials Courts are generally consistent in holding that the Fourth Amendment does not protect students at private colleges and universities from searches conducted by school officials. For example, in *Duarte v. Commonwealth*, 407 S.E.2d 41 (Va. App. 1991), a college official at a private university, acting at the direction of the dean of students, conducted a search of a student's room. The dean of students had been advised by police that the student was suspected of having participated in a burglary and that stolen property might be found in the student's dormitory room. Even though the police specifically asked the dean to refrain from taking any action, including searching the student's room, until the police had completed their investigation, the dean instructed two college officials to search the student's dormitory room "and to confiscate any contraband or stolen items, pursuant to the guidelines for searches and seizures set forth in the [college's] Student Handbook." 407 S.E.2d at 42. The search yielded several bags of marijuana and drug paraphernalia that the college turned over to police, which, in turn, resulted in the student being charged with possession of a controlled substance with intent to distribute. The court upheld the search and seizure finding that the Fourth Amendment was "wholly inapplicable 'to a search or seizure, even an unreasonable one, effected by a private individual not acting as an agent of the Government or with the participation or knowledge of any governmental official.'" 407 S.E.2d at 42.

State v. Burroughs, 926 S.W.2d 243 (Tenn. 1996), similarly upheld a search of a student's room at a private college by a residence director (RD) who acted pursuant to school policy that allowed unannounced, unscheduled entries into student rooms for the purpose of ensuring compliance with school policies. The RD had been told that a particular student was engaged in selling cocaine from his dorm room, so the RD went to the student's room and knocked. Receiving no response, the RD "used a master key to gain entry. He searched and discovered a set of electronic scales and a cigar box containing a quantity of 'white powdery substance.'" 926 S.W.2d at 245. The residence director contacted a dean, who, in turn, contacted the college's liaison at the local police department. The officer arrived on the scene, identified the substance as cocaine, and seized the evidence which was then used in the student's criminal prosecution. The court held the search and seizure valid because it had been conducted by the RD "not as an agent of the state, but as a college official whose purpose and actions were in furtherance of college policy, not state policy." 926 S.W.2d at 246.

Actions by Public College or University Officials The Fourth Amendment clearly applies to searches and seizures conducted on the campuses of public colleges and universities. While school officials have some latitude to enforce campus disciplinary regulations, they may not act as instruments of law enforcement. The purpose and intent of their search-related activities is key to the legality of their actions.

Smyth v. Lubbers, 398 F. Supp. 777 (D. Mich. 1975), involved the search of several students' dormitory rooms by officials at a public college. The college had a written policy that allowed students' rooms to be entered and searched if school officials had "reasonable cause to believe that students" were violating federal, state, or local laws. Pursuant to that policy, two campus police officers and several residential life staff members searched several students' rooms and discovered marijuana. In reviewing the college's actions, the court began by stating that students' interest in the privacy of their rooms was "not at the 'outer limits,' . . . but on the contrary . . . , at the very core of the Fourth Amendment's protections." 398 F. Supp. at 786. The court then went on to reject the college's contention that the search qualified as a special needs search:

> This case clearly involves a full search which focused upon the room of a specific individual who was suspected of criminal activity, and which aimed at

discovering specific evidence. The search was not 'administrative' in the sense of a generalized or routine inspection for violations of housing, health, or other regulatory code. Since the College authorities were looking for marijuana in Smith's room, the search was specifically for instrumentalities of crime, defining 'instrumentalities' here as contraband. . . . 398 F. Supp. at 786-87.

Notably, the court refused to rely on the consent search doctrine (see Chapter 9) because the students had agreed to abide by certain residence life policies as a precondition to living on campus. The court found such consent was ineffective because it was contained in a contract of adhesion to which students were forced to agree; and, therefore, any alleged waiver of their privacy rights was not truly voluntary. 398 F. Supp. at 788. The court therefore concluded that the college needed a search warrant, duly supported by probable cause, to search the student's rooms. The court specifically stated that the fact that campus police officers were involved in the search was of no consequence, as the same result would have occurred if the search had been solely conducted by college residence life staff. *See, e.g., Morale v. Grigel*, 422 F. Supp. 988 (D.N.H. 1976) (finding that repeated searches of a student's dormitory room by a student-resident advisor searching for evidence of criminal drug use constituted state action for Fourth Amendment purposes).

In *State v. Kappes*, 550 P.2d 121, 122 (Ariz. App. 1976), a state university had a housing regulation that provided university officials could enter dormitory rooms and "inspect for cleanliness, safety, or the need for repairs and maintenance." Once per month, students who were employed by the university as resident advisors (RAs) inspected all rooms at a time announced by a posting one day in advance of the inspections. During one such inspection, two RAs found marijuana in the defendant's dormitory room. They called campus police to the room and admitted the officers into the room. In upholding the validity of the search, the court held that:

> [W]here the entry is made by a student advisor conducting a routine dormitory inspection announced in advance, we cannot say that the intrusion is the result of government action which will invoke the Fourth Amendment, and, consequently, the exclusionary rule. The purpose of the room inspection is not to collect evidence for criminal proceedings against the student, but to insure that the rooms are used and maintained in accordance with the university regulations. 550 P.2d 124.

Moreover, the court held that the subsequent seizure of the drugs by police did not violate the Fourth Amendment because they were in plain view (see Chapter 10). While the logic of *Kappes* with respect to the search is still good law, its holding with respect to the subsequent warrantless seizure under the plain view doctrine is suspect in light of more recent case law.

In *Washington v. Chrisman*, 455 U.S. 1 (1982), a campus police officer observed what he believed to be an underage student in possession of alcohol. When the student was asked for identification, he could not produce it and therefore asked the officer if they could go back to his dormitory room to retrieve it. When the student opened the door and admitted the officer with him, the police officer saw the student's roommate in possession of drugs and drug paraphernalia. The U.S. Supreme Court upheld the warrantless seizure of the drugs that were in plain view because the police officer was lawfully admitted to the dormitory room. But the plain view doctrine does not apply to a police seizure when officers are not lawfully present in the dormitory room at the time they make a plain view observation. *See, e.g., Commonwealth v. Lewin*, 555 N.E.2d 551 (1990).

In *Commonwealth v. Neilson*, 666 N.E.2d 984 (Mass. 1996), college officials lawfully entered and searched a room looking for a cat, which residence hall rules forbade. Once inside the dorm room, however, they discovered marijuana. They notified police, who then entered the room and seized the contraband. The court ruled that while it was perfectly appropriate for university officials to have notified law enforcement, police should not have entered the room and seized the contraband without a warrant. Of course, a warrant could easily have been issued in *Neilson* based upon the statements provided by the university officials. But the police failed to obtain such a warrant before entering a dormitory room and seizing evidence contained therein. This violated the Fourth Amendment because no other warrant exception, such as exigent circumstances, was deemed to have been applicable in the case. Notably, the state argued that the student had given consent for such a warrantless entry by police since he had signed a residence hall contract authorizing university officials to enter his room. The court rejected this argument:

> [T]here was no consent to the police entry and search of the room. The defendant's consent was given, not to police officials, but to the University and the latter cannot fragmentize, share, or delegate it. While the college officials were entitled to conduct a health and safety inspection, they clearly . . . had no authority to consent to or join in a police search for evidence of crime. 666 N.E.2d at 987 (internal quotations and citations omitted).

In *Smyth*, the search was clearly motivated by criminal investigatory purposes. *Kappes* and *Neilson*, in contrast, concerned searches motivated by a desire to enforce campus disciplinary and safety regulations. That distinction is clearly what differentiated the legality of the searches. But not all cases are so clear-cut, as illustrated by *State v. Hunter*, 831 P.2d 1033 (Utah App. 1992). A wave of vandalism in a particular residence hall prompted university officials to call meetings of the residents and inform them that room-to-room inspections would be conducted as a way of combating the vandalism. During one such inspection, college officials found both a sign and a banner that had been stolen from the university. The court upheld the search because it was "a reasonable exercise of the university's authority to maintain an educational environment"—a responsibility "incumbent upon the university to . . . provide a clean, safe, well-disciplined environment in its dormitories." 831 P.2d at 1036. While the court found the enforcement of disciplinary rules to have been the motivation for the searches, the fact that the searches had been instituted in response to criminal actions could have led a court to conclude that university officials were searching for criminal evidence connected to the acts of vandalism.

Border Searches

Border searches are arguably the ultimate special needs search. Accordingly, there is no reasonable expectation of privacy at any of the U.S. borders or their functional equivalents, such as international airline terminals, cruise ship terminals, or some other place where someone may be stopped for the first time upon entering the country. Not only are border searches a part of maintaining the sovereignty of the country by controlling the flow of both people and articles into or out of the country, but also they play a vital role in maintaining national security. *United States v. Montoya de Hernandez*, 473 U.S. 531, 538 (1985). As a result, **"routine searches of the persons and effects of entrants are not subject to any requirement of reasonable suspicion, probable cause, or warrant."** *United States v. Flores-Montano*, 541 U.S. 149 (2004). Border patrol or U.S. customs officials may "search carry-on bags and checked luggage, conduct canine sniffs or pat-downs, photograph and fingerprint travelers, and even disassemble the gas tank on a vehicle without an independent trigger for the search" (Gilmore, 2007: 767); *see also, e.g., Bradley v. United States*, 299 F.3d 197 (3d Cir. 2002) (pat-downs); *United States v. Hernandez*, 424 F.3d 1056, 1057 (9th Cir. 2005) They may also x-ray luggage and people. *United States v. Okafor*, 285 F.3d 842 (9th Cir. 2002). Given the scope of permissible searches at borders, the only substantive restraint on the searches of objects is that they be conducted in a reasonable manner. Thus, for example, searches conducted in a "particularly offensive manner," such as one that is unnecessarily destructive, may violate the Fourth Amendment. *Flores-Montano*, 541 U.S. at 154 n.2 & 156.

In contrast to routine border searches, more invasive searches of people—such as strip searches, body cavity searches, or extended periods of detention—do require reasonable suspicion, although they do not require a warrant. *Montoya de Hernandez*, 473 U.S. at 541. However, these invasive searches still need to be executed in a reasonable manner. (For more detailed information on physically invasive searches, see the section on "Searches on or in the Body" in Chapter 8).

Other Special Needs Searches

In addition to those named above, there are other special needs searches. These include searches at airports, courthouses, and public transit systems, as well as searches of DNA databases.

Airport and Courthouse Searches Starting in the mid-1960s and increasing through the 1970s, a "wake of unprecedented airport bombings, aircraft piracy and courtroom violence" befell the nation. *Wheaton v. Hagan*, 435 F. Supp. 1134, 1362 (M.D.N.C. 1977). As a result, the federal government began to implement a series of screening mechanisms to make public access to planes and courthouses safer. Courts recognized the special needs for increased security in these areas, and therefore allowed warrantless, suspicionless searches of both airports and courtrooms. *E.g., United States v. Albarado*, 495 F.2d 799 (2d Cir. 1974).

Multiple Justifications Courts use several constitutional theories to justify warrantless, suspicionless searches at airports, courthouses, and other public places with special security needs. First, given the public safety issues at stake, routine searches at these locations can be justified as special needs searches. Second, given how highly regulated airline travel is, some courts have justified steps taken during pre-boarding searches under the administrative search doctrine. *E.g., United States v. Davis*, 482 F.2d 893 (9th Cir. 1973); *United States v. Hartwell*, 436 F.3d 174 (3d Cir. 2006). But the most common theory courts use is consent. People seeking to enter a place with special security needs (like a courthouse or the boarding areas of an airport) voluntarily place themselves in a position where they know they will be subject to a search. By doing so, they give implied consent to be subjected to routine screening procedures. *See United States v. Hartwell*, 296 F. Supp. 2d 596 (E.D. Pa. 2003). Moreover, once this implied consent is given, it cannot be revoked. Thus, for example, a person who attempts to pass through an airport security checkpoint cannot then decline secondary screening procedures by revoking consent. *See United States v. Aukai*, 440 F.3d 1168 (9th Cir. 2006).

Scope of Search and Requirement of Reasonability An airport screening search is reasonable if: (1) it is no more extensive or intensive than necessary, in light of current technology, to detect weapons or explosives; (2) it is confined in good faith to that purpose; and (3) passengers may avoid the search by electing not to fly. *Torbet v. United Airlines, Inc.*, 298 F.3d 1087, 1089 (9th Cir. 2002).

▶ **Requesting Identification** Requesting identification is not a "seizure" within the meaning of the Fourth Amendment, especially because a passenger is normally able to leave the airport if they cannot or elect not to comply with the request. *See Gilmore v. Gonzales*, 435 F.3d 1125 (9th Cir. 2006), *cert. denied*, 127 S. Ct. 929 (2007).

▶ **Routine Initial Screening Processes** Under the test as set forth in *Torbet*, the usual screening process of having would-be passengers pass through magnetometers as their carry-on luggage passes through x-ray machines easily passes constitutional muster:

> The scan and subsequent search involves only a slight privacy intrusion as long as the scope of the search is limited to the detection of weapons, explosives, or any other dangerous devices, and is conducted in a manner which produces negligible social stigma. Given these circumstances, a visual inspection and limited hand search of luggage which is used for the purpose of detecting weapons or explosives, and not in order to uncover other types of contraband, is a privacy intrusion we believe free society is willing to tolerate. *United States v. Figueroa Cruz*, 822 F. Supp. 853 (D.P.R. 1993).

▶ **Random Manual Searches of "Selectees"** Random manual searches of a would-be passenger and his or her belongings for weapons or explosives does not violate the Fourth Amendment. *Torbet*, 298 F.3d at 1090; *United States v. Marquez*, 410 F.3d 612 (9th Cir. 2005).

▶ **Advance Routine Screening Processes** If magnetic and/or x-ray scans yield inconclusive results, further searches are warranted so long as they are reasonably conducted. But, at that point, because of the inconclusive results, security personnel have reasonable suspicion to conduct a patdown of a person and/or a more extensive search of one's carry-on luggage. And, depending what is found, probable cause to do an even more extensive search may then exist. For example, in *United States v. Hartwell*, 436 F.3d 174 (3rd Cir. 2006), the defendant set off an alarm when he passed through a metal detector. Transportation Security Administration (TSA) agents then used a magnetic wand to pinpoint any metal on his person. When they detected something in Hartwell's pocket, they asked to see it. When he refused, a TSA agent reached into the defendant's pocket and pulled out a package that contained crack cocaine. In upholding the search as reasonable under the Fourth Amendment, the court concluded the intrusions of privacy were minimal when compared to the gravity of the public interests that are served by warrantless, administrative searches.

▶ **The Limits of a Search** Some courts have found that by agreeing to be searched at an airport or courthouse, people grant a limited form of consent to be searched for weapons, explosives, or other items that pose a danger to public safety. *E.g., United States v. $124,570 U.S. Currency*, 873 F.2d 1240 (9th Cir. 1989). When, as in *Hartwell,* routine screening yields contraband such as drugs, there is no Fourth Amendment violation. However, when preliminary screening fails to identify the presence of something that is the legitimate target of a special needs search—namely weapons or explosives—then a further search of the person and/or the person's belongings may not be constitutionally permissible. For example, if an initial screening yields the presence of large amounts of money, that does not permit screeners to conduct a full search of the person's belongings for contraband. *See also United States v. Doe*, 61 F.3d 107 (1st Cir. 1995); *United States v. Williams*, 267 F. Supp. 2d 1130 (M.D. Ala. 2003).

DNA Searches Federal law and the law of all fifty states now provide for collection of DNA samples from criminal offenders.

> Some states (like Indiana, Massachusetts, Virginia, and Wyoming) collect DNA profiles from all felons, but not from misdemeanants; other states (like California, Florida, New Jersey, and Ohio) collect samples from both felons and misdemeanants; and a small number of states (e.g., California, Louisiana, Texas, and Virginia) allow samples to be collected from people arrested for certain crimes. Most states include collection of DNA from juveniles, but in approximately twenty states, juveniles are excluded from collection efforts. A small number of states (like Hawaii, Michigan, and Nebraska) only permit DNA samples collected from suspects to be maintained in their databases during the time in which the individual is considered a suspect, while other states retain samples in their databases even after a suspect is acquitted (Owen & Burke, 2007: 619–20).

Thus far, each appellate court that has addressed the constitutionality of a state or federal DNA testing statute has upheld the constitutionality of the law. *State v. O'Hagen*, 914 A.2d 267, 273 (N.J. 2007). The courts, however, are split as to the underlying constitutional theory that justifies such DNA searches. Some courts apply a reasonableness balancing test examining the totality of the circumstances, relying on the Supreme Court's holding in *United States v. Knights*, 534 U.S. 112 (2001). *See, e.g., United States v. Sczubelek*, 402 F.3d 175 (3d Cir.2005), *cert. denied*, 126 S. Ct. 2930 (2006). Other courts consider DNA searches under the special needs approach. *E.g., Nicholas v. Goord*, 430 F.3d 652 (2d Cir.2005), *cert. denied*, 127 S. Ct. 384 (2006). The special needs approach is a more difficult test to satisfy in light of the fact that it requires a showing that "there is a special governmental need beyond the normal need for law enforcement that justifies [DNA] testing without individualized suspicion." *O'Hagen*, 914 A.2d at 277. However, even under the more stringent special needs approach, DNA testing laws have been upheld on the basis that they serve a number of permissible special needs, such as:

> [I]dentification; development of a population database; support of identification research and protocol development of forensic DNA analysis methods; identi-

fication of human remains from mass disasters or for other humanitarian purposes; research, administrative, and quality control purposes; judicial proceedings; criminal defense purposes; and such other purposes as may be required under federal law as a condition for federal funding. *O'Hagen*, 914 A.2d at 278.

Even though several of these purposes "may involve law enforcement to some degree, the central purposes of the DNA testing are not intended to subject the donor to criminal charges. That is, the DNA test result is not intended to directly aid in the prosecution of the donor." 914 A.2d at 278. When these needs are balanced against the minimal invasion of privacy that an oral DNA swab engenders, courts routinely conclude that laws allowing for the warrantless, suspicionless seizure of a DNA sample from persons charged or convicted of criminal offenses comply with the requirements of the Fourth Amendment. *United States v. Amerson*, 483 F.3d 73 (2d Cir. 2007) (upholding DNA collection requirements under the federal Crime Control and Law Enforcement Act of 1994, Pub. L. No. 103-322, 108 Stat. 1796 (1994)).

Public Transit System Searches In response to the terrorist attacks on September 11, 2001, cities across the United States took steps to increase security. Of particular concern to New York City was the vulnerability of its subway system to attack. This concern was due, in large part, to terrorist attacks on a number of urban subway systems around the world, including one using nerve gas that killed twelve people and injured 6,000 more on a Tokyo subway in 1995, and two others in 2004 that killed approximately 230 and injured over 1,500 in Moscow and Madrid. Since that time, an attack on the London Underground was thwarted; but one in Mumbai in 2006 killed more than 200 and wounded another 800 people (Martin, 2007: 1286). To help prevent such attacks on the New York subway system, the city implemented a checkpoint system in which police would randomly stop every fifth or tenth person as they attempted to enter the transit system and ask for permission to conduct a visual search of any bags or packages the would-be subway riders were carrying. The inspection program the city designed was upheld as a valid special needs search in *MacWade v. Kelly*, 460 F.3d 260 (2d Cir. 2006).

According to the City of New York, its goal in establishing the subway screening checkpoints was "to deter terrorists from carrying concealed explosives onto the subway system and, to a lesser extent, to uncover any such attempt." 460 F.3d at 264. The scope of the inspections was limited as follows:

> As to scope, officers search only those containers large enough to carry an explosive device, which means, for example, that they may not inspect wallets and small purses. Further, once they identify a container of eligible size, they must limit their inspection "to what is minimally necessary to ensure that the . . . item does not contain an explosive device," which they have been trained to recognize in various forms. They may not intentionally look for other contraband, although if officers incidentally discover such contraband, they may arrest the individual carrying it. Officers may not attempt to read any written or printed material. Nor may they request or record a passenger's personal information, such as his name, address, or demographic data. 460 F.3d at 265.

Anyone who refused to grant consent to have the containers they were carrying searched by police were denied access to the transit system, but they were allowed to leave the subway without any further questioning. 460 F.3d at 266.

Both a federal district court and the U.S. Court of Appeals for the Second Circuit upheld the city's subway checkpoint scheme under the special needs doctrine. Analogizing the checkpoints to those in airports, the courts found that the searches were designed to advance public safety—a need "distinct from ordinary post-hoc criminal investigation." 460 F.3d at 271. Moreover, the courts found that the city's need to prevent attacks on its subway system was enormous and compelling; that even though the searches infringe on a full privacy interest, the nature of the intrusion into that privacy was minimal; and that the program was reasonably effective as a deterrent. 460 F.3d at 272-74.

A few months after the decision, *MacWade* was applied to a similar screening process that had been implemented on a commuter ferry system serving the Lake Champlain area of Vermont. Pursuant to the authority granted by the Maritime Transportation Security Act of 2002 (MTSA), *see* 46 U.S.C. §§ 70101-70119 (2006), the U.S. Coast Guard conducted random, warrantless searches of ferry commuter's carry-on baggage and motor vehicles. Coming to the same conclusions about the specific requirement of special needs searches that were reached in *MacWade*, the court upheld the search program. *Cassidy v. Chertoff*, 471 F.3d 67 (2d Cir. 2006). The court emphasized that although such screening programs may not be the perfect way to stop a terrorist attack, they are a reasonable, minimally intrusive method that "may well stymie an attack, disrupt the synchronicity of multiple bombings, or at least reduce casualties." 471 F.3d at 87.

If *MacWade* and *Cassidy* are applied consistently on a nationwide basis, it is clear that random, warrantless, suspicionless searches may become commonplace as part of law enforcement efforts to protect buses, trains, ferries, and other forms of public transportation from terrorist attack.

key points

- An exception to the warrant and probable cause requirements of the Fourth Amendment exists where "special needs" of the government, beyond the normal need for law enforcement gathering evidence for crime investigation, make the warrant and probable cause requirements impracticable.
- "Special needs" exceptions are evaluated under the "reasonableness" standard of the Fourth Amendment, by balancing (1) the weight and immediacy of the government interest; (2) the nature of the privacy interest allegedly compromised by the search; (3) the character of the intrusion imposed by the search; and (4) the efficacy of the search in advancing the government interest. Applying this balancing test allows for warrantless searches based on reasonable suspicion in some circumstances, while in other circumstances warrantless, suspicionless searches may be appropriate.

►ELECTRONIC SURVEILLANCE WARRANTS

Electronic surveillance—searches conducted using wiretaps, bugs, or other devices to overhear conversations or obtain other kinds of information—is a relatively recent concern of criminal and constitutional law. Certainly the Framers could not have imagined the possibilities for gathering information on crime created by the marvels of twentieth-century technology. Nor could they, when they drafted the Constitution, have contemplated the potential invasions of privacy brought about by the new technology. It is not surprising, then, that the Constitution gives little guidance for balancing privacy interests against the need for effective law enforcement in the area of electronic surveillance.

On the one hand, electronic listening, tracking, and recording devices provide a very powerful tool for law enforcement officials in investigating and prosecuting crime. On the other hand, the potential for the abuse of individual rights can be far greater with electronic surveillance than with any ordinary search or seizure. The task of resolving these competing interests has fallen on state legislatures, the U.S. Congress, and, ultimately, the courts. This section traces the early development of the law of electronic surveillance; examines legislative and judicial responses to the problem; and concludes with a discussion of Title III of the Omnibus Crime Control and Safe Streets Act of 1968, which provided authority for electronic surveillance pursuant to a court order.

Early Developments in Electronic Interceptions Law

Although electronic eavesdropping has been used as an information-gathering technique since the mid-1800s, the U.S. Supreme Court did not decide its first electronic eavesdropping case until 1928. In *Olmstead v. United States*, 277 U.S. 438 (1928), involving interception of telephone conversations by means of a wiretap, the Court held that wiretapping was not covered by the Fourth Amendment. One reason for this decision was that without physical trespass into the defendant's premises, there was no search. The other reason was that all the evidence had been obtained by hearing only; as the Fourth Amendment referred only to the seizure of tangible items, the interception of a conversation could not qualify as a seizure.

As discussed in Chapter 3, *Katz v. United States*, 389 U.S. 347 (1967), rendered invalid the first rationale of *Olmstead* by changing the focus of Fourth Amendment analysis from a "property" approach to a "privacy" approach. *Berger v. New York*, 388 U.S. 41 (1967), disposed of the second rationale of *Olmstead* by holding that conversations were protected by the Fourth Amendment and that the use of electronic devices to capture conversations was a search within the meaning of the Fourth Amendment.

Once the premise was established that electronic surveillance is a search and seizure within the meaning of the Fourth Amendment, the U.S. Supreme Court had to decide what kinds of electronic surveillance the Fourth Amendment allowed and prohibited and to what extent. The guidelines for these constitutional limitations on electronic surveillance were worked out in a series of decisions in the mid-1960s.

The Supreme Court first explicitly considered the constitutionality of electronic surveillance conducted under authority of a warrant in *Osborn v. United States*, 385 U.S. 323 (1966). In that case, federal law enforcement officials had information that labor leader Jimmy Hoffa's attorney was trying to bribe a prospective juror. The officials obtained a warrant authorizing an undercover agent with a concealed tape recorder to record a specific conversation with the attorney. The tape of the conversation was admitted at trial, and the attorney was convicted of attempting to bribe a juror. The Court upheld the conviction, emphasizing that "[t]he issue here is . . . the permissibility of using such a device under the most precise and discriminate circumstances. . . ." 385 U.S. at 329.

The Supreme Court's limited grant of constitutional permissibility for electronic surveillance was tested again the next year in *Berger v. New York*, 388 U.S. 41 (1967). In *Berger*, the issue was the constitutionality of a New York statute that authorized electronic surveillance pursuant to a judicial warrant. Ultimately, the Court invalidated the law because it failed to properly limit the nature, scope, or duration of the electronic surveillance. The Court pointed out that the availability of an initial two-month surveillance period under the law was "the equivalent of a series of intrusions, searches, and seizures pursuant to a single showing of probable cause." 388 U.S. at 59. The Court also stressed that the statute placed no termination requirement on the eavesdropping, even after the desired conversation had been obtained. Furthermore, the statute had two major deficiencies with respect to probable cause. First, an eavesdropping warrant could be issued without probable cause that a particular crime had been committed and without a particular description of "the property" (conversations in this context) to be seized. Second, an eavesdropping order could be extended or renewed without a showing of probable cause for continuation of the eavesdrop. Finally, in contrast to conventional search warrant procedures, the statute permitted electronic eavesdropping without prior notice or a showing of exigency excusing notice.

Despite the Supreme Court's invalidation of the statute in *Berger*, the possibility that a properly circumscribed warrant procedure for electronic surveillance could be created was left open. This possibility was given further credence by *Katz v. United States*, 389 U.S. 347, 354 (1967), in which FBI agents attached an electronic listening device to a public telephone booth and recorded the defendant's calls. The Court held that the interception was an unlawful search and seizure because there was no warrant, but strongly indicated that a proper warrant could have been issued:

> [T]he surveillance was limited, both in scope and in duration, to the specific purpose of establishing the contents of the petitioner's unlawful telephonic communications. The agents confined their surveillance to the brief periods during which he [Katz] used the telephone booth, and they took great care to overhear only the conversation of the petitioner himself. Accepting this account of the Government's actions as accurate, it is clear that this surveillance was so narrowly circumscribed that a duly authorized magistrate, properly notified of the need for such investigation, specifically informed of the basis on which it was to proceed, and clearly apprised of the precise intrusion it would entail, could constitutionally have authorized, with appropriate safeguards, the very limited search and seizure that the Government asserts in fact took place. 389 U.S. at 354.

The possibility that a constitutionally permissible warrant procedure for electronic surveillance could be set up paved the way for congressional action.

Omnibus Crime Control and Safe Streets Act of 1968

Wiretapping and other forms of electronic surveillance can be invaluable tools to law enforcement officials. However, these forms of gathering information represent a significant intrusion into arenas in which people have reasonable expectations of privacy. To balance these competing interests, Congress enacted the Omnibus Crime Control and Safe Streets Act of 1968—the year following the *Berger* and *Katz* opinions. Title III of that act superseded earlier statutory prohibitions against intercepted communications and provided authorization for electronic surveillance pursuant to warrant.

Enactment of Title III The passage of **Title III of the Omnibus Crime Control and Safe Streets Act**, following so closely on the heels of the *Berger* and *Katz* decisions, was not simply a matter of Congress enacting legislation in response to the guidelines of those decisions. Concern had long been expressed about the inadequacy of existing electronic surveillance legislation. Defense lawyers and civil libertarians complained of governmental violations of the privacy rights of American citizens. Proponents of electronic surveillance argued that wiretapping and bugging were essential tools for law enforcement officials to combat the modern sophisticated criminal, especially in the area of organized crime.

The belief that electronic surveillance was the only way to deal with the unique problems of investigating and prosecuting organized crime prompted the President's Crime Commission to recommend legislation authorizing electronic surveillance. Political pressures were exerted in a national climate of fear brought about by intense social unrest and the assassinations of Martin Luther King, Jr., and Robert Kennedy, and crystallized in the "law and order" presidential campaign of Richard Nixon. The result was a bipartisan effort to balance modern society's conflicting demands for privacy and more effective law enforcement through the enactment of Title III in 1968.

The discussion now turns to an examination of Title III and cases interpreting it. Because of the length of the law, this discussion is necessarily general in nature. Also, the discussion points out how the USA PATRIOT Act, enacted in response to the terrorist attacks of September 11, 2001, affects electronic surveillance in general and Title III in particular.

Scope and Terminology The reach of Title III is much broader than the Fourth Amendment's. Title III applies to private searches and seizures of wire, oral, or electronic communications as well as those involving governmental actors. As a result, Title III provides remedies that go beyond the usual Fourth Amendment remedy of suppressing evidence illegally obtained by a state actor. Title III also provides for suppression of evidence for private conduct as well as statutory criminal and civil penalties for violations of its commands aimed at protecting privacy. For example, *United States v. Councilman*, 418 F.3d 67, 71 (1st Cir. 2005) upheld criminal charges against an Internet service provider for the illegal interception and copying of e-mail messages.

Before discussing the details of applications for and judicial supervision of electronic surveillance, it is necessary to define some important terms.

▶ **Aural Transfer:** "A transfer containing the human voice at any point between and including the point of origin and the point of reception." 18 U.S.C. § 2510(18).

▶ **Electronic Communication:** "[A]ny transfer of signs, signals, writing, images, sounds, data, or intelligence of any nature transmitted in whole or in part by a wire, radio, electromagnetic, photo-electronic or photo-optical system that affects interstate or foreign commerce but does not include (A) any wire or oral communication; (B) any communication made through a tone-only paging device; (C) any communication from a tracking device . . . ; or (D) electronic funds transfer information stored by a financial institution in a communications system used for the electronic storage and transfer of funds." 18 U.S.C. § 2510(12).

▶ **Intercept:** "[T]he aural or other acquisition of the contents of any wire, electronic, or oral communication through the use of any electronic, mechanical, or other device." 18 U.S.C. § 2510(4).

▶ **Oral Communication:** "Any oral communication uttered by a person exhibiting an expectation that such communication is not subject to interception under circumstances justifying such expectation, but such term does not include any electronic communication." 18 U.S.C. § 2510(2).

▶ **Wire Communication:** "[A]ny aural transfer made in whole or in part through the use of facilities for the transmission of communications by the aid of wire, cable, or other like connection between the point of origin and the point of reception (including the use of such connection in a switching station) furnished or operated by any person engaged in providing or operating such facilities for the transmission of interstate or foreign communications or communications affecting interstate or foreign commerce and such term includes any electronic storage of such communication." 18 U.S.C. § 2510(1).

Application for Interception Orders Title III establishes specific procedures for the application for, the issuance of, and the execution of court orders for the interception of wire, oral, or electronic communications.

Who May Apply Only the U.S. Attorney General or a select group of his or her deputies specified by Title III may authorize an application for a federal "wire communication" or "oral communication" interceptions order. 18 U.S.C. § 2516(1). However, any attorney authorized to prosecute Title III offenses may make an application for a federal "electronic communication" interception order. See 18 U.S.C. § 2516(3).

Application Must Be Based on a Predicate Offense Interception orders may only be issued for specified crimes including, but not limited to, espionage, treason, labor racketeering, murder, kidnapping, robbery, extortion, bribery of public officials, gambling, drug trafficking, escape, and counterfeiting. 18 U.S.C. § 2516. These crimes are called **Title III predicate offenses**. The USA PATRIOT Act added crimes "relating to terrorism" and crimes "relating to chemical weapons" to the list of predicate offenses. The USA PATRIOT Act also added violations of 18 U.S.C.A. § 1030 (Computer Fraud and Abuse) as predicate offenses. Before the enactment of the Patriot Act, interception orders for wire communications in computer hacking investigations were not permitted.

Contents of Standard Application Courts must only rely on the factual assertions in a written application and all supporting affidavits. Under 18 U.S.C. § 2518, these documents must be sworn to under oath and must include:

▶ the identity of the investigative or law enforcement officer making the application, and the officer authorizing the application;

▶ a full and complete statement of the facts and circumstances relied upon by the applicant, to justify his belief that an order should be issued, including the details as to the particular predicate offense that has been, is being, or is about to be committed;

▶ a particular description of the nature and location of the facilities from which or the place where the communication is to be intercepted, unless a roving wiretap is sought (see below);

▶ a particular description of the type of communications sought to be intercepted, including the identity of the person (if known) committing the offense and whose communications are to be intercepted;

▶ a full and complete statement as to whether or not other investigative procedures have been tried and failed or why they reasonably appear to be unlikely to succeed if tried or to be too dangerous;

▶ a statement of the period of time for which the interception is required to be maintained. If the nature of the investigation is such that the authorization for interception should not automatically terminate when the described type of communication has been first obtained, a particular description of facts establishing probable cause to believe that additional communications of the same type will occur thereafter;

▶ a full and complete statement of the facts concerning all previous applications known to the individual authorizing and making the application, made to any judge for authorization to intercept, or for approval of interceptions of, wire, oral, or electronic communications involving any of the same persons, facilities, or places specified in the application, and the action taken by the judge on each such application; and

▶ where the application is for the extension of an order, a statement setting forth the results thus far obtained from the interception, or a reasonable explanation of the failure to obtain such results.

With respect to the requirement of identifying the person whose communications are to be intercepted, *United States v. Donovan*, 429 U.S. 413 (1977), held that the applicant must name all persons who the government has probable cause to believe are committing the offense for which the application is made. However, failure to comply with this identification requirement does not require the exclusion of evidence obtained by the interception. Thus, for example, in *United States v. Urban*, 404 F.3d 754, 773 (3d Cir. 2005), an intercepted conversation involving the defendant showed his involvement in a drug distribution ring. Even though he had not been named in the application, the intercepted conversation was nonetheless admissible against him.

Contents of Roving Wiretaps The requirement that an application contain a particular description of the nature and location of the facilities from which or the place where the communication is to be intercepted is not applicable if the application is for a **roving wiretap**. 18 U.S.C. § 2518(11) allows for the authorization of roving taps that target a particular suspect's communications wherever they are made, thereby dispensing with the normal requirement that interceptions be limited to a fixed location. Roving taps on either landline or cellular phones do not violate the particularity requirement of the Fourth Amendment if the surveillance is limited to communications involving an identified speaker and relates to crimes in which the speaker is a suspected participant. *See United States v. Wilson*, 237 F.3d 827, 831 (7th Cir. 2001); *United States v. Petti*, 973 F.2d 1441 (9th Cir. 1991).

Veracity Requirements of Applications and Affidavits As with any other type of search warrant, the contents of an application for an interception order and the affidavits in support thereof must be true. If the contents of these documents contain material falsehoods, material omissions, or were made with reckless disregard for the truth, the warrants may be challenged in a *Franks* hearing (see *Franks v. Delaware*, 438 U.S. 154 (1978), as any other search warrant may be. *See, e.g., United States v. Shryock*, 342 F.3d 948 (9th Cir. 2003). (See Chapter 4 for a further discussion of *Franks* hearings.)

Issuance of Interception Orders One important characteristic of Title III, designed to protect against governmental abuses of citizens' privacy rights, is the law's provision for judicial supervision of all aspects of electronic surveillance. Federal law enforcement officials may not intercept wire, oral, or electronic communications without prior judicial approval

United States v. Denman, 100 F.3d 399 (5th Cir. 1996), held that, for jurisdictional purposes, an interception involving a wiretap takes place at both the location of the tapped telephone and the original listening post. Therefore, judges in either jurisdiction have authority under Title III to issue interception orders. Before issuing an interception order, the court must find all of the following:

▶ Probable cause to believe that the person whose communication is to be intercepted is committing, has committed, or is about to commit one of the specified crimes. "The probable cause showing required . . . for electronic surveillance does not differ from that required by the Fourth Amendment for a search warrant." *United States v. Macklin*, 902 F.2d 1320, 1324 (8th Cir. 1990), *cert. denied*, 498 U.S. 1031 (1991).

▶ Probable cause to believe that particular communications concerning that offense will be obtained through the interception.

▶ That normal investigative procedures have been tried and have failed, or reasonably appear to be unlikely to succeed if tried, or reasonably appear to be too dangerous. This condition—often referred to as the "necessity requirement"—is intended to ensure that electronic surveillance is not used unless normal investigative procedures are inadequate. For example, in *United States v. Wagner*, 989 F.2d 69 (1993), the necessity for a wiretap was established because (1) the rural location of the house and the presence of dogs made surveillance difficult, (2) the confidential informant was unable to determine the source of supply and method of delivery of marijuana, and (3) the government did not think it could infiltrate the marijuana distribution network with undercover agents.

▶ Probable cause to believe that the facilities from which, or the place where, the wire, oral, or electronic communications are to be intercepted are being used (or are about to be used) in connection with the commission of the specified offense; or are leased to, listed in the name of, or commonly used by the suspect. 18 U.S.C. § 2518(3).

Other aspects of judicial supervision of electronic surveillance are the court's power to require, at any time, reports on the progress of the interception toward the achievement of authorized objectives; the requirement of court approval for any extension of the surveillance; and the requirement that the recordings of any communications be sealed under directions of the court immediately on the order's expiration.

Judicial sanctions for violations of Title III include criminal penalties, penalties for contempt of court, and awards of civil damages. In addition, 18 U.S.C. § 2515 provides for the exclusion of evidence obtained in violation of Title III. *United States v. Spadaccino*, 800 F.2d 292 (2d Cir. 1986), held that the good-faith exception to the exclusionary rule did not apply to violations of Title III. The court said that when the legislature has spoken clearly on the issue, "it is appropriate to look to the terms of the statute and the intentions of the legislature, rather than to invoke judge-made exceptions to judge-made rules." 800 F.2d at 296.

If, on the basis of the application, the judge makes the required findings, the judge may issue an order authorizing or approving the interception of wire, oral, or electronic communications. Pursuant to 18 U.S.C. § 2518(4), each judicially authorized interception order must specify all of the following:

▶ the identity of the person, if known, whose communications are to be intercepted;

▶ the nature and location of the communications facilities as to which, or the place where, authority to intercept is granted;

▶ a particular description of the type of communication sought to be intercepted, and a statement of the particular offense to which it relates;

▶ the identity of the agency authorized to intercept the communications, and of the person authorizing the application; and

▶ the period of time during which such interception is authorized, including a statement as to whether or not the interception shall automatically terminate when the described communication has been first obtained.

Execution of Interception Orders

Orders Must Be Executed as Soon as Practicable Under 18 U.S.C. § 2518(5), every order to intercept wire, oral, or electronic communications must be executed "as soon as practicable." *United States v. Martino*, 664 F.2d 860 (2d Cir. 1981), held that delay in the execution of an interception order did not require the suppression of evidence obtained if the delay was not willful and if the information on which probable cause was initially based had not become stale. *United States v. Gallo*, 863 F.2d 185 (2d Cir. 1988), held that suppression of the intercepted communications was not required because of a five-month delay in installing the interception devices, when the government adequately explained that the installation was extremely difficult and the crime was one of continuing conduct, in which probable cause was "freshened" by visual surveillance.

Separate Order for Covert Entry Not Necessary Although law enforcement officials must obtain a judicial order to intercept wire, oral, or electronic communications, neither Title III nor the Fourth Amendment requires them to obtain judicial authorization to covertly enter premises to install a listening device. In *Dalia v.*

United States, 441 U.S. 238 (1979), a federal court authorized the interception of all oral communications concerning an interstate stolen-goods conspiracy at the defendant's office. Although the interception order did not explicitly authorize entry into the defendant's office, FBI agents secretly entered the office and installed a listening device in the ceiling. Six weeks later, after the surveillance had terminated, the agents reentered the office and removed the device. The defendant was convicted, partly on the basis of intercepted conversations. The Supreme Court considered the legislative history of Title III and concluded:

> [O]ne simply cannot assume that Congress, aware that most bugging requires covert entry, nonetheless wished to except surveillance requiring such entries from the broad authorization of Title III, and that it resolved to do so by remaining silent on the subject. On the contrary, the language and history of Title III convey quite a different explanation for Congress' failure to distinguish between surveillance that requires covert entry and that which does not. Those considering the surveillance legislation understood that, by authorizing electronic interception of oral communications in addition to wire communications, they were necessarily authorizing surreptitious entries. 441 U.S. at 252.

With respect to the Fourth Amendment, the Court found that nothing in the language of that Amendment or the Court's decisions suggested that search warrants must include a specification of the precise manner in which those warrants must be executed. "[I]t is generally left to the discretion of the executing officers to determine the details of how best to proceed with the performance of a search authorized by warrant—subject of course to the general Fourth Amendment protection 'against unreasonable searches and seizures.'" 441 U.S. at 257.

Minimization Requirements Title III requires that authorized interceptions be conducted so as to minimize the interception of communications not otherwise subject to interception under Title III. This **minimization** effort must be objectively reasonable under the circumstances. *See, e.g., United States v. McGuire*, 307 F.3d 1192, 1199-1200 (9th Cir. 2002). *Scott v. United States*, 436 U.S. 128 (1978), held an interception reasonable although only 40 percent of the intercepted conversations related to crimes specified in the order, because the remaining conversations were ambiguous and brief. *United States v. Smith*, 909 F.2d 1164 (8th Cir. 1990), held that minimization efforts were reasonable despite failure to minimize interceptions of the defendant's sister's phone conversations with his ex-girlfriend, because the officers suspected the defendant's family of aiding in drug activities but did not know which family members were doing so.

Interceptions Beyond Scope of Order Under 18 U.S.C. § 2517(5), when law enforcement officers intercept communications that relate to offenses other than those specified in the interception order, the government may use the evidence of these other crimes only if another application is made to a court "as soon as practicable" for a determination that the interception complied with Title III requirements. *See United States v. Angiulo*, 847 F.2d 956 (1st Cir. 1988).

Termination Upon Achieving Objective Authorized interceptions must terminate on attainment of the authorized objective, or in any event in thirty days. *United*

States v. Carneiro, 861 F.2d 1171 (9th Cir. 1988), held that suppression of communications intercepted after the discovery of a drug source was not required, because the objective of the wiretap was to investigate the entire drug operation, not merely to discover a drug source. Extensions of an interception order may be granted, but only on reapplication in accordance with the same procedures as for an original application.

Confidentiality Requirements

▶ **Disclosures** Law enforcement officers who learn information by listening to intercepted communications have an obligation to keep the content of what they hear confidential. They are only permitted to disclose the contents of what they learned from hearing an intercepted communication under limited circumstances.

▶ Information may be disclosed to another law enforcement officer "to the extent such disclosure is appropriate." 18 U.S.C § 2517(1). For example, in *United States v. Correa*, 220 F. Supp.2d 61(D. Mass. 2002), a prison routinely recorded telephone conversations of inmates other than those made to their attorneys or clergy members. Prison authorities disclosed the contents of some such tapes to police for use in the criminal investigation of an inmate. In upholding the disclosure over a Title III challenge, the court ruled that the sharing of the recorded conversations between correctional law enforcement officers and police was within the permissible scope of Section 2517(1). Key to the court's decision was that the recordings were lawfully intercepted by correctional officials and then disclosed to other law enforcement authorities. *See also United States v. Lewis*, 406 F.3d 11 (1st Cir. 2005). Similarly, when state authorities, pursuant to a valid wiretap order, discovered evidence of illegal gambling in *United States v. Williams*, 124 F.3d 411 (3d Cir. 1997), the court upheld their disclosure of their lawfully obtained recordings to Criminal Investigation Division agents of the Internal Revenue Service for potential prosecution of tax-related charges stemming from the gambling operation.

▶ Information learned may be used by a law enforcement officer in the performance of his or her official duties. For example, a law enforcement officer may briefly quote and/or paraphrase an intercepted communication to establish probable cause for defendant's arrest. *United States v. VanMeter*, 278 F.3d 1156 (10th Cir. 2002). Such information may also be disclosed in state or federal court while giving testimony related to the intercepted communication.

▶ Information may be disclosed to any federal "law enforcement, intelligence, protective, immigration, national defense, or national security official" if it assists them with a matter of foreign intelligence or counter-terrorism. 18 U.S.C. § 2517(6).

▶ Information may be disclosed to a foreign law enforcement officer (i.e., police in countries other than the United States) if it is necessary to assist the foreign officer in the performance of his or her official duties. 18 U.S.C. § 2517(7).

▶ If the information learned concerns a threat of attack or other hostile act by terrorists or a foreign power, it may be disclosed to any appropriate governmental official of the United States or a foreign country in order to allow the government to prevent or help respond to such an attack. 18 U.S.C. § 2517(8).

▶ **Seal Upon Expiration of Order** Immediately upon the expiration of an interception order (meaning without unnecessary or unreasonable delay), both the interception order and all recordings made pursuant to it are required to be delivered to the judge who issued the order to be sealed under the judge's directions. Putting material **under seal** means it is not accessible to anyone without a special court order. The purposes of the sealing requirement are to prevent tampering, aid in establishing the chain of custody, protect confidentiality, and establish judicial control over the surveillance. A failure to comply with the sealing requirement renders intercepted communications inadmissible. *United States v. Mora*, 821 F.2d 860, 866 (1st Cir. 1987); *State v. Oster*, 922 A.2d 151 (R.I. 2007). Before ordering such suppression, however, courts will examine all the circumstances, including whether the defendant has been prejudiced by tampering or other governmental misconduct. *United States v. Rodriguez*, 786 F.2d 472 (2d Cir. 1986).

If there is a delay in sealing, the statute requires **"that the Government explain not only why a delay occurred, but also why it is excusable."** *United States v. Ojeda Rios*, 495 U.S. 257, 265 (1990). Courts consider the following factors in determining whether the government has satisfactorily explained its failure to seal or delay in sealing: "the length of any delay before sealing, the care taken in handling the recordings, prejudice to the defendants, any tactical advantage accruing to the government, and whether deliberate or gross dereliction of duty or honest mistake caused the failure to file." *United States v. Suarez*, 906 F.2d 977, 982 (4th Cir. 1990).

Inventory and Notice Requirements Within a reasonable time, but not later than ninety days after the termination of the period of an order, an inventory must be served on the persons named in the order and on such other parties to intercepted communications as the judge determines in the interest of justice. An inventory must also be served after emergency interceptions are carried out. It must include a notice of the fact of the order, the date of approval of the application, the period of the authorized interception, and a statement of whether or not wire, oral, or electronic communications were intercepted during the period. Failure to serve the inventory is not grounds for suppression unless the failure causes actual, incurable prejudice. *United States v. Donovan*, 429 U.S. 413, 438-39 (1977); *United States v. Armendariz*, 922 F.2d 602, 608-09 (10th Cir. 1990).

The USA PATRIOT Act amended 18 U.S.C.A. § 3103a to permit law enforcement officers to delay notice of the execution of a search warrant or interception order in certain circumstances. Specifically, that section now permits delaying notice when "the court finds reasonable cause to believe that providing immediate notification of the execution of the warrant may have an adverse result (as defined in Section 2705)." Recall that Section 2705 defines an "adverse result" as "(A) endangering the life or physical safety of an individual; (B) flight from prosecution; (C) destruction of or tampering with evidence; (D) intimidation of potential witnesses; or (E) otherwise seriously jeopardizing an investigation or unduly delaying a trial." See the discussion of covert entry warrants in Chapter 4.

Exigent Circumstances Exception Finally, Title III provides authority for designated federal or state officials to intercept wire, oral, or electronic communications without a prior interception order if (1) an emergency situation exists that involves immediate danger of death or serious physical injury to any person, conspiratorial activities threatening the national security interest, or conspiratorial activities characteristic of organized crime; and (2) an interception order cannot be obtained in sufficient time. The determination of emergency must be made by the U.S. Attorney General or one of the other few governmental officials specified in Title III. The law enforcement officer carrying out the emergency surveillance must apply for an interception order under Section 2518 within forty-eight hours after the interception has occurred or begins to occur. If an order is not obtained, the interception must immediately terminate when the sought-after communication is obtained or when the application is denied, whichever is earlier.

Title III and Its Applicability to the States

Title III specifically authorizes state law enforcement officials to apply for, obtain, and execute orders authorizing or approving the interception of wire, oral, or electronic communications. The procedures are similar to those governing federal interception orders. The primary difference is that the state procedure must be authorized by a separate state statute. If a state statute so authorizes, the principal prosecuting attorney of the state, or of a political subdivision of the state, may apply to a state court judge of competent jurisdiction for an interception order. In granting the order, the judge must comply with both the applicable state statute and Title III. The interception order may be granted only when the interception may provide or has provided:

> [E]vidence of the commission of the offense of murder, kidnapping, gambling, robbery, bribery, extortion, or dealing in narcotic drugs, marihuana or other dangerous drugs, or other crime dangerous to life, limb, or property, and punishable by imprisonment for more than one year, designated in any applicable State statute authorizing such interception, or any conspiracy to commit any of the foregoing offenses. 18 U.S.C. § 2516(2).

"Generally speaking, insofar as wiretapping is concerned, states are free to superimpose more rigorous requirements upon those mandated by the Congress . . . but not to water down federally-devised safeguards." *United States v. Mora*, 821 F.2d 860, 863 n.3 (1st Cir. 1987). Federal courts are not obliged to adhere to more restrictive state laws, however, and generally admit evidence that violates such a law, as long as the evidence was not obtained in violation of Title III. *See, e.g., United States v. Charles*, 213 F.3d 10, 19 (1st Cir. 2000). For example, even if a consensual interception of a conversation without a search warrant violated state law, the evidence might still be admissible in federal court since Title III does not require a warrant when one of the parties to the intercepted conversation consents to the interception. *See, e.g., United States v. Goodapple*, 958 F.2d 1402, 1410 n.3 (7th Cir. 1992).

Suppression of Illegally Obtained Interceptions

Violations of Title III concerning oral and wire communications result in the broad suppression of illegally obtained evidence far beyond that normally prescribed by the exclusionary rule. Aggrieved persons may also move to suppress.

Statutory Exclusionary Rule of Title III Notably, and quite differently from the Fourth Amendment's exclusionary rule, Title III provides its own statutory exclusionary rule that applies to oral and wire communications that were illegally intercepted by government actors as well as by private persons. Under 18 U.S.C. § 2515:

> [N]o part of the contents of such communication and no evidence derived therefrom may be received in evidence in any trial, hearing, or other proceeding in or before any court, grand jury, department, officer, agency, regulatory body, legislative committee, or other authority of the United States, a State, or a political subdivision thereof if the disclosure of that information would be in violation of this chapter. *See also Gelbard v. United States*, 408 U.S. 41 (1972).

It should be noted, however, that this statutory exclusionary rule only applies to wire or oral communications. It does not apply to illegally intercepted electronic communications, the remedies for which include criminal penalties and civil suits. *See* 18 U.S.C. §§ 2510(12), 2511, 2515, 2518(10)(c).

In spite of the broad language of the statutory exclusionary rule in Title III, suppression is seldom imposed for inadvertent, unavoidable, or unintentional violations. A violation of Title III does not require suppression of evidence if the provision violated is not central to the statute's underlying purpose of guarding against unwarranted use of wiretapping or electronic surveillance. *United States v. Chavez*, 416 U.S. 562 (1974). For example, *United States v. Callum*, 410 F.3d 571, 576 (9th Cir. 2005), held that a failure to properly meet identification requirements in Title III did not require suppression of an otherwise properly executed interception order since it otherwise complied with all statutory requirements. On the other hand, a major violation of Title III, such as failing to obtain proper authorization from the Attorney General's designee, warrants suppression. *United States v. Reyna*, 218 F.3d 1108, 1111 (9th Cir. 2000).

Standing Any "aggrieved person" may move to suppress the contents of or evidence derived from oral or wire intercepts that were obtained in violation of Title III in either a state or federal proceeding. 18 U.S.C.. §§ 2515, 2518(10) (a). An **aggrieved person** means "a person who was a party to any intercepted" wire or oral communication or "a person against whom the interception was directed." 18 U.S.C. § 2510(11). The Supreme Court held that the term aggrieved person should be construed in accordance with existing standing rules. Therefore:

> [A]ny petitioner would be entitled to the suppression of government evidence originating in electronic surveillance violative of his own Fourth Amendment right to be free of unreasonable searches and seizures. Such violation would occur if the United States unlawfully overheard conversations of a petitioner himself or conversations occurring on his premises, whether or not he was present or participated in those conversations.
> *Alderman v. United States*, 394 U.S. 165, 176 (1969).

Thus, to have standing to challenge the admissibility of any evidence allegedly obtained in violation of Title III's wire or oral communications requirements, the person must have been either a party to the illegally intercepted conversation or the owner of the premises where the illegal interception occurred. *Alderman*, 394 U.S. at 176-78; *United States v. Gonzalez, Inc.*, 412 F.3d 1102, 1116-17 (9th Cir. 2005).

Exemptions from Title III

Many types of interceptions of wire, oral, or electronic communications are either not covered by provisions of Title III or are specifically exempted from coverage. Some of the most important exceptions to Title III's requirement of an interception order are discussed here.

Willful and Voluntary Disclosure A party to an oral communication who has no reasonable expectation of privacy with respect to the communication is not protected by either Title III or the Fourth Amendment. Other than certain privileged communications (such as between attorney and client, psychotherapist and patient, or clergy and penitent), people generally have no reasonable expectation of privacy that what they tell another person in conversation will not, in turn, be disclosed by the person to whom they were talking.

> In the course of conversing with others, persons assume certain risks that may bear on the viability of any Fourth Amendment rights they subsequently assert. Inescapably, one contemplating illegal activities must realize and risk that his companions may be reporting to the police. If he sufficiently doubts their trustworthiness, the association will very probably end or never materialize. But if he has no doubts, or allays them, or risks what doubt he has, the risk is his. *In re Askin*, 47 F.3d 100, 105 (4th Cir. 1995).

In other words, no matter how confidential one may think a discussion is, the person to whom one reveals information may elect not to keep such information confidential. If that person then voluntarily discloses information to others, including law enforcement or other governmental authorities, the Fourth Amendment will not serve as a basis to prevent such third-party disclosure. The same principle applies to Title III for electronic communications. Thus, one has no reasonable expectation of privacy that the recipient of an e-mail, instant messenger, or electronic chat room communication will not voluntarily disclose its contents to authorities. *See, e.g., United States v. Meek*, 366 F.3d 705 (9th Cir. 2004).

Eavesdropping As defined earlier, 18 U.S.C. § 2510(2) limits the meaning of "oral communication" for Title III purposes to material spoken by a person "exhibiting an expectation that such communication is not subject to interception under circumstances justifying such expectation." In other words, a person must have a reasonable expectation of privacy in their conversations for Title III to apply. If a conversation takes place in public where other parties can overhear the conversation, there is no reasonable expectation of privacy, because the participants exposed their conversation to the ears of others. *Katz v. United States*, 389 U.S. 347 (1967). Thus, any recording of such a conversation would not violate Title III. For example, in *Kee v. City of Rowlett*, 247 F.3d 206 (5th Cir. 2001), the court upheld the use of recordings of conversations and prayers made at a graveside burial service. The public nature of the outdoor conversations rendered them outside of the definition of an "oral communication" for Title III purposes since there was no reasonable expectation of privacy in such a setting.

Similarly, if a conversation takes place in an area where the participants ought not expect any privacy, such as in a correctional facility or in the back of a police car, then neither the Fourth Amendment nor Title III would serve to stop any recording of such a conversation from being used as evidence in court. *See, e.g., United States v. Harrelson*, 754 F.2d 1153, 1170 (5th Cir. 1985) (prison conversation) ("Mistaking the degree of intrusion of which probable eavesdroppers are capable is not at all the same thing as believing there are no eavesdroppers."); *United States v. McKinnon*, 985 F.2d 525 (11th Cir. 1993) (backseat of police car).

A somewhat unusual exception to Title III is the "business extension exception" contained in 18 U.S.C. § 2510(5)(a). Under it, neither telephones nor extension telephones are considered intercepting devices when they are used in the ordinary course of business. *O'Sullivan v. NYNEX Corp.*, 687 N.E.2d 1241 (Mass. 1997). Thus, what an employer overhears while monitoring phone conversations over extensions for legitimate business reasons will not implicate Title III. Courts have extended this exception to cover what family members overhear while eavesdropping on the conversations of other family members using an extension telephone. *E.g., Commonwealth v. Vieux*, 671 N.E.2d 989 (Mass. App. 1996), *cert. denied*, 520 U.S. 1245 (1997).

Consent Sections 2511(2)(c) and 2511(2)(d) exclude **consent surveillance** from the regulatory scheme established by Title III for court-ordered surveillance. Therefore, when one party to a communication consents to the interception of the communication, neither Title III nor the Fourth Amendment prevents the use of the communication in court against another party to the communication. Thus, a law enforcement officer or a private citizen who is a party to a communication may intercept the communication or permit a law enforcement official to intercept the communication without violating Title III or the Fourth Amendment. *United States v. Caceres*, 440 U.S. 741 (1979). This exception allows a law enforcement officer or agent, an informant, an accomplice or co-conspirator, or a victim to wear a body microphone; act as an undercover agent without being wired; or eavesdrop and/or record a telephone conversation with the permission of the person receiving the call even though the person making the call has no knowledge of this activity.

In *United States v. Capo*, 693 F.2d 1330 (11th Cir. 1982), the government's interception of a conversation between a consenting informant and the defendant was held not to be a violation of the Fourth Amendment, because the defendant willingly projected his voice outside the privacy of his home and his voice was intercepted at the other end. A private citizen, however, may not intercept a communication "for the purpose of committing any criminal or tortious act in violation of the Constitution or laws of the United States or of any State." 18 U.S.C. § 2511(2)(d).

Miscellaneous Statutory Exceptions

Provider Exception Under the **provider exception** an employee or agent of a communications service provider may intercept and disclose communications to protect the rights or property of the provider as part of the ordinary course of business. 18 U.S.C. § 2511(2)(a)(I). Under this exception, a system administrator of a computer network may monitor a hacker intruding into the network and then disclose the evidence obtained to law enforcement officials without violating Title III. A college or university could monitor e-mail communications of students to ensure compliance with student access agreements, such as not using the school's Internet service to run a business. *Hall v. EarthLink Network, Inc.*, 396 F.3d 500 (2d Cir. 2005), held that an Internet service provider's interception and storage of a suspected spammer's e-mails were permissible under this exception because it occurred as part of the provider's ordinary course of business. If, however, such interception of communications is not a part of the provider's ordinary course of business, then the surveillance would not be authorized under this exception. *Adams v. City of Battle Creek*, 250 F.3d 980 (6th Cir. 2001), for example, disallowed a police department's monitoring of an officer's pager when it suspected that the officer was involved in illegal activity, because the department did not routinely monitor the pagers that it issued to its employees. This violation of Title III gave rise to the officer having a claim for damages against the police department.

Computer Trespasser Exception Under the **computer trespasser exception**, victims of computer attacks by hackers may authorize law enforcement officials to intercept wire or electronic communications of a computer trespasser, if specific statutory requirements are satisfied. 18 U.S.C. § 2511(2)(i).

Public Access Exception Under the **accessible to the public exception**, 18 U.S.C. § 2511(2)(g)(I), any person may intercept an electronic communication made through a system "that is configured so that . . . [the] communication is readily accessible to the general public." This section allows for access to public web sites, but prohibits access to web sites protected from public access via usernames and passwords. *See, e.g., Konop v. Hawaiian Airlines, Inc.*, 302 F.3d 868 (9th Cir. 2002), *cert. denied*, 537 U.S. 1193 (2003). Similarly, it allows for public access to publicly broadcast radio and television programs. But 18 U.S.C.A. § 2510 (16) specifically defines "readily accessible to the general public" as meaning radio communications that are not:

(A) scrambled or encrypted;

(B) transmitted using modulation techniques whose essential parameters have been withheld from the public with the intention of preserving the privacy of such communication;

(C) carried on a sub-carrier or other signal subsidiary to a radio transmission;

(D) transmitted over a communication system provided by a common carrier, unless the communication is a tone-only paging system communication; or

(E) transmitted on [frequencies specially regulated by the Federal Communication Commission].

Trap-and-Trace Devices and Pen Registers A **trap-and-trace device** records incoming addressing information (such as caller ID information). A **pen register** records outgoing addressing information (such as numbers dialed from a particular, monitored telephone). Neither device "intercepts" communications, because it does not record or otherwise allow someone to listen to the contents of a wire, oral, or electronic communication. Title III, therefore, does not apply to the use of these devices. They are, however, regulated by both the Fourth

Amendment and by other provisions of federal law; namely, the **Electronic Communications Privacy Act of 1986 (ECPA).**

Fourth Amendment *Smith v. Maryland*, 442 U.S. 735 (1979), held that the installation and use of a pen register is not a search and is therefore not subject to the Fourth Amendment. The Court reasoned that the defendant had no reasonable expectation of privacy in the destination of his outgoing phone calls because the telephone company routinely monitors these calls to check billing, detect fraud, and prevent other violations of law.

The Supreme Court has not yet addressed the Fourth Amendment implications of the use of trap-and-trace devices. Because telephone companies do not routinely monitor incoming calls, the rationale of the *Smith* case may not apply to the use of those devices.

ECPA Since the *Smith* decision, Congress enacted the Pen Registers and Trap and Trace Devices chapter of Title 18 (18 U.S.C. §§ 3121–3127), prohibiting the installation or use of a pen register or a trap-and-trace device except by court order. Because the use of these devices does not constitute a "search" for Fourth Amendment purposes, neither probable cause nor a warrant is necessary to use either type of device. Quite unlike wiretaps under Title III, the use of pen registers and trap-and-trace devices only requires certification from a government attorney that "the information likely to be obtained by such installation and use is relevant to an ongoing criminal investigation." See 18 U.S.C. § 3123(a). Upon such a showing, a court may issue an *ex parte* order for the use of either or both types of devices. This order must specify, if known:

▶ the owner and location of the phone to which the device will be attached and the identity of the person who is the subject of the criminal investigation; and

▶ a statement of the offense to which it relates.

Before the enactment of the USA PATRIOT Act, the statutory definitions of pen registers and trap-and-trace devices did not explicitly allow them to be used to capture Internet communications (such as the "To" and "From" information in an e-mail). The USA PATRIOT Act broadened the definitions, allowing them to be used on Internet and other electronic communications.

Tracking Devices

Tracking Beepers Title III does not apply to the use of electronic devices emitting signals that enable law enforcement officials to track the location of objects and persons. These devices are incapable of transmitting speech and, therefore, do not intercept any communications. As a result, use of these devices, sometimes called tracking transmitters or **tracking beepers**, is governed solely by the Fourth Amendment and the Electronic Communications Privacy Act of 1986 (ECPA).

In *United States v. Knotts*, 460 U.S. 276 (1983), the U.S. Supreme Court held that the warrantless monitoring of one of these devices placed inside a container of chemicals did not violate the Fourth Amendment when it revealed no information that could not have been obtained through visual surveillance. The Court specified that the mere *monitoring* of such devices constitutes "neither a 'search' nor a 'seizure' within the contemplation of the Fourth Amendment." 460

U.S at 285. The *Knotts* Court did not, however, reach the question regarding the constitutionality of the installation of a tracking beeper, nor did it consider the constitutionality of monitoring such a device in areas that could not have been achieved by visual surveillance alone. The Supreme Court did, however, answer both of these questions the year after *Knotts* in *United States v. Karo*, 468 U.S. (1984).

As for the first question, the installation of a tracking beeper *may* implicate the Fourth Amendment, depending on where it was installed. If it was installed in a place in which a person has a reasonable expectation of privacy, then probable cause and a warrant are required before a tracking device may be installed in such a location. On the other hand, if a tracking device is to be installed in some object or container in which a person has no reasonable expectation of privacy, then, consistent with *Knotts*, the Fourth Amendment is not implicated.

The Court's answer to the second question follows the same line of reasoning. *Knotts* held that if the monitoring of a tracking device merely assists law enforcement in "seeing" where they could use visual surveillance, then the Fourth Amendment is not implicated. *Karo,* in contrast, held that if the monitoring of a tracking device allows law enforcement to "see" where they could not without the device (such as inside a private residence, as was the case in *Karo* itself), then the Fourth Amendment prohibits the use of such a device without probable cause and a warrant.

Since most of the legal issues involving limitations on the use of tracking devices relate to the attachment of the devices to vehicles and containers, these issues are discussed more fully in Chapter 11. However, the *Karo* case is notable here in terms of its effect on statutory law. A particular provision in the ECPA was enacted in response to the *Karo* decision. The act specifically authorized the monitoring of tracking devices which may move across district lines by providing:

> If a court is empowered to issue a warrant or other order for the installation of a mobile tracking device, such order may authorize the use of that device within the jurisdiction of the court, and outside that jurisdiction if the device is installed in that jurisdiction. 18 U.S.C. § 3117(a).

Thus—using the usual search warrant procedure in Federal Rule of Criminal Procedure 41 (or an equivalent state rule)—upon a showing of probable cause, courts may authorize the installation of tracking devices within their jurisdiction and the subsequent monitoring of those devices wherever they may roam. *United States v. Gbemisola*, 225 F.3d 753 (D.C. Cir. 2000).

Pagers Title III specifically exempts **tone-only pagers** from its requirements. 18 U.S.C § 2510(12)(B). Therefore, law enforcement officials do not need a warrant to activate a suspect's pager to confirm an identity or location. See, *e.g., United States v. Diaz-Lizaraza*, 981 F.2d 1216 (11th Cir. 1993).

Cell Phones, Cell Sites When the government seeks to intercept conversations in which a party is using a cellular telephone, the usual requirements of Title III must be followed. However, a cellular phone may also be used to track the location of a person using **real-time, cell site data searching**. This process was described by one court as follows:

> When a cell phone is powered up, it acts as a scanning radio, searching through a list of control channels for the strongest signal. The cell phone re-scans every

seven seconds or when the signal strength weakens, regardless of whether a call is placed. The cell phone searches for a five-digit number known as the System Identification Code assigned to service providers. After selecting a channel, the cell phone identifies itself by sending its programmed codes which identify the phone, the phone's owner, and the service provider. These codes include an Electronic Serial Number (a unique 32-bit number programmed into the phone by the manufacturer), and a Mobile Identification Number, a 10-digit number derived from the phone's number. . . . The cell site relays these codes to the mobile telecommunications switching office in a process known as registration. . . . [Thus], a cell phone is (among other things) a radio transmitter that automatically announces its presence to a cell tower via a radio signal over a control channel which does not itself carry the human voice. By a process of triangulation from various cell towers, law enforcement is able to track the movements of the target phone, and hence locate a suspect using that phone. *In re Application for Pen Register and Trap/Trace Device with Cell Site*, 396 F.Supp.2d 747, 750 (S.D. Tex. 2005).

The few courts that have addressed the constitutionality of using real-time cell site data to track the user's physical location have held that such information qualifies as tracking device information under the Electronic Communica-

key points

- Electronic surveillance by agents of the government is a search and seizure governed by the Fourth Amendment.
- Electronic surveillance is permissible only if conducted pursuant to the authority of an interception order affording protections similar to those present in the use of conventional warrants authorizing the seizure of tangible evidence.
- A warrant procedure authorizing electronic surveillance must carefully circumscribe the search in nature, scope, and duration and must not permit a trespassory invasion of the home or office by general warrant, contrary to the command of the Fourth Amendment.
- Title III of the Omnibus Crime Control and Safe Streets Act prohibits the interception of wire, oral, or electronic communications by both private persons and state actors unless such interceptions were conducted with the procedures duly authorized under the provisions of Title III.
- Title III balances the need to use electronic surveillance for effective law enforcement against the need to protect the privacy rights of individuals by providing for judicial supervision of all aspects of electronic surveillance and establishing warrant procedures based on probable cause similar to those required for the search and seizure of tangible objects. Special exigent circumstances provisions, however, allow for emergency interceptions that must be judicially supervised within forty-eight

hours after the interception has occurred or begins to occur.
- Although a judicially issued interception order is required to lawfully intercept wire, oral, or electronic communications, separate judicial approval is not required to covertly enter premises to install a listening device.
- Judicially authorized interceptions must terminate on attainment of the authorized objective, or on the expiration of the intercept order.
- Information gained through the lawful execution of a judicially authorized intercept order is highly regulated. As a rule, law enforcement officers must keep such information confidential unless one of the specific provisions of Title III authorizes disclosure.
- Immediately upon the expiration of an interception order (meaning without unnecessary or unreasonable delay), both the interception order and all recordings made pursuant to it are required to be delivered to the judge who issued the order to be sealed under the judge's directions. Failure to comply with the sealing requirement may render intercepted communications inadmissible.
- Within a reasonable time, but not later than ninety days after the termination of the period of an order, an inventory must be served on the persons named in the order and on such other parties to intercepted communications as the judge determines in the interest of justice. Such notice, however, may

tions Privacy Act (ECPA). The government must therefore demonstrate probable cause pursuant to Rule 41 to obtain a search warrant that authorizes obtaining such information. *In re Application for Pen Register and Trap/Trace Device with Cell Site*, 396 F. Supp. 2d 747 (S.D. Tex. 2005); *In re Application of the U.S. for an Order (1) Authorizing the Use of a Pen Register and a Trap and Trace Device and (2) Authorizing Release of Subscriber Information and/or Cell Site Information*, 396 F. Supp. 2d 294 (E.D.N.Y. 2005). However, other courts have disagreed. They have held that a court may issue an order authorizing the disclosure of a cell phone user's location without a probable cause showing or a warrant, so long as the government does not seek triangulation information or location information other than that transmitted at the beginning and end of particular calls. *See In re Application of U.S. for an Order for Prospective Cell Site Location Information on a Certain Cellular Telephone*, 460 F. Supp. 2d 448 (S.D.N.Y. Oct 23, 2006); *In re Application of U.S.*, 415 F. Supp.2d 663 (S.D. W. Va. 2006) (allowing time tracking information based on specific and articulable facts). Either an act of Congress or consistent rulings of higher courts will be necessary to resolve this conflict.

be delayed if "the court finds reasonable cause to believe that providing immediate notification of the execution of the warrant may have an adverse result." A failure to comply with the inventory and notice requirements usually does not give rise to the suppression of evidence unless such failure causes actual, incurable prejudice to the defendant.

- States are free to superimpose more rigorous requirements for electronic surveillance than those mandated by Congress in Title III, but they must not water down the federally mandated safeguards contained in Title III.

- Violations of Title III concerning oral and wire communications by private or state actors result in the broad suppression of illegally obtained evidence far beyond that normally prescribed by the exclusionary rule. This statutory exclusionary rule, however, does not apply to illegally intercepted electronic communications, the remedies for which include criminal penalties and civil suits.

- Title III does not cover: wire, oral, or electronic communications in which a person has no reasonable expectation of privacy; surveillance conducted with the consent of a party to an intercepted wire, oral, or electronic communication; interceptions and disclosures of communications by communications service providers conducted as part of the ordinary course of business; interceptions of wire or electronic communications of a computer trespasser; interceptions of wire or electronic communications made through a system "that is configured so that . . . [the] communication is readily accessible to the general public"; tone-only pagers; and video surveillance that records only images and not aural communications.

- Although Title III does not regulate trap-and-trace devices or pen registers, as neither "intercepts" a communication covered by Title III, the Communications Privacy Act of 1986 prohibits the installation or use of either device except by court order. Unlike search warrants or Title III intercept orders, however, the use of pen registers and trap-and-trace devices does not require a warrant supported by probable cause. Rather, these devices may be authorized by court order upon the certification of a government attorney that "the information likely to be obtained by such installation and use is relevant to an ongoing criminal investigation."

- Tracking devices are not covered by Title III because they do not "intercept" a communication. However, the communications Privacy Act of 1986 provides that these devices may be installed and monitored by court order issued in accordance with usual Rule 41 procedures—i.e., the issuance of a warrant upon a showing of probable cause.

- E-mail and voice mail are "electronically stored communications" that are not covered by Title III. Both may be accessed by law enforcement using the usual Rule 41 procedures—i.e., the issuance of a warrant upon a showing of probable cause.

E-mail and Voice Mail Although e-mail is ubiquitous and has replaced telephone communication in many spheres, it is not considered a "wire communication" for Title III purposes. Under the **Stored Wire and Electronic Communications and Transactional Records Access Act**, 18 U.S.C. § 2703(a), e-mail, like other forms of stored electronic communications, may be obtained by law enforcement authorities using normal search warrant procedures subject to various date/time limitations.

Prior to the enactment of the USA PATRIOT Act, voice mail was considered to be a stored wire communication. As such, in order to retrieve a stored voice mail message, law enforcement authorities had to comply with the requirements of Title III to access stored voice mail messages. But Section 209 of the USA PATRIOT Act changed that by deleting the phrase "electronic storage" of wire communications from the definition of "wire communication." As a result, voice mail is no longer covered by Title III. Voice mail, like e-mail, is now accessible under the Stored Wire and Electronic Communications and Transactional Records Access Act using a standard search warrant subject to various date/time limitations. 18 U.S.C. § 2703(a).

Video Surveillance Title III does not cover **video surveillance**—the use of video cameras that record only images and not aural communications. Thus, surreptitious video surveillance without any audio component is analyzed under state invasion of privacy laws and under the Fourth Amendment. Legal analysis under the latter, of course, depends on whether the video surveillance violated an aggrieved person's reasonable expectation of privacy:

> [T]he Fourth Amendment forbids warrantless videotaping of a private office and hotel rooms. However, video surveillance does not in itself violate a reasonable expectation of privacy. Indeed, videotaping of suspects in public places, such as banks, does not violate the Fourth Amendment; the police may record what they normally may view with the naked eye. We have not defined the precise contours of Fourth Amendment protection in the video context. However, in this case, given the public nature of the mailroom in a community hospital where individuals—even DEA agents—strolled nearby without impediment during the transaction, we conclude the defendant had no objectively reasonable expectation of privacy that would preclude video surveillance of activities already visible to the public." *United States v. Gonzalez*, 328 F.3d 543 (9th Cir. 2003).

In *United States v. Corona-Chavez*, 328 F.3d 974 (8th Cir. 2003), police officers conducted silent video surveillance of an informant with suspected drug dealers in a hotel room. Such video surveillance did not implicate Title III since it did not "intercept" any aural communication. Moreover, the video surveillance was held to be constitutionally permissible under the Fourth Amendment—the participants in the hotel-room drug transaction had no reasonable expectation of privacy when meeting with others who could have been, and in fact were, government informants. Had covert video surveillance caught someone alone in the privacy of a hotel room, however, a reasonable expectation of privacy may have been violated.

If surveillance contains *both* audio and video components, then the video sections are controlled by the Fourth Amendment (and state privacy laws) and audio portions are reviewed under Title III and the Fourth Amendment. *See United States v. Shryock*, 342 F.3d 948, 977-79 (9th Cir. 2003).

Foreign Intelligence Surveillance Act

Title III did not regulate foreign intelligence electronic communications. For more than forty years prior to the enactment of Title III, the U.S. government conducted warrantless electronic surveillance of foreign powers and their agents under a broad and amorphous "national security exception" to the warrant requirement of the Fourth Amendment. That changed in the 1970s, when the Watergate scandal illustrated all too clearly the governmental abuses of that power. Congress responded by passing the **Foreign Intelligence Surveillance Act (FISA)** in 1978. FISA authorizes and regulates the electronic surveillance of foreign powers and their agents within the United States. 50 U.S.C. §§ 1801 *et seq.* Additionally, pursuant to amendments made to the law in 2004, FISA authorizes surveillance of so-called "lone wolves"—any individual or group that is not linked to a foreign government but who "engages in international terrorism or activities in preparation therefore," 50 U.S.C. §1801(b)(1)(C), or engages in acts of "sabotage." 50 U.S.C. §1801(c)(3)(C).

FISA does not regulate U.S. governmental intelligence operations outside of the United States, such as operations conducted by the Central Intelligence Agency. Extra-territorial investigations remain within the scope of the national security exemption to the warrant requirement of the Fourth Amendment. *United States v. Bin Laden*, 126 F. Supp. 2d 264 (S.D.N.Y. 2000).

> There is an exception to the warrant requirement for searches conducted abroad for purposes of foreign intelligence collection, but this exception is narrowly drawn to include only those overseas searches, authorized by the President or the Attorney General, which are conducted primarily for foreign intelligence purposes and which target foreign powers or their agents, including American citizens believed to be agents of a foreign power. 126 F. Supp. 2d at headnote 2.

FISA Applications FISA permits federal agents to conduct electronic surveillance and physical searches for national defense purposes. While any federal agent may apply for such a warrant, an application must first be approved by the U.S. Attorney General. Additionally, 50 U.S.C. § 180 also requires that the application contain information similar to what Title III requires for other electronic surveillance warrants, including:

▶ the identity, if known, or a description of the specific target of the electronic surveillance;

▶ a statement of the facts and circumstances relied upon by the applicant to justify his belief that—

　(A) the target of the electronic surveillance is a foreign power or an agent of a foreign power; and

　(B) each of the facilities or places at which the electronic surveillance is directed is being used, or is about to be used, by a foreign power or an agent of a foreign power;

▶ a statement of the proposed minimization procedures;

▶ a detailed description of the nature of the information sought and the type of communications or activities to be subjected to the surveillance;

▶ a certification or certifications by the Assistant to the President for National Security Affairs or an executive branch official or officials designated by the President from among those executive officers employed in the area of national security or defense and appointed by the President with the advice and consent of the Senate—

   (A) that the certifying official deems the information sought to be foreign intelligence information;

   (B) that a significant purpose of the surveillance is to obtain foreign intelligence information;

   (C) that such information cannot reasonably be obtained by normal investigative techniques;

   (D) that designates the type of foreign intelligence information being sought according to the categories described in section 1801(e) of this title; and

   (E) including a statement of the basis for the certification that—

      (i) the information sought is the type of foreign intelligence information designated; and

      (ii) such information cannot reasonably be obtained by normal investigative techniques;

▶ a statement of the means by which the surveillance will be effected and a statement whether physical entry is required to effect the surveillance;

▶ a statement of the facts concerning all previous applications that have been made to any judge under this subchapter involving any of the persons, facilities, or places specified in the application, and the action taken on each previous application;

▶ a statement of the period of time for which the electronic surveillance is required to be maintained, and if the nature of the intelligence gathering is such that the approval of the use of electronic surveillance under this subchapter should not automatically terminate when the described type of information has first been obtained, a description of facts supporting the belief that additional information of the same type will be obtained thereafter; and

▶ whenever more than one electronic, mechanical or other surveillance device is to be used with respect to a particular proposed electronic surveillance, the coverage of the devices involved and what minimization procedures apply to information acquired by each device.

Notably, the above provisions of FISA, unlike normal search warrants or Title III intercept orders, do not require a showing of probable cause to believe that a crime has been or is being committed. Rather, the statute only requires probable cause that the surveillance is of an authorized person or group for purposes relating to the gathering of foreign intelligence or preventing terrorism. Additional findings, however, are required if the targets of the investigation are U.S. citizens or lawful resident aliens.

In addition to electronic surveillance, FISA authorizes physical searches of "premises, information, material, or property used exclusively by, or under the open and exclusive control of, a foreign power or powers." 50 U.S.C. § 1822. Unlike either regular search warrants or covert entry warrants, the fact that such physical searches take place need not be disclosed unless and until the U.S. "Attorney General determines there is no national security interest in continuing to maintain the secrecy of the search." 50 U.S.C. § 1825(b).

Approval by the Foreign Intelligence Surveillance Court Congress created a special Article III court to review FISA applications called the **Foreign Intelligence Surveillance Court (FISC)**. 50 U.S.C. § 1803(a). The composition of the court is determined by the Chief Justice of the U.S. Supreme Court who:

> [S]hall publicly designate 11 district court judges from seven of the United States judicial circuits of whom no fewer than 3 shall reside within 20 miles of the District of Columbia who shall constitute a court which shall have jurisdiction to hear applications for and grant orders approving electronic surveillance anywhere within the United States under the procedures set forth in [FISA].

Prior to the enactment of the USA PATRIOT Act (and assuming that all of the requirements of a valid FISA application were otherwise present), the FISC was authorized to issue a FISA warrant only if the court determined that the "primary purpose" of the warrant was to engage in the collection of foreign intelligence collection and not criminal prosecution. But the USA PATRIOT Act amended FISA so that the intelligence gathering need only be a "significant purpose" of such surveillance, thereby expanding the government's ability to use FISA warrants for investigative purposes. *In re Sealed Case*, 310 F.3d 717 (Foreign Intel. Surv. Ct. Rev. 2002), upheld this change over a Fourth Amendment challenge, finding that the law constitutionally balances the government's need to gather information for national security purposes and an individual's privacy rights. If the "significant purpose" test is met, then any information gathered during the execution of a duly-authorized FISA warrant may be used in subsequent criminal prosecutions, including those involving domestic crimes. *See, e.g., United States v. Ning Wen*, 477 F.3d 896 (7th Cir. 2007). This applies even to defendants who were not named in the FISA warrant. *United States v. Duggan*, 743 F.2d 59 (2d Cir. 1984).

If the FISC denies an application, that denial may be appealed by the Department of Justice to the Foreign Intelligence Surveillance Court of Review. The Court of Review is a three-judge panel. Since its creation (and as of the writing of this text), this court has only come into session once, in 2002. 50 U.S.C. § 1803(b).

Alternate Executive Approval Procedures FISA does not require compliance with the procedures detailed above under all circumstances. The President, through the U.S. Attorney General, is authorized under 50 U.S.C.A. § 1802(a) to approve an application for FISA surveillance for periods up to one year without FISC approval if the following conditions are met:

▶ the electronic surveillance is solely directed at—

   (i) the acquisition of the contents of communications transmitted by means of communications used exclusively between or among foreign powers; or

   (ii) the acquisition of technical intelligence, other than the spoken communications of individuals, from property or premises under the open and exclusive control of a foreign power,

▶ there is no substantial likelihood that the surveillance will acquire the contents of any communication to which a United States person is a party; and

▶ proper minimization procedures are used.

If this executive authorization procedure is used, the U.S. Attorney General must certify that he or she has made the requisite statutory findings and has followed all procedures mandated by FISA. This certification must be provided to the intelligence committees of both the U.S. House of Representatives and the U.S. Senate, as well as filed under seal with the FISC.

Notably, the executive authorization provisions in Section 1802(a)(1)(A) of FISA are limited exclusively to intelligence information targeting foreign powers or their agents. Thus, executive authorization to monitor individuals or groups that may be engaged in sabotage or international terrorism is not authorized under FISA. Approval of the surveillance of such individuals or groups is supposed to be the exclusive province of the FISC. Yet, the *New York Times* disclosed that President George W. Bush had "secretly authorized the National Security Agency (NSA) to eavesdrop on Americans and others inside the United States to search for evidence of terrorist activity without the court-approved warrants ordinarily required for domestic spying" (Risen & Lichtblau, 2005: A1).

A number of bills were introduced in Congress following the discovery of the NSA surveillance program; but, as of the writing of this text, no laws have been enacted changing the scope of executive authority regarding FISA. This may be due, in part, to the fact that the NSA surveillance program was challenged and declared unconstitutional in *American Civil Liberties Union v. Nat'l Sec. Agency*, 438 F. Supp. 2d 754 (E.D. Mich. 2006). Since then, the Bush Administration reversed its position and agreed to comply with FISA requirements mandating the judicial supervision of antiterrorism domestic surveillance efforts by the FISC (Lichtblau & Johnston, 2007).

However, FISA does permit the Attorney General to authorize domestic surveillance in an emergency situation in which seeking FISC approval would unnecessarily delay the gathering of necessary evidence. 50 U.S.C. § 1805(f). If this emergency provision is used, however, the Attorney General must (1) notify the FISC within seventy-two hours of his or her authorization to conduct an emergency search and (2) have the FISC approve his or her actions after the fact and authorize any continued surveillance, if necessary. The statute provides for special notice procedures if the FISC denies the Attorney General's request, but that has only happened six times out of the nearly 20,000 applications the FISC has received and reviewed since it was created (Adler, 2007: 407).

Challenging FISA Surveillance Warrants Normally, when defendants challenge the legality of a search warrant, they do so in a *Franks* hearing or in other adversarial proceedings that are conducted in open court. Motions to suppress evidence "obtained or derived" from surveillance conducted pursuant to FISA work differently.

A defendant may certainly challenge the admissibility of such evidence on the grounds that "the information was unlawfully acquired" or that "the surveillance was not made in conformity with an order of authorization or approval." However, given the sensitive nature of information that may be at stake in an espionage or terrorism case, FISA authorizes courts to conduct *ex parte, in camera* **reviews** of surveillance materials if the U.S. Attorney General certifies under oath that "disclosure or an adversary hearing would harm the national security of the United States." 50 U.S.C. § 1806(f). This means that a judge may review the relevant information on his or her own, without all of the information being disclosed to defense counsel or being revealed in open court. Defendants have challenged *ex parte, in camera* reviews on due process, equal protection, and Sixth Amendment Confrontation Clause and right-to-counsel grounds, but courts have routinely rejected these challenges and have uniformly upheld closed review procedures by FISC judges. *See, e.g., United States v. Nicholso*n, 955 F. Supp. 588 (E.D. Va. 1997).

key points

- Title III does not regulate foreign intelligence electronic communications. Rather, the Foreign Intelligence Surveillance Act (FISA) authorizes and regulates the electronic surveillance and physical searches of foreign powers and their agents, as well as any individual or group that is not linked to a foreign government but who "engages in international terrorism or activities in preparation therefore.

- "FISA does not regulate U.S. governmental intelligence operations outside of the United States. Extraterritorial investigations remain within the scope of the national security exemption to the warrant requirement of the Fourth Amendment.

- Although any federal agent may apply for a FISA warrant, each application must first be approved by the U.S. Attorney General. Moreover, such an application must contain information similar to what Title III requires for other electronic surveillance warrants with one notable exception. Unlike normal search warrants or Title III intercept orders, FISA warrants may be issued without any showing of probable cause to believe that a crime has been or is being committed. Rather, FISA only requires probable cause that the surveillance is of an authorized person or group and that a "significant purpose" of the surveillance relates to the gathering of foreign intelligence or preventing terrorism.

- Normally, applications for FISA warrants are reviewed by a special Article III court called the Foreign Intelligence Surveillance Court (FISC). If the FISC denies an application, that denial may be appealed by the U.S. Department of Justice to the Foreign Intelligence Surveillance Court of Review. However, the president, through the U.S. Attorney General, is authorized to approve an application for FISA surveillance for periods up to one year without FISC approval under certain circumstances; namely, to gather intelligence from foreign governments or their agents in the U.S. If this executive authorization procedure is used, the U.S. Attorney General must certify that he or she has made the requisite statutory findings and has followed all procedures mandated by FISA. This certification must be provided to the intelligence committees of both the U.S. House of Representatives and the U.S. Senate, as well as filed under seal with the FISC.

- The validity of a FISA warrant may be challenged in any federal court. However, any judge reviewing a FISA warrant is authorized to do so *ex parte* and *in camera* if the U.S. Attorney General certifies under oath that "disclosure or an adversary hearing would harm the national security of the United States."

Summary

An administrative search is a routine inspection of a home or business to determine compliance with codes and licensing provisions dealing with fire, health, safety, housing, and so on. Although administrative searches are not directed toward convicting a person of a crime, they are still subject to the warrant requirement of the Fourth Amendment. However, the probable cause standard for administrative search warrants is less stringent than the standard for criminal searches. If, however, an administrative search takes on the characteristics of a criminal search, the traditional probable cause standard applies. Exceptions to the administrative search warrant requirement are similar to the exceptions for a criminal search warrant with less stringent standards. Also, warrantless searches are allowed for certain licensed and closely regulated enterprises.

An exception to the warrant and probable cause requirements of the Fourth Amendment exists where "special needs" of the government, beyond the normal need for law enforcement, make the warrant and probable cause requirements impracticable. Special needs searches are evaluated under the "reasonableness" standard of the Fourth Amendment. Some special needs searches may be lawfully conducted without a warrant upon a showing of reasonable suspicion. Other special needs searches justify warrantless, suspicionless searches in light of the important governmental needs at stake when balanced against the intrusiveness of the search upon a person's reasonable expectation of privacy.

Electronic surveillance was originally considered beyond the coverage of the Fourth Amendment because it involved no trespass into the defendant's premises and no seizure of tangible items. In a series of U.S. Supreme Court decisions in the mid-1960s, the Court reversed this approach and held that electronic surveillance by agents of the government is a search and seizure governed by the Fourth Amendment. The leading case adopting this new approach was *Katz v. United States*, which held that the Fourth Amendment protects people, not places, thereby shifting the focus of the Fourth Amendment from property to privacy. In addition, the Court held that electronic surveillance is permissible only if conducted pursuant to a warrant that carefully limits the surveillance in nature, scope, and duration.

In 1968, Congress enacted Title III of the Omnibus Crime Control and Safe Streets Act, which attempts to balance the need to use electronic surveillance for effective law enforcement against the need to protect individuals' privacy rights. Title III provides for judicial supervision of all aspects of electronic surveillance and establishes warrant procedures similar to those required for the search and seizure of tangible objects. These procedures are designed to limit who can authorize an application for an interception order, who can apply for an order, the duration of electronic surveillance allowed, and various aspects of the execution of an interception order.

The coverage of Title III has many exceptions. Title III does not protect a party to a conversation who has no reasonable expectation of privacy with respect to that conversation. If one party to a conversation consents to the interception of that conversation, the conversation may be used against the other party. Title III does not apply to the use of electronic devices such as beepers, trap-and-trace devices, and pen registers, although the installation and use of these devises is regulated by other federal laws.

Although an interception order is required to intercept wire, oral, or electronic communications, judicial approval is not required to covertly enter premises to install a listening device. Neither is an interception order required to intercept wire, oral, or electronic communications in emergencies involving immediate danger of death or serious physical injury, or conspiracies threatening national security or involving organized crime, although an interception order must be applied for within forty-eight hours of the emergency interception.

An illegal search and seizure by either a private or state actor under Title III, whether caused by a failure to comply with warrant procedures or by a failure to satisfy one of the exceptions to the warrant requirement, results in application of the exclusionary rule to illegally intercepted wire or oral communications. Thus, evidence obtained from an illegal interception of a wire or oral communication is inadmissible in court, often resulting in termination of the prosecution and release of the person charged. And while the exclusionary rule does not apply to illegally intercepted electronic communications, people, including law enforcement officers, who conduct an illegal search or seizure of a wire, oral, or electronic communication may be civilly or criminally liable for their actions.

Searches and seizures concerning foreign intelligence and antiterrorism efforts are authorized and regulated by the Foreign Intelligence. Surveillance Act (FISA). FISA applies to domestic electronic surveillance and physical searches of foreign powers and their agents, as well as any individual or group that is not linked to a foreign government but who "engages in international terrorism or activities in preparation therefore." FISA warrants need not be supported by probable cause in the traditional sense, but rather may be issued upon certification from the U.S. Attorney General that the surveillance is of an authorized person or group and that a "significant purpose" of the surveillance relates to the gathering of foreign intelligence or preventing terrorism. Although FISA warrant applications are normally reviewed by a special Article III court called the Foreign Intelligence Surveillance Court (FISC), the president, through the U.S. Attorney General, is authorized to approve an application for FISA surveillance for periods up to one year without FISC approval under certain circumstances so long as FISA procedures are followed and such surveillance is reported to Congress and filed under seal with the FISC.

Key Terms

accessible to the public exception, 287
administrative search, 248
aggrieved person, 284
aural transfer, 275
computer trespasser exception, 287
consent surveillance, 286
electronic communication, 275
Electronic Communications Privacy Act of 1986, 288

electronic surveillance, 272
ex parte, in camera reviews, 296
Foreign Intelligence Surveillance Act (FISA), 293
Foreign Intelligence Surveillance Court (FISC), 295
intercept, 276
minimization requirements, 280
Oral Communication, 276

pen register, 287
provider exception, 286
real-time, cell site data searching, 289
roving wiretaps, 277
sealing/putting under seal, 282
special needs doctrine, 252
Stored Wire and Electronic Communications and Transactional Records Access Act, 292

Title III of the Omnibus Crime Control and Safe Streets Act of 1968, 275
Title III predicate offenses, 276
tone-only pagers, 289
tracking beepers, 288
trap-and-trace device, 287
video surveillance, 292
Wire Communication, 276

Review and Discussion Questions

1. What are the differences between conventional search warrants (directed toward gathering evidence for a criminal prosecution), administrative search warrants, and "special needs" searches?

2. What is the justification for requiring an administrative search warrant to conduct certain administrative searches, but allowing for other types of administrative searches to be conducted without a warrant?

3. Under what circumstances are random, warrantless, and suspicionless searches of high school students permitted? What is the underlying rationale of these searches? Critique this rationale.

4. What are the differences between the limitations on searches that may be conducted of passengers arriving by plane at an international airport and those that may be conducted of boarding passengers on a domestic flight? Explain and critique the rationale for the differences you identify.

5. What are the special needs that justify the warrantless seizure of DNA samples from people arrested and/or convicted of certain crimes? Compare and contrast the arguments that these justifications fit within the usual scope of the special needs doctrine with the arguments that these justifications fail to conform to the usual requirements of special needs searches.

6. How is a Title III interception order different from a standard search warrant?

7. Name and discuss four types of electronic surveillance that are either not covered by or are specifically exempted from coverage of Title III of the Omnibus Crime Control and Safe Streets Act of 1968.

8. How did the Communications Privacy Act of 1986 and the Stored Wire and Electronic Communications and Transactional Records Access Act alter the use of pen registers, trap-and-trace devices, and tracking beepers?

9. Explain the controversy in the courts concerning the use of real-time, cell site data searching in order to track the location of a cell phone's user.

10. Compare and contrast the standards for issuance of a Title III interception order and a FISA warrant that authorizes electronic surveillance.

11. Under what circumstances must applications for FISA warrants be reviewed and issued by the FISC as opposed to ones that may be initially authorized by the executive branch of the federal government?

Applications of the Law in Real Cases

1 Simons was employed as an electronic engineer at the Foreign Bureau of Information Services (FBIS), a division of the Central Intelligence Agency (CIA). FBIS provided Simons with an office, which he did not share with anyone, and a computer with Internet access.

In June 1998, FBIS instituted a policy regarding Internet usage by employees. The policy stated that employees were to use the Internet for official government business only. Accessing unlawful material was specifically prohibited. The policy explained that FBIS would conduct electronic audits to ensure compliance:

Audits. Electronic auditing shall be implemented within all FBIS unclassified networks that connect to the Internet or other publicly accessible networks to support identification, termination, and prosecution of unauthorized activity. These electronic audit mechanisms shall be capable of recording:

- access to the system, including successful and failed login attempts, and logouts;
- inbound and outbound file transfers;
- terminal connections (telnet) to and from external systems;
- sent and received e-mail messages;
- web sites visited, including uniform resource locator (URL) of pages retrieved;
- date, time, and user associated with each event.

The policy also stated that "[u]sers shall . . . [u]nderstand FBIS will periodically audit, inspect, and/or monitor the user's Internet access as deemed appropriate."

FBIS contracted with Science Applications International Corporation (SAIC) for the management of FBIS's computer network, including monitoring for any inappropriate use of computer resources. On July 17, 1998, Clifford Mauck, a manager at SAIC, began exploring the capabilities of a firewall recently acquired by SAIC. Mauck believed that SAIC needed to become more familiar with the firewall to service the FBIS contract properly.

He entered the keyword "sex" into the firewall database for July 14 and 17, 1998, and found a large number of Internet "hits" originating from Simons' computer. It was obvious to Mauck from the names of the sites that they were not visited for official FBIS purposes.

Mauck reported this discovery to his contact at FBIS, Katherine Camer. Camer then worked with another SAIC employee, Robert Harper, to further investigate the apparently unauthorized activity. Camer instructed Harper to view one of the web sites that Simons had visited. Harper complied and found that the site contained pictures of nude women.

At Camer's direction and from his own workstation, Harper examined Simons' computer to determine whether Simons had downloaded any picture files from the Internet; Harper found over 1,000 such files. Again from his own workstation, Harper viewed several of the pictures and observed that they were pornographic in nature. Also at Camer's request and from his own workstation, Harper printed a list of the titles of the downloaded picture files. Harper was then asked to copy all of the files on the hard drive of Simons' computer; Harper accomplished this task, again, from his own workstation.

On or about July 31, 1998, two representatives from the CIA Office of the Inspector General (OIG), one of whom was a criminal investigator, viewed selected files from the copy of Simons' hard drive; the pictures were of minors. Later that day, Harper physically entered Simons' office, removed the original hard drive, replaced it with a copy, and gave the original to the FBIS Area Security Officer. The Security Officer turned it over to the OIG criminal investigator the same day. This last assignment was the only one that required Harper to physically enter Simons' office.

On August 5, 1998, FBI Special Agent John Mesisca viewed over fifty of the images on the hard drive that had been removed from Simons' office; many of the images contained child pornography. Mesisca, Harper, the two OIG representatives, and Assistant United States Attorney Tom Connolly worked together to prepare an application for a warrant to search Simons' office and computer. An affidavit from Mesisca supported the warrant application. The affidavit stated, *inter alia*, that Simons had connected a zip drive to his computer. The affidavit also expressed a "need" to conduct the search in secret.

The warrant was issued on August 6, 1998. It stated that the executing officers were to leave at Simons' office a copy of the warrant and a receipt for any property taken. The warrant mentioned neither permission for, nor prohibition of, secret execution.

Mesisca and others executed the search during the evening of August 6, 1998, when Simons was not present. The search team copied the contents of Simons' computer; computer diskettes found in Simons' desk drawer; computer files stored on the zip drive or on zip drive diskettes; videotapes; and various documents, including personal correspondence. No original evidence was removed from the office. Neither a copy of the warrant nor a receipt for the property seized was left in the office or otherwise given to Simons at that time, and Simons did not learn of the search for approximately forty-five days. When Mesisca reviewed the computer materials copied during the search, he found over fifty pornographic images of minors.

In September 1998, Mesisca applied for a second search warrant. The supporting affidavit, like the affidavit that supported the August application, stated that Simons had connected a zip drive to his computer. The September affidavit described the August application as an application for a surreptitious search warrant.

A second search warrant was obtained on September 17, 1998 and executed on September 23, 1998, with Simons present. Original evidence was seized and removed from the office. The executors left Simons with a copy of the warrant and an inventory of the items seized. Simons subsequently was indicted on one count of knowingly receiving child pornography that had been transported in interstate commerce, see 18 U.S.C.A. § 2252A(a)(2)(A), and one count of knowingly possessing material containing images of child pornography that had been transported in interstate commerce, see 18 U.S.C.A. § 2252A(a)(5)(B). Simons moved to suppress the evidence, arguing that the searches of his office and computer violated his Fourth Amendment rights. Should the motion to suppress be granted? *United States v. Simons*, 206 F.3d 392 (4th Cir. 2000).

2 On April 3, 2003, following an undercover operation, Pennsylvania State Liquor Control Enforcement (LCE)

Officers and the West Chester Police (WCP) issued underage drinking citations to a group of students who were attending a party at Sigma Pi fraternity. On this night, Sigma Pi fraternity opened their fraternity house to the public for a party by selling tickets for admission. The tickets were required to be presented before a person could gain entry to the party, and allowed students to purchase alcoholic beverages once inside the fraternity house. The undercover LCE officers, who were dressed in plain clothing, obtained their tickets from the West Chester Police Department a few days before the party. The Department had obtained them from a student. The LCE officers were able to enter the party with relative ease. Upon entry, the LCE officers presented their tickets to a person seated behind a table who then checked the tickets against a list. The person seated behind the desk then marked the officers' hands, and allowed them to enter the party. The LCE officers then made their way to the basement of the fraternity house where they observed a makeshift bar where people who appeared to be students were being served and were consuming alcoholic beverages. From their observations, the LCE officers generally gathered that many of the students, who seemed youthful in appearance, were under the age of twenty-one. The LCE officers had not procured a search warrant before entering the fraternity house.

As the crowd in the basement began to multiply, the LCE officers believed it was necessary, for safety purposes, to call in the detail of the WCP. The WCP were uniformed police officers, and they did not procure a search warrant before entering the fraternity house. When the WCP arrived, the LCE officers stopped the party and began to "card" each student by checking their drivers' licenses for identification. Based on their ages, LCE officers divided the students into two groups: those who were over the age of twenty-one, and those who were under the age of twenty-one. Those who were over the age of twenty-one were told that they were free to leave; the under twenty-ones were further detained. The WCP and the LCE officers then administered preliminary alcohol breath tests to the under twenty-one group, and began to question students concerning whether or not they had been drinking. Based on the tests, students' admissions that they had been drinking, and LCE officers' observations, LCE officers issued under-age drinking citations to fifty-six students.

A group of the students charged with underage drinking filed a motion to suppress, challenging the constitutionality of the detention of a large group of people regardless of individualized suspicion. Should their motion be granted? *See Commonwealth v. Mistler*, 912 A.2d 1265 (Pa. 2006).

3 In order to protect school grounds from expanding violence, or to prevent an increase in drug use among students, John C. Fremont High School instituted a program to conduct random, warrantless, and suspicionless searches of students for contraband. Pursuant to the program, five two-member teams of school officials were each randomly assigned ten classrooms by the administrator in charge of student discipline. The teams visited each classroom and randomly selected ten students to be searched from among those whose last names began with certain predetermined letters. On the day in question, Freddy A. was one of the students randomly chosen to be searched. During the search, Foster Allen, the dean of students, removed a four-inch locking-blade knife from Freddy A.

The district attorney filed a petition alleging Freddy A., then fourteen years old, had unlawfully possessed a weapon on school grounds. Following the denial of his motion to suppress evidence, Freddy A. admitted the allegations in the petition. The juvenile court sustained the petition, adjudicated Freddy A. a delinquent, and placed him on probation. Freddy A. appealed, contending that the search that uncovered the knife violated his rights under the Fourth Amendment to the United States Constitution because it was conducted without individualized suspicion that he possessed a weapon, had engaged in other criminal activity, or had broken a school rule. Should his conviction be overturned on appeal? Why or why not? See *In re Freddy A.*, 2007 WL 1139955 (Cal. App. 2007).

4 A duly-authorized Title III wiretap had been placed on the phone of Shawn Bullitt. During a recorded conversation with Reginald Shantez Rice, the two spoke of the imminent arrival of "a hundred." FBI Special Agent Scott Wenther thought this was a reference to a large quantity of cocaine. Within ten days of hearing this conversation, the government applied for and was granted a separate Title III interception order for Rice's phone. As a result of that wiretap, the government ultimately collected evidence leading to Rice being indicted on drug charges.

In the affidavit used in support of the application to tap Rice's phone, Special Agent Wenther stated the following:

> All normal avenues of investigation have been carefully evaluated for use or have been attempted with minimal results. The traditional investigative techniques utilized thus far have included the use of confidential sources (against known members of the Shawn Bullitt organization), obtaining toll records

for other phone lines and for the target telephone, and physical surveillance. Also closely considered, but not deemed likely to succeed for reasons set forth below, include the use of undercover agents, use of a Federal Grand Jury, the serving of search warrants, interviews of subjects or associates, and the use of "trash pulls."

> Physical surveillance of the subjects of this investigation has been conducted and is presently being conducted with only limited success. Physical surveillance has identified locations and vehicles utilized by members of this organization. Physical surveillance has also corroborated information provided by [a confidential source]. . . . The risk of conducting long-term physical surveillance in this investigation is two-fold. As previously outlined, this organization utilizes violence and/or the threat of violence as intimidation to further their drug trafficking activities. Members of this criminal organization with known violent histories routinely carry firearms and wear bullet-resistant vests, which poses an unreasonable danger to law enforcement personnel attempting to conduct physical surveillance.

Rice subsequently challenged the interception order based upon the false or deliberately misleading allegations made in Wenther's affidavit. At the suppression hearing, the district court found that, based on Wenther's affidavit, an issuing judge would mistakenly think that agents had conducted physical surveillance on Rice and/or his associates, and that Wenther had information leading him to believe that "Rice and/or his associates had used violence or threats of violence, had violent histories, carried firearms, and wore bullet-proof vests." In fact, the later testimony of Wenther at the suppression hearing revealed that agents had not conducted any physical surveillance on Rice and that they had no specific information on whether Rice carried a firearm. Further, the district court found that "the bald statement that '[m]embers of this criminal organization . . . routinely carry firearms and wear bullet-resistant vests' does not provide sufficient information to the magistrate about Rice to determine whether physical surveillance was too dangerous to be attempted." Accordingly, the district court found that the misleading statement pertaining to physical surveillance was made recklessly.

The district court found that the government was using the wiretap in a forbidden manner as the first step in its investigation against Rice. Because the district court found that the Wenther Affidavit failed to satisfy the requirements under Title III, it granted the defendants' motion to suppress the fruits of the unlawful wiretap. The government appealed. Should the appellate court affirm or reverse the district court's opinion? Explain your reasoning. *See United States v. Rice*, 478 F.3d 704 (6th Cir. 2007).

5 Defendants Steven J. Rosen and Keith Weissman are charged with espionage for conspiring to communicate national defense information to persons not entitled to receive it. Specifically, certain government officials with authorized possession of classified national defense information communicated that information to Rosen and Weissman, who were employed at the time as lobbyists for the American-Israel Public Affairs Committee (AIPAC). It is further alleged that Rosen and Weissman then communicated the information received from their government sources to members of the media, other foreign policy analysts, and certain foreign officials, none of whom were authorized to receive this information.

In the course of its investigation of the alleged conspiracy, the government sought and obtained orders issued by the FISC pursuant to FISA that authorized certain physical searches and electronic surveillance. As the investigation pertained to national security, these applications and orders were classified. Because the government intends to offer evidence obtained or derived from physical searches and electronic surveillance authorized by these orders, defendants seek by motion (1) to obtain disclosure of the classified applications submitted to the FISC, the FISC's orders, and related materials; and/or (2) to suppress the evidence obtained or derived from any searches or surveillance conducted pursuant to the issued FISA orders.

Defendants seek disclosure of the FISA applications, orders, and related materials at issue in this case so they may effectively participate in the review process. On this point, FISA is clear: It allows a reviewing court to disclose such materials "only where such disclosure is necessary to make an accurate determination of the legality of the surveillance." Defendants claim this condition is met, by arguing (1) that the FISC's determination that they were agents of a foreign power was surely wrong; and (2) that evidence of the government's evident failure to comply with FISA's minimization procedures requires disclosure. In response to defendants' motion, the government filed: (1) a classified, *ex parte* brief in opposition to the defendants' motion; (2) an unclassified, redacted brief in opposition to the defendants' motion; (3) a declaration and claim of privilege of the Attorney General of the United States; (4) a classified Declaration of an Assistant Director of the FBI concerning the classified minimization procedures; and (6) certified copies of the FISA applications, orders and related materials at issue in this case.

As a threshold matter, should the court grant the defendants' motion for an order disclosing the applications submitted to the FISC and the FISA warrants issued pursuant to that application? Why or why not?

As for the substance of the defendants' complaint, they attack the lawfulness of the FISA surveillance in this case on the grounds that the FISC did not have probable cause to believe that they, as the targets of the sanctioned surveillance, were "agents of a foreign power" as required by FISA. Based on the U.S. government's allegations of the defendant's conduct, do you think that the defendants have alleged a *prima facie* case that the FISC erred in finding that the defendants were "agents of a foreign power," as required by FISA? Explain your reasoning. *See United States v. Rosen*, 447 F. Supp. 2d 538 (E.D. Va. 2006).

6

Arrest

Learning Objectives

▶ Define the elements of a formal arrest.

▶ Understand the distinctions among a seizure, a stop, and a seizure tantamount to arrest (*de facto* arrest).

▶ Understand the difference between arrest warrant and a summons; explain why arrests made pursuant to a warrant are preferred.

▶ Differentiate between the warrantless arrest authority for misdemeanors and for felonies.

▶ Know the procedures for making a formal arrest.

▶ Know the law relating to citizen's arrest, arrest in "hot pursuit," and arrest in "fresh pursuit."

▶ Know the limitations on the use of force in making arrests, self-defense, and entry of dwellings.

▶ Know the legal requirements and procedures for dealing with an arrested person after the arrest is made.

▶ Understand the consequences of an illegal arrest.

The authority to arrest is the most important power a law enforcement officer possesses. An officer who arrests a person deprives that person of the freedom to carry out daily personal and business affairs. Also, an arrest initiates against that person the process of criminal justice, which may ultimately result in that person being fined or imprisoned. Because of the potential extremely detrimental effect on a person's life, liberty, and privacy, the law governing arrest provides many protections to ensure that persons are arrested only when it is reasonable and necessary. These protections take the form of severe limitations and restrictions on the law enforcement officer's exercise of the power of arrest. The law governing arrest is based on guarantees in the Fourth Amendment to the U.S. Constitution:

> The right of the people to be secure in their *persons,* houses, papers and effects, against unreasonable searches and *seizures,* shall not be violated and no Warrants shall issue, but upon probable cause, supported by Oath or affirmation, and particularly describing the place to be searched and the *persons* or things to be *seized.* U.S. Const., Amend. 4 (italics added).

Because the Fourth Amendment does not specifically mention arrest, some believe that it applies only to searches and seizures of material things and not to people. The word "persons" is italicized in the preceding passage to indicate clearly that the Fourth Amendment protects individuals from illegal seizures of their persons. *An arrest is a type of seizure.* It clearly is governed by the Fourth Amendment. The discussion now turns to defining arrest and exploring the law enforcement officer's arrest powers and duties.

►TYPES OF ARRESTS

Arrest is difficult to define because it is used in different ways. In its narrow sense, sometimes called a formal or technical arrest, arrest is defined as "the taking of a person into custody for the commission of an offense as the prelude to prosecuting him for it." *State v. Murphy*, 465 P.2d 900, 902 (Or. App. 1970). In its broader sense, sometimes called a seizure tantamount to arrest, a *de facto* arrest, the functional equivalent of arrest, or an arrest for constitutional purposes, arrest means any seizure of a person significant enough to resemble a formal arrest in important respects. This chapter refers to the narrow sense as a formal arrest, and to the broad sense as a seizure tantamount to arrest, or simply an arrest. (Seizures tantamount to arrest are discussed in the next section.)

Formal Arrest

Four basic elements are necessary for a formal arrest:

1. a law enforcement officer's purpose or intention to take a person into the custody of the law;
2. the officer's exercise of real or pretended authority;

3. that the arrestee be taken into custody either by physical force or by submission to assertion of authority; and

4. understanding by the person to be arrested of the officer's intention to arrest.

Intention to Arrest To satisfy the first element of formal arrest, a law enforcement officer must intend to take a person into the custody of the law. This element distinguishes a formal arrest from lesser forms of detention, such as restraining a person who is acting dangerously; stopping a person to seek information or to render assistance; serving a subpoena or summons; asking a suspect or witness to appear at the station house for questioning; or stopping a vehicle to inspect license, equipment, or load. Thus, if a law enforcement officer does not intend to take a person into custody, there is no formal arrest.

The brief seizure of a person for investigation based on an officer's reasonable suspicion of criminal activity—commonly referred to as a **stop**—is another detention that does not involve an intention to arrest. Because a separate body of law governs stops, they are discussed separately in Chapter 7.

Real or Pretended Authority to Arrest A law enforcement officer's seizure of a person must be under real or pretended authority. Real authority means the officer has the legal right to make a formal arrest with or without a warrant. Pretended authority means the officer has no legal right to make a formal arrest, but erroneously assumes that right. The arrest is still technically a formal arrest despite the officer's error. The authority requirement distinguishes arrests from seizures for which no authority is claimed, such as a kidnapping.

Custody through Detention or Restraint According to the U.S. Supreme Court, a formal arrest requires that a person be taken into custody either through the actual use of physical force, **"or, where that is absent, submission to the assertion of authority."** *California v. Hodari D.*, 499 U.S. 621, 626 (1991).

Physical Force **"To constitute an arrest, . . . the quintessential 'seizure of the person' under our Fourth Amendment jurisprudence—the mere grasping or application of physical force with lawful authority, whether or not it succeeded in subduing the arrestee, [is] sufficient."** *Hodari D.*, 499 U.S. at 624. Thus, the slightest application of physical force results in an arrest even if the force was unsuccessful in ultimately taking a person into custody. Therefore, a person who escapes immediately after an officer's intentional application of the slightest force has still been arrested, because a seizure is a single act and not a continuous fact.

Constructive Seizures Through a Show of Authority An arrest may occur without any physical touching if the officer makes a **show of authority** and the person to be arrested submits to this authority. Words alone (e.g., "Stop, in the name of the law!") do not constitute an arrest by a show of authority. In contrast, if an officer's words and actions convey to a reasonable person that his freedom of movement is being restricted such that the person is not free to leave, and the person then submits to the officer's authority, an arrest has been made. For example, an officer yelling "Stop or I'll shoot" while drawing a weapon and pointing it at

Discussion

↑ POINT

When Is a Fleeing Suspect Chased at Gunpoint "Seized"?

State v. Harbison, 156 P.3d 30 (N.M. 2007).

On the evening of June 13, 2003, detectives organized and executed an undercover "buy-bust" operation in a northeast Albuquerque, New Mexico, neighborhood after receiving reports of the prevalence of drugs and drug dealing in that area. Posing as a drug purchaser, a detective drove into the parking lot of an apartment complex and purchased a rock of crack cocaine for twenty dollars from a subject later identified as Lawrence Clark. As he drove away, the detective radioed the other members of his team to inform them of the buy and gave a description of Clark. Within one minute of the cocaine purchase, the remaining members of the "arrest team" arrived in two vehicles and observed a group of eight to ten people gathered in front of a building at the far end of the parking lot from where the drug transaction had occurred. In addition to this group standing outside, there were two cars with a total of four people in them in the immediate vicinity of the group. Detective Soto, the officer who ultimately arrested Defendant Harbison, testified that as he approached he could see a subject who fit the description of Clark among the group. Harbison was also in this group, though not immediately next to Clark. The officers did not observe any interaction between Harbison and Clark as they approached.

As the detectives got out of their cars, the group began to scatter. Clark attempted to run but was quickly overtaken and placed under arrest. Harbison also split off from the group, in the opposite direction from Clark, in what Detective Soto described as a "slow run." This caught the detective's attention, and he pursued Harbison with his gun drawn, yelling for the suspect to stop. Harbison did not stop immediately, and the detective continued following him and told him to get down on the ground. The detective told Harbison to stop three or four times before Harbison responded by stopping in front of a vehicle parked in the lot. When he finally stopped, he went to his knees and threw something underneath the car. The detective placed him in handcuffs and looked under the car to see what Harbison had thrown. He found a broken glass crack pipe, a lighter, and a small piece of what was later identified as crack cocaine. The detective testified

a suspect has, by a combination of words and actions, demonstrated a show of authority designed to get a suspect to comply with the officer's orders. If the suspect submits to the show of authority, an arrest has been made. If, however, the suspect does not submit to the officer's show of authority and attempts to flee, then no arrest occurs, as illustrated by the Discussion Point "When is a fleeing suspect chased at gunpoint 'seized'?"

Understanding of Arrestee The final element of formal arrest is the arrested person's understanding that an arrest is being made. Usually, the officer's noti-

When is a Fleeing Suspect Chased at Gunpoint "Seized"? *(Continued)*

that, as he turned back around to face Harbison, he noticed that Harbison "had his finger in his coin pocket" and was attempting to remove something, at which point the detective reached into Harbison's pocket and retrieved a second rock of crack cocaine. Harbison was formally arrested and charged with possession of crack cocaine, tampering with evidence, and possession of drug paraphernalia.

Harbison subsequently filed a motion to suppress evidence, claiming that Officer Soto lacked reasonable suspicion when he pursued and seized Harbison. When Harbison was "seized" became an important issue because if he had not been seized at the time he discarded the drugs, then they would be considered abandoned property and, as such, the protections of the Fourth Amendment would not apply (see Chapter 12).

> In determining whether Defendant was seized in violation of the Fourth Amendment, our first inquiry is at what moment Defendant was seized: when Detective Soto pursued Defendant ordering him to stop, or when Defendant in fact stopped? . . . [T]here is no question of a show of authority at the time the detectives drew their weapons and gave orders for people to stop moving. If Defendant had immediately submitted to this show of authority, then he would have been seized at that time and we would apply a reasonable suspicion analysis as of that time. However, Defendant did not immediately submit to Detective Soto's show of authority; instead, he fled when the officers arrived and continued to move away from Detective Soto at a "slow run." Pursuing Defendant with his gun drawn, Detective Soto had to repeat his command for Defendant to stop three or four times before Defendant finally dropped to his knees behind the car where he threw the drugs and paraphernalia.

Based on the U.S. Supreme Court's holding in *Hodari D.,* the New Mexico Supreme Court held that no seizure of the defendant had occurred until he yielded to the detective commands to stop.

Do you agree with the logic of *Hodari D.* and *Harbison* that someone must actually submit to a show of authority before a seizure takes place? Why or why not? Don't you think that a reasonable person would know that he or she is not "free to leave" when police order the person to "freeze" while chasing him with a drawn weapon? Why, then, do you think courts in *Hodari D.* and *Harbison* decided that no arrest takes place until someone actually submits to a show of authority?

fying the person of the arrest conveys this understanding. However, handcuffing or other physical restraint or confinement may satisfy the understanding requirement, even though the officer never says a word. If the arrested person is unconscious, under the influence of drugs or alcohol, or mentally impaired, the understanding requirement may be delayed or eliminated.

The understanding requirement presents problems when an encounter between the police and a person does not quite fit the description of a formal arrest, but the intrusion on the person's freedom of action is significantly greater than an ordinary, brief investigative detention or minimal street encounter. The next section discusses such seizures. Although not formal arrests, they may be tantamount to arrests for the purposes of Fourth Amendment protection.

Seizures Tantamount to Arrest

Law enforcement officers have varying degrees of contact with members of the public. These contacts range in intensity from a brief observation or questioning to a formal arrest accompanied by force. With respect to the most minimal of these police contacts, the U.S. Supreme Court said:

> [L]aw enforcement officers do not violate the Fourth Amendment by merely approaching an individual on the street or in another public place, by asking him if he is willing to answer some questions, by putting questions to him if the person is willing to listen, or by offering in evidence in a criminal prosecution his voluntary answers to such questions. . . . Nor would the fact that the officer identifies himself as a police officer, without more, convert the encounter into a seizure requiring some level of objective justifications. . . . The person approached, however, need not answer any question put to him; indeed, he may decline to listen to the questions at all and may go on his way. . . . He may not be detained even momentarily without reasonable, objective grounds for doing so; and his refusal to listen or answer does not, without more, furnish those grounds. . . . If there is no detention—no seizure within the meaning of the Fourth Amendment—then no constitutional rights have been infringed. *Florida v. Royer*, 460 U.S. 491, 497-98 (1983).

Furthermore:

> Even when law enforcement officers have no basis for suspecting a particular individual, they may pose questions, ask for identification, and request consent to search luggage—provided they do not induce cooperation by coercive means. . . . If a reasonable person would feel free to terminate the encounter, then he or she has not been seized. *United States v. Drayton*, 536 U.S. 194, 201 (2002).

Other encounters between the police and members of the public are more intrusive than those described above and involve greater encroachments on freedom of movement and privacy. An example is a stop (mentioned earlier), which is sometimes accompanied by a limited search for weapons called a **frisk**. (Stops and frisks are discussed in Chapter 7.)

At a still higher level of intrusiveness are police contacts that restrain a person's freedom of action more than a stop but do not satisfy the four elements of a formal arrest. The missing element is usually the officer's intention to arrest. In these instances, courts hold that the seizure is so similar to a formal arrest in important respects that it should be allowed only if supported by probable cause to believe a crime has been or is being committed. These seizures are called "seizures tantamount to arrest," *de facto* arrests, or the "functional equivalents of arrest." Regardless of terminology, each and every seizure of a person that has **"the essential attributes of a formal arrest, is unreasonable unless it is supported by probable cause."** *Michigan v. Summers*, 452 U.S. 692, 700 (1981).

In *Dunaway v. New York*, 442 U.S. 200 (1979), the defendant was picked up at his neighbor's home by the police and taken to the police station for questioning about an attempted robbery and homicide. Although the defendant was not told that he was under arrest, he would have been physically restrained had he attempted to leave. The police did not have probable cause to arrest the defendant. The police gave him *Miranda* warnings, and he waived his right to counsel. The police then questioned him, and he eventually made statements and drew sketches incriminating himself. His motions to suppress the statements and sketches were denied.

The Supreme Court held that the police violated Dunaway's constitutional rights under the Fourth and Fourteenth Amendments. The seizure was much more intrusive than a traditional stop and frisk (see Chapter 7) and could not be justified on the mere grounds of "reasonable suspicion" of criminal activity. Whether or not technically characterized as a formal arrest, the seizure was, in important respects, indistinguishable from a formal arrest. Instead of being questioned briefly where he was found, the defendant was taken from a neighbor's home to a police car, transported to a police station, and placed in an interrogation room. He was never informed that he was free to go and would have been physically restrained had he refused to accompany the officers or tried to escape their custody. That he was not formally arrested, was not booked, and would not have had an arrest record if the interrogation had proven fruitless did not make his seizure something less than an arrest for purposes of Fourth Amendment protections. Because it was unsupported by probable cause, Dunaway's seizure was illegal. Therefore, even though an officer does not intend to formally arrest a person, a seizure or detention of the person that is indistinguishable from a formal arrest in important respects is illegal unless supported by probable cause.

In *Hayes v. Florida*, 470 U.S. 811, 816 (1985), police took a burglary-rape suspect against his will from his home to the police station for fingerprinting. The Court reiterated the principles set out in *Dunaway*:

> [W]hen the police, without probable cause or a warrant, forcibly remove a person from his home or other place in which he is entitled to be and transport him to the police station, where he is detained, although briefly, for investigative purposes . . . such seizures, at least where not under judicial supervision, are sufficiently like arrests to invoke the traditional rule that arrests may constitutionally be made only on probable cause. 470 U.S. at 816.

The Court did not, however, rule out the possibility that an investigative seizure on less than probable cause might be permissible if judicially authorized:

> [U]nder circumscribed procedures, the Fourth Amendment might permit the judiciary to authorize the seizure of a person on less than probable cause and his removal to the police station for the purpose of fingerprinting. . . . [S]ome States . . . have enacted procedures for judicially authorized seizures for the purpose of fingerprinting. The state courts are not in accord on the validity of these efforts to insulate investigative seizures from Fourth Amendment invalidation. 470 U.S. at 817.

Many issues involving seizures tantamount to arrest arise as a result of detentions of suspected drug law violators at airports. In *Florida v. Royer*, 460 U.S. 491 (1983), narcotics agents had adequate grounds to suspect the defendant of carrying drugs: he was traveling under an assumed name and his appearance and conduct fit the "drug courier profile." Therefore, the agents had the right to temporarily detain the defendant to confirm or dispel their suspicions. The agents, however, went beyond requesting identification and asking the defendant to accompany them to another room. They told him they were narcotics agents and had reason to believe he was carrying illegal drugs; and they kept his identification and airline ticket, They then took him to a small room, where he found himself alone with two police officers. They also retrieved his checked luggage from the airline without his consent; they never informed him he was free to board his plane if he so chose; and they would not have allowed him to leave the interrogation room even if he had asked to do so.

Under these circumstances, the Court found the officers' conduct much more intrusive than a stop, which might have been justified on the basis of reasonable suspicion. The detention was instead a seizure tantamount to an arrest; and because the officers did not have probable cause to arrest, it was an illegal seizure. The defendant's consent to search his luggage in the interrogation room was tainted by the illegal seizure and was also ruled illegal as a "fruit of the poisonous tree" (see Chapter 3).

United States v. Hill, 91 F.3d 1064 (8th Cir. 1996), held that "a *de facto* arrest occurs when the officers' conduct is more intrusive than necessary for an investigative stop. . . . We must consider such factors as the duration of a stop, whether the suspect was handcuffed or confined in a police car, whether the suspect was transported or isolated, and 'the degree of fear and humiliation that the police conduct engenders.'" 91 F.3d at 1070.

key points

- The requirements for a formal arrest are a law enforcement officer's intention to take a person into the custody of the law to answer for an alleged crime, under real or pretended authority, accompanied by detention or restraint of the person and an understanding by the person that an arrest is being made.
- The "custody by detention or restraint" requirement of a formal arrest may be satisfied either by actually touching the person to be arrested or by the person's submitting to an officer's show of authority.
- A seizure of a person that is substantially indistinguishable from a formal arrest is illegal unless it is supported by probable cause to believe that the person has committed or is committing a crime.

▶ AUTHORITY TO ARREST

Although law enforcement officers have long been authorized to make warrantless arrests, arrests made under the authority of a warrant have always been preferred. This section discusses the details involved with arrests pursuant to a warrant, warrantless arrests, and citizens' arrests by police officers.

Arrests Pursuant to a Warrant

The U.S. Supreme Court said that **"the informed and deliberate determinations of magistrates empowered to issue warrants . . . are to be preferred** over the hurried action of officers . . . who may happen to make arrests." *Aguilar v. Texas*, 378 U.S. 108, 110-11 (1964). In other words, impartial judicial authorities are better suited to determining probable cause than law enforcement officers who, in their eagerness to enforce the law and investigate crime, may be tempted to violate constitutional rights.

Although law enforcement officers often consider warrants a hindrance, arrest warrants protect officers in an important way. If a warrant is proper on its face and officers do not abuse their authority in obtaining or executing the warrant, they have qualified immunity against civil liability for damages, even though the warrant is later determined to be invalid. In *Malley v. Briggs*, 475 U.S. 335 (1986), a state trooper applied for a warrant to arrest the defendants for marijuana possession, the judge issued the warrant, and the defendants were arrested. The charges were subsequently dropped, however, when the grand jury failed to find probable cause to indict. The defendants then brought a civil action for damages under 42 U.S.C. § 1983, alleging that the officer violated their rights under the Fourth and Fourteenth Amendments when he applied for the warrant. The U.S. Supreme Court held that a law enforcement officer applying for a warrant has qualified immunity from liability for damages if the officer's actions were "objectively reasonable." Under that standard, "[o]nly where the warrant application is so lacking in indicia of probable cause as to render official belief in its existence unreasonable . . . will the shield of immunity be lost." 475 U.S. at 344-45. In short, the question is:

> [W]hether a reasonably well-trained officer in petitioner's position would have known that his affidavit failed to establish probable cause and that he should not have applied for the warrant. If such was the case, the officer's application for a warrant was not objectively reasonable, because it created the unnecessary danger of an unlawful arrest." 475 U.S. at 345.

Issuance of Arrest Warrants

Complaints As explained in Chapter 2, the criminal process against a defendant usually begins with the filing of a complaint. (Recall from Chapter 2 that a complaint may also function as the charging instrument in misdemeanor cases.) According to Federal Rule of Criminal Procedure 3, a **complaint** is "a written statement of the essential facts constituting the offense charged." A complaint serves as the basis for determining whether an arrest warrant should be issued. The complaint must be made on oath or affirmation, must state the essential facts of the offense being charged, must be in writing, and must be made before a neutral judicial officer authorized to issue process in criminal cases. This judicial officer is usually a **magistrate** or a justice of the peace, although a judge may also authorize a complaint. The information in the complaint may come from a law enforcement officer's personal observation or experience or it may come from victims, witnesses, or informants. Nevertheless, the evidence put forth in the complaint must be strong enough to convince the magistrate that there is probable cause that an offense has been committed and that the defendant committed it (see Chapter 3 for an in-depth discussion of probable cause). (See Figure 2.5 in Chapter 2 for a typical form of a criminal complaint.)

Information not contained in the body of the complaint or that comes from witnesses other than the complainant may be brought to the court's attention in the form of an **affidavit**: a sworn written statement of the facts relied on in seeking the issuance of a warrant. An affidavit need not be prepared with any particular formality. It is filed with the complaint. Together, the complaint and affidavit provide a written record for a reviewing court to examine in determining whether probable cause existed for the issuance of a warrant.

Warrants or Summons Issued on a Complaint Once the magistrate has determined from a sworn complaint (and accompanying affidavits, if any) that there is probable cause to believe that an offense has been committed and that the defendant committed it, the magistrate may issue a summons or an arrest warrant.

▶ Summons A **summons** is a court order that commands someone to appear before a court to respond to charges. (See Figure 2.6 in Chap-ter 2.) Court rules and statutes usually provide that, if a defendant fails to appear in response to a summons, then a warrant will issue for his or her arrest.

   ▶ When Used: A summons is typically issued when the offense charged in a complaint is a **misdemeanor,** a violation of a municipal ordinance, or some other petty offense. If the alleged offender is a citizen with "roots firmly established in the soil of the community" and can be easily found if the summons is ignored, the summons procedure is more efficient and less intrusive than formal arrest as a means of inducing the defendant to appear in court.

   ▶ Required Contents: The requirements for a summons are generally the same as those for an arrest warrant (described below), except that a summons directs the defendant to appear before a court at a stated time and place rather than ordering the defendant's arrest.

   ▶ Different from Citations: The term summons may be confusing because it is often used to describe a citation, ticket, or notice to appear issued by a law enforcement officer, especially in traffic cases. Such a notice is not a summons in the legal sense, because it is not issued by a magistrate on the basis of a complaint. A citation, ticket, or notice to appear merely gives notice to offenders that they may be arrested if they do not voluntarily appear in court to answer the charges against them.

   ▶ Service and Return of Process: A summons is served by personally delivering a copy to the defendant, or by leaving it at the defendant's home or usual place of abode with a person of suitable age and discretion who resides there. Depending on the rules of a particular jurisdiction, mailing a summons to the defendant's last known address with a return receipt may be permitted as service. As with an arrest warrant, most states provide that a summons for a violation of state law may be served at any place within the state. In addition, the officer serving the summons must return it to the proper judicial authority before the return date on the summons.

▶ Arrest Warrant An **arrest warrant** is a written order directing the arrest of a particular person or persons. Figure 2.6 in Chapter 2 contains a typical form for an arrest warrant. (In some jurisdictions, a form is used that combines a complaint, a summons, an arrest warrant, and/or an order of detention.) An arrest warrant may only be issued on a sworn complaint. If an arrest warrant is issued on an unsworn complaint, it is void; an arrest made under such a warrant is illegal. An arrest warrant must conform to additional requirements, which vary by jurisdiction. In general, an arrest warrant must contain the following information:

▶ The caption of the court or division of the court from which the warrant issues.

▶ The name of the person to be arrested, if known; if not known, any name or description by which the person can be identified with reasonable certainty. The warrant must show on its face that it is directed toward a particular, identifiable person to satisfy the Fourth Amendment requirement that a warrant particularly describe the person to be seized.

▶ A description of the offense charged in the complaint. The description should be in the language of the appropriate statute or ordinance. More important, the description must be specific enough for the defendant to readily understand the charge. Charging the defendant merely with a "felony" or a "misdemeanor," for example, is insufficient and will invalidate the warrant.

▶ The date of issuance.

▶ The officer or officers to whom the warrant is directed, together with a command that the defendant be brought before the proper judicial official.

▶ The signature of the issuing magistrate, together with a statement of the magistrate's official title.

An officer to whom an arrest warrant is directed should read the warrant carefully. If the warrant satisfies the above requirements, the officer may execute the warrant without fear of civil liability.

key points

- An arrest warrant is a written order to arrest a person, issued by a proper judicial authority on the basis of a sworn complaint charging the commission of a crime, supported by a statement of facts and circumstances establishing probable cause.

- A summons is similar to an arrest warrant, except that it directs a person to appear in court rather than ordering the person's arrest.

Warrantless Arrests

Law enforcement officers are often faced with the decision of whether to apply for an arrest warrant or to arrest without a warrant. *United States v. Watson*, 423

U.S. 411 (1976), held that the Fourth Amendment permits warrantless arrests in a public place under certain circumstances. Generally, authority to arrest without a warrant depends on the difference between a felony and a misdemeanor.

In most jurisdictions, a **felony** is defined as any crime that may be punished by death or imprisonment in a state prison. This means that a crime is probably not a felony unless the penalty is at least one year of incarceration. Note that the punishment that *may* be imposed under the statute defining the crime determines whether a crime is a felony or misdemeanor, not the penalty that *actually* is imposed. Therefore, a felony can be defined as any crime for which the punishment could possibly be imprisonment for a term of one year or more.

All crimes that do not amount to a felony are classified as misdemeanors. Jurisdictions differ greatly as to which crimes are classified as felonies and misdemeanors. Thus, law enforcement officers must familiarize themselves with the classifications of crimes in their respective jurisdictions.

Felonies As a matter of federal constitutional law, a law enforcement officer may make a warrantless public arrest for a felony if, at the time of arrest, the officer has probable cause to believe that a felony has been committed and that the person to be arrested is committing or has committed the felony. The U.S. Supreme Court said:

> **Law enforcement officers may find it wise to seek arrest warrants where practicable to do so, and their judgments about probable cause may be more readily accepted where backed by a warrant issued by a magistrate. . . . But we decline to transform this judicial preference into a constitutional rule when the judgment of the Nation and Congress has for so long been to authorize warrantless public arrests on probable cause rather than to encumber criminal prosecutions with endless litigation with respect to the existence of exigent circumstances, whether it was practicable to get a warrant, whether the suspect was about to flee, and the like.** *United States v. Watson*, 423 U.S. 411, 423-24 (1976).

Requirement of Probable Cause to Arrest

▶ Majority Approach Before making a warrantless felony arrest, nearly all U.S. jurisdictions require that a law enforcement officer have probable cause to make such an arrest. That is to say that the arresting officer must have specific facts or circumstances that the person to be arrested has committed, or is committing, a particular felony. *E.g.*, *Qualls v. State*, 947 So.2d 365 (Miss. App. 2007). An officer who is unable to justify an arrest by articulating the facts and circumstances supporting probable cause risks having the arrest declared illegal. An arrest without a warrant is valid if the arresting officer has probable cause to believe a felony has been committed, and probable cause to believe the suspect to be arrested committed the felony.

If an officer has probable cause to believe that a felony has been committed and that the defendant committed it, it makes no difference whether the officer turns out to be wrong or whether the defendant is later acquitted. Probable cause justifies the arrest and makes it legal. On the other hand, if an officer makes a warrantless felony arrest on mere suspicion or chance, the arrest is illegal whether the defendant is guilty or not. Therefore, probable cause is the main consideration in determining the validity of a warrantless felony arrest.

▶ **Minority Approach** A minority of U.S. jurisdictions require that law enforcement officers obtain an arrest warrant before making an arrest for any felony that did not occur in the officer's presence, unless exigent circumstances make it impracticable to obtain an arrest warrant first. *E.g., Akins v. State*, 202 S.W.3d 879 (Tex. App. 2006) (citing VERNON'S ANN. TEXAS C.C.P. art. 14.04); *People v. Casias*, 563 P.2d 926 (Colo. 1977); *Payne v. State*, 343 N.E.2d 325 (Ind. App. 1976). Exigent circumstances include situations when the suspect would be able to destroy evidence, flee or otherwise avoid capture; or when the suspect might, during the time necessary to procure a warrant, endanger the safety or property of others. *State v. Canby*, 252 S.E.2d 164 (W. Va. 1979).

Timing of Arrest Unlike warrantless arrests for misdemeanors, warrantless arrests for a felony may be delayed, whether or not it was committed in the officer's presence. *United States v. Drake*, 655 F.2d 1025 (10th Cir. 1981). Delay may be justified for a variety of reasons, as long as the delay is not designed to prejudice a person's constitutional rights. Reasons justifying delay include inability to locate the defendant, need to complete additional undercover investigation, desire to avoid alerting other potential offenders, and need to protect the identity of undercover agents or informants:

> **The police are not required to guess at their peril the precise moment at which they have probable cause to arrest a suspect, risking a violation of the Fourth Amendment if they act too soon, and a violation of the Sixth Amendment if they wait too long. Law enforcement officers are under no constitutional duty to call a halt to a criminal investigation the moment they have the minimum evidence to establish probable cause, a quantum of evidence which may fall far short of the amount necessary to support a criminal prosecution.** *Hoffa v. United States*, 385 U.S. 293, 310 (1966).

The safest procedure for the law enforcement officer is to arrest soon after a crime is committed unless there are good reasons for delay:

> [A] point can be reached where the delay is so great that the prejudice to the defendant caused by it—due to faded memories of parties and witnesses, loss of contact with witnesses, and loss of documents—becomes so great that due process and fundamental fairness require that the charges be dismissed. *People v. Hall*, 729 P.2d 373, 375 (Colo. 1986).

Misdemeanors

Requirement of Probable Cause to Arrest

▶ **Minority Approach** Some states follow the same rules for warrantless misdemeanor arrests as for warrantless felony ones. Thus, in a handful of states, warrantless misdemeanor arrests may be made if supported by probable cause; in a few others, a warrant is required to make a misdemeanor arrest unless exigent circumstances are present. Compare, *e.g., State v. Martin*, 268 S.E.2d 105 (S.C. 1980) (applying probable cause approach), with *State v. Remy*, 711 A.2d 665 (Vt. 1998) (requiring exigent circumstances for warrantless misdemeanors arrests).

▶ **Majority Approach** The overwhelming number of U.S. jurisdictions follow a variation of the common law rule that a law enforcement officer may make a warrantless arrest on a misdemeanor charge only when the misdemeanor is committed *in the officer's presence*. (Note: The **common law** is a body of unwritten law developed in England and based on court decisions. It receives its binding force from traditional usage, custom, and universal acceptance.) At common law, the misdemeanor had to be one that caused a "breach of the peace." One or two jurisdictions still follow that rule precisely. *Commonwealth v. Lockridge*, 810 A.2d 1191 (Pa. 2002). But in *Atwater v. City of Lago Vista*, 532 U.S. 318 (2001), the U.S. Supreme Court ruled that the "breach of the peace" rule was not required by the Fourth Amendment. Thus, unless otherwise provided by statute, most states permit law enforcement officers to make an arrest without a warrant for *any* misdemeanor so long as the misdemeanor was committed in the officer's presence. *See In re R.P.*, 918 A.2d 115 (Pa. Super. 2007); *Higbee v. City of San Diego*, 911 F.2d 377 (9th Cir. 1990).

The requirement that a misdemeanor occur "in the officer's presence" ordinarily means that the officer must personally perceive the misdemeanor being committed before making an arrest. Sight, of course, is the primary sense used to perceive the commission of a crime, but it is not the only one. For example, *People v. Nitz*, 863 N.E.2d 817(Ill. App. 2007), upheld the warrantless arrest of a defendant when a police officer smelled marijuana coming from the driver's vehicle. *See also Harding v. State*, 641 S.E.2d 285 (Ga. App. 2007). And *Sharp v. State*, 621 S.E.2d 508 (Ga. App. 2005), upheld a warrantless arrest for hunting without a license and obstruction of law enforcement officers when park rangers heard shots being fired, followed by the defendant's flight from the rangers as soon as he observed them.

The "presence" requirement may even be satisfied by the defendant's admission of guilt. *Jaegly v. Couch*, 439 F.3d 149 (2d Cir. 2006). But information from victims, witnesses, or informants may not be used to satisfy the presence requirement. The officer must present such evidence to a magistrate and seek an arrest warrant. Moreover, officers may enhance their senses in various ways to satisfy the "presence" requirement:

> Permissible techniques of surveillance include more than just the five senses of officers and their unaided physical abilities. Binoculars, dogs that track and sniff out contraband, search lights, fluorescent powders, automobiles and airplanes, burglar alarms, radar devices, and bait money contribute to surveillance without violation of the Fourth Amendment in the usual case. *United States v. Dubrofsky*, 581 F.2d 208, 211 (9th Cir. 1978).

However, law enforcement officers may not use devices that allow them to sense things in areas that would otherwise be unobservable. Thus, although using binoculars, telescopic lenses on cameras, and radar guns do not violate the Fourth Amendment, the same cannot be said for devices that actual invade the privacy of the home. For example, in *Kyllo v. United States*, 533 U.S. 27, 34 (2001), the Supreme Court invalidated a search of a private residence using a thermal imaging device that revealed the presence of marijuana plants. **"We think that obtaining by sense-enhancing technology any information regarding the interior of the home that could not otherwise have been obtained without physical 'intrusion into a constitutionally protected area' constitutes a search—at least where . . . the technology in question is not in *general public use*."** *Kyllo* clearly implies that advances in technology that allow the previously unknowable to be known—such as ultrasound and infrared radiation sensors, laser listening devices, and handheld "sniffing" devices that use gas chromatography and mass spectrometry, just to name a few—will certainly be subject to Fourth Amendment scrutiny. Thus, it is highly doubtful that the use of advanced technologies not in widespread, "general public use" (as opposed to being available to military, law enforcement, and scientific personnel) can be used to satisfy the "in the officer's presence" requirement for warrantless arrests.

Timing of Arrest Unlike warrantless arrests for felonies, an arrest without a warrant for a misdemeanor committed in an officer's presence must be made promptly and without unnecessary delay. For example, *State v. Warren*, 709 P2d 194 (N.M. App. 1985), held that a delay of two and a half hours before making an arrest for drinking in public was untimely. Accordingly, the officer must set out to make the arrest at the time the offense is perceived and must continue until the arrest is accomplished or abandoned. Any delay in making the arrest must be due to some reason concerning the arrest itself. Thus, if there is a delay in making a warrantless misdemeanor arrest because the offender fled, or because the officer thought it reasonably necessary to seek assistance before making the arrest, then such delays would be constitutionally permissible. If, however, the delay is unrelated to the process of making the arrest, then any subsequent warrantless arrest would be unlawful. Instead, other types of delay require the officer to obtain a warrant and to arrest in accordance with the warrant. *See, e.g., Torres v. State*, 807 A.2d 780 (Md. App. 2002).

Citizen's Arrests

Unless altered by the statutory law of a particular jurisdiction, private citizens and law enforcement officers outside of their law jurisdiction may make lawful arrests under certain circumstances. When such an arrest is made, it is referred to as a **citizen's arrest**.

Arrests by Private Persons

Felonies Under the common law rule in force in most states, a private citizen may arrest a person if the citizen has probable cause to believe that the person has committed a felony. *Tekle ex rel. Tekle v. United States*, 457 F.3d 1088 (9th Cir. 2006) (citing CAL. PENAL CODE § 834). This includes, of course, felonies committed in the presence of the private citizen. *Miles v. State*, 194 S.W.3d 523 (Tex. App. 2006) (citing VERNON'S ANN. TEXAS CODE CRIM PRO. art. 14.01).

Misdemeanors A law enforcement officer may arrest a person without a warrant when he or she has probable cause to believe that the arrestee committed a misdemeanor in his presence. A private person, however, may only arrest someone for a misdemeanor when the offense actually has been committed or attempted in his or her presence. *Hamburg v. Wal-Mart Stores, Inc.*, 10 Cal. Rptr.3d 568, 580 (Cal. App. 2004). Reasonable cause to believe that a misdemeanor has been committed is not sufficient. Many states, however, limit the power to conduct a citizen's arrest for misdemeanor offenses to those committed in the citizen's presence that constitute a "breach of the peace"—crimes that present "an imminent threat to the public security or morals to justify a citizen taking immediate action." *Johnson v. Barnes & Noble Booksellers, Inc.*, 437 F.3d 1112, 1116 (11th Cir. 2006).

Use of Force A private citizen may use the same degree of force as a law enforcement officer in making an arrest. As with law enforcement, only force that is reasonable under the circumstances may be used to restrain the individual arrested. *Patel v. State*, 620 S.E.2d 343 (Ga. 2005). (See the discussion of use of force later in this chapter.)

Effect of Mistake If the private citizen arresting for a felony is mistaken and no felony was actually committed, the citizen may be civilly liable for damages. In contrast, law enforcement officers who arrest in their jurisdiction for a felony based on probable cause are protected from civil liability, even if they are mistaken.

Citizen's Arrests by Police outside Jurisdictional Power

Extra-Territorial Citizen Arrest Power Law enforcement officers outside their territorial jurisdiction generally have the same authority as private citizens to arrest without a warrant. *United States v. Atwell*, 470 F. Supp. 2d 554 (D. Md. 2007). Thus (unless neighboring states have modified the common law rule regarding citizen's arrests by statute), when law enforcement officers are beyond the territorial limits of their jurisdiction, they may make a warrantless felony arrest if they have probable cause to believe that a felony has occurred; and they may make a warrantless misdemeanor arrest if a misdemeanor was committed or attempted in their presence (and, in some jurisdictions, the misdemeanor must be one that constitutes a breach of the peace). Like private citizens, however, officers making an arrest as private citizens risk civil liability if they cannot prove that a felony was actually committed or that a misdemeanor constituting a breach of the peace was committed or attempted in their presence.

Under Color of Office Limitation When law enforcement officers make arrests outside their jurisdiction as private citizens, they may not use the powers of their office that are unavailable to private citizens; they may not utilize their power of office to gather evidence or ferret out criminal activity not otherwise observable. *People v. Olson*, 361 Ill. App. 3d 62 (2005). This limitation:

> [R]efers not to the *modus operandi* of the arrest, but whether official authority was used to gain access to the information that lead to the belief that an arrest should be made. . . . Courts are widely split as to what constitutes exercise of the "under the color of office" authority inconsistent with a citizen's arrest. Some courts hold that . . . "under the color of office" refers to a law enforcement officer actually holding himself out as a police officer, by either wearing his uniform or in some other manner openly asserting his official position [such as using lights and sirens], in order to observe the unlawful activity involved or the contraband seized. Other courts do not focus on the status of the police officer as a police officer but whether he uses the indicia or powers as a police officer to gain the probable cause for the arrest. . . . [But we think] what is most essential in a determination regarding the validity of a citizen's arrest and the impact of the "under the color of office" doctrine is whether the arresting officer acting outside of his jurisdiction had probable cause for the arrest *based*

solely on evidence that a private citizen might observe and have the ability to interpret. Atwell, 470 F. Supp. 2d at 567-69 (internal citations and alterations omitted) (italic added).

key points

- In most jurisdictions, a law enforcement officer may make a warrantless public arrest for a felony if, at the time of arrest, the officer has probable cause to believe that a felony has been committed and that the person to be arrested is committing or has committed the felony.
- A law enforcement officer may arrest without a warrant for a misdemeanor only when the misdemeanor is committed in the officer's presence, unless otherwise provided by statute or state constitution. All five senses may be used to satisfy the "in the officer's presence" requirement. Devices that enhance the senses may also be used to meet this requirement if they are in general public use and do not allow officers to sense things that would otherwise be unknowable without the use of technology.
- An arrest without a warrant for a misdemeanor committed in a law enforcement officer's presence must be made as quickly after commission of the offense as circumstances permit. An arrest without a warrant for a felony on probable cause, however, may be delayed for various reasons, as long as the delay is not designed to prejudice a person's constitutional rights.

- A private person may make a valid citizen's arrest if he or she has probable cause to believe that the person to be arrested (1) has committed a felony, or (2) actually committed or attempted to commit a misdemeanor that constitutes a breach of the peace in the presence of the person seeking to make the citizen's arrest. A private citizen may use the same degree of force as a law enforcement officer in making an arrest. Unlike law enforcement officers, who are protected by qualified immunity from civil liability for good-faith mistakes made while arresting someone in their jurisdiction, private citizens who are mistaken when they make a citizen's arrest may be civilly liable for damages.
- Law enforcement officers outside their jurisdiction generally have the same authority as private citizens to arrest without a warrant so long as they do not use the powers of their office that are unavailable to private citizens when making a citizen's arrest. Law enforcement officers making arrests outside their jurisdiction are subject to civil liability for their mistakes in the same way a private citizen would be.

▶MAKING AN ARREST

To make a formal arrest, a law enforcement officer must satisfy the basic requirements of a formal arrest. To summarize, these requirements are a law enforcement officer's intention to take a person into the custody of the law to answer for an alleged crime, under real or pretended authority, accompanied by detention or restraint of the person and an understanding by the person that an arrest is being made.

Provisions for All Arrests

In addition to the requirements noted above, there are other aspects of making an arrest. These include notice, time of day, assistance, and discretion. Additional considerations are involved in executing an arrest warrant.

Notice As a matter of constitutional law, someone being arrested does not have to be informed that he or she is under arrest. *Kladis v. Brezek*, 823 F.2d 1014

POINT

Should Police Conduct a Citizen's Arrest?

People v. Williams, 829 N.E.2d 1203 (N.Y. 2005).

While patrolling a housing project, two peace officers employed by the Buffalo Municipal Housing Authority observed the defendant driving an automobile on a public street adjacent to the project. The officers stopped the defendant because he allegedly was not wearing a seat belt. After the defendant informed the officers that he did not have a valid driver's license, the officers ordered him to step out of his vehicle. In response to questioning by an officer, the defendant replied in a manner that led the officer to suspect that the defendant had an object in his mouth. The defendant opened his mouth, revealing what appeared to be a plastic bag protruding from underneath his tongue. When asked to lift his tongue, the defendant shoved the officer and fled. Upon being apprehended after a brief chase, the defendant spit the bag onto the ground. The bag, which was recovered by the officers, appeared to contain crack cocaine.

As a result of this incident, the defendant was indicted for criminal possession of a controlled substance in the fifth degree and several violations of the Vehicle and Traffic Law. Before trial, the defendant moved to dismiss the charges, arguing that the initial seizure for a traffic infraction was unlawful because the Housing Authority peace officers lacked jurisdiction outside the boundaries of the housing project and the officers were not acting pursuant to their special duties as Housing Authority peace officers when they stopped him for a seat belt violation. The People countered that the seizure was lawful because the peace officers were within their geographical jurisdiction and, even if they were not, the stop was justified as a "citizen's arrest."

The trial court agreed with the defendant and dismissed the charges. The court concluded that there was no statutory authority for the peace officers to apprehend the defendant for an offense committed outside their geographic area of employment, and the People had failed to demonstrate that the officers were acting pursuant to their special duties when they stopped the defendant for a seat belt violation. The court further rejected the People's contention that the traffic stop was a valid citizen's arrest. An appeals court affirmed. The highest court in the State of New York accepted discretionary appellate jurisdiction and affirmed, reasoning that the alleged traffic infractions and the seizure of the defendant occurred outside the geographical jurisdiction of the Buffalo Municipal Housing Authority peace officers. The court also rejected the assertion that the apprehension of the defendant was the equivalent of a citizen's arrest because the Housing Authority peace officers were not "acting other than as a police officer or a peace officer" at the time of the stop and subsequent arrest.

Do you think that the officers in this case were acting "under color of law and with all the accoutrements of official authority"? Why or why not?

Assume, for the sake of argument, the officers were acting under color of law. Do you think that should deprive them of the authority to have made the arrest in this case? Explain your answer and your underlying reasoning.

(7th Cir. 1987). However, a law enforcement officer may be required to give notice when making an arrest under the statutory law of a particular jurisdiction. *E.g.*, N.Y. Crim. Pro. L. § 140.15 (McKinney 1970). But regardless of whether notice is legally required, it is a good idea that an officer tell a suspect that he or she is under arrest so that the person being taken into custody is aware that the detention is legal, and therefore the suspect is unlikely to resist arrest. *See Pullins v. State*, 256 N.E.2d 553, 556 (Ind. 1970). This becomes especially important if the arresting officer's authority is not already known to the arrestee due to an obvious display of a badge, uniform, or other indicia of authority. *See State v. Erdman*, 292 N.W.2d 97 (S.D. 1980).

Time of Day An arrest, with or without a warrant, may be made on any day of the week and at any time of the day or night, unless otherwise provided in the warrant or by statute. *See, e.g., Robinette v. Jones*, 476 F.3d 585 (8th Cir. 2007) (citing Mo. Rev. Stat. § 544.210). Unlike the execution of a search warrant, generally no specific provision in an arrest warrant is required to authorize a nighttime arrest. Note, however, that some states limit the time during which a misdemeanor warrant may be served, unless another time period is specifically authorized in the warrant. *See, e.g., People v. Dinneen*, 119 Cal. Rptr. 186 (Cal. App. Super. 1974) (citing West's Ann. Cal. Penal Code § 840); *State v. McCoy*, 131 N.E.2d 679 (Ohio App. 1955).

Entry in Dwellings *Payton v. New York*, 445 U.S. 573 (1980), held that, absent exigent circumstances or consent, a law enforcement officer may not make a warrantless entry into a suspect's home to make a routine felony arrest. *See also Kyllo v. United States*, 533 U.S. 27, 40 (2001) ("We have said that the Fourth Amendment draws a 'firm line at the entrance to the house.' That line, we think, must be not only firm, but also bright . . . ."). The Supreme Court said that physical entry of the home is the chief evil against which the Fourth Amendment is directed and that the warrant procedure minimizes the danger of needless intrusions into a person's home. The Court went on to say that an arrest warrant requirement, although providing less protection than a search warrant requirement, was sufficient to interpose the magistrate's determination of probable cause between a zealous officer and a citizen. The Court concluded that "an arrest warrant founded on probable cause implicitly carries with it the limited authority to enter a dwelling in which the suspect lives when there is reason to believe the suspect is within." 445 U.S. at 603. Thus, entry into a home to make an arrest usually requires a warrant executed in accordance with the special procedures discussed below in the section dealing with the "Place of Execution" of an arrest warrant.

Assistance Law enforcement officers may request private citizens to aid them in making an arrest. The laws of some jurisdictions require that any person called on by a law enforcement officer to assist the officer in executing his or her official duties, including the arrest of another person, is legally obligated to obey the officer. Refusal to aid an officer may be punishable under state law.

Private citizens who aid a known law enforcement officer have the same rights and privileges as the officer, including the right to use force and to enter property. If a person aiding an officer acts in good faith, he or she is protected from liability even if the officer was acting illegally. "It would be manifestly unfair to impose civil liability upon a private person for doing that which the law declares it a misdemeanor for him to refuse to do." *Peterson v. Robison*, 277 P.2d 19, 24 (Cal. 1954).

If, however, a third party is not assisting police with making an arrest, the third party's presence during the execution of an arrest warrant might violate the Fourth Amendment. Recall from Chapter 4 that *Wilson v. Layne*, 526 U.S. 603, 614 (1999), held **"it is a violation of the Fourth Amendment for police to bring members of the media or other third parties into a home during the execution of a warrant when the presence of the third parties in the home was not in aid of the execution of the warrant."** Thus, officers should not permit a third party to accompany them inside a residence for any purpose unless (1) the resident voluntarily consents to the third party's entry, or (2) the third party's presence is reasonably necessary for police to carry out their duties. If third parties are enlisted to help in the execution of a warrant, the purpose of their presence should be spelled out in the application for the warrant and in the warrant itself.

Discretion Even though a law enforcement officer clearly has the ability and authority to arrest, good police practice may call for the arrest to be delayed or not to be made at all. It is beyond the scope of this book to give detailed guidelines in this area, but a brief discussion is necessary to set out general principles.

A law enforcement officer's primary duty is to protect the public at large. Therefore, when an arrest would create a great risk of public harm or would cause embarrassment to a person who poses no real threat to the community, proper police practice may call for delay or restraint in exercising the power of arrest. For example, when a crowd is present, it is often unwise to arrest a person who is creating a minor disturbance. An arrest may aggravate the disturbance and possibly precipitate a riot or civil disorder. Less drastic ways to handle the matter should be explored, even though legal grounds for an arrest may exist. The same considerations apply to minor squabbles and disturbances by intoxicated persons who are creating no danger and may need no more than help in getting home.

An arrest is a significant restraint on a person's freedom and should always be justified by circumstances. Law enforcement agencies generally have policies covering discretion to arrest. Where no policies exist, officers must use their common sense and good judgment. Authority to arrest does not necessarily mean duty to arrest.

Additional Procedures for Executing an Arrest Warrant

Executing an arrest warrant involves additional considerations in addition to those applicable to making a warrantless arrest. First, when officers are directed to execute an arrest warrant, their belief in the guilt of the defendant or their personal knowledge of facts pertaining to the offense is immaterial. The offense need not be committed in their presence and they need not have probable cause to believe that the defendant committed the offense. Officers are simply required to carry out the command of the warrant in a constitutionally reasonable manner if the warrant is valid on its face.

Determining the Facial Validity of a Warrant When the accused is identified in the warrant by name or description, a law enforcement officer is required to exercise reasonable diligence to make sure only the person designated in the warrant is arrested. If the person being arrested claims not to be the person identified in the warrant, the arresting officer should make a reasonable effort to verify the claim or the officer risks civil liability for damages.

A warrant that is invalid on its face gives the officer executing it no protection and no authority to arrest. An officer must examine the warrant if it is available and risks civil liability for damages for executing a warrant obviously invalid on its face. An arrest warrant is invalid on its face if one or more of the following are true:

▶ The court issuing the warrant clearly has no jurisdiction.

▶ The warrant fails to adequately indicate the crime charged.

▶ The warrant fails to name or describe any identifiable person.

▶ The warrant is not signed by the issuing magistrate.

▶ The warrant is not directed to the officer who is about to execute it. (If a warrant is directed to all law enforcement officers in a jurisdiction, any officer may execute it. If, however, the warrant is directed only to the sheriff of a particular county, only that sheriff or a deputy sheriff may execute it.)

Once an officer determines that a warrant is valid on its face, the officer must carry out the warrant's commands and arrest the person identified in the warrant. The officer no longer has any personal discretion and is merely carrying out an order of the court.

Place of Execution

Territorial Limits Most states allow arrest warrants for violations of state law to be executed at any place within the boundaries of the state. However, a law enforcement officer of one state may not go into another state to arrest under a warrant except in fresh pursuit (discussed later in this chapter).

Entry into a Suspect's Home Under *United States v. Watson*, 423 U.S. 411 (1976), police may make a warrantless arrest in a public place based on probable cause. *See also McClish v. Nugent*, 483 F.3d 1231 (11th Cir. 2007). But, as stated earlier, *Payton v. New York* held that absent consent or exigent circumstances, law enforcement officers must have at least an arrest warrant to lawfully enter a suspect's home to arrest the suspect. Moreover, at the time of the execution of such an arrest warrant, an officer must have "reason to believe the suspect is within" the dwelling that officers seek to enter. 445 U.S. at 603.

> [I]n order for law enforcement officials to enter a residence to execute an arrest warrant for a resident of the premises, the facts and circumstances within the knowledge of the law enforcement agents, when viewed in the totality, must warrant a reasonable belief that [1] the location to be searched is the suspect's dwelling, and that [2] the suspect is within the residence at the time of entry. . . .
> In evaluating this on-the-spot determination, as to the second *Payton* prong, courts must be sensitive to common sense factors indicating a resident's presence. For example, officers may take into consideration the possibility that the

resident may be aware that police are attempting to ascertain whether or not the resident is at home, and officers may presume that a person is at home at certain times of the day—a presumption which can be rebutted by contrary evidence regarding the suspect's known schedule. *United States v. Magluta*, 44 F.3d 1530, 1535 (11th Cir. 1995).

The Supreme Court has repeatedly reinforced *Payton*'s holding that, absent consent or exigent circumstances, **"the firm line at the entrance to the house may not reasonably be crossed without a warrant."** *Kirk v. Louisiana*, 536 U.S. 635, 636 (2002); *cf. United States v. Santana*, 427 U.S. 38 (1976) (arrest without a warrant in the doorway of a dwelling upheld since no Fourth Amendment expectation of privacy existed in such a location). However, some courts have held that the *Payton* rule does not apply to vestibules and common areas of multiple-tenant buildings. *See, e.g., United States v. Nohara*, 3 F.3d 1239, 1241 (9th Cir.1993); *United States v. Holland*, 755 F.2d 253 (2d Cir. 1985). These courts upheld non-consensual, non-emergency arrests of defendants who answered the doorbell in the vestibule of his apartment building because the arresting officer had probable cause to believe that the defendant was involved in criminal activity. Other courts, however, have limited the vestibule/common area exception only to *large* apartment buildings, reasoning that a tenant in a small multiple-tenant building (such as a duplex or multiple-family home) has a reasonable expectation of privacy in their common areas. *United States v. King*, 227 F.3d 732 (6th Cir. 2000); *Logan v. Commonwealth*, 616 S.E.2d 744 (Va. App. 2005). Law enforcement officers should verify the law controlling this issue in their jurisdiction.

Entry into a Third Party's Home *Steagald v. United States*, 451 U.S. 204 (1981), held that an arrest warrant does not authorize law enforcement officers to enter the home of a third person to search for the person to be arrested, in the absence of consent or exigent circumstances. To protect the Fourth Amendment privacy interests of persons not named in an arrest warrant, a search warrant must be obtained to justify the entry into the home of any person other than the person to be arrested. The Court said:

> In the absence of exigent circumstances, we have consistently held that [law enforcement officers' determinations of probable cause] are not reliable enough to justify an entry into a person's home to arrest him without a warrant, or a search of a home for objects in the absence of a search warrant. We see no reason to depart from this settled course when the search of a home is for a person rather than an object.
>
> A contrary conclusion—that the police, acting alone and in the absence of exigent circumstances, may decide when there is sufficient justification for searching the home of a third party for the subject of an arrest warrant—would create a significant potential for abuse. Armed solely with an arrest warrant for a single person, the police could search all the homes of that individual's friends and acquaintances. . . . Moreover, an arrest warrant may serve as the pretext for entering a home in which the police have suspicion, but not probable cause to believe, that illegal activity is taking place. 451 U.S. at 215.

If police have probable cause to believe that someone for whom they have an arrest warrant is located in the home of a third person, *Steagald* requires that law enforcement seek a search warrant to enter the third party's home. The

Supreme Court suggested that in most instances the police may avoid altogether the need to obtain a search warrant simply by waiting for a suspect to leave the third person's home before attempting to arrest the suspect. When the suspect leaves either the home of a third person or his or her own home and is in a public place, officers may arrest on probable cause alone. Neither an arrest warrant nor a search warrant is required to support an arrest made in a public place.

A handful of courts have carved out some minor exceptions to *Steagald*'s requirement of a search warrant to enter a third person's home to arrest a suspect. *United States v. Donaldson*, 793 F.2d 498 (2d Cir. 1986), held that a search warrant was not required when the third party homeowner knowingly allowed a fleeing felon to enter his home, and therefore the search of the residence could be justified as a search incident to the arrest of the homeowner for harboring a fugitive. And *United States v. Riis*, 83 F.3d 212 (8th Cir. 1996), held that a search warrant was not required to arrest a suspect at the home of a third party when police reasonably believed that the suspect was the third party's girlfriend and that she possessed common authority over the home they shared. *See also Watts v. County of Sacramento*, 256 F.3d 886 (9th Cir. 2001).

Exigent Circumstances In neither *Payton* nor *Steagald* did the Supreme Court specify the nature of the **exigent circumstances** that would justify a warrantless entry of a home to make an arrest. *Welsh v. Wisconsin*, 466 U.S. 740, 753 (1984), however, held:

> **[A]n important factor to be considered when determining whether any exigency exists is the gravity of the underlying offense for which the arrest is being made. Moreover, although no exigency is created simply because there is probable cause to believe that a serious crime has been committed . . . application of the exigent-circumstances exception in the context of a home entry should rarely be sanctioned when there is probable cause to believe that only a minor offense . . . has been committed.**

Thus, *Welsh* appears to have held that for an exigent circumstance exception to apply, thereby allowing a warrantless home arrest, the underlying crime for which the arrest will be made needs to be a serious one. As a result, even when emergency circumstances exist, such as the threat of removal or destruction of evidence from a home, warrantless home arrests for misdemeanors are highly suspect under *Welsh*.

In the wake of *Welsh*, courts have established several categories of exigent circumstances that have been held to authorize a law enforcement officer's warrantless entry into a home:

▶ a risk that evidence will be destroyed;

▶ hot pursuit of a fleeing felon;

▶ a threat to the safety of a suspect or others; and

▶ a likelihood that the suspect will flee and thereby escape.

Let's look at these types of exigencies in more detail.

▶ Destruction of Evidence: A warrantless entry into a dwelling may be made if there is a strong likelihood that evidence or contraband will be lost, destroyed, or removed from premises if police fail to take immediate action.

E.g., United States v. Martins, 413 F.3d 139 (1st Cir.), *cert. denied*, 126 S. Ct. 644 (2005). In *Welsh v. Wisconsin*, the warrantless arrest of the defendant in his home for a "non-jailable" traffic offense (fleeing the scene of an accident) was held illegal. The driver in *Welsh* had lost control of his car and ended up in a field, causing no injury or damage. But a witness told police that the man who walked away from the car was either intoxicated or sick. They went to his home (not in hot pursuit) and made a warrantless arrest on the theory that they needed to quickly obtain a blood sample from him for blood-alcohol testing. When he refused to give the sample, his license was suspended for violating the state's implied consent law. He challenged the license suspension on the grounds that the police violated *Payton* in entering his home to arrest him without a warrant. The Supreme Court sided with the driver and held that there was no exigency that justified violating *Payton*'s command that a warrant is necessary to enter a home to make an arrest. Key to the Court's rationale, however, was the nature of the underlying offense—one that under relevant state law was merely a civil forfeiture traffic violation, not a criminal offense for which any imprisonment was possible. *See also United States v. Mikell*, 102 F.3d 470 (11th Cir. 1996).

In the wake of *Welsh*, some states upheld warrantless entries when the underlying crime was a serious one. For example, *State v. Lamont*, 631 N.W.2d 603 (S.D. 2001), upheld a warrantless entry into a suspect's home to obtain a blood-alcohol sample from him after a felony hit-and-run accident caused a vehicular homicide. And in *Illinois v. McArthur*, 531 U.S. 326 (2001), the Court held that the need to preserve evidence of "jailable offenses" (possession of marijuana and drug paraphernalia in *McArthur*) was sufficiently urgent or pressing to justify the police in keeping the defendant from entering his home. The Court noted, however, that **"[t]emporarily keeping a person from entering his home, a consequence whenever police stop a person on the street, is considerably less intrusive than police entry into the home itself in order to make a warrantless arrest or conduct a search."** 531 U.S. at 336. Note that the Court did not decide whether the need to preserve evidence would have justified a greater allowance for a "jailable offense" than a "non-jailable" offense (although *Welsh* clearly implies that more latitude will be given for warrantless home entries to preserve evidence for "jailable offenses"). A more definite resolution of these issues awaits a case that presents them.

In *Minnesota v. Olson*, 495 U.S. 91 (1990), the U.S. Supreme Court approved the Minnesota Supreme Court's standard for determining whether exigent circumstances exist. The Minnesota court held that "a warrantless intrusion may be justified by hot pursuit of a fleeing felon, or imminent destruction of evidence . . . or the need to prevent a suspect's escape, or the risk of danger to the police or to other persons inside or outside the dwelling." 436 N.W.2d at 97. Furthermore, **"in the absence of hot pursuit there must be at least probable cause to believe that one or more of the other factors justifying the entry were present and that in assessing the risk of danger, the gravity of the crime and likelihood that the suspect is armed should be considered."** 495 U.S. at 100.

Applying this standard, exigent circumstances justifying the warrantless entry into a home to make an arrest were determined not to exist in the *Olson* case, in which:

▶ although a grave crime was involved, the defendant was known not to be the murderer;

▶ the police had already recovered the murder weapon;

▶ there was no suggestion of danger to the two women with whom the defendant was staying;

▶ several police squads surrounded the house;

▶ the time was 3 P.M. Sunday;

▶ it was evident the suspect was not going anywhere; and

▶ if he came out of the house, he would have been promptly apprehended.

▶ **Hot Pursuit** *Warden v. Hayden*, 387 U.S. 294 (1967), held that **hot pursuit** of the perpetrator of a serious crime constituted exigent circumstances. In that case, police officers had reliable information that an armed robbery had taken place and that the perpetrator had entered a certain house five minutes earlier. The Court held that the officers:

[a]cted reasonably when they entered the house and began to search for a man of the description they had been given and for weapons which he had used in the robbery or might use against them. The Fourth Amendment does not require police officers to delay in the course of an investigation if to do so would gravely endanger their lives or the lives of others. Speed here was essential, and only a thorough search of the house for persons and weapons could have insured that Hayden was the only man present and that the police had control of all weapons which could be used against them or to effect an escape. 387 U.S. at 298-99; *see also United States v. Williams*, 354 F.3d 497, 503 (6th Cir. 2003).

When the arrest of a suspect is set in motion in a public place, but the suspect retreats into his or her home, the right of officers to enter the home in hot pursuit is governed by *United States v. Santana*, 427 U.S. 38 (1976). In that case, police officers drove to the defendant's house after receiving information that she had in her possession marked money used to make a heroin buy arranged by an undercover agent. The defendant was standing in the doorway of her house holding a paper bag as the police pulled up within fifteen feet of her. The officers got out of the car, shouting "Police!" and the defendant retreated into her house, where she was then apprehended. When the defendant tried to pull away, envelopes containing heroin fell to the floor from the paper bag. Some of the marked money was found on her person.

The Court held that, while standing in the doorway of her house, the defendant was in a "public place" for purposes of the Fourth Amendment. She had no expectation of privacy since she was exposed to public view, speech, hearing, and touch, the same as if she had been standing completely outside her house. When police sought to arrest her, they merely intended to make a warrantless arrest in a public place based on probable cause. Under *United States v. Watson*, 423 U.S. 411 (1976), such an arrest would not violate the Fourth Amendment. By retreating into a private place, the defendant could not defeat an otherwise proper arrest that had been set in motion in a public place. The officers needed to act quickly to prevent the destruction of evidence, and so a true hot pursuit took place, even though it entailed only a very short chase. Thus, the warrantless entry to make the arrest was justified, as was the search incident to that arrest. Key to *Santana*'s logic was the fact that the defendant was outside of the confines of her home when the arrest process began. When a defendant is inside, however, law enforcement may not reach in, even by a few inches, to remove someone so that they are then technically outside of the confines of their home, such as on a porch. *See McClish v. Nugent*, 483 F.3d 1231 (11th 2007).

▶ **Threats to Safety:** A real and imminent threat to the safety of a suspect, to officers, or to others justifies an entry into a dwelling to make an arrest without a warrant. *United States v. Martins*, 413 F.3d 139 (1st Cir.), *cert. denied*, 126 S. Ct. 644 (2005). The primary motive for such a warrantless entry must be to render emergency aid and assistance, not to find evidence. *E.g., State v. Frankel*, 847 A.2d 561 (N.J.), *cert. denied*, 543 U.S. 876 (2004). Courts have upheld such warrantless entries in a number of situations, including:

> ▶ to extinguish a fire in a burning building, *see Michigan v. Tyler*, 436 U.S. 499 (1978).
>
> ▶ to break up a violent fight, *see Brigham City v. Stuart*, 126 S. Ct. 1943 (2006).
>
> ▶ to stop acts of domestic violence, *see United States v. Martinez*, 406 F.3d 1160 (9th Cir. 2005).
>
> ▶ to rescue a kidnapped infant, *see United States v. Laboy*, 909 F.2d 581, 586 (1st Cir.1990).
>
> ▶ to attend to a shooting or stabbing victim, *see United States v. Gillenwaters*, 890 F.2d 679, 682 (4th Cir. 1989).

While warrantless entry to a dwelling that is the scene of a homicide or potential homicide may be justified under the "safety/exigent circumstances" rationale when police reasonably believe that a person within is in need of immediate aid, there is no "murder scene exception" to the warrant requirement. *Thompson v. Louisiana*, 469 U.S. 17 (1984). Thus, while a warrantless entry may be made to give aid to victims, and a protective sweep may then be conducted to see if there are other victims or if a killer is still on premises (see Chapter 8), a full search of the premises is not permissible without a warrant.

▶ **Escape:** A warrantless entry into a dwelling to make an arrest may be justified to prevent the imminent escape of the person within during the time it would take to obtain a warrant authorizing entry and arrest. *E.g., United States v. Amburn*, 412 F.3d 909 (8th Cir. 2005). However, if police surround a home to make escape impossible, then they must wait for a warrant to enter and seize people and evidence inside the dwelling unless other exigent circumstances justify entry. *State v. Bowe*, 557 N.E.2d 139 (Ohio App. 1988).

Exigency May Not Be Police-Created Officers may not deliberately create exigent circumstances to subvert the warrant requirements of the Fourth Amendment. *State v. Carter*, 160 S.W.3d 526 (Tenn. 2005), *cert. denied*, 126 S. Ct. 1797 (2006). In considering claims of manufactured exigency, courts "distinguish between cases where exigent circumstances arise naturally during a delay in obtaining a warrant and those where officers have deliberately created the exigent circumstances." *United States v. Webster*, 750 F.2d 307, 327 (5th Cir. 1984); *see also Robinson v. Commonwealth*, 625 S.E.2d 651 (Va. App. 2006) (upholding delayed warrantless entry into backyard party until after officers saw teenagers engaged in underage drinking). *United States v. Hultgren*, 713 F.2d 79 (5th Cir. 1983), held that exigent circumstances arose naturally when the transmitter worn by a confidential informant participating in a drug buy suddenly failed. Concern for the confidential informant's safety justified a warrantless entry. *See also Buchanan ex rel. Estate of Buchanan v. Maine*, 417 F. Supp. 2d 45 (D. Me. 2006). In contrast, *United States v. Scheffer*, 463 F.2d 567 (5th Cir.), *cert. denied*, 409 U.S. 984 (1972), found a manufactured exigency where government agents enlisted the aid of co-defendants who had already been arrested to help them catch other members of a drug conspiracy. The agents sent the cooperating defendants into a residence to consummate a drug deal, and then made a warrantless entry to arrest the residents. The court refused to accept the government's argument that the agents lacked the time to obtain a warrant, because the agents controlled the timing of the drug buy. *See also United States v. Duchi*, 906 F.2d 1278 (8th Cir. 1990).

Manner of Execution

Notice Officers executing an arrest warrant should give the same notice, discussed earlier, they would give in making any arrest. In addition, officers should have the warrant in their possession at the time of arrest and should show the warrant to the person arrested. Failure to have the warrant in the arresting officer's possession does not affect the legality of the arrest. Officers must, however, inform the defendant of the offense charged and the existence of the warrant. If the defendant requests, officers must produce the warrant as soon as possible.

Timing Like a warrantless felony arrest, an arrest made under a warrant (for a felony or misdemeanor) need not be made immediately. Officers have considerable discretion in deciding the time to make an arrest under a warrant. They may have lawful strategic reasons for delay, or they may wish to select a time when the arrest can be accomplished with the least difficulty. "[T]he general rule is that, while execution should not be unreasonably delayed, law enforcement officers have a reasonable time in which to execute a warrant and need not arrest at the first opportunity." *United States v. Drake*, 655 F.2d 1025, 1027 (10th Cir. 1981).

Forced Entry As with the execution of search warrants, before making a forcible entry to execute an arrest warrant at a dwelling, officers must knock-and-announce their presence and authority; demand entry into the home; and be actually or constructively denied entry. *Wilson v. Arkansas*, 514 U.S. 927 (1995). As with search warrants, there are a number of exceptions to the knock-and-announce rule. The issues regarding the knock-and-announce rule, its exceptions, and the rules regarding forced entry are discussed in great detail in Chapter 4.

Return of the Warrant An officer executing an arrest warrant must make a return of the warrant. The return is made by entering on the warrant the date of the arrest, signing the warrant, and filing the warrant with the court. (See the arrest warrant forms in Figure 2.6.) Failure to return an arrest warrant may invalidate the arrest and subject the officer to civil liability for damages.

Place of Arrest

Territorial jurisdiction limits where someone may actually be arrested. However, a widely recognized exception to this rule allows law enforcement officers to arrest someone they began to pursue while within their territorial jurisdiction.

Territorial Limits In most states, law enforcement officers acting under authority of a warrant may make an arrest at any place within the state where the defendant may be found. Similarly, officers may serve a summons at any place within the state.

With respect to warrantless arrests, however, law enforcement officers acting outside the jurisdiction for which they were elected or appointed do not have any official power to arrest. *People v. Williams*, 829 N.E.2d 1203 (N.Y. 2005). Thus, sheriffs may not arrest without a warrant beyond the counties in which they have been elected, nor may municipal police officers arrest without a warrant beyond the limits of the cities in which they have been appointed. On the other hand, the authority of state law enforcement officers is statewide, and their power to arrest without a warrant runs throughout the state. Generally, a law enforcement officer of one state has no authority to arrest in another state.

There are two exceptions to the rule that officers may not arrest without a warrant outside their jurisdiction. The first, explored earlier, is when police make arrests outside their jurisdiction as private persons governed by the law of citizen's arrest. The other exception is when an extra-territorial arrest is made in fresh pursuit, a concept similar to hot pursuit, but used to describe the pursuit of a suspect across jurisdictional lines.

Fresh Pursuit Exception Under the common law and most statutes, law enforcement officers may make a lawful arrest without a warrant beyond the borders of their jurisdiction in **fresh pursuit**. Fresh pursuit means an officer's immediate pursuit of a criminal suspect into another jurisdiction after the officer has attempted to arrest the suspect in the officer's jurisdiction. The common law allowed a warrantless arrest in fresh pursuit only in felony cases; but today most state statutes allow warrantless arrests for both felonies and misdemeanors (subject to *Welsh*'s limitation on warrantless misdemeanor arrests at a suspect's home as described earlier). For a warrantless arrest in fresh pursuit to be legal, all of the following conditions must be met:

▶ The officer must have authority to arrest for the crime in the first place.

▶ The pursuit must be of a fleeing criminal attempting to avoid immediate capture.

▶ The pursuit must begin promptly and be maintained continuously.

The main requirement is that the pursuit be fresh. The pursuit must flow out of the act of attempting to make an arrest and must be a part of the continuous process of apprehension. The pursuit need not be instantaneous, but it must be made without unreasonable delay or interruption, and there should be no side trips or diversions, even for other police business. The continuity of pursuit is not legally broken by unavoidable interruptions connected with the act of apprehension, such as eating, sleeping, summoning assistance, or obtaining further information.

Fresh pursuit may lead a law enforcement officer outside the boundaries of his or her state. Ordinarily, an officer has no authority beyond that of a private citizen to make arrests in another state. Most states, however, have adopted the Uniform Act on Fresh Pursuit or similar legislation, which permits law enforcement officers from other states, entering in fresh pursuit, to make an arrest. The Uniform Fresh Pursuit Law of Iowa is typical:

> Any member of a duly organized state, county, or municipal law-enforcing unit of another state of the United States who enters this state in fresh pursuit, and continues within this state in such fresh pursuit, of a person in order to arrest the person on the ground that the person is believed to have committed a felony in such other state, shall have the same authority to arrest and hold such person in custody, as has any member of any duly organized state, county, or municipal law-enforcing unit of this state, to arrest and hold in custody a person on the ground that the person is believed to have committed a felony in this state. Iowa Code Ann. § 806.1; *see also, e.g.*, Ariz Rev. Stat. § 13-3832; West's Ann. Cal. Penal Code § 852.2; Vernon's Ann. Texas Code Crim Pro. art. 14.051.

Because some states extend the privilege to make an arrest in fresh pursuit to out-of-state officers only on a reciprocal basis, law enforcement officers must be familiar with not only the fresh pursuit statutes in their own state but also those of all neighboring states.

A law enforcement officer who makes an arrest in fresh pursuit under such a statute in a neighboring state must take the arrested person before an appropriate judicial officer in that state without unreasonable delay. Some states, however, allow an arresting officer from another state to take a person arrested in fresh pursuit back to the officer's home state after the arrested person is brought before an appropriate judicial officer. Other states allow this only by means of **extradition** or waiver of extradition. Extradition is a procedure whereby authorities in one state (the demanding state) demand from another state (the asylum state) that a fugitive from justice in the demanding state, who is present in the asylum state, be delivered to the demanding state. Federal law requires extradition of a "fugitive from justice." *See* 18 U.S.C. § 3182. Additionally, forty-eight states have adopted the Uniform Criminal Extradition Act, which provides uniform extradition procedures among the states, including the extradition of persons who commit criminal acts in states where they were never physically present.

Use of Force

A law enforcement officer's right to use force to arrest depends on the degree of force used and the context in which it is used. The basic rule covering the use of force while making an arrest is that law enforcement personnel may use whatever force is necessary to make the arrest, but may not use excessive

key points

- Unless there are extenuating circumstances, an officer arresting a person should give notice that the person is under arrest as well as notice of the officer's authority and the cause of arrest.
- Warrantless arrests are discretionary and should always be justified by the circumstances.
- If an arrest warrant is valid on its face, a law enforcement officer must execute the warrant within a reasonable time according to its terms, and the officer has no personal discretion in this matter.
- In general, law enforcement officers have no authority to make warrantless arrests outside the geographic limits of the jurisdiction for which they have been elected or appointed.
- Law enforcement officers may arrest outside their jurisdiction in "fresh pursuit." Fresh pursuit means an officer's immediate and continuously maintained pursuit of a criminal suspect into another jurisdiction after the officer has attempted to arrest the person in the officer's own jurisdiction.
- Absent exigent circumstances or consent, law enforcement officers may not make a warrantless entry into a suspect's home to make a routine felony arrest. Officers must have at least an arrest warrant to lawfully enter a suspect's home to arrest the suspect.
- Absent exigent circumstances or consent, an arrest warrant does not authorize law enforcement officers

- to enter the home of a third person to search for the person to be arrested. A search warrant must be obtained to justify the entry into the home of any person other than the person to be arrested.
- Exigent circumstances that would justify a warrantless entry of a dwelling to arrest are hot pursuit of a fleeing felon, imminent destruction of evidence, the need to prevent a suspect's escape, and the risk of danger to the police or to other persons. In assessing the risk of danger, the gravity of the crime and the likelihood that the suspect is armed should be considered.
- If an arrest is begun in a public place, officers in hot pursuit may enter a dwelling without a warrant to complete the arrest.
- Before law enforcement officers may lawfully force their way into a dwelling to arrest someone inside (absent extenuating circumstances), they should first knock on the door, announce their authority and purpose, and then demand admittance and be refused admittance.
- An officer executing an arrest warrant must make a return of the warrant. The return is made by entering on the warrant the date of the arrest, signing the warrant, and filing the warrant with the court. Failure to return an arrest warrant may invalidate the arrest and subject the officer to civil liability for damages.

force. *E.g., Papineau v. Parmley*, 465 F.3d 46 (2d Cir. 2006); *Smith v. District of Columbia*, 882 A.2d 778 (D.C. 2005). This section is devoted to exploring the limitations the Fourth Amendment places on the use of force in contextually differentiating reasonable force under the totality of the circumstances from that which is "excessive."

Resisting Arrest When a suspect submits to the authority of law enforcement and offers no resistance, officers may not use any force to make such an arrest other than the minor levels of physical force needed to apply handcuffs and escort the arrestee to a police vehicle or station. *See, e.g., Couden v. Duffy*, 446 F.3d 483 (3d Cir. 2006). It is only when a suspect is not cooperative that the use of force will be deemed "reasonable" under the Fourth Amendment. But there is a difference between a suspect who is merely not cooperative and one who is truly resisting arrest. *See Sheehan v. State*, 201 S.W.3d 820 (Tex. App. 2006).

Defining the Crime of Resisting Arrest **Resisting arrest** is a crime consisting of a person's interference with a law enforcement officer's lawful ability to take the person into custody. The following statute is a typical one defining the crime of resisting arrest:

> (a) A person commits the crime of resisting arrest if he knowingly prevents or attempts to prevent a police officer, acting under color of his official authority, from effecting an arrest of the actor or another, by: (1) using or threatening to use physical force or violence against the police officer or another; or (2) using any other means which creates a substantial risk of causing bodily injury to such police officer or another. MASS. GEN. LAWS ch. 268, § 32B.

As the language of the above-quoted statutes implies, active opposition such as shooting, striking, pushing, or some other form of actively resisting the officer is usually required. *Commonwealth v. Grandison*, 741 N.E.2d 25 (Mass. 2001). Struggling to prevent being handcuffed, for example, is sufficient active resistance to justify a resisting arrest charge. *State v. Briggs*, 894 A.2d 1008 (2006). Actual injury to the officer, however, is not an element of the crime. *Sampson v. State*, 640 S.E.2d 673 (Ga. Ct. App. 2006).

In contrast, mere flight, concealment, other avoidance or evasion of arrest usually do not constitute the crime of resisting arrest, although state laws differ on the issue of flight. Some states consider flight to constitute resisting arrest if the defendant fled with the knowledge that the officer had intended to lawfully arrest him or her. *See, e.g., Jean-Marie v. State*, 947 So. 2d 484 (Fla. Dist. Ct. App. 2006); *Whaley v. State*, 843 N.E.2d 1 (Ind. App. 2006). Other states make flight a separate offense if the evasion is done in a manner that creates a risk of death or injury. *See State v. Turner*, 193 S.W.3d 522 (Tenn. 2006) (applying TENN. CODE ANN. § 39-16-603(b)(3)). And still other states would consider flight as satisfying the elements of some other crime like eluding or reckless endangerment. *See, e.g., State v. Ferebee*, 630 S.E.2d 460 (N.C. App. 2006).

Similarly, verbal objections—even loud protests that use curse words—or threats unaccompanied by force usually do not constitute the crime of resisting arrest. *See, e.g., Woodward v. Gray*, 527 S.E.2d 595 (2000). However, a minority of states do allow strictly verbal conduct to constitute the crime of resisting arrest. *See, e.g., People v. Christopher*, 40 Cal. Rptr. 3d 615 (Cal. App. 2006); *People v. Vasquez*, 612 N.W.2d 162 (Mich. App. 2000). However, even in states that follow the majority approach that mere words, without more, are insufficient, a serious, imminent threat that prevents an officer from acting because of reasonable fear of serious bodily injury may constitute the crime of resisting arrest. *See State v. Wozniak*, 486 P.2d 1025 (1971); *Wise v. Commonwealth*, 641 S.E.2d 134 (Va. App. 2007).

Common Law Approach to Resisting Arrest Under the common law rule, the crime of resisting arrest required that the arrest be lawful. Thus, if the arrest was unlawful, a person had the right to resist the unlawful arrest using what amount of force was reasonably necessary for self-defense and prevention of impending injury. *See, e.g., Bad Elk v. United States*, 177 U.S. 529 (1900) (holding a defendant had the right to use such force as was necessary to resist an attempted illegal arrest). As a result of these rules, it was always important for arresting officers to: establish their identity, if not already known or obvious; and to explain their purpose and authority.

The right to resist an unlawful arrest extended to arrests that were being executed in an unlawful manner, such as when police used excessive force to effectuate what would have otherwise been a legal seizure of a person.

> Simply stated, the law recognizes that liberty can be restored through legal processes but life or limb cannot be repaired in a courtroom. And so it holds

that the reason for outlawing resistance to an unlawful arrest and requiring disputes over its legality to be resolved in the courts has no controlling application on the right to resist an officer's excessive force. . . .

Two qualifications on the citizen's right to defend against and to repel an officer's excessive force must be noticed. He cannot use greater force in protecting himself against the officer's unlawful force than reasonably appears to be necessary. If he employs such greater force, then he becomes the aggressor and forfeits the right to claim self-defense to a charge of assault and battery on the officer. . . . Furthermore, if he knows that if he desists from his physically defensive measures and submits to arrest the officer's unlawfully excessive force would cease, the arrestee must desist or lose his privilege of self-defense. *State v. Mulvihill*, 270 A.2d 277, 280 (N.J. 1970).

Modern Approach to Resisting Arrest While some states continue to use the common law rule allowing resistance to an illegal arrest, an increasing number of states have adopted a modern trend that began in the 1960s. Modern law rejects the common law rule in light of the dangers inherent in its approach, and because the consequences of an illegal arrest are at most a brief period of detention during which arrested persons can resort to nonviolent legal remedies for regaining their liberty. However, even in those states that hold an arrestee has no right to resist an unlawful arrest, all states adhere to the common law's approach on the right to use force in self-defense against an arresting officer's excessive force. Thus, for example, the court in *Shoultz v. State*, 735 N.E.2d 818 (Ind. Ct. App. 2000), held that because an officer had used excessive force in making a misdemeanor arrest, the defendant was privileged to offer reasonable resistance to the excessive force without running afoul of the state's resistance statute. Key to the court's reasoning was that the defendant never threatened the officer with any force or violence, nor had anyone touched the officer before he used pepper spray and a flashlight to subdue defendant. Moreover, the officer neither informed the defendant that he was under arrest nor attempted to handcuff him before using force.

The Common Law Approach to Using Force to Make an Arrest If a suspect resisted arrest, the common law differentiated the permissible levels of force that could be used in making an arrest based upon the underlying crime. Thus, there was one rule governing the use of force for misdemeanor arrests, and another rule for felony arrests.

Misdemeanors At common law, law enforcement officers were permitted to use any reasonably necessary *non-deadly* force to arrest for a misdemeanor. However, an officer was not justified in using *deadly* force to arrest for a misdemeanor. *E.g., State v. Wall*, 286 S.E.2d 68 (N.C. 1982). The rationale underlying the common law rule was that it would be better for a misdemeanant to escape than for a human life to be taken in the pursuit of a minor lawbreaker. Thus, the common law held that the use of deadly force on a misdemeanant was excessive force constituting an assault and/or battery. Moreover, an officer who killed a suspected misdemeanant could be held criminally liable for murder or manslaughter, as well as civilly liable for damages.

Felonies Under the common law rule, a law enforcement officer could use any reasonably necessary *non-deadly* force to arrest for a felony. But unlike with misdemeanor arrests, deadly force could be used to make a felony arrest if the suspect fled.

> If persons that are pursued by these officers for felony or the just suspicion thereof . . . shall not yield themselves to these officers, but shall either resist or fly before they are apprehended or being apprehended shall rescue themselves and resist or fly, so that they cannot be otherwise apprehended, and are upon necessity slain therein, because they cannot be otherwise taken, it is no felony." 2 M. Hale, Historia Placitorum Coronae 85 (1736).

Under the rule, an officer was not required to retreat from making an arrest to avoid extreme measures, but was required to press on and use all necessary force to bring the offender into custody. The use of deadly force was therefore permitted as a last resort if the only alternative was to abandon the attempt to arrest.

Self-Defense and Defense of Others It should be noted that the common law's felony/misdemeanor distinction to the use of force applied only to making an arrest when the would-be arrestee fled or resisted arrest; it did not apply when the arrestee used or attempted to use unlawful force against the police officer or a third party. If such unlawful force was being used against the officer or a third party, then the rules of self-defense or defense of others came into play, and the arresting officer was not bound by the usual rules for the use of force in making arrests.

▶ **Self-Defense**—A law enforcement officer may use a reasonable amount of non-deadly force to defend himself or herself against the imminent, unlawful application of non-deadly force to the officer. If, however, the officer is faced with imminent, unlawful deadly force, then the officer is privileged to use deadly force to defend himself or herself against such unlawful deadly force.

▶ **Defense of Others**—A law enforcement officer may use a reasonable amount of non-deadly force to defend a third party against an imminent, unlawful attack involving non-deadly force. If, however, the third party is faced with imminent, unlawful deadly force, then an officer is privileged to use deadly force to defend the third party against such unlawful deadly force.

When making an arrest, if someone begins to assault or batter a law enforcement officer, then the arrestee has transformed the situation into a self-defense one, thereby making it lawful for the officer to use any force reasonably necessary under the circumstances, including deadly force, if the officer reasonably believes that the person to be arrested is about to commit an assault and that the officer is in danger of death or serious bodily injury. The law enforcement officer's duty is to be the aggressor and to press forward to bring the person under restraint. This cannot be accomplished by purely defensive action on an officer's part. Therefore, if an officer has lawful authority to arrest, the officer is not required to back down in the face of physical resistance to the arrest. An officer faced with the choice of abandoning an arrest or using deadly force in self-defense has the right to use deadly force in response to an immediate threat of death or serious bodily injury. *See, e.g., Salim v. Proulx*, 93 F.3d 86 (2d Cir. 1996).

The Modern Approach The common law's approach to a law enforcement officer's privilege to use force, even deadly force, in self-defense or in defense of others remains the law today in nearly all U.S. jurisdictions. However, the common law's distinction between felonies and misdemeanors in the lawful use of force to make an arrest over a suspect's flight or resistance has become "untenable" in modern times. *Tennessee v. Garner*, 471 U.S. 1, 14 (1985). The common law rule originated in an era when all felonies were capital crimes punishable by death, all felons were considered dangerous, defendants had meager rights, and few of those arrested and tried for felonies escaped conviction and death. Consequently, the use of deadly force to apprehend fleeing felons was viewed merely as a more timely and less costly implementation of the eventual penalty for their offenses. In addition, professional police forces did not exist at that time; the responsibility for apprehending fleeing felons fell to unarmed and untrained citizens who responded to the hue and cry. Weapons were primitive, and the use of force often meant hand-to-hand combat, which was seldom deadly, although it posed significant danger to the arresting person.

In modern times, most felonies are not punishable by death; fewer felons are convicted or executed; and police are organized, trained, equipped with sophisticated weapons, and capable of killing accurately at a distance and under circumstances posing little danger to officers or others, especially if the felon is unarmed. Operation of the common law rule under these circumstances would allow police to kill persons merely suspected of offenses that, on conviction, would very likely result in only brief imprisonment or even probation. Thus, today, the misdemeanor/felony distinction has been replaced by a balancing test that analyzes the use of force for its "reasonableness" under the Fourth Amendment, applying a totality-of-the-circumstances approach. *Graham v. Connor*, 490 U.S. 386 (1989).

In *Graham*, the U.S. Supreme Court set forth the following factors as the three primary ones to be examined when making a reasonableness inquiry about the use of force:

▶ the severity of the crime at issue;

▶ whether the suspect poses an immediate threat to the safety of the officers or others; and

▶ whether he is actively resisting arrest or attempting to evade arrest by flight.

The application of this balancing test has produced rules that are similar, but not identical, to the common law's approach.

Non-Deadly Force A law enforcement officer making an arrest—whether for a felony or a misdemeanor—has the right to use a reasonable amount of non-deadly force to make the arrest.

> The officer has discretion to determine the degree of force required under the circumstances as they appear to the officer at the time. The reasonableness of the force used is a question for the trier of facts. The test to determine the actual amount of force necessary is not one of hindsight. The degree of force used may be reasonable even though it is more than is actually required. The officer may not, however, use an unreasonable amount of force or wantonly

or maliciously injure a suspect. *Clark v. Thomas*, 505 F.Supp.2d 884 (D. Kan. 2007).

Under this approach, only minimal force, such as that necessary to apply handcuffs, would be necessary to make an arrest of a cooperative suspect. However, the more a suspect resists, the more non-deadly force could be lawfully used to make the arrest.

Deadly Force The modern parameters for the use of deadly force were established by the U.S. Supreme Court in *Tennessee v. Garner*, 471 U.S. 1 (1985). In *Garner*, a woman called the police to report that a "prowler" was attempting to break in to her neighbor's home. When police arrived on the scene, the woman gestured toward an adjacent property and told police that she had heard glass breaking. When officers went to investigate, they heard a door slam and saw someone, later identified as Edward Garner, running across the backyard until he came to a stop at a six-feet-high chain link fence.

> With the aid of a flashlight, [the officer] was able to see Garner's face and hands. He saw no sign of a weapon, and, though not certain, was "reasonably sure" and "figured" that Garner was unarmed. He thought Garner was 17 or 18 years old and about 5'5" or 5'7" tall. While Garner was crouched at the base of the fence, [the officer] called out "police, halt" and took a few steps toward him. Garner then began to climb over the fence. Convinced that if Garner made it over the fence he would elude capture, [the officer] shot him. The bullet hit Garner in the back of the head. Garner was taken by ambulance to a hospital, where he died on the operating table. Ten dollars and a purse taken from the house were found on his body. 471 U.S. at 3-4.

The officer's use of deadly force to seize Garner would have been permissible under the common law since burglary is a felony and, therefore, Garner was a fleeing felon. And, at the time, both the laws of the State of Tennessee and the relevant police regulations governing the use of deadly force both were in accord with the common law. Thus, according to the law in effect at the time of the shooting, the use of deadly force to stop Garner was justified. 471 U.S. at 3-4 (citing TENN. CODE ANN. § 40-7-108 (1982)).

Garner's father filed a suit under 42 U.S.C. § 1983 asserting that his son was unconstitutionally seized in violation of the Fourth Amendment because the use of deadly force against him was unreasonable under the facts and circumstances of the case. The Supreme Court ultimately agreed with Garner's father and declared that the **"use of deadly force to prevent the escape of all felony suspects, whatever the circumstances, is constitutionally unreasonable."** 471 U.S. at 11. In so ruling, the Court overruled the centuries-old common law approach governing the use of deadly force in making arrests and, accordingly, the Tennessee statute based upon the common law rule. In its place, the Court reasoned that the "reasonableness" command of the Fourth Amendment required the following approach:

> **It is not better that all felony suspects die than that they escape. Where the suspect poses no immediate threat to the officer and no threat to others, the harm resulting from failing to apprehend him does not justify the use of deadly force to do so. It is no doubt unfortunate when a suspect who is in sight escapes, but the fact that the police arrive a little late or are a little slower afoot does not always justify killing the suspect.**

> **A police officer may not seize an unarmed, non-dangerous suspect by shooting him dead. . . .**
>
> **Where the officer has probable cause to believe that the suspect poses a threat of serious physical harm, either to the officer or to others, it is not constitutionally unreasonable to prevent escape by using deadly force. Thus, *if the suspect threatens the officer with a weapon or there is probable cause to believe that he has committed a crime involving the infliction or threatened infliction of serious physical harm, deadly force may be used if necessary to prevent escape*, and if, where feasible, some warning has been given.** 471 U. S. at 11-12 (italics added).

In effect, the *Garner* decision constitutionalized the common law approach to misdemeanants, as even violent misdemeanors rarely involve the inflection of *serious* bodily harm. Thus, just as it was under the common law, police are not justified in using deadly force to arrest for a misdemeanor. But *Garner* altered the common law rule regarding fleeing felons. Today, deadly force may only be used by law enforcement officers:

▶ in defense of their own lives (i.e., to prevent an imminent, unlawful attack that poses a risk of death or serious bodily harm to the officer);

▶ in defense of the lives of others (i.e., again to prevent an imminent, unlawful attack that poses a risk of death or serious bodily harm to a third party);

▶ to stop the escape of a fleeing suspect if there is probable cause to believe that the suspect has committed a crime involving the infliction or threatened infliction of serious physical harm.

Excessive Force under the Fourth Amendment Using unnecessary force against a cooperative suspect is nearly always unreasonable. For example, in *Couden v. Duffy*, 446 F.3d 483 (3d Cir. 2006), police set up a surveillance team outside a home based on a tip that a fugitive wanted on drug and weapons-related charges might be staying at that address. At approximately 8:30 P.M., the occupant of the home pulled up in a car in front of the house and let her fourteen-year-old son, carrying a skateboard, out of the vehicle. The boy was supposed to put his skateboard in the garage and then get his sister from the house so the family could then all go out to dinner together. But the boy then "saw a man charging towards him with a gun. Frightened, he slammed the garage door shut, remaining inside." 446 F.3d at 490. Mistakenly believing the boy was the fugitive they wanted, four police officers pursued the boy into the house. They jumped on him to subdue him; one officer put his knee into the boy's back; other officers pointed guns at the boy's head, handcuffed him, and sprayed him with mace. Because the boy was cooperative and police had no reason to believe that the boy was armed, dangerous, or that any accomplice was present, the court held that police officers used **excessive force** to seize the boy in violation of the Fourth Amendment. When police use unnecessary force against a cooperative suspect, they expose themselves to liability. In refusing to apply the doctrine of qualified immunity to the facts of one such case, *Payne v. Pauley*, 337 F.3d 767, 780 (7th Cir. 2003), held that it was "well established" that applying handcuffs unusually tightly and then violently yanking the arms of arrestees "who were not resisting arrest, did not disobey the orders of a police officer, did not pose a threat to the safety of the officer or others" constituted excessive force prohibited by the Fourth Amendment.

On the other hand, when police have reason to believe someone is armed and dangerous, then their use of even deadly force is justified. In *Boyd v. Baeppler*, 215 F.3d 594 (6th Cir. 2000), for example, police officers used deadly force against a suspect who had a gun in his hand and who pointed it at officers and others. This rule applies even when the police are mistaken, so long as their mistake is both honest and reasonable. For example, in *Bell v. City of East Cleveland*, 125 F.3d 855 (6th Cir. 1997), the court upheld the actions of a police officer who shot a young boy who was carrying only a toy gun. The officer thought the gun was real. When the boy did not follow the officer's command to put the gun down, and the boy pointed the gun at the officer, the officer shot the boy.

There are countless situations, however, that lie in between a cooperative suspect who submits to the authority of an arresting officer and one who resists using actual or perceived deadly force. These are the "tough cases" that need to be judged under the totality of the circumstances under *Graham*'s balancing test. While a comprehensive review of the use of force by law enforcement is beyond the scope of this book, several scenarios in the "gray area" receive much attention in the courts and are therefore summarized in a general manner here.

Non-Deadly Force and Special Medical Circumstances If the use of non-deadly force by law enforcement while making an arrest inadvertently causes the death of a suspect or bodily injury to a suspect, courts usually find in favor of the police unless the officer either knew or had objective reasons to know of a suspect's particular susceptibility to the tactic used. For example, in *Hendon v. City of Piedmont*, 163 F. Supp. 2d 1316 (N.D. Ala. 2001), police arrested a seventy-four-year-old woman in connection with her behavior while driving. The woman had disregarded a police roadblock for a funeral procession and was pulled over accordingly. However, she drove away from the scene before the officer could finish issuing a traffic citation to her, having told the officer she was "smothering" and needed to get to her physician's office. The officer pursued her and used his car to block hers. He then used minor force to remove the woman from her car, whereupon she slapped him. He then handcuffed her in a manner that resulted in minor bruising and bleeding on her wrists. As her breathing became more labored, she was transported to a hospital where she subsequently died of a heart attack. Her family sued, claiming that her verbal protestations about her breathing coupled with the fact that she had disabled license tags on her car should have been sufficient to put the officer on notice that even the minor force he used would have been excessive for someone in her condition. The court rejected this assertion and held that the officer's actions were objectively reasonable under the Fourth Amendment. *See also Estate of Smith v. Marasco*, 430 F.3d 140 (3d Cir. 2005).

In contrast, law enforcement officers must be careful about the level of force they use against a suspect who has visible signs of an injury or special medical condition that might establish the reasonable likelihood of a suspect's vulnerable condition and thereby counsel against the use of a level of force that might otherwise have been lawfully employed. For example, in *Guite v. Wright*, 147 F.3d 747 (8th Cir. 1998), police went to a suspect's home to arrest him. The suspect was at home recovering from surgery on his left shoulder. In spite of the fact that he was wearing a sling on his left arm, officers grabbed his wrist, pushed him backwards, and held him up against the open door inside the house. The court ruled that the suspect had a valid claim for excessive force under the circumstances. The same result was reached in *Howard v. Dickerson*, 34 F.3d 978 (10th Cir. 1994), when a suspect wearing a neck brace advised officers that she had just undergone surgery, yet police handcuffed her with her hands behind her back in spite of requests not to put her arms in that position. *See also Aceto v. Kachajian*, 240 F. Supp. 2d 121 (D. Mass. 2003).

Conducted Energy Devices Starting in approximately the year 2001, a number of law enforcement organizations began to use conducted energy devices (CEDs), more commonly referred to as "stun-guns" or by the brand-name Tasers.® CEDs, which have a range of approximately twenty-one feet, deliver a shock to the recipient, thereby incapacitating him or her, and thereby obviating the need for deadly force. But CEDs have been linked to well over 150 deaths since 2001 (see Amnesty Int'l, 2006). One court described CEDs as follows:

> [T]he Taser is designed to deliver a 50,000-volt shock; the shock overrides the body's central nervous system, causing total incapacitation of the muscles and instant collapse; on the use-of-force continuum, the Taser falls in the highest category of force, just one step down from the use of deadly force; the Taser can cause severe muscle contractions that may result in injuries to muscles, tendons, ligaments, backs and joints, and stress fractures; and in a number of cases, individuals have died in custody after being Tased. *Parker v. City of South Portland*, ___ F. Supp. 2d ___, 2007 WL 1468658 (D. Me. 2007).

Given its characteristics, at least one court has called the use of CEDs "a significantly violent level of force." *DeSalvo v. City of Collinsville*, 2005 WL 2487829, at *4 (S.D. Ill. 2005). In light of this, some courts have held that the use of a CED can constitute excessive force under certain circumstances, such as when used against "an unarmed arrestee who is suspected of having committed a minor crime; not actively resisting arrest; not trying to flee; and not posing an imminent threat of harm to officers or others. *Parker*, 2007 WL 1468658, at *22. Other courts have held that misuse of CEDs can give rise to liability not only for the individual officers who use them, but also to the municipalities who employ them for failing to properly train officers in the use of such devices. *See, e.g., Lieberman v. Marino*, ___ F. Supp. 2d ___, 2007 WL 789436 (E.D. Pa. 2007).

In the wake of calls for a moratorium on the use of CEDs by Amnesty International, the U.S. Department of Justice and the Police Executive Research Forum conducted a study of the use of these devices. These two organizations jointly issued formal guidelines for the use of CEDs in November of 2006. Some of their recommendations include:

▶ *CEDs should only be used against persons who are actively resisting or exhibiting active aggression, or to prevent individuals from harming themselves or others. CEDs should not be used against a passive suspect.*

▶ No more than one officer at a time should activate a CED against a person.

▶ When activating a CED, law enforcement officers should use it for one standard cycle and stop to evaluate the situation (a standard cycle is five seconds). If subsequent cycles are necessary, agency policy should restrict the number and duration of those cycles to the minimum activations necessary to place the subject in custody.

▶ Training protocols should emphasize that multiple activations and continuous cycling of a CED appear to increase the risk of death or serious injury and should be avoided where practical.

▶ That a subject is fleeing should not be the sole justification for police use of a CED. Severity of offense and other circumstances should be considered before officers' use of a CED on the fleeing subject.

▶ *CEDs should not generally be used against pregnant women, elderly persons, young children, and visibly frail persons unless exigent circumstances exist.*

▶ CEDs should not be used on handcuffed persons unless they are actively resisting or exhibiting active aggression, and/or to prevent individuals from harming themselves or others.

▶ CEDs should not generally be used when a subject is in a location where a fall may cause substantial injury or death.

▶ Officers should avoid firing darts at a subject's head, neck, and genitalia.

▶ All persons who have been exposed to a CED activation should receive a medical evaluation. Agencies shall consult with local medical personnel to develop appropriate police-medical protocols.

▶ Following a CED activation, officers should use a restraint technique that does not impair respiration.

▶ The CED "Probe Mode" should be the primary setting option, with "Drive Stun Mode" generally used as a secondary option.

▶ CEDs should not be used in the known presence of combustible vapors and liquids or other flammable substances including but not limited to alcohol-based Oleoresin Capsicum (O.C.) Spray carriers. Agencies utilizing both CEDs and O.C. Spray should use a water-based spray.

▶ A warning should be given to a person prior to activating the CED unless to do so would place any other person at risk (Cronin & Ederheimer, 2006: 23-26) (emphasis added).

Police Dogs Police have used trained canines as part of law enforcement for quite some time. The manner in which officers use police dogs as instrumentalities of force is governed by the Fourth Amendment's reasonableness requirement. One of the leading cases in this area is *Robinette v. Barnes*, 854 F.2d 909 (6th Cir. 1988). In that case, police had probable cause to believe that a man suspected of burglary was hiding inside a darkened building. After police commands for the suspect to exit the building were disregarded, they warned that they had a police dog that they would turn loose if the suspect did not come out of the building. After the initial warning produced no suspect, the police repeated their warning. When the second warning went unheeded, they released the canine. The dog subsequently apprehended the suspect by biting him on the neck, and the suspect died shortly thereafter. His estate filed a civil suit, arguing that the use of the police dog constituted the impermissible use of deadly force in violation of *Tennessee v. Garner*. The court rejected that claim:

[W]e find that the use of a properly trained police dog to apprehend a felony suspect does not carry with it a substantial risk of causing death or serious bodily harm. Although we cannot ignore the fact that, in this case, the use of a police dog did result in a person's death, we also cannot ignore the evidence in the record which indicates that this tragic event was an extreme aberration from the outcome intended or expected. [The evidence] was unequivocal on the fact that the dogs are trained to seize suspects by the arm and then wait for an officer to secure the arrestee. 854 F.2d at 912.

Many police dogs are specially trained to attack using a technique known as the "bite and hold." Most courts that have considered this technique are in accord with the decision in *Robinette v. Barnes*, and have held that the technique does not, in and of itself, constitute deadly force. *See, e.g., Jarrett v. Town of Yarmouth*, 331 F.3d 140 (1st Cir. 2003). However, the use of canines as weapons can nonetheless constitute excessive force under the facts of a particular case. For example, *Watkins v. City of Oakland*, 145 F.3d 1087, 1093 (9th Cir. 1998), held that when police improperly encouraged the continuation of an attack by a police dog, the use of force was unreasonable and therefore violated the Fourth Amendment. *See also Priester v. City of Riviera Beach*, 208 F.3d 919 (11th Cir. 2000).

Car Chases When police engage in high-speed chases of suspects, their vehicles can become deadly weapons that, if negligently or recklessly operated, can inflict injuries upon innocent third parties. *See, e.g., Day v. State ex rel. Utah Dept. of Public Safety*, 980 P.2d 1171 (Utah 1999). As a rule, law enforcement officers have a duty "to avoid driving in reckless disregard for the safety of others and to exercise due care for the safety of others once pursuit is undertaken." 57 AM. JUR. 2d *Municipal, County, School, and State Tort Liability* § 439 (Supp. 2007). As a result of the potential injuries to innocent third parties, many police departments have developed policies that prohibit high-speed chases under a number of circumstances. In addition to the tort liability such chases engender, there is also potential Section 1983 liability that a seizure that occurs as part of such a chase violates the Fourth Amendment. *See Albright v. Oliver*, 510 U.S. 266 (1994) (illegal seizure may subject officer to Section 1983 liability). Indeed, there is an argument to be made that high-speed chases might constitute deadly force under *Tennessee v. Garner*. But in *Scott v. Harris*, 127 S. Ct. 1769 (2007), the U.S. Supreme Court rejected such an argument, at least as it applied to the suspect fleeing police at high speed.

In *Scott v. Harris*, police attempted to pull over a car for speeding. Rather than yielding to police authority, the car accelerated to more than thirty miles per hour over the posted speed limit. "Six minutes and nearly 10 miles after the chase had begun, [an officer] decided to attempt to terminate the episode by employing a 'Precision Intervention Technique' ('PIT') maneuver, which causes the fleeing vehicle to spin to a stop." 127 S. Ct. at 1773. After being given radio permission to execute the maneuver by his supervisor, "the officer applied his push bumper to the rear of [the driver's] vehicle" causing the driver to lose "control of his vehicle, which left the roadway, ran down an embankment, overturned, and crashed." 127 S. Ct. at 1773. The driver was rendered a quadriplegic as a result of the injuries he sustained in the crash. He subsequently sued on the grounds that the maneuver constituted excessive force that violated the Fourth Amendment under *Tennessee v. Garner*. The entire episode was caught on videotape. The Supreme Court described the videotape as follows:

> There we see respondent's vehicle racing down narrow, two-lane roads in the dead of night at speeds that are shockingly fast. We see it swerve around more than a dozen other cars, cross the double-yellow line, and force cars traveling in both directions to their respective shoulders to avoid being hit. We see it run multiple red lights and travel for considerable periods of time in the occasional center left-turn-only lane, chased by numerous police cars forced to engage in the same hazardous maneuvers just to keep up. Far from being the cautious and controlled driver the lower court depicts, what we see on the video more closely resembles a Hollywood-style car chase of the most frightening sort, placing police officers and innocent bystanders alike at great risk of serious injury. 127 S. Ct. at 1775-76.

In light of the danger the driver posed by driving in that manner, the Supreme Court held that the officer's maneuver constituted a reasonable seizure of the driver's vehicle. Concurring justices wrote to specially note, however, that the case did not create a *per se* rule authorizing high-speed chases under the Fourth Amendment. "The inquiry . . . is situation specific. Among relevant considerations: Were the lives and well-being of others (motorists, pedestrians, police officers) at risk? Was there a safer way, given the time, place, and circumstances, to stop the fleeing vehicle?" 127 S. Ct. at 1779 (Ginsburg, J., concurring). As a result, law enforcement officers are well-advised to consider alternatives to high-speed chases that pose a risk of danger to others whose "seizure" would not be so easily deemed "reasonable" under the facts of another case.

key points

- In general, a law enforcement officer may not use deadly force to arrest or prevent the escape of a felon, unless the felon poses a threat of serious physical harm to either the officer or others.
- Law enforcement officers may use any reasonably necessary non-deadly force, but may never use deadly force to arrest for a misdemeanor. It is better that a misdemeanant escape than to take a human life.
- A law enforcement officer making a lawful arrest (for either a misdemeanor or a felony) may use

any force reasonably necessary under the circumstances in self-defense, including deadly force, if the officer reasonably believes that the person to be arrested is about to commit an assault and that the officer is in danger of death or serious bodily injury.
- Resisting arrest is a crime involving a person's opposition by direct and often forcible means against a law enforcement officer to prevent being taken into custody.

▶ AFTER MAKING AN ARREST

An arrest initiates a series of administrative and judicial procedures dealing with the arrested person and his or her property. These procedures vary among jurisdictions, but all basically deal with the same issues: the protection of the person and property of the arrestee, notification of and opportunity to exercise certain rights, safety and security of law enforcement officials and places of confinement, identification, further investigation, record keeping, and avoidance of civil liability. Booking is usually the first of these procedures to take place after arrest.

Booking

Booking is a police administrative procedure officially recording an arrest in a police register. At a minimum, booking involves recording the name of the person arrested; the name of the officer making the arrest; and the time of, place of, circumstances of, and reason for the arrest. The meaning of booking, however, is sometimes expanded to include other procedures that take place in the station house after an arrest. For more serious offenses, booking may include a search of the arrested person (including in some cases a search of body cavities), fingerprinting, photographing, a lineup, or other identification procedures. The arrested person may be temporarily detained in a jail or lockup until release on bail can be arranged. For less serious offenses, the arrested person may be released on personal recognizance, under which the person agrees to appear in court when required but is not required to pay or promise to pay any money or property as security.

Booking is usually completed before the arrested person's initial appearance before the magistrate, but not necessarily. Booking procedures vary among different jurisdictions and among different law enforcement agencies within a particular jurisdiction.

Initial Appearance

After arresting a person, with or without a warrant, a law enforcement officer must take the person before a magistrate or deliver the person according to the mandate of the warrant. Statutes in different jurisdictions require that this be done promptly, using terms such as immediately, without unnecessary delay, forthwith, within a specified time period, or other similar language. These statutes confer a substantial right on the defendant and create a corresponding duty on law enforcement officers.

The reasons for requiring an **initial appearance** without unnecessary delay are:

▶ To verify that the person arrested is the person named in the complaint

▶ To advise arrested persons of the charges, so that they may prepare a defense

▶ To advise arrested persons of their rights, such as the right to a preliminary hearing, the right to counsel, and the right to remain silent

▶ To protect arrested persons from being abandoned in jail and forgotten by, or otherwise cut off from contact with, people who can help them

▶ To prevent secret and extended interrogation of arrested persons by law enforcement officers

▶ To give arrested persons an early opportunity to secure release on bail while awaiting the final outcome of the proceedings. If the person has been bailed earlier, the magistrate simply reviews that bail. Release on personal recognizance may also be granted at the initial appearance.

▶ To give arrested persons an opportunity to speedily conclude proceedings on charges of minor offenses by pleading guilty to the charges, paying fines, and carrying on with their lives

▶ To obtain a prompt, neutral "judicial determination of probable cause as a prerequisite to extended restraint of liberty following arrest." *Gerstein v. Pugh*, 420 U.S. 103, 114 (1975). Not all states, however, provide for a judicial determination of probable cause at the initial appearance before a magistrate:

> There is no single preferred pretrial procedure, and the nature of the probable cause determination usually will be shaped to accord with a State's pretrial procedure viewed as a whole. . . . It may be found desirable, for example, to make the probable cause determination at the suspect's first appearance before a judicial officer, . . . or the determination may be incorporated into the procedure for setting bail or fixing other conditions of pretrial release. In some States, existing procedures may satisfy the requirement of the Fourth Amendment. Others may require only minor adjustment, such as acceleration of existing preliminary hearings. Current proposals for criminal procedure reform suggest other ways of testing probable cause for detention. Whatever procedure a State may adopt, it must provide a fair and reliable determination of probable cause as a condition for any significant pretrial restraint of liberty, and this determination must be made by a judicial officer either before or promptly after arrest. *Gerstein*, 420 U.S. at 123-25.

County of Riverside v. McLaughlin, 500 U.S. 44 (1991), held that, to satisfy the "promptness" requirement of *Gerstein*, a jurisdiction that chooses to combine probable cause determinations with other pretrial proceedings must do so as soon as reasonably feasible, but not later than forty-eight hours after arrest. Note that a probable cause hearing provided within forty-eight hours might not pass constitutional muster if it is unreasonably delayed. As the Court said:

> Such a hearing may nonetheless violate *Gerstein* if the arrested individual can prove that his or her probable cause determination was delayed unreasonably. Examples of unreasonable delay are delays for the purpose of gathering additional evidence to justify the arrest, a delay motivated by ill will against the arrested individual, or delay for delay's sake. In evaluating whether the delay in a particular case is unreasonable, however, courts must allow a substantial degree of flexibility. Courts cannot ignore the often unavoidable delays in transporting arrested persons from one facility to another, handling late-night bookings where no magistrate is readily available, obtaining the presence of an arresting officer who may be busy processing other suspects or securing the premises of an arrest, and other practical realities. 500 U.S. at 56-57.

When an arrested person does not receive a probable cause determination within forty-eight hours, the burden shifts to the government to demonstrate the existence of a bona fide emergency or other extraordinary circumstance. The Court specifically stated that neither intervening weekends nor delays related to consolidating pretrial proceedings qualify as extraordinary circumstances.

Safety Considerations

Just because a suspect has been subdued does not necessarily mean that police officers or others are free from danger. The Supreme Court has therefore given law enforcement officers some latitude in protecting themselves, the arrestee, third parties, and the crime scene, if applicable.

> [I]t is not "unreasonable" under the Fourth Amendment for a police officer, as a matter of course, to monitor the movements of an arrested person, as his judgment dictates, following the arrest. The officer's need to ensure his own safety—as well as the integrity of the arrest—is compelling. Such surveillance is not an impermissible invasion of the privacy or personal liberty of an individual who has been arrested. *Washington v. Chrisman*, 455 U.S. 1, 7 (1982).

Protection and Welfare of Arrested Person and Arresting Officer When delay in taking an arrested person before a magistrate is unavoidable, the officer must keep the arrested person safely in custody for the period of the delay. The officer may reasonably restrain the person to prevent escape and may even confine the person in a jail or other suitable place. Handcuffs may be used at the officer's discretion, depending on the person's reputation or record for violence, the time of day, the number of other persons in custody, and the duration of the detention.

The officer is responsible for the health and safety of the arrested person, including providing adequate medical assistance, if necessary. Any unnecessary use of force or negligent failure to prevent the use of force by others against the arrested person may subject the officer to criminal or civil liability.

Inventory Search When a person is arrested and taken into custody, police may search the person and any container or item in his or her possession as part of the routine administrative procedure incident to booking and jailing the person. *Illinois v. Lafayette*, 462 U.S. 640 (1983), held that station-house **inventory searches** are an incidental step following arrest and preceding incarceration, and are reasonable under the Fourth Amendment without any further justification. The Court said that the governmental interests justifying a station-house inventory search are different from, and may in some circumstances be even greater than, those supporting a search incident to arrest (see Chapter 8). Among those interests are prevention of theft of the arrested person's property; deterrence of false claims regarding that property; prevention of injury from belts, drugs, or dangerous instruments such as razor blades, knives, or bombs; and determination or verification of the person's identity. Furthermore, station-house searches are valid even though less intrusive means of satisfying those governmental interests might be possible. The Court said:

> It is evident that a stationhouse search of every item carried on or by a person who has lawfully been taken into custody by the police will amply serve the important and legitimate governmental interests involved. Even if less intrusive means existed of protecting some particular types of property, it would be unreasonable to expect police officers in the everyday course of business to make fine and subtle distinctions in deciding which containers or items may be searched and which must be sealed as a unit. 462 U.S. at 648.

If special circumstances exist, a station-house inventory search need not be conducted immediately on the arrested person's arrival at the station house. *United States v. Edwards*, 415 U.S. 800 (1974), held that a seizure of a prisoner's clothing in the morning, several hours after his arrest and incarceration the previous evening, was reasonable. Since no substitute clothing had been available at the time of arrest, the normal processes incident to arrest and custody had not been completed:

> [O]nce the accused is lawfully arrested and is in custody, the effects in his possession at the place of detention that were subject to search at the time and place of his arrest may lawfully be searched and seized without a warrant even though a substantial period of time has elapsed between the arrest and subsequent administrative processing, on the one hand, and the taking of the property for use as evidence, on the other. 415 U.S. at 807.

Note that in *Edwards*, the later seizure and search of the suspect's clothing was permissible, even though a considerable amount of time had passed since the suspect's arrest and arrival at the stationhouse, because initially there was no substitute clothing available, the clothing itself had evidentiary value (i.e., particular paint chips on the clothing), and the suspect could have destroyed that value.

Sometimes, especially when a vehicle is involved, officers must take positive action to protect an arrested person's property or risk civil liability for damages for failure to do so. Many law enforcement agencies have adopted standard procedures for impounding arrested persons' vehicles and making an inventory of their contents. (For a discussion of impoundment and inventory of vehicles, see Chapter 11.)

Identification and Examination of an Arrested Person

Typical Identification Procedures at Booking Law enforcement officers may take fingerprints, footprints, or photographs of an arrested person for purposes of identification or evidence. Officers may also obtain voice exemplars or have a dentist examine a defendant's mouth for a missing tooth for identification purposes:

> [T]he Fourth Amendment does not protect "what a person knowingly exposes to the public even in his home or office. . . . Like a man's facial characteristics, or handwriting, his voice is repeatedly produced for others to hear. No person can have a reasonable expectation that others will not know the sound of his voice, any more than he can reasonably expect that his face will be a mystery to the world." This doctrine is applicable as well to a missing tooth. *United States v. Holland*, 378 F. Supp. 144, 155 (E.D. Pa. 1974).

Law enforcement officers may physically examine arrested persons for measurements, scars, bruises, tattoos, and so on:

> Such procedures and practices and tests may result in freeing an innocent man accused of crime, or may be part of a chain of facts and circumstances which help identify a person accused of a crime or connect a suspect or an accused with the crime of which he has been suspected or has been accused. The law is well settled that such actions, practices, and procedures do not violate any constitutional right. *Commonwealth v. Aljoe*, 216 A.2d 50, 52-53 (Pa. 1966).

(See Chapter 14 for a discussion of the Fifth Amendment issues regarding fingerprinting, voice exemplars, and other pre-trial identification procedures.)

If necessary, force may be used to identify and examine arrested persons, but the methods used may not "shock the conscience," offend a "sense of justice," or run counter to the "decencies of civilized conduct." *Rochin v. California*, 342 U.S. 165 (1952). In *Rochin*, three officers, suspecting that Rochin was selling narcotics, entered his home and forced their way into a bedroom occupied by him and his wife. When asked about two capsules on a bedside stand, he put them in his mouth. After an unsuccessful struggle to extract them by force, the three officers took him to a hospital. There, a medicine to induce vomiting was forcibly administered, and Rochin vomited the two capsules, which later were found to contain morphine. This evidence was admitted at trial over Rochin's objection and he was convicted. The Supreme Court, finding that the conduct of the officers "shocked the conscience" and thereby violated the due process clause of the Fourteenth Amendment, reversed the conviction.

Breithaupt v. Abram, 352 U.S. 432 (1957), held, however, that there is no denial of due process of law in taking a blood sample with proper medical supervision from a person who is unconscious and unable to give consent. Also, *Schmerber v. California*, 384 U.S. 757 (1966), held that there is no violation of the Fifth Amendment privilege against self-incrimination or the Fourth Amendment protection against unreasonable searches and seizures when a blood sample is taken without consent from an arrested person in lawful custody. The Court explained that the privilege against self-incrimination **"protects an accused only from being compelled to testify against himself, or otherwise provide the State with evidence of a testimonial or communicative nature, and that the withdrawal of blood and use of the analysis in question in this case did not involve compulsion to these ends."** 384 U.S. at 761. The Court found that the Fourth Amendment standard of reasonableness was satisfied when (1) "there was plainly probable cause for the officer to arrest petitioner and charge him with driving an automobile under the influence of intoxicating liquor," and (2) the facts "suggested the required relevance and likely success of a test of petitioner's blood for alcohol. . . ." The blood sample was taken in a hospital by a physician following accepted medical procedures. Also, the officer "might reasonably have believed that he was confronted with an emergency" because the sample was needed to measure the blood's alcohol content, which would quickly dissipate. The Court said:

> [W]e reach this judgment only on the facts in the present record. The integrity of an individual's person is a cherished value of our society. That we today hold that the Constitution does not forbid the State's minor intrusions into an individual's body under stringently limited conditions in no way indicates that it permits more substantial intrusions or intrusions under other conditions. 384 U.S. at 772.

Winston v. Lee, 470 U.S. 753 (1985), involved a more substantial intrusion, and the Supreme Court refused, on Fourth Amendment grounds, to allow the prosecution to compel an armed robbery suspect to undergo a surgical procedure under a general anesthetic for removal of a bullet lodged in his chest. The Court applied the balancing test used in *Schmerber* and found that the potential threat to the suspect's health and safety, combined with the extensive intrusion on the suspect's personal privacy and bodily integrity, were not counterbalanced by a compelling need for evidence. Of particular importance was the Court's finding that the prosecution had substantial additional evidence connecting the suspect to the robbery. The Court said:

> The Fourth Amendment is a vital safeguard of the right of the citizen to be free from unreasonable governmental intrusions into any area in which he has a reasonable expectation of privacy. Where the Court has found a lesser expectation of privacy . . . or where the search involves a minimal intrusion on privacy interests . . . the Court has held that the Fourth Amendment protections are correspondingly less stringent. Conversely, however, the Fourth Amendment's command that searches be "reasonable" requires that when the State seeks to intrude upon an area in which our society recognizes a significantly heightened privacy interest, a more substantial justification is required to make the search "reasonable." Applying these principles, we hold that the proposed search in this case would be "unreasonable" under the Fourth Amendment. 470 U.S. at 767.

Strip Searches and Body Cavity Searches As a rule, an individual who has been arrested "may be strip searched as part of the booking process only if officers have reasonable suspicion that he is either armed or carrying contraband." *See also Wood v. Hancock County Sheriff's Dept.*, 354 F.3d 57, 62 (1st Cir. 2003); *Arpin v. Santa Clara Valley Transp. Agency*, 261 F.3d 912 (9th Cir. 2001). If there is reasonable suspicion to believe a weapon or contraband might be hidden in body cavities, a more invasive visual search of body cavities may be justified "to protect prisons and jails from smuggled weapons, drugs, or other contraband which pose a threat to the safety and security of penal institutions." *Fuller v. M.G. Jewelry*, 950 F.2d 1437, 1447 (9th Cir. 1991).

Pretrial Confrontations for Identification Pretrial procedures for identifying and examining an arrested person take many different forms. One form is confrontation of the arrested person with victims or witnesses of the crime, sometimes accomplished through the use of a police lineup or showup. The arrested person may not object to being viewed by witnesses for identification purposes and also may not demand to be placed in a lineup. (For a discussion of pretrial identification procedures and the right to counsel, see Chapter 14.)

key points

- A state must provide a fair and reliable judicial determination of probable cause as a condition for any significant pretrial restraint on liberty either before arrest or as soon as is reasonably feasible after arrest, but not later than 48 hours after arrest absent extraordinary circumstances justifying any further delay.
- A law enforcement officer may monitor the movements of an arrested person, as judgment dictates, to ensure the officer's safety and the arrest's integrity.
- Once a person is lawfully arrested and in custody, police may, as part of the routine administrative procedure incident to booking and jailing the person, search the person and any containers or items in his or her possession.
- An arrested person may be subjected to various identification and examination procedures, including the obtaining of fingerprints and, if circumstances warrant, a blood sample, so long as the reasonableness requirement of the Fourth Amendment is satisfied. Reasonable force may be used for these purposes if the methods do not "shock the conscience," offend a "sense of justice," or run counter to the "decencies of civilized conduct."

▶ EFFECT OF AN ILLEGAL ARREST

If an arrest is illegal, this does not affect trial jurisdiction. It may, however, have an adverse affect on the trial.

Effect on Jurisdiction

Jurisdiction to try a person for a crime is not affected by an illegal arrest:

> [T]he power of a court to try a person for crime is not impaired by the fact that he had been brought within the court's jurisdiction by reason of a "forcible abduction." . . . [D]ue process of law is satisfied when one present in court is convicted of crime after having been fairly apprised of the charges against him and after a fair trial in accordance with constitutional procedural safeguards. There is nothing in the Constitution that requires a court to permit a guilty person rightfully convicted to escape justice because he was brought to trial against his will. *Frisbie v. Collins*, 342 U.S. 519, 522 (1952).

This doctrine is known as the *Ker-Frisbie* doctrine after *Ker v. Illinois*, 119 U.S. 436, 444 (1886), which declared that "forcible abduction is no sufficient reason why the party should not answer when brought within the jurisdiction of the court which has the right to try him for such an offense, and presents no valid objection to his trial in such a court."

Although an illegal arrest does not affect jurisdiction to try an offender, the exclusionary rule may affect the trial adversely. The exclusionary rule, as applied to arrest, states that any evidence obtained by exploitation of an unlawful arrest is inadmissible in court in a prosecution against the person arrested. If the only evidence the government has against an armed robbery suspect is a gun, a mask, and a roll of bills taken during a search incident to an unlawful arrest, the offender will very likely go free because these items will be inadmissible in court. (The exclusionary rule is discussed in detail in Chapter 3. For more details about the exclusionary rule's applicability to searches incident-to-arrest, see Chapter 8.)

A confession obtained by exploitation of an illegal arrest is also inadmissible in court. In *Brown v. Illinois*, 422 U.S. 590 (1975), the defendant was illegally arrested in a manner calculated to cause surprise, fright, and confusion and then taken to a police station. He was given *Miranda* warnings, waived his rights, and made incriminating statements, all within two hours of the illegal arrest. The Court held that *Miranda* warnings alone could not avoid the effect of the illegal arrest:

> The *Miranda* warnings are an important factor, to be sure, in determining whether the confession is obtained by exploitation of illegal arrest. But they are not the only factor to be considered. The temporal proximity of the arrest and the confession, the presence of intervening circumstances, . . . and, particularly, the purpose and flagrancy of the official misconduct are all relevant. . . . And the burden of showing admissibility rests, of course, on the prosecution. 422 U.S. at 603-04.

If evidence is not the product of illegal arrest, however, the exclusionary rule does not apply. Indirect fruits of an illegal arrest should be suppressed only when they bear a sufficiently close relationship to the underlying illegality. In *New York v. Harris*, 495 U.S. 14 (1990), police officers, who had probable cause to believe that the defendant committed murder, entered his home without first obtaining an arrest warrant in violation of *Payton v. New York* (discussed earlier in this chapter). The officers administered *Miranda* warnings and obtained an admission of guilt. After the defendant was arrested, taken to the police station, and again given *Miranda* warnings, he signed a written incriminating statement. The first statement was ruled inadmissible because it was obtained in the defendant's home by exploitation of the *Payton* violation. The statement taken at the police station, however, was ruled admissible. That statement was not the product of being in unlawful custody; nor was it the fruit of having been arrested in the home rather than someplace else.

The police had justification to question the defendant prior to his arrest. Therefore, his subsequent statement was not an exploitation of the illegal entry into his home. Moreover, suppressing a station-house statement obtained after a *Payton* violation would have minimal deterrent value, because police would not be motivated to violate *Payton* just to obtain a statement from a person they have probable cause to arrest. The Court therefore held that **"where the police have probable cause to arrest a suspect, the exclusionary rule does not bar the State's use of a statement made by the defendant outside of his home, even though the statement is taken after an arrest made in the home in violation of *Payton*."** 495 U.S. at 21. (For more details about the exclusionary rule's applicability to confession evidence, see Chapter 13.)

Finally, law enforcement officers may be subject to civil or criminal liability for making illegal arrests or for using excessive or unreasonable force.

key points

- Jurisdiction to try a person for a crime is not affected by an illegal arrest.
- In general, evidence that is obtained by exploitation of an illegal arrest and is a product of that arrest will be inadmissible in court in a prosecution against the person arrested.

Summary

A formal arrest is the taking of a person into custody for the commission of an offense as the prelude to prosecuting him or her for it. The basic elements constituting a formal arrest are (1) a law enforcement officer's purpose or intention to take a person into the custody of the law; (2) the officer's exercise of real or pretended authority; (3) detention or restraint of the person to be arrested, whether by physical force or by submission to assertion of authority; and (4) understanding by the person to be arrested of the officer's intention to arrest. Even when these basic elements are not all present, courts may find that an encounter between a law enforcement officer and a person entails such a significant intrusion on the person's freedom of action that it is in important respects indistinguishable from a formal arrest. Such an encounter, sometimes called a seizure tantamount to arrest or a *de facto* arrest, must be supported by probable cause or it is illegal. The test to determine whether a seizure is tantamount to arrest is whether, in view of all the circumstances surrounding the encounter, a reasonable person would have believed that he or she was not free to leave.

Although warrantless arrests on probable cause are permitted, courts always prefer arrests made under the authority of an arrest warrant. An arrest warrant is a written judicial order directing a law enforcement officer to arrest a particular person. An arrest warrant is issued by a magistrate on the basis of a complaint stating the essential facts constituting the offense charged, if the magistrate has probable cause to believe that the offense was committed and that the person to be arrested committed it. The magistrate may also issue a summons that merely directs the defendant to appear rather than ordering an arrest.

Law enforcement officers may make a warrantless public arrest for a felony if they have probable cause to believe that a felony has been or is being committed and that the person to be arrested has committed or is committing the felony. Officers may make a warrantless public arrest for a misdemeanor, however, only if (1) the misdemeanor was committed in their presence; or (2) a state statute or constitution allows warrantless arrests on probable cause for certain misdemeanors. A warrantless misdemeanor arrest for offenses committed in the officer's presence must be made immediately; but a warrantless felony arrest may be delayed for various reasons, as long as the defendant's rights are not prejudiced by the delay.

When law enforcement officers make arrests, they should notify the arrested person that he or she is under arrest and notify the person of the officers' authority and the cause of the arrest. If the arrest is made under authority of a warrant, officers should examine the warrant to make sure it is valid on its face before carrying out its commands. When an arrest warrant is executed, officers should return the warrant as directed and explain what they have done in carrying out its commands.

Officers have no official authority to arrest without a warrant outside their jurisdiction—the geographic area for which they were elected or appointed. Nevertheless, outside their jurisdiction they have the same authority as any private citizen to arrest for breach of the peace misdemeanors committed in their presence and for felonies on probable cause. They may also arrest outside their jurisdiction in fresh pursuit of a criminal who has fled their jurisdiction, if the pursuit is begun promptly inside the jurisdiction and maintained continuously.

Officers may use only the amount of force reasonably necessary under the circumstances to make an arrest. Deadly force may be used only as a last resort and then only in specifically limited circumstances. Deadly force may never be used to accomplish an arrest for a misdemeanor. Officers may, however, use deadly force in self-defense to protect themselves from death or serious bodily injury, and need not abandon an attempt to arrest in the face of physical resistance to the arrest.

Officers may not enter a dwelling to arrest a person without a warrant unless there is consent or exigent circumstances exist. An arrest warrant is required to enter a suspect's home to arrest the suspect. A search warrant is required to enter a third person's home to arrest a suspect. Exigent circumstances that would justify a warrantless entry of a dwelling to arrest are hot pursuit of a fleeing felon, imminent destruction of evidence, the need to prevent a suspect's escape, and the risk of danger to police or other persons. In assessing the risk of danger, the gravity of the crime and the likelihood that the suspect is armed should be considered. If an arrest is begun in a public place, officers in hot pursuit may enter a dwelling without a warrant to complete the arrest.

Before officers may lawfully enter a dwelling forcibly to arrest a person, they must be refused admittance after knocking, announcing their authority and purpose, and demanding admittance. Failure to knock-and-announce is excused if an officer's purpose is already known, or if the officer has reasonable suspicion that knocking-and-announcing would cause danger to the officer or other persons, permit the escape of the suspect, or result in the loss or destruction of evidence.

Duties of an officer after an arrest is made include the following: booking; bringing the arrested person before a magistrate without unnecessary delay; ensuring the health and safety of the arrested person while in the officer's custody; conducting a station-house inventory search of the prisoner, which may include searching and seizing any container or object in the prisoner's possession; and conducting identification procedures, including fingerprinting, photographing, physical examinations, and lineups.

Although an illegal arrest does affect the jurisdiction of the court to try a person, any evidence obtained as the product of the exploitation of an illegal arrest is inadmissible in a criminal proceeding against the defendant. In addition, a law enforcement officer may be civilly or criminally liable for making an illegal arrest or using unreasonable or excessive force.

Key Terms

affidavit, 314	complaint, 313	fresh pursuit, 332	misdemeanor, 314
arrest, 306	excessive force, 340	frisk, 310	resisting arrest, 334
arrest warrant, 314	exigent circumstances,	hot pursuit, 329	show of authority, 307
booking, 346	327	initial appearance, 346	stop, 307
citizen's arrest, 319	extradition, 333	inventory search, 348	summons, 314
common law, 318	felony, 316	magistrate, 313	

Review and Discussion Questions

1. Is it possible to formally arrest a mentally ill or mentally retarded person? Explain.

2. Name several ways in which a law enforcement officer or officers can prevent a routine encounter with a person on the street from being considered a seizure tantamount to arrest.

3. Give three practical reasons why a law enforcement officer should obtain an arrest warrant if possible.

4. How is a law enforcement officer's authority to arrest affected by time?

5. Is it valid to say that if an officer has strong probable cause to arrest someone, the officer may arrest the person anywhere in the country? Explain.

6. What are the major differences between an officer's felony arrest powers and an officer's misdemeanor arrest powers?

7. What is meant by a "citizen's arrest"? Explain the legal limitations on making a citizen's arrest.

8. Under what circumstances may a law enforcement officer use deadly force, and what are the potential consequences of an illegal use of deadly force? Name several circumstances under which little or no force should be used to make an arrest.

9. Do law enforcement officers have a broader right to self-defense when they are assaulted while making an arrest than when they are assaulted while simply walking or cruising their beats?

10. Assume that a law enforcement officer has probable cause to arrest a defendant for armed assault and probable cause to believe that the person is hiding in a third person's garage, which is attached to the house. What warrants, if any, does the officer need to enter the garage to arrest the defendant? What if the officer is in hot pursuit of the defendant? What if the defendant is known to be injured and unarmed?

11. Give reasons to support an argument that a law enforcement officer should never have to knock-and-announce before entering a dwelling to arrest a dangerous felon or a drug offender.

12. If a law enforcement officer has probable cause to arrest, does the officer have to make an arrest? If not, what alternatives to arrest are available, and under what circumstances should they be used?

13. Discuss in detail four different things a law enforcement officer must do after he or she has arrested a person.

Applications of the Law in Real Cases

1 Officer Jerry Symonds, a police officer with the Village of Woodridge in Du Page County, testified that he was on duty on May 23, 1999, at approximately 1:40 A.M. when he saw a car traveling southbound on Lemont Road at a high rate of speed. Defendant was driving the car Officer Symonds observed, and Officer Symonds was outside of Woodridge when he saw the defendant. Officer Symonds testified that the defendant was "perhaps" in Woodridge at the time he first observed him. Specifically, Officer Symonds testified that he "[did not] know if [defendant] was in town or out of town. It was that close." Officer Symonds watched as the car got closer to him, and he activated his radar when no other cars were around defendant's car. At the time the radar was activated, the defendant was not in any municipality.

The radar showed that the defendant was driving 67 miles per hour, and the posted speed limit was 45 miles per hour. Officer Symonds made a U-turn, activated his emergency equipment, drove approximately 80 miles per hour to catch him, and eventually stopped the defendant approximately a half mile away in Cook County. After the stop, Officer Symonds notified his dispatch and conducted an investigation. Based on this investigation, Officer Symonds placed the man under arrest for driving while under the influence of alcohol.

The trial court denied the defendant's petition and found that Officer Symonds had properly arrested him. The court stated that, assuming the defendant was outside Woodridge, Officer Symonds was acting as a private citizen when he arrested the defendant for speeding; and Officer Symonds only made the arrest after he observed the defendant traveling at a high rate of speed. The trial court noted that after making that observation, Officer Symonds activated his radar to determine the defendant's precise speed. This timely appeal followed.

The defendant argues that Officer Symonds lacked the authority to arrest him because Symonds was outside his jurisdiction at the time he made the arrest—the officer did not have any statutory authority to make the arrest outside his jurisdiction. The State contends that the arrest was a proper citizen's arrest. Specifically, the State argues that the arrest was proper because Officer Symonds first observed the defendant driving at a high rate of speed, an observation that a private citizen could make, and then used his radar to determine the defendant's precise speed. The State claims that an officer's use of the powers of his office after observing criminal activity does not invalidate the arrest. Did Officer Symonds have the authority to arrest the defendant? *People v. Kirvelaitis*, 734 N.E.2d 524 (Ill. App. 2000).

2 The controversy concerns a full-time City of Overland Park police officer, Kevin Duncan, who was working off-duty as a security guard at the Oak Park Mall in his spare time. His duties at the mall included patrolling the parking lot, responding to calls for assistance or emergency-type situations, and doing routine security activities such as locking the doors. During the time Officer Duncan was employed at the mall, he was armed and dressed as an Overland Park police officer. The evidence indicates that Officer Duncan received no money from the City of Overland Park for working off-duty. The only exception would be an occasion when circumstances required him to make an arrest.

On the day in question, Officer Duncan was working at his mall job when he was dispatched to Nordstrom's department store. At Nordstrom's, another security guard showed him a photograph of the defendant and informed him that the man was currently in the store. The other security guard had been informed by an Overland Park detective that there was a warrant outstanding for the defendant's arrest. The security guard was asked to notify the police if he saw the defendant. After receiving this information, Officer Duncan contacted the Overland Park police dispatch and verified there was an outstanding misdemeanor warrant for the defendant's arrest.

Officer Duncan then watched the defendant until he left the store, approached him, and identified himself as an Overland Park police officer. He informed the defendant of the outstanding warrant and asked for identification. The man refused to identify himself, whereupon Officer Duncan handcuffed him and removed his wallet. After verifying that the defendant was the same individual who was wanted in the misdemeanor warrant, Officer Duncan placed him under arrest. During the search incident to the arrest, he removed a $20 bill from the defendant's wallet. When the bill was unfolded, it was found to contain a white powdery substance that was later confirmed to be cocaine. After finding the cocaine, Officer Duncan called for an on-duty police officer to respond to the scene, and that officer took the defendant into custody.

The defendant filed a motion to suppress introduction of the cocaine into evidence at his trial. The motion was based on the fact that the police officer was acting as a security guard or as a private citizen, and had no authority to arrest or to search the defendant.

The record contains the Overland Park Police Department policy manual guidelines for off-duty employment. The guidelines say, among other things, that an officer who is working off duty is not acting in his or her capacity as a law enforcement officer. The guidelines go on to provide that officers employed as security personnel are not to provide on-duty response when the matter can be handled by requesting the assistance of an on-duty law enforcement officer. Officer Duncan testified that he did not know about this provision of the manual guidelines. The trial court found that Officer Duncan was acting as a police officer, that he had the authority to arrest the defendant, and that the cocaine found during the search incident to the arrest should not be suppressed. Should the cocaine be suppressed? *State v. Epps*, 9 P.3d 1271 (Kan. App. 2000).

3 In March 1996, Gutierrez entered a fast-food restaurant in Bay City, Texas. Using a receipt that belonged to another customer, he asked to be given free food. When he was told he could not have the food, he cursed one of the managers, who was black, and called her a racial epithet. The manager told him to leave and then called the police, who arrived after Gutierrez already had departed.

Gutierrez returned to the restaurant about an hour later, and the manager again called the police. This time, Officer Hadash arrived and recognized the man as Gutierrez. He approached Gutierrez, and an altercation ensued. According to Hadash, Gutierrez jumped off a stool and started swinging his fists, striking Hadash several times. Hadash apparently did not strike Gutierrez at this time, because he was busy blocking his assailant's blows. Other witnesses also said Gutierrez struck Hadash, and it is undisputed that Hadash and Gutierrez eventually ended up struggling on the floor.

Officer Mirelez arrived and tried to assist Hadash. The two officers struggled to restrain Gutierrez, who continued fighting. Although different witnesses provided slightly varying accounts as to the sequence of events, it is undisputed that one or both of the officers dragged Gutierrez outside and sprayed him with pepper spray. It is uncertain how many times he was sprayed or how much spray was used. And although one witness stated that the officers sprayed Gutierrez while inside the restaurant, all other witnesses stated that this occurred after Gutierrez was taken outside.

Next, the officers placed Gutierrez face down on the pavement and eventually were able to handcuff him. According to the officers, Gutierrez was still struggling at that point. But, according to one witness, Maria

Juarez, Gutierrez did not appear to be struggling at the time he was dragged outside. Juarez stated that after Gutierrez was taken outside, she watched the incident from the store and saw Gutierrez on the ground, face down, handcuffed.

One of the officers had his knee on Gutierrez's back and "kept pushing Mr. Gutierrez [sic] neck and head to the ground" with a stick. Mirelez confirmed placing his right shin across Gutierrez's back while attempting to restrain Gutierrez. Neither Hadash nor Mirelez mentioned using a baton, however.

After Gutierrez was cuffed, three other officers arrived—Sergeant Garcia, Officer Hempel, and Officer Sherrill. According to Garcia, when he arrived he observed Hadash and Mirelez on top of Gutierrez. Then, when Sherrill and Hempel arrived, Garcia told them to put Gutierrez into a patrol car. Garcia advised Hadash that Gutierrez could go to the hospital to be decontaminated from the pepper spray, but Hadash declined, because the jail was closer and more secure, and because Gutierrez had been combative.

When Sherrill and Hempel arrived, Gutierrez was lying on his stomach and was no longer struggling. The officers had to carry him to place him in the car; he did not walk on his own. The officers placed him in the car head-first. Sherrill had to go to the other side of the vehicle to pull Gutierrez through, placing him on his stomach with his head turned toward the front of the vehicle. Sherrill reported that Gutierrez appeared to have passed out. According to Garcia, he did not attempt to assess whether Gutierrez was injured, nor did he speak to him.

Hadash then drove Gutierrez to the county jail. He recalled hearing "a couple of groans and grunts" during the trip but did not speak to Gutierrez during that time. When Hadash arrived, he was met by two jailers, who again had to assist Gutierrez out of the car. Gutierrez was not combative; indeed, Hadash did not know whether he was even conscious at that point. The jailers carried Gutierrez into the jail, half dragging him, and laid him face down. At that point, Hadash looked at Gutierrez and told Garcia that it appeared Gutierrez was not breathing. The officers removed Gutierrez's handcuffs and turned him over, and Hadash began CPR. Once his breathing was revived, Gutierrez was transported to the hospital, where he slipped into a coma and eventually died.

Gutierrez's sister (Wagner) and his daughter (Irma Gutierrez) sued the city and the officers, alleging violations of Gutierrez's civil rights pursuant to § 1983. The complaint set forth claims of, inter alia, excessive force and a failure to respond to Gutierrez's medical needs. Although the original complaint named Bay City and every male officer of the Bay City police force, the claims eventually were dismissed against all but Bay City and Mirelez, Sherrill, Garcia, Hadash, and Hempel, the officers involved in the arrest. The officers moved for summary judgment on the basis of qualified immunity, and the court granted summary judgment on the excessive force claims as to Sherrill, Garcia, and Hempel, because they arrived after the altercation was over. The court denied summary judgment in all other respects. Should officers Mirelez and Hadash be protected from liability for damages because of qualified immunity? *Wagner v. Bay City*, Tex., 227 F.3d 316 (5th Cir. 2000).

4 On October 29, 1998, Lieutenant Alvin Pair of the Greensville County Sheriff's Department sent a confidential informant to Room 117 of the Dixie Motel in order to make a controlled purchase of cocaine. Pair searched the informant beforehand to determine that he had no drugs on his person, and gave him a marked twenty dollar bill to use to purchase cocaine. Police surveillance was positioned outside the motel room while the informant knocked on the door. Robert Ferguson, a codefendant, opened the door, stepped outside the room, looked around, and allowed the informant to enter, closing the door after the informant was inside.

Soon thereafter, Ferguson walked out of the room again and looked around, whereupon the informant exited the room, got into his car, drove a short distance away, and met the police. The informant gave the police the crack cocaine he had just purchased, and a search of his person established that he no longer had possession of the marked twenty dollar bill.

Pair and two other officers "immediately went back to Room 117." Pair knocked on the door. One of the occupants asked who was there. Pair identified himself and said, "Police, open the door." The immediate reply from inside the room was, "wait a minute." Pair then heard voices, movements, and a commode being flushed, whereupon he knocked on the door again. Ferguson opened the door and, after he and Weathers exited the room and were placed in custody, the officers entered. They searched the room and found cocaine located in and around the commode. The marked bill was found on Weathers' person, together with additional cash and a single-edged razor.

On July 22, 1999, Weathers was tried for possession of cocaine with intent to distribute and was convicted on that charge. This appeal followed. Should Weathers' motion to suppress the seized evidence be granted? *Weathers v. Commonwealth*, 529 S.E.2d 847 (Va. App. 2000).

5 On September 10, 1997, at approximately 7:15 P.M., Milwaukee Police Officer Diane Arenas, Wauwatosa Police Detective Keith Werner, and two other Milwaukee police officers arrived at an apartment building located at 2867 South Kinnickinnic Avenue in the City of Milwaukee. The officers believed that Blanco was staying in apartment 118 at that location. The officers had an arrest warrant for Blanco for the crime of attempted first-degree homicide, while armed. The officers did not directly proceed to the apartment where Blanco was believed to be, but conducted further investigation. An officer showed Blanco's picture to the apartment manager, who stated that Blanco might be staying in apartment 118. An occupant of the apartment building told an officer that Blanco had just been outside the apartment building smoking a cigarette before the police arrived. Another occupant told the police that he had seen Blanco enter apartment 118 just before the police arrived.

At approximately 8:00 P.M., the officers knocked on the apartment door, announced that they were police officers, and that they were there to arrest Blanco, pursuant to a felony arrest warrant. A female, later identified as Al-Shammari, refused to allow the officers to enter. During this time period, another officer observed Blanco attempt to leave the apartment through a window. Blanco aborted the attempt, however, when he saw the police. The police called for assistance from the Tactical Enforcement Unit.

The immediate area was secured, surrounding apartments were evacuated, and the police were granted entry to an apartment immediately above and identical to the Al-Shammari apartment. As a result of this access and a review of the layout of the apartment, police were aware that there was a crawl space above the bathtub where someone could hide. Communications were repeatedly attempted with Al-Shammari to have Blanco turn himself over to the police. During this time, the police heard noises and activity coming from Al-Shammari's bathroom, including an inordinate amount of toilet flushing, and voices and sounds near the crawl space above the bathtub. The police also heard repeated use of the garbage disposal in Al-Shammari's kitchen. As a result, the water was turned off to the Al-Shammari apartment.

At approximately 10:30 P.M., after their unsuccessful efforts to have Al-Shammari consent to entry, or Blanco voluntarily submit to arrest, the six-man Tactical Enforcement Unit entered the apartment by use of a key obtained from the building manager. Officer Gilbert Carrasco was the first to enter. He held his shield in front of him in anticipation of some type of resistant force. Upon entry, three individuals were located: Al-Shammari, Blanco, and Rogelio Fuentez. The three were handcuffed and taken into custody. Carrasco proceeded to the bathroom to perform a protective sweep of that room. He testified that he was concerned that someone may have been hiding in the crawl space located above the bathtub. The board covering the crawl space was secured to the ceiling with four screws. Carrasco asked another officer for a screwdriver and he then removed the panel. Upon doing so, a bag containing marijuana fell on his head. He checked the crawl space for suspects, but it was empty.

As a result of the discovery of the contraband, the police obtained a search warrant for the premises and discovered additional marijuana, a total of 20.4 pounds, scales, $1,745 in cash, three pagers, a cellular telephone, and a .380 caliber pistol. After being properly charged for the drug offenses, Blanco and Al-Shammari both filed motions seeking to suppress the evidence. Should the evidence be suppressed? *State v. Blanco*, 614 N.W.2d 512 (Wis. App. 2000).

6 Officer Dave Tertipes of the Moline, Illinois, police department responded to a call on June 25, 1998, to meet the manager of an apartment complex concerning "pictures of naked children." On his arrival, the manager gave Tertipes a magazine entitled *Ophelia Editions*, which had been found in the hallway of the apartment complex where Moore lived. The magazine was addressed to "Chris Moore."

The cover of the magazine featured a drawing of a clothed girl in a provocative pose who appeared to be about ten to twelve years old and described the contents as "Fine Art—Photography—Literature—Non-Fiction." The twenty-eight page magazine was a catalogue accompanied by descriptions and sample photos of about eighty other publications, including picture books of nude children and stories of children engaged in sex. The magazine contained a disclaimer purportedly affirming that the contents had been reviewed by an attorney and did not contain "lascivious exhibition[s]" of persons under eighteen. Tertipes, who had no special training in identifying child pornography, found at least three photographs that he considered illegal under the state child pornography law. The catalogue also contained many written descriptions of sexual contact with and among minors.

Based on this review, Tertipes knocked on Moore's apartment door and identified himself to Moore, who invited him to enter. Tertipes asked Moore about the magazine, and Moore admitted to ordering the magazine over the Internet. Moore characterized himself as a nudist who "likes to view the human body in its natural state." Tertipes asked Moore to come to the police station, and Moore initially complied voluntarily. Once in the car, Moore asked if he could leave. Tertipes consulted with his supervisor who said, "He doesn't have a choice. Bring him down." Tertipes placed Moore under arrest.

Once Moore arrived at the station, Lt. Steve Brockway took over the investigation. Brockway, who had previous training and experience in child sexual abuse and pornography cases, reviewed the magazine and concluded that it contained child pornography. Brockway read Moore his *Miranda* rights. Following a detailed explanation of his rights, Moore agreed to waive his rights and signed a voluntary waiver form. During questioning, which lasted about two hours, Moore referred to himself as a nudist but eventually admitted that he had a proclivity toward sex with children and possessed other depictions of child pornography at his apartment.

Brockway informed Moore that he thought he had probable cause to obtain a search warrant and asked Moore if he would consent to a search of his apartment and vehicle. Moore agreed and signed a form consenting to the warrantless search of his home and vehicle. No evidence indicated that Moore was incapable of voluntary consent or that Moore was threatened or coerced in any way. After signing the form, Moore ceased the interview.

The police executed the warrant and found an album containing 89 photographs of minor boys posed provocatively or engaged in sexual acts and a stack of computer-generated photos of boys engaged in sexual acts. Police seized Moore's computer, which contained images of child pornography and e-mail correspondences detailing Moore's efforts to arrange meetings with children for the purpose of engaging in sex. Other publications, including some that were advertised in *Ophelia Editions*, were also found.

Subsequently, Moore challenged the legality of the search under the Fourth Amendment. Moore presents two reasons why the search should be suppressed. First, he argues that police lacked probable cause to arrest him, and therefore, his consent to the search of his apartment was involuntary. Second, he contends that as a matter of law, the police should seek probable cause review from a neutral magistrate before executing an arrest. Should the fruits of the search be suppressed? *United States v. Moore*, 215 F.3d 681 (7th Cir. 2000).

7

Stops and Frisks

Learning Objectives

▶ Understand the distinctions among a stop, a formal arrest, a seizure tantamount to an arrest, and minimal non-intrusive contact between a citizen and a law enforcement officer.

▶ Understand the distinctions between a frisk and a full search.

▶ Understand how to balance competing interests when determining the reasonableness of a stop and frisk.

▶ Know what justifies a law enforcement officer in stopping a person and what interference with the person's freedom of action the law permits.

▶ Know what justifies a law enforcement officer in frisking a person and the scope of the search the law permits.

▶ Apply the legal principles governing stops and frisks to analogous situations, such as detentions and examinations of luggage, mail, and other property.

In Chapter 6, a formal **arrest** was defined as "the taking of a person into custody for the commission of an offense as the prelude to prosecuting him for it." *State v. Murphy*, 465 P.2d 900, 902 (Or. App.1970). Also discussed were **seizures tantamount to arrest**—encounters between a law enforcement officer and a person that intrude on the person's freedom of action to the degree that it is indistinguishable from an arrest in important respects. A stop involves an even less intrusive **seizure** of a person; and a frisk involves a limited search of that person.

A **stop** is a police practice involving the temporary detention and questioning of a person initiated on a **reasonable suspicion** (less than **probable cause**) of criminal activity for the purposes of crime prevention and investigation. A **frisk** is a limited search of a stopped person who is reasonably believed to be armed and dangerous for the protection of the law enforcement officer carrying out the investigation.

Stops and frisks are not contacts in which a law enforcement officer approaches a person in a public place and asks if the person is willing to answer questions. These contacts should involve a legitimate law enforcement purpose, but they do not require the reasonable suspicion associated with a stop and frisk. The officer may not detain the person, even momentarily, whether or not the person chooses to cooperate. If, however, an initially friendly and neutral encounter somehow provides the officer with reason to suspect criminal activity or danger, the officer may be justified in making the more significant intrusions of a stop and a frisk.

▶THE FOUNDATIONS FOR STOPS AND FRISKS

Law enforcement has employed stops and frisks for centuries. This section looks briefly at that history, and then explores the legal foundations for this practice.

History

A law enforcement officer's power to detain and question suspicious persons dates back to the common law of England, where constables had the power to detain suspicious persons overnight to investigate their suspicious activities. In the United States, until the mid-1960s, police-initiated contacts with citizens that did not amount to arrests were generally left to the discretion of individual officers, and were not subject to constitutional protections or judicial oversight. In the mid-1960s—a period of expanding constitutional rights for citizens— reform-minded individuals called for the extension of constitutional protections to all police-citizen encounters and review of these encounters by the courts. Some in law enforcement argued that, because of their experience and professionalism, street encounters should be subject to their discretion rather than formal rules.

The reformers maintained that a free society requires that constitutional safeguards protect every citizen, especially minorities and dissidents, at all times and places. In response, the U.S. Supreme Court adopted formal guidelines governing street encounters amounting to less than arrests or full searches in three cases decided in 1968. In those three foundational cases—*Terry v. Ohio, Sibron v. New York*, and *Peters v. New York*—the Court attempted to resolve the conflicting interests by applying a balancing test under the **reasonableness** requirement of the Fourth Amendment.

The Foundational Case

The discussion of the modern law regulating stops and frisks begins with a summary of *Terry v. Ohio*, 392 U.S. 1 (1968).

Terry v. Ohio The facts of the case were stated by the U.S. Supreme Court:

> At the hearing on the motion to suppress this evidence, Officer McFadden testified that while he was patrolling in plain clothes in downtown Cleveland at approximately 2:30 in the afternoon of October 31, 1963, his attention was attracted by two men, Chilton and Terry, standing on the corner of Huron Road and Euclid Avenue. He had never seen the two men before, and he was unable to say precisely what first drew his eye to them. However, he testified that he had been a policeman for 39 years and a detective for 35 and that he had been assigned to patrol this vicinity of downtown Cleveland for shoplifters and pickpockets for 30 years. He added: "Now, in this case when I looked over they didn't look right to me at the time."
>
> His interest aroused, Officer McFadden took up a post of observation in the entrance to a store 300 to 400 feet away from the two men. "I get more purpose to watch them when I seen their movements," he testified. He saw one of the men leave the other one and walk southwest on Huron Road, past some stores. The man paused for a moment and looked in a store window, then walked on a short distance, turned around and walked back toward the corner, pausing once again to look in the same store window. He rejoined his companion at the corner, and the two conferred briefly. Then the second man went through the same series of motions, strolling down Huron Road, looking in the same window, walking on a short distance, turning back, peering in the store window again, and returning to confer with the first man at the corner. The two men repeated this ritual alternately between five and six times apiece—in all, roughly a dozen trips. At one point, while the two were standing together on the corner, a third man approached them and engaged them briefly in conversation. This man then left the two others and walked west on Euclid Avenue. Chilton and Terry resumed their measured pacing, peering and conferring. After this had gone on for 10 to 12 minutes, the two men walked off together, heading west on Euclid Avenue, following the path taken earlier by the third man.
>
> [His suspicions aroused and fearing Terry and Chilton had a gun which they intended to use to rob the store, Officer McFadden followed them. Observing that the two men stopped in front of another store called "Zucker's," Officer McFadden intervened. He] identified himself as a police officer and asked for their names. At this point his knowledge was confined to what he had observed. . . . When the men "mumbled something" in response to his inquiries, Officer McFadden grabbed petitioner

Terry, spun him around so that they were facing the other two, with Terry between McFadden and the others, and patted down the outside of his clothing. In the left breast pocket of Terry's overcoat Officer McFadden felt a pistol. He reached inside the overcoat pocket, but was unable to remove the gun. At this point, keeping Terry between himself and the others, the officer ordered all three men to enter Zucker's store. As they went in, he removed Terry's overcoat completely, removed a .38-caliber revolver from the pocket and ordered all three men to face the wall with their hands raised. Officer McFadden proceeded to pat down the outer clothing of Chilton and the third man, Katz. He discovered another revolver in the outer pocket of Chilton's overcoat, but no weapons were found on Katz. The officer testified that he only patted the men down to see whether they had weapons, and that he did not put his hands beneath the outer garments of either Terry or Chilton until he felt their guns. So far as appears from the record, he never placed his hands beneath Katz' outer garments. Officer McFadden seized Chilton's gun, asked the proprietor of the store to call a police wagon, and took all three men to the station. . . . 392 U.S. at 5–7.

Terry and Chilton were formally charged and convicted of carrying concealed weapons. They appealed, claiming that the weapons were obtained by means of an unreasonable search and should not have been admitted into evidence at their trial. The U.S. Supreme Court affirmed the convictions holding that, even though stops and frisks represent a lesser restraint than traditional arrests and searches, the procedures are still governed by the Fourth Amendment. However, stops and frisks are not subject to as stringent a limitation as are traditional full arrests and searches. Instead of applying the probable cause standard to stops and frisks, the Court applied the fundamental test of the Fourth Amendment: the reasonableness under all the circumstances of the particular governmental invasion of a citizen's personal security.

In discussing the reasonableness of Officer McFadden's actions, the Court recognized that law enforcement officers need to protect themselves when suspicious circumstances indicate possible criminal activity by potentially dangerous persons, even though probable cause for an arrest is lacking. It would be unreasonable to deny an officer the authority to take steps to determine whether a suspected person is armed and to neutralize the threat of harm. The Court concluded that:

[W]here a police officer observes unusual conduct which leads him reasonably to conclude in light of his experience that criminal activity may be afoot and that the persons with whom he is dealing may be armed and presently dangerous, where in the course of investigating this behavior he identifies himself as a policeman and makes reasonable inquiries, and where nothing in the initial stages of the encounter serves to dispel his reasonable fear for his own or other's safety, he is entitled for the protection of himself and others in the area to conduct a carefully limited search of the outer clothing of such persons in an attempt to discover weapons which might be used to assault him. 392 U.S. at 30.

The Reasonableness Standard

Stop-and-frisk procedures are serious intrusions on a person's privacy. They are governed by the Fourth Amendment to the Constitution, which prohibits unreasonable searches and seizures.

> It is quite plain that the Fourth Amendment governs "seizures" of the person which do not eventuate in a trip to the station house and prosecution for crime—"arrests" in traditional terminology. It must be recognized that whenever a police officer accosts an individual and restrains his freedom to walk away, he has "seized" that person. And it is nothing less than sheer torture of the English language to suggest that a careful exploration of the outer surfaces of a person's clothing all over his or her body in an attempt to find weapons is not a "search." Moreover, it is simply fantastic to urge that such a procedure performed in public by a policeman while the citizen stands helpless, perhaps facing a wall with his hands raised, is a "petty indignity." It is a serious intrusion upon the sanctity of the person, which may inflict great indignity and arouse strong resentment, and it is not to be undertaken lightly. *Terry*, 392 U.S. at 16–17.

Nevertheless, because a stop is more limited in scope than an arrest and a frisk is more limited in scope than a full search, stops and frisks are judged by a less rigid standard than the probable cause standard applicable to an arrest and search. Terry made clear that stops and frisks are governed not by the warrant clause of the Fourth Amendment but by the reasonableness clause:

> [W]e deal here with an entire rubric of police conduct—necessarily swift action based upon the on-the-spot observations of the officer on the beat—which historically has not been, and as a practical matter could not be, subjected to the warrant procedure. Instead, the conduct involved in this case must be tested by the Fourth Amendment's general proscription against unreasonable searches and seizures. *Terry*, 392 U.S. at 20.

The question for the law enforcement officer is whether it is reasonable, in a particular set of circumstances, for the officer to seize a person (e.g., make a "stop") and subject the person to a limited search (e.g., a "frisk") when there is no probable cause to arrest.

The determination of reasonableness involves a balancing of the competing interests involved in a stop-and-frisk situation. On one side are a person's right to privacy and right to be free from unreasonable searches and seizures. As *Terry* indicated, "Even a limited search of the outer clothing for weapons constitutes a severe, though brief, intrusion upon cherished personal security, and it must surely be an annoying, frightening, and perhaps humiliating experience." 392 U.S. at 24–25. On the other side are the governmental interests: effective crime prevention and detection and protection of law enforcement officers and others from armed and dangerous persons. Balancing these competing interests of individual privacy and effective law enforcement in a particular situation requires an evaluation of:

▶ whether *any* police interference at all is justified by the circumstances; and

▶ if so, *how extensive* an interference those circumstances justify.

In this regard, the Supreme Court has also said that the reasonableness determination for a stop-and-frisk involves a "weighing of the gravity of the public concerns served by the seizure, the degree to which the seizure advances the public interest, and the severity of the interference with individual liberty." *Brown v. Texas*, 443 U.S. 47, 51 (1979).

Stops and frisks are discussed separately in this chapter because they have different purposes, different sets of circumstances that justify them, and different consequences for the person subjected to the procedure. The remainder of this chapter discusses in detail a law enforcement officer's authority to conduct stops and frisks and the allowable scope of that authority.

key point

- The determination of the reasonableness of stops and frisks involves balancing a person's right to privacy and right to be free from unreasonable searches and seizures against the governmental in-terests of effective crime prevention and detection and the safety of law enforcement officers and others from armed and dangerous persons.

 ## STOPS

The U.S. Supreme Court recognized that stopping persons for the purpose of in-vestigating possible criminal activity can be, at times, necessary to the government's interest in effective crime prevention and detection. "**[I]t is this interest which underlies the recognition that *a police officer may in appropriate circumstances and in an appropriate manner approach a person for pur-poses of investigating possibly criminal behavior even though there is no probable cause to make an arrest.*" *Terry v. Ohio*, 392 U.S. 1, 22 (1968) (em-phasis added).

Differentiating Stops as Seizures from Non-Seizures

A stop is the least intrusive type of seizure of the person governed by the Fourth Amendment. However, not every approach of a person by a law enforcement officer for purposes of investigating possible criminal activity is considered a seizure under the Fourth Amendment. In *Terry*, the Court noted, "**Obviously not all personal intercourse between policemen and citizens involves 'sei-zures' of persons. Only when the officer, by means of physical force or show of authority, has in some way restrained the liberty of a citizen may we conclude that a 'seizure' has occurred.**" 392 U.S. at 19 n.16. Chapter 6 explored in detail the tests courts employ to determine when someone is under arrest or its functional equivalent. This chapter explores the criteria courts use to determine when a stop has occurred, and, therefore, whether a seizure of a person has taken place for Fourth Amendment purposes.

The "Free-to-Leave" Test In *United States v. Mendenhall*, 446 U.S. 544 (1980), the U.S. Supreme Court found no seizure (and therefore no stop) on the follow-ing facts:

> **The events took place in the public concourse [of an airport]. The agents wore no uniforms and displayed no weapons. They did not summon the respondent to their presence, but instead approached her and identified themselves as federal agents. They requested, but did not demand to see the respondent's identification and ticket. Such conduct without more, did not amount to an intrusion upon any constitutionally protected**

> interest. The respondent was not seized simply by reason of the fact that the agents approached her, asked her if she would show them her ticket and identification and posed to her a few questions. Nor was it enough to establish a seizure that the person asking the questions was a law enforcement official. In short, nothing in the record suggests that the respondent had any objective reason to believe that she was not free to end the conversation in the concourse and proceed on her own way, and for that reason we conclude that the agents' initial approach to her was not a seizure. 446 U.S. at 555.

The Supreme Court in *Mendenhall* set forth a test for determining whether a person has been seized within the meaning of the Fourth Amendment. The Court used a "totality of circumstances" approach in formulating its test for "seizures":

> *[A] person has been "seized" within the meaning of the Fourth Amendment only if, in view of all of the circumstances surrounding the incident, a reasonable person would have believed that he was not free to leave.* **Examples of circumstances that might indicate a seizure, even where the person did not attempt to leave, would be the threatening presence of several officers, the display of a weapon by an officer, some physical touching of the person of the citizen, or the use of language or tone of voice indicating that compliance with the officer's request might be compelled. . . . In the absence of some such evidence, otherwise inoffensive contact between a member of the public and the police cannot, as a matter of law, amount to a seizure of that person.** 446 U.S. at 554–55 (emphasis added).

Under this test, certain "shows of authority" by officers, such as a display of a weapon or the use of a certain language, would lead a reasonable person to believe he or she is not free to leave (therefore satisfying the *Mendenhall* definition for a "seizure"). It is important to note that the test in *Mendenhall* is objective: it is **"not whether the [particular] citizen perceived that he was being ordered to restrict his movement, but whether the officer's words and actions would have conveyed that to a reasonable person."** *See California v. Hodari D.*, 499 U.S. 621, 628 (1991).

Florida v. Rodriguez, 469 U.S. 1 (1984), also found no seizure (and hence no stop) when an officer approached a man in an airport and asked him to move to a nearby, public location within the airport so that the officer could speak with him. The facts leading up to the officer-citizen encounter in *Rodriguez* are as follows: The officer followed the defendant because he and his two companions behaved in an unusual manner at an airline ticket counter. At some point, the defendant realized he was being followed, and made a half-hearted attempt to flee. He then confronted the officer and "uttered a vulgar exclamation." The officer showed his badge, and asked to speak with him. The defendant agreed, and the officer recommended that they move approximately fifteen feet to another location, where another police officer was meeting with the man's companions. In holding that this encounter between the defendant and the officer was not a seizure (and hence not a stop) for Fourth Amendment purposes, the Court said: "The initial contact between the officers and [defendant], where they simply asked if he would step aside and talk with them, was clearly the sort of consensual encounter that implicates no Fourth Amendment interest." 469 U.S. at 5–6. In 2004, the Supreme Court reaffirmed its rule that asking basic investigatory questions, including a request for identification and a request to search, do not implicate the Fourth Amendment (and hence are not "stops"): **"Asking questions is an essential part of police investigations. In the ordinary course a police officer is free to ask a person for identification without implicating the Fourth Amendment."** *See Hiibel v. Sixth Judicial Dist. Ct. of Nev., Humboldt County,* 542 U.S. 177, 185 (2004).

However, in *Florida v. Royer,* 460 U.S. 491 (1983), yet another case occurring in an airport, the Court did find a seizure for Fourth Amendment purposes because of the intrusiveness of the conduct on the part of the officers. In particular, the officers made a "show of authority"; as a result, a reasonable person in the defendant's position would not feel free to leave. In *Royer,* the defendant purchased a one-way airline ticket under an assumed name, and checked luggage under this assumed name. As the defendant walked toward the boarding area within the concourse, two detectives approached him because his characteristics and actions fit a "drug courier profile." Upon request, he showed the detectives his airline ticket and driver's license, which carried his correct name. The defendant explained the discrepancy in names by pointing out that a friend had placed the ticket reservation in the assumed name. The detectives, who identified themselves as narcotics investigators, told the defendant that they suspected him of transporting narcotics. The detectives did not return the defendant's ticket or his license, but asked him to accompany them to a small room near the concourse. The Court concluded that on these facts, there was a seizure (and hence a stop) for Fourth Amendment purposes:

> **Asking for and examining Royer's ticket and his driver's license were no doubt permissible in themselves, but when the officers identified themselves as narcotics agents, told Royer that he was suspected of transporting narcotics, and asked him to accompany them to the police room, while retaining his ticket and driver's license and without indicating in any way that he was free to depart, Royer was effectively seized for the purposes of the Fourth Amendment. These circumstances surely amount to a show of official authority such that "a reasonable person would have believed he was not free to leave."** 460 U.S. at 501–02.

The Court distinguished *Mendenhall* (the other airport case discussed above where no seizure occurred) in the following way:

> **Here, Royer's ticket and identification remained in the possession of the officers throughout the encounter; the officers also seized and had possession of his luggage. As a practical matter, Royer could not leave the airport without them. In Mendenhall, no luggage was involved, the ticket and identification were immediately returned, and the officers were careful to advise that the suspect could decline to be searched. Here, the officers had seized Royer's luggage and made no effort to advise him that he need not consent to the search [i.e., that he could refuse to accompany the officers to the small room where a subsequent search of his luggage would be conducted].** 460 U.S. at 503.

The Supreme Court has also decided cases in the "seizure" context in other environments outside airports. For example, when immigration authorities enter a factory to determine if any employees are undocumented aliens, and question individuals regarding their citizenship status, no Fourth Amendment seizure occurs: This was the holding of *I.N.S. v. Delgado,* 466 U.S. 210 (1984). In *Delgado,* the Court described the "factory surveys" by immigration authorities in the following way:

> At the beginning of the surveys several agents positioned themselves near the buildings' exits, while other agents dispersed throughout the factory to question most, but not all, employees at their work stations. The agents displayed badges, carried walkie-talkies, and were armed, although at no point during any of the surveys was a weapon ever drawn. Moving systematically through the factory, the agents approached employees and, after identifying themselves, asked them from one to three questions relating to their citizenship. If the employee gave a credible reply that he was a United States citizen, the questioning ended, and the agent moved on to another employee. If the employee gave an unsatisfactory response or admitted that he was an alien, the employee was asked to produce his immigration papers. During the survey, employees continued with their work and were free to walk around within the factory. 466 U.S. at 212–13.

In response to the defendants' argument that the entire work force of the factory was "seized" during the survey because immigration officers were stationed at the exits, the Court said:

> But it was obvious from the beginning of the surveys that the INS agents were only questioning people. Persons such as [defendants] who simply went about their business in the workplace were not detained in any way; nothing more occurred than that a question was put to them. While persons who attempted to flee or evade the agents may eventually have been detained for questioning, [defendants] did not do so and were not in fact detained. The manner in which defendants were questioned, given its obvious purpose, could hardly result in a reasonable fear that [defendants] were not free to continue working or to move about the factory. [Defendants] may only litigate what happened to them, and our review of their description of the encounters with the INS agents satisfies us that the encounters were classic consensual encounters rather than Fourth Amendment seizures. 466 U.S. at 220–21.

Application of this objective "free to leave" test was also the basis for the Supreme Court's decision in *Michigan v. Chesternut*, 486 U.S. 567 (1988). In that case, officers in a patrol car chased the defendant after they observed him run when he saw the patrol car. The chase consisted of a brief acceleration to catch up with the defendant, followed by a short drive alongside him.

The Court in *Chesternut* found no stop because the defendant could not have reasonably believed that he was not free to disregard the police presence and go about his business. The Court noted that the police did not activate a siren or flasher, did not command the defendant to halt, did not display any weapons, and did not operate the patrol car in an aggressive manner to block the defendant's course or otherwise control the direction or speed of the defendant's movement. *The Court recognized that* "[w]hile the very presence of a police car driving parallel to a running pedestrian could be somewhat intimidating, this kind of police presence does not, standing alone, constitute a seizure." 486 U.S. at 575. Referring to *Mendenhall*'s objective test, the Court said:

> The [*Mendenhall*] test is necessarily imprecise, because it is designed to assess the coercive effect of police conduct, taken as a whole, rather than to focus on particular details of that conduct in isolation. Moreover, what constitutes a restraint on liberty prompting a person to conclude that he is not free to "leave" will vary, not only with the particular police conduct at issue, but also with the setting in which the conduct occurs. 486 U.S. at 573.

A case with facts similar to *Chesternut* also found no "seizure" (and hence no stop) for Fourth Amendment purposes. In *United States v. Dockter*, 58 F.3d 1284 (8th Cir. 1995), the court held that the defendants were not seized within the meaning of the Fourth Amendment when a deputy sheriff pulled his vehicle behind their automobile, which was parked off the traveled portion of the road and had its parking lights on, and activated his amber warning lights. The deputy sheriff did not block their vehicle in any manner to preclude them from leaving, did not draw his weapon, and spoke to them in a tone that was inquisitive rather than coercive.

The "Free to Decline Requests or Terminate Encounter" Test Cases decided since *Mendenhall* have attempted to refine its test for "seizure" (e.g., whether a reasonable person feels free to leave). For example, the Court in *Florida v. Bostick*, 501 U.S. 429, 435 (1991), established that *law enforcement officers may ask a person basic investigatory questions, including requests to examine identification or search luggage, and there is no seizure for Fourth Amendment purposes* **"as long as the police do not convey the message that compliance with their requests is required."** In particular, *Bostick* suggested that there is no seizure when two law enforcement officers walk up to a person, who is seated on a bus, ask him a few questions, and ask whether they can search his bags. The Court said that, although the defendant in this case may not have felt free to leave, his freedom of movement was restricted by a factor independent of police conduct:

> [T]he mere fact that Bostick did not feel free to leave the bus does not mean that the police seized him. Bostick was a passenger on a bus that was scheduled to depart. He would not have felt free to leave the bus even if the police had not been present. Bostick's movements were "confined" in a sense, but this was the natural result of his decision to take the bus; it says nothing about whether or not the police conduct at issue was coercive. 501 U.S. at 436.

The Court in *Bostick* went on to refine the test for "seizure" it had first set forth in *Mendenhall:*

> *[I]n order to determine whether a particular encounter constitutes a seizure, a court must consider all the circumstances surrounding the encounter to determine whether the police conduct would have communicated to a reasonable person that the person was not free to decline the officers' requests or otherwise terminate the encounter.* That rule applies to encounters that take place on a city street or in an airport lobby, and it applies equally to encounters on a bus. 501 U.S. at 439–40 (emphasis added).

In another case involving a request by law enforcement officials to search a bus passenger, the Supreme Court examined the totality of the circumstances, and determined that the passenger was not seized:

> There was no application of force, no intimidating movement, no overwhelming show of force, no brandishing of weapons, no blocking of exits, no threat, no command, not even an authoritative tone of voice. It is beyond question that had this encounter occurred on the street, it would be constitutional. The fact that an encounter takes place on a bus does not on its own transform standard police questioning of citizens into an

> **illegal seizure. . . . Indeed, because many fellow passengers are present to witness officers' conduct, a reasonable person may feel even more secure in his or her decision not to cooperate with police on a bus than in other circumstances.** *United States v. Drayton*, 536 U.S. 194, 204 (2002).

Drayton also held that the officer's display of a badge did not convert an otherwise non-coercive encounter into a seizure. Note that on these same facts, the Court found that the defendant bus passengers' consent to a search of their luggage and their persons was voluntary. (See Chapter 9 on Consent Searches.)

However, in *Brendlin v. California*, 127 S.Ct. 2400 (2007), the Supreme Court found that not only the driver but also passengers are seized for Fourth Amendment purposes when an officer makes a routine *traffic stop of a private vehicle:*

> **A traffic stop necessarily curtails the travel a passenger has chosen just as much as it halts the driver, diverting both from the stream of traffic to the side of the road, and the police activity that normally amounts to intrusion on "privacy and personal security" does not normally (and did not here) distinguish between passenger and driver. An officer who orders one particular car to pull over acts with an implicit claim of right based on fault of some sort, and a sensible person would not expect a police officer to allow people to come and go freely from the physical focal point of an investigation into faulty behavior or wrongdoing. If the likely wrongdoing is not the driving, the passenger will reasonably feel subject to suspicion owing to close association; but even when the wrongdoing is only bad driving, the passenger will expect to be subject to some scrutiny, and his attempt to leave the scene would be so obviously likely to prompt an objection from the officer that no passenger would feel free to leave in the first place. It is also reasonable for passengers to expect that a police officer at the scene of a crime, arrest, or investigation will not let people move around in ways that could jeopardize his safety.** 127 S.Ct. at 2409–10.

Acknowledging that passengers of non-private vehicles (i.e., taxicabs and buses) may be treated differently under Fourth Amendment seizure law than passengers of private vehicles, the Court said that the **"the crucial question would be whether a reasonable person in the passenger's position would feel free to take steps to terminate the encounter,"** and go about his business: **"[T]he issue is whether a reasonable passenger would have perceived that the show of authority [by the officer] was at least partly directed at him, and that he was thus not free to ignore the police presence and go about his business."** 127 S.Ct. at 2409–10. Thus, with this caveat, the Court's statements in *Bostick* and *Drayton* that bus passengers were not seized under the facts of those cases, remain valid.

In addition, the Court has been clear that more intrusive actions by police will amount to a seizure under the Fourth Amendment. In *Kaupp v. Texas*, 538 U.S. 626 (2003), in the company of five other officers, an officer named Pinkins went to the defendant's house at approximately 3 A.M. After being let in by the defendant's father, Officers Pinkins went to the defendant's bedroom, awakened him with a flashlight, identified himself, and stated, "We need to go and talk." The defendant, a seventeen-year-old boy, agreed. He was handcuffed and then, without shoes, was led by the officers out of his house and into a patrol car. The patrol car stopped for five or ten minutes at the location where the victim's body in a recent murder had been found, and then the car proceeded to police headquarters. The defendant was taken to an interview room. After having been given *Miranda* warnings and in response to police questioning, he admitted having a role in the murder.

The Court held that these actions by officers not only amounted to a seizure, but also constituted a full arrest:

> A 17-year-old boy was awakened in his bedroom at three in the morning by at least three police officers, one of whom stated "'we need to go and talk.'" He was taken out in handcuffs, without shoes, dressed only in his underwear in January, placed in a patrol car, driven to the scene of a crime and then to the sheriff's offices, where he was taken into an interrogation room and questioned. This evidence points to arrest even more starkly than the facts in *Dunaway v. New York*, 442 U.S. 200, 212 (1979), where the petitioner 'was taken from a neighbor's home to a police car, transported to a police station, and placed in an interrogation room.' There we held it clear that the detention was "in important respects indistinguishable from a traditional arrest" and therefore required probable cause or judicial authorization to be legal. The same is, if anything, even clearer here. 538 U.S. at 631.

In particular, the Court found that a reasonable person in the defendant's position would not be free to terminate the encounter and "go about his business": **"It cannot seriously be suggested that when the detectives began to question Kaupp, a reasonable person in his situation would have thought he was sitting in the interview room as a matter of choice, free to change his mind and go home to bed."** 538 U.S. at 632.

"Means Intentionally Applied" Test For purposes of the Fourth Amendment, a seizure requires an intentional acquisition of physical control. For example, if a parked and unoccupied police car slips its brake and pins an innocent passerby against a wall, it is likely that a tort has occurred but not a violation of the Fourth Amendment. And the situation would not change if the passerby happened, by lucky chance, to be a serial murderer for whom there was an outstanding felony arrest warrant—even if, at the time he was pinned by the unoccupied car, he was in the process of running away from two pursuing police officers. In this regard, *Brower v. County of Inyo*, 489 U.S.593, 596–97 (1989), held that:

> [A] Fourth Amendment seizure does not occur whenever there is a governmentally caused termination of an individual's freedom of movement (the innocent passerby), nor even whenever there is a governmentally caused and governmentally *desired* termination of an individual's freedom of movement (the fleeing felon), but only when there is a governmental termination of freedom of movement *through means intentionally applied* (italics in original).

Accordingly, the Court has held that **"no Fourth Amendment seizure would take place where a 'pursuing police car sought to stop the suspect only by the show of authority represented by flashing lights and continuing pursuit,' but accidentally stopped the suspect by crashing into him."** *Sacramento v. Lewis*, 523 U.S. 833, 844 (1998).

"Halting or Submission" Requirement As discussed in Chapter 6, the Supreme Court has established a related principle regarding seizures: if a **show of**

authority by a law enforcement officer does not result in a halting or submission by the person being confronted, there is no seizure under the Fourth Amendment. For example, in *California v. Hodari D.*, 499 U.S. 621 (1991), the defendant was fleeing the approach of an unmarked police car and was surprised when he confronted an officer on foot pursuing him from another direction. The defendant immediately tossed away a small rock and was soon tackled by the officer. The rock was recovered and proved to be crack cocaine. The Court held that, in the absence of any physical contact or submission to the officer's show of authority, the defendant was not seized until he was tackled. The cocaine abandoned while he was running could not, therefore, be the fruit of a seizure and subject to exclusion.

Summary of Criteria Used to Determine Whether a Stop/Seizure Occurred To summarize, three basic questions must be answered to determine if a seizure or stop has occurred for Fourth Amendment purposes. First, did the law enforcement officer, by means of physical force or a show of authority, restrain a person's liberty? In other words, under the totality of the circumstances, would a reasonable person believe that he or she was not free to leave as a result of the officer's actions? Did the police conduct communicate to a reasonable person that the person was not free to decline the officers' requests or otherwise terminate the encounter and go about his business? Second, did the police force or show of authority resulting in the termination or restriction of the person's movement, come about through governmental means intentionally applied? Third, did the physical force or show of authority result in an actual halting or submission by the person being confronted? If all three inquiries are answered in the affirmative, there has been a seizure for Fourth Amendment purposes.

Note that a seizure of a suspect can, at some point, evolve beyond a "stop" and become an arrest requiring probable cause. Arrests and seizures tantamount to arrest were discussed in Chapter 6.

key point

- A "stop" is the least intrusive type of seizure of a person under the Fourth Amendment. If, in view of all of the circumstances surrounding the incident, a reasonable person would have believed that he or she was not free to leave, decline the officer's requests or otherwise terminate the encounter, the person has been "seized" within the meaning of the Fourth Amendment. Only when an officer intentionally, by means of physical force or show of authority, has restrained a person's liberty has a "seizure" occurred. Also, for a seizure to occur, the person being confronted by the officer must have submitted to the officer's authority or force.

Authority to Stop

It is important for law enforcement officers to know when they have authority to stop. The details of the reasonable suspicion standard are discussed in this section.

The Reasonable Suspicion Standard A law enforcement officer may stop and briefly detain a person for investigative purposes if the officer has a **reasonable**

suspicion *supported by articulable facts that criminal activity "may be afoot,"* even if the officer lacks probable cause. (Indications of criminal activity are discussed in Chapter 3.) Reasonable suspicion is **"considerably less than proof of wrongdoing by a preponderance of the evidence"** and **"is obviously less demanding than that for probable cause."** *United States v. Sokolow*, 490 U.S. 1, 7 (1989). The concept of reasonable suspicion, like probable cause, is not "readily, or even usefully, reduced to a neat set of legal rules." *Illinois v. Gates*, 462 U.S. 213, 232 (1983). In evaluating the validity of a stop, courts consider the totality of the circumstances:

> **The totality of the circumstances—the whole picture—must be taken into account. Based upon that whole picture the detaining officers must have a particularized and objective basis for suspecting the particular person stopped of criminal activity. . . . The analysis proceeds with various objective observations, information from police reports, if such are available, and consideration of the modes or patterns of operation of certain kinds of lawbreakers. From these data, a trained officer draws inferences and makes deductions—inferences and deductions that might well elude an untrained person.**
>
> **The process does not deal with hard certainties, but with probabilities. Long before the law of probabilities was articulated as such, practical people formulated certain common-sense conclusions about human behavior; jurors as fact-finders are permitted to do the same—and so are law enforcement officers.** *United States v. Cortez,* 449 U.S. 411, 417–18 (1981).

The U.S. Supreme Court has also said that **"officers [can] draw on their own experience and specialized training to make inferences from and deductions about the cumulative information available to them that 'might well elude an untrained person.'"** *United States v. Arvizu*, 534 U.S. 266, 273 (2002).

Hunches vs. Articulable Suspicions Though an officer may certainly make logical deductions from human activity based on his experience and training, the officer must still be able to give valid reasons to justify a stop. As the Supreme Court said in *Terry,* **"[I]n justifying the particular intrusion the police officer must be able to point to specific and articulable facts which, taken together with rational inferences from those facts, reasonably warrant that intrusion."** 392 U.S. at 21. A court will not accept an officer's mere statement or conclusion that criminal activity was suspected. The officer must be able to back up the conclusion by reciting the specific facts that led to that conclusion. *United States v. Pavelski*, 789 F.2d 485 (7th Cir. 1986), held that an officer who testified to a "gut feeling that things were really wrong" failed to articulate any objective facts indicative of criminal activity.

In *United States v. Golab*, 325 F.3d 63 (1st Cir. 2003), the court found the officer stopped a car based on a hunch and not reasonable suspicion, as required. The officer also failed to give valid reasons for his stop. The court said:

> [W]e agree with the district court that there was no objectively reasonable suspicion to justify a *Terry* stop of the car in light of the totality of the circumstances. The basis for the stop amounted to no more than an impermissible hunch. First, the car was not in the . . . office parking lot [next to the office where the alleged crime of alien smuggling was occurring], which contained a

number of vehicles as well as many empty spaces. Rather, it was in a different lot associated with a commercial office building, separated by a grassy area and a lengthy access road. Also, a very short time elapsed between when [the officer] first saw the car and when he stopped it, somewhere between fifteen seconds and a minute. This was not enough time, the government conceded, to discern whether the driver was sitting and waiting in the car [for one of the alleged perpetrators of the crime in the office], or had just gotten in the car to leave. Further, the car's license plates were from Vermont. Such plates, the district court found, are a common sight in Concord, New Hampshire and by themselves raise no suspicion. Moreover, the earlier alien smuggling with which [the officer] was familiar involved individuals driving to New Hampshire in vans, not cars, from the New York City area. Furtado testified that the Vermont plate had no 'special significance' to him with regard to the earlier smuggling rings. It is objectively unreasonable to say that this prior smuggling ring justified the suspicion of all vehicles with out-of-state plates, regardless of their origin. . . . Under these circumstances, reasonable suspicion is not established by the fact that a car in a remote parking lot associated with another building has out-of-state license plates and is occupied. Based on that rationale, no person would be protected from a *Terry* stop. 325 F.3d at 66–67.

However, in *United States v. Arvizu*, 534 U.S. 266 (2002), the U.S. Supreme Court found a law enforcement officer had reasonable suspicion to stop a vehicle under the totality of the circumstances. The officer made logical deductions based on his knowledge, training, and experience, and provided valid reasons for the stop. In *Arvizu*, Agent Clinton Stoddard was working at a border patrol checkpoint designed to detect illegal immigration and smuggling across the international border. Border patrol agents also used roving patrols as well as electronic sensors to detect illegal immigration in rural areas around the checkpoint. Agent Stoddard received two reports that an electronic sensor had been triggered. The reports happened at a time of day when the area where the sensor was located experienced less human surveillance because agents routinely made a shift change at that time.

While driving toward the sensors to investigate, Agent Stoddard spotted a vehicle. Based on the timing of the reports he had previously received from the sensors, the location of the vehicle, and the fact that he had not seen any other vehicles in the area, Stoddard believed that this was the vehicle originally detected by the sensors. He pulled to the side of the road for the purpose of observing the vehicle as it passed by. He saw a minivan, a type of automobile that Stoddard knew, from his training, smugglers used. As the minivan approached, it decreased its speed significantly. Officer Stoddard saw five individuals inside the vehicle. Two adults, one of whom was driving, were in the front and three children were in the back. The driver appeared "stiff" and his posture "very rigid." He did not look at Office Stoddard. Based on his experience, Stoddard thought this particular fact was suspicious—most drivers acknowledge border patrol agents in that area by waving. He also noticed that the knees of the two children sitting in the back seat were "unusually high," which indicated to him that their feet may be resting on a container below.

The officer decided to follow the vehicle. As he did so, the children in the back, while facing forward, simultaneously began to wave at Stoddard in an unusual fashion. They waved for about five minutes. Stoddard thought the children had been instructed by someone to do so. As the vehicle approached an intersection near the fixed checkpoint, it put its signal light on, then turned it off and then signaled again. The vehicle then turned quickly. Stoddard thought this turn was significant because it was the last place that would have allowed the minivan to avoid the checkpoint. Also, the van turned onto a road that, because of its poor condition, Stoddard knew was mostly used by four-wheeled vehicles as opposed to minivans. Also, as an agent who patrolled this area frequently, Stoddard did not recognize this particular minivan. He also did not think this was a family headed for a picnic because he was unaware of picnic grounds in the direction the vehicle was headed.

Stoddard radioed headquarters to check the vehicle's registration, and discovered that the minivan was registered to an address in an area known for illegal immigration and drug smuggling. After receiving the information, Stoddard stopped the vehicle. Defendant, the driver of the vehicle, gave Agent Stoddard permission to inspect the vehicle. Stoddard found marijuana in a bag under the feet of the children in the back seat. Another bag containing marijuana was also found behind the rear seat.

Characterizing Stoddard's confrontation with the vehicle and its occupants as "a brief investigative stop," the Supreme Court found that Officer Stoddard had reasonable suspicion to justify the stop:

> Having considered the totality of the circumstances and given due weight to the factual inferences drawn by the law enforcement officer and District Court Judge, we hold that Stoddard had reasonable suspicion to believe that respondent was engaged in illegal activity. It was reasonable for Stoddard to infer from his observations, his registration check, and his experience as a border patrol agent that respondent had set out from [the nearby town where the vehicle was registered] along a little-traveled route used by smugglers to avoid the [fixed] checkpoint. Stoddard's knowledge further supported a commonsense inference that respondent intended to pass through the area at a time when officers would be leaving their backroads patrols to change shifts. The likelihood that respondent and his family were on a picnic outing was diminished by the fact that the minivan had turned away from the known recreational areas. . . . Corroborating this inference was the fact that recreational areas farther to the north would have been easier to reach by taking [a different road], as opposed to the 40-to-50-mile trip on unpaved and primitive roads. The children's elevated knees suggested the existence of concealed cargo in the passenger compartment. Finally, for the reasons we have given, Stoddard's assessment of respondent's reactions upon seeing him and the children's mechanical-like waving, which continued for a full four to five minutes, were entitled to some weight. 534 U.S. at 277.

Reasonable, Articulable Suspicion Is an Objective Standard *Arvizu* illustrates that an officer's decision to initiate a stop is judged against the following objective standard: "[W]ould the facts available to the officer at the moment of the seizure or the search 'warrant a man of reasonable caution in the belief' that the action taken was appropriate?" *Terry*, 392 U.S. at 21–22; *see also Arvizu*, 534 U.S. at 273. ("When discussing how reviewing courts should make reasonable-suspicion determinations, we have said repeatedly that they must look at the 'totality of the circumstances' of each case to see whether the detaining officer has a 'particularized and objective basis' for suspecting legal wrongdoing.")

This objective standard is similar to the standard imposed on law enforcement officers in traditional search and seizure or arrest situations. For example, assume that an officer is attempting to obtain a warrant for a person's arrest. Because probable cause is required to obtain the warrant, the officer must have specific facts sufficient to support a fair probability that a specific crime has been or is being committed. In the stop situation, the officer must have specific facts sufficient to support a reasonable suspicion of ongoing, impending, or past criminal activity to justify the initial intrusion. The common element in the two situations is that officers must be able to justify their actions with specific facts related to criminal activity. The only difference is in the amount of information the officer must have; for an investigative stop, the officer need only show facts indicating the possibility that criminal behavior is afoot (e.g., a "reasonable suspicion" that criminal activity is afoot).

Additional examples of facts and circumstances supporting a reasonable suspicion to stop are discussed in the section "Specific Circumstances Justifying Stops and Frisks," later in this chapter.

Applies to Suspicion of Previous Criminal Activity An officer's authority to stop is not limited to crimes about to be committed or crimes in the process of being committed. The U.S. Supreme Court authorized the stop of a person whom officers suspected of being involved in a *completed felony*:

> [W]here police have been unable to locate a person suspected of involvement in a past crime, the ability to briefly stop that person, ask questions, or check identification in the absence of probable cause promotes the strong government interest in solving crimes and bringing offenders to justice. Restraining police action until after probable cause is obtained would not only hinder the investigation, but might also enable the suspect to flee in the interim and to remain at large. Particularly in the context of felonies or crimes involving a threat to public safety, it is in the public interest that the crime be solved and the suspect detained as promptly as possible. The law enforcement interests at stake in these circumstances outweigh the individual's interest to be free of a stop and detention that is no more extensive than permissible in the investigation of imminent or ongoing crimes. *United States v. Hensley*, 469 U.S. 221, 229 (1985).

Discontinuation of Reasonable Suspicion An officer has a duty to discontinue an investigation and not make a stop of a person if, at the time of the intended stop, justification for the initial suspicion has disappeared. "An officer cannot continue to press his investigation when he discovers new evidence demonstrating that his original interpretation of his suspect's actions was mistaken." *State v. Garland*, 482 A.2d 139, 144 (Me. 1984). In a similar vein, once the purpose of a valid stop ends (i.e., a driver is issued a warning or citation following a valid stop for a traffic infraction), any further continuation of the stop must be justified by reasonable suspicion. *See United States v. Beck*, 140 F.3d 1129, 1136 (8th Cir. 1998). ("Because the purposes of Officer Taylor's initial traffic stop of [defendant] had been completed by this point, Officer Taylor could not subsequently detain [defendant] unless events that transpired during the traffic stop gave rise to reasonable suspicion to justify Officer Taylor's renewed detention of [defendant].")

Bases for Forming Reasonable Suspicion

Information from Known Informants In *Adams v. Williams*, 407 U.S. 143 (1972), a law enforcement officer on patrol in his cruiser was approached by a person known to him and was told that a man seated in a nearby vehicle had a gun at his waist and was carrying narcotics. The officer approached the vehicle, tapped on the window, and asked the occupant (the defendant) to open the door. When the defendant rolled down the window instead, the officer reached in, removed a pistol from the defendant's waistband, and then arrested the defendant.

The U.S. Supreme Court held that the officer acted justifiably in responding to the informant's tip:

> The informant was known to him personally and had provided him with information in the past. This is a stronger case than obtains in the case of an anonymous telephone tip. The informant here came forward personally to give information that was immediately verifiable at the scene. Indeed, under Connecticut law, the informant herself might have been subject to immediate arrest for making a false complaint had Sgt. Connolly's investigation proven the tip incorrect. Thus, while the Court's decisions indicate that this informant's unverified tip may have been insufficient for a narcotics arrest or search warrant, the information carried enough indicia of reliability to justify the officer's forcible stop of Williams.
>
> In reaching this conclusion, we reject respondent's argument that reasonable cause for a stop and frisk can only be based on the officer's personal observation, rather than on information supplied by another person. Informants' tips, like all other clues and evidence coming to a policeman on the scene, may vary greatly in their value and reliability. One simple rule will not cover every situation. Some tips, completely lacking in indicia of reliability, would either warrant no police response or require further investigation before a forcible stop of a suspect would be authorized. But in some situations—for example, when the victim of a street crime seeks immediate police aid and gives a description of his assailant, or when a credible informant warns of a specific impending crime—the subtleties of the hearsay rule should not thwart an appropriate police response. 407 U.S. at 146–47.

Under *Adams v. Williams*, an officer may stop a person based on an informant's tip if the tip carries "enough indicia of reliability" to provide reasonable suspicion of criminal activity. This requires an officer to have specific reasons why he or she believes a tip to be reliable. As the quoted material indicates, an anonymous telephone tip might not be sufficiently reliable without corroboration.

As suggested by the Supreme Court in *Adams*, when an informant personally communicates the tip to police, and the tip contains recent information that is then corroborated by police, courts will be more willing to find reasonable suspicion to stop based on the tip. In particular, *United States v. Valentine*, 232 F.3rd 350 (3rd Cir. 2000), held that police officers had reasonable suspicion to stop the defendant after an informant made a face-to-face report to police that he had seen a man fitting the description of the defendant moments before with a gun at 1:00 A.M. in a high-crime area known for shootings. Based on the report, two police officers stopped the defendant by force and found a gun. The court found the informant's tip distinguishable from the tip in *Florida v. J. L.*, an anonymous tipster case discussed below, in several ways:

> First, unlike *J. L.*, the officers in our case knew that the informant was reporting what he had observed moments ago, not what he learned from stale or secondhand sources. At the suppression hearing, Officer Woodard was asked, "Did [the informant] say how long ago that he saw the individual carrying a gun?" Woodard replied, "About—maybe a second ago, two seconds ago." . . . So the officers could expect that the informant had a reasonable basis for his beliefs. The Supreme Court has recognized the greater weight carried by a witness's recent report, such as when "the victim of a street crime seeks immediate police aid and gives a description of the assailant."
>
> Second, the officers had more reason to believe that the informant was credible than the officers did in *J. L.*, for a tip given face to face is more reliable than an anonymous telephone call. . . . [W]hen an informant relates information to the police face to face, the officer has an opportunity to assess the informant's credibility and demeanor. . . . And when an informant gives the police information about a neighbor . . . or someone nearby (as in our case), the informant is exposed to a risk of retaliation from the person named, making it less likely that the informant will lie. . . . Similarly . . . "citizens who personally report crimes to the police thereby make themselves accountable for lodging false complaints." 232 F.3d at 354 (internal citations omitted).

Information from Anonymous Informants *Alabama v. White*, 496 U.S. 325 (1990), illustrates the minimum level of corroboration needed to support an anonymous tip and provide reasonable suspicion to justify an investigatory stop. In that case, police received an anonymous telephone tip that the defendant would be leaving a particular apartment at a particular time in a particular vehicle, that she would be going to a particular motel, and that she would be in possession of cocaine. Police went immediately to the apartment building and saw a vehicle matching the caller's description. They observed the defendant leave the building and enter the vehicle, followed her along the most direct route to the motel, and stopped her vehicle just short of the motel. A consensual search of the vehicle revealed marijuana and, after the defendant was arrested, cocaine was found in her purse.

The U.S. Supreme Court held that the anonymous tip, as corroborated by independent police work, exhibited sufficient *indicia* of reliability to provide reasonable suspicion to make the stop. The Court applied the totality-of-the-circumstances approach of *Illinois v. Gates* (see Chapter 3) in determining whether the informant's tip established reasonable suspicion:

> **Gates made clear . . . that those factors that had been considered critical under *Aguilar* and *Spinelli*—an informant's "veracity," "reliability," and "basis of knowledge"—remain "highly relevant in determining the value of his report." . . . These factors are also relevant in the reasonable suspicion context, although allowance must be made in applying them for the lesser showing required to meet that standard.** 496 U.S. at 328–29.

Like the tip in *Gates*, the anonymous tip in *White* provided virtually nothing indicating that the caller was either honest or had reliable information, nor did the tip give any indication of the basis for the caller's predictions regarding the defendant's activities. As in *Gates*, however, there was more than the tip itself.

And although the tip was not as detailed and the corroboration not as complete as in *Gates*, the required degree of suspicion was not as high:

> **Reasonable suspicion is a less demanding standard than probable cause not only in the sense that reasonable suspicion can be established with information that is different in quantity or content than that required to establish probable cause, but also in the sense that reasonable suspicion can arise from information that is less reliable than that required to show probable cause. . . . Reasonable suspicion, like probable cause, is dependent upon both the content of information possessed by police and its degree of reliability. Both factors—quantity and quality—are considered in the "totality of the circumstances—the whole picture," . . . that must be taken into account when evaluating whether there is reasonable suspicion. Thus, if a tip has a relatively low degree of reliability, more information [from the tipster and police corroboration] will be required to establish the requisite quantum of suspicion than would be required if the tip were more reliable. The *Gates* Court applied its totality of the circumstances approach in this manner, taking into account the facts known to the officers from personal observation, and giving the anonymous tip the weight it deserved in light of its indicia of reliability as established through independent police work [e.g., corroboration]. The same approach applies in the reasonable suspicion context, the only difference being the level of suspicion that must be established.** 496 U.S. at 330–31.

After explaining the totality-of-the-circumstances approach to determine if an informant's tip can serve as a basis for reasonable suspicion, the Court in *White* held that in that case, the tip could serve as a reliable basis for reasonable suspicion: **"Contrary to the court below, we conclude that when the officers stopped the respondent, the anonymous tip had been sufficiently corroborated to furnish reasonable suspicion that respondent was engaged in criminal activity and that the investigative stop therefore did not violate the Fourth Amendment."** 496 U.S. at 331.

The Court's analysis of corroboration illustrates how corroboration works to supplement an anonymous tip in providing reasonable suspicion. First, although not every detail mentioned by the tipster was verified—such as the name of the woman leaving the building or the precise apartment from which she left—the officers did corroborate that a woman left the building and got into the particularly described vehicle. Because the officers proceeded to the building immediately after the call and the defendant emerged not too long thereafter, the defendant's departure was within the time frame predicted by the caller. Furthermore, because her four-mile route was the most direct way to the motel but nevertheless involved several turns, the caller's prediction of the defendant's destination was significantly corroborated even though she was stopped before she reached the motel. Moreover, the caller's ability to predict the defendant's future behavior demonstrated inside information—a special familiarity with her affairs. When significant aspects of the caller's predictions were verified, the officers had reason to believe not only that the caller was honest but also that he was well informed. Under the totality of the circumstances, the anonymous tip, as corroborated, exhibited sufficient *indicia* of reliability to justify the stop of the defendant's car.

Florida v. J. L., 529 U.S. 266 (2000), held that an anonymous tip that a person is carrying a gun is, without more, insufficient to justify a police officer's stop and frisk of that person. In *J. L.*, an anonymous caller reported to the police that a young black male standing at a particular bus stop and wearing a plaid shirt was carrying a gun. Soon thereafter, two officers arrived at the bus stop and saw three black males, one of whom was wearing a plaid shirt. Apart from the tip, the officers had no reason to suspect any of the three of illegal conduct. The officers did not see a firearm and J. L made no threatening or otherwise unusual movements. One of the officers approached J. L., told him to put his hands up, frisked him, and seized a gun from his pocket.

The U.S. Supreme Court found that the contention that the tip was reliable because its description of the suspect proved accurate misapprehended the reliability needed for a tip to justify a *Terry* stop:

> **An accurate description of a subject's readily observable location and appearance is of course reliable in this limited sense: It will help the police correctly identify the person whom the tipster means to accuse. Such a tip, however, does not show that the tipster has knowledge of concealed criminal activity. The reasonable suspicion here at issue requires that a tip be reliable in its assertion of illegality, not just in its tendency to identify a determinate person.** 529 U.S. at 272.

Comparing the anonymous tip in *J. L.* to that in *White*, the Court said:

> **Although the Court held that the suspicion in *White* became reasonable after police surveillance, we regarded the case as borderline. Knowledge about a person's future movements indicates some familiarity with that person's affairs, but having such knowledge does not necessarily imply that the informant knows, in particular, whether that person is carrying hidden contraband. We accordingly classified *White* as a "close case." . . . The tip in the instant case lacked the moderate indicia of reliability present in White and essential to the Court's decision in that case.** 529 U.S. at 271.

The Court also rejected a so-called "firearm exception" under which a tip alleging an illegal gun would automatically justify a stop and frisk even if the tip failed standard reliability testing. Such an exception would enable any person seeking to harass another to set in motion an intrusive, embarrassing police search of the other person merely by placing an anonymous call falsely reporting that the person was carrying a gun. Also, the Court found that the *Terry* rule permitting protective police searches on the basis of reasonable suspicion adequately responded to the serious threat that armed criminals pose to public safety. The Court went on to say:

> **The facts of this case do not require us to speculate about the circumstances under which the danger alleged in an anonymous tip might be so great as to justify a search even without a showing of reliability. We do not say, for example, that a report of a person carrying a bomb need bear the indicia of reliability we demand for a report of a person carrying a firearm before the police can constitutionally conduct a frisk. Nor do we hold that public safety officials in quarters where the reasonable expectation of Fourth Amendment privacy is diminished, such as airports . . . and schools . . . cannot conduct protective searches on the basis of information insufficient to justify searches elsewhere.** 529 U.S. at 273–74.

Note that nothing in the *J. L.* decision limits the right of a law enforcement officer, upon receiving an anonymous tip alleging criminal behavior, to investigate the situation further. For example, the officer may observe the suspect or ask the suspect basic questions related to identifying the suspect or obtaining the suspect's consent for a search of her person and belongings. These observations or the suspect's responses to questions may, in turn, provide the reasonable suspicion to justify a stop. This was the case in *United States v. Jacob*, 377 F.3d 573 (6th Cir. 2004), where police received information of possible criminal behavior from a confidential informant, and proceeded to corroborate the veracity and basis of that information through their own investigation:

> The district court took into consideration a number of factors that, in their entirety, give rise to reasonable suspicion. Investigators learned from an informant that [the co-defendant and accomplice] had checked into a hotel, paid cash, and displayed Arizona identification. The district court noted that Arizona is a source state of narcotics that enter the Cleveland area. Investigators further learned that [the co-defendant] had been previously arrested for transportation of narcotics [in California]. In addition, a drug detection dog gave a positive indication to the Camry [outside the hotel with California plates] and showed interest in the right wheel tire area, an indication of the possible existence of a hidden compartment. Moreover, the district court found that it was reasonable for an investigator to conclude that the defendants engaged in countersurveillance. Investigators observed [the co-defendant] constantly scan the street, driveway, and parking lot as he waited at [defendant's] hotel. They further observed the defendants engage in countersurveillance after they drove to a gas station for no apparent reason. Finally, the defendants appeared to engage in countersurveillance as they drove erratically on the freeway. We agree with the district court that these facts provided a sufficient basis upon which the investigators conducted a Terry stop [of defendants' vehicle]. Based upon these facts, a well-trained officer could reasonably conclude that criminal activity was possibly afoot. Therefore, the investigators were permitted to conduct a stop to investigate their suspicion. 377 F.3d at 577–78.

Information from Police Flyers, Bulletins, or Radio Dispatches Officers may stop a person or vehicle on the basis of a police flyer, bulletin, or radio dispatch. Because criminal suspects are increasingly mobile and more likely to flee across jurisdictional boundaries, police in one jurisdiction need to be able to act promptly on the basis of information contained in a bulletin or flyer from another jurisdiction. The leading Supreme Court case in this area that supports this notion is *United States v. Hensley*, 469 U.S. 221 (1985)

In *Hensley*, two armed men robbed a tavern. Later, an informant provided information to the St. Bernard police department that defendant Hensley had driven the getaway car. As a result, Officer Davis of the St. Bernard police department issued a "wanted flyer" for Hensley to other local police departments. It stated that Hensley was wanted for investigation of an aggravated robbery, provided a description of Hensley, the date and location of the robbery, and requested that other police departments retrieve and hold Hensley on behalf of St. Bernard. The flyer also warned that Hensley may be armed and dangerous.

Another police department, Covington, located about five miles from St. Bernard, received the flyer. Some officers in Covington knew Hensley, and began to monitor places he frequented. Officer Cope from Covington, who had seen or heard about the flyer, found Hensley driving in his vehicle, and stopped him. Cope recalled that the flyer sought a stop for investigation only, and that in his experience the issuance of such a flyer was usually followed by the issuance of an arrest warrant. A police dispatcher was contacted to verify if there was an outstanding arrest warrant for Hensley. The dispatcher was unable to verify this information before Officer Cope's stop of Hensley's vehicle. As Cope approached Hensley's vehicle with his gun drawn, Officer Cope requested that Hensley and another passenger exit the car. A search of the car uncovered three weapons. Hensley was arrested. 469 U.S. at 223–25.

The Court found that officers may rely on a bulletin from another police department to stop a suspect *as long as* the bulletin itself is based on facts providing reasonable suspicion (for a stop):

> Neither [Hensley] nor the Court of Appeals suggests any reason why . . . a police department should not be able to act on the basis of a flyer indicating that another department has a reasonable suspicion of involvement with a crime. It could be argued that police can more justifiably rely on a report that a magistrate has issued a warrant than on a report that another law enforcement agency has simply concluded that it has a reasonable suspicion sufficient to authorize an investigatory stop. We do not find this distinction significant. The law enforcement interests promoted by allowing one department to make investigatory stops based upon another department's bulletins or flyers are considerable, while the intrusion on personal security is minimal. The same interests that weigh in favor of permitting police to make a *Terry* stop to investigate a past crime support permitting police in other jurisdictions to rely on flyers or bulletins in making stops to investigate past crimes. *We conclude that, if a flyer or bulletin has been issued on the basis of articulable facts supporting a reasonable suspicion that the wanted person has committed an offense, then reliance on that flyer or bulletin justifies a stop to check identification, to pose questions to the person, or to detain the person briefly while attempting to obtain further information. . . . Assuming the police make a Terry stop in objective reliance on a flyer or bulletin, we hold that the evidence uncovered in the course of the stop is admissible if the police who issued the flyer or bulletin possessed a reasonable suspicion justifying a stop, and if the stop that in fact occurred was not significantly more intrusive than would have been permitted the issuing department.* 469 U.S. at 681–82 (emphasis added).

After articulating the relevant test, the Court in *Hensley* first found that the St. Bernard police had the required reasonable suspicion to issue the bulletin for Hensley's stop:

> We agree with the District Court that the St. Bernard police possessed a reasonable suspicion, based on specific and articulable facts, that Hensley was involved in an armed robbery. The District Judge heard testimony from the St. Bernard officer who interviewed the informant. On the strength of the evidence, the District Court concluded that the wealth of detail concerning the robbery revealed by the informant, coupled with her admission of tangential participation in the robbery, established that the informant was sufficiently reliable and credible "to arouse a reasonable suspicion of criminal activity by [Hensley] and to constitute the specific and articulable facts needed to underly a stop." Under the circumstances, "the information carried enough indicia of reliability," to justify an investigatory stop of Hensley. 469 U.S. at 233–34 (internal citations omitted).

The Court then held that officers in the Covington police department could objectively rely on the flyer issued by the other police department:

> **Turning to the flyer issued by the St. Bernard police, we believe it satisfies the objective test announced today. An objective reading of the entire flyer would lead an experienced officer to conclude that Thomas Hensley was at least wanted for questioning and investigation in St. Bernard. Since the flyer was issued on the basis of articulable facts supporting a reasonable suspicion, this objective reading would justify a brief stop to check Hensley's identification, pose questions, and inform the suspect that the St. Bernard police wished to question him. As an experienced officer could well assume that a warrant might have been obtained in the period after the flyer was issued, we think the flyer would further justify a brief detention at the scene of the stop while officers checked whether a warrant had in fact been issued.** 469 U.S. at 234.

Thus, because police who issued the flyer had reasonable suspicion to stop Hensley, and the officers from the other department validly relied on the flyer, Hensley's stop was constitutional under the Fourth Amendment, and the weapons found during the stop were admissible. 469 U.S. at 236.

Officers may also rely on a police radio dispatch, or bulletin, to stop a person or vehicle. Officers may rely on such a dispatch to stop a person or vehicle when the dispatch itself originates from a fellow officer who has knowledge of facts supporting reasonable suspicion for a stop. For example, in *United States v. Nelson*, 284 F.3d 472 (3rd Cir. 2002), an officer received a tip from an informant that a particular vehicle's occupants were involved in armed hold-ups. He conveyed this information over radio dispatch to fellow officers on patrol, who actually stopped the vehicle. The Court stated that the relevant question was whether the officer issuing the bulletin had reasonable suspicion to stop the vehicle:

> Against the backdrop of Supreme Court guidance and our precedents, we assess whether the communications to the police [dispatcher from the informant] possessed sufficient indicia of reliability, when considering the totality of the circumstances, for us to conclude that the [patrolling] officers possessed an objectively reasonable suspicion sufficient to justify a *Terry* stop. We find that they do. In order for the stop of the car to be justified, the officers stopping the car must have had reasonable suspicion. Because the officers stopping the car did so based on the fact that the car and individuals matched the description broadcast over the police radio, the reasonableness of the stop in this case depends on the reliability of the tip itself. Did [the dispatching officer] have sufficient grounds to view the tip as reliable and issue the radio bulletin pursuant to which the car was stopped? 284 F.3d at 481.

If, however, it is later determined the dispatcher had no facts supporting reasonable suspicion, a stop made by officers in the field relying on the dispatcher's information may be ruled illegal. This was the holding of *Feathers v. Aey*, 319 F.3d 843 (6th Cir. 2003), where the dispatcher received a tip from an anonymous informant that was determined to be both unreliable and without a proper basis, and later communicated the information in the tip to officers in the field. The officers in the field, in turn, made a stop based on the information provided by the dispatcher:

> The officers [in the field] did not know that the dispatcher's information was from an anonymous tipster who offered no evidence of reliability, but for

purposes of determining whether the *Terry* stop was reasonable, we must impute to the individual officers the dispatcher's knowledge that the tip was anonymous [and lacked sufficient reliability or basis]. 319 F.3d at 849.

Thus, the court in *Feathers* held that the stop by the officers in the field violated the Fourth Amendment because "the authorities' collective information," including the information provided by the dispatcher, "did not amount to reasonable suspicion." 319 F.3d at 851.

Note, however, that if officers in the field rely in good faith on unreliable, insufficient, or incorrect information provided by a dispatcher to justify a stop, some courts may find the stop by officers valid, at least where these officers possess other valid information that justifies the stop. In *United States v. DeLeon Reyna*, 930 F.2d 396 (5th Cir. 1991), an officer stopped a vehicle based on both personal observations he made about unusual aspects of the vehicle and on incorrect license plate information he received from the dispatcher. The court found that the officer relied in good faith on the license plate information he received, and when this information was combined with his personal observations, knowledge and experience, the officer had reasonable suspicion to stop the vehicle:

> Here we determine that it was objectively reasonable for an officer in Agent Martinez's position to conclude that under all the circumstances there was a particularized and objective basis for reasonable suspicion that defendant's vehicle was engaged in criminal activity—in other words, that a stop of the vehicle was lawful. . . . Martinez's decision to pull the truck over—including his good-faith reliance on the license plate information—was not unreasonable in the face of all of the surrounding circumstances: the road's common use by drug traffickers and close proximity to the border; the Border Patrol reference manual warning of smuggling efforts via false compartments in plywood cargo; the incongruity of the truck and the cargo it carried; and his evaluation of the circumstances and defendant's conduct, based on four years of experience in the same area of Texas. His reliance on the license plate check is all the more unexceptionable given the district court's acknowledgment that a "license plate switcheroo" is not uncommon in smuggling cases. 930 F.2d at 401.

A quote from *United States v. Robinson*, 536 F.2d 1298, 1299–1300 (9th Cir. 1976), summarizes how courts deal with reasonable suspicion in the context of police dispatches:

> We recognize that effective law enforcement cannot be conducted unless police officers can act on directions and information transmitted by one officer to another and that officers, who must often act swiftly, cannot be expected to cross-examine their fellow officers about the foundation for the transmitted information. The fact that an officer does not have to have personal knowledge of the evidence supplying good cause for a stop before he can obey a direction to detain a person or a vehicle does not mean that the Government need not produce evidence at trial showing good cause to legitimate the detention when the legality of the stop is challenged. If the dispatcher himself had had founded suspicion, or if he had relied on information from a reliable informant who supplied him with adequate facts to establish founded suspicion, the dispatcher could properly have delegated the stopping function to [the officer in the field]. But if the dispatcher did not have such cause, he could not create justification simply by relaying a direction to a fellow officer to make the stop.

key points

- A law enforcement officer may stop and briefly detain a person for investigative purposes if the officer has a reasonable suspicion supported by articulable facts of ongoing, impending, or past criminal activity. In determining reasonable suspicion, an officer may make logical deductions from human activity based on his observations, knowledge, experience, and training. The officer must be able to provide valid reasons for his determination of reasonable suspicion, and may not base his suspicion on a mere hunch.
- Reasonable suspicion is a less demanding standard than probable cause, not only in the sense that it can be established with information that is different in quantity or content than that for probable cause, but also in the sense that reasonable suspicion can arise from information less reliable than that required to show probable cause.
- A law enforcement officer's decision to initiate a stop based on reasonable suspicion is judged against the objective standard: Would the facts available to the officer at the moment of the seizure or the search warrant a person of reasonable caution in believing that the action taken was appropriate?
- A law enforcement officer may stop a person based on an informant's tip if, under the totality of the circumstances, the tip, plus any corroboration of the tip by independent police investigation, carries enough *indicia* of reliability to provide reasonable suspicion of criminal activity.
- An anonymous tip that a particular person at a particular location is carrying a gun is not, without more information, sufficient to justify law enforcement officers in stopping and frisking that person.
- A law enforcement officer may stop a person on the basis of a flyer, bulletin, or radio dispatch issued by another law enforcement agency as long as the issuing law enforcement agency has a reasonable suspicion that the person named in the flyer, bulletin, or dispatch is or was involved in criminal activity.

Permissible Scope of a Stop

Once an officer determines that a stop is justified, to what extent may the officer interfere? In other words, how long may the person be detained, how much force may be used, and how much questioning may be employed? The U.S. Supreme Court in *Florida v. Royer*, 460 U.S. 491, 500 (1983), addressed the issue:

> The predicate permitting seizures on suspicion short of probable cause is that law enforcement interests warrant a limited intrusion on the personal security of the suspect. The scope of the intrusion permitted will vary to some extent with the particular facts and circumstances of each case. This much, however, is clear: *an investigative detention must be temporary and last no longer than is necessary to effectuate the purpose of the stop.* Similarly, the investigative methods employed should be the least intrusive means reasonably available to verify or dispel the officer's suspicion in a short period of time. . . . It is the State's burden to demonstrate that the seizure it seeks to justify on the basis of a reasonable suspicion was sufficiently limited in scope and duration to satisfy the conditions of an investigative seizure (emphasis added).

Twenty years later in *Hiibel v. Sixth Judicial Dist. Ct. of Nev.*, 542 U.S. 177, 185–86 (2004), the Court described the scope of a stop in this way:

> Beginning with *Terry v. Ohio*, the Court has recognized that a law enforcement officer's reasonable suspicion that a person may be involved in criminal activity permits the officer to stop the person for a brief time and take additional steps to investigate further. To ensure that the resulting seizure is constitutionally reasonable, a *Terry* stop must be limited. The officer's action must be "justified at its inception, and reasonably related in scope to the circumstances which justified the interference in the first place." For example, the seizure cannot continue for an excessive period of time, or resemble a traditional arrest.

Ordering Driver and Passengers Out of a Vehicle During a Stop Recall from the previous discussion of Fourth Amendment seizures that when an officer makes a traffic stop of a private vehicle, both the driver and passengers are "seized" within the meaning of that Amendment. Therefore, for the officer to make a lawful traffic stop of a vehicle and its occupants, the officer needs to possess at least reasonable suspicion that the vehicle and its occupants have committed a traffic infraction.

An officer who has lawfully stopped a motor vehicle may, for personal safety reasons, order the driver out of the vehicle, even though the officer has no reason to suspect foul play from the driver at the time of the stop. The U.S. Supreme Court said:

> We think this additional intrusion can only be described as *de minimis*. The driver is being asked to expose to view very little more of his person than is already exposed. The police have already lawfully decided that the driver shall be briefly detained; the only question is whether he shall spend that period sitting in the driver's seat of his car or standing alongside it. Not only is the insistence of the police on the latter choice not a "serious intrusion upon the sanctity of the person," but it hardly rises to the level of a "'petty indignity.'" . . . What is at most a mere inconvenience cannot prevail when balanced against legitimate concerns for the officer's safety. *Pennsylvania v. Mimms*, 434 U.S. 106, 111 (1977).

Maryland v. Wilson, 519 U.S. 408, 415 (1997), extended the *Mimms* rule, holding that **"an officer making a traffic stop may order passengers to get out of the car pending completion of the stop."** The Court found that the danger to an officer from a traffic stop is likely to be greater when there are passengers in addition to the driver in the stopped car. Although the justification for ordering passengers out of the car is different than that for the driver, the additional intrusion on passengers is minimal:

> [A]s a practical matter, the passengers are already stopped by virtue of the stop of the vehicle. The only change in their circumstances which will result from ordering them out of the car is that they will be outside of, rather than inside of, the stopped car. Outside the car, the passengers will be denied access to any possible weapon that might be concealed in the interior of the passenger compartment. It would seem that the possibility of a violent encounter stems not from the ordinary reaction of a motorist stopped for a speeding violation, but from the fact that evidence of a more serious crime might be uncovered during the stop. And the motivation of a passenger to employ violence to prevent apprehension of such a crime is every bit as great as that of the driver. 519 U.S. at 413–14.

By implication, an officer may also order a driver or passengers to remain in a vehicle or to get back into a vehicle. An officer working alone may find it safer for the driver and passengers to remain in a vehicle where the officer can more easily control them for safety purposes.

Frisks of car occupants who have been ordered out of a vehicle are governed by the same standards as frisks of other individuals. (See "Protective Search for Weapons within Reach of Person Being Frisked," later in this chapter.)

Reasonable Investigative Methods during a Stop The permissible scope of an officer's interaction with a person is, in part, determined by the person's answers to investigative questions posed by the officer. An officer's initial questioning of a suspect may assure the officer that no further investigation is necessary. For example, a law enforcement officer in a patrol car observed a young man, carrying a flashlight and a small box, walking on the sidewalk of a residential street at 2:40 A.M. The officer drove up to him and asked what he was doing. He replied that he was collecting nightcrawlers for fishing bait. The officer wished him luck and drove on.

On the other hand, evasive or implausible answers to routine investigative questions may give an officer reasonable suspicion that criminal activity is afoot and justify stopping the person for further investigation. In *United States v. Sterling*, 909 F.3d 1078 (7th Cir. 1990), the court held that narcotics investigators at the airport had reasonable suspicion to stop a woman and detain her luggage, in part, because she gave implausible answers to their questions:

> The issue now becomes whether the agents had reasonable suspicion of criminal activity by this time. We hold that they did. Although the fact that [the woman named Sterling] met the drug courier profile alone does not support a finding of reasonable suspicion, the agents gained enough information during the course of the consensual [investigative] questioning to justify a finding of reasonable suspicion. Our determination must be based on the 'totality of the circumstances.' The agents identified . . . [Sterling] initially because she arrived from a drug source city, deplaned among the last passengers, and looked around repeatedly. Once the officers had asked Sterling a few questions, they gleaned more facts that led them to suspect criminal activity. First, they learned that [the woman] purported to have no identification on her person and that she had gone to Miami to see her cousin . . . without knowing his address or telephone number. She then told them that after she arrived in Miami, she learned that [her cousin] was driving to Chicago to visit her. Moreover, the officers learned that [the woman] met her cousin's sister in Miami, but was uncertain at first whether [her cousin's] sister was also her own cousin. Finally, the agents learned that [the woman] could not tell them the name of her hotel in Miami. The officers were entitled to interpret these answers in light of their experience. Here [the woman] had an improbable story; the officers appropriately assessed, and the district court properly found, that her answers were an effort to conceal the truth. When she voluntarily produced her airplane ticket receipt, the officers were not only able to verify an outright lie [e.g., the ticket was not purchased at a travel agency as the woman had said but bore a stamp indicating it had been purchased at an airline ticket counter], they were also able to establish that [the woman] had conformed to a 'standard operating procedure for drug smugglers.' (that is, purchase of airplane ticket with cash); We thus conclude that the consensual encounter ripened into an investigative stop when the agents told [the woman] they intended to detain her suitcases. . . . Moreover, we find that the agents had a reasonable suspicion for this detention. 909 F.2d at 1083–84.

Note that if an officer has reasonable suspicion to justify a stop of a person (i.e., based on a person giving implausible answers, information from informants, etc.), and then that person refuses in violation of state law to identify herself, the officer may be permitted to expand the scope of the detention by arresting the person. For example, in *Hiibel v. Sixth Judicial Dist. Ct. of Nev.*, 542 U.S. 177 (2004), police received a call reporting an assault of a woman by a man in a particular truck on a particular road. Sheriff Dove was sent to investigate. Upon his arrival at the scene, Dove saw a man was standing by a truck parked on the side of the road, and a young woman sitting inside the truck. Dove saw skid marks behind the vehicle, leading him to believe it stopped suddenly. When Dove approached the man and informed him of his investigation into a possible fight, Dove noticed that the man appeared to be intoxicated.

The Court described the exchange between Officer Dove and the man in this way:

> The officer asked him if he had "any identification on [him]," which we understand as a request to produce a driver's license or some other form of written identification. The man refused and asked why the officer wanted to see identification. The officer responded that he was conducting an investigation and needed to see some identification. The unidentified man became agitated and insisted he had done nothing wrong. The officer explained that he wanted to find out who the man was and what he was doing there. After continued refusals to comply with the officer's request for identification, the man began to taunt the officer by placing his hands behind his back and telling the officer to arrest him and take him to jail. This routine kept up for several minutes: The officer asked for identification 11 times and was refused each time. After warning the man that he would be arrested if he continued to refuse to comply, the officer placed him under arrest. [The man was convicted under the state of Nevada's stop and identify statute for failing to identify himself by providing his name]. 542 U.S. at 177–81.

The Court began its analysis by explaining the importance to an officer of obtaining a suspect's identification during a stop:

> Obtaining a suspect's name in the course of a *Terry* stop serves important government interests. Knowledge of identity may inform an officer that a suspect is wanted for another offense, or has a record of violence or mental disorder. On the other hand, knowing identity may help clear a suspect and allow the police to concentrate their efforts elsewhere. Identity may prove particularly important in cases such as this, where the police are investigating what appears to be a domestic assault. Officers called to investigate domestic disputes need to know whom they are dealing with in order to assess the situation, the threat to their own safety, and possible danger to the potential victim. 542 U.S. at 186.

Next, the Court determined that a state may require a suspect who has been lawfully stopped to identify oneself:

> The principles of *Terry* permit a State to require a suspect to disclose his name in the course of a *Terry* stop. The reasonableness of a seizure under the Fourth Amendment is determined "by balancing its intrusion on the individual's Fourth Amendment interests against its promotion of legitimate government interests." The Nevada statute satisfies that standard. The request for identity has an immediate relation to the purpose, rationale, and practical demands of a *Terry* stop. The threat of criminal sanction helps ensure that the request for identity does not become a legal nullity. On the other hand, the Nevada statute does not alter the nature of the stop itself: it does not change its duration, or its location. A state law requiring a suspect to disclose his name in the course of a valid *Terry* stop is consistent with Fourth Amendment prohibitions against unreasonable searches and seizures. 542 U.S. at 187–88.

In response to the defendant's argument that the state law impermissibly sanctioned his arrest on a simple refusal to identify himself, the Court said:

> These are familiar concerns. [Defendant's] concerns are met by the requirement that a *Terry* stop must be justified at its inception and "reasonably related in scope to the circumstances which justified" the initial stop. Under these principles, an officer may not arrest a suspect for failure to identify himself if the request for identification is not reasonably related to the circumstances justifying the stop. [An officer may require identification if there is] "a reasonable basis for believing that [providing the identification] will establish or negate the suspect's connection with that crime." It is clear in this case that the request for identification was "reasonably related in scope to the circumstances which justified" the stop. The officer's request was a common-sense inquiry, not an effort to obtain an arrest for failure to identify after a *Terry* stop yielded insufficient evidence. The stop, the request, and the State's requirement of a response did not contravene the guarantees of the Fourth Amendment. 542 U.S. at 188–89.

Thus, an officer may request identification during a stop if it will help the officer connect the suspect to a crime he is investigating, and the request is reasonably related to the circumstances justifying the stop. An officer must not ask for identification if the officer's only purpose for doing so is to arrest the suspect for possible failure to identify.

As to the defendant's Fifth Amendment claim that disclosure of his name was a violation of his Fifth Amendment right against self-incrimination, the Court said:

> In this case petitioner's refusal to disclose his name was not based on any articulated real and appreciable fear that his name would be used to incriminate him. . . . As best we can tell, petitioner refused to identify himself only because he thought his name was none of the officer's business. 542 U.S. at 190.

Note that if disclosure of a suspect's name could subject him or her to criminal liability for another crime, the Court suggested that the suspect would not have to disclose:

> Still, a case may arise where there is a substantial allegation that furnishing identity at the time of a stop would have given the police a link in the chain of evidence needed to convict the individual of a separate offense. In that case, the court can then consider whether the privilege applies, and, if the Fifth Amendment has been violated, what remedy must follow. We need not resolve those questions here. 542 U.S. at 191.

During a traffic stop, "reasonable investigation includes asking for the driver's license and registration, requesting that the driver sit in the patrol car, and asking the driver about his destination and purpose." *United States v. Bloomfield*, 40 F.3d 910, 915 (8th Cir. 1994). Likewise, an officer may engage in similar routine questioning of the vehicle's passengers to verify information provided by the driver. Moreover, "if the responses of the detainee and the circumstances give rise to suspicions unrelated to the traffic offense, an officer may broaden his inquiry and satisfy those suspicions." *United States v. Barahona*, 990 F.2d 412, 416 (8th Cir. 1993). Once the purposes of an initial traffic stop are completed, however, the officer may not further detain the vehicle or its occupants unless something that occurs during the traffic stop generates reasonable suspicion to justify further detention. *United States v. Mesa*, 62 F.3d 159 (6th Cir. 1995). The same rules apply at fixed vehicle checkpoints set up and conducted by the police: "When an officer seeks to expand the investigation of a motorist beyond the reasons stated for the checkpoint, he or she must have a particularized and objective basis for suspecting the particular person stopped of criminal activity." *United States v. Galindo-Gonzales*, 142 F.3d 1217, 1221 (10th Cir. 1998).

Time Issues during a Stop "[T]he brevity of the invasion of the individual's Fourth Amendment interests is an important factor in determining whether the seizure is so minimally intrusive as to be justifiable on reasonable suspicion." *United States v. Place*, 462 U.S. 696, 709 (1983). An investigative stop is not subject to any rigid time limitation, but at some point an extended stop that has not developed probable cause for an arrest can no longer be justified as reasonable. For example, the Court in *Place*, while acknowledging that there was no precise time limitation for a valid stop, refused to sanction a ninety-minute detention of a suspect's luggage. (For further discussion of this case, see section entitled "Detention of Containers and Other Property" on page 416).

Factors Considered in Reasonableness of Length of Stop In determining the reasonableness of the duration of a stop, courts consider the law enforcement purposes to be served by the stop as well as the time reasonably needed to effectuate those purposes:

> **In assessing whether a detention is too long in duration to be justified as an investigative stop, we consider it appropriate to examine whether the police diligently pursued a means of investigation that was likely to confirm or dispel their suspicions quickly, during which time it was necessary to detain the defendant. . . . A court making this assessment should take care to consider whether the police are acting in a swiftly developing situation and in such cases the court should not indulge in unrealistic second-guessing. . . . The question is not simply whether some other alternative was available, but whether the police acted unreasonably in failing to recognize or to pursue it.** *United States v. Sharpe*, 470 U.S. 675, 686–87 (1985).

In *Sharpe*, the Court approved a twenty-minute detention of a driver made necessary by the driver's own evasion of a drug agent and the decision of a state police officer, who had been called to assist in making the stop, to hold the driver until the agent could arrive on the scene. The Court found that it was reasonable for the state police officer to hold the driver for the brief period pending the drug agent's arrival because (1) the state police officer could not be certain that he was aware of all of the facts that had aroused the drug agent's suspicions, and (2) as a highway patrolman, he lacked the agent's training and experience in dealing with narcotics investigations.

In contrast to *Sharpe*, when there is an unjustified delay in an investigation that is not caused by the suspect, courts may find that the continued detention of the suspect was unreasonable under the Fourth Amendment. For example, in *United States v. Dortch*, 199 F.3d 193 (5th Cir. 1999), officers waited nine to ten minutes into a valid traffic stop to request drug-detecting dogs, the dogs did not arrive until after the lawful traffic stop ended, and the canine search took an additional 10 minutes. Based on this, the court found that the stop was unreasonable.

The court first took issue with the fact that officers waited approximately ten minutes to contact the canine unit after having stopped the defendant: "The delay for the canine unit to arrive cannot be attributed to any of [defendant's] actions. In fact, it was approximately 9–10 minutes into the stop before the officers first requested that the dispatcher send the canine unit. The officers offered no justification for this delay. . . ." 199 F.3d at 200. The court also found the prolonged stop involving the canine search unreasonable because it occurred *after* the lawful traffic stop had ended:

> [T]he justification for [the traffic] detention ceased once the computer check came back negative [for a stolen car or outstanding warrants], and the canine search was not performed until after that completed check. Admittedly, that search, if performed *during* the detention, would not have violated [defendant's] constitutional rights, because it is not a search at all under the Fourth Amendment. 199 F.3d at 200.

Finally, the length of the canine search itself was a factor in the court's finding of unreasonableness: "This conclusion is bolstered by the fact that the canine search took another ten minutes, with the dogs first circling the car for a few moments before a dog alerted to the driver-side door." 199 F.3d at 200.

Other reasons that might justify an officer's prolonging a suspect's detention include the following: attempting to obtain further information in the context of a complex and rapidly developing situation; summoning assistance; traveling to the scene of suspected criminal activity; caring for injured persons or responding to other emergency circumstances; and dealing with evasive tactics or other delays caused by the suspect. *United States v. Quinn*, 815 F.2d 153 (1st Cir. 1987), held that a defendant's detention for investigation for twenty to twenty-five minutes did not transform the initial lawful stop into a seizure tantamount to arrest. Although several police officers were present, they made no threats, displayed no weapons, and exerted no physical restraint on the defendant. Moreover, the officers had a strong suspicion of criminal activity, and there was no way they could have significantly shortened the inquiry.

In most cases, twenty to twenty-five minutes is probably the outside time limit, beyond which a stop becomes a seizure tantamount to arrest, requiring a justification of probable cause. However, a few courts have permitted slightly longer stops if there is adequate cause for the delay. For example, *United States v. Mayo*, 394 F.3d 1271 (9th Cir. 2005), permitted a forty-minute stop because reasonable suspicion gradually developed over time, and the officers acted as diligently as they could in the context of complex and rapidly unfolding circumstances:

> Here, the officers conducted the investigation in a constitutional manner. The period of detention was permissibly extended because new grounds for suspicion of criminal activity continued to unfold. The officers pursued their multiple inquiries promptly as they arose: they questioned [defendant] regarding their suspicion of narcotics activity; investigated the vehicle code violation; investigated [defendant's] attempted use of another's credit card; investigated the connection between [defendant] and [another individual], who returned to the scene while officers were questioning [defendant]; searched [this other individual's] Dodge Caravan; and questioned [defendant] about the chemical odor associated with methamphetamine. A maximum of forty minutes to pursue all of these inquiries was not unreasonable. Therefore, the *Terry* detention did not exceed constitutional limits. 394 F.3d at 1276.

Delays in Making a Stop Under ordinary circumstances, an officer who has a reasonable suspicion that a person may be engaged in criminal activity should initiate a stop of the person immediately. Nevertheless, a short delay in making the stop may be justified in certain situations. However, as the delay between the development of reasonable suspicion on the part of the officer and the actual stop grows longer, courts may find that the suspicion has "evaporated."

For example, in *State v. Cyr*, 501 A.2d 1303 (Me. 1985), an officer had grounds to stop a truck parked in an area of recent burglaries after observing the person in the driver's seat duck down to avoid detection. However, because the officer was transporting an arrested person, he continued driving slowly past the truck. In his rearview mirror, the officer observed the truck leave its parking place and follow his cruiser. After being informed that no other police unit was available to intercept the truck, the officer stopped the truck some two to three minutes after the first observation. The court held that the suspicion had not evaporated because of the delay, as the truck remained within the officer's sight at all times and the delay was caused by an arrested person's presence in the officer's vehicle.

A longer delay, however, may cause a stop to be held illegal. For example, *United States v. Posey*, 663 F.2d 37 (7th Cir. 1981), held that suspicion had evaporated when the defendant was stopped fifteen minutes after suspicion arose and fifteen miles away from the place where the defendant was originally seen. In *Posey*, there was an armed robbery of a bank by four men wearing Halloween masks. One of the men was armed with a rifle and another was armed with a semiautomatic revolver. No definitive eyewitness descriptions of the robbers were available. About three months after the robbery, a police officer observed the defendant and a male companion drive an automobile several times past a bank in another town. The officer noted that the defendant and his companion were observing both the bank and the officer in a "suspicious manner." Other surrounding businesses were closed at that time, and the bank itself had been recently robbed. The officer than issued a radio bulletin which provided a description of the automobile and instructing anyone spotting it to "check the passengers out and see what they were up to." Approximately fifteen minutes later, the defendant was stopped about fifteen miles outside of the town by another police officer. A search of the automobile revealed the revolver used in the armed bank robbery three months before as well as other weapons.

After expressing doubt that the police officer observing the defendant outside the bank had reasonable suspicion to stop the defendant's vehicle (or instruct other officers to do so), the court stated that even if the officer initially possessed reasonable suspicion to justify a stop, this suspicion had evaporated by the time the defendant's vehicle was actually stopped:

> Even assuming arguendo that [defendant's] conduct in [the town] constituted justification for a *Terry* stop, that justification had evaporated by the time of the stop. Presumably, the criminal activity of which [defendant] was suspected by [the officer] was preparing to rob the . . . bank. Once [defendant] was fifteen miles outside of [the town] traveling away from that town it cannot fairly be contended that [defendant's] conduct gave rise to a reasonable suspicion that a crime had been committed or was about to be committed. 663 F.2d at 41.

As a result of the court's finding that reasonable suspicion had "evaporated" by the time of the traffic stop, the court suppressed the weapons found in the defendant's vehicle.

And though *United States v. Feliciano*, 45 F.3d 1070 (7th Cir. 1995), cast some doubt on the scope of the "evaporation" doctrine first adopted in *Posey*, it appears to have retained the concept of evaporation by positing that in some cases, reasonable suspicion that a person will commit a crime in the future may not suffice to justify a stop—at least where the future is a distant one. In *Feliciano*, an officer on patrol one night near a train station noticed three men at the station. One, later identified as a college student, was standing close to the train tracks and held a suitcase. The other two, including the defendant and a companion, were walking toward a particular corner of the station's parking lot while looking at the third man. The officer considered this activity "odd" because there were no cars in that part of the parking lot. His suspicions aroused, he radioed for assistance and provided descriptions of the suspects. Two patrolling officers responded.

Moments after radioing for assistance, the officer observed the defendant's companion walk over to the third man near the train tracks, speak to him briefly, then return to the defendant, who was waiting in the corner of the parking lot. At that point, the defendant and his companion left the parking lot, walking east on a nearby street. The third man also left the area, walking on the same street but in the opposite direction of the defendant and his companion. The officer told the two responding officers to monitor the defendant and his companion while he tried to find out from the third man—the college student—what had happened. When the officer caught up with this man, the man explained his belief that the defendant and his companion had been planning to rob him. In particular, the man explained how the defendant's companion tried to get him to walk to a secluded location at the train station; when the man refused, he asked him for money.

After hearing this explanation, the officer immediately contacted the two responding officers, and instructed them to stop and frisk the defendant and his companion. They did so. The frisk of the defendant revealed a pistol, and the frisk of the companion uncovered a meat cleaver and a folding knife, along with marijuana. When they were stopped, both of the suspects were walking towards their homes. In finding that the officer had reasonable suspicion to radio the responding officers and instruct them to stop the defendant and his companion, the court relied, in part, on the fact that the officer had reasonable suspicion that the pair may commit a future crime; namely, a robbery:

> The officers were independently justified, moreover, in stopping [defendant and his companion] on suspicion that they might try to rob some other hapless passerby. It is true that they were walking toward their homes and that by this time the downtown area . . . , where the station was located, was deserted except for [the college student], and he was walking in the opposite direction. But the officers could not have any confidence that [defendant and his companion] were finished with crime for the night. They were walking toward a residential area and might encounter a pedestrian; even in [the town where the station was located], not everyone is in bed or even at home by midnight. [Defendant and his companion] apparently had tried and failed to rob one person, and should they chance on another the probability of a repetition could not be reckoned trivial. 45 F.3d at 1073.

In response to the defendant's argument that even if there is a reasonable suspicion that "the person stopped is en route to the commission of a crime, he may not be stopped if the crime is not expected to occur within a few minutes," the court rejected this argument but said that suspicion of crime to be committed in the distant future may not justify a stop:

> Our more recent cases cast considerable doubt on the existence, or at least scope, of an "evaporation" doctrine; for they do not cite *Posey*, or refer to such a doctrine, even though they involve intervals of hours. *Terry* itself involved an open time frame. The suspects [in *Terry*] had cased one store, and were in front of another when they were stopped. It was unclear whether they meant to rob the second store forthwith or to return at nightfall and hit both. It did not matter; the stop was lawful. The metaphor of evaporation is not a happy one. Water evaporates at a more or less constant rate (holding temperature constant); suspicion does not. The metaphor may not even help defendants. . . . Yet in defense of *Posey*—not of its formula or metaphor, but of its animating idea—it can be argued that an articulable suspicion of a crime to be committed in the distant future would not justify a stop. The long incubation period of the crime would both attenuate the probability that the crime would actually be committed and give the police ample time by further investigation to obtain a better "fix" on that probability. The difficult question is what is "distant" for these purposes. We need not try to answer it here. The probability that [defendant and his companion] would mug someone before they went home, which is to say within minutes or at most a few hours, was sufficient under *Terry* to justify the stop. 45 F.3d at 1074.

Use of Force during a Stop Law enforcement officers making stops may take steps **"reasonably necessary to protect their personal safety and to maintain the status quo during the course of the stop."** *United States v. Hensley*, 469 U.S. 221, 235 (1985). Use of force in making a stop is governed by the Fourth Amendment standard of reasonableness, judged from the perspective of a reasonable officer on the scene rather than from hindsight. The nature and quality of the intrusion on the suspect's Fourth Amendment interests must be balanced against the countervailing governmental interests. The reasonableness inquiry is an objective one—**"whether the officers' actions are 'objectively reasonable' in light of the facts and circumstances confronting them, without regard to their underlying intent or motivation."** *Graham v. Connor*, 490 U.S. 386, 397 (1989). Furthermore, **"[t]he calculus of reasonableness must embody allowance for the fact that police officers are often forced to make split-second judgments—in circumstances that are tense, uncertain, and rapidly evolving—about the amount of force that is necessary in a particular situation."** 490 U.S. at 396–97.

United States v. Seelye, 815 F.2d 48, 50 (8th Cir. 1987), listed six facts and circumstances to be considered in determining the amount and kind of force that is reasonable and consistent with an investigative stop:

(1) the number of officers and police cars involved;

(2) the nature of the crime and whether there is reason to believe the suspect is armed;

(3) the strength of the officer's articulable, objective suspicions;

(4) the need for immediate action by the officer;

(5) the presence or lack of suspicious behavior or movement by the person under observation; and

(6) whether there was an opportunity for the officer to have made the stop in less threatening circumstances.

United States v. Bullock, 71 F.3d 171 (5th Cir. 1995), held that law enforcement officers were justified in drawing their weapons on the defendant after stopping his vehicle for speeding. The officers had been informed over the radio that the defendant was a suspect in a bank robbery committed just hours before, and the officers were familiar with the defendant from previous encounters and knew him to be a dangerous man, who had previously resisted arrest and threatened police. *United States v. Melendez-Garcia*, 28 F.3d 1046, 1053 (10th Cir. 1994), however, held that it was unreasonable, after stopping drug suspects' vehicles, for officers to aim their guns at the suspects and handcuff them "when they outnumbered the defendants, executed the stop on an open highway during the day, had no tips or observations that the suspects were armed or violent, and the defendants had pulled their cars to a stop off the road and stepped out of their cars in full compliance with police orders." *United States v. Romain*, 393 F.3d 63 (1st Cir. 2004), held that officers were justified in temporarily placing a man against a wall because there was reasonable suspicion he was armed, and he acted belligerently and charged toward the officers upon seeing them, thereby putting others in danger. ("We conclude, without serious question, that the temporary detention—placing the [defendant] up against the wall—was justified at its inception because the officers had a reasonable suspicion that the [defendant] was armed and had acted in such a way as to threaten the person who placed the 911 call.") Also, in *United States v. Fisher*, 364 F.3d 970 (8th Cir. 2004), the court held that officers could approach a man with guns drawn because they had information that he committed an armed assault minutes before, and the location where they stopped the man was known for gun violence:

> The decision to approach Fisher with guns drawn was reasonably necessary to the investigative stop. Although Fisher had been cooperative in his initial encounter with the officers, this cooperation did not negate the risk that Fisher was armed and potentially dangerous. After their first contact with Fisher, the officers received specific information that an assailant matching Fisher's description had used a gun in connection with an assault only minutes earlier. Moreover, the officers were approaching Fisher in a neighborhood known for gun violence. Under these circumstances, the officers were entitled to exercise a great degree of control over the investigative stop. 364 F.3d at 973–74.

See Table 7.1 for a comparison of a stop and a formal arrest.

key points

- An investigative stop must last no longer than is reasonably necessary and must use the least intrusive methods reasonably available to confirm or dispel an officer's suspicions of criminal activity.
- An officer who has lawfully stopped a motor vehicle may order both the driver and passengers out of the vehicle pending completion of the stop.

- If an officer has reasonable suspicion to justify a stop of a person, and that person subsequently refuses in violation of state law to identify herself, the officer may be permitted to expand the scope of the detention by arresting the person.
- An officer making a stop must use an objectively reasonable degree of force or threat of force.

TABLE 7.1

COMPARISON OF A STOP WITH AN ARREST

	Stop	Arrest
Purpose	Brief, limited investigatory detention	To bring a suspect into custody for the commission of an offense as the prelude to criminal prosecution
Justification	Reasonable suspicion supported by articulable facts that criminal activity may be afoot	Probable cause to believe that the person to be arrested has committed or is committing a crime
Warrant	Not needed	Preferred but not needed for arrests in public places. Required to enter a suspect's home. Search warrant also needed to enter a third party's home to arrest a suspect therein.
Notice	None required	Officer usually must give notice that the person is under arrest and that the officer has the authority to arrest.
Force	Officer may use a reasonable degree of force judged from the perspective of the reasonable officer on the scene. Officer may never use deadly force to make a stop, but may use deadly force if, during the stop, it becomes necessary to act in self-defense or defense of others. Officer must use the least intrusive methods reasonably available to confirm or dispel the officer's suspicions of criminal activity.	Officer may use any reasonably necessary non-deadly force to arrest for a misdemeanor or a felony. Officer may use deadly force if, during the process of arrest, it becomes necessary to act in self-defense or defense of others. Office may also use deadly force to stop a fleeing felon from escaping if the officer has probable cause to believe that the suspect poses a threat of serious bodily harm either to the officer or to others. Deadly force may not be used to stop a fleeing misdemeanant or a fleeing felon who poses no risk of danger.
Time Limit	Must be temporary and last no longer than is necessary to effectuate the purpose of the stop	Whatever time is reasonably necessary to make the arrest and bring the suspect into custody for booking and further processing
Judicial Review	Someone stopped by police does not have an automatic right to prompt judicial review of the legality of the stop. If a citation is issued, it may be challenged in subsequent court proceedings.	Someone who is arrested has the right to prompt judicial review of the legality of the arrest by a neutral judicial officer, usually within forty-eight hours of the time of arrest.
Search Allowed	Protective pat-down frisk of outer clothing for weapons may be conducted if, and only if, the officer has reason to believe that the person stopped is armed and dangerous.	A full body search of the arrestee for weapons and evidence may be conducted as a search incident to any valid, custodial arrest. Officers may also search the areas into which the arrestee might reach to grab weapons, contraband, or other evidentiary items.

Frisks

A frisk is a limited search of a person's body consisting of a careful exploration or pat-down of the outer surfaces of the person's clothing in an attempt to discover weapons. The law enforcement officer's determination of whether to frisk a suspect is a separate issue from determination of whether to stop. A frisk serves a different governmental interest and is justified by a different set of factors. The governmental interest served is the protection of the officer and others from possible violence by persons being investigated for crime. "[W]e **cannot blind ourselves to the need for law enforcement officers to protect themselves and other prospective victims of violence in situations where they may lack probable cause for an arrest.**" *Terry v. Ohio*, 392 U.S. 1, 24 (1968).

Balanced against this interest is the citizen's right to privacy, which is necessarily invaded by giving police the right to frisk suspects. "**We must still consider, however, the nature and quality of the intrusion on individual rights which must be accepted if police officers are to be conceded the right to search for weapons in situations where probable cause to arrest for crime is lacking.**" 392 U.S. at 24. As noted earlier, the Court considers the frisk procedure to be a serious intrusion on a person's rights, possibly inflicting great indignity and arousing strong resentment.

Balancing these competing interests, the Supreme Court in *Terry* gave law enforcement officers the following limited frisk authority:

> **Our evaluation of the proper balance that has to be struck in this type of case leads us to conclude that there must be a narrowly drawn authority to permit a reasonable search for weapons for the protection of the police officer, where he has reason to believe that he is dealing with an armed and dangerous individual, regardless of whether he has probable cause to arrest the individual for a crime.** 392 U.S. at 27.

Limited Authority to Frisk

A law enforcement officer's authority to frisk is limited and narrowly drawn. An officer may not frisk everyone that he or she stops to investigate possible criminal activity. Before conducting a frisk, an officer must have "reason to believe that he is dealing with an armed and dangerous individual." An officer need not be absolutely certain that the individual is armed. Rather, the issue is "**whether a reasonably prudent man in the circumstances would be warranted in the belief that his safety or that of others was in danger.**" 392 U.S. at 27. *An officer must be able to justify a frisk of a person by pointing to specific facts and* "**specific reasonable inferences which he is entitled to draw from the facts in light of his experience.**" 392 U.S. at 27. Thus, frisks are governed by the same objective reasonable suspicion standard as stops.

The Supreme Court has held that this standard is not met when officers, armed with a warrant authorizing a search of a bar and bartender for narcotics, frisk the customers in that bar. An officer cannot frisk a customer, or any individual for that matter, unless the officer has reasonable suspicion that the individual is armed and dangerous:

> The "narrow scope" of the *Terry* exception does not permit a frisk for weapons on less than reasonable belief or suspicion directed at the person to be frisked [i.e., a bar customer], even though that person happens to be on premises where an authorized narcotics search is taking place. *Ybarra v. Illinois*, 444 U.S. 85 (1979).

Justification to frisk usually requires a combination of one or more factors, evaluated in the light of an officer's experience and knowledge. The more factors present, the more likely a reviewing court will find that the officer had reasonable suspicion to frisk. The following is a partial list of factors that may be considered in deciding to frisk a person:

▶ The suspected crime involves the use of weapons.

▶ The suspect is nervous or edgy about being stopped.

▶ There is a bulge in the suspect's clothing.

▶ The suspect's hand is concealed in his or her clothing.

▶ The suspect does not present satisfactory identification or an adequate explanation for suspicious behavior.

▶ The suspect behaves in a secretive, or furtive, fashion.

▶ The area in which the officer is operating is known to contain armed persons.

▶ The suspect exhibits belligerent behavior upon being stopped.

▶ The officer believes that the suspect may have been armed on a previous occasion.

Many of these factors will be discussed in more detail in the section entitled "Specific Circumstances Justifying Stops and Frisks."

Note that special considerations may apply when frisking someone of the opposite sex. Frisking a person of the opposite sex presents a delicate situation for which few specific guidelines are available. On the one hand, law enforcement officers could reasonably fear danger to themselves or others from a person of the opposite sex. On the other hand, use of routine frisk procedures on a person of the opposite sex may subject an officer to civil or criminal liability. Therefore, other protective alternatives should be explored. If an officer of the same gender as the suspect to be frisked can be summoned to the scene in a reasonable amount of time without jeopardizing the safety of the officers present, this alternative should be explored. Alternatively, officers at the scene may request stopped persons to remove outer clothing.

Scope of a Frisk

This section will explore the permissible scope of a frisk under *Terry* and other cases. In particular, it will address the scope of a frisk in the context of both persons and vehicles.

Pat-Down of the Person's Outer Clothing The U.S. Supreme Court in *Terry* emphasized that a frisk is "a *reasonable* search for weapons for the protection of the police officer." 392 U.S.at 27. Because the only justifiable purpose of a frisk is the protection of the officer and others, the search must be strictly **"limited to that which is necessary for the discovery of weapons which might be used to harm the officer or others nearby."** 392 U.S. at 26. If the protective search goes beyond what is necessary to determine if the suspect is armed, it is no longer valid under *Terry*, and its fruits are inadmissible.

Therefore, a frisk must initially be limited to a pat-down of the *outer* clothing. An officer has no authority to reach inside clothing or into pockets in the *initial* stages of a frisk. During the pat-down, if the officer detects an object that feels like a weapon, the officer may then reach inside the clothing or pocket and seize it. If the object is not a weapon but is some other implement of crime (such as a burglar's tool), that implement is admissible in evidence for the crime to which it relates (for example, attempted burglary).

If an officer feels no weapon-like object during the course of the pat-down, the officer can no longer have a reasonable fear that the person is armed. Any further search without probable cause would exceed the purpose of the frisk—the protection of the officer and others—and would be unreasonable under the Fourth Amendment. Evidence obtained from an unlawful frisk is inadmissible. For example, the Court in *United States v. Miles*, 247 F.3d 1009 (9th Cir. 2001), found that the officer exceeded the permissible scope of a frisk when he manipulated a small box in the defendant's pocket that did not initially feel like a weapon or weapon-like object. By manipulating the box, the officer believed that it contained bullets. He removed the box from the defendant's pocket, and after opening it, found bullets. The Court in *Miles* describes the invalid frisk in this way:

> [The officer] felt a small box in [defendant's] pocket. The box was no bigger than a large package of chewing gum and was one-half the size of a package of cigarettes. While the officer may have been patting down for a weapon, he had reached the outer limits of his pat-down authority when it was clear that the object was a small box and could not possibly be a weapon. [T]he officer here did not immediately recognize the box as contraband. Rather, . . . "the officer determined that the object was contraband only after squeezing . . . and otherwise manipulating the contents of the defendant's pocket." At that point, the officer's further manipulation of the box was impermissible. He had no cause to shake or manipulate the tiny box on the pretext that he was still looking for a weapon. The government suggests that the officer might legitimately have been looking for a tiny pen knife, needle, or other slender weapon. But the officer did not testify to such a motivation. Under the government's logic there would be no limit to the bounds of a *Terry* stop. Rather, looking for the proverbial "needle in a haystack" would become the norm. "Shake, rattle, and roll" would take on new meaning in the context of a *Terry* pat-down. It must also be remembered that this search took place while [defendant] was handcuffed. Having already used significant force to secure the scene for safety purposes, the officers cannot leverage the safety rationale into a justification for a full-scale search. The search exceeded the "strictly circumscribed" limits of *Terry*. 247 F.3d at 1014–15.

Thus, since the small box did not initially feel like a weapon or weapon-like object, the officer could not further manipulate the box, or remove the box from the defendant's pocket and open it. As a result, the court excluded from trial the bullets found in the box.

However, in *United States v. Majors*, 328 F.3d 791 (5th Cir. 2003), the court found that the officer's more intrusive "frisk" of the defendant's pocket was permissible because the officer could not initially discern whether or not the bulge he felt in the defendant's pocket was a weapon. The court described the officer's actions in this way:

> [Officer] Rush felt a large bulge in the left pocket of baggy shorts. Unable to identify the bulge, Rush pulled up the outside of [defendant's] pocket to see what was inside. He testified that there was no other reasonable way to verify that the bulge was not a weapon. Inside the pocket, Rush saw a plastic bag filled with smaller plastic bags containing white powder. [The powder was cocaine]. 328 F.3d at 794.

The court found the frisk permissible because the bulge may have been a weapon; as a result, the cocaine was admissible into evidence against the defendant:

> Rush did not rule out the possibility that the bulge in [defendant's] pocket was a weapon; his continued search of [defendant's] pocket was therefore justified under *Terry* for the protection of himself and the other officers in the house. The bulge in [defendant's] pocket was 'bigger than a softball' and 'in between hard and soft.' Although Rush could not feel a knife in [defendant's] pocket, he could not tell if there was another weapon in the bulge, [such as a grenade]. Rush testified that apart from looking inside [defendant's] pocket, there was no other reasonable way to determine if a weapon was present. . . . Rush had not ruled out the possibility that the bulge was a weapon, nor had he ruled out that the softball size item in [defendant's] pocket might conceal a weapon. Consequently, he could continue the search beyond the initial "plain feel." 328 F.3d at 795.

Protective Search for Weapons within Reach of Person Being Frisked *Michigan v. Long*, 463 U.S. 1032 (1983), approved an extension of the permissible scope of a protective search for weapons beyond the person of a suspect to include the passenger compartment of an automobile. In *Long*, two police officers patrolling at night observed a car traveling erratically and at excessive speed. When the car swerved into a ditch, the officers stopped to investigate. The driver, the only occupant of the car, met the officers at the rear of the car. He did not respond to initial requests to produce his license and registration, but after the request was repeated, he began walking toward the car to obtain the papers. Note that at this point, while the officers had sufficient grounds for a stop, they did not have sufficient grounds to conduct a frisk for weapons. However, as the officers approached the car, they saw a hunting knife on the floorboard of the driver's side of the car. The Supreme Court held that the officers then had sufficient grounds to conduct a pat-down search of the driver and a limited search of the passenger compartment of the car for weapons:

> **[T]he search of the passenger compartment of an automobile, limited to those areas in which a weapon may be placed or hidden, is permissible if the police officer possesses a reasonable belief based on "specific and articulable facts which, taken together with the rational inferences from those facts, reasonably warrant" the officers in believing that the suspect is dangerous and the suspect may gain immediate control of weapons.** 463 U.S. at 1049.

Thus, if officers lawfully stop a vehicle, and then develop in the course of that stop reasonable suspicion that the occupants or recent occupants are armed and dangerous, they may not only frisk the occupants, but they may also conduct a limited search of the passenger compartment of the vehicle for weapons. As part of this search, officers can look anywhere a weapon could be hidden in the vehicle.

In reaching its decision, the Court in *Long* recognized that roadside encounters between police and suspects are especially hazardous and that danger may arise from the possible presence of weapons in the area surrounding a suspect. The Court emphasized, however, that its decision does not mean that the police may conduct automobile searches whenever they make stops. Because the sole justification for a frisk is the protection of police officers and others nearby, officers may frisk an occupant of an automobile (both the driver and any passengers, as well as the automobile's passenger compartment) only when they have reasonable suspicion that the occupant is armed and dangerous. Unlike a warrantless search incident to a lawful arrest (see Chapter 8), a frisk is not justified by any need to prevent the disappearance or destruction of evidence of crime.

However, "[i]f, while conducting a legitimate *Terry* search of the interior of the automobile, the officer should . . . discover contraband other than weapons, he clearly cannot be required to ignore the contraband, and the Fourth Amendment does not require its suppression in such circumstances." *Long*, 463 U.S. at 1050. In *Long*, one of the officers shined a flashlight into the car and saw a pouch protruding from under the armrest of the front seat. Since the pouch could have contained a weapon, the officer was justified in lifting the armrest, revealing an open pouch containing marijuana. Having discovered the marijuana pursuant to a legitimate frisk, the officer was justified in seizing the marijuana under the plain view doctrine. Under that doctrine, "if police are lawfully in a position from which they view an object, if its incriminating character is apparent, and if the officers have a lawful right of access to the object, they may seize it without a warrant." *Minnesota v. Dickerson*, 508 U.S. 366, 375 (1993). If, however, the police lack probable cause to believe that an object in plain view is an item subject to seizure without conducting some further search of the object (such as manipulating the object to look for a serial number or some other identifying characteristic), the plain view doctrine does not justify its seizure. The plain view doctrine is discussed in detail in Chapter 10.

Relying on the plain view doctrine, the Supreme Court in *Dickerson* further expanded the scope of a permissible frisk by approving a so-called plain touch (or plain feel) exception to the rule allowing only the seizure of weapons or weapon-like objects discovered in the course of a frisk. That exception allows the seizure of non-threatening contraband, such as drugs, if its identity as contraband is immediately apparent to the sense of touch as the result of the pat-down search (e.g., the officer, upon immediately feeling the object, has probable cause based on his or her sense of "touch" that the object is non-threatening contraband).

In *Dickerson* itself, the Court did not approve of the seizure of the crack cocaine found in the defendant's pocket because the officer did not have probable cause, upon feeling the object, that it was cocaine. Thus, the officer went beyond the permissible scope of a frisk when he manipulated the object to determine if it was, indeed, an illegal drug:

> Although the officer was lawfully in a position to feel the lump in respondent's pocket, because *Terry* entitled him to place his hands upon respondent's jacket [as part of a valid "pat-down"], the court below determined that the incriminating character of the object was not immediately apparent to him. Rather, the officer determined that the item was contraband only after conducting a further search [involving manipulation of the object], one not authorized by *Terry* or by any other exception to the warrant requirement. Because this further search of respondent's pocket was constitutionally invalid, the seizure of the cocaine that followed is likewise unconstitutional. 508 U.S. at 379.

The plain touch, or plain feel, exception is further discussed in Chapter 10.

key points

- A law enforcement officer may conduct a reasonable limited protective search (frisk) for weapons when the officer has reasonable suspicion that he or she is dealing with an armed and dangerous person, whether or not the officer has probable cause to arrest.
- A frisk must initially be limited to a pat-down of a person's outer clothing. If a weapon or weapon-like object is detected, or if a non-threatening object's identity as contraband is immediately apparent to an officer's sense of touch, the officer may reach inside clothing or a pocket and seize the object. For an object's identity as non-threatening contraband (i.e., drugs) to be immediately apparent to an

officer's sense of touch, the officer must have probable cause, upon feeling the object, that the object is this kind of contraband.
- If a law enforcement officer has a reasonable, articulable suspicion that a motor vehicle's occupant is armed and dangerous, the officer may frisk the occupant and search the passenger compartment of the vehicle for weapons. The officer may look in any location in the passenger compartment that a weapon could be found or hidden. The officer may also seize items of evidence other than weapons, if discovered in plain view during the course of such a search.

►SPECIFIC CIRCUMSTANCES JUSTIFYING STOPS AND FRISKS

Stops and frisks encompass an infinite variety of possible situations. General guidelines may not be sufficient to clearly indicate what behavior is appropriate for a law enforcement officer in a given situation. This section presents actual cases involving stops and frisks to show how courts evaluate the reasonableness of the actions of law enforcement officers. The cases are grouped under various headings indicating major factors influencing the court decisions.

Behavioral Cues

A law enforcement officer should evaluate reasonable suspicion of criminal activity under the totality of circumstances—that is, the officer should consider all of the behaviors exhibited by the suspect when judging whether reasonable suspicion to stop and frisk exists. This section will address the types of behaviors that may provide the officer with the necessary reasonable suspicion of criminal activity to stop and/or frisk the suspect.

Flight and other Forms of Evasive Behavior In *Illinois v. Wardlow*, 528 U.S. 119, 124 (2000), the U.S. Supreme Court recognized that "nervous, evasive behavior is a pertinent factor in determining reasonable suspicion." The Court said, "Headlong flight—wherever it occurs—is the consummate act of evasion: it is not necessarily indicative of wrongdoing, but it is certainly suggestive of such." In *Wardlow*, the defendant fled when he saw a caravan of police vehicles converge on his street, which was known for heavy narcotics trafficking. Officers in one of the vehicles pursued the defendant and eventually cornered him. An officer exited the vehicle, stopped the defendant, and immediately conducted a pat-down search for weapons. The officer discovered a handgun and arrested the defendant.

The U.S. Supreme Court held that the stop was lawful because the suspect's presence in a high-crime area, coupled with his sudden flight, constituted reasonable suspicion to detain and investigate further:

> Such a holding is entirely consistent with our decision in *Florida v. Royer*, 460 U.S. 491 (1983), where we held that when an officer, without reasonable suspicion or probable cause, approaches an individual, the individual has a right to ignore the police and go about his business. . . . And any "refusal to cooperate, without more, does not furnish the minimal level of objective justification needed for a detention or seizure." *Florida v Bostick*, 501 U.S. 429, 437 (1991). But unprovoked flight is simply not a mere refusal to cooperate. Flight, by its very nature, is not "going about one's business"; in fact, it is just the opposite. Allowing officers confronted with such flight to stop the fugitive and investigate further is quite consistent with the individual's right to go about his business or to stay put and remain silent in the face of police questioning. 528 U.S. at 125.

Note that unprovoked flight, standing alone, does not automatically provide reasonable suspicion to stop a suspect. Relying on *Wardlow*, *United States v. Jordan*, 232 F.3d 447 (5th Cir. 2000), held that the totality of the circumstances, including the defendant's "running at full sprint" from the direction of a nearby grocery store, his "looking back over his shoulder, left and right," the time (6:45 P.M. on a January evening), and place (a high-crime area), justified the officer's decision to stop the defendant. The court said:

> *Wardlow* did not establish a bright-line test in cases where a defendant is seen to be running. Instead, citing *Terry*, *Wardlow* examined the totality of circumstances to determine whether the officer had a "reasonable, articulable suspicion that criminal activity is afoot." . . . *Wardlow* noted that an individual's presence in a "high-crime area" is a relevant consideration, as is "nervous, evasive behavior." 232 F.3d at 449.

The court in *United States v. Baskin*, 401 F.3d 788 (2005), examined flight in the context of time of day and location in reaching its conclusion that police had reasonable suspicion to stop the defendant's vehicle:

> [I]t is highly relevant to the reasonable suspicion analysis that the approaching vehicle's acceleration occurred in such close proximity to a newly discovered methamphetamine lab in an otherwise remote county park at a time when most people are asleep. Therefore, it was appropriate for the district court to consider the proximity to the methamphetamine lab in performing the analysis. It was also reasonable for [the police officer] to interpret the vehicle's sudden acceleration as evidence of unprovoked flight. 401 F.3d at 793.

Evasive behavior may include other actions besides flight that are collectively referred to as **furtive gestures**. For example, before reaching a police roadblock, if a vehicle brakes abruptly, turns into a private driveway and comes to a stop, this action may constitute evasive behavior capable of contributing to an officer's determination of reasonable suspicion to stop:

> Having concluded that evasive behavior by a motorist approaching a police roadblock may contribute to a reasonable suspicion of criminal activity, we now consider whether, based on the totality of the circumstances here, the officers possessed a reasonable suspicion that [defendant] was engaged in criminal activity. For the reasons that follow, we conclude that they did. The officers observed [defendant's] vehicle brake abruptly and turn suddenly into a private gravel driveway [before reaching the roadblock]. [Defendant's] erratic driving and the nature of the road onto which he turned could have reasonably suggested to the officers that [defendant] was attempting to evade the roadblock rather than simply "going about [his] business." Upon further investigation, [the officer] observed [defendant's] vehicle stopped in the middle of the driveway, more than 200 feet from the public road but still some distance from the residence. [The officer] could have reasonably inferred from this observation that [defendant] was attempting to evade the police checkpoint by hiding in the driveway and was not simply turning into the driveway because he lived there or because he was turning around to avoid the checkpoint for innocent reasons, such as a belief that an accident was ahead. And although [the officer] had activated his police lights, [defendant's] vehicle did not remain stopped—as one would expect of a driver who turned away from the roadblock for innocent reasons—but instead proceeded around the curve in the driveway. As the district court recognized, this additional evasive behavior gave [the officer] further reason to believe that [defendant] might be engaged in criminal activity. Thus, by the time [defendant] finally submitted to [the officer's] display of authority by stopping at the end of the driveway, [the officer] had observed [defendant] engage in a series of evasive actions—all inconsistent with innocent reasons for avoiding the roadblock. And, all of this conduct occurred at 3:05 A.M., compounding the suspiciousness of [defendant's] behavior. We conclude that these facts, viewed in their totality, provided the officers with reasonable suspicion that [defendant] may have been engaged in criminal activity, thus permitting them to stop his vehicle to investigate that suspicion. See *United States v. Smith,* 396 F.3d 579, 585–87 (4th Cir. 2005).

There are many types of furtive gestures that may be considered by officers as part of the totality of circumstances analysis for reasonable suspicion. Some examples that courts have considered as evidence of evasive behavior include:

▶ multiple suspects providing conflicting answers to questions posed by police officers, see, e.g., *United States v. Edwards*, 424 F.3d 1106 (D.C. Cir. 2005);

▶ avoiding eye contact with officers, see, e.g., *United States v. Owens*, 167 F.3d 739 (1st Cir. 1999);

▶ attempting to hide something out of an officer's line of vision, see, e.g., *People v. Carvey*, 680 N.E.2d 150 (N.Y. 1997);

▶ attempting to swallow something so an officer cannot find it, see, e.g., *State v. Thomas*, 483 N.W.2d 527 (Neb. 1992); and

▶ continually looking over one's shoulder in a manner that suggests someone is trying to make sure that no one is watching, see, e.g., *United States v. Jordan*, 232 F.3d 447 (5th Cir. 2000).

Finally, suspects may exhibit a form of evasive behavior by placing their hands in their pockets when approached by police. In *United States v. Mayo*, 361 F.3d 802 (4th Cir. 2004), while two officers were traveling through a high crime area, they observed the defendant standing in a street talking with another person. When the defendant saw the approaching police car, he "put his left hand into his left hand jacket pocket, turned 180 degrees, walked out of the street and onto the [apartment] complex property. . . ." One of the officers observed that defendant "'either . . . had something heavy in [his] pocket or he was pushing his hand down' into the pocket, a movement that [the officer] believed was consistent with an individual's effort to maintain control of a weapon while moving." The officers drove to the other side of the apartment complex, and saw the defendant emerge. When the defendant again saw the officers in the police car, he first stopped but then continued walking. At this point, one of the officers approached the defendant, showed his badge, and asked if he could speak with him. The other officer requested that he remove his left hand from his pocket, and the defendant complied. In response to the officer's question if he lived in the apartment complex, the defendant did not respond and appeared "shocked." The officer also observed that the defendant appeared to be shaking. When asked if he had a weapon, the defendant failed to respond, and averted his eyes. At this point, one of the officers frisked him. The officer found a semi-automatic pistol in one of the defendant's pockets—the same pocket into which the defendant had earlier inserted his hand. The officer seized the pistol, and arrested the man for carrying a concealed weapon without a permit. 361 F.3d at 803, 804.

Based, in part, on the defendant inserting his hand into his pocket upon seeing the officers for the first time, the court found that the officers had a reasonable suspicion to both stop and frisk him:

> When we evaluate the circumstances found in this case to determine whether the . . . police officers had a reasonable suspicion to stop [defendant] under the principles of *Terry v. Ohio*, we conclude that they did. First, we note that [the officer's] encounter with [defendant] occurred in a high-crime area that had been targeted for special enforcement. . . . Although standing alone this factor may not be the basis for reasonable suspicion to stop anyone in the area, it is a factor that may be considered along with others to determine whether police have a reasonable suspicion based on the totality of the circumstances. Second, [defendant's] activity upon viewing the marked patrol car suggested that he might be carrying a gun. The way [defendant] put his hand in his pocket and the appearance of something heavy in his pocket suggested to the officers that [defendant] had put his left hand onto a gun to protect it while he was moving. Third, upon seeing the police, [defendant] sought to evade their scrutiny. When he saw the approaching police car, [defendant] 'turned 180 degrees' and walked from the street into an adjacent apartment complex. And when he came out the other side, only to view the police again, he reacted in a shocked manner, thereafter proceeding to walk away. Fourth and finally, when the officers confronted [defendant], he evinced an unusually nervous behavior. He averted his eyes to avoid those of the officers, and his nervousness was palpable. . . . Because the officers' suspicion was reasonable and was

supported by articulable facts, the officers had a right to stop [defendant] and, because they reasonably believed [defendant] was armed, to pat him down in the interest of their personal safety. 361 F.3d at 807–8.

Association with Known Criminals/Prior Criminal Record *United States v. Cruz*, 909 F.2d 422 (11th Cir. 1989), found adequate grounds, based partially on the suspect's association with known drug dealers, for both a stop and frisk under the following circumstances:

> First, the appellant was seen walking together with a known drug dealer who had negotiated with one of the agents for the delivery of fifteen grams of cocaine. Second, the agents certainly understood that the crime of drug trafficking has a particularly violent nature. Finally, the appellant's male companion was seen speaking to one of the dealers whom the agents knew was present to exchange a kilogram of cocaine. While none of these factors, by themselves, necessarily justifies an investigative stop, they are each relevant in the determination of whether the agents had reasonable suspicion to stop the appellant. . . . Thus under all the circumstances known to the officers at the time of the stop, we hold that the officers had reasonable suspicion to stop the appellant who had walked away from the scene of the original arrests.
>
> Because the detective had reasonable suspicion to stop the appellant, she also had the right to make a limited protective search for concealed weapons in order to secure the safety of herself and the safety of those around her. The factors articulated above indicated that the appellant was likely involved in narcotics trafficking and, as is judicially recognized, such individuals are often armed. . . . In addition, in an area known for heavy drug trafficking, the appellant was walking down the street and stopping before a car of known dealers who were at the scene to exchange some cocaine. Under these circumstances, a limited protective search, including a search of the purse, was reasonable. 909 F.2d at 424.

In *United States v. Sprinkle*, 106 F.3d 613 (4th Cir. 1997), the court found that the defendant's presence with a known drug criminal did not, in conjunction with other factors, provide reasonable suspicion for officers to stop him:

> [The officer's] curiosity was understandably aroused when he spotted [defendant's companion], who had recently served time for a narcotics offense, in a neighborhood with a high incidence of drug traffic. But for these factors to support reasonable suspicion there must be (other) particularized evidence that indicates criminal activity is afoot. 106 F.3d at 618.

The court then turned its attention to the other factors the government claimed supported reasonable suspicion to stop defendant:

> When [defendant's companion] and [defendant] huddled with their hands close together, [the officer] was able to see into the car: he saw their hands, he did not see anything pass between them, and they did not try to conceal any object. In other words, [the officer] could actually see that nothing of a criminal nature was happening in the car. Of course, after [the officer] looked into the car, [defendant's companion] did try to hide his face. We agree that this appears suspicious. Nevertheless, without some stronger indication of criminal activity, this act cannot tip this case to reasonable suspicion. Nor does the final factor, driving away in a normal, unhurried fashion, lend itself to a finding of reasonable suspicion here. [Defendant] had just gotten into the car, so a prompt departure could be expected. Together, [these factors] did not give

the officers the necessary reasonable, articulable suspicion of criminal activity. The district court was therefore correct to conclude that the initial stop was unjustified. 106 F.3d at 618–19.

A related issue directly addressed by the court in *Sprinkle* is whether an officer's knowledge of a person's criminal record can give rise to reasonable suspicion to stop. The court found that a person's criminal record alone cannot support reasonable suspicion to stop:

> [Defendant's companion] first got [the officer's] attention because the officer knew [the companion] had a criminal record and that he had recently finished a sentence for a drug conviction. [The officer], however, had no information that [the companion] had returned to crime since his release. A prior criminal record "is not, standing alone, sufficient to create reasonable suspicion." Nevertheless, an officer can couple knowledge of prior criminal involvement with more concrete factors in reaching a reasonable suspicion of current criminal activity. 106 F.3d at 617.

"Innocent" Conduct A series of individual lawful acts may provide reasonable suspicion of criminal activity sufficient to justify a stop, if the overall pattern of those acts is indicative of criminal activity. Officers should evaluate all circumstances in their totality rather than evaluate each act or circumstance in isolation:

> **When discussing how reviewing courts should make reasonable suspicion determinations, we have said repeatedly that they must look at the "totality of the circumstances" of each case to see whether the detaining officer has a "particularized and objective basis" for suspecting legal wrongdoing. . . . This process allows officers to draw on their own experience and specialized training to make inferences from and deductions about the cumulative information available to them that "might well elude an untrained person."** *United States v. Arvizu*, 534 U.S. 266, 273 (2002) (internal citations omitted).

As may be recalled from the previous discussion of *Arvizu* ("Authority to Stop: Reasonable Suspicion Standard," earlier in this chapter), the U.S. Supreme Court in that case found that the officer had reasonable suspicion to stop a vehicle under the totality of the circumstances, all of which were innocent when considered individually:

> **[Defendant] argues that we must rule in his favor because the facts suggested a family in a minivan on a holiday outing. A determination that reasonable suspicion exists, however, need not rule out the possibility of innocent conduct. Undoubtedly, each of these factors alone is susceptible of innocent explanation, and some factors are more probative than others. Taken together, we believe they sufficed to form a particularized and objective basis for [the officer] stopping the vehicle, making the stop reasonable within the meaning of the Fourth Amendment.** 534 U.S. at 277–78.

In *Reid v. Georgia*, 448 U.S. 438 (1980), the U.S. Supreme Court found an officer could not infer reasonable suspicion to stop a person from the following facts: (1) the defendant had arrived from Fort Lauderdale, which a Drug Enforcement Administration (DEA) agent testified is a principal place of origin of cocaine sold elsewhere in the country; (2) the defendant arrived in the early morning, when law enforcement activity is diminished; (3) he and his companion appeared to the agent to be trying to conceal the fact that they were traveling together; and (4) they apparently had no luggage other than their shoulder bags:

> **We conclude that the agent could not, as a matter of law, have reasonably suspected the petitioner of criminal activity on the basis of these observed circumstances. Of the evidence relied on, only the fact that the petitioner preceded another person and occasionally looked backward at him as they proceeded through the concourse relates to their particular conduct. The other circumstances describe a very large category of presumably innocent travelers, who would be subject to virtually random seizures were the Court to conclude that as little foundation as there was in this case could justify a seizure. Nor can we agree, on this record, that the manner in which the petitioner and his companion walked through the airport reasonably could have led the agent to suspect them of wrongdoing. Although there could, of course, be circumstances in which wholly lawful conduct might justify the suspicion that criminal activity was afoot . . . this is not such a case. The agent's belief that the petitioner and his companion were attempting to conceal the fact that they were traveling together, a belief that was more an "inchoate and unparticularized suspicion or 'hunch,'" . . . than a fair inference in the light of his experience, is simply too slender a reed to support the seizure in this case.** 448 U.S. at 441.

Similarly, in *Johnson v. Campbell*, 332 F.3d 199 (3d Cir. 2003), a lower court found that officers could not infer reasonable suspicion to stop a person who drank coffee and read a newspaper while exhibiting "agitated" behavior:

> But [nothing] can turn the simple, objective facts that Johnson was drinking coffee, flipping through a newspaper, pacing, and rubbing his head into articulable suspicion that Johnson was about to commit a crime. Furthermore, by the time that [the officer] reached him, Johnson was doing nothing more than sitting in a van with another man and reading a paper—activities that, even when done on a cold night in December, do not add any cause for particularized suspicion, and that a citizen must be allowed to do unhindered by the police. 332 F.3d at 209–10.

In contrast, *United States v. Sokolow*, 490 U.S. 1 (1989), found an overall pattern indicating criminal activity from a similar but more specific and detailed set of facts. In that case, DEA agents stopped the defendant on his arrival at Honolulu International Airport. The agents found 1,063 grams of cocaine in his carry-on luggage. When the defendant was stopped, the agents knew that (1) he paid $2,100 for two airplane tickets from a roll of $20 bills; (2) he traveled under a name that did not match the name under which his telephone number was listed; (3) his original destination was Miami, a source city for illicit drugs; (4) he stayed in Miami for only forty-eight hours, even though a round-trip flight from Honolulu to Miami takes twenty hours; (5) he appeared nervous during his trip; and (6) he checked none of his luggage. The Court found reasonable suspicion to justify the stop, even though there was no evidence of ongoing criminal activity. Applying a totality-of-the-circumstances test, the Court said that **"[a]ny of these factors is not by itself proof of any illegal conduct and is quite consistent with innocent travel. But we think taken together they amount to reasonable suspicion."** 490 U.S. at 9.

Admissions by Defendant In *State v. Hall*, 476 P.2d 930, 931 (Or. App. 1970), after an officer stopped the defendant's vehicle for speeding, the defendant got out of the vehicle, holding his right hand in the pocket of his knee-length coat. The pocket was baggy and sagging. When the officer grabbed the defendant's arm and asked him whether he had a gun, the defendant answered yes. The officer then removed the gun and arrested the defendant. The court assumed without discussion that the stop was reasonable because it was a routine traffic stop. Upholding the frisk, the court said, "Here the officer did not merely think he was dealing with an armed person—he knew he was." 476 P.2d at 931.

Recall from the earlier discussion of *United States v. Chhien*, 266 F.3d 1 (1st Cir. 2001), that after the officer made a lawful traffic stop, the defendant consented to being frisked. Upon feeling a large bulge in defendant's pocket, the officer asked what it was. The defendant responded that the bulge was a wad of cash totaling $2,000. The court held that the defendant's response provided reasonable suspicion for the officer to detain him for additional questioning. 266 F.3d at 10.

Possible Evidentiary Cues

Certain types of evidentiary cues associated with a suspect may provide a law enforcement officer with the necessary reasonable suspicion of criminal activity to stop and/or frisk the suspect. This section will address several types of these evidentiary cues (for example, the observation by an officer of a bulge underneath the suspect's clothing). Recall that a law enforcement officer should evaluate reasonable suspicion of criminal activity under the totality of circumstances—that is, the officer should consider all of the evidentiary cues associated with the suspect in determining whether reasonable suspicion to stop and frisk exists.

Observation of Bulge or Heavy Object Recall that in *Pennsylvania v. Mimms*, 434 U.S. 106 (1977), the U.S. Supreme Court held that an officer may order a driver to exit a vehicle if the officer makes a lawful traffic stop of the driver's vehicle. Once the driver in *Mimms* did exit his vehicle, the officer saw a large bulge under the defendant's jacket. Based on this observation, the Court concluded that the officer had reasonable suspicion to frisk the driver: **"The bulge in the jacket permitted the officer to conclude that [the driver] was armed and thus posed a serious and present danger to the safety of the officer. In these circumstances, any man of 'reasonable caution' would likely have conducted the pat-down."** 434 U.S. at 112.

The observation of a bulge also helped justify a frisk in *State v. Simmons*, 818 P.2d 787 (Idaho App. 1991). In *Simmons*, a sheriff's department notified local pawnshops to be alert for a described person suspected of burglarizing a home and stealing silver dollars. When a pawnshop reported a person matching the description trying to sell silver dollars, detectives went to the pawnshop and observed the suspect apparently attempting to sell coins. He was wearing a long wool coat, which seemed out of place for the day's weather, appeared nervous, and was sweating. A detective observed a bulge in an exterior pocket of the suspect's coat. When another detective frisked the suspect, he felt a hard object in the coat pocket that possibly felt like a small gun or knife. He reached his hand in and pulled out a pipe that appeared to be one used for smoking illegal drugs.

Discussion

POINT

Interpreting *Arvizu*: When Does "Innocent" Conduct Support Reasonable Suspicion to Stop?

United States v. Townsend, 305 F.3d 537 (6th Cir. 2002).

In the early morning hours of June 16, 1999, Ohio highway patrolmen Douglas Eck and John Chesser stopped an automobile traveling Eastbound on Interstate 70 in excess of the speed limit. The officers testified that, from the beginning of the stop, they found several things unusual. As they approached the vehicle, Townsend, who had been driving the car, put his hands in the air without prompting. When told that the radar indicated that they had been speeding at 76 miles per hour, Townsend immediately admitted that he had been traveling at 85 miles per hour. Townsend had his license, registration, and proof of insurance ready when Officer Eck arrived at his window. Officer Eck testified that he found this behavior reflective of an unusual eagerness to end the stop quickly.

Officer Eck returned to his patrol car, where another officer, James Myers, had arrived. At the suppression hearing, the three officers testified that the defendants acted nervously in the car, frequently looking back at the officers while they were processing the paperwork. Although Townsend's name matched the name listed on the proof of insurance for the car, the registered owner was different. Eck returned to the car and asked Townsend whether the owner of the automobile was present. Townsend said no. As it turns out, the car was registered to Townsend's mother. At the suppression hearing, Eck testified that he found the absence of the recorded owner suspicious as drug couriers often do not own the cars that they are driving.

Eck then questioned Townsend and Green regarding the purpose of their journey. Townsend claimed that they were traveling from Chicago to visit his sister in Columbus. Eck then questioned Townsend and Green (another passenger in the vehicle) regarding the purpose of their journey. Townsend said that he could not remember his sister's address in Columbus, but claimed that he had planned to call his sister once he reached the Columbus area. At the suppression hearing, Eck testified that he believed Townsend to be lying about the purpose of his journey, as he found it odd that Townsend had planned to call his sister in the early morning hours. Eck also testified that he believed Chicago to be a source city and Columbus a destination city for narcotics. The defendants' traveling between those destinations made Eck suspect that they were transporting drugs, Eck testified.

The officers observed three cellular telephones and a Bible in the passenger compartment. According to Eck, the large number of cellular telephones were typical of drug couriers. In addition, Eck testified that, in his experience, drug couriers often prominently display religious symbols in their cars in order to deflect suspicion of drug smuggling.

The officers asked the defendants to exit their vehicle, and then frisked them for weapons. The officers found no weapons, but did detect what felt like a large roll of cash. Eck testified that

(Continued)

Interpreting *Arvizu*: When Does "Innocent" Conduct Support Reasonable Suspicion to Stop? *(Continued)*

he knew that drug couriers, engaging in a largely cash-based business, often carried large amounts of currency. The officers also searched the passenger compartment for weapons, but found none.

Finding no contraband in the passenger area of the car or on the person of the defendants, the officers ordered the defendants to sit in the back of the patrol car and called for a canine unit. Over thirty minutes later, another officer arrived with a drug-sniffing dog. The dog alerted on the trunk of the car. Because of the dog's indication, the officers opened and searched the trunk. They found nothing in the main luggage compartment of the trunk. The officers also dismantled a compact-disc changer mechanism that was in the back of the trunk. Lodged inside the device were ten, apparently counterfeit, one-hundred dollar bills. The officers never found any trace of narcotics of any kind in the trunk. The officers arrested the defendants for possession of counterfeit currency.

The defendants moved to suppress the ten counterfeit bills seized during the officers' search of the trunk, arguing that the search violated the Fourth Amendment. The appeals court agreed with the defendants, and suppressed the counterfeit bills. The court found that the totality of circumstances failed to support the reasonable suspicion necessary to detain the defendants while police summoned a canine unit. After examining each factor upon which the officers based their reasonable suspicion to detain the defendants beyond the time necessary to conduct the routine traffic stop, the court said:

> Although the government has pointed to several factors, present in this case, which we have recognized as valid considerations in forming reasonable suspicion, they are all relatively minor and, in many cases, are subject to significant qualification. The fact of the matter is that this case lacks any of the stronger indicators of criminal conduct that have accompanied these minor factors in other cases. We hold that the officers lacked reasonable suspicion to detain the defendants until the canine unit arrived. We, therefore, [affirm] the district court's order suppressing the counterfeit bills seized in the officers' search of defendants' trunk. . . . 305 F.3d at 545.

Specifically, the court found that the following facts did not amount to reasonable suspicion to detain the defendants in order to conduct the canine search of their trunk, which revealed the counterfeit bills:

The court upheld both the stop and the frisk. The court found that the facts gave the detectives a reasonable, articulable basis to believe that the person in the store was the burglar of the home. Therefore, they had sufficient grounds to stop the suspect and resolve their suspicions. When they noticed the bulge in the suspect's overcoat pocket, they had reasonable grounds to be concerned for their safety and to conduct a frisk for weapons. The defendant claimed that wearing a long wool coat on a warm day and being nervous were not suspicious

Interpreting *Arvizu*: When Does "Innocent" Conduct Support Reasonable Suspicion to Stop? *(Continued)*

(1) The defendant raised his hands in the air upon being stopped for the speeding violation.

(2) The defendant had his license, registration, and other documentation ready when the officer arrived to the car.

(3) The defendant admitted to traveling at a higher speed than the officer indicated he was traveling.

(4) The defendant explained that he was traveling from Chicago to visit his sister in Columbus but did not know her address.

(5) The defendants were traveling from a source city for narcotics to a destination city for narcotics.

(6) The defendants had three cellular telephones in the car.

(7) The defendants had a Bible in the car.

(8) The defendants apparently had rolls of currency in their pockets which were detected by police during their frisk of defendants (Note: Police had reasonable suspicion to frisk defendants and search the passenger compartment of the car for weapons because police learned that one of the defendants had been previously arrested for a weapons charge, though he never had been convicted).

(9) The defendants appeared nervous, constantly looking back at the car while officers completed the citation for speeding.

(10) The defendants' car was "cluttered" with food wrappers and clothing.

(11) The defendant's mother, who was not present, was the registered owner of the car.

Do you agree with the court that these facts do not support a reasonable suspicion to detain the defendants for "over 30 minutes" while a canine unit could be summoned to examine the trunk of the car for drugs? What distinguishes this case from the Supreme Court's decision in *Arvizu* (discussed earlier), where the Court found that the circumstances—though innocent in nature when considered individually—supported reasonable suspicion for a stop when evaluated in their totality? Are all of the facts listed above from *Townsend* really innocent when considered individually? In their totality? More generally, in evaluating reasonable suspicion, how much deference should courts give to officers' experience, training, and knowledge? How much do you think this consideration played into the court's holding in *Townsend*? In *Arvizu*?

behaviors and that the officers had no reason to fear him. Nevertheless, the court said that "taken together . . . all of the information the police had about the case generated a reasonable, articulable suspicion, and a concern for their safety which warranted the intrusion." 818 P.2d at 792.

United States v. Barnes, 909 F.2d 1059 (7th Cir. 1990), upheld the seizure of a pistol discovered as the result of a pat-down of a person lawfully stopped for having altered temporary license plates. The frisk was justified because the officer observed a "heavy object" protruding from the person's jacket and the person attempted to reach for his pocket before the initial pat-down.

In *United States v. Chhien*, 266 F.3d 1, 10 (1st Cir. 2001), when the officer felt a bulge in the suspect's pocket while conducting a lawful frisk, and the suspect explained that the bulge was $2,000 in cash, the court held that this combination of events provided the officer with reasonable suspicion to continue the suspect's detention long enough to ask additional questions: "Since the trooper lawfully learned about the cash—the appellant, after all, consented to the pat-down search and voluntarily described the composition of the discerned bulge—that discovery elevated his suspicions to a degree sufficient to continue the detention briefly and in a minimally intrusive way."

Presence in a High-Crime Area In *Brown v. Texas*, 443 U.S. 47 (1979), police on patrol in an area with a high incidence of drug traffic stopped the defendant in an alley while he was walking away from another person. The officer later testified that the situation "looked suspicious and we had never seen that subject in that area before." The U.S. Supreme Court invalidated the stop: **"The fact that appellant was in a neighborhood frequented by drug users, standing alone, is not a basis for concluding that appellant himself was engaged in criminal conduct. In short, the appellant's activity was no different from the activity of other pedestrians in that neighborhood."** 443 U.S. at 52.

Illinois v. Wardlow, 528 U.S. 119 (2000) (discussed above, in "Flight and Other Forms of Evasive Behavior"), reiterated the holding in *Brown*, but added that presence in a high-crime area combined with other specific suspicious information, such as unprovoked flight, may justify a stop:

> **An individual's presence in an area of expected criminal activity, standing alone, is not enough to support a reasonable, particularized suspicion that the person is committing a crime [citing *Brown v. Texas*]. But officers are not required to ignore the relevant characteristics of a location in determining whether the circumstances are sufficiently suspicious to warrant further investigation. Accordingly, we have previously noted the fact that the stop occurred in a "high-crime area" among the relevant contextual considerations in a *Terry* analysis.** 528 U.S. at 124.

Suspect Matches Description in a Report of Violent Crime In *People v. Anthony*, 86 Cal. Rptr. 767 (Cal. App. 1970), police officers on patrol received a radio report of an armed robbery in their vicinity at about 3:30 A.M., minutes after the robbery happened. The officers had seen only one moving car in the vicinity, and they approached it. Noticing that a passenger fit the description of the robber given on the radio, they stopped the car and instructed its two occupants to get out. Without asking any questions, an officer immediately conducted a pat-down search of the defendant for weapons. He found bullets and arrested the defendant. The court held that both the stop and the frisk were justified:

> If the reason for the stop is an articulate suspicion of a crime of violence, and the officer has reason to fear for his personal safety, he may immediately proceed to make a pat-down search for weapons without asking any prior questions. . . . There is no reason why an officer, rightfully but forcibly con-

fronting a person suspected of a serious crime, should have to ask one question and take the risk that the answer might be a bullet. 86 Cal. Rptr. at 773.

In *United States v. Fisher*, 364 F.3d 970 (8th Cir. 2004), when police officers learned from a victim that he had been assaulted by a particular man with a gun, the officers were justified in stopping a man minutes later, with their guns drawn, who fit the description provided by the victim:

> The [victim] approached the officers, telling them he had been assaulted in that area by someone matching [defendant's] distinctive description moments earlier. Although the officers did not know the [victim's] name or why he was at the location, they were nonetheless confronted with an in-person report of a serious street crime and a description of the perpetrator that matched [defendant]. The [victim's] report was corroborated by the fact that [defendant] was in close proximity to the scene of the alleged assault at or around the time it was alleged to have occurred. Based on this information, the officers had reasonable suspicion that Fisher committed a crime, and that he was armed and dangerous.
>
> The decision to approach [defendant] with guns drawn was reasonably necessary to the investigative stop. [T]he officers received specific information that an assailant matching [defendant's] description had used a gun in connection with an assault only minutes earlier. Moreover, the officers were approaching [defendant] in a neighborhood known for gun violence. 364 F.3d at 973.

After the officers stopped the defendant, he blurted out, without being questioned by the officers, that he had a gun. The court also upheld the subsequent frisk of defendant to find the gun, which was in the defendant's pocket.

key points

- Officers should evaluate the following circumstances in their totality rather than evaluate each act or circumstance in isolation, before deciding whether to stop or frisk someone:

  1. The suspected crime involves the use of weapons or is otherwise a violent crime.
  2. There is a bulge in the suspect's clothing.
  3. The suspect's hand is concealed in his or her clothing.
  4. The suspect does not give an adequate explanation for suspicious behavior (i.e., provides implausible or incorrect answers).
  5. The suspect behaves in an evasive or furtive fashion (i.e., the suspect flees upon seeing police).
  6. The area in which the officer is operating is a high-crime area.
  7. The officer believes that the suspect may have been armed on a previous occasion.
  8. The officer knows the suspect has a prior criminal record.

  9. The suspect admits to possessing a weapon or to some other type of criminal activity.
  10. The suspect is present with another individual known to be a criminal.
  11. The suspect is unusually nervous, edgy, or belligerent about being stopped.

Note that in deciding whether reasonable suspicion exists to frisk a suspect, officers should consider only those factors listed above relevant to determining whether the suspect is armed and dangerous.

- A series of individual lawful acts may provide reasonable suspicion of criminal activity sufficient to justify a stop, if the overall pattern of those acts is indicative of criminal activity.
- If an officer stops a person on a reasonable, articulable suspicion of a violent crime, and the officer has reason to fear for his or her personal safety, the officer may immediately make a pat-down search for weapons without asking any questions.

Detentions of Containers and Other Property

Smith v. Ohio, 494 U.S. 541 (1990), stated the general rule regarding the investigatory detention of property:

> Although the Fourth Amendment may permit the detention for a brief period of property on the basis of only "reasonable, articulable suspicion" that it contains contraband or evidence of criminal activity . . . it proscribes—except in certain well-defined circumstances—the search of that property unless accomplished pursuant to judicial warrant issued upon probable cause. 494 U.S. at 542.

United States v. Place, 462 U.S. 696 (1983), held that *Terry v. Ohio* applied to the warrantless seizure and limited investigation of personal luggage. In *Place*, based on information from law enforcement officers in Miami, DEA agents at a New York airport suspected that the defendant was carrying narcotics. When the defendant arrived at the airport, the agents approached him, informed him of their suspicion, and requested and received identification from him. When the defendant refused to consent to a search of his luggage, an agent told him that they were going to take the luggage to a federal judge to try to obtain a search warrant.

Instead, the agents took the luggage to another airport, where they subjected it to a sniffing by a trained narcotics detection dog, a procedure commonly referred to as a **canine sniff** or a **dog sniff**. The dog reacted positively to one of the bags. At this point, approximately ninety minutes had elapsed since the seizure of the luggage. The agents later obtained a search warrant for the luggage and found cocaine.

As in *Terry*, the *Place* Court balanced the nature and quality of the intrusion on the individual's Fourth Amendment interests against the importance of the governmental interests alleged to justify the intrusion. The Court found a substantial governmental interest in detecting drug trafficking, a unique problem because it is highly organized and conducted by sophisticated criminal syndicates, the profits are enormous, and drugs are easily concealed:

> The context of a particular law enforcement practice, of course, may affect the determination whether a brief intrusion on Fourth Amendment interests on less than probable cause is essential to effective criminal investigation. Because of the inherently transient nature of drug courier activity at airports, allowing police to make brief investigative stops of persons at airports on reasonable suspicion of drug trafficking substantially enhances the likelihood that police will be able to prevent the flow of narcotics into distribution channels. 462 U.S. at 704.

The *Place* Court also found that some brief detentions of personal effects may be so minimally intrusive that strong, countervailing governmental interests will justify a seizure based only on specific, articulable facts that the property contains contraband or evidence of a crime. The Court therefore held that **"when an officer's observations lead him reasonably to believe that a traveler is carrying luggage that contains narcotics, the principles of *Terry* and its progeny would permit the officer to detain the luggage briefly to investigate the circumstances that aroused his suspicion, provided that the investigative detention is properly limited in scope."** 462 U.S. at 706. In addition, the Court specifically found that the brief investigation of the luggage could include a "canine sniff" by a well-trained narcotics detection dog. This procedure was found to be uniquely limited in nature because it does not require opening the luggage, it does not expose non-contraband items to view, and it discloses only the presence or absence of narcotics. *See also Illinois v. Caballes*, 543 U.S. 405, 410 (2005). ("**A dog sniff conducted during a concededly lawful traffic stop that reveals no information other than the location of a substance that no individual has any right to possess [i.e., drugs] does not violate the Fourth Amendment.**")

Nevertheless, the Court in *Place* found that the scope of the investigative detention of the luggage exceeded the limits established in *Terry*, primarily because of the length of the detention:

> **Although the 90-minute detention of respondent's luggage is sufficient to render the seizure unreasonable, the violation was exacerbated by the failure of the agents to accurately inform respondent of the place to which they were transporting his luggage, of the length of time he might be dispossessed, and of what arrangements would be made for return of the luggage if the investigation dispelled the suspicion. In short, we hold that the detention of respondent's luggage in this case went beyond the narrow authority possessed by police to briefly detain luggage reasonably suspected to contain narcotics.** 462 U.S. at 710.

Although the Court did not establish any rigid time limitation on an investigative detention, it clearly indicated that efforts of officers to minimize the intrusion on Fourth Amendment rights would be considered in determining the reasonableness of the detention. For example, the court in *United States v. Avery*, 137 F.3d 343 (6th Cir. 1997), found reasonable the detention of the suspect's luggage for twenty-five minutes at the airport while officers conducted, in a diligent and efficient manner, a canine sniff. The court first found that reasonable suspicion existed to detain the suspect's bag:

> At the point the officers seized the bag in this case, in addition to Avery's actions, which the officers believed to be suspicious, they knew the following: (1) only a brief moment after he boarded the plane, Avery stated he had thrown his ticket away; (2) Avery lied about the origin of his trip, stating it was Orlando, when in fact it was San Juan; (3) Avery misrepresented the nature of his business in Orlando, stating that he was visiting friends on vacation, when in fact Orlando was a stop-over on his way to Washington, D.C.; (4) Avery stated he could not remember the name of his hotel and had no receipts; (5) Avery's ticket was issued in a name different than his own; (6) Avery did not have any identification, although he was traveling from San Juan to Washington; (7) Avery consented to a search of his person, but not his carry-on bag; and (8) Avery was traveling on a cash one-way ticket purchased only thirty-five minutes before departure. While it is true that none of these facts alone is incriminating or illegal, and we are very reluctant to ascribe criminal intent to scenarios that are similar to innocent acts of the general public, we must look at the totality of the circumstances in determining whether or not the detention of the bag was supported by reasonable suspicion. We believe the combined factors in this case provided the officers with sufficient suspicion to hold the bag briefly in order to allow a police dog to sniff it. 137 F.3d at 350.

In addition, the court found reasonable the twenty-five-minute detention of the suspect's luggage while police conducted the canine sniff because police acted diligently, and kept the suspect informed regarding the handling of his luggage:

> Upon deplaning the aircraft, the officers immediately contacted the airport canine handler and arranged for a meeting at the airport police department with a drug-sniffing dog. The entire process from the time the bag was detained to the time it was sniffed took twenty-five minutes. Before leaving the plane, the officers offered Avery the opportunity to accompany his bag or in the alternative they would return the bag to Avery's . . . address if no drugs were discovered or if they were unable to obtain a warrant. 137 F.3d at 350–51.

The court also distinguished this case from the Supreme Court's decision in *Place* invalidating a ninety-minute detention of luggage:

> In *Place*, a luggage detention case, the court found the detention was unreasonable because there was a ninety-minute gap from seizure to sniff, the officers failed to obtain a canine sniffer expeditiously, and the officers did not inform the defendant what they were doing with his luggage. Here, the officers informed Avery what they intended to do with his bag; they quickly obtained a canine to sniff the luggage and did so within twenty-five minutes. 137 F.3d at 351.

United States v. Ganser, 315 F.3d 839 (7th Cir. 2003) also involved a detention of property that did not also detain a person. In *Ganser*, postal authorities removed a certain envelope from the mail stream because it matched a description provided by an informant of an envelope that allegedly contained drugs. The court found that there was reasonable suspicion to detain the envelope based on this corroboration by postal authorities. In addition, the court found reasonable a one-day detention of this envelope while law enforcement authorities conducted a canine sniff (and indicated that a two-day detention would also be reasonable under the circumstances):

> In the present case, the first letter was detained based on reasonable suspicion as discussed above from Thursday until Friday, at which time a narcotics-trained canine alerted to it. Once the canine alerted to the letter, reasonable suspicion was elevated to probable cause. We have previously held that a two-day detention of letters in order to subject them to a canine sniff test was brief enough to be sustained by reasonable suspicion. Furthermore, postal authorities in the present case acted diligently. 315 F.3d at 844.

Note that detention and search of carry-on luggage at airline security checkpoints are a special case because of the severe danger presented by the possibility of allowing weapons or explosives on a plane. (For more details about detentions of containers at airports, see the discussion of the special needs doctrine in the section "Airport and Courthouse Searches" in Chapter 5).

In a case involving the equivalent of a "frisk" of luggage on a bus as opposed to at an airline security checkpoint, the U.S. Supreme Court held that a law enforcement officer's physical manipulation of a bus passenger's carry-on luggage violated the Fourth Amendment's proscription against unreasonable searches. In *Bond v. United States*, 529 U.S. 334 (2000), a border patrol agent in Texas boarded a bus to check the immigration status of its passengers. As the agent walked from the rear to the front of the bus, he squeezed the soft luggage in the overhead storage space above the seats. He noticed that a canvas bag above the defendant's seat contained a "bricklike" substance. After the defendant admitted ownership of the bag and consented to its search, the agent discovered a "brick" of methamphetamine.

The Court likened the level of intrusion of squeezing the defendant's luggage to that of a frisk of his person. **"Although Agent Cantu did not 'frisk' petitioner's person, he did conduct a probing tactile examination of petitioner's carry-on luggage. Obviously, petitioner's bag was not part of his person. But travelers are particularly concerned about their carry-on luggage; they generally use it to transport personal items that, for whatever reason, they prefer to keep close at hand."** 529 U.S. at 337–38. The Court found the "frisk" of the luggage unreasonable:

> Our Fourth Amendment analysis embraces two questions. First, we ask whether the individual, by his conduct, has exhibited an actual expectation of privacy; that is, whether he has shown that "he [sought] to preserve [something] as private." *Smith v. Maryland*, 442 U.S. 735, 740 (1979). . . . Here, petitioner sought to preserve privacy by using an opaque bag and placing that bag directly above his seat. Second, we inquire whether the individual's expectation of privacy is "one that society is prepared to recognize as reasonable." . . . When a bus passenger places a bag in an overhead bin, he expects that other passengers or bus employees may move it for one reason or another. Thus, a bus passenger clearly expects that his bag may be handled. He does not expect that other passengers or bus employees will, as a matter of course, feel the bag in an exploratory manner. But this is exactly what the agent did here. We therefore hold that the agent's physical manipulation of petitioner's bag violated the Fourth Amendment. 529 U.S. at 338–39.

Note that *Bond* does not prevent law enforcement officers from boarding buses or other means of public transportation and talking to passengers. Nor does it prevent officers from asking passengers for consent to search their belongings. *Bond* merely holds that it is illegal for a law enforcement officer to squeeze a passenger's belongings absent at least reasonable suspicion to believe a container has criminal evidence within it. If an officer possessing this reasonable suspicion feels the container and detects something that he or she has probable cause to believe is contraband, the officer should, absent an emergency such as the threat of an exploding bomb, obtain a judicial warrant before opening and searching the container. This is especially the case in a stop and frisk situation since the suspect has not yet been arrested. *See, generally, United States v. Chadwick*, 433 U.S. 1 (1977). (See the section in Chapter 6 entitled "Container Searches" for more information.)

Traffic Stops and Roadblocks

An ordinary traffic stop is governed by the same standards as any other stop. "[A] traffic stop is valid under the Fourth Amendment . . . if the police officer has reasonable articulable suspicion that a traffic or equipment violation has occurred or is occurring." *United States v. Botero-Ospina*, 71 F.3d 783, 787 (10th Cir. 1995); *see also United States v. Arvizu*, 534 U.S. 266, 273 (2002) (evaluating ordinary traffic stop under reasonable suspicion standard). Minor traffic or equipment violations are so common that law enforcement officers are often tempted to use them to justify an investigation based on vague suspicion that the motorist may be engaging in more serious illegal activity. For example, an officer who observes a burned-out taillight, cracked windshield, or failure to signal when changing lanes may stop a vehicle even if a hypothetical "reasonable officer" would not have been motivated by a desire to enforce the traffic laws. This particular officer may actually be interested in investigating a crime more serious than the minor traffic or equipment violation. A stop made under such pretenses is often called a **pretextual stop.**

In *Whren v. United States*, 517 U.S. 806 (1996), plainclothes police officers patrolling a high-drug crime area in an unmarked vehicle observed a truck driven by the defendant waiting at a stop sign for an unusually long time. Suddenly, the truck turned without signaling and drove off at an unreasonable speed. One of the officers stopped the vehicle, supposedly to warn the driver about traffic violations, and on approaching the truck, the officer observed plastic bags of crack cocaine in the defendant's hands. The defendant argued that the traffic stop was pretextual and that the evidence seized should be suppressed. The U.S. Supreme Court held that police officers with probable cause to believe that a traffic violation has occurred may stop a vehicle even though the stop is a pretext to search for drugs or some other, more serious crime. **"Subjective intentions play no role in ordinary, probable-cause Fourth Amendment analysis."** 517 U.S. at 813. The Court emphasized, however, the distinction between its holding in *Whren* and cases involving police intrusion without probable cause. The Court indicated its pretext analysis would not apply to such cases, which lack the "'quantum of individualized suspicion' necessary to ensure that police discretion is sufficiently contained." 517 U.S. at 817–18. Therefore, pretext (the subjective motive for stopping a vehicle) is irrelevant when probable cause exists to support a stop, but pretextual stops made without probable cause are not justified.

The *Whren* decision adopted the so-called *could* test and overrode previous law in some jurisdictions that subscribed to the more narrow *would* test. In other words, the question for the officer is "Could I stop the vehicle?" (because there is probable cause to believe a traffic violation has occurred), not "Would I stop the vehicle?" (because, under normal circumstances, a stop would not be made for a minor violation). The *Whren* decision essentially legitimizes pretextual stops and disregards the subjective intent of the officer in favor of judging the constitutionality of a vehicle stop on the basis of objective data: was there probable cause to believe a violation of law occurred?

Note, however, that random stops of vehicles, based on whim, hunch, or rumor, to check licenses, registrations, or equipment are not allowed. *Delaware v. Prouse*, 440 U.S. 648, 663 (1979), held that:

> [E]xcept in those situations in which there is at least articulable and reasonable suspicion that a motorist is unlicensed or that an automobile is not registered, or that either the vehicle or an occupant is otherwise subject to seizure for violation of law, stopping an automobile and detaining the driver in order to check his driver's license and the registration of the automobile are unreasonable under the Fourth Amendment.

The *Prouse* Court expressed its concern that random vehicle checks present a potential danger of arbitrary or discriminatory enforcement of the law. *See also United States v. Brignoni-Ponce*, 422 U.S. 873 (1975) (officers conducting roving patrol near border need at least reasonable suspicion that vehicle contains undocumented persons before stopping it). Nevertheless, the Court in *Prouse* specifically held open the possibility for states to develop methods for spot checks that involve less intrusion or that do not involve the unconstrained exercise of discretion. The Court suggested as one possible alternative the questioning of *all* oncoming traffic at roadblock-type stops.

Recall from Chapter 5 that *Michigan Department of State Police v. Sitz*, 496 U.S. 444 (1990), approved a highway **sobriety checkpoint** program with guidelines governing checkpoint operations, site selection, and publicity. During the only operation of the checkpoint at the time of the Court decision, 126 vehicles had passed through the checkpoint, the average delay per vehicle was twenty-five seconds, and two drivers were arrested for driving under the influence. Applying the special needs doctrine, the Court found that although a Fourth Amendment "seizure" occurs when a vehicle is stopped at a checkpoint, police may stop a vehicle at a valid checkpoint without reasonable suspicion that the occupants are engaging in criminal activity.

Recall, however, that *Indianapolis v. Edmond*, 531 U.S. 32 (2000), held that a highway checkpoint program—the primary purpose of which was the discovery and interdiction of illegal narcotics—violated the Fourth Amendment. What distinguished this checkpoint program from those previously approved by the Court in *Sitz* is that its primary purpose was to detect evidence of criminal wrongdoing, as opposed to the public safety goals at issue in *Sitz* that made the sobriety checkpoint constitutional under the special needs doctrine (see Chapter 5).

Illinois v. Lidster, 540 U.S. 419 (2004) involved a roadblock set up by police to locate witnesses to a hit-and-run accident that had killed a bicyclist a week earlier. The roadblock was located on the same portion of highway, in the same direction, and at about the same time of day as the accident. The Court described the roadblock as follows:

> **Police cars with flashing lights partially blocked the eastbound lanes of the highway. The blockage forced traffic to slow down, leading to lines of up to 15 cars in each lane. As each vehicle drew up to the checkpoint, an officer would stop it for 10 to 15 seconds, ask the occupants whether they had seen anything happen there the previous weekend, and hand each driver a flyer.** 540 U.S. at 422.

The defendant approached the checkpoint in a minivan, swerved, and nearly hit one of the officers. Officers determined that he was driving under the influence, and arrested him.

The defendant contended that the roadblock was an unlawful detention, because officers were prohibited by *Indianapolis v. Edmond* from establishing roadblocks intended to apprehend motorists who were using or transporting drugs. The Court, however, pointed out that there is a big difference between an *Edmond* crime-control roadblock and an information-seeking roadblock intended to locate witnesses to a crime. The main difference is that a crime-control roadblock is essentially a stop, which must be justified by reasonable articulable suspicion that a driver or occupant is involved in criminal activity. An information-seeking roadblock, however, falls into the category of "special needs" detentions that are justified by a legitimate law enforcement objective other than the need to stop and question a suspect temporarily. Such detentions

# POINT

Interpreting *Lidster*: Are "Safety Checkpoints" Permitted?

Ex parte Jackson, 886 So.2d 155 (Ala. 2004).

The Mobile Housing Authority entered into a contract with the Mobile County Sheriff's Department that permitted the Sheriff's Department to enter housing areas governed by the Housing Authority at the request of the Housing Authority and perform such policing activities as rolling patrols, foot patrols, community policing, and safety checkpoints to establish some sort of "police presence." Pursuant to that contract, the Mobile County Sheriff's Department entered the R.V. Taylor housing project in Mobile on the evening of May 10, 2001, to set up what they called a "safety checkpoint" at a major intersection in the housing community. The Housing Authority had made no particular request for a roadblock-type stop in this instance; a captain in the Sheriff's Department made the decision to set up the roadblock-type stop. The officers checked driver's licenses, automobile insurance documentation, and vehicle "safety devices" (e.g., seat belts, child restraints, etc.) at the roadblock-type stop. They put in place seven marked Sheriff's Department vehicles at the intersection and stopped every vehicle that came through the intersection. They followed guidelines established by the Sheriff's Department while conducting the roadblock-type stop; those guidelines required that they perform no random searches and that the officers' activities be supervised by superior officers in the Sheriff's Department.

An officer stopped Jackson's vehicle at the roadblock. He discovered marijuana and two rolls of cash on Jackson's person, and a larger quantity of marijuana in the console between the driver's seat and the passenger's seat. Hidden under the tire cover in the trunk of Jackson's vehicle was an Old Navy store shopping bag that contained more marijuana, scales, and numerous plastic sandwich bags. At trial, Jackson filed a motion to suppress the marijuana found on his person and in his vehicle, on the basis that the roadblock-type stop was an unreasonable seizure that violated the Fourth Amendment to the United States Constitution. The court refused to suppress the marijuana in light of its finding that this was a reasonable stop designed to check driver's licenses, insurance information, and safety devices. According to the court, the stop, described by police as a "safety checkpoint," was brief; minimally intrusive; neutral (e.g., involved no "random" checks—every driver was checked); conducted pursuant to guidelines set by superior officers; and involved limited discretion on the part of the officers actually conducting the stop:

> [T]he roadblock-type stop was to be conducted in accordance with guidelines for such stops established by the . . . Sheriff's Department. For example, in compliance with the

Interpreting Lidster: Are "Safety Checkpoints" Permitted? *(Continued)*

guidelines, the officers checked the driver of every vehicle for a driver's license, proof of automobile liability insurance, and safety equipment; there were no random checks. Therefore, the officers in the field had no discretion in deciding whom to stop. Each stop lasted approximately one minute, unless the officers found problems with the paperwork or safety equipment. "Superior officers" were involved in the planning, placement, and timing of the roadblock. The officers' discretion was limited by the guidelines established by the sheriff's department for conducting such stops, thereby creating a neutral and objective plan, which limited the officers' discretion. The intrusion upon the drivers was minimal because it involved only checking to determine whether the driver had the paperwork drivers are required to carry in their vehicles, and the stops lasted only about one minute. The presence of seven marked law-enforcement vehicles gave adequate warning to oncoming drivers that the stop was authorized and organized by law-enforcement personnel. 886 So.2d at 163-64.

In sum, the court concluded that "the roadblock-type stop was a valid and constitutional means of protecting the public from unlicensed drivers and unsafe vehicles." 886 So.2d at 163.

As to the defendant's argument that this was an impermissible roadblock constructed for the purpose of combating crime more generally (e.g., a "general law enforcement purpose"), the court said:

> Other than the inferential suspicion based on the word "presence" in Sgt. Cassidy's testimony and the contract between the sheriff's department and the housing authority, [defendant] presented no evidence to prove that this particular roadblock-type stop was for a general law-enforcement purpose. Therefore, we hold that [defendant] has not sufficiently proven that the license checkpoint was a subterfuge for "a general law-enforcement checkpoint stop." 886 So.2d at 165.

Do you agree with the court that the police constructed this roadblock in an urban housing community for the purpose of checking driver's licenses, insurance documentation, and whether seat belts and child restraints were being worn? Or did this stated purpose only serve to mask the real purpose of combating crime more generally (i.e., illegal drugs and weapons detection)? When the superior officer involved in planning the roadblock testified, he indicated that the reason for the roadblock was to maintain a "police presence" in the housing community. Do you agree with this assessment? In your opinion, what should constitute a permissible purpose, if any, for a police roadblock?

are evaluated by the same standard as the highway sobriety checkpoint in *Sitz*. Balancing the need for the roadblock against its intrusiveness, the Court found:

▶ The relevant public concern was grave—a serious crime resulting in death. Also, the need for information was great, because the investigation had apparently stalled.

▶ The police advanced this grave public concern by tailoring the stops to fit important investigatory needs. **"The stops took place about one week after the hit-and-run accident, on the same highway near the location of the accident, and at about the same time of night. And police used the stops to obtain information from drivers, some of whom might well have been in the vicinity of the crime at the time it occurred."** 540 U.S. at 427.

▶ The stops interfered only minimally with motorists' Fourth Amendment liberties. **"Viewed objectively, each stop required only a brief wait in line—a very few minutes at most. Contact with the police lasted only a few seconds. . . . Police contact consisted simply of a request for information and the distribution of a flyer. . . . Viewed subjectively, the contact provided little reason for anxiety or alarm. The police stopped all vehicles systematically. . . . And there is no allegation here that the police acted in a discriminatory or otherwise unlawful manner while questioning motorists during stops."** 540 U.S. at 427.

Consequently, the Court held that the roadblock in *Lidster* was lawful.

Racial Profiling

An issue causing great controversy and concern in recent years is the law enforcement practice of **racial profiling**. Although definitions of racial profiling vary greatly, the following broad definition taken from a racial profiling study design guide produced for the U.S. Department of Justice is useful for a general discussion. Racial profiling is "any police-initiated action that relies upon: the race, ethnicity, or national origin of an individual rather than [1] the behavior of that individual, or [2] information that leads the police to a particular individual who has been identified as being engaged in or having been engaged in criminal activity."

One of the reasons racial profiling has become a volatile issue is *Whren v. United States*, 517 U.S. 806 (1996), which gives police wide discretion in enforcing traffic laws if they have probable cause to believe that a traffic violation is occurring or has occurred. Recall that *Whren* authorizes an officer who observes a minor traffic violation—a burned-out taillight, a cracked windshield, or failure to signal when changing lanes—to legally stop the driver even if the officer's actual intent is to look for evidence of drug offenses or other more serious offenses. Because minor traffic violations are so common, some commentators have suggested that *Whren* gives police virtually unlimited authority to stop any vehicle they wish to stop.

The basic premise of *Whren* was re-affirmed by the Supreme Court in *Arkansas v. Sullivan*, 532 U.S. 769 (2001). There, the officer stopped a vehicle driven by defendant for speeding and for having improperly tinted windshields. When the officer examined defendant's license, he recognized his name as a person under investigation for narcotics. When the officer subsequently saw in plain view in the car a roofing hatchet, he arrested defendant for "speeding, driving without his registration and insurance documentation, carrying a weapon (the roofing hatchet), and improper window tinting." A later inventory search of the car uncovered drugs and drug paraphernalia. In response to defendant's argument that his stop and arrest by the officer was merely a pretext for the officer to search for drugs, the Supreme Court upheld its decision in *Whren* finding that pretextual seizures are not prohibited by the Fourth Amendment:

> The Arkansas Supreme Court's holding to that effect [e.g., the officer's pretextual stop and arrest violated the Fourth Amendment] cannot be squared with our decision in *Whren*, in which we noted our "unwilling[ness] to entertain Fourth Amendment challenges based on the actual motivations of individual officers," and held unanimously that "[s]ubjective intentions play no role in ordinary, probable-cause Fourth Amendment analysis." That *Whren* involved a traffic stop, rather than a custodial arrest, is of no particular moment; indeed, *Whren* itself relied on *United States v. Robinson*, for the proposition that "a traffic-violation arrest . . . [will] not be rendered invalid by the fact that it was 'a mere pretext for a narcotics search.'" 532 U.S. at 771–72.

Note that though *Whren* allows pretextual stops when an officer has probable cause that a traffic violation is being or has been committed, the Court in *Whren* did say that:

> We of course agree with petitioners that the Constitution prohibits selective enforcement of the law based on considerations such as race. But the constitutional basis for objecting to intentionally discriminatory application of laws is the Equal Protection Clause, not the Fourth Amendment. Subjective intentions play no role in ordinary, probable-cause Fourth Amendment analysis. 517 U.S. at 813.

In *United States v. Brignoni-Ponce*, 422 U.S. 873 (1975), the Court refused to allow the apparent observation by the officer that the occupants of a car were of Mexican ancestry, by itself, justify a stop of that car near the U.S.-Mexican border. The Court did say, however, that Mexican ancestry could be one factor considered by an officer in deciding whether there is reasonable suspicion to stop a car near the U.S.-Mexican border to question occupants about their citizenship status:

> In this case the officers relied on a single factor to justify stopping respondent's car: the apparent Mexican ancestry of the occupants. We cannot conclude that this furnished reasonable grounds to believe that the three occupants were aliens. At best the officers had only a fleeting glimpse of the persons in the moving car, illuminated by headlights. Even if they saw enough to think that the occupants were of Mexican descent, this factor alone would justify neither a reasonable belief that they were aliens, nor a reasonable belief that the car concealed other aliens who were illegally in the country. Large numbers of native-born and naturalized citizens have the physical characteristics identified with Mexican ancestry, and even in the border area a relatively small proportion of them are aliens. The likelihood that any given person of Mexican ancestry is an alien is high enough to make Mexican appearance a relevant factor, but standing alone it does not justify stopping all Mexican-Americans to ask if they are aliens. 422 U.S. at 886–87.

Many members of racial and ethnic groups and organizations that represent their interests claim that police are abusing their broad discretion by targeting members of these groups in the unequal enforcement of traffic laws. A rash of articles, speeches, and other commentary condemn the practice of racial profiling and what have sarcastically been described as the "new" crimes of driving while black/brown (DWB) and, by extension, walking, idling, standing, shopping, and breathing while black/brown (*e.g.*, Harris, 1997; Kowalski & Lundman, 2007). The issue of racial profiling has engendered much anger, fear, resentment, and mistrust on the part of minorities and has contributed to disintegrating police–community relations in many areas of the country.

The extent of the racial profiling problem is in dispute. Recent polls indicate that the majority of Americans, black and white, believe the problem is real and widespread. Also, some studies support the notion that racial profiling exists. For example, an investigation of racial profiling by the Attorney General of New Jersey resulted in the conclusion that "minority motorists have been treated differently [by New Jersey State Troopers] than non-minority motorists during the course of traffic stops on the New Jersey Turnpike." (Interim Report of State Police Review Team, 1994: 4). Also, a 2006 study in Missouri showed that African-American and Hispanic drivers were stopped more frequently than their White counterparts, given their representation in the overall state population:

> Whites were stopped, in other words, at slightly below the rate we would expect based on their fraction of the estimated population age 16 and older. The same is not the case for several of the other groups. African-Americans were stopped at a rate 49 percent greater than expected based solely on their proportion of the population 16 and older. Hispanics were stopped at a rate slightly above their population proportion. . . . The values on the disparity index for the groups can be compared directly to one another. For example, the likelihood that an African-American motorist was stopped is 1.57 times that of a white motorist. . . . In other words, African-Americans were 57 percent more likely than Whites to be stopped in [Missouri] in 2006 (Missouri Vehicle Stops, 2006).

However, in reports entitled "Contacts between Police and the Public," the U.S. Department of Justice found that White, African-American and Hispanic drivers were stopped at similar rates, though African-American and Hispanic drivers were more frequently searched after being stopped:

> The 2002 and 2005 surveys found that Whites, Blacks, and Hispanics were stopped at similar rates. In both 2002 and 2005 police searched about 5 percent of stopped drivers. In 2005 police searched 9.5 percent of stopped Blacks and 8.8 percent of stopped Hispanics, compared to 3.6 percent of White motorists. While the survey found that Black and Hispanic drivers were more likely than Whites to be searched, such racial disparities do not necessarily demonstrate that police treat people differently based on race or other demographic characteristics. This study did not take into account other factors that might explain these disparities (U.S. Dept. of Justice, 2005: 5).

To more accurately determine the extent of the problem, many state legislatures have enacted statutes providing for the collection of statistical data on racial profiling. These laws require law enforcement agencies to collect information on vehicle stops, including number of persons stopped, race and ethnicity of persons stopped, reasons for the stops, and actions taken by officers as a result of the stops. For example, the Missouri report on racial profiling discussed above was issued in response to a state statute requiring the collection of statistical data on racial profiling. If a law enforcement agency in Missouri fails to collect and report the required data, the Governor can withhold state funds from the agency. In addition, law enforcement agencies throughout the country are establishing official policies against racial profiling and are integrating discussion about racial profiling into diversity and refresher training for their officers.

At the federal level, the U.S. Department of Justice issued guidelines in 2003 which prohibit federal law enforcement agents from using race or ethnicity in making routine traffic stops.

> In making routine or spontaneous law enforcement decisions, such as ordinary traffic stops, Federal law enforcement officers may not use race or ethnicity to any degree, except that officers may rely on race and ethnicity in a specific suspect description [that is trustworthy]. This prohibition applies even where the use of race or ethnicity might otherwise be lawful (U.S. Dept. of Justice, 2003: 1).

As part of the guidelines, the Department of Justice also prohibited racial or ethnic profiling in protecting national security and patrolling the border:

> In investigating or preventing threats to national security or other catastrophic events (including the performance of duties related to air transportation security), or in enforcing laws protecting the integrity of the Nation's borders, Federal law enforcement officers may not consider race or ethnicity except to the extent permitted by the Constitution and laws of the United States (U.S. Dept. of Justice, 2003: 1).

In February 2004, members of the U.S. Congress introduced bipartisan legislation called the "End Racial Profiling Act" directed toward ending racial bias in law enforcement. This legislation was still pending before Congress in June of 2007. It seeks to ban racial profiling at all levels of law enforcement and conditions the receipt of federal money by law enforcement agencies on their making efforts to eliminate the practice. The legislation provides grants to police departments for data collection systems and racial profiling prevention training. It also provides victims of racial profiling with legal tools to hold law enforcement agencies accountable. Finally, the Attorney General is required by the legislation to report regularly to Congress on the data collection results. *See* 108th Congress, 2d Session, S. 2131, "To prohibit racial profiling" (2004); 108th Congress, 2d Session, H.R. 3847, "To prohibit racial profiling" (2004).

Increasingly, citizens who claim to be the subjects of racial profiling are bringing lawsuits against the police, alleging violations of their constitutional rights as guaranteed by the Fourth, Fifth, and Fourteenth Amendments. One example is *Stewart v. City and County of Denver*, 203 F.3d 836 (10th Cir. 2000), an unpublished disposition of the Tenth Circuit Court of Appeals in January 2000. Although the circuit court upheld the trial court's grant of summary judgment for the defendants, including the municipality that employed the police officers involved in the traffic stop, the case suggested what may be necessary to establish a claim of racial profiling by a city's police force. The plaintiff, an African American, argued that the police stopped him in Denver, Colorado, not because one of his vehicle's headlights was out as the police claimed, but because he was African American. The plaintiff raised claims of violations of his equal protection rights through racial discrimination, violation of his Fourth Amendment rights to be free from unlawful searches and seizures, and violation of his Fifth Amendment due process rights.

The circuit court upheld the finding of the trial court that the plaintiff was unable to make a specific showing of a police custom or practice in the municipality to treat African Americans differently than others, beyond the vague testimony offered by the plaintiff and others that traffic stops in the particular neighborhood appeared to them to be racially motivated. In particular, the plaintiff failed to present sufficient evidence regarding the existence of a continuing, persistent, and widespread practice of unconstitutional conduct by the city's employees. In other words, the plaintiff's claims failed as a result of a lack of empirical evidence of racial profiling by the Denver police. The case is important, though, because it establishes a potential framework in which later successful suits may be brought by others aggrieved in a similar fashion. And though the plaintiff in this case was not successful in proving a discriminatory practice or custom by the city, the circuit court, in a related action, upheld the denial of qualified immunity for two individual officers involved in the traffic stop, thereby paving the way for these officers to be subject to a civil lawsuit by the plaintiff for violation of his equal protection rights. *See Stewart v. City and County of Denver*, 203 F.3d 836 (10th Cir. 2000). ("If [plaintiff's] allegations are believed by the ultimate fact finder, this evidence could support a determination that defendants fabricated a reason to stop him, but in fact stopped him merely because he was an African American and then wrongly issued him a citation for invalid insurance cards. [Plaintiff] has alleged facts which are sufficient to preclude summary judgment for defendants on qualified immunity grounds.")

In addition to individuals filing suits, organizations (such as the American Civil Liberties Union and the National Association for the Advancement of Colored People) have filed class-action suits seeking significant monetary damages for violations of constitutional rights. *See, e.g., Maryland State Conference of NAACP Branches v. Md. Dept. State Police*, 72 F. Supp. 2d 560 (D. Md. 1999); *Rodriguez v. Cal. Highway Patrol*, 89 F. Supp. 2d 1131 (N.D. Cal. 2000). Law enforcement officers should therefore be aware that targeting a person solely on the basis of race or ethnicity could result in suppression of evidence or civil liability.

Indeed, in *United States v. Jones*, 242 F.3d 215 (4th Cir. 2001), the court suppressed drug evidence because an officer stopped a car based on his observation that the car had four African-American occupants. In *Jones*, the officer had received an anonymous tip that several African-American males were drinking and "causing a disturbance" at a particular traffic intersection. Upon reaching the intersection, the officer found no activity matching the activity described by the anonymous informant. After the officer left the intersection, he subsequently observed a car some distance from the intersection occupied by four African-American males. The officer stopped the car, and a subsequent search revealed drugs. The court suppressed the drugs because the officer lacked reasonable suspicion of criminal activity necessary to justify the stop:

> The anonymous tip in this case . . . lacks sufficient indicia of reliability. In fact, the tip here was so barren of detail about the alleged culprits' physical descriptions that it was even less reliable. . . . The 911 caller told the . . . police dispatcher that several black males were drinking and causing a disturbance at a certain intersection. The caller said nothing else. Specifically, he did not identify himself, did not give his location or vantage point, and did not explain how he knew about the disturbance. The tipster did not say exactly how many men were present, and apart from mentioning their race, gave no information

about their appearance. The caller did not mention whether the men were residents of the neighborhood or outsiders. Finally, he did not say whether the men were in an automobile or whether they had access to one. [P]olice went to the intersection and saw no one. They undertook an inspection of the immediate area and still found no one and saw no signs that there had been a disturbance. At that point, the anonymous tip was totally uncorroborated.

In this case, the anonymous tip became essentially useless once the police found no one and no illegal activity at the intersection. If the police wished to investigate any further, they were relegated to looking for several African-American men, who had not been described or otherwise identified. Indeed, as [the officer who stopped the men] admitted, when he met the white Chevrolet two-tenths of a mile from the empty intersection, he 'saw four black guys . . . and stopped them for that.' Officer Hart saw no traffic or equipment violations or any suspicious activity. He stopped the car simply because the earlier, uncorroborated tip mentioned several black men. Because Officer Hart had not been able to confirm the 911 'informant's knowledge or credibility,' the tip was not a reliable accusation against the men in the white Chevrolet. In short, the uncorroborated tip and [the officer's] . . . sighting of four African-American men in a car were insufficient to establish reasonable suspicion for a stop. The stop was therefore illegal, and the crack cocaine that [the officer] discovered during his search . . . should have been excluded at trial. 242 F.3d at 218–19.

With these potential consequences in mind, this discussion of racial profiling concludes with a passage from *Washington v. Lambert*, 98 F.3d 1181 (9th Cir. 1996), in which the court held that a police officer was not entitled to qualified immunity from two arrestees' civil action for damages under 42 U.S.C. § 1983. The officer had arrested the two African-American men with the assistance of at least three other officers, a police dog, a spotlight, and drawn weapons, after the officer decided that the men, who had stopped at a restaurant after a professional baseball game, resembled a vague description of serial robbery suspects. At the time of the arrest, the law was clearly established concerning the permissible degree of intrusiveness of a stop, and a reasonable officer could not have believed it reasonable to employ such highly intrusive means of making a stop. The court said:

In balancing the interests in freedom from arbitrary government intrusion and the legitimate needs of law enforcement officers, we cannot help but be aware that the burden of aggressive and intrusive police action falls disproportionately on African American, and sometimes Latino, males. Notwithstanding the views of some legal theoreticians, as a practical matter neither society nor our enforcement of the laws is yet color-blind. Cases, newspaper reports, books, and scholarly writings all make clear that the experience of being stopped by the police is a much more common one for black men than it is for white men. . . . Although much of the evidence concerns the disproportionate burden police action imposes on African-American males who are young and poor, there is substantial evidence that the experience of being stopped by police is also common both for older African Americans and for those who are professionals—lawyers, doctors, businessmen, and academics. For example, Deval Patrick, formerly a partner in a prestigious Boston law firm and now an Assistant Attorney General of the United States and head of the Civil Rights Division at the Department of Justice, recently reported that "I still get stopped if I'm driving a nice car in the 'wrong' neighborhood." Christopher Darden, a . . . well-known prosecutor, recently wrote that he is stopped by police five times a year because "I always seem to get pulled over by some cop who is suspicious of a black man driving a Mercedes." Henry L. Gates, Jr. has written, poignantly, "[n]or does [University of Chicago Professor] William Julius Wilson . . . wonder why he was stopped near a small New England town by a policeman who wanted to know what he was doing in those parts. There's a moving violation that many African Americans know as D.W.B.: Driving While Black." These encounters are humiliating, damaging to the detainees' self-esteem, and reinforce the reality that racism and intolerance are for many African Americans a regular part of their daily lives. 98 F.3d at 1187–88 (internal citations omitted).

Detentions, the USA PATRIOT Act, and the War on Terror

The USA PATRIOT Act has broadened the government's power to detain individuals within the United States for long periods of time on apparently nothing more than reasonable suspicion once such persons have been classified by the U.S. government as an enemy combatant.

Enemy Combatants In response to the terrorist attacks on the United States on September 11, 2001, both the legislative and executive branches of the U.S. government took actions to prevent future attacks on the country. Congress enacted the "Authorization for Use of Military Force" in which Congress authorized the President:

> [T]o use all necessary and appropriate force against those nations, organizations, or persons he determines planned, authorized, committed, or aided the terrorist attacks that occurred on September 11, 2001, or harbored such organizations or persons, in order to prevent any future acts of international terrorism against the United States by such nations, organizations, or persons." Pub. L. 107–40, 115 Stat. 224 (2001).

Pursuant to this grant of war authority, President George W. Bush signed an executive order authorizing the indefinite detention and military trial of people who are suspected terrorists at "an appropriate location" outside of the United States as determined by the U.S. Secretary of Defense. *See* Detention, Treatment, and Trial of Certain Non-Citizens in the War Against Terrorism, 3 C.F.R. § 918 (2002). The people detained under this executive order came to be known as **enemy combatants**, although the technical definition of that term has evolved since then to include "an individual who was part of or supporting Taliban or al Qaeda forces, or associated forces that are engaged in hostilities against the United States or its coalition partners (Wolfowitz Memorandum, 2004: ¶ a).

The Geneva Conventions

A body of international law collectively referred to as the **Geneva Conventions** has developed over the centuries to set rules for the treatment of civilians, the sick, and prisoners of war ("POW") captured on the battlefield in war time (*See* Schindler & Toman, 2004).

> The designation of an individual as a POW is highly relevant because POWs are afforded significant protection. Upon receiving POW status, one can no longer be considered a target and receives full combat immunity. In particular, POWs cannot be transferred by the detaining power to another power, which is itself not a party to the Convention (Article 12). Moreover, POWs must 'at all times be humanely treated' and cannot be denied medical treatment (Article 13). At the beginning of captivity, a POW is required to provide only her or his name, rank, date of birth and army, regimental, personal or serial number,

or equivalent information (Article 17). Significantly, Article 17 also states: 'no physical or mental torture, nor any other form of coercion, may be inflicted on prisoners of war to secure from them information of any kind whatever.' They cannot be held in danger in a combat zone (Article 19), cannot be used as human shields (Article 23), and must be quartered under the same, or as favourable, conditions as forces of the detaining power who are in the same area (Article 25).

Common Article 3 of the Geneva Conventions, which applies to armed conflicts 'not of an international character' (which can be interpreted literally to mean all conflicts not between sovereign states, that is, unconventional conflicts) that occur 'in the territory of one of the High Contracting Parties,' requires that 'each Party to the conflict' shall be bound to treat all individuals rendered *hors de combat* humanely. Common Article 3 also requires that such actions as violence and the taking of hostages are prohibited, and further provides that the wounded and sick shall be cared for. Importantly, Common Article 3 demands minimal humanitarian guarantees for those detained or placed *hors de combat*, and thus specifically prohibits all kinds of murder, cruel treatment, and torture. Finally, although the wording does not expressly require fair hearings, the 'passing of sentences and the carrying out of executions without previous judgment pronounced by a regularly constituted court affording all the judicial guarantees which are recognized as indispensable by civilized peoples,' suggests a high-level of procedural fairness (Falk, 2007: 33–34).

From the outset of the War on Terror, however, the administration of George W. Bush has steadfastly refused to apply the protections of the Geneva Conventions to enemy combatants, arguing that they are qualitatively different from prisoners of war for a number of reasons.

▶ Prisoners of war are not normally considered criminals because being a soldier is not a criminal act. Enemy combatants, on the other hand, are involved in criminal conspiracies to commit criminal offenses, many of which target civilians—one of the core prohibitions of the Geneva Conventions.

▶ The Geneva Conventions set forth rules to govern more traditional wars between nations. In contrast, acts of terrorism are committed by individuals who commit crimes against specific targets outside the traditional scope of state-sponsored warfare. As such, the theoretical underpinnings of the Geneva Conventions are inapplicable to terrorists.

▶ By treating enemy combatants not as soldiers, but as captured criminals, interrogation beyond that provided for by the Geneva Conventions could produce intelligence that could help the U.S. combat terrorism.

If the Geneva Conventions are inapplicable to enemy combatants for any of the above reasons, then it would stand to reason that those being detained in the War on Terror are criminals. As such, the normal criminal procedures that are guaranteed to those charged with crimes should be applicable to enemy combatants. However, the Bush Administration has disputed this classification as well, arguing that enemy combatants are in a class by themselves that effectively puts them beyond the reach of both the guarantees of Geneva Conventions and the guarantees of the U.S. Constitution applicable to the criminally accused. Instead, the USA PATRIOT Act apparently authorizes the indefinite detention of enemy combatants under the circumstances described in the next section.

Detention by Certification upon "Reasonable Grounds to Believe . . ." Pursuant to Section 412 of the USA PATRIOT Act, someone who is not a citizen of the United States, including permanent resident aliens living in the United States, can be detained indefinitely if the United States Attorney General certifies that he has "reasonable grounds to believe" that the non-citizen has engaged in terrorist activity. Significantly, the definition of "engaging in terrorist activity" is quite broad, and encompasses activities that may not even be associated with "terrorism," at least as that term is commonly understood.

> Section 412 of the USA PATRIOT Act also raises serious due process concerns. It gives the Attorney General new power to detain aliens without a hearing and without a showing that they pose a danger or a flight risk. He need only certify that he has "reasonable grounds to believe" that the alien is "described in" various anti-terrorism provisions of the [Immigration and Nationality Act], and the alien is then subject to potentially indefinite detention. The [Immigration and Nationality Act's] anti-terrorism provisions in turn include persons who are mere members of designated "terrorist organizations," persons who have supported only the lawful activities of such organizations, and persons who have used, or threatened to use, any weapon with intent to endanger person or property. Thus, the law defines as a terrorist subject to unilateral executive detention a permanent resident alien who the [Immigration and Naturalization Service] has reasonable grounds to believe threatened her husband with a kitchen knife in a domestic dispute. Surely all such persons do not pose a danger or flight risk necessitating preventive detention, but the USA PATRIOT Act empowers the Attorney General to detain them without any showing that they in fact pose a danger or flight risk (Cole, 2002: 1026).

At first, most enemy combatants were held as prisoners at the U.S. Military Base in Guantanamo Bay, Cuba. The U.S. maintained that enemy combatants being held at Guantanamo had no right to have their detentions reviewed by the courts of the United States. However, in *Hamdi v. Rumsfeld*, 542 U.S. 507 (2004), the U.S. Supreme Court ruled that enemy combatants who are U.S. citizens have the right to have their detentions reviewed by an impartial judge as part of the guarantees of both due process and *habeas corpus*. *Rasul v. Bush*, 542 U.S. 466 (2004), decided by the U.S. Supreme Court the same day as *Hamdi*, held that non-U.S. citizens held at Guantanamo also had the right to use *habeas corpus* to have federal courts review the legality of their detentions as enemy combatants.

In response to *Hamdi* and *Rasul*, the Department of Defense created Combatant Status Review Tribunals (CSRTs) to review the legality of enemy combatant detentions at Guantanamo (Parry, 2006). These *ex parte* proceedings (meaning they took place without the accused or his/her counsel present), were declared unconstitutional by the U.S. Supreme Court in *Hamdan v. Rumsfeld*, 126 S. Ct. 2749 (2006). In response to that ruling, Congress enacted the Detainee Treatment Act of 2005 (DTA) which legislatively authorized the use of CSRTs with the addition of certain procedural safeguards that were not originally included by the Department of Defense when they initially created the tribunals. The DTA specifically provided that the decisions of CSRTs are not reviewable by means of *habeas corpus*, but that the D.C. Circuit Court of Appeals has the limited power to judicially review "whether the decision of the CSRT was consistent with standards and procedures developed by the Secretary of Defense, and whether those standards and procedures are themselves consistent with federal law" (Parry, 2006: 772, citing Pub. L. No. 109–48, § 1005(e)(2), 119 Stat. 2680, 2742 (2006)).

In addition to the detention of enemy combatants at Guantanamo Bay, Cuba, the United States has also been detaining enemy combatants at numerous covert detention centers around the world, some of which are run as secret prisons by the CIA (Hafetz, 2006). The people being held outside the United States are now subject to the same procedures applicable to enemy combatants at Guantanamo Bay because Congress enacted the Military Commissions Act in 2006. This law extended the procedures of CSRTs to all non-U.S. citizens being held as enemy combatants anywhere in the world. (Parry, 2006: 772, citing Pub. L. No. 109–366, §§ 7(a), 10, 120 Stat. 2600, 2635–36 (2006)). The U.S. Supreme Court agreed to hear arguments on the constitutionality of the Military Commissions Act and its effect on the suspension of *habeas corpus* for enemy combatants in late June of 2007. *See Boumediene v. Bush*, 2007 WL 1854132 (Jun. 29, 2007); *Al Odah v. United States*, 2007 WL 1582961 (Jun. 29, 2007). A ruling is expected by June of 2008.

key points

- A law enforcement officer may not stop a motor vehicle and detain the driver to check license and registration unless the officer has reasonable, articulable suspicion of criminal activity or unless the stop is conducted in accordance with a properly conducted highway checkpoint program.
- The test to determine the reasonableness of stopping a vehicle at a highway checkpoint involves balancing the gravity of the public concerns served by the seizure, the degree to which the seizure advances the public interest, and the severity of the interference with individual liberty.
- Police may not conduct a checkpoint for general law enforcement purposes (i.e., to detect the presence of narcotics or weapons). However, sobriety and border checkpoints have been upheld by the Supreme Court. The Court has also upheld a checkpoint designed to find witnesses to a crime involving a fatality.
- A law enforcement officer may detain property for a brief time if the officer has a reasonable, articulable suspicion that the property contains items subject to seizure. The officer may not search the property without a search warrant but may subject the property to a properly conducted "canine sniff."

- A law enforcement officer's physical manipulation of a person's belongings absent at least reasonable suspicion that a container has criminal evidence within it is an unreasonable search under the Fourth Amendment. If an officer does detect something in the container that he or she has probable cause to believe is contraband, the officer should, absent an emergency, obtain a judicial warrant before opening and searching the container.
- Many states and the federal government have rules prohibiting racial profiling by law enforcement officers. Many states require law enforcement agencies to collect statistical data on racial profiling. Courts are increasingly receptive to arguments by plaintiffs that they have been targets of racial profiling, and may exclude evidence or subject offending officers to civil rights lawsuits.
- The USA PATRIOT Act permits the indefinite detention of enemy combatants who are non-U.S. citizens, including permanent resident aliens, if the United States Attorney General certifies that he has "reasonable grounds to believe" that the noncitizen has engaged in terrorist activity.

Summary

A law enforcement officer may stop a person for purposes of investigating possible criminal behavior even though the officer does not have probable cause to arrest the person, so long as the officer has reasonable suspicion to believe that the person is involved in criminal activity. A "stop" is the least intrusive type of seizure of a person under the Fourth Amendment. Only when an officer intentionally, by means of physical force or show of authority, has restrained a person's liberty has a "seizure" occurred. Also, for a "seizure" to occur, the person confronted by the officer must submit to the officer's force or show of authority. If, in view of all of the circumstances surrounding the incident, a reasonable person would have believed that he or she was not free to leave, decline an officer's requests, or otherwise terminate the encounter, the person has been "seized" within the meaning of the Fourth Amendment.

The officer making a stop must be able to justify the stop with specific facts and circumstances indicating possibly criminal behavior. This is sometimes called "reasonable, articulable suspicion of criminal activity." Reasonable suspicion is measured objectively in light of the totality of circumstances. For a valid stop, reasonable suspicion must exist as to a present, past, or impending crime. The investigative detention, or stop, must be reasonable at its inception and last no longer than necessary to achieve its purpose. The investigative methods used must be the least intrusive means reasonably available to verify or dispel the officer's suspicion. The officer, in making a stop, should use no more force than is necessary to carry out the stop, and in all cases the force used should be reasonable.

If an officer has reasonable suspicion to justify a stop of a person, and that person subsequently refuses in violation of state law to identify herself, the officer may be permitted to expand the scope of the detention by arresting the person. An officer who has lawfully stopped a motor vehicle may order both the driver and passengers out of the vehicle pending completion of the stop.

A law enforcement officer may stop a person based on an informant's tip if, under the totality of the circumstances, the tip, plus any corroboration of the tip by independent police investigation, carries enough indicia of reliability to provide reasonable suspicion of criminal activity. An anonymous tip that a particular person at a particular location is carrying a gun is not, without more information, sufficient to justify law enforcement officers in stopping and frisking that person. A law enforcement officer may stop a person on the basis of a flyer, bulletin, or radio dispatch issued by another law enforcement agency as long as the issuing law enforcement agency has reasonable suspicion that the person named in the flyer, bulletin, or dispatch is or was involved in criminal activity.

A law enforcement officer may conduct a protective search for weapons, also called a frisk, if the officer has reasonable suspicion that a person is armed and dangerous. A frisk is not automatically authorized whenever there is a stop. The officer must be able to demonstrate, by specific facts and circumstances, a reasonable suspicion that the person is armed and dangerous. Because a frisk may only be performed for protective purposes, it must be limited initially to a pat-down of outer clothing. If a weapon or weapon-like object is detected, or if a non-threatening object's identity as contraband is immediately apparent to the officer's sense of touch, the officer may reach inside the clothing or pocket and seize the object. For an object's identity as non-threatening contraband (i.e., drugs) to be immediately apparent to the officer's sense of touch, the officer, upon immediately feeling the object, must have probable cause to believe the object is this type of contraband.

If a law enforcement officer has a reasonable, articulable suspicion that a motor vehicle's occupant is armed and dangerous, the officer may frisk the occupant and search the passenger compartment of the vehicle for weapons. The officer may look in any location in the passenger compartment that a weapon could be found or hidden. The officer may also seize items of evidence other than weapons, if discovered in plain view during the course of such a search. Evidence of crime seized as the result of a properly conducted frisk is admissible in court.

The test to determine the reasonableness of stopping a vehicle at a highway checkpoint involves balancing the gravity of the public concerns served by the seizure, the degree to which the seizure advances the public interest, and the severity of the interference with individual liberty. Police may not conduct a checkpoint for general law enforcement purposes (i.e., to detect the presence of narcotics or weapons). However, properly conducted checkpoints to detect drunk driving, illegal aliens, and drivers without a valid license have been upheld by courts. The Supreme Court has also upheld a checkpoint designed to find witnesses to a crime involving a fatality.

A law enforcement officer may detain property for a brief time if the officer has a reasonable, articulable suspicion that the property contains items subject to seizure. The officer may not search the property without a search warrant but may subject the property to a properly conducted "canine sniff." A law enforcement officer's physical manipulation of a person's belongings absent at least reasonable suspicion that a container has criminal evidence within it is an unreasonable search under the Fourth Amendment. If an officer with reasonable suspicion to manipulate a container does detect something in the container that he or she has probable cause to believe is contraband, the officer should, absent an emergency, obtain a judicial warrant before opening and searching the container.

Many states and the federal government have rules prohibiting racial profiling by law enforcement officers. Many states require law enforcement agencies to collect statistical data on racial profiling. Courts are increasingly receptive to arguments by plaintiffs that they have been targets of racial profiling, and may exclude evidence or subject offending officers to civil rights lawsuits.

The USA PATRIOT Act permits the indefinite detention of enemy combatants who are non-U.S. citizens, including permanent resident aliens, if the United States Attorney General certifies that he or she has "reasonable grounds to believe" that the non-citizen has engaged in terrorist activity.

Key Terms

arrest, 362	furtive gestures, 405	reasonableness , 363	show of authority, 372
canine sniff/dog sniff, 416	Geneva Conventions, 430	reasonable suspicion, 362, 373	sobriety checkpoint/roadblock, 421
enemy combatants, 430	pretextual stop, 420	seizure, 362	stop, 362
flight, 404	probable cause, 362	seizures tantamount to arrest, 362	
frisk, 362	racial profiling, 424		

Review and Discussion Questions

1. Name some of the factors or circumstances that might distinguish a *Terry*-type investigative stop from police action that would not amount to a seizure under the Fourth Amendment. From your reading of Chapter 6 on arrests and this chapter, what factors or circumstances might distinguish a *Terry* stop from a seizure tantamount to arrest and a full-blown arrest?

2. In determining whether an officer has a reasonable suspicion that criminal activity is afoot, must the officer have a particular crime in mind?

3. Is less evidence required to support an investigative stop for a suspected violent crime than for a minor misdemeanor?

4. Can a lawfully stopped suspect be transported by the police to a crime scene for identification by victims or witnesses? Or would this action convert the stop into a seizure tantamount to arrest?

5. How does the *indicia*-of-reliability test for evaluating an informant's tip in the stop-and-frisk situation differ from the totality-of-the-circumstances test of the *Gates* case discussed in Chapter 3? Why should there be different tests?

6. Must there be an immediate possibility of criminal activity to justify a stop, or would a possibility of criminal activity at some time in the future suffice? What about when an officer has reasonable suspicion of criminal activity as to a past crime?

7. Assuming that a frisk of a person is warranted, how extensive a search is permitted? Can the officer look for razor blades, nails, vials of acid, or Mace containers? Can the officer look into brief-

cases, shopping bags, purses, hatbands, and other containers?

8. Should an officer conducting a roadblock-type stop to check licenses and registrations be allowed to order every driver stopped out of his or her vehicle? What factors might provide justification to frisk a driver or passengers in this situation?

9. Assuming that a law enforcement officer reasonably believes that a suspect is dangerous and may gain immediate control of weapons from an automobile, how extensive a protective search of the automobile may be made? May the officer look into suitcases and other containers?

10. Assume that police receive an anonymous telephone tip that a Middle Eastern woman in her thirties is carrying anthrax and is about to board a train to New York City. Can potential passengers fitting the description be detained? To what extent? Can they be frisked? Can the train be prevented from leaving the station?

11. Would it be reasonable under the Fourth Amendment to subject to a canine sniff every piece of luggage to be carried on a flight to Miami, Florida? Does it matter if the dog is trained as a drug-sniffing dog or a bomb-sniffing dog?

12. If an officer reasonably suspects that an object he feels in a suspect's pocket during a valid frisk is cocaine, may he reach into the pocket and seize it?

13. May police set up a valid roadblock to check for illegal drugs? To find persons without valid documentation to be in the country? To locate eyewitnesses to any crime?

Applications of the Law in Real Cases

1 On August 22, 1996, Metropolitan Police Sgt. Gregory Wilson received a call at his desk. Although Sgt. Wilson had been out of the particular police district since May 1994, he immediately recognized the caller as a tipster with whom he had personally spoken five or six times prior to May 1994, but whose name or other identifying characteristics he did not know. The caller told Sgt. Wilson that a tall, dark-complected black man, wearing dark shorts and a white tee-shirt, was "working" out of the trunk of a car parked at the intersection of Fourth and L Streets, S.E. Sgt. Wilson took this description to mean that the man was selling drugs.

The informant described the car as a blue Datsun Z with damage to the left rear and District plates. At Sgt. Wilson's direction, Officer Seth Weston and two other officers arrived at Fourth and L about fifteen minutes later and confirmed the innocent details of the tip, in particular the presence of a car matching the description and a man nearby matching the description. However, the man was not sitting in the car or involved in any suspicious activity when the officers arrived, and when he was unable to produce identification the officers decided not to detain him.

Soon thereafter, one of the officers asked loudly whether anyone owned the car and received no answer. The officers then searched the car. (The officers did not need to use force to access the car because it had an open top and the keys were lying inside on the floor.) Inside the trunk they found seventeen small bags of cocaine inside a larger bag. They immediately impounded the car.

Subsequently, during an inventory search, a Maryland learner's permit and District identification card belonging to appellant, the owner of the car, were recovered from the glove compartment. The officers recognized appellant's picture on the documents as portraying the man to whom they had spoken at the scene. The appellant moved to have the cocaine suppressed on the ground that the police lacked probable cause to search. Should the appellant's motion be granted? *Sanders v. United States*, 751 A.2d 952 (D.C. App. 2000).

2 The only witness who testified at the suppression hearing was Officer Larry Gill, who conducted the investigatory stop and the pat-down search of James. Officer Gill testified that, on February 17, 1995, about 6:00 P.M. or 6:30 P.M., he was patrolling Dauphin Island Parkway, a known high-drug-crime area, when he noticed a van pulled off on the shoulder of the road on Cedar Downs Drive located off Dauphin Island Parkway. Officer Gill observed "two or three subjects talking into the window of the van," but he could not see what the driver or the subjects were doing.

As Officer Gill approached the van, the "subjects" standing beside the van ran, and James, the driver of the van, drove away. Officer Gill followed the van and signaled his patrol lights for James to stop. After James pulled over at a Chevron gasoline station, he exited his van and met Officer Gill as he approached the van. Officer Gill told James he stopped him because Gill saw his van parked on the street "where those subjects ran from [his] van." Gill asked James whether he had any weapons in his possession, and James responded that he did not. Nevertheless, Officer Gill informed James that he needed to conduct a pat-down search of James for safety reasons. Officer Gill testified that, as he was conducting the pat-down, James "went to put his hands in his left front pants pocket and I kind of tapped his hand and told him to pull his hand out and I put my hand in [James's] pocket after his hand coming out [and] I found the marijuana cigarettes in his pocket." Officer Gill testified that he did not pat-down the outside of James's pants pocket before he reached into it and that he did not feel anything that appeared to be a weapon during his pat-down of James. James moved to suppress the marijuana on the ground that the marijuana was seized during an illegal Terry stop and pat-down search. Should his motion be granted? *Ex parte James*, 797 So.2d 413 (Ala. 2000).

3 Officers Carlos Torres and Steven Stretmater of the United States Secret Service Uniform Division were stopped at the intersection of Columbia Road and Ontario Road, N.W., when they noticed appellant in the 1700 block of Columbia Road, a block Torres described as an "open air drug market," and where he had previously made drug-related arrests. They observed appellant and a homeless man engaged in what appeared to be a narcotics transaction. Torres witnessed appellant take two small plastic-wrapped objects from inside a larger piece of plastic in his cupped left hand and hand them to the homeless man, who inspected the objects. Torres testified that he had stopped this homeless person earlier that day after receiving a complaint that he was smoking narcotics in the 3100 block of 16th Street, N.W., and that the person had possessed a crack pipe at that time.

The officers proceeded through the light and made a U-turn when it was safe to do so. By the time they stopped, appellant had walked some distance along the street, and the homeless man had gone down an alley. The officers got out of their car and Officer Torres told appellant he wanted to talk to him. Appellant stopped. Officer Torres said: "Come over here." Appellant turned toward the officer and put his hands in his pants pockets, but did not come toward the officers. Officer Torres told appellant twice to take his hands out of his pockets, based on what Torres testified was a concern for his safety since appellant could have had a weapon in his pocket. Appellant eventually took his right hand out of his pocket. Torres then told appellant, in English and Spanish, to remove his other hand, and when appel-

lant did not respond, the officers grabbed appellant and pulled him over to the police cruiser. After Torres again told appellant to take his left hand out of his pocket, appellant took his clenched left fist out of his pocket. The officers put appellant's hands on the car, and Torres told appellant to open his fist. At some point, a small bag of cocaine fell out of appellant's hand. Thereafter, appellant opened his left hand, revealing several small plastic wrappings containing a white-colored substance wrapped in a larger piece of clear plastic wrapping, and immediately stated that he had just purchased them and they were for his personal use. In total, appellant had in his possession thirty-three small packages of what tests later showed was crack cocaine. Should the appellant's motion to suppress the cocaine be granted? *Reyes v. United States*, 758 A.2d 35 (D.C. App. 2000).

4 On the afternoon of March 4, 1998, in Laurens, South Carolina, Kenneth Burton was standing at a pay telephone outside the Green Street Mini-Mart when he was approached by four police officers who were in the area serving outstanding warrants. When one of the officers, Detective Tracy Burke, identified himself as a policeman and requested identification from Burton, Burton did not respond. The officers repeated their request several times, but Burton remained mute. The officers then asked Burton to remove his right hand from his coat pocket. When Burton failed to do so, the officers repeated their request. Burton still did not respond.

While the other officers remained facing Burton, Officer Burke moved behind Burton, reached around him, thrust his hand into Burton's coat, and grabbed his right hand. Burton resisted, and a struggle ensued, during which the officers wrestled Burton to the ground. While on the ground, Officer Burke claims that Burton "raised his left side of his body up" and pointed a handgun at Officer Burke, who was lying on top of him. Burton squeezed the trigger three or four times, but the gun was jammed and did not fire. The officers subdued Burton and removed the weapon.

Burton was indicted for unlawful possession of a firearm by a felon, in violation of 18 U.S.C. § 922(g). He moved to suppress the firearm as the fruit of an illegal search. At the evidentiary hearing before the district court, Officer Burke testified that at the time he approached Burton, he had no reason to suspect that Burton was engaged in criminal activity, but Burton's refusal to remove his hand from his coat made Officer Burke feel "uneasy about our safety being there with him with his hand and no response, you know, towards us." Officer Burke thought that Burton "possibly had a weapon in his pocket or in his hand or in his coat that he was holding on to. It could have been narcotics or maybe [an] alcoholic beverage or something." Should Burton's motion to suppress the firearm be granted? *United States v. Burton*, 228 F.3d 524 (4th Cir. 2000).

5 At 2:53 A.M., on August 17, 1998, Orono Police Officer William Sheehan watched a car drive into the Med Now parking lot and stop. Med Now is an emergency care medical facility that only operates during the day. Sheehan was concerned that the occupants of the car might be looking for emergency medical treatment. He followed the car into the lot, and parked about ten feet behind it. He did not activate his blue lights or his siren and did not block the vehicle's exit from the parking lot.

Upon approaching the car, Sheehan spoke briefly with the driver and asked if everything was okay. The driver, Tanner Gulick, responded that everything was fine and asked how far it was to Portland. Sheehan informed Gulick that the trip would take approximately two hours. He then asked to see Gulick's driver's license. Sheehan testified that, at the point that he requested Gulick's license, he was no longer concerned that Gulick or his passenger had a medical emergency.

Gulick did not have his license with him. Suspicious of Gulick's explanation for the missing license, Sheehan obtained Gulick's name and date of birth and checked on the status of Gulick's license to operate in Maine. Upon learning that Gulick's license was suspended, Sheehan issued him a summons for operating after suspension.

Gulick moved to suppress all evidence resulting from Sheehan's request for his license . . . claiming that Sheehan lacked a reasonable articulable suspicion to justify detaining Gulick. Should the motion to suppress be granted? *State v. Gulick*, 759 A.2d 1085 (Me. 2000).

6 On February 12, 1997, at approximately noon, Sergeant Herman Badger of the New Haven police department received an anonymous telephone call from a citizen complaining about a drug transaction taking place on the steps of a church at 246 Dixwell Avenue. Badger was stationed at the police substation on Charles Street around the corner from the church when he received the call. The caller indicated that two black males, one taller than the other, were selling drugs. The caller also described the color of the jackets that the two individuals were wearing. The caller was excited and upset by the fact that drug dealing was occurring on the church steps. Badger was familiar with the area and testified that it was an area known for frequent drug transactions.

Badger contacted Officer Richard Zasciurinskas by radio and dispatched him in his patrol car to the area of the church to look for the suspects described in the anonymous tip. At the time that Zasciurinskas was dispatched, he was a very short distance from the area in a marked patrol car. Badger, accompanied by Officer Samuel Bagley, left the substation and walked approximately 100 to 200 feet to the intersection of Charles Street and Dixwell Avenue. All three officers were in full uniform. Just prior to reaching the intersection, Badger and Bagley observed two black males standing in front of the church. One male was taller than the other, and their jackets matched the description given by the caller. The officers did not observe any conduct indicating that a drug transaction was taking place. The two men, however, fled when they saw the officers approach.

The two men walked across Dixwell Avenue and proceeded north, away from the officers. Badger radioed Zasciurinskas and ordered him to stop the two individuals. Badger and Bagley then proceeded across Dixwell Avenue and followed the two men at a distance of approximately thirty to fifty feet. Zasciurinskas, who was traveling south on Dixwell Avenue, drove his car across the northbound lane of traffic in front of the suspects and partially blocked traffic. As Zasciurinskas exited his vehicle, the two suspects reacted by turning and proceeding south on Dixwell Avenue. Zasciurinskas yelled to them to stop. Zasciurinskas then observed one of them drop a bundle on the ground.

Zasciurinskas picked up the bundle, which consisted of nine glassine envelopes. On the basis of his almost twenty years of police experience, Zasciurinskas determined that the bags contained a possible narcotic substance. Badger and Bagley were about eight to ten feet from the two suspects, and Zasciurinskas was about ten to fifteen feet on the other side of them.

The two men were detained by Badger and Bagley, and transported to the police substation. There, the contents of one of the nine envelopes tested positive for the presence of heroin. The defendant was placed under arrest. A search of the defendant incident to the arrest revealed a single plastic bag containing a white powder also believed to be a narcotic substance. At the substation, the defendant indicated that the single bag of cocaine was for his personal use. Should the defendant's motion to suppress the evidence seized be granted? *State v. Hammond*, 759 A.2d 133 (Conn. App. 2000).

8

Searches Incident to Arrest and Protective Sweeps

Learning Objectives

▶ Understand the law's preference for search warrants and why exceptions to the warrant requirement are allowed.

▶ Understand the allowable purposes of a search incident to arrest as set forth in *Chimel v. California*.

▶ Know the limits on the allowable scope of a search incident to arrest with respect to the following: property that may be searched for and seized; search and seizure of an arrestee's body and items in or on the body or associated with or carried on the body; search of the area into which the arrestee might reach, including motor vehicles.

▶ Know the limits on the allowable scope of a search incident to arrest with respect to the search of the arrestee's companions and the search of other areas of the premises for accomplices and destructible evidence.

▶ Understand the other requirements of a valid search incident to arrest, including: lawful custodial arrest; contemporaneous nature of arrest and search; who may conduct the search; limitations on use of force.

▶ Understand the limitations on a search incident to detention.

Chapters 3, 4, 5, and 6 of this book highlighted the law's preference for warrants based on probable cause. Warrants are the chief means of balancing the need for efficient and effective law enforcement against the need to protect the rights of individual citizens to be secure against unreasonable searches and seizures. *See, e.g., Katz v. United States*, 389 U.S. 347, 357 (1967). (:"[S]earches conducted outside the judicial process, without prior approval by judge or magistrate, are per se unreasonable under the Fourth Amendment—subject only to a few specifically established and well-delineated exceptions.") In *Aguilar v. Texas*, 378 U.S. 108 (1964), the U.S. Supreme Court stated that the preference for warrants is so strong that less persuasive evidence will justify the issuance of a warrant than would justify a warrantless search or warrantless arrest. The warrant procedure is preferred because it places responsibility for deciding the delicate question of probable cause with a neutral and detached judicial officer. *See Katz*, 389 U.S. at 357. Law enforcement is served by this procedure, because law enforcement officers may search certain persons or places and seize certain persons or things when the officers can show that it is more likely than not that a person, place, or thing is connected with criminal activity. The Fourth Amendment rights of citizens are also protected by warrants, because the decision to allow a search and seizure is removed from the hurried judgment of possibly overzealous law enforcement officers engaged in the competitive enterprise of investigating crime.

Situations often arise, however, in which the time and effort needed to obtain a warrant would unjustifiably frustrate enforcement of the laws. To ensure that the delicate balance between individual rights and law enforcement is maintained, courts have carved out various exceptions to the warrant requirement and have allowed warrantless searches and seizures in certain situations. One of the most important exceptions is a search incident to arrest. The leading case governing search incident to arrest is *Chimel v. California*, 395 U.S. 752 (1969).

► SEARCHES OF PEOPLE AND AREAS INCIDENT TO ARREST

This section will first discuss the **search incident to arrest** doctrine as established in the landmark case of *Chimel v. California*. Following this discussion, the protective sweep doctrine will be explored in detail.

Chimel v. California

Since 1969, the law governing search incident to arrest has been controlled by the U.S. Supreme Court case of *Chimel v. California*. In that case, law enforcement officers arrived at the defendant's home with a warrant for his arrest for the burglary of a coin shop. The defendant was not at home, but his wife let the officers in to wait for him. When the defendant arrived, the officers arrested him under the warrant and asked whether they could look around. Over his objections the officers searched the entire house on the basis of the lawful arrest.

The officers found coins and other items that were later admitted into evidence against the defendant.

The U.S. Supreme Court found the search of the entire house unreasonable:

> When an arrest is made, it is reasonable for the arresting officer to search the person arrested in order to remove any weapons that the latter might seek to use in order to resist arrest or effect his escape. Otherwise, the officer's safety might well be endangered, and the arrest itself frustrated. In addition, it is entirely reasonable for the arresting officer to search for and seize any evidence on the arrestee's person in order to prevent its concealment or destruction. And the area into which an arrestee might reach in order to grab a weapon or evidentiary items must, of course, be governed by a like rule. A gun on a table or in a drawer in front of one who is arrested can be as dangerous to the arresting officer as one concealed in the clothing of the person arrested. There is ample justification, therefore, for a search of the arrestee's person and the area "within his immediate control"—construing that phrase to mean the area from within which he might gain possession of a weapon or destructible evidence. There is no comparable justification, however, for routinely searching any room other than that in which an arrest occurs—or, for that matter, for searching through all the desk drawers or other closed or concealed areas in that room itself. Such searches, in the absence of well-recognized exceptions, may be made only under the authority of a search warrant. 395 U.S. at 762–63.

Chimel drastically changed the area allowed to be searched incident to arrest from that allowed under previous law. Under pre-*Chimel* law, an officer was allowed to search incident to arrest the area considered to be in the "possession" or under the "control" of the arrested person. Courts interpreted these vague standards to include areas that were not necessarily under the defendant's "physical control" but were within his or her "constructive possession." Under this interpretation, law enforcement officers could, without a search warrant, search an entire residence incident to a valid arrest made in the residence, and they had almost unlimited discretion in deciding what would be searched. Furthermore, because neither a written application for a search warrant nor a determination of probable cause was required, law enforcement officers found the search incident to arrest administratively more convenient and used it frequently. *Chimel* changed all of that, although neither a search warrant nor probable cause is needed to conduct a search incident to arrest today. However, search incident to arrest is clearly more limited under *Chimel* than it was before the case was decided. This chapter explores the ways in which the doctrine has evolved since the *Chimel* decision.

Protective Sweeps

Under *Chimel*, when officers make an arrest in a home or other location, they may not conduct a full search of any areas of the premises other than the limited area within the arrestee's immediate control (e.g., "armspan"). However, the protective sweep doctrine provides a limited exception to the *Chimel* rule. This section will explore that doctrine and discuss protective sweeps in more detail.

The Protective Sweep Doctrine Under the **protective sweep** doctrine, officers may conduct a quick and limited search of premises incident to an arrest to protect their own safety and the safety of others from potential accomplices linked to the arrestee. Also, if officers believe evidence is about to be destroyed or removed as they make a home arrest, they may also conduct a limited search of the premises to prevent this destruction or removal. Finally, officers may need to pass through other rooms when entering or leaving premises to make an arrest. These movements into other areas of the premises are not considered full-blown searches, because the officer's purpose is not to look for weapons or incriminating evidence but to make the arrest. If one of these exceptions applies, an officer who observes a weapon or other seizable item lying open to view may seize it. The item is admissible in court if the seizure satisfies the requirements of the plain view doctrine (see Chapter 10).

The exception to the *Chimel* rule allowing protective sweeps for accomplices during home arrests was developed in *Maryland v. Buie*, 494 U.S. 325 (1990). This case also addresses the idea that officers may pass through other areas of the home if it is necessary to make an arrest. In *Buie*, two men, one of whom was wearing a red running suit, committed an armed robbery. The same day, police obtained an arrest warrant for the defendant and his suspected accomplice and executed the warrant for the defendant at his home. After the defendant was arrested as he emerged from the basement, one of the officers entered the basement "in case there was someone else" there and seized a red running suit lying in plain view.

In determining the reasonableness of the search of the basement leading to the plain view seizure, the U.S. Supreme Court balanced the officer's need to search against the invasion of privacy caused by the search. Possessing an arrest warrant and probable cause to believe the defendant was in his home, the officers were entitled to enter and search anywhere in the house in which the defendant might be found. Once he was found, however, the search for him was over, and the officers no longer had that particular justification for entering any rooms that had not yet been searched. Those rooms, however, were not immune from entry simply because of the defendant's expectation of privacy with respect to them. That privacy interest must be balanced against the:

> [I]interest of the officers in taking steps to assure themselves that the house in which a suspect is being or has just been arrested is not harboring other persons [e.g., accomplices] who are dangerous and who could unexpectedly launch an attack. The risk of danger in the context of an arrest in the home is as great as, if not greater than, it is in an on-the-street or roadside investigatory encounter. 494 U.S. at 333.

The Court in *Buie* held that the police officers had a limited right to conduct a protective sweep for their own protection after arresting the defendant:

> [A]s an incident to the arrest the officers could, as a precautionary matter and without probable cause or reasonable suspicion, look in closets and other spaces immediately adjoining the place of arrest from which an attack could be immediately launched. Beyond that, however, . . . there must be articulable facts which, taken together with the rational inferences from those facts, would warrant a reasonably prudent officer in believing that the area to be swept harbors an individual posing a danger to those on the arrest scene. 494 U.S. at 334.

Thus, when the officer makes an in-home arrest, the officer may conduct a protective sweep of the room in which he or she makes the arrest to look for possible accomplices. The officer may do this without probable cause or even reasonable suspicion that an actual accomplice exists.

Protective Sweeps for Accomplices The officer may also make a protective sweep of rooms and other spaces in a home that are immediately adjacent to the room where the officer makes the arrest, looking for possible accomplices (as an attack could be "immediately launched" from these areas). This limited sweep for accomplices can also be made without probable cause or reasonable suspicion. However, in the case of rooms and other spaces in a home that are *not* adjacent to the room where the officer makes an arrest, the standard to justify a protective sweep is the same as the standard to justify an investigatory *Terry*-type stop: reasonable suspicion based on specific and articulable facts. The Supreme Court in *Buie* emphasized that a protective sweep of areas beyond the area immediately adjoining the place of arrest permits only a cursory inspection of those spaces where a person may be found; it does not permit a full search of the premises. The sweep may last no longer than is necessary to dispel the reasonable suspicion of danger and in any event no longer than it takes to complete the arrest and depart from the premises.

This last point regarding the duration of a protective sweep was nicely illustrated in *United States v. Paradis*, 351 F.3d 21 (1st Cir. 2003). In *Paradis*, at the time police searched the bedroom and found a gun, the defendant had already been arrested in that bedroom, a protective sweep of that room for accomplices had already happened, and defendant had been removed from the apartment. Id. at 25, 26, 29–30. Also, police had no reasonable suspicion that accomplices remained in other areas of the apartment because they had seen all of the other occupants leave the apartment prior to defendant's arrest, including the person to whom the apartment was rented. They had also searched the other rooms in their efforts to find the defendant, whom they ultimately found in the bedroom. Id. at 29. As a result, the court in *Paradis* declined to uphold the extended "protective sweep" of the bedroom, and therefore excluded the gun.

Various courts have also addressed the issue of whether a protective sweep of premises is permitted when a person is arrested outside those premises. *United States v. Soria*, 959 F.2d 855 (10th Cir. 1992) approved a protective sweep of the defendant's auto shop after the defendant was arrested during a drug transaction near the shop. The officers reasonably believed that drug-dealing activities had taken place in the shop and that others may have been hiding inside. Also, in *United States v. Cavely*, 318 F.3d 987 (10th Cir. 2003), the court upheld a protective sweep for accomplices within defendant's home, even though defendant was arrested in an area just outside his residence:

> The evidence showed specific facts that would warrant a reasonable officer to believe that appellant's home harbored an individual posing a danger to the officers or others on the arrest scene. Among other things, [the police] knew that [defendant's] house had previously been used to manufacture methamphetamine and that [defendant] had just come out of the house carrying an explosive fuel sometimes used to manufacture methamphetamine. Moreover, appellant admitted he had "a friend" inside the house, but the friend did not appear or answer when officers knocked on the front door. The officers also knew that firearms had been found in the house during a prior search. They were just outside of the back door in an area where they could have been vulnerable to an attack from someone inside. There was no evidence that the

officers entered the house merely for the purpose of gathering incriminating evidence. Under these circumstances, the officers had a compelling interest in assuring themselves that the house was not harboring other persons who posed a danger to them. In response, they engaged in a cursory visual inspection of the areas of the house where a person could be found. . . . [T]his search was reasonable under the Fourth Amendment. 318 F.3d at 996.

United States v. Hogan, 38 F.3d 1148 (10th Cir. 1994), however, invalidated a protective sweep of the defendant's residence after the defendant was arrested outside the residence. He was not home when the police first arrived, and the only possible danger to the police was the hypothetical possibility that the defendant's accomplice to the murder committed a month earlier might be in the residence. And in *United States v. Colbert*, 76 F.3d 773 (6th Cir. 1996), the court found that the defendant's arrest outside of a home did not justify a protective sweep of that home because there was no reasonable suspicion that the residence harbored accomplices who might harm the arresting officers. The fact that a resident of the home left the home unexpectedly and in an enraged manner, and approached the location where the defendant had been arrested, did not provide reasonable suspicion for the police to conduct a protective sweep of the home:

> [I]t is altogether incredible that an officer would be surprised by the fact that a resident of a home would come out of his or her house upon seeing a large group of undercover police officers arresting an individual who just left that resident's apartment. In addition, there is no indication that [the resident] herself posed any kind of a threat to the officers. 76 F.3d at 777.

Protective Sweeps to Prevent the Destruction of Evidence Some courts also allow police to conduct a warrantless search of premises incident to an arrest on those premises if police believe evidence is about to be destroyed or removed. Although the U.S. Supreme Court has never directly addressed the appropriate legal standard for premise arrests and destructible evidence, it has decided one case in this area: *Vale v. Louisiana*, 399 U.S. 30 (1970). In *Vale*, officers arrested a defendant on an arrest warrant outside his home. Because police had observed conduct prior to the arrest which made them believe defendant was engaging in a drug transaction, they entered the home after arresting defendant and conducted a search without a warrant. This search revealed narcotics. The Louisiana Supreme Court upheld the search on the basis that evidence such as narcotic drugs could be destroyed inside the home had police taken the time to get a warrant. The U.S. Supreme Court disagreed with Louisiana Court and invalidated the search:

> **Such a rationale [that drug evidence could be destroyed] could not apply to the present case, since by their own account the arresting officers satisfied themselves that no one else was in the house when they first entered the premises. But entirely apart from that point, our past decisions make clear that only in 'a few specifically established and well-delineated' situations may a warrantless search of a dwelling withstand constitutional scrutiny, even though the authorities have probable cause to conduct it. The burden rests on the State to show the existence of such an exceptional situation. And the record before us discloses none. 399 U.S. at 34.**

The Supreme Court also found that it was feasible for the police to get a warrant before searching a defendant's house:

> The goods ultimately seized were not in the process of destruction. . . .
> The officers were able to procure two warrants for [defendant's] ar-
> rest. They also had information that he was residing at the address
> where they found him. There is thus no reason, so far as anything before
> us appears, to suppose that it was impracticable for them to obtain a
> search warrant as well. 399 U.S. at 35.

After *Vale*, lower courts require police officers to have either reasonable suspicion or a probable cause belief that evidence is about to be destroyed or removed from a home before they allow police to conduct a warrantless search
for evidence incident to a home arrest (see Whitebread & Slobogin, 2000: 189).
In *United States v. Rubin*, 474 F.2d 262, 269 (3rd Cir. 1973), the court said that:

> When Government agents, however, have probable cause to believe contra-
> band is present and, in addition, based on the surrounding circumstances or
> the information at hand, they reasonably conclude that the evidence will be
> destroyed or removed before they can secure a search warrant, a warrantless
> search is justified.

The court outlined the following considerations police may weigh in deciding
whether a search incident to an arrest on premises is justified because of a
threat of evidence destruction or removal:

▶ "the degree of urgency involved and the amount of time necessary to obtain a warrant;

▶ reasonable belief that the contraband is about to be removed;

▶ the possibility of danger to police officers guarding the site of the contraband while a search warrant is sought;

▶ information indicating the possessors of the contraband are aware that the
  police are on their trail; and

▶ the ready destructibility of the contraband and the knowledge that efforts
  to dispose of narcotics and to escape are characteristic behavior of persons
  engaged in the narcotics traffic." 474 F.2d at 268–69.

In other cases, courts have permitted a warrantless search after a home arrest if police have only an articulable, reasonable suspicion that evidence is about
to be destroyed or removed from the home. *See United States v. Hoyos*, 868 F.2d
1131, 1138 (9th Cir. 1989). ("The testimony credited by the district court establishes sufficient articulable facts that an entry into the residence was necessary
to protect the officers and to avoid the destruction of evidence.")

Occasionally, events and circumstances surrounding an arrest will justify officers going into other parts of an arrestee's residence for reasons unrelated to
their safety or evidence destruction. In a bank robbery case, the defendant was
arrested while unclothed in his girlfriend's dark apartment. When an officer went
to get clothing for the defendant, he found two jackets resembling those report-
edly worn by the bank robbers. When an officer turned on the kitchen light to
see his way out, he observed money taken during the robbery on the kitchen
floor. The court held that both the jackets and the money were admissible in
evidence:

> Since they were bound to find some clothing for Titus rather than take him
> nude to FBI headquarters on a December night, the fatigue jackets were

properly seized under the "plain view" doctrine. Welch was entitled to turn on the kitchen lights, both to assist his own exit and to see whether the other robber might be about; when he saw the stolen money, he was permitted to seize it. Everything the agents took was in their "plain view" while they were where they had a right to be; there was no general rummaging of the apartment. *United States v. Titus,* 445 F.2d 577, 579 (2d Cir. 1971).

key points

- When an arrest is made, it is reasonable for the arresting officer to search the person arrested and the area within his or her immediate control—the area from within which the person might gain possession of a weapon or destructible evidence.
- As a general rule, law enforcement officers may not conduct a full search of any areas of the premises other than the limited area within the arrestee's immediate control. However, incident to an arrest on premises, an arresting officer may look in closets and other spaces immediately adjoining the place of arrest from which an attack could be immediately launched. This protective sweep for accomplices may be done without probable cause or reasonable suspicion, and includes not only the room where the arrest occurred but also immediately adjoining rooms and spaces.

- Incident to an arrest on premises, an officer may conduct a protective sweep for accomplices in other rooms and spaces not adjacent to the room where the arrest occurred when the searching officer possesses a reasonable, articulable suspicion that these rooms or spaces harbor an individual posing a danger to those on the arrest scene. The officer can only look in places where a person could be.
- Also, if police have reasonable suspicion or probable cause that evidence is about to be destroyed or removed from the premises, they may, incident to an arrest on those premises, conduct a limited search of the premises to prevent this destruction or removal.

▶ REQUIREMENTS FOR A VALID SEARCH INCIDENT TO ARREST

This section will explore in detail the two major requirements for a valid search incident to arrest: (1) a lawful, custodial arrest; and (2) contemporaneousness.

Lawful, Custodial Arrest

To justify a full search incident to arrest, there first must be a **lawful custodial arrest**. This type of arrest involves taking the person into custody and transporting him or her to a police station or other place to be dealt with according to the law. *See United States v. Robinson,* 414 U.S. 218, 234–35 (1973). ("[t]he **danger to an officer is far greater in the case of the extended exposure which follows the taking of a suspect into custody and transporting him to the police station than in the case of the relatively fleeting contact resulting from the typical *Terry*-type stop.") The word *custodial* is important here. In some states, the term *arrest* applies when an officer stops a person and issues a ticket, citation, or notice to appear in court, instead of taking the person into custody and transporting the person to a police station or other place to be dealt with according to the law. A full search is not authorized unless the officer takes the arrestee into custody.

Traffic Citation Stops Are Insufficient The U.S. Supreme Court reaffirmed its requirement of a lawful custodial arrest as a prerequisite to a search incident to arrest in *Knowles v. Iowa*, 525 U.S. 113 (1998). In *Knowles*, a police officer with probable cause to believe the defendant was speeding stopped the defendant and issued a citation. The officer could have arrested the defendant because Iowa law permitted law enforcement officers to immediately arrest traffic violators and take them before a magistrate. Iowa law also permitted officers to issue a citation in lieu of arrest if it "does not affect the officer's authority to conduct an otherwise lawful search." 525 U.S. at 115. After issuing the citation, the officer searched the defendant's car, without probable cause or the defendant's consent, but based solely on Iowa's so-called "search-incident-to-citation" exception to the warrant requirement. The officer found marijuana.

The *Knowles* Court held that Iowa's search-incident-to-citation exception to the Fourth Amendment was unconstitutional. The search incident to arrest exception is a "bright-line rule," justified only by a lawful full custodial arrest. The issuance of a citation alone is not sufficient to justify a search. Basing its decision on the two historic rationales for a search incident to arrest (e.g., officer safety and evidence destruction), the Court first discussed officer safety:

> The threat to officer safety from issuing a traffic citation, however, is a good deal less than in the case of a custodial arrest. In *Robinson*, we stated that a custodial arrest involves "danger to an officer" because of "the extended exposure which follows the taking of a suspect into custody and transporting him to the police station." . . . We recognized that "[t]he danger to the police officer flows from the fact of the arrest, and its attendant proximity, stress, and uncertainty, and not from the grounds for arrest." . . . A routine traffic stop [resulting in the issuance of a citation], on the other hand, is a relatively brief encounter and "is more analogous to a so-called '*Terry* stop' . . . than to a formal arrest." . . . This is not to say that the concern for safety is absent in the case of a routine traffic stop. It plainly is not. . . . But while the concern for officer safety in this context may justify the "minimal" additional intrusion of ordering a driver and passengers out of the car, it does not by itself justify the often considerably greater intrusion attending a full field-type search. 525 U.S. at 117.

With respect to the second rationale, the need to discover and preserve evidence, the Court said: "Once *Knowles* was stopped for speeding and issued a citation, all the evidence necessary to prosecute that offense had been obtained. No further evidence of excessive speed was going to be found either on the person of the offender or in the passenger compartment of the car." 525 U.S. at 118.

Thus, after *Knowles*, when an officer merely issues a driver a traffic citation for failure to obey a traffic law, the officer may not, incident to issuing that citation, conduct a full search of the driver, other occupants within the vehicle, or the vehicle itself. However, if the officer instead lawfully arrests the occupants of the vehicle, then the officer (incident to those arrests) can search the occupants and the passenger compartment of their vehicle. This is discussed in more detail in the section "Search of Motor Vehicles," later in this chapter.

Note that in some cases involving vehicles and detained occupants, courts have been reluctant to find the requirement of "custodial arrest" satisfied. When this happens, a full search of the occupants and their vehicle would not be permitted. For example, *United States v. Parr*, 843 F.2d 1228 (9th Cir. 1988) found no custodial arrest of a defendant who was merely stopped on suspicion of driving with a suspended driver's license and placed briefly in a patrol car, without any other restraint or questioning. The court observed that "sitting in the patrol car for several minutes was merely a normal part of traffic police procedure for identifying delinquent drivers and did not constitute custodial arrest." 843 F.2d at 1230.

Custodial Arrests for Minor Crimes Justify Search Incident to Arrest "If an officer has probable cause to believe that an individual has committed even a very minor criminal offense in his presence, he may, without violating the Fourth Amendment, arrest the offender." *Atwater v. City of Lago Vista*, 532 U.S. 318, 354 (2001). If an officer makes such a custodial arrest, even if it is for minor crimes unlikely to involve the use of weapons or destructible evidence, officers are permitted to conduct a full search incident to the arrest. For example, in *United States v. Robinson*, 414 U.S. 218 (1973), the police officer stopped the defendant for driving his vehicle without a valid operator's permit. The officer then told the defendant he was under arrest for driving without the required permit. At this point, the officer conducted a full search of the defendant's person that uncovered a cigarette package containing capsules of heroin. The Court in *Robinson* upheld the search incident to the defendant's arrest, and allowed the heroin into evidence:

> Since it is the fact of custodial arrest which gives rise to the authority to search, it is of no moment that [the police officer] did not indicate any subjective fear of the [defendant] or that he did not himself suspect that [defendant] was armed. Having in the course of a lawful search [incident to arrest] come upon the crumpled package of cigarettes, he was entitled to inspect it; and when his inspection revealed the heroin capsules, he was entitled to seize them as 'fruits, instrumentalities, or contraband' probative of criminal conduct. 414 U.S. at 236.

The Court found unimportant the fact that the search incident to the defendant's arrest for failure to possess a valid operator's permit was unlikely to involve weapons or destructible evidence:

> The authority to search the person incident to a lawful custodial arrest, while based upon the need to disarm and to discover evidence, does not depend on what a court may later decide was the probability in a particular arrest situation that weapons or evidence would in fact be found upon the person of the suspect. 414 U.S. at 235.

The Court continued by explaining that all custodial arrests, even those for minor crimes, present dangers for the law enforcement officer justifying a subsequent search:

> "Nor are inclined, on the basis of what seems to us to be a rather speculative judgment, to qualify the breadth of the general authority to search incident to a lawful custodial arrest on an assumption that persons arrested for the offense of driving while their licenses have been revoked are less likely to possess dangerous weapons than are those arrested for other crimes. It is scarcely open to doubt that the danger to an officer is far greater in the case of the extended exposure which follows the taking of a suspect into custody and transporting him to the police station

> than in the case of the relatively fleeting contact resulting from the typical *Terry*-type stop. This is an adequate basis for treating *all* custodial arrests alike for purposes of search justification." *Robinson*, 414 U.S. at 234–35 (1973) (italics supplied).

Gustafson v. Florida, 414 U.S. 260 (1973), also found that an arrest for failure to operate a motor vehicle with a valid driver's license justified a full search of defendant's person incident to the arrest. The search in *Gustafson* revealed a cigarette package containing marijuana. The Court allowed the marijuana into evidence as part of a valid search incident to arrest. For the Supreme Court, it did not matter that the arrest justifying the search was for a crime unlikely to involve weapons or destructible evidence:

> We hold, therefore, that upon arresting [defendant] for the offense of driving his automobile without possession of a valid operator's license, and taking him into custody, [the police officer] was entitled to make a full search of [defendant's] person incident to that lawful arrest. Since it is the fact of custodial arrest which gives rise to the authority to search, it is of no moment that [the police officer] did not indicate any subjective fear of the [defendant] or that he did not himself suspect that the [defendant] was armed. Having in the course of his lawful search come upon the box of cigarettes, [the officer] was entitled to inspect it; and when his inspection revealed the homemade cigarettes which he believed to contain an unlawful substance [e.g., the marijuana], he was entitled to seize them as 'fruits, instrumentalities or contraband' probative of criminal conduct. 414 U.S. at 266.

A Valid Search Incident to Arrest Allows for Seizure of Items Found A lawful custodial arrest is all that is needed to validate the seizure of an item in conjunction with a search incident to arrest. "For an item to be validly seized during a search incident to arrest, the police need not have probable cause to seize the item, nor do they need to recognize immediately the item's evidentiary nature." *United States v. Holzman*, 871 F.2d 1496, 1505 (9th Cir. 1989). Also, from the discussion of the Supreme Court opinion in *Robinson* above, once the officer developed the probable cause to arrest the defendant for driving without a valid permit, the officer could search the defendant and seize any contraband on the defendant (in this case, heroin) without probable cause or even reasonable suspicion.

key points

- The lawful custodial arrest that justifies a search incident to arrest is an arrest that involves taking the person into custody and transporting him or her to a police station or other place to be dealt with according to the law.
- The issuance of a traffic citation alone is not a lawful custodial arrest sufficient to justify a search incident to arrest.

- A lawful custodial arrest for minor crimes not likely to involve weapons or destructible evidence, still allows police officers to conduct a search incident to the arrest.

Contemporaneousness

A search "can be incident to an arrest only if it is substantially **contemporaneous** with the arrest. . . ." *James v. Louisiana*, 382 U.S. 36, 37 (1965). The reason for this rule is that officers may search incident to arrest only (1) to protect themselves and (2) to prevent the destruction or concealment of evidence. A delayed search may indicate that the officers conducted the search for some other impermissible purpose.

The Meaning of "Contemporaneous" Generally speaking, *a search is said to be contemporaneous with an arrest if the search is at the same time probable cause to arrest develops or is conducted shortly thereafter.* Though searches incident to arrest should ideally be conducted immediately following the suspect's arrest, allowing a short time to pass between the arrest and the subsequent search will usually not result in the search being invalidated for failure to satisfy the contemporaneous requirement.

United States v. McLaughlin, 170 F. 3d 889 (9th Cir. 1999), approved a search of the passenger compartment of a vehicle that occurred five minutes after the arrest of the driver. The search was essentially contemporaneous with the arrest in that "the arrest, the filling out of the impound paperwork before searching the car, and the initial search were all one continuous series of events closely connected in time." 170 F.3d at 891. And in *Curd v. City Court of Judsonia, Ark.*, 141 F.3d 839, 843–44 (8th Cir. 1998), the court permitted a search of defendant's purse at the stationhouse even though it occurred fifteen minutes after defendant's arrest in her home: "The search of [defendant's] purse at the station house fifteen minutes after her arrest fell well within the constitutionally acceptable time zone for searches of persons and objects "immediately associated" with them incident to arrest." However, in *United States v. Chaves*, 169 F.3d 687 (11th Cir. 1999), when approximately forty-five minutes passed between the arrest of defendants outside a warehouse and a protective sweep of that warehouse by police officers, the court invalidated the sweep, in part, because of the length of time that had transpired:

> It is undisputed that the sweep in this case did not immediately follow the arrest of Garcia and Torres outside the locked warehouse, but occurred a substantial time after the agents arrested Garcia and Torres. During the interim period, approximately forty-five minutes, the officers simply sat in their cars outside the warehouse. The agents, thus, saw no immediate need to enter the warehouse to protect themselves or other persons in the area. 169 F.3d.at 692.

The *Edwards* "Good Reason" Exception to the Contemporaneous Rule Longer delays may be permitted between arrests and searches if it is not practically feasible to search an arrested person at, or near, the time of arrest. The U.S. Supreme Court made such an exception to the contemporaneousness rule in *United States v. Edwards*, 415 U.S. 800 (1974). In that case, the defendant was arrested shortly after 11:00 P.M. for attempting to break into a building and was taken to jail. Law enforcement officials had probable cause to believe that the defendant's clothing contained paint chips from the crime scene. Because the police had no substitute clothing for the defendant, they waited until the next morning to seize his clothing, on which they found paint chips matching those at the crime scene.

The Court in *Edwards* held that, despite the delay, the clothing was lawfully seized incident to the defendant's arrest. The administrative process and the mechanics of arrest had not yet come to a halt the next morning. The police had custody of the defendant and the clothing and could have seized the clothing at the time of arrest. However, in this case, it was reasonable to delay the seizure until substitute clothing was available:

> [O]nce the accused is lawfully arrested and is in custody, the effects in his possession at the place of detention that were subject to search at the time and place of his arrest may lawfully be searched and seized without a warrant even though a substantial period of time has elapsed between the arrest and subsequent administrative processing, on the one hand, and the taking of the property for use as evidence on the other. 415 U.S. at 807.

Edwards does not allow law enforcement officers to delay a search incident to arrest for as long as they wish. Nor does it sanction all delays in searching and seizing evidence incident to arrest. Officers must be able to provide *good reasons* for delaying a search incident to arrest, and the duration of a delay must be reasonable under the circumstances; otherwise, the search and seizure may be declared illegal. For example, in *Edwards* itself, the Court made clear that it was not practically feasible to search defendant's clothing at the time of his arrest or immediately after bringing him to the stationhouse because no substitute clothing was available at that particular hour of the night. The Court also pointed out that the defendant's "clothes could have been brushed down and vacuumed while [he] had them on in the cell, and it was similarly reasonable to take and examine them as the police did, particularly in view of the existence of probable cause linking the clothes to the crime." 415 U.S. at 806. Thus, after *Edwards*, police should only conduct searches long after the defendant's arrest if it is not practically feasible to conduct an earlier search (i.e., no substitute clothing is available), and the later search is needed to prevent destruction of crucial evidence (i.e., paint chips on the defendant's clothing). In general, officers should be prepared to provide the prosecutor with good reasons why they delayed the search.

Sometimes, circumstances simply prevent an officer from conducting an immediate search incident to arrest. For example, practical considerations usually mandate that body cavity searches and searches of persons of the opposite sex be delayed. In these situations, the officer should remove the arrested person from the scene and conduct the search as soon as favorable circumstances prevail. In *United States v. Miles*, 413 F.2d 34 (3d Cir. 1969), an arrest for an armed bank robbery took place in a crowded hotel lobby, which was lit only by candles because of a power failure. Under these circumstances, the court held that it was proper for officers to make a cursory search for weapons at the hotel and to make a more thorough search later at the station. In *United States v. Willis*, 37 F.3d 313 (7th Cir. 1994), the fact that the officer, after arresting the defendant but before searching his car, needed to walk back to his patrol car to retrieve a camera in order to photograph evidence, did not invalidate the search.

Searches Preceding Arrest The Supreme Court has said that, as a general rule, "an incident search may not precede an arrest and serve as part of its justification." *Sibron v. New York*, 392 U.S. 40, 63 (1968). The Court elaborated on this point in *Smith v. Ohio*, 494 U.S. 541 (1990). In *Smith*, the defendant threw a bag he was carrying onto the hood of his car in response to the officer's command to approach him. When the defendant did not respond to the officer's question as to what was in the bag, the officer retrieved the bag by pushing away the defendant's hand, and opened it. The officer found drug paraphernalia inside the bag, and arrested the defendant. The U.S. Supreme Court reversed the state court's decision, and excluded the drug paraphernalia evidence from trial. It did not agree with the state court's finding that the search incident to arrest could both precede the defendant's arrest and serve to justify it. The Court held that the exception for searches incident to arrest **"does not permit the police to search any citizen without a warrant or probable cause so long as an arrest immediately follows."** 494 U.S. at 543.

However, there is a narrow exception to *Sibron* that allows a search to precede an arrest and still be a valid search incident to arrest. In *Rawlings v. Kentucky*, 448 U.S. 98, 111 (1980), the Supreme Court held that an arrest need not always precede a search if:

▶ probable cause to *arrest* existed at the time of the search and did not depend on the fruits of the search, and

▶ the **"formal arrest followed quickly on the heels of the challenged search."**

In *Rawlings*, the defendant Rawlings placed drugs into Cox's purse for safekeeping. When police arrived at the home where the defendant was present, they made Cox remove the contents of her purse, including the drugs Rawlings had placed there. At this point, Rawlings claimed ownership of the drugs. Once he admitted ownership, police searched Rawlings' person and discovered $4,500 in cash and a knife. He was then placed under arrest. Even though the search of Rawlings' person preceded his formal arrest, the Court upheld the search as incident to his arrest because probable cause to arrest developed before the search, and the formal arrest followed immediately after the search:

> **[W]e have no difficulty upholding this search as incident to petitioner's formal arrest. Once petitioner admitted ownership of the sizable quantity of drugs found in Cox's purse, the police clearly had probable cause to place petitioner under arrest. Where the formal arrest followed quickly on the heels of the challenged search of petitioner's person, we do not believe it particularly important that the search preceded the arrest rather than vice versa.** 448 U.S. at 111.

United States v. Montgomery, 377 F.3d 582 (6th Cir. 2004), similarly upheld a search of a defendant immediately before he was placed under formal arrest. The court found the search revealing cocaine on the defendant's person valid under the search incident to arrest doctrine because probable cause to arrest the defendant existed prior to the search, and the arrest occurred right after the search. The probable cause to arrest the defendant developed independently of the search revealing cocaine on the defendant's person because officers had earlier found a marijuana stem and a scale used for weighing drugs in a car in which the defendant was a passenger.

key points

- In general, a search incident to arrest must be contemporaneous with the arrest. A search is contemporaneous with the arrest if the search occurs at the same time probable cause to arrest develops or is conducted shortly thereafter. Short delays between a formal arrest and an incident search are generally permitted but if the delay becomes prolonged, officers must be prepared to provide good reasons for the delay.

- A search incident to arrest may not both precede an arrest and serve as part of the arrest's justification. However, when probable cause to arrest exists before a search is conducted, a search can precede the formal arrest as long as the arrest follows immediately after the search.

▶ PERMISSIBLE SCOPE OF A SEARCH INCIDENT TO A LAWFUL ARREST

Generally, the allowable scope of a search incident to arrest depends on its purpose. *Chimel* allows a law enforcement officer to search a person incident to arrest for only two purposes:

▶ To search for and remove weapons that the arrestee might use to resist arrest or effect an escape; or

▶ To search for and seize evidence to prevent its concealment or destruction.

Thus, for searches of persons incident to their arrest, officers may search anywhere on the person that weapons or evidence may be found. The following are examples of types of property that may be seized:

▶ evidence of a crime;

▶ contraband, fruits of crime, or other items illegally possessed; and

▶ property designed for use, intended for use, or used in committing a crime.

See FED. R. CRIM. P. 41(c). In addition, an officer may seize evidence of crimes other than the crime for which the arrest was made. For example, in *United States v. Jackson*, 377 F.3d 715 (2004), an officer pulled over a driver of an automobile when he changed lanes without signaling. When the driver failed to produce a license and therefore could not properly be identified, the officer handcuffed the driver and placed him in the patrol car. The court characterized this action as a lawful custodial arrest. In the process of placing the driver in the patrol car, the officer searched the driver and found a large amount of crack cocaine in his crotch area. Even though the officer arrested the driver for failure to possess a valid license, the search and seizure of the cocaine was still valid:

> It would have been foolhardy to trundle [the driver] into the squad car without ensuring that he was unarmed. [The officer] was entitled to reduce danger to himself before securing [the driver] in the back seat for however long it took to find out who he really was. Likewise [the officer] was entitled to preserve any evidence that [the driver] may have been carrying. That the search turned up drugs rather than a gun (or bogus identification) does not make it less valid. 377 F.3d at 717–18.

Discussion

POINT

Do These Actions by Officers—Issuance of Citations vs. Arrests for Minor Crimes—Make a Difference for Search Incident to Arrest Doctrine?

State v. Barros, 48 P.3d 584 (Haw. 2002).

On September 29, 1999, at approximately 2:50 P.M., Officer Rafael Hood (Officer Hood), while on patrol in the Kalihi-Palama-Chinatown-A'ala Street area, observed Barros jaywalk from the mauka side of North King Street to A'ala Park, then from A'ala Park back to North King Street. At 2:56 P.M., Officer Hood approached Barros, intending to issue Barros a citation for jaywalking. Officer Hood forgot his citation book in his patrol car, and decided not to retrieve it. Officer Hood identified himself to Barros, explained the reason for the stop, and informed Barros that he was going to cite Barros for jaywalking. In response to Officer Hood's request for identification, Barros presented his State of Hawai'i Identification Card.

Officer Hood used his shoulder-mounted police radio to request a warrant check. He requested a warrant check because "this was a high drug activity area." Officer Hood also stated that Barros was "acting funny" because "he started shifting from one foot to the other . . . trying to circle me." Officer Hood interpreted his conduct as leading to a possible attack or that Barros "just didn't wanna be there." In addition, Officer Hood generally requests warrant checks to determine "if the person has any unfinished business with the court." At that time, Officer Hood began to write down the salient information to issue a citation. Because he did not have his citation book with him, Officer Hood recorded the necessary information in his notebook. Within a couple of minutes, dispatch confirmed that Barros had outstanding warrants. Officer Hood placed Barros under arrest for contempt of court. Barros was not aware of the outstanding traffic warrants.

Thereafter, Officer Hood conducted a pat-down search of Barros's person for "contraband, means of escape, [and] fruits of the crime." Officer Hood recovered from Barros's pockets a metallic stick, flattened at one end and burned at the other end. Based on his training and experience, Officer Hood believed the stick to be a "scraper" used to extract rock cocaine from the inside of pipes. Officer Hood recovered from Barros's left front pocket a hard cylindrical object believed to be a "crack pipe." As Officer Hood was removing the pipe from Barros's left front pocket, an unraveled napkin also came out, revealing a piece of rock cocaine inside.

As a result of the arrest for Contempt of Court and seizure of the items, Officer Hood did not issue a jaywalking citation to Barros. Had Officer Hood not forgotten his citation book, it would have taken approximately five minutes to issue the citation.

Barros moved to suppress the evidence seized, arguing that the pat-down search was conducted incident to an unlawful citation arrest. The Supreme Court of Hawai'i disagreed with Barros, and allowed the search of Barros's person, revealing cocaine and drug paraphernalia. According to the court, this search was a valid search incident to Barros's lawful arrest on an

Do These Actions by Officers—Issuance of Citations vs. Arrests for Minor Crimes—Make a Difference for Search Incident to Arrest Doctrine? *(Continued)*

outstanding traffic warrant (e.g., for contempt of court). Concerning the constitutional issues, the Court first characterized the initial stop for jaywalking as a brief, investigative stop that was conducted lawfully: "Barros committed the offense in Officer Hood's presence, and there appears to be no doubt that Officer Hood could lawfully stop Barros to cite him for the [jaywalking] offense." Id. at 589. Furthermore, though police may not generally prolong an investigative stop for the purpose of checking for outstanding warrants, the delay here was permissible. Also, according to the court, the investigative stop for jaywalking was not pretextual:

> Evidence in the record also demonstrates that Officer Hood neither used the stop as a pretext to allow him to request the warrant check, nor did he prolong impermissibly the stop in order to allow dispatch to complete the warrant check he requested. Moreover, there is no indication that Officer Hood requested any information other than what was necessary to facilitate the warrant check. Thus, Officer Hood's detention of Barros to run the warrant check did not constitute an unreasonable intrusion. 48 P.3d at 590.

Lastly, the court found that once Hood lawfully arrested Barros for the outstanding traffic warrant, he could search him incident to the arrest: "[T]he pat-down search was justified under the 'search incident to a lawful arrest' exception to the warrant requirement." 48 P.3d at 590.

As a general matter, should we allow full searches of individuals like Barros after they have been lawfully arrested for a crime not likely to involve weapons or destructible evidence (i.e., an arrest for an outstanding traffic warrant)? Were there any facts about Barros that may have led Hood to believe Barros was armed or about to destroy evidence?

On another note, had Hood cited Barros for jaywalking only, would he have been able to conduct a full search of Barros incident to that citation? Explain.

Key to the court's finding that Officer Hood could conduct the warrant check leading to the lawful arrest was that Hood's initial stop of Barros for jaywalking was not pretextual (e.g., Hood did not stop Barros with the intent of checking him for outstanding warrants). Do you agree with the court's conclusion here that Officer Hood's investigative stop for jaywalking was not pretextual? What other information might we like to know either about Officer Hood's prior practices regarding jaywalkers or the practices among Hood's fellow officers regarding jaywalkers? Does the fact that the citation for jaywalking occurred in a high drug area mean the stop was more or less likely to be pretextual? Explain. Even if we conclude that the stop was pretextual, does this matter for Fourth Amendment purposes? (See the discussion of the *Whren* case later in this chapter, in the section entitled "State Departures from the Rule Allowing a Full Search of Suspect's Body Incident to Lawful Custodial Arrest.")

Full Search of the Arrestee's Body

Chimel gives few guidelines as to the allowable extent of a search of an arrestee's body. However, the later cases of *United States v. Robinson*, 414 U.S. 218 (1973), and *Gustafson v. Florida*, 414 U.S. 260 (1973), held that a law enforcement officer may conduct a full search of a person's body incident to the custodial arrest of the person. In these cases, it will be remembered, the U.S. Supreme Court upheld an inspection of the contents of a cigarette package seized incident to the arrest of the defendant for a traffic violation. Illegal drugs were found in both cases. The following language from *Robinson* was quoted with approval in *Gustafson*:

> A police officer's determination as to how and where to search the person of a suspect whom he has arrested is necessarily a quick ad hoc judgment which the Fourth Amendment does not require to be broken down in each instance into an analysis of each step in the search. The authority to search the person incident to a lawful custodial arrest, while based upon the need to disarm and to discover evidence, does not depend on what a court may later decide was the probability in a particular arrest situation that weapons or evidence would in fact be found upon the person of the suspect. A custodial arrest of a suspect based on probable cause is a reasonable intrusion under the Fourth Amendment; that intrusion being lawful, a search incident to the arrest requires no additional justification. It is the fact of the lawful arrest which establishes the authority to search, and we hold that in the case of lawful custodial arrest a full search of the person is not only an exception to the warrant requirement of the Fourth Amendment, but is also a "reasonable" search under that Amendment. 414 U.S. at 235.

Therefore, under the *Robinson–Gustafson* rule, whenever an officer makes a lawful custodial arrest, the officer may make a **"full search" of the arrestee's body** incident to the arrest. But what constitutes a "full search" of the arrestee's body? The following principles can be derived from court decisions dealing with this issue.

Searches On or In the Body Searches on or in the body include the following:

Non-Intrusive Searches of the Body A full search of an arrestee's body usually allows for the search and seizure of evidence on the body. For example, relatively non-intrusive seizures, such as obtaining hair samples and fingernail clippings, are usually upheld if reasonable and painless procedures are employed. *Commonwealth v. Tarver*, 345 N.E.2d 671 (Mass. 1975), upheld a seizure of hair samples from the head, chest, and pubic area of a person incident to his arrest for murder and sexual abuse of a child. More intrusive searches and seizures, such as obtaining blood samples or comparable intrusions into the body, require stricter limitations as discussed below.

Strip Searches and Body Cavity Searches The "full search" that may be effectuated as a valid search incident to arrest does not automatically extend to a strip search or any search that involves bodily intrusion. *Fuller v. M.G. Jewelry*, 950 F.2d 1437 (9th Cir. 1991); *Mary Beth G. v. City of Chicago*, 723 F.2d 1263 (7th Cir.1983). "Strip searches" are visual inspections of a naked human body without any intrusion into a person's body cavities. *Peckham v. Wisconsin Dep't of*

Corrections, 141 F.3d 694, 695 (7th Cir.1998). If body cavities are penetrated, then a "body cavity search" has occurred. Both types of searches are "intrusive and degrading and, therefore, should not be unreservedly available to law enforcement officers." *Wood v. Hancock County Sheriff's Dept.*, 354 F.3d 57 (1st Cir. 2003). Accordingly, courts have established strict limitations to when these types of searches may be conducted incident to an arrest, and, if authorized under the particular circumstances, how they are to be carried out. The guiding principle is always the "reasonableness" of the search at issue.

In *Bell v. Wolfish*, 441 U.S. 520, 559 (1979), the U.S. Supreme Court held that strip searches and visual body cavity searches may be conducted on people in custody with less than probable cause. However, there must be a need for such an intrusion of privacy. To determine if any such search was "reasonable" within the meaning of the Fourth Amendment: **"the scope of the particular intrusion, the manner in which it is conducted, the justification for initiating it, and the place in which it is conducted"** all need to be balanced.

As a rule, an individual who has been arrested "may be strip searched as part of the booking process only if officers have reasonable suspicion that he is either armed or carrying contraband." *Wood*, 354 F.3d at 62; *Arpin v. Santa Clara Valley Transp. Agency*, 261 F.3d 912 (9th Cir. 2001). If there is reasonable suspicion to believe a weapon or contraband might be hidden in body cavities, a more invasive visual search of body cavities may be justified "to protect prisons and jails from smuggled weapons, drugs or other contraband which pose a threat to the safety and security of penal institutions." *Fuller v. M.G. Jewelry*, 950 F.2d at 1447.

Evans v. Stephens, 407 F.3d 1272, 1279 (11th Cir. 2005), involved an unusual strip search that was not targeted at safety or security concerns in a jail upon an arrestee's booking, but rather concerned "a post-arrest investigatory strip search by the police looking for evidence (and not weapons)." The court was unsure whether reasonable suspicion would be sufficient to justify such a search, stating that the standard of proof might be "higher than reasonable suspicion, especially where, as here, the search includes touching genitalia and penetrating anuses." 407 F.3d at 1280. The court found it unnecessary to resolve that question because the officer did not even have reasonable suspicion to believe the people searched possessed drugs on their persons. Although the court refused to create a categorical rule that a search incident to arrest involving the penetration of body cavity orifices are unconstitutional, the court clearly implied that such searches would typically not withstand constitutional scrutiny without some compelling justification.

Even when there are reasonable grounds to conduct a sexually invasive search, the manner in which the search is executed must still be reasonable. As the Supreme Court stated in *Illinois v. Lafayette*, 462 U.S. 640, 645 (1983), **"the interests supporting a search incident to arrest would hardly justify disrobing an arrestee on the street."** Courts consider the following factors when judging the reasonableness, and therefore constitutionality, of the way a strip search or body cavity search was performed:

▶ the amount of force used;

▶ whether sanitary conditions were employed;

▶ the use of threatening or abusive language;

▶ the degree of respect shown for the privacy of the person searched;

▶ whether there is actual physical penetration of cavities or orifices; and

▶ the presence of exigent circumstances.

Recall that in *Evans v. Stephens*, the court found unlawful a post-arrest strip search of body cavities for drugs in light of the absence of reasonable suspicion that the arrestees had drugs on their person. The court also invalidated the search in light of the excessive force used during the search.

> The physical aspects of the searches are also disturbing. Unnecessary force was used. Evans was thrown into Jordan, causing both men to collapse. As Jordan tried to stand back up, Officer Stephens hit him with a baton-like object. It matters that a body cavity search was undertaken. In addition, while conducting the search, Stephens inserted the same baton or club—without intervening sanitation—in each Plaintiff's anus and used the same baton or club to lift each man's testicles. Apart from other issues, this last practice is highly unsanitary. 407 F.3d at 1281.

The officer in *Evans*, a white male, also used "threatening and racist" language towards the arrestees, who were both African-American males, as he conducted the search.

> [I]n this case, the totality of the circumstances—for example, the physical force, anal penetration, unsanitariness of the process, terrifying language, and lack of privacy—collectively establish a constitutional violation, especially when the search was being made in the absence of exigent circumstances requiring the kind of immediate action that might make otherwise questionable police conduct, at least arguably, reasonable. 407 F.3d at 1282.

Thompson v. State, 824 N.E.2d 1265 (Ind. App. 2005), also invalidated a strip search that occurred incident to arrest because of the way it was conducted. Unlike in *Evans,* where the court found no reason to have justified the strip search under the facts of that case, the court in *Thompson* held that law enforcement officers had reasonable suspicion to conduct a strip search. "It was more than reasonable for the officers to believe that Thompson had cocaine somewhere on his person because he had told [an undercover officer] that he was on his way to the motel with the crack cocaine she had requested." 824 N.E.2d at 1268. The search was nonetheless ruled unconstitutional because of the way it was conducted.

> The circumstances of this case include that a camerawoman with no affiliation with law enforcement was present during the search and that she filmed portions of the search. Indeed, our review of the videotape reveals that after [officers had handcuffed the arrestee] and taken him into the motel bathroom, [one officer] told the camerawoman, "You don't want to film that." [The officer] then explained on camera that the other officers would be looking for "the crack that they [drug dealers] usually keep in the crack." Thereafter, when [the officer] went to retrieve gloves, the camerawoman stood at the threshold of the bathroom door and filmed Thompson, who was bent over with his pants pulled down and his buttocks exposed. [Another officer] was standing next to Thompson holding him down. Then, the camerawoman zoomed in on Thompson's bare buttocks, which revealed a white substance between his buttocks [which officers then recovered]. 824 N.E.2d at 1269–70.

Intrusive Searches within the Body A full search of an arrestee's body may also, under limited circumstances, allow for the search and seizure of items within, or inside, the arrestee's body. *Schmerber v. California*, 384 U.S. 757 (1966), held that a more intrusive search and seizure to obtain items within the suspect's body (i.e., blood), will be upheld only if:

(1) the process was a reasonable one performed in a reasonable manner (in *Schmerber*, blood was taken from a person arrested for drunk driving by a physician in a hospital environment according to accepted medical practices);

(2) there was a clear indication in advance that the evidence sought would be found (in *Schmerber*, the arrestee had glassy, bloodshot eyes and the smell of alcohol emanated from his breath); and

(3) there were exigent circumstances and hence insufficient time to obtain a warrant (in *Schmerber*, the blood test had to be taken before the percentage of alcohol in the blood diminished).

Though the routine blood test in *Schmerber* was upheld under this three-pronged inquiry, other, more invasive procedures may be constitutionally unreasonable. For example, in *Rochin v. California*, 342 U.S. 165, 172 (1952), the Supreme Court, under particular circumstances, refused to sanction the act of pumping an arrestee's stomach in a hospital environment as part of a search for pills believed to be drugs. (**"This is conduct that shocks the conscience. Illegally breaking into the privacy of the petitioner, the struggle to open his mouth and remove what was there, the forcible extraction of his stomach's contents—this course of proceeding by agents of government to obtain evidence is bound to offend even hardened sensibilities."**) And in *Winston v. Lee*, 470 U.S. 753 (1985), the Court prohibited the surgical removal under general anesthesia of a bullet from the suspect's chest area.

Searches Immediately Associated with the Arrestee's Body A full search of the arrestee's body allows the seizure and search of items of evidence or weapons immediately associated with the arrestee's body, such as clothing, billfolds, jewelry, wristwatches, and weapons strapped or carried on the person. In this context, "immediately associated" means attached in a permanent or semi-permanent way to the arrestee's body or clothing. A search of items seized might include going through the pockets of clothing; examining clothing for bloodstains, hair, or dirt; and examining weapons for bloodstains, fingerprints, or serial numbers. In *Michigan v. DeFillippo*, 443 U.S. 31 (1979), the U.S. Supreme Court upheld a search incident to an arrest when the police officer inspected the suspect's shirt pockets following his lawful arrest. Drugs found in two of the suspect's shirt pockets were allowed into evidence. *United States v. Molinaro*, 877 F.2d 1341 (7th Cir. 1989), held that a person's wallet may be validly seized and its contents immediately searched incident to the person's arrest to prevent the destruction or concealment of evidence. In *United States v. Ortiz*, 84 F.3d 977 (7th Cir. 1996), officers arrested the defendant and seized an electronic pager incident to the arrest. One of the officers pushed a button on the pager, revealing the telephone numbers stored in the pager. The court upheld the activation of the pager, and the retrieval of the telephone numbers, as a valid search incident to arrest. 84 F.3d at 984.

A full search of the arrestee's body may allow the seizure and search of other personal property and containers that are not immediately associated with the arrestee's body but are in the immediate control of the arrestee (e.g., "proximate" to the arrestee). *United States v. Johnson*, 846 F.2d 279 (5th Cir. 1988). Property that might be seized and searched in this context includes luggage, attaché cases, bundles, or packages. As a general rule, luggage and similar containers are not in the immediate control of the arrestee if the arrestee could not access them for some reason (e.g., the arrestee was handcuffed or the container was secured with locks or by some other means that made it inaccessible to the arrestee). For example, in *United States v. $639,558 in U.S. Currency*, 955 F.2d 712, 716–17 (D.C. Cir. 1992), a search of the suspect's luggage following his arrest was not considered a valid search because the suspect was handcuffed to a chair, and could not gain access to the luggage to retrieve a weapon or destroy evidence. Thus, since the suspect could not harm anyone with a weapon or destroy evidence contained inside the luggage, no exigency existed. (See below for further discussion of this topic.)

Containers Proximate to Arrestee

United States v. Chadwick, 433 U.S. 1 (1977), held that the search of seized luggage or other containers not immediately associated with an arrestee's body is not allowed if the search is remote in time and place from the arrest, or if there is no exigency.

Container Searches Remote in Time and/or Place   In *Chadwick*, the defendants arrived in Boston from San Diego by train. They loaded a large, double-locked footlocker, which they had transported with them, into the trunk of their waiting car. Federal narcotics agents, who had probable cause to arrest and to search the footlocker but no warrants, arrested the defendants. The agents took exclusive control of the footlocker and transported it and the defendants to the federal building in Boston. An hour and a half later, without the defendants' consent and without a search warrant, the agents opened the footlocker and found large amounts of marijuana. The U.S. Supreme Court held that the search of the footlocker was illegal:

> **The potential dangers lurking in all custodial arrests make warrantless searches of items within the "immediate control" area reasonable without requiring the arresting officer to calculate the probability that weapons or destructible evidence may be involved. . . . However, warrantless searches of luggage or other property seized at the time of an arrest cannot be justified as incident to that arrest either if the "search is remote in time and place from the arrest," . . . or no exigency exists. Once law enforcement officers have reduced luggage or other personal property not immediately associated with the person of the arrestee to their exclusive control, and there is no longer any danger that the arrestee might gain access to the property to seize a weapon or destroy evidence, a search of that property is no longer an incident of the arrest.** 433 U.S. at 14–16.

The search of the footlocker by police officers had occurred more than an hour after they gained exclusive control of it. Therefore, the search of the footlocker was remote, and not a valid search incident to the defendants' arrest. Moreover, the defendants were securely in custody at the time of the search, and therefore could not gain access to the footlocker to destroy evidence or retrieve a weapon. As a result, no exigency existed.

Likewise, in *United States v. Bonitz*, 826 F.2d 954, 956 (10th Cir. 1987), a gun case located near the suspect could not validly be searched incident to the suspect's arrest because the suspect had been handcuffed, and thus could not gain access to the contents of the case. There was no danger to the arresting officers that the suspect would gain access to the gun or other weapon inside the case, and harm the officers. There was also no danger that the suspect could destroy the contents of the case (e.g., the gun).

In *United States v. $639,558 in U.S. Currency*, 955 F.2d 712, 716–17 (D.C. Cir. 1992), discussed above, the search of the suspect's luggage incident to his arrest was invalid not only because he was handcuffed to a chair at the time of the search and therefore could not gain access to the luggage, but also because the search occurred at least thirty minutes after his arrest. As a result of this delay, the search of the luggage incident to the suspect's arrest was "remote" in time from the actual arrest:

> Before searching [the suspect's] luggage, the officers had "reduced" the luggage "to their exclusive control." [The suspect] had been arrested and was handcuffed to a chair. The officers did not fear for their safety; there was no possibility that [the suspect] could destroy any evidence. Any need for swift action had by that time disappeared. [The suspect], like the arrestees in Chadwick, no longer had access to the luggage. To be sure, the search of the footlocker in Chadwick took place some ninety minutes after the arrests, whereas the search of [this suspect's] suitcases occurred somewhat sooner [e.g., at least 30 minutes after the arrest]. But the fact remains that this search did not "follow [ ] immediately upon" [the suspect's] arrest, or only a few minutes later. 955 F.2d at 716 (citing *New York v. Belton*, 453 U.S. at 462).

To summarize, law enforcement officers may seize and search luggage and other containers not immediately associated with an arrestee's body if that property is within the arrestee's immediate control and if the search is not remote in time and place from the arrest. Once officers have the property under their exclusive control, however, and there is no further danger that the arrestee might gain access to the property to seize a weapon or destroy evidence, officers may not search the property without a warrant or consent.

Container Searches Based on Exigent Circumstances Other exigency factors need to be considered when determining whether police can make a warrantless search of a suspect's luggage or other containers as part of a valid search incident to arrest. The Supreme Court in *Chadwick* commented that **"if officers have reason to believe that luggage contains some immediately dangerous instrumentality, such as explosives, it would be foolhardy to transport it to the stationhouse without opening the luggage and disarming the weapon."** 433 U.S. at 15 n.9.

In *United States v. Johnson*, 467 F.2d 630 (2d Cir. 1972), police officers were notified by a reliable informant that a recent arrestee's suitcase containing a shotgun could be found near the rear door of an apartment building. The officers knew that the building was located in a transient and high-crime area and that the suitcase was probably visible to passersby. The officers rushed to the apartment building, opened the suitcase, and found the shotgun. The court upheld both the seizure and search of the suitcase:

> [I]n opening the suitcases, the police were not acting in violation of the Fourth Amendment. The "exigencies of the situation made that course imperative." . . . The officers were holding a suitcase which they had probable cause to believe contained a contraband sawed-off shotgun. There was a substantial possibility the gun was loaded. As they stood in that transient and high-crime area, their

own safety and the safety of others required that they know whether they were holding a dangerous weapon over which they had no control. . . . Under these circumstances, we cannot hold that the police were required to carry the suitcase, unopened, to the police station to obtain a warrant or that an officer should have stood near or held the unopened suitcase as a warrant was obtained. The police were entitled to know what they were holding in their possession. 467 F.2d at 639.

Search of Area into Which the Arrestee Might Reach

As may be apparent from the above discussion of container searches, in addition to a search of an arrestee's person or body, a search-incident-to-a-lawful-arrest may also extend into the area within the **immediate control** of the suspect, sometimes referred to as the suspect's **"armspan,"** **"wingspan,"** "lunge area," "wingspread," or "grabbing distance." The Supreme Court in *Chimel* provided a clear definition of the "area within the immediate control of the suspect": **"There is ample justification, therefore, for a search of the arrestee's person and the area 'within his immediate control'—construing that phrase to mean the area from within which he might gain possession of a weapon or destructible evidence."** 395 U.S. at 763.

This passage from *Chimel* gives definite guidelines regarding the extent of the area around an arrestee that is "within his immediate control" and is therefore subject to search by an officer following an arrest. The determination of the permissible area of search depends on several factors, such as the size and shape of the room, the size and agility of the arrestee, whether the arrestee was handcuffed or otherwise subdued, the size and type of evidence being sought, the number of people arrested, and the number of officers present. The following cases illustrate the *Chimel* guidelines.

▶ In *James v. Louisiana*, 382 U.S. 36 (1965), officers lawfully arrested the defendant for narcotics possession on a downtown street corner and took him to his home some distance away where an intensive search yielded narcotics. The Court held the search unreasonable:

> **In the circumstances of this case . . . the subsequent search of the petitioner's home cannot be regarded as incident to his arrest on a street corner more than two blocks away. A search "can be incident to an arrest only if it is substantially contemporaneous with the arrest and is confined to the immediate vicinity of the arrest."** 382 U.S. at 37 (1965).

▶ *United States v. Tarazon*, 989 F.2d 1045 (9th Cir. 1993), however, held that the drawers of the desk at which the defendant was sitting when he was arrested were clearly within the defendant's control and could be searched incident to the arrest moments after the arrest.

▶ In *People v. Spencer*, 99 Cal. Rptr. 681 (Cal. App. 1972), officers went to the defendant's trailer home to arrest him for armed robbery and found him lying in bed. One officer immediately searched under the blankets for a gun as other officers attempted to subdue the defendant, who was resisting. Two revolvers were found in a box at the foot of the bed. The court held that this box was within the area of the defendant's reach and that the revolvers were admissible in evidence.

▶ Though many courts prohibit a search of the area around the suspect if he or she is handcuffed or otherwise secured (see discussion of cases dealing with container searches in previous two sections), the fact that the suspect is handcuffed after arrest does not always prevent a search of the area around the suspect (e.g., a search within the suspect's armspan). In *United States v. Helmstetter*, 56 F.3d 21 (5th Cir. 1995), the suspect was arrested, handcuffed, and placed in a chair. The court allowed the search and seizure of a gun under the chair incident to the suspect's arrest because of the possibility that the suspect could still gain access to it. "The limited restraint placed on [the suspect] impeded but did not prevent him from reaching the readily accessible weapon. In taking possession of the weapon the arresting officers did not conduct an illegal search and the court did not err in declining to suppress the evidence." 56 F.3d at 23.

▶ A few courts may go even further and permit a search of the area within the suspect's reach had he or she not been handcuffed or restrained in some other way. For example, in *United States v. Poole*, 407 F.3d 767, 773 (6th Cir. 2005), the court permitted a search incident to a valid arrest to extend to the area that would have been within the suspect's reach had he not been handcuffed:

> After [the police officer] had handcuffed [the suspect] . . . , [the officer's] seizure of the crack cocaine and razors found on the dresser near [the suspect] was the product of a permissible search incident to arrest, because the dresser would have been within [the suspect's] reach had he not been handcuffed. A search incident to arrest may encompass the areas that would be within the defendant's reach, even when the defendant is restrained.

▶ In addition, if it is necessary for an arrested person to go into a different area of the premises from the area where he or she was arrested, the officer may, for protective purposes, accompany the person and search and seize evidence within the person's armspan. The following quotation from *Washington v. Chrisman*, 455 U.S. 1, 7 (1982), reflects this notion:

> [I]t is not "unreasonable" under the Fourth Amendment for a police officer, as a matter of course, to monitor the movements of an arrested person, as his judgment dictates, following the arrest. The officer's need to ensure his own safety—as well as the integrity of the arrest—is compelling. Such surveillance is not an impermissible invasion of the privacy or personal liberty of an individual who has been arrested.

In *Washington v. Chrisman*, the officer arrested the suspect on suspicion of underage drinking, and then asked the suspect for his identification. When the suspect, accompanied by the officer, went to retrieve identification from his dorm room, the area within the immediate control of the arrested suspect (e.g., his "armspan") moved with him. Therefore, when the officer observed marijuana seeds and a pipe on a desk in the suspect's dorm room, the officer could search and seize this evidence incident to the suspect's arrest. (Note: This evidence could also be searched and seized under the plain view doctrine, discussed in Chapter 10.)

▶ *Giacalone v. Lucas*, 445 F.2d 1238 (6th Cir. 1971), sheds additional light on the flexibility of the armspan rule when the arrested suspect travels from the initial place of arrest. In *Giacalone*, the court held that "if immediately after a lawful arrest, the arrestee reads the arrest warrant and without coercion consents to go to his bedroom to change into more appropriate clothing, the arresting officers—incident to that arrest—may search the areas upon which the arrestee focuses his attention and are within his reach to gain access to a weapon or to destroy evidence." 445 F.2d at 1247. Officers may not, however, deliberately move an arrested person near an object or place they want to search in order to activate the search incident to arrest exception. *United States v. Perea*, 986 F.2d 633 (2d Cir. 1993).

STATE DEPARTURES FROM THE RULE ALLOWING A "FULL SEARCH" INCIDENT TO LAWFUL CUSTODIAL ARREST

The *Robinson* case has been criticized on the ground that it facilitates "pretext" or "subterfuge" arrests for minor offenses and searches incident to those arrests for evidence of more serious crimes for which probable cause to arrest or search is lacking. In *Whren v. United States*, 517 U.S. 806 (1996), the U.S. Supreme Court clearly stated that an officer's ulterior motives do not invalidate the officer's conduct that is justifiable on the basis of probable cause to believe that a violation of law has occurred. In short, if police conduct is justified by probable cause, subjective intent or pretext is irrelevant for Fourth Amendment purposes. The Court went on to say that:

> [O]f course . . . the Constitution prohibits selective enforcement of the law based on considerations such as race. But the constitutional basis for objecting to intentionally discriminatory application of laws is the Equal Protection Clause [of the Fourteenth Amendment], not the Fourth Amendment. Subjective intentions play no role in ordinary, probable-cause Fourth Amendment analysis. 517 U.S. at 813.

Nevertheless, based on interpretations of their state constitutions, some state courts have refused to follow the *Robinson–Gustafson* rule allowing a full-body search incident to a lawful custodial arrest. Several states, including Alaska, California, Colorado, Hawaii, and New York, have placed various limitations on the *Robinson–Gustafson* rule. The Supreme Court of Hawaii limited the warrantless search of an arrestee's person incident to a lawful custodial arrest (1) to disarming the arrested person when there is reason to believe from the facts and circumstances that the person may be armed; and (2) to discovering evidence related to the crime for which the person was arrested. *State v. Kaluna*, 520 P.2d 51, 60 (Haw. 1974). Under this more restrictive rule, officers may not search for evidence incident to an arrest when arresting a suspect for an offense that would not produce evidence (such as loitering and minor traffic offenses), and officers may not search for weapons unless they can point to specific facts and circumstances indicating the likelihood that the arrested person is armed and dangerous.

New York provides another example of a state that has prohibited, in certain cases, full searches of an arrestee incident to his arrest. Generally, when a suspect in New York is arrested for an ordinary traffic violation, such as speeding, the suspect may not be searched incident to his arrest. *See People v. Marsh*, 228

N.E.2d 783 (N.Y. 1967). However, under limited circumstances, a police officer in New York can search a suspect following his arrest for a traffic violation:

> [T]he Legislature never intended to authorize a search of a traffic offender [who has been arrested] unless, when the vehicle is stopped, there are reasonable grounds for suspecting that the officer is in danger or there is probable cause for believing that the offender is guilty of a crime rather than merely a simple traffic infraction. 228 N.E.2d at 786.

key points

- The allowable purposes of a search incident to arrest are: (1) to search for and remove weapons that the arrestee might use to resist arrest or effectuate an escape; and (2) to search for and seize evidence to prevent its concealment or destruction.
- A law enforcement officer may conduct a full search of a person's body incident to the arrest of the person.
- A full search of the arrestee's body allows the seizure and search of weapons or evidence immediately associated with the body. It also usually allows for the search and seizure of evidence on the body. In addition, a full search of the arrestee's body may, under certain circumstances, allow for searches and seizures inside, or within, the body.

- A full search of the arrestee's body allows the seizure and search of other personal property such as luggage or other containers not immediately associated with the arrestee's body but under the immediate control of the arrestee. This property may not be searched, however, if the search is remote in time and place from the arrest or no exigency exists (e.g., the suspect cannot gain access to the luggage to obtain a weapon or destroy evidence).
- If police conduct is justified by probable cause to believe that a violation of law has occurred, subjective intent or pretext is irrelevant for Fourth Amendment purposes.

►MOTOR VEHICLE SEARCHES INCIDENT TO ARREST

In *New York v. Belton*, 453 U.S. 454 (1981), the leading U.S. Supreme Court case on search incident to arrest of motor vehicles, a police officer stopped a vehicle for speeding. In the process of inspecting the vehicle's registration and other documentation, the officer discovered that none of the four male occupants of the vehicle owned the vehicle or was related to its owner. The officer also smelled burnt marijuana and noticed on the floor of the vehicle an envelope marked "Supergold" that he associated with marijuana. The officer directed the occupants to get out of the vehicle, and placed them under arrest for the unlawful possession of marijuana. After patting down each of the four men, he then picked up the envelope from the floor of the vehicle marked "Supergold" and found that it contained marijuana. At that point, the officer gave *Miranda* warnings to the men, and searched them. He then searched the vehicle's passenger compartment. On the back seat he found a black leather jacket belonging to one of the vehicle's former occupants. After unzipping one of the jacket's pockets, the officer found cocaine. He then seized the jacket.

At his trial, Belton moved to suppress the cocaine the trooper seized from his jacket pocket. The Court held:

> **[W]hen a policeman has made a lawful custodial arrest of the occupant of an automobile, he may, as a contemporaneous incident of that arrest,**

> search the passenger compartment of that automobile. It follows from this conclusion that the police may also examine the contents of any containers found within the passenger compartment, for if the passenger compartment is within the reach of the arrestee, so also will containers in it be within his reach. . . . Such a container may, of course, be searched whether it is open or closed. 453 U.S. at 460–61.

Thus, once a police officer has arrested an occupant of a vehicle, the officer may search the passenger compartment of that vehicle and its containers, regardless of whether the occupant has been removed from the vehicle and secured with handcuffs or in some other way. *See United States v. Wesley*, 293 F.3d 541, 549 (D.C. 2002) (finding that officer could lawfully search passenger compartment of vehicle and its containers after arresting car occupant even though, at time of search, occupant was handcuffed and removed from the vehicle).

A footnote in *Belton* defined a "container" for the purposes of motor vehicle searches incident to arrest. A **container** is any object capable of holding another object. A container thus includes "**closed or open glove compartments, consoles or other receptacles located anywhere within the passenger compartment, as well as luggage, boxes, bags, clothing, and the like.**" 453 U.S. at 460–61 n.4. The Court also pointed out that only the interior of the passenger compartment of an automobile, and not the trunk, may be searched incident to arrest.

In vehicles that do not have a traditional "trunk," such as vans, hatchbacks, station wagons, and sport utility vehicles (SUVs), courts have consistently defined "a 'passenger compartment' for *Belton* purposes . . . 'as including all space reachable without exiting the vehicle,' excluding areas that would require dismantling the vehicle." *United States v. Pino*, 855 F.2d 357, 364 (6th Cir. 1988). Therefore, a search of these areas incident to the arrest of a vehicle's occupant is permissible under *Belton*. According to the First Circuit Court of Appeals, the only relevant question in these situations is whether "the area to be searched is generally 'reachable without exiting the vehicle, without regard to the likelihood in the particular case that such a reaching was possible.'" *United States v. Doward*, 41 F.3d 789, 794 (1st Cir. 1994). Therefore, "officers may search the entire passenger compartment, including the interior cargo or luggage area, of sport utility vehicles or similarly configured automobiles, whether covered or uncovered." *United States v. Olguin-Rivera*, 168 F.3d 1203, 1207 (10th Cir. 1999). Incident to an arrest of a vehicle's occupant, officers may even search compartments hidden by a trap door if these compartments are themselves within the passenger compartment of a vehicle, and potentially accessible to a vehicle's occupant. In *United States v. Poggemiller*, 375 F.3d 686, 688 (8th Cir. 2004), the court stated that "the search incident to arrest permissibly extended to the trap door compartment, since it was accessible to [the arrested occupant] and therefore within [the] rule that all areas 'within reach' of an occupant of the passenger compartment are subject to search."

Thornton v. United States, 541 U.S. 615 (2004), held that *Belton* is not limited to situations in which the officer initiated contact with an arrestee while the arrestee was still an occupant of the car. In *Thornton*, the officer had probable cause to arrest a car's driver, but before the officer had an opportunity to pull him over, he drove into a parking lot, parked, and got out of the vehicle. When the officer initiated contact with him, he was in close proximity, both temporally and spatially, to his car. The Court said:

> In all relevant aspects, the arrest of a suspect who is next to a vehicle presents identical concerns regarding officer safety and the destruction of evidence as the arrest of one who is inside the vehicle. An officer may search a suspect's vehicle under *Belton* only if the suspect is arrested. . . . A custodial arrest is fluid and "[t]he danger to the police officer flows from the fact of the arrest, and its attendant proximity, stress, and uncertainty." . . . The stress is no less merely because the arrestee exited his car before the officer initiated contact, nor is an arrestee less likely to attempt to lunge for a weapon or to destroy evidence if he is outside of, but still in control of, the vehicle. In either case, the officer faces a highly volatile situation. It would make little sense to apply two different rules to what is, at bottom, the same situation. 541 U.S. at 621.

Therefore, the Court held that *"Belton allows police to search the passenger compartment of a vehicle incident to a lawful custodial arrest of both 'occupants' and 'recent occupants.'"* 541 U.S. at 622. The Court also indicated that the concept of "recent occupant" should be thought of in terms of time and distance away from the vehicle (not in terms of whether the officer first approached the suspect to arrest him while he was inside or outside of the vehicle):

> [W]hile an arrestee's status as a "recent occupant" may turn on his temporal or spatial relationship to the car at the time of the arrest and search, it certainly does not turn on whether [the arrestee] was inside or outside the car at the moment that the officer first initiated contact with him. 541 U.S. at 622.

Belton deals only with the search incident to arrest exception to the warrant requirement and has nothing to do with the so-called automobile exception under the *Carroll* doctrine (see Chapter 11). *Belton* specifically referred to *Chimel*, stating that the relatively narrow compass of the passenger compartment of an automobile is within "the area into which an arrestee might reach in order to grab a weapon or evidentiary item." 395 U.S. at 763. Therefore, the holding in *Belton* does not apply unless there has been a custodial arrest of the occupant or recent occupant of an automobile. It is the custodial arrest that provides the justification for examining articles and containers seized from the passenger compartment of the automobile. Moreover, as the previously quoted passage from *Belton* indicates, the searching of any containers found in the automobile must be substantially contemporaneous with the arrest of the automobile's occupant. If a container is seized and then searched some time later, after it is in the exclusive control of the police, the *Chadwick* case requires that a warrant be obtained. This is both because the later container search is remote in time from the car occupant's arrest and the occupant/arrestee would not be able to obtain a weapon or destroy evidence from the container once it is in the exclusive control of police.

key point

- When a law enforcement officer has made a lawful custodial arrest of either an occupant or recent occupant of a vehicle, the officer may contemporaneously search the passenger compartment of that vehicle and may also examine the contents of any containers found within the passenger compartment, whether the containers are open or closed.

Discussion POINT

How Should We Interpret *Thornton*'s Extension of *Belton* to Include "Recent Occupants" of Vehicles?

United States v. Bush, 404 F.3d 263 (4th Cir. 2005).

In the wake of the U.S. Supreme Court's recent decision in *Thornton,* lower courts must interpret the case in a way that is consistent with both its holding and rationale. The case of *United States v. Bush* is an example of a lower court doing just that. In *Bush*, a female suspect named Yvette Canty, under surveillance by police detective Ellsworth Jones for possible loan fraud, exited a Jeep in front of a Maryland bank. Canty entered the bank accompanied by the driver of the Jeep, Larry Bush. After identifying herself as someone other than Yvette Canty to a bank employee, Canty proceeded to complete the loan application process while Bush waited in the lobby of the bank. Once this process was completed, Canty and Bush exited the bank. The duo was followed, without their knowledge, by Detective Jones. As Canty was in the process of entering the Jeep (she had even opened its door and placed her purse on the floor of the passenger side), Jones arrested Canty. Jones and another officer also detained Bush. At this point, Jones conducted a search of the vehicle and found documents related to the fraudulent loan application, including a credit report in the name by which Canty had introduced herself to the bank employee. After uncovering this information, Jones also placed Bush under arrest.

Bush was later convicted of various charges related to bank fraud. Bush appealed the decision, arguing that the evidence found in the Jeep at the bank should have been suppressed. The appeals court agreed with the lower court and refused to suppress the evidence of loan fraud found in the Jeep. The appeals court believed that the *Thornton* rule should apply to this decision: that is, a search of a vehicle incident to an arrest made outside of the vehicle should be allowed as long as the arrested individual was a recent occupant of the vehicle. The appeals court then explained the rationale of *Thornton*, including the threat to the safety of the officer and the possible destruction of evidence posed by a recent vehicle occupant arrested outside the vehicle:

▶ SEARCHES OF THE ARRESTEE'S COMPANIONS

When an arrest is made, other persons besides the arrested person are often in the vicinity. Some courts allow an immediate frisk for weapons of the arrestee's companions without any further justification. This is sometimes called the **automatic companion rule**. These courts believe that the protection of arresting officers from hidden weapons that could be carried by companions of an arrestee outweighs the minimal intrusion imposed on the companion during a brief patdown for weapons:

How Should We Interpret *Thornton*'s Extension of *Belton* to Include "Recent Occupants" of Vehicles? *(Continued)*

[T]he arrest of Canty as she prepared to enter the [Jeep] presented the same concerns of officer safety and destruction of evidence recognized by the [Supreme] Court in *Thornton*. Accordingly, because officers had seen Canty exit the Jeep just before entering the [bank], and because Canty was in the process of reentering the Jeep at the time of her arrest, Jones was permitted to search the Jeep incident to Canty's arrest.

Thus, Bush's motion to suppress the evidence in the Jeep was denied because this evidence was lawfully searched and seized incident to Canty's arrest.

This case shows how lower courts must strictly follow U.S. Supreme Court precedent that is closely "on point" factually and legally to the case they are deciding (e.g., the lower court case presents facts and legal issues that are identical or similar to the Supreme Court precedent—*Thornton*). Do you agree with the court's application of the *Thornton* case to this case? How far from the Jeep was Ms. Canty at the time she was arrested and the vehicle searched? What if Canty had been ten feet from the Jeep? One hundred feet? In addition, would it be helpful to know how much time Ms. Canty spent in the bank (e.g., outside the vehicle)? The court did not analyze this issue. Why might this fact be important after *Thornton*? Would the result in this case be the same if we were told that Canty spent fifteen minutes in the bank? What about two hours?

More generally, does the search incident doctrine for motor vehicles make sense in light of its stated rationale? In other words, when a vehicle occupant is removed from the vehicle and arrested outside the vehicle, how much sense does it make to say, as the Supreme Court did in *Belton* and *Thornton*, that the entire passenger compartment of a vehicle and its containers can be searched by a police officer because the occupant can reach these areas in order to gain access to a weapon or destroy evidence?

It is inconceivable that a peace officer effecting a lawful arrest . . . must expose himself to a shot in the back from a defendant's associate because he cannot, on the spot, make the nice distinction between whether the other is a companion in crime or a social acquaintance. All companions of an arrestee within the immediate vicinity, capable of accomplishing a harmful assault on the officer, are constitutionally subjected to the cursory "pat-down" reasonably necessary to give assurance that they are unarmed. *United States v. Berryhill*, 445 F.2d 1189, 1193 (9th Cir. 1971).

Also, in *Perry v. State*, 927 P.2d 1158, 1163 (Wyo. 1996), the court allowed an automatic frisk for weapons of the companion of the arrestee because of a concern for officer safety: "This justifiable concern for officer safety in the context of a lawful arrest of [one suspect] leads to our holding that Officer Kirby's frisk of [the suspect's companion] was lawful under the "automatic companion" rule.

Other courts reject the automatic companion rule, requiring instead that arresting officers have reasonable suspicion to believe the companion of the arrestee is armed and dangerous, based on the totality of the circumstances, before allowing the companion to be frisked for weapons. Under this approach, companionship is one factor among many to consider in deciding whether to frisk. *United States v. Flett*, 806 F.2d 823 (8th Cir. 1986), upheld a pat-down search of an arrestee's companion, even though the companion made no threatening moves toward the officer and the officer noticed no bulge in the companion's clothing. The court found that "the officer reasonably perceived the subject of the frisk as potentially dangerous," justifying a frisk of the companion in the following circumstances:

▶ The arrestee was the subject of an arrest warrant for narcotics violations.

▶ The arrestee was a known member of a national motorcycle gang with violent propensities.

▶ The arrestee was the "enforcer" of the local chapter of the motorcycle gang and had been previously charged with a firearms violation.

▶ The companion was in the arrestee's house, was dressed in attire similar to that of gang members, and physically resembled known gang members.

▶ The officer had fifteen years' experience in law enforcement.

In addition, in *United States v. Garcia*, 459 F.3d 1059, 1067 (10th Cir. 2006), after officers armed with a warrant arrested one woman outside her apartment, they proceeded to conduct a frisk of the defendant, who happened to be another occupant of the apartment. The court held that this frisk was permissible since officers had the necessary reasonable suspicion:

> We nonetheless conclude that it was reasonable for the officers to believe that the persons present in the front room, who were all apparently connected to drug transactions involving known and suspected gang members, all had some degree of gang affiliation. Although not necessarily determinative by itself, that gang connection further supports the reasonableness of a weapons frisk of those present, including [defendant]. . . . [W]e conclude that [circumstances] did not eliminate the officers' reasonable suspicion that one or more of the persons present in the front room was armed and dangerous or make the weapons frisk of [defendant] unreasonable.

The area within the reach of the defendant's companions may also be subject to search. *United States v. Lucas*, 898 F.2d 606 (8th Cir. 1990), held that a search of a cabinet in a small kitchen, immediately after officers had handcuffed the defendant and while they were removing him from the kitchen, was a valid search incident to arrest. The defendant had attempted to reach the cabinet door immediately before his struggle with the arresting officers and two of the defendant's friends, who were not handcuffed, were still at the kitchen table when the search took place. A revolver found in the cabinet was held admissible in evidence against the defendant.

key point

- A law enforcement officer may conduct a frisk of an arrestee's companion in the immediate area of the arrest, when the arresting officer reasonably believes that the companion is armed and dangerous.

▶RELATED ISSUES

This section deals with several issues related to the search incident to arrest doctrine, including: (1) who may conduct a search incident to arrest; (2) the use of force during a search incident to arrest; and (3) the limited, emergency search incident to detention doctrine.

Who May Conduct Searches Incident to Arrest

If possible, the law enforcement officer making the arrest should conduct the search incident to the arrest. An officer who does not immediately search an arrestee, but allows another officer to do so later, risks having the later search invalidated. It would not meet the requirement of contemporaneousness, nor would it indicate a concern for the arresting officer's protection or the prevention of the destruction or concealment of evidence.

Nevertheless, if the arresting officer transfers an arrested person to the custody of another officer, the second officer may again search the arrested person. This second search is allowed because the second officer is entitled to take personal safety measures and need not rely on the assumption that the arrestee has been thoroughly searched for weapons by the arresting officer. *United States v. Dyson*, 277 A.2d 658 (D.C. App. 1971). This principle was reaffirmed in *State v. Cooney*, 149 P.3d 554 (Mont. 2006). In *Cooney,* two officers conducted a search of the defendant outside a residence after he was arrested. Another officer then was assigned to transport the defendant. The court found that the officer responsible for transporting the defendant was allowed to conduct an additional search:

> Officer Brodie's and Officer Lewis's testimony indicates that their initial search of [defendant] outside the residence was sufficient only to ensure safety in what was a relatively secure situation. . . . Officer Kelly did not act on his own initiative [in re-searching defendant prior to transporting him]. Officer Brodie advised Officer Kelly that he should perform a more thorough search before placing [defendant] in the back seat of his police cruiser. Officer Brodie and Officer Lewis testified that they did not believe that their initial search of [defendant] outside the residence was thorough enough to ensure that [defendant] would be secured in the back seat of a police cruiser. Officer Kelly would be alone with [defendant] in this less controlled environment where [defendant] might have a greater opportunity to retrieve a hidden weapon. We agree with the District Court that under these circumstances Officer Kelly's search was commensurate with preventing Cooney from retrieving any hidden weapons that he may have had on his person. We do not read [the applicable state statute] to require a police officer to trust his personal safety to a perfunctory search performed by other officers when those same officers have advised him that their initial search was insufficient to ensure the safe transport of a prisoner. 149 P.3d at 556–57.

Use of Force

Law enforcement officers searching a person incident to arrest may use the degree of force reasonably necessary to protect themselves, prevent escape, and prevent the destruction or concealment of evidence. Courts review the use of force strictly, and require officers to use as little force as necessary to accomplish their legitimate purpose. *Salas v. State*, 246 So.2d 621 (Fla. Dist. Ct. App.

1971) upheld a seizure of drugs incident to arrest even though the arresting officer put a choke hold on the arrestee and forced him to spit out drugs he was attempting to swallow. However, as may be recalled from the above discussion of *Evans v. Stephens*, 407 F.3d 1272, 1281 (11th Cir. 2005), courts will not sanction unnecessary levels of force in searching an arrestee. In *Evans*, the court invalidated a post-arrest strip search of body cavities for drugs, in part because of the excessive force used during the search. The officer in *Evans* threw one of the arrestees, hit one of them with a baton, inserted the same baton in each arrestee's anus and used this same baton to lift each arrestee's testicles.

In addition—even though the U.S. Supreme Court refused to uphold the stomach pumping of an arrestee in *Rochin*, discussed above—if officers use no unnecessary force in effecting an arrest, a subsequent stomach pump of the arrestee in a hospital environment to extract swallowed drugs *may* be permissible:

> The case at bar is not comparable to *Rochin*. The original actions by the police in this case were lawful, as set out above. The original actions by the police in *Rochin* were apparently unlawful [because they illegally broke into Rochin's apartment and attempted to open his mouth forcefully to remove the drugs]. The emergency room physician in our case made a medically sound decision to pump [the arrestee's] stomach based on patient history and [the arrestee's] condition at the time. [The physician's] decision prevented a potentially lethal ingestion of cocaine and may well have saved [the arrestee's] life. Pumping [the arrestee's] stomach in this situation does not offend normal sensibilities. *State v. Green*, 89 P.3d 940 (Kan. 2004).

But even if police act lawfully in arresting a suspect, the act of pumping the suspect's stomach may still constitute unnecessary force if there were other possible means to obtain the ingested evidence:

> We cannot but conclude that the forceful placing of a tube into the nostrils and down the esophagus of defendant which by reason of the pain inflicted upon her coerced her to agree to swallow the emetic, and the consequent regurgitation were more than 'minor intrusions into an individual's body' and that the high statistical probability that the balloons would 'pass through' constituted a condition other than the emergency situation [as] in *Schmerber* [where alcohol in the suspect's blood could dissipate before a warrant was obtained for the blood test]. *People v. Bracamante*, 540 P.2d 624, 631, (Cal. 1975).

Limited, Emergency Search Incident to Detention

In *Cupp v. Murphy*, 412 U.S. 291 (1973), the U.S. Supreme Court held that a law enforcement officer may conduct a limited, warrantless search of a person merely detained for investigation, which is often referred to as a **limited search incident to detention**. In that case, the defendant, after being notified of his wife's strangulation, voluntarily came to police headquarters and met his attorney there. Police noticed a dark spot on the defendant's finger and asked permission to take a scraping from his fingernails. The defendant refused. Under protest and without a warrant, police proceeded to take the samples, which included particles of the wife's skin and blood and fabric from her clothing. The defendant was not formally arrested until approximately one month after the samples were taken.

The Court held that the momentary detention of the defendant to get the fingernail scrapings constituted a seizure governed by the Fourth Amendment. Citing *Chimel*, the Court also recognized that under prescribed conditions, warrantless searches incident to an arrest are constitutionally valid. Without an arrest or search warrant, however, a full *Chimel* search of the defendant's body and the area within his immediate control was not permissible. Nevertheless, the Court validated the search under a limited application of the *Chimel* rule based on the unique facts of the case:

▶ The defendant was not arrested but was detained only long enough to take the fingernail scrapings.

▶ The search was very limited in extent, involving only the scraping of fingernails. (A full *Chimel* search of the defendant's body and the area within his immediate control would not have been justified without an arrest.)

▶ The evidence—blood and skin on the fingernails—was readily destructible.

▶ The defendant made attempts to destroy the evidence, creating exigent circumstances.

▶ The officers had probable cause to arrest the defendant, even though he was not actually arrested.

key points

- As a general rule, the arresting officer should conduct the search at the time of arrest or shortly thereafter. However, if the arresting officer transfers an arrested person to the custody of another officer, the second officer may again search the arrested person for the purpose of protecting this officer's safety.
- Law enforcement officers searching a person incident to arrest may use the degree of force reasonably necessary to protect themselves, prevent escape, and prevent the destruction or concealment of evidence. Courts review the use of force strictly, and require officers to use as little force as necessary to accomplish their legitimate purpose.
- Law enforcement officers may conduct a limited warrantless search of a person detained for investigation, if they have probable cause to arrest the person and if there is an imminent danger that crucial evidence will be destroyed if the search is not made immediately.

Summary

Search incident to arrest is a recognized exception to the warrant requirement of the Fourth Amendment. The U.S. Supreme Court case of *Chimel v. California* permits the search of a person who has been subjected to a lawful custodial arrest for the purposes of removing weapons and preventing the concealment or destruction of evidence. A full search for weapons and seizable evidence is permitted, whether or not there is any likelihood of danger from weapons or any reason to believe evidence will be found.

Full searches of areas of the premises beyond the immediate control of the arrestee or companions are prohibited. Nevertheless, an officer may look in closets and other spaces immediately adjoining the place of arrest from which an attack could be immediately launched. Also, an officer may conduct a properly limited protective sweep of the area beyond the spaces immediately adjoining the place of arrest when the officer has reasonable articulable suspicion that the area to be swept harbors a person posing a danger to those on the arrest scene. Also, if police have reasonable suspicion or probable cause that evidence is about to be destroyed or removed from a home, they may (incident to a home arrest) conduct a limited search of the home to prevent this destruction or removal.

There must be a lawful custodial arrest before police can conduct a search incident to an arrest. A lawful custodial arrest is an arrest that involves taking the person into custody and transporting him or her to a police station or other place to be dealt with according to the law. The issuance of a citation alone is not a lawful custodial arrest; however, if there is a lawful custodial arrest, a search incident to that arrest can occur even if the crime for which the person was arrested is a minor one (i.e., the crime is unlikely to involve the use of weapons or destructible evidence).

Also, a search incident to arrest must be substantially contemporaneous with the arrest. Generally speaking, a search is said to be contemporaneous with an arrest if the search is at the same time probable cause to arrest develops or is conducted shortly thereafter. Short delays between an arrest and an incident search are generally permitted but if the delay becomes prolonged, officers must be prepared to provide good reasons for the delay. Generally, an incident search may not precede an arrest and serve to justify it. However, if probable cause to arrest develops before the challenged search and the arrest follows quickly after the search, then a search preceding a formal arrest may be permissible.

The scope of a search incident to a lawful arrest may extend to the arrestee's body and to the area, and to all items and containers, within his or her immediate control—the area from which the arrestee might gain possession of a weapon or destructible evidence. Any weapon or seizable evidence found within this area may be seized. If, however, police seize luggage or other personal property not immediately associated with the person of the arrestee, they may not conduct a delayed search of the property after it has come within their exclusive control without a warrant or exigent circumstances.

If the search is contemporaneous with the arrest, a search incident to the arrest of an occupant of a motor vehicle may extend to the passenger area of the vehicle and may include a search of containers found in the vehicle. Officers may conduct pat-down searches of companions of the arrested person if the officers have reasonable articulable suspicion that the companions are armed and dangerous.

Generally, the officer making the arrest should conduct the search incident to the arrest. Officers should use as little force as necessary to protect themselves, prevent escape, and prevent the destruction or concealment of evidence. The U.S. Supreme Court has approved a limited warrantless search of a person merely detained for investigation. Law enforcement officers may conduct such a search, however, only if they have probable cause to arrest the suspect and there is an imminent danger that crucial evidence will be destroyed if the search is not made immediately.

Key Terms

automatic companion rule, 470

containers, 468

contemporaneous, 452

full search of arrestee's body, 458

immediate control (arm-span/wingspan rule), 464

lawful custodial arrest, 448

limited search incident to detention, 474

protective sweep, 443

search incident to arrest, 442

Review and Discussion Questions

1. Assume that while riding in the first-class section of an airplane, a person is legally arrested for transporting illegal drugs. Can the arresting officers immediately conduct searches of the following items and places incident to the arrest?

   a. The person's clothing

   b. The person's suitcase
   c. The entire first-class section of the airplane
   d. The person's body cavities

   If you approved any of the preceding searches, consider whether each search should be made. What are the possible alternatives?

2. If a defendant is arrested in an automobile for stealing the automobile, may the arresting officer search other passengers in the automobile incident to the defendant's arrest?

3. In a typical search incident to arrest situation, the arrest is followed by a search and then by a seizure. Is a search followed by a seizure and then by an arrest valid? Is a seizure followed by an arrest and then by an additional search valid?

4. What problems relative to search incident to arrest arise when the individual arrested is a person of the opposite sex?

5. Does the nature of the offense arrested for have any effect on the scope of a search incident to arrest?

6. Assume that a defendant is arrested in his kitchen for the armed robbery of a bank earlier that day. The arresting officers have an arrest warrant but no search warrant. The defendant is one of three persons wanted in the robbery. The defendant's automobile, the suspected getaway car, is parked in his driveway. Indicate the full extent of the arresting officers' authority to search the defendant, his premises, and his automobile under the search incident to a lawful arrest doctrine.

7. Assume the same facts as in question 6, except that the defendant is arrested while running from his house to his automobile. Indicate the full extent of the arresting officers' authority to search the defendant, his premises, and his automobile. What if the officers have only a search warrant for the defendant's house, and no arrest warrant? What if it is raining heavily?

8. Is the scope of a search incident to arrest affected by any of the following circumstances?

   a. The defendant is handcuffed and chained to a pole.
   b. The defendant is unconscious.
   c. The defendant is surrounded by a group of friends.
   d. The defendant is arrested on a dark street.

9. Under *New York v. Belton*, the search of containers in the passenger compartment of an automobile is allowed incident to a custodial arrest. Should law enforcement officers wait until a defendant is in an automobile before making an arrest, when possible? Should officers make custodial arrests for offenses for which they would ordinarily not make custodial arrests?

10. Discuss the meaning of this statement: "It is not at all clear that the 'grabbing distance' authorized in the *Chimel* case is conditioned upon the arrested person's continued capacity 'to grab.'" *People v. Fitzpatrick*, 300 N.E.2d 139, 143 (N.Y.1973).

11. Under what circumstances might a strip search or a body cavity search be justified as a search incident to arrest? What about blood tests, stomach pumping, or surgery (i.e., to remove a bullet)?

12. Should a law enforcement officer who has arrested the driver of a vehicle automatically be allowed to frisk all the passengers in the vehicle? Should the officer automatically be allowed to conduct a full search of these passengers incident to the driver's arrest? Why or why not?

Applications of the Law in Real Cases

1 Amaechi and her husband, a guard at the Lorton correctional facility, lived in a townhouse in Dumfries, Virginia. Amaechi's young children sometimes played music in the townhouse too loudly, causing neighbors to complain. On August 10, 1997, Officer Stephen Hargrave, of the Dumfries Police Department, responded to a complaint from one of the Amaechis' neighbors about the loud music coming from the Amaechis' townhouse. Hargrave instructed Amaechi to turn down the music, and she did so. At that time, Hargrave told Amaechi that he would not arrest her unless he received another complaint about the noise level. Believing that Hargrave was unnec-

essarily impolite in his handling of the matter, Amaechi called the Prince William County Police Department and complained about Hargrave's conduct. Hargrave discovered that Amaechi had registered a complaint against him later that afternoon. On August 12, 1997, without any further complaints about the noise level, Hargrave secured an arrest warrant charging Amaechi for the two-day-old violation of the Town of Dumfries's misdemeanor noise ordinance.

After 9:00 P.M. that night, Officer Pfluger took his trainee, West, and other officers to the Amaechis' townhouse to execute the arrest warrant. When Pfluger and

West knocked on the door, a nude Amaechi was in her bathroom preparing for bed. She covered herself with a housedress and followed her husband downstairs.

When Amaechi answered the door with her husband, Pfluger told her she was under arrest. Amaechi fully cooperated during the arrest, but when told that she was to be handcuffed, Amaechi pointed out to the officers that she was completely naked under the dress and requested permission to get dressed because she would no longer be able to hold her dress closed once handcuffed. This request was denied, and Amaechi's hands were secured behind her back, causing her dress to fall open below her chest.

Pfluger then turned to West, who was at the door with Pfluger, and told him to complete Amaechi's processing. West escorted Amaechi to the police car in her semi-clad state, walking past several officers on the way to the car. Amaechi proceeded to enter the back door of the car, which West had opened. West stopped her and told her that he would have to search her before she entered the car. Amaechi protested that she was not wearing any underwear, and West said,

> "I still have to search you." . . . West then stood in front of Amaechi, squeezed her hips, and inside her opened dress, "swiped" one ungloved hand, palm up, across her bare vagina, at which time the tip of his finger slightly penetrated Amaechi's genitals. Amaechi jumped back, still in handcuffs, and exclaimed, "I told you I don't have on any underwear." . . . West did not respond and proceeded to put his hand "up into [her] butt cheeks," kneading them. . . . West then allowed Amaechi to enter the car. This search took place directly in front of the Amaechis' townhouse, where the other police officers, Amaechi's husband, her five children, and all of her neighbors had the opportunity to observe.

On June 2, 1999, Amaechi filed a seven-count complaint in federal district court, claiming money damages against West in his individual capacity, the Town of Dumfries, and Pfluger under 42 U.S.C.A. § 1983 and under state law for West's alleged sexually invasive search. Amaechi contends that West's search, including the touching and penetration of her genitalia, was unreasonable in light of the circumstances surrounding the arrest. West argues, on the other hand, that Supreme Court precedent allows an officer, conducting a search incident to arrest, to effectuate a "full search of the person." Should West's motion for summary judgment arguing he is entitled to a legal judgment in his favor be granted? *See Amaechi v. West,* 237 F.3d 356 (4th Cir. 2001).

2 West Virginia State Police in Rainelle, West Virginia, responded to a 911 dispatch during the early evening hours of May 10, 1998, which indicated that "a domestic altercation [was] in progress on Backus Mountain Road [in Meadow Bridge, West Virginia] with weapons involved." The 911 dispatcher had received a call from Anna Terry who stated: "[M]y daughter is living up there with a guy named Dennis Gwinn, and she just called me real fast and told me to call the police. . . . And she told me that he's got a gun in there by the door and he told her he was going to kill her." Terry also told the 911 dispatcher that her daughter had her baby with her.

State Trooper Ron Thomas was dispatched to respond to the call and was later joined by State Police Sergeant Scott Moore and another trooper. When Trooper Thomas arrived at 485 Backus Road, a remote location in Fayette County, he pulled his cruiser to within twenty-five yards of a small, "single-wide" trailer with a front porch. He drew his weapon from its holster and yelled for Dennis Gwinn to come out. Gwinn exited the trailer, wearing only a pair of blue jeans. Trooper Thomas conducted a pat-down search of Gwinn, handcuffed him, and placed him in the backseat of his cruiser. Trooper Thomas then asked Gwinn "where his wife was at so [Thomas] could speak to her." Gwinn responded that the woman was his girlfriend, not his wife, and that she was inside the trailer.

Trooper Thomas then entered the trailer—the door was open and the screen door shut—where he found Diane Harrah, crying and holding her baby. Sergeant Moore, who had just joined Trooper Thomas, conducted a protective sweep of the trailer while Thomas questioned Harrah. Harrah reported that Gwinn was drunk and had prevented her from leaving the trailer.

She related that Gwinn had gone to the bedroom, obtained a pistol, and brandished it, telling her that "if you try to leave, I'll kill you." She described the handgun as a blue-colored pistol but did not know where Gwinn had put it. She had last seen him with it in the living room. Trooper Thomas and Sergeant Moore searched for the handgun, but discovered instead a loaded shotgun under the couch. They failed to find the handgun.

The officers left the trailer, placed the shotgun in the trunk of Trooper Thomas' cruiser, and prepared to transport Gwinn to the "regional jail." Because Gwinn was wearing no shirt or shoes, Trooper Thomas went back into the trailer and said to Harrah, "Where's his shoes? And we need to get a shirt for him." Harrah directed Thomas to Gwinn's boots in the living room, and she then went back to the bedroom to retrieve a shirt. While Harrah was getting the shirt, Trooper Thomas picked up Gwinn's mid-calf work boots, which "seemed awful[ly] heavy," and heard something "flop inside." When he opened the boot and looked inside, he discovered a pistol. He showed it to Harrah, and Harrah identified it as the weapon with which Gwinn had threatened her earlier that evening.

Gwinn was charged as a felon in possession of a Smith & Wesson .38 caliber revolver and a Winchester 12-gauge shotgun, in violation of 18 U.S.C. § 922. Gwinn moved to suppress the evidence of the two guns because they were obtained pursuant to a warrantless search. Should the guns be suppressed? *See United States v. Gwinn*, 219 F.3d 326 (4th Cir. 2000).

3 Belfield police officer Michael Gant and Belfield police chief Eric Ahrens responded to a complaint from an employee of the Super Pumper Station Store in Belfield, North Dakota. The employee's complaint alleged a customer in the store's parking lot was making "fist gestures" at employees. When the officers arrived, they attempted to speak to Haverluk, who was seated in a car in the store's parking lot. Haverluk responded by cursing at the officers.

Officer Gant, who was stationed on the passenger side of Haverluk's vehicle, observed Haverluk place his right hand between the driver's seat and console. Gant informed Chief Ahrens of Haverluk's actions; the officers drew their weapons and ordered Haverluk to step out of the car.

The officers noticed several indications of intoxication and ultimately arrested Haverluk for being in actual physical control (APC) of a motor vehicle while under the influence of intoxicating liquor, drugs, or other substances. Shortly after Haverluk was ordered out of the car, Gant entered the car and reached between the driver's seat and console, where he found a set of keys, one of which was the vehicle's ignition key. Ahrens advised Haverluk he was under arrest. Haverluk then struck Ahrens in the face.

After a preliminary hearing, Haverluk moved to suppress the keys, based on the testimony presented at the preliminary hearing. Should his motion to suppress be granted? *See State v. Haverluk*, 617 N.W.2d 652 (N.D. 2000).

4 Canyon County Deputy Sheriff Donia Ballard received a call from dispatch shortly after 7 P.M. on a May evening. Dispatch relayed that a caller, who wished to remain anonymous, reported seeing a vehicle parked on a road in a field near the intersection of Farmway and Ustick Roads in early morning and late evenings several times in the preceding weeks. The caller reported that the vehicle was currently in the area and opined that its occupant might be "doing drugs," but did not articulate any reason for this suspicion.

Ballard responded to the dispatch and arrived in the area shortly before dusk. A vehicle was parked on a muddy dirt road surrounded by agricultural fields. The road paralleled a concrete irrigation ditch and came to a dead end in the fields of a farm belonging to Zelda Nickel. Three houses were in the general vicinity.

Ballard parked behind the vehicle. James Nickel was sitting in the driver's seat with the window rolled down. Ballard approached Nickel and explained that she had received a call about a suspicious vehicle and was checking out the report. Nickel told her his name and stated that he was "watching the corn grow." He told Ballard that he was on the property of his mother, Zelda Nickel, and pointed in the direction of his mother's house. Ballard later testified that she believed that Nickel was under the influence of something because he was uncooperative, his eyes seemed wild, and he was shaky. Although Ballard knew that Zelda Nickel lived in the vicinity, she did not believe Nickel when he told her he was on his mother's property.

Ballard asked Nickel for identification, and he handed her a copy of an expired temporary permit, issued pursuant to Section 18–8002 of the Idaho Code. The record does not reveal how long Ballard kept the form or whether she returned it to Nickel. Nickel made no attempt to drive or walk away. Ballard returned to her patrol car and ran a check on Nickel's name. Her backup, Deputy William Adams, arrived about this time. The check with dispatch revealed an outstanding arrest warrant from the City of Caldwell. Ballard and Adams returned to the vehicle and Ballard asked Nickel to step out. He refused. After she asked several more times, Nickel eventually complied. Ballard then told him that he was under arrest. A brief scuffle ensued during which Adams used pepper spray to subdue Nickel.

After handcuffing Nickel, Ballard placed him in the back seat of her patrol car. As she was doing this, Adams searched the vehicle. On the passenger seat, Adams found a one-dollar bill wrapped around an off-white substance. The substance was removed from the vehicle. A field test indicated positive for methamphetamine; later tests at the Bureau of Forensic Services identified the substance as cocaine. Although Adams testified at the suppression hearing that his search of Nickel's vehicle was done as an inventory search, he did not fill out an inventory form.

After the search, deciding that a tow truck would not be able to get the vehicle off the muddy road, Ballard and Adams decided to leave the vehicle where it was.

Ballard issued a misdemeanor citation to Nickel for resisting arrest. The Canyon County prosecutor filed a criminal information charging Nickel with possession of methamphetamine. Nickel pleaded not guilty to both charges. The district court later granted the State's motion to amend the information to charge Nickel with possession of cocaine. Nickel moved to suppress all evidence stemming from the search of the vehicle. Should his motion be granted? *See State v. Nickel*, 7 P.3d 219 (Idaho 2000).

5 On the evening of September 26, 1995, three undercover Boston police officers were investigating drug activity in the Roxbury section of Boston. A woman attempted to flag down one of the officers, who was driving an unmarked vehicle. He did not stop, but reported by radio to nearby officers that he believed that the woman was interested in selling narcotics to him. He also communicated his location as well as the woman's description and requested backup.

When the other officers reported that they were in place, the officer returned to the street where he had seen the woman and stopped as she approached the vehicle. The woman asked him if he was "looking for something." The officer responded in the affirmative. She then asked him how many he wanted, and the officer said "a couple." The woman told him to wait, and she walked away from the rear of the officer's vehicle, which was parked on the side of the street. The woman crossed the street and met briefly with a black male, later identified as the defendant. The officer observed the woman and the defendant gesture to one another, then the woman put her hand to her mouth as she walked back toward him. When the woman returned to the officer's vehicle, he indicated that he wanted two, at which point she opened her mouth and removed two small plastic bags. The officer told her that "they were too small" so he would purchase only one. He gave her two marked five-dollar bills, and she handed to him a plastic bag that appeared to contain crack cocaine. The woman then walked away from the vehicle toward the defendant. As the officer drove off, he radioed to the other officers that the transaction was complete. He told them they should observe the defendant and the woman and retrieve the money.

One of the assisting officers saw the defendant and the woman standing on the steps of a building. He approached them to conduct a "field interrogation observation." The officer asked the defendant for his name and address. The officer then asked whether the defendant had any money on him. The defendant produced the two marked bills from his pocket. The officer placed the defendant under arrest.

The defendant was taken to a police station and booked. Immediately after booking, officers escorted the defendant to a corridor in the cellblock area to search him for weapons and contraband. As the defendant removed his pants and underpants, he reached behind his back and retrieved a plastic bag that appeared to contain crack cocaine. The officer then ordered the defendant to turn around and bend over. As the defendant did so, another plastic bag fell to the floor. The officer observed yet another plastic bag in the area between the defendant's buttocks and removed the bag.

In his motion to suppress, the defendant argued that the money was seized pursuant to an illegal stop. He further argued that the cocaine was seized as the fruit of his unlawful arrest and also as a result of an illegal strip search. Should the defendant's motion to suppress be granted? *See Commonwealth v. Thomas*, 708 N.E.2d 669 (Mass. 1999).

6 On January 9, 1997, Tumwater Police Detective Anthony Gianesini observed Porter driving her van on Trosper Road in Tumwater. Porter's adult son, Charles, sat in the passenger seat next to her. Gianesini recognized both of them from prior incidents, and he suspected that Charles had an outstanding warrant for his arrest. A computer warrants check confirmed Detective Gianesini's suspicion. Gianesini did not attempt to stop the van himself. At the time, he was dressed in civilian clothes and was driving an unmarked police car. Instead, he called for a uniformed Tumwater police officer to make the arrest.

Meanwhile, Porter drove to a gas station, legally parked the van next to a pay telephone, and got out to place a call. Gianesini then saw the two occupants go to the rear of the van, do "something which [he] really couldn't see," and close the van doors. According to Gianesini, Porter and Charles looked directly at him. Charles then reentered the van, emerged with a leashed dog, and began walking along Trosper Road. Gianesini did not follow Charles. He chose to maintain his position, keeping both Charles and the van within sight.

A uniformed police officer arrived approximately twenty-five to thirty seconds later. The officer arrested Charles on the side of the road about 300 feet from the van. The officer searched Charles and discovered a small plastic bag containing methamphetamine. Charles was then handcuffed and placed in the back of the officer's patrol car. Porter observed the arrest and walked from the van to the arrest location. She retrieved the dog from

Charles and continued to walk it along the road away from the van. She did not return to the van.

The uniformed officer then drove to Porter's van where Gianesini was waiting. Acting without a warrant, Gianesini opened the van and saw items consistent with the manufacture of methamphetamine. The van was impounded and later, based upon Gianesini's observations, a search warrant was obtained authorizing a full search. The subsequent search revealed glass vials and plastic bags, which were later found to contain amounts of pseudoephedrine, a precursor to methamphetamine.

The State charged Porter with possession of pseudoephedrine with the intent to manufacture methamphetamine. Porter moved to suppress the evidence seized from the van, arguing Gianesini's initial search could not be justified as a search incident to the arrest of her son. Should the motion to suppress be granted? *State v. Porter*, 6 P.3d 1245 (Wash. App. 2000).

9

Consent Searches

Learning Objectives

▶ Explain the benefits, to the law enforcement officer and to the person being searched, of a consent search.

▶ Understand the circumstances that are considered in determining whether a consent search is voluntary.

▶ Know the difference between consent to enter premises and consent to search premises.

▶ Understand how the scope of a consent search is limited by: the person giving consent; the area to which consent to search is given; time; and the expressed object of the search.

▶ Understand when a third person may be authorized to consent to a search of a person's property and how third-party consent is affected by the person's reasonable expectation of privacy.

Another well-established exception to the search warrant requirement is the **consent search**. A consent search occurs when a person *voluntarily* waives his or her Fourth Amendment rights and allows a law enforcement officer to search his or her body, premises, or belongings:

> Police officers act in full accord with the law when they ask citizens for consent. It reinforces the rule of law for the citizen to advise the police of his or her wishes and for the police to act in reliance on that understanding. *United States v. Drayton*, 536 U.S. 194, 207 (2002).

Voluntary consent prohibits the consenting person from later protesting the search on constitutional grounds. Also, evidence seized as a result of a search for which valid consent is obtained becomes admissible in court, even though there was no warrant and no probable cause to search.

A consent search can benefit a consenting party who is innocent of any wrongdoing. For example, such a search may convince police that it is unnecessary to subject a citizen to the inconvenience and embarrassment of an arrest or more extensive search. *See Schneckloth v. Bustamonte*, 412 U.S. 218, 228 (1973).

Similarly, consent searches can be an effective way for law enforcement authorities to investigate potential misconduct. Officers frequently use consent searches because they are faster than warrant procedures and do not require often difficult determinations of whether there is probable cause, either to search or to arrest. Consent searches, however, present many opportunities for abuse of Fourth Amendment rights by law enforcement officers. To protect those rights, courts closely examine the circumstances surrounding every consent search to determine whether the consent was truly voluntary.

The U.S. Supreme Court has stated that "the Fourth and Fourteenth Amendments require that consent not be coerced, by explicit or implicit means, by implied threat or covert force." *Schneckloth v. Bustamonte*, 412 U.S. 218, 228 (1973). To date, the Supreme Court has resolved the tension between the effectiveness of consent searches for law enforcement and the potential for governmental abuse and coercion inherent in these searches by requiring that all consent searches be conducted voluntarily:

> To approve such searches without the most careful scrutiny would sanction the possibility of official coercion; to place artificial restrictions upon such searches would jeopardize their basic validity. Just as was true with confessions the requirement of "voluntary" consent reflects a fair accommodation of the constitutional requirements involved. In examining all the surrounding circumstances to determine if in fact the consent to search was coerced, account must be taken of subtly coercive police questions, as well as the possibly vulnerable subjective state of the person who consents. Those searches that are the product of police coercion can thus be filtered out without undermining the continuing validity of consent searches. In sum, there is no reason for

us to depart in the area of consent searches, from the traditional definition of "voluntariness." *Schneckloth*, 412 U.S. at 228–29.

In *Schneckloth*, Officer Rand stopped a vehicle when he noticed one of its headlights and license plate light were burnt out. Joe Alcala and defendant Robert Bustamonte were in the front seat along with Joe Gonzales, the driver. Three other passengers were in the rear. Only one of the passengers, Joe Alcala, produced identification upon the officer's request. Alcala explained that the car belonged to his brother. After all of the passengers exited the vehicle, Officer Rand asked Alcala for permission to search the car. Alcala responded, "Sure, go ahead." 412 U.S. at 220. Alcala proceeded to assist Officer Rand and two other officers in the search of the car, by opening the trunk and glove compartment. In their search, police officers discovered three stolen checks under the left rear seat.

The U.S. Supreme Court in *Schneckloth* agreed with the California state appellate court that Alcala consented voluntarily to the search of the car. Therefore, the stolen checks found by police could be admitted into evidence, and the defendant, Bustamonte, was convicted of check fraud:

> Our decision today is a narrow one. We hold only that when the subject of a search is not in custody and the State attempts to justify a search on the basis of his consent, the Fourth and Fourteenth Amendments require that it demonstrate that the consent was in fact voluntarily given, and not the result of duress or coercion, express or implied. Voluntariness is a question of fact to be determined from all the circumstances. . . . Because the California court followed these principles in affirming the respondent's conviction, and because the Court of Appeals for the Ninth Circuit in remanding for an evidentiary hearing required more, its judgment must be reversed. 412 U.S. at 221, 248–49.

A prosecuting attorney who attempts to introduce into court evidence obtained as a result of a consent search must prove by a preponderance of the evidence that the consent was voluntary and not the result of duress or coercion, express or implied. *Lego v. Twomey*, 404 U.S. 477, 489 (1972); *United States v. Matlock*, 415 U.S. 164, 177–78 (1974). The prosecutor's proof will consist almost entirely of the law enforcement officer's testimony about the circumstances surrounding the obtaining of the consent and the conducting of the search. The remainder of this chapter is devoted to explaining in detail the meaning of the

key points

- Law enforcement officers may, without a warrant or probable cause, conduct a search based on a person's voluntary consent. Any evidence discovered within the permissible scope of the search may be seized and admitted into evidence against the person in court.
- Before evidence seized as the result of a consent search may be admitted in court, the court must find from the totality of the circumstances that the consent was voluntary and not the result of duress or coercion, express or implied.
- The prosecutor attempting to introduce into court evidence obtained as a result of a consent search must show by a preponderance of the evidence that the consent was voluntary.

voluntariness requirement and providing guidelines for law enforcement officers in conducting consent searches.

►VOLUNTARINESS OF CONSENT

There are no set rules for determining whether a consent to search is voluntary. Courts examine the totality of the circumstances surrounding the giving of the consent in making this decision. The following examples illustrate the circumstances courts consider important in deciding the question of voluntariness of consent.

Force, Threats of Force, and Other Threats

Courts find consent involuntary if law enforcement officers use force, threats of force, or other types of threats to obtain the consent. In *United States v. Al-Azzawy*, 784 F.2d 890 (9th Cir. 1985), the defendant, while kneeling outside his trailer with his hands on his head, gave permission to search the trailer as numerous police officers approached him with guns drawn. The court found that these coercive conditions rendered the consent to search involuntary. Likewise, when police officers ordered suspects to open a door to a warehouse, entered with guns drawn, and demanded that all of the occupants lie on the floor, the court found that the subsequent consent to search the warehouse was involuntary. *See United States v. Morales*, 171 F.3d 978, 983 (5th Cir. 1999). Similar conditions led to a finding of involuntary consent when law enforcement officials, with guns drawn, handcuffed the defendant and took him to his apartment for the purpose of searching it. At the time of the search, the defendant was surrounded by five federal narcotics agents and lacked any freedom of movement. *United States v. Whitock*, 418 F. Supp. 138, 145 (E.D. Mich. 1976).

Also, in *United States v. Hatley*, 15 F.3d 856, 858 (9th Cir. 1994), the Court found involuntary the defendant's consent given after an officer threatened to take the defendant's child into custody. Likewise, involuntary consent was found when officers told the defendant that if he did not consent, the officers could and would get a search warrant that would allow them to tear the paneling off his walls and ransack his house. *United States v. Kampbell*, 574 F.2d 962 (8th Cir. 1978). Lastly, involuntary consent resulted when law enforcement officials threatened defendants with jail time, monetary fines, foreclosure, or property damage. *See United States v. Waupekenay*, 973 F.2d 1533, 1536 (10th Cir. 1992) (consent found involuntary after officers threatened defendant's wife with jail time); *Jones v. Unknown Agents of the Fed. Elec. Comm'n*, 613 F.2d 864, 879–80 (D.C. Cir. 1979) (consent to search and seize financial records found involuntary when defendant threatened with ten years of jail time, $10,000 fine, and foreclosure of his home if he did not provide authorities with financial information); *Lightford v. State*, 520 P.2d 955, 956–57 (Nev. 1974) (consent to search found involuntary when officer threatened to "kick in" defendant's door if the defendant did not provide the officer with the key).

However, a mere statement by police that they will attempt to obtain a warrant if consent is withheld is usually not considered threatening behavior. On the other hand, if the police officer indicates that a search warrant can actually be obtained, then the officer's claim should be well founded. For example, the officer should know that probable cause to obtain a search warrant exists. *See United States v. Kaplan*, 895 F.2d 618, 622 (9th Cir. 1990).

Sometimes the initial encounter between a law enforcement officer and a suspect requires the officer to use force or threat of force for personal or public safety. Despite the coercive nature of the initial confrontation, an officer may still obtain a valid consent to search if the consent itself is obtained without coercion. For example, in *United States v. Alfonso*, 759 F.2d 728 (9th Cir. 1985), police with guns drawn arrested the defendant in his motel room. After determining that no weapons or other persons were in the room, the officers holstered their guns. The officers informed the defendant of the purpose of their investigation and requested consent to search his luggage. The defendant, who was not handcuffed or otherwise restrained, responded that he had "nothing to hide." The court held that the defendant's consent was voluntary, despite the initial armed confrontation.

Submission to a Fraudulent or Mistaken Claim of Authority

A law enforcement officer's false assertion of a right to search is a more subtle form of coercion. A person's submission to a false assertion of authority does not constitute a voluntary consent. Allowing a search under these circumstances does not reflect free will on the part of the consenter, but rather a mistaken demonstration of respect for the law. The consent to search is invalid, whether the officer's assertion of authority was mistaken or was deliberately designed to deceive the person.

In *Bumper v. North Carolina*, 391 U.S. 543 (1968), officers went to the home of a rape suspect to look for evidence. The home was owned and occupied by the suspect's grandmother, who let the officers in after they told her that they had a search warrant. The officers found a rifle. At the hearing on the motion to suppress the rifle, the prosecutor relied on the grandmother's consent rather than on the warrant to support the legality of the search. (In fact, no warrant was ever returned, nor was there any information about the conditions under which it was issued.) On these facts, the U.S. Supreme Court held that a search cannot be justified on the basis of consent when that consent is obtained only after an untruthful announcement by the officers conducting the search that they have a valid search warrant:

> When a prosecutor seeks to rely upon consent to justify the lawfulness of a search, he has the burden of proving that the consent was, in fact, *freely and voluntarily given*. This burden cannot be discharged by showing no more than acquiescence to a claim of lawful authority. A search conducted in reliance upon a warrant cannot later be justified on the basis of consent if it turns out that the warrant was invalid [or non-existent]. When a law enforcement officer claims authority to search a home under a warrant, he announces in effect that the occupant has no right to resist the search. The situation is instinct with coercion—albeit colorably lawful coercion. Where there is coercion there cannot be consent. 391 U.S. at 548–50 (emphasis added).

Similarly, when police merely announce themselves and their intention to search, any subsequent consent they obtain will be deemed involuntary in the

POINT

Espionage and Computer Files: Do Certain Claims to Have a Search Warrant Represent a "Show of Authority?"

Trulock v. Freeh, 275 F.3d 391 (4th Cir. 2001).

Plaintiff Notra Trulock served as the Director of the Office of Intelligence of the U.S. Department of Energy (DOE) from 1994 to 1998. From 1995 to 1998, Trulock also served as the DOE's Director of the Office of Counter Intelligence. Trulock alleges that he uncovered evidence that Chinese spies had systematically penetrated U.S. weapons laboratories—most significantly, the Los Alamos Nuclear Laboratory.

Trulock contends that the White House, the FBI, and the Central Intelligence Agency (CIA) ignored his repeated warnings about the espionage. Congress eventually learned of the security breach, and in 1998 invited Trulock to testify, which he did on several occasions. That same year, Trulock was demoted within the DOE; he was ultimately forced out in 1999. In early 2000, Trulock wrote an account of his findings, which criticized the White House, the DOE, the FBI, and the CIA for turning a blind eye to the security breach. Trulock claims that the manuscript did not include any classified information. Nonetheless, in March of 2000, Trulock submitted the manuscript to the DOE for a security review, but the DOE declined to examine it. Afterward, Trulock sent the manuscript to the *National Review*, which published an excerpt in an edition that was circulated in early July of 2000. Although neither side placed the article in the record, the parties agree that it charged the administration with incompetence.

Co-plaintiff Linda Conrad has been the Executive Assistant to the Director of the Office of Intelligence at the DOE for more than six years, and reported to Trulock during his tenure. Conrad now reports to Trulock's successor, Lawrence Sanchez. Also, Trulock and Conrad live together in a Falls Church, Virginia, townhouse, which Conrad owns. Conrad alleges that on the morning of July 14, 2000, when she arrived at work, Sanchez took her aside to say that the FBI wanted to question her about Trulock. Sanchez warned her that the agents had a warrant to search the townhouse and would break down the front door in the presence of the media, if she refused to cooperate.

Although the plaintiffs allege that Sanchez made this statement to Conrad "on behalf of the FBI," the complaint does not recite a factual basis for this assertion. Nor does the complaint allege that any of the five individual defendants, all agents or officials within the FBI, either directed Sanchez to make the threat or knew about it.

Later that day, around 4:00 P.M., FBI Special Agents Brian Halpin and Steven Carr arrived at DOE headquarters and escorted Conrad to a conference room. Although the complaint states that they were armed, Conrad does not contend that the agents displayed their weapons, raised their voices, or otherwise threatened her during the three-hour interview.

According to the complaint, Conrad was able to receive two incoming telephone calls, one of which was from Trulock, but that the agents "would not let [her] take either telephone call in

Espionage and Computer Files: Do Certain Claims to Have a Search Warrant Represent a "Show of Authority?" *(Continued)*

private." The complaint further alleges that the agents refused to allow Conrad to make any outgoing calls. The complaint implies that Conrad was not at liberty to leave the conference room. When questioned on this point during oral argument, however, Conrad's attorney could not assert that she ever tried to leave the room (e.g., to place a call in private) or that the agents told her that she was not free to terminate the interview and leave.

The FBI agents queried Conrad about Trulock's personal records and computer files. Conrad responded that she shared a computer with Trulock, but that each of them maintained separate, password-protected files on the hard drive. Conrad and Trulock did not know each other's passwords and could not, therefore, access each other's private files, Conrad stated. The agents questioned Conrad for about three hours. Toward the end of the interview, the agents gave Conrad a form, which they asked her to sign. The complaint alleges that the agents did not explain the form to Conrad and that Conrad did not read it, learning only afterwards that she had consented to a search of her house.

The complaint does not allege that the FBI agents claimed to have a search warrant, threatened to break down Conrad's door if she refused to sign, or mentioned the media. Conrad does maintain, however, that she was fearful, crying and shaking. At the end of the questioning, the agents followed Conrad to her townhouse, where Trulock was waiting. When Trulock asked to see the search warrant, the agents responded that they had no warrant but that Conrad had consented to the search. The complaint does not contend that Conrad tried to withdraw her consent or that Trulock tried to bar the search on the ground that his consent, as a resident of the house, was also necessary.

The agents located the computer in the bedroom. Special Agent Carr and an unidentified FBI computer specialist (named in the complaint as Jane Doe I) searched the computer's files for about ninety minutes. The complaint alleges that Agent Carr looked at Trulock's password-protected files. When the search was over, the specialist, after giving Conrad a receipt, took the hard drive away.

Two weeks later, Conrad and Trulock filed the instant lawsuit. Count one of the complaint, brought under the Fourth Amendment, alleges two consent-related issues: (1) the defendants violated Conrad and Trulock's rights by coercing Conrad's consent to search their home; and (2) that Conrad's consent, even if voluntary, was insufficient to permit the search of Trulock's private computer files. 275 F.3d at 397-99.

As to the first issue, the court found Conrad's consent to be coerced, or involuntary, under a "show of authority" rationale. Because Sanchez, Conrad's immediate superior at the DOE, told her that the FBI had a search warrant, Conrad would have felt compelled to consent to the

(Continued)

Espionage and Computer Files: Do Certain Claims to Have a Search Warrant Represent a "Show of Authority?" *(Continued)*

search of her home by the FBI agents. The important fact for the court was that although the FBI agents did not claim to have a search warrant, "Conrad believed that Sanchez was conveying this information [about the existence of a warrant] on behalf of the FBI." 275 F.3d at 402. As to the second issue, the court found that even if Conrad's consent to search her home was voluntary, she still could not have validly consented to a search of Trulock's computer files since she lacked common authority and control over these files. The court commented:

> We conclude that, based on the facts in the complaint, Conrad lacked authority to consent to the search of Trulock's files. Conrad and Trulock both used a computer located in Conrad's bedroom and each had joint access to the hard drive. Conrad and Trulock, however, protected their personal files with passwords; Conrad did not have access to Trulock's passwords. Although Conrad had authority to consent to a general search of the computer, her authority did not extend to Trulock's password-protected files.

The court reasoned that since Trulock did not share the password to his computer files with Conrad or anyone else, Trulock maintained a reasonable expectation of privacy in these files. Moreover, by not sharing the password, Trulock did not assume the risk that Conrad or other individuals would, in turn, share the password with law enforcement authorities. Thus, Conrad did not have common authority over the files and could not consent to their search by the FBI. 275 F.3d at 403.

Do you agree with the court's finding that Sanchez's "show of authority" (e.g., by telling Conrad that the FBI had a warrant to search her home) renders her consent involuntary under the Fourth Amendment? Should the inquiry rather be focused on the behavior of the FBI agents who actually obtained Conrad's consent later that same day? If so, did the FBI agents impermissibly coerce Conrad under the facts described above?

Lastly, does it make any sense to say, as the court appears to do, that while Conrad could have consented to a search of other parts of the computer, including parts on the hard drive, she could not validly consent to a search of certain files on that hard drive. Is the court "splitting hairs" here? Or does modern technology, including the availability of password protection, make it possible to logically conclude that while a person may have a reasonable expectation of privacy and "common authority" over certain parts of a particular computer, that same person may lack a privacy expectation and authority over other parts of that computer?

absence of a warrant or other valid authorization to search. In *Johnson v. United States*, 333 U.S. 10, 13 (1948), police officers began their search by merely identifying themselves. They later announced their intention to arrest the defendant and search her hotel room. As part of its finding that the defendant did not give a valid consent under these circumstances, the Court said that "[e]ntry to defendant's living quarters, which was the beginning of the search, was demanded under color of office. It was granted in submission to authority rather than as an understanding and intentional waiver of a constitutional right." 333 U.S. at 13. Also, in *Amos v. United States*, 255 U.S. 313, 317 (1921), the Court found invalid the consent of defendant's wife to search the defendant's home after law enforcement officers arrived at the home, identified themselves, and then announced their intention to search for violations of the law. The Court said:

> The contention that the constitutional rights of defendant were waived when his wife admitted to his home the government officers, who came, without warrant, demanding admission to make search of it under government authority, cannot be entertained. [I]t is perfectly clear that under the implied coercion here presented, no such waiver was intended or effected. 333 U.S. at 268.

However, not all "shows of authority" by police officers will result in a finding of involuntary consent. For example, when an individual who is shown to be educated and intelligent clearly indicates to officers his willingness to allow them to view a videotape, then voluntary consent may be found despite an officer's "claim of authority." This was the holding of *United States v. Raibley*, 243 F.3d 1069 (7th Cir. 2001), where the officer told an incarcerated suspect "we are going to be viewing that tape." Though the Court characterized this language on the part of the officer as a "show of authority," the Court found the suspect's consent to view the tape voluntary because the suspect called the officer to his prison cell to watch the tape. The Court also noted that the officer did not harass the suspect in any way, and that the suspect was an educated and intelligent man who had even published several scholarly articles. 243 F.3d at 1077.

Misrepresentation or Deception

Coercion may also take the form of misrepresentation or deception on matters other than the officer's authority. A person's consent to search based on false impressions created by a law enforcement officer is not voluntary. In *Commonwealth v. Wright*, 190 A.2d 709 (Pa. 1963), officers arrested the defendant for robbery and murder and questioned him at police headquarters, but they obtained no incriminating statements. The next day officers, without a search warrant, went to the defendant's apartment to conduct a search. They falsely told the defendant's wife that the defendant had admitted the crime and had sent the police for the "stuff." The frightened and upset wife admitted the officers to the apartment and led them to money taken in the robbery. The court held that the consent given by the wife for this search by police was not voluntary: "[I]t is well established that the consent may not be gained through stealth, deceit, or misrepresentation, and that if such exists this is tantamount to implied coercion." 190 A.2d at 711. If, however, the deceit is carried out by an undercover officer and concerns only the officer's identity as a governmental agent, a person's misplaced confidence in the agent does not make the person's consent involuntary:

> Entry of an undercover agent is not illegal if he enters a home for the "very purposes contemplated by the occupant." . . . If the occupant reveals private information to the visitor under such circumstances, he or she assumes the risk the visitor will reveal it. *United States v. Goldstein*, 611 F. Supp. 624, 626 (N.D. Ill. 1985).

In *Goldstein*, the undercover officer gained entrance to the defendant's home for the purpose understood by the defendant's wife: to discuss the possible purchase of a stolen emerald. The wife voluntarily showed the officer the emerald. The court held this was the result of her misplaced trust in the officer and did not implicate any Fourth Amendment privacy interest. In short, the wife's consent regarding the inspection of the emerald did not result from any official deceit or misrepresentation apart from the officer's concealed identity.

In this regard, lower courts have held that "[a] government agent may obtain an invitation onto property by misrepresenting his identity, and if invited, does not need probable cause nor warrant to enter so long as he does not exceed the scope of his invitation." *United States v. Scherer*, 673 F.2d 176, 182 (7th Cir. 1982). This is primarily because the U.S. Supreme Court has held that entries onto premises by undercover agents do not generally implicate Fourth Amendment privacy interests at all, so long as the owner of the premises permits the entry. *See On Lee v. United States*, 343 U.S. 747, 751–52 (1952); *Hoffa v. United States*, 385 U.S. 293, 302 (1966).

Arrest or Detention

Even if the consenting party is in custody or is detained, the voluntariness of the consent is still determined by the totality of the circumstances. In *United States v. Watson*, 423 U.S. 411 (1976), the Supreme Court held that a consent to search is not involuntary solely because the person giving the consent is under arrest or otherwise in custody. Similarly, in *Davis v. United States*, 328 U.S 582, 592–94 (1946), the fact that the defendant was under arrest when he consented to a search of his office for ration coupons by authorities, did not convert an otherwise voluntary consent into an involuntary one. In addition, in *United States v. Mendenhall*, 446 U.S. 544 (1980), the Supreme Court held that a person subjected to a legal *Terry*-type stop was capable of giving a valid consent to search.

Nevertheless, courts examine very carefully any consent given under circumstances of custody or detention. An arrested or detained person is believed to be "more susceptible to duress or coercion from the custodial officers." *United States v. Richardson*, 388 F.2d 842, 845 (6th Cir. 1968). As a result, it is generally more difficult to prove voluntary consent when the person giving the consent is in custody. For example, if the law enforcement officer subjects the person in custody to additional coercive action, such as handcuffing, display of weapons, incarceration, or if the officer interrogates the person without giving *Miranda* warnings, a subsequent consent to search is very likely to be ruled involuntary. *United States v. Chan-Jimenez*, 125 F.3d 1324 (9th Cir. 1997) found involuntary a consent to search a truck on an unpopulated desert highway obtained by an officer who requested permission to search with one hand resting on his gun.

Another issue arising in this area is that if an arrest or detention is *illegal*, courts generally hold that consent to search obtained by exploitation of the illegal conduct is "fruit of the poisonous tree," unless the causal chain between the illegal arrest and the obtaining of consent has been attenuated, or weakened. Courts determine whether the causal chain has been attenuated by considering:

▶ the time elapsed between the illegal arrest and the giving of consent;

▶ the presence of intervening circumstances between the arrest and the consent;

▶ the purpose and flagrancy of the police misconduct surrounding the arrest; and

▶ whether *Miranda* warnings are given prior to any questioning surrounding the giving of consent.

See, e.g., Brown v. Illinois, 422 U.S. 590, 603–4 (1975).

In *Florida v. Royer*, 460 U.S. 491 (1983) (discussed earlier, in Chapter 7), the defendant purchased a one-way airline ticket under an assumed name and then checked his luggage under this assumed name. As the defendant walked toward the boarding area within the concourse, two detectives approached him because his characteristics and actions fit a "drug courier profile." Upon request, the defendant showed the detectives his airline ticket and driver's license, which carried his correct name. The defendant explained the discrepancy in names by pointing out that a friend had placed the ticket reservation in the assumed name. The detectives, who identified themselves as narcotics investigators, told the defendant that they suspected him of transporting narcotics. Still holding his ticket and license, the detectives asked the defendant to accompany them to a small room near the concourse. Without the defendant's consent, one of the detectives brought the defendant's checked luggage to the room. The defendant did not respond to a request by detectives to consent to a search of the luggage, but he did use a key to unlock one of the suitcases (thereby indicating his consent). Marijuana was found in this suitcase. After the defendant claimed he did not know the combination to a lock on a second suitcase belonging to him, the officers pried it open. The defendant did not object to this action by the detectives. More marijuana was found in the second suitcase. The detectives informed the defendant he was under arrest.

The U.S. Supreme Court in *Royer* found that the defendant was illegally arrested at the time he consented to the search of his luggage because the detectives lacked probable cause for the arrest. They also held that the consent itself was tainted by this illegality and therefore was involuntary:

> Because . . . [defendant] was being illegally detained when he consented to the search of his luggage, we agree that the consent was tainted by the illegality and was ineffective to justify the search. *Royer*, 460 U.S. at 507–8.

Also, in *United States v. Robles-Ortega*, 348 F.3d 679 (7th Cir. 2003), the Court found that an illegal entry into an apartment without a warrant "tainted" the subsequent written consent to search provided by an individual within that apartment. The Court determined that the consent must be excluded as a result of the illegal entry because: (1) insufficient time passed between the illegal entry and consent; (2) the police entered the apartment in a flagrant manner by forcibly breaking down the door, drawing their guns, and ordering all occupants to the floor; and (3) the written consent provided was not an intervening circumstance weakening the taint because it was provided within minutes of the sudden and forceful illegal entry. 348 F.3d at 683, 684.

However, in *United States v. Wellins*, 654 F.2d 550 (9th Cir. 1981), despite an illegal arrest of the defendant, the court held that a consent to search obtained one and one-quarter hours after the illegal arrest, was valid. The court found that the causal chain between the illegal arrest and consent was weakened by giving the defendant *Miranda* warnings and allowing him to consult with his attorney and codefendant before signing a form granting consent to search.

In *United States v. Cherry*, 794 F.2d 201 (5th Cir. 1986), the Court held that the passage of a significant amount of time between an illegal arrest and defendant's consent, an absence of flagrant misconduct by police, the provision of warnings, and sufficient intervening circumstances helped purge the taint of the initial illegal arrest. Specifically, in *Cherry,* about twenty-four hours passed between defendant's illegal arrest and his consent to search his cubicle. The police also did not threaten or intimidate the defendant in any way that would suggest they acted flagrantly. In addition, the police provided the defendant with *Miranda* warnings and informed him of his right to refuse consent to search. Finally, after the illegal arrest but before defendant's consent, intervening circumstances developed which indicated that police had probable cause to detain the defendant. Thus, the consent search in *Cherry* was found valid despite the previous illegal arrest. 794 F.2d at 205–7.

Knowledge of the Right to Refuse Consent

This section will discuss the landmark case of *Schneckloth v. Bustamonte*, which puts forth the current legal test in the consent to search context.

The *Schneckloth* Rule Before the U.S. Supreme Court decision in *Schneckloth v. Bustamonte* (discussed earlier), some courts held that, to prove voluntary consent to search, the prosecution had to show that the person giving consent knew of the right to refuse consent. Other courts ruled that knowledge of the right to refuse consent was only one factor to be considered in determining voluntariness. In *Schneckloth*, the U.S. Supreme Court adopted the latter view, in which knowledge of the right to refuse consent constitutes one factor among others in the overall determination of voluntary consent. In particular, the Court commented that: **"Voluntariness is a question of fact to be determined from all the circumstances, and while the subject's knowledge of a right to refuse is a factor to be taken into consideration, the prosecution is not required to demonstrate such knowledge as a prerequisite to establishing a voluntary consent."** 412 U.S. at 248–49.

Strictly speaking, a law enforcement officer seeking to obtain a valid consent to search from a person need not warn that person of his or her right to refuse consent. Nevertheless, even though formal warnings are not required for consent searches, the U.S. Supreme Court still considers a person's knowledge of the right to refuse consent as very persuasive evidence of voluntariness. For example, in *United States v. Mendenhall*, 446 U.S. 544 (1980), the Court placed special emphasis on the officers warning the defendant of her right to refuse consent in reaching its holding that defendant voluntarily consented to a search of her person and handbag. In particular, the Court commented that:

> [I]t is especially significant that the respondent was twice expressly told that she was free to decline to consent to the search, and only thereafter explicitly consented to it. Although the Constitution does not require [knowledge of the right to refuse consent], such knowledge was highly relevant to the determination that there had been consent. And, perhaps more important for present purposes, the fact that the officers themselves informed the respondent that she was free to withhold her consent substantially lessened the probability that their conduct could reasonably have appeared to her to be coercive. 446 U.S. at 558, 559.

Lower courts have also noted the importance of warning defendants of their right to refuse consent. In the case of *In re Joe R.*, 612 P.2d 927 (Cal. 1980), the court found voluntary consent to search despite the presence of several officers with drawn guns, because the officers explained the right to refuse consent. But in contrast, *United States v. Jones*, 846 F.2d 358 (6th Cir. 1988), found the consent involuntary in similar circumstances, because the police failed to apprise the defendant of his *Miranda* rights or his right to refuse consent.

Though the warning of the right to refuse consent is not a controlling or determinative factor in the voluntariness inquiry, it remains important. Here is an example of what constitutes an adequate warning in this context:

> I am a law enforcement officer. I would like to request permission from you to search your premises (person, belongings).

> You have an absolute right to refuse to grant permission for me to search unless I have a search warrant.

> If you do grant permission to search, anything found can be used against you in a court of law. If you refuse, I will not make a search at this time.

A court is likely to rule as voluntary a consent to search given by a person who received such a warning, assuming no other coercive circumstances.

Alternatively, if an officer has clear indications that a consenting person already knows of the right to refuse consent, warnings need not be given. In *United States v. Manuel*, 992 F.2d 272 (10th Cir. 1993), the court held that the defendant's steadfast, repeated refusals to consent to the search of a gift-wrapped package demonstrated his knowledge of the right to refuse consent. When he finally did consent under non-coercive circumstances, the court found the consent voluntary.

Applying *Schneckloth* to People in Police Custody This section will discuss the application of *Schneckloth* to individuals in custody by federal and state law enforcement officials.

The Federal Approach A person who is in police custody can also voluntarily consent to a search without being warned of the right to refuse consent, though the warning remains a factor in the overall voluntariness inquiry. In *United States v. Watson*, 423 U.S. 411 (1976), the U.S. Supreme Court found a consent to search given by a defendant arrested in public valid, even though the defendant received no formal warnings of his right to refuse consent. In particular, the Court in *Watson* commented that "the absence of proof that [the arrested defendant] knew he could withhold his consent, though it may be a factor in the overall judgment, is not to be given controlling significance." 423 U.S at 424. For the *Watson* Court, the lack of any explicit or implicit threats by police against defendant, the public nature of the arrest, and defendant's personal characteristics and background, all contributed to its finding of voluntary consent.

State Approaches Although nearly all states follow the *Schneckloth v. Bustamonte* totality-of-the-circumstances test (and therefore conform to the "federal approach" discussed above), a handful of states require that consenting persons be aware of their right to refuse consent in addition to requiring that the consent be voluntary. For example, the New Jersey Supreme Court held that their state constitution demands that:

> [T]he validity of a consent to search, even in a non-custodial situation, must be measured in terms of waiver; i.e., where the state seeks to justify a search on the basis of consent it has the burden of showing that the consent was voluntary, an essential element of which is knowledge of the right to refuse consent. State v. Johnson, 346 A.2d 66, 68 (N.J. 1975).

Mississippi law is in accord with New Jersey's requirement that the would-be subject of a search must be aware of the right to refuse consent. *See Penick v. State*, 440 So. 2d 23 (Miss. 1991).

The New Jersey Supreme Court expanded its holding in *Johnson* in 2002, when it set a requirement that reasonable, articulable suspicion exist before an officer may request consent to search in the context of a traffic stop. *State v. Carty*, 790 A.2d 903, 905 (N.J. 2002).

Still other states take a different approach. Oklahoma, for example, requires that individuals be given *Miranda* warnings before their consent to search can be obtained. Yet, Oklahoma does not require that persons in custody be specifically told that they have the right to refuse consent to search. *Case v. State*, 519 P.2d 523 (Okla. Crim. App. 1974).

Informing Suspects That They Are Free to Go

In *Ohio v. Robinette*, 519 U.S. 33 (1996), the defendant was legally stopped for speeding and the officer asked for and was handed the defendant's license. The officer ran a computer check, which indicated that the defendant had no previous violations. The officer then asked the defendant to step out of his car, turned on his mounted video camera, issued a verbal warning, and returned his license. After receiving a negative response to questions about the defendant's possession of drugs or weapons, the officer requested and obtained consent to search his car. The officer found drugs in the car. The defendant contended that a lawfully seized person must be advised that he is "free to go" before his consent to search will be recognized as voluntary. The U.S. Supreme Court disagreed with the defendant, holding that:

> **[J]ust as it "would be thoroughly impractical to impose on the normal consent search the detailed requirements of an effective warning," . . . so too would it be unrealistic to require police officers to always inform detainees that they are free to go before a consent to search may be deemed voluntary.** 519 U.S. at 39–40.

Thus, whether police inform suspects that they are "free to go" is just one factor that can be considered by courts in the overall determination of whether a suspect voluntarily consented to a search. After *Ohio v. Robinette*, courts can still find voluntary consent in the absence of police informing suspects that they are "free to go."

⬆ POINT

How Should One Interpret *Robinette's* "Free to Leave" Test?

Commonwealth v. Strickler, 757 A.2d 884 (Pa. 2000).

On May 26, 1995, at approximately 12:40 A.M., a uniformed officer of the Upper Allen Township Police Department was on routine patrol in a marked vehicle. He was traveling on Fisher Road in a rural area when he saw a car parked at the side of the road, alongside the lawn in front of a farmhouse and barn. Standing about fifteen feet from the parked car were two men who appeared to be urinating. The officer pulled in behind the parked car with the intent, as he explained at the suppression hearing, to ascertain what was happening and whether anything was wrong. He stepped out of his vehicle and approached the individuals—noticing, as he passed their car, that it contained a cooler containing unopened beer cans. When the officer asked the men what they were doing, they replied that they were coming from the races at the Williams Grove Speedway and had stopped to urinate. The officer asked to see their driver's licenses, which they produced, and returned to his vehicle to check on the validity of the licenses and to determine whether there were outstanding warrants for either of the men. As he was conducting the license check, a fellow officer arrived and parked his vehicle behind the patrol car. After verifying that the licenses were valid and that there were no warrants for either of the two men, the officer stepped back out of his cruiser; called defendant/appellant Brett Strickler (the owner and operator of the parked car) over to him; returned Strickler's driver's license to him; advised him that it was not appropriate to stop along the road and urinate on someone else's property; thanked him for his cooperation; and began walking toward his cruiser. At that point, he later testified, Strickler was free to leave, although there is no evidence that he informed Strickler of that fact.

After taking a few steps toward his car, the officer turned around and asked Strickler if he had anything illegal in his car. When Strickler answered that he did not, the officer then asked him "if he wouldn't mind if I took a look through his car." As the officer testified at the suppression hearing, he had no reason to suspect Strickler of having any form of contraband in the car.

Nevertheless, his reason for requesting Strickler's consent to search was "[t]o see if there was anything illegal in his car." In response to the request, [Strickler] hesitated. "He stood there and looked at me and looked at [the officer] who assisted me at the scene, and I explained to him, you know, he didn't have to say yes, you know, and then I asked him again. After saying that, I said, Do you mind. Is it okay with you if we just take a quick search of your vehicle[?]"

At that point, Strickler consented to a search. Upon searching the car, the officer found, between the console and the front passenger seat, an object that looked and smelled like a marijuana smoking pipe. Strickler was arrested and charged with possession of drug paraphernalia.

Strickler filed a pretrial motion to suppress the marijuana pipe on the grounds that the arresting officer, having had no reasonable belief that a crime had occurred or was occurring, had impermissibly requested his consent to a search, and, in addition, that any search for drug paraphernalia was outside the scope of the consent that he gave.

(Continued)

How Should One Interpret *Robinette's* "Free to Leave" Test? *(Continued)*

The Supreme Court of Pennsylvania refused to suppress the marijuana pipe. It found that Strickler was not illegally seized under the Fourth Amendment when the officer asked him for permission to search the car. The court also found that Strickler consented voluntarily to the search of the car. For both the seizure and consent inquiries, the court relied on the totality of circumstances approach, and considered the fact of a suspect being told he or she is "free to leave" as one circumstance, among others, in the overall determination of voluntary consent. In particular, the Court considered the following factors in reaching its finding that Strickler was not illegally seized, and voluntarily consented to the search of his car, revealing the drug paraphernalia:

- ▶ Aggressive behavior or language by officer
- ▶ Show of weapons by officer
- ▶ Whether suspect is told to exit the vehicle or allowed to remain in the vehicle
- ▶ Time of day
- ▶ Suspect's familiarity with the area in which the traffic stop or other type of seizure occurred
- ▶ Whether officer returns documentation to suspect, such as a driver's license
- ▶ Whether officer turns away from suspect prior to re-initiating the contact, resulting in consent
- ▶ Whether officer thanks suspect prior to re-initiating the contact, resulting in consent
- ▶ Whether officer touches suspect or directs suspect's movements in any way
- ▶ Whether officer advises suspect of the right to refuse consent to search
- ▶ Suspect's personal characteristics such as age, mental state, and maturity

For the court, though the officer never directly told Strickler he was "free to leave," the officer's actions did indicate an "end-point" to the routine traffic stop, and suggested to Strickler that he was free to leave. For example, the officer returned Strickler's driver license, thanked Strickler for his cooperation in the traffic stop, and physically turned away from Strickler prior to re-initiating the contact that ultimately led to his consent. Also, the officer's language and actions towards Strickler were not aggressive, and the officer did not show his weapon. Finally, the court noted that the officer told Stickler, who appeared mature and of sound mental judgment, that he could refuse consent to the search of his vehicle.

In light of *Ohio v. Robinette*, do you agree with the court's handling in *Strickler* of the "free to leave" factor? How much weight, if any, should be given to this particular factor in evaluating whether a consent to search is voluntary? Do you agree with the court's assessment that the officer's actions should have suggested to Strickler that he was free to leave? Or should officers have to explicitly tell suspects that they are "free to leave" before this factor is even considered in the voluntariness/totality of circumstances analysis?

Suspect's Attitude about the Likelihood of Discovering Evidence

United States v. Crespo, 834 F.2d 267 (2d Cir. 1987), found a voluntary consent to search, largely on the basis of the trial judge's finding that "having observed Jose Crespo, I believe he is arrogant and self-assured and that it is quite likely that he believed that the agents would not find the materials which were in a closet on a shelf hidden in a bag." 834 F.2d at 272. In *United States v. Gonzalez-Basulto*, 898 F.2d 1011 (5th Cir. 1990), one of the considerations that led the court to find a voluntary consent was that the defendant "may well have believed that no drugs would be found because the cocaine was hidden in boxes toward the front of the trailer and there was little crawl space in the trailer." 898 F.2d at 1013. And in *United States v. Hernandez*, 279 F.3d 302, 308 (2002), the court found voluntary consent, in part, because defendant likely knew contraband would be found in her suitcase, though she first admitted that she was not aware of the contraband's presence. For the court, the defendant's admitted lack of awareness of the contraband meant she had no reason to deny consent to a search of her suitcase.

These cases illustrate that when a suspect indicates verbally or nonverbally to police that they are unlikely to find relevant evidence, their attitude toward the search may lead to a finding of voluntary consent under the totality of circumstances.

Clearness and Explicitness of Consent

Another issue in determining the voluntariness of consent is whether the expression of consent is clear, explicit, and unequivocal. Hesitation or ambiguity in giving consent could indicate that the consent is not voluntary. On the other hand, when a suspect clearly cooperates with law enforcement in their efforts to search a particular place, courts will be more inclined to find voluntary consent.

Both written and oral consent to search are equally effective in waiving a person's right to later object to the search on constitutional grounds. A signed and witnessed writing or an electronically recorded oral statement provides the best proof of a clear, voluntary waiver of a known right. A written or recorded consent is also the best way to refute challenges later raised by the defendant.

Consent need not be expressed in words but may be implied from a person's gestures or conduct. For example, in *United States v. Benitez*, 899 F.2d 995 (10th Cir. 1990), the defendant never verbally consented to a search of his vehicle. Nevertheless, the court found valid consent because the defendant exited his vehicle, opened the trunk, and opened a suitcase contained in the trunk. *United States v. Williams*, 754 F.2d 672 (1985), found that the defendant's assisting the officer in opening the suitcase by twice setting the tumbler on its combination lock was indicative of voluntariness. In addition, in *United States v. Solis*, 299 F.3d 420, 436–37 (5th Cir. 2002), the court found voluntary consent, in part, because defendant's wife cooperated with police in searching defendant's home and showed police the exact location of the contraband.

Moreover, in *United States v. Acosta*, 363 F.3d 1141 (11th Cir. 2004), the court found that verbal permission to search combined with particular actions on the part of the defendant, was sufficient to indicate voluntary consent to search defendant's duffle bag. In *Acosta*, when the police officer asked the defendant for the key to the duffle bag and consent to search it, the defendant replied, "Yes, of course," and provided the officer with the keys. This non verbal action contributed to the court's finding of voluntary consent. Likewise, in *United States v. Garcia*, 339 F.3d 116, 119–20 (2d. Cir. 2003), defendant's wife was found to have voluntarily consented to a search of defendant's apartment because after opening the door to the apartment and allowing the officers to enter, she verbally consented to a search of the apartment.

Verbal consent to search was found insufficiently clear or explicit, however, when defendant's fiancée simply said "okay" after a police officer announced he was going to search a laundry room. *See United States v. Weidul*, 325 F.3d 50 (1st Cir. 2003). The court in *Weidul* pointed out that police had already entered the fiancée's home and conducted a search without permission. Also, at the point when defendant's fiancée said "okay," an officer had already begun walking towards the laundry room. According to the court, this statement was "not a consent to search—it was a simple acquiescence to what any reasonable person would have perceived . . . as police conduct tantamount to a claim of lawful authority to search for weapons." 325 F.3d at 54.

Notification of Counsel

A defendant has no Sixth Amendment right to counsel until after the initiation of adversarial judicial criminal proceedings. *Kirby v. Illinois*, 406 U.S. 682 (1972). Thus, before the filing of formal charges, police are not required to notify retained counsel before soliciting a person's consent, even if the person is under arrest. Police refusal to allow a person to consult with counsel after that person has requested counsel, however, may be indicative of involuntariness of consent.

Also, though neither the Fifth Amendment nor *Miranda* require counsel to be notified before consent to search is obtained, a person in custody who is asked to provide consent should be given *Miranda* warnings. In fact, some states require *Miranda* warnings before a person in custody can grant valid consent to conduct a search. *See Case v. State*, 519 P.2d 523 (Okla. Crim. App. 1974) (discussed earlier). If the arrested person wishes to remain silent or asks for attorney, police attempts to obtain consent should cease.

Conversely, consent given after consultation with counsel is very likely to be found voluntary. *Cody v. Solem*, 755 F.2d 1323, 1330 (8th Cir. 1985). Furthermore, if police have agreed with a suspect's counsel (whenever retained) not to communicate with the suspect, a breach of that agreement may invalidate consent. *Hall v. Iowa*, 705 F.2d 283, 289–90 (8th Cir. 1983).

Individual Factors and Personal Characteristics

Voluntariness of consent may be affected by the physical, mental, or emotional condition of the person giving consent. These personal characteristics must be balanced against police pressures and tactics used to induce cooperation; the length of the police contact; the general conditions under which the contact occurs; excessive physical or psychological pressure; and inducements, threats, or other methods used to compel a response. If a person is sick, injured, mentally ill, under the influence of alcohol or drugs, or otherwise impaired, his or her vulnerability to subtle forms of coercion may affect the voluntariness of consent. Likewise, if a person is immature, inexperienced, mentally retarded, illiterate, or emotionally upset, the impairment of perception and understanding may render any consent to search a mere submission to authority. *See United States v. Gallego-Zapata*, 630 F. Supp.665 (D. Mass. 1986).

The existence of any one of these conditions or states of mind alone usually does not invalidate an otherwise uncoerced consent. "[T]he mere fact that one has taken drugs, or is intoxicated, or mentally agitated, does not render consent involuntary." *United States v. Rambo*, 789 F.2d 1289, 1297 (8th Cir. 1986). The U.S. Supreme Court also appears to support this notion that personal characteristics alone, such as being young or less educated, will not generally render a consent involuntary (see Discussion Point below on *United States v. Mendenhall*).

Intoxication In *United States v. Gay*, 774 F.2d 368 (10th Cir. 1985), the court examined a defendant's ability to consent while intoxicated. The court said that the issue was whether the defendant was so intoxicated that his consent to search was not the product of a rational intellect and a free will. "The question is one of mental awareness so that the act of consent was that of one who knew what he was doing. It is elementary that one must know he is giving consent for the consent to be efficacious." 774 F.2d at 377. In *Gay,* the court found voluntary consent to search the defendant's automobile glove compartment despite his intoxication, based on evidence that the defendant was able to answer questions addressed to him; produced his driver's license on request; responded when asked if he had been drinking; emptied his pockets on request; and denied access to the automobile's trunk, which was found to contain cocaine in a later search.

Intelligence and Educational Level Courts also consider a person's intelligence and educational level in determining the voluntariness of consent. In *United States v. Bates*, 840 F.2d 858, 861 (11th Cir. 1988), the court found a valid consent when "[t]he defendant, an educated man, had 'been informed of [his] right to refuse to consent to such a search.'" And in *United States v. Kaplan*, 895 F.2d 618, 622 (9th Cir. 1990), one of the court's reasons for finding voluntary consent was that the defendant, a doctor, "was not a person lacking in education and understanding."

In addition, even if a person has a low I.Q., minimal education, and certain psychological problems, these characteristics do not necessarily result in a finding of involuntariness. For example, in *United States v. Hall*, 969 F.2d 1102, 1107–9 (D.C. Cir. 1992), a defendant with these characteristics was held to have voluntarily consented to a search of her person and tote bag because the police officer did not threaten or apply pressure to the defendant, the officer confronted defendant for a short time, and the defendant herself exhibited behavior indicating she could make decisions on her own.

Language Barriers Although a person's unfamiliarity with the English language is not an indication of intelligence or educational level, language barriers make determining voluntariness more difficult. In *State v. Xiong*, 504 N.W.2d 428, 432 (Wis. App. 1993), the court said:

> It is incumbent upon the police to effectively communicate their objectives when seeking consent to search. Merely providing an interpreter is not enough. The interpretation must convey what is intended to be communicated. Communication is effective only if it clearly and accurately relates all pertinent information to the listener. If effective communication is not provided, then that is a form of coercion.

For example, in *United States v. Lee*, 317 F.3d 26, 33–34 (1st Cir. 2003), the court found that though English was defendant's second language, he could voluntarily consent to a search of his vehicle because he had lived in the United States for many years and had prior experience with the U.S. judicial system. However, in *United States v. Guerrero*, 374 F.3d 584, 589 (8th Cir. 2004), though the officer provided the defendant with a consent to search form in Spanish, his first language, the court found the consent involuntary because defendant may not have read Spanish and had tremendous difficulty communicating in English with the officer. Though the officer did attempt to obtain defendant's verbal consent, the court concluded that defendant's statement merely reflected his inability to understand the officer—the defendant was simply repeating what the officer said.

Voluntary Production of Evidence

Some people confuse the voluntariness test for consent with a purely voluntary production of evidence. If a person voluntarily produces incriminating evidence, without any attempt by police to obtain consent and without coercion, deception, or other illegal police conduct, there is no search and seizure, and the evidence is admissible in court. In *Coolidge v. New Hampshire*, 403 U.S. 443 (1971), two officers went to the defendant's home, while the defendant was at the police station under investigation for murder, to check out the defendant's story with his wife. The officers asked the wife whether the defendant owned any guns, and she replied, "Yes, I will get them in the bedroom." She then took four guns out of a closet and gave them to the officers. The officers then asked her what her husband had been wearing on the night in question, and she produced several pairs of trousers and a hunting jacket. The police seized the evidence, and it was used against the defendant in court.

The Court found no objection to the introduction of the evidence in court. In fact, the Court found that the actions of the police did not even amount to a search and seizure. Because the Court discussed in detail the significance of the actions of the police, and because of the importance of the issue, the Court's opinion is quoted here at length:

> [I]t cannot be said that the police should have obtained a warrant for the guns and clothing before they set out to visit Mrs. Coolidge, since they had no intention of rummaging around among Coolidge's effects or of dispossessing him of any of his property. Nor can it be said that they

should have obtained Coolidge's permission for a seizure they did not intend to make. There was nothing to compel them to announce to the suspect that they intended to question his wife about his movements on the night of the disappearance or about the theft from his employer.

Once Mrs. Coolidge had admitted them, the policemen were surely acting normally and properly when they asked her, as they asked those questioned earlier in the investigation, including Coolidge himself, about any guns there might be in the house. The question concerning the clothes Coolidge had been wearing on the night of the disappearance was logical and in no way coercive. Indeed, one might doubt the competence of the officers involved had they not asked exactly the questions they did ask. And surely when Mrs. Coolidge of her own accord produced the guns and clothes for inspection, rather than simply describing them, it was not incumbent on the police to stop her or avert their eyes. . . .

In assessing the claim that this course of conduct amounted to a search and seizure, it is well to keep in mind that Mrs. Coolidge described her own motive as that of clearing her husband, and that she believed that she had nothing to hide. She had seen her husband himself produce his guns for two other policemen earlier in the week, and there is nothing to indicate that she realized that he had offered only three of them for inspection on that occasion. The two officers who questioned her behaved, as her own testimony shows, with perfect courtesy. There is not the slightest implication of an attempt to coerce or dominate her, or for that matter, to direct her actions by the more subtle techniques of suggestion that are available to officials in circumstances like these. To hold that the conduct of the police here was a search and seizure would be to hold, in effect, that a criminal suspect has constitutional protection against the adverse consequences of a spontaneous, good-faith effort by his wife to clear him of suspicion. 403 U.S. at 488–90.

key points

- Consent to search given in submission to force, threat of force, or other show of authority is not voluntary.
- Consent to search obtained by misrepresentation or deception is not voluntary, except that a person's misplaced trust in an undercover police agent will not alone invalidate an otherwise voluntary consent.
- Knowledge of the right to refuse consent is only one factor among others to be considered in determining the voluntariness of a consent search.
- The Fourth Amendment does not require that a lawfully seized person be advised that he or she is "free to go" before the person's consent to search will be ruled voluntary.
- Voluntary consent to search may be given in writing, orally, or by a person's conduct so long as the expression of consent is clear and unequivocal. Consent need not be expressed in words but may be implied from a person's gestures or conduct.
- Voluntariness of consent may be affected by the physical, mental, or emotional condition and the intelligence or educational level of the person giving consent. These personal characteristics alone, however, are generally not enough to render consent involuntary.
- If a person voluntarily produces incriminating evidence, without any attempt by police to obtain consent and without coercion, deception, or other illegal police conduct, there is no search and seizure, and the evidence is admissible in court.

▶ SCOPE OF CONSENT

Determination of the allowable scope of a consent search involves issues of whether permission to actually search, rather than merely enter, has been given and what limits are placed on the search in terms of area, time, and expressed object of the search. A discussion of revocation of consent is also included in this section.

Consent Merely to Enter

A person's consent to an officer's request to enter his or her home does not automatically give the officer a right to search. There is a vital distinction between granting admission to one's home for the purposes of conversation and granting permission to thoroughly search the home.

In *Duncan v. State*, 176 So.2d 840 (Ala. 1965), officers investigating a murder knocked on the defendant's hotel room door and the defendant invited them in. They did not advise the defendant that they were police officers, nor did they make any request to search the defendant's room. Nevertheless, the officers conducted a search and found incriminating evidence. The court held that the defendant's invitation to enter his room to the person who knocked on the door did not constitute consent to search his room. The court said:

> To justify the introduction of evidence seized by a police officer within a private residence on the ground that the officer's entry was made by invitation, permission, or consent, there must be evidence of a statement or some overt act by the occupant of such residence sufficient to indicate his intent to waive his rights to the security and privacy of his home and freedom from unwarranted intrusions therein. An open door is not a waiver of such rights. 176 So. 2d at 853.

Initial Consent vs. Subsequent Consent

Even if police are granted consent to conduct a search after being granted consent to enter a residence, such consent is limited to search on that particular occasion. Consent to enter and search on one occasion does not automatically translate into consent to enter and search premises on a subsequent occasion. For example, in *Shamaeizadeh v. Cunigan*, 338 F.3d 535, 548 (6th Cir. 2003), the court found that defendant's initial, valid consent to police officers to search his home for a possible burglar did not authorize these officers to conduct two additional warrantless searches of his home for drugs. The court separated the initial search from the other searches because with the subsequent searches, officers were summoned with particular experience in detecting drugs.

Area of Search

Assuming that an officer obtains a valid consent not only to enter premises, but also to search the premises, "the standard for measuring the scope of a suspect's consent under the Fourth Amendment is that of 'objective reasonableness'—what would the typical reasonable person have understood by the exchange between the officer and the suspect?" *Florida v. Jimeno*, 500 U.S. 248, 251 (1991). As a general rule, if an officer asks for and obtains consent to search a specific area, whether in a place or on a person, the officer is limited to that specific area. If the search goes beyond that area, evidence seized is inadmissible in court.

Grants of General Consent to Search Places In *Jimeno*, the Supreme Court found a police officer acted reasonably in searching a particular container within the defendant's automobile for drugs after the defendant had consented generally to a search of his automobile. The Court noted that the officer in *Jimeno* had explained to the defendant that he wanted to search for drugs prior to obtaining his consent to search the car. Moreover, the defendant did not place any restriction on the officer's search. Under these circumstances, the Court concluded that **"it was objectively reasonable for the police to conclude that the general consent to search [defendant's] car included consent to search containers within that car which might bear drugs. A reasonable person may be expected to know that narcotics are generally carried in some form of container."** 500 U.S. at 251.

Similarly, in *United States v. Jones*, 356 F.3d 529, 533–35 (4th Cir. 2004), the court found that the officer acted reasonably when he searched a locked container within defendant's duffle bag after the defendant had told the officer he could search the bag. The court reasoned that the defendant did not qualify his consent in any way that would indicate to the officer that the locked container was "off-limits." For example, the defendant did not state that the officer could not use keys located in the bag to open the locked container. Also, the defendant failed to make any objection when the officer opened the locked box in defendant's presence. Finally, because the officer stated that he was looking for drugs and the defendant communicated to the officer that drugs were present in the bag, "it was reasonable to conclude that Jones was referring [and consenting] to [a search of] the contents of the [locked container]." 356 F.3d at 534–35.

And in *United States v. Kapperman*, 764 F.2d 786, 794 (11th Cir. 1985), a consent to search form that authorized officers to search the defendant's car and remove "whatever documents or items of property whatsoever, which they deem pertinent to the investigation," was held to grant authority for a general, exploratory search. Therefore, officers did not exceed the scope of the consent by opening an unlocked suitcase found in the car's trunk.

Restricted Grants of Consent to Search Places When a defendant restricts his consent in some way, courts may reach a different result. For example, in *State v. Johnson*, 427 P.2d 705 (Wash. 1967), consent was given to officers to search the trunk of a car. The court held that this consent did not extend to search of the passenger area of the car and that evidence found in the passenger area was inadmissible in court. Likewise, in *United States v. Wald*, 216 F.3d 1222, 1228 (10th Cir. 2000), when the police officer received permission from the defendant during a routine traffic stop to "take a quick look" inside his vehicle, the court concluded that the scope of this consent did not extend to the trunk of defendant's car. As a result, the court excluded from trial the drugs found within defendant's trunk.

Restrictions on grants of consent need not be explicit; restrictions may be implied. For example, in *People v. Cruz*, 395 P.2d 889 (Cal. 1964), an officer obtained permission to "look around" an apartment but was informed that certain property at that apartment belonged to individuals not present at the time of the search. The court held that this type of verbal consent did not authorize the officer to open and search boxes and suitcases that he had been told were the property of persons other than the person giving consent. In other words, an officer can search only the parts of premises over which the person giving consent has some possessory right or control, and not personal property that the officer knows belongs to some other person.

General vs. Restricted Grants to Search People The limitation on the area of search allowed by consent applies equally to searches of people as to searches of premises or vehicles. In a case involving both a nonverbal consent and a limitation on the area to be searched by consent, a police officer asked the defendant whether he was still using or carrying narcotics. When the defendant replied that he was not, the officer asked permission to check him for needle marks. The defendant said nothing but put his arms out sideways. Instead of checking the defendant's arms, the officer patted down his coat and found marijuana cigarettes. The court held that the search went beyond the area of search to which the defendant had consented:

> Bowens' putting out his arms sideways in response to a query whether he minded allowing the officer to check "if he had any marks on him" could hardly be said to be naturally indicative or persuasive of the giving of an intended consent to have the officer switch instead to a general search of his pockets—in which he had two marijuana cigarettes. *Oliver v. Bowens*, 386 F.2d 688, 691 (9th Cir. 1967).

Time of Search

A consent to search may also be limited with respect to time. For example, in *United States v. Alcantar*, 271 F.3d 731, 738 (2001), the court found an hour-long search of defendant's vehicle for drugs and weapons permissible because: (1) the defendant did not object to a search of this length; and (2) one hour was reasonable in light of the fact that drugs and weapons can easily be concealed inside a vehicle.

In *State v. Brochu*, 237 A.2d 418 (Me. 1967), officers investigating the death of the defendant's wife obtained a valid consent from the defendant to search his home. The officers conducted a search and found nothing. At that time, the defendant had not been accused of anything. Later in the day, however, police received information giving them probable cause to arrest the defendant for his wife's murder and to obtain a search warrant for his premises. They arrested the defendant that evening and executed the search warrant the next day. The defendant successfully challenged the validity of this warrant by asserting that certain items seized by police were not mentioned in the warrant, and the prosecution attempted to justify the second search on the basis that the defendant's earlier consent continued in effect after his arrest to the next day. The court rejected this contention because the defendant's status had changed between the two searches from that of a concerned husband to that of the accused in his wife's murder:

> The consent [from the first search] in our view should be measured on the morning of the [following day] by the status of the defendant as the accused. There is no evidence whatsoever that the consent [for the first search] was ever discussed with the defendant at or after his arrest, or that he was informed of the State's intent to enter and search his home [a second time] on the strength of a continuing consent. We conclude, therefore, that consent of the defendant had ended by [the time of the second search], and accordingly the officers were not protected thereby on the successful [second] search. . . . 237 A.2d 421.

Therefore, if a significant period of time passes after consent to search is given, a new consent should be obtained before continuing to search, especially if intervening events suggest that a second consent might not be given so readily as the original consent. If the suspect does not renew his or her consent, a search warrant should be obtained.

Object of Search

If the consenting person places no limit on the scope of a search, the scope is "generally defined by its expressed object." *Florida v. Jimeno*, 500 U.S. 248, 251 (1991). Therefore, a search may be as broad as the officer's previously acquired knowledge about the crimes likely to have been committed and the items of evidence likely to be discovered. *United States v. Sealey*, 630 F. Supp. 801 (E.D. Cal. 1986).

The U.S. Supreme Court's opinion in *Jimeno*, discussed earlier, provides an example of how the stated object, or purpose, of a search can determine that search's scope. In *Jimeno*, a police officer was following the defendant's car after overhearing the defendant arranging what appeared to be a drug transaction. The officer stopped the defendant's car for a traffic infraction and declared that he had reason to believe that the defendant was carrying narcotics in the car. The officer asked permission to search the car for drugs, and received the defendant's consent. During the search, the officer found cocaine inside a folded paper bag on the car's floorboard.

The Court held that a criminal suspect's Fourth Amendment right to be free from unreasonable searches is not violated when, after he gives a police officer consent to search his automobile, the officer opens a closed container found within the car that might reasonably hold the object of the search. In other words, the Court believed that in light of the stated object of the consent search—a search for drugs—the officer was permitted to look for drugs in a paper bag since this bag could contain drugs. On the other hand, if the stated object of the automobile search had been a person or another object of equal size, the Court would likely have held that the search of the bag was unconstitutional.

United States v. Rodney, 956 F.2d 295 (D.C. Cir. 1992), held that a request to conduct a body search for drugs reasonably includes a request to conduct some search of the crotch area. The court noted that drug dealers frequently hide drugs near their genitals.

Note that the "objective reasonableness" standard depends on the facts of each case. A general consent to search a particular area of a vehicle does not necessarily allow the search of all containers in that area of the vehicle. For example, consent to search the trunk of a car may not include authorization to pry open a locked briefcase found inside the trunk. As the Court noted in *Jimeno*, "[i]t is very likely unreasonable to think that a suspect, by consenting to the search of his trunk, has agreed to the breaking open of a *locked* briefcase within the trunk, but it is otherwise with respect to a closed paper bag." 500 U.S. at 251–52 (emphasis added).

Lower courts, however, have permitted searches of locked containers within vehicles when the defendant provides consent to both a complete search of his vehicle and to the seizure of any property contained within it. For example, in *United States v. Reeves*, 6 F.3d 660, 662 (9th Cir. 1993), the defendant signed a consent form allowing police to "'conduct a complete search' of the car," and seize papers and other items contained within it. On these facts, the court found that a search of a locked briefcase in the hatchback area of the car and the removal of contraband from that briefcase was within the scope of defendant's consent.

Of course, the consenting person may specifically limit the scope of a consent search to a search for a particular object. In *People v. Superior Court (Arketa)*, 89 Cal. Rptr. 316 (Cal. App. 1970), a person gave officers consent to search his house for a crime suspect. The officers instead conducted a thorough search of the house and its closets for a crowbar without advising the person that they wanted to look for a crowbar. The court invalidated the search because it went beyond the scope of the consent granted. Also, in *United States v. Turner*, 169 F.3d 84, 87–89 (1999), the police, prior to obtaining defendant's consent, explained that they wanted to search places in his home that might contain physical evidence left by an intruder who had committed a recent assault. Under these circumstances, the court found that the police officers' search of defendant's computer files fell outside the scope of his consent. The court explained that "it obviously would have been impossible to abandon physical evidence [such as a knife or clothing] in a personal computer hard drive, and bizarre to suppose . . . that the suspected intruder stopped to enter incriminating evidence into the Turner computer." 169 F.3d at 88. Similarly, in *People v. Rice*, 66 Cal. Rptr. 246, 249 (Cal. App. 1968), where defendant consented to a search of his body for weapons, the court found that the seizure of marijuana from a plastic bottle in defendant's pocket was illegal as beyond the scope of the consent granted.

In sum, law enforcement officers should confine their search to only those areas where the object for which they have consent to search could possibly be located, taking into consideration the size, shape, and character of the object.

Revocation of Consent

The person giving consent to search may revoke or withdraw that consent at any time after the search has begun. In *State v. Lewis*, 611 A.2d 69 (Me.1992), after arresting the defendant for drunk driving and releasing him on personal recognizance, a state trooper offered to drive the defendant to a nearby motel. When the defendant retrieved a carry-on bag from his car, the trooper asked for and received permission to check the bag for guns. The trooper immediately observed two large brown bags inside the carry-on bag, smelled marijuana, and asked permission to examine the bags. The defendant refused and attempted to return the carry-on bag to his car. The trooper intervened and searched the brown bags, finding marijuana. The court found that the defendant had revoked his consent to search the carry-on bag before the trooper opened the brown bags.

> Even though defendant consented to the trooper's looking inside his carry-on bag, he at no time consented to the trooper's looking into the brown bags contained therein. Rather, by expressly terminating his consent when the trooper requested to open the brown bags and by seeking to return them to his car, defendant most certainly manifested a subjective expectation of privacy with respect to those inside bags. Because those bags were always closed and their contents shielded from the trooper's view, society would regard defendant's expectation of privacy in them to be reasonable. 611 A.2d at 70.

Similarly, in *United States v. Bily*, 406 F. Supp. 726 (E.D. Pa. 1975), the defendant consented to a search of his house for pornographic films. After an investigation of approximately two hours, during which certain films were discovered, the defendant stated, "That's enough, I want you to stop." The court held that this was a revocation of consent that took immediate effect. Only the seizures of films that took place before the revocation were held valid.

Likewise, *United States v. Ibarra*, 731 F. Supp. 1037 (D. Wyo. 1990), held that a motorist's closing and locking the trunk of his car after a police officer's consensual search of the trunk constituted a revocation of that consent and barred any further search. However, if the motorist, after revoking her consent by closing the trunk, reopens it, a court may find that this motorist has voluntarily renewed her consent. *See United States v. Flores*, 48 F.3d 467, 468–69 (10th Cir. 1995) (absence of threats and other coercive actions by officer significant for finding that renewed consent was voluntary).

For a revocation of consent to be valid, the suspect must clearly communicate that he or she is revoking consent. Ambiguous revocations may be held to be insufficient to have accomplished the intended revocation. For example, if a suspect merely complains about the length of the search, this fact alone may not constitute revocation of that suspect's consent. *See United States v. Brown*, 345 F.3d 574, 580–81 (8th Cir. 2003). Similarly, in *United States v. West*, 321 F.3d 649 (7th Cir. 2003), after the driver of an automobile provided a blanket consent to officers to search a car, the defendant, a passenger in the car, claimed ownership of a particular duffel bag located within the car. The police subsequently found cocaine in the bag. The court held that defendant's claim of ownership, without more, did not revoke the driver's consent to search the car, including the duffel bag:

> To say he owned [the duffel bag] and not couple that statement with a revocation of the driver's consent could well be thought an affirmation that the officers had his consent to search it. In any event the officer was not unreasonable in failing to interpret [the passenger's] response as a denial of consent to search the bag. . . . 321 F.3d at 652.

United States v. West also stands for the principle that revocation of consent will not be inferred from mere silence:

> [T]he question on which the lawfulness of the seizure of the cocaine turns . . . is whether [the passenger] revoked the driver's consent to search the entire car, necessarily including the bag. By his silence in the face of her consent he forfeited any right to claim that her consent was ineffective to authorize the search because the bag was his. His silence was confirmation or ratification of her authority to consent. 321 F.3d at 651–52.

key points

- An invitation to enter premises is not the equivalent of consent to search the premises. Also, a person found to have provided valid consent to one search has not necessarily provided valid consent for additional searches.
- The scope of a consent search depends on what the typical reasonable person would have understood by the exchange between the officer and the suspect.
- A person giving consent to search may place a time limitation on the search. Also, a court may infer a time limitation on the person's consent if the role or status of the person changes significantly (e.g., from that of concerned spouse to that of murder suspect).
- If the consenting person places no limit on the scope of a consent search, the scope is generally defined by its expressed object.
- The person giving consent to search may revoke or withdraw that consent at any time after the search has begun, although such revocations of consent should be clear and unambiguous.

►WHO MAY GIVE CONSENT?

In general, the only person able to give a valid consent to a search is the person whose constitutional protection against unreasonable searches and seizures would be invaded by the search if it were conducted without consent. This means, for example, that when the search of a person's body or clothing is contemplated, only that person can consent to the search. The same rule applies to searches of property, except that when several people have varying degrees of interest in the same property, more than one person may be qualified to give consent to search.

Third-Party Consent under Actual or Apparent Authority

In certain situations, the law recognizes the authority of third persons to consent to a search of property even though they are not the persons against whose interests the search is being conducted. *United States v. Matlock*, 415 U.S. 164 (1974), stated the test for determining whether a third person can consent to a search of premises or effects:

> [W]hen the prosecution seeks to justify a warrantless search by proof of voluntary consent, it is not limited to proof that consent was given by the defendant, but may show that permission to search was obtained from a third party who possessed *common authority over or other sufficient relationship to the premises or effects sought to be inspected.* 415 U.S. at 171 (emphasis added).

Actual Common Authority In a footnote of the *Matlock* decision, the Supreme Court defined what it meant when it used the term **common authority**:

> Common authority is, of course, not to be implied from the mere interest a third party has in the property. The authority which justifies the third-party consent does not rest upon the law of property, with its attendant historical and legal refinements, . . . but rests rather on mutual use of the property by persons generally having joint access or control for most purposes, so that it is reasonable to recognize that any of the co-inhabitants has the right to permit the inspection in his own right and that the others have assumed the risk that one of their number might permit the common area to be searched. 415 U.S. at 171 n.7.

From this, we discern that someone with **actual authority** over property has the legal capacity to grant consent to search the property over which they have access or control.

Apparent Common Authority In addition to a third party having actual authority to consent to a search of another person's property or effects, a third party may also have **apparent authority** to do so. For example, a warrantless entry and search is valid when based on the consent of a third party whom the police, at the time of the entry, reasonably believe to possess common authority over the premises but who in fact does not have such authority. This does not suggest that law enforcement officers may always accept a person's invitation to enter premises:

> Even when the invitation is accompanied by an explicit assertion that the person lives there, the surrounding circumstances could conceivably be such that a reasonable person would doubt its truth and not act upon it without further inquiry. As with other factual determinations bearing upon search and seizure, determination of consent to enter must "be judged against an objective standard: would the facts available to the officer at the moment . . . 'warrant a man of reasonable caution in the belief'" that the consenting party had authority over the premises? . . . If not, then warrantless entry without further inquiry is unlawful unless authority actually exists. But if so, the search is valid. *Illinois v. Rodriguez*, 497 U.S. 177, 188–89 (1990).

Rodriguez has been construed as "appli[cable] to situations in which an officer would have had valid consent to search if the facts were as he reasonably believed them to be." *United States v. Whitfield*, 939 F.2d 1071, 1074 (D.C. Cir. 1991). *Rodriguez* would not validate, however, a search based on an erroneous view of the law. For example, an officer's erroneous belief that landlords are generally authorized to consent to a search of a tenant's premises could not provide the authorization necessary for a warrantless search.

Proving Actual or Apparent Common Authority The prosecution has the burden of showing that someone consented and that the person had actual or apparent authority to do so. Therefore, law enforcement officers must provide sufficient evidence of both consent and authority to the prosecuting attorney for presentation in court. Mutual, or common, authority involving third parties generally comes from spouses and persons involved in similar partnerships, but also occurs in roommate, parent-child, employee-employer, and other relationships. The law enforcement officer should ask reasonable questions designed to show a relationship of such common authority that either party has the right to consent to the shared real or personal property. And, of course, the answers received must reasonably show such a relationship. Reasonableness, not perfection, is the standard on which the officer's behavior is measured. Officers are not required to be correct in their deductions concerning one's authority to consent, but they must act in good faith and reasonably, based on training and experience.

Note that a person with common authority may consent to a search only in the absence of other persons with equal or superior authority. In *State v. Leach*, 782 P.2d 1035 (Wash. 1989), a co-owner of a travel agency consented to a search of the agency office. The defendant, the other owner of the agency with a superior interest, was arrested at the office and was present during the search, but his consent was not sought. The court invalidated the search:

> Where the police have obtained consent to search from an individual possessing, at best, equal control over the premises, that consent remains valid against a cohabitant, who also possesses equal control, only while the cohabitant is absent. However, should the cohabitant be present and able to object, the police must also obtain the cohabitant's consent. Any other rule exalts expediency over an individual's Fourth Amendment guarantees. Accordingly, we refuse to beat a path to the door of exceptions. 782 P.2d at 1040.

Questions of who may give valid consent are often confusing and complicated, and courts carefully scrutinize any waiver of a person's constitutional rights. The remainder of this chapter examines examples of consent search situations in which the person giving the consent is not the person against whose interests the search is being conducted. Therefore, in each of these examples, the central question is whether the person providing consent has common authority, whether actual or apparent, over the searched premises or effects such that the person is capable of providing valid consent.

Specific Types of Third-Party Consent

Since the U.S. Supreme Court's 1967 decision in *Katz v. United States*, 389 U.S. 347 (1967), courts pay particular attention to a person's reasonable expectation of privacy as a major factor in determining whether a third party has authority to consent to search of another's property. If a person has a reasonable expectation of privacy in a place, a third party may not be able to consent to a search of that place.

For example, in *State v. Fitzgerald*, 530 P.2d 553 (Or. App. 1974), the court relied on a defendant's reasonable expectation of privacy to invalidate the search of a bedroom in a private residence that the defendant occupied under a rental agreement. A father and his two daughters leased and occupied the residence along with the defendant. The defendant was the only occupant of a private room under an agreement with the father. One of the daughters gave consent to search the defendant's room, where incriminating evidence was found. The court held that the daughter could not consent to a search of the defendant's room. The defendant had a reasonable expectation of privacy in the room because he rented it, was its sole occupant, and had never given anyone permission to enter it.

With *Katz* in mind, the following sections are devoted to explaining how courts have balanced people's reasonable expectations of privacy against the actual or apparent authority of third parties in common types of relationships.

Persons Having Equal Rights or Interests in Property It is well settled that, when two or more persons have substantially equal rights of ownership, occupancy, or other possessory interest in property to be searched or seized, any one of the persons may legally authorize a search and any evidence found may be used against any of the other persons. For example, the court in *United States v. Kelley*, 953 F.2d 562 (9th Cir. 1992), found authority to consent to a search of the defendant's bedroom and closet under the following circumstances: the person giving consent had rented the apartment together with the defendant and had signed the lease; she described herself as the defendant's roommate; and she had joint access not only to the common areas of the apartment but also to the defendant's separate bedroom, where the apartment telephone was located.

In determining whether a person is a joint occupant of premises, courts consider a number of factors: whether the person paid rent; how long the person stayed; whether the person left belongings on the premises; whether the person possessed a key; and whether there was any written or oral agreement among other parties as to the person's right to use and occupy the premises. *Illinois v. Rodriguez*, 497 U.S. 177 (1990), held that the defendant's former co-tenant did not have actual authority to grant police consent to enter the defendant's premises without a warrant, even though she had some furniture and household effects in the premises and sometimes spent the night at the premises after moving out a month before the search at issue. Her name was not on the lease; she did not contribute to the rent; she was not allowed to invite others to the apartment on her own; she never went to the premises when the defendant was not at home; she had moved her clothing and that of her children from the premises; and she had taken a key to the premises without the defendant's knowledge. These facts convinced the Court that the former co-tenant did not possess *actual* authority to consent to the search of defendant's apartment, though the Court did remand the case to the lower court to determine if the co-tenant had *apparent* authority to consent (e.g., whether the officers could have reasonably believed the former co-tenant had authority to consent).

However, in *United States v. Matlock*, 415 U.S. 164, 175–76 (1975), discussed above, when the person providing consent to search a room slept there regularly with defendant and stored her clothing there, the Court found that this person had actual authority to consent to a search of that room, including containers within that room.

Consent to search given by a person with common authority over the premises is not invalidated because that person gave consent with the expectation of receiving a reward. In *Bertolotti v. State*, 476 So.2d 130 (Fla. 1985), a woman who knew of the possibility of a reward through a crime watch program consented to a search of an apartment she shared with the defendant. The court said:

> A community-wide, regularly advertised program which rewards any citizen who provides information useful to the police in their criminal investigations is not tantamount to recruiting police agents; the state should not be penalized in the use of information so obtained. Mrs. Griest's consent to the search was not vitiated by the possibility of financial reward. 476 So.2d at 132.

In *Frazier v. Cupp*, 394 U.S. 731 (1969), involving equal rights to *personal effects*, the defendant, at his murder trial, objected to the introduction into evidence of clothing seized from his duffel bag. At the time of the seizure, the duffel bag was being used jointly by the defendant and his cousin and had been left in the cousin's home. When police arrested the cousin, they asked him whether they could have his clothing. The cousin directed them to the duffel bag, and both the cousin and his mother consented to its search. During the search, the officers came upon the defendant's clothing in the bag and seized it as well. The Court upheld the legality of the search over the defendant's objections:

> **Since Rawls (the cousin) was a joint user of the bag, he clearly had authority to consent to its search. The officers therefore found evidence against [defendant] while in the course of an otherwise lawful search . . . . [Defendant] argues that Rawls only had actual permission to use one compartment of the bag and that he had no authority to consent to a search of the other compartments. We will not, however, engage in such metaphysical subtleties in judging the efficacy of Rawls' consent. [Defendant], in allowing Rawls to use the bag and in leaving it in his house, must be taken to have assumed the risk that Rawls would allow someone else to look inside. We find no valid search and seizure claim in this case.** 394 U.S. at 740.

A third party who has common authority to use premises may give consent to a search of the premises even if not actually using the premises at the time of the search. In *United States v. Cook*, 530 F.2d 145 (7th Cir. 1976), the defendant's landlady consented to a search of a poultry house on her property. The poultry house consisted of a large room in which the landlady had segregated an area with wire fence for her exclusive use. She gave the defendant permission to use the remaining space, but she retained the right to use the space if necessary.

The defendant claimed that because neither the landlady nor her family *actually* used the defendant's area, there was no common authority. The court upheld the search, however, ruling that the defendant had assumed the risk that the landlady would permit others to inspect the premises, including his shared area of the room.

A third party cannot consent to a search of more than that over which he or she has common authority. *United States v. Gilley*, 608 F. Supp. 1065 (S.D. Ga. 1985), held that a consent to search a home given by the home's occupant did not authorize a search of a guest's travel bag found in the living room. The guest had done nothing to diminish his natural expectation of privacy in the contents of the bag. The host lacked common authority over the bag, as she had not been authorized to open or use the bag, and had not in fact opened the bag.

United States v. Jaras, 86 F.3d 383, 389–90 (5th Cir. 1996) also stands for the principle that a third party cannot consent to a search of more than that over which he or she has common authority. In *Jaras*, the court found that the driver of an automobile lacked authority to consent to a search of a passenger's suitcases located in the trunk of the car. The court noted that there was no evidence that the driver had joint access or control over the suitcases to support a claim of actual authority. Also, the court explained that the officer could not have a reasonable belief that the suitcases belonged to the driver since the driver clearly explained to the officer that they were not his suitcases but rather belonged to the passenger. As a result, the driver also lacked apparent authority over the suitcases.

Landlords and Tenants A landlord has *no implied actual or apparent authority* to consent to a search of a tenant's premises or a seizure of the tenant's property during the period of the tenancy, even though the landlord has the authority to enter the tenant's premises for the limited purposes of inspection, performance of repairs, or housekeeping services. *Chapman v. United States*, 365 U.S. 610 (1961). Once the tenant has abandoned the premises or the tenancy has otherwise terminated, however, and the landlord has regained the primary right to occupation and control, the landlord may consent to a search of the premises, even though the former tenant left personal belongings on the premises. *United States v. Sledge*, 650 F.2d 1075, 1077–78 (9th Cir. 1981). Furthermore, because a landlord clearly has joint authority over, and access to, common areas of an apartment building, a landlord may give valid consent to search those areas. *United States v. Kelly*, 551 F.2d 760 (8th Cir. 1977); *see also United States v. Elliott*, 50 F.3d 180, 187 (1995).

Hotel Management and Guests The U.S. Supreme Court held that the principles governing a landlord's consent to a search of tenant's premises apply to consent searches of hotel rooms allowed by hotel managers. In *Stoner v. California*, 376 U.S. 483 (1964), police investigating a robbery went to the defendant's hotel and, in his absence, obtained permission from the hotel clerk to search his room. The police found items of evidence in the room incriminating the defendant in the robbery. The Court held that the search was illegal and that the items seized were inadmissible. The defendant's constitutional right was at stake here—not the clerk's or the hotel's right. Therefore, only the defendant, either directly or through an agent, could waive that right. The police had no basis whatsoever to believe that the defendant authorized the night clerk to permit the police to search his room:

> It is true . . . that when a person engages a hotel room he undoubtedly gives "implied or express permission" to "such persons as maids, janitors, or repairmen" to enter his room "in the performance of their duties." . . . But the conduct of the night clerk and the police in the present case was of an entirely different order. . . . No less than a tenant of a house, or the occupant of a room in a boarding house . . . a guest in a hotel room is entitled to constitutional protection against unreasonable searches and seizures. . . . That protection would disappear if it were left to depend upon the unfettered discretion of an employee of the hotel. 376 U.S. at 489–90.

Moreover, the concept of "hotel guest' has been given a broad interpretation by courts. For example, in *United States v. Kimoana*, 383 F.3d 1215 (10th Cir. 2004), the court found that although the defendant had not registered or paid for the hotel room, he could still validly consent to a search of that room since "he had stayed there overnight, left his possessions there, and carried a key to the room." According to the court, these facts "support a finding that Defendant had joint access or control over the room, and thus had actual authority to consent." 383 F.3d at 1222; see also *United States v. Rodriguez*, 414 F.3d 837, 844 (8th Cir. 2005) (person who had neither paid for nor registered for motel room could validly consent to search of room since she "was the only person who lived there").

When the term of a hotel guest's occupancy of a room expires, however, the guest loses the exclusive right to privacy in the room, whether or not the guest remains in the room. The hotel manager then has the right to enter the room and may consent to a search of the room and a seizure of items found in the room. *United States v. Larson*, 760 F.2d 852 (8th Cir. 1985).

Hosts and Guests In general, the owner or primary occupant of the premises (the host) may validly consent to a search of the premises, and any evidence found is admissible against a guest on the premises. In *United States v. Hall*, 979 F.2d 77 (6th Cir. 1992), the owner of a residence gave consent to search the room of the defendant, whom he had allowed to stay at his residence in exchange for farm work. The court held that the owner had authority to consent to the search when he owned all the furniture in the room, he had personal items stored in an adjacent room accessed through the defendant's room, the room was never locked, and there was no agreement between him and the defendant that he was not to go in the room.

If, however, the person against whom a search is directed is a long-term guest and has a section of the premises set aside for exclusive personal use, the host may not consent to a search of that area of the premises. *Reeves v. Warden*, 346 F.2d 915 (4th Cir. 1965). The host's authority to consent to a search of the guest's area of the premises depends on the length of time of the guest's stay, the exclusiveness of the guest's control of a particular area of the premises, and the guest's reasonable expectation of privacy in that area of the premises.

Also, a host may not consent to a search of an item that is obviously the exclusive personal property of the guest. *State v. Edwards*, 570 A.2d 193 (Conn. 1990), held that although a lessee of an apartment could consent to a search of her apartment, she could not consent to a search of a guest's backpack.

Employers and Employees This section will first discuss an employer's ability to consent to a search of certain parts of the employer's premises. Next, it will explore an employee's ability to consent to a search of his or her employer's premises.

Employer's Ability to Consent In general, an employer may consent to a search of any part of the employer's premises over which the employer has exclusive or joint authority and control. *State v. Robinson*, 206 A.2d 779 (N.J. Super. 1965), held that an employer could validly consent to the search of an employee's locker in the employer's plant. The employer owned the premises; further, under the terms of a contract between the employer and the employee's union, the employer retained a master key to all employee lockers. Likewise, *United States v. Carter*, 569 F.2d 801 (4th Cir. 1977), validated an employer's consent to search a company vehicle in an employee's temporary custody. The employer not only owned the vehicle but also could tell the employee what and what not to do with it and could designate any other use of it.

An employer may not, however, validly consent to search an area set aside for use by an employee and within the employee's exclusive control. *United States v. Blok*, 188 F.2d 1019 (D.C. Cir. 1951), held that an employee's boss could not validly consent to a search of a desk assigned for the employee's exclusive use:

> In the absence of a valid regulation to the contrary, [the employee] was entitled to, and did keep private property of a personal sort in her desk. Her superiors could not reasonably search the desk for her purse, her personal letters, or anything else that did not belong to the [employer] and had no connection with the work of the office. Their consent did not make such a search by the police reasonable. 188 F.2d at 1021.

Employee's Ability to Consent An employee's ability to consent validly to a search of the employer's premises depends on the scope of the employee's authority. The average employee, such as a clerk, janitor, maintenance person, driver, or other person temporarily in charge, may not give such consent. *United States v. Block*, 202 F. Supp. 705 (S.D.N.Y. 1962).

If, however, the employee is a manager or other person of considerable authority who is left in complete charge for a substantial period of time, the employee may validly consent to a search of the employer's premises. *See United States v. Antonelli Fireworks Co.*, 155 F.2d 631 (2d Cir. 1946). Under this standard, typical babysitters have insufficient authority over the premises of their employers to give a valid consent to search the premises. *People v. Litwin*, 355 N.Y.S.2d 646 (N.Y. App. Div. 1974). And though "live-in" babysitters who reside in the home to care for special-needs children may be able to validly consent to a search of common areas of the home, they generally cannot consent to a search of the homeowner's bedroom. This was the holding of *United States v. Dearing*, 9 F.3d 1428 (9th Cir. 1993), where the babysitter had a room in the home and lived there for approximately six months. The court in *Dearing* found that the "live-in" babysitter could not consent to a search for a machine gun in the homeowner's bedroom since the babysitter did not have "mutual use and joint access or control for most purposes" over the bedroom. 9 F.3d at 1430. A reasonable officer should have known that the babysitter lacked this kind of use and access or control over the bedroom.

School Officials and Students A police search of a high school student's locker, based on consent given by a school official, is valid because of the relationship between school authorities and students. The school authorities have an obligation to maintain discipline over students, and usually they retain partial access to the students' lockers so that neither has an exclusive right to use and possession of the lockers. In a case in which police opened the locker of a student suspected of burglary with the consent of school authorities and found incriminating evidence, the court said:

> Although a student may have control of his school locker as against fellow students, his possession is not exclusive against the school and its officials. A school does not supply its students with lockers for illicit use in harboring pilfered property or harmful substances. We deem it a proper function of school authorities to inspect the lockers under their control and to prevent their use in illicit ways or for illegal purposes. We believe this right of inspection is inherent in the authority vested in school administrators and that the same must be retained and exercised in the management of our schools if their educational functions are to be maintained and the welfare of the student bodies preserved. *State v. Stein*, 456 P.2d 1, 3 (Kan. 1969).

Though not squarely a consent to search case, *Zamora v. Pomeroy*, 639 F.2d 662, 670 (1981), held that high school officials have a right to inspect student lockers, and relied explicitly on language from the consent to search context when it said that "[i]nasmuch as the school had assumed joint control of the locker[,] it cannot be successfully maintained that the school did not have a right to inspect it." *Zamora* found no Fourth Amendment violation when school officials permitted police to enter a school to conduct searches of lockers using drug-sniffing dogs. 639 F.2d at 670. (Acknowledging in dicta that school officials may consent to a locker inspection by law enforcement officers.)

However, consent searches of college dormitory rooms are treated similarly to searches of hotel rooms. In *Commonwealth v. McCloskey*, 272 A.2d 271 (Pa. Super. 1970), police, with the consent of the dean, searched the defendant's room at a university and found marijuana. The evidence was held inadmissible in court:

> A dormitory room is analogous to an apartment or a hotel room. It certainly offers its occupant a more reasonable expectation of freedom from governmental intrusion than does a public telephone booth. The defendant rented the dormitory room for a certain period of time, agreeing to abide by the rules established by his lessor, the University. As in most rental situations, the lessor, Bucknell University, reserved the right to check the room for damages, wear, and unauthorized appliances. Such right of the lessor does not mean [defendant] was not entitled to have a "reasonable expectation of freedom from governmental intrusion," or that he gave consent to the police search, or gave the University authority to consent to such search. 272 A.2d at 273.

Principals and Agents A person clearly may give someone else authority to consent to a search of the person's property. The person giving the authority is called the **principal**; the person acting for the principal is called an **agent**. For example, an attorney may consent to a search of a client's premises if the attorney has been specifically authorized to do so by the client. *Brown v. State*, 404 P.2d 428 (Nev. 1965), upheld a search of the defendant's premises and a seizure of his farm animals because consent to search had been given by the defendant's attorney after consultation with the defendant. Without a specific authorization to consent to search, however, the mere existence of an attorney–client relationship gives an attorney no authority to waive a client's personal rights.

Another case involving a principal–agent relationship is *State v. Kellam*, 269 S.E.2d 197 (N.C. App. 1980). In *Kellam*, homeowners gave their next-door neighbor the key to their house with instructions to "look after their house" while the owners were away. The court held that the neighbor's consent to search the house was valid. And in *United States v. Novello*, 519 F.2d 1078 (5th Cir. 1975), the defendant (the "principal") rented an enclosed storage area that was accessible only to the rental agent and to those working with the agent. The defendant stored his truck containing marijuana in the area. Acting on an informant's tip, law enforcement officers obtained consent to enter the enclosed area from one of the persons having access and discovered marijuana in the truck. The court held that the defendant had no reasonable expectation of privacy in the storage area and upheld the search. "One who knows that others have of right general and untrammeled access to an area, a right as extensive as his own, can scarcely have much expectation of secrecy in it or confidence about whom they may let inspect it." 519 F.2d at 1080.

A principal has the power to limit the authority of his or her agent with respect to the principal's property; for example, an employer could limit an employee's authority to show business records to certain persons and not to others. A principal may not, however, limit an agent's authority for the purpose of obstructing justice. Therefore, in a case in which a doctor told his employee to take business records and hide them from the authorities, the court said that "when an employer gives an employee access to documents intentionally and knowingly in order to obstruct justice, that employee is a custodian of those records for the purposes of a valid subpoena or seizure." *United States v. Miller*, 800 F.2d 129, 135 (7th Cir. 1986).

Spouses "Where two persons, such as a husband and wife, have equal rights to the use and occupation of certain premises, either may give consent to a search, and the evidence thus disclosed can be used against either." *United States v. Ocampo*, 492 F. Supp. 1211, 1236 (E.D.N.Y. 1980). In *Roberts v. United States*, 332 F.2d 892 (8th Cir. 1964), officers questioned the defendant's wife as part of a murder investigation. The wife volunteered information that the defendant had fired a pistol into the ceiling of their home some time ago. She later validly consented to a search for and seizure of the bullet in the ceiling. The court sustained the search on the basis that the consent was voluntary, the place of the search was the home of the defendant's wife, and the premises were under the wife's immediate and complete control at the time of the search. Furthermore, the bullet could not be considered a personal effect of the husband, for which the wife would have no authority to consent to search. "It is not a question of agency, for a wife should not be held to have authority to waive her husband's constitutional rights. This is a question of the wife's own rights to authorize entry into premises where she lives and of which she had control." 332 F.2d at 896–97.

Some courts have even allowed estranged spouses to consent to the search of marital premises they have vacated. *United States v. Long*, 524 F.2d 660 (9th Cir. 1975), held that an estranged wife, as a joint owner of a house she had vacated, could give consent to search the house even though her husband (the temporarily absent current occupant) had changed the locks on the doors. And in another estranged husband and wife case, the court found that the wife had common authority to consent to the search of the marital home even though the wife had moved out one week prior to the search. *See United States v. Shelton*,

337 F.3d 529 (5th Cir. 2003). In *Shelton,* the husband and wife had been married for six years; they lived in the marital home for at least these six years; neither husband nor wife attempted to file for divorce; the wife maintained a key to the house; and after moving out of the home, the wife visited frequently without the husband present. The court explained its holding that the wife had common authority to consent in this way:

> [The husband's] decision to solicit [the wife's] assistance in the [illegal] bingo operation, and at the same time to perpetuate her essentially unrestricted access to the house, on par with the access that she had enjoyed while residing there as his spouse, is what vested [the wife] with common authority to consent to a search. 337 F.3d at 534.

Also, and quite appropriately, a wife does not lose the ability to consent to the search of the marital home even though an abusive husband has forced her away from the home. This was the holding of *United States v. Backus,* 349 F.3d 1298 (11th Cir. 2003), where the wife had lived in the marital house she owned jointly with her husband for five years before leaving as a result of the abuse. Though the wife remained away from the house continuously for six months and the husband changed the locks in her absence, the Court held that the wife could validly consent to the search of the home for contraband:

> Where a wife is driven by an abusive husband from the home she jointly owns and jointly occupied, the duration of her absence is likely to be influenced by the nature and extent of her fear. The greater the fear, the longer the absence. We are not willing to extend to violently abusive husbands something akin to a rule of repose against the authority of their wives to consent to a search of jointly owned property. To do so would reward unlawful behavior in direct proportion to the amount of terror it inflicts. One month or six, [the wife] still had enough [common authority over the home to consent to a search of it.] 349 F.3d at 1305.

Parents and Children This section will first discuss a parent's ability to consent to a search of premises owned by the parent. Following this discussion, the section will explore a child's ability to consent to a search of family premises.

Parental Consent to Search A parent's consent to search premises owned by the parent will usually be effective against a child who lives on those premises:

> Hardy's father gave his permission to the officers to enter and search the house and the premises which he owned and in which his son lived with him. Under the circumstances presented here the voluntary consent of Hardy's father to search his own premises is binding on Hardy and precludes his claim of violation of constitutional rights. *Commonwealth v. Hardy,* 223 A.2d 719, 723 (Pa. 1966).

Likewise, in *United States v. Rith,* 164 F.3d 1323, 1331 (10th Cir. 1999), the consent given by parents to police to search their son's bedroom for weapons, was considered valid because the parents maintained control over the home as owners:

> There is no evidence to rebut this presumption [of control over the home by the parents]: no lock on [the son's] bedroom door; no agreement with [the]

parents that they not enter [the son's] room without his consent; no payment of rent. Because the presumption of control is unrebutted, [the] parents had authority to consent to the search of [their son's] bedroom.

As suggested by the court in *Rith,* however, a parent may not consent to a search of an area of the parent's home occupied by the child if the child pays rent, uses the room exclusively, has sectioned it off by using locks or in some other way, has furnished it with his or her own furniture, or otherwise establishes an expectation of privacy. *See also State v. Peterson*, 525 S.W.2d 599 (Mo. App. 1975).

Furthermore, parents may not consent to a search of a child's room in their home if the child has already refused to grant such consent. "Constitutional rights may not be defeated by the expedient of soliciting several persons successively until the sought-after consent is obtained." *People v. Mortimer*, 361 N.Y.S.2d 955, 958 (N.Y. 1974).

Child's Consent to Search The Supreme Court of Georgia identified certain factors to be considered in determining whether a minor's consent to search family premises is valid:

> [W]hether the minor lived on the premises; whether the minor had a right of access to the premises and the right to invite others thereto; whether the minor was of an age at which he or she could be expected to exercise at least minimal discretion; and whether officers acted reasonably in believing that the minor had sufficient control over the premises to give a valid consent to search. *Davis v. State*, 422 S.E.2d 546, 549 (Ga. 1992).

United States v. Clutter, 914 F.2d 775, 778 (6th Cir. 1990), helps to illustrate how these factors are applied in practice. In *Clutter*, two children, one twelve years of age and the other fourteen years of age, consented to the search of their parents' home. The court found this consent valid given the amount of access and control the children exercised over the premises:

> Under the circumstances of this case, where children twelve and fourteen years of age routinely were left in exclusive control of the house, and defendants' possession of large quantities of marijuana was so open and patently non-exclusive that its odor pervaded the house, the government satisfied its burden of demonstrating the initial warrantless search of the bedroom was by consent, since the boys enjoyed that degree of access and control over the house that afforded them the right to permit inspection of any room in the house, and defendants assumed that risk. 914 F.2d at 778.

Bailors and Bailees A **bailee** is a person in possession of someone else's personal property with the lawful permission of the rightful owner, also referred to as a **bailor**. Depending on the level of control a bailee has over the personal property of another person, the bailee may be able to give legal consent for a search of that property.

Bailee in Full Possession and Control of Personal Property A bailee of personal property may consent to a search of the property if the bailee has full possession and control. In *United States v. Eldridge*, 302 F.2d 463 (4th Cir. 1962), the defendant loaned his car to a friend for the friend's personal use. Police investigating a theft asked the friend for permission to search the trunk of the car. The friend opened the trunk, and the police found evidence incriminating the defendant. The court held that the search was legal and that the evidence found was admissible. The defendant gave his friend rightful possession and control over the automobile and he could do with it whatever was reasonable under the circumstances. The defendant reserved no exclusive right to the trunk when he gave his friend the key. The friend's opening of the trunk for the police was a resonable exercise of his control over the car for the period during which he was permitted to use it.

Likewise, in *United States v. Beshore*, 961 F.2d 1380, 1382–83 (8th Cir. 1992), the court found that defendant's girlfriend could provide valid consent to search defendant's car because the defendant had given his girlfriend permission to use the car and she had placed her own license plates on the car. The court reasoned that the defendant had "thus assumed the risk that [his girlfriend] would permit the vehicle to be searched."

Bailee with Mere Custody of Personal Property If a bailor gives a bailee only limited control over the bailor's property, such as for shipment, storage, or repair purposes, evidence found by law enforcement officers would not be admissible in court against the owner of the property. For example, in *United States v. Jacobsen*, 466 U.S. 109 (1984), the Court found that delivery package employees cannot consent to a search of packages they were moving within the company's warehouse. Also, an airline cannot validly consent to the search of a package that a person has wrapped, tied, and delivered to the airline solely for transportation purposes. *Corngold v. United States*, 367 F.2d 1 (9th Cir. 1966). Nor can the owner of a boat who agrees to store another person's property on his boat give a valid consent to police to search and seize the property. *Commonwealth v. Storck*, 275 A.2d 362 (Pa. 1971). In addition, *State v. Farrell*, 443 A.2d 438, 442 (R.I. 1982), held that "one who entrusts his automobile to another for the purposes of repair, or periodic inspection as required by law, does not confer the kind of mutual use or control which would empower that person to consent to a warrantless search and seizure."

United States v. Most, 876 F.2d 191 (D.C. Cir. 1989), held that a store clerk who was asked by the defendant to watch a package could not give valid consent to search the package. The court said, "We see no basis for holding that delivery people who move packages may not consent to a search, but that store clerks who watch packages may." 876 F.2d at 200 n.18.

key points

- In general, the only person able to give a valid consent to a search is the person whose constitutional interest against unreasonable searches and seizures would be invaded by the search if it were conducted without consent.
- If a person establishes a reasonable expectation of privacy in property, another person may not consent to a search of the property.

- A person may specifically authorize another to consent to a search of the person's property.
- Consent to search may be obtained from a third party whom the police, at the time of entry, reasonably believe to possess common authority over or other sufficient relationship to the premises or effects sought to be inspected.

Discussion
POINT

When May a Bailee Validly Consent to a Search of the Bailor's Property?

United States v. James, 353 F.3d 606 (8th Cir. 2003).

The defendant, Mr. James (the "bailor"), gave one Mr. Laschober (the "bailee") certain computer discs for safekeeping and storage. Before giving the discs to Laschober, James sealed the envelopes containing the discs and packaged the discs inside the envelope with tape. He also marked the discs themselves with the words "confidential" and "private."

By intercepting a letter James sent from prison while detained on another charge, law enforcement authorities learned of both the existence and location of these discs at the home of Laschober. These authorities then proceeded to the home of Mr. Laschober, and requested his permission to open the envelope believed to contain the discs. After receiving this permission, the authorities opened the envelopes and found the discs. They then obtained Laschober's consent to transport the discs to police headquarters where they could be read. The discs were found to contain child pornography.

James was subsequently charged with possession of child pornography. Before trial, James moved to suppress the discs, arguing that the authorities obtained the discs in violation of his Fourth Amendment rights. The district court denied this motion, and James was convicted. He then appealed his conviction.

The court considered whether James's action of handing over, or "bailing," the computer disks to Laschober meant that Laschober could validly consent under the Fourth Amendment to a search of those discs by authorities. The court began its analysis with the following statement:

> A review of our case law and the law of other circuits shows that although a bailee of a concealed item [like Mr. Laschober] may have potential physical access to the inner contents of the item (he can pick the lock; break the seal; open up the storage bin), this kind of access does not mean the bailee has actual authority to look at the contents of the items, or to consent to another's searching them. Put another way, [a bailor like Mr. James] does not cede dominion over an item to another just by putting him in possession. 353 F.3d at 614.

In explaining that Laschober lacked dominion, or common authority and control, over the computer disks even though he possessed them, the court pointed out that James had sealed the envelopes, packaged the discs in a secure fashion, and instructed Laschober to only store the discs (as opposed to actually use them). In addition, the court noted that James had a reasonable expectation of privacy in the discs because he marked them "private" and "confidential," and utilized a disc that could only be read by an advanced computer. Id. at 614-615. Furthermore, the court found that it was unreasonable for the authorities to believe that Laschober had authority to consent to a search of the computer discs. Since there was no valid consent for

When May a Bailee Validly Consent to a Search of the Bailor's Property? *(Continued)*

Fourth Amendment purposes and the authorities had no warrant to view the discs, the court excluded the discs from evidence and overturned James's conviction on child pornography charges. 353 F.3d at 615-17.

Do you agree with the court's finding that Laschober lacked common authority and control over the discs such that he could not consent to a search of those discs by law enforcement authorities? Does it make any sense to say that Laschober lacked "common authority and control" over the computer discs when he literally had them in his hands (i.e., possessed them)? If James really wanted to maintain an exclusive privacy interest in the discs, why does the law not require him to avoid handing over, or "bailing," the discs to another person? Finally, what kinds of questions might a law enforcement official ask to ensure that a bailee like Mr. Laschober can validly consent to a search?

Summary

A consent search occurs when a person allows a law enforcement officer to search his or her body, premises, or belongings. Consent searches are convenient for law enforcement officers, requiring no justification, such as probable cause or a warrant; but consent searches also present many opportunities for abuse. For this reason, courts exercise a strong presumption against consent searches and place a heavy burden on prosecutors to prove that they are voluntary.

Voluntariness depends on the totality of circumstances surrounding the giving of consent. Among the circumstances considered are:

▶ Force or threat of force by police
▶ Fraudulent or mistaken claim of police authority
▶ Misrepresentation or deception by police
▶ Arrest or detention of consenting person

▶ Consenting person's awareness of the right to refuse consent to search
▶ Police informing consenting person that she is free to go
▶ Consenting person's attitude about the likelihood of discovery of evidence
▶ Clearness and explicitness of consent
▶ Physical, mental, emotional, and educational status of consenting person

The Fourth Amendment does not require that a lawfully seized person be advised that he or she is free to go before the person's consent to search will be recognized as voluntary.

Consent to enter premises is not the equivalent of consent to search the premises. The standard for measuring the scope of a suspect's consent is that of "objective reasonableness": What would the typical reasonable person have understood by the exchange between the officer and the suspect? The scope of a consent search may be limited by area, by time, and by the object for which the search is allowed. If the consenting person places no limit on the scope of a search, the scope is generally defined by its expressed object. The person giving consent to search may revoke it at any time.

The constitutional right to refuse to consent to a search is a personal right of the individual against whom the search is directed. A person other than the person against whose interests the search is being conducted cannot effectively consent to a search of property unless (1) the person has been specifically authorized to do so; (2) the person possesses common authority over, or has other sufficient relationship to, the premises or effects sought to be inspected; or (3) police reasonably believe the person has sufficient authority to consent, even though the person in fact does not have such authority. If a person establishes an exclusive reasonable expectation of privacy in property, another person may not consent to a search of the property.

Key Terms

actual authority, 510	bailee, 520	common authority, 510	principal, 517
agent, 517	bailor, 520	consent search, 484	voluntariness, 486
apparent authority, 510			

Review and Discussion Questions

1. If a person is deprived of freedom of action in a significant way by a law enforcement officer, is it necessary for that person to be given warnings of the right to refuse consent before being asked for consent to search? Explain.

2. If a law enforcement officer asks a person for consent to search his or her home for stolen jewelry when the officer's real purpose is to look for marked money, is the consent voluntary?

3. Assume that law enforcement officers have obtained a valid consent to search an arrested defendant's automobile for drugs, and an intial search proves fruitless. Can the officers search the automobile again two hours later without obtaining a new consent to search? What about two days later? What about two weeks later? What changes in the defedant's status might render the intial consent no longer valid?

4. If, after giving consent to search, a person becomes nervous and revokes or limits the scope of the search, can this reaction be used by the officers as an indication of probable cause to obtain a search warrant? Can a person validly revoke or limit the scope of their initial consent to search?

5. Are third-party consents to search the defendant's premises valid in the following circumstances?

   a. A husband, out of anger at his wife, the defendant, invites the police into the house and points out evidence incriminating the wife.
   b. The defendant's girlfriend, who lives with him part-time, consents to a search of the defendant's apartment.
   c. A wife disobeys the instructions of her husband, the defendant, not to allow a search of their home. Does it matter whether the police know of the instructions? Does it matter whether the husband is present at the time of the search?

6. Is it proper for a law enforcement officer to deliberately avoid attempting to obtain consent to search from the defendant and instead attempt to obtain consent from someone with equal authority over the defendant's premises? Does it matter whether the law enforcement officer had an op-

portunity to attempt to obtain consent from the defendant and deliberately failed to take it? What if the defendant was deliberately avoiding the police?

7. The dissenting opinion in *Florida v. Jimeno* stated, "Because an individual's expectation of privacy in a container is distinct from, and far greater than, his expectation of privacy in the interior of his car, it follows that an individual's consent to a search of the interior of his car cannot necessarily be understood as extending to containers in the car." 500 U.S. at 254. Discuss.

8. Should a person be able to limit the number of officers conducting a consent search? Should a person be able to choose which officer or officers conduct the consent search? Should a person be allowed to follow around the officer conducting the search?

9. Can the following persons give a valid consent to search?

   a. A highly intoxicated person
   b. A five-year-old, a seven-year-old, or a ten-year-old child
   c. A mentally retarded or senile person
   d. An emotionally upset person
   e. An uneducated person

10. Can the driver of a motor vehicle consent to a search of the vehicle even though a passenger objects? Can the owner of a store consent to a search of the store even though an employee objects? Can a parent consent to a search of his or her home even though a child objects?

11. In *Florida v. Bostick*, 501 U.S. 429, 438 (1991), the defendant contended "that no reasonable person would freely consent to a search of luggage that he or she knows contains drugs." Should there be a presumption of involuntariness when incriminating evidence is readily found pursuant to the "consent" of a person who denies guilt?

12. Assume that consent to obtain a blood sample from a rape suspect is obtained by telling him that the sample will be tested to determine the percentage of alcohol in his blood. Is his consent voluntary if the blood sample is actually used to match his blood with fluids found at the rape scene? *See Graves v. Beto*, 424 F.2d 524 (5th Cir. 1970).

Applications of the Law in Real Cases

1 Shortly after midnight on April 28, 2002, North Dakota Highway Patrolman Jody Skogen received a report that an intoxicated driver was operating a motor vehicle in a remote area of North Dakota. While investigating the report, Skogen observed a vehicle proceeding east on Highway 52 near Harvey, North Dakota. The vehicle's tires were on the centerline.

When asked to step out of the vehicle and to produce identification, the driver complied. Based on the identification presented to him, Skogen determined Mancias to be the driver of the vehicle. After being informed he was stopped for erratic driving, Mancias attributed such driving to being sleepy. When asked about his intended destination, Mancias gave details that conflicted with Skogen's knowledge of the area. Skogen patted Mancias down and asked him to sit inside his patrol car. While verifying whether Mancias had a valid driver's license, Skogen informed Mancias that he would receive a citation for "care required." After he learned Mancias had a valid Minnesota driver's license and a suspended North

Dakota driver's license, Skogen informed Mancias that he would receive an additional citation for driving with a suspended license. After telling Mancias that he would not be allowed to drive, Skogen offered to drive Mancias to Harvey, North Dakota, where he could spend the night. Skogen indicated he would direct another officer to follow them in Mancias' vehicle to Harvey, North Dakota. Mancias agreed to this arrangement.

Skogen placed Mancias under arrest for driving under a suspended North Dakota driver's license. Skogen informed Mancias that he would be jailed if he could not post a cash bond of $200. Meanwhile, Wells County Deputy Sheriff Hoyt arrived to assist Skogen. In order to move things along more quickly, Skogen continued the paperwork while Hoyt conducted a search of Mancias' vehicle. During the course of his search, Hoyt noticed the rear seat of the vehicle was not bolted down. When Hoyt put his weight on the rear seat, the backrest of the rear seat slid out of position. Hoyt moved the backrest and noticed a cutout. Looking through the cutout and into the trunk of Mancias' vehicle, Hoyt saw several suspicious-looking bundles.

While Hoyt was conducting his search, Skogen finished the necessary paperwork, conducted an alcohol-screening breath test, and collected the $200 cash bond. As Mancias stepped out of the patrol car to receive a final pat-down, Hoyt approached Skogen and Mancias. Hoyt informed Skogen there was something in the trunk area of the vehicle that they needed to check out. Upon hearing what Hoyt had to say, Skogen returned to Mancias to pat him down and to place handcuffs on him. After putting Mancias in the rear seat of the patrol car, Skogen asked Mancias on at least two separate occasions if he would consent to a search of his vehicle. Each time, Mancias consented to the search. After securing Mancias inside the patrol car, Hoyt and Skogen continued the search of the vehicle pursuant to Mancias' consent. Skogen observed a digital scale on the rear seat and the cutout behind the backrest. Ultimately, the officers seized twenty-six pounds of marijuana from the trunk of Mancias' vehicle. Mancias moved to suppress the evidence, contending that the totality of the circumstances surrounding his consent rendered it involuntary because at the time he gave his consent: (1) he was suffering from extreme fatigue; (2) he was handcuffed and sitting in the back of the patrol car; and (3) he was not advised of his *Miranda* rights. Was his consent voluntary? See *United States v. Mancias*, 350 F.3d 800 (8th Cir. 2003).

2 While observing traffic on a major interstate highway passing through Nebraska, Officer Leroy Jones of the Nebraska State Patrol "clocked" a vehicle traveling above the posted speed limit. After stopping the vehicle for this traffic infraction, Jones approached the car from the passenger's side. He immediately noticed an individual in the front passenger's seat as well as the driver. After receiving the driver's license and registration, he noticed the name on the registration did not match the name on the license. Jones had also learned before approaching the vehicle that the Indiana license plates on the vehicle were listed as "not on file" in his patrol car database.

At this point, Officer Jones asked the driver, Charles Brown, to accompany him to the patrol car, where Brown provided conflicting stories as to his travel plans and as to who owned the vehicle. Jones informed Brown that he would need to conduct a further, investigatory "stop" of the vehicle.

Jones next approached the passenger in the front passenger seat, Larry Walden, and proceeded to ask him questions about his travel plans. Walden's description of his travel plans conflicted with those provided by Jones. His suspicions aroused, Officer Jones called for "back-

up" and also requested a background check of both of the vehicle's occupants. This "check" revealed that both occupants had criminal records, including prior drug offenses.

At this juncture, Officer Jones gave the driver, Brown, his license back, and issued him a warning for speeding. Jones then requested Brown's permission to search the vehicle. Brown gave his consent orally and then signed a form indicating his consent in writing. After receiving Brown's consent, Officer Jones, with the help of another police officer who arrived on the scene, searched Brown's vehicle for about thirty minutes. Though Brown complained about the long duration of the search, he did not withdraw his consent. When Officer Jones noticed evidence of a "false ceiling" in the vehicle, he arranged for a dog trained in drug detection to enter the vehicle. Once the dog indicated the presence of contraband in the ceiling, the officers removed the ceiling and found large quantities of cocaine.

At the trial court level, Brown entered a conditional guilty plea to drug possession with intent to distribute, after the District Court denied his motion to suppress the drugs. Brown now appeals the District Court's ruling, arguing that (1) his detention was unlawful; (2) his consent to search the vehicle was not given voluntarily, and (3) the search exceeded the scope of his consent. Should the Court of Appeals reverse the District Court's ruling and suppress the drugs because either Brown did not voluntarily consent to the search or because Officer Jones exceeded the scope of Brown's consent (e.g., by searching the vehicle for 30 minutes despite Brown's complaints and by entering the ceiling area of the car)? See *United States v. Brown*, 345 F.3d 574 (8th Cir. 2003).

3 On the evening of September 15, 1999, officers from the Muldrow, Oklahoma, police department, accompanied by Damon Tucker, an Oklahoma Highway Patrol officer, established a checkpoint on Treat Road within the city limits of Muldrow. The impetus for establishing the checkpoint was the officers' suspicion that Holt, who lived in the area, was transporting illegal drugs along Treat Road.

At the checkpoint, the officers stopped all vehicles traveling along Treat Road and checked drivers' licenses. At approximately 10:30 P.M., Tucker observed a Ford Ranger truck approach the checkpoint. Tucker noted that the driver of the truck, defendant Holt, was not wearing a seatbelt. After asking to see Holt's driver's license, Tucker asked Holt why he was not wearing a seatbelt. Holt stated that he lived in the area and pointed toward his house. At some point thereafter, officers from the Muldrow police department informed Tucker that Holt was the person they were seeking. Tucker asked Holt to pull over to the side of the road and join Tucker in his patrol car.

After Holt got into the patrol car, Tucker asked for Holt's driver's license and proceeded to write a warning for the seatbelt violation. While doing so, Tucker asked Holt if "there was anything in [Holt's] vehicle [Tucker] should know about such as loaded weapons." According to Tucker, he asks that question "on a lot of [his] stops." Holt stated there was a loaded pistol behind the passenger seat of his vehicle. Holt did not indicate whether he had a permit to carry a loaded gun (which was required under Oklahoma law), and Tucker did not ask whether Holt possessed such a permit. Tucker asked Holt if "there was anything else that [Tucker] should know about in the vehicle." Holt stated, "I know what you are referring to" but "I don't use them anymore." Upon further questioning by Tucker, Holt indicated that he had previously used drugs, but "hadn't been involved with them in about a year or so." Tucker then asked Holt for consent to search his vehicle. Holt agreed. It is unclear from the record whether Tucker issued the warning to Holt for the seatbelt violation at that point, or if Tucker ever returned Holt's driver's license to him. It is undisputed that Tucker had Holt's driver's license in his possession during the above-outlined questioning. According to Tucker, approximately three to four minutes elapsed between the time he and Holt got into the patrol car and the time that Holt consented to the search of his vehicle.

Tucker and Holt got out of the patrol car, and Tucker again asked Holt if there was anything else in the vehicle. Holt responded that the gun was all that Tucker would find. Tucker proceeded to search the cab of the truck and, as described by Holt, found a loaded pistol behind the passenger seat. One of the Muldrow police officers, when informed by Tucker that Holt had given consent to have his vehicle searched, began looking through a camper shell on the back of the truck. During the course of his search, this officer found a small bag containing spoons, syringes, loose matches, and a white powdery substance in separate bags. Based upon the discovery of this evidence, Tucker arrested Holt and transported him to the Muldrow jail.

Shortly after Holt's arrest, Tucker contacted an assistant district attorney for Sequoyah County regarding the possibility of obtaining a search warrant for Holt's residence based upon the evidence recovered from Holt's vehicle. The assistant district attorney concluded the evidence was not sufficient to support a search warrant for Holt's residence. He did, however, advise Tucker to utilize "a knock and talk" technique. In accordance with this advice, police officers went to Holt's residence and Holt's mother gave verbal consent to search the premises. During the search, officers found chemical glassware in a room where Holt stayed, as well as drugs and drug-making equipment in an outbuilding. Should Holt's motions to suppress the evidence seized from his vehicle and from his residence be granted? *See United States v. Holt*, 229 F.3d 931 (10th Cir. 2000).

4 On June 29, 1999, at about 10:00 P.M., three Colorado Springs police officers responded to a disturbance at a mobile home park in the 3600 block of North Cascade. A neighbor had reported that men and women were yelling and screaming at that address. When they arrived at the scene, officers found a man heavily intoxicated, yelling and knocking on the door of the residence where the disturbance was reported. They placed the intoxicated man in one of the police cars. The officers then knocked on the residence door of the defendant, Kenneth Garcia (Garcia), to inquire about the reported disturbance. Garcia stepped approximately ten feet outside the residence to speak with the officers and left the door open behind him. The officers questioned Garcia. He denied there was any disturbance.

As the officers spoke with Garcia, they saw a small pipe on the ground next to him of a type used for smoking methamphetamine or crack cocaine. They also noticed a picture of a marijuana plant on the wall inside the residence.

The officers placed Garcia in the back seat of a different police car from where the intoxicated man was sitting. Officers testified at the suppression hearing that they had placed the intoxicated individual and Garcia in two separate police cars because they didn't know what was happening inside, if there are or were other individuals that were yelling—officer safety purposes. Officer testimony about Garcia's detention also included the following:

Q. And is there any reason that you could tell the Court why you decided to put him in the car versus having him stand outside?

A. Officer safety issues, that's the only reason he was in the patrol car.

The officers did not handcuff Garcia when they placed him in the police car, but he could not open the car doors from the inside. A cage separated Garcia from an officer who was sitting in the front seat of the police car. This officer told Garcia that he would be held in the police car during the investigation, and he asked Garcia whether there was anyone in the residence. Garcia replied that two women were inside. While Garcia sat in the police car, the two women exited the residence. One of the women told the officers that Garcia offered her a blast from his crack pipe. Based on the pipe, the picture of the marijuana plant inside Garcia's residence, and the statement that Garcia had offered the woman crack to smoke, the officers decided to ask Garcia for consent to search his residence.

The officer who was sitting in the front of the police car with Garcia filled out the top portion of a search waiver form and handed it to him. Garcia read the search waiver aloud to the officer, then signed the bottom portion. The officers searched Garcia's residence and found several items of drug paraphernalia and crack cocaine. They then told Garcia that he was under arrest. Should Garcia's motion to suppress the evidence be granted? In particular, should the officers have read Garcia the *Miranda* warnings prior to obtaining his consent? Also, did Garcia's detention in the patrol car constitute an illegal arrest that may have tainted his subsequent consent to search the home? *See People v. Garcia,* 11 P.3d 449 (Colo. 2000).

5 On April 17, 1998, Jeff Thorp called the Lawrence Police Department and reported he was living at 1405 East 15th Street and that one of the other occupants of the residence was growing marijuana in the home. Thorp spoke with Dispatch Officer Tom Moore. Officer Moore relayed the information to Officer David Axman, who went to the residence to check out the tip. In his affidavit, Officer Axman related that Officer Moore told him that Thorp had said Lyzeme Savage was growing approximately fourteen small marijuana plants on a window sill in the kitchen. Thorp also told Officer Moore that he had free access to the kitchen area of the house and he would show a police officer the plants if they would come by.

When Officer Axman arrived at the residence, he knocked on the back door, which led directly into the kitchen. Thorp answered the door. At the suppression hearing, evidence was presented that Thorp was 17 years old at the time of the search. Officer Axman asked the man his name, and he replied he was Jeff Thorp. Officer Axman asked Thorp if he lived at the residence and Thorp replied he did. Thorp stated he had lived there for approximately two months.

However, later in direct testimony, Officer Axman gave a slightly different sequence of the events. He testified that before he entered the residence, he identified himself as a Lawrence police officer, he asked Thorp his name, and then Thorp invited Officer Axman into the kitchen. It did not appear to Officer Axman that anyone else was present in the home. Officer Axman saw what appeared to be marijuana plants in the kitchen window sill. Officer Axman then asked Thorp if he lived at the

residence and Thorp replied he did and had been there for approximately two months. Thorp told Officer Axman that he lived there with Savage, Savage's girlfriend Mary Thorp (Thorp's sister), and Mary Thorp's son. Thorp told Officer Axman that Mary and Savage slept in an upstairs bedroom and he slept on the couch in the living room.

Based on the information he gathered during his visit with Thorp, Officer Axman applied for a search warrant for 1405 East 15th Street. As additional information in his affidavit, Officer Axman stated that Thorp told him he had previously smoked marijuana at the residence, had seen Savage smoking marijuana at the residence, and that Savage had a small silver smoke pipe with a black-colored neck. The district judge granted a search warrant for the residence. As a result of the search, Savage was charged with cultivation of marijuana, individual counts of possession of marijuana, cocaine, methamphetamine, and two counts of possession of drug paraphernalia. Should Savage's motion to suppress the evidence obtained in the search be granted? In particular, could Officer Axman reasonably believe that Thorp had authority to consent to the search of the home? Also, could Thorp give valid consent to search the home as a seventeen-year-old minor? *See State v. Savage,* 10 P.3d 765 (Kan. App. 2000).

6 On the evening of January 29, 1999, at about 11:30 P.M., the Jamestown Police Department responded to a call to investigate a loud party at an apartment in Jamestown. Officer Nagel was the first to arrive. He noticed an unusual number of cars parked nearby, as well as loud music and talking coming from the top floor apartment. Officer Nagel climbed the stairs to the upstairs apartment and knocked on the door. He heard people warning, "It's the cops. The cops are here." By this time there were three officers around the apartment.

Officer Nagel continued to knock and could hear people scrambling around inside. He also heard people making comments, and what he believed to be a window breaking. He directed another officer to go and make sure no one was jumping out of the windows. By this time a fourth officer had arrived. Officer Nagel requested assistance from the county sheriff's department and continued to knock on the apartment door.

A young woman opened the door. Officer Nagel testified he could smell the odor of alcohol coming from inside the apartment and could see a number of young people inside. From the door, Officer Nagel could see a short hallway with three open doors to adjoining rooms. There is conflict in the testimony about whether or not Officer Nagel stepped into the apartment at this point. The trial court found the officer walked into the apartment once the door was opened. Officer Nagel asked the young woman who opened the door if she lived in the apartment; she said she did not. Officer Nagel asked if she knew who did live there, and said he needed to talk to the person who lived in the apartment. The legal resident of the apartment, John Dardis, came out of the bedroom. Officer Nagel told Dardis he could smell the odor of alcohol and asked if anyone in the apartment was twenty-one years old or older. Dardis shook his head to indicate no. Dardis walked toward Officer Nagel and Officer Nagel established Dardis' breath smelled of alcohol. Officer Nagel asked for some identification from Dardis, who turned to go to another room and then turned back to answer loudly that he did not have any identification. Officer Nagel observed Dardis's eyes were heavily bloodshot.

At this point, Officer Nagel testified Dardis became very obnoxious and disorderly. Dardis turned and walked away from Officer Nagel, who told Dardis to stop and come back. Officer Nagel repeated this twice and Dardis continued walking away. A young man grabbed hold of Dardis in an attempt to calm Dardis down, which Officer Nagel said resulted in a shoving match. Officer Nagel called for assistance. Dardis broke away from the young man and continued to walk away. At this point Officer Nagel stepped further into the apartment and grabbed hold of Dardis to stop him from walking away. Dardis grabbed hold of Officer Nagel's wrist. Officer Nagel told Dardis to let go of his hand, which he did. Officer Nagel then arrested Dardis for consumption of alcohol and disorderly conduct. Should Dardis's motion to suppress the evidence obtained from his apartment be granted? Specifically, did the officer have valid consent to enter Dardis's apartment? *See City of Jamestown v. Dardis*, 618 N.W.2d 495 (N.D. 2000).

10

The Plain View Doctrine

Learning Objectives

▶ Understand the rationale for the plain view doctrine.

▶ Understand the requirements of the plain view doctrine.

▶ Give examples of prior valid intrusions into zones of privacy.

▶ Understand the various ways officers are permitted to develop probable cause for plain view searches and seizures.

▶ Know the distinction between a plain view observation and a search, especially with respect to closer examinations of items and examinations of containers.

▶ Understand that a plain view seizure need not be inadvertent.

▶ Understand the so-called plain touch or plain feel doctrine.

The U.S. Supreme Court stated the basic **plain view doctrine** in *Harris v. United States*: "It has been settled that objects falling in the plain view of an officer who has a right to be in a position to have that view may be introduced in evidence." 390 U.S. 234, 236 (1968). Under this doctrine, "if police are lawfully in a position from which they view an object, if its incriminating character is apparent, and if the officers have a lawful right of access to the object, they may seize it without a warrant." *Minnesota v. Dickerson*, 508 U.S. 366, 375 (1993).

The plain view doctrine permits law enforcement officers to observe, search, and/or seize evidence without a warrant or other justification. It is a recognized exception to the warrant requirement of the Fourth Amendment, even though a plain view observation technically does not constitute a **search**. A search occurs only if a person's reasonable expectation of privacy is infringed. If a law enforcement officer merely observes an item of evidence from a position in which the officer has a right to be, this is ordinarily not considered an infringement of a person's privacy rights. *See, e.g., Texas v. Brown*, 460 U.S. 730, 739 (1983): "It is important to distinguish "plain view" . . . to justify **seizure** of an object, from an officer's mere observation of an item left in plain view. Whereas the latter (e.g., mere observation) generally involves no Fourth Amendment search, the former (e.g., seizure of an item) generally does implicate the Amendment's limitations upon seizures of personal property.")

But the Fourth Amendment prohibits unreasonable *seizures* as well as unreasonable searches. The plain view doctrine, while applicable to Fourth Amendment searches, is primarily concerned with *seizures* under that Amendment:

> The right to security in person and property protected by the Fourth Amendment may be invaded in quite different ways by searches and seizures. A search compromises the individual interest in privacy; a seizure deprives the individual of dominion over his or her person or property. . . . The "plain view" doctrine is often considered an exception to the general rule that warrantless searches are presumptively unreasonable, but this characterization overlooks the important difference between searches and seizures. If an article is already in plain view, neither its observation nor its seizure would involve any invasion of privacy. . . . A seizure of the article, however, would obviously invade the owner's possessory interest. . . . If "plain view" justifies an exception from an otherwise applicable warrant requirement, therefore, it must be an exception that is addressed to the concerns that are implicated by seizures rather than by searches. *Horton v. California*, 496 U.S. 128, 133–34 (1990).

Thus, if the plain view doctrine is found to apply, it will justify a warrantless seizure of an item belonging to an individual despite the apparent intrusion into that individual's possessory interest. The plain view doctrine extends the longstanding authority of the police to make warrantless seizures in public places of incriminating objects (such as weapons and contraband) to zones of privacy (such as the home), where searches and seizures without a warrant are presumptively unreasonable:

> [T]he practical justification for that extension is the desirability of sparing police, whose viewing of the object in the course of a lawful search is as legitimate as it would have been in a public place, the inconvenience and the risk—to themselves or to preservation of the evidence—of going to obtain a warrant. *Arizona v. Hicks*, 480 U.S. 321, 327 (1987).

Thus, the plain view doctrine is predicated not on any sort of exigency, but is permitted in the interest of police convenience:

> The reason so light and transient a justification as police convenience is deemed reasonable is because of the absolutely minimal risk posed by the Plain View Doctrine to either of the two traditional Fourth Amendment values or concerns. . . . In terms of the initial intrusion or breach into the zone of privacy, the Plain View Doctrine, by definition, poses no threat whatsoever. It does not authorize the crossing of a threshold or other initiation of an intrusion. It does not even come into play until the intrusion is already a valid fait accompli. . . .
>
> In terms of the other traditional Fourth Amendment concern, preventing even a validly initiated search from degenerating into an exploratory fishing expedition or general rummaging about, the Plain View Doctrine, again by definition, poses no threat whatsoever, for it authorizes not even the most minimal of further searching. It authorizes only the warrantless seizure by the police of probable evidence already revealed to them, with no further examination or searching being involved. *State v. Jones*, 653 A.2d 1040, 1045 (Md. Ct. Spec. App. 1995).

▶REQUIREMENTS OF THE PLAIN VIEW DOCTRINE

The plain view doctrine does not give law enforcement officers a license to look around anywhere, at any time, and under any circumstances, and to seize anything they wish. The doctrine has carefully prescribed requirements developed through court decisions over the years. These requirements can be summarized as follows:

1. The officer must not unreasonably intrude on any person's reasonable expectation of privacy. If a person's reasonable expectation of privacy was invaded, then to satisfy the Fourth Amendment's mandate of reasonableness, the officer must have had a valid justification for having intruded upon or into a zone of privacy.
2. The incriminating character of the object to be seized must be immediately apparent to the officer. In particular, the officer must have probable cause to believe that the item he or she is observing, and intends to seize, is incriminating in nature.
3. The discovery of the item of evidence by the officer need not be inadvertent.

In order to justify a seizure of evidence under the plain view doctrine, the law enforcement officer seizing the item must satisfy the above three requirements. The remainder of this chapter is devoted to a discussion of these requirements.

Valid Justifications for Intrusions into a Zone of Privacy

The U.S. Supreme Court has provided several examples of valid justifications for prior intrusions into a zone of privacy that is protected by the Fourth Amendment:

> What the "plain view" cases have in common is that the police officer in each of them had a prior justification for an intrusion in the course of which he came . . . across a piece of evidence incriminating the accused. The doctrine serves to supplement the prior justification— whether it be a warrant for another object, hot pursuit, search incident to lawful arrest, or some other legitimate reason for being present unconnected with a search directed against the accused—and permits the warrantless seizure. *Coolidge v. New Hampshire*, 403 U.S. 443, 466 (1971).

For purposes of this chapter, a valid justification for a prior intrusion simply means that a law enforcement officer has made a legal encroachment into a constitutionally protected area or has otherwise legally invaded a person's reasonable expectation of privacy. Stated otherwise: "It is . . . an essential predicate to any valid warrantless seizure of incriminating evidence that the officer did not violate the Fourth Amendment in arriving at the place from which the evidence could be plainly viewed." *Horton v. California*, 496 U.S. 128, 136 (1990). Each section that follows will address this first requirement for the plain view doctrine: What is a valid justification for a prior intrusion into an individual's privacy?

Effecting a Lawful Arrest, Search Incident to Arrest, or Protective Sweep A law enforcement officer may lawfully seize an object that comes into view during a *lawfully executed arrest, search incident to arrest, or protective sweep.* The law of search incident to arrest and the plain view doctrine must be clearly distinguished. Under *Chimel v. California* (see Chapter 8), a law enforcement officer may search a person incident to arrest only for weapons or to prevent the destruction or concealment of evidence. The extent of the search is limited to the arrestee's body and the area within the arrestee's immediate control, "construing that phrase to mean the area from within which he might gain possession of a weapon or destructible evidence." 395 U.S. 752, 763.

The plain view doctrine does not extend the permissible area of search incident to arrest. In *Chimel,* the Supreme Court specifically said:

> There is no comparable justification, however, for routinely searching any room other than that in which an arrest occurs—or for that matter, for searching through all the desk drawers or other closed or concealed areas in that room itself. Such searches, in the absence of well-recognized exceptions, may be made only under the authority of a search warrant. 395 U.S. at 763.

Nevertheless, the law of search incident to arrest does not require law enforcement officers to ignore or avert their eyes from objects readily visible in the room where the arrest occurs. If the arresting officer observes an item of incriminating evidence open to view but outside the area under the immediate control of the arrestee, the officer may seize it—so long as the observation was made in the course of a lawful arrest or an appropriately limited search incident to arrest. For example, in *Washington v. Chrisman*, 455 U.S. 1, (1982) (also discussed in Chapter 8), the officer arrested the suspect on suspicion of underage drinking, and then asked the suspect for his identification. When the suspect went to retrieve identification from his dorm room, the officer accompanied him to the room. From the doorway of the suspect's room, the officer observed marijuana seeds and a pipe on a desk. The Court in *Chrisman* concluded that the officer was lawfully in the doorway to the dorm room because he had previously arrested the suspect, and was therefore permitted to accompany the arrestee to the room:

> [I]t is not "unreasonable" under the Fourth Amendment for a police officer, as a matter of routine, to monitor the movements of an arrested person, as his judgment dictates, following the arrest. The officer's need to ensure his own safety – as well as the integrity of the arrest – is compelling. Such surveillance is not an impermissible invasion of the privacy or personal liberty of an individual who has been arrested. 455 U.S. at 9.

Because the officer possessed a valid justification for being in the arrestee's doorway, the officer was permitted, under the plain view doctrine, to seize the marijuana seeds and pipe he saw on the arrestee's desk:

> Accordingly, [the officer] had the right to act as soon as he observed the seeds and pipe. This is a classic instance of incriminating evidence found in plain view when a police officer, for unrelated but entirely legitimate reasons, obtains lawful access to an individual's area of privacy. The Fourth Amendment does not prohibit seizure of evidence of criminal conduct found in these circumstances. 455 U.S. at 9.

This same rule applies to items of evidence observed during the course of a properly limited protective sweep (see Chapter 8). Accordingly, if officers are conducting a valid protective sweep of premises, the plain view doctrine does not extend the permissible scope of the sweep but rather it allows officers to seize incriminating evidence that comes naturally into their view from a location they are permitted to be. *United States v. Ford*, 53 F.3d 265 (D.C. Cir. 1995), nicely illustrates this point. The court in *Ford* described the following facts:

> On the morning of January 10, 1992, six law enforcement officers, including a special agent of the FBI, arrived at the home of [defendant's] mother with an arrest warrant for [the defendant]. Upon entering the apartment, the FBI agent observed [the defendant] in the apartment hallway and arrested him. The agent then conducted what the Government characterizes as a "protective sweep." He walked into the bedroom immediately adjoining the hallway in which appellant was arrested, purportedly to check for individuals who might pose a danger to those on the arrest scene. Once in the bedroom, the agent spotted a gun clip in plain view on the floor, and, although he realized that there were no people in the bedroom, the agent nevertheless continued to search. He lifted a mattress under which he found live ammunition, money, and crack cocaine, and he lifted the window shades and found a gun on the windowsill. 53 F.3d at 266.

The Court of Appeals allowed the gun clip into evidence under the plain view doctrine, but excluded the evidence found under the mattress and behind the window shades:

> [T]he agent was justified in looking in the bedroom [under the protective sweep doctrine], which was a space immediately adjoining the place of arrest. And once in the bedroom, the agent could legitimately seize the gun clip which was in plain view. The agent could not, however, lawfully search beyond that—neither under the mattress nor behind the window shades—because these were not spaces from which an attack could be immediately launched, and there were no exigent circumstances justifying the warrantless search. We hold that the evidence taken from under the mattress and from behind the window shades was seized in violation of the Fourth Amendment and therefore was inadmissible at trial. 53 F.3d at 266.

Thus, the court excluded the evidence found under the mattress and behind the window shades because this evidence was discovered in places where the officer did not have a valid justification to be under the protective sweep doctrine. Recall that under that doctrine discussed in Chapter 8, the officer may only look in places where a person could be (e.g., spaces from where an attack could be immediately launched). However, the court admitted into evidence the gun clip found in plain view on the floor of the adjacent bedroom because it was located in an area within the valid scope of the protective sweep doctrine.

Conducting a Valid Stop and Frisk An officer may seize without a warrant items of evidence observed while conducting a lawful stop and frisk. (See Chapter 7 for a discussion of stops and frisks.) Again, the plain view doctrine does not extend the area of search permissible under stop-and-frisk law, but it does give the officer authority to seize readily visible objects conducted during a valid stop and frisk.

In *United States v. Ridge*, 329 F.3d 535 (6th Cir. 2003), the court permitted a plain view seizure of a gun during a valid investigative stop of a vehicle. The court described the facts in *Ridge* as follows:

> Officers stopped a van driven by [defendants] as it approached the site of a known methamphetamine laboratory where the officers were [already] conducting a [valid] search. One officer had intercepted a phone call twenty minutes earlier, and was told, "[One of the defendants is] on the way with the money." After [a co-defendant] was removed from the van, officers seized a firearm that was sitting on [that defendant's] seat. 329 F.3d at 537.

On these facts, the court held "[t]he officers had a reasonable, articulable suspicion sufficient to justify a stop, which led naturally to the discovery of the weapon in plain view when [defendant] exited the van." 329 F.3d at 542.

The U.S. Supreme Court case of *Texas v. Brown*, 460 U.S. 730 (1983), involved a plain view seizure during a stop at a valid police roadblock, or checkpoint. In *Brown*, police officer Harold Maples assisted in setting up a routine driver's license checkpoint. Around midnight, Maples stopped an automobile driven by defendant Brown. While Maples asked Brown for his driver's license, Maples shined his flashlight into the car and saw Brown remove his right hand from his right pants pocket. Maples noticed that an opaque, green party balloon, knotted about one half inch from the tip, was caught between the two middle fingers of Brown's hand. Maples' experience as a police officer frequently involved in drug arrests made him aware that these types of balloons are typically used in transporting narcotics. Brown let the balloon fall to the seat near his leg, and then reached to open the glove compartment. Upon seeing the balloon, Maples shifted his position to obtain a better view of the glove compartment. Maples then noticed several small plastic vials, quantities of loose white powder, and an open bag of party balloons in the glove compartment. After Brown could not find his license, Maples instructed him to get out of the car, which Brown did. Officer Maples reached into the car and picked up the green balloon. Maples noticed what appeared to be a powdery substance within the tied-off portion of the balloon (lab tests later determined this powder to be heroin). Brown was placed under arrest. 460 U.S. at 734–35.

The Supreme Court in *Brown* found that Officer Maples' actions leading to the plain view seizure of the balloon were lawful: "**Applying these principles, we conclude that Officer Maples properly seized the green balloon from Brown's automobile. The Court of Criminal Appeals stated that it did not "question . . . the validity of the officer's initial stop of appellant's vehicle as a part of a license check," and we agree.** 460 U.S. at 739–40.

Recall that under "stop and frisk" law, the passenger compartment of an automobile may be lawfully searched for weapons if the officer has developed reasonable suspicion that the automobile's driver or one of its passengers is armed and dangerous. Any illegal objects found in plain view during this lawful search for weapons may also be seized:

> **If while conducting a legitimate *Terry* search of the interior of the automobile [e.g., a search with the necessary reasonable suspicion], the officer should . . . discover contraband other than weapons, he clearly cannot be required to ignore the contraband, and the Fourth Amendment does not require its suppression in such circumstances.** *Michigan v. Long*, 463 U.S. 1032, 1050 (1983).

Executing a Valid Search Warrant In *Coolidge v. New Hampshire*, 403 U.S. 443, 465 (1971), the U.S. Supreme Court said that an "example of the applicability of the 'plain view' doctrine is the situation in which the police have a warrant to search a given area for specified objects, and in the course of the search come across some other article of incriminating character." And in *Cady v. Dombrowski*, 413 U.S. 433 (1973), the U.S. Supreme Court held that an officer executing a *valid search warrant* of an automobile could legally seize items of evidence lying in plain view (e.g., a sock and a floor mat) even though they were not particularly described in the warrant:

> **The seizures of the sock and the floor mat occurred while a valid warrant was outstanding, and thus could not be considered unconstitutional under the theory advanced below. As these items were constitutionally seized, we do not deem it constitutionally significant that they were not listed in the return of the warrant.** 413 U.S. at 449.

In addition, in *United States v. Gamble*, 388 F.3d 74 (2d Cir. 2004), the court held that a valid warrant authorizing seizure of cocaine and drug paraphernalia at defendant's apartment, permitted police to seize an ammunition clip found in plain view in a dresser drawer:

> [T]he district court properly concluded that the "plain view" exception to the warrant requirement permitted law enforcement officers to seize the ammunition clip found in [defendant's] dresser drawer. The "plain view" exception

"authorizes seizure of illegal or evidentiary items visible to a police officer whose access to the object has some prior Fourth Amendment justification. . . ." The officers in this case had a Fourth Amendment justification for searching the contents of [defendant's] drawer because they had a warrant authorizing them to search for and seize cocaine and drug paraphernalia—items that could plausibly be found in a dresser drawer. And there is no dispute that the ammunition clip was found in plain view in the drawer. 388 F.3d at 76–77.

Once officers have discharged their duties under a warrant, however, the warrant no longer provides valid justification for their presence on premises. Officers may not seize items of evidence observed in plain view after a warrant is fully executed. *See, e.g., United States v. Limatoc*, 807 F.2d 792 (9th Cir. 1987). In a similar vein, if a warrant is later found to be invalid for failing to meet the particularity requirement (or for any other reason), items seized in plain view while police executed the warrant will be excluded from evidence unless a valid exception to the warrant requirement applies:

> [T]he government's argument that the seizure of the additional items was proper under the 'plain view' doctrine, fails. The "plain-view" doctrine does not apply unless the initial entry is lawful, either pursuant to a valid warrant or under one of the recognized exceptions to the warrant requirement. Neither of these circumstances was present in this case. *United States v. Hotal*, 143 F.3d 1223, 1228 (9th Cir. 1998).

Making "Controlled Deliveries" The plain view doctrine is also implicated during a controlled delivery. After a brief discussion of controlled deliveries, the leading Supreme Court case in this area, *Illinois v. Andreas*, 463 U.S. 765 (1983), will be addressed.

The U.S. government has the right to inspect all incoming goods from foreign countries at the port of entry. In addition, common carriers have a common-law right to inspect packages they accept for shipment, based on their duty to refrain from carrying contraband. Although the sheer volume of goods in transit prevents systematic inspection of all or even a large percentage of these goods, common carriers and customs officials inevitably discover contraband in transit in a variety of circumstances. When such a discovery is made, it is routine procedure to notify law enforcement authorities, so that they may identify and prosecute the person or persons responsible for the contraband's movement. The arrival of law enforcement authorities on the scene to confirm the presence of contraband and to determine what to do with it does not convert the otherwise legal search by the common carrier or customs official into a government search subject to the Fourth Amendment. *United States v. Edwards*, 602 F.2d 458 (1st Cir. 1979). *See also United States v. Jacobsen*, 466 U.S. 109 (1984) (discussed later in this chapter).

Law enforcement authorities, rather than simply seizing the contraband, often make a so-called **controlled delivery** of the container, monitoring the container on its journey to the intended destination. Then they can identify the person dealing in the contraband when the person takes possession of and asserts control over the container. The typical pattern of a controlled delivery has been described as follows:

> They most ordinarily occur when a carrier, usually an airline, unexpectedly discovers what seems to be contraband while inspecting luggage to learn the

identity of its owner, or when the contraband falls out of a broken or damaged piece of luggage, or when the carrier exercises its inspection privilege because some suspicious circumstance has caused it concern that it may unwittingly be transporting contraband. Frequently, after such a discovery, law enforcement agents restore the contraband to its container, then close or reseal the container, and authorize the carrier to deliver the container to its owner. When the owner appears to take delivery he is arrested and the container with the contraband is seized and then searched a second time for the contraband known to be there. *United States v. Bulgier*, 618 F.2d 472, 476 (7th Cir. 1980).

In *Illinois v. Andreas*, 463 U.S. 765 (1983), the leading Supreme Court case involving a controlled delivery, a large, locked metal container was shipped by air from a foreign location to the defendant in the United States. When the container arrived at a Chicago airport, a Customs inspector opened it and found a wooden table. Upon further inspection, marijuana was discovered hidden inside this table. The inspector informed federal drug enforcement authorities, and a federal agent arrived to the airport to chemically test the substance. The agent confirmed the substance as marijuana. The table with the marijuana was then resealed inside its container.

The following day, the federal agent drove to the defendant's apartment with the container. Posing as delivery men, the agent and another officer attempted to deliver the package to the defendant. In response to the agent's remark about the weight of the package, the defendant answered that it "wasn't that heavy; that he had packaged it himself, that it only contained a table." After leaving the container in a hallway at the defendant's request, the agent remained outside in the hallway, and subsequently observed the defendant pull the package into his apartment. When the other officer left to get a warrant for the defendant's apartment, the agent, still in the hallway, observed the defendant leave his apartment with the container. The agent arrested the defendant. At the stationhouse, the officers reopened the container and seized the marijuana. No search warrant was obtained prior to reopening the container.

Relying on the plain view doctrine, the Supreme Court held that the controlled delivery of the container to the defendant did not violate the Fourth Amendment. According to the Court, no protected privacy interest remains in contraband in a container once government officers have lawfully opened that container and observed in plain view its illegal contents. Simply put, at this point the plain view doctrine would allow the seizure of the contraband in the container.

Furthermore, the simple act of resealing the container to enable the police to make a controlled delivery does not operate to revive or restore the lawfully invaded privacy rights. As a result, reopening the container after the controlled delivery is not a Fourth Amendment search, and therefore does not require a warrant. The Court said:

> The plain view doctrine is grounded on the proposition that once police are lawfully in a position to observe an item first-hand, its owner's privacy interest in that item is lost; the owner may retain the incidents of title and possession but not privacy. . . . [O]nce a container has been found to a certainty to contain illicit drugs, the contraband becomes like objects physically within the plain view of the police, and the claim to privacy is lost. Consequently, the subsequent reopening of the container [after it has been re-sealed by police] is not a "search" within the intendment of the Fourth Amendment. 463 U.S. at 771–72.

In *Andreas*, the Court acknowledged that there are often unavoidable interruptions of control or surveillance of a container. At some point after such an interruption, courts should recognize that the container may have been put to other uses, thereby reinstating a person's legitimate expectation of privacy in the container. The Court established an objective test to limit the risk of intrusion on legitimate privacy interests when such an interruption occurs: whether there is a substantial likelihood that the contents of the container have been changed during the gap in surveillance. If there is no such likelihood, an officer may legally reopen the container without a warrant. Applying this test to the facts in *Andreas*, the Court found that:

> [T]here was no substantial likelihood here that the contents of the shipping container were changed during the brief period that it was out of sight of the surveilling officer. The unusual size of the container, its specialized purpose, and the relatively short break in surveillance, combine to make it substantially unlikely that the respondent removed the table or placed new items inside the container while it was in his apartment. Thus, reopening the container did not intrude on any legitimate expectation of privacy and did not violate the Fourth Amendment. 463 U.S. at 773.

Hot Pursuit of a Fleeing Suspect Law enforcement officers who are lawfully on premises in **hot pursuit** of a fleeing suspect may seize items of evidence observed open to their view. For example, the U.S. Supreme Court in *Coolidge v. New Hampshire*, said:

> Where the initial intrusion that brings the police within plain view of such an article is supported, not by a warrant, but by one of the recognized exceptions to the warrant requirement, the seizure is also legitimate. Thus the police may . . . come across evidence while in "hot pursuit" of a fleeing suspect. 403 U.S. 443, 465 (1971).

In addition, *Warden v. Hayden*, 387 U.S. 294 (1967), although not relying directly on plain view doctrine, provides an example of how that doctrine may be implicated when police are in hot pursuit of a suspect. In *Hayden*, the police were informed that an armed robbery had taken place and that a suspect wearing a light cap and dark jacket had entered a certain house less than five minutes before the officers arrived. Several officers entered the house and began to search for the described suspect and weapons that he had used in the robbery and might be used against them. One officer, while searching the cellar, found in a washing machine clothing of the type that the fleeing man was said to have worn.

The Court in *Hayden* first held that the entry into the house and subsequent search for the suspect, and any weapons he may use, was justified without a warrant since police were in "hot pursuit":

> We agree with the Court of Appeals that neither the entry without warrant to search for the robber, nor the search for him without warrant was invalid. Under the circumstances of this case, 'the exigencies of the situation made that course imperative.' The police were informed that an armed robbery had taken place, and that the suspect had entered [the home] less than five minutes before they reached it. They acted reasonably when they entered the house and began to search for a man of the description they had been given and for weapons which he had used in the robbery or might use against them. The Fourth Amendment does not require police officers to delay in the course of an investigation if to do

> so would gravely endanger their lives or the lives of others. Speed here was essential, and only a thorough search of the house for persons and weapons could have insured that [the suspect] was the only man present and that the police had control of all weapons which could be used against them or to effect an escape. 387 U.S. at 299.

The Court next held that the seizure of the clothing observed by the officer in the washing machine was lawful because a police officer, while in hot pursuit of a suspect, is permitted to look in places where he may find a weapon:

> [T]he seizures occurred . . . as part of an effort to find a suspected felon, armed, within the house into which he had run only minutes before the police arrived. The permissible scope of search must, therefore, at the least, be as broad as may reasonably be necessary to prevent the dangers that the suspect at large in the house may resist or escape. . . . [The officer] knew that the robber was armed and he did not know that some weapons had been found at the time he opened the [washing] machine. In these circumstances the inference that he was in fact also looking for weapons is fully justified. 387 U.S. at 299–300.

Because the officer found the clothing in a place he was permitted to be (e.g., inside the washing machine), the plain view doctrine would support its seizure. If, however, the suspect had already been taken into custody when the officer looked into the washing machine, the seizure of the clothing would have been unlawful. This is because there would no longer be any danger of the fleeing suspect's using a weapon against the officers and, therefore, no valid justification for searching the washing machine for such a weapon.

To summarize, officers who enter a zone of privacy in hot pursuit of a fleeing suspect have a valid justification to be there and may seize items of evidence observed lying open to view during the hot pursuit and the protective search for weapons. For a further discussion of the hot pursuit doctrine, see Chapter 6 on arrests.

Responding to Certain Emergencies Related to the hot pursuit situation is an officer's observation of items open to view when responding to an **emergency**. In *United States v. Gillenwaters*, 890 F.2d 679 (4th Cir. 1989), a police officer responded to a report of a stabbing at the defendant's home. The victim was a visiting friend, and the officer arrived while paramedics were still tending her wounds. The officer briefly questioned the victim and also observed several incriminating items open to view in the room where the victim lay. Based on these observations, the officer obtained a warrant to search the premises. The court held that the observations were not an improper warrantless search:

> Hager [the officer] was responding to an emergency call; he arrived while the victim was still receiving emergency medical treatment on the scene; he attempted to obtain evidence from her concerning her assailant. His presence was unquestionably justified by exigent circumstances, and his observations— made in the room where the victim lay bleeding—fall within the scope of the plain view doctrine. 890 F.2d at 682.

Law enforcement officers may be tempted to justify otherwise illegal searches by resorting to this combination of the plain view doctrine and response to an emergency. Courts carefully examine these situations and invalidate searches or seizures of items of evidence if a genuine emergency did not exist, or if the officer's actions go beyond what is necessary to respond to the emergency. For example, in *Arizona v. Hicks*, 480 U.S. 321 (1987) (discussed further later in this chapter), the officer's search of suspected stolen stereo equipment went beyond what was necessary to respond to a shooting incident. Therefore, in the absence of probable cause to justify the additional search or to seize the object, the plain view doctrine did not apply.

Mincey v. Arizona, 437 U.S. 385, 393 (1978), also discussed the limited nature of warrantless searches conducted in response to emergencies, and hence the limited applicability of the plain view doctrine in this context. It stated that **"a warrantless search must be 'strictly circumscribed by the exigencies which justify its initiation, . . .'"** In *Mincey*, the prosecution attempted to justify an extensive four-day warrantless search of a murder suspect's apartment on the basis of a "murder scene exception" to the warrant requirement. The search occurred when there was no emergency threatening life or limb and after all persons in the apartment had been located.

The Court in *Mincey* first explained the parameters of entries and searches in response to emergencies such as a homicide. The Court said that police may make warrantless entries into premises when they reasonably believe that a person within needs immediate aid. In addition, police may also make a prompt warrantless protective search of the area to see whether other potentially dangerous persons are still on the premises (e.g., police may "secure" the premises). Any items of evidence observed in plain view during the course of these legitimate emergency activities may be seized.

However, once the emergency justifying the initial warrantless entry has ended, and the premises have been secured, police may not continue to search and seize evidence under the plain view doctrine or any other doctrine without a warrant. In this regard, the Court in *Mincey* refused to recognize a "murder scene exception" to the Fourth Amendment warrant requirement. The Court held that the **"'murder scene exception' . . . is inconsistent with the Fourth and Fourteenth Amendments—that the warrantless search of Mincey's apartment was not constitutionally permissible simply because a homicide had recently occurred there."** 437 U.S. at 395.

Thompson v. Louisiana, 469 U.S. 17 (1984), reiterated that even a two-hour, general, non-emergency search of a murder scene remains a significant intrusion on a person's privacy and may not be conducted without a warrant. Hence, the plain view doctrine has no applicability during these types of invalid, warrantless searches conducted after an emergency has come to an end, and the premises have been secured. In *Thompson*, several officers arrived at defendant's home in response to a report by defendant's daughter of a homicide. The officers entered the house, made a quick search and found "[defendant's] husband dead of a gunshot wound in a bedroom and the defendant lying unconscious in another bedroom due to an apparent [attempted suicide by] drug overdose." The deputies immediately transported defendant to a hospital, and secured the home.

Thirty-five minutes later, two members of a homicide unit entered the home to conduct a follow-up investigation. The detectives apparently were conducting a "general exploratory search for evidence of a crime." This search lasted two hours, and the detectives searched every room of the house.

The Court found the plain view doctrine inapplicable to the subsequent two-hour search by the detectives; as a result, the Court excluded the evidence, including a gun and a suicide note, discovered by the detectives:

> To be sure, [the call for assistance] would have justified the authorities in seizing evidence under the plain view doctrine while they were in petitioner's house to offer her assistance. In addition, the same doctrine may justify seizure of evidence obtained in the limited [search for a] 'victim-or-suspect' . . . discussed in *Mincey*. However, the evidence at issue here was not discovered in plain view while the police were assisting [defendant] to the hospital, nor was it discovered during the 'victim-or-suspect' search [necessary to secure premises] that had been completed by the time the homicide [detectives] arrived. 469 U.S. at 22.

Also, in *Flippo v. West Virginia*, 528 U.S. 11 (1999), the defendant and his wife, while on vacation in a state park, called emergency personnel to report an apparent attack. When the police arrived, they discovered the defendant next to the cabin where he had been staying with his wife. He had noticeable injuries to various parts of his body. An officer then entered the cabin and found the body of the defendant's wife with fatal head wounds. After the officers secured the area and transported the defendant to the hospital, they:

> [S]earched the exterior and environs of the cabin for footprints or signs of forced entry. When a police photographer arrived at about 5:30 A.M., the officers reentered the [cabin] and proceeded to process the crime scene. For over 16 hours, they took photographs, collected evidence, and searched through the contents of the cabin. [T]he investigating officers found on a table in Cabin 13, among other things, a briefcase, which they, in the ordinary course of investigating a homicide, opened, wherein they found and seized various photographs and negatives. 528 U.S. at 12 (internal quotations omitted).

Citing *Mincey*, the *Flippo* Court rejected the trial court's finding that after the homicide crime scene was secured for investigation, a warrantless search of "anything and everything found within the crime scene area" was "within the law." 528 U.S. at 14. The Court elaborated:

> This position squarely conflicts with *Mincey v. Arizona*, where we rejected the contention that there is a murder scene exception to the Warrant Clause of the Fourth Amendment. We noted that police may make warrantless entries onto premises if they reasonably believe a person is in need of immediate aid and may make prompt warrantless searches of a homicide scene for possible other victims or a killer on the premises, but we rejected any general murder scene exception as inconsistent with the Fourth and Fourteenth Amendments—the warrantless search of Mincey's apartment was not constitutionally permissible simply because a homicide had recently occurred there. 528 U.S. at 14 (internal quotations omitted).

Thus, *Mincey–Thompson–Flippo* support the principle that when police are investigating an emergency such as a homicide, they may offer assistance to victims, and conduct a brief, limited search of premises without a warrant to find other potential victims or suspects. The goal in finding other potential suspects should be narrowly tailored to "securing" the premises from dangerous persons who may harm the police or third parties. In the course of these actions, police may seize objects in plain view if they have probable cause to believe these objects are illegal contraband. Police may not, however, continue searching premises beyond the brief, limited search for victims or suspects; if they do, any evidence they find in plain view will be excluded. Of course, police may use the evidence they lawfully find in plain view as a basis for obtaining a warrant to more fully search the premises.

Another type of emergency that may support a valid, warrantless entry onto premises is a fire. Evidence of arson found in plain view as firefighters battle a fire may be seized. In *Michigan v. Tyler*, 436 U.S. 499 (1978) the Court said:

> **A burning building clearly presents an exigency of sufficient proportions to render a warrantless entry "reasonable." Indeed, it would defy reason to suppose that firemen must secure a warrant or consent before entering a burning structure to put out the blaze. And once in a building for this purpose, firefighters may seize evidence of arson that is in plain view. Thus, the Fourth and Fourteenth Amendments were not violated by the entry of the firemen to extinguish the fire . . . , nor by [the] removal of the two plastic containers of flammable liquid found on the floor of one of the showrooms.** 436 U.S. at 509.

United States v. Thomas, 372 F.3d 1173 (10th Cir. 2004), involved yet one more type of emergency. In *Thomas*, the emergency justifying a warrantless entry was a threat of guns in an apartment that could be used against police by unknown suspects. The court described the following facts:

> [P]olice officer Ron Kawano was on patrol near a four-unit apartment building after midnight. . . . Kawano observed a man run from the apartment building to a car, say something to the effect of "go ahead and kill me," and run back to the stairwell of the apartment building. Kawano concluded that the man had gone upstairs, and he decided to investigate the situation. As he approached the apartments, Kawano heard loud voices arguing in one of the two upstairs units. He walked up a stairway to determine where the argument was taking place, and as he did so the fight grew louder. Kawano heard a female voice say "you better put that gun away before I call the police" in a tone he described as angry, scared, and loud. At that point, Kawano drew his weapon. When he reached the top of the stairs, the door to one of the apartment units was open and Kawano could see about six or seven people inside. Among them was Defendant Thomas, who was holding a gun. Thomas then started to move, and Kawano ordered him to stop. Thomas did not comply. Instead, Thomas ran with the gun towards a hallway near the back of the apartment, stashed the gun in a "closet type storage area," and continued to run down the hallway into a bedroom. Meanwhile, a screaming woman ran across the apartment in the opposite direction. Kawano ordered all of the occupants out of the apartment. Everyone whom he had observed in the apartment, including Thomas, obeyed that order. He and other officers then conducted a warrantless search of the apartment [for other potential suspects]. During the search of the apartment, . . . the officers saw the gun in plain view and seized it. 372 F.3d at 1175–76.

The court found that on these facts, police could enter the apartment without a warrant to confirm that other suspects were not present who could pose a danger to police by accessing the gun:

> [T]he officers in the instant case faced a situation in which there were firearms inside the home, it was unclear how many people were inside the home, and the circumstances gave rise to a reasonable fear that the firearms might be used against the officers or others. The officers had just broken up a heated argument in which a firearm had been brandished, one of the participants in that argument had defied police orders and stashed the gun in a rear area of

the apartment, and the officers had no way of knowing if there were others in the apartment with access to the gun. 372 F.3d at 1177–78.

After finding that a valid emergency existed justifying the warrantless entry, the court concluded that the gun found in plain view in the apartment could be validly seized by police:

> [O]nce lawfully present in the home due to exigent circumstances, the plain view doctrine applies, and police may seize incriminating evidence found in plain view within the officer's lawful right of access. In the instant case, officers were lawfully within the apartment for [emergency reasons], and [Defendant] Thomas concedes that the gun was then in their plain view. There was probable cause to believe that Thomas had used the gun to commit one or more state law offenses during the preceding argument, and the gun served as evidence of those crimes. Finally, nothing impeded the officers' lawful right of access to the firearm. Because all of the elements of the plain view exception are satisfied, it was proper to seize the gun at that time. 372 F.3d at 1178–79.

Consent Searches When police obtain valid consent from a person to enter or search premises, they may seize any evidence in plain view that they have probable cause to believe is illegal in nature. For example, in *United States v. Garner*, 338 F.3d 78 (1st Cir. 2003), police obtained permission to enter a home from one of its residents. After entering, an officer asked another resident for permission to enter a room where the officer wanted to question this resident. The resident agreed. The court held that six bags of cocaine observed by this officer in plain view in the room were admissible in evidence:

> Here, the officers had defendant's permission to enter the apartment, and his girlfriend's permission to enter the bedroom. They had a legal right to be present at the location. It follows that they had the authority, without a warrant, to seize any obviously illegal material in plain view. The finding that the six bags of crack cocaine were in plain view is not clearly erroneous. They became obvious to [the officer] when [defendant's girlfriend] accidentally knocked over a bottle of nail polish remover supporting a picture frame which had partly hidden the drugs. 338 F.3d at 80.

Also, in *United States v. Santiago*, 410 F.3d 193 (5th Cir. 2005), officers obtained valid consent to enter and search a residence; as a result, the court found that the officers' seizure of illegal weapons in plain view was also valid. The court first explained the facts related to defendant's consent:

> When the deputies arrived at his residence, [defendant] opened the door allowing them to enter. Upon entering the residence, the deputies observed a firearm in plain view on a mantle in an adjacent room. [Defendant] acquiesced to the deputies' request to search his home for items that [defendant] may have received from [a suspected burglar]. 410 F.3d at 196.

After finding that the defendant validly consented to the entry and search of his residence by police, the court determined that the firearm police observed on the mantle was admissible under the plain view doctrine:

> [I]t is also clear . . . that the firearm was seen in plain view [on the mantle]. Though we do not get the sense from the record that deputies entered into the home operating under the belief that they would discover a cache of weapons, we have never asked law enforcement "to ignore the significance of items

[observed] in plain view . . . ." [T]he incriminating character of the firearm was readily apparent, as we have often recognized the interrelatedness between the possession of firearms and criminality. [F]inally, we conclude that the deputies had a lawful right of access to the firearm. [T]he gun was located in a place where the deputies had a lawful right to be. Therefore, with the foregoing considerations addressed, we find that the discovery of the first firearm, the .38 Taurus, fell within the ambit of the plain view doctrine. 410 F.3d at 201.

Vehicle Inventory Searches and VIN Searches Evidence may be seized that is observed by police in plain view during a valid inventory search of a vehicle. In *South Dakota v. Opperman*, 428 U.S. 364 (1976), police conducting a routine inventory search of an impounded vehicle seized both valuables belonging to the owner as well as drugs in plain view in the vehicle's glove compartment:

> **The inventory was not unreasonable in scope. Respondent's motion to suppress in state court challenged the inventory only as to items inside the car not in plain view. But once the policeman was lawfully inside the car to secure the personal property in plain view, it was not unreasonable to open the unlocked glove compartment, to which vandals would have had ready and unobstructed access once inside the car.** 428 U.S. at 376, n.10.

The police were lawfully in the vehicle as part of an inventory search, so their seizure of valuables in the passenger compartment and marijuana in the glove compartment was justified under the plain view doctrine.

One other, rather narrow instance in which the plain view doctrine applies is when police conduct a valid search for a vehicle's identification number (VIN). The one case decided by the Supreme Court in this area is *New York v. Class*, 475 U.S. 106 (1986). In *Class*, a law enforcement officer stopped an automobile for a traffic infraction. After the driver voluntarily got out of the vehicle, the officer entered the vehicle and removed some papers from the dashboard in order to ascertain the vehicle identification number (VIN). (Federal law requires the VIN to be placed in the plain view of someone outside the automobile to facilitate the VIN's usefulness for various governmental purposes such as research, insurance, safety, theft prevention, and vehicle recall.) The Court held that there was no reasonable expectation of privacy in the VIN because of the important role played by the VIN in the pervasive governmental regulation of the automobile and because of the efforts of the federal government to ensure that the VIN is placed in plain view. Furthermore, the placement of papers on top of the VIN was insufficient to create a privacy interest in the VIN, because efforts to restrict access to an area do not generate a reasonable expectation of privacy where none would otherwise exist. The mere viewing of the formerly obscured VIN was not, therefore, a violation of the Fourth Amendment. Moreover, because the officer's entry into the vehicle to uncover the VIN did not violate the Fourth Amendment, the officer had a prior valid justification to be where he was when he saw a gun under the seat. The gun was thus in plain view; and, because the officer had probable cause to believe that the gun was evidence of a crime, he could seize it under the plain view doctrine.

Note that *New York v. Class* also supports this principle: if police are not conducting a "search" or "seizure" for Fourth Amendment purposes because an individual lacks a privacy expectation in a particular area or object (e.g., a "VIN"), then police may intrude upon that area or object without implicating the Fourth Amendment. If police have probable cause to believe that an item observed from their lawful vantage point is incriminating in nature, they may search or seize the object under the plain view doctrine without a warrant. (See below for a further discussion of the probable cause requirement for plain view searches and seizures.)

key points

- The plain view doctrine allows the warrantless seizure of items of evidence observed open to view after a prior valid justification for an intrusion into a zone of privacy, whether that justification is a warrant for another object, hot pursuit, search incident to arrest, an emergency, a consent search, a stop and frisk, certain vehicular searches, a controlled delivery, or some other legitimate reason.

- Once police are lawfully in a position to observe an item firsthand, its owner's privacy interest in that item is lost, although the owner may retain the incidents of title and possession. If the plain view doctrine applies, police may seize an object though the owner retains incidents of title and possession.

- A warrantless search of a murder scene is not constitutionally permissible simply because a homicide has recently occurred there. When police are investigating an emergency such as a homicide, they may offer assistance to victims, and conduct a brief, limited search of premises without a warrant to find other potential victims or suspects. In the course of these actions, police may seize objects in plain view if they have probable cause to believe these objects are illegal contraband. Police may not, however, continue searching premises beyond the brief, limited search for victims or suspects; if they do, any evidence they find in plain view will be excluded. Of course, police may use the evidence they lawfully find in plain view as a basis for obtaining a warrant to more fully search the premises.

- If police are not conducting a "search" or "seizure" for Fourth Amendment purposes because an individual lacks a privacy expectation in a particular area or object, then police may intrude upon that area or object without implicating the Fourth Amendment. If police have probable cause to believe that an item observed from their lawful vantage point is incriminating in nature, they may seize the object under the plain view doctrine. (See below for a further discussion of the probable cause requirement for plain view searches and seizures.)

Probable Cause to Believe That the Observed Object Is Incriminating in Character

This requirement of the plain view doctrine means that before an item may be seized, the police must have **probable cause** that the item is incriminating in character and hence subject to seizure, *without conducting some further search of the item. See Arizona v. Hicks*, 480 U.S. 321 (1987). *See also Minnesota v. Dickerson*, 508 U.S. 366, 375 (1993) (emphasis added). ("If . . . the police lack probable cause to believe that an object in plain view is contraband without conducting some further search of the object—i.e., if 'its incriminating character [is not] "immediately apparent,"' . . . the plain-view doctrine cannot justify its seizure." *Minnesota v. Dickerson*, 508 U.S. 366, 375 (1993). In *Coolidge v. New Hampshire*, 403 U.S. 443, 466 (1971), the U.S. Supreme Court said that a seizure of an item in plain view is justified "only where it is immediately apparent to the police that *they* have evidence before them." *See also Horton v. California*, 496 U.S. 128, 136 (1990) ("[an item's] incriminating character must also be 'immediately apparent'" for the plain view doctrine to apply).

For example, in *United States v. Santiago*, 410 F.3d 193 (5th Cir. 2005), discussed above, police officers were justified in entering and searching defendant's

Discussion

POINT

Should Recently Burglarized Premises be Treated as Emergencies?

State v. Faretra, 750 A.2d 166 (N.J. Super. 2000).

On March 22, 1997, at 1:00 A.M., while on patrol, Officer Edward Sousa of the Bloomfield Police Department was flagged down at the corner of Bloomfield and Belmont Avenues by an individual named Angelo DiGiacomo. DiGiacomo advised Officer Sousa that another individual had broken into a garage located at 5 Columbus Street and left that location carrying a cardboard box. He then pointed down the street at the individual to whom he was referring. Officer Sousa observed the individual and stopped him at the corner of Bloomfield Avenue and North 10th Street.

Upon walking up to the individual, later identified as Louis Gillick, Officer Sousa observed the cardboard box Gillick was carrying, and noticed that it was filled with car radios. Officer Sousa questioned Gillick about where he had found the radios. Gillick responded that he had found the box on the street corner, and then advised Officer Sousa that his brother worked in the garage. Because Officer Sousa had observed Gillick walking down the street with the box in hand, he determined that the man was a suspect in the burglary of the garage that DiGiacomo had previously told him about.

At that time, Officer Sousa read Gillick his *Miranda* rights, and DiGiacomo identified Gillick as the individual he had seen leaving the garage. Officer Sousa then brought Gillick back to the exterior of the garage, where he was identified by a second witness, Edgar Villaneuva. Villaneuva had advised Officer Sousa that he had seen the light in the garage and had seen one person walking around inside. Both witnesses, DiGiacomo and Villaneuva, lived at 7 Columbus, next door to the subject garage.

After Mr. Gillick was placed under arrest for burglary and theft, Officer Sousa went to the front of the garage. He observed that a door panel to the garage door had been pushed in, leading him to determine that there had been a forcible entry into the building. Officer Sousa, accompanied by Officers Dwyer and Motsch, who came to the scene pursuant to a burglary-in-progress call, entered the garage in search of additional suspects. Upon entering the garage, the officers observed a large number of car parts from what appeared to be newer model cars. The search did not produce any additional suspects, nor did it produce any cars being repaired.

Based on Officer Sousa's six-month experience with the Auto Theft Task Force and his fifteen years with the Bloomfield Police Department, he believed that the parts were stolen and that the garage was being used as a "chop shop." Officer Sousa then wrote down the Vehicle Identification Numbers (VINs) for three of the car doors he observed in the garage and radioed those numbers to his dispatcher, who ran the numbers through a computerized database. As a result of the database search, the dispatcher advised Officer Sousa that the car doors were from cars

Should Recently Burglarized Premises be Treated as Emergencies? *(Continued)*

that had been reported stolen. Upon getting the results, Officer Sousa secured the garage as a crime scene and obtained a search warrant based on the information that he had gained from his entry into the building.

A few hours after the initial incident, at approximately 8:00 A.M. on March 22, 1997, a warrant to search the garage at 5 Columbus, Bloomfield, New Jersey, was obtained from Municipal Court Judge John Bukowsky. Officer Sousa participated in the search of the garage pursuant to the warrant, and the auto parts that were housed at that location were seized. Additionally, during the search, a tool box that was believed to contain "other property connected with the crime of chop shop operation," as detailed in the warrant, was searched.

The "other property" referenced in the warrant was interpreted by Officer Sousa to mean registrations, licenses, insurance policies, and any other items that would show ownership of the cars to which the car parts went. In one of the drawers of the tool box, Officer Sousa found license plates that had been folded and placed in a small bag through which the contents could be seen. In continuing to search the tool box, Officer Sousa removed a black pouch from the tool box. Believing that other folded license plates and pieces of identification could be found inside the pouch, Officer Sousa opened the pouch and found a white powdery substance believed to be heroin along with green vegetation believed to be marijuana. These items were later tested and proved to be controlled dangerous substances.

The court in *Faretra* first found that the warrantless entry and search of the garage by the officers was justified under the emergency exception to the warrant requirement:

> We are satisfied that the application of this [emergency] exception to the requirement for a warrant is justified in this case. There is no suggestion that the police entered the garage as a ruse to search for evidence of a crime committed by the lessee [who was defendant's brother]. The police were flagged down by a citizen who told them of the burglary. The quick capture of Gillick near the scene clearly indicated that a burglary had just occurred. 750 A.2d at 170.

As part of its finding that the emergency exception to the warrant requirement applied to the facts of the case, the court explained that the officer's entry and search did not fall under the "crime scene exception" to the warrant requirement that had been previously rejected by the U.S. Supreme Court. Rather, the officers' actions, including plain view observations, were justified as valid activities following an emergency like a burglary:

> We hold that the rejection of a crime scene exception does not affect the authority of the police to enter private premises when the police reasonably believe that a crime is taking place or has just

(Continued)

Should Recently Burglarized Premises be Treated as Emergencies? *(Continued)*

taken place, for the limited purposes of rendering aid to a possible victim of the crime or seeking or apprehending the perpetrators or taking any necessary steps to secure the premises. The established and well-delineated exception to the requirement for a warrant in circumstances involving recently burglarized premises is discussed in numerous cases. . . . Here, the police had a right to enter the premises and, consequently, to make plain view observations. Those observations did not constitute a proscribed search of a crime scene. Here, we are not presented with an extensive crime scene search. The officers entered private premises which had just been burglarized for the purpose of determining whether there were any burglars on the premises. They immediately recognized that the garage was a "chop shop" . . . This record demonstrates a permissible entry followed by a plain-view observation of incriminating evidence. Thus, the proscribed crime-scene exception does not apply to these facts. 750 A.2d at 169–71.

Because the warrant obtained by the officer was valid, the court allowed all of the evidence seized under it. Do you agree with the court in *Faretra* that police should be able to conduct a warrantless, "emergency" search of premises that have recently been burglarized? If the suspected burglar has been apprehended and arrested, as was the case in *Faretra*, what dangers do these premises continue to pose for police? Apart from any perceived dangers to police, are there any other justifications for allowing limited searches of premises that have recently been burglarized? To what extent do you think the officers in *Faretra* were looking for other suspects and victims as part of a permissible search of premises following an emergency? To what extent do you think the officers in this case were looking for evidence of a crime, such as stolen auto parts? How do your answers to these last two questions affect your answer as to the first question above—that is, should there ultimately be an emergency exception allowing a limited, warrantless search of recently burglarized premises for victims and suspects? Finally, what if the burglary is less "recent"; for example, should the exception apply if the burglary happened five hours before police arrive? What about five days before?

residence because defendant consented to both the entry and search. Upon entering the residence, the officers observed a firearm in plain view on a mantle. The court found the plain view seizure of the firearm valid not only because the police were justified in entering the apartment but also because police had *probable cause* to believe that the firearm was illegal contraband (i.e., the firearm's incriminating nature was immediately apparent):

[T]he incriminating character of the firearm was readily apparent, as we have often recognized the interrelatedness between the possession of firearms and criminality. Given that the deputies went to [defendant's] home because they believed that he had information related to . . . recent burglaries—as [the defendant] had acted as a "fence" [to store stolen goods] for [a suspected burglar]—and because the deputies were also aware that [the defendant] had prior criminal convictions, the incriminating character of the firearm was immediately apparent. 410 F.3d at 201.

In addition, in *United States v. Gamble*, 388 F.3d 74 (2d Cir. 2004), discussed above, police officers were justified in entering and searching the defendant's apartment because they had a valid warrant authorizing the seizure of cocaine and drug paraphernalia. Police seized an ammunition clip found in plain view during the search of a dresser drawer. The court in *Gamble* authorized the plain view seizure of the ammunition clip not only because police were justified in searching the drawer as a result of the warrant but also because they had probable cause to believe the clip was illegal contraband: "[T]he officers had probable cause to believe that the ammunition clip was connected with criminal activity because ammunition is a recognized tool of the drug-dealing trade." 388 F.3d at 77.

Courts will not always find that the incriminating character of an object observed by police in plain view is "immediately apparent"; that is, courts may find that an officer lacks the probable cause necessary to seize or search an object under the plain view doctrine. For example, in *United States v. Wilson*, 36 F.3d 1298, 1306 (5th Cir. 1994), because police had to make a telephone call before learning of the incriminating character of particular bank checks, the court found that the plain view seizure of these checks was unlawful: "the incriminating character of the checks did not become apparent until their stolen nature was verified by the telephone call. The incriminating character of the evidence was not immediately apparent. The checkbook was not admissible under the plain view doctrine."

Similarly, in *United States v. McLevain*, 310 F.3d 434 (6th Cir. 2002), officers executing a search warrant for a residence authorizing the seizure of two individuals, one of whom did not live at the residence, found the following items in plain view: a twist tie and a cut cigarette filter under the bed in the master bedroom; a spoon with residue on a tackle box in a sink in the garage (an officer "seized" this residue at the scene and conducted a test to determine if it was an illegal drug); and a prescription bottle, with no label, filled with a clear liquid that looked like water (the bottle was found on a mantle in the home). The court found that none of the above objects was "immediately apparent" as illegal contraband; hence, the officers could not rely on the plain view doctrine to seize or search these items:

> [T]he items found in [defendant's] home might be found under beds, in sinks, and on mantels in many homes, and not exclusively those where methamphetamine is being used. While the cut cigarette filter and the prescription bottle with fluid in it might be out of the ordinary, the police are not authorized to seize odd items. We do not care what the explanation is for the items, but we care that there may be some other explanation for the items. Defense counsel pointed out at oral argument that sometimes smokers who do not want filters in their cigarettes remove them. The "plain view" exception authorizes seizure of only those items that "immediately app[ear]" to be contraband. 310 F.3d at 442.

Furthermore, the court in this case did not agree with the officer that, based on his experience, he had probable cause to believe that the four items were illegal in nature:

> [The officer] also testified that from his experiences as a narcotics officer he suspected that the twist tie, cigarette filter, spoon, and prescription bottle with liquid were being used with methamphetamine. The connection between these items and illegal activities, however, is not enough to render these items intrinsically incriminating. The connection is not enough to make their intrinsic nature such that their mere appearance gives rise to an association with criminal activity. 310 F.3d at 442.

Though an officer's experience may not always support a finding of probable cause to believe an object is incriminating in character, officers may certainly use their background and experience to evaluate the facts and circumstances in determining probable cause. For example, in *Texas v. Brown*, 460 U.S. 730 (1983) (discussed above in the context of the "prior valid justification" requirement for plain view seizures), an officer stopped the defendant's automobile at night at a routine driver's license checkpoint, asked the defendant for his license, and shined a flashlight into the car. The officer observed an opaque green party balloon, knotted about one-half inch from the tip. After shifting his position, the officer also observed several small vials, quantities of loose white powder, and an open bag of party balloons in the open glove compartment. Based, in part, on the officer's prior experience, the Court in *Brown* held that the officer had probable cause to believe that the opaque green balloon contained an illicit substance:

> **[The officer] testified that he was aware, both from his participation in previous narcotics arrests and from discussions with other officers, that balloons tied in the manner of the one possessed by [the defendant] were frequently used to carry narcotics. This testimony was corroborated by that of a police department chemist who noted that it was "common" for balloons to be used in packaging narcotics. In addition, [the officer] was able to observe the contents of the glove compartment of [the defendant's] car, which revealed further suggestions that [the defendant] was engaged in activities that might involve possession of illicit substances. The fact that [the officer] could not see through the opaque fabric of the balloon is all but irrelevant: the distinctive character of the balloon itself spoke volumes as to its contents—particularly to the trained eye of the officer.** 460 U.S. at 742–43.

Therefore, since the officer (1) was justified in stopping the car at the routine checkpoint; and (2) had probable cause to believe the balloon was illegal contraband, he could validly seize the balloon under the plain view doctrine.

Courts interpret the term immediately apparent broadly to give officers a reasonable time within which to make the *probable cause* determination. For example, *United States v. Johnston*, 784 F.2d 416 (1st Cir. 1986), held that an item's incriminating nature need not be determined by the first officer who observes the item, but may be based on the collective knowledge of all officers lawfully on the premises after all have observed the item. In *Johnston*, an officer came across torn pages from a notebook while executing a search warrant for narcotics. Probable cause to seize the pages as incriminating evidence did not develop, however, until the team of searching officers completed a search of the rest of the premises and discovered related evidence of narcotics violations. The court found that as long as the officers had probable cause to believe the items were incriminating by the time of completion of the execution of the search warrant, the *immediately apparent* requirement was held to be satisfied:

> If the plain view doctrine's immediate apparency requirement were taken literally, it would mean that unless searching officers had probable cause to grasp the incriminating character of an item not specifically covered by a search warrant at the precise moment they first spotted it, its seizure would become unlawful for the duration of the search, regardless of information lawfully acquired later in the search. Such an approach would condition the lawfulness of a seizure on the fortuity of whether the item was discovered early or late in the search: if officers entered premises under a warrant, and first saw a kitchen knife and then a corpse with its throat slit, they could not take the knife; but they could if the sequence were reversed. Thus, although the phrase immediately apparent sounds temporal, its true meaning must be that the incriminating nature of the item must have become apparent in the course of the search, without the benefit of information from any unlawful search or seizure. *United States v. Garces*, 133 F.3d 70, 75 (D.C. Cir. 1998).

This principle—that an item's incriminating nature need not be determined by the first officer who observes the item but may be based on the collective knowledge of all officers lawfully on the premises after all have observed the item—also finds support in *United States v. Wells*, 98 F.3d 808 (4th Cir. 1996). In *Wells*, officers executed a warrant for a residence authorizing a search for evidence related to bank fraud. In the course of the search, one of the officers discovered a loaded firearm on the headboard of the defendant's bed. Following established procedures, the agent unloaded the weapon and then replaced it on the headboard. He informed fellow officers on the scene that he had found the weapon. Upon learning about the weapon, the supervising officer ordered the firearm seized as evidence. Another officer then seized the weapon. Although the warrant did not list weapons among the objects to be seized, a "criminal records review by the supervising agent prior to the search indicated that [defendant] had a prior felony conviction; the weapon, therefore, was evidence of a violation of [federal law]." 98 F.3d at 809.

Although the officer who seized the weapon in plain view lacked specific knowledge regarding the defendant's prior conviction (and therefore individually lacked probable cause to believe the weapon was illegal contraband), the court found that the plain view doctrine nonetheless justified the seizure of the weapon because the officers lawfully on the scene collectively had probable cause:

> [A]lthough the agent who actually seized the weapon pursuant to the supervising agent's instructions had no personal knowledge that [defendant] was a convicted felon, it is sufficient that the agents collectively had probable cause to believe the weapon was evidence of a crime at the time of the seizure. As a result, the incriminating nature of the firearm was immediately apparent. Thus, the seizure of the firearm was proper under the plain view doctrine. 98 F.3d at 810 (internal quotations omitted).

In certain instances, an officer wants to search rather than seize items found in plain view. As is the case for a plain view seizure, an officer, before searching an item in plain view, must have probable cause to believe that the item being observed is incriminating in nature. For example, in *Arizona v. Hicks*, 480 U.S. 321 (1987) (discussed in further detail later), an officer conducting an emergency search of an apartment after a shooting incident observed stereo equipment that he suspected was stolen. He searched the equipment by moving it for closer examination, and obtained the serial numbers. Based on these serial numbers, he determined that the equipment was stolen and seized some equipment immediately and some later under the authority of a warrant. The Supreme Court held that the same probable cause standard applies to plain view searches as applies to plain view seizures. The officer had only a suspicion that the stereo equipment was stolen before searching it; therefore, his search was not based on probable cause and was unreasonable under the Fourth Amendment.

► MECHANICAL OR ELECTRICAL AIDS TO DETERMINE PROBABLE CAUSE FOR PLAIN VIEW SEARCHES AND SEIZURES

Flashlights Although the plain view doctrine does not allow a law enforcement officer to conduct a further search of an object to determine its incriminating nature, it is well settled that an officer may use mechanical or electrical aids to assist in observing items of evidence. Of course, the officer must have a valid justification for a prior intrusion into a zone of privacy and must not unreasonably intrude on someone's reasonable expectation of privacy. For example, in *Texas v. Brown*, 460 U.S. 730 (1983), discussed above, the U.S. Supreme Court found that the officer validly seized an opaque green balloon under the plain view doctrine after stopping defendant's vehicle at a police checkpoint. The Court also found that shining a flashlight into the passenger compartment of the vehicle to enable the officer to see objects in plain view, did not violate the Fourth Amendment:

> **It is likewise beyond dispute that Maples' action in shining his flashlight to illuminate the interior of Brown's car trenched upon no right secured to the latter by the Fourth Amendment. . . . Numerous other courts have agreed that the use of artificial means to illuminate a darkened area simply does not constitute a search, and thus triggers no Fourth Amendment protection.** 460 U.S. at 739–40.

Similarly, in *United States v. Dunn*, 480 U.S. 294, 305 (1987), the U.S. Supreme Court found that a plain view observation by police using a flashlight could serve as a valid basis for issuing a search warrant:

> **Here, the officers' use of the beam of a flashlight, directed through the essentially open front of [the defendant's] barn, did not transform their observations [of a drug manufacturing lab] into an unreasonable search within the meaning of the Fourth Amendment. The officers lawfully viewed the interior of [the defendant's] barn, and their observations were properly considered by the Magistrate in issuing a search warrant for [the defendant's] premises.**

See also United States v. Desir, 257 F.3d 1233 (11th Cir. 2001). ("[T]he crack cocaine was in plain view when [the officer] shined his flashlight through the windshield of [the defendant's] car. Under the plain view doctrine, this was a sufficient alternative basis [to admit the drugs].")

Night Vision Devices Courts have approved the use of night vision goggles to make plain view observations. Similar to the use of a flashlight, these devices do not implicate the Fourth Amendment:

> The night vision goggles used in this case are not infrared or heat-sensing; instead, they merely amplify light. The goggles are commonly used by the military, police, and border patrol, and they are available to the public via Internet. More economical night vision goggles are available at sporting goods stores. Therefore, night vision goggles which merely amplify light are available for general public use. District courts addressing the use of night vision goggles . . have determined that there are significant technological differences between the thermal imaging device . . . and night vision goggles such as those used herein. Night vision goggles do not penetrate walls, detect something that would otherwise be invisible, or provide information that would otherwise require physical intrusion. The goggles merely amplify ambient light to see something that is already exposed to public view. This type of technology is no more "intrusive" than binoculars or flashlights, and federal courts have routinely approved the use of binoculars and flashlights by law enforcement officials. . . . For these reasons, the Court finds that . . . the use of night vision goggles by [the officer] to observe the inside of Defendant's vehicle did not constitute a "search" in violation of the Fourth Amendment. *United States v. Vela*, 486 F. Supp. 2d 587, 590 (W.D. Tex. 2005).

Binoculars Although an argument can be made that binoculars should be treated like flashlights for Fourth Amendment purposes because they amplify the ability to see what is already in plain view, they are somewhat different. Unlike flashlights, binoculars allow areas to be viewed that may not otherwise have been viewable without an impermissible intrusion into a protected zone of privacy. Thus, courts judge the constitutional permissibility of using binoculars by scrutinizing the strength of the binoculars and the distance from which they are used in relation to whether their use infringed upon the defendant's reasonable expectation of privacy. For example, in *United States v. Grimes*, 426 F.2d 706 (5th Cir. 1970), the court held that viewing the defendant's actions using common binoculars from fifty yards away did not constitute an illegal search. In contrast, police observations into an eighth-floor window from a vantage point 200 to 300 yards away using high-powered binoculars was held to unreasonably intrude on the defendant's reasonable expectation of privacy in *People v. Arno*, 153 Cal. Rptr. 624 (Cal. App. 1979). Key to the court's rationale was that it would have been impossible for police to see into this area without using high-powered binoculars:

> We . . . view the test of validity of the surveillance as turning upon whether that which is perceived or heard is that which is conducted with a reasonable expectation of privacy and not upon the means used to view it or hear it. So long as that which is viewed or heard is perceptible to the naked eye or unaided ear, the person seen or heard has no reasonable expectation of privacy in what occurs. Because he has no reasonable expectation of privacy, governmental authority may use technological aids to visual or aural enhancement of whatever type available. However, the reasonable expectation of privacy

extends to that which cannot be seen by the naked eye or heard by the unaided ear. While governmental authority may use a technological device to avoid detection of its own law enforcement activity, it may not use the same device to invade the protected right. 153 Cal. Rptr. at 627.

Uncommon Devices Whether a device is commonly available to the general public (as opposed to not being generally available) clearly plays a role in the determination of the constitutionality of using that device to obtain probable cause based on the plain view doctrine. However, that criterion is clearly not determinative. The nature of the device's ability to intrude into protected zones of privacy (e.g., the device's ability to penetrate walls) lies at the heart of the constitutional analysis, as illustrated by the following cases involving a number of devices that are not commonly available:

▶ In *Kyllo v. United States*, 533 U.S. 27 (2001), the U.S. Supreme Court found the use of thermal imagers to detect invisible infrared radiation emanating from a home to be unconstitutional. The Court said that the use of thermal imagers constituted a "search" for Fourth Amendment purposes because these devices—which are "not in general public use"—impermissibly allow law enforcement **"to explore details of the home that would previously have been unknowable without physical intrusion for this purpose."** 533 U.S. at 40.

> *It would be foolish to contend that the degree of privacy secured to citizens by the Fourth Amendment has been entirely unaffected by the advance of technology.* **For example, as the cases discussed above make clear, the technology enabling human flight has exposed to public view (and hence, we have said, to official observation) uncovered portions of the house and its curtilage that once were private. . . . The question we confront today is what limits there are upon this power of technology to shrink the realm of guaranteed privacy. . . . While it may be difficult to refine** *Katz* **when the search of areas such as telephone booths, automobiles, or even the curtilage and uncovered portions of residences is at issue,** *in the case of the search of the interior of homes – the prototypical and hence most commonly litigated area of protected privacy – there is a ready criterion, with roots deep in the common law, of the minimal expectation of privacy that exists, and that is acknowledged to be reasonable. To withdraw protection of this minimum expectation would be to permit police technology to erode the privacy guaranteed by the Fourth Amendment.* **We think that obtaining by sense-enhancing technology any information regarding the interior of the home that could not otherwise have been obtained without physical "intrusion into a constitutionally protected area" constitutes a search – at least where (as here) the technology in question is not in general public use. This assures preservation of that degree of privacy against government that existed when the Fourth Amendment was adopted. On the basis of this criterion, the information obtained by the thermal imager in this case was the product of a search.** 533 U.S. at 33–35 (internal citations omitted) (emphasis added).

Having determined that the use of a thermal imaging device to "see" inside a private residence constituted a "search" under the Fourth Amendment, the Court concluded its opinion by holding that the use of such devices **"is presumptively unreasonable without a warrant."** 533 U.S. at 40.

▶ *Dow Chemical Company v. United States*, 476 U.S. 227 (1986) upheld the use of a standard precision aerial mapping camera to photograph an industrial plant complex from an aircraft flying in navigable airspace. Key to the Court's rationale was that the photographs that had been taken had not been accomplished by a physical trespass onto the company's private property, but rather had been taken using a camera to see an area that was "more comparable to an open field" because, from the sky, **"it is open to the view and observation of persons in aircraft lawfully in the public airspace immediately above or sufficiently near the area for the reach of cameras."** 476 U.S. at 239.

▶ *United States v. Knotts*, 460 U.S. 276 (1983), upheld the use of a tracking beeper to monitor a container in a car traveling on a highway to a cabin. Key to the Court's rationale was that the beeper simply allowed law enforcement to monitor the movement of a vehicle on public roadways—something that could have been achieved using the human eye as part of typical surveillance efforts.

> A person travelling in an automobile on public thoroughfares has no reasonable expectation of privacy in his movements from one place to another. When [the driver] travelled over the public streets he voluntarily conveyed to anyone who wanted to look the fact that he was travelling over particular roads in a particular direction, the fact of whatever stops he made, and the fact of his final destination when he exited from public roads onto private property. . . . Visual surveillance from public places along [the driver's] route or adjoining [the defendant's] premises would have sufficed to reveal all of these facts to the police. The fact that the officers in this case relied not only on visual surveillance, but on the use of the beeper to signal the presence of [the driver's] automobile to the police receiver, does not alter the situation. Nothing in the Fourth Amendment prohibited the police from augmenting the sensory faculties bestowed upon them at birth with such enhancement as science and technology afforded them in this case. 460 U.S. at 281–82.

▶ *United States v. Karo*, 468 U.S. 705 (1984), stands in sharp contrast to the way in which a tracking beeper had been used in *Knotts*. In *Karo*, the Supreme Court refused to uphold the monitoring of a tracking beeper in areas that were not open to visual surveillance. The beeper at issue in *Karo* allowed law enforcement to monitor movement within a private home. The Court said:

> At the risk of belaboring the obvious, private residences are places in which the individual normally expects privacy free of governmental intrusion not authorized by a warrant, and that expectation is plainly one that society is prepared to recognize as justifiable. Our cases have not deviated from this basic Fourth Amendment principle. Searches and seizures inside a home without a warrant are presumptively unreasonable absent exigent circumstances. . . . In this case, had a DEA agent thought it useful to enter the Taos residence to verify that the ether was actually

> in the house and had he done so surreptitiously and without a warrant, there is little doubt that he would have engaged in an unreasonable search within the meaning of the Fourth Amendment. For purposes of the Amendment, the result is the same where, without a warrant, the Government surreptitiously employs an electronic device to obtain information that it could not have obtained by observation from outside the curtilage of the house. 468 U.S. at 714–15.

Shifting Position to Determine Probable Cause for Plain View Searches and Seizures The U.S. Supreme Court in *Texas v. Brown*, 460 U.S. 730 (1983), held that a police officer's changing of position to get a better vantage point to look inside a vehicle did not invalidate an otherwise lawful plain view observation:

> [T]he fact that [Officer] Maples "changed [his] position" and "bent down at an angle so [he] could see what was inside" Brown's car . . . is irrelevant to Fourth Amendment analysis. The general public could peer into the interior of Brown's automobile from any number of angles; there is no reason Maples should be precluded from observing as an officer what would be entirely visible to him as a private citizen. *There is no legitimate expectation of privacy . . . shielding that portion of the interior of an automobile which may be viewed from outside the vehicle by either inquisitive passersby or diligent police officers. In short, the conduct that enabled Maples to observe the interior of Brown's car and of his open glove compartment was not a search within the meaning of the Fourth Amendment.* 460 U.S. at 740 (emphasis added).

Closer Examination of Items to Determine Probable Cause for Plain View Searches and Seizures How far may an officer go in examining an item more closely before the examination constitutes a plain view search rather than a mere plain view observation? (Recall that a plain view search requires probable cause; mere observation of an object in plain view from a place the officer has a lawful right to be, would not ordinarily implicate the Fourth Amendment—it is not a "search"). The U.S. Supreme Court provided some guidelines in a case in which police, investigating a shooting, entered the defendant's apartment to search for the shooter, other victims, and weapons. One officer noticed stereo components and, suspecting they were stolen, read and recorded their serial numbers, moving some of the equipment in the process. After checking with headquarters and learning that the components were stolen, the officer seized some of the components and obtained warrants for others. The Court said:

> [T]he mere recording of the serial numbers did not constitute a seizure. . . . [I]t did not "meaningfully interfere" with respondent's possessory interest in either the serial numbers or the equipment, and therefore did not amount to a seizure. . . . Officer Nelson's moving of the equipment, however, did constitute a "search" separate and apart from the search for the shooter, victims, and weapons that was the lawful objective of his entry into the apartment. Merely inspecting those parts of the turntable that came into view during the latter search would not have constituted an independent search because it would have produced no additional invasion of respondent's privacy interest. . . . But taking action, unrelated to the objectives of the authorized intrusion, which exposed to view concealed portions of the apartment or its contents, did produce a

> new invasion of respondent's privacy unjustified by the exigent circumstance that validated the entry. *Arizona v. Hicks*, 480 U.S. 321, 324–25 (1987).

Thus, the Court excluded from evidence the stolen stereo equipment because Officer Nelson lacked probable cause to search the equipment before he moved it to record certain serial numbers. At the time of the search, the officer only suspected that the stereo equipment was stolen; he did not have probable cause to believe the equipment was stolen before he moved it.

The lesson of *Hicks* is that an officer's examination of an item of property is a *plain view search* requiring probable cause rather than a *plain view observation* if:

▶ the officer produces a new invasion of the person's property by taking action that exposes to view concealed portions of the premises or its contents; and

▶ the officer's action is unrelated to, and unjustified by, the objectives of his or her valid intrusion.

In *United States v. Silva*, 714 F. Supp. 693 (S.D.N.Y. 1989), an officer executing a search warrant for fruits and instrumentalities of the crime of bank robbery discovered a notebook in plain view. The government argued that once the notebook was in plain view, the officer was justified in opening and reading it to ascertain its value as evidence. The court rejected that contention, specifically referring to *Hicks*:

> This court can hardly imagine a less intrusive action than moving a stereo turntable to view its serial number. By comparison, the opening of a notebook or document is, if anything, a more significant intrusion since it is bound to reveal something of much greater personal value than the bottom of a turntable. Accordingly, the court is constrained to conclude that, after Hicks, even the minor investigation of a notebook beyond inspecting what is visible must constitute a search. 714 F. Supp. at 696.

The court further elaborated in a footnote:

> The court does not hold that an officer cannot read a document or book if it is plainly visible without opening or disturbing it in any way. The holding is limited to finding that if the incriminating nature of the document cannot be readily ascertained without moving or disturbing it, an officer may not, absent probable cause move or further search the book or document. 714 F. Supp. at 696 n.6.

However, if the officer has particular information that provides him with a probable cause belief that a notebook contains evidence of crime, then the officer can seize the notebook under the plain view doctrine. For example, in *United States v. Pindell*, 336 F.3d 1049 (D.C. Cir. 2003), officers had knowledge from victims of a string of robberies that the suspect recorded information while committing the robberies in a particular kind of notebook. The court held that under the plain view doctrine, the officers could seize similar notebooks they found during searches they conducted with a warrant of defendant's car and home:

> At the time he conducted the search [under warrant] of [defendant's] car, Detective Paci had already interviewed [one robbery victim], who had told him that [defendant] had been dressed as a police officer and had recorded personal information in a notebook. When [Detective] Paci found a notebook lying next to a police uniform in [defendant's] car, he had probable cause to believe that it was the same notebook that [defendant] had used to record that information just two weeks before. At a minimum, he had probable cause to

believe that the notebook could have evidentiary value because it might contain a chronology of [defendant's] daily whereabouts.

Moreover, because it was by then clear to Detective Paci that [defendant] had committed at least one other similar robbery, it was also reasonable for him to believe that the notebook might include information regarding other crimes that could be relevant in proving the offenses already under investigation. As we discuss in Part III, evidence of other robberies would likewise have been admissible at a trial for the robbery of [other victims].

For the same reason, we conclude that Detectives Griffin and Williams had probable cause to seize the notebooks ...that they discovered in defendant's house [while executing another warrant]. The detectives had been briefed by Detective Paci regarding the particulars of the [other victims'] robberies, including the fact that [defendant] had used a notebook to record personal information during the former crime. When Detective Williams flipped through the notebooks to see whether they contained the currency and identification cards specified in the warrant, she discovered names, dates, addresses, and other personal details. At that point, she had probable cause to believe that the information contained therein might constitute evidence of crimes similar to those she was investigating. We therefore conclude that the district court properly denied the motion to suppress because the seizures [of the notebooks] were lawful under the plain view doctrine. 336 F.3d at 1055–56.

key points

- Before a law enforcement officer may seize or search an item of property that is observed open to view, the officer must have probable cause to believe that the property is incriminating in character (i.e., illegal contraband). An officer is allowed a reasonable time within which to make the probable cause determination and the determination may be based on the collective knowledge of all officers lawfully on the scene after all have observed the item. An officer, however, may not conduct a further search of the object to make the probable cause determination.
- Law enforcement officers may use mechanical or electrical devices, such as binoculars and flash-

lights, to assist in observing items of evidence, so long as they do not unreasonably intrude on someone's reasonable expectation of privacy.
- An officer's examination of an item of property will be a search rather than a plain view observation if the officer produces a new invasion of the property by taking action that exposes to view concealed portions of the premises or its contents and the officer's action is unrelated to and unjustified by the objectives of his or her valid intrusion. Before searching an item in plain view, an officer must possess probable cause to believe that the item is incriminating in nature.

Containers and Probable Cause for Plain View Searches and Seizures Ordinarily, the opening and examining of closed containers by government agents are considered searches requiring a warrant because they are serious invasions of privacy. *See generally United States v. Chadwick*, 433 U.S. 1 (1977) (discussed further in Chapter 11). Nevertheless, courts have held that these actions are either not searches under the Fourth Amendment, nor are justified under the plain view doctrine, under one of the following two circumstances:

▶ the contents of a container can be inferred from its outward appearance, distinctive configuration, transparency, or other characteristics. *See Arkansas v. Sanders*, 442 U.S. 753, 765, n.13 (1979): **"Not all containers . . . deserve the full protection of the Fourth Amendment. [S]ome containers (for example a kit of burglar tools or a gun case) by their very nature cannot support any reasonable expectation of privacy because their contents**

can be inferred from their outward appearance. Similarly, in some cases the contents of a package will be open to "plain view," thereby obviating the need for a warrant," *rev'd on other grounds by California v. Acevedo,* 500 U.S. 565 (1991). *See also Robbins v. California,* 453 U.S. 420, 427 (1981) (no Fourth Amendment protection for a container **"if the distinctive configuration of a container proclaims its contents, …if the container were transparent, or otherwise clearly revealed its contents,"** *rev'd on other grounds by United States v. Ross,* 456 U.S. 798 (1982).

▶ a container has already been opened and its contents examined by a private party. *See United States v. Jacobsen,* 466 U.S. 109 (1984), discussed in detail below.

The remainder of this section explores these two criteria governing the applicability of the plain view doctrine to container searches in greater detail.

Contents Can Be Inferred from Appearance, Configuration, Transparency, or Other Characteristics If the contents of a container can be inferred from its outward appearance, distinctive configuration, transparency or other characteristic, the container may be opened and searched by law enforcement officers. If the officer has probable cause to believe items in the container constitute illegal contraband, the officer may seize the container along with these items. For example, in *United States v. Blair,* 214 F.3d 690 (6th Cir. 2000), an officer observed a hard, off-white substance in a clear plastic bag, which itself was contained within a pill vile. The court held that that the officer could, without a warrant, validly seize and conduct a field test on the substance in the bag he believed to be drugs: "Because the drugs legitimately fell into the plain view exception, their warrantless seizure was permissible." 214 F.3d at 698.

Also, in *United States v. Eschweiler,* 745 F.2d 435 (7th Cir. 1984), the court held that the removal of a key from an envelope that said "safe-deposit box key" and had the name of a bank on it was not an additional search of the envelope, which was found in plain view:

> [A] container that proclaims its contents on the outside is not a private place. This point would be obvious if the envelope had been transparent; then its contents would have been literally in plain view. The inscription and other characteristics that unequivocally revealed its contents made it transparent in the contemplation of the law. 745 F.2d at 440.

Thus, since the contents of the envelope were essentially in "plain view" as a result of the inscription on the outside of the envelope, the envelope could be seized and its contents searched without violating the Fourth Amendment. Moreover, since it was reasonable for the officers to conclude that the objects of the search conducted under warrant—drugs and money—could be found within the safety deposit box, the key could also be seized.

However, closed containers that do not reveal their contents may not generally be searched absent a warrant. In *United States v. Donnes,* 947 F.2d 1430 (10th Cir. 1991), the court held that defendant had a reasonable expectation of privacy in a closed, opaque camera lens case:

> The container at issue was a closed camera lens case made of black leather and therefore opaque. The case was placed inside a glove. The glove was found on the living room floor of the house. The district court found that the defendant

had a reasonable expectation of privacy in the surrounding area when it ruled that defendant had standing to assert his Fourth Amendment claim. Given these circumstances, the defendant clearly manifested a reasonable expectation of privacy in the contents of the camera lens case. 947 F.2d at 1435–36.

Next, the court found that the plain view doctrine did not permit a warrantless search of the container by a police officer:

> The "incriminating character" of the contents of a closed, opaque, innocuously shaped container, such as a camera lens case, is not "immediately apparent." The contents of such a container come into plain view only when the container is opened. Therefore, the plain view exception cannot be relied upon to justify a warrantless search of a container such as the one at issue in the present case. 947 F.2d at 1438.

Since the plain view doctrine did not apply, the court excluded the drugs found by the officer during the warrantless search of the lens case:

> [B]y removing the lens case from the glove, and then opening the lens case, the officer exceeded the scope of the private search. The officer should have obtained a warrant, issued by a neutral and detached magistrate, prior to opening the lens case. The evidence discovered inside the camera lens case must be suppressed. 947 F.2d at 1439.

Containers Already Opened and Examined by a Private Party *United States v. Jacobsen*, 466 U.S. 109 (1984), allowed a warrantless examination of a partially closed container by government agents after the container had been opened and its contents examined by a private party. Employees of a freight carrier examined a damaged cardboard box wrapped in brown paper and found a white powdery substance in the innermost of four plastic bags that had been concealed in a tube inside the package. The employees notified the Drug Enforcement Administration (DEA), replaced the plastic bags in the tube, and placed the tube back in the box. A DEA agent arrived and removed the tube from the box and the plastic bags from the tube. When he saw the white powder, he opened the bags and removed a small amount of the powder and subjected it to a field chemical test. The test indicated that the powder was cocaine.

The U.S. Supreme Court found that the initial invasion of the package by the freight carrier employees did not violate the Fourth Amendment, because it was a private rather than a governmental action. The Court then analyzed the additional invasions of privacy by the DEA agent in terms of the degree to which they exceeded the scope of the private search. The Court found that even if the white powder was not itself in plain view because it was enclosed in so many containers and covered with papers, the DEA agent could be virtually certain that nothing else of significance was in the package and that a manual inspection of the tube and its contents would not tell him anything more than the freight carrier employees had already told him. The agent's reexamination of the contents of the package merely avoided the risk of a flaw in the employees' recollection, rather than further infringing on someone's privacy. Had the DEA agent's conduct significantly exceeded that of the freight carrier's employees, then he would have conducted a new and different search that would have been subject to Fourth Amendment protections. The Court said:

> Respondents could have no privacy interest in the contents of the package, since it remained unsealed and since the Federal Express employees had just examined the package and had, of their own accord, invited the federal agent to their offices for the express purpose of viewing its contents. The agent's viewing of what a private party had freely made available for his inspection did not violate the Fourth Amendment. . . . Similarly, the removal of the plastic bags from the tube and the agent's visual inspection of their contents enabled the agent to learn nothing that had not previously been learned during the private search. It infringed no legitimate expectation of privacy and hence was not a "search" within the meaning of the Fourth Amendment. 466 U.S. at 119-20.

The Court further held that the agent's assertion of dominion and control over the package and its contents was a seizure; but the seizure was reasonable because the agent had probable cause to believe that the tube and plastic bags contained contraband and little else. The Court said: "[I]t is well-settled law that it is constitutionally reasonable for law enforcement officials to seize 'effects' that cannot support a justifiable expectation of privacy without a warrant, based on probable cause to believe they contain contraband." 466 U.S. at 121–22.

The Court then addressed the question of whether the additional intrusion occasioned by the field test, which had not been conducted by the freight carrier employees and therefore exceeded the scope of the private search, was an unlawful search or seizure within the meaning of the Fourth Amendment. The Court held that a chemical test that merely discloses whether a particular substance is cocaine, and no other arguably "private" fact, compromises no legitimate privacy interest. Furthermore, even though the test destroyed a quantity of the powder and thereby permanently deprived its owner of a protected possessory interest, the infringement was constitutionally reasonable. The Court reasoned that the law enforcement interests justifying the procedure were substantial and, because only a trace amount of material was involved, the seizure could have, at most, only a minimal effect on any protected property interest.

To summarize, a law enforcement officer may examine, without a warrant, a container whose contents are not open to view, if (1) a private party has already compromised any privacy interest in the contents of the container, and (2) the private party has informed the officer about the contents. In addition, the officer may seize the container, if the officer has probable cause to believe the contents are contraband, and may conduct a chemical field test as long as only a trace amount of the substance is destroyed by the test.

Note, however, if the subsequent search by police of a container exceeds the scope of the earlier private search, the evidence discovered during the police search will be suppressed in the absence of a warrant. For example, in *United States v. Donnes*, 947 F.2d 1430 (10th Cir. 1991), discussed above, the officer's opening and examination of the camera lens case exceeded the earlier actions by a private individual named Bertrand:

> In *United States v. Jacobsen,* the Supreme Court recognized a standard for evaluating the actions of law enforcement officials when presented with evidence uncovered during a private search. The Court stated that "[t]he additional invasions of [defendant's] privacy by the Government agent must be tested by the degree to which they exceeded the scope of the private search." The district

court found that Bertrand gave the glove and its contents to the officer immediately after seeing the syringe inside the glove. Bertrand did not himself open the camera lens case which was also inside the glove. Here, . . . Bertrand never opened the camera lens case or viewed its contents prior to turning it over to the officer. This is not the case in which the conduct of the law enforcement official enabled him "to learn nothing that had not previously been learned during the private search." The officer's warrantless search of the camera lens case exceeded the scope of the private search. 947 F.2d at 1435.

key points

- A law enforcement officer may open and examine the contents of a closed container found in open view if the contents of the container can be inferred from its outward appearance, distinctive configuration, transparency, or other characteristics.
- A law enforcement officer may open and examine, without a warrant, a container whose contents

are not open to view if a private party has already compromised any privacy interest in the contents of the container and the private party has informed the officer about the contents.

▶ THE DISCOVERY OF THE ITEM OF EVIDENCE BY AN OFFICER NEED NOT BE INADVERTENT

In *Horton v. California*, 496 U.S. 128 (1990), a police officer investigating an armed robbery determined that there was probable cause to search the defendant's home for stolen property and weapons used in the robbery. His affidavit for a search warrant referred to police reports that described both the weapons and the stolen property, but the warrant issued by the magistrate only authorized a search for the stolen property. In executing the warrant, the officer did not find the stolen property but did find the weapons in plain view and seized them. The officer testified that, while he was searching for the named stolen property, he was also interested in finding other evidence connecting the defendant to the robbery. Thus, the seized evidence was not discovered "inadvertently."

In holding that inadvertence was not a necessary condition of a legitimate plain view seizure, the Court discussed *Coolidge v. New Hampshire*, 403 U.S. 443 (1971). Justice Stewart's opinion in *Coolidge* stated that "the discovery of evidence in plain view must be inadvertent." 403 U.S. at 469. Nevertheless, Justice Stewart's analysis of the plain view doctrine did not command a majority, and a plurality of the Court has since made clear that this analysis is not a binding precedent. *See Texas v. Brown*, 460 U.S. 730, 737 (1983). Justice Stewart concluded that the inadvertence requirement was necessary to avoid a violation of the express constitutional requirement that a valid warrant must particularly describe the things to be seized. *Horton* found two flaws in this reasoning:

> **First, evenhanded law enforcement is best achieved by the application of objective standards of conduct, rather than standards that depend upon the subjective state of mind of the officer. *The fact that an officer is interested in an item of evidence and fully expects to find it in the course of a search should not invalidate its seizure if the search is confined in area and duration by the terms of a warrant or a valid exception to the warrant requirement.* If the officer has knowledge approaching certainty**

that the item will be found, we see no reason why he or she would deliberately omit a particular description of the item to be seized from the application for a search warrant. Specification of the additional item could only permit the officer to expand the scope of the search. On the other hand, if he or she has a valid warrant to search for one item and merely a suspicion concerning the second, whether or not it amounts to probable cause, we fail to see why that suspicion should immunize the second item from seizure if it is found during a lawful search for the first. . . .

Second, the suggestion that the inadvertence requirement is necessary to prevent the police from conducting general searches, or from converting specific warrants into general warrants, is not persuasive because that interest is already served by the requirements that no warrant issue unless it "particularly describ[es] the place to be searched and the persons or things to be seized," . . . and that a warrantless search be circumscribed by the exigencies which justify its initiation. . . . Scrupulous adherence to these requirements serves the interests in limiting the area and duration of the search that the inadvertence requirement inadequately protects. Once those commands have been satisfied and the officer has a lawful right of access, however, no additional Fourth Amendment interest is furthered by requiring that the discovery of evidence be inadvertent. *If the scope of the search exceeds that permitted by the terms of a validly issued warrant or the character of the relevant exception from the warrant requirement, the subsequent seizure is unconstitutional without more.* 496 U.S. at 138–40 (emphasis added).

In *Horton*, the omission of any reference to the weapons in the warrant did not enlarge the scope of the search in the slightest. In fact, if the stolen property named in the warrant had been found or surrendered at the outset, no search for weapons could have taken place:

[T]he seizure of an object in plain view does not involve an intrusion on privacy. If the interest in privacy has been invaded, the violation must have occurred before the object came into plain view and there is no need for an inadvertence limitation on seizures to condemn it. The prohibition against general searches and general warrants serves primarily as a protection against unjustified intrusions on privacy. But reliance on privacy concerns that support that prohibition is misplaced when the inquiry concerns the scope of an exception that merely authorizes an officer with a lawful right of access to an item to seize it without a warrant. 496 U.S. at 141–42.

Following the *Horton* rule, *United States v. Ribeiro*, 397 F.3d 43 (1st Cir. 2005), found the fact that a search warrant authorized a search for cash, drug-related documents and drug paraphernalia, did not preclude the seizure of drugs in plain view in defendant's apartment:

First, in a familiar note, [the defendant] dismisses the documentary search warrant as a mere pretense because the police intended to search for drugs from the outset. [The defendant] emphasizes that the police asked him where his drugs were immediately upon arrest, and the officers in the apartment asked his girlfriend the same question. As the district court correctly noted, however, this argument is a dead-end. As long as the search was within the scope of the warrant, it is no matter that the officers may have hoped to find drugs. The fact that an officer is interested in an item of evidence and fully expects to find it in the course of a search should not invalidate its seizure if the search is confined in area and duration by the terms of a warrant or a valid exception to the warrant requirement. 397 F.3d at 52–53 (internal quotations omitted).

Although federal courts would appear to be bound by *Horton*'s abandonment of the inadvertence requirement, at least two circuit courts apparently do not follow *Horton*. Instead, they continue to require that the discovery of evidence be inadvertent (e.g., not intentional or deliberate). *See, e.g., United States v. Murphy*, 261 F.3d 741 (8th Cir. 2001) ("A law enforcement officer is permitted to seize evidence without a warrant when the initial intrusion is lawful, the discovery of the evidence is inadvertent, and the incriminating nature of the evidence is immediately apparent. Because [the defendant] voluntarily showed his wallet to [the officer], he cannot, and does not, argue that [the officer's] discovery of his driver's license was the result of an unlawful intrusion or that the discovery was deliberate.") (internal quotations omitted); *United States v. Blair*, 214 F.3d 690, 698 (6th Cir. 2000) ("It is well established that law enforcement agents may seize items in plain view, so long as the agent is lawfully present, the discovery is inadvertent, and the incriminating nature of the item is 'immediately apparent.'")

In addition, several state courts retain the inadvertence requirement based on interpretations of their state constitutions. *See, e.g., Commonwealth v. Balicki*, 762 N.E. 2d 290, 298 (Mass. 2002) ("We decline to eliminate the inadvertence requirement from our [constitutional] jurisprudence."); *State v. Meyer*, 893 P.2d 159, 165 n.6 (Haw. 1995). ("We note that in *Horton* . . . , the United States Supreme Court eliminated inadvertence as a requirement of a plain view sighting. However, because we continue to believe that the factor of inadvertence is necessary for the protection of our citizens in order to foster the objective of preventing pretextual . . . activity, we decline to follow *Horton* to the extent it eliminated inadvertence as a requirement of a plain view sighting.")

key point

- Plain view seizures need not be inadvertent. Even though a law enforcement officer is interested in an item of evidence and fully expects to find it in the course of a search, a plain view seizure of the item is not invalidated if the search is confined in its scope by the terms of a warrant or a valid exception to the warrant requirement.

▶ EXTENSION OF PLAIN VIEW TO OTHER SENSES

The plain view doctrine has been expanded to include other senses. The U.S. Supreme Court extended the plain view doctrine to include the sense of touch, while lower courts have extended the doctrine to cover smell, taste, and hearing. An analysis of each of these extensions of the plain view doctrine follows.

Plain Touch or Plain Feel

Minnesota v. Dickerson, 508 U.S. 366 (1993), applied the principles of the plain view doctrine to a situation in which a law enforcement officer discovered contraband through the sense of touch during an otherwise lawful search. This is sometimes called the **plain touch** or **plain feel** doctrine. In *Dickerson*, officers on patrol observed the defendant leaving a building known for cocaine traffic. When the defendant attempted to evade the officers, they stopped him and ordered him to submit to a pat-down search. The search revealed no weapons, but the officer conducting the search felt a small lump in the defendant's jacket. The officer examined the lump with his fingers, it slid, and the officer believed it to be a lump of crack cocaine in cellophane. The officer then reached into the pocket and retrieved a small plastic bag of crack cocaine. The Court said:

> We think that this [plain view] doctrine has an obvious application by analogy to cases in which an officer discovers contraband through the sense of touch during an otherwise lawful search. The rationale of the plain view doctrine is that if contraband is left in open view and is observed by a police officer from a lawful vantage point, there has been no invasion of a legitimate expectation of privacy and thus no "search" within the meaning of the Fourth Amendment— or at least no search independent of the initial intrusion that gave the officers their vantage point. . . . The warrantless seizure of contraband that presents itself in this manner is deemed justified by the realization that to resort to a neutral magistrate under such circumstances would often be impracticable and would do little to promote the objectives of the Fourth Amendment. . . . The same can be said of tactile discoveries of contraband. **If a police officer lawfully pats down a suspect's outer clothing and feels an object whose contour or mass makes its identity immediately apparent, there has been no invasion of the suspect's privacy beyond that already authorized by the officer's search for weapons; if the object is contraband, its warrantless seizure would be justified by the same practical considerations that inhere in the plain view context.** 508 U.S. at 375–76.

Dickerson, however, held the seizure of the package of cocaine illegal, because the contraband contents of the defendant's pocket were not immediately apparent to the officer. Only after the officer squeezed, slid, and otherwise manipulated the pocket's contents did he determine that it was cocaine.

> Although the officer was lawfully in a position to feel the lump in respondent's pocket, because *Terry* entitled him to place his hands upon respondent's jacket, the court below determined that the incriminating character of the object was not immediately apparent to him. Rather, the officer determined that the item was contraband only after conducting a further search [by manipulating the object], one not authorized by *Terry* or by any other exception to the warrant requirement. Because this further search of respondent's pocket was constitutionally invalid, the seizure of the cocaine that followed is likewise unconstitutional. 508 U.S. at 379.

United States v. Bustos-Torres, 396 F.3d 935 (8th Cir. 2005), however, permitted a seizure of cash found in "plain touch" during a valid stop and frisk following a drug transaction:

> We have established the officers in this case lawfully stopped the Lumina and conducted the pat-down search of its occupants. In the course of frisking Mr. Alfaro for weapons, Sergeant Pavlak came across two wads of bills in Mr. Alfaro's pockets. There is no evidence, nor do the defendants argue, that Sergeant Pavlak rummaged through Mr. Alfaro's pockets or otherwise expanded the

circumscribed protective search beyond the scope authorized by *Terry*. Rather, in the course of properly frisking Mr. Alfaro for weapons, the Sergeant came across the objects which turned out to be the stash. The only question remaining, therefore, is whether he was justified in seizing these objects as they came into "plain touch."

Dickerson requires the officer conducting a pat-down search have probable cause to believe the item in plain touch is incriminating evidence. To give rise to probable cause, the incriminating character of the object must be immediately identifiable. That is to say, the object must be one "whose contour or mass makes its identity immediately apparent."

We have now distilled the question to its very essence: Were the bills, by their mass and contour, immediately identifiable to the Sergeant's touch as incriminating evidence? Pondering the question with a dose of common sense, we believe they were. Sergeant Pavlak testified he found $6,000 in one of Mr. Alfaro's pockets and $4,000 in another. Officers also testified the cash consisted of twenty, fifty, and one-hundred dollar bills. Supposing Sergeant Pavlak first discovered the $4,000 wad and the money consisted entirely of one-hundred dollar bills, he would have come across a collection of forty bills, all in one pocket. We now recall the circumstances which justified the *Terry* stop in the first instance: The officers saw the defendants leave the scene of a suspected drug buy in an area known for drug traffic. Under these circumstances, Sergeant Pavlak had probable cause to believe the wad of papers he came across with his hand was indeed cash, and was likely evidence of the drug trade. As a result, we affirm the district court's denial of the defendants' motion to suppress the evidence. 396 F.3d at 945–46 (internal quotations omitted).

Plain Smell

In *United States v. Barry*, 394 F.3d 1070 (8th Cir. 2005), the court found probable cause for the warrantless search of defendant's vehicle based, in part, on the smell of drugs emanating from the vehicle's interior:

As events unfolded, Sergeant Brothers gained the authority to make a warrantless search of Barry's vehicle based on probable cause because, "given the totality of the circumstances, a reasonable person could believe there [was] a fair probability that contraband or evidence of a crime would be found in" Barry's vehicle. After Barry and his companion exited the vehicle and answered a few questions, the evidence became overwhelmingly supportive of probable cause to search the vehicle. Sergeant Brothers (1) had observed a mist inside the parked vehicle; (2) had smelled marijuana and air freshener emanating from the vehicle; (3) observed Barry's and his companion's eyes were glassy and bloodshot, and both men were swaying and slowly responding to questions; (4) heard Barry and his companion give different stories for being in the alley behind closed stores at 11:18 P.M.; and (5) knew Verus, the drug dog, had alerted to the driver-side door handle. This conclusion is undoubtedly consistent with our court's long-standing precedent. *See, e.g., United States v. Winters*, 221 F.3d 1039, 1042 (8th Cir. 2000) (finding probable cause supported the search of a vehicle in which a state trooper smelled raw marijuana); *United States v. Peltier*, 217 F.3d 608, 610 (8th Cir. 2000) (concluding "the smell of marijuana gave the deputy probable cause to search [the defendant]'s truck for drugs"); *United States v. Caves*, 890 F.2d 87, 89–91 (8th Cir.1989) (holding the totality of the circumstances, including the smell of marijuana on the defendant's person, allowed a warrantless search of the defendant's vehicle based on probable cause). 394 F.3d at 1078.

United v. Humphries, 372 F.3d 653 (4th Cir. 2004), used "plain smell" to justify the search of a residence. The court said that:

> [W]hen marijuana is believed to be present in an automobile based on the odor emanating therefrom, we have found probable cause to search the automobile, and when the odor of marijuana emanates from an apartment, we have found that there is "almost certainly" probable cause to search the apartment. 372 F.3d at 658.

The court in *Humphries* also confronted the issue of whether a "plain smell" could provide an officer with probable cause to arrest defendant in public without a warrant. The court found that the officer's "plain smell" of marijuana, along with other factors, provided the officer with probable cause to make the arrest:

> [I]f an officer smells the odor of marijuana in circumstances where the officer can localize its source to a person, the officer has probable cause to believe that the person has committed or is committing the crime of possession of marijuana. In this case, Officers Venable and Carr smelled a strong odor of marijuana immediately upon exiting their patrol car about 20 feet from Humphries. Humphries was not alone on the street, however, so the odor could not initially be tied to Humphries alone. But when Officer Venable followed Humphries as Humphries quickly walked away, getting to within 5 to 10 feet of Humphries, he continued to smell 'the same strong odor of marijuana . . . coming off his person.' Officer Venable also smelled the odor of marijuana coming off Humphries as he knocked on the door of the residence that he entered to evade the officer.
>
> [T]he odor of marijuana emanating from Humphries was sufficient to provide Officer Venable with probable cause to believe that marijuana was present on Humphries' person. And because Officer Venable had probable cause to believe Humphries was presently possessing marijuana, he had probable cause to arrest him for the crime of possession.
>
> Other factors strengthen the conclusion that Officer Venable had probable cause to arrest Humphries. Officer Venable's probable-cause calculation properly considered Humphries' evasive conduct, even if it fell short of "headlong flight." Humphries immediately walked away as the officers approached, and although he did not run, he walked away at a quick pace, ignoring the officer's commands to stop. He also ignored the officer's command to stop before he entered a residence. Such evasive conduct would suggest culpability to a reasonable officer.
>
> In addition, as the police officers approached in their marked patrol car, Humphries patted his waist, which Officer Venable interpreted as a "security check," an instinctive check by Humphries to see that his weapon was in place. Also, the entire encounter with Humphries took place in an area known for drug trafficking. As an experienced police officer, Officer Venable properly considered these circumstances in his probable-cause calculation, because the increased possibility that Humphries was carrying a weapon and was in an area known for drug trafficking increased the possibility that Humphries was possessing marijuana or other contraband. Because Officer Venable had probable cause to believe that Humphries was in possession of marijuana, he had authority to arrest him without a warrant in a public place. 372 F.3d at 659–60.

And *United States v. Haley*, 669 F.2d 201, 203 (4th Cir. 1982), upheld the search of a container based on "the odor given off by [its] contents."

It should be noted that warrantless "plain smell" providing probable cause for a search may be accomplished by both humans and animals.

> [T]he use of a well-trained narcotics-detection dog—one that does not expose non-contraband items that otherwise would remain hidden from public view—during a lawful traffic stop, generally does not implicate legitimate privacy interests. . . . A dog sniff conducted during a concededly lawful traffic stop that reveals no information other than the location of a substance that no individual has any right to possess does not violate the Fourth Amendment. *Illinois v. Caballes*, 543 U.S. 405, 409–10 (2005) (internal quotations omitted).

Plain Hearing

United States v. Ceballos, 385 F.3d 1120 (7th Cir. 2004), relying on the "plain hearing" doctrine, permitted the comparison of defendants' voices recorded during a valid wiretap, to their spoken voices during a post-arrest booking interview:

> [T]he comparison of the defendants' voices with those on the tapes falls within the "plain hearing" exception to the search warrant requirement. The plain view exception to the search requirement applies where an officer is: (1) lawfully present, (2) sees something in plain view not named in the warrant, and (3) whose incriminating nature is immediately present. We have recognized that the plain view doctrine applied in the context of overheard speech, creating a "plain hearing" doctrine. Because the defendants did not have a reasonable expectation of privacy in their voices during their booking interviews, their voices fall within the exception of the plain hearing exception to the search warrant requirement; the district court did not err in finding their Fourth Amendment claim [as to the comparison of voices] invalid. 385 F.3d at 1124.

See also United States v. Moncivais, 401 F.3d 751 (6th Cir. 2005).

key points

- If a law enforcement officer is lawfully in a position from which he or she feels an object, if the object's incriminating character is immediately apparent, and if the officer has a lawful right of access to the object, the officer may seize it without a warrant under a doctrine analogous to plain view commonly referred to as the "plain touch" or "plain feel" doctrine.
- Lower courts have permitted seizures based on "plain smell" and "plain hearing" analogies to the plain view doctrine.

Summary

Under the plain view doctrine, an observation of items lying open to view by a law enforcement officer who has a right to be in a position to have that view is not a search, and the officer may seize or search the evidence without a warrant provided the requirements of the doctrine are satisfied. The doctrine has three requirements, all of which must be satisfied before seizure of an item of evidence can be legally justified.

First, the officer must have a valid justification for a prior intrusion into a zone of privacy. Examples of valid justifications include effecting an arrest or search incident to an arrest, conducting a stop and frisk, executing a search warrant, making controlled deliveries, hot pursuit of a fleeing suspect, consent searches, and responding to an emergency.

Second, the incriminating character of the item to be seized or searched must be immediately apparent to the officer. This simply means that before an item may be seized or searched, the officer must have *probable cause* that the item is incriminating in character without conducting some further search of the object.

Officers may use their experience and background in determining whether a particular item is seizable. Officers may use mechanical or electrical aids, such as a flashlight or binoculars, to assist in observing an item, so long as this does not unreasonably intrude on someone's reasonable expectation of privacy. The officer may also examine items more closely, unless:

▶ the officer produces a new invasion of the person's property by taking action that exposes to view concealed portions of the premises or its contents; and

▶ the officer's action is unrelated to, and unjustified by, the objectives of his or her valid intrusion.

If the officer's examination of an item produces a new invasion and is unrelated to, and unjustified by, the objectives of his valid intrusion, the officer has conducted a plain view search. Such a search must be based upon probable cause (as is the case for plain view seizures).

Furthermore, opening and examining a closed container to determine whether incriminating evidence is inside is prohibited without a warrant, unless:

▶ the contents of the container can be inferred from its outward appearance, distinctive configuration, transparency, or other characteristics; or

▶ a private party has already compromised any privacy interest in the contents of the container, and the private party has informed the officer about the contents.

If, after opening and examining a container under the circumstances described above, an officer has probable cause to believe that the items within the container are incriminating in nature, the officer may seize the container along with the items.

Third, under the plain view doctrine, the discovery of the item of evidence by the officer need not be inadvertent. Even though a law enforcement officer is interested in an item of evidence and fully expects to find it in the course of a search, a plain view seizure of the item is not invalidated if the search is confined in its scope by the terms of a warrant or a valid exception to the warrant requirement. Nevertheless, even though the officer is interested in finding a particular item of evidence, the officer may not expand the scope of the search beyond the original justification for the search, whether that justification is a search warrant for other items of evidence, an exception to the search warrant requirement, or some other justification.

Analogizing to the plain view doctrine, the U.S. Supreme Court allows the seizure of an object discovered through "plain touch" rather than "plain view." Therefore, if police are lawfully in a position from which they feel an object, if its incriminating character is *immediately apparent*, and if the officers have a lawful right of access to the object, they may seize it without a warrant. If, however, the police lack probable cause to believe that the object felt is incriminating in character without conducting some further search of the object (e.g., its incriminating character is not "immediately apparent"), its seizure is not justified.

Lower courts have established "plain smell" and "plain hearing" analogies to the "plain view" doctrine.

Key Terms

Review and Discussion Questions

1. If law enforcement officers have a valid justification for a prior intrusion into a zone of privacy and they observe bottles that appear to contain illegal drugs, may they open the bottles and examine the contents further? May law enforcement officers use their senses of smell, taste, or touch to determine whether items are subject to seizure when they are not sure?

2. Assume that law enforcement officers have a warrant to arrest the defendant for stealing guns four months ago. The officers suspect that the guns are at the defendant's home, but that suspicion is based on stale information insufficient to obtain a search warrant. May the officers seize guns found in plain view when they arrest the defendant? Would it make any difference if the officers could have easily found out whether the guns were still at the defendant's home by contacting a reliable informant?

3. May law enforcement officers take an item off the shelf in an antique store and examine it to determine whether it is stolen? May officers do the same thing in a private home into which they have been invited by a person who does not know they are law enforcement officers?

4. Discuss the meaning of the following statement of the U.S. Supreme Court: "'Plain view' is perhaps better understood . . . not as an independent 'exception' to the warrant clause, but simply as an extension of whatever the prior justification for an officer's 'access to an object' may be." *Texas v. Brown*, 460 U.S. 730, 738–39 (1983).

5. An officer executing a search warrant for specified obscene materials seizes some magazines that are in plain view but were not specified in the warrant. What problems are presented by this scenario?

6. What are the limits on protective searches following an emergency (for example, a homicide)? May officers routinely look throughout a house for other suspects or victims whenever they are called to a scene to respond to an emergency? May officers go into other buildings on the premises? May officers go into neighboring homes?

7. Does the plain view doctrine authorize a warrantless entry into a dwelling to seize contraband visible from outside the dwelling? Why? What if an officer observes contraband from the hallway of a motel through the open door to one of the rooms? What if an officer observes contraband lying on the desk in someone's office?

8. Would it be proper for officers executing a search warrant for stolen property to bring along victims of the theft to aid the officers in seizing other stolen items not named in the warrant that might be in plain view? Why?

9. If law enforcement officers are legitimately on premises, may they record the serial numbers of any objects that they suspect are stolen property? May they take photographs of these objects?

10. Discuss the following statement from *Texas v. Brown*, 460 U.S. 730, 741 (1983): "Decisions by this Court since *Coolidge* indicate that the use of the phrase 'immediately apparent' was very likely an unhappy choice of words, since it can be taken to imply that an unduly high degree of certainty as to the incriminatory character of evidence is necessary for an application of the 'plain view' doctrine."

11. Make an argument for and against the proposition that a package emitting a strong odor of marijuana should be immediately seizable under a "plain smell" extension of the plain view doctrine.

Applications of the Law in Real Cases

1 The defendant lived in a house in north Portland. The front of the house faced North Michigan Avenue. Behind the house, and detached from it, was a garage that faced the opposite direction, fronting on a public alley that ran parallel to North Michigan Avenue. A chain-link fence, with a gate, separated the backyard from the alley. . . .

In the late spring of 1997, an unknown informant told Portland Police Officer Peter McConnell that people were working on cars in the defendant's garage "until all hours of the night" and that "they" were on methamphetamine. Several weeks later, at about 11 P.M. on the night of July 3, 1997, as McConnell and his partner drove down the alley behind defendant's house, they saw light coming out of the open side door of the garage. They stopped and got out of their car.

The officers walked through the gate in the chain-link fence and proceeded up the path adjacent to the side of the garage. As the officers passed the open side door of the garage, McConnell looked in and saw the defendant in the corner of the garage "kneeling down and lighting something beneath a glass flask that . . . had a piece of brown surgical tubing coming out of it." There was smoke or steam coming from around the glass. From what he saw, McConnell believed that the defendant was operating a methamphetamine lab.

McConnell knocked on the open door. When the defendant turned around, he looked "worried." McConnell asked if he could come in, and the defendant refused. The defendant then came outside to speak to McConnell, closing the door behind him. In response to McConnell's questions, the defendant said that he had been heating up varnish for antlers. When McConnell suggested that the defendant might be operating a methamphetamine lab and asked if he could confirm that the substance in the flask was varnish, the defendant refused.

The defendant then said that he needed to use the bathroom, went into the house, and did not return. McConnell, concerned that the garage might explode, called in other officers. Five to ten minutes after the defendant entered the house, McConnell went to the back door of the house and knocked. The defendant's wife answered and told the officers that the defendant was not at home. She agreed that the officers could search the house for the defendant, but the ensuing search merely confirmed that the defendant was gone.

Either during or after the search of the house, Mc-Connell asked the defendant's wife for consent to search the garage. She refused, saying that she did not have access to the garage and was afraid that the defendant would learn that she had consented. McConnell then told the defendant's wife that he believed that there was a methamphetamine laboratory in the garage; that such operations were highly dangerous; and that, if she did not consent, he could obtain a search warrant. The defendant's wife then consented to a search of the garage, which yielded evidence of methamphetamine production. Should the defendant's motion to suppress that evidence be granted? See *State v. Somfleth*, 8 P.3d 221 (Or. App. 2000).

2 On February 12, 1999, Detective James Davis of the Emporia Police Department was advised that Dorothea Smith, a suspect in a forgery case he was investigating, was in a taxi en route to the bus station. Detective Davis arrived at the bus station, and Officer Stormont also arrived at the same time in another vehicle. Upon arrival, the officers noticed a parked taxi occupied by two backseat passengers, Smith and the appellant.

Detective Davis approached the taxi, removed Smith, and arrested her. He then patted her down for weapons. He directed Officer Stormont to remove the appellant from the taxi and pat him down.

The officers testified that they had no reason to believe Smith was armed and dangerous or that any evidence of the forgery would be found in the taxi or on Smith's person. Further, the appellant was not a suspect in the forgery or any other investigation. The appellant complied peaceably and without resistance to Officer Stormont's direction that he get out of the taxi and submit to a pat-down search. Nothing was found on his person as a result of the search. When the appellant was patted down, Smith was already under arrest and in handcuffs on the other side of the car.

After patting down the appellant, Officer Stormont reached into the taxi to retrieve the appellant's jacket. He intended to return the jacket to the appellant and allow him to go on his way. Before giving the jacket to the appellant, however, Officer Stormont felt it for weapons. In doing so, he felt something hard that was about the size of an ink pen. He testified at both the suppression hearing and at trial that he had no idea what the object was. He further testified that it was not immediately apparent to him that the object was either a weapon or contraband.

The object turned out to be three small metal pipes, which later were determined to contain cocaine residue. The appellant was placed under arrest for possession of drug paraphernalia. He later admitted that the pipes belonged to him and that he had smoked them.

The appellant filed a motion to suppress, claiming the officer was not justified in searching him or his jacket. The trial court denied the motion to suppress. Was the trial court correct? See *State v. Davis*, 11 P.3d 1177 (Kan. App. 2000).

3 Officer Cyr responded to a report that Thomson had made threatening remarks to his co-workers at Alcatel, a business located in Salt Lake City, Utah. The employees of Alcatel had locked themselves in the ground-level office. Officer Cyr located the ground-level office and he was allowed to enter after identifying himself. He interviewed the manager, Mr. Panza, and two witnesses. Panza informed Cyr that Thomson had been terminated a few days earlier but had remained in the building for two and a half days. Panza further indicated Thomson was on the fifth floor, where he was purportedly cleaning out his office. Panza informed the officer that Thomson had a history of drug abuse and was known to carry a handgun. Officer Cyr next spoke with one of the witnesses, Mr. Hutchinson, who informed him that earlier in the day he had heard Thomson say the words "fire storm" and "this place is going to burn." Hutchinson also informed Cyr that a few weeks earlier, he had a phone conversation with Thomson during which Thomson said to Hutchinson that the conversation was "just between you and me. If you tell anyone else, I'll kill you." In addition, Hutchinson told Cyr that Thomson carried a gun in a green canvas bag.

The other witness, Mr. Stott, told Cyr about an incident in Thomson's office. Stott had noticed a large bullet on Thomson's desk and asked, "[w]hat is that for?" According to Stott, Thomson replied, "[i]t's for all you mother F'ers. You're all the same." Officer Cyr also noted that all of the employees appeared to be frightened.

At some point during Officer Cyr's interview of the employees, Officer Hill arrived. The two policemen went to the fifth floor and found Thomson sitting at the desk in his office. Cyr asked Thomson to place his hands on his desk and Thomson complied. Cyr asked Thomson if he had any weapons on his person, and Thomson replied that he did not. Cyr patted Thomson down and asked if he had weapons nearby. Thomson indicated that there was a weapon in a green canvas bag on the floor next to him. Cyr took the bag and carried it over to the other side of the desk away from Thomson. Cyr opened the bag and immediately found a handgun and three magazines of ammunition. Should Thomson's motion to suppress the handgun be granted? *See United States v. Thomson*, 354 F.3d 1197 (10th Cir. 2003).

4 [O]n November 9, 2000, at 10:45 A.M., a man wearing a red and white wind-suit and a ski mask over his face and carrying a .380 pistol walked into the Trustmark Bank in Southaven, Mississippi, a town situated on the state line between Tennessee and Mississippi and a suburb of Memphis, Tennessee. Upon entering the bank, he shot a single round from his weapon into the ceiling and proceeded to the teller counter. He yelled to the lone teller behind the counter, Glenda Wheeler, to get down on the floor, and kicked in the gate accessing the area behind the counter. Once he was behind the counter he located Wheeler's teller drawer and removed $17,097 in cash. Because the robber was covered from head to toe,

neither Wheeler nor law enforcement officers (who later viewed the bank's videotape of the robbery) were able to identify his race or other identifying characteristics.

After recovering the money, the robber ran out of the bank and jumped into the passenger side of a maroon Mazda 626 that had been waiting for him in the bank parking lot. As the Mazda attempted to pull out of the parking lot, a dye pack placed by the teller into the wads of stolen money exploded. Eyewitnesses reported that, after the dye pack exploded, both the driver and passenger of the vehicle opened the car doors to let the smoke escape. As they did so, the car hit a parked vehicle in the parking lot, and the jolt caused the passenger to drop currency onto the ground. As he leaned down to pick up the money, witnesses heard a pop and observed the passenger grab his chest or stomach area. Then both individuals exited the vehicle and ran across the lot to a waiting black SUV and got into that car. The SUV left the lot and headed north, toward Memphis.

From the parking lot, agents recovered several thousand dollars with red stain on it. They also took samples from the interior of the Mazda, which they observed was splattered with red dye. The only evidence recovered from inside the bank was the bullet in the ceiling, a small crowbar, and a .380 casing from the spent round.

A few minutes after the robbery, a 911 call came in from the Tulane Apartments in Memphis, roughly four and a half miles from the bank. The caller reported that an individual in apartment two, a second-story apartment, had sustained a gunshot wound to his chest. An ambulance and police personnel responded to the call and arrived to find Neely wounded and lying in the kitchen of the apartment. The ambulance workers quickly secured Neely and transported him to the Regional Medical Center, also known as "The Med," in Memphis. At the foot of the rear stairs leading to the apartment police seized a banking bag and an empty plastic ice bag, both stained with red dye.

At The Med, emergency personnel rushed Neely to the Shock Trauma Unit. During treatment, the medical workers found it necessary to remove Neely's clothing, which included a royal blue t-shirt and a pair of blue jeans. They placed the clothing in a plastic bag. Kerry Kirkland, the patient care coordinator for The Med's 7 A.M. shift, testified that when someone such as Neely is brought into the trauma unit suffering from a gunshot wound and covered with blood, and medical personnel finds it necessary to cut his clothing off of his body, it is inventoried, placed in a plastic bag, and put into the clothing storeroom at the back of the unit.

The clothing is maintained in the storeroom for five to six days and, if the owner does not claim it, it is thrown away. Kirkland further affirmed that the hospital considered such clothing to belong to the patient even while in the hospital's possession; that the staff at The Med does not consider the hospital to be an owner of the clothes.

While Neely was in surgery or shortly thereafter, a detective captain at the Southaven Police Department, acting on information from the Memphis Police Department, dispatched an officer to The Med to retrieve Neely's clothing. Although the officer had no warrant for the clothing, and police were then in the process of procuring an arrest warrant for Neely, medical personnel gave him Neely's clothes upon the officer's request. Lab analysis of the seized clothes revealed tear gas and red dye consistent with substances deployed in a dye pack.

Neely argued that the clothing and the lab results were inadmissible products of a warrantless search and seizure subject to no exception to the warrant requirement. Is Neely correct? *See United States v. Neely*, 345 F.3d 366 (5th Cir. 2003).

5 Beginning in approximately 1992, George Blair and Connie Blair (aka Launa Miakowski) operated several prostitution houses in Detroit, Michigan. As a part of their operation, the Blairs sold drugs—typically crack cocaine or heroin—to the prostitutes who worked in the houses, most of whom had serious drug addictions. In addition to requiring the prostitutes to buy their drugs from them, the Blairs sold drugs to the prostitutes' clients. The Blairs also sold drug paraphernalia such as syringes and pipes at their houses. During a routine "shift" at a house, the Blairs sold approximately $1,000 worth of drugs.

In April 1997, IRS Special Agent Thomas Kraft, having information that the Blairs were engaged in narcotics trafficking, provided an affidavit in order to obtain a search warrant for the Blairs' residence and one of the prostitution houses. A federal magistrate judge issued the warrant, which authorized law enforcement agents to seize records "relating to the transportation, importation, ordering, sale, and distribution of controlled substances." Detroit police officers assisted in the execution of the warrant to search the Blairs' residence. In that capacity, a Detroit police officer who was also a DEA Task Force Agent, Sergeant James Raby, aided in the search. Raby observed on top of a dresser an open pill vial that contained a plastic bag in which there was "a white substance [that appeared] to be narcotics." Raby conducted a field test on the substance which revealed the presence of cocaine.

At this point, Raby left the Blairs' residence to obtain a state search warrant authorizing agents to seize "[a]ll suspected controlled substances, all items used in the [sic] connection with the sales, manufacture, use, storage, distribution, transportation, delivery or concealment of controlled substances." Raby then returned to the Blairs' residence with the state warrant.

Law enforcement agents ultimately seized 350 grams of crack cocaine, 50 grams of heroin, drug paraphernalia, four loaded firearms, and approximately $13,000 in cash. Should the defendants' motion to suppress the evidence seized during the search of their residence be granted? *See United States v. Blair*, 214 F.3d 690 (6th Cir. 2000).

6 On December 28, 1999, Gary Cauley failed to return from work release at the Daviess County Detention Center in Daviess County, Kentucky. Based on information from a confidential informant, the Daviess County Jailer Harold Taylor sought a search warrant for Roger Dale McLevain's house at 8865 Sacra Drive, Maceo, Kentucky, in the early afternoon of December 29. McLevain is the defendant now before us.

The affidavit supporting the search warrant suggested a connection between McLevain and Cauley's girlfriend, Lydia Bell. The informant told the police that Bell had been staying at McLevain's residence, and she had been picked up from there by a friend on the night Cauley escaped. She went to Cauley's mother's house, where she received a call from Cauley at the Detention Center. Bell then borrowed Cauley's mother's car and returned it about an hour and a half later. The affidavit contained no information as to McLevain himself, but Cauley and McLevain were known to be friends. On the basis of this information, Taylor sought a search warrant for McLevain's house.

A state court judge determined that Taylor had probable cause to believe that Cauley could be at McLevain's residence, and he issued the warrant to search the residence. The warrant described the residence to be searched, including the detached garage and the outbuilding, and named Cauley and McLevain to be seized. It has never been explained why McLevain was included.

Taylor sought assistance from the Daviess County Sheriff's Department. That department was aware that McLevain had a criminal record with a narcotics offense. Officers of both the Daviess County Detention Center and the Daviess County Sheriff's Department executed the warrant at McLevain's home at about 2:00 P.M. on December 29. Law enforcement officers surrounded the home and forcibly entered through both the front and the back doors. The officers at the front door immediately seized McLevain in the hallway and gained control over his girlfriend and two children in the front room. The officers then began searching for Cauley. Narcotics Detective Jim Acquisito went into the master bedroom, from where

McLevain had just emerged, and looked under the bed for Cauley. Acquisito saw there a twist tie and a cut cigarette filter. He suspected these items to be drug paraphernalia. He informed his supervisor and took photographs of this evidence, although he left it undisturbed.

Later in the search for Cauley, who was never found at McLevain's home, another officer drew Acquisito's attention to a spoon with residue on a tackle box in a sink in the garage. Acquisito conducted a field test on the residue, and he found it to be residue of methamphetamine. At about the same time, Acquisito noticed on the mantel of the fireplace in the garage a prescription bottle, with no label, filled with a clear liquid that looked like water. Acquisito identified these four items as drug paraphernalia, and he used them to establish probable cause in seeking a second warrant. Upon returning with the second warrant, the officers discovered, concealed inside a kerosene heater in the garage, approximately eighty-five grams of methamphetamine; $5,710 in cash; and various plastic bags, syringes, twist ties, and electronic scales. These items formed the basis for the charges against McLevain.

McLevain filed a motion to suppress, objecting to the plain view discovery of the evidence in the first search. He argued that none of the first four pieces of evidence was immediately incriminating. He also argued that the discovery took the officers beyond the scope of a search for an escapee. Should McLevain's motion to suppress be granted? *See United States v. McLevain*, 310 F.3d 434 (6th Cir. 2002).

11

Search and Seizure of Vehicles and Containers

Learning Objectives

▶ Understand the rationale for and the scope of searches allowed under the *Carroll* doctrine (automobile exception to the search warrant requirement).

▶ Understand the requirements that must be met for the automobile exception to apply.

▶ Understand how the differences between a motor vehicle and a movable container with respect to expectation of privacy affect a law enforcement officer's warrantless search authority.

▶ Understand the circumstances under which a motor vehicle may be impounded and the requirements that must be met before law enforcement officers may conduct an inventory of the vehicle's contents.

▶ Be able to analyze a search and seizure situation involving a motor vehicle in terms of the reasonable expectation of privacy of the vehicle's occupants (e.g., these occupants' "standing" to challenge a search of the vehicle).

I t is well settled that an automobile is a personal effect, a place, or a thing within the meaning of the Fourth Amendment, and is therefore protected against unreasonable searches and seizures. Accordingly, law enforcement officers should obtain a warrant whenever they want to search a motor vehicle unless a recognized exception to the warrant requirement applies. The courts, however, have created an exception to the warrant requirement for motor vehicles that applies under certain circumstances. This chapter is devoted to exploring that so-called automobile exception.

► THE *CARROLL* DOCTRINE

The *Carroll* doctrine holds that a warrantless **search** of a **readily mobile motor vehicle** by a law enforcement officer who has **probable cause** to believe that the vehicle contains incriminating items subject to seizure is not unreasonable under the Fourth Amendment. The *Carroll* doctrine originated in *Carroll v. United States*, 267 U.S. 132 (1925), and is sometimes referred to as the **automobile exception** to the search warrant requirement.

In *Carroll*, federal prohibition agents had convincing evidence that the defendants were bootleggers who plied their trade on a certain road in a certain automobile. The agents later unexpectedly encountered the two men in the automobile on that road. They pursued the automobile, stopped it, and thoroughly searched it—without a warrant—finding several bottles of illegal liquor concealed in its upholstery. The U.S. Supreme Court held: "**On reason and authority the true rule is that** *if the search and seizure without a warrant are made upon probable cause, that is upon a belief, reasonably arising out of circumstances known to the seizing officer, that an automobile or other vehicle contains that which by law is subject to seizure and destruction, the search and seizure are valid.*" 267 U.S. at 149 (emphasis added).

Rationale for the Automobile Exception

Courts have created numerous exceptions to the warrant requirement for motor vehicles. Some of these exceptions were discussed in other chapters (e.g., Chapter 7, discussing *Terry* searches of lawfully stopped vehicles; and Chapter 8, discussing searches of vehicles incident to a suspect's arrest). The automobile exception to the warrant requirement is yet another exception justifying the search of a vehicle without a warrant.

In general, courts have allowed warrantless searches of vehicles under doctrines such as the automobile exception because they are mobile and may be quickly moved out of a particular jurisdiction. The Court in *Carroll* said:

> We have made a somewhat extended reference . . . to show that the guaranty of freedom from unreasonable searches and seizures by the Fourth Amendment has been construed, practically since the beginning of the government, as recognizing a necessary difference between a search of a store, dwelling house, or other structure in respect of which a proper official warrant readily may be obtained and a search of a ship, motor boat,

> wagon, or automobile for contraband goods, where it is not practicable to secure a warrant, because the vehicle can be quickly moved out of the locality or jurisdiction in which the warrant must be sought. 267 U.S. at 153.

In addition, courts allow the warrantless searches of automobiles because a person has a lessened expectation of privacy in a motor vehicle for the following reasons: (1) an automobile travels public thoroughfares where its occupants and contents are open to view; (2) it seldom serves as a residence or permanent place for personal effects; (3) it is required to be registered and its occupant is required to be licensed; (4) it is extensively regulated with respect to the condition and manner in which it is operated on public streets and highways; (5) it periodically undergoes an official inspection; and (6) it is often taken into police custody in the interests of public safety.

In *United States v. Chadwick*, 433 U.S. 1 (1977), the U.S. Supreme Court summarized the twin rationales for the automobile exception in the following passage:

> [A]utomobiles are "effects" under the Fourth Amendment, and searches and seizures of automobiles are therefore subject to the constitutional standard of reasonableness. But this Court has recognized significant differences between motor vehicles and other property which permit warrantless searches of automobiles in circumstances in which warrantless searches would not be reasonable in other contexts.
>
> Our treatment of automobiles has been based in part on their inherent mobility, which often makes obtaining a judicial warrant impracticable. Nevertheless, we have also sustained "warrantless searches of vehicles . . . in cases in which the possibilities of the vehicle's being removed or evidence in it destroyed were remote, if not nonexistent.
>
> The answer lies in the diminished expectation of privacy which surrounds the automobile: One has a lesser expectation of privacy in a motor vehicle because its function is transportation and it seldom serves as one's residence or as the repository of personal effects. It travels public thoroughfares where both its occupants and its contents are in plain view.
>
> Other factors reduce automobile privacy. All States require vehicles to be registered and operators to be licensed. States and localities have enacted extensive and detailed codes regulating the condition and manner in which motor vehicles may be operated on public streets and highways. Automobiles periodically undergo official inspection, and they are often taken into police custody in the interests of public safety. 433 U.S. at 12–13 (internal quotations omitted); *see also New York v. Class*, 475 U.S. 106, 112 (1986) ("the Federal and State Governments are amply justified in making [the vehicle identification number] a part of the web of pervasive regulation that surrounds the automobile").

Other Supreme Court cases have also expounded upon an individual's diminished expectation of privacy in the case of motor vehicles. For example, *Cardwell v. Lewis*, 417 U.S. 583 (1974), in holding that the warrantless examination of the exterior of the defendant's automobile upon probable cause was reasonable, commented in the following way with respect to the diminished privacy expectation for motor vehicles:

> One has a lesser expectation of privacy in a motor vehicle because its function is transportation and it seldom serves as one's residence or as

> the repository of personal effects. A car has little capacity for escaping public scrutiny. It travels public thoroughfares where both its occupants and its contents are in plain view. . . . This is not to say that no part of the interior of an automobile has Fourth Amendment protection; the exercise of a desire to be mobile does not, of course, waive one's right to be free of unreasonable governmental intrusion. But insofar as Fourth Amendment protection extends to a motor vehicle, it is the right to privacy that is the touchstone of our inquiry. 417 U.S. at 590–91.

And in *South Dakota v. Opperman*, 428 U.S. 364 (1976), in approving a warrantless inventory by police of an automobile impounded for parking violations, the Court said:

> Besides the element of mobility, less rigorous warrant requirements govern because the expectation of privacy with respect to one's automobile is significantly less than that relating to one's home or office. In discharging their varied responsibilities for ensuring the public safety, law enforcement officials are necessarily brought into frequent contact with automobiles. Most of this contact is distinctly non-criminal in nature. . . . Automobiles, unlike homes, are subjected to pervasive and continuing governmental regulation and controls, including periodic inspection and licensing requirements. As an everyday occurrence, police stop and examine vehicles when license plates or inspection stickers have expired, or if other violations, such as exhaust fumes or excessive noise, are noted, or if headlights or other safety equipment are not in proper working order. 428 U.S. at 367–68.

Furthermore, a person does not necessarily have a greater expectation of privacy in a vehicle merely because the vehicle is capable of functioning as a home:

> In our increasingly mobile society, many vehicles used for transportation can be and are being used not only for transportation, but for shelter, i.e., as a "home" or "residence." To distinguish between respondent's motor home and an ordinary sedan for purposes of the vehicle exception would require that we apply the exception depending upon the size of the vehicle and the quality of its appointments. Moreover, to fail to apply the exception to vehicles such as a motor home ignores the fact that a motor home lends itself easily to use as an instrument of illicit drug traffic and other illegal activity. . . . We decline . . . to distinguish between "worthy" and "unworthy" vehicles which are either on the public roads and highways, or situated such that it is reasonable to conclude that the vehicle is not being used as a residence. *California v. Carney*, 471 U.S. 386, 393–94 (1985).

(*Carney* is discussed later in this chapter in reference to the "readily mobile" requirement of the automobile exception.)

Nevertheless, even though the reasonable expectation of privacy in a vehicle is less than that in a home or office, law enforcement officers must not violate that expectation when conducting searches or inventories of vehicles. The U.S. Supreme Court stated that "a search, even of an automobile, is a substantial invasion of privacy. To protect that privacy from official arbitrariness, the Court always has regarded probable cause as the minimum requirement for a lawful search." *United States v. Ortiz*, 422 U.S. 891, 896 (1975).

Requirements of the Automobile Exception

For the automobile exception to the warrant requirement to apply, two criteria must be met:

1. An officer must have probable cause to believe the motor vehicle contains items that are incriminating in character (e.g., illegal contraband).
2. The vehicle must be readily mobile such that it is capable of being moved outside the jurisdiction (*Note*: No other emergency/exigent circumstance is required).

If these two requirements for the automobile exception are satisfied, then an officer may search the vehicle without a warrant. This chapter will first turn its attention to each of the two requirements listed above before addressing the permissible scope of a vehicle search under the automobile exception.

Probable Cause The controlling consideration in a warrantless search of a motor vehicle is probable cause. Therefore, if a law enforcement officer has a fair probability that a readily mobile motor vehicle contains items that are incriminating in character, the officer may search the vehicle. *See, e.g., United States v. Ross*, 456 U.S. 798, 809 (1982). ("In short, the exception to the warrant requirement established in *Carroll* . . . applies only to searches of vehicles that are supported by probable cause.")

In the *Carroll* decision itself, discussed at the beginning of the chapter, the Supreme Court examined whether the officers in that case had probable cause to search defendants' vehicle. The Court discussed the following facts in finding that probable cause existed to search the defendants' vehicle for evidence related to the crime of bootlegging:

> **Finally, was there probable cause? We know in this way that Grand Rapids is about 152 miles from Detroit, and that Detroit and its neighborhood along the Detroit River, which is the international boundary, is one of the most active centers for introducing illegally into this country spirituous liquors for distribution into the interior. It is obvious from the evidence that the prohibition agents were engaged in a regular patrol along the important highways from Detroit to Grand Rapids to stop and seize liquor carried in automobiles. They knew or had convincing evidence to make them believe that the Carroll boys, as they called them, were so-called 'bootleggers' in Grand Rapids; i.e., that they were engaged in plying the unlawful trade of selling such liquor in that city. The officers had soon after noted their going from Grand Rapids halfway to Detroit, and attempted to follow them to that city to see where they went, but they escaped observation. Two months later these officers suddenly met the same men on their way westward presumably from Detroit. The partners in the original combination to sell liquor in Grand Rapids were together in the same automobile they had been in the night when they tried to furnish the whisky to the officers, which was thus identified as part of the firm equipment. They were coming from the direction of the great source of supply for their stock to Grand Rapids, where they plied their trade. That the officers, when they saw the defendants, believed that they were carrying liquor, we can have no doubt, and we think it is equally clear that they had reasonable cause for thinking so.** 267 U.S. at 160.

In *United States v. Swanson*, 341 F.3d 524 (6th Cir. 2003), the court also found probable cause sufficient to justify a warrantless search of defendant's vehicle under the automobile exception:

> We conclude that the agents had both probable cause and justification for . . . searching [defendant's] automobile without a warrant. First, the agents had probable cause to . . . search the vehicle. [Defendant's companion] had used the Grand Am to deliver an automatic weapon thirty days earlier to a confidential informant; thus the vehicle was used as an instrumentality of the crime. The agents also had ample facts at their disposal to support their belief that there was further evidence of a crime inside the car. Only two days earlier, [defendant's companion] had received a Federal Express package from the confidential informant containing money as payment for automatic weapons and silencers that [defendant's companion] was to deliver by United Parcel Service. The agents had seen [defendant's companion] arrive for work at the tattoo parlor in the Grand Am that day. When they searched the tattoo parlor, the empty Federal Express package was found in the trash. They also found three handguns, but not any automatic weapons that might be the ones that were to be delivered to the confidential informant. Moreover, the agents had just spoken with [defendant]. [Defendant] had given evasive answers only to questions about guns. When asked if there was anything in the car that could get him into trouble, he replied yes. There was "a fair probability that contraband or evidence of a crime" would be found inside the automobile. 341 F.3d at 532 (internal citations omitted).

However, in *United States v. Edwards*, 242 F.3d 928 (10th Cir. 2001), the court found that probable cause to search the vehicle was lacking because police officers previously received information that the relevant crime had not actually occurred:

> [Defendant and defendant's girlfriend] were not arrested in or near the vehicle and, although they were carrying what appeared to be contraband in [defendant's girlfriend's] camera bag, there was no testimony presented at the suppression hearing that would support a belief by the police that additional contraband or evidence could be found in the vehicle. Furthermore, by the time the police decided to search the rental car, the police were aware that the City National Bank had not been robbed, making it even less likely that traditional tools of robbery (such as guns or disguises) might be found in the vehicle. In short, we see no evidence from which the police could have deduced a "fair probability" that a search of the car would reveal contraband or further evidence of criminal activity. 242 F.3d at 939.

Although the *Carroll* doctrine allows the warrantless *search* of a motor vehicle on the basis of probable cause to believe it contains items of an incriminating character, a warrantless **seizure** of the *vehicle itself* is allowed when police have probable cause to believe that the vehicle itself is contraband. In *Florida v. White*, 526 U.S. 559 (1999), police officers on several occasions observed the defendant using his car to deliver cocaine. Therefore, they had probable cause to believe that his car was subject to forfeiture under the Florida Contraband Forfeiture Act, which provided that any vehicle used in violation of the act "may be seized and shall be forfeited." When the defendant was later arrested at his workplace on unrelated charges, the arresting officers seized his car in accordance with the provisions of the Act. During a subsequent inventory search, the police found crack cocaine in the car.

The Supreme Court held that the warrantless seizure of the automobile did not violate the Fourth Amendment:

> **Although . . . the police lacked probable cause to believe that respondent's car contained contraband . . . they certainly had probable cause to believe that the vehicle *itself* was contraband under Florida law. Recognition of the need to seize readily movable contraband before it is spirited away undoubtedly underlies the early federal laws relied upon in *Carroll*. . . . This need is equally weighty when the *automobile*, as opposed to its contents, is the contraband that the police seek to secure.** 526 U.S. 564–65.

The Court noted that because the police seized the car from a public place—the defendant's employer's parking lot—the warrantless seizure did not invade the defendant's privacy. **"[O]ur Fourth Amendment jurisprudence has consistently accorded law enforcement officials greater latitude in exercising their duties in public places."** 526 U.S. at 565.

Readily Mobile Vehicle For a number of years, the automobile exception as set forth in *Carroll* was interpreted by the courts as requiring some **exigent circumstance** to conduct a search of a vehicle once it was stopped (i.e., no longer mobile). In other words, after lawfully stopping a vehicle, police were expected to apply for a warrant to search the vehicle unless some emergency situation justified the warrantless search and/or seizure of an automobile. For example, *Cardwell v. Lewis*, 417 U.S. 583 (1974), upheld the warrantless search and seizure of a car after determining that evidence could have been removed from the vehicle by family members of the defendant if the police had delayed in seizing the car. *See also, Chambers v. Maroney*, 399 U.S. 42 (1970). **("Only in exigent circumstances will the judgment of the police as to probable cause serve as a sufficient authorization for a search.")** But a showing of exigent circumstances is no longer required. All that is necessary today to search and/or seize a readily-mobile motor vehicle stopped on the road is probable cause. In *Michigan v. Thomas*, 458 U.S. 259, 261 (1982), the U.S. Supreme Court said:

> **In *Chambers v. Maroney* . . . we held that when police officers have probable cause to believe there is contraband inside an automobile that has been stopped on the road, the officers may conduct a warrantless search of the vehicle, even after it has been impounded and is in police custody. We firmly reiterated this holding in *Texas v. White*, 423 U.S. 67 (1975). . . . It is thus clear that the justification to conduct such a warrantless search does not vanish once the car has been immobilized; nor does it depend upon a reviewing court's assessment of the likelihood in each particular case that the car would have been driven away, or that its contents would have been tampered with, during the period required for the police to obtain a warrant.**

In short, any requirement that exigent circumstances must exist before the police's judgment as to probable cause will justify a warrantless search, is automatically satisfied in the case of a motor vehicle that is "readily mobile." **"If a car is readily mobile and probable cause exists to believe it contains contraband, the Fourth Amendment . . . permits police to search the vehicle without more."** *Pennsylvania v. Labron*, 518 U.S. 938, 940 (1996); see also *Maryland v. Dyson*, 527 U.S. 465, 467 (1999) (reaffirming *Labron's* holding that the automobile exception does not require **"a separate finding of exigency in addition to a finding of probable cause"**).

In *California v. Carney*, 471 U.S. 386 (1985), the U.S. Supreme Court provided some guidance as to what constitutes a "readily mobile vehicle." In *Carney*, Drug Enforcement Agency (DEA) agents had probable cause to search a mobile motor home parked in a lot in a large city's downtown area. The Court applied the standard that a search of a vehicle is justified under the automobile exception if the vehicle "is being used on the highways, or if it is readily capable of such use and is found stationary in a place not regularly used for residential purposes—temporary or otherwise." 471 U.S. at 392. In *Carney*, the Court found that the warrantless search of the mobile home was valid because the vehicle was readily mobile by the turn of the ignition key, and was so situated that an objective observer would conclude that it was being used not as a residence but as a vehicle. In a footnote, the Court listed some factors that would indicate whether a mobile home was being used as a residence as opposed to a readily mobile vehicle:

> Among the factors that might be relevant in determining whether a warrant would be required in such a circumstance is its location, whether the vehicle is readily-mobile or instead, for instance, elevated on blocks, whether the vehicle is licensed, whether it is connected to utilities, and whether it has convenient access to a public road. 471 U.S. at 394 n.3.

In contrast to *Carney*, the court in *United States v. Levesque*, 625 F. Supp. 428 (D.N.H. 1985), found that the motor home in that case was not readily mobile, and therefore disallowed a warrantless search by police:

> The trailer at issue . . . was situated in a trailer park and on a lot, objectively indicating that it was being used as a residence. Although the truck which tows the trailer was only a few feet from the trailer, the trailer was not readily mobile in light of the fact that one end of the trailer was elevated on blocks and that the trailer was connected to utilities at the campground, and also because of the three quarters of an hour lead time to connect the trailer and truck. The mobile home exception to the warrant requirement thus would appear to have no application herein. 625 F. Supp. at 450–51.

In determining whether a vehicle is readily mobile, courts look to whether the vehicle is inherently capable of movement and not to whether the vehicle is actually mobile at a particular moment in time. For example, in *United States v. Mercado*, 307 F.3d 1226 (10th Cir. 2002), the court found that a vehicle that is temporarily immobile due to mechanical problems is still readily-mobile for purposes of the automobile exception to the warrant requirement:

> The present case presents a unique circumstance because the car was not immobile as the result of a justifiable police stop but simply because it was having mechanical problems. Regardless, Appellant's car had not lost its inherent mobility. Additionally, the repair shop was open all night and the mechanic had indicated that the van would be operable again before morning. The shop was open to the public, including to the Appellant, all night. We are of the view that mere temporary immobility due to a readily repairable problem while at an open public repair shop does not remove the vehicle from the category of "readily-mobile." 307 F.3d at 1229.

See also United States v. Maggard, 221 F.3d 1345 (8th Cir. May 26, 2000) (unpublished decision). ("[T]he pickup truck did not appear to have lost its inherent mobility. It was merely stuck in a ditch. Inasmuch as there was no evidence of any permanent immobility, it was reasonable for the officers who conducted the search to conclude that all the truck needed was to be towed out of the ditch and then it could have been driven away.")

United States v. Brookins, 345 F.3d 231 (4th Cir. 2003), is another case shedding light on how modern courts address the readily mobile requirement of the automobile exception. As the court in *Brookins* explains, the inquiry is focused primarily on whether the vehicle is inherently mobile as opposed to a dwelling, or residence, which would not qualify under this test:

> [Defendant] seeks additional support for this theory in *California v. Carney*, where the Supreme Court held that a mobile home, on the facts presented, was more characteristic of an automobile than a fixed residence. The Court [in *Carney*] did look to the nature of the location where the vehicle was discovered, but only to ascertain whether the vehicle itself was, in an ontological sense, in use as a 'movable vessel' or as a fixed residence. [In addition,] [i]n light of the Supreme Court's holding in *Dyson*, we find the "automobile exception" applicable to the case before us. First, the motor vehicle at issue was clearly operational and therefore readily movable. Second, as discussed in greater detail above, the police officers had probable cause to conclude that there was contraband in the vehicle. . . . Given these facts, the warrantless search of [the defendant's] vehicle by law enforcement officers did not violate his Fourth Amendment rights. 345 F.3d at 238.

As the cases discussed above show, unless it has become clear to police that a vehicle is no longer being used for the purpose of movement or mobility (i.e., it has been elevated "on blocks," many or all of its essential parts have been permanently removed, etc.), modern courts will not hesitate to find the readily mobile requirement of the automobile exception satisfied.

Apart from courts addressing whether automobiles and mobile homes qualify as "readily mobile vehicles," some courts have examined whether other vessels fit this category. For example, in *United States v. Tartaglia*, 864 F.2d 837 (D.C. Cir. 1989), police had probable cause to search a train roomette for drugs. The court found a warrantless search of the roomette justified under the circumstances:

> Because the police did not have sufficient time to procure a warrant before train 98 left Union Station and because there was more than a reasonable likelihood that the train, and therefore the roomette and its contents, would be moved before a warrant could be obtained, the warrantless search of defendant's roomette was justified. . . . 864 F.2d at 843.

One plurality decision by the U.S. Supreme Court that has seemingly survived *Labron* and *Dyson*, both mentioned above, is *Coolidge v. New Hampshire*, 403 U.S. 443 (1971). *Coolidge* appears to stand for the principle that even though a vehicle is readily mobile and police have the necessary probable cause, it may not be searched absent a warrant if it is located on private property and there is sufficient time to get a warrant. In *Coolidge*, the Court pointed out that there was no real possibility that someone would move the car located on the defendant's property or conceal or destroy evidence within it. Also, the police had known for some time of the probable role of the defendant's automobile in a crime. They went to his home, arrested him, and escorted his wife and children to another town to spend the night. No other adults resided in the house, and the automobile was unoccupied and parked in defendant's driveway. Police towed it to the station house and searched it there without a warrant. The Court invalidated the search under the automobile exception because there was sufficient time to obtain a warrant: "**In short, by no possible stretch of the legal imagination can this be made into a case where 'it is not practicable to secure a warrant,' and the 'automobile exception,' despite its label, is simply irrelevant.**" 403 U.S. at 462.

At least one federal circuit decision, however, casts doubt on the continuing viability of *Coolidge*. In *United States v. Brookins*, 345 F.3d 231 (4th Cir. 2003), also discussed above, the court upheld the warrantless search of a vehicle parked in the driveway of a private residence. The court rejected defendant's argument that the vehicle could not be searched under the automobile exception because of its location on private property:

> [Defendant] proposes an interpretation of the "automobile exception," which he grounds largely in *Coolidge v. New Hampshire*. In *Coolidge*, the Supreme Court, by the opinion of a four-justice plurality, declined to apply *Carroll* under circumstances evincing no exigency whatsoever. Specifically, the defendant's automobile was parked in his own driveway and contained no contraband. Additionally, the police had developed probable cause well in advance of the warrantless search. [Defendant] maintains that *Coolidge* represents the sole Supreme Court decision to address "head-on" the warrantless search of an automobile at a private residence. Based upon the facts of *Coolidge*, [defendant] would posit a bright-line rule, whereby the automobile exception may never apply when a vehicle is stationed on private, residential property.
>
> We decline to adopt this construction of *Coolidge*. Nor do we find it necessary to determine the contours of the expectation of privacy in and around one's private property. Although heightened privacy interests may be triggered when a vehicle is encountered on private property, the *Coolidge* plurality opinion cannot be fairly read to create a bright-line rule precluding warrantless searches on private property under all circumstances. 345 F.3d at 237 n.8.

Until the U.S. Supreme Court decides a case that more clearly articulates the parameters of the readily mobile requirement to the automobile exception, officers should obtain a warrant before searching a vehicle they have probable cause to search when:

1. the vehicle is clearly not being used for movement (e.g., it is elevated "on blocks"); or
2. the vehicle is located on private property and there is time to obtain a warrant.

Delay in Search If possible, warrantless searches under the *Carroll* doctrine should be conducted immediately at the scene where the vehicle is stopped. If, however, surrounding circumstances make an immediate search on the highway unsafe or impractical, the vehicle may be removed to a more convenient location. If a search is conducted without unreasonable delay after the vehicle's arrival at the new location, the probable cause factor existing on the highway remains in force, and the warrantless search is constitutionally permissible. This was the holding of *Chambers v. Maroney*, 399 U.S. 42 (1970). In *Chambers*, the police had information that armed robbers had fled the robbery scene in a light blue compact station wagon. Four men were said to be in the vehicle, one wearing a green sweater and another wearing a trench coat. The police stopped a vehicle fitting the description, arrested the four occupants, and drove the vehicle to the police station. There, police thoroughly searched the vehicle and seized

How Should We Interpret *Dyson* and *Labron*?

State v. Pederson-Maxwell, 619 N.W.2d 777 (Minn. App. 2000).

On July 10, 1998, at approximately 8:00 P.M., a confidential informant met with Crookston Police Department Detective Gerardo Moreno and other law enforcement officers. The informant stated that he or she had met with individuals the previous day at the Polk County Fair in Fertile, Minnesota, who stated they could supply the informant with controlled substances. The informant was supplied with $450 of "buy money" and an electronic transmitter to record the purchase. This informant met with Brian Christopher Johnson at the fair, and Johnson introduced the informant to Raymond Richard Krebs. Johnson and Krebs agreed to sell the informant two ounces of marijuana for $300 later in the evening.

The informant subsequently met with Krebs and Johnson. The three proceeded to a white four-door Dodge Spirit, which was registered to the appellant, Tamara Gay Pederson-Maxwell. Krebs entered the vehicle and told a female sleeping in the front seat (later identified as appellant) to open the trunk so he could get the "weed." Krebs instead grabbed a pair of boots from the back seat of the vehicle and took approximately two ounces of marijuana out of one of the boots. The informant, Krebs, and Johnson then entered a different vehicle and drove around for a short time.

The informant, after being dropped off, met with Deputy Helget. The informant told Deputy Helget that Krebs and Johnson smoked a marijuana joint while they were in the car, and that Krebs provided the informant with approximately two ounces of marijuana in exchange for $300. A short time later, the informant identified Krebs to Detective Moreno as the man who sold him the marijuana. The informant also identified appellant as the woman who was sleeping in the Dodge Spirit when Krebs obtained the marijuana. Krebs and appellant were placed under arrest. Johnson was also subsequently arrested.

The officers searched Krebs and found $517 in cash, $290 of which was marked buy money that the informant stated was paid in exchange for the marijuana. The appellant's purse was found to contain approximately two ounces of marijuana and $2,675 in cash. At trial, the evidence established that the actual amount of marijuana in appellant's purse totaled 39.9 grams.

Detective Moreno asked the appellant for permission to search the Dodge Spirit, but she refused. She agreed to allow Detective Moreno to drive the vehicle from the fairgrounds to the Fertile Police Department. Once at the police department, a trained drug-detection dog reacted to the presence of controlled substances in the vehicle and in the trunk. The vehicle was impounded and transported to the Northwest Regional Corrections Center in Crookston.

On July 13, 1998, officers searched the Dodge Spirit without a warrant. Three Tupperware containers filled with marijuana, a weight scale, a cellular phone, a pager, a .380 caliber semiautomatic handgun and an ammunition clip, a .38 caliber semiautomatic handgun with one loaded and one unloaded ammunition clip, an interchangeable .45 caliber barrel, ammunition, and

(Continued)

How Should We Interpret *Dyson* and *Labron*? (*Continued*)

other items were found in the trunk of the vehicle. The appellant was charged with, and convicted of, two counts of fifth-degree controlled substance crime and one count of failing to affix a controlled substance tax stamp.

The court in *Pedersen-Maxwell* began its discussion by finding that there was probable cause to search the appellants' automobile: "In the present case, the dog's reaction did establish probable cause that there was contraband in the trunk of the car." 619 N.W.2d at 781.

In response to appellant's argument that the warrantless search of her automobile required both probable cause and an emergency, the court said:

> Appellant points to language in *Pennsylvania v. Labron* for the proposition that something more than probable cause is required to search a vehicle without a warrant[.] Appellant would have us interpret "readily mobile" as equivalent to exigent circumstances above and beyond mere probable cause. [But] *Labron* validated automobile searches based on probable cause, without requiring separate exigency requirements.
>
> The second case, *Maryland v. Dyson*, is equally unhelpful to appellant. [T]he Supreme Court in *Dyson* noted: "In this case, the Court of Special Appeals found that there was 'abundant probable cause' that the car contained contraband. This finding alone satisfies the automobile exception to the Fourth Amendment's warrant requirement." Based on the language of these two cases, the automobile exception to the Fourth Amendment's warrant requirement "does not have a separate exigency requirement." 619 N.W.2d at 781, 782.

The court then held that the drugs found in appellant's trunk by police were admissible under the automobile exception.

Do you agree with the appellant in *Pedersen-Maxwell* that there should be a separate finding of exigent circumstances before courts find the warrantless search of a vehicle by police based on probable cause valid? Or does an impending search of a readily mobile motor vehicle inherently support a finding of exigency because these vehicles can easily be driven out of a particular jurisdiction? Should the fact that individuals have a reduced expectation of privacy in vehicles justify the elimination of the exigency requirement (as many courts have concluded)? Explain your responses fully.

evidence leading to the defendant's conviction. The U.S. Supreme Court upheld the search:

> In enforcing the Fourth Amendment's prohibition against unreasonable searches and seizures, the Court has insisted upon probable cause as a minimum requirement for a reasonable search permitted by the Constitution. As a general rule, it has also required the judgment of a magistrate on the probable cause issue and the issuance of a warrant before a search is made. Only in exigent circumstances will the judgment of the police as

> to probable cause serve as a sufficient authorization for a search. *Carroll . . .* holds a search warrant unnecessary where there is probable cause to search an automobile stopped on the highway; the car is movable, the occupants are alerted, and the car's contents may never be found again if a warrant must be obtained. Hence an immediate search is constitutionally permissible. Arguably, because of the preference for a magistrate's judgment, only the immobilization of the car should be permitted until a search warrant is obtained; arguably, only the "lesser" intrusion is permissible until the magistrate authorizes the "greater." But which is the "greater" and which the "lesser" intrusion is itself a debatable question and the answer may depend on a variety of circumstances. *For constitutional purposes, we see no difference between on the one hand seizing and holding a car before presenting the probable cause issue to a magistrate and on the other hand carrying out an immediate search without a warrant. Given probable cause to search, either course is reasonable under the Fourth Amendment.* On the facts before us, the blue station wagon could have been searched on the spot when it was stopped since there was probable cause to search and it was a fleeting target for a search. The probable cause factor still obtained at the station house and so did the mobility of the car unless the Fourth Amendment permits a warrantless seizure of the car and the denial of its use to anyone until a warrant is secured. In that event there is little to choose in terms of practical consequences between an immediate search without a warrant and the car's immobilization until a warrant is obtained. 399 U.S. at 51–52 (emphasis added).

Florida v. Meyers, 466 U.S. 380 (1984), upheld a warrantless search of an impounded automobile eight hours after it had been impounded and despite the fact that the automobile had already been subject to an initial, valid search on the highway. *Meyers* relied on *Michigan v. Thomas*, 458 U.S. 259 (1982), which upheld a warrantless search of an automobile after it had been stopped on the road, taken into police custody (e.g., "impounded"), and subjected to a valid inventory search. (Impoundment and inventory searches are discussed later in this chapter).

And *United States v. Johns*, 469 U.S. 478 (1985), upheld a warrantless search of containers in an impounded vehicle three days after it had been impounded. In particular, *United States v. Johns*, 469 U.S. 478 (1985), held that, when officers have probable cause to search a vehicle for a specific object, the search of a container in the vehicle that could contain that object need not be conducted at the same time as the initial seizure or search of the vehicle. Customs agents in *Johns* had seized and impounded a vehicle under the *Carroll* doctrine on the basis of probable cause to believe it contained marijuana. The Court approved a warrantless search of plastic bags found in the vehicle conducted three days later.

In the aftermath of *Johns*, officers should obtain a warrant for searches to be made more than three days after impounding a vehicle. Note again that courts have a strong preference for warrants. Law enforcement officers should consider applying for a warrant to search an automobile once it has been taken into police custody, especially when the facts and circumstances supporting probable cause may be weak or questionable. Note also that officers may validly detain a vehicle they have probable cause to search while they seek a warrant. *See United States v. Kimberlin*, 805 F.2d 210, 229 (7th Cir. 1986). ("[An] agent was sent to secure [the vehicle] until the search warrant could be obtained and the search conducted. Defendant's lawyer arranged to have the car towed, but the agent did not permit the removal. Defendant argues that this interference with his control of the car was an unreasonable seizure in violation of the Fourth Amendment, requiring suppression of the results of the search. We think it clear that when an officer has probable cause to search a vehicle, it is reasonable under the Fourth Amendment to prevent removal while obtaining a warrant.")

key points

- Under the *Carroll* doctrine, if a car is readily mobile and probable cause exists to believe it contains contraband, the Fourth Amendment permits police to search the vehicle without a warrant or other justification. The *Carroll* doctrine, also known as the automobile exception to the warrant requirement, stems from the inherent mobility of motor vehicles as well as the diminished expectation of privacy possessed by occupants of motor vehicles.

- To satisfy the readily mobile requirement of the automobile exception, the vehicle must be inherently capable of movement. No separate showing of exigency is generally needed for the automobile exception to apply.

- Officers should obtain a warrant before searching a vehicle they have probable cause to search in the following circumstances: (1) the vehicle is clearly not being used for movement (i.e., it is elevated

"on blocks"); or (2) the vehicle is located on private property and there is time to obtain a warrant.

- The justification to search a motor vehicle under the *Carroll* doctrine does not vanish once the vehicle has been immobilized, impounded, and taken into police custody; nor does it depend on the likelihood that the vehicle would have been driven away or that its contents would have been tampered with during the period required for the police to obtain a warrant.

- If circumstances make an immediate search of a vehicle on the highway unsafe or impractical, the vehicle may be removed to a more convenient location. If a search is conducted without unreasonable delay after the vehicle's arrival at the new location, the probable cause factor existing on the highway remains in force, and the warrantless search is constitutionally permissible.

Scope of a Vehicle Search under the Automobile Exception

The discussion related to the scope of a search of a vehicle under the *Carroll* doctrine is divided into two sections: (1) when an officer has probable cause to search the entire vehicle or a particular area of that vehicle (e.g., the trunk); and (2) when an officer has probable cause to search a container located within a vehicle. At times, of course, officers may have probable cause to search both a vehicle and containers within it; in those cases, the relevant principles discussed in both sections would apply.

Search of an Entire Vehicle or of a Particular Area in a Vehicle *United States v. Ross*, 456 U.S. 798 (1982), established the permissible scope of a warrantless search of a motor vehicle under the *Carroll* doctrine. In that case, police stopped and searched an automobile they had probable cause to believe contained narcotics. During the search, an officer found and opened a closed brown paper bag and a zippered leather pouch in the automobile's trunk, revealing heroin and a large amount of money. The Court held the search was legal:

> [T]he scope of the warrantless search authorized by [the *Carroll*] exception is no broader and no narrower than a magistrate could legitimately

> **authorize by warrant. If probable cause justifies the search of a lawfully stopped vehicle, it justifies the search of every part of the vehicle and its contents that may conceal the object of the search.** 456 U.S. at 825.

In other words, the scope of the search depends entirely on the object of the search:

> **The scope of a warrantless search of an automobile thus is not defined by the nature of the container in which the contraband is secreted. Rather, it is defined by the object of the search and the places in which there is probable cause to believe that it may be found. Just as probable cause to believe that a stolen lawnmower may be found in a garage will not support a warrant to search an upstairs bedroom, probable cause to believe that undocumented aliens are being transported in a van will not justify a warrantless search of a suitcase. Probable cause to believe that a container placed in the trunk of a taxi contains contraband or evidence does not justify a search of the entire cab.** 456 U.S. at 824.

Because the scope of a search depends, in part, on the object of that search, an officer with probable cause to believe an illegal alien is present within a vehicle could not search in that vehicle's glove compartment or in a similar area that is too small to conceal a person.

In addition, as the Court indicated in *Ross,* the scope of a search depends on the location in which there is probable cause to believe items of an incriminating character will be found. For example, if an officer has probable cause to believe the trunk of the vehicle contains incriminating items, the officer may only search that particular area of the vehicle. Likewise, if an officer has probable cause to believe the passenger compartment of a vehicle contains incriminating items, he or she could only search that particular area of the vehicle. But if the officer validly possessed probable cause that the entire vehicle contained items of an incriminating character, the officer could search anywhere in the vehicle those items could fit.

A case that nicely illustrates these issues related to scope is *United States v. Wald,* 216 F.3d 1222 (10th Cir. 2000). In *Wald,* the court found that the officer had developed probable cause to search the passenger compartment of a vehicle for contraband but not the trunk:

> Had [the officer] testified that he detected the odor of raw methamphetamine, such evidence, if based upon proper foundation, would have sufficed to provide probable cause for the trunk search. In the instant case, however, [the officer] testified that he smelled only burnt methamphetamine, not raw methamphetamine, and that burnt methamphetamine has a distinctively pungent odor. Following [precedent case law], the strong odor of burnt methamphetamine, whether or not it can permeate trunks, does not provide probable cause to search a trunk, because it is unreasonable to think someone smoked drugs in the trunk of a car. 216 F.3d at 1228.

The court in *Wald* essentially held that because the officer smelled burnt methamphetamine, which supported a belief that individuals had recently used the drug, the officer lacked probable cause to search the trunk of the car given the improbability of current or recent use of the drug in that area of the car. Thus, the court excluded drugs the officer found during his search of the trunk.

In contrast to odors detected by humans, sniffs by police dogs supporting probable cause to search a vehicle are not subjected to as much precision. For example, in *United States v. Rosborough*, 366 F.3d 1145 (10th Cir. 2004), when a dog trained in drug detection alerted police to the presence of drugs in the passenger area of a vehicle, the court permitted police to search the trunk of that vehicle without a warrant. According to the court, the canine sniff provided the necessary probable cause to search the trunk:

> [I]n the case of an alert by a trained drug-sniffing dog with a good record, we would not require corroboration to establish probable cause. The dog would have no reason to make a false alert. . . . [F]or a human sniffer, an officer with an incentive to find evidence of illegal activities and to justify his actions when he had searched without consent, we believe constitutional rights are endangered if limitations are not imposed. Thus, [a precedent case] clearly implies that a canine alert toward the passenger compartment of a vehicle would give rise to probable cause to search the vehicle's trunk. Our holdings with regard to drug-dog alerts do not lend themselves to that level of exactness. A dog alert creates general probable cause to search a vehicle; it does not implicate the precision of a surgeon working with scalpel in hand. Thus, we hold that a canine alert toward the passenger area of a vehicle gives rise to probable cause to search the trunk as well; the search [of defendant's] vehicle subsequent to the canine alert was therefore supported by probable cause. 366 F.3d at 1153.

And in *United States v. Carter*, 300 F.3d 415 (4th Cir. 2002), though the court required more precision for the canine sniff than in *Rosborough*, the court found that a particular sniff by a dog trained in drug detection supported probable cause for police to search the trunk when the dog alerted in the "vicinity of the trunk" area:

> The government argues that the K-9 drug dog's "alerting" on the driver side of the car gave [the officer] probable cause to search the entire vehicle: including the trunk and the suitcase [located in the trunk]. We think that overstates the matter. Because probable cause must be tailored to specific compartments and containers within an automobile, the key is whether the dog "alerted" in the precise vicinity of the trunk. That is a question of fact that the district court resolved in favor of the government, finding that the dog's "alerting" was sufficiently close to the trunk to give [the officer] probable cause to believe it contained contraband. We review the district court's findings of fact in a suppression hearing only for clear error. And it was not clearly erroneous for the district court to conclude that the dog's "alerting" was prompted by the contents of the trunk. 300 F.3d at 422.

(For further discussion of canine sniffs in the context of motor vehicles, see the section entitled "Searches by Dogs" at the end of this chapter.)

The scope of a *Carroll* doctrine search may even extend to dismantling part of the vehicle, or looking into hidden compartments within the vehicle. In *United States v. Zucco*, 71 F.3d 188 (5th Cir. 1995), police had probable cause to search an entire recreational vehicle because cocaine had been found in a cabinet during a valid consent search. When a drug-sniffing dog alerted to another part of the vehicle, police were authorized to remove a wall panel, where they discovered a large cache of cocaine. *See also United States v. Thornton*, 197 F.3d 241, 249 (7th Cir. 1999). (Once the first police officer lawfully discovered a package in a vehicle containing cocaine, a second officer was permitted to search two hidden compartments in the car's interior because "[t]he discovery of the 1-kilogram brick of cocaine created probable cause to search the rest of [defendant's] car.")

Search of a Container Found in a Vehicle When officers have probable cause to search only a particular container placed in a vehicle, they may search that container without a warrant but not the entire vehicle. In *California v. Acevedo*, 500 U.S. 565 (1991), police observed the defendant leave an apartment known to contain marijuana with a brown paper package the same size as marijuana packages they had seen earlier. He placed the bag in the trunk of his car and started to drive away. Fearing the loss of evidence, officers in an unmarked car stopped him, opened his trunk and the bag, and found marijuana.

The Court in *Acevedo* held that the Fourth Amendment does not compel separate treatment for an automobile search that extends only to a container within the vehicle. The Court said:

> The interpretation of the *Carroll* doctrine set forth in *Ross* now applies to all searches of containers found in an automobile. In other words, the police may search without a warrant if their search is supported by probable cause. The Court in *Ross* put it this way: 'The scope of a warrantless search of an automobile . . . is not defined by the nature of the container in which the contraband is secreted. Rather, it is defined by the object of the search and the places in which there is probable cause to believe that it may be found.' [The Court in *Ross*] went on to note: 'Probable cause to believe that a container placed in the trunk of a taxi contains contraband or evidence does not justify a search of the entire cab.' We affirm that principle. In the case before us, the police had probable cause to believe that the paper bag in the automobile's trunk contained marijuana. That probable cause now allows a warrantless search of the paper bag. The facts in the record reveal that the police did not have probable cause to believe that contraband was hidden in any other part of the automobile and a search of the entire vehicle would have been without probable cause and unreasonable under the Fourth Amendment. 500 U.S. at 579–80.

Thus, if police have probable cause to believe a particular container contains items of an incriminating character, they may search that container. But they may not search other areas of the vehicle unless they have probable cause that those areas contain incriminating items.

Note that if police have probable cause to search an entire vehicle, they may conduct a warrantless search of the vehicle and any containers in the vehicle capable of holding the object of their search. For example, in *United States v. Pinela-Hernandez*, 262 F.3d 974 (9th Cir. 2001), police developed probable cause to search a vehicle for drugs by corroborating an informant's tip and as a result of certain actions by defendant. They did not obtain a warrant to search the vehicle. Citing the U.S. Supreme Court's decision in *Ross*, the court in *Pinela-Hernandez* said:

> The Supreme Court has held that if "probable cause justifies the search of a lawfully stopped vehicle, it justifies the search of every part of the vehicle and its contents that may conceal the object of the search." Because there was probable cause to search the car [for drugs], there was probable cause to open the trunk and to search the packages that turned out to contain marijuana. 262 F.3d at 979.

Also, in *Ross* itself, discussed earlier for its relevance to the overall scope inquiry for automobile searches, the Supreme Court found that "police officers had probable cause to search [the defendant's] entire vehicle" for drugs. 456 U.S.

at 817. The Court in *Ross* overturned the lower court's holding, thereby sanctioning police actions in opening and searching without a warrant a closed paper bag and leather pouch located in the trunk of the vehicle.

Furthermore, *Wyoming v. Houghton*, 526 U.S. 295, 307 (1999), extended warrantless automobile container searches to a passenger's belongings. The Court in *Houghton* held that "**police officers with probable cause to search a car may inspect passengers' belongings found in the car that are capable of concealing the object of the search.**" The Court found that passengers, like drivers, have a reduced expectation of privacy with regard to property that they transport in motor vehicles. Police examination of an item of a passenger's personal property is unlikely to produce the annoyance, fear, and humiliation that a search of one's body is likely to produce. In contrast, the Court found the government's interests in inspecting passengers' belongings substantial:

> **Effective law enforcement would be appreciably impaired without the ability to search a passenger's personal belongings when there is reason to believe contraband or evidence of criminal wrongdoing is hidden in the car. As in all car-search cases, the "ready mobility" of an automobile creates a risk that the evidence or contraband will be permanently lost while a warrant is obtained. . . . In addition, a car passenger—unlike the unwitting tavern patron in *Ybarra*—will often be engaged in a common enterprise with the driver, and have the same interest in concealing the fruits or the evidence of their wrongdoing. . . . A criminal might be able to hide contraband in a passenger's belongings as readily as in other containers in the car . . . perhaps even surreptitiously, without the passenger's knowledge or permission.** 526 U.S. at 304–05.

A few other considerations apply to the scope of searches under the automobile exception. For example, if an officer obtains probable cause to search a container after the container has been removed from a vehicle, the *Carroll* doctrine does not apply—even if the container is in the process of being returned to the vehicle. The officer must have probable cause to believe that items subject to seizure are contained *somewhere inside the vehicle.* In *State v. Lewis*, 611 A.2d 69 (Me. 1992), after the defendant was arrested for operating a vehicle under the influence of drugs or alcohol, the officer released him on personal recognizance and offered him a ride to a motel. The defendant voluntarily retrieved from his car a carry-on bag containing two smaller bags; the officer, smelling the odor of marijuana, asked to see inside the smaller bags. When the defendant attempted to return the carry-on bag to his car, the officer opened the smaller bags and found marijuana. The court invalidated the search, holding that "the fact that the bags came from the car and were in the process of being returned to the car does not trigger the automobile exception." 611 A.2d at 71. (Searches of containers not associated with vehicles will be discussed further below.)

In addition, searches under the automobile exception do not extend to the body of an occupant of the vehicle. The U.S. Supreme Court in *Houghton* cited *United States v. Di Re*, 332 U.S. 581 (1948), for the principle that officers may not conduct searches of a car occupant's person under the automobile exception:

> *United States v. Di Re* held that probable cause to search a car did not justify a body search of a passenger. [This] case turned on the unique, significantly heightened protection afforded against searches of one's person. Even a limited search of the outer clothing . . . constitutes a severe, though brief,

intrusion upon cherished personal security, and it must surely be an annoying, frightening, and perhaps humiliating experience. Such traumatic consequences are not to be expected when the police examine an item of personal property found in a car. 526 U.S. at 303 (internal quotations omitted).

Of course, if an officer has probable cause to arrest one or more occupants of a motor vehicle, the officer may search all arrested occupants and the passenger compartment incident to that arrest. As part of a search incident to a vehicle occupant's arrest, the officer may search for weapons and destructible evidence on the arrested person and in the passenger compartment. (See the discussion of *New York v. Belton* in Chapter 8 on searches incident to arrest.) Also, if an officer has reasonable suspicion that an occupant of a vehicle is armed and dangerous, the officer may conduct a limited frisk of that person for weapons as well as a limited search of the passenger compartment of the vehicle for weapons. (See Chapter 7 on stops and frisks.)

Search of a Container Not Found in a Vehicle The rationale justifying a warrantless search of a container in an automobile believed to be harboring items of an incriminating nature arguably applies with equal force to any movable container believed to be carrying such an item. *United States v. Chadwick*, 433 U.S. 1 (1977), however, squarely rejected that argument. In *Chadwick*, federal railroad officials became suspicious when they noticed that a large, unusually heavy footlocker loaded onto a train was leaking talcum powder, a substance often used to mask the odor of marijuana. Narcotics agents met the train at its destination, and a trained police dog signaled the presence of a controlled substance inside the footlocker. Instead of seizing the footlocker at that time, the agents waited until the defendant arrived and placed the footlocker in the trunk of his automobile. Before he started the engine, the officers arrested him and his two companions. The agents then removed the footlocker from the trunk, moved it to a secure place in a government building, and opened it there without a warrant. They discovered a large quantity of marijuana inside the footlocker.

On appeal, the prosecution did not argue that the locker's brief contact with the automobile's trunk made the *Carroll* doctrine applicable. Rather, the prosecution argued that the warrantless search was "reasonable" because a footlocker has some of the mobile characteristics that support warrantless searches of automobiles. The Supreme Court rejected the argument:

> **The factors which diminish the privacy aspects of an automobile do not apply to respondents' footlocker. Luggage contents are not open to public view, except as a condition to a border entry or common carrier travel; nor is luggage subject to regular inspections and official scrutiny on a continuing basis. Unlike an automobile, whose primary function is transportation, luggage is intended as a repository of personal effects. In sum, a person's expectations of privacy in personal luggage are substantially greater than in an automobile.** 433 U.S. at 13.

The *Chadwick* Court noted that the practical problems associated with the temporary detention of a piece of luggage during the period of time necessary to obtain a warrant are significantly less than those associated with the detention of an automobile. By invalidating the warrantless search of the footlocker, the Court reaffirmed the general principle that closed packages and containers may not be searched without a warrant. Thus, the Court declined to extend the rationale of the automobile exception to permit a warrantless search of any movable container found in a public place. *See generally California v. Acevedo*, 500 U.S. 565 (1991).

Other Container Searches Investigatory detentions of containers are discussed in Chapter 7 on stops and frisks. Seizures and searches of containers incident to arrest are discussed in Chapter 8. Plain view container searches and seizures are discussed in Chapter 10. Searches and seizures of abandoned containers are discussed in the next chapter, Chapter 12. Inventory searches of containers are discussed in the next section of this chapter.

key points

- When an officer has probable cause to search a vehicle for a particular object under the *Carroll* doctrine, the officer may look anywhere in the vehicle in which there is probable cause to believe the object may be found, including containers that could hold the object.
- If an officer has probable cause to search only a particular container placed in a vehicle, the officer may search that container without a warrant, but may not search the entire vehicle.
- Law enforcement officers with probable cause to search a motor vehicle may inspect passengers' be-

longings found in the vehicle that are capable of concealing the object of the search.
- The *Carroll* doctrine does not permit the warrantless search of any movable container found in a public place, even if the searching officer has probable cause. Closed containers and packages located outside of a vehicle may not be searched without a warrant or justification under some other exception to the warrant requirement.

▶IMPOUNDMENT AND INVENTORY SEARCHES

The police may **impound** motor vehicles for a variety of reasons. Accompanying a vehicle's impoundment, police routinely inventory the vehicle's contents for reasons of safety, liability, and convenience. This section explores the legal issues involved in impounding and inventorying motor vehicles.

Impoundment

Impoundment usually involves the police taking possession of a vehicle that would otherwise be left unattended and moving it to a garage or police lot for safekeeping. The main justifications for impoundment are to protect threats to public safety posed by the vehicle and to ensure the efficient movement of traffic:

> In the interests of public safety and as part of what the Court has called "community caretaking functions," . . . automobiles are frequently taken into police custody. Vehicle accidents present one such occasion. To permit the uninterrupted flow of traffic and in some instances to preserve evidence, disabled or damaged vehicles will often be removed from the highways or streets in caretaking and traffic control activities. Police will also frequently remove and impound automobiles which violate parking ordinances and which thereby jeopardize both the public safety and the

Discussion
↑POINT

Does the Scope of a Search under the Automobile Exception Extend to a Passenger's Belongings?

People v. Hart, 86 Cal. Rptr. 2d 762 (Cal. App. 3d Dist. 1999).

On May 8, 1997, the Sacramento Sheriff's Department received a report at about 1:30 A.M. that a Chevrolet van was parked in a residential area. The caller, a resident in the area, thought the van was suspicious and "believed that there was possible burglary activity about to take place." Deputy Donald Bricker and another deputy responded to a dispatch and went to investigate. Deputy Bricker observed the right front and rear tires of the van were on the sidewalk, in violation of Vehicle Code section 22500, subdivision (f). When he knocked on the side door of the van, the defendant opened the door.

The deputy looked inside the van and saw the defendant (by the side door) and Scott LeBlanc (in the rear of the van). There was a bed in the rear of the van, and the deputy was concerned someone could have hidden under it. Deputy Bricker asked the defendant and LeBlanc what they were doing in the neighborhood, but neither responded. He then asked for their identification to determine whether either was subject to an arrest warrant or had a valid license to drive the vehicle. The deputy was concerned about his safety because of the possibility of a concealed weapon. The defendant looked around on the floor of the van and stated she was searching for her identification. However, after she searched for several minutes without finding it, the deputy asked them to step out of the van. There was no indication the defendant was under the influence of alcohol or narcotics.

Deputy Bricker patted them down for weapons and placed them in the rear of the patrol car. The defendant gave the deputy her name and birth date and claimed ownership of the van. She told him her identification was in the van, either on the floorboard or in the visor, despite the fact that she had previously searched those areas. When Deputy Bricker told the defendant he was going to look in the van for her identification, she told him she did not want him to search the van. Choosing now to respond to Deputy Bricker's original inquiry as to her purpose in the neighborhood, she told Deputy Bricker that she and LeBlanc were "on a rendezvous because they didn't want to be seen together." Deputy Bricker initially went into the van for just a moment, looking for weapons or other people, and saw a purse on the floor in the back of the van. After a discussion with the other deputy, he reentered the van and opened the purse. Inside, he found a glass pipe, marijuana, methamphetamine, and the defendant's California identification card.

The court in *Hart* allowed the search of the van by Deputy Bricker for defendant's identification. According to the court, the search was justified by the existence of probable cause to believe defendant had violated a local parking ordinance, the defendant's refusal to provide identification as required by law, and by the overall suspicious circumstances of the encounter:

(Continued)

Does the Scope of a Search under the Automobile Exception Extend to a Passenger's Belongings? *(Continued)*

The encounter between Deputy Bricker and the defendant was justified by the defendant's Vehicle Code violation. Since Deputy Bricker had probable cause to believe there had been a violation, the defendant had to produce satisfactory identification. When she deliberately failed to produce identification and acted suspiciously (including a failure to explain her and her van's presence in another neighborhood at 1:30 A.M.), Deputy Bricker, for his own safety, was justified in retrieving the identification himself. Therein lies the justification for the search and the holding of our opinion. It was a search for identification. The narrow question is whether the officer had to risk his safety by allowing an uncooperative detainee to purport to try yet again to retrieve it. In such circumstances, an officer is not required merely to default to the machinations of an anonymous detainee. As a matter of officer safety, we hold that Deputy Bricker's retrieval of the identification was consistent with the Vehicle Code, [precedent] cases . . . , and the Fourth Amendment.

This is not a case, as posited by the defendant, of the detention of a citizen and search of her property "on the basis of a minor parking infraction alone. Had the defendant answered the officer's inquiry of the reason for her presence and produced the identification in her purse, there would have been no reason for any search. But that was far from the case here: the defendant did not explain her presence in the van at 1:30 in the morning or produce her identification. Instead, she rummaged in places she knew her identification was not. She never asserted she had no identification, she simply chose not to provide it to Deputy Bricker. This was not her prerogative. Deputy Bricker did not have to put his safety at risk by permitting her to renew her earlier, deliberately unsuccessful, search for identification, but instead could retrieve it himself.

[T]he search was legal. 86 Cal. Rptr. 2d at 769–70.

Moreover, the court found that under the principles established by the U.S. Supreme Court in *Wyoming v. Houghton*, Deputy Bricker's search of defendant's purse was within the permissible scope of a vehicle search:

This was a vehicle search. Since it is well established that containers in a vehicle are searchable if the vehicle is searchable, especially when, as here, the container searched was a likely place for

efficient movement of vehicular traffic. The authority of police to seize and remove from the streets vehicles impeding traffic or threatening public safety and convenience is beyond challenge. *South Dakota v. Opperman*, 428 U.S. 364, 368-69 (1976).

Other reasons to impound vehicles include:

▶ The driver has been arrested and taken into custody. *United States v. Lyles*, 946 F.2d 78 (8th Cir. 1991); *Colorado v. Bertine*, 479 U.S. 367 (1987) (discussed below in section entitled "Scope of Inventory Search").

Does the Scope of a Search under the Automobile Exception Extend to a Passenger's Belongings? *(Continued)*

the object of the search (see *Wyoming v. Houghton*), we will focus on whether Deputy Bricker's search of those places in the van likely to hold defendant's identification was legal.

Deputy Bricker's search was limited to a search for identification. "The critical element in a reasonable search is . . . that there is reasonable cause to believe that the specific 'things' to be searched for and seized are located on the property to which entry is sought." While the defendant told him her identification was in the visor or on the floorboard, in light of her inability to produce any identification, it was reasonable for the deputy to conclude that her identification could be elsewhere and that some form of identification would likely be found in her purse. She claimed she was searching for the identification while she was in the van. The defendant certainly had not established any reason for the deputy to think she was credible. There was no evidence he was searching for anything but her identification. 86 Cal. Rptr. 2d at 766–68.

Thus, because both the search of defendant's vehicle was valid and the officer properly limited the scope of the search, the drugs and drug paraphernalia found in defendant's purse were admissible at trial. The search was valid because it was supported by probable cause; the scope of the search was permissible because a purse could hold defendant's identification (i.e., the object of the search).

Do you agree that police should be able to search the personal belongings of vehicle occupants as part of a valid search under the automobile exception? Why or why not? Does the limitation that the container, or belonging, be able to hold the object of the search, serve as a sufficient constraint on discretion by police officers in this area? If officers had probable cause to believe a vehicle contained illegal aliens, would they be able to search the personal belongings of vehicle occupants? What about probable cause to believe a vehicle contained illegal weapons? Would your answer to this last question depend on the size of the weapon or the nature of the occupant's belongings? Explain.

▶ The driver is incapacitated by intoxication, injury, illness, or some other condition. *United States v. Ford*, 872 F.2d 1231 (6th Cir. 1989).

▶ The vehicle is seized as evidence of or an instrument of a crime. *United States v. Cooper*, 949 F.2d 737 (5th Cir. 1991).

▶ The vehicle is forfeited pursuant to a state or federal forfeiture law. *United States v. Bizzell*, 19 F.3d 1524 (4th Cir. 1994).

▶ The vehicle has been reported stolen.

In many jurisdictions, the right of police to impound vehicles is defined by statute or departmental policy or both. If an officer impounds a vehicle in violation of statute or policy, or for an illegitimate reason such as harassment of the driver or searching for evidence, the impoundment may be held illegal under the Fourth Amendment. For example, in *United States v. Ibarra*, 955 F.2d 1405 (10th Cir. 1992), the court found that the officer impounded a vehicle unlawfully in violation of a state statute and the Fourth Amendment:

> Specifically, the district court found that defendant's vehicle did not obstruct the normal flow of traffic. . . . This finding is supported by the undisputed fact that the police officers at the scene did not request defendant to move his car while the officers waited forty-five minutes for the wrecker to arrive. The district court also found that defendant's situation did not justify removal of the vehicle under [the relevant statute] for the following reasons: 1) there was no report that the vehicle had been stolen; 2) the person in charge of the vehicle was able to provide for the custody of the vehicle but was never given the opportunity to do so by [the officer]; and 3) defendant was not under arrest at the time [the officer] elected to have the vehicle removed.
>
> We hold that the district court's factual findings regarding the lack of justification for the impoundment pursuant to [statute] are not clearly erroneous.
>
> The government argues that [the officer's] decision to impound defendant's vehicle was reasonable because defendant could not provide for the custody or removal of his vehicle and therefore [the officer] was authorized to remove the vehicle to a place of public safety under [the statute]. Because we hold that the district court's finding that defendant was in fact able to provide for the removal and custody of his vehicle was not clearly erroneous, we conclude that [the officer's] decision to impound the vehicle was made without proper authority under [the statute]. Therefore his decision was not reasonable and in conformance with the Fourth Amendment. . . . 955 F.2d at 1409.

The *Ibarra* court, citing the U.S. Supreme Court's decision in *Opperman*, also concluded that the officer was not justified in impounding the vehicle for public safety reasons:

> Although [the officer] did not conform to [state] law when seizing defendant's vehicle, the much closer question in this case is whether reasons of public safety dictated that [the officer] impound the car as allowed under *Opperman*. Clearly, police officers must have a certain amount of discretion in determining what threatens public safety. Indeed, [the officer] testified that he elected to have the car impounded because it posed a safety hazard. It appears that if the position of the vehicle would have been a true threat to public safety, the officers would have moved the vehicle to the side of the road while waiting for the tow truck to arrive. Furthermore, the potential existed that the real reason the officers wished to remove the vehicle to a more secure location was to conduct a more intensive investigatory search. We conclude that the government failed to carry its burden of showing that the impoundment of defendant's vehicle was authorized by [state] law or *Opperman*. Therefore, we affirm the district court's holding that the seizure of defendant's vehicle was unreasonable. 955 F.2d at 1409–10.

Law enforcement officers are not constitutionally required to offer a person an opportunity to make other arrangements for the safekeeping of his or her vehicle, nor must they always choose methods of dealing with vehicles that are less intrusive than impoundment. As the U.S. Supreme Court stated, "[t]he reasonableness of any particular governmental activity does not necessarily or invariably turn on the existence of alternative 'less intrusive' means." *Illinois v. Lafayette*, 462 U.S. 640, 647 (1983). Therefore, nothing prohibits the exercise of police discretion to impound a vehicle rather than to lock and park it in a safe place, **"so long as that discretion is exercised according to standard criteria and on the basis of something other than suspicion of evidence of criminal activity."** *Colorado v. Bertine*, 479 U.S. 367, 375 (1987).

For example, in *United States v. Mayfield*, 161 F.3d 1143 (8th Cir. 1998), the court concluded that the officer's decision to impound a car rather than allow a passenger to drive it away, was reasonable under the Fourth Amendment:

> Here, the arrestee was Mayfield, who did not own the car. The logical person to take custody of the car, its owner, was Mayfield's passenger. She informed the officers she could not drive because of her medication, and she lacked a driver's license. Rather than objecting to impoundment, she asked for a ride to a doctor's appointment and received one. Under these circumstances, we conclude the decision to impound the vehicle "did not so exceed the [state patrol] policy as to warrant suppression." It appears the troopers applied the impoundment policy in good faith. The troopers were not constitutionally required to choose a less intrusive way of securing the car. We conclude the decision to impound the car was reasonable, and thus did not violate the Fourth Amendment. 161 F.3d at 1144.

Some states, however, require officers to consider reasonable alternatives to impoundment. "Although an officer is not required to exhaust all possibilities, the officer must at least consider alternatives; attempt, if feasible, to obtain a name from the driver of someone in the vicinity who could move the vehicle; and then reasonably conclude from this deliberation that impoundment is proper." *State v. Coss*, 943 P.2d 1126, 1130 (Wash. App.1997). *Coss* held that the impoundment of a stopped vehicle was unreasonable when the driver had a suspended license but a properly licensed passenger could have driven the vehicle away.

Inventory Searches

Assuming a lawful impoundment, may the vehicle then be searched for incriminating evidence without a warrant? Unless the situation satisfies the requirements of the automobile exception, police have no authority to conduct a warrantless investigatory search of a lawfully impounded motor vehicle. In other words, police must obtain a search warrant to search an impounded vehicle unless they have probable cause to search the vehicle and the vehicle is readily mobile.

Nevertheless, *South Dakota v. Opperman*, 428 U.S. 364 (1976), approved a more limited search of a lawfully impounded motor vehicle: the routine practice of local police departments of securing and inventorying the vehicle's contents. This limited type of warrantless search is allowed:

▶ to protect the owner's property while it remains in police custody;

▶ to protect the police against claims or disputes over lost, stolen, or vandalized property; and

▶ to protect the police from potential danger.

See Colorado v. Bertine, 479 U.S. 367, 372 (1987). ("We found [in *Opperman*] that inventory procedures serve to protect an owner's property while it is in the custody of the police, to insure against claims of lost, stolen, or vandalized property, and to guard the police from danger.")

Apart from collecting and securing valuables left in the vehicle, officers should record, as part of an inventory search, the vehicle identification number, the motor number, and the make, model, and license plate number of the car so that it may be easily identified later. *Cotton v. United States*, 371 F.2d 385 (9th Cir. 1967), *overruled on other grounds by United States v. Cunag*, 386 F.3d 888 (9th Cir. 2004); *see also South Dakota v. Opperman*, 428 U.S. 364, 372 (1976). ("[C]ases have recognized that standard inventories often include an examination of the glove compartment, since it is a customary place for documents of ownership and registration, as well as a place for the temporary storage of valuables.")

No Warrant or Probable Cause Required for Inventory Searches This inventory procedure is not considered a search for Fourth Amendment purposes because its object is not to find incriminating evidence as part of a criminal investigation. Rather, it is considered a routine administrative, custodial procedure made for the purpose of creating an inventory of a vehicle's contents. An inventory search neither requires a warrant nor probable cause:

> **The policies behind the warrant requirement are not implicated in an inventory search, nor is the related concept of probable cause: The standard of probable cause is peculiarly related to criminal investigations, not routine, non-criminal procedures. . . . The probable-cause approach is unhelpful when analysis centers upon the reasonableness of routine administrative caretaking functions.** *Bertine*, 479 U.S. at 371 (internal quotations omitted).

However, an inventory search "must not be a ruse for a general rummaging in order to discover incriminating evidence." *Florida v. Wells*, 495 U.S. 1, 4 (1990). For example, in *United States v. Edwards*, 242 F.3d 928 (10th Cir. 2001), police impounded a car rented by the defendant's girlfriend after finding incriminating evidence in the car related to an alleged armed robbery committed by the defendant and his girlfriend. The court determined that the warrantless search of the vehicle that revealed the incriminating evidence could not be considered a valid inventory search in light of the investigatory motives of the police:

> In this case, it is clear that the search of the rental vehicle was conducted for investigatory, rather than administrative, purposes. The officer testified that he "was assigned to the suspects' vehicle to search for any additional evidence or anything that would indicate this is their vehicle and indicate anything that would suffice that a crime occurred." He also admitted on cross-examination that he was "searching for evidence of the crime." In addition, the decision to impound the car was not made until after the search revealed incriminating evidence against [defendant], which makes it exceedingly difficult to believe that this was an inventory search conducted to protect the police from liability after the decision was made to impound the car. Based upon the foregoing facts, we have no trouble determining that this search was conducted for investigative rather than administrative purposes and cannot be justified as a mere inventory search. 242 F.3d at 938–39.

Nevertheless, an investigatory motive will not invalidate an inventory search if there is also a genuine administrative motive:

It would be disingenuous of us to pretend that when the agents opened Judge's bag, they weren't hoping to find some more evidence to use against him. But, they could have also reasonably had an administrative motive, which is all that is required under *Bertine*. While there are undoubtedly mixed motives in the vast majority of inventory searches, the constitution does not require and our human limitations do not allow us to peer into a police officer's "heart of hearts." *United States v. Judge*, 864 F.2d 1144, 1147 n.5 (5th Cir. 1989).

Likewise, in *United States v. Lumpkin*, 159 F.3d 983 (6th Cir. 1998), the court found that an officer's suspicion that a particular area of the vehicle had illegal contraband did not invalidate an otherwise valid inventory search:

> An inventory search may not be conducted for purposes of investigation and must be conducted according to standard police procedures. However, the fact that an officer suspects that contraband may be found does not defeat an otherwise proper inventory search. Therefore, the fact that [the officers] may have suspected that the truck contained evidence of drug trafficking does not render their inventory search invalid if otherwise found to be lawful. 159 F.3d at 987.

The "Standard Procedures" Requirement for Inventory Searches

Each law enforcement agency must have standard procedures for inventorying impounded vehicles, or the inventories will be declared an illegal search. In upholding the validity of an inventory of an impounded car, *South Dakota v. Opperman* emphasized that the police were using a standard inventory form pursuant to standard police procedures. The Court said, **"The decisions of this Court point unmistakably to the conclusion reached by both federal and state courts that inventories pursuant to standard police procedures are reasonable."** 428 U.S. at 372.

In *Florida v. Wells*, 495 U.S. 1 (1990), a state trooper stopped defendant for speeding. After the officer smelled alcohol on defendant's breath, he arrested defendant. After the car was impounded, an inventory search of a locked suitcase in the car's trunk revealed marijuana. The Court found that in the absence of a policy or procedure by police to regulate this particular inventory search, it was invalid:

> **In the present case, the Supreme Court of Florida found that the Florida Highway Patrol had no policy whatever with respect to the opening of closed containers encountered during an inventory search. We hold that absent such a policy, the instant search was not sufficiently regulated to satisfy the Fourth Amendment and that the marijuana which was found in the suitcase, therefore, was properly suppressed by the Supreme Court of Florida.** 495 U.S. at 4–5.

The Court, however, did posit examples of valid police procedures for inventory searches of closed containers: **"Thus, while policies of opening all containers or of opening no containers are unquestionably permissible, it would be equally permissible, for example, to allow the opening of closed containers whose contents officers determine they are unable to ascertain from examining the containers' exteriors."** 495 U.S. at 4. Indeed, individual police departments may develop their own procedures for inventory searches and as long as they are reasonable and administered in good faith (i.e., not for the purpose of criminal investigation), the fact that a reviewing court might conceive of an alternative procedure is not controlling:

> The Supreme Court of Colorado also expressed the view that the search in this case was unreasonable . . . because [defendant] himself could have been offered the opportunity to make other arrangements for the safekeeping of his property. We conclude that here . . . reasonable police regulations relating to inventory procedures administered in good faith satisfy the Fourth Amendment, even though courts might as a matter of hindsight be able to devise equally reasonable rules requiring a different procedure. *Bertine*, 479 U.S. at 373–74.

For example, in *United States v. Wimbush*, 337 F.3d 947 (7th Cir. 2003), the court sanctioned an inventory search of an automobile revealing an illegal weapon because it was conducted pursuant to established police policy:

> [T]he warrantless search was valid as a routine post-arrest inventory search, which authorizes police to search vehicles in lawful custody in order to secure or protect the car and its contents. Here, police lawfully arrested [defendant] for driving without a license and for driving with an open container of alcohol, and it was undisputed that the car was searched in a manner consistent with the police department's inventory policy. [T]he district court did not clearly err by denying [defendant's] motion to suppress [the weapon] based on the search of his vehicle. 337 F.3d at 951.

However, courts will invalidate an inventory search in violation of existing procedures. For example, in *United States v. Johnson*, 936 F.2d 1082, 1084 (9th Cir. 1991), because police violated an established procedure under state law in opening the locked trunk of defendant's car during an inventory search, the court suppressed an illegal weapon found in the trunk during the search:

> Under [state] law, "an officer may not examine the locked trunk of an impounded vehicle in the course of an inventory search absent a manifest necessity for conducting such a search." The government has made absolutely no showing of manifest necessity in this case. That failure to comply with governing state procedures renders the search of the trunk of [defendant's] car unconstitutional. . . . We vacate [defendant's] conviction and remand with instructions to suppress evidence obtained from the inventory search of the car's trunk. 936 F.2d at 1084.

As long as a police department has established reasonable procedures for inventory searches and administers them in good faith (i.e., not for the purpose of investigating crime), minor variations from police procedures may not invalidate an otherwise lawful impoundment and inventory search. In *United States v. Kimes*, 246 F.3d 800 (6th Cir. 2001), the officer's failure to call defendant's relatives or friends to retrieve defendant's vehicle before impounding it did not invalidate the subsequent search of the vehicle by police revealing illegal weapons:

> In this connection [Defendant] points out that on some occasions the [police department] permitted family members or friends to remove a vehicle if its owner or operator was unable to do so. The defendant's arguments are not persuasive. Discretion as to impoundment [and inventorying] is permissible 'so long as that discretion is exercised according to standard criteria and on the basis of something other than suspicion of evidence of criminal activity.' Here, as we gather, [departmental] police sometimes permitted vehicles to be picked up by a driver's friends and relations if they were already present or if

the driver could contact them and get them to come to the facility promptly. [Defendant] suggests that rather than towing his truck, the officers should have taken it upon themselves to call his wife and ask her to get the vehicle. He cites no authority compelling such a conclusion, and we are aware of none. 246 F.3d at 804–5.

Finally, standard inventory procedures need not be written. *United States v. Feldman*, 788 F.2d 544 (9th Cir. 1986), approved a procedure under which officers are instructed orally that stolen vehicles must be impounded and their contents inventoried on a standard printed form. *See also United States v. Hawkins*, 279 F.3d 83, 86 (1st Cir. 2002). ("A warrantless search is permitted under the Fourth Amendment if it is carried out pursuant to a standardized inventory policy. Such a standardized inventory policy may be unwritten. Because the district court found that there was a standardized, albeit unwritten, inventory policy compelling officers to open containers to determine their contents during an inventory, the drug evidence was properly obtained.")

Permissible Scope of Inventory Searches

Officers should follow standard departmental procedures regarding the allowable scope of a vehicle inventory. So long as the officer follows these procedures in good faith, and does not conduct an inventory solely for investigatory purposes, the officer has some discretion regarding the administration of an inventory search. *See, e.g., Bertine*, 479 U.S. at 375. (**"Nothing in [our precedent cases] prohibits the exercise of police discretion so long as that discretion is exercised according to standard criteria and on the basis of something other than suspicion of evidence of criminal activity."**) In *Bertine* itself, the Court permitted an inventory search of the passenger compartment of defendant's van. Furthermore, when the search revealed drugs and drug paraphernalia in a closed backpack, the Court permitted the government to rely on this evidence in defendant's trial on drug charges. 479 U.S. at 368–69.

Also, a lawful inventory search may extend to a vehicle's glove compartment:

> **The inventory was not unreasonable in scope. [Defendant's] motion to suppress in state court challenged the inventory only as to items inside the car not in plain view. But once the policeman was lawfully inside the car to secure the personal property in plain view, it was not unreasonable to open the unlocked glove compartment, to which vandals would have had ready and unobstructed access once inside the car.** *Opperman*, 428 U.S. at 375 n.10.

In addition, courts permit the search of a vehicle's trunk if it is part of an inventory search conducted pursuant to police procedures. For example, in *United States v. Rankin*, 261 F.3d 735 (8th Cir. 2001), an inventory search of defendant's trunk revealed drugs. The court found the search valid:

> We next turn to [the defendant's] argument concerning the suppression of the evidence found in the trunk of his vehicle. We conclude that the district court did not err in its finding that the search of [the defendant's] vehicle was a valid inventory search. [The officer] testified that he seized and towed the vehicle pursuant to department guidelines on asset forfeiture. There is no indication that the search was a subterfuge for a 'general rummaging' for incriminating evidence. Accordingly, the district court did not err in allowing the items from the trunk to be admitted into evidence. 261 F.3d at 740.

Indeed, most courts allow the opening of a *locked* trunk by police during a valid inventory search conducted pursuant to police procedures:

> In support of his position that the search of the [locked] trunk itself was unreasonable, the defendant cites *United States v. Wilson*. In *Wilson*, the Eighth Circuit held that 'the needs of the Government in conducting an inventory search may be ordinarily accomplished without the serious intrusion into the locked trunk of an automobile.' However, . . . other circuits have not adopted this position.
>
> We agree with and adopt the following language by the district court below: To protect themselves against spurious claims of lost or stolen property, the authorities must know the contents of any vehicle which they impound. This is especially true in this case since the . . . authorities did not have their own impoundment facility and relied on private contractors to tow and store impounded vehicles.
>
> The inventory form which the sheriff's deputy was required to complete prior to releasing the vehicle for impoundment asked him to determine if the vehicle had a spare tire. To obtain that information, it was necessary to open the trunk of the car. The Court is persuaded that under the circumstances of this case, opening the locked trunk with the keys obtained from defendant was reasonable under the Fourth Amendment as an inventory search conducted pursuant to the standard policy and practice of the sheriff's department. *United States v. Duncan*, 763 F.2d 220, 223 (6th Cir. 1985).

Moreover, various courts have permitted inventory searches of the engine compartments of vehicles. *See United States v. Lumpkin*, 159 F.3d 983, 988 (6th Cir. 1998). ("We agree with the position taken by the Eighth and Tenth Circuits and, therefore, hold that a valid inventory search conducted by law enforcement officers according to standard procedure may include the engine compartment of a vehicle. Accordingly, the district court did not err in denying the motion to suppress evidence [e.g., drugs] obtained from the warrantless search of the [engine compartment] of the pickup truck.")

Colorado v. Bertine, 479 U.S. 367 (1987), expanded the allowable scope of an inventory search to include the opening of closed containers found in the impounded vehicle and the examination of their contents. Recall that in *Bertine*, discussed above, the Court permitted an inventory search of a closed backpack in the defendant's van. The search revealed drugs in the backpack, which were admissible at the defendant's trial. Of course, police departments must have standardized criteria regulating the opening of containers found during inventory searches, both to narrow the latitude of individual police officers and to prevent the inventory search from becoming a general rummaging to discover incriminating evidence:

> **But in forbidding uncanalized discretion to police officers conducting inventory searches, there is no reason to insist that they be conducted in a totally mechanical "all or nothing" fashion. . . . A police officer may be allowed sufficient latitude to determine whether a particular container should or should not be opened in light of the nature of the search and characteristics of the container itself. Thus, while policies of opening all containers or of opening no containers are unquestionably permissible, it would be equally permissible, for example, to allow the opening of closed containers whose contents officers determine they are unable to ascertain from examining the containers' exteriors. The allowance of the exercise of judgment based on concerns related to the purposes of an inventory search does not violate the Fourth Amendment.** *Florida v. Wells*, 495 U.S. 1, 4 (1990).

United States v. Lozano, 171 F.3d 1129 (7th Cir. 1999), applied *Bertine* in upholding an inventory search of closed duffel bags that revealed marijuana in the bed of a defendant's truck.

> In the present case, the district court judge found that the inventory search was conducted pursuant to the Peoria Police Department's standard routine of opening all closed containers that might contain valuables and, therefore, was a valid inventory search. We agree with this conclusion. The record establishes that officer Krider followed the Peoria Police Department's practice of filling out the inventory tow sheet at the site of the vehicle impoundment. The record also shows that Krider discovered the five duffel bags in the bed of Lozano's truck during his inventory search. Krider then followed the department's policy of opening all closed containers within the car that could possibly contain valuable items. Krider further testified that he routinely opens closed containers that might contain valuable items to protect himself, the other officers involved, and the citizens being arrested. Officer Roegge corroborated Krider's testimony and we find no evidence to the contrary. Because we believe that the district court did not commit clear error in determining that the Peoria Police Department followed standard procedure while conducting an inventory search of Lozano's automobile, we affirm the district court's denial of Lozano's motion to suppress the evidence found within five duffel bags located in the bed of his truck. 171 F.3d at 1132.

The importance of following established department guidelines or procedures addressing the scope of an inventory search cannot be overstressed. For example, if department procedures prohibit searching inside of containers, any evidence obtained in that manner is inadmissible in court. *United States v. Ramos-Oseguera*, 120 F.3d 1028 (9th Cir. 1997), overruled on other grounds by *United States v. Nordby*, 225 F.3d 1053 (9th Cir. 2000), suppressed heroin found in the pockets of a pair of jeans discovered during an inventory search of an automobile. The court said:

> Inventory searches have been held constitutional if they are conducted in accordance with the standard procedures of the agency conducting the search or come under another exception to the Fourth Amendment warrant requirement. . . . These regulations specifically provide for cataloging and/or safekeeping visible property. They do not permit searching the inside of containers. The government argues that the jeans were visible and they might have contained something valuable. The regulations, however, do not provide authority to look inside of things to find valuable items. 120 F.3d at 1036.

Moreover, *United States v. Khoury*, 901 F.2d 948 (11th Cir. 1990), held that a second examination of a diary found in a briefcase during an inventory of the defendant's impounded car exceeded the permissible scope of a lawful inventory search. As a result, the court excluded the diary as evidence from defendant's trial on drug charges. In *Khoury*, the officer's initial examination consisted of flipping through a notebook to look for items of value. He determined that the notebook was a diary but not that it had evidentiary value. He later examined the notebook again and decided that it had evidentiary value. The court said:

> [Agent] Simpkins' initial inspection of the notebook was necessary and proper to ensure that there was nothing of value hidden between the pages of the notebook. Having satisfied himself that the notebook contained no discrete items of value and having decided that the diary entries themselves would have intrinsic value to [the defendant], Simpkins had satisfied the requisites of

the inventory search and had no purpose other than investigation in further inspecting the notebook. Such a warrantless investigatory search may not be conducted under the guise of an inventory. 901 F.2d at 959.

In *United States v. Andrews*, 22 F.3d 1328 (5th Cir. 1994), however, the court allowed into evidence a notebook discovered during an inventory search that contained both individuals' names and a diagram relevant to a drug investigation, because the officer conducting the search observed this information, and recognized its evidentiary value, during the initial search and not during any subsequent examination:

> [The police department's] policy did allow [the officer] to open [defendant's] notebook, in order to determine whether it contained personal property which should have been included on a [departmental] inventory form. Opening a notebook, to determine whether valuables might be found between its pages, is consistent with [departmental] policy requiring an inventory search to protect the city from claims of lost property. Cash, credit cards, negotiable instruments, and any number of other items could be hidden between the pages of a notebook, and could give rise to a claim against the city if lost.
>
> ***
>
> *United States v. Khoury*, upon which [defendant] relies, is distinguishable. In *Khoury* a DEA agent examined the defendant's notebook in the course of an inventory search, but did not discover that the notebook had evidentiary value. The purposes of the inventory search being fulfilled, the inventory exception to the warrant requirement was no longer available; but the agent examined the notebook again, this time determining that it had evidentiary value. The [court in *Khoury*] held that the agent's second look at the notebook, without a warrant, violated the Fourth Amendment.
>
> [In the present case,] [i]n the course of his inventory search of [defendant's] car, [the officer] determined that the diagram and various names in the notebook had evidentiary value pertinent to the federal agents' investigation. *Khoury* is distinguishable, therefore, because [the officer] was aware of the evidentiary value of the notebook before a second look was taken by federal agents. [Defendant] has not demonstrated that his rights under the Fourth Amendment were violated, or that the district court erred by denying his motion to suppress. 22 F.3d at 1335–37.

Note that, as officers may not conduct inventory searches for the purpose of investigating and finding evidence of crime, officers would generally not have reason to dismantle the vehicle—including ripping apart its upholstery. Such actions exceed the scope of a valid inventory search to protect and secure the vehicle's contents.

Time Limitations for Inventory Searches

A vehicle inventory should be conducted as soon as possible after the impoundment, taking into consideration the police agency's personnel resources, facilities, workload, and other circumstances. An unreasonably delayed inventory indicates that police were not really concerned about safeguarding the owner's property or protecting themselves against claims or from danger but rather were primarily interested in looking for evidence:

> [T]he Fourth Amendment requires that, without a demonstrable justification based upon exigent circumstances other than the mere nature of automobiles, the inventory be conducted either contemporaneously with the impoundment

or as soon thereafter as would be safe, practical, *and* satisfactory in light of the objectives for which this exception to the Fourth Amendment warrant requirement was created. In other words, to be valid, there must be a sufficient temporal proximity between the impoundment and the inventory. When the inventory must be postponed, each passing moment detracts from the full effectuation of the objectives of the inventory, and indeed, disserves those objectives; at some point, the passage of time requires, to uphold the validity of the inventory, proof of some immediate and exigent circumstances (other than the mere nature of automobiles) the attention to which is more important than protecting the arrestee's property and protecting the police from false claims or danger associated with that property. *Ex Parte Boyd*, 542 So.2d 1276, 1279 (Ala. 1989).

Thus, *Ex Parte Boyd* stands for the principle that, unless emergency circumstances exist, an inventory search of a vehicle must generally be conducted at the time of impoundment or shortly thereafter. In *Ex Parte Boyd,* the court invalidated an inventory search conducted by police four days after they had impounded the vehicle: "We hold that the warrantless search in this case can not be upheld as an inventory search because of the insufficient temporal proximity between the impoundment and the search, with a lack of demonstrable justification based on exigent circumstances." 542 So.2d at 1281.

Young v. Commonwealth, 2001 WL 1356395 (Va. App. 2001) (unpublished decision), citing the rule from *Ex Parte Boyd* regarding the timing of an inventory search, found that a police officer's failure to conduct an inventory search immediately at the scene did not render the search invalid under the Fourth Amendment:

> The fact that [the officer] used a private towing company to transport [defendant's] car to the sheriff's department and conducted the inventory search only after the vehicle had been transported did not render the search unreasonable under the Fourth Amendment. A business near the scene of the stop had recently been vandalized, and [the officer] testified he believed conducting the search at the sheriff's department would be safer. As in [a precedent case], [the officer] also testified that he would have had better lighting at the sheriff's department, permitting the inference that conducting the search at that location was more likely to result in an accurate inventory. 2001 WL 1356395 at *2.

Thus, because conditions at the scene where the vehicle was impounded were not conducive to an accurate inventory search, the court permitted the officer in *Young* to conduct the search upon arriving at the sheriff's department.

In sum, police should conduct an inventory search as soon as possible after impounding a vehicle. Unless there is a genuine emergency, long delays between an impoundment and an inventory search will result in a court invalidating the search, and excluding any relevant evidence found by police in the course of inventorying the vehicle.

Inventory Searches and the Plain View Doctrine

Although officers may not look for evidence of crime while conducting legitimate inventories, they may seize contraband or other items subject to seizure that they observe open to view. Under the *plain view doctrine*, an officer lawfully conducting an inventory of a vehicle has valid justification for a prior intrusion into a zone of privacy. If an officer then observes in the course of a valid inventory search items that the officer has probable cause to believe are incriminating in character, the officer may seize these items under the plain view doctrine. In both *Opperman* and *Bertine*, officers discovered drugs in plain view while lawfully conducting inventories of impounded vehicles. (For further discussion of valid plain view seizures of evidence during a lawful inventory search, see Chapter 10.)

Table 11.1 shows a comparison of a *Carroll* doctrine search and an inventory search.

TABLE 11.1 COMPARISON OF A *CARROLL* DOCTRINE SEARCH AND AN INVENTORY SEARCH

	Search under *Carroll* Doctrine	Inventory Search
Justification	Probable cause to search vehicle combined with exigent circumstances. (Exigent circumstances requirement is satisfied if vehicle is readily mobile.)	Impoundment of vehicle by police.
Purpose	To obtain evidence of crime.	To protect the owner's property while it remains in police custody; to protect the police against claims or disputes over lost, stolen, or vandalized property; and to protect the police from potential danger.
Scope of search of entire vehicle	If there is probable cause to search the entire vehicle, the search may extend to every part of the vehicle and its contents that may conceal the object of the search, including the opening of containers. If there is probable cause to search only a container in the vehicle, then only the container and not the entire vehicle may be searched.	If standard departmental procedures are followed, inventory may extend to all areas of the vehicle in which the owner's or occupant's personal belongings might be vulnerable to theft or damage.
Scope of search of containers found in vehicle	If there is probable cause to search the entire vehicle, a container that may contain the object of the search may be searched. If there is probable cause to search only a container in a vehicle, then only the container may be searched.	If standard departmental procedures are followed, the inventory may include the opening of closed containers found within the vehicle and the examination of their contents.
Time	Search should be conducted without unreasonable delay, but vehicle may be removed to another location for the search, and searches up to three days later have been upheld.	Inventory should be conducted as soon as possible after the impoundment of the vehicle, taking into consideration the police agency's human resources, facilities, workload, and other circumstances, such as an emergency requiring the inventory to be delayed.
Plain view doctrine	If items subject to seizure other than the object of the search are observed open to view during a search under the *Carroll* doctrine, the items may be lawfully seized and are admissible in evidence. (The requirements of the plain view doctrine must be satisfied.)	If items subject to seizure are observed open to view during a bona fide inventory, the items may be lawfully seized and are admissible in evidence. (The requirements of the plain view doctrine must be satisfied.)

key points

- Police may impound motor vehicles when they impede traffic or threaten public safety and convenience, or when their drivers or owners are taken into custody or are incapacitated. Police may also impound vehicles after seizing them as evidence of a crime, after the vehicle has been forfeited pursuant to state law, or after a vehicle has been reported stolen.

- Police may inventory the contents of lawfully impounded vehicles according to standardized procedures to protect the owner's property; to protect the police against claims regarding lost, stolen, or vandalized property; and to protect the police from potential danger.

- A valid inventory search requires neither probable cause nor a warrant.

- Police may not conduct an inventory search based on an investigatory motive alone. Police must follow all established procedures governing inventory searches in their jurisdiction. These procedures

must be reasonable and administered in good faith (e.g., not for the purpose of criminal investigation).

- The allowable scope of an inventory search of an impounded vehicle is determined by established police procedures. When conducted pursuant to these procedures, courts have upheld inventory searches of the passenger compartment, glove compartment, trunk, and engine compartment of vehicles. Courts have also upheld opening closed containers found within the vehicle and examining their contents when police do so in accordance with valid police procedure for inventory searches.

- Unless emergency circumstances exist, an inventory search of a vehicle must be conducted at the time of impoundment or shortly thereafter.

- An officer may not look for evidence of crime while conducting a bona-fide inventory; nonetheless, if contraband or other incriminating items subject to seizure are observed open to view, those items may lawfully be seized under the plain view doctrine.

▶ STANDING FOR OBJECTING TO VEHICLE SEARCHES

Whether a driver or passenger can challenge a particular search by police of a vehicle under the automobile exception (for lack of probable cause, or for any other reason) depends on whether that driver or passenger has a reasonable expectation of privacy in the vehicle. Not all drivers and passengers have such an expectation of privacy, and hence under the Fourth Amendment these vehicle occupants would be said to lack **standing** to challenge a particular vehicle search by police.

For example, in *United States v. Haywood*, 324 F.3d 514 (7th Cir. 2003), the court found that an unauthorized, unlicensed driver of a vehicle did not have a reasonable expectation of privacy in the vehicle under the Fourth Amendment. As a result, the driver lacked standing to challenge the search of that vehicle by police:

> Haywood was not simply an unauthorized driver, he was also an unlicenced one. Haywood should not have been driving any car, much less a rental car that Enterprise never would have given him permission to drive. As a result, Haywood's expectation of privacy was not reasonable. Unlike the defendant in [another precedent case], there was nothing unique about Haywood's situation that suggests an exception should be made. Therefore, Haywood lacked standing to challenge the search. 324 F.3d at 516.

Applying similar reasoning, *United States v. Riazco*, 91 F.3d 752 (5th Cir. 1996), held that a driver lacked standing to challenge a search by police because the driver of a rental car was not authorized to drive the car under the rental agreement and did not have the authorized renter's permission to drive.

> Under this analysis, Riazco lacked standing to challenge the validity of the search. Riazco, the driver of the car, did not assert a property or possessory interest in the vehicle. He neither owned nor rented it. The rental agreement specifically stated that the car was to be driven only by persons authorized by the car rental company, and Riazco was not so authorized. In fact, he admitted at the suppression hearing that he did not even have the renter's permission to drive it. 91 F.3d at 754.

From the court's discussion in *Riazco* of the standing issue, it should be apparent that drivers who either legitimately own or rent a vehicle would have standing under the Fourth Amendment to challenge a search by police of that vehicle. Also, a driver of a rental vehicle who has been authorized by the rental company to drive the vehicle may have a reasonable expectation of privacy in the vehicle even if the rental agreement has expired. *See United States. v. Cooper*, 133 F.3d 1394, 1402 (11th Cir. 1998). ("[W]e hold that society is prepared to accept as reasonable [the driver's] expectation of privacy in the overdue rental car and, therefore, he has standing to challenge law enforcement's search of the glove compartment, the trunk, and the items therein.")

Unlike drivers who validly own or rent a vehicle, passengers in a vehicle generally have no reasonable expectation of privacy in the vehicle's interior area. Therefore, passengers may not challenge warrantless searches by police of areas such as the glove compartment, the spaces under the seats, and the trunk. Such a search invades no Fourth Amendment interest of the passengers, even if it turns up evidence implicating the passengers. In this regard, the U.S. Supreme Court in *Rakas v. Illinois*, 439 U.S. 128 (1978), stated:

> We have on numerous occasions pointed out that cars are not to be treated identically with houses or apartments for Fourth Amendment purposes. But here [the defendants'] claim is one which would fail . . . , since they made no showing that they had any legitimate expectation of privacy in the glove compartment or area under the seat of the car in which they were merely passengers. Like the trunk of an automobile, these are areas in which a passenger qua passenger simply would not normally have a legitimate expectation of privacy. 439 U.S. at 148–49.

In *Rakas*, the Court commented that it was immaterial to the standing issue that the defendants who were passengers in the vehicle were present with the consent of the owner. "The fact that [the defendants] were 'legitimately on [the] premises' in the sense that they were in the car with the permission of its owner is not determinative of whether they had a legitimate expectation of privacy in the particular areas of the automobile searched." 439 U.S. at 148; *see also United States v. Pulliam*, 405 F.3d 782 (9th Cir. 2005) (holding, relying on *Rakas*, that a passenger who did not have a possessory interest in the car—i.e., was not its owner—lacked standing under the Fourth Amendment to challenge a search by police that revealed a gun under the passenger seat).

Note that though passengers in a vehicle generally lack standing to challenge a warrantless search of that vehicle by police, they are "seized" for Fourth Amendment purposes when a police officer stops a vehicle in which they are passengers. *See Brendlin v. California*, 127 S. Ct. 2400 (2007). As a result, passengers may challenge a stop of a vehicle in which they are traveling. The ability to challenge a vehicular stop may also affect the standing issue for passengers who also want to challenge a subsequent search by police of the vehicle in which they are traveling. This is because any potentially incriminating items obtained during the search may be considered poisonous fruit of any illegal stop. (See Chapter 3 for further discussion of the fruit of the poisonous tree doctrine.) Thus, in *Brendlin*, because the initial stop of the vehicle in which the defendant had been a passenger was illegal (the officer lacked reasonable suspicion to pull over the car), the defendant-passenger had standing to challenge a subsequent search, as he had been "seized" for Fourth Amendment purposes. 127 U.S. at 2406-07.

key point

- In order to challenge an illegal search by police under the automobile exception, a vehicle occupant must have a reasonable expectation of privacy in the areas of the vehicle that are searched. If this expectation of privacy exists, the vehicle occupant is said to have "standing" under the Fourth Amendment to challenge the search. Drivers who either legitimately own or rent a vehicle have standing under the Fourth Amendment to challenge a search by police of that vehicle. Mere passengers in a vehicle, however, generally have no reasonable expectation of privacy in the vehicle's interior area; hence, these passengers would lack standing.

▶ OTHER ISSUES RELATED TO VEHICLE SEARCHES

This section will discuss the constitutionality under the Fourth Amendment of the use of tracking devices by police to monitor the movement of vehicles. Following this discussion, the section will explore the application of the Fourth Amendment to vehicle searches by dogs.

Tracking Vehicles Using Electronic Devices

A **beeper** is a radio transmitter, usually battery operated, that emits periodic signals that can be picked up by a radio receiver. A beeper neither records nor transmits any sounds other than its signal; but the signal can be monitored by directional finders, enabling law enforcement officers to determine the beeper's location. The U.S. Supreme Court dealt with the Fourth Amendment implications of the use of beepers for the first time in *United States v. Knotts*, 460 U.S. 276 (1983). With the consent of a chemical company, officers installed a beeper in a five-gallon container of chloroform, a substance used to manufacture illicit drugs. One of the defendants purchased the container of chloroform and transported it by automobile to a codefendant's secluded cabin in another state. Law enforcement officers monitored the progress of the automobile carrying the chloroform all the way to its destination. After three days of visual surveillance of the cabin, officers obtained a search warrant, searched the cabin, and found evidence of the illegal manufacture of drugs.

The *Knotts* Court held that the warrantless monitoring of the beeper by law enforcement officers to trace the location of the chloroform container did not violate the defendant's legitimate expectation of privacy:

> **The governmental surveillance conducted by means of the beeper in this case amounted principally to the following of an automobile on public streets and highways. . . . *A person travelling in an automobile on public thoroughfares has no reasonable expectation of privacy in his movements from one place to another. When [the codefendant] travelled over the public streets he voluntarily conveyed to anyone who wanted to look the fact that he was travelling over particular roads in a particular direction, the fact of whatever stops he made, and the fact of his final destination when he exited from public roads onto private property.* 460 U.S. at 281 (emphasis added).**

The owner of the cabin and surrounding premises undoubtedly had a justifiable expectation of privacy within the cabin. But this expectation did not extend to the visual observation of his codefendant's automobile arriving on his premises after leaving a public highway, or to movements of objects such as the container of chloroform outside the cabin. That the officers relied not only on visual surveillance but also on the use of the beeper to locate the automobile did not alter the situation. **"Nothing in the Fourth Amendment prohibited the police from augmenting the sensory faculties bestowed upon them at birth with such enhancement as science and technology afforded them in this case."** 460 U.S. at 282.

The *Knotts* Court emphasized the limited use the officers made of the signals from the beeper. There was no indication that the beeper signal was received or relied on after it had indicated that the chloroform container had ended its automotive journey at the defendant's cabin. Moreover, there was no indication that the beeper was used in any way to reveal information as to the container's movement within the cabin, or in any way that would not have been visible to the naked eye from outside the cabin.

United States v. Karo, 468 U.S. 705 (1984), addressed whether monitoring a beeper in a private residence, a location not generally open to visual surveillance by the public, violates the Fourth Amendment rights of those who have a justifiable interest in the privacy of the residence. In that case, government agents installed a beeper in a container of chemicals with the consent of the original owner, who sold the container to the defendant. The agents saw the defendant pick up the container from the owner, followed the defendant to his house, and determined that the container was inside the house, where it was monitored. The Court found that the government's warrantless surreptitious use of an electronic device to obtain information it could not have obtained by observation from outside the area surrounding the house (e.g., the "curtilage") was the same, for purposes of the Fourth Amendment, as a law enforcement officer's warrantless surreptitious entry of the house to verify that the beeper was in the house. Even though the monitoring of a beeper inside a private residence is less intrusive than a full-scale search, it is illegal unless conducted under authority of a warrant. The Court said:

> **Requiring a warrant will have the salutary effect of ensuring that use of beepers is not abused, by imposing upon agents the requirement that they demonstrate in advance their justification for the desired search.**

> This is not to say that there are no exceptions to the warrant rule, because *if truly exigent circumstances exist no warrant is required under general Fourth Amendment principles.* 468 U.S. at 717–18 (emphasis added).

Therefore, warrantless monitoring of a beeper in a house is permissible only if the beeper or its container could have been observed from outside the curtilage of the house. Monitoring a beeper located in a place not open to such visual surveillance is illegal without a warrant or exigent circumstances.

Although *Karo* ruled the *monitoring* of the beeper illegal, the Court held that warrantless *installation* of a beeper in a manner that does not violate reasonable expectations of privacy is generally permissible. "**It is the exploitation of technological advances that implicates the Fourth Amendment, not their mere existence.**" 468 U.S. at 712. Furthermore, *United States v. Jones*, 31 F.3d 1304 (4th Cir. 1994), held that "the Fourth Amendment does not prohibit the placing of beepers in contraband and stolen goods because the possessors of such articles have no legitimate expectation of privacy in substances which they have no right to possess at all." 31 F.3d at 1311.

In *State v. Jackson*, 46 P.3d 257 (Wash. App. 2002), the court found that both under its state constitution and the Fourth Amendment, police did not need warrants to monitor a vehicle on public highways with a **Global Positioning System (GPS) tracking device**. The police officer in *Jackson*, however, had obtained a warrant before attaching the GPS devices to defendant's vehicles. The court described the facts related to the GPS devices as follows:

> [The officer] applied for and received a 10-day warrant (warrant #2) to attach GPS tracking devices to [defendant's] 1995 Ford pickup and 1985 Honda Accord while they remained in police impound. [Another officer] installed the devices to the vehicles' 12-volt electrical systems . . . without [the defendant's] knowledge, and the vehicles were returned to him. The position of the vehicles could be precisely tracked every five seconds and become known upon device recovery and computer analysis. 46 P.3d at 261.

By tracking defendant's vehicles with the GPS devices, police were able to gather evidence linking defendant to the murder of his daughter.

The court in *Jackson* first found that the use of the GPS devices by police to track defendant's vehicles on public roads was not a search requiring a warrant under the state constitution:

> Monitoring [the defendant's] public travels in his truck by use of the GPS device is reasonably viewed as merely sense augmenting, revealing open-view information of what might easily be seen from a lawful vantage point without such aids. In other words, a law officer could legally follow [the defendant's] vehicles on public thoroughfares or see his travels from his home, to his mini-storage unit, and to the . . . sites [where relevant evidence was found]. In another sense, the GPS devices made [the defendant's] vehicles visible or identifiable as though the officers had merely cleaned his license plates, or unobtrusively marked his vehicles and made them plain to see.
>
> Thus, this case is distinguishable from cases involving the warrantless use of technical aids or enhancement devices to unlawfully intrude upon private affairs. [The defendant's] case does not involve an invasion of the home or use of enhancements to monitor what could not already have been plainly seen by any member of the public.

> Accordingly, under these facts, we hold that police use of the GPS devices did not offend the Washington Constitution because the State did not impermissibly intrude upon private affairs when attaching and monitoring the devices. Here, [defendant's] privacy interests were ultimately insufficient to require warrants. 46 P.3d at 269–70.

The court in *Jackson,* relying upon the U.S. Supreme Court decisions in *Karo* and *Knotts* (discussed above), also found that the use of the GPS devices to monitor defendant's vehicles was also valid under the Fourth Amendment to the U.S. Constitution:

> In *Knotts*, the warrantless placing of a "beeper" device into a chemical drum carried in the defendant's vehicle and police monitoring of the beeper signals was not a Fourth Amendment search or seizure when the drum was not monitored once it moved indoors. The court considered the activity tantamount to the following of an automobile on public streets and highways. The beeper trace was not a search because a person has a lesser expectation of privacy in a car because it seldom serves as one's residence.
>
> This latter concept likewise appears in Washington case law. Here, [the defendant] did not use his vehicles as a residence. And moreover, he did not attempt to conceal his private property, i.e., the vehicles, from public view until after the crucial GPS monitoring was completed and he borrowed [a third party's] truck instead of using his own.
>
> In *Karo*, on the other hand, the court held that the monitoring of a beeper in a private residence not open to visual surveillance violated the Fourth Amendment rights of those with a justifiable interest in the privacy of the residence. Consequently, the court found no reason to deviate from the general rule that the search of a house should be conducted pursuant to a warrant. Here, [defendant's] vehicles were not garaged or moved indoors; the monitoring disclosed only public locations and did not infringe upon the sanctity of protected areas. In this regard, [the defendant's] case falls within the ambit of *Knotts*, not *Karo*. 46 P.3d at 271.

The court in *Jackson* concluded that "[u]nder the facts, we find no Fourth Amendment violation in the State's employment of the GPS devices to track [defendant's] vehicles." The court also found that "no search warrant was required under the state or federal constitution to use the GPS devices here." 46 P.3d at 272.

Vehicle Searches by Dogs

Whether conducted on vehicles or other objects, such as luggage, the U.S. Supreme Court has generally not considered canine sniffs to be "searches" under the Fourth Amendment. *See Illinois v. Caballes*, 543 U.S. 405, 410 (2005). ("A dog sniff conducted during a concededly lawful traffic stop that reveals no information other than the location of a substance that no individual has any right to possess [i.e., drugs] does not violate the Fourth Amendment.") *United States v. Place*, 462 U.S. 696, 707 (1983). ("[W]e conclude that the particular course of investigation that the agents intended to pursue here—exposure of [the defendant's] luggage, which was located in a public place, to a trained canine—did not constitute a 'search' within the meaning of the Fourth Amendment.")

In *Caballes*, an officer stopped the defendant's car for speeding. A second officer then arrived on the scene. While the first officer completed a warning ticket for the defendant's speeding violation, the second officer escorted a dog trained in drug detection around the perimeter of the vehicle. When the dog signaled, or "alerted," to the presence of possible drugs in the trunk of the defendant's vehicle, the officer searched the trunk. He discovered marijuana, and arrested the defendant.

The U.S. Supreme Court in *Caballes* found that the canine sniff of the defendant's vehicle did not constitute a search for Fourth Amendment purposes; therefore, the marijuana found in the trunk of the defendant's vehicle was admissible at the defendant's subsequent trial on drug charges:

> **In this case, the dog sniff was performed on the exterior of [the defendant's] car while he was lawfully seized for a traffic violation. Any intrusion on [the defendant's] privacy expectations does not rise to the level of a constitutionally cognizable infringement. A dog sniff conducted during a concededly lawful traffic stop that reveals no information other than the location of a substance [e.g., marijuana] that no individual has any right to possess does not violate the Fourth Amendment.** 543 U.S. at 409–10.

Thus, if police lawfully stop a vehicle for a traffic violation such as speeding, they may conduct a canine sniff of that vehicle. Though police should use discretion in deciding whether to conduct a canine sniff on any particular vehicle, they do not need additional suspicion or probable cause to conduct this type of law enforcement activity (apart from the reasonable suspicion or probable cause of a traffic violation that is necessary to stop the vehicle in the first place). If the canine sniff by a dog trained in drug detection alerts to the presence of drugs in a vehicle, the officers may search that vehicle without a warrant. This is because such a canine sniff provides the probable cause necessary to search a readily mobile vehicle under the automobile exception. *See Caballes*, 543 U.S. at 409 (agreeing with the **"the trial judge['s] [finding] that the dog sniff was sufficiently reliable to establish probable cause to conduct a full-blown search of the trunk"**).

It should be noted, however, that in contrast to vehicles and luggage, the sniffing of *persons* by dogs constitutes a search protected by the Fourth Amendment.

> [S]ociety recognizes the interest in the integrity of one's person, and the Fourth Amendment applies with its fullest vigor against any intrusion on the human body. . . . [W]e hold that sniffing by dogs on the students' persons . . . [i.e., sniffing around each child, putting his nose on the child and scratching and manifesting other signs of excitement in the case of an alert] . . . is a search within the purview of the Fourth Amendment. *Horton v. Goose Creek Indep. School Dist.*, 690 F.2d 470, 478–79 (5th Cir. 1982).

See also B.C. v. Plumas Unified School Dist., 192 F.3d 1260, (9th Cir. 1999). ("We agree with the Fifth Circuit in [*Horton*] that 'close proximity sniffing of the person is offensive whether the sniffer be canine or human.' Because we believe that the dog sniff [of students] in this case infringed [plaintiff's] reasonable expectation of privacy, we hold that it constitutes a search.")

- The warrantless monitoring of a beeper or GPS device in a motor vehicle to trace the movement of the vehicle over public thoroughfares does not violate the reasonable expectation of privacy of the occupant of the vehicle. However, monitoring the beeper or GPS device in a motor vehicle after it enters a private home or business would generally be prohibited under the Fourth Amendment absent a warrant or emergency circumstances.

- The use of specially trained dogs to detect the smell of drugs in a vehicle does not violate the reasonable expectation of privacy of the vehicle's owner; as a result, the use of dogs in this way by a police officer is not a "search" under the Fourth Amendment. If the specially trained dog alerts to the presence of contraband in the vehicle, this may provide the officer with the probable cause necessary to search a readily mobile vehicle under the automobile exception.

Summary

Although the search and seizure of motor vehicles are generally governed by the warrant requirement of the Fourth Amendment, courts have created certain exceptions to the warrant requirement for motor vehicles, based on the differences between motor vehicles and fixed premises. A motor vehicle is mobile and is used to transport criminals, weapons, and fruits and instrumentalities of crime. It seldom serves as a residence or a permanent repository of personal effects. Furthermore, a person has a reduced expectation of privacy in a motor vehicle because the vehicle travels public thoroughfares where its occupants and contents are open to view, and because the vehicle is subject to extensive governmental regulation, including periodic inspection and licensing.

One of the principal exceptions to the warrant requirement is the automobile exception as embodied in the *Carroll* doctrine. Under the *Carroll* doctrine, law enforcement officers may conduct a warrantless search of a motor vehicle if they have probable cause to believe that a readily mobile vehicle contains incriminating items subject to seizure. A search under the *Carroll* doctrine need not be conducted immediately, but may be delayed for a reasonable time and may be performed even after the vehicle has been impounded and is in police custody.

The scope of a search under the automobile exception is defined by the object of the search and the places in which there is probable cause to believe the object may be found. If officers have probable cause to believe that a particular seiz-

able item is located somewhere in a vehicle that is readily mobile, they may search the vehicle as if they had a search warrant for the item. This means they may open and search closed, opaque containers and passengers' belongings located inside the vehicle, in which the seizable item might be contained. If, however, police do not have probable cause to search the entire vehicle, but only probable cause to search a particular container or area inside the vehicle, they may search only that container or area but not the entire vehicle.

Warrantless searches of movable, closed, opaque containers *unassociated with a vehicle* are not allowed under the rationale of the *Carroll* doctrine, even if there is probable cause to believe they contain items subject to seizure. Closed, opaque containers may only be searched under authority of a warrant or some other exception to the warrant requirement. For example, if a closed, opaque container is seized incident to the arrest of an occupant of a motor vehicle, the search and seizure of the contents of the container are governed by *New York v. Belton* (discussed in Chapter 8 dealing with Searches Incident to Arrest).

Motor vehicles may be removed from the highways and streets and impounded in the interests of public safety and as part of a law enforcement agency's community caretaking function. An inventory search of an impounded vehicle may be conducted without a warrant. This procedure is not considered to be a search for Fourth Amendment purposes, but merely an administrative procedure. The officer making the inventory may not have the purpose of looking for incriminating evidence, but may be concerned only with protecting the owner's property, protecting the police against claims or disputes over lost or stolen property, and protecting the police from potential danger. The inventory of a vehicle must be limited in scope and intensity by the purposes for which it is allowed and must conform to standard police procedures. Nevertheless, incriminating items subject to seizure found in plain view during an inventory may be seized and are admissible in court.

Not every vehicle occupant has constitutional standing to challenge a search by police under the automobile exception. This is because some vehicle occupants, such as mere passengers in a vehicle, lack a reasonable expectation of privacy in areas within the interior of the vehicle.

Courts generally approve tracing the location of motor vehicles on public thoroughfares by means of electronic devices, and detection of drugs in motor vehicles by means of sniffing by specially trained dogs. Both these limited types of intrusion are allowed without a warrant because of the reduced expectation of privacy in motor vehicles.

Key Terms

automobile exception, 580

beeper, 615

Carroll doctrine, 580

exigent circumstances, 585

Global Positioning System (GPS) tracking device, 617

impound, 598

inventory, 604

probable cause, 580

readily mobile motor vehicle, 580

search, 580

seizure, 584

standing, 613

Review and Discussion Questions

1. Are there any situations in which a warrant is required to search a motor vehicle? In reality, isn't the warrant requirement the exception rather than the rule in automobile cases? Fully explain your answer.

2. Do the legal principles in this chapter apply to vehicles such as bicycles, rowboats, motor homes, trains, or airplanes?

3. If a law enforcement officer has probable cause to believe a vehicle contains small concealable items, such as drugs, jewels, or rare coins, to what extent can he or she search the vehicle without a warrant under the *Carroll* doctrine? Can the upholstery be ripped open? Can the vehicle be dismantled? Can the tires be taken off to look inside them? Can pillows, radios, clothing, and other potential containers be dismantled or ripped apart?

4. Under the *Carroll* doctrine, an officer with probable cause to search a motor vehicle has the choice to either conduct the search immediately or impound the vehicle and search it later at the station house. What factors should the officer consider in making this choice?

5. Describe three situations in which there would be probable cause to search a vehicle that is readily mobile.

6. If the postal service turns over to the police plastic bags believed to contain illegal drugs, may the police conduct chemical tests on the contents of the bags without a warrant?

7. Assume that a person is arrested for drunk driving late at night while driving alone on a city street. He tells the police that he does not want his car impounded and that a friend will pick up the car some time the next day. He says he will sign a statement absolving the police from any liability for any loss of or damage to the car or its contents. Can the police still impound the car? Should they?

8. Under the *Carroll* doctrine, must the police have probable cause to search a vehicle at the time it is stopped on the highway in order to search it later

at the station? Suppose a person is arrested on the highway for drunk driving and is told to accompany officers to the station to post bond. A routine check at the station reveals that the vehicle is stolen. May the officers search it without a warrant?

9. If officers have probable cause to search a vehicle stopped on the highway but no probable cause to arrest the passengers of the vehicle, can they search the passengers also? Are the passengers "containers" under the ruling of the *Ross* case? Does the answer depend on the nature of the evidence for which the officers are looking?

10. Is a warrantless installation of a beeper proper in any of the following circumstances?

   a. Attaching a beeper to the outside of an automobile
   b. Placing a beeper somewhere inside an automobile
   c. Opening a closed package or luggage to install a beeper
   d. Attaching a beeper to the outside of a package or luggage
   e. Placing a beeper with money taken in a bank robbery

11. If a law enforcement officer has reasonable articulable suspicion that an automobile contains dangerous weapons, can the officer "frisk" the automobile, even though there is no person in it?

12. If a person's only home is a motor home and the person travels all year long, should the *Carroll* doctrine apply to a search of the motor home? What are the relevant factors from the *Carney* case that should be considered in answering this question? Assuming the *Carroll* doctrine does apply, should there be any limits on the scope of the search allowed?

13. What if police develop probable cause to believe a readily mobile vehicle parked on private property contains incriminating items subject to seizure? Should police obtain a warrant before searching such a vehicle? What if police knew the owner of the vehicle was about to leave on a cross-country journey to visit family? What if police knew the owner was planning to begin the journey in about a week?

Applications of the Law in Real Cases

1 A one-car accident occurred near Byron, Nebraska, in rural Thayer County. Later in the day, after a passerby reported seeing a weapon in the car, Nebraska State Patrol Trooper Kyle Johansen was dispatched to the scene. Johansen had visited the accident scene earlier in the day, and had briefly discussed the accident with Thayer County Deputy Sheriff Gordon Downing. At that time, Johansen observed an individual in the back of Downing's car, whom Downing identified as the driver of the car in the accident and whom Johansen later learned was Scovill. Johansen talked to Downing a second time about the accident while at the sheriff's station later that same day, but before Johansen was dispatched to the scene on the weapons call.

When Johansen responded to the dispatch, he looked inside and immediately observed a handgun on the front passenger seat. At the time he responded to the call, no one else was present at the accident scene. Johansen testified that he did not remember whether he reached through a broken window to pick up the gun, but that he did eventually open the passenger door of the car. Upon closer examination of the gun,

Johansen realized it was a BB gun. After making this determination, Johansen continued searching for other weapons and for the registration of the vehicle. He testified that although he had seen the person identified as the driver, he was curious as to who owned the car. Johansen opened the glove box and found the car's registration, which listed Scovill as the owner. He also found a piece of broken mirror and small medical forceps that were burnt on the ends, which Johansen believed were drug paraphernalia.

Johansen then searched the remainder of the car for contraband before focusing his search on the items strewn about the accident scene. Johansen first found a Crown Royal whiskey bag about thirty feet in front of the vehicle. He picked it up, felt a small box inside, opened the bag, and removed the box. He then opened the box and found a small grain scale. Johansen also found a closed six-pack cooler, which he opened. Inside the cooler was a cardboard tube. Johansen opened the tube and found short plastic straws, which he believed were used for inhaling illegal drugs. Finally, Johansen found a bong (a pipe used for smoking marijuana) in a corn row in the harvested corn field adjacent to the ditch, which was "a considerable distance" from the other items that were strewn about.

Johansen collected the paraphernalia and other items strewn about the scene. He placed the paraphernalia in his patrol car, and the rest of the items in the trunk of Scovill's car. He then called Downing back to the scene to discuss what he had found. Downing informed Johansen that he could probably find Scovill at a truckstop in Hebron, Nebraska. While Downing remained at the scene, Johansen went to the truckstop and found Scovill leaning against an outside wall of the building. Johansen testified that he, while in uniform, approached Scovill and asked if he was Scovill. After Scovill nodded that he was, he informed Johansen that he was the only occupant in the car at the time of the accident and that the items in the car belonged to him.

Johansen then explained to Scovill that he had found drug paraphernalia at the scene, and asked whether Scovill had any weapons or contraband on his person. Scovill stated that he did not have any weapons. Johansen patted Scovill down nonetheless. Specifically, Johansen testified that he conducted the pat-down search because, based on what Johansen had found at the scene, he believed Scovill "still could have had drugs on him or possibly a weapon." On cross-examination, Johansen admitted he conducted the pat-down "basically to search him to see if [he] could find anything else." Johansen also testified that he did not have any reason to believe Scovill was armed and dangerous other than the fact that Johansen did not know him, a possibility that exists with virtually anyone. Johansen was also curious because Scovill only answered that he did not have any weapons, and said nothing about whether he had any contraband. Johansen testified that he thought he could not have arrested Scovill at that point because he had only found drug paraphernalia, which he knew to be an infraction that would justify only the delivery of a citation in lieu of arrest.

Johansen started with the right front pocket of Scovill's ski jacket and, without manipulation, felt what he believed to be a pipe used for smoking marijuana. He then asked Scovill to remove the item from his pocket, which he did. Johansen found that it was a marijuana pipe that still had residue inside. Johansen next patted the right front change pocket of Scovill's jeans and felt a small bulge. Johansen manipulated the bulge a little to see if it was soft and then removed it from the pocket. Johansen discovered that the item was a wad of plastic wrap containing some marijuana. There was also a cellophane wrapper containing part of a pill later determined to be alprazolam (sold under the brand name Xanax).

As Johansen continued his pat-down search on the right side of Scovill's coat, he felt a pocket with a small

rectangular box inside. Johansen asked Scovill what the box contained, to which Scovill replied, "[S]ome meth." Johansen then removed the box, opened it, and found a razor and a small baggie containing a yellowish white powder, which Johansen believed to be methamphetamine. Johansen testified that he did not arrest Scovill until he completed searching him. He then placed Scovill under arrest for possession of methamphetamine, possession of marijuana, and possession of drug paraphernalia. Should Scovill's motion to suppress the drugs and paraphernalia be granted? *See State v. Scovill*, 608 N.W.2d 623 (Neb. App. 2000).

2 [O]n June 12, 1999, Sergeant John Cox brought his patrol car to a halt directly behind Gibson's van, which was stopped at a red traffic light. Sergeant Cox then conducted a random computer check of Gibson's license plate, which indicated that Gibson had an outstanding warrant for his arrest from Brown County, Indiana. However, Sergeant Cox did not initiate a traffic stop of Gibson's van.

Instead, Sergeant Cox followed Gibson as he drove into the parking lot of a convenience store. As Gibson exited the van and walked toward the convenience store, Sergeant Cox got out of his patrol car, stopped Gibson, and requested his driver's license. After examining the driver's license, Sergeant Cox handcuffed Gibson. Officer Bradley Meyers, who had responded to Sergeant Cox's call for assistance, then asked Gibson if he had any weapons or contraband in his van. Gibson informed Officer Meyers that marijuana was located in the center console of his van. Neither Sergeant Cox nor Officer Meyers informed Gibson of his *Miranda* rights before Officer Meyer began questioning Gibson. A plastic bag containing a green leafy substance later determined to be marijuana was retrieved from Gibson's vehicle.

Consequently, the State charged Gibson with possession of marijuana, a Class A misdemeanor. Gibson filed with the trial court a motion to suppress the statements made by him after his arrest, and the marijuana obtained from the warrantless search of his vehicle. Should Gibson's motion to suppress be granted? *See Gibson v. State*, 733 N.E.2d 945 (Ind. App. 2000).

3 On August 21, 1997, Officer Alex Hodge, a trooper for the Mississippi Highway Patrol, pulled over a red Ford Taurus traveling at the rate of 75 miles per hour in a 70 miles per hour zone in Jones County. The driver of the vehicle was the appellant, James B. Millsap. Forty-six kilograms of marijuana were found in the trunk of his car. A trial was held on February 23, 1999, and Millsap was found guilty and sentenced to twenty years in the custody of the Mississippi Department of Corrections, with eight years suspended and twelve years to serve.

The State's first witness was Officer Alex Hodge. Lieutenant Tony Sarrow, a lieutenant with the Harrison County Sheriff 's Department, was riding along with Officer Hodge on the day in question. Officer Hodge testified that he pulled Millsap over and asked him for his license and registration. Officer Hodge testified that he became suspicious when he noticed that the vehicle was a Hertz rental and Millsap's name did not appear on the rental contract. He asked Millsap if he had any handguns, contraband, or dead bodies in the vehicle. Officer Hodge testified that Millsap's response was "Of course not. My father would kill me if I was involved in anything like that." Then Officer Hodge testified that he asked Millsap, "What are you talking about when you refer to that?" and stated that Millsap's response was "You know, drugs and stuff." Then Officer Hodge asked if he could search the vehicle, and Millsap stated that he did not want the vehicle searched because the last time it was searched the police had damaged his vehicle. Officer Hodge testified that he took this statement as an indicator that Millsap did not want him searching his trunk. This caused him to get his patrol dog to do an exterior walk around the vehicle, which resulted in the dog making an aggressive alert to the back of the car by scratching on the trunk. The officer explained that at this point he asked Mr. Millsap if there would be any reason the dog would have indicated on the vehicle or if there were any illegal narcotics in the vehicle. He testified that Millsap's response was "Yes" and after asking how much Millsap responded with "A lot." Officer Hodge then asked what he meant by a lot, and Millsap responded with "Well, it should be between 104 and 106 pounds."

Officer Hodge stated that he handcuffed Millsap and the passenger in the car, Alicia Stone, in order to safely search the car. When he opened the trunk, he found two duffel bags filled with a "green leafy substance, compressed and wrapped in clear plastic wrap," later determined to be marijuana with a weight of 46 kilograms, or approximately 101 pounds. Officer Hodge arrested Millsap and brought him to the Highway Patrol Office in Hattiesburg. At the station, Officer Don Sumrall advised Millsap of his *Miranda* rights and gave him his rights advisement form. Millsap signed the waiver and explained to the officers that he had traveled from Severeville, Tennessee, to Houston, Texas to pick up the marijuana.

Millsap testified that he was not speeding on the day in question and that he gave a phone number to the officer to verify that he was driving the rental car with his friend's permission. He stated that he did not want the officer to search the car because he had some personal items in the car, and that he never stated anything about the trunk or any drugs. He further testified that he was not allowed to observe the dog sniff the vehicle. He also stated that Officer Hodge never asked him if he had any drugs, guns, or weapons in the car. Millsap also testified that during the questioning he asked for a lawyer and the officer replied, "Everybody in jail has a lawyer," but did not provide him with one. Should Millsap's motion to suppress the evidence seized from his vehicle be granted? *See Millsap v. State*, 767 So.2d 286 (Miss. App. 2000).

4 Nevada State Trooper Scott Cobel heard a report over his police radio that shots had been fired at the Saddle West Hotel & Casino in Pahrump, Nevada. Trooper Cobel immediately responded to the casino, where he was flagged down by a security guard, who gave a license plate number and description of the vehicle in which the shooting suspects had left.

Trooper Cobel proceeded southbound on State Route 160, caught up with the vehicle, and pulled it over. Cobel drew his weapon and ordered the four occupants of the vehicle to raise their hands. At the time of the stop, the appellant was sitting in the back seat of the vehicle, behind the driver. With the assistance of another Trooper, Cobel then conducted a felony traffic stop, ordering each of the vehicle's occupants at gunpoint to step out of the car, one at a time. As each occupant stepped out of the vehicle, Cobel performed a quick pat-down search, handcuffed the individual, and sat him or her down on the side of the road. Trooper Cobel then searched the vehicle for weapons. Cobel testified that when he searched the vehicle, officer safety was not an issue because the four suspects were temporarily restrained and had been patted down for weapons.

Beneath the driver's seat, Cobel found a Beretta semiautomatic handgun. The Beretta was located behind a metal bar that adjusts the seat, with the barrel pointed toward the front of the car and the hammer pulled back. Cobel also found marijuana in a black duffel bag. A casino security guard reported seeing the appellant outside the casino carrying a black duffel bag. Methamphetamine and a second handgun were also recovered by police, as well as a third handgun that had been thrown from the vehicle prior to the stop.

The appellant and the other occupants of the vehicle were arrested. Sergeant Steve Huggins of the Nye County Sheriff's Office informed Trooper Cobel that the sheriff's office would be handling the case, including gathering the evidence, and asked Cobel to return the Beretta, marijuana, and other evidence to the vehicle. Cobel placed the evidence back inside the vehicle.

The appellant was charged and tried on three counts of being an ex-felon in possession of a firearm (one count for the Beretta, and two counts for the other two handguns) and two counts of possession of a controlled substance (one count for the marijuana in the black duffel bag, and one count for the methamphetamine found in the car). Prior to trial, the appellant filed a motion to suppress the evidence obtained in the warrantless search of the vehicle. Should the motion be granted? *See Hughes v. State*, 12 P.3d 948 (Nev. 2000).

5 Early in the morning on July 19, 1998, two Philadelphia police officers noticed a car with its headlights on behind an abandoned building in Philadelphia. The officers investigated and found Prenice Bolden standing outside his car, urinating. The officers asked Bolden for some identification. He reached into his car and removed a driver's license from above the driver's side sun visor.

While the officers checked the validity of Bolden's license, they also determined that he was intoxicated. The officers conducted field sobriety tests, which Bolden failed. The officers noticed that Bolden had two containers of beer in the front seat of his car, one of which was open. The officers arrested Bolden for violation of Philadelphia's open container law. Bolden was not arrested for DUI because the officers had not seen him driving his car.

After the arrest, one of the officers sought to secure any valuables that may have been in Bolden's car. The officers testified that this was standard policy for the police department in order to decrease liability for items that could be stolen from an unattended automobile. As the officer reached above the sun visor from which Bolden had removed his license, a clear bag containing what the officer thought was cocaine fell to the floorboard of the car.

After Bolden was taken to the police station, the officers informed him of his *Miranda* rights. He indicated that he understood them. Bolden was then asked where he had purchased the drugs. Bolden identified the street on which he bought the cocaine, as well as the make and color of the automobile of the person from whom he bought it and the amount he paid. Bolden was charged with possession of cocaine.

Bolden appealed his subsequent conviction for possession of the drugs, asserting that the search of his car that revealed the cocaine was illegal and that he was unable to validly waive his Miranda rights because of his intoxicated state. Was the search legal? *See Bolden v. State*, 767 So.2d 315 (Miss. App. 2000).

6 Except as specifically noted, the following facts are uncontroverted. At about eleven o' clock on the morning of May 25, 1997, Stayton Police Officer Jim Krieger received a dispatch that an unidentified informant had called 911 to report that a car was driving erratically near Sublimity. The caller described the car and gave its license plate number; a records check showed that the car was registered to the defendant. Krieger waited for the car, saw it run a stop sign, and then made a traffic stop based on that infraction. Krieger asked the defendant, who was driving, for his license, registration, and proof of insurance, and then ran another records check, which confirmed that the car was registered to the defendant.

Krieger then returned the defendant's documents, issued him a citation for failing to obey a traffic control device, ORS 811.265, and told him that he was free to leave. After serving the defendant with the citation, Krieger clearly informed him he did not have to remain at the scene of the stop. However, the defendant agreed to remain there so officer Krieger could investigate further the citizen's report of the reckless and intoxicated operation of the vehicle.

Before pursuing that investigation, Krieger returned to his patrol car, turned off his overheads, and confirmed with Stayton dispatch that a backup officer would be there in minutes. He then re-contacted the defendant and his passenger, both of whom had remained seated in the vehicle. In the ensuing discussion, the defendant acknowledged that he had been driving erratically due to mechanical problems. During that conversation, the defendant and his passenger remained seated in the car.

As Krieger and the defendant spoke, Sergeant Stai of the Marion County Sheriff's Office arrived to provide backup. After Stai arrived, Krieger asked defendant if he would consent to a search of his car. When the defendant refused, Krieger walked away to confer with a third officer. Meanwhile, Stai, who had been standing on the passenger side of defendant's car, noted that the door lock on the passenger door was completely missing, as if it had been "punched out." Based on his experience investigating stolen vehicles, Stai became curious and suspicious that the car might be stolen: "[T]hat got my suspicions up and my curiosity and concern."

Stai, who was unaware that Krieger had already confirmed defendant's registration, asked the defendant for his registration. After he complied, Stai then attempted to compare the Vehicle Identification Number (VIN) on the registration with the VIN on the car's dashboard by looking through the windshield, but was unable to see clearly. Stai then "advised the two occupants that I wanted them to step from the vehicle so that I could check the federal trade sticker on the driver's door post, which would be another location for a VIN."

After the defendant and his passenger opened their doors and got out, Stai bent down to examine the now-visible VIN sticker on the driver's-side door post. From that vantage point through the open door, Stai saw a stack of credit cards on the center console. Stai's "suspicions were aroused because people don't normally carry credit cards unprotected, or unconcealed I should say." Stai asked defendant and his passenger whether the cards were theirs, and both denied any ownership of them. Stai then seized the cards, which proved to have been stolen during the theft and burglary with which the defendant was subsequently charged. In the ensuing search of the defendant's car, police found other items, including checks, a baseball autographed by Barry Bonds, and baseball caps. Like the credit cards, all of these items had been stolen from the offices of the Salem-Keizer Volcanoes.

Before trial, the defendant moved to suppress the items, including the credit cards, found in the car. Should the defendant's motion to suppress be granted? *See State v. Finlay*, 12 P.3d 999 (Or. App. 2000).

12

Open Fields and Abandoned Property

Learning Objectives

▶ Understand how the concepts of open fields, curtilage, and reasonable expectation of privacy interrelate and their importance to the law of search and seizure.

▶ Be able to analyze a fact situation involving a description of a place, and determine whether the place is located in the open fields or is within the curtilage.

▶ Know the differences among the open fields doctrine, the plain view doctrine, and observations into the curtilage from a vantage point in the open fields or a public place.

▶ Know the factors considered by courts in determining whether premises, objects, or vehicles have been abandoned, and the significance of abandonment in the law of search and seizure.

As you know by now, the Fourth Amendment to the U.S. Constitution guarantees "the right of the people to be secure in their persons, *houses, papers,* and effects, against unreasonable *searches* and seizures . . ." (emphasis added). The words *houses* and *searches* are italicized because the meaning of open fields depends on court interpretation of the word *houses,* and the meaning of abandoned property depends on court interpretation of the word *searches. Hester v. United States,* 265 U.S. 57 (1924), established the concepts of open fields and abandoned property in the law of search and seizure.

As described in *Hester v. United States,* as revenue officers investigating suspected bootlegging went to Hester's father's house, they saw Henderson drive up to the house. They concealed themselves and observed Hester come out of the house and hand Henderson a quart bottle. An alarm was given. Hester went to a nearby car and removed a gallon jug, and he and Henderson fled across an open field. One of the officers pursued, firing his pistol. Henderson threw away his bottle, and Hester dropped his jug, which broke, retaining about one quart of its contents. A broken jar, still containing some of its contents, was found outside the house. The officers examined the jug, the jar, and the bottle, and determined that they contained illicitly distilled whiskey. The officers had neither a search warrant nor an arrest warrant.

The defendant contended on appeal that the testimony of the two officers was inadmissible because their actions constituted an illegal search and seizure. The U.S. Supreme Court said:

> It is obvious that even if there had been a trespass, the above testimony was not obtained by an illegal search or seizure. The defendant's own acts, and those of his associates, disclosed the jug, the jar, and the bottle—and there was no seizure in the sense of the law when the officers examined the contents of each after it had been *abandoned.* . . . The only shadow of a ground for bringing up the case is drawn from the hypothesis that the examination of the vessels took place upon Hester's father's land. As to that, it is enough to say that, apart from the justification, the special protection accorded by the Fourth Amendment to the people in their "persons, houses, papers, and effects," is not extended to the *open fields.* The distinction between the latter and the house is as old as the common law. 265 U.S. at 58–59 (emphasis added).

The remainder of this chapter is devoted to a discussion of the law of search and seizure applied to open fields and abandoned property.

▶ OPEN FIELDS

Hester stated the basic open fields doctrine: "[T]he special protection accorded by the Fourth Amendment to the people in their 'persons, houses, papers and effects' is not extended to the open fields." 265 U.S. at 59. The **open fields** doctrine allows law enforcement officers to search for and seize evidence in the open fields without a warrant, probable cause, or any other legal justification. Even if officers trespass while searching the open fields, the trespass does not render the evidence admissible. *Oliver v. United States*, 466 U.S. 170 (1984).

The key issue under the open fields doctrine is the determination of the demarcation line between the area protected by the Fourth Amendment and the open fields. This depends on court interpretations of the word **houses** in the Fourth Amendment. "Houses" has been given a very broad meaning by the courts. The term "houses" includes homes (whether owned, rented, or leased), and any other place in which a person is staying or living, permanently or temporarily. Examples of protected living quarters are hotel and motel rooms, apartments, rooming and boarding house rooms, and even hospital rooms. The term "houses" extends to places of business. *See v. City of Seattle*, 387 U.S. 541 (1967). This protection is limited, however, to areas or sections that are not open to the public:

> [A] private business whose doors are open to the general public is also to be considered open to entry by the police for any proper purpose not violative of the owner's constitutional rights—e.g., patronizing the place or surveying it to promote law and order or to suppress a breach of the peace. *State v. LaDuca*, 214 A.2d 423, 426 (N.J. Super. App. Div. 1965); *see also State v. DeMarco*, 384 A.2d 1113, 1116 (N.J. Super. App. Div. 1978).

For convenience, the remainder of this chapter uses the word *house* to refer to either residential or commercial premises covered by the Fourth Amendment. Courts have further extended the meaning of *houses* to include **curtilage**— the "ground and buildings immediately surrounding a dwelling house." *State v. Sindak*, 774 P.2d 895, 898 (Idaho 1989), *overruled on other grounds by State v. Clark*, 16 P.3d 931, 934 (Idaho 2000); *see also United States v. Cousins*, 455 F.3d 1116, 1121–22 (10th Cir. 2006). ("The curtilage concept originated at common law to extend to the area immediately surrounding a dwelling house the same protection under the law . . . as was afforded the house itself.") The concept of curtilage is vital to the open fields doctrine because the open fields are considered to be all the space not contained within the curtilage. The following discussion focuses on the facts and circumstances that courts use in determining the extent of the curtilage.

Determining Curtilage

To determine whether property falls within a house's curtilage, the law enforcement officer must consider **"the factors that determine whether an individual reasonably may expect that an area immediately adjacent to the home will remain private."** *Oliver v. United States,* 466 U.S. 170, 180 (1984). *United States v. Dunn*, 480 U.S. 294, 301 (1987), described those factors:

> **[W]e believe that curtilage questions should be resolved with particular reference to four factors:** *the proximity of the area claimed to be curtilage to the home, whether the area is included within an enclosure surrounding the home, the nature of the uses to which the area is put, and the steps taken by the resident to protect the area from observation by people passing by* **(emphasis added).**

These factors are not a rigid formula. Rather, they are useful analytical tools to help determine whether the area in question should be placed under the same Fourth Amendment protection as the home. For example, if the area is determined to be "curtilage," it will be provided full Fourth Amendment protection similar to a home (e.g., a warrant supported by probable cause would be required for police to search the "curtilage"); on the other hand, an open field would not be afforded such protection. The Court emphasized that **"the primary focus is whether the area in question harbors those intimate activities associated with domestic life and the privacies of the home."** 480 U.S. at 301 n.4. The four factors are discussed below.

Residential Yard   The backyard of a house is ordinarily within the curtilage of a house and is thereby protected from a warrantless search under the Fourth Amendment. *United States v. Van Dyke*, 643 F.2d 992 (4th Cir. 1980). For example, in *United States v. Boger*, 755 F. Supp. 333, 338 (E.D. Wash. 1990), the court said:

> [I]t is clear that the area of Mr. Boger's backyard . . . is within the curtilage of the home. The area was enclosed with sight-obscuring fences on the east and west, and by the house on the south. An unoccupied field was to the north. The area in question was obviously used by the resident as part of the home. An outside patio was located on the rear of the home and the backyard was in grass and landscaping. Clearly the resident had taken appropriate steps to protect the area from observation on three sides and an unoccupied open field was on the fourth side.

If a residential yard is accessible to the public, however, and the owner takes no steps to protect it from observation, it may not qualify for Fourth Amendment protection. For example, in *United States v. Titemore*, 335 F. Supp. 2d 502 (D. Vt. 2004), the court found that a police officer could approach the porch area of defendant's house through a path on a portion of his yard used as a garden. The officer wished to speak with defendant about his possible involvement in an act of vandalism. The court described the officer's approach to defendant's house, from Patten Shore Road, in the following way:

> The porch area is clearly visible from the road. There is a rail fence along Patten Shore Road that partially restricts access to the porch. The rail fence is essentially decorative. There is also a garden in the area of the path from Patten Shore Road to the porch, although due to that time of year little vegetation would restrict access. There was a dysfunctional doorbell and a lamp converted to a plant holder on opposite sides of the sliding door. The [porch] was used as an outside sitting area by the defendant. Although some views from the porch were restricted by trees, there were unrestricted views of a neighbor's house and the lake. Some neighbors had approached the residence by invitation in the past by following the same path taken by [the officer]. There were no signs restricting access to the porch in any way. 335 F. Supp. 2d at 504–5.

Thus, because this area of defendant's yard containing the path to the porch was accessible to the public, and defendant had not restricted access to this area, the officer could make a warrantless entry into this area without violating the Fourth Amendment:

> In this case, it was reasonable for [the officer] to approach the residence at the sliding door. Many factors support this conclusion. The sliding door at the porch is clearly visible from two public streets. In fact, the sliding door is more open to public view than the door on the west side of the house. Moreover, there is no barrier between the porch and [another road adjacent to defen-

dant's home]. The Supreme Court has noted that whether the area is included within an enclosure surrounding the home and whether the resident has taken steps to protect the area from observation by people passing by are both important factors to consider when deciding whether an area is curtilage. Thus, these factors are highly relevant to whether it was reasonable for [the officer] to approach the sliding door for a knock and talk visit [with the defendant]. 335 F. Supp. 2d at 506 (quotations omitted).

The court in *Titemore* distinguished other cases where police were prohibited from entering backyards enclosed with fences, to gain access to a home:

> This case presents very different facts. [The officer] did not approach a back door in an enclosed yard. He was confronted by a house with no front door and simply chose one of the side doors. Moreover, unlike the back doors at issue in the cases cited by [the defendant], the sliding door in this case was not enclosed or blocked from public view. 335 F. Supp. 2d at 506.

Law enforcement officers should consider the residential yard of a house as curtilage, unless there are clear indications that the person residing in the house allowed members of the public access to the yard and had no **reasonable expectation of privacy** in the yard. (Recall from Chapter 3 the discussion of the U.S. Supreme Court's decision in *Katz* that the Fourth Amendment "search" question is determined by whether or not an individual's reasonable expectation of privacy is violated. If no such privacy expectation has been violated, then police have not conducted a "search" under the Fourth Amendment requiring a warrant.)

Fences If the area immediately surrounding a house is enclosed by a fence, the area within the fence is usually defined as the curtilage. *United States v. Swepston*, 987 F.2d 1510 (10th Cir. 1993), found that a chicken shed located a hundred feet from the defendant's house was within the curtilage of the house. A barbed wire fence enclosed the shed and the house and *no fence separated the two structures*. In addition, the defendant maintained a path between the house and the shed and visited the shed regularly, neither the house nor the shed could be seen from a public road or adjoining property, and there was no evidence that the shed was not being used for intimate activities of the home.

In contrast, marijuana gardens located about three hundred feet from the co-defendant's house in *Swepston* were found to be outside the curtilage:

> [A]lthough the gardens were encircled by a barbed wire fence, *they were outside the fence that encircled [the codefendant's] house, and they were separated from [his] house by the chainlink fence. . . .* [T]he area within the barbed wire fence contained numerous chickens and chicken huts and was used primarily for the raising of game chickens. These huts were visible to the . . . officers as they overflew the area, and indicated to them that the area was not being used for intimate activities of the home. Finally, [the codefendant] did little to protect the marijuana gardens from observation by those standing in the open fields surrounding [his] property. 987 F.2d at 1515 (emphasis added).

Because the marijuana gardens were located outside the curtilage in the "open fields," police would not need a warrant to search this area. (Note that a later case by the same court that decided *Swepston*—*United States v. Cousins*, 455 F.3d 1116 (10th Cir. 2006)—overruled *Swepston* in part, but continued to apply the *Swepston* facts related to the curtilage concept. The overruling dealt only with the technical legal standard by which appellate courts review lower court decisions on issues related to curtilage. *See Cousins*, 455 F.3d at 1121. ("In the past, we have reviewed district courts' curtilage determinations for clear error. *See, e.g., United States v. Swepston*, 987 F.2d 1510, 1513 [10th Cir. 1993].) ("However, based on the [U.S] Supreme Court decision in *Ornelas v. United States*, 517 U.S. 690 [1996], we now conclude that ultimate curtilage conclusions are to be reviewed under a *de novo* standard although we continue to review findings of historical facts for clear error.")

If a piece of land is already outside the curtilage, erecting fences around it or taking other steps to protect its privacy does not establish that the expectation of privacy in the land is legitimate and bring the land within the curtilage. In *Oliver v. United States*, 466 U.S. 170 (1984), to conceal their criminal activities, the defendants planted marijuana on secluded land and erected fences and "No Trespassing" signs around the property. The Court said:

> **[I]t may be that because of such precautions, few members of the public stumbled upon the marijuana crops seized by the police. Neither of these suppositions demonstrates, however, that the expectation of privacy was *legitimate* in the sense required by the Fourth Amendment. *The test of legitimacy is not whether the individual chooses to conceal asserted "private" activity. Rather, the correct inquiry is whether the government's intrusion infringes upon the personal and societal values protected by the Fourth Amendment. . . .* [W]e find no basis for concluding that a police inspection of open fields accomplishes such an infringement.** 466 U.S. at 182–83 (emphasis added).

Whether a fence defines the curtilage of a home may depend on the nature of the fence. *United States v. Brady*, 734 F. Supp. 923 (E.D. Wash. 1990), found that the fence was not sufficient to define the curtilage:

> There was no "no trespassing" sign posted on or near the gate. The fence was not a sight-obstructing fence. The fence did not completely enclose the property in that there was a wide gap on either side of the gate which could reasonably be construed to be a pedestrian path. The fence was not of a type which evidenced an intent to exclude strangers. 734 F. Supp. at 928.

Also, recall from *United States v. Titemore*, 335 F. Supp. 2d 502 (D. Vt. 2004), discussed above, that even though defendant had erected a decorative "rail" fence between the public road and the yard area surrounding his porch, the court found that the officer could make a warrantless entry into this area without violating the Fourth Amendment.

Distance from the Dwelling The definitive trend among lower courts after the Supreme Court's decision in *Dunn*, discussed above, is to use a totality of circumstances approach in determining the extent of the curtilage, with the distance from an individual's dwelling as one of many factors to be weighed in making the determination:

> It is of course true, as the Government argues, that a bright-line rule would be easier to administer than the fact-specific rule announced by *Dunn*. The Seventh Circuit, writing in 1976, before *Dunn*, did try to establish the "clear rule" that any outbuilding or area within 75 feet of the house is within the curtilage and any outbuilding or area further than 75 feet is outside the curtilage. But this decision cannot be reconciled with the Supreme Court's warning in *Dunn*

against mechanistic application of any one factor, and has not been accepted by other Circuits. Thus the Ninth Circuit has stated: There is not . . . any fixed distance at which curtilage ends. And the Fourth Circuit, even before *Dunn*, explicitly criticized the [clear] rule [approach], and pointed out that distance is just one of many factors to be weighed when determining the reach of the curtilage. The Seventh Circuit itself has not mentioned [the "clear rule" approach] in the past twelve years, and its last discussion of the case implicitly challenged [that approach]. *United States v. Reilly*, 76 F.3d 1271, 1277 (2d Cir. 1996).

In *Reilly*, quoted above, the court found that defendant's cottage located 375 feet away from defendant's main dwelling, and a wooded area located 125 feet from the cottage, was still within defendant's curtilage, and hence protected from a warrantless search by police under the Fourth Amendment. During a warrantless search of the wooded area near the cottage, police discovered marijuana:

> The court below found that the cottage was 375 feet away from the main residence and that the wooded area was 125 feet away. The cottage distance, taken alone, could support a finding that the search did not take place within the curtilage. But the distance between the main house and the cottage does not, in the circumstances of this case, require such a finding. The distance between the marijuana plants and the main residence in the case before us is admittedly large. But that is just the beginning of the inquiry. 76 F.3d at 1277.

The court found that because the cottage and woods were in a secluded area, private activities occurred there and defendant had taken steps to enclose the property, such as erecting fences and planting hedgerows, these areas were within the curtilage of defendant's main dwelling:

> We have examined each of the *Dunn* factors individually and at substantial length. In the end, however, they must be evaluated as a whole. When that is done, we readily conclude that the court below correctly defined curtilage and that it did not clearly err in its findings that the cottage and wooded area were within [the defendant's] curtilage. We therefore affirm the district court's determination of these issues. 76 F.3d at 1280.

Because the cottage and woods were within defendant's curtilage, and the police had no warrant when initially searching these areas, the marijuana discovered there was inadmissible at trial.

Also, in *State v. Silva*, 509 A.2d 659 (Me. 1986), the court held that a marijuana patch located roughly 250 feet behind the defendant's house was within the curtilage and was entitled to Fourth Amendment protection. The marijuana patch was within a cultivated lawn extending from the house to a tree-studded bog just beyond the patch; a swath of trees stood between the patch and the house but was not long enough to cut the back lawn completely in half; and the lawn was dotted with fruit trees, fruit bushes, two gardens, a shed, and flowers.

Multiple-Occupant Dwellings Multiple-occupancy dwellings are treated differently than single-occupancy dwellings for purposes of determining the extent of the curtilage. Generally, the shared areas of multiple-occupancy buildings (such as common corridors, passageways, driveways, parking lots, and yards) are not entitled to the protection of the Fourth Amendment because individual tenants do not have a reasonable expectation of privacy with respect to those areas. *United*

States v. Nohara, 3 F.3d 1239 (9th Cir. 1993). Nevertheless, multiple-occupancy dwellings are all different and courts examine all the facts and circumstances in determining the curtilage.

In *Fixel v. Wainwright*, 492 F.2d 480 (5th Cir. 1974), two law enforcement officers who had been informed that narcotics were being sold on the defendant's premises observed the defendant's residence in a four-unit apartment building. Over a forty-five-minute period, several people entered the defendant's apartment. Each time, the defendant went into his backyard and removed a shaving kit from beneath some rubbish under a tree. One officer went into the backyard and seized the shaving kit, while the other officer arrested the defendant. Chemical analysis revealed that the shaving kit contained heroin. The court held that the backyard was a protected area and that the seizure and search of the shaving kit were illegal:

> The backyard of Fixel's home was not a common passageway normally used by the building's tenants for gaining access to the apartments. . . . Nor is the backyard an area open as a corridor to salesmen or other businessmen who might approach the tenants in the course of their trade. . . . This apartment was Fixel's home, he lived there, and the backyard of the building was completely removed from the street and surrounded by a chainlink fence. . . . While the enjoyment of his backyard is not as exclusive as the backyard of a purely private residence, this area is not as public or shared as the corridors, yards, or other common areas of a large apartment complex or motel. Contemporary concepts of living such as multi-unit dwellings must not dilute Fixel's right to privacy anymore than is absolutely required. We believe that the backyard area of Fixel's home is sufficiently removed and private in character that he could reasonably expect privacy. 492 F.2d at 484.

In contrast, *United States v. Soliz*, 129 F.3d 499 (9th Cir. 1997), held that a parking area adjacent to an apartment complex was not within the curtilage:

> First (proximity): The parking area was adjacent to the residence, although the record does not reveal the distance between the parked cars and the apartment units. . . . Proximity is not determinative as there is no fixed distance at which curtilage begins or ends. . . . Here, the proximity is certainly close enough to support a finding of curtilage, if other factors support such a finding. . . .
>
> Second (enclosure): A fence surrounded the entire property. However, it was a chainlink fence through which the public could easily see—it was not intended to shield the property from public view. The mere existence of such a fence does not necessarily demonstrate enclosure of curtilage. . . .
>
> Third (use): The use factor is helpful in determining whether the parking lot was an area which contained activities associated with the "sanctity of a man's home and the privacies of life." . . . There is no evidence that the parking lot was used for private activities connected with the sanctity of the home. . . . Rather, it was a shared area used by the residents and guests for the mundane, open, and notorious activity of parking. This is not the type of area which we have determined in the past to have the requisite expectation of privacy required to bring it within the protections of the Fourth Amendment. . . . We doubt whether, in the absence of evidence of intimate activities, a shared common area in a multi-unit dwelling compound is sufficiently privacy oriented to constitute curtilage. . . .
>
> Fourth (steps taken to prevent observation): No steps were taken here to prevent outside observation of the parking area. The fence surrounding the property did not prevent people from peering in, the gate was strewn on the

CHAPTER 12 | OPEN FIELDS AND ABANDONED PROPERTY

ground, and the property could be viewed from both the street and the alley. . . . Additionally, there were no "No Trespassing" signs posted. . . . Unlike the defendant in *Depew* who went to great lengths to ensure his privacy, Soliz took no such steps. *See Depew*, 8 F.3d at 1428 (defendant chose residence because it was in a remote, secluded area not visible from the highway; defendant maintained post office box in town and read his own meter so that no postal worker or meter reader came to his premises). [See Applications of the Law in Real Cases, item 2, for the details of the *Depew* case.]

Analysis of the four factors supports the district court's finding that there was no violation of the curtilage in this case. 129 F.3d at 502–3.

See also United States v. Johnson, 256 F.3d 895, 913 (9th Cir. 2001) (changing standard of review for appellate courts like court in *Soliz*). ("[W]e hold that the determination that a particular search did (or did not) occur within the curtilage must be reviewed de novo on appeal [and not under the clearly erroneous standard applied in *Soliz*].")

Porches and fire escapes outside an apartment or unit in a multiple-occupancy dwelling fall within the curtilage of the apartment or unit. *See, e.g., State v. Johnson*, 793 A.2d 619 (N.J. 2002) (finding that porch of multi-occupancy dwelling was part of curtilage). Note that though the court in *Johnson* found that the porch was part of the curtilage, it also found that a police officer, who observed defendant place an object in a hole by a post on the porch, could enter the porch to view the object more closely. The officer was permitted to enter the porch without a warrant because this area was accessible to members of the public visiting the dwelling, and was an area shared by all tenants of the dwelling:

> Viewed in that context, the porch involved in this case, although part of the curtilage, has a diminished expectation of privacy. We agree with the [lower court] that [t]he curtilage concept has limited applicability with respect to multi-occupancy premises because none of the occupants can have a reasonable expectation of privacy in areas that are also used by other occupants. Here, [the officer] and his partner went to 695 Martin Luther King Boulevard to investigate a report of drug activity. They were there for a legitimate investigative purpose. [The officer] did not go beyond the porch, thus restricting his movements to the places that any other visitor could be expected to go. Defendant's diminished expectation of privacy on the porch was further indicated by the fact that when he placed the package in a hole beside the post on the porch of the multiple-family row house, a portion of the home which all residents and visitors must use to enter, there were four other people on the porch that evening. In short, the conduct that enabled [the officer] to observe the object in the hole was not a search within the meaning of the Fourth Amendment. Any object in the hole could have been observed by inquisitive passersby or any other member of the public. There is no reason why a diligent police officer should not be allowed to observe that which he or she could have observed as a private citizen. We conclude, therefore, that the "light-colored" object was in plain view because Officer Wilson had a right to be in a position where he could observe that object in defendant's hand as defendant placed it beside the post. 793 A.2d at 629–30 (internal citations omitted).

Because the officer was permitted to be on the porch, he could seize the object in plain view, which he believed to be cocaine:

> We conclude, therefore, that all three elements of the plain view doctrine were met in this case. [The Officer] was lawfully on the porch of 695 Martin Luther

King Boulevard. He did not know that evidence would be found in a hole by a porch post at this address, and thus discovered the evidence inadvertently. Finally, the incriminating nature of this "light-colored" object was immediately apparent based on probable cause after the object was visualized in the hole by Officer Wilson. Thus, we hold that the conduct of the police in seizing the clear plastic bag [containing cocaine] from the hole was reasonable under the plain view doctrine and violated neither the federal nor the New Jersey Constitution. 793 A.2d at 636.

If a porch of a particular apartment in a multi-occupancy dwelling was *not* generally accessible to other tenants or members of the visiting public, police would, in such a case, need a warrant to enter and search this area.

Public halls or stairs are public areas used in common by tenants and their guests or others lawfully on the property. A fire escape in a non-fireproof building, however, is different: it is required outside of each apartment as a secondary means of egress for the occupants of that particular apartment. Although it is true that, in the event of fire, people might have occasion to lawfully pass over the fire escape of an apartment other than their own, this would be the only time that one might be lawfully on the fire escape of another. *People v. Terrell*, 277 N.Y.S.2d 926, 933 (N.Y. 1967). Therefore, fire escapes are generally considered part of the curtilage of a dwelling, and police must generally obtain a warrant before entering these areas. The court in *Terrell* said:

A fair determination and analysis of the decisions leads this court to the unalterable conclusion that a fire escape outside of a man's residence is in law part of the curtilage of his apartment and as such is entitled to the protection of the Fourth Amendment. Accordingly, the observations [of drugs and drug paraphernalia] surreptitiously made by the police from the fire escape which created the probable cause were made in the course of a trespass and were consequently illegal; probable cause having been illegally acquired. The entrance into the residential apartment without a warrant was illegal and violative of the Fourth Amendment and all evidence and admissions obtained as a result thereof must be suppressed. 277 N.Y.S. at 938.

See also People v. Toodle, 400 N.W.2d 670, 675 (Mich. App. 1986) (citing with approval *Terrell's* holding that fire escapes are part of the curtilage).

Garages A garage, and the area immediately surrounding it, is ordinarily considered part of the curtilage, especially if the garage is near or attached to the dwelling house and used in connection with it. In *State v. Ross*, 959 P.2d 1188, 1192 (Wash. App. 1998), where the garage was located within twenty-five to forty yards from a street abutting defendant's home, the court prohibited the warrantless entry by police into the area immediately surrounding the garage:

We hold that the unannounced, plain-clothed, after-dark, warrantless, side-entries onto the curtilage of [the defendant's] garage to investigate a marijuana grow were unreasonable under the Fourth Amendment; the search warrant based thereon was invalid; and the evidence seized with the warrant [e.g., the marijuana] should have been suppressed. 959 P.2d at 1192.

The court found the particular warrantless entry unconstitutional because of the manner in which police accessed the area by the garage where they detected marijuana:

The discovery here was not accidental; rather the officers entered [the defendant's] property specifically to investigate an informant's tip about a marijuana grow operation. They acted secretly by going on the property at night, in an unmarked car, in plain clothes, and without identifying themselves to [the defendant]. They did not use the most direct access to the front door, from Woodbourne [Street], the locus of [the defendant's] address and front gate. Rather they accessed the driveway and garage from Luzader [Street], abutting the side of the house. According to [the defendant], to reach the spot where they smelled the marijuana, the officers had to deviate nearly ten feet from a direct route between their patrol car and the gate to the side path to the front door. Moreover, they made no attempt to talk to [the defendant], but instead clearly tried to avoid him. 959 P.2d at 1190–91.

Also, in *Commonwealth v. Murphy*, 233 N.E.2d 5 (Mass. 1968), where a garage and a house were surrounded on three sides by a fence and the garage was close to the house (e.g., fifty to seventy-five feet from the street), the court found that the garage was within the curtilage. A garage not used by its owner in connection with the residence, however, was held to be outside the curtilage. *People v. Swanberg*, 255 N.Y.S.2d 267 (N.Y. 1964). Furthermore, a garage used in connection with a multiunit dwelling was held to be outside the curtilage because it was used in common by many tenants of the dwelling. *People v. Terry*, 454 P.2d 36 (Cal. 1969); *see also People v. Galan*, 209 Cal. Rptr. 837 (1985) (finding that police could make a warrantless entry into a garage shared by tenants in order to investigate a shooting incident because this garage was used in common by tenants, and outside visitors could freely pass through this area); *People v. Bermudez*, 2006 WL 6091793 (Cal. App. 1st Dist. 2006) (warrantless search by police permitted of a garage accessible to both other tenants and outside visitors).

Other Outbuildings In determining whether an outbuilding is part of the curtilage, courts consider factors such as distance from the dwelling house, presence and location of fences or other enclosures, family use of the building, and attempts to protect the area from observation. In *United States v. Dunn*, 480 U.S. 294 (1987), discussed above, a barn located fifty yards from a fence surrounding a house and sixty yards from the house itself was held to be outside the curtilage. The Court found that the owner had done little to protect the barn area from observation by those standing in the open fields. The Court also found it especially significant that law enforcement officials possessed objective data indicating that the barn was not being used for intimate activities of the home. Rather, they knew that a truck carrying a container of phenylacetic acid was backed up to the barn, a strong odor of the acid emanated from the barn, and the sound of a pump-like motor could be heard from within the barn. These activities suggested the barn was being used for the manufacture of drugs.

United States v. Calabrese, 825 F.2d 1342 (9th Cir. 1987), found that a structure located about fifty feet from a main residence and its two *attached* garages were not within the curtilage. Significant to the court's determination was law enforcement officials' knowledge, obtained during a previous legal search, that the detached structure was being used to manufacture methamphetamine and not for domestic activities.

United States v. Van Damme, 823 F. Supp. 1552 (D. Mont. 1993), *vacated on other grounds, United States v. Van Damme*, 48 F.3d 461 (9th Cir. 1995), held that a greenhouse compound located more than two hundred feet from the defendant's house and surrounded by a twelve-foot stockade fence was not part of the house's curtilage:

> [B]ecause of the isolation of the greenhouse compound from the rest of the property, the lack of nearby buildings or facilities, and the absence of any indicia of activities commonly associated with domestic life, the investigating officers had no reason to deem the greenhouse compound as part of the Defendant's home. Additionally, the citizen informant's report provided the officers with some "objective data indicating that the [compound] was not being used for intimate activities of the home." 823 F. Supp. at 1558.

In contrast, the court in *United States v. Johnson*, 256 F.3d 895 (9th Cir. 2001) indicated that a shed located forty to fifty yards from defendant's main residence could fall within the curtilage of defendant's home:

> Based on the combination of the (1) the rural setting, (2) the fence around the home and shed, (3) the lack of objective data pointing to illegal activity [in the shed] prior to entry, and (4) the inability to see the shed from the "open fields," one could find that the shed was so intimately tied to the home itself that it should be placed under the home's 'umbrella' of Fourth Amendment protection. 256 F.3d at 904 (internal quotations omitted).

Unoccupied Tracts An unoccupied, uncultivated, remote tract of land is generally held to be outside the curtilage and in the open fields:

> **[T]he term "open fields" may include any unoccupied or undeveloped area outside of the curtilage. An open field need be neither "open" nor a "field" as those terms are used in common speech. For example . . . a thickly wooded area nonetheless may be an open field as that term is used in construing the Fourth Amendment.** *Oliver v. United States*, 466 U.S. 170, 180 n.11 (1984).

In *Oliver v. United States*, 466 U.S. 170 (1984), involving a warrantless police seizure of marijuana from a secluded, unoccupied plot of land surrounded by fences and "No Trespassing" signs, the Court stated that **"an individual may not legitimately demand privacy for activities conducted out of doors in fields, except in the area immediately surrounding the home."** 466 U.S. 170, 178. The Court in *Oliver* upheld the warrantless police search and seizure of marijuana on the defendant's unoccupied, remote tract of land because it was located in the "open fields," an area where individuals lack any reasonable expectation of privacy. The Court said:

> **[O]pen fields do not provide the setting for those intimate activities that the [Fourth] Amendment is intended to shelter from government interference or surveillance. There is no societal interest in protecting the privacy of those activities such as the cultivation of crops, that occur in open fields. Moreover, as a practical matter these lands usually are accessible to the public and the police in ways that a home, an office, or commercial structure would not be. It is not generally true that fences or "No Trespassing" signs effectively bar the public from viewing open fields in rural areas. And . . . the public and police lawfully may survey lands from the air. For these reasons, the asserted expectation of privacy in open fields is not an expectation that "society recognizes as reasonable."** 466 U.S. at 179.

In *Maine v. Thornton* (decided in the same opinion as *Oliver v. United States*), police officers received a tip that marijuana was being grown in the woods behind the defendant's residence and entered the woods by a path between the residence and a neighboring house. They followed the path until they reached two marijuana patches that were fenced with chicken wire and displayed "No Trespassing" signs. When the officers determined that the patches were on the defendant's property, they obtained a search warrant and seized the marijuana. The Court held that the officers' initial actions were not an unreasonable search and seizure, because the area was an open field. *Conrad v. State*, 218 N.W.2d 252, 257 (Wis. 1974), held that the Fourth Amendment did not apply to a local sheriff's warrantless digging in a field about 450 feet from the defendant's house to find the body of the defendant's wife, who had disappeared:

> Under the "open fields" doctrine, the fact that evidence is concealed or hidden is immaterial. The area [the open field] is simply not within the protection of the Fourth Amendment. If the field where the body was found does not have constitutional protection, the fact that the sheriff, rather than observing the evidence that might have been in plain view, dug into the earth to find the body and committed a trespass in so doing does not confer protection.

Also, in *State v. Dixson*, 766 P.2d 1015 (Or. 1988), the court found that police officers, without a warrant, could enter the defendant's remote and undeveloped land to view marijuana plants. The court described the officers' actions in this way:

> The officers drove onto the property by way of a public road until they reached a dirt logging road the informant had described as leading to the marijuana. Unknown to the officers, this road extended onto property being purchased by defendants . . . , and on which they lived. The dirt road had fallen into disuse and no longer was passable by car. The trunk of a large tree lay across the road and, a little further on, a wire cable with a "No Hunting" sign on it stretched across the road. The officers left their car and walked past the fallen tree and wire cable. Just past the cable was another dirt road running along a fence line. This road also had a wire cable and "No Hunting" sign stretched across it. The officers continued walking down this second road. At a bend in the road, they encountered another "No Hunting" sign. The area was rural and covered with thick brush. The officers were able to see marijuana plants only after pushing aside the brush. The plants, which were on the [defendants'] property, were not visible at ground level except from that property. 766 P.2d at 1016.

The court found that the defendants did not make sufficient efforts to exclude others from their undeveloped land:

> In the present case, the defendants (or someone) had blocked access to their property with cables and posted "No Hunting" signs. However, on this record there was no objective reason for the officers to believe that, in addition to the restriction on hunting, other uses such as hiking were forbidden. In this state, with its expanses of rough and open country, hiking, camping and the like commonly occur on land that is owned by large companies and individuals. Unless they intended to hunt, neither the officers nor anyone else would have understood the posted signs to be intended to exclude them from the property entirely. The state carried its burden of showing that there was no [constitutional] violation. . . . 766 P.2d at 1024.

Plain View, Open Fields, and Observations into Constitutionally Protected Areas

Law enforcement officers often confuse the open fields and plain view doctrines. The *plain view doctrine* (discussed in Chapter 10) states that a law enforcement officer with a valid justification for a prior intrusion into a zone of privacy may seize items of evidence observed open to view, if their incriminating character is immediately apparent (i.e., the officer has probable cause to seize the items). On the other hand, under the open fields doctrine, an officer need not be concerned with the validity of the justification for the prior intrusion into a zone of privacy or a person's reasonable expectation of privacy. Open fields are not a zone of privacy; therefore, they do not support any reasonable expectation of privacy. Accordingly, the officer may not only seize items that are open to view in the open fields, but also may search for items hidden from view and seize them. Of course, all seizures must be based on probable cause that the items are subject to seizure.

In addition, from a vantage point in the open fields or a public place, officers may, without a warrant, make observations into constitutionally protected areas. "[A] law enforcement 'officer's observations from a public vantage point where he has a right to be' and from which the activities or objects he observes are 'clearly visible' do not constitute a search within the meaning of the Fourth Amendment." *United States v. Taylor*, 90 F.3d 903, 908 (4th Cir. 1996). These observations may be enhanced by electrical or mechanical means such as flashlights or binoculars. *United States v. Dunn*, 480 U.S. 294 (1987). In *Dunn*, the U.S. Supreme Court allowed the use of flashlight by officers to see inside the defendant's barn from their position in the open fields. Also, *United States v. Taft*, 769 F. Supp. 1295 (D. Vt. 1991), found no constitutional violation when police, standing in the open fields, observed the defendant's cabin from about fifty yards with the aid of binoculars. Information obtained from such observations may be used as a basis for probable cause to arrest or to obtain a search warrant.

Using Mechanical or Electronic Devices to Obtain Plain View Observations Observations into constitutionally protected areas may not, however, violate the reasonable expectation of privacy of the person whose premises or activities are being observed. *Raettig v. State*, 406 So.2d 1273 (Fla. App. 1981), held that a person in lawful possession of a camper truck established a reasonable expectation of privacy by painting over the windows, locking the doors, and refusing access to the police. That expectation was violated when an officer shined a flashlight through a minute crack to observe the contents of the truck. The defendant's failure to seal the crack "could hardly be regarded as an implied invitation to any curious passerby to take a look." 406 P.2d at 1278. Also, *State v. Ward*, 617 P.2d 568, 573 (Haw. 1980), found that:

> The Constitution does not require that in all cases a person, in order to protect his privacy, must shut himself off from fresh air, sunlight, and scenery. And as a corollary, neither does the Constitution hold that a person, by opening his curtains, thereby opens his person, house, papers, and effects to telescopic scrutiny by the government.

In particular, *Ward* held that the viewing with binoculars of a crap game in a seventh-story apartment from a vantage point an eighth of a mile away was an illegal search. "[If] the purpose of the telescopic aid is to view that which could not be seen without it, it is a constitutional invasion." 617 P.2d 573.

However, if mechanical or electronic devices allow police to see persons and objects associated with them that could otherwise be readily seen with the naked eye by any member of the public, the reasonable expectation of privacy of the person being observed has not been violated. For example, in *State v. Augafa*, 992 P.2d 723 (Haw. 1999), a video recorder mounted on a public sidewalk captured images of the defendant who appeared to be carrying out a drug transaction. The court in *Augafa* determined the captured image did not violate defendant's privacy expectation:

> [W]e conclude that Defendant did not have a reasonable expectation of privacy in his location or arguendo in the purported transaction at the area involved. Defendant was on a public street fronting a bar in a heavily trafficked area. The police video camera was mounted on a pole protruding from the public sidewalk across the street from the bar. The videotape revealed Defendant on Hotel Street at approximately 6:30 in the evening among numerous pedestrians and several passing buses. Defendant cannot transform the "public street" into a "private sphere" by arguing that a right of expected privacy is invoked by his "unilateral action" of engaging in a drug deal. Further, as seen on the videotape, Defendant exposed and shifted objects from hand to hand and engaged in what appeared to be an open and obvious drug transaction. Defendant himself was in an "open view situation" and the alleged transaction was conducted in public. The observations preserved on videotape could easily have been viewed by anyone on the street; in this case, the police observed Defendant from the "outside looking outside." Therefore, considering the nature of Defendant's location, we conclude society would not view Defendant's expectation of privacy as objectively reasonable. 992 P.2d at 734.

See Chapter 10 for a further discussion of the use of mechanical or electronic devices to obtain evidence in plain view.

Aerial Observations

In two major cases, the U.S Supreme Court has found that warrantless police surveillance from the air of curtilage does not violate the Fourth Amendment. First, in *California v. Ciraolo*, 476 U.S. 207 (1986), the Court held that the Fourth Amendment was not violated by a warrantless aerial observation from an altitude of 1,000 feet of a fenced-in backyard within the curtilage of a home. The Court found that the defendant clearly manifested an intent and desire to maintain privacy by placing a ten-foot fence around his backyard. His expectation of privacy from observation from the air was found not to be reasonable, however:

> **That the area is within the curtilage does not itself bar all police observation. The Fourth Amendment protection of the home has never been extended to require law enforcement officers to shield their eyes when passing by a home on public thoroughfares. Nor does the mere fact that an individual has taken measures to restrict some views of his activities preclude an officer's observations from a public vantage point where he has a right to be and which renders the activities clearly visible.** 476 U.S. at 213.

Because the observations took place from public navigable airspace, from which any member of the public flying in that airspace could have observed everything the officers observed, the defendant's expectation that his backyard was protected from such observation was not an expectation that society was prepared to honor:

> In an age where private and commercial flight in the public airways is routine, it is unreasonable for respondent to expect that his marijuana plants were constitutionally protected from being observed with the naked eye from an altitude of 1,000 feet. The Fourth Amendment simply does not require the police traveling in the public airways at this altitude to obtain a warrant in order to observe what is visible to the naked eye. 476 U.S. at 215.

Second, and applying the same reasoning as in *Ciraolo*, the Court in *Florida v. Riley*, 488 U.S. 445, 451–52 (1989), held that police observation of the defendant's greenhouse from a helicopter flying at 400 feet did not violate the defendant's reasonable expectation of privacy and was therefore not a search:

> [T]he helicopter in this case was *not* violating the law, and there is nothing in the record or before us to suggest that helicopters flying at 400 feet are sufficiently rare in this country to lend substance to respondent's claim that he reasonably anticipated that his greenhouse would not be subject to observation from that altitude. Neither is there any intimation here that the helicopter interfered with respondent's normal use of the greenhouse or of other parts of the curtilage. As far as this record reveals, no intimate details connected with the use of the home or curtilage were observed, and there was no undue noise, no wind, dust, or threat of injury. In these circumstances, there was no violation of the Fourth Amendment.

And in *Dow Chemical Co. v. United States*, 476 U.S. 227 (1986), the U.S. Supreme Court held that a government agency's aerial photography of a chemical company's 2,000-acre outdoor industrial plant complex from navigable airspace was not a search prohibited by the Fourth Amendment. The Court analogized this particular complex to an "open field":

> [T]he open areas of an industrial plant complex with numerous plant structures spread over an area of 2,000 acres are not analogous to the "curtilage" of a dwelling for purposes of aerial surveillance; such an industrial complex is more comparable to an open field and as such it is open to the view and observation of persons in aircraft lawfully in the public airspace immediately above or sufficiently near the area for the reach of cameras. 476 U.S. at 239.

Driveways and Other Means of Access to Dwellings In *Robinson v. Commonwealth*, 612 S.E.2d 751 (Va. App. 2005), the court described the officer's warrantless approach to defendants' dwelling through a driveway in the following way:

> [The police] received three separate telephone calls reporting an alleged underage drinking party at the [defendants'] home. [A police officer] was dispatched to investigate these allegations, and he arrived at the defendants' home at approximately 11:00 P.M. From the state road in front of the house, [the officer] could see ten to twenty cars parked on the state road, as well as two to three parked cars on the left-hand side of the driveway. From that position, [the officer] could also see the house, the front porch, the front door, and the front yard, although he could not see the backyard or the entire driveway. The floodlights above the front door were turned on, and the lights along the

sidewalk leading to the front door were also turned on. [The officer], who was driving a marked police car with its headlights on, turned into the driveway and started to drive towards the house. While proceeding up the driveway, [the officer] saw several additional parked vehicles near the right side of the driveway, as well as several parked vehicles near the side of the house straight in front of him.

[The officer] continued up the driveway in his police car. From his position inside the police car, he began to see some "activity" in the backyard. Before reaching the point where the walkway to the front door intersects with the [defendants'] driveway, [the defendant] saw two individuals holding clear beer bottles. The individuals, both of whom appeared to be underage, were standing by a pine tree about seven or eight yards away from [the officer's] police car. The two juveniles looked at [the officer], looked at the house, yelled 'cops,' dropped the beer bottles, and ran down a fence line toward the woods. [The officer] pulled his police car behind one of the parked cars and looked to his left. From that vantage point, [the officer] saw juveniles running toward the woods. Also, [the officer] could see a patio table covered with beer bottles and noticed beer bottles strewn about the backyard. [The officer] then got out of his car, yelled for people to stop running, and radioed other officers who were waiting off the property that kids were running east into the woods. 612 S.E. 2d at 755.

The court determined that the area of the driveway from where the officer made his observations was "curtilage" under the Fourth Amendment:

Applying the factors [from the U.S. Supreme Court's decision in *Dunn*] to this case, we conclude that the portion of the driveway from which [the officer] observed the juveniles drinking beer—the area next to the bush—falls within the curtilage of the [defendants'] home. First, the area next to the bush is within a few feet of the home itself. Second, the [defendants] testified that they used the area for washing cars and unloading groceries, home-related activities that evidence the nature of the uses to which the area is put. Third, although the area next to the bush is not included within an enclosure surrounding the home, the area is protected from public observation. Specifically, although the [defendants] did not erect a fence or post any no-trespassing signs, the trees and layout of the driveway obscure the area from public view. It is evident, therefore, that the area next to the bush is protected from observation by people passing by. Given that three out of the four *Dunn* factors are satisfied, we are compelled to conclude that the area next to the bush is intimately tied to the home itself and, thus, falls within the curtilage of the [the defendants'] home. 612 S.E. 2d at 758.

Interestingly, even though the police officer in *Robinson* was found to be on the curtilage, which is an area generally protected from warrantless entry by police, the court admitted the officer's observations as evidence at trial because defendants had opened their house (and driveway) to members of the public on the particular night when the underage drinking party occurred:

[W]e therefore conclude that the [defendants] extended an implied invitation to the public to enter their driveway on the night of the party. We further conclude that, when [the officer] entered the curtilage with the purpose of "investigating" the allegations of underage drinking, he did not exceed the scope of this implied invitation because, at the point in time when he viewed the illicit activity, he had gone no further than an ordinary member of the public would have gone in an attempt to contact the occupants of the property. Accordingly, because the [defendants] extended an implied invitation to enter the property [on the particular night of the underage drinking party], and because [the officer] did not exceed the scope of that invitation, the [defendants] had no reasonable expectation of privacy in the area of the driveway by the bush, and [the officer's] actions neither implicated nor violated the Fourth Amendment. 612 S.E. 2d at 419–20.

Lorenzana v. Superior Court of Los Angeles County, 511 P.2d 33 (Cal. 1973) involved an officer's approach to a dwelling not through a driveway but by an alternate means of access. In *Lorenzana,* a narcotics officer investigating a tip about heroin dealing went to the alleged crime scene, a single-family dwelling, seventy feet from the sidewalk, with access from the west. There were no doorways or defined pathways on the east side of the house, and a strip of land covered with grass and dirt separated the east side of the house from the driveway of the apartment next door. The officer went to the east side of the house, peeked through a two-inch gap under the partially drawn shade of a closed window, and observed indications of criminal activity.

The court held that the officer's observations constituted an illegal search because the officer was standing on a part of the property surrounding the house that had not been opened, expressly or implicitly, to public use. The court also discussed the officer's actions in terms of the defendant's reasonable expectation of privacy, a concept first addressed in the Fourth Amendment "search" context by the U.S. Supreme Court in *Katz* (see Chapter 3 for further discussion of this foundational case in the Fourth Amendment "search" area):

> [T]he generic *Katz* rule permits the resident of a house to rely justifiably upon the privacy of the surrounding areas as a protection from the peering of the officer unless such residence is "exposed" to that intrusion by the existence of public pathways or other invitations to the public to enter upon the property. This justifiable reliance on the privacy of the property surrounding one's residence thus leads to the *particular* rule that searches conducted without a warrant from such parts of the property *always* are unconstitutional unless an exception to the warrant requirement applies. . . .
>
> Pursuant to the principles of *Katz,* therefore, we do not rest our analysis exclusively upon such abstractions as "trespass" or "constitutionally protected areas" or upon the physical differences between a telephone booth and the land surrounding a residence; we do, however, look to the conduct of people in regard to these elements. Taking into account the nature of the area surrounding a private residence, we ask whether that area has been opened to public use; if so, the occupant cannot claim he expected privacy from all observations of the officer who stands upon that ground; if not, the occupant does deserve that privacy. Since the eavesdropping officer in the case before us stood upon private property and since such property exhibited no invitation to public use, we find that the officer violated petitioner Lorenzana's expectations of privacy, and hence, his constitutional rights. 511 P.2d at 42.

In general, if an officer gathers information while situated in a public place or a place where an ordinary citizen with legitimate business might be expected to be, the officer does not invade anyone's reasonable expectation of privacy. Therefore, an observation by a police officer from an ordinary means of access to a dwelling, such as a driveway, walkway, front porch or side door, may not violate a person's reasonable expectation of privacy if a member of the public could have also made a similar observation. For example, in *Robinson v. Com-*

monwealth, 612 S.E. 2d 751 (Va. App. 2005), discussed above, the court found that the officer was permitted to make observations from defendants' driveway. Though the court determined that the driveway was part of the curtilage of defendant's dwelling, the observations of underage drinking made by the officer were admissible as evidence because any member of the public could have also made them:

> [B]ecause the [defendants] had extended an implied invitation to the public to use the driveway to access the front door of their home, they had no reasonable expectation of privacy in that area. And, because the [defendants] had no reasonable expectation of privacy in the illicit activities that were clearly visible from their driveway, the Fourth Amendment does not apply to any observations made by a police officer who was present in the driveway and complying with the terms of that implied invitation. Because the Fourth Amendment does not apply, no warrant is required and, therefore, no exception to the warrant requirement is needed. Because [the officer's] observations do not implicate the Fourth Amendment, those observations are admissible in their entirety. 612 S.E. 2d at 621.

See also State v. Harris, 919 S.W.2d 619, 623–24 (Tenn. Crim. App. 1995). ("A sidewalk, pathway, or similar passageway leading from a public sidewalk or roadway to the front door of a dwelling represents an implied invitation to the general public to use the walkway for the purpose of pursuing legitimate social or business interests with those who reside within the residence. Police officers conducting official police business [such as serving a summons and complaint] are considered members of the general public. What an officer [conducting such business] sees from a vantage point along the walkway between the public road and the front door is not protected by either the Fourth Amendment or the state constitution.")

Furthermore, officers in a place where they have a right to be may listen at doors or gather evidence with their other senses:

> The general rule is that information obtained by an officer using his natural senses, where the officer has a right to be where he is, is admissible evidence. The fact that the information is in the form of conversations emanating from a private space, such as a hotel room, is not a bar to its admissibility. *United States v. Perry*, 339 F. Supp. 209, 213 (S.D. Cal. 1972).

Although it may be permissible, without a warrant, for police officers to overhear conservations from a place they have a right to be, *Kyllo v. United States*, 533 U.S. 27, 34 (2001), held that **"obtaining by sense-enhancing technology any information regarding the interior of the home that could not otherwise have been obtained without physical "intrusion into a constitutionally protected area,"** . . . **constitutes a search—at least where** . . . **the technology in question is not in general use."** In *Kyllo*, federal agents were suspicious that marijuana was being grown in Kyllo's home in a triplex. They used a thermal imaging device to scan the triplex to determine if the amount of heat emanating from it was consistent with the high-intensity lamps typically used for indoor marijuana growth. The scan showed that his garage roof and a side wall were relatively hot compared to the rest of his home, and substantially warmer than neighboring units. Based in part on the thermal imaging, a warrant was issued to search Kyllo's home, where agents found marijuana growing.

The Court, reiterating the primacy of the home in the array of protected places, held, **"Where, as here, the Government uses a device that is not in general public use, to explore details of the home that would previously have been unknowable without physical intrusion, the surveillance is a 'search' and is presumptively unreasonable without a warrant."** 533 U.S. at 40. The government claimed that there was a fundamental difference between "off-the-wall" observations and "through-the-wall" observations, arguing that thermal imaging must be upheld because it detected "only heat radiating from the external surface of the house." The Court rejected this argument:

> **[J]ust as a thermal imager captures only heat emanating from a house, so also a powerful directional microphone picks up only sound emanating from a house—and a satellite capable of scanning from many miles away would pick up only visible light emanating from a house. We rejected such a mechanical interpretation of the Fourth Amendment in *Katz*, where the eavesdropping device picked up only sound waves that reached the exterior of the phone booth. Reversing that approach would leave the homeowner at the mercy of advancing technology—including imaging technology that could discern all human activity in the home. While the technology used in the present case was relatively crude, the rule we adopt must take account of more sophisticated systems that are already in use or in development.** 533 U.S. at 35–36.

The Court also rejected the government's contention that thermal imaging did not violate the Constitution because it did not reveal any "intimate details" or "detect private activities occurring in private areas." The Court said, **"In the home, our cases show, all details are intimate details, because the entire area is held safe from prying government eyes."** 533 U.S. at 37.

Regardless of which sense an officer uses to detect criminal activity occurring in a constitutionally protected area, the officer does not have authority to enter into the area to make a search or seizure without a warrant. Only a search warrant gives this authority, unless there is an emergency or a recognized exception to the search warrant requirement applies:

> An officer is not entitled to conduct a warrantless entry and seizure of in-criminating evidence simply because he has seen the evidence from outside the premises. "Incontrovertible testimony of the senses that an incriminating object is on premises belonging to a criminal suspect may establish the fullest possible measure of probable cause. But even where the object is contraband, this Court has repeatedly stated and enforced the basic rule that the police may not enter and make a warrantless seizure," absent exigent circumstances. *United States v. Wilson*, 36 F.3d 205, 209 n.4 (1st Cir. 1994).

In *United States v. Taylor*, 90 F.3d 903 (4th Cir. 1996), in which both probable cause and exigent circumstances were found, an officer approached the defendant's front door, looked through his picture window adjacent to the door, and observed a large amount of money and what appeared to be illegal drugs on the dining room table. When someone inside the house quickly closed the blinds, the officer "had a reasonable basis for concluding that there was probable cause to believe that criminal activity was in progress in the house and that there was an imminent danger that evidence would be destroyed unless the officers immediately entered the house and took possession of it." 90 F.3d at 909–10.

Discussion
↑POINT

Are Warrants Based on Information Obtained from Thermal Imaging Devices Always Unconstitutional?

State v. Mordowanec, 788 A.2d 48 (Conn. 2002).

On February 9, 1996, a Superior Court judge issued a warrant to search the business premises of L & M Home Improvement (L & M) at 151 Main Street in Seymour. When Seymour police officers executed that warrant, they discovered on L & M's second floor nineteen marijuana plants, lights used to grow the plants, and other items relating to indoor marijuana cultivation and sales. As a result, the defendant and his brother, Daniel Mordowanec, the operators of L & M, were arrested and charged.

Prior to trial, the defendant moved to suppress all evidence seized pursuant to the search warrant, arguing that the warrant was obtained in violation of his rights under the Fourth and Fourteenth Amendments to the United States Constitution. In the trial court, the defendant argued that the evidence seized in the execution of the warrant should be suppressed because the affidavit in support of the warrant did not present sufficient evidence for a finding of probable cause. The defendant's motion to suppress included a request for a hearing pursuant to *Franks v. Delaware*, 438 U.S. 154 (1978). The trial court noted that although it "felt that the [defendant] initially failed to sufficiently demonstrate that the affiants acted with 'deliberate falsehood or reckless disregard for the truth,' the court nevertheless gave the [defendant] the benefit of the doubt and allowed preliminary testimony in a *Franks*-type hearing."
The trial court found the following facts:

> The application for the warrant was supported by the affidavit of Det./Sgt. James Hayes of the Seymour police department and Special Agent David Hoyt of the [United States] Drug Enforcement Administration. The application and affidavit contained several basic allegations. First, Officer Hayes received an anonymous [tele]phone call from an unknown male caller who stated that he observed approximately twenty to twenty-five six-foot tall marijuana plants growing inside a room under tubular, purplish lights on the second floor of the building housing [L & M]. The caller stated that he made the observation through a slightly opened door from the rear fire escape of the building while taking a cigarette break from a karate class, which is located on the third floor of the building, in which his child was enrolled. The caller also indicated that he detected a strong odor of marijuana, claiming that he 'knows marijuana citing the fact that he is a "Vietnam vet."' The caller described two males located on the second floor who he believed to be 'the guys from L & M,' one heavy-set and balding and the other with glasses and his hair tied back in a ponytail. He also stated that he did not think the males saw him and that "you better move quick or [you're] gonna lose it." Officer Hayes indicated that from his personal knowledge the descriptions of the two males fit Daniel [Mordowanec] and [the defendant]. He further verified by a visit to the third floor of 151/153 Main Street that there was an enclosed fire escape stairway in the rear of the building. In addition, assessor's records were obtained which showed that the building was owned by the [defendant's] mother.

(Continued)

Are Warrants Based on Information Obtained from Thermal Imaging Devices Always Unconstitutional? *(Continued)*

The second affiant, Special Agent Hoyt, attested to his knowledge from "training and experience that individuals who grow marijuana indoors commonly utilize 1,000 watt metal halide or high-pressure sodium lights to" grow marijuana, and that the lights appear "bluish in color."

The second allegation relied upon in the application for the search warrant was a claimed increase in the electrical power usage at the property. On February 7, 1996, an administrative subpoena was obtained and executed at Northeast Utilities for records of kilowatt electrical usage covering two years of service for 151 Main Street. The records revealed 'a clear kilowatt hour usage increase [of 474 kilowatt hours] . . . for the period covering December 1995 to January of 1996 as compared to the previous one-month period, and more significantly, when compared to the same one-month period one year ago.'

The final allegations relied upon in the application were the results of an external inspection of the heat emanating from the building at 151/153 Main Street through employment of a thermal imaging device. On February 9, 1996, at approximately 12:30 A.M., two Seymour police detectives and a Connecticut state police trooper fixed an 'Agema' Model 210 thermal imaging device on the building. The device measured 'a significantly higher surface temperature on the second floor than that of the first and third floors and adjacent buildings.' The affiant concluded that '[t]his is consistent with the heat that would be generated by the high-power artificial lighting systems commonly used in the indoor cultivation of marijuana.' Furthermore, upon inspection of the town of Seymour building permits and assessor's field card, it was evident that 'only one oil-fired hot water furnace [was] being used to heat said structure and . . . this furnace is located in the basement of the building and would not explain a high amount of heat emanating from the second floor."

The court in *Mordowanec* declined to suppress the marijuana and marijuana paraphernalia discovered by police pursuant to the search warrant. The court found that even though the use of a thermal imaging device to detect heat in defendant's business may have been illegal in light of the U.S. Supreme Court's decision in *Kyllo,* the search warrant itself was still valid based on evidence contained in the affidavit not related to the use of this device:

The Kyllo decision did not address the question of whether a search warrant would be required to conduct a thermal imaging scan of premises other than a home, such as a commercial property. The court emphasized, however, the heightened expectation of privacy in one's home and distinguished that heightened expectation from the lesser expectation of privacy in a commercial property. We need not decide that issue because we conclude, . . . that even without the results of the thermal imaging scan there were other sufficient facts in the affidavit to establish probable cause. 788 A.2d at 54.

The *Mordowanec* court determined that based on the information provided to police by the anonymous informant's telephone call from the fire escape, there was sufficient evidence of drug activity to support the necessary probable cause for the search warrant.

In effect, *Elstad* refused to apply the traditional "fruit of the poisonous tree" doctrine developed in Fourth Amendment cases, even though a violation of *Miranda* is a violation of a constitutional rule, as the Court declared in *Dickerson v. United States*, 530 U.S. 428 (2000). The "fruit of the poisonous tree" doctrine applies only if the previous *Miranda* violation is accompanied by deliberately coercive or improper tactics in obtaining the initial statement (i.e., there was a due process violation during the initial interrogation).

Sufficiency of *Miranda* Warnings

The warnings that a law enforcement officer must give to a suspect before conducting a custodial interrogation are stated in the *Miranda* decision:

> **He must be warned prior to any questioning that he has the right to remain silent, that anything he says can be used against him in a court of law, that he has the right to the presence of an attorney, and that if he cannot afford an attorney one will be appointed for him prior to any questioning if he so desires.** 384 U.S. at 479.

These warnings must be given regardless of the nature of the offense. Thus, whether the suspect is being investigated for a felony or a minor misdemeanor, *Miranda* warnings must be given prior to beginning any custodial interrogation. *Berkermer v. McCarty*, 468 U.S. 420 (1984). However, *Miranda* does not apply to any civil proceedings such as customs procedures, civil commitments, extradition proceedings, and license revocation proceedings.

The warnings need not be given in the exact form used in the *Miranda* decision. *California v. Prysock*, 453 U.S. 355 (1981), held that no "talismanic incantation" of *Miranda* warnings are required; rather, all that is necessary is that the words used reasonably convey to a suspect his or her *Miranda* rights. For example, the standard *Miranda* warnings used by the Federal Bureau of Investigation are:

> Before we ask you any questions, you must understand your rights.
>
> You have the right to remain silent.
>
> Anything you say can be used against you in court.
>
> You have the right to talk to a lawyer for advice before we ask you any questions and to have a lawyer with you during questioning.
>
> If you cannot afford a lawyer, one will be appointed for you before any questioning if you wish.
>
> If you decide to answer questions now without a lawyer present, you will still have the right to stop answering at any time. You also have the right to stop answering at any time until you talk to a lawyer. *Duckworth v. Eagan*, 492 U.S. 195, 202 n.4 (1989).

No matter how the warnings are issued, the warnings will be deemed invalid if one or more of the essential *Miranda* rights are omitted. For example, in *Watson v. Detella*, 122 F.3d 450, (7th Cir. 1997), the warnings given were held to be inadequate because they merely informed the suspect of a right to counsel without explaining a lawyer would be appointed to assist the suspect during interrogation if the suspect could not afford one for himself. Similarly in *United States v. Tillman*, 963 F.2d 137 (6th Cir. 1992), warnings were also determined to be inadequate because the suspect was not told that if he gave up his right to silence, whatever he said could be used against him. To avoid such problems, most law enforcement agencies distribute *Miranda* warning cards for their officers to use when informing persons subjected to custodial interrogation of their rights.

Although it is clearly not required by *Miranda* or the U.S. Constitution, some jurisdictions have added another right that must be communicated to suspects prior to commencing custodial interrogation: suspects are advised that if they answer some questions without a lawyer, they have the right to stop the questioning at any time and to ask to speak with an attorney (Kahn, Zapf & Cooper, 2006).

Manner of Giving Warnings *Miranda* rights are supposed to be given to *all* suspects before they are subjected to custodial interrogation. Thus, law enforcement officers should not assume that a suspect knows his rights just because the suspect may have some prior experience with the criminal justice system. *Miranda*, 384 U.S. at 468-69. Nor should police assume that a suspect has the financial means to be able to afford an attorney, and therefore think that they need not advise the suspect of the right to appointed counsel for a suspect who cannot afford an attorney for himself. *Miranda*, 384 U.S. at 473. In fact, most courts require the full *Miranda* warnings to be provided to all suspects regardless of how knowledgeable the suspect may be about their rights.

Thus, for example, the fact that a suspect was a police officer with twenty years of law enforcement experience did not obviate the need for full and complete *Miranda* warnings to be given to him in *United States v. Street*, 472 F.3d 1298 (11th Cir. 2006). Similarly, *Miranda* warnings have been required for suspects who are skilled, practicing attorneys. *United States v. Farinacci-Garcia*, 551 F. Supp. 465, 476 (D.P.R. 1982). However, the *Miranda* opinion implies that the warnings do not need to be given to suspects who already have an attorney present with them, because the lawyer's "presence would insure that statements made in the government-established atmosphere are not the product of compulsion." 384 U.S. at 466. To be on the safe side, however, *Miranda* warnings should always be given to all suspects regardless of their background and regardless of whether they have an attorney present.

When *Miranda* warnings are given, they must be stated clearly in a language understood by the suspect. Moreover, the warnings must be delivered in an unhurried manner so that the person being warned understands his or her rights and feels free to claim them without fear. The warnings should not be given in a careless, indifferent, or superficial manner. When warnings are given to an immature, illiterate, or mentally impaired person, the warnings must be given in language that the person can comprehend and on which the person can intelligently act. If necessary, the officer should explain and interpret the warnings. The test is whether the words used by the officer, in view of the age, intelligence, and demeanor of the person being interrogated, convey a clear understanding of all *Miranda* rights. *North Carolina v. Butler*, 441 U.S. 369, 374–75 (1979); *United States v. Rodriguez-Preciado*, 399 F.3d 1118, 1127 (9th Cir. 2005).

Timing of Warnings It is clear that *Miranda* warnings must be given prior to beginning custodial interrogation. But the passage of time can complicate matters.

Initial Interrogation To comply with the mandate to give suspects their *Miranda* rights b*efore* they are subjected to custodial interrogation, police sometimes read

Miranda rights to a suspect upon taking the suspect into custody. This is clearly not required, as *Miranda* rights do not attach when someone is taken into custody, but rather attach only when someone in custody is subjected to interrogation or its functional equivalent. When this occurs, a significant amount of time might pass before custodial interrogation takes place. Although it is always a good idea to re-warn a suspect before starting any custodial interrogation, the passage of time usually does not compromise a *Miranda* warning.

Courts have consistently upheld the integrity of *Miranda* warnings even when several hours have elapsed between the reading of the warning and the interrogation. In *United States v. Frankson*, 83 F.3d 79 (4th Cir. 1996), the defendant contended that *Miranda* requires the police to re-advise suspects of their rights when the interrogation does not immediately follow the *Miranda* warning or when an interrogation in progress is delayed. The court held that the defendant's "initial *Miranda* warning was in no way compromised by the passage of two and one-half hours between the issuance of his warning and the point at which he began to confess his crimes and cooperate with the police." 83 F.3d at 83.

Subsequent Interrogations Sometimes a suspect waives *Miranda* rights and submits to interrogation; then, after an interval of time, police want to interrogate the suspect again. The general rule is that *Miranda* rights do not need to be repeated "so long as the circumstances attending any interruption or adjournment of the process [are] such that the suspect has not been deprived of the opportunity to make an informed and intelligent assessment of his interest involved in the interrogation, including his right to cut off questioning." *Bivins v. State*, 642 N.E.2d 928, 939 (Ind. 1994). In other words, so long as the initial warnings have not "gone stale," they do not need repeating. *United States v. Ferrer-Montoya*, 483 F.3d 565, 569 (8th Cir. 2007). Determining when warnings have "gone stale," however, is not always easy.

When there is only a lapse of several hours between the administration of Miranda warnings and the interrogation, "there is no need for repeated warnings before the second interrogation." *Commonwealth v. Scott*, 752 A.2d 871 (Pa. 2000). However, when the continuity of the interrogation is interrupted by time and other factors, then staleness may be an issue. In *Commonwealth v. Wideman*, 334 A.2d 594, 598 (Pa. 1975), the court listed five factors relevant to determining whether an accused must be re-informed of his or her *Miranda* rights:

> (1) the time lapse between the last *Miranda* warnings and the accused's statement; (2) interruptions in the continuity of the interrogation; (3) whether there was a change of location between the place where the last *Miranda* warnings were given and the place where the accused's statement was made; (4) whether the same officer who gave the warnings also conducted the interrogation resulting in the accused's statement; and (5) whether the statement elicited during the complained-of interrogation differed significantly from other statements which had been preceded by *Miranda* warnings.

Applying these factors, the *Wideman* court held that the *Miranda* warnings had "gone stale" because twelve hours had passed between the warnings and the time of interrogation; the defendant had been moved to another location; and a different set of police officers conducted the interrogation. But more recent cases have upheld statements made much longer than twelve hours after *Miranda* warnings were given under circumstances when other factors may have also contributed to the staleness of warnings. *Jones v. State*, 119 S.W.3d 766, 800-01 (Tex.

Ct. Crim. App. 2003), for example, upheld statements made two days after the warnings, even though "the interrogation was conducted by a different person (belonging to a different law enforcement agency)" in a different location and the statement "involved different events than earlier statements made immediately after *Miranda* warnings." Key to the court's rationale was that there was "no reason to believe appellant suffered from any emotional state that would have impaired his understanding of the earlier-given warnings." 119 S.W.3d at 801.

It is clear that the passage of time is among the most important of the factors considered when determining if *Miranda* warnings have gone stale. In *Maguire v. United States*, 396 F.2d at 331 (9th Cir. 1968), the court held that *Miranda* warnings remained effective for a statement made three days later. But *Ex Parte J.D.H.*, 797 So.2d 1130 (Ala. 2001), invalidated a confession made sixteen days after *Miranda* warnings were given. And in *State v. DeWeese*, 582 S.E.2d 786 (W. Va. 2003), the court invalidated a confession made seven days after the administration of warnings. The *DeWeese* court used the same criteria listed nearly thirty years earlier by the *Wideman* court, but added an additional component: the "apparent intellectual and emotional state of the suspect." 582 S.E.2d at 799.

To avoid staleness problems, law enforcement officials should always re-administer *Miranda* warnings whenever there has been a break in the continuity of interrogation.

key points

- *Miranda* requirements apply regardless of the nature or severity of the offense being investigated.
- *Miranda* is inapplicable to civil proceedings such as customs procedures, civil commitments, extradition proceedings, and license revocation proceedings.
- Before custodial interrogation of a person, a law enforcement officer must warn the person (1) of the right to remain silent; (2) that anything said can be used against the person in a court of law; (3) of the right to the presence of an attorney; and (4) that if the person cannot afford an attorney, one will be appointed prior to any questioning.
- *Miranda* warnings need not be given in the exact form described in the *Miranda* decision, so long as the warnings reasonably convey to a suspect his or her *Miranda* rights.

- Law enforcement officers should give complete *Miranda* warnings before conducting custodial interrogations, even if they believe that the suspect knows his or her rights or that the suspect is not indigent.
- *Miranda* warnings do not need to be given to suspects repeatedly if a short time has passed from the time of initial warnings to the time of interrogation. However, if warnings have "gone stale," then they need to be administered again. To avoid staleness problems, law enforcement officials should always re-warn suspects of the *Miranda* rights whenever there has been a break in the continuity of interrogation.

Waiver of *Miranda* Rights

Like most constitutional rights, the rights that flow from the Firth Amendment's Self-Incrimination Clause can be waived. The *Miranda* case stated that, after *Miranda* warnings have been given to a person about to be subjected to custodial interrogation, and the person has had an opportunity to exercise the rights, **"the individual may knowingly and intelligently waive these rights and agree to answer questions or make a statement. But unless and until such warnings and waiver are demonstrated by the prosecution at trial no evidence obtained as a result of interrogation can be used against him."** 384

U.S. at 478–79. In the *Miranda* context, a **waiver** is a voluntary and intentional relinquishment of a known right. *See generally Johnson v. Zerbst*, 304 U.S. 458 (1938). A valid waiver of *Miranda* rights means that a suspect has voluntarily given up the right to silence and/or the right to counsel.

The dissenting justices in *Miranda* worried that requiring law enforcement officers to give warnings to suspects prior to interrogation would severely impact the ability of police to investigate and solve crimes because if suspects were aware of these rights, they would not voluntarily choose to waive them. Many commentators, including police, prosecutors, politicians, scholars, and the media echoed these concerns (*see* Leo, 1996: 622). But these fears were not well founded. *Miranda* has had "only a negligible effect on the ability of police to elicit confessions, solve crimes, and secure convictions" (645; *see also* Thomas & Leo, 2002). In fact, more than three-quarters of all suspects waive their *Miranda* right to remain silent and agree to talk to the police (Leo, 1996: 659). Some studies report even higher numbers, finding that 84 percent of suspects waive their *Miranda* rights at the initial stages of an interrogation (Cassell & Hayman, 1996). And once interrogation begins, few suspects who originally waive their *Miranda* rights subsequently assert them, with studies placing the percentage of suspects who do so between 1.1 percent (Leo, 1996) and 4 percent (Cassell & Hayman, 1996). And when suspects confess, "confessions are very rarely excluded from evidence in court as a result of *Miranda*," as research suggests this occurs in less than one percent of all cases (Leo, 1996: 677).

Express vs. Implied Waivers There are two ways in which a suspect can validly waive their *Miranda* rights: expressly or impliedly. **Express waivers** occur when a suspect says, writes, or otherwise acknowledges that he or she is aware of his or her *Miranda* rights and voluntarily elects to give up those rights with knowledge of the consequences of doing so. To obtain an express waiver, after *Miranda* warnings have been administered, a law enforcement officer should ask the suspect whether he or she understands the rights that have been explained. The officer should then ask the suspect whether he or she wishes to talk without first consulting a lawyer or having a lawyer present during questioning. If the officer receives an affirmative answer to both questions, the officer should carefully record the exact language in which the answer was given, preserving it for possible future use in court. The officer may then proceed with the interrogation.

If possible, the officer should always try to obtain a written waiver of rights from the suspect before questioning. A written waiver is almost always ruled by courts to be sufficient if the suspect is literate and there is no evidence of police coercion. *E.g., Hart v. Attorney General of State of Florida*, 323 F.3d 884, 893 (11th Cir. 2003). Figure 13.1 is a suggested form for obtaining a written waiver of *Miranda* rights.

Implied Waivers Law enforcement officers may not always be able to obtain express written or oral waivers of *Miranda* rights. *North Carolina v. Butler*, 441 U.S. 369 (1979), held that express waivers are not required. **Implied waivers** are valid if, under the totality of the circumstances, evidence shows that a suspect knew of his or her *Miranda* rights and then voluntarily waived them.

Some of the factors that are used to determine whether a defendant impliedly waived his rights are (1) whether the defendant understood his rights, (2) the

Case File _____ Police Dept. _____

Date _____ Time _____ Place _____

STATEMENT OF RIGHTS

THE FOLLOWING SEVEN STATEMENTS MUST BE FULLY UNDER-STOOD BY YOU BEFORE WE CAN CONTINUE. IF YOU DO NOT UNDERSTAND A STATEMENT, ASK THAT IT BE EXPLAINED:

1. You have the right to remain silent.
2. Anything you say can and will be used against you in a court of law.
3. You have the right to talk to a lawyer and have the lawyer present with you while you are being questioned.
4. If you cannot afford to hire a lawyer, one will be appointed to represent you before any questioning, if you wish.
5. You can decide at any time to exercise these rights and not answer any questions or make any statements.
6. Do you understand each of these rights I have explained to you?
7. Having these rights in mind, do you wish to talk to us now without a lawyer present?

ACKNOWLEDGEMENT AND WAIVER OF RIGHTS

THE ABOVE STATEMENT OF MY RIGHTS HAS BEEN READ AND EX-PLAINED TO ME AND I FULLY UNDERSTAND WHAT MY RIGHTS ARE. KNOWING THIS I AM WILLING TO ANSWER QUESTIONS OR TO MAKE A STATEMENT WITHOUT A LAWYER PRESENT.

Witness _____ Signed _____
    (Advising Officer or Witness)   (Individual Advised of Rights)

Witness _____ Education _____
    (Officer or Witness)   (Name of school and last grade completed)

STATEMENT

Page No. ____ of _____ Page Statement

I have read the above statement, have signed each page of the statement, and acknowledge receipt of a true copy of the statement.

    I give this statement without threat, coercion or promise of any kind.

Witness _____

Witness _____ Signed _____

Page No. ____ of _____ Page Statement Date _____

Page No. ____ of _____ Page Statement

I have read the above statement, have signed each page of the statement, and acknowledge receipt of a true copy of the statement.

    I give this statement without threat, coercion or promise of any kind.

Witness _____

Witness _____ Signed _____

▶**Figure 13.1** SUGGESTED FORM FOR WAIVER OF *MIRANDA* RIGHTS

defendant's willingness to speak, (3) whether the defendant expressed any desire to remain silent, (4) whether the defendant's answers were in a narrative form rather than monosyllabic responses, (5) whether there are any facts that cast doubt on the voluntariness of the waiver, and (6) whether the defendant subsequently exercises his *Miranda* rights. *State v. Stephenson*, 915 A.2d 327 (Conn. Ct. App. 2007).

The following is a summary of some of the guiding principles courts utilize in examining whether a valid implied waiver of *Miranda* rights occurred.

Silence Is Not a Waiver The *Miranda* opinion made it clear that "a valid waiver will not be presumed simply from the silence of the accused after warnings are given[;] . . . there must be an allegation and evidence which show that an accused was offered counsel but intelligently and understandably rejected the offer. Anything less is not a waiver." 384 U.S. at 475.

Words Indicating a Waiver Any comprehensible oral statements of understanding and willingness to speak are usually acceptable as a waiver of *Miranda* rights. Examples of valid waivers are a suspect saying, "I might as well tell you about it," *United States v. Boykin*, 398 F.2d 483, 484 (3d Cir. 1968); "I want to say some things," *United States v. Castro-Higuero*, 473 F.3d 880, 886 (8th Cir. 2007); "That means I ain't got to say nothing right now, 'til I talk to my lawyer [but] . . . I can talk to you if I want to." *State v. Murphy*, 747 N.E.2d 765, 778 (Ohio 2001). Courts have also approved nonverbal waivers, including nods, *Ragland v. Commonwealth*, 191 S.W.3d 569 (Ky. 2006); *United States v. Chapa-Garza*, 62 F.3d 118 (5th Cir. 1995), and shrugs *State v. Brammeier*, 464 P.2d 717 (Or. App. 1970). And, if the suspect indicates his or her desire to invoke *Miranda* rights in the future, rather than the present, such an invocation will not be valid. Thus, in *Thompson v. State*, 235 So.2d 354 (Fla. App. 1970), the court ruled that a suspect impliedly waived his right to counsel under *Miranda* when he indicated his desire to talk to a lawyer at some time in the future, but agreed to answer questions by police first without a lawyer being present. *See also Bruni v. Lewis*, 847 F.2d 561 (9th Cir. 1988) (holding that suspect had not invoked his present right to counsel when he said he would answer some questions now, and other questions later only after talking with his attorney, and thus had impliedly waived that right for the questions he agreed to answer at the time of interrogation).

Actions Indicating a Waiver Sometimes a suspect will indicate an understanding of *Miranda* rights and then simply begin to make a statement without any other verbal or nonverbal indication of waiver. Most courts hold that, once the suspect has been informed of *Miranda* rights and indicates an understanding of those rights, choosing to speak without a lawyer present is sufficient evidence of a knowing and voluntary waiver of the rights. "A defendant's 'subsequent willingness to answer questions after acknowledging [his] *Miranda* rights is sufficient to constitute an implied waiver.'" *United States v. Frankson*, 83 F.3d 79, 82 (4th Cir. 1996); *United States v. Cardwell*, 433 F.3d 378, 389-90 (4th Cir. 2005) ("Because [defendant] had been fully informed and indicated his understanding of his *Miranda* rights, his willingness to answer [police] questions is as clear an indicia of his implied waiver of his right to remain silent as we can imagine."); *State v. Kirtdoll*, 136 P.3d 417 (Kan. 2006).

Defendants have argued that a number of other actions or behaviors constitute either an invocation of *Miranda* rights, or evidence that an implied waiver was not knowing, intelligent, and voluntary. In spite of the fact that courts are supposed to presume a lack of waiver in the *Miranda* context, it is clear that courts often construe the actions of suspects as implied waivers. Consider the following cases.

▶ **Requests to See Someone Other Than an Attorney** A request to see or talk with someone other than an attorney is not an assertion of *Miranda* rights, although a denial of such a request may have some bearing on the voluntariness of the statements. *Watkins v. Callahan*, 724 F.2d 1038 (1st Cir. 1984), found a valid waiver of *Miranda* rights when the defendant indicated he was ready to make a statement after calling his family instead of calling an attorney. *Fare v. Michael C.*, 442 U.S. 707 (1979), held that a juvenile waived his *Miranda* rights even though he had been denied a request to speak to his probation officer. The Court found that the request, made by an experienced older juvenile with an extensive prior record, did not constitute an invocation of the right to remain silent, nor was it tantamount to a request for an attorney. However, some states (like Colorado, Connecticut, Illinois, Indiana, and North Dakota), require a parent, guardian, or other interested adult, such as an attorney, to be notified before a juvenile may be found to have waived *Miranda* rights. *See, e.g., Commonwealth v. Juvenile*, 449 N.E.2d 654 (Mass. 1983); Colo. Rev. Stat. § 19-2-511 (limiting the admissibility of statements made by a juvenile suspect to those made in the presence of a parent or guardian after both juvenile and adult have been apprised of the juvenile's *Miranda* rights).

▶ **Requests for Counsel Not Made to Police**   A request for counsel made by a suspect to a friend or relative is not the same as a request to the police. Thus, in a case in which a suspect told his brother to post bond for him and to get him a lawyer, the suspect's request to his brother did not operate as an exercise of his *Miranda* rights even though the police were aware of the request. Moreover, the suspect's subsequent statements to the police indicated that he had impliedly waived his *Miranda* rights. *People v. Smith*, 246 N.E.2d 689 (Ill. App. 1969).

Implied Waiver Through "Initiating" Further Communication   *Oregon v. Bradshaw*, 462 U.S. 1039 (1983), attempted to explain what would constitute the initiation of further communication with the police by a suspect after the suspect had invoked his or her *Miranda* rights:

> [T]here are undoubtedly situations where a bare inquiry by either a defendant or by a police officer should not be held to "initiate" any conversation or dialogue. There are some inquiries, such as a request for a drink of water or a request to use a telephone that are so routine that they cannot be fairly said to represent a desire on the part of an accused to open up a more generalized discussion relating directly or indirectly to the investigation. Such inquiries or statements, by either an accused or a police officer, relating to routine incidents of the custodial relationship, will not generally "initiate" a conversation in the sense in which that word was used in *Edwards*. 462 U.S. at 1045.

In contrast to requests for water or to use a phone, when a suspect "initiates" conversation with regard to substantive or procedural matters concerning the crime, *Bradshaw* considers such initiation to constitute a waiver of *Miranda* rights. *Bradshaw* involved a suspect who was in custody who had invoked the right to counsel. The suspect subsequently asked a police officer, "Well, what is going to happen to me now?" 462 U.S. at 1045-46. The Supreme Court ruled that the suspect's question "evinced a willingness and a desire for a generalized discussion about the investigation; it was not merely a necessary inquiry arising out of the incidents of the custodial relationship." 462 U.S. at 412. Accordingly, the incriminating statements that the suspect made over the course of the discussion he had with the police officer were deemed admissible.

Selective Waivers   Sometimes, suspects specifically invoke their *Miranda* rights in a narrow way, while acting in a manner that suggests they impliedly waive their *Miranda* rights with regard to other aspects of a case. These are referred to as selective waivers or qualified waivers. Most courts give little weight to selective waivers. They find that so long as a suspect understands that they do not have to talk to law enforcement authorities without the assistance of counsel, a suspect's attempt to carve out a partial exception to an otherwise knowing and voluntary waiver will usually be ineffective. *United States v. Frazier,* 476 F.2d 891 (D.C. Cir. 1973) is a typical example of this. In *Frazier,* the defendant agreed to talk with police without an attorney being present, but he refused to allow police to take notes during the interrogation. Although this indicated that he may have misunderstood that his oral statements could, in fact, be used as evidence against him in court, the court upheld his waiver and allowed his oral statements to be used against him at trial.

Similarly, once a suspect has been given *Miranda* warnings, the suspect's refusal to give a written statement outside the presence of his or her attorney does not render ineffective the suspect's clear waiver of rights for the purpose of giving an oral statement. In *Connecticut v. Barrett,* 479 U.S. 523 (1987), the suspect, who was in custody on a sexual assault charge, was given the *Miranda* warnings and indicated to the police that he would not make a written statement outside the presence of his attorney. He then clearly expressed his willingness to speak with the police without an attorney, and made an oral statement admitting his involvement in the sexual assault. The Court held that the defendant's exercise of his right to counsel was limited by its terms to the making of written statements and did not prohibit further police questioning leading to the oral confession. *See also Crosby v. State,* 784 A.2d 1102 (Md. 2001). The same result has occurred when suspects agreed to talk, but refused to have sessions recorded. *E.g., State v. Bell,* 745 S.W.2d 858 (Tenn. 1988).

Other examples of valid selective waivers are a statement that "it would depend on the questions and he would answer some questions if he thought it appropriate." . . . *United States v. Eaton,* 890 F.2d 511, 513 (1st Cir. 1989), and the statement, "Well, ask your questions and I will answer those I see fit." *Bruni v. Lewis,* 847 F.2d 561, 564 (9th Cir. 1988). In spite of the suspects' attempts to limit the scope of their waivers, courts upheld the admissibility of their statements because their willingness to engage in a dialogue with police constituted valid implied waivers.

There are, however, cases in which defendants can make selective waivers of their rights for some purposes while preserving their rights to silence and counsel for other purposes as illustrated by *State v. Jones,* 607 S.E.2d 498 (W. Va. 2004). The defendant, a juvenile, and his attorney agreed to allow police to administer a polygraph test to the defendant. After the test was concluded, however, police interrogated the defendant without his lawyer being present with regard to the answers he provided during the polygraph examination even though the defendant requested consultation with his attorney. The court ruled that *Miranda* was violated because the selective waiver as to the polygraph examination did not extend to being an implied waiver for any subsequent interrogation.

The Requirements for Valid Waivers of *Miranda* Rights Regardless of whether the alleged waiver of *Miranda* rights in any particular case was express or implied, the *Miranda* Court made it clear that suspects may waive the rights conveyed in the *Miranda* warnings only if the "waiver is made voluntarily, knowingly and intelligently." 384 U.S. at 475. Courts begin their evaluation of purported waivers by presuming that a defendant did not waive his or her rights. Courts will not presume that suspects waived their *Miranda* rights just because they ultimately confessed. 384 U.S. at 475. Rather, courts examine the totality of the circumstances surrounding the alleged waiver by examining two distinct lines of inquiry as set forth by the U.S. Supreme Court in *Moran v. Burbine*:

> First the relinquishment of the right must have been voluntary in the sense that it was the product of a free and deliberate choice rather than intimidation, coercion or deception. Second, the waiver must have been made with a full awareness both of the nature of the right being abandoned and the consequences of the decision to abandon it. Only if "the totality of the circumstances surrounding the interrogation" reveal both an uncoerced choice and the requisite level of comprehension may a court properly conclude that the *Miranda* rights have been waived. *Moran v. Burbine*, 475 U.S. 412, 421 (1986).

Proof The prosecution then bears the burden of persuasion of proving, by a preponderance of the evidence, that the words and actions of the suspect evidenced a knowing, intelligent, and voluntary implied waiver of his or her *Miranda* rights. *Colorado v. Connelly*, 479 U.S. 157 (1986). Moreover, the absence of any evidence of waiver will result in a finding of no waiver and the exclusion of any statement obtained. *Tague v. Louisiana*, 444 U.S. 469 (1980). Therefore, when no written waiver or unambiguous oral waiver can be obtained, law enforcement officers should record all circumstances surrounding the attempt to obtain an implied waiver so that the prosecution will have evidence to prove that the waiver was voluntary, knowing, and intelligent.

Burbine **Prong 1: Voluntariness of the Waiver** *Colorado v. Connelly*, 479 U.S. 157 (1986), held that the voluntariness of waiver inquiry under first prong of *Moran v. Burbine* is exclusively concerned with the absence of police coercion. 479 U.S. at 170.

Colorado v. Connelly involved a defendant who, of his own accord and without any prompting, approached a police officer and said that he had murdered someone and wanted to talk to the police about it. The officer immediately advised Connelly of his *Miranda* rights. Connelly responded by saying that he understood his rights, but he wanted to talk about the murder anyway "because his conscience had been bothering him." 479 U.S. at 160. It turned out that Connelly was mentally ill, suffering from schizophrenia. During an actively psychotic phase, he went to the police to confess because auditory hallucinations which he believed to be "the voice of God" commanded him to do so. 479 U.S. at 161. The central question in the case was whether Connelly's waiver of his *Miranda* rights was "voluntary," in light of the fact that his severe mental illness made him feel compelled to confess. In deciding that the confession was voluntary, the Supreme Court said:

> The sole concern of the Fifth Amendment, on which *Miranda* was based, is governmental coercion. Indeed, the Fifth Amendment privilege is not concerned "with moral and psychological pressures to confess emanating from sources other than official coercion." The voluntariness of a waiver of this privilege has always depended on the absence of police overreaching, not on "free choice" in any broader sense of the word. 479 U.S. at 170.

Thus, the fact that Connelly's confession may have been compelled by mental illness was irrelevant because the compulsion did not flow from any police actions.

Burbine **Prong 2: Requisite Level of Comprehension** The second requirement of *Moran v. Burbine* is that a waiver must be made with full awareness of both the right being abandoned and the consequences of the decision to abandon that right. Normally, this prong is satisfied by careful administration of the *Miranda* warnings to a suspect. As stated in *Colorado v. Spring*, 479 U.S. 564, 574 (1987):

> **The Constitution does not require that a criminal suspect know and understand every possible consequence of a waiver of the Fifth Amendment privilege. . . . The Fifth Amendment's guarantee is both simpler and more fundamental: A defendant may not be compelled to be a witness against himself in any respect. The *Miranda* warnings protect this privilege by insuring that a suspect knows that he may choose not to talk to law enforcement officers, to talk only with counsel present, or to discontinue talking at any time. The *Miranda* warnings ensure that a waiver of these rights is knowing and intelligent by requiring that the suspect be fully advised of this constitutional privilege, including the critical advice that whatever he chooses to say may be used as evidence against him.**

Courts vary in their interpretations of the effect on the voluntariness of waiver of police use of psychological tactics, such as playing on the suspect's sympathies or explaining that honesty is the best policy. Some courts apply a totality-of-the-circumstances test to determine whether the suspect's will was overborne or the suspect's capacity for self-determination was critically impaired. *United States v. Pelton*, 835 F.2d 1067, 1073 (4th Cir. 1987), said: "Agents may properly initiate discussions on cooperation, and may indicate that they will make this cooperation known. . . . General encouragement to cooperate is far different from specific promises of leniency." With respect to the use of psychological tactics, *Miller v. Fenton*, 796 F.2d 598, 605 (3d Cir. 1986), *cert. denied sub nom*, 479 U.S. 989, said:

> These ploys may play a part in the suspect's decision to confess, but so long as that decision is a product of the suspect's own balancing of competing considerations the confession is voluntary. The question . . . is whether . . . statements were so manipulative or coercive that they deprived [the defendant] of his ability to make an unconstrained, autonomous decision to confess.

Applying this principle, *Miller v. Fenton* upheld a confession as voluntary even though the police officer engaged in a number of psychological tactics that were alleged to have overborne the will of the defendant. Specifically, the police officer feigned extreme sympathy towards the defendant; encouraged the defendant to "unburden" himself by confessing to murder; promised to get the defendant psychological help; and lied to the defendant that the victim was still alive at the time the interrogation began and then, during the interview, told the suspect that the victim had died. The court ruled that these tactics did not produce psychological pressure strong enough to render the confession involuntary.

Specific Factors Considered When Applying the *Burbine* Test for Waivers

This section presents a list of factors that courts commonly considered when examining the validity of a waiver of *Miranda* rights. The list should not be consider exhaustive since courts must consider the totality of the circumstances surrounding an interrogation to determine if a waiver was knowing, intelligent, and voluntary.

Competency of the Suspect The inquiry as to whether a suspect has the requisite level of comprehension to validly waive *Miranda* rights is directed at the **competency** of the suspect. In determining competency to waive *Miranda* rights, courts examine the totality of the circumstances surrounding the waiver, with no single factor controlling.

▶ **Intelligence** No specific level of intelligence constitutes a minimum threshold for suspects to be considered competent to waive their *Miranda* rights. Thus, suspects with below-average IQs may be competent to waive their rights. *United States v. Rosario-Diaz*, 202 F.3d 54 (1st Cir. 2000) (upholding waiver by a defendant with an I.Q. in mid-70s). This is even the case for suspects who are mentally retarded (Fulero & Everington, 1995). *Smith v. Mullin*, 379 F.3d 919, 933 (10th Cir. 2004), for example, upheld a waiver by a defendant with the cognitive abilities of a twelve-year-old because he had prior experience with the criminal justice system and understood *Miranda* warnings). *Young v. Walls*, 311 F.3d 846, 849-50 (7th Cir. 2002), did the same for a defendant with an I.Q. of only 56 because he was a "career criminal" who had a general understanding of his rights. But, when law enforcement personnel are dealing with an impaired suspect whose cognitive abilities are low, they must take special care to insure that the language they use is understood by the suspect. *See United States v. Garibay*, 143 F.3d 534 (9th Cir. 1998).

▶ **Education** As with intelligence, there is no specific level of education that constitutes a minimum threshold for suspects to be considered competent to waive their *Miranda* rights. *United States v. Bautista-Avila*, 6 F.3d 1360 (9th Cir. 1993), upheld a waiver by a defendant with a sixth-grade Mexican education because the officer read him his rights in Spanish and the defendant said that he understood his rights.

▶ **Age** Suspects who may be too young to understand *Miranda* warnings pose special problems for the criminal justice system.

> The United States Supreme Court has decided more cases involving the interrogation of juveniles than any other aspect of juvenile justice administration. Although it has cautioned trial judges to be especially sensitive to the effects of youthfulness and immaturity on a defendant's ability to waive or to invoke her *Miranda* rights and to make voluntary statements, the Court has not mandated any special procedural protections for immature suspects. Instead, it endorsed the adult waiver standard—"knowing, intelligent, and voluntary" under the "totality of the circumstances"—to gauge the validity of a juvenile's waiver of *Miranda* rights (Feld, 2006: 27).

Developmental psychology has demonstrated that reasoning and decision-making skills continue to develop throughout childhood and early adolescence (Larson, 2003: 649). In fact, research has consistently shown that most teenagers under the age of sixteen do not understand either the language of *Miranda* rights or some of the concepts underlying those rights, such as the role of defense counsel in criminal prosecutions (Feld, 2006; Beyer, 2000; Grisso, 1997). For example, Grisso (1981: 129) found that one-third of children "with few or no prior felony referrals believed that defense attorneys defend the interests of the innocent but not the guilty." In spite of these facts, courts routinely uphold waivers by teenagers between the ages of fourteen and eighteen. *E.g., Gachot v. Stadler*, 298 F.3d 414 (5th Cir. 2002). Courts, however, often find that juveniles who are preteens or younger lack the intellectual development to make a knowing, intelligent, and voluntary waiver of *Miranda* rights. *E.g., Murray v. Earle*, 405 F.3d 278 (5th Cir. 2005) (invalidating waiver by eleven-year-old). Recall, however, that approximately thirteen states have laws that require a parent, guardian, or other interested adult, such as an attorney, to be notified before a juvenile may be found to have waived *Miranda* rights (Feld, 2006: 36).

▶ **Familiarity with the Justice System** A complete lack of familiarity with the justice system certainly does not call into question a suspect's competency to invoke or waiver *Miranda* rights. Nonetheless, courts usually find that suspects who have some prior experience in the justice system are less likely to be susceptible to mild forms of psychological tactics used by police to get suspects to confess. Thus, in a close case, prior criminal justice experience weighs toward the validity of a waiver of *Miranda* rights. For example, *United States v. Palmer*, 203 F.3d 55 (1st Cir. 2000), held a waiver to be valid—even though the defendant was going through heroin withdrawal at the time of the interrogation—because the defendant had sixteen prior arrests. *Hardaway v. Young*, 302 F.3d 757 (7th Cir. 2002), upheld a waiver by a fourteen-year-old defendant because he had had been arrested at least nineteen times in the past and appeared to understand his *Miranda* rights as a result of his prior experience with the justice system, in spite of his relative youth.

▶ **Physical and Mental Condition** *Mincey v. Arizona*, 437 U.S. 385, 399 (1978), ruled that *Miranda* was violated when a police officer interrogated a hospitalized patient who was in "unbearable pain" after having been seriously wounded.

> It is hard to imagine a situation less conducive to the exercise of "a rational intellect and a free will" than Mincey's. He had been seriously wounded just a few hours earlier, and had arrived at the hospital "depressed almost to the point of coma," according to his attending physician. Although he had received some treatment, his condition at the time of Hust's interrogation was still sufficiently serious that he was in the intensive care unit. He complained to Hust that the pain in his leg was "unbearable." He was evidently confused and unable to think clearly about either the events of that afternoon or the circumstances of his interrogation, since some of his written answers were on their face not entirely coherent. Finally, while Mincey was being questioned he was lying on his back on a hospital bed, encumbered by tubes, needles, and breathing apparatus. He was, in short, "at the complete mercy" of Detective Hust, unable to escape or resist the thrust of Hust's interrogation. 437 U.S. at 398–99.

Yet, courts have upheld waivers under many circumstances in which suspects were injured or in pain, so long as they were alert and responsive during questioning. *Reinert v. Larkins*, 379 F.3d 76, 88–89 (3d Cir. 2004), for example, upheld the defendant's implied waiver even though the interrogation was taking place in an ambulance as the defendant was being taken to a hospital because he was "alert and coherent" during questioning. *United States v. Cristobal*, 293 F.3d 134, 142 (4th Cir. 2002), upheld a waiver by a defendant suffering from postsurgical pain in spite of being on narcotic painkiller because the medication apparently did not affect his thinking. And *United States v. Huerta*, 239 F.3d 865, 873 (7th Cir. 2001), upheld a waiver even though the defendant was tired and had taken medication on an empty stomach.

▶ **Drug and/or Alcohol Use** Although drugs or alcohol certainly impair cognitive functioning, suspects under the influence of drugs or alcohol may nonetheless validly waive their *Miranda* rights. The critical question in such cases is the degree of impairment. If the suspect is functioning reasonably well, then courts usually uphold their waivers. For example, although the defendant was intoxicated in *Clagett v. Angelone*, 209 F.3d 370 (4th Cir. 2000), because he did not slur his speech or have trouble walking, the court upheld his waiver. A *Miranda* waiver was similarly upheld in *United States v. Walker*, 272 F.3d 407, 412–13 (7th Cir. 2001), in spite of the fact that the defendant was vomiting during the interrogation due to heroin withdrawal, because a doctor said the defendant was alert and "with the program."

Explicitness of the Waiver The more explicit a waiver, the more likely it is to be ruled valid. For example, *Wilcher v. Hargett*, 978 F.2d 872, 877 (5th Cir. 1992), upheld a waiver even though the interrogation involved repeated questioning of the suspect over a six-day day period because the defendant received *Miranda* warnings and signed written waivers before each questioning period. However, even a meticulously obtained written waiver cannot overcome other misconduct that calls into question the legitimacy of the waiver. *Hart v. Att'y Gen. of Fla.*, 323 F.3d 884, 893–94 (11th Cir. 2003), for example, invalidated a written waiver obtained after careful explanation of *Miranda* because the interrogating officer contradicted the written warnings by saying that signing the waiver form "honesty will not hurt you" in response to the defendant's questions regarding the benefits of having counsel present during the interrogation.

Language Barriers *Miranda* warnings must be given in a language understood by the suspect. Thus, providing warnings in English to non-English-speaking suspects, or to suspects whose knowledge of the English language is minimal, will not suffice. *E.g., United States v. Garibay*, 143 F.3d 534 (9th Cir. 1998). But if *Miranda* rights are translated into a language that a suspect can understand, even if the translation is imperfect due to misspellings or grammar errors, then a waiver of those rights is usually upheld. *E.g., Thai v. Mapes*, 412 F.3d 970 (8th Cir. 2005); *United States v. Yunis*, 859 F.2d 953 (D.C. Cir. 1988).

Failures to Disclose Information about the Interrogation

▶ **Failure to State True Purpose and Scope of Interrogation** In *Colorado v. Spring*, 479 U.S. 564 (1987), the defendant contended that police failure to inform him of the potential subjects of interrogation constituted police trickery and deception as condemned in *Miranda*, and rendered his waiver of *Miranda* rights invalid. The U.S. Supreme Court disagreed. Citing *Burbine,* the Court said that a valid waiver does not require that police supply a suspect with all useful information to help calibrate his or her self-interest in deciding whether to speak or to stand by his or her rights. The Court held that "a suspect's awareness of all the possible subjects of questioning in advance of interrogation is not relevant to determining whether the suspect voluntarily, knowingly, and intelligently waived his Fifth Amendment privilege." 479 U.S. at 577.

▶ **Failure to Inform Suspect that He OR She is Target of Investigation**
United States v. Tapp, 812 F.2d 177 (5th Cir. 1987), held that the interrogating officer's failure to inform the defendant that he was the target of the investigation did not render his waiver of *Miranda* rights involuntary.

Failures to Disclose Outside Information and Events In *Moran v. Burbine*, the police failed to let the defendant, Moran, know that his public defender had been trying to contact him. Although Moran otherwise made a voluntary waiver and confessed, he later challenged the validity of his waiver on the grounds that it was not "knowing" because he did not know that his lawyer had been trying to contact him. The Supreme Court rejected this claim, reasoning that: **"Events occurring outside of the presence of the suspect and entirely unknown to him surely can have no bearing on the capacity to comprehend and knowingly relinquish a constitutional right. . . . We have never read the Constitution to require that the police supply a suspect with a flow of information to help him calibrate his self-interest in deciding whether to speak or stand by his rights."** 475 U.S. at 422. Thus, a suspect need not know all of the facts and circumstances surrounding a case to validly waive his or her *Miranda* rights. Rather, a suspect only needs to know the "nature of his rights and the consequences of abandoning them." 475 U.S. at 424.

In spite of upholding the actions of the police, the Supreme Court warned that a more flagrant violation by the police might rise to the level of a due process violation. Therefore, police should not interpret *Burbine* as generally approving dishonest or shady dealings with defense attorneys in interrogation situations occurring before the initiation of formal charges. In fact, some states have explicitly rejected *Burbine* on the basis of state constitutional law. Consider the rationale for the California Supreme Court's rejection of *Burbine:*

> [W]hether or not a suspect in custody has previously waived his rights to silence and counsel, the police may not deny him the opportunity, before questioning begins or resumes, to meet with his retained or appointed counsel who has taken diligent steps to come to his aid. If the lawyer comes to the station before interrogation begins or while it is still in progress, the suspect must promptly be told, and if he then wishes to see his counsel, he must be allowed to do so. Moreover, the police may not engage in conduct, intentional or grossly negligent, which is calculated to mislead, delay, or dissuade counsel in his efforts to reach his client. Such conduct constitutes a denial of a California suspect's *Miranda* rights to counsel, and it invalidates any subsequent statements. *People v. Houston*, 724 P.2d 1166, 1174–75 (Cal. 1986).

key points

- After warnings of *Miranda* rights have been given to a person subjected to custodial interrogation and the person has been given an opportunity to exercise the rights, the person may voluntarily, knowingly, and intelligently waive the rights, either explicitly or impliedly, and then agree to answer questions or make a statement. But unless and until such warnings and waiver are demonstrated by the prosecution at trial, no evidence obtained as a result of interrogation can be used against the person.

- To constitute a full and effective waiver of *Miranda* rights, (1) the relinquishment of the right must have been voluntary in the sense that it was the product of a free and deliberate choice rather than police intimidation, coercion, or deception; and (2) the waiver must have been made with a full awareness both of the nature of the right being abandoned and the consequences of the decision to abandon

(Continued)

key points

it. This second requirement is satisfied by careful administration of the *Miranda* warnings to a competent suspect.

- Before formal criminal proceedings are instituted against a particular suspect (such as an indictment, preliminary hearing, or arraignment), undercover agents do not need to administer *Miranda* warnings to suspects before obtaining statements. This applies even of they are in custody, as questioning by someone undercover is not inherently coercive in the way that routine custodial interrogations by known police officers can be.

- A request to see someone other than a lawyer is not an assertion of *Miranda* rights, although a denial of such a request may have some bearing on the voluntariness of the statements.

- Police are not required to inform uncharged suspects of attorneys' attempts to reach them, or to otherwise keep them abreast of the status of their legal representation or of other information that may be useful to their defense, before giving *Miranda* warnings and obtaining a waiver of *Miranda* rights.

Effect of *Miranda–Edwards* in Court

Recall that *Dickerson v. United States*, 530 U.S. 428 (2000), held that *Miranda* warnings are constitutionally required. In spite of this holding, violation of a suspect's *Miranda* rights produces few consequences compared to those that are normally triggered by other constitutional violations, such as the Fourth Amendment's guarantees against unreasonable searches and seizures or the Eighth Amendment's prohibition on cruel and unusual punishment.

Miranda Violations Are Barred Only in Prosecution Case-in-Chief Statements taken in violation of *Miranda* requirements are inadmissible in court as substantive evidence in the prosecution's case-in-chief to prove the defendant's guilt of crime. Statements taken in violation of *Miranda* may, however, be admissible for purposes other than the proof of a defendant's guilt. *Harris v. New York*, 401 U.S. 222 (1971), and *Oregon v. Hass*, 420 U.S. 714 (1975), admitted testimony of previous inconsistent statements taken from a defendant in violation of his *Miranda* rights solely for the purpose of impeaching the defendant's testimony at trial. Stressing that the trustworthiness of the defendant's earlier conflicting statements must satisfy legal standards, the Court said: **"The shield provided by *Miranda* cannot be perverted into a license to use perjury by way of a defense, free from the risk of confrontation with prior inconsistent utterances. We hold, therefore, that petitioner's credibility was appropriately impeached by use of his earlier conflicting statements."** 401 U.S. at 226.

Similarly, a statement taken in violation of *Edwards v. Arizona* may be used to impeach a defendant's false or inconsistent testimony at trial, even though the same statement may not be used as substantive evidence. *Michigan v. Harvey*, 494 U.S. 344 (1990). And *Michigan v. Tucker*, 417 U.S. 433 (1974), held that a *Miranda* violation that resulted in the discovery of a witness did not preclude the government from later calling that witness to testify at trial. The witness was named in the defendant's alibi during an interrogation that followed incomplete *Miranda* warnings. The witness not only contradicted the defendant's alibi but also provided additional incriminating information. The Supreme Court denied the defendant's attempt to exclude the witness's testimony at trial, concluding that, although statements taken without benefit of full *Miranda* warnings generally could not be admitted at trial, identification of witnesses is an acceptable use of the statements.

Criminal justice professionals should not interpret the *Harris, Hass, Harvey,* and *Tucker* cases as an opportunity to evade the requirements of *Miranda–Edwards*. An admission or confession obtained in compliance with those cases is much more valuable to the prosecution than an illegally obtained voluntary statement to be used only for impeachment or discovery of witnesses. In addition, involuntary statements obtained from a defendant cannot be used for any purpose in a criminal trial. *Mincey v. Arizona*, 437 U.S. 385, 398 (1978), stated that **"any criminal trial use against a defendant of his involuntary statement is a denial of due process of law, 'even though there is ample evidence aside from the confession to support the conviction.'"** The only exception to this rule allows admission of an involuntary statement if the admission is found to be harmless error. *Arizona v. Fulminante*, 499 U.S. 279 (1991).

Effect of Silence Pre- and Post-Warnings

United States v. Hale, 422 U.S. 171 (1975), and *Doyle v. Ohio*, 426 U.S. 610 (1976), held that a defendant's silence after receiving *Miranda* warnings could not be used against the defendant at trial either in the prosecution's case-in-chief or for the purpose of impeachment.

> **[W]hen a person under arrest is informed as *Miranda* requires, . . . it does not comport with due process to permit the prosecution during the trial to call attention to his silence at the time of arrest and to insist that because he did not speak about the facts of the case at that time, as he was told he need not do, an unfavorable inference might be drawn as to the truth of his trial testimony. . . .** 426 U.S. at 619.

The *Doyle* bar on discussing post-warning silence does not apply, however, to a defendant's silence before *Miranda* warnings are given:

> [T]he Constitution does not prohibit the use for impeachment purposes of a defendant's silence prior to arrest . . . or after arrest if no *Miranda* warnings are given. . . . Such silence is probative and does not rest on *any implied assurance by law enforcement authorities that it will carry no penalty. Brecht* v. Abrahamson, 507 U.S. 619, 628 (1993).

Fruit of the Poisonous Tree Doctrine Inapplicable

The fruit of the poisonous tree doctrine (see Chapter 3) is usually applied to prevent the "fruits" of a constitutional violation from being used in court. However, the Supreme Court has limited the applicability of this doctrine in two important ways in the Fifth Amendment context.

Subsequent Admission or Confession After Initial Taint *Oregon v. Elstad*, 470 U.S. 298 (1985), limited the applicability of the fruit of the poisonous tree doctrine to admissions and confessions made after an initial *Miranda* violation. When a suspect being subjected to custodial interrogation makes incriminating statements without having been given his or her *Miranda* rights, but subsequently repeats those incriminating statements after having been read his or her *Miranda* rights, defendants cannot argue that the fruit of the poisonous tree doctrine bars the admissibility of their second admission or confession as being tainted by the first if the initial statements were knowingly and voluntarily given. The fruit of the poisonous tree doctrine will only operate to prevent the use of the second admission or confession if the initial, un-Mirandized statements were obtained involuntarily (i.e., a due process violation occurs because deliberately coercive or improper tactics were used to obtain the initial statement).

Inapplicable to Physical Evidence The fruit of the poisonous tree doctrine does not apply to physical evidence derived from statements made in violation of *Miranda*. In *United States v. Patane*, 304 F.3d 1013 (10th Cir. 2002), *rev'd*, 542 U.S. 630 (2004), statements made by a suspect in response to police questions that were designed to elicit an incriminating response were suppressed because the defendant had not been read his *Miranda* rights. In response to being asked if he had any firearms, the defendant told police he had a handgun in his bedroom. The gun was suppressed as fruit of the poisonous tree because it was discovered as a result of the defendant's unwarned statements. On appeal, the U.S. Supreme Court reversed, holding that the failure to properly advise a suspect of *Miranda* rights does not trigger the fruit of the poisonous tree doctrine so long as the suspect's unwarned statements were voluntary. 542 U.S. 643–64. Some states, however, have declined to follow *Patane* on state law grounds. *E.g., Com-*

Can *Chavez* be Applied to the War on Terror?

A plurality of four U.S. Supreme Court justices in *Chavez v. Martinez* made it clear that the Fifth Amendment privilege against self-incrimination is only a trial right. In their view, the Self-Incrimination Clause merely prevents coerced statements from being used against a suspect at criminal trial. It does not provide an independent right that, if violated, gives rise to a claim for damages. Two of the concurring justices in the case—Justices Souter and Breyer—agreed that the plaintiff in that case had no claim for damages, but they did not rule out a claim for damages in the future in "extreme cases in which plaintiffs made 'powerful showings'" (Parry, 2007: 815-16, quoting *Chavez*, 538 U.S. at 777–78 [Souter, J., concurring]).

Assume, for the sake of argument, that a Canadian citizen lawfully entered the United States on business, but was detained upon his arrival because he was mistakenly believed to be a terrorist. Further assume that he was covertly sent to a secret CIA prison camp in the Middle East, where he was subjected to three months of custodial interrogation that involved torture. He was never Mirandized or provided with any of the rights associated with *Miranda*. Once it was discovered that a case of mistaken identity had taken place (i.e., the man had no connections to terrorism at all), he was then returned to Canada.

Do you think the man should be permitted to sue under Section 1983 for damages under the possible "powerful showing" exception mentioned in Justice Souter's concurring opinion in *Chavez*? Or do you think the *Chavez* plurality's bar on damages for *Miranda* violations should prevent him from recovering any monetary compensation for what he went through? Might there be other constitutional theories under which this plaintiff could collect damages other than the Fifth Amendment's Self-Incrimination Clause, thereby circumventing the holding in *Chavez*? What are they?

monwealth v. Martin, 827 N.E.2d 198 (Mass. 2005); State v. Knapp, 700 N.W.2d 899 (Wis. 2005).

Section 1983 Claims Barred for Miranda Violations In *Chavez v. Martinez*, 538 U.S. 760 (2003), a suspect was interrogated by police while he was in the hospital being treated for gunshot wounds he sustained during an altercation with the police. In spite of the fact that the interrogation interrupted the suspect's medical care, the officer refused to stop the questioning of the suspect (over the objections of medical personnel) until the suspect admitted that he had pointed a gun at an officer. He eventually made such an admission. However, at no time during the interrogation had the suspect been given his *Miranda* rights. The suspect was never charged with a crime, but he subsequently sued the police under 42 U.S.C. § 1983 for a number of claims. The district court ruled in his favor that the police had violated his Fifth Amendment rights. The U.S. Court of Appeals for the Ninth Circuit affirmed, but the Supreme Court reversed in a highly fractured plurality opinion. As a result of *Chavez v. Martinez*, suspects have no constitutional right to be free from custodial interrogations that violate *Miranda*. Thus, if they are interrogated without having been given *Miranda* warnings, the only remedy is that their unwarned statements may not be admitted at trial as substantive evidence against them. They have no viable § 1983 claim against the officers who failed to honor their *Miranda* rights.

key points

- Statements taken in violation of *Miranda–Edwards* requirements are inadmissible in court as substantive evidence in the prosecution's case-in-chief to prove the defendant's guilt of crime; but they may be used to impeach the defendant's testimony at trial or to discover witnesses, so long as the statements were voluntarily given.
- Involuntary statements obtained from a defendant cannot be used for any purpose in a criminal trial.
- A defendant's silence after receiving the *Miranda* warnings may not be used against the defendant at trial for any purpose.
- Silence in response to questions asked prior to *Miranda* warnings (i.e., responses to questions that were not the product of custodial interroga-

tions) may be used to impeach a defendant's testimony at trial.
- The fruit of the poisonous tree doctrine does not apply to physical evidence derived from statements made in violation of *Miranda*; nor does it bar the use of a second statement that was voluntarily given after a valid waiver of *Miranda* was obtained following an initial *Miranda* violation.
- If suspects are interrogated without having been given *Miranda* warnings, the only remedy is that their unwarned statements may not be admitted at trial as substantive evidence against them. They have no viable Section 1983 claim against the officers who failed to honor their *Miranda* rights.

▶ INTERROGATION AND THE SIXTH AMENDMENT

The Sixth Amendment to the U.S. Constitution provides that "[i]n all criminal prosecutions, the accused shall enjoy the right . . . to have the Assistance of Counsel for his defense." Recall that *Escobedo v. Illinois*, 378 U.S. 478 (1964), tied the Sixth Amendment right to counsel to pretrial criminal proceedings once the suspect had become the focus of the investigation. Also recall that the focus of the investigation test espoused in *Escobedo* was short-lived. However, the core holding of *Escobedo*—that the Sixth Amendment right to counsel has application at pretrial stages of criminal prosecutions—remains a vital principle in constitutional criminal procedure. *See United States v. Wade*, 388 U.S. 218 (1967) (holding that the Sixth Amendment right to counsel extended to pretrial proceedings whenever such assistance was necessary to guarantee a fair trial).

Attachment of Sixth Amendment Right to Counsel

The right to counsel under the Sixth Amendment differs from the right to counsel under *Miranda* that flows from the Fifth Amendment. The sole purpose of the right under *Miranda* is to insure that a suspect's will is not overborne by coercive police interrogation tactics while the suspect is in custody. Thus, it exists to prevent compulsory self-incrimination only when a suspect is subject to custodial interrogation. *Miranda*, 384 U.S. at 474. In contrast, the Sixth Amendment is not concerned with compulsion in the self-incrimination context. Rather, the Sixth Amendment concerns the protection of someone who will face criminal adversarial proceedings in court. Thus, the modern rule is that *the Sixth Amendment right to counsel is triggered ("attaches") when formal criminal proceedings have begun. Kirby v. Illinois*, 406 U.S. 682 (1972). As a result, **"a person is entitled to the help of a lawyer at or after the time that judicial proceedings have been initiated against him 'whether by way of formal charge, preliminary hearing, indictment, information, or arraignment.'"** *Fellers v. United States*, 540 U.S. 519, 523 (2004) (quoting *Brewer v. Williams*, 430 U.S. 387, 398 (1977)).

Once the Sixth Amendment right to counsel attaches and is invoked or asserted, authorities may not engage in any conduct that is designed to elicit an incriminating response from the defendant without the presence or waiver of counsel. *Brewer v. Williams*, 430 U.S. 387, 399 (1977). This means that a defendant may not be questioned without his or her lawyer being present unless a valid waiver of the Sixth Amendment right to counsel is first obtained. Recall that in *Moran v. Burbine*, no Fifth Amendment violation was found when the police failed to disclose to the suspect that his family had retained a lawyer for him and that lawyer had been trying to reach the defendant. Had formal criminal proceedings begun, and thus, the right to counsel under the Sixth Amendment would have attached, there would have been a constitutional violation. *Patterson v. Illinois*, 487 U.S. 285, 296 n. 9 (1988).

Fifth Amendment "Interrogation" vs. Sixth Amendment "Deliberate Elicitation" Because the Sixth Amendment right to counsel attaches under circumstances that are qualitatively different from those giving rise to a Fifth Amendment right to counsel under *Miranda*, *Miranda*'s focus on custodial interrogation is inapplicable when examining Sixth Amendment rights. *Michigan v. Jackson*, 475 U.S. 625, 632, n.5 (1986), stated: **"The Sixth Amendment provides a right to counsel . . . even when there is no interrogation and no Fifth Amendment applicability."** Rather than using the interrogation standard of the Fifth Amendment, the Sixth Amendment bars the use of any statements made by a defendant in response to the actions of law enforcement that might deliberately elicit an incriminating response. *United States v. Henry*, 447 U.S. 264, 270 (1980). **Deliberate elicitation** occurs when state officials create "a situation likely to induce . . . incriminating statements without the assistance of counsel . . . ." *United States v. Henry*, 447 U.S. 264, 274-75 (1980). The deliberate elicitation standard is broader than the protections afforded suspects under the Fifth Amendment because it prohibits authorities from engaging in conduct that would not be considered "interrogation" or its functional equivalent under *Miranda*. Perhaps one of the most notable differences between the two amendments' approaches is that the Sixth Amendment bars the use of any secret investigatory techniques, while the Fifth Amendment does not. Consider the following leading cases.

Deliberate Elicitation Violates Right to Counsel Once the Sixth Amendment right to counsel attaches, the state must not do anything that deliberately or knowingly interferes with that right.

▶ In *Massiah v. United States*, 377 U.S. 201 (1964), after the defendant was indicted, federal agents obtained incriminating statements from him in the absence of his counsel. While the defendant was free on bail, his co-defendant, in cooperation with the federal agents, engaged the defendant in conversation in the presence of a hidden radio transmitter located in the co-defendant's car. Because the defendant was not in custody, no Fifth Amendment rights under *Miranda* were applicable. But, because he had already been indicted, the defendant's Sixth Amendment right to counsel had attached. The Supreme Court determined that the statements were inadmissible because the government violated the defendant's Sixth Amendment rights by using "his own incriminating words, which federal agents had deliberately elicited from him after he had been indicted and in the absence of his counsel." 377 U.S. at 206.

▶ The Supreme Court affirmed the continuing validity of *Massiah* in *Brewer v. Williams*, 430 U.S. 387 (1977), a case often referred to as the "Christian Burial Speech" case. In *Brewer v. Williams*, the defendant, Williams, had been arrested, arraigned, and jailed in Davenport, Iowa, for abducting a ten-year-old girl in Des Moines, Iowa. He needed to be transported by police from where he was captured in Davenport to Des Moines where his trial would take place. His lawyer in Davenport was denied permission to ride in the back seat of the police car with Williams during the 160-mile drive. Accordingly, both that lawyer and the one who was representing Williams in Des Moines advised him not to make any statements during the trip. Pursuant to their instructions, "[a]t no time during the trip did Williams express a willingness to be interrogated in the absence of an attorney." 430 U.S. at 392. The police officers transporting Williams agreed not to question him during the trip. However, soon after the police began their trip with the defendant from Davenport to Des Moines, one officer engaged the defendant in "a wide-ranging conversation covering a variety of topics, including the subject of religion." 430 U.S. at 392. One of the officers then said the following to Williams, whom he addressed as "Reverend":

> **"I want to give you something to think about while we're traveling down the road. . . . Number one, I want you to observe the weather conditions, it's raining, it's sleeting, it's freezing, driving is very treacherous, visibility is poor, it's going to be dark early this evening. They are predicting several inches of snow for tonight, and I feel that you yourself are the only person that knows where this little girl's body is, that you yourself have only been there once, and if you get snow on top of it you yourself may be unable to find it. And,**

> since we will be going right past the area on the way into Des Moines, I feel that we could stop and locate the body, that the parents of this little girl should be entitled to a Christian burial for the little girl who was snatched away from them on Christmas Eve and murdered. And I feel we should stop and locate it on the way in rather than waiting until morning and trying to come back out after a snow storm and possibly not being able to find it at all." Williams asked [the officer] why he thought their route to Des Moines would be taking them past the girl's body, and [he] responded that he knew the body was in the area of Mitchellville, a town they would be passing on the way to Des Moines. [The officer] then stated: "I do not want you to answer me. I don't want to discuss it any further. Just think about it as we're riding down the road."
>
> As the car approached Grinnell, a town approximately 100 miles west of Davenport, Williams asked whether the police had found the victim's shoes. When [an officer] replied that he was unsure, Williams directed the officers to a service station where he said he had left the shoes; a search for them proved unsuccessful. As they continued towards Des Moines, Williams asked whether the police had found the blanket, and directed the officers to a rest area where he said he had disposed of the blanket. Nothing was found. The car continued towards Des Moines, and as it approached Mitchellville, Williams said that he would show the officers where the body was. He then directed the police to the body of [the victim]. 430 U.S. at 392–93.

Because Williams had already been arraigned, formal adversarial proceedings had commenced against him; he therefore had a Sixth Amendment right to have legal representation during the time in which he made incriminating statements in response to the officer's "Christian Burial Speech." The Court said that there could be no doubt that the officer "deliberately and designedly set out to elicit information from Williams just as surely as and perhaps more effectively than if he had formally interrogated him." 430 U.S. at 399. Thus, relying on *Massiah*, the Court ruled that Williams' statements were inadmissible because they had been obtained by police in violation of his Sixth Amendment right to counsel.

▶ *United States v. Henry*, 447 U.S. 264 (1980), upheld the suppression of statements made by an indicted and imprisoned defendant to a paid, undisclosed government informant who was in the same cell block. Although the informant did not question the defendant, the informant "stimulated" conversations with him and developed a relationship of trust and confidence with him. As a result, the defendant made incriminating statements without the assistance of counsel. This indirect and surreptitious type of interrogation was an impermissible interference with the Sixth Amendment in violation of *Massiah* because the government "intentionally created a situation likely to induce [the defendant] to make incriminating statements without the assistance of counsel." 447 U.S. at 274 (1980). Key to the Court's rationale was the fact that the government had: "singled out" the defendant as the informant's target; used an informant whose "apparent status [was that of] a person sharing a common plight" with the defendant; and agreed to pay the informant only if he provided useful information. *See also Randolph v. California*, 380 F.3d 1133 (9th Cir. 2004); *Manning v. Bowersox*, 310 F.3d 571 (8th Cir. 2002).

▶   Furthermore, even when a confrontation between an accused and a police agent is initiated by the accused, the government may not deliberately attempt to elicit information without counsel present. In *Maine v. Moulton*, 474 U.S. 159 (1985), two codefendants had been indicted on several theft-related offenses. During a meeting in which the two defendants met to discuss strategy for their upcoming trial, Moulton suggested that the two kill one of the state's witnesses against them. The codefendant and his lawyer subsequently met with police and confessed to his participation in a series of thefts that included the charges for which he and Moulton had already been indicted, as well as other thefts. In exchange for a promise that no further charges would be brought against him, the defendant agreed to testify against Moulton and otherwise cooperate in the ongoing police investigation. As part of that agreement, the codefendant allowed a recording device to be placed on his telephone line so that police could record conversation that he had with Moulton. During several telephone conversations, the codefendant got Moulton to make several incriminating statements. He also got Moulton to make incriminating statements during meetings between the two defendants while the codefendant was wired with a recording device.

The state attempted to distinguish the actions of the police in this case from those in *Massiah* and *Henry* on the grounds that in those cases, "the police set up the confrontation between the accused and a police agent at which incriminating statements were elicited." 474 U.S. at 175. In contrast, Moulton had initiated the recorded telephone conversations and had requested the in-person meeting in which another conversation was recorded. The Supreme Court rejected this distinction and held that the guarantee of the Sixth Amendment includes the government's affirmative obligation not to circumvent the protections accorded the accused who invokes his or her right to rely on counsel as a "medium" between the accused and the government. The Court continued:

> [T]he Sixth Amendment is not violated whenever—by luck or happenstance—the State obtains incriminating statements from the accused after the right to counsel has attached. . . . However, knowing exploitation by the State of an opportunity to confront the accused without counsel being present is as much a breach of the State's obligation not to circumvent the right to assistance of counsel as is the intentional creation of such an opportunity. Accordingly, the Sixth Amendment is violated when the State obtains incriminating statements by knowingly circumventing the accused's right to have counsel present in a confrontation between the accused and a state agent. 474 U.S. at 176.

Thus, it was not the use of the recording device or even the use of an informant that was problematic in *Moulton,* as authorities may be the passive recipients of information. *See United States v. Gunn*, 369 F.3d 1229 (11th Cir. 2004) (finding no Sixth Amendment violation when police recorded an incriminating conversation between co-defendants in a police car because officers just listened). Rather, the constitutional violation in *Moulton* occurred because a state informant deliberately elicited incriminating information from the defendant without his attorney being present, thereby violating the Sixth Amendment.

▶ In *Franklin v. Fox*, 312 F.3d 423, 442 (9th Cir. 2002), the court ruled that the Sixth Amendment had been violated when the defendant's daughter had agreed with the government to meet with her father and attempt to persuade him to confess to a murder without his lawyer being present after the father had been formally charged with the homicide.

▶ *Powell v. Texas*, 492 U.S. 680 (1989), held that the Sixth Amendment is violated when a psychiatric or psychological examination of the defendant is performed, but defense counsel is not given adequate notice of the examination, its scope, and nature. *See also Delguidice v. Singletary*, 84 F.3d 1359 (11th Cir. 1996). However, there is no Sixth Amendment violation when defense is notified of a psychiatric or psychological exam and chooses not to attend. *Re v. Snyder*, 293 F.3d 678 (3d Cir. 2002).

In *Fellers v. United States*, 540 U.S. 519 (2004), the defendant had been indicted by a grand jury on charges related to the distribution of methamphetamine. When police subsequently arrested him in his home, they told him he had been charged with distributing methamphetamine. In response, the defendant made incriminating statements. In holding that the police violated his Sixth Amendment right to counsel, the Court stated:

> [T]here is no question that the officers in this case "deliberately elicited" information from petitioner. Indeed, the officers, upon arriving at petitioner's house, informed him that their purpose in coming was to discuss his involvement in the distribution of methamphetamine and his association with certain charged co-conspirators. Because the ensuing discussion took place after petitioner had been indicted, outside the presence of counsel, and in the absence of any waiver of petitioner's Sixth Amendment rights, the Court of Appeals erred in holding that the officers' actions did not violate the Sixth Amendment standards established in *Massiah* . . . and its progeny. 540 U.S at 524–25.

Passive Receipt of Information Does Not Violate the Right to Counsel The cases summarized in the last section collectively illustrate that courts carefully examine any attempts to circumvent the right of any formally charged person to have counsel present at a confrontation between the person and police agents. But a defendant's Sixth Amendment rights are not violated when an informant, either through prior arrangement or voluntarily, reports the defendant's incriminating statements to the police. "[T]he defendant must demonstrate that the police and their informant took some action, beyond merely listening, that was designed deliberately to elicit incriminating remarks." *Kuhlmann v. Wilson*, 477 U.S. 436, 459 (1986). For example:

▶ In *United States v. LaBare*, 191 F.3d 60 (1st Cir. 1999), the court ruled that a defendant's incriminating statements to a cellmate were admissible when the cellmate simply reported the statements to federal authorities under a general agreement to report what he might hear from other prisoners about violations of law, but was instructed not to directly question anyone. "Where a jail mate simply agrees to report whatever he learns about crimes from other inmates in general, . . . there is not enough to trigger *Massiah*." 191 F.3d at 65-66.

▶ *United States v. Li*, 55 F.3d 325 (7th Cir. 1995), found no Sixth Amendment violation when an accomplice deliberately elicited information from the defendant without any governmental direction and then later disclosed what he had learned to the police. *See also United States v. Danielson*, 325 F.3d 1054 (9th Cir. 2003).

Offense-Specific Nature of the Sixth Amendment Right to Counsel The Sixth Amendment right to counsel, unlike the right to counsel under *Miranda* flowing from the Fifth Amendment's privilege against self-incrimination, is *offense specific*. Thus, invocation of the Sixth Amendment right to counsel right bars police from deliberately eliciting incriminating information regarding only the offense at issue; it does not bar police-initiated interrogation or other activities designed to elicit an incriminating response on unrelated charges:

> **The purpose of the Sixth Amendment counsel guarantee—and hence the purpose of invoking it—is to "protec[t] the unaided layman at critical confrontations" with his "expert adversary," the government, after "the adverse positions of government and defendant have solidified" with respect to a particular alleged crime. . . . The purpose of the *Miranda– Edwards* guarantee, on the other hand—and hence the purpose of invoking it—is to protect a quite different interest: the suspect's "desire to deal with the police only through counsel," . . . . This is in one respect narrower than the interest protected by the Sixth Amendment guarantee (because it relates only to custodial interrogation) and in another respect broader (because it relates to interrogation regarding any suspected crime and attaches whether or not the "adversarial relationship" produced by a pending prosecution has yet arisen).** *McNeil v. Wisconsin*, 501 U.S. 171, 177–78 (1991).

The prohibition against deliberate attempts to elicit information in the absence of counsel is not intended to hamper police investigation of crimes other than the crime for which adversary proceedings have already commenced. The police need to investigate crimes for which formal charges have already been filed as well as new or additional crimes. Either type of investigation may require surveillance of persons already indicted. Moreover, police who are investigating a person suspected of committing one crime and formally charged with having committed another crime may seek to discover evidence of either crime. In seeking evidence relating to pending charges, however, police investigators are limited by the Sixth Amendment rights of the accused. Therefore, incriminating statements relating to pending charges will be inadmissible at the trial of those charges—even though police were also investigating other crimes—if, in obtaining the evidence, the government violated the Sixth Amendment by knowingly circumventing the accused's right to the assistance of counsel. On the other hand, evidence relating to charges to which the Sixth Amendment right to counsel had not attached at the time the evidence was obtained will not be inadmissible merely because other charges were pending at the time. *Maine v. Moulton*, 474 U.S. 159 (1985).

In *Texas v. Cobb*, 532 U.S. 162 (2001), the defendant confessed to a home burglary but denied knowledge of a woman and child's disappearance from the home. He was indicted for the burglary, and counsel was appointed to represent him on that charge. He later confessed to his father that he had killed the woman and child in the course of the burglary, and his father contacted the police. After police arrested him and administered *Miranda* warnings, he waived his *Miranda* rights and confessed to the murders. On appeal of his capital murder conviction, he argued that his confession should have been sup-

Discussion
⬆POINT

Are Conversations with Friends Who Are Police Officers "Interrogations"?

People v. McRae, 678 N.W.2d 425 (Mich. 2004).

Defendant McRae was charged with first-degree murder after the remains of fifteen-year-old Randy Laufer were found on the grounds of defendant's previous residence. After McRae was arrested, he was Mirandized and invoked both his Fifth Amendment right to be free from compelled self-incrimination and his Sixth Amendment right to counsel. After arraignment, while McRae was in custody awaiting trial, he requested to speak to an old neighbor, Dean Heintzelman. It had been ten years since McRae had seen Heintzelman. He was, therefore, completely unaware that Heintzelman had become a reserve police officer and, moreover, that both Heintzelman and his son were part of the police team present at the scene when Randy Laufer's body was recovered.

Heintzelman visited McRae one night after 11:00 P.M. while he was dressed in full uniform, including his badge. When he arrived at McRae's cell, the two talked about many topics. Eventually, Heintzelman asked McRae some questions concerning the murder charge he was facing, including a direct question if he had committed the murder, to which McRae did not respond. Heintzelman then informed McRae that the police believed McRae's son, who was being held as an accessory to the murder, was also involved in the murder. McRae responded: "Well, if they try to pin it on [my son], I'll let 'em fry my ass." This response prompted Heintzelman to ask McRae again: "Did you do it?" In response, McRae hung his head down and said, "Dean, it was bad. It was bad."

Heintzelman testified against McRae at his murder trial because the trial court denied McRae's motion to suppress Heintzelman's testimony. The court ruled that that even though Heintzelman had not reissued *Miranda* warnings to McRae, there was no violation of the Sixth Amendment because McRae had initiated the conversation. After a series of appeals, the Supreme Court of Michigan overturned McRae's conviction, relying, in part, on *Fellers v. United States*, 540 U.S. 519 (2004). Key to the court's decision was the fact that Heintzelman was acting in his position as a state actor, not as McRae's friend. Do you agree with the court's finding that Heintzelman was a state actor during his discussion with McRae? Why or why not?

Assuming, for the sake of argument, that the court's conclusion that Heintzelman was acting as a state actor is correct, do you think that McRae's having asked to speak to Heintzelman, and then his willingness to do so even though Heintzelman was clearly a police officer, constitutes a waiver of his right to counsel under *Edwards v. Arizona* and *Michigan v. Jackson*? Explain your reasoning, paying particular attention to *Fellers*.

pressed because it was obtained in violation of his Sixth Amendment right to counsel. He claimed that the right attached when counsel was appointed in the burglary case, which was "factually related" to the capital murder charge. The

Court rejected the claim and held that, because burglary and capital murder are not the *same offense* under Texas law, and because the Sixth Amendment right to counsel is "offense specific," the failure to obtain the defendant's counsel's permission did not bar the police from interrogating him regarding the murders. His confession was therefore admissible.

Waiver of Sixth Amendment Right to Counsel

As with the Fifth Amendment right to counsel under *Miranda*, a defendant may waive his or her right to counsel under the Sixth Amendment. Also, as it is with the Fifth Amendment, there is a strong presumption against implied waivers of counsel in the Sixth Amendment context, given the essential function that defense counsel plays in the administration of justice.

> [It is] incumbent upon the State to prove "an intentional relinquishment or abandonment of a known right or privilege." That standard has been reiterated in many cases. We have said that the right to counsel does not depend upon a request by the defendant, . . . and that courts indulge in every reasonable presumption against waiver. This strict standard applies equally to an alleged waiver of the right to counsel whether at trial or at a critical stage of pretrial proceedings. *Brewer v. Williams*, 430 U.S. 387, 404 (1977) (internal citations omitted).

Thus, to show that a valid waiver of counsel for Sixth Amendment purposes exists, the prosecution must prove that: (1) the defendant was aware of the right to counsel; and (2) the defendant knowingly, intelligently, and voluntarily relinquished the right. This is qualitatively no different from waivers in the Fifth Amendment context under *Miranda*.

> While our cases have recognized a "difference" between the Fifth Amendment and Sixth Amendment rights to counsel, and the "policies" behind these constitutional guarantees, we have never suggested that one right is "superior" or "greater" than the other, nor is there any support in our cases for the notion that because a Sixth Amendment right may be involved, it is more difficult to waive than the Fifth Amendment counterpart. *Patterson v. Illinois*, 487 U.S. 285, 297–98 (1988).

Miranda Warnings Sufficient to Provide Knowledge of Right to Counsel

Miranda warnings were created by the Supreme Court to safeguard the Fifth Amendment privilege against self-incrimination. In spite of this, *Patterson v. Illinois*, 487 U.S. 285 (1988), held that the *Miranda* warnings are also sufficient to inform a defendant of the right to have counsel present during questioning once the Sixth Amendment right to counsel has attached, as well as the consequences of a decision to waive the Sixth Amendment right during such questioning:

> [W]hatever warnings suffice for *Miranda*'s purposes will also be sufficient in the context of post-indictment questioning. The State's decision to take an additional step and commence formal adversarial proceedings against the accused does not substantially increase the value of counsel to the accused at questioning, or expand the limited purpose that an attorney serves when the accused is questioned by authorities. With respect to this inquiry, we do not discern a substantial difference between the usefulness of a lawyer to a suspect during custodial interrogation, and his value to an accused at post-indictment questioning. 487 U.S. at 298–99.

Waiver after Miranda Warnings Once a defendant suspect has been informed of his right to counsel under the Sixth Amendment by having been "admonished with the warnings prescribed by [the Supreme] Court in *Miranda*" and has been sufficiently apprised of the nature and consequences of abandoning his or her Sixth Amendment rights, the defendant's "waiver on this basis will be considered a knowing and intelligent one." *Patterson*, 487 U.S. at 296.

> Once it is determined that a suspect's decision not to rely on his rights was uncoerced, that he at all times knew he could stand mute and request a lawyer, and that he was aware of the State's intention to use his statements to secure a conviction, the analysis is complete and the waiver is valid as a matter of law." **487 U.S. at 296 (quoting** *Moran v. Burbine*, 475 U.S. at 422–23).

Subsequent Waiver after Initial Invocation of the Sixth Amendment Rights Recall that under *Edwards v. Arizona*, 451 U.S. 477 (1981), after a knowing and voluntary waiver of *Miranda* rights, law enforcement officers may continue questioning until and unless the suspect clearly requests an attorney. Ambiguous or equivocal references to an attorney are insufficient to invoke a suspect's right to counsel: Although a suspect need not "'speak with the discrimination of an Oxford don,' . . . he must articulate his desire to have counsel present sufficiently clearly that a reasonable police officer in the circumstances would understand the statement to be a request for an attorney. If the statement fails to meet the requisite level of clarity, *Edwards* does not require that the officers stop questioning the suspect." *Davis v. United States*, 512 U.S. 452, 459 (1994).

Following the rule in *Edwards* for Fifth Amendment purposes, the Supreme Court has held that once a defendant has clearly and unambiguously invoked his or her right to counsel under the Sixth Amendment at or after the initiation of adversary judicial proceedings, any further interrogation of the defendant without counsel actually being present is not permitted if the police initiate the discussion. *Patterson v. Illinois*, 487 U.S. 285 (1988). If police violate this principle by initiating **"interrogation after a defendant's assertion, at an arraignment or similar proceeding, of his right to counsel, any waiver of the defendant's right to counsel for that police-initiated interrogation is invalid."** *Michigan v. Jackson*, 475 U.S. 625, 636 (1986).

In *Michigan v. Jackson*, several defendants requested counsel at their arraignments on murder charges. Before counsel had been provided to them, police officers questioned the defendants after advising them of their *Miranda* rights. The defendants waived their *Miranda* rights and agreed to talk with police who, in turn, were able to obtain confessions from the defendants. The Supreme Court held that the confessions were obtained in violation of the Sixth Amendment right to counsel because police initiated contact with the defendants after they had invoked their right to counsel and, in so doing, sought a waiver of that right before counsel had actually been provided to the defendants. 475 U.S. at 635.

If, however, a defendant re-initiates contact with police after requesting that counsel be provided under the Sixth Amendment (i.e., after formal criminal proceedings have been commenced against the suspect), and the defendant is re-advised of his or her *Miranda* rights and then knowingly and voluntarily waives them, following the parallel *Edwards* rule for the Fifth Amendment, such a waiver of the Sixth Amendment right to counsel will likely be upheld as valid. *See Michigan v. Jackson*, 475 U.S. at 635.

Remedies for Violations of the Sixth Amendment Right to Counsel Violations of the Sixth Amendment right to counsel in the interrogation context are treated in much the same way *Miranda* violations are treated. Thus, any incriminating statements made by a defendant that are obtained in violation of the Sixth Amendment are inadmissible at trial in the prosecution's case-in-chief. *Michigan v. Harvey*, 494 U.S. 344 (1990). However, such statements are admissible for impeachment purposes if they were obtained voluntarily (i.e., to show inconsistencies in a defendant's statements). 494 U.S. at 350–51; *see also McGriff v. Dept. of Corr.*, 338 F.3d 1231 (11th Cir. 2003). Such statements may also be used if an exception to the exclusionary rule applies (see Chapter 3).

Subsequent Waiver after Initial Violation of the Sixth Amendment Recall that, under *Oregon v Elstad*, 470 U.S. 298 (1985), if a suspect being subjected to custodial interrogation makes incriminating statements without having been given his or her *Miranda* rights, subsequent reiterations of those incriminating statements after having been properly Mirandized can purge the taint of the initial constitutional violation so long as the initial statements were knowingly and voluntarily given. Thus, *Elstad* held that the "fruit of the poisonous tree" doctrine applies only if the initial *Miranda* violation was accompanied by deliberately coercive or improper tactics in obtaining the initial statement. While the Supreme Court has not yet ruled on whether the *Elstad* would similarly disallow the fruit of the poisonous tree doctrine to Sixth Amendment violations, at least one U.S. Circuit Court of Appeals has extended *Elstad* to the Sixth Amendment realm.

In *Fellers v. United States*, 540 U.S. 519 (2004), the Supreme Court determined that post-indictment statements made by a defendant in response to police statements while being arrested on methamphetamine charges violated the defendant's Sixth Amendment right to counsel. There was no indication, however, that the defendant's statements were anything other than purely voluntary. The Court ended its decision in *Fellers* by remanding the case for consideration of the question of whether the Sixth Amendment required suppression of Feller's "jailhouse statements on the ground that they were the fruits of previous questioning conducted in violation of the Sixth Amendment deliberate-elicitation standard." On remand, the Eighth Circuit answered that question in the negative.

> In contrast with the statements made at Fellers's home, Fellers's jailhouse statements were given after a proper administration of *Miranda* warnings and a proper oral and written waiver of his *Miranda* rights. The *Miranda* warnings fully informed Fellers of "the sum and substance" of his Sixth Amendment rights, and his waiver of his *Miranda* rights operated as a knowing, intelligent, and voluntary waiver of his right to counsel [under *Patterson*, 487 U.S. at 293-94]. He was thus given all of the information he needed to decide whether to invoke his Sixth Amendment rights. Furthermore, no evidence indicates that either Fellers's initial statements or his subsequent jailhouse statements were coerced, compelled, or otherwise involuntary. As a result, the condition that made his prior statements inadmissible—the inability to have counsel present or to waive the right to counsel—was removed. *United States v. Fellers*, 397 F.3d 1090 (8th Cir.) (citing *Elstad*, 470 U.S. at 314), *cert denied*, 426 S. Ct. 415 (2005).

key points

- The Sixth Amendment, the right to counsel, is triggered ("attaches") when formal criminal proceedings have begun. As a result, a person is entitled to the help of a lawyer at or after the time that judicial proceedings have been initiated against him, whether by way of formal charge, preliminary hearing, indictment, information, or arraignment.

- Once the Sixth Amendment right to counsel has attached, providing a defendant with *Miranda* warnings, coupled with informing the person that she has been formally charged with a crime, is sufficient to provide adequate notice to the person of his or her Sixth Amendment rights.

- Once a suspect has invoked the right to counsel at an arraignment or similar proceeding, police may not interrogate the defendant further without counsel present unless the defendant initiates further communication with the police. If the defendant initiates further communication, interrogation may proceed if the defendant makes a voluntary, know-

ing, and intelligent waiver of the right to counsel and the right to silence.

- After a person has been formally charged (indicted, arraigned, etc.) and has requested counsel, law enforcement authorities may not deliberately elicit incriminating statements from the person either directly or by surreptitious methods concerning the crimes for which the defendant has been charged. The Sixth Amendment, however, does not bar police-initiated interrogation or other activities designed to elicit an incriminating response on unrelated crimes for which the defendant has not been charged or has not invoked the right to counsel.

- Any incriminating statements made by a defendant that are obtained in violation of the Sixth Amendment are inadmissible at trial in the prosecution's case-in-chief, but such statements are admissible for impeachment purposes if they were obtained voluntarily.

Summary

An admission or confession obtained by a law enforcement officer is inadmissible in court unless (1) it is voluntary, and (2) the requirements of *Miranda v. Arizona* are satisfied. A statement is involuntary if it is a product of police coercion, whether by force or by subtler forms of coercion, and if, in the totality of the circumstances, the statement is not the result of a person's free and rational choice. In determining voluntariness, courts consider the personal characteristics of the defendant, such as age, mental capacity, physical or mental impairment, and experience with the police, in establishing the setting in which coercion might operate to overcome the defendant's will.

Miranda held that a statement obtained by police during a custodial interrogation of a defendant is inadmissible unless the police used certain procedural safeguards to secure the defendant's privilege against self-incrimination. Those procedural safeguards are (1) giving warnings of rights and (2) obtaining a valid waiver of those rights, before an interrogation is begun. Therefore, the major issues of *Miranda* fall into four categories: custody, interrogation, warnings, and waiver.

A person is in custody if there is a formal arrest or restraint on freedom of movement of the degree associated with a formal arrest. Custody is determined by

examining, from a reasonable person's point of view, the totality of facts and circumstances surrounding an encounter between a person and law enforcement authorities. These include the place; the time; the presence of family, friends, or other persons; physical restraint; and coercion or domination by the police.

Interrogation refers not only to express questioning but also to any words or actions on the part of police that the police should know are reasonably likely to elicit an incriminating response. Nevertheless, clarifying questions, spontaneous questions, and routine questions are not considered to be interrogation for *Miranda* purposes. In addition, volunteered statements are not the product of interrogation and are not subject to the *Miranda* requirements. Multiple attempts at interrogation are permitted after a defendant's invocation of the right to silence; but the defendant's right to cut off questioning must be scrupulously honored, fresh warnings must be given, and no coercion or other pressures may be employed. If the defendant has exercised the right to counsel, further interrogation without counsel may be conducted only upon the initiation of the defendant and the waiver of *Miranda* rights. After a defendant has been formally charged and has requested counsel, law enforcement authorities are prohibited under the Sixth Amendment from using any methods, however surreptitious or indirect, to elicit incriminating evidence from the defendant in the absence of counsel.

Before persons in custody may be interrogated, they must be given the familiar *Miranda* warnings:

▶ You have the right to remain silent.

▶ Anything you say can and will be used against you in a court of law.

▶ You have the right to consult with a lawyer and to have the lawyer present with you while you are being questioned.

If you cannot afford to hire a lawyer, a lawyer will be appointed to represent you before any questioning, if you wish.

These warnings must be recited clearly and unhurriedly in a language understood by the suspect. Spe-

cial care must be taken to carefully explain the meaning of the warnings to immature, illiterate, or mentally impaired persons. *Miranda* requirements apply regardless of the nature or severity of the offense being investigated. *Miranda* does not apply to civil proceedings, such as customs procedures, civil commitments, extradition proceedings, and license revocation proceedings.

A person who waives the *Miranda* rights to remain silent and to have an attorney may be questioned. To be effective, a waiver of *Miranda* rights must be voluntary and made with a full awareness of both the nature of the right being abandoned and the consequences of the decision to abandon it.

Waiver will not be inferred from mere silence but may be expressed by a great variety of words and gestures. If possible, an officer should obtain a written waiver of rights, because a written waiver provides the best evidence of a voluntary and intentional relinquishment of a known right.

Key Terms

admission, 676
competency, 721
confession, 676
custodial interrogation, 678
custody, 688
deliberate elicitation, 730
express waiver, 715

implied waiver, 715
incommunicado interrogation, 679
interrogation, 676, 688
Miranda warnings, 679
public safety, 703

reasonably likely to elicit an incriminating response, 696
selective waiver/qualified waiver, 718
state actor, 704
statement, 676

voluntariness, 677
waiver, 688, 715
warning, 688

Review and Discussion Questions

1. Would any of the following actions cause a statement of a suspect to be involuntary?

   a. Making an appeal to the suspect's moral or religious beliefs

   b. Confronting the suspect with the deceased or seriously injured victim of the crime in question

   c. Starting an argument with, challenging, or baiting the suspect

2. Does a person need a lawyer to help decide whether to waive *Miranda* rights? Is the compelling atmosphere of a custodial setting just as likely to influence a person's decision to waive rights as it is to influence the decision to confess?

3. Is a person's giving of consent to search an inculpatory or exculpatory statement? Should a person

in custody be given *Miranda* warnings before being asked for consent to search? Why must police give elaborate warnings before custodial interrogation but no warnings before obtaining consent to search?

4. Assume that a person has been formally arrested for one crime, and police want to question that person about another, unrelated crime. Are *Miranda* warnings required to be given before the questioning? If the answer is no, what additional circumstances might cause *Miranda* warnings to be required?

5. It is reasonable to assume that a person under investigation for a crime might think that complete silence in the face of an accusation might not look good to a judge or a jury. Should the *Miranda*

warnings include a statement that a person's silence may not be used against the person in any way?

6. Should suspects be told the nature and seriousness of the offense for which they are being interrogated? What if a person believes that he or she is being investigated for an accident caused by driving while intoxicated but does not know that a person in the other vehicle has died?

7. What would be the advantages and disadvantages of requiring law enforcement officers to tape-record the entire process of administration of *Miranda* warnings and the suspect's invocation or waiver of rights?

8. Is it proper for a law enforcement officer to inform a suspect who has just invoked the *Miranda* right to counsel that the case against the suspect is strong and that immediate cooperation with the authorities would be beneficial in the long run? If the suspect says, "What do you mean?" would this be considered an initiation of further communication by the suspect and a waiver of the right to counsel?

9. Considering the confusion and pressures associated with being arrested and transported to a police station, should arrested persons be advised, in addition to the *Miranda* warnings, of where they are being taken, what is going to happen to them, how long they will be held, and with whom they may communicate?

10. Would the *Massiah* rule be violated if conversations of an indicted and imprisoned person were obtained by means of a listening device installed in that person's cell?

11. In *New York v. Quarles*, the Court said, "We think police officers can and will distinguish almost instinctively between questions necessary to secure their own safety or the safety of the public and questions designed solely to elicit testimonial evidence from a suspect." Do you agree or disagree with this statement? Describe three situations in which the distinction might not be so easy for a police officer to make.

Applications of the Law in Real Cases

1. Police officers in Phoenix, Arizona, stopped the defendant after receiving a complaint from a restaurant that he had paid for his food with a counterfeit $20 bill. Before questioning the defendant, Officer Kulesa read the *Miranda* rights to him in English. The defendant, speaking in English with a Japanese accent, said that he understood his rights. Then Kulesa questioned him about his driver's license and the license plate on his car. During that conversation, the defendant told Kulesa that he was from Japan. The officers arrested the defendant when they learned that his driver's license was suspended and that the license plate on his car was stolen. During an inventory of his car (the lawfulness of which is not at issue here), the officers found $360 in counterfeit bills.

Officers took the defendant to a police precinct, where Special Agent Thurling of the Secret Service questioned him about the manufacture and use of counterfeit currency. Before that questioning began, Thurling advised him again, in English, of the *Miranda* rights. The defendant then signed a standard-form waiver of *Miranda* rights. That form, which is printed in English, said that the defendant understood his rights

and was willing to speak to the agent without having a lawyer present. Thereafter, the defendant made oral statements (in English) that he had made and used counterfeit currency, and signed a written statement (also in English) to the same effect. He also signed a form, which was printed in English, authorizing a search of his apartment.

Neither Kulesa nor Thurling informed the defendant of his right to contact the Japanese consulate, nor did they ask him whether he needed an interpreter. Both officers testified, however, that the defendant appeared to have no difficulty understanding and conversing in English. Moreover, he did not request an interpreter at any time during Kulesa's or Thurling's questioning.

After obtaining written consent, the Secret Service searched the defendant's apartment. There they found computer equipment with which he had made counterfeit bills, $13,000 in counterfeit bills, and schedules for making and passing counterfeit bills. Those schedules were written in English. The officers also discovered computer manuals and books written in English, as well as check registers in which notations had been made in English.

The defendant was indicted on two counts: manufacturing counterfeit obligations and uttering counterfeit obligations, in violation of 18 U.S.C. §§ 472 and 474. He filed a motion to suppress his written statement and the evidence found during the search of his apartment. Should his motion be granted? *See United States v. Amano*, 229 F.3d 801 (9th Cir. 2000).

2 On August 13, 1997, shortly after 5:00 A.M., an anonymous caller telephoned the Anchorage Police Department and reported that there was a dead body in Room 222 of the Mush Inn, an Anchorage motel. Anchorage Police Officers Kevin Iverson and Steven Hebbe responded to the call. When the officers arrived at the Mush Inn, the door to Room 222 was open. The officers told a security guard on the scene and Murray, the occupant of Room 222, that they were responding to the dead body report. The officers asked to enter the room to look for the dead body. Murray consented. While the officers were checking the room, they told Murray to sit down on the bed with his hands in view. Someone at the Mush Inn front desk called the room to ask Murray about payment for the room charges. Murray asked to leave to take care of his bill, but the officers told Murray he had to wait until they were finished searching. The officers found no body.

The officers questioned Murray while they were in the room, but they did not advise him of the *Miranda* warnings or tell him he was free to leave. The officers questioned Murray for twenty to thirty minutes. Murray told the officers that: (1) he was on felony probation for a prior drug offense (Officer Iverson ran a check that confirmed this); (2) he had only recently returned to the room; (3) his housemate and girlfriend, Jeannie Joy, and two other people had been in the room earlier; (4) Joy was a drug user, but he did not know whether she had drugs; (5) he had given Joy money to buy cocaine; (6) he had consumed some cocaine, and a urinalysis for cocaine would probably be positive; and (7) Joy still had the cocaine and was driving his Chevy Blazer around town. The officers asked to search the room for drugs and Murray agreed to a search of the room for that purpose.

The officers found a single-serving plastic alcohol bottle with a hole cut in it that could be used to smoke crack cocaine. The officers departed to look for Joy. They left Murray behind. The officers hoped to recover the Blazer for Murray and to search it for drugs.

Officer Hebbe spotted Murray's Blazer and stopped it at Third Avenue and Ingra Street. Joy and another person were inside the Blazer. Officer Iverson returned to the Mush Inn and told Murray that the police found his Blazer and asked Murray for his consent to search

the Blazer. Murray gave that consent. Officer Iverson relayed the consent to Officer Hebbe.

Meanwhile, Joy was talking with the police and reported (1) that there was marijuana in the Blazer; (2) that Murray had given her the marijuana to sell; (3) that Murray grew marijuana; and (4) that Murray owned a firearm and had a prior drug conviction. The officers searched the Blazer and found marijuana and a crack pipe. About this time, Murray drove to Third and Ingra in his truck and parked behind the line of vehicles. The officers questioned Murray about Joy's claims. Murray admitted that he had given marijuana to Joy to sell and that he had about a quarter of a pound of marijuana and a handgun at his home. Murray drove to his home and the officers followed. The officers asked Murray to consent to a search of his home. At first, Murray agreed, but when the officers presented him with a consent-to-search form, he asked for an attorney. Because Murray withdrew his consent, the officers obtained a search warrant for Murray's residence.

During the execution of the warrant, the police found the following items: (1) a bag containing 170.9 grams (approximately six ounces) of "bud" marijuana in a living room closet; (2) a screening tin (used to separate "bud" from "shake") and a gram scale in the kitchen; (3) marijuana residue in a bedroom drawer and in the screening tin; (4) a loaded .44 magnum handgun inside a "fur-lined case" in the bedside table drawer; and (5) a gun cleaning kit and boxes of ammunition in a bucket in the bedroom. In the handgun case, the officers later found a marijuana "bud."

The grand jury indicted Murray for the following offenses: one count of fourth-degree misconduct involving a controlled substance for possession of one ounce of marijuana with intent to deliver; another count of fourth-degree misconduct involving a controlled substance for maintaining a dwelling for keeping or distributing controlled substances; one count of second-degree misconduct involving weapons for possession of the .44 magnum handgun during the commission of a felony drug offense; one count of third-degree misconduct involving weapons for being a felon in possession of a firearm capable of being concealed on one's person; and another count of third-degree misconduct involving weapons for being a convicted felon and living in a dwelling knowing that a firearm was present in the dwelling.

Murray moved to suppress the evidence acquired in Room 222, including his statements to the police, claiming that the police violated the Fourth Amendment and did not advise him of his *Miranda* rights. He also claimed that evidence obtained after the police left the room should be suppressed as the fruit of this police illegality. Should Murray's motion to suppress be granted? *See Murray v. State*, 12 P.3d 784 (Alaska App. 2000).

3 According to the uncontradicted testimony of the detectives, the defendant was arrested shortly after witnesses claimed that he assaulted a man with a bat, pointed a gun at the witnesses, and fired several rounds in their direction. He was taken into custody at the Greeley Police Department. Because he was a juvenile at the time, the defendant's father was contacted and asked to come to the police station. (By statute in Colorado, the Fifth Amendment privilege of juveniles is further protected by requiring the presence of a parent or guardian during custodial interrogation.)

After arriving, the father was read a Spanish translation of the *Miranda* rights, and the defendant was read his *Miranda* rights in English in his father's presence. Following a private consultation with his father, the defendant told Detective Connell that he wanted to speak with a lawyer because either way, he was going to jail. Detective Connell then told the father that the defendant would in fact be going to jail and escorted the father out.

The defendant was re-handcuffed and left in the interviewing room while Detective Connell worked on the attendant bonding paperwork in his office. About ten minutes later, Connell gave the completed paperwork to Detective Schrimpf for the purpose of taking the defendant to jail. However, Schrimpf returned in a moment and notified Connell that the defendant wanted to tell his side of the story. Connell testified that he did not initially respond because the defendant's father had already left. However, after another five minutes and several more requests by the defendant, including shouting out to him by name, Connell went to the interview room. When Connell reached the doorway, the defendant asked him what charges were being filed.

The detective responded by reciting the charges, at which point the defendant began talking about the incident and continued for about thirty seconds. The defendant acknowledged that he was present at the confrontation and had a pellet gun, but he claimed that he was not shooting at anybody and was just trying to scare people. Detective Connell testified that he then tried to find the defendant's father because he wanted to pursue the defendant's statement with follow-up questions. When it was clear that the father was already gone, the defendant was taken to jail without being questioned. Should the defendant's statements be suppressed? *See People v. Rivas*, 13 P.3d 315 (Colo. 2000).

4 Reyes, a known narcotics dealer, was arrested during an undercover heroin bust. The officers had specific information that Reyes routinely carried a firearm while conducting business. Before conducting a search incident to arrest, the arresting officer—fearing the presence of a gun or sharp objects that are routinely used in the drug trade business, such as syringes or blades—asked Reyes if he had anything on him that could hurt the officer or anyone on his field team. Reyes responded that he had a gun in his pocket. The officer then asked Reyes, "Do you have anything inside your pocket that could hurt me?" Reyes, who did not speak English well, responded that there were more drugs in his car. The officer did not advise Reyes of his *Miranda* rights before asking either of these questions. Should Reyes' statements be suppressed? *See United States v. Reyes*, 2003 WL 346450 (S.D.N.Y. 2003), rev'd 353 F.3d 148 (2nd Cir. 2003).

5 At 4:00 A.M. on April 17, 1999, Officer Bradley Deaver of the Brookings Police Department was dispatched to the local emergency room. Taylor Roberts was being treated there for what appeared to be a severe beating. Roberts had cuts and abrasions on his face. His left eye was swollen shut. He had a deep wound on his forehead. According to the medical personnel, Roberts had a "blow-out fracture of the left orbit with [a] buckle fracture of the left lateral sinus wall." Deaver thought Roberts' injuries had been caused by a blunt object.

Deaver attempted an interview, but Roberts could not remember much of what occurred. He told Deaver that he had been walking through Normandy Village, a Brookings trailer court, on his way to a friend's home when a white Chevy S-10 pickup pulled up alongside him. He recognized Keith Whitehead and recalled that Whitehead stepped from the vehicle and confronted him. After that, all he could remember was being on the ground, having been beaten.

Deaver returned to the police department and discussed the case with Officer Even. Even recalled that earlier, he had seen Keith Whitehead speaking with an individual in a white "lowrider" pickup with Florida license plates. Another officer had run a license plate check on the white pickup. Deaver obtained the license plate number from the police dispatch log and ran another check on the vehicle: the white pickup truck was registered to Pedro Morato.

Officer Even told Deaver that Keith Whitehead was living at 920 Southland Lane. Deaver had a patrol officer drive by the residence to see whether the white pickup with Florida license plates was parked there. It was. Deaver and another officer drove to the apartment complex and looked through the truck window. They spotted a jack handle lying on the floor of the pickup. The two officers proceeded to Whitehead's apartment. A female answered the door. She told the officers that Keith was home and invited them in. As he walked into the apartment, Deaver saw a man sleeping in an easy chair. He asked the man who owned the pickup. The man, later identified as Morato, responded that it was his vehicle. Keith Whitehead came out of the bedroom, and the officers asked both men to accompany them outside. Morato was escorted to Deaver's patrol car while Whitehead was taken to another patrol car.

Once Deaver and Morato were seated in the car, Deaver started a tape recorder. In the initial moments of the recording, the following exchange took place:

> Deaver: Hey listen, man, I also want you to understand you don't have to talk to me if you don't want to, alright?
> Morato: Yeah, I know, I know.
> Deaver: You're free to leave, um, you're not under arrest.
> Morato: Well, I just can't even talk right now cause you know I'm probably still, you know, messed up and stuff and that's the way it is.

In addition to commenting on his intoxicated state, Morato said that he did not remember anything of an altercation the night before. Morato did not say that he wished to leave the car or that he refused to talk; instead, his comments indicated only an inability to talk at that time because he was "drunk or halfway drunk." Deaver noticed an odor of alcoholic beverage on Morato and saw that his eyes were slightly bloodshot. Morato had no difficulty walking from the apartment to the car, however. Deaver later described Morato's speech as "slightly slurred," but explained that he did not know whether this was attributable to Morato's alcohol consumption or his unfamiliar accent. Deaver exited the vehicle for a few minutes, leaving Morato alone in the car. When Deaver returned, the following conversation took place:

> Deaver: Pedro.
> Morato: Yeah.
> Deaver: Here's what's going to happen, Pedro. We're going to tow your truck. Okay? Cause we believe that you and Keith and John were involved in an assault last night, and we believe, uh, the weapon that was used to assault the subject is in that vehicle right now. So, we're going to have to tow it, secure it, so we can obtain a search warrant and go through the vehicle. Okay? You understand?
> Morato: Yeah.
> Deaver: You know why we're doing this, right?
> Morato: Yeah, I know.
> Deaver: You know what happened last night?
> Morato: Yeah, I know what happened.
> Deaver: Okay. You wanna tell me about it?

At this point, Morato explained that he used "the bar" to hit the victim because the victim took a swing at him: "I had to defend myself." After this admission Morato was told he was no longer free to leave. Deaver read Morato the *Miranda* warnings and Morato invoked his right to counsel. Deaver told Morato that he needed to remove the jack handle from the pickup, and requested Morato's permission to obtain it. Morato responded that he had the keys in his pocket and indicated which key would unlock the vehicle. Should Morato's motion to suppress his statements and the jack handle be granted? *State v. Morato*, 619 N.W.2d 655 (S.D. 2000).

14 Pretrial Visual Identification Procedures

Learning Objectives

▶ Understand the terms confrontation, showup, lineup, and photo array.

▶ Understand how perception is a selective and interpretive process that can contribute to mistakes in identification procedures that can, in turn, lead to wrongful convictions.

▶ Explain the three phases of memory.

▶ Explain both the estimator variables (including event factors and individual witness factors) that influence our ability to remember events accurately; and understand how these factors can contribute to mistakes in identification procedures that can, in turn, lead to wrongful convictions.

▶ Understand why the presence of counsel is required at a pretrial confrontation with witnesses conducted after the initiation of adversary judicial proceedings.

▶ Know when a law enforcement officer may use a one-person showup and the ways in which the inherent suggestiveness of the showup may be reduced.

▶ Know the factors that indicate accuracy or reliability of an identification even if the identification procedure was unnecessarily suggestive.

▶ Know the proper procedures for conducting a lineup and a photographic identification procedure.

You have undoubtedly heard the phrase "seeing is believing." Juries accept this adage as a truism when they consider the testimony of an eyewitness. But there are serious problems with the accuracy of pretrial confrontation techniques that lead to most eyewitness identifications.

A **confrontation** is any presentation of a suspect to a victim of or witness to a crime for the purpose of identifying the perpetrator of the crime. Pretrial confrontation of a suspected criminal with witnesses or victims has long been an accepted law enforcement technique to identify perpetrators of crime and also to clear innocent suspects. Most eyewitness identifications occur as a result of one of two pretrial confrontation techniques: showups or lineups.

A **showup** is the presentation of a single suspect to a victim of or witness to a crime for the purpose of identifying the perpetrator of the crime. A **lineup** is the presentation of several persons at one time to a victim of or witness to a crime for the purpose of identifying the perpetrator of the crime. A lineup gives the victim or witness several choices (a suspect may or may not be included). Both procedures can also be conducted using photographs. A **photographic showup** is a presentation of a single photograph of a suspect to a victim of or witness to a crime; and a **photographic lineup** (also called a **photo array**) is a presentation at one time of several photographs, including that of a suspect, to a victim of or witness to a crime.

Decades of research have demonstrated that eyewitness identifications, regardless of the technique used, are remarkably unreliable. This chapter will explore the many factors that contribute to the unreliability of eyewitness identifications and the ways in which criminal justice professionals can conduct pretrial confrontations to minimize identification errors. The discussion begins with matters related to human memory and perception in the context of pretrial identification procedures, and moves on to the legal issues related to pretrial identification procedures.

▶MISTAKEN IDENTIFICATIONS:THE ROLE OF PERCEPTION AND MEMORY

Unreliability of eyewitness identification testimony may have many causes.[1] First, of course, it is possible that an eyewitness is lying. Concerns about truthful witnesses can be traced back to the time of Moses: "Thou shalt not bear false witness against thy neighbour" (Exodus 20:16). Juries are expected to assess the veracity of all witnesses; and cross-examination is presumed to reveal when eyewitnesses have motivation to lie, just as it would with any other witness. More troubling, however, is the eyewitness who honestly believes his or her

---

[1] The section is derived from the following article: Fradella, H.F. (2006). Why Judges Should Admit Expert Testimony on the Unreliability of Eyewitness Testimony. *Federal Law Review, 2006(3)*, 1–29. Reprinted with the gracious permission of the *Federal Courts Law Review*.

testimony is the truth, but is incorrect. Even back in Ancient Greece, Plato (1938: 99) cautioned, "have sight and hearing any truth in them? Are they not, as the poets are always telling us, inaccurate witnesses?" (orig. 360 B.C.E.)

Although there is no truly accurate way to know how often mistaken identifications result in wrongful convictions, decades of research on the topic point to it as the leading cause (Huff et al, 2003; Goss, 1999; Sporer, 1966). In fact, it is so common that it practically rivals the sum of all other errors that lead to wrongful conviction (Medwed, 2006; Rattner, 1988). For example, between 75 percent and 85 percent of the convictions overturned by DNA evidence have involved a mistaken eyewitness (Scheck, Neufeld & Dwyer, 2000). This is likely due to the fact, as the Supreme Court has observed, that "despite its inherent unreliability, much eyewitness identification evidence has a powerful impact on juries . . . . All evidence points rather strikingly to the conclusion that there is almost nothing more convincing than a live human being who takes the stand, points a finger at the defendant, and says, 'That's the one!'" *Watkins v. Sowders*, 449 U.S. 341, 352 (1981). Yet, studies have repeatedly shown a roughly forty percent rate of mistaken identifications (see Vrij, 1998, for a review of studies). Figure 14.1 shows mistaken ID as the major factor leading to wrongful convictions.

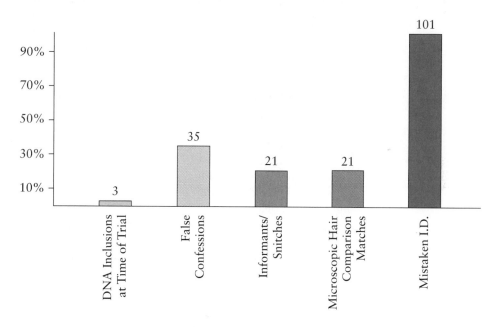

▶Figure 14.1 **FACTORS LEADING TO WRONGFUL CONVICTIONS**
Source: The Innocence Project. Available at http://www.innocenceproject.org/understand/
Figure represents data from first 130 exonerations won by the Innocence Project.

Perception

Given the many causes of misidentification, the United States Supreme Court has held that identifications that occur under questionable circumstances should not be admitted at trial. "[R]eliability is the linchpin in determining the admissibility of identification testimony. . . ." *Manson v. Brathwaite*, 432 U.S. 98, 114 (1977). The Supreme Court's demand for reliability in identification procedures is a result of its conclusion that "the vagaries of eyewitness identification are well known; the annals of criminal law are rife with instances of mistaken identification." 432 U.S. at 119 (quoting *United States v. Wade*, 388 U.S. 218, 228 [1967]). To prevent such misidentifications, the Court in *Manson v. Brathwaite* reiterated its belief in the criteria for examining the reliability of identifications set down in *Neil v. Biggers*, 409 U.S. 188 (1972). The criteria includes "the opportunity of the witness to view the criminal at the time of the crime, the witness's degree of attention, the accuracy of the witness's prior description of the criminal, the level of certainty demonstrated by the witness at the confrontation, and the length of time between the crime and the confrontation." 409 U.S. at 199–200. All of these legal factors seem straightforward; but they depend on complex psychological issues pertaining to perception and memory.

Unintentional inaccuracy of eyewitness testimony stems from the fact that memories are not exact recordings of events. First and foremost, memory is dependent on perception. We tend to think of **perception** as the recognition and interpretation of stimuli received through our basic senses—sight, hearing, touch, taste, and smell. But perception is really a complicated neurological process: "the total amalgam of sensory signals received and then processed by an individual at any one time" (Friedland, 1990: 181). This process is highly selective. It is as dependent upon psychological factors as it is on physical senses because it is an "interpretive process" (Buckhout, 1976: 76). In fact, the "actual" sensory data we perceive is "processed in light of experience, learning, preferences, biases, and expectations" (Chemay, 1985: 724).

One of the most important factors that affects our ability to perceive is the sheer volume of sensory stimulation that bombards us. "Perception is highly selective because the number of signals or amount of information impinging upon the senses is so great that the mind can process only a small fraction of the incoming data" (Friedland, 1990: 181). We focus on certain stimuli while filtering out others (Cowan, 2000). This results not only in incomplete acquisition of sensory data, but also in differential processing (i.e., interpretation) of events. Even when lighting and distance conditions are good for observation, a person experiencing **sensory overload**—"overwhelmed with too much information in too short a period of time" (Chemay, 1985, 726)—may still experience incomplete acquisition.

Another important factor that affects perception is **incomplete sensory acquisition,** and the human mind's ability to fill these gaps to make a logical story. Unfortunately, the details often fit logically, but inaccurately (Roberts, 2004).

Finally, the type of stimuli involved also affects perception. In particular, people are poor perceivers of duration (we tend to overestimate how long something takes), time (it "flies by" or "drags on"), speed, distance, height, and weight (Friedland, 1990, 181–82). It is important to keep in mind that people are not aware of their individual variations in the process of perception. How we perceive and synthesize sensory data are unconscious processes.

Memory

Memory is another unconscious process that concerns the acquisition, retention, and recall of past experience. All three component phases of the process of memory are affected by a number of physical and psychological factors that can taint the accuracy of memories. Even someone's mood can taint the accuracy of a memory (Forgas et al., 2005). Yet, juries often fail to comprehend the complexities of memory when assessing the testimony of an eyewitness, which can, in turn, lead to conviction of an innocent person.

Acquisition Phase The first phase in the development of memory is the **acquisition phase** (also called the **encoding phase**) During this phase, sensory data, as perceived by the individual, are encoded in the appropriate areas of the cerebral cortex (Haber & Haber, 2000). Accordingly, the acquisition of memories depends on perception. Perception, however, depends on a number of individualized factors, and this phase in the process of developing memories is affected by those same factors. Sensory overload is particularly important. It can lead to so many gaps in memory that **confabulation**—"the creation or substitution of false memories through later suggestion"—can occur (Chemay, 1985: 726; *see also* Mazzoni, 1999).

Perceptual variability aside, one more important factor affects memory acquisition. A person's expectations influence the way in which details about an event are encoded. An observer tends to seek out some information and avoid other information, an effect called the **confirmation bias** (Risinger, 2002)—we see what we're expecting to see.

Retention Phase The next part of the memory process is the **retention phase** (also called the **storage phase**). During this phase, the brain stores the memory until it is called upon for retrieval. Clearly, the amount of data being encoded and retained affects this phase. The greater the amount of data presented, especially in shorter periods of time, the less that will be retained. The other important factor is the retention interval—how much time passes between storage of the memory and retrieval of it. But a third, far less obvious factor than the amount of data or the retention interval has the most potentially negative effect on memory retention: the **post-event misinformation effect**. Exposure to subsequent information affects the way in which earlier memories are retained (Patterson, 2006). This means that an eyewitness exposed to post-event misinformation can accept misinformation as if it were an accurate account (Brigham et al., 1999).

> For example, a witness to a traffic accident may later read a newspaper article which stated that the driver had been drinking before the accident. "Post-event information can not only enhance existing memories but also change a witness's memory and even cause nonexistent details to become incorporated into a previously acquired memory." When witnesses later learn new information which conflicts with the original input, many will compromise between what they saw and what they were told later on (Cohen, 1996: 246–47).

Retrieval Phase Finally, during the **retrieval phase**, "the brain searches for the pertinent information, retrieves it, and communicates it" (Chemay, 1985: 725; *see also* Haber & Haber, 2000). This process occurs when eyewitnesses describe what they observed to police, when they participate in lineup or photo array identifications, and when they testify in court. Several factors affect retrieval.

Time is a very important factor in memory retrieval. As a rule, the longer the time period between acquisition, retention, and retrieval, the more difficulty we have retrieving the memory (Bartol & Bartol, 2004).

It has also been repeatedly demonstrated that retrieval of memories can be affected by **unconscious transference**. In this phenomenon, different memory images may become combined or confused with one another (Bingham, 1999; Geiselman et al., 1996). For example, this can manifest itself when an eyewitness accurately recalls an innocent bystander at the scene of a crime but incorrectly identifies him as the perpetrator (Perfect & Harris, 2003).

Estimator Variables Impacting Perception and Memory

Memory is also affected by a number of phenomena that collectively are referred to as **estimator variables**—factors over which the criminal justice system has no control. Estimator variables can be broken down into two categories: event factors and witness factors.

Event factors include time, "lighting conditions, changes in visual adaptation to light and dark, duration of the event, speed and distance involved, and the presence or absence of violence" (Cohen, 1996: 242; *see also* Haber & Haber 2000). **Witness factors** include stress, fear, physical limitation on sensory perception (e.g., poor eyesight, hearing impairment, alcohol or drug intoxication), expectations, age (the very young and very old have unique problems), and gender (Cohen, 1996: 242; *see also* Haber & Haber 2000).

Time as an Event Factor Both common sense and our own experience inform us about how time affects memory. First and foremost, the longer one has to examine something, the better the memory formation will be and the more accurate recall will be. Conversely, the less time someone has to witness an event, the less complete—and less accurate—both perception and memory will be (Memon, 2003). The rate at which events happen is a related factor. Given the limitations of human perception, when things happen very quickly, memory can be negatively affected. This is true even when an eyewitness has a reasonable period of time to observe an event: attention is focused on processing a fast-moving series of events, rather than on a particular aspect of the occurrence (Haber & Haber, 2000).

We all know that memories tend to fade over time. Research has confirmed that time delay impacts the accuracy of identification, but to a much smaller degree than might be expected. This may be due to the fact that memory does not disappear in increments, over time. Instead, it fades fairly rapidly immediately following the event—a phenomenon referred to as the **forgetting curve** (Sikstrom, 2002). After the initial fade, there is a greater likelihood of confabulation. Such filling and/or alteration of memory by post-event discussions has a much more powerful negative impact on the accuracy of recall than does the passage of time alone (Haber & Haber, 2000).

Event Significance and Violence as Event Factors Overall event significance plays an important role in the accuracy of memory recall. When people fail to perceive that a significant event is transpiring, their attention is not focused on the event. This lack of attention leads to poorer perception and memory of the event. Conversely, when people are aware that a significant event is taking place, their attention is better focused. Correspondingly, perception and memory of the event is improved (Leippe et al., 1975).

In terms of eyewitness accuracy, this often translates into high levels of inaccuracy in identifications for the perpetrator of a petty theft, and higher rates

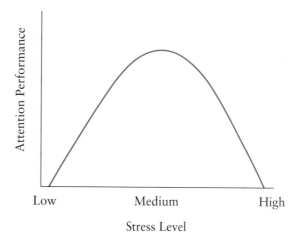

▶Figure 14.2 THE YERKES–DODSON CURVE

of accuracy for a more significant nonviolent crime (Chemay, 1985: 728). The use of the limiting phrase "nonviolent crime" here is important: the seriousness of the crime is not a determinative factor of event significance and the corresponding attention being paid to the event. The *violence* level of the crime is also important. Even when witnesses understand that they are watching a significant event, "the more violent the act, the lower will be the accuracy and completeness of perception and memory" (Chemay, 1985: 728). This is a function of the negative impact high levels of arousal and stress can produce.

Arousal and Stress as Event Factors Many people believe that stress heightens perception and memory. In fact, research suggests that perception and memory acquisition function most accurately when the subject is exposed to a moderate amount of stress (Loftus, 1986; Clifford, 1979). This is often referred to as the **Yerkes–Dodson law**. This law holds that when stress levels are too low, people do not pay sufficient attention; and when stress levels are too high, the ability to concentrate and perceive are negatively impacted (Loftus, 1986).

The Yerkes–Dodson law (see Figure 14.2) has a strong effect on people's ability to perceive and remember certain details of an event. Detail significance refers to the minutia of a crime scene, as opposed to its overall significance. When people are concerned about personal safety, they tend to focus their attention on the details that most directly affect their safety, such as "blood, masks, weapons, and aggressive actions" (Bartol & Bartol, 1994: 221). While focusing on these details, they pay less attention to the other details of the crime scene, such as characteristics of the perpetrator (e.g., facial features, hair color and style, clothing, height, weight), the crime scene, and other important details (Deffenbacher et al., 2004; Morgan et al., 2004). This phenomenon manifests itself particularly when a weapon is present. The so-called **weapons effect** describes crime situations in which a weapon is used, and witnesses spend more time and psychic energy focusing on the weapon rather than on other aspects of the event. The weapons effect results in incomplete or inaccurate information about the crime scene and the perpetrator. This effect is magnified when the use of a weapon comes as a surprise to a witness (Pickel, 1999; Steblay, 1992).

Expectancies and Stereotypes as Witness Factors "A person's expectations and stereotypes can also affect both perception and memory: what he perceives and encodes is, to a large extent, determined by cultural biases, personal prejudices, effects of training, prior information, and expectations induced by motivational states, among others" (Chemay, 1985: 72627). Whether the hunter is looking for deer, or one is searching for Bigfoot or the Loch Ness Monster, what we expect to see clearly influences what we think we have seen (Bartol & Bartol, 1994: 227). Unfortunately, stereotypes affect expectations in terms of who looks like a criminal. For example:

> [I]n one experiment a "semi-dramatic" photograph was shown to a wide variety of subjects, including whites and blacks of varying backgrounds. The photograph showed several people sitting in a subway car, with a black man standing and conversing with a white man, who was also standing, but holding a razor. Over half of the subjects reported that the black man had been holding the razor, and several described the black man as "brandishing it wildly." Effectively, expectations and stereotypes cause people to see and remember what they want or expect to see or to remember. This phenomenon should be of concern to the criminal justice system as "[t]here is evidence that some people may in fact incorporate their stereotype of 'criminal' in their identification of suspects. . . ." (Chemay, 1985: 727).

Age and Gender as Witness Factors Age is an important factor affecting witnesses' memories. Children usually fail to retain as many details as adults, but the percentage of "correct" information that children are able to recall is proportionally similar to that of adults (Bingham et al., 1999). In terms of making accurate identifications, preschoolers are much less likely than adults to make a correct identification. But after the age of five or six, children do not differ significantly from adults in their ability to make an accurate identification. (Pozzulo & Lindsay, 1998). However, children up to the age of thirteen are more likely than adults to correctly reject a target-absent lineup (i.e., a lineup that does not contain an actual suspect, but rather contains all foils) (Pozzulo & Lindsay, 1998). In contrast, elderly witnesses are much less reliable than younger ones (Yarmey, 1996). The elderly frequently believe events they imagined were actually perceived, a mistake known as a **reifying error** (Memon & Gabbert, 2003). And both children and the elderly are particularly "susceptible to the effects of suggestive questioning or post-event misinformation" (Pozzulo & Lindsay, 1998: 16).

Gender has much less significance on memory accuracy than age. Some studies suggest that women might have slightly higher accuracy rates in facial recognition; and other studies suggest that recall is consistent with gender stereotypes (Lindholm & Christianson, 1998; *cf.* Herrmann et al., 1992). For example, a woman might pay more attention to clothing, while a man might take notice of the make of a car (Loftus et al., 1987). These gender differences, however, are generally considered to have little significance on the overall accuracy of eyewitness identifications (Vrij, 1998).

Characteristics of the Offender as Witness Factors An eyewitness is much more likely to identify accurately someone of his or her own race than someone of a different race (Kleider & Goldinger, 2001; Golby et al., 2001). The same is true, although arguably to a lesser extent, for cross-ethnic identifications (Sporer, 2001). Because of **cross-racial identification bias**, people apply more lenient criteria in identifying someone of a different race or ethnicity and use more stringent requirements when identifying someone of the same racial or ethnic group (Doyle, 2001). The result of cross-racial bias is a higher rate of false positive identifications, especially when a Caucasian eyewitness identifies an African-American suspect (Doyle, 2001; Golby et al., 2001). Combinations of event factors (e.g., duration and conditions of viewing) interact with cross-racial bias to further inhibit the reliability of cross-racial identifications (MacLin, 2001). Courts have begun to take notice of this significant limitation on identification accuracy. The Supreme Court of New Jersey, for example, has mandated that juries be instructed on the risks of inaccuracies in cross-racial identifications when an "identification is a critical issue in the case, and an eyewitness's cross-racial identification is not corroborated by other evidence giving it independent reliability." *New Jersey v. Cromedy*, 727 A.2d 457, 467 (N.J. 1999).

Another variable that affects the accuracy of an eyewitnesse's identification of a suspect is the facial distinctiveness of the suspect. Suspects with faces that an eyewitness perceives as either highly attractive or highly unattractive are much more likely to be remembered accurately than faces that lack distinctiveness (Sarno & Alley, 1997). A complicating matter, however, is that some characteristics of facial distinctiveness are easily changed. For example, a suspect can disguise himself or herself during the perpetration of a crime, or change his or her appearance after it by altering hairstyle, hair color, the presence or absence of facial hair, the wearing of glasses, and so on (Vrij, 1998). These easily changed facial features are called **malleable characteristics**. While some distinctive facial features might increase subsequent recognition of a person, to be accurate, the two comparisons must use non-malleable characteristics—such as the shape of someone's nose, the distinctiveness of eyes, dimples, scars, etc. That, however, is often easier said than done.

Discussion
⬆ POINT

How Can We Reduce Mistaken Identifications?

The Innocence Project: The Case of Antonio Beaver
Source: http://www.innocenceproject.org/Content/470.php

The Innocence Project is a national organization devoted to helping wrongfully convicted prisoners prove their innocence using DNA evidence. Since it was founded in 1992, the Innocence Project has helped to exonerate more than two hundred people, including over fifteen who were on death row. According to the Innocence Project, mistaken identification is the leading cause of wrongful convictions. In fact, mistaken identification accounts for upwards of three out of every four exonerations (see Figure 14.1). The case of Antonio Beaver illustrates how the psychological phenomena described earlier in this chapter contribute to wrongful convictions based on mistaken identifications.

(Continued)

How Can We Reduce Mistaken Identifications? (*Continued*)

On August 15, 1996, a twenty-six-year-old white woman drove into a St. Louis parking lot planning to park her car and return to work. After parking, she approached a man in the lot, thinking he was the parking attendant. The man told her that she had to move her car immediately or it would be towed, and he followed her back to the car. As she got in the car to leave, the man told her she could stay. As she got back out, the man attacked her with a screwdriver and told her to give him the keys and her purse. She struggled with him and then decided to flee; she threw her purse on the seat and jumped out of the car. As she was exiting the car, she noticed that the man was bleeding and that there was blood inside the driver's side door. She ran into a nearby parking garage and called the police.

The victim described her attacker to police as a clean-shaven African-American man wearing a baseball cap. She said the man was 5'10" tall, with a "David-Letterman-like" gap between his teeth. The next day, the victim helped police draw a composite sketch of the attacker and police recovered the victim's car in East St. Louis. Latent fingerprints and swabs of the blood stain inside the driver's side door were collected.

Six days later, a detective arrested Antonio Beaver because he thought Beaver resembled the composite sketch in this case. However, Beaver had a full mustache, was 6'2" tall, and had chipped teeth.

The same detective then prepared a live lineup, including Beaver and three other men—two of them police officers. Beaver and the other non-officer were the only two to wear baseball caps, and Beaver was the only one with noticeable defects to his teeth. The victim identified Beaver.

Beaver was charged with first-degree robbery and tried in April 1997. The victim testified that Beaver was the man who attacked her; the prosecution argued that the victim's clear memory of the crime meant that she was better able to identify the perpetrator. The defense presented evidence showing that fingerprints collected from the victim's car—including prints from the driver's side and the rearview mirror—did not match the victim or Beaver. They argued that prints left on the rearview mirror indicated that the person who left them must have driven the car.

After several hours of deliberations over two days, the jury convicted Beaver of first-degree robbery. He was sentenced to eighteen years in prison. In 2001, Beaver filed a motion on his own behalf requesting DNA testing. The state opposed the motion, but the court granted a hearing on the issue in 2005. The Innocence Project accepted Beaver's case and filed another brief on his behalf in 2006. The state agreed to testing in October 2006, and the results proved that Beaver could not have committed this crime. He was exonerated on March 29, 2007. He was forty-one years old at the time of his exoneration and had served more than a decade in prison.

What factors described in the section of this chapter entitled "Mistaken Identifications: The Role of Perception and Memory" do you think contributed to the wrongful conviction of Antonio Beaver? How could the police have improved the reliability of the identification in this case?

Systemic Variables Impacting Perception and Memory

In addition to the various witness and situational factors affecting the accuracy of identifications, there are a number of factors under the control of the criminal justice system that impact the reliability of eyewitness identifications. These variables primarily concern the ways in which pretrial confrontations between suspects and victims or witnesses occur, including the conduct of law enforcement officers during the administration of a showup, lineup, or photo array. We will return to these systemic factors in more detail later in this chapter. First, however, we will review the requirements that the law imposes on justice system professionals when conducting pretrial identification procedures.

key points

- A confrontation is any presentation of a suspect to a victim of or witness to a crime for the purpose of identifying the perpetrator of the crime.
- A showup is the presentation of a single suspect to a victim of or witness to a crime for the purpose of identifying the perpetrator of the crime. A photographic showup is a presentation of a single photograph of a suspect to a victim of or witness to a crime.
- A lineup is the presentation at one time of several persons, which may or may not include a suspect, to a victim of or witness to a crime for the purpose of identifying the perpetrator of the crime. A lineup gives the victim or witness several choices. A photographic lineup (also called a photo array) is a presentation at one time of several photographs, including that of a suspect, to a victim of or witness to a crime.
- Perception is a highly selective, unconscious process that depends on both the acuity of the physi-

cal senses and a number of psychological factors—because the sensory data we perceive is processed in light of experience, learning, preferences, biases, and expectations.
- Memory is a highly selective, unconscious process that has three critical phases: acquisition/encoding, retention, and recall/retrieval. All three phases are affected by a number of physical and psychological factors that can taint the accuracy of a memory. These include time, lighting conditions, changes in visual adaptation to light and dark, duration of the event, speed and distance involved, the presence or absence of violence, stress, fear, physical limitation on sensory perception (e.g., poor eyesight, hearing impairment, alcohol or drug intoxication), expectations, age (the very young and very old have unique problems), and gender.

▶SIXTH AMENDMENT REQUIREMENTS FOR PRETRIAL IDENTIFICATIONS

Recall that the Sixth Amendment guarantees defendants the right to the effective assistance of counsel at "critical stages" in all criminal prosecutions. *Kirby v. Illinois*, 406 U.S. 682, 689 (1972). In 1967, the Supreme Court decided several important cases dealing with pretrial identifications.

The Wade–Gilbert Rule

United States v. Wade, 388 U.S. 218 (1967), and *Gilbert v. California*, 388 U.S. 263, 272 (1967), both held that a post-indictment, pretrial lineup is a "critical stage" of a criminal prosecution that triggers the right to counsel. The Court reached this conclusion in light of its determination that counsel is needed to prevent suggestive techniques that could lead to wrongful convictions. *Wade*, 388 U.S. at 228–29. The *Wade* court listed a number of such suggestive procedures that had been documented in numerous published judicial opinions:

> [T]hat all in the lineup but the suspect were known to the identifying witness, that the other participants in a lineup were grossly dissimilar in appearance to the suspect, that only the suspect was required to wear distinctive clothing which the culprit allegedly wore, that the witness is told by the police that they have caught the culprit after which the defendant is brought before the witness alone or is viewed in jail, that the suspect is pointed out before or during a lineup, and that the participants in the lineup are asked to try on an article of clothing which fits only the suspect. 388 U.S. at 233 (internal citation omitted).

To combat such suggestive practices, the Court held that *conducting a post-indictment lineup* "without notice to and in the absence of his counsel denies the accused his Sixth Amendment right to counsel and calls in question the admissibility at trial of the in-court identifications of the accused by witnesses who attended the lineup." *Gilbert*, 388 U.S. at 272. As with other critical stages of criminal prosecutions, if a suspect is unable to afford a lawyer, he or she is entitled to have one appointed by the court to assist at the confrontation (see Chapter 1).

The Rationale Underlying the Court's Decision in *Wade–Gilbert*

The Supreme Court's reasoning in *Wade* and *Gilbert* was based on (1) the inherent unreliability of eyewitness identifications and (2) the possibility of improper suggestions being made to witnesses during the confrontation procedure:

> [T]he confrontation compelled by the State between the accused and the victim or witnesses to a crime to elicit identification evidence is peculiarly riddled with innumerable dangers and variable factors which might seriously, even crucially, derogate from a fair trial. The vagaries of eyewitness identification are well-known; the annals of criminal law are rife with instances of mistaken identification. . . . The identification of strangers is proverbially untrustworthy. . . . A major factor contributing to the high incidence of miscarriage of justice from mistaken identification has been the degree of suggestion inherent in the manner in which the prosecution presents the suspect to witnesses for pretrial identification. A commentator has observed that "[t]he influence of improper suggestion upon identifying witnesses probably accounts for more miscarriages of justice than any other single factor—perhaps it is responsible for more such errors than all other factors combined." . . . Suggestion can be created intentionally or unintentionally in many subtle ways. And the dangers for the suspect are particularly grave when the witness's opportunity for observation was insubstantial, and thus his susceptibility to suggestion the greatest.
>
> Moreover, "[i]t is a matter of common experience that, once a witness has picked out the accused at the lineup, he is not likely to go back on his word later on, so that in practice the issue of identity may (in the absence of other relevant evidence) for all practical purposes be determined there and then, before the trial." 388 U.S. at 228–29.

The Court was concerned that it would be difficult to determine what happened at a lineup or other identification confrontation conducted in secret:

> [T]he defense can seldom reconstruct the manner and mode of lineup
> identification for judge or jury at trial. Those participating in a lineup
> with the accused may often be police officers; in any event, the partici-
> pants' names are rarely recorded or divulged at trial. The impediments
> to an objective observation are increased when the victim is the witness.
> Lineups are prevalent in rape and robbery prosecutions and present
> a particular hazard that a victim's understandable outrage may excite
> vengeful or spiteful motives. In any event, neither witnesses nor lineup
> participants are apt to be alert for conditions prejudicial to the suspect.
> And if they were, it would likely be of scant benefit to the suspect since
> neither witnesses nor lineup participants are likely to be schooled in the
> detection of suggestive influences. Improper influences may go unde-
> tected by a suspect, guilty or not, who experiences the emotional tension
> which we might expect in one being confronted with potential accusers.
> Even when he does observe abuse, if he has a criminal record he may be
> reluctant to take the stand and open up the admission of prior convic-
> tions. Moreover any protestations by the suspect of the fairness of the
> lineup made at trial are likely to be in vain; the jury's choice is between
> the accused's unsupported version and that of the police officers present.
> In short, the accused's inability effectively to reconstruct at trial any un-
> fairness that occurred at the lineup may deprive him of his only oppor-
> tunity meaningfully to attack the credibility of the witness's courtroom
> identification. 388 U.S. at 230–32.

The Court believed that the presence of counsel at the pretrial confrontation
with witnesses would prevent misconduct by those conducting the confrontation. In addition, counsel would have firsthand knowledge of what occurred at
the confrontation and could cross-examine witnesses later at a suppression hearing or trial and point out improprieties that might have occurred:

> Since it appears that there is grave potential for prejudice, intentional or
> not, in the pretrial lineup, which may not be capable of reconstruction at
> trial, and since presence of counsel itself can often avert prejudice and
> assure a meaningful confrontation at trial, there can be little doubt that
> for Wade the post-indictment lineup was a critical stage of the prosecu-
> tion at which he was "as much entitled to such aid [of counsel] . . . as at
> the trial itself." . . . Thus both Wade and his counsel should have been
> notified of the impending lineup, and counsel's presence should have
> been a requisite to conduct of the lineup, absent an "intelligent waiver."
> 388 U.S. at 236–37.

The Court's ruling recognizes the defendant's need for assistance at critical stages
of the prosecution, when the absence of counsel might result in an unfair trial:

> When the Bill of Rights was adopted, there were no organized police forces as
> we know them today. The accused confronted the prosecutor and the witnesses
> against him, and the evidence was marshalled, largely at the trial itself. In
> contrast, today's law enforcement machinery involves critical confrontations of
> the accused by the prosecution at pretrial proceedings where the results might
> well settle the accused's fate and reduce the trial itself to a mere formality. In
> recognition of these realities of modern criminal prosecution, our cases have
> construed the Sixth Amendment guarantee to apply to "critical" stages of the
> proceedings. The guarantee reads: "In all criminal prosecutions, the accused
> shall enjoy the right . . . to have the Assistance of Counsel for his defence." The
> plain wording of this guarantee thus encompasses counsel's assistance when-
> ever necessary to assure a meaningful "defence." 388 U.S. at 224–25.

When the *Wade–Gilbert* Right to Counsel Attaches The right to counsel guaranteed under *Wade–Gilbert* does not apply at the outset of criminal case. Rather, the right must "attach" upon a triggering event.

Applies to Live Showups and Lineups at or after Initiation of Adversarial Criminal Proceedings Although the language of *Wade* and *Gilbert* concerned post-indictment pretrial identifications, an indictment per se is not necessary to trigger the right to counsel under *Wade–Gilbert*. *Kirby v. Illinois*, 406 U.S. 682, 689 (1972), held that the right to counsel attaches to pretrial identification procedures that are conducted "at or after the initiation of adversary judicial criminal proceedings—whether by way of formal charge, preliminary hearing, indictment, information or arraignment. . . ."

> The initiation of judicial criminal proceedings is far from a mere formalism. It is the starting point of our whole system of adversary criminal justice. For it is only then that the government has committed itself to prosecute, and only then that the adverse positions of government and defendant have solidified. It is then that a defendant finds himself faced with the prosecutorial forces of organized society, and immersed in the intricacies of substantive and procedural criminal law. It is this point, therefore, that marks the commencement of the "criminal prosecutions" to which alone the explicit guarantees of the Sixth Amendment are applicable. 406 U.S. at 689–90.

Thus, for example, the *Wade–Gilbert* rule for counsel was held to have attached during a preliminary hearing in *Moore v. Illinois*, 434 U.S. 220 (1977), since that process began adversarial proceedings under the applicable Illinois statute.

In contrast, there is no Sixth Amendment right to counsel at any pretrial confrontation *before* adversary judicial criminal proceedings begin. So, when someone is merely a suspect and has not been formally charged with any crime, *Wade–Gilbert* does not apply—and, therefore, suspects need not be advised of any right to counsel at pretrial identification. However, because state laws differ regarding what process begins formal adversarial judicial proceedings, law enforcement officers conducting pretrial identification procedures must determine at what point in the criminal justice process the right to counsel attaches in their jurisdiction. For example, police filing a complaint that seeks an arrest warrant is not a critical state of criminal proceeding that triggers the right to counsel under *Kirby*. *Anderson v. Alameida*, 397 F.3d 1175, 1180 (9th Cir. 2005). As in the federal system, the law of many states reflects the notion that when police make an arrest pursuant to an arrest warrant issued upon the filing of a complaint, they need not advise suspects of their right to counsel because arrest has never been held by the U.S. Supreme Court to qualify as a "critical stage" giving rise to any Sixth Amendment right to counsel. *See United States v. Gouveia*, 467 U.S. 180, 190 (1984); *Beck v. Bowersox*, 362 F.3d 1095, 1101–2 (8th Cir. 2004); *State v. Pierre*, 890 A.2d 474 (Conn. 2006). Some states, however, do consider the issuance of an arrest warrant as instituting formal adversarial judicial proceedings. *E.g., Cannaday v. State*, 455 So.2d 713 (Miss. 1984), *cert. denied*, 469 U.S. 122 (1985); *People v. Bustamante*, 634 P.2d 927 (Cal. 1981); *People v. Jackson*, 217 N.W.2d 22 (Mich. 1974); *Commonwealth v. Richman*, 320 A.2d 351 (Pa. 1974); *People v. Blake*, 320 N.E.2d 625 (N.Y. 1974).

Does Not Apply for Preparatory Steps *Wade* stated that there is no right to counsel at preparatory steps in the gathering of the prosecution's evidence, such as "systematized or scientific analyzing of the accused's fingerprints, blood sample, clothing, hair, and the like":

> We think there are differences which preclude such stages being character- ized as critical stages at which the accused has the right to the presence of his counsel. Knowledge of the techniques of science and technology is sufficiently available, and the variables in techniques few enough, that the accused has the opportunity for a meaningful confrontation of the Government's case at trial through the ordinary processes of cross-examination of the Government's expert witnesses and the presentation of the evidence of his own experts. The denial of a right to have his counsel present at such analyses does not there- fore violate the Sixth Amendment; they are not critical stages since there is minimal risk that his counsel's absence at such stages might derogate from his right to a fair trial. 388 U.S. at 227–28.

Does Not Apply to Photo Arrays In *United States v. Ash*, 413 U.S. 300 (1973), the Court held that there is no right under the Sixth Amendment to have counsel present to observe a photographic array, even after indictment. The Court reasoned that "since the accused is not present at the time of the photographic array, there is no possibility that he might be misled by his lack of familiarity with the law or over- powered by his professional adversary." 413 U.S. at 317. The same logic applies to the showing of videotaped lineups, *State v. Jones*, 849 So.2d 438 (Fla. Ct. App. 2003); *United States v. Amrine*, 724 F.2d 84 (8th Cir. 1983), and the playing of tape-recorded voice arrays. *United States v. Dupree*, 553 F.2d 1189 (8th Cir. 1977).

Substitute Counsel

If a suspect requests the advice and presence of his or her own lawyer and that lawyer is not immediately available, a substitute lawyer may be called for the purpose of the confrontation. *Zamora v. Guam*, 394 F.2d 815 (9th Cir. 1968). *United States v. Wade* said:

> **Although the right to counsel usually means a right to the suspect's own counsel, provision for substitute counsel may be justified on the ground that the substitute counsel's presence may eliminate the hazards which render the lineup a critical stage for the presence of the suspect's own counsel.** 388 U.S. at 237 n.9.

Waiver of the *Wade–Gilbert* Right to Counsel

Post-indictment pretrial identifications that are conducted in violation of the *Wade–Gilbert* mandates pertaining to counsel are inadmissible unless a valid waiver of Sixth Amendment rights was obtained before the confrontation. *Gil- bert*, 388 U.S. at 272; *Moore v. Illinois*, 434 U.S. 220, 231 (1977). As with most other waivers of constitutional rights, waivers of the right to the presence of counsel at pretrial identification procedures must be knowing, intelligent, and voluntary. Whether this standard is met is determined under the totality of the circumstances of each case "including the background, experience, and con- duct of the accused." *Johnson v. Zerbst*, 304 U.S. 458, 464 (1938). This standard is identical to the one used to determine the validity of waivers of the Sixth Amendment right to the presence of counsel at interrogations (see Chapter 13). However, given the rights involved, a form with the warning contained in Figure 14.3 is suggested for the purpose of obtaining a waiver of the **Wade–Gilbert right to counsel** at confrontations since providing *Miranda* warnings in their

---

Pretrial Identification Warning and Waiver

Name: _____ Address: _____

Age: _____ Place: _____

Date: _____ Time: _____

Warning

Before appearing at any confrontation with any witnesses being conducted by (Name of Police Department) in relation to (Description of Offense), you are entitled to be informed of your legal rights.

The results of the confrontation can and will be used against you in court.

You have the right to the presence and advice of an attorney of your choice at any such confrontation.

If you cannot afford an attorney and you want one, an attorney will be appointed for you at no expense, before any confrontation is held.

Waiver

I have been advised of my right to the advice of an attorney and to have an attorney present at any confrontation with witnesses, and that if I cannot afford an attorney, one will be appointed for me before any such confrontation occurs. I understand these rights.

I do not want an attorney and I understand and know what I am doing.

No promises have been made to me and no pressures of any kind have been used against me.

_____
Signature of Suspect

Certification

I, (Name of Officer), hereby certify that I read the above warning to (Name of Suspect) on (Date), that this person indicated an understanding of the rights, and that this person signed the WAIVER form in my presence.

_____
Signature of Officer

_____
Witness

▶**Figure 14.3** **PRETRIAL IDENTIFICATION WARNING AND WAIVER** standard form would not adequately advise defendants of their rights at pretrial identification procedures.

The information contained in the form shown in Figure 14.3 should be more than sufficient to establish a valid waiver. *Dallio v. Spitzer*, 343 F.3d 553, 555 (2d Cir. 2003), for example, upheld a waiver of Sixth Amendment rights under *Wade–Gilbert* even though the warning provided to the suspect did not explicitly warn him of the dangers and disadvantages of consenting to participation in a lineup. All that is necessary is that the defendant be warned that the results of the confrontation can and will be used against the defendant in court; that the defendant has the right to the presence and assistance of counsel at the confrontation; and that if the defendant cannot afford an attorney to be present at the confrontation, one will be provided at no cost before any confrontation is conducted. *See United States v. Sublet*, 644 F.2d 737 (8th Cir. 1981) (upholding knowing and intelligent waiver of the right to counsel even though the defendant refused to sign the waiver form because the defendant consented to being placed in the lineup after its purpose was explained). Of course, while having the suspect sign an explicit waiver is the best evidence of the validity of a waiver, the form need not be signed. *Paulino v. Castro*, 371 F.3d 1083 (9th Cir. 2004), for example, upheld a waiver even though the defendant refused to sign a waiver. The defendant had been informed of his rights and never unambiguously requested counsel. Yet, because he agreed to participate in the lineup after having been informed of his rights, his refusal to sign the waiver form was irrelevant to his having knowingly, intelligently, and voluntarily waived his rights under *Wade–Gilbert*.

key points

- A suspect's right to counsel at a pretrial confrontation with witnesses attaches at or after the initiation of adversary judicial criminal proceedings—whether by way of formal charge, preliminary hearing, indictment, information, or arraignment. Before such a lineup is conducted, police must inform the accused of the right to counsel at the lineup, the right to have counsel appointed if the suspect cannot afford one, and the fact that the results of the confrontation can and will be used against the suspect in court.
- There is no right to counsel at preparatory steps in the gathering of the prosecution's evidence, such as "systematized or scientific analyzing of the ac-

cused's fingerprints, blood sample, clothing, hair, and the like."
- There is no right to have counsel present for the administration of a photographic identification procedure, whether that procedure is held before or after the initiation of adversary judicial criminal proceedings, because photo arrays are not a "critical stage" of a criminal prosecution in which an accused might be misled or overpowered by his professional adversary.
- In the absence of a knowing, intelligent, and voluntary waiver of the right to counsel, counsel must be present at the lineup.

▶DUE PROCESS AND PRETRIAL IDENTIFICATIONS

The Due Process Clause of the Fifth and Fourteenth Amendments guarantees all suspects the right to have all identification procedures conducted in a fair and impartial manner. *Kirby*, 406 U.S. at 690. These due process rights during confrontations apply regardless of whether the pretrial procedures occur before or after the attachment of the Sixth Amendment right to counsel under *Wade–Gilbert*.

The *Stovall v. Denno* Rule

Even before *Kirby* was decided, the Supreme Court held in *Stovall v. Denno*, 388 U.S. 293 (1967), that due process forbids any pretrial identification procedure that is unnecessarily suggestive and conducive to irreparable mistaken identification.

> As the Court pointed out in *Wade* itself, it is always necessary to "scrutinize any pretrial confrontation. . . ." 388 U.S. 227. The Due Process Clause of the Fifth and Fourteenth Amendments forbids a lineup that is unnecessarily suggestive and conducive to irreparable mistaken identification. *Stovall v. Denno*, 388 U.S. 293 (1967). When a person has not been formally charged with a criminal offense, *Stovall* strikes the appropriate constitutional balance between the right of a suspect to be protected from prejudicial procedures and the interest of society in the prompt and purposeful investigation of an unsolved crime. *Kirby*, 406 U.S. at 690–91.

Whether a confrontation violates due process because it is unnecessarily suggestive is evaluated by courts under the totality of the circumstances surrounding the pretrial identification. *Stovall*, 388 U.S. at 302.

Showups under *Stovall* Showups are highly suggestive and, accordingly, produce high levels of false identifications (Yarmey, 1998). Moreover, showups have a biasing effect on any subsequent identification at a lineup or in court (Behrman & Vayder, 1994). Showups should, therefore, not be used unless there is some extenuating circumstance that prevents a photo array or lineup from being used. In fact, some courts have ruled that showups that occur without some showing as to the necessity of having conducted the showup will be inadmissible. *E.g.*, *State v. Dubose*, 699 N.W.2d 582 (Wis. 2005); *State v. Ramirez*, 817 P.2d 774 (Utah 1991). The impending death or blindness of an eyewitness, for example, is an emergency situation that would justify a showup. Another exigent circumstance is when police lack probable cause to arrest someone, but have temporarily detained a suspect who matches a general eyewitness description under *Terry v. Ohio*. A showup under such a situation would allow police to conduct an identification procedure rather than simply releasing a potentially guilty perpetrator.

When a showup does occur, either because it is unplanned (i.e., not prearranged) or due to some exigent circumstance, law enforcement officers must exercise great care to ensure that the identification procedures are not unnecessarily suggestive and conducive to irreparable mistaken identification. When officers do so, the following types of showups have been held to be admissible.

Spontaneous Showups Unarranged, spontaneous showups are not considered impermissibly suggestive. For example, in *United States v. Boykins*, 966 F.2d 1240 (8th Cir. 1992), an unaccompanied witness, while walking toward the courtroom on the day of trial, recognized the defendant as one of the armed intruders who had previously broken into her home. She told the prosecuting attorney, who accompanied her down the hall to confirm the identification. She later identified the defendant in court. The court allowed the in-court identification, finding that the witness recognized the defendant without any suggestion from the government. "While a lineup is certainly the preferred method of identification, a witness who spontaneously recognized a defendant should be allowed to testify to that fact." 966 F.2d at 1243.

Cruising Crime Area Showups resulting from a crime victim or witness cruising the area of the crime in a police car also rarely present problems of suggestiveness. Cruising the area is an accepted investigative technique when police have no suspect for a crime that has just occurred. Witness memories are still fresh, and perpetrators are still likely to be in the area with their clothes or appearance unaltered. Of course, police should not coach witnesses by suggesting that certain persons look suspicious or have bad reputations.

Certain Arranged, "On-the-Scene" Showups A more common type of showup is the arranged on-the-scene showup, in which a suspect is arrested or apprehended at or near the scene of a crime and is immediately brought before victims or witnesses by a law enforcement officer for identification purposes. If adversary judicial criminal proceedings have not been initiated, the suspect has no right to counsel at this type of confrontation. But does an on-the-scene showup satisfy the *Stovall* requirements regarding suggestiveness? Although courts differ, the prevailing view is that practical considerations may justify a prompt on-the-scene showup under the *Stovall* test. In *Russell v. United States*, 408 F.2d 1280 (D.C. Cir. 1969), the court said that the delay required to assemble a lineup "may not only cause the detention of an innocent suspect; it may also diminish the reliability of any identification obtained." 480 F.2d at 1284. The court also suggested that only "fresh" on-the-scene identifications that occur within minutes of the witnessed crime would satisfy the *Stovall* standard. In *Johnson v. Dugger*, 817 F.2d 726 (11th Cir. 1987), the court said:

> Although show-ups are widely condemned . . . immediate confrontations allow identification before the suspect has altered his appearance and while the witness's memory is fresh, and permit the quick release of innocent persons. . . . Therefore, showups are not unnecessarily suggestive unless the police aggravate the suggestiveness of the confrontation. 817 F.2d at 729.

In *Bates v. United States*, 405 F.2d 1104 (D.C. Cir. 1968), the court said:

> There is no prohibition against a viewing of a suspect alone in what is called a "one-man showup" when this occurs near the time of the alleged criminal act; such a course does not tend to bring about misidentification but rather in some circumstances to insure accuracy. The rationale underlying this is in some respects not unlike that which the law relies on to make an exception to the hearsay rule, allowing spontaneous utterances a standing which they would not be given if uttered at a later point in time. An early identification is not error. Of course, proof of infirmities and subjective factors, such as hysteria of a witness, can be explored on cross-examination and in argument. Prudent police work would confine these on-the-spot identifications to situations in which possible doubts as to identification needed to be resolved promptly; absent such need the conventional lineup viewing is the appropriate procedure. 405 F.2d at 1106.

The following fact statement from *United States v. Watson*, 76 F.3d 4, 6 (1st Cir. 1996), illustrates an on-the-scene showup that was not found unnecessarily suggestive:

> As Alexander Milette was bicycling home to the Cathedral Project, a Porsche drove past him and stopped in front of his house. Trevor Watson got out of the car, carrying a loaded pistol of the type favored by the Boston police, a Glock 9mm semi-automatic. After accusing Milette of liking "hitting on" women, Watson aimed the gun at Milette's stomach. Someone said "Don't shoot him." Instead, Watson pistol-whipped Milette's head, causing the gun to fire into a building and then to jam. Milette, bleeding, ran while Watson unjammed the gun and fired again, hitting the building Milette ran behind. Milette sought sanctuary at a friend's house and was helped with his bleeding head.
>
> Watson had jumped back into the Porsche, only to have it stall out in a deep puddle. A nearby off-duty Boston Police officer, Officer Christopher Shoulla, heard the shots, drove to the project, and put out a call on his police radio. Officer Shoulla saw Watson and asked him to stop. Watson instead fled, clutching his right pocket, and, ironically, ran right past Milette and past another youth.
>
> Two other Boston officers arrived and gave chase. Watson threw the gun, as he ran, into a small garden. Officer Shoulla stopped Watson at gunpoint. When the officers patted down Watson and determined he had no gun, they retraced Watson's steps and found it within forty seconds.
>
> One officer saw Milette, still holding a bloody towel to his head, and had the others bring Watson over. Watson was brought over by patrol car and Milette was asked by the police, "What's the story?" Milette looked, and identified Watson as his assailant. He later testified he was 100% sure of that identification. Watson was also identified by the other youth past whom he had run.

Law enforcement officers should use on-the-scene showups only when a suspect can be shown to a witness minutes after the crime has occurred. Furthermore, officers should not add in any way to the already inherent suggestiveness of the on-the-scene identification. For example, the officer should not say or do anything to lead the witness to believe that the suspect is believed to be the perpetrator or that the suspect has been formally arrested, has confessed, or has been found in possession of incriminating items. If there is a significant delay between the commission of the crime and the confrontation, officers should take the suspect to the station and conduct a lineup.

Photographic Evidence from a Crime Scene Photographs of suspects in the act of committing the crime (such as bank robbery surveillance photographs) do not present any problems of suggestiveness and mistaken identification. Presenting such photographs to witnesses shows the actual perpetrator of the crime in the act rather than suggesting a number of possible perpetrators. The photographs refresh the witness's memory of the actual crime and thereby strengthen the reliability of a witness's subsequent in-court identification. *United States v. Browne*, 829 F.2d 760 (9th Cir. 1987).

Lineups and Photo Arrays under *Stovall* Lineups and photo arrays must be conducted in ways that are not unnecessarily suggestive or otherwise conducive to irreparable mistaken identification. Nothing should be done, therefore, that makes the suspect (or his or her photo) "stand out" from the other people used in a lineup or from the other pictures used in a photo array. Following the procedures set forth later in this chapter under the heading "Guidelines for Lineups and Photo Arrays" should not only help to ensure that the due process mandates of *Stovall* are met, but also should help increase the reliability of any identification made as a result of these confrontation procedures.

Reliability Trumps *Stovall*

If a pretrial confrontation is not unnecessarily suggestive, then the identification is admissible. If, however the confrontation is deemed to have been impermissibly suggestive, that fact alone does not necessarily mean that the identification will be inadmissible. Such an identification may still be able to be used in court if it were reliably made in spite of the suggestive nature of the confrontation. Thus, an evaluation of the reliability of an identification will become necessary if a court rules that a confrontation was tainted by impermissible suggestion. The goal of this reliability evaluation is to ensure that valuable evidence is not discarded unless using an identification would violate a defendant's due process rights.

The Reliability Factors of *Neil v. Biggers* and *Manson v. Brathwaite* In 1972, the U.S. Supreme Court decided *Neil v. Biggers*, 409 U.S. 188, which focused on whether the identification was accurate or reliable despite the suggestiveness of the identification procedure. The Court said, **"It is the likelihood of misidentification that violates a defendant's right to due process. . . . Suggestive confrontations are disapproved because they increase the likelihood of misidentification, and unnecessarily suggestive ones are condemned for the further reason that the increased chance of misidentification is gratuitous."** 409 U.S. at 198. *Biggers* involved a defendant who had been convicted of rape on evidence consisting, in part, of a victim's visual and voice identification of the defendant at a stationhouse showup seven months after the crime. At the time of the crime, the victim was in her assailant's presence for nearly a half hour, and the victim directly observed her assailant indoors and under a full moon outdoors. The victim testified at trial that she had no doubt that the defendant was her assailant. Immediately after the crime, she gave the police a thorough description of the assailant that matched the description of the defendant. The victim had also made no identification of others presented at previous showups or lineups or through photographs.

Despite its concern about the seven-month delay between the crime and the confrontation, the Supreme Court held that the central question was **"whether under 'the totality of the circumstances' the identification was reliable even though the confrontation procedure was suggestive."** 409 U.S. at 199. The Court listed the following five factors to be considered in evaluating the likelihood of misidentification:

1. Witness's opportunity to view the criminal at the time of the crime
2. Witness's degree of attention
3. Accuracy of the witness's prior description of the criminal
4. Level of certainty demonstrated by the witness at the confrontation
5. Length of time between the crime and the confrontation

Applying these factors, the Court found no substantial likelihood of misidentification and held the evidence of the identification admissible in court.

Five years after the decision in *Biggers*, the Supreme Court decided *Manson v. Brathwaite*, 432 U.S. 98, 114 (1977), in which the Court said: "**[R]eliability is the linchpin in determining the admissibility of identification testimony . . . .**" In *Manson*, the Court reiterated the five reliability factors of *Biggers* and emphasized that they should be balanced against the corrupting effect of the suggestive identification itself. In *Manson*, two days after a drug sale, an undercover drug officer viewed a single photograph of a suspect that had been left in his office by a fellow officer. After finding that the single photographic display was unnecessarily suggestive, the Court considered the five *Biggers* factors affecting reliability and found that the undercover officer made an accurate identification. The Court noted that the officer was no casual observer but a trained police officer, that he had sufficient opportunity to view the suspect for two or three minutes in natural light, that he accurately described the suspect in detail within minutes of the crime, that he positively identified the photograph in court as that of the drug seller, and that he made the photographic identification only two days after the crime.

Then the Court analyzed the corrupting effect of the suggestive identification and weighed it against the factors indicating reliability:

> These indicators of Glover's ability to make an accurate identification are hardly outweighed by the corrupting effect of the challenged identification itself. Although identifications arising from single-photograph displays may be viewed in general with suspicion, . . . we find in the instant case little pressure on the witness to acquiesce in the suggestion that such a display entails. D'Onofrio had left the photograph at Glover's office and was not present when Glover first viewed it two days after the event. There thus was little urgency and Glover could view the photograph at his leisure. And since Glover examined the photograph alone, there was no coercive pressure to make an identification arising from the presence of another. The identification was made in circumstances allowing care and reflection. 432 U.S. at 116.

Therefore, under the totality of the circumstances, the Court held the identification reliable and the evidence admissible.

The lesson of the *Biggers* and *Manson* cases is that, even though a pretrial confrontation may have been unnecessarily suggestive, the evidence may still be admissible in court if the identification was otherwise reliable. These cases, however, should not be interpreted as evidencing a lack of concern about conducting fair and impartial identification procedures. As the Court stated in *Manson*:

> [I]t would have been better had D'Onofrio presented Glover with a photographic array including "so far as practicable . . . a reasonable number of persons similar to any person then suspected whose likeness is included in the array." . . . The use of that procedure would have enhanced the force of the identification at trial and would have avoided the risk that the evidence would be excluded as unreliable. 432 U.S. at 117.

Applying the Reliability Factors

In spite of the fact that psychological research and the number of wrongful convictions based on mistaken eyewitness identification attest to the fact that the *Biggers–Mason* reliability test is not "a satisfactory method of measuring reliability," the five factors set forth in both opinions remain the test for determining the admissibility of identifications that were initially tainted by some level of being impermissibly suggestive (Rosenberg, 1991:

292). Despite heavy criticism of *Biggers–Mason* as being outdated, the Supreme Court "has yet to confront the need to overhaul" the test (O'Toole & Shay, 2006: 116). Yet, several jurisdictions have taken it upon themselves to refine the test:

> Some state courts have attempted to respond to the criticism of [*Biggers–Mason*] by interpreting their state constitution or other state law to provide more protection than [*Biggers–Mason*]. Utah and Kansas have adopted a refined version of the [*Biggers–Mason*] test on state law grounds, using reliability factors that have a firmer grounding in the social science. New York and Massachusetts require the automatic suppression of **unnecessarily suggestive identification** procedures. Wisconsin requires suppression of show-up identifications, in which a single suspect is presented to the witness, unless the use of the procedure was necessary under the circumstances (O'Toole & Shay, 2006: 115) (emphasis added).

Cases Upholding Identifications as Reliable As the following cases illustrate, courts are loathe to exclude eyewitness identifications as unreliable even when they were made under highly suggestive circumstances.

▶ *United States v. Thody*, 978 F.2d 625 (10th Cir. 1992), applied the *Biggers–Manson* factors to find an identification of a bank robber reliable despite an impermissibly suggestive lineup.

> Each witness had an adequate opportunity to observe Thody closely during the two robberies. All three witnesses testified at the suppression hearing that at least once they were within a few feet of Thody, and that they were able to observe McIntosh and him for several minutes. Woods and Harshfield were within arm's reach of Thody while complying with his instructions. The light was good, and there is no question that the attention of these three employees was riveted on Thody and his companion. Dillard testified that she had been trained to remember the descriptions of robbers. When the second robbery took place Harshfield immediately recognized Thody from the July 12 robbery, exclaiming to Woods, "It's him!" The descriptions of the robbers given by Harshfield, Woods, and Dillard after the robberies also corroborated one another to the degree that descriptions of subtleties in nose size, presence or lack of facial hair, and hair color corresponded significantly. The witnesses were unequivocal in their testimony, both at trial and at the suppression hearing. Despite attempts by defense counsel to unearth inconsistencies, no significant inconsistencies materialized. Also, only one week separated the confrontation from the robbery. 978 F.2d at 629.

▶ *United States v. Wong*, 40 F.3d 1347 (2d Cir. 1994), also found an identification to be reliable in spite of suggestive techniques. A witness to a restaurant shooting was shown three photo arrays from which she selected the defendant's photo because it "looked like the shooter." The police then held a lineup that featured the defendant along with five or six other "Asian males of similar general appearance." 40 F.3d 1359. The witness identified the defendant as someone who "looked like" the shooter, but added that she could not be sure because he appeared to be "taller than she remembered the gunman to be" by six to eight inches. Police then dimmed the lights to recreate the lighting conditions in the restaurant at the time of the shooting and told the witness that they could not accept "a possibly." She then identified the defendant even though "he was taller than she remembered the gunman to be [because he] had 'the same facial features, fair skin, [and] rather big, huge eyes.'" 40 F.3d 1358. The court found that although the police statements to the witness at the time of the lineup "involved some element of suggestiveness," the conduct of law enforcement was not unduly suggestive because although "the detective's comment created the risk of prompting an identification on something less than total certainty, it did not suggest that [the witness] choose any particular participant, nor did it confirm the correctness of her choice after it had been made." 40 F.3d at 1358–59. Moreover, to the extent that the lineup was unnecessarily suggestive, the court ruled the identification was reliable nonetheless in spite of the height difference between the witness's initial description of the shooter and the height of the defendant. The court reasoned:

> The circumstances of this case seem to indicate that [the witness] chose Wong *despite* his height, not because of it. In any event, [her] testimony was that Wong was in a crouched position, shooting, when she observed him in the restaurant, rendering a misestimate of his height understandable without significantly undercutting the reliability of her identification. 40 F.3d at 1359.

Because the witness observed the shooter "after she ducked under the table at the restaurant, staring him in the face for two to three seconds before he turned away, thereby allowing her to accurately identify the defendant's facial features," the court concluded the identification was reliable enough to be admissible.

▶ In *Clark v. Caspari*, 274 F.3d 507 (8th Cir. 2001), the court ruled that a showup following the robbery of a liquor store was unnecessarily suggestive for the following reasons:

> The circumstances surrounding [witnesses'] identifications indicate that the procedures used were improperly suggestive. The record reveals that prior to the identifications, [the witnesses] were asked to identify several suspects that had been apprehended by the police. When they arrived on the scene, [they] saw only [the two African-American defendants]. Both individuals were handcuffed, and were surrounded by white police officers, one of whom was holding a shotgun. Under these circumstances, [the witnesses] may have felt obligated to positively identify [the defendants], so as not to disagree with the police, whose actions exhibited their belief that they had apprehended the correct suspects. Essentially, [the witnesses] were given a choice: identify the apprehended suspects, or nobody at all. This coercive scenario increased the possibility of misidentification. 274 F.3d at 511.

The court, however, ruled that the witnesses' identifications were reliable and therefore admissible even though neither of the two witnesses had been able to provide a description of the robbers. Key to the court's rationale was that both witnesses "had the opportunity to clearly view the perpetrators at the time of the robbery" and the fact that only thirty minutes had passed from the time of the robbery to the time of the showup. 274 F.3d at 512.

▶ *Howard v. Bouchard*, 405 F.3d 459 (6th Cir. 2005), upheld an identification of a shooting suspect even though the identifying witness had seen the defendant in court, sitting with his lawyer at the defense table, just an hour before a lineup was conducted. In addition, the defendant stood out in the lineup due to his height (he was at least three inches taller than the foils) and his hairstyle—a "high-fade haircut that the witnesses later said was so distinctive." 405 F.3d at 471. The court found that these factors were only minimally suggestive. Moreover, the court found that the suggestiveness was outweighed by the reliability of the identification. This conclusion, however, is somewhat remarkable because the eyewitness initially only "got a glance" at the shooter while passing by the scene in a moving truck at a distance of three to six feet, and then viewed the shooter for "a split-second again" when he heard the sound of shots being fired at a distance of approximately fifteen feet. The witness then viewed the shooter a third time as he was picking up shells from 60 to 90 seconds at a distance of thirty to forty feet. All three opportunities to view the shooter from the truck occurred in the early morning hours while the area was lit by street lamps. The court was nonetheless persuaded that the opportunity for the witness to have viewed the shooter was sufficient because the witness was "participating in a repossession, which by its stressful nature generally de-mands heightened attention" and because the witness expressed certainty as to the identification. 405 F.3d at 473.

▶ In *State v. Thompson*, 839 A.2d 622 (Conn. App. Ct. 2004), during the time that police transported a witness to a shooting to a showup, one officer told the witness that the person they were holding was "probably the shooter"; that they believed they "have the person"; and that police "need[ed the wit-ness] to identify him." 839 A.2d at 271. Although the court found the con-frontation to be "highly and unnecessarily suggestive," the court ruled the identification was reliable because the witness had a "good, hard look" at the shooter in daylight; the identification occurred less than two hours after the shooting, and the witness was sure of his identification. 839 A.2d at 272.

▶ In *State v. Johnson*, 836 N.E.2d 1243 (Ohio Ct. App. 2005), the wife of a murder victim had been unable to identify the defendant from a photo array conducted approximately one month following the homicide. Seven months later, however, she identified the defendant in court at a prelimi-nary hearing. During that proceeding, the defendant "was dressed in cloth-ing from the Department of Youth Services and may have been handcuffed and . . . he was the only young African-American male seated at the de-fense table." 836 N.E.2d 1258. The court nonetheless ruled that the identifi-cation was reliable because the witness had observed the gunman for over a minute at the time of the shooting from a distance of only a few feet, and because she had an opportunity to stare into his eyes. When she identified the defendant in court, she testified: "Those eyes, those eyes. I will never forget those eyes." 836 N.E.2d at 1250. Given her level of certainty, the court dismissed her initial inability to identify the defendant at the photo array and admitted her subsequent in-court identification.

Cases Excluding Identifications as Unreliable As the following cases illustrate, courts usually only exclude an impermissibly suggestive identification under highly limited circumstances. To warrant exclusion, either none of the *Biggers–Manson* factors provide a basis for the reliability of the identification, or the factors that do provide such indicia of reliability have to be significantly outweighed by a glaring inconsistency in one of the important *Biggers–Manson* factors.

▶ *United States v. De Jesus-Rios*, 990 F.2d 672 (1st Cir. 1993), found that a boat captain's identification of a woman who had contracted for cargo transport was not otherwise reliable after an impermissibly suggestive one-person showup. The court had no problem with the first, second, and fifth *Biggers-Manson* factors but was troubled by application of the third and fourth factors (the accuracy of the witness's prior description of the criminal and the level of certainty the witness demonstrated at the confrontation):

> Agent Marti testified that, on the date the cocaine was discovered, February 8, 1991, Rivera [the boat captain] described the suspect as "white" and approximately five feet, two inches tall. Rivera's testimony at the suppression hearing and Agent Dania's trial testimony revealed that during his February 11, 1991, interview with Agent Dania, Rivera again described her as "white." It was not until after the February 16, 1991, showup that Rivera described the suspect as having "light brown" skin. Moreover, Rivera also failed to provide an accurate description of her height (five feet, six inches) at either of his pre-showup descriptions.
>
> The record also contains uncontroverted evidence that, despite having been asked at the February 16, 1991, showup to signal the agents when he positively identified Eva Rios, Rivera waited until after she approached the agents and began speaking with them (as scheduled) to signal. We hardly think that this constitutes a high degree of certainty on Rivera's part, particularly in light of the showup procedure at issue here. Prior to that showup, Rivera was informed that the agents were meeting the suspect in front of the customs building at a specific time. While a few other women also may have walked by the customs building that morning, only Eva Rios stopped to speak with the agents. 990 F.2d at 678.

▶ *Raheem v. Kelly*, 257 F.3d 122 (2d Cir. 2001), two witnesses to a shooting gave police a description of the perpetrator that included mention of a distinctive article of clothing: a three-quarter length black leather coat. The defendant was placed in a lineup in which he was the only person in a black leather coat. The court ruled the lineup was unduly suggestive. But the court also excluded the identification as unreliable because almost all of the *Biggers–Manson* criteria weighed in favor of the unreliability of the identification. Specifically, the witnesses had an opportunity to see a variety of people in a dimly lit bar prior to the shooting, during which time their degree of attention was low, as they were watching football, drinking, and talking with others. Moreover, after a shot had been fired, the witnesses admitted that they focused their attention on the gun, not at the person holding it. Other than the witnesses' description of the shooter's coat, they had been able to provide only "general information as to the shooter's age, height, and weight" while being unable to provide any details about the shooter's face. 257 F.3d at 138. And, the witnesses were not confident in their identifications. Given the lack of indicia of reliability under so many of the *Biggers–Manson* factors, added to "the fact that both witnesses repeatedly cited the coat worn by [the shooter] as influential in their selection of [the defendant]," the court stated that it could not conclude that the identifications "had reliability independent of the black leather coat" and therefore excluded the identification on due process grounds. 257 F.3d at 140.

Law enforcement officers have control over the conduct of the identification procedures, but they have little or no control over the five factors determining the reliability of the identification. Therefore, officers should conduct all identification procedures fairly and impartially. To avoid the risk that identification evidence will be excluded as unreliable, officers should follow the guidelines for lineups and/or photo array identifications that appear later in this chapter.

Discussion POINT

Was the Lineup in Antonio Beaver's Case Unnecessarily Suggestive?

The Innocence Project: The Case of Antonio Beaver
Source: http://www.innocenceproject.org/Content/470.php

Recall the case of Antonio Beaver from the first Discussion Point in this chapter. Applying the law of *Stovall v. Denno*, do you think the lineup in Beaver's case was unnecessarily suggestive? Why or why not?

Assume for the sake of argument that a court were to rule that the lineup in Beaver's case had been unnecessarily suggestive. Applying the *Biggers–Manson* factors, do you think the pretrial identification should be admitted into evidence anyway on reliability grounds? Explain your answer.

key points

- Due process requires that the totality of the circumstances surrounding any identification must not be so overly suggestive as to cause a substantial likelihood of irreparable misidentification. All lineups and showups must be conducted in a fair and impartial manner.
- The central question surrounding any identification is whether under the totality of the circumstances it was reliable, even though the confrontation procedure was suggestive. Factors to be considered in evaluating the reliability of an identification are (1) the witness's opportunity to view the criminal at the time of the crime; (2) the witness's degree of attention; (3) the accuracy of the witness's prior description of the criminal: (4) the level of certainty demonstrated by the witness at the confrontation; (5) the length of time between the crime and the confrontation; and (6) the corrupting effect of the suggestive identification.

▶ EXIGENT CIRCUMSTANCES EXCEPTION

In an emergency, courts are more likely to condone highly suggestive identification procedures such as one-person showups, or excuse violations of the *Wade–Gilbert* right-to-counsel rule, because an immediate identification by a witness may be the only identification possible. For identification purposes, an emergency can be defined as a witness in danger of death or blindness or a suspect in danger of death. The leading case on emergency identifications is *Stovall v. Denno*, 388 U.S. 293 (1967), in which the defendant was arrested for stabbing a doctor to death and seriously wounding his wife, who was hospitalized for major surgery. Without affording the defendant time to retain counsel, police arranged with the wife's surgeon to bring the defendant to her hospital room, where she identified the defendant as her assailant. The Court held that "a claimed violation of due process of law in the conduct of a confrontation depends on the totality of the circumstances surrounding it, and the record in the present case reveals that the showing of the defendant to the wife in an immediate hospital confrontation was imperative":

> Here was the only person in the world who could possibly exonerate Stovall. Her words, and only her words, "He is not the man" could have resulted in freedom for Stovall. The hospital was not far distant from the courthouse and jail. No one knew how long Mrs. Behrendt might live. Faced with the responsibility of identifying the attacker, with the need for immediate action, and with the knowledge that Mrs. Behrendt could not visit the jail, the police followed the only feasible procedure and took Stovall to the hospital room. Under these circumstances, the usual police station lineup, which Stovall now argues he should have had, was out of the question. 388 U.S. at 302.

In *Trask v. Robbins*, 421 F.2d 773 (1st Cir. 1970), the defendant, who was in jail on a store robbery charge, was brought before a hospitalized victim of a separate assault and robbery and was spontaneously and positively identified as his assailant. It was uncertain whether the defendant had retained a lawyer on the store robbery charge, but no lawyer was contacted for the identification proceeding for the separate assault and robbery. The defendant claimed that he should have been represented by a lawyer at this confrontation.

Applying the *Stovall* totality-of-the-circumstances test, the court found that the circumstances surrounding the identification were not unnecessarily suggestive and conducive to irreparable mistaken identification: (1) no preliminary statements were made to the victim; (2) the victim's words of identification were spontaneous and positive; (3) the defendant said nothing in the presence of the victim; (4) the case was merely in the investigatory stage; and (5) the critically injured victim (thought to be dying) was about to be moved to a distant hospital. Under these emergency conditions, the fact that a lawyer was not present did not void the identification. (Note that identification procedures involving critically injured persons should only be conducted with the approval of medical authorities. The importance of obtaining an identification is secondary in importance to the treatment and care of an injured person.)

key point

- Emergency situations sometimes require that police conduct a confrontation in a manner that would otherwise be considered too suggestive, such as a one-on-one showup. Given exigent circumstances such as the impending death or blindness of a witness, such a confrontation is not *unnecessarily* suggestive, but rather is driven out of the necessity of the emergency situation. So long as a suggestive confrontation was conducted because of exigent circumstances, and assuming it is reliable, courts will admit an identification into evidence even if a suspect's right to counsel under *Wade–Gilbert* was violated.

▶GUIDELINES FOR LINEUPS AND PHOTO ARRAY IDENTIFICATION PROCEDURES

The police and the prosecution have discretion to conduct lineups. Although the police, the prosecution, or the court may grant a suspect's request for a lineup, a suspect has no right to a lineup. *Sims v. Sullivan*, 867 F.2d 142 (2d Cir. 1989); *United States v. Harvey*, 756 F.2d 636 (8th Cir. 1985). The following are guidelines for the law enforcement officer in conducting lineup identification procedures.

Special Considerations before the Administration of a Lineup Law enforcement officers should consider the following before conducting a lineup:

▶ A law enforcement officer should not conduct a lineup without first discussing with a prosecuting attorney the legal advisability of a lineup.

▶ A lineup should be conducted as soon after the arrest of a suspect as practicable. Promptly conducted lineups enable innocent arrestees to be released, guarantee that witnesses' memories are fresh, and ensure that crucial identification evidence is obtained before the suspect is released on bail or for other reasons. When possible, lineup arrangements (such as contacting witnesses and locating innocent participants) should be completed before the arrest of the suspect.

▶ A person in custody may be compelled to participate in a lineup without violating Fourth or Fifth Amendment rights. Most courts hold that once a person is in custody, his or her liberty is not further infringed under the Fourth Amendment by being presented in a lineup for witnesses to view. *State v. Wilks*, 358 N.W.2d 273 (Wis. 1984); *People v. Hodge*, 526 P.2d 309 (Colo. 1974). Furthermore, the Fifth Amendment is not violated by "**compelling the accused merely to exhibit his person for observation by a prosecution witness prior to trial [which] involves no compulsion of the accused to give evidence having testimonial significance. It is compulsion of the accused to exhibit his physical characteristics, not compulsion to disclose any knowledge he might have.**" *United States v. Wade*, 388 U.S. 218, 222 (1967).

Compelling people who are not in custody to appear in a lineup involves a much greater intrusion on liberty, and therefore implicates the Fourth Amendment. Forcing someone who is not in custody to appear for a lineup is usually accomplished by order of a court or grand jury, although some states have enacted statutes that create special procedures for doing so. Regardless of the procedure used, U.S. jurisdictions are split on whether such orders to appear require reasonable suspicion, probable cause, or some other standard.

> [A] number of states have . . . adopt[ed] "temporary detention orders" which may be issued for the detention of persons to obtain fingerprints, photographs, blood samples, and other physical evidence when reasonable grounds exist. The "reasonable grounds" standard generally requires that reasonable suspicion exist that the person from whom the evidence is sought is connected to the commission of an offense. Some states, however, require only that there be reasonable cause to believe a crime has been committed and that the ordered identification procedure "may contribute to the identification of the individual who committed such of-

fense." One court has held that appearance similar to that of the alleged perpetrator or similarity in modus operandi between a previously committed offense and the one under investigation is insufficient, standing alone, to meet the latter standard (Ringel, 2007: § 18:4).

Some courts have upheld the ordering of a person not in custody to appear in a lineup in serious cases, in which the public interest in law enforcement outweighed the privacy interests of the person. *State v. Hall*, 461 A.2d 1155 (N.J. 1983); *Wise v. Murphy*, 275 A.2d 205 (D.C. App. 1971). Other courts have held that a person not in custody cannot be ordered to participate in a lineup unless there is probable cause to arrest. *In re Armed Robbery, Albertson's, on August 31, 1981*, 659 P.2d 1092 (Wash. 1983); *Alphonso C. v. Morgenthau*, 376 N.Y.S.2d 126 (N.Y. 1975).

► If the suspect has a right to counsel at a lineup, the suspect should be informed of that right. If the suspect chooses to waive the right to counsel, a careful record should be made of the suspect's waiver and agreement to voluntarily participate in the lineup. (See Figure 14.3.)

► If the suspect chooses to have an attorney present at the lineup, the lineup should be delayed a reasonable time to allow the attorney to appear. The attorney must be allowed to be present from the beginning of the lineup, or "the moment [the suspect] and the other lineup members were within the sight of witnesses." *United States v. LaPierre*, 998 F.2d 1460, 1464 (9th Cir. 1993). The attorney should be allowed to consult with the suspect before the lineup and to observe all the proceedings, take notes, and tape-record the identification process in whole or in part. If the attorney has suggestions that might improve the fairness of the proceedings, the officer in charge may follow them if they are reasonable and practicable. The suspect's attorney should not be allowed to control the proceedings, however.

► Even when the suspect's counsel is not required at a lineup because formal criminal proceedings have not yet been instituted or the suspect has knowingly, intelligently, and voluntarily waived the right to counsel, the officer conducting the lineup should consider allowing counsel to be present to minimize subsequent challenges to the fairness of the lineup. *State v. Taylor*, 210 N.W.2d 873 (Wis. 1973).

► The names of all persons participating in the lineup, the names of the officers conducting the lineup, and the name of the suspect's attorney, if any, should be recorded and preserved.

► Witnesses should not be allowed to view photographs of the suspect before the lineup. If a witness has viewed such photographs before the lineup, the officer conducting the lineup should inform the suspect's counsel and the court of any identification of the suspect's photograph, any failure to identify the suspect's photograph, and any identification of a photograph of someone other than the suspect.

► Before viewing the lineup, each witness should be required to give to the officer in charge of the lineup a written description of the perpetrator of the crime. A copy should be made available to the suspect's counsel.

Guidelines for Administering Lineups and Photo Arrays In light of the empirical research demonstrating systemic problems with eyewitness identification, the American Psychology and Law Society (Wells et al., 1998) and the U.S. Department of Justice (1999) both published guides for reforming the way the criminal justice system approaches eyewitness evidence. Following the issuance of those reports, the American Bar Association issued the following "Statement of Best Practices for Promoting the Accuracy of Eyewitness Identification Procedures" (2004). The procedures they recommend apply to both the live administration of lineups and to photo arrays.

One Suspect per Lineup or Array Only one suspect should appear in the lineup. If there are two or more suspects, no two should appear together in the same lineup or photo array.

Double-Blind Administration Whenever practicable, the person who conducts a lineup or photo array and all others present (except for defense counsel, when his or her presence is constitutionally required) should be unaware of which of the participants is the suspect.

▶ The person who administers a lineup or photo array affects the reliability of any identification. The procedure should be **double-blind**—that is, neither the witness nor the person administering the lineup or photo array should know who the suspect is and who the foils are (Wells & Seelau, 1995). That procedure greatly reduces, if not eliminates, suggestive questioning by the administrator and other possibilities of the administrator unduly influencing the witness, either consciously or unconsciously (Steblay, 1997). To enhance the reliability of the double-blind procedure, eyewitnesses should be instructed that they should not assume that the person administering the lineup knows who the suspect is. Doing so helps to decrease the likelihood of witnesses looking for cues from the administrator of the identification procedure.

▶ If a double-blind procedure is not used, the administrator of the lineup should not engage in unnecessary conversation with witnesses. Most importantly, the administrator should not indicate by word, gesture, or other means of communication any opinion as to the identity or guilt of the suspect. This means, especially, that the administrator should not coax, coach, or tell witnesses that they have chosen the person suspected of the crime or have made the "correct" decision.

▶ If more than one witness is called to view a lineup, those who have already viewed the lineup should not be allowed to converse with persons who have not yet viewed the lineup. Witnesses who have viewed the lineup should be kept in a room separate from witnesses who have not yet viewed the lineup. Furthermore, only one witness at a time should be present in the room where the lineup is being conducted.

Witness Instructions Upon entering the room in which the lineup is being conducted, each witness should be handed a form for use in the identification. The form should be signed by the witness and the law enforcement officer conducting the lineup. Many police departments use lineup forms like the one that appears as Figure 14.4. A copy of the witness identification form should be given to the suspect's attorney at the time each witness completes viewing the lineup. It

Lineup Identification Form for Witnesses

Your Name: _____ Date of Birth: _____

Address: _____

Telephone Number: _____ Case Number: _____

Place Viewed: _____ Officer: _____

Agency: _____

TO THE WITNESS: You have been asked to look at a lineup. This is either a presentation in person of several individuals or a presentation of several photographs. You may or may not be able to identify a person in the lineup. Please look at all the persons before making any choice. If you do not identify a person in the lineup, please indicate below. If you do identify a person, please indicate the number of the person on this form.

You must look at this display and make an independent identification *without assistance*. Do not ask any questions about the people being shown. You may, however, ask the officer to have persons in the lineup say certain words, do certain things, or wear certain clothing, if you think it will aid you. Do not ask anyone for help or discuss this with anyone except the officer. There is no "right" answer, so do not ask whether you have made the "right" choice.

Please mark your choice with an "X":

I do not identify anyone

I identify   1   2   3   4   5   6   7   8

COMMENTS: _____

_____

_____

_____

Thank you for your cooperation.

_____ Date and Time _____
Viewer's Signature

_____ Date and Time _____
Officer's Signature/Badge Number

▶**Figure 14.4** LINEUP IDENTIFICATION FORM FOR WITNESSES

should be noted, however, that many lineup forms are missing two key instructions that the ABA recommends be provided to all witnesses before the lineup is conducted. If the form does not contain the following two instructions, they should be orally told to witnesses:

▶ Eyewitnesses should be instructed that the perpetrator may or may not be in the lineup. Explicitly informing a witness that the suspect may not be in the lineup or array reduces the pressure on the witness to make an identification. This, in turn, decreases the risk that the witness will make a questionable identification by selecting "the person who best resembles the culprit relative to the others in the lineup" or array (Wells & Seelau, 1995: 778–79).

▶ Eyewitnesses should be instructed that they need not identify anyone, but, if they do so, they will be expected to state in their own words how certain they are of any identification they make or the lack thereof. This procedure reduces a witness's use of relative decision making by encouraging a witness to use an absolute threshold (Levi & Lindsay, 2001; Steblay, 1997).

Specific Guidelines for Foil Selection, Number, and Presentation Methods

The American Psychology and Law Society (Wells et al., 1998) and the U.S. Department of Justice (1999) also recommended specific guidelines regarding the selection and presentation of foils.

Appearance of Foils The people who appear in a lineup or photo array other than the suspect are called **foils** or **fillers.** Foils should be chosen for their similarity to the witness's description of the perpetrator. For a lineup or photo array to be fair, the actual suspect should not stand out from the other participants in a lineup or photo array (Wells & Seelau, 1995). But constructing a truly fair lineup or photo array can be difficult. Although the participants should not be clones of each other, they should generally be of the same race; should be similarly dressed (although preferably not in clothing matching witnesses' descriptions of clothing worn by the culprit); should not be of substantially differing height and weight; and should not have visible distinctive features (e.g., all should have similar or absent facial hair; either all or none should have tattoos, etc.) (Judges, 2000; Wells & Seelau, 1995).

Number of Foils Lineups and photo arrays should use a sufficient number of foils to reasonably reduce the risk of an eyewitness selecting a suspect by guessing rather than by recognition. The witness should not know how many individuals will be shown to them in a lineup or photo array.

The number of foils presented along with the suspect is also important to lineup or photo array fairness. The more people who participate in a lineup, the less likely a suspect will be identified merely by chance. The same is true of photo arrays; the more photographs presented to the witness, the less likely it is the suspect will be identified by chance.

Accordingly, most experts recommend that at least six people be in a lineup or photo array (Wells et al., 1998; Levi, 1998). To decrease chance identifications, England routinely uses nine or ten people; and Canada uses twelve (Levi & Lindsay, 2001).

Sequential vs. Simultaneous Presentation of Foils Historically, all of the participants in a photo array or lineup were presented to the witness at the same time—a practice that continues to this day. But research has demonstrated that **sequential** viewing of photographs or lineup participants one after another, rather than

simultaneous presentation of foils (viewing of all participants at once), is preferable. As with the previous precaution, this procedure reduces a witness's use of relative decision making by encouraging a witness to use an absolute threshold (Levi & Lindsay, 2001; Steblay, 1997). "Critical tests of this hypothesis have consistently shown that a sequential procedure produces fewer false identifications than does a simultaneous procedure with little or no decrease in rates of accurate identification" (Wells & Seelau, 1995: 772; *see also* Klobuchar et al., 2006).

Foil Behavior at Lineups Suspects should be allowed to choose their position in the lineup and to change that position after each viewing. This promotes fairness and eliminates any claim that the positioning of the suspect in the lineup was unduly suggestive.

Lineup participants may be compelled to speak for purposes of voice identification. As stated in the *Wade* opinion, "**[C]ompelling Wade to speak within hearing distance of the witnesses, even to utter words purportedly uttered by the robber, was not compulsion to utter statements of a 'testimonial' nature; he was required to use his voice as an identifying physical characteristic, not to speak his guilt.**" 388 U.S. at 222–23. Hence, there is no Fifth Amendment violation when a lineup participant is compelled to speak in this way. Each person in the lineup, however, should be asked to speak the same words in roughly the same tone of voice (e.g., all should whisper, all should shout, or all should talk "normally").

If any body movement or gesture is necessary, it should be made one time only by each person in the lineup and repeated only at the express request of the observing witness or victim. Again, the officer conducting the lineup should keep a careful record of any person's failure to cooperate.

Additional Considerations for Photographic Arrays Photo arrays bring their own set of cautions concerning suggestibility. Law enforcement officers should pay attention to the following concerns when assembling a photo array.

▶ "In the absence of exigent circumstances, presentation of a single photograph to the victim of a crime amounts to an unnecessarily suggestive photographic identification procedure." *United States v. Jones*, 652 F. Supp. 1561, 1570 (S.D.N.Y. 1986); *see also Simmons v. United States*, 390 U.S. 377 (1968); *United States v. Smith*, 429 F. Supp.2d 440, 450 (D. Mass. 2006) ("It is axiomatic that identifications achieved through the use of a single photo are highly problematic. A single photo shown to an eyewitness [the proverbial "Is this the man you saw?" question] plainly suggests the guilt of the person pictured.") Thus, photos should be sequentially presented in arrays of at least six pictures.

▶ Photos should either all be color pictures or all black-and-white. Arrays that mix color and black-and-white photos might be held to be unnecessarily suggestive. *E.g., O'Brien v. Wainwright*, 738 F.2d 1139 (11th Cir. 1984).

▶ If possible, mug shot photos should not be used. Mug shots may prejudice the suspect by implying that he or she has a criminal record. If the use of mug shots is unavoidable, only frontal views should be used and their identity as mug shots should be disguised such that arrest information, height markings, and the like are not visible. *E.g., Cikora v. Dugger*, 840 F.2d 893, 894 (11th Cir. 1988).

Discussion
POINT

How Do Foil Selection, Number, and Presentation Affect Suggestibility?

The Innocence Project: The Case of Antonio Beaver
Source: http://www.innocenceproject.org/Content/470.php

Recall the case of Antonio Beaver from the first Discussion Point in this chapter. Critique the lineup procedures used in Beaver's case using the material in the section entitled "Specific Guidelines for Foil Selection, Number, and Presentation Methods." What specific measures could police have taken to have reduced the suggestibility of the lineup in Beaver's case and increased the reliability of the lineup procedure?

► If mug shot photos are used, they should not be displayed in a photographic array alongside ordinary photographs. *Perry v. Lockhart*, 871 F.2d 1384, 1391 (8th Cir.), *cert. denied*, 493 U.S. 959 (1989).

► If police have no suspect, the display of a mug book to a witness or victim presents no problems of being suggestive. A reasonable number of photographs should be shown and careful records kept of all pictures shown and pictures identified.

► A photograph in a photographic display may be altered (to show what the person would look like with a beard or a hat, for example) so long as all other photographs in the display are altered in the same way. *United States v. Dunbar*, 767 F.2d 72 (3d Cir. 1985).

Recording Procedures Whenever practicable, the police should videotape or digitally video-record identification procedures, including the witness's confidence statements and any statements made to the witness by the police.

► Absent videotaping or digital video recording, a photograph should be taken of each lineup or photo array, and a detailed record made describing with specificity how the entire procedure (from start to finish) was administered, also noting the appearance of the foils and of the suspect and the identities of all persons present. Some courts hold that a failure to properly photograph or record an identification procedure allows courts to presume that the procedure was unduly suggestive. *Smith v. Campbell*, 781 F. Supp. 521 (M.D. Tenn. 1991).

► Regardless of the way in which a lineup is memorized, and for all other identification procedures, including photo arrays, the police shall, immediately after completing the identification procedure and in a non-suggestive manner, request witnesses to indicate their level of confidence in any identification and ensure that the response is accurately documented.

Obtaining a statement of confidence level before other information can prevent contamination of a witness's judgment increases the reliability of an identification (Wells & Seelau, 1995). Because confidence level at the time of initial identification is a powerful force in determining both the admissibility of an out-of-court identification and the weight accorded to it by the trier-of-fact, it should be self-evident why an uncontaminated statement of high confidence should be obtained at the time of an initial identification (Weber & Brewer, 2006; Smith, Lindsay & Pryke, 2000). But the importance of initial confidence goes beyond the obvious in light of a phenomenon called **confidence malleability**: "the tendency for an eyewitness to become more or less confident in his or her identification as a function of events that occur after the identification" (Wells & Seelau, 1995: 774; see also Penrod & Cutler, 1995).

Immediate Post-Lineup or Post-Photo-Array Procedures The American Psychology and Law Society (Wells et al., 1998) and the U.S. Department of Justice (1999) recommend that the following procedures be followed after a lineup or photo array is conducted.

▶ Police and prosecutors should avoid at any time giving the witness feedback on whether he or she selected the "right" person—the person believed by law enforcement to be the culprit. Not only does this procedure help to reduce confidence malleability, it also helps to avoid both confabulation and the post-event misinformation effect.

▶ The officer conducting the lineup should take complete notes of everything that takes place at the lineup and should prepare an official report of all the proceedings, to be filed in the law enforcement agency's permanent records. The report should include the time, location, identity of persons present, statements made, photographs or videotapes of the lineup, and the lineup identification form (see Exhibit 14.2) for each witness viewing the lineup. A copy of the report should be sent to the prosecuting attorney and made available to the suspect's attorney.

▶ A defendant has no right to have counsel present at a post-lineup police interview with an identifying witness. *Sams v. Walker*, 18 F.3d 167 (2d Cir. 1994); *Hallmark v. Cartwright*, 742 F.2d 584 (10th Cir. 1984).

Multiple Lineups or Photo Arrays Special procedures were recommended by the American Psychology and Law Society (Wells et al., 1998) and the U.S. Department of Justice (1999) when multiple identification procedures are used.

Avoid Multiple Identification Procedures Using the Same Witness and Suspect Multiple lineups or photo arrays involving the same suspect and witness are inherently suggestive and strongly discouraged. In *Foster v. California*, 394 U.S. 440 (1969), the eyewitness was unable to make a positive identification at the first lineup, in which Foster was placed with considerably shorter men. After meeting Foster one-on-one, the witness made a tentative, uncertain identification. At a second lineup, the eyewitness was finally convinced that Foster committed the crime and positively identified him. Foster was the only person who appeared in both lineups. The U.S. Supreme Court reversed the conviction:

> The suggestive elements in this identification procedure made it all but inevitable that the witness] would identify petitioner whether or not he was in fact "the man." In effect, the police repeatedly said to the witness, "This is the man." . . . This procedure so undermined the reliability of the eyewitness identification as to violate due process. 394 U.S. at 443.

Vary Position of Participants When Multiple Lineups Are Used for Multiple Witnesses Place the people in a lineup or photos in a photo array in different positions each time a lineup or array is administered to multiple witnesses for the same case. In theory, witnesses should have no contact with each other. Nonetheless, in case one witness manages to communicate to another the position of the person whom they believe to be the suspect, varying the positions of the suspect and the foils will help to eliminate the possibility of such a contamination of the identification procedures.

Use Different Foils for Different Suspects for the Same Witness When showing a new suspect to a witness in a second or subsequent lineup or photo array, avoid reusing the same people as foils. That way, the witness should not have seen any of the people previously used in subsequent lineups or photo arrays.

Discussion

POINT

Can Identifications be Improved Using Double-blind Administration?

The Innocence Project: The Case of Anthony Michael Green
Source: http://www.innocenceproject.org/Content/163.php

In June 1998, a Caucasian woman was attacked in her room at the Cleveland Clinic Inn, where she was staying following cancer treatment at the Cleveland Clinic Hospital. On the night of the crime, she had responded to a knock at her door. When she opened the door, a hand reached inside and grabbed her by the throat. The assailant held a knife near her face, pushed her into the room, and demanded money from her. After the victim gave him some money, the perpetrator ordered her to sit on the bed and to undress. The assailant then told her to put her clothing back on and went toward the door. After he arrived at the door, however, the assailant walked back over to the victim and ordered her to undress again. He pushed the victim onto the bed and raped her. The victim testified at trial that the perpetrator said his name was Tony during the attack.

Approximately an hour and a half after the perpetrator left her room, the victim called the Cleveland Clinic security, who notified the Cleveland Police Department, and both agencies responded to the scene. The victim's initial description of the assailant was an African-American

(Continued)

Can Identifications be Improved Using Double-blind Administration? *(Continued)*

male, around twenty-three years old, 5'8", 165 pounds, medium build, brown eyes, black short afro, pockmarked face with pimples, wearing a black ski cap–type hat and a "doo rag," a black t-shirt with cut-off sleeves, and gray pleated pants.

A few days after the attack, the victim was shown a photo array which depicted young African-American males and included Green's former work identification photograph. After viewing this first array, the victim stated that she saw one person "that resembled [her] attacker, but just not enough." The following day, she was shown a photo array comprised of booking photographs. Green's photograph was the only photograph repeated in both arrays. The booking photographs contained biographical placards on them, including the subject's height, weight, and age. The card on Green's photograph gave a height, weight, and age description that matched the description given by the victim to the police. She identified Green as her assailant from this second photo array.

Mr. Green's subsequent conviction was based almost exclusively on the eyewitness identification made by the victim. He served thirteen years in prison for a crime that DNA evidence later proved he did not commit. Since his release, the real perpetrator of this crime confessed and was convicted.

(1) What factors described in the section of this chapter entitled "Mistaken Identifications: The Role of Perception and Memory" do you think contributed to the wrongful conviction of Anthony Michael Green? (2) The Innocence Project asserts that: "It is unlikely that a 'blind' administrator would have decided to perform two lineups and include pedigree information in the second. Since the victim lacked confidence in her first identification, it is improbable that Mr. Green would have been identified through a double-blind sequential procedure had it been employed." Do you agree with this statement? Why or why not?

key points

- Only one suspect should appear in any lineup or photo array.
- Whenever possible, lineups and photo arrays should be administered using a double-blind procedure—that is, neither the witness nor the person administering the lineup or photo array should know who the suspect is and who the foils are.
- Eyewitnesses should be instructed that the perpetrator may or may not be in the lineup; that they need not identify anyone; and, if they do make an

identification, then they will be expected to state in their own words how certain they are of any identification they make.
- Foils should be chosen for their similarity to the witness's description of the perpetrator, without the suspect standing out in any way from the foils and without other factors drawing undue attention to the suspect. While the participants should not be clones of each other, they should generally be of the same race, should be similarly dressed (although

key points

- preferably not in clothing matching witnesses' descriptions of clothing worn by the culprit), should not be of substantially differing height and weight, and should not have visible distinctive features (e.g., all should have similar or absent facial hair; either all or none should have tattoos, etc.).

- A minimum of six people should appear in any lineup or photo array; seven to nine people is preferable.

- Sequential viewing of photographs or lineup participants one after another, rather than simultaneous viewing of all participants, is preferable.

- Immediately after completing an identification procedure, police must, in a non-suggestive manner, request witnesses to indicate their level of confidence in any identification, and ensure that the response is accurately documented and record their responses.

- Whenever practicable, the police should videotape or digitally video-record identification procedures, including the witness's confidence statements and any statements made to the witness by the police.

- Lineups and photo arrays must be properly documented in a detailed record that describes with specificity how the entire procedure (from start to finish) was administered, also noting the appearance of the foils and of the suspect and the identities of all persons present.

- Before, during, and after an identification procedure, police and prosecutors should avoid giving witnesses any feedback on whether they feel they have made a "good" or "correct" identification.

- Multiple lineups or photo arrays involving the same suspect and witnesses are inherently suggestive and strongly discouraged.

- Place the people in a lineup or photos in a photo array in different positions each time a lineup or array is administered to multiple witnesses for the same case.

- When showing a new suspect to a witness in a second or subsequent lineup or photo array, avoid re-using the same people as foils.

▶ EFFECT OF IMPROPER IDENTIFICATION PROCEDURES

To enforce the standards set out by the U.S. Supreme Court with respect to pretrial identifications, rules have been established for the admission of identification evidence in court. Rule 12 of the Federal Rules of Criminal Procedure require a defendant to file a pretrial motion to suppress identification evidence before a trial begins. If the motion is granted either because a confrontation was made in violation of the defendant's right to counsel, or because an identification is unreliable and thereby violates a defendant's right to due process of law, the court must exclude at trial:

▶ any evidence of the pretrial identification presented as a part of the prosecutor's case-in-chief; and

▶ any identification made by a witness in court who participated in the tainted pretrial identification.

Independent Source Doctrine If a pretrial identification is ruled to be inadmissible on either Sixth Amendment or due process grounds, an eyewitness may still be allowed to make an in-court identification. *Coleman v. Alabama*, 399 U.S. 1 (1970). In *Gilbert v. California*, 388 U.S. 263 (1967), the Supreme Court held that such an in-court identification would be constitutionally permissible if the identification were based on a source independent of the illegally tainted pretrial identification procedure. Courts will rule that an in-court identification has an **independent source** when the identifying witness, by drawing on personal memory of the crime and observations of the defendant during the crime, has such a clear and definite image of the defendant that the witness can make an identification unaffected by the illegal confrontation. The prosecution bears the burden of persuasion to prove, by clear and convincing evidence, that a witness has a source independent from the illegal confrontation for identifying the perpetrator of the crime. *Tomlin v. Myers*, 30 F.3d 1235 (9th Cir. 1994); *Frisco v. Blackburn*, 782 F.2d 1353 (5th Cir. 1986). Factors to be considered by judges in determining an independent source are set out in *Wade*:

> **Application of [the independent source test] requires consideration of various factors; for example, the prior opportunity to observe the alleged criminal act, the existence of any discrepancy between any pre-lineup description and the defendant's actual description, any identification prior to the lineup of another person, the identification by picture of the defendant prior to lineup, failure to identify the defendant on a prior occasion, and the lapse of time between the alleged act and the lineup identification. It is also relevant to consider those facts which, despite the absence of counsel, are disclosed concerning the conduct of the lineup.** 388 U.S. at 241.

McKinon v. Wainwright, 705 F.2d 419 (11th Cir. 1983), found an independent source for the identification of an accused at trial when the witness had known the accused long before the crime was committed and had spent several hours with the accused on the day of the crime. Law enforcement officers should gather and record information on these factors from witnesses. Officers should obtain as much detail as possible because strong evidence of an independent source for identification of a criminal can salvage an improperly conducted identification procedure. Of course, if the defendant does not meet the threshold requirement of showing that the in-court identification was tainted by impermissible suggestiveness, then "independent reliability [of the in-court identification] is not a constitutionally required condition of admissibility . . . and the reliability of the identification is simply a question for the jury." *Jarrett v. Headley*, 802 F.2d 34, 42 (2d Cir. 1986).

Courts use the same independent-source factors to determine the admissibility of in-court identifications that are based on pretrial identification procedures administered in violation of a defendant's Fourth Amendment rights. *United States v. Crews*, 445 U.S. 463 (1980); *United States v. Meyer*, 359 F.3d 820 (6th Cir. 2004). For example, in *United States v. Slater*, 692 F.2d 107 (10th Cir. 1982), the photograph used for an out-of-court identification had been obtained through an illegal arrest. The court held that the in-court identification of the defendant was admissible, however, because "the witnesses . . . had each actually seen the crime committed at close hand, there was little discrepancy between the pretrial descriptions and the defendant's actual description, there was no identification of another person or failure to identify the defendant, and the person who committed the crime made no attempt to conceal his face." 692 F.2d at 108. *See also United States v. Foppe*, 993 F.2d 1444, (9th Cir. 1993) (admitting an in-court identification even though an out-of-court photo identification was the inadmissible fruit of illegal arrest because the eyewitness had a chance to observe the defendant indoors at close range under good lighting conditions).

Summary

Both human perception and memory are complicated, highly selective, unconscious processes that can be negatively affected by a number of factors. Perception depends both on the acuity of the physical senses and a number of psychological factors that affect how sensory data is processed in light of experience, learning, preferences, biases, and expectations. Memory has three critical stages: acquisition/encoding, retention, and recall/retrieval. All three stages are affected by physical and psychological factors that can taint the accuracy of a memory. These factors include time; lighting conditions; changes in visual adaptation to light and dark; duration of the event; speed and distance involved; the presence or absence of violence; stress; fear; physical limitation on sensory perception (e.g., poor eyesight, hearing impairment, alcohol or drug intoxication); expectations; age (the very young and very old have unique problems); and gender.

A criminal suspect has a right to counsel at all lineups and showups conducted at or after the initiation of adversary judicial criminal proceedings against the suspect. The emergency showup is the only exception to this rule. In every other case, the suspect should be warned of the right to counsel in accordance with the form appearing as Figure 14.2.

If a lineup or showup is conducted before adversary judicial criminal proceedings are initiated against a suspect, the suspect is not entitled to the presence or advice of counsel. Nevertheless, all pretrial identification procedures, whether lineups or showups, must be conducted in accordance with due process, which forbids any pretrial identification procedure that is unnecessarily suggestive and conducive to irreparable mistaken identification. As further interpreted by the U.S. Supreme Court, due process simply requires that all pretrial identifications be reliable in the totality of the circumstances; otherwise, evidence of the identification is inadmissible in court.

The following factors should be considered in determining reliability: the witness's opportunity to view the criminal at the time of the crime; the witness's degree of attention; the accuracy of the witness's prior description of the criminal; the level of certainty demonstrated by the witness at the confrontation; and the length of time between the crime and the confrontation. These factors are weighed against the corrupting effect of a suggestive identification.

Officers conducting lineups or photo arrays are advised to follow the guidelines for these identification procedures presented in this chapter.

A criminal suspect is not entitled to the presence or advice of counsel at photographic identification procedures no matter when those procedures are held. Nevertheless, such procedures must be conducted as fairly and impartially as possible, and identifications are evaluated by the reliability test described in the preceding paragraph. Officers are advised to follow the guidelines for photographic identifications provided in this chapter.

If a pretrial identification is excluded on either Sixth Amendment or due process grounds, a subsequent in-court identification may be permissible under the following circumstances: if the prosecution proves, by clear and convincing evidence, that the in-court identification is not the product of the tainted pretrial confrontation, but rather stems from an independent source, such as the witness's personal observations and memory of the defendant at the scene of the crime.

Key Terms

acquisition stage/encoding phase, 751

confabulation, 751

confidence malleability, 782

confirmation bias, 751

confrontation, 748

cross-racial identification bias, 754

double-blind administration of lineup/photo array, 777

Review and Discussion Questions

1. What are some of the factors that affect perception in the "normal" human adult who is free from
   any physical perceptual impairments? How might
   these factors affecting perception interfere with
   the accuracy of an eyewitness identification?

2. Describe the three phases of memory and at least
   one psychological factor that might impair the accuracy of memory in each phase.

3. Estimator variables—those variables concerning
   the accuracy of an eyewitness identification over
   which the criminal justice system has no control—
   include both "event factors" and "witness factors."
   Describe the significance of at least three event
   factors and three witness factors, explaining how
   each estimator variable might negatively affect the
   accuracy of an eyewitness identification.

4. Why should a person not have a right to demand
   an immediate lineup to clear himself or herself
   and avoid the many inconveniences associated
   with being arrested?

5. State three ways in which a law enforcement officer conducting a lineup can decrease the suggestibility of the lineup. State three ways in which a
   law enforcement officer can decrease the suggestibility of a one-person showup.

6. Assume that a suspect is about to be placed in a
   lineup and is told by a law enforcement officer
   that she has a right to counsel at the lineup. If
   the suspect asks, "Why do I need a lawyer?" what
   should the officer say?

7. Why should photographic identification procedures not be used first when a subsequent physical lineup is contemplated?

8. What arguments would a defense attorney make
   at a suppression hearing under each of the following circumstances?

   a. The witness identified the defendant's photo-
      graph at a pretrial photographic display but
      failed to identify the defendant at a later physi-
      cal lineup.
   b. The witness failed to identify the defendant's
      photograph at a pretrial photographic display
      but identified the defendant at a later physical
      lineup.
   c. The witness identified the defendant's photo-
      graph at a pretrial photographic display and
      also identified the defendant at a later physical
      lineup.

9. Is it possible to conduct a fair lineup when the
   suspect is unusually tall or short or has very distinctive features or deformities?

10. Would an emergency one-person showup be justi-
    fied if the suspect and not the victim were seri-
    ously injured? In what ways could the suggestibil-
    ity of the showup be decreased?

11. Would certain suggestive pretrial identification
    procedures be excusable in a small rural police
    department as opposed to a large urban police
    department? What procedures might be excus-
    able, and why?

12. Discuss the following quotation from Justice Wil-
    liam J. Brennan's dissenting opinion in *United
    States v. Ash*, 413 U.S. 300, 344 (1973), in which the
    U.S. Supreme Court held that there is no right to
    counsel at any photographic identification proce-
    dure: "There is something ironic about the Court's
    conclusion today that a pretrial lineup identifica-

tion is a 'critical stage' of the prosecution because counsel's presence can help to compensate for the accused's deficiencies as an observer, but that a pretrial photographic identification is not a 'critical stage' of the prosecution because the accused is not able to observe at all."

13. Would there be any need for counsel at a lineup if the entire lineup procedure were recorded on both audiotape and videotape?

14. A person subject to interrogation who is under "formal arrest or restraint on freedom of movement of the degree associated with a formal ar-

rest" is entitled to an attorney. Why isn't a person subject to a pretrial identification procedure entitled to an attorney when he or she is under the same type of restraint?

15. Assume that a victim of a rape or other sexual assault recalled that her assailant had a distinctive smell. What legal issues are presented by conducting a lineup for the purposes of smell identification? Are the issues different if a showup between the victim and a suspect is conducted shortly after the crime?

Applications of the Law in Real Cases

1 On the night of March 18, 1997, Thomas Rund ("Rund"), a detective with the City of St. Louis Police Department, arrested the appellant on a misdemeanor warrant. At the time of his arrest, Rund verbally advised the appellant of his *Miranda* rights. The appellant indicated he understood those rights, and he did not ask for a lawyer.

After arriving at the police station, Rund informed the appellant about an investigation concerning five robberies occurring near the area in which he was arrested. In particular, Rund questioned appellant for about ten minutes regarding a robbery occurring the night before involving a victim named Bridgette Sinar. The appellant stated that he did approach a woman at the robbery location and ask her for some money.

Subsequently, Rund contacted Sinar to request her presence at the police station to view a physical lineup. Rund selected four individuals with a similar description as the appellant who were already incarcerated in a holdover to participate in the lineup with the appellant. Rund informed Sinar that she would see five individuals in the lineup, and if she recognized one of the individuals as the person who approached her during the robbery in question, she should identify the individual by an assigned number.

Prior to the lineup, Rund advised the appellant that he was going to be placed in the lineup. At this time, approximately 1:30 A.M., the appellant provided Rund with the name of an attorney whom he requested Rund contact. Rund attempted to contact the attorney prior to the lineup, but he was unsuccessful. Later in the morning, after the lineup, Rund left a message with the attorney's secretary.

Initially, the appellant refused to stand up for the lineup, even after he was requested to do so. Thus, two officers brought the appellant to his feet. During the lineup, they stood behind the appellant so that he could be viewed. Sinar identified the appellant as her assailant. Following Sinar's identification, Rund again advised the appellant of his *Miranda* rights. The appellant completed a warning and waiver form, indicating that he understood and waived those rights. He did not ask for a lawyer at this time. Part of the warning and waiver form included a written statement by the appellant confessing to the robberies. He signed the form, which was dated March 19, 1997, at 2:30 A.M. No threats or promises were made to him for completing this statement.

Subsequently, Rund conducted lineups for each of the other robbery victims, each of whom identified the appellant as their assailant. Should the appellant's motion to suppress statements and motion to suppress identification be granted? *State v. Lanos*, 14 S.W.3d 90 (Mo. App. 1999).

2 On March 31, 1999, a white male wearing sunglasses and a blue hat resembling those issued by the LaPrairie Mutual Insurance Company approached Denise Brown, the walk-up teller at Heritage Bank. He told Brown to remove all of the money from the drawer. Then, speaking in a low voice, he altered his instructions and indicated that he wanted only bundles and $1 bills. Brown later said that she paid close attention to his mouth and lower face, because she was concerned that the robber might become agitated if she had difficulty understanding him. In the fifty-some seconds she had to observe him, she also formed the impression that he was lightly unshaven, between 5'6" and 5'8" tall, about 150 pounds, and between thirty-five and forty-five years old. The other teller on duty, Karen Jones, was serving drive-up customers, and thus caught only a glimpse of the robber; her description of him was similar to Brown's.

The next day, someone gave Peoria police officers and FBI agents a tip that a woman named Kim Salzman could help them. Salzman was cooperative. She told the officers that the person in the surveillance video from the bank strongly resembled her brother, Randy Downs. Her statement, along with her account that Downs's gambling problems had led him to break into her printing business and steal a compressor in order to pawn it, increased the suspicions of the investigators. They decided to assemble a photo array and show it to both Brown and Jones. They did so, but neither was able positively to identify Downs as the robber from the pictures. Brown suggested that it would be more helpful to see people wearing hats and sunglasses.

Later that day, the officers interviewed Downs himself, first on a gambling boat and then later in a security office. The next day, they talked to Richard Downs, his father. The elder Mr. Downs told the officers that he had given Randy a hat from LaPrairie Mutual Insurance very similar to the one that appeared on the video. He also volunteered that when he had refused to loan Randy $2,000, Randy had responded, "You leave me little choice." After this, the officers searched Randy's apartment, with his consent; they found nothing there.

On April 5, the officers held the lineup that is the focus of this appeal. On that day, they had finally arrested Downs and brought him to the police station. One officer telephoned Jones and asked her to come to the station, and he informed Jones that they had arrested someone. Another officer called Brown and asked her to come, but it is unclear whether or not she was told there had been an arrest. For the lineup, each person was given a LaPrairie Mutual hat and a pair of sunglasses. They entered the room one after the other; each man stepped in, walked around, and said, "No, put the money in the envelope, hurry." Downs was the second to walk in. As the exhibits Downs later introduced make crystal clear, the other four all sported heavy moustaches; only Downs had no facial hair at all. Otherwise (but it is a big "otherwise"), they were similar in body build.

At the lineup, both Brown and Jones identified Downs as the robber. Jones was not very confident in her choice, describing her certainty as a seven out of ten, if ten meant absolutely sure. Brown, in contrast, jumped behind one of the detectives the minute she saw Downs enter the room, and exclaimed "Oh my God, that's him." She was crying and trembling, according to the testimony of another officer. Brown then viewed the last three

lineup participants, and at the end reiterated that she was "positive" the robber was Downs, based on "the lower half of his face" and his "stocky upper body." Should Downs's motion to suppress both the lineup and any in-court identification by Brown or Jones be granted? *United States v. Downs*, 230 F.3d 272 (7th Cir. 2000).

3 On the morning of October 30, 1998, Tim Seese, a delivery man for Grady Sims d/b/a Sims Distributing Company, a distributor of Tom's snack foods, parked the company delivery van in front of Laird's Hospital in Union, Mississippi. Seese left the doors of the van open as he was inside of the hospital making an inventory of the snack machines and refilling them. Sherry Whinery and Faye Walker, two of the hospital's employees, approached Seese to inform him that they had witnessed two individuals take something from the delivery van driven by Seese. Upon returning to the van, Seese ascertained that between $500 to $600 in coins and one-dollar bills was missing from the van.

Following a call to the police by the witnesses, an investigation of this incident took place. The investigation led to the questioning of Whinery and Walker. They provided a detailed description of the thieves to the police, including the fact that they were two black men. Whinery and Walker also gave a detailed description of the car in which the perpetrators drove away, including the make and color of the car and the Alabama license plate number. A report was then radioed out to all nearby law enforcement agents. Soon after, the police pulled over a vehicle matching the description given by Whinery and Walker. The car was occupied by Stradford and Richards Burks. Burks and Stradford were immediately apprehended and a search of the vehicle ensued. No money was found in the car at the time of the search; however, it was later recovered by a highway maintenance worker along a roadside, apparently having been dumped there after the crime.

About two hours after Burks and Stradford were arrested, Whinery and Walker were shown photographs of six black men. At that time, they identified Burks and Stradford as the men they saw robbing the delivery van at the hospital. Before the trial began, Burks filed a motion to suppress the identification testimony of Whinery and Walker. (Stradford claims that the photographs of him and Burks were the only photographs where there was not present an identification tag worn by criminals who had been arrested.) At trial, both Burks and Stradford objected to this identification testimony. A hearing was conducted outside the presence of the jury regarding the motion and objections. The trial judge denied the motion and overruled the objections, allowing the testimony to be heard by the jury. Stradford cites error on the part of the trial court for failing to suppress such testimony. Should the court have suppressed the testimony? *Stradford v. State*, 771 So.2d 390 (Miss. App. 2000).

4 As two female pedestrians were walking across the Duke Ellington Bridge from Adams Morgan to Connecticut Avenue shortly after midnight on August 23, 1996, a car approached. Men in the car made harassing comments to the women, which they ignored. As the women continued to walk away, the car cut in front of them. A man alighted from the vehicle, brandishing a weapon. One pedestrian, Ms. Moriconi, ran across the street to avoid the car, and hid behind a street light. But the other pedestrian, Ms. Dizon, remained and was faced by the assailant directly. The assailant pointed the gun at her and grabbed her clutch purse away from her. The man then hit her in the face with the gun, saying "I don't like your attitude, bitch," and got back into the car. The car drove away, passing within seven feet of Ms. Moriconi.

Police responded shortly thereafter and were given descriptions of the assailant and the driver, as well as the car they drove. The police broadcast a lookout for the car and for the two men, one of whom was said to be armed. In a matter of minutes, an officer spotted a car matching the description, heading the wrong way with its lights off on California Street, in the vicinity of the crime. The officer tried to pull the car over, but the car sped away. After a short chase, the car was eventually stopped by another police cruiser at Kalorama Circle. Several officers were on the scene as the car was stopped and the passenger, who was appellant Maddox, and the driver, who was appellant Davis, were removed from the vehicle.

While Maddox and Davis were secured, another officer, Officer Felicia Toronto, searched the car for weapons. The glove compartment was open, so the officer looked inside and removed a clutch purse that was obstructing her view of the compartment. The officer placed the purse on the passenger seat and continued to search, but did not find a weapon. She left the purse, apparently open, on the seat.

Detective Hugh Carew then came to the scene and observed, through the window of the car, the open purse and an exposed identification card of Debra Dizon. He called an officer at the scene of the crime to confirm whether one of the complainants' names matched that of the identification on the passenger seat. After finding that the identification did indeed match the name of the victim, he seized the purse.

While Ms. Dizon was taken to a local emergency room for treatment for a serious gash inflicted by the assailant's weapon which required at least 40 stitches, Ms. Moriconi was escorted from the crime scene to the spot where the car was stopped to determine whether the men stopped could be identified as the perpetrators. Prior to arriving, she was informed that two men fitting the general description she had given had been found. There, she identified appellant Maddox as the assailant and appellant Davis as the driver of the car involved in the incident. Approximately an hour later, the police brought Maddox to the hospital where Ms. Dizon was being treated. There, she identified Maddox as the assailant. Should appellants' motions to suppress evidence of these identifications by the two victims and to suppress the clutch purse and its identification card be granted? *Maddox v. United States*, 745 A.2d 284 (D.C. App. 2000).

5 On April 6, 1993, at approximately 4:30 A.M., the victim drove to the Econo Foods supermarket in Iron Mountain, Michigan, in order to pick up doughnuts for the guests of the Super Eight Motel. After coming out of the supermarket, the victim was abducted by a man hiding in the back seat of her car. The man brandished a knife and instructed the victim to drive to a secluded spot along a dirt road, where he ordered her to climb into the back seat. The man then forced the victim to disrobe, to kiss him on the lips, and to perform oral sex. Shortly thereafter, the headlights of a police car appeared behind the victim's car. The man instructed the victim to put her shirt back on, climb back into the front seat, and drive away from the area.

After driving around for a while, the man instructed the victim to park along a residential street in Iron Mountain and once again had her climb into the back seat. This time he forced the victim to perform oral and vaginal intercourse. He then had her drive to a point near a gas station where he got out of the car. The victim returned to the Super Eight Motel and reported the incident to the police. She described her attacker as an unshaven, dark-complexioned white man of medium build, about six feet tall, forty to fifty years old, with uncombed, dirty dishwater blond hair and odd-looking lips. He had been drinking, smelled bad, and smoked a darker than normal cigarette.

The defendant ultimately became the prime suspect. The police took the defendant into custody and arranged a corporal lineup. The victim tentatively identified the defendant as her assailant at the lineup. She made the following statement after the lineup:

> I was called at 2:00 P.M. to come down to look at a lineup. I looked at eight people. Number six looked like him, but I can't be sure. His eyes and face fit, but his lips were what threw me off. His eyes really look like the eyes I remember. I can't be positive, but there is something about his eyes and face.

The police arrested and charged the defendant with one count of kidnapping and two counts of third-degree CSC after the lineup. Later that evening, Officer Revord went to the victim's home to inform her that the police had arrested a suspect. During the visit, Officer Revord showed the victim a single photograph of the defendant. After seeing the photograph, she became sure that the defendant was the one who attacked her. As she testified at the hearing on the defendant's motion to suppress the identification:

> When I was relaxed after the lineup and I was at home, Officer Revord came over and he showed me the picture and it was at that time that I had no doubts that it was him.

The trial court denied a motion by the defendant to prohibit an in-court identification of defendant by the victim, holding that although the use of the photograph by Officer Revord was improper, there was a sufficiently independent basis for the victim to identify Mr. Gray at trial. Pursuant to his plea agreement, the defendant appealed the denial of his motion. Should his appeal be granted? *People v. Gray,* 577 N.W.2d 92 (Mich. 2000).

6 At approximately 10:00 P.M. on June 6, 1999, a man entered Eileen Olson's apartment through a patio door and robbed her. According to Olson, the man was in her apartment for about ten to fifteen minutes. The man hit Olson, cut her with a knife, and threatened to kill her. Olson described her assailant as a forty-five-year-old white male wearing a baseball hat, a dark plaid shirt, and blue jeans. Olson was treated for her injuries at a Fargo hospital, where police officers showed her a picture of Norrid, a suspect they had detained and photographed near her apartment. Olson did not have her glasses at the hospital, and she was unable to positively identify Norrid as her assailant. After officers retrieved her glasses from her apartment, she was still unable to positively identify Norrid as her assailant, and she indicated "It was hard for me to look at those pictures cause my glasses were so bent out of shape." At approximately 12:30 A.M., Olson was taken to a location near the scene of the crime to personally view Norrid. Olson indicated "[t]hey put a spotlight on him and asked me if that was the man that had assaulted me. And I said I was 99 percent sure, I said I just—I just—I hated to think that I would get an innocent man or anything and I wanted to stay and make sure. So we sat for a long time until I was positive it was him."

Prior to Olson's identification of Norrid as her assailant, police officers detained him and gave him warnings required by *Miranda v. Arizona,* 384 U.S. 436 (1966). After Olson identified Norrid, he was taken to the police station at approximately 3:00 A.M. and again given

Miranda warnings. Detective Jim LeDoux interviewed Norrid at the police station. Norrid initially denied involvement in the incident, but at 6:15 A.M., he signed a written statement implicating himself in the incident.

The State charged Norrid with burglary, aggravated assault, and terrorizing. Norrid moved to suppress Olson's identification of him, arguing it was unduly suggestive and violated his due process rights under the Fourteenth Amendment of the United States Constitution. Norrid also moved to suppress statements he made to police officers, arguing the statements were extracted through deception and coercion and violated his privilege against self-incrimination under the Fifth and Fourteenth Amendments. Should Norrid's motions be granted? *State v. Norrid,* 611 N.W. 2d 866 (N.D. 2000).

7 The following events were a part of a highly publicized series of rapes and related felonies collectively referred to as the "Belmont Shores rapes" that occurred over eighteen months in the City of Long Beach.

During the late night hours of September 18, 1998, Carolyn Ronlov was raped by a man she described as white with an ethnic accent. From a scent pad created at the crime scene, a police bloodhound attempted to track the assailant. The dog, named Tinkerbelle, eventually led the officers to a twenty-unit apartment building almost two miles away from the crime scene. Tinkerbelle went directly to the second floor of the building, attempted to track the scent for ten more minutes, and then gave up after failing to identify any particular unit or individual. At the time, Jeffery Allen Grant lived in a unit on the first floor. Tinkerbelle did not show any interest in Grant's unit or in the first floor at any point.

The officers sought to gather more information by questioning residents awakened by the commotion. Officer Bahash focused his attention on Grant's particular unit because inside lights appeared to be on but no one answered when he knocked. With Bahash's permission, two other officers picked the locks on Grant's apartment door with the intention of drawing the occupant outside. When the door did not open, the police testified that they grew even more suspicious and left with Grant as a possible suspect in their minds. Officer Bahash then obtained a copy of Grant's photograph from the DMV and placed it in a six-person photograph array (also known as a "six-pack") for possible identification by two earlier victims. Of the nine victims identified at that point, only Jennifer Haines and Amyjo Dale felt confident enough to make a positive identification from the photo spread.

On the night of July 3, 1998, Jennifer Haines woke to the sound of someone trying to break into her home. She called 911 and described the individual as a 5'7" Hispanic man with dark skin tone and short hair. On July 22, approximately two weeks after the incident and before Grant was ever a suspect, Officer Bahash showed Haines a six-pack containing the photograph of a man (Hernandez) who police considered to be the possible assailant at the time. Haines tentatively identified Hernandez, stating, "It looks like number 2, but I'm not real sure. But real close." A police forensic expert subsequently matched a latent fingerprint found at the Haines residence to one of Hernandez's rolled fingerprints. The police dropped Hernandez as a suspect shortly thereafter, although neither trial testimony nor the parties' briefs indicate a reason. On September 26, almost three months after the attempted break-in, Officer Bahash asked Haines to view another six-pack, this time with a photograph of Grant. She selected Grant, stating "It's number 3, if the hair were shorter. It's him." Officer Bahash never followed up by having Haines choose between the two photographs of Grant and Hernandez after she had identified both as her assailant.

On the night of May 25, 1998, Amyjo Dale woke to discover a man crawling on her bedroom floor. They struggled, and the assailant succeeded in throwing a blanket over Dale's head. Just as he was leaving her bedroom, Dale removed the blanket and caught a glimpse of his face. He told her to look away and then fled the scene. She dialed 911 and described her assailant as a Caucasian male with olive-toned skin, about 5'10" to 6' tall. On June 19, three weeks after her attack, Officer Watson showed Dale eight separate photographs. Dale made a tentative identification of an individual named Oliver, stating his features were very close to her assailant.

On September 30, almost four months after her attack, Officer Watson presented Dale with the array containing Grant's photograph created by Officer Bahash. At this point, both officers were coordinating their investigation efforts and sharing information. Upon viewing the array, Dale tentatively selected Grant and stated that she was "pretty sure," but would be more positive with a live identification. On that same day, the police arrested Grant without a warrant for all nine of the Belmont Shores rapes and related felonies. When forensic evidence found at several crime scenes failed to match Grant's DNA, the prosecutor dropped all charges and released Grant from jail, where he had been sitting for over three months awaiting trial. Grant then sued the City of Long Beach, the Long Beach Police Department, and the two police officers who spearheaded the investigation under 42 U.S.C. § 1983 for false arrest and false imprisonment. He alleged that the defendants' conduct violated his Fourth Amendment protection from arrest without probable cause and his Fourteenth Amendment right to due process. Should Grant succeed in his claim for damages for false arrest and false imprisonment? *Grant v. City of Long Beach*, 315 F.3d 1081 (9th Cir. 2002).

Glossary

abandoned property Property whose owner has voluntarily discarded or left it behind; or has otherwise relinquished his or her interest in it and no longer retains a **reasonable expectation of privacy** with regard to it. Law enforcement officers may lawfully seize abandoned property without a warrant or probable cause because the Fourth Amendment does not apply.

abuse of discretion Discretionary decisions of courts of original jurisdiction are reviewed on appeal using the *abuse of discretion* standard. This highly deferential standard of review invalidates a discretionary decision only if it can be shown to have been made in an arbitrary, capricious, or unreasonable manner. See **standard of review**.

acquittal A judgment of a court that the defendant is not guilty of the offense for which he or she has been tried. It is based either on the verdict of a jury or of a judicial officer in a bench trial. An acquittal on all charges is a final court disposition terminating criminal jurisdiction over the defendant.

administrative law The rules and regulations promulgated by a governmental agency that is empowered through statutory law to make such rules.

administrative search A routine inspection of a home or business by governmental authorities responsible for determining compliance with various statutes and regulations (e.g., fire, health, safety, and housing codes).

admission An admission or acknowledgment of a fact by a person that tends to incriminate the person; it is not sufficient of itself to establish guilt of a crime. An admission, alone or in connection with other facts, that tends to show the existence of one or more, but not all, of the elements of a crime. See **confession**.

affidavit A written statement sworn to or affirmed before an officer authorized to administer an oath or affirmation. Unlike a **deposition**, an affidavit requires no notice to the adverse party or opportunity for cross-examination. In the criminal law, law enforcement officers and others use affidavits to provide information to a magistrate in order to establish probable cause for the issuance of an arrest warrant or a search warrant.

affirmative defense A defense, such as insanity or entrapment, in which the defendant bears the burden of persuasion to prove the existence of all elements of the defense.

allocute/allocution Allocution is the process of meeting the requirement under Federal Rule of Criminal Procedure 11 that a criminal defendant provides a "factual basis" for a plea of guilty. To allocute, the defendant must admit in open court to the conduct central to the criminality of crimes charged. This is accomplished at an allocution hearing, sometimes referred to as a "change of plea" proceeding.

anticipatory search warrant A warrant to search a particular place for a particular seizable item that has not yet arrived there. The **affidavit** submitted in application for the warrant must establish probable cause that evidence of a certain crime will be located at a specific place in the future. If some **triggering condition** (other than the mere passage of time) is necessary for probable cause to search and seize to exist, then probable cause must also presently exist to believe the triggering condition will, in fact, occur.

appeal An application to or proceeding in an appellate court for review or rehearing of a judgment, decision, or order of a lower court or other tribunal in order to correct alleged errors or injustices or *plain errors*. Plain errors are those defects in a trial that so seriously affect the rights of the accused that a failure to correct them—even those that were not objected to at trial—would undermine the fundamental fairness of the trial and bring about a miscarriage of justice. See **harmless error doctrine**.

appellate jurisdiction Lawful authority or power of a court to review a decision made by a lower court or to hear an appeal from a judgment of a lower court.

appurtenant property Property that is incident to, belonging to, or going with the principal property. This includes buildings on the land (such as sheds), and other things attached to or annexed to the land that may be searched during the execution of a warrant for the search of the principal property. For example, a detached garage, even if not named in a warrant, can be searched as an appurtenant building to a house.

arraignment The hearing before a court having jurisdiction in a criminal case, in which the identity of the defendant is established, the defendant is informed of the charge and of his or her rights, and the defendant is required to enter a plea. The defendant's entering of a plea is the crucial distinguishing element of the arraignment.

arrest A seizure of a person in which the person is taken into governmental custody for the purpose of charging the person with a criminal offense (or, for juveniles, a delinquent act or status offense). See **show of authority**.

arrest warrant A written order issued by a magistrate or other proper judicial officer, upon probable cause for a particularly described offense, that directs a law enforcement officer to arrest a particular person described in the warrant by name and/or other unique characteristics.

attenuation of taint An exception to the **fruit of the poisonous tree doctrine** that allows the admission of tainted evidence if that evidence was obtained in a manner that is sufficiently removed or "attenuated" from unconstitutional search or seizure, thereby rendering the evidence admissible at trial.

aural transfer An electronic transfer containing the human voice at any point between and including the point of origin and the point of reception, such as over telephone lines or via cellular telephone.

automatic companion rule A rule that allows a law enforcement officer to frisk the companion of an arrestee for weapons because of a concern for officer safety, without any further justification.

automobile exception See *Carroll* **doctrine**.

bail To obtain the release from custody of an arrested or imprisoned person by pledging money or other prop-

erty as a guarantee of the person's appearance in court at a specified date and time.

bailee/bailor A bailee is a person in possession of someone else's personal property with the lawful permission of the rightful owner—the bailor. A bailee of personal property may consent to a search of the property if he or she has full possession and control. In contrast, a bailee who has only mere custody of a bailor's property could not lawfully consent to a search of that property.

beeper A radio transmitter, usually battery operated, which emits periodic signals that can be picked up by a radio receiver.

bench trial A trial in which there is no jury, and in which a judicial officer determines all issues of fact and law.

bill of attainder A special act of a legislature that declares a person or group of persons has committed a crime, and imposes punishment without a court trial. Under our system of separation of powers, only courts may try a person for a crime or impose punishment for violation of the law. Article I, Section 9 of the U.S. Constitution restrains Congress from passing bills of attainder; Article I, Section 10 of the U.S. Constitution restrains the states.

Bill of Rights The first ten amendments to the U.S. Constitution added to guarantee basic individual liberties, including freedom of speech, freedom of the press, freedom of religion, and freedom to assemble and petition the government. The guarantees of the Bill of Rights originally applied only to acts of the federal government. By operation of the Fourteenth Amendment's Due Process Clause (added in 1868), all fundamental rights specified in the Bill of Rights have been selectively incorporated such that they are applicable to the states as well. See **selective incorporation**.

booking A police administrative procedure that officially records an arrest in a police register. Booking involves, at the minimum, recording the names of the person arrested and the officer making the arrest; and the time of, place of, circumstances of, and reason for the arrest. Sometimes booking also means other procedures that take place in the stationhouse after an arrest, such as fingerprinting and/or photographing the arrested person.

burden of proof A generic term that encompasses both the burdens of production and persuasion. See **burden of production** and **burden of persuasion**.

burden of persuasion The duty to establish a particular issue or proposition by the quantity of evidence required by law (e.g., probable cause, preponderance of the evidence, clear and convincing evidence, or beyond a reasonable doubt). In criminal cases, the prosecution's burden of persuasion is to prove every element of the crime charged beyond a reasonable doubt.

burden of production The duty of the party presenting an issue or fact to produce or "come forward" with sufficient evidence to support a favorable finding on that issue or fact; also referred to as the burden of coming forward.

***Carroll* doctrine** Sometimes referred to as the automobile exception to the search warrant requirement, this search and seizure doctrine originated in *Carroll v. United States*, 267 U.S. 132 (1925). It states that a warrantless search of a motor vehicle under exigent circumstances by a law enforcement officer who has probable cause to believe that the vehicle contains items subject to seizure is not unreasonable under the Fourth Amendment.

challenge for cause A formal objection to a prospective juror based on the assumption that the juror cannot reach a fair and impartial verdict on the particular case. These may be *fact-partial challenges* (based on the person's background, opinions, biases, or personal knowledge of the facts of a case), or *principal challenges* (the prospective juror has personal knowledge of the participants in the case).

citizen's arrest Under the common law rule in force in most states, a private citizen may arrest a person if the citizen (1) has probable cause to believe that the person has committed a felony; or (2) actually witnessed a suspect commit or attempt to commit a misdemeanor. Law enforcement officers outside their territorial jurisdiction generally have the same authority as private citizens to arrest without a warrant.

civil rights Generally, the constitutionally guaranteed rights of a person by virtue of the person's status as a member of civil society, except those rights involving participation in the establishment, support, or management of the government.

clearly erroneous The Standard of Review that an appellate court applies to factual determinations made by a court of original jurisdiction. Under this deferential standard, an appellate court will not overturn any factual decisions made by the lower court unless the factual determinations are *clearly erroneous*. See **standard of review**.

closing argument A statement made by each party at the end of a trial, after all the evidence has been presented and the jury has been instructed. Each side recapitulates the facts and evidence it has presented and attempts to convince the judge or jury of the correctness of its position.

collateral estoppel doctrine An issue of ultimate fact that has once been determined by a valid and final judgment cannot again be litigated between the same parties in any future lawsuit.

common authority The authority that justifies third-party consent to search based on mutual use of the property by those who have joint access or control for most purposes. It may be based on *actual common authority* (the official legal capacity to grant consent to search the property over which someone has lawful access or control), or *apparent common authority* (someone whom police reasonably believe to possess actual common authority over the premises, but who, in fact, does not have such authority).

common law The system of law, originated and developed in England, based on court decisions and on custom and usage, rather than on written laws created by legislative enactment; judge-made law that evolves based on the principles of precedent and *stare decisis*.

competency In criminal procedure, a judicial determination that a criminal defendant understands his or her situation and has the intellectual wherewithal to stand trial or waive certain constitutional rights. Competency to stand trial, for example, requires defendants to have (1) a rational as well as factual understanding of the proceedings against them; and (2) sufficient present ability to consult an attorney with a reasonable degree of rational understanding in order to assist in their own defense.

complaint A sworn written statement presented to a proper judicial officer alleging that a specified person has committed a specified crime and requesting prosecution.

compulsory process Coercive means, such as subpoenas and arrest warrants, used by courts to procure the attendance in court of persons wanted as witnesses or otherwise; the right of a criminal defendant as set forth in the Sixth Amendment to the U.S. Constitution to compel competent, material witnesses to appear in court and testify as part of the defense's case.

concurrent jurisdiction When both the state and federal courts (or when two courts within the same court system) both have original jurisdiction over the same matter.

confabulation The creation or substitution of false memories through later suggestion that incorrectly fills in the gaps in a person's memory.

confession A statement in which a person admits facts revealing his or her guilt as to all elements of a particular crime. See **admission**.

confirmation bias The tendency to search for or interpret new information in a way that confirms one's preconceptions, and to avoid information and interpretations that contradict prior beliefs.

confrontation 1. The right of an accused person to come face to face with an adverse witness in court, to object to the testimony of the witness, and to cross-examine the witness. The Sixth Amendment to the U.S. Constitution guarantees the right of confrontation to defendants in federal criminal prosecutions. The due process clause of the Fourteenth Amendment makes this Sixth

Amendment guarantee applicable to the states. 2. Any presentation of a suspect to a victim or witness of a crime for the purpose of identifying the perpetrator of the crime. The term confrontation includes showups, lineups, and photo arrays.

consent search A search of a person's body, premises, or belongings conducted by a law enforcement officer after the person has given voluntary permission.

constitutional law 1. The study of foundational or basic laws of nation states and other political organizations. 2. The interpretation and application of the provisions of the U.S. Constitution and/or the constitutions of the states.

containers Any object capable of holding another object. A container thus includes "closed or open glove compartments, consoles or other receptacles located anywhere within the passenger compartment of a vehicle, as well as luggage, boxes, bags, clothing, and the like."

contraband Items whose possession is prohibited by law.

controlled delivery Monitoring a container known or reasonably believed to contain contraband while on its journey to the intended destination. A controlled delivery may qualify as a **triggering event** for the purposes of an **anticipatory search warrant**.

correctional system/corrections The variety of agencies, institutions, and programs that seek to punish and/or rehabilitate someone convicted of a crime using such tools as fines, **probation, intermediate sanctions, incarceration**, and **parole**.

corroborate Present additional information that confirms or strengthens the truthfulness of a fact or assertion to support or enhance its believability.

court of general jurisdiction A criminal court that has trial jurisdiction over all criminal offenses, including all felonies, and that may or may not hear appeals. It also has original jurisdiction over all felonies, and frequently has appellate jurisdiction over the decisions of a **court of limited jurisdiction**.

court of limited jurisdiction A criminal court whose trial jurisdiction is limited to adjudicating particular types of offenses, such as misdemeanors, traffic cases, drunk-driving cases, etc.

covert entry warrant A search warrant that specifically authorizes officers to enter unoccupied premises, search for specified evidence, and then leave—without seizing the evidence they find, and without leaving a trace that an entry has been made. Officers usually photograph or videotape the evidence, or otherwise document exactly what they saw and its exact location. However, under the USA PATRIOT Act, items discovered during the execution of a covert entry warrant may be seized if there is

a "reasonable necessity for the seizure." The practice has come to be known as a "sneak-and-steal" search.

crime control model The repression of criminal conduct through prevention, and by the swift apprehension, conviction, and punishment of offenders. One of Herbert Packer's two competing conceptualizations of value systems that function in the U.S. system of criminal justice. Compare to **due process model**.

critical stages of criminal prosecutions Proceedings during criminal prosecutions at which the accused is entitled to the assistance of counsel because his or her substantial rights may be affected by what transpires. Critical stages include: pre-indictment preliminary hearings, bail hearings, post-indictment pretrial lineups, post-indictment or post-arraignment interrogations, arraignments, felony trials, misdemeanor trials involving a potential jail sentence, first appeals as a matter of right, juvenile delinquency proceedings involving potential confinement, sentencing hearings, and hearings regarding psychiatric examinations.

cross-examination The questioning of one party's witness by the opposing party after **direct examination**. The purpose of cross-examination is to discredit the witness's information and impeach the witness's credibility as a means of testing the accuracy of his or her testimony. The scope of cross-examination is usually limited to matters covered during direct examination.

cruel and unusual punishment Punishments that are prohibited under the Cruel and Unusual Punishment Clause of the Eighth Amendment. This clause limits the punishment that may be imposed on conviction of a crime in two ways: (1) by imposing substantive limits on what can be made criminal and punished as such; and (2) by prohibiting certain kinds of punishment, such as torture and divestiture of citizenship, that violate "evolving standards of decency that mark the progress of a maturing society." *Trop v. Dulles*, 356 U.S. 86, 101 (1958).

curtilage The grounds and buildings immediately surrounding a dwelling that are used for domestic purposes in connection with the dwelling. Areas within the curtilage of a home are protected against unreasonable searches and seizures by the Fourth Amendment to the U.S. Constitution.

custodial arrest An arrest in which the person arrested is taken into **custody** and not merely given a ticket, citation, or notice to appear.

custody 1. Legal or physical control of a person or thing; legal, supervisory, or physical responsibility for a person or thing. 2. A person is in custody for purposes of *Miranda v. Arizona* when the person is deprived of freedom of action in any significant way.

defamation A false, public statement of fact (not opinion) that injures or damages a person's reputation.

Defamation in writing is called libel; spoken defamation is called slander. Defamation is a class of speech that is not protected by the First Amendment to the U.S. Constitution.

de novo In appellate review of the decisions of courts of original jurisdiction, *de novo* grants no deference to the lower court. Rather, the appellate court reviews the legal issues presented in the case anew. See **trial de novo** and **standard of review**.

deposition A witness's out-of-court testimony, taken under oath prior to trial and recorded and/or transcribed. Depositions are usually taken orally and require notice to the adverse party so that the adverse party may attend the deposition and cross-examine the witness. Depositions are used to preserve the testimony of a prospective witness who may be unable to attend or be prevented from attending a trial or hearing. A deposition may also be used as part of the discovery process to gain information about a case. Deposition testimony may be used to contradict or impeach the testimony of the deponent when the deponent later testify as a witness at a hearing or trial. See **discovery**.

derivative evidence Tainted evidence that is directly derived from an unconstitutional search or seizure and is, therefore, inadmissible under the **fruit of the poisonous tree doctrine** unless one of the exceptions to that doctrine (such as attenuation, inevitable discovery, good faith, etc.) is applicable.

determinate sentencing See **sentence/sentencing**.

direct examination The initial examination of a witness in a trial by the party on whose behalf the witness is called. The attorney asks specific questions, and the witness is expected to give testimony favorable to the party calling the witness. See **cross-examination**.

discovery A procedure by which a party obtains a legal right to compel the opposing party to permit access to information in order to promote the orderly ascertainment of the truth during trial. Discovery in criminal cases usually involves allowing the moving party to obtain, inspect, copy, or photograph items within the possession or control of the opposing party. The process can also be used to compel access to witnesses for the purpose of conducting a **deposition**.

double-blind administration of lineup/photo array An identification procedure in which neither the witness nor the person administering the lineup or photo array should know who the suspect is and who the **foils** are.

double jeopardy A legal command of the Fifth Amendment to the U.S. Constitution that prohibits the same sovereign (e.g., the federal government or a state government) from prosecuting someone for the same offense after acquittal or conviction, and from imposing multiple punishments on someone for the same offense. See **dual sovereignty doctrine**.

dual sovereignty doctrine The doctrine under which, "[w]hen a defendant in a single act violates the 'peace and dignity' of two sovereigns [e.g., two different state governments] by breaking the laws of each, he has committed two distinct 'offences.'" *Heath v. Alabama*, 474 U.S. 82, 88 (1985). Double jeopardy does not arise when a single act exposes a defendant to prosecution by two separate sovereigns, such as the federal government and a state government, or the governments of two different states.

due process model Crime prevention through **due process of law** vis-à-vis formal, adjudicative, adversary fact-finding processes that are concerned with legal guilt. One of Herbert Packer's two competing conceptualizations of value systems that function in the U.S. system of criminal justice. Compare to **crime control model**.

due process revolution The U.S. supreme court's ideological shift during the 1960s civil rights era towards "constitutionalizing" criminal procedure with a focus on individual rights and liberties.

due process of law The legal notion, guaranteed by the Fifth and Fourteenth Amendments to the U.S. Constitution, that laws and legal procedures will conform to the rules and principles established in our system of justice for the enforcement and protection of individual rights. Due process is traditionally associated with the principles of adequate and fair notice and the right to be heard. It also protects against the exercise of arbitrary governmental power, and guarantees equal and impartial dispensation of law according to the settled course of judicial proceedings or in accordance with fundamental principles of distributive justice.

effective assistance of counsel The principle that merely providing the accused with an attorney is not enough; that attorney must defend the accused in a reasonably competent manner. The Sixth Amendment's guarantee of the right to counsel to assist the accused in all criminal prosecutions is meaningless if counsel's representation falls below an objective standard of reasonableness.

electronic communication Any transfer of signs, signals, writing, images, sounds, data, or intelligence of any nature transmitted in whole or in part by a wire, radio, electromagnetic, photo-electronic or photo-optical system that affects interstate or foreign commerce but does not include (1) any **wire communication** or **oral communication**;. (2) any communication made through a tone-only paging device; (3) any communication from a tracking device; or (4) electronic funds transfer information stored by a financial institution in a communications system used for the electronic storage and transfer of funds.

electronic surveillance/intercept Searches conducted using wiretaps, bugs, or other electronic or mechanical devices to overhear conversations or obtain other kinds of information.

emergency See **exigent circumstances**.

eminent domain The power of the government to take private property for "public use" so long as the owner of such property is fairly compensated for the seizure of his or her property.

en banc A special session of a court in which all the judges of the court participate, as opposed to a session presided over by a single judge or a mere quorum of judges.

enemy combatants A designation given to individuals who were captured by the United States on suspicion of being involved in terrorist activities by being a part of or supporting Taliban or al Qaeda forces, or associated forces that are engaged in hostilities against the United States or its coalition partners. The USA PATRIOT Act apparently authorized the indefinite detention of enemy combatants who are not citizens of the United States, including permanent resident aliens living in the United States, if the U.S. Attorney General certifies that he or she has "reasonable grounds to believe" that the non-citizen has engaged in "terrorist activity." The constitutionality of the indefinite detention of enemy combatants has yet to be decided by the U.S. Supreme Court.

equal protection of the laws The Fourteenth Amendment to the U.S. Constitution provides, in part, that no state shall "deny to any person within its jurisdiction the equal protection of the laws." This constitutional guarantee prohibits states from denying any person or class of persons the same protection of the law enjoyed by other persons or other classes of persons in similar circumstances. Thus, no state may adopt laws, regulations, or policies that establish categories of people receiving unequal treatment on the basis of race, religion, or national origin. No clause in the U.S. Constitution specifically guarantees that equal protection applies to actions of the federal government; but the federal government is prohibited from denying a person equal protection of federal laws by judicial interpretations of the Due Process Clause of the Fifth Amendment.

Establishment Clause The provision in the First Amendment to the U.S. Constitution that provides that neither Congress nor a state legislature (by virtue of the Fourteenth Amendment) may "make any law respecting an establishment of religion." This means that no legislature may enact a law that establishes an official church that all Americans must accept and support, or to whose tenets all must subscribe, or that favors one church over another.

estimator variables Variables that affect the memory of a witness, and over which the criminal justice system has no control. Estimator variables include *event factors* (e.g., time, lighting conditions, changes in visual adaptation to light and dark, duration of the event, speed and distance involved, and the presence or absence of violence); and *witness factors* (e.g., stress, fear, physical limitation on sensory perception—poor eyesight, hearing impairment, alcohol or drug intoxication—expectations, age, and gender).

evidence Anything offered to a court or jury through the medium of witnesses, documents, exhibits, or other objects, to demonstrate or ascertain the truth of facts at issue in a case; the means by which facts are proved or disproved in court. *Direct evidence* is firsthand evidence that does not require a **presumption** to be made or an **inference** to be drawn in order to establish a proposition of fact. *Circumstantial evidence* is indirect evidence of some fact in dispute that requires the trier-of-fact to presume or infer the existence of some fact to reach some logical conclusion. Subtypes of evidence include: *testimonial evidence* (oral testimony given under oath); *real/physical evidence* (tangible objects that have evidentiary value); *scientific evidence* (the formal results of forensic investigatory techniques); and *demonstrative evidence* (visual or auditory aids created for use at trial to assist the trier-of-fact in understanding evidence). See also **judicial notice**.

excessive force The use of more force than is reasonably necessary to make an arrest, prevent an escape, stop a fleeing suspect, subdue someone in lawful custody, or to lawfully defend oneself, another person, or property. The use of excessive force gives rise to both criminal and civil liability for assault, battery, and other crimes against the person (including homicide and attempted homicide charges), as well as for civil rights lawsuits for deprivations of constitutional rights under the Fourth, Fifth, Eighth, and Fourteenth Amendments to the U.S. Constitution.

exclusionary rule A rule, developed by the U.S. Supreme Court, stating that evidence obtained in violation of a person's constitutional rights by law enforcement officers or agents will be inadmissible in a criminal prosecution against the person whose rights were violated. Subject to several exceptions, the exclusionary rule usually also prohibits the introduction of derivative evidence, both tangible and testimonial, that is the product of the primary evidence, or that is otherwise acquired as an indirect result of an unlawful search or seizure.

exculpatory evidence Any evidence that may be favorable to the defendant at trial either by tending to cast doubt on the defendant's guilt or by tending to mitigate the defendant's culpability, thereby potentially reducing the defendant's sentence. Under *Brady v. Maryland*, 373 U.S. 83, 87 (1963), "the suppression by the prosecution of evidence favorable to an accused upon request violates due process where the evidence is material either to guilt or punishment, irrespective of the good faith or bad faith of the prosecution."

exigent circumstances A serious situation developing suddenly and unexpectedly that demands immediate action rather than conformity with the usual requirements of law. They usually include emergency situations that have given rise to imminent danger to life, serious damage to property, imminent escape of a suspect, or the imminent destruction of evidence.

ex post facto From Latin, meaning "after the fact." An *ex post facto* law is "one which makes that criminal which was not so at the time the action was performed, or which increases the punishment, or, in short, in relation to the offense or its consequences, alters the situation of a party to his disadvantage." *Lindsey v. Washington*, 301 U.S. 397 (1937). *Ex post facto* laws are prohibited by Article I, Sections 9 and 10, of the U.S. Constitution and similar provisions of state constitutions.

extradition The surrender of an accused or convicted person by the state to which the person has fled (the asylum state), to the state with jurisdiction to try or punish the person (the demanding state), upon demand of the latter state, so that the person may be dealt with according to its laws. The governor of the demanding state issues an extradition warrant. The delivery of the person to the demanding state occurs under the executive or judicial authorization of the asylum state. The U.S. Constitution, Article IV, Section 2, requires the officials of a state to arrest and return an accused fugitive to another state for trial upon demand of the governor of the latter state. Most states have adopted the Uniform Criminal Extradition Act, which provides uniform extradition procedures among the states.

fact-partial challenge See **challenge-for-cause**.

federalism The constitutional division of power between the state and federal governments in which certain powers were granted the federal government concerning national matters, while all other governmental powers were reserved for the states.

felony In general, a crime of a more serious nature than those designated as misdemeanors. Felonies are distinguished from misdemeanors by place of punishment and possible duration of punishment, as defined by statute. The statutory definition of felony may differ between states and between the federal government and various states. Typically, a felony is a crime with a possible punishment of death or imprisonment in a state or federal prison facility for a period of one year or more.

fighting words Words that are so highly inflammatory they are likely to provoke the average person to retaliation and thereby cause a breach of the peace. Such speech is not protected by the First Amendment to the U.S. Constitution.

foils/fillers The people who appear in a lineup or photo array other than the suspect.

Foreign Intelligence Surveillance Act ("FISA") A statute enacted by the U.S. Congress that authorizes and regulates the electronic surveillance of foreign powers and their agents within the United States, as well as any individual or group that is not linked to a foreign government but who "engages in international terrorism or activities in preparation therefore." FISA permits federal agents to conduct electronic surveillance and physical searches for national defense purposes. Unlike normal search warrants or Title III intercept orders, FISA warrants do not require a showing of probable cause to believe that a crime has been or is being committed. Rather, FISA only requires probable cause that the surveillance is of an authorized person or group for purposes relating to the gathering of foreign intelligence or preventing terrorism. Additional findings, however, are required if the targets of the investigation are U.S. citizens or lawful resident aliens. FISA warrants are usually issued by Foreign *Intelligence Surveillance Court* ("FISC"), although the U.S. Attorney General may authorize FISA surveillance for periods up to one year without FISC approval under certain circumstances. See **Title III of the Omnibus Crime Control and Safe Streets Act of 1968**.

forgetting curve The phenomenon in which memory declines with the passage of time, but not at a linear rate. Rather, memory tends to fades fairly rapidly immediately following a stressful event.

Franks* hearing** An adversarial judicial proceeding named after the U.S. Supreme Court's decision in *Franks v. Delaware*, 438 U.S. 154 (1978). It holds that a court must conduct an evidentiary hearing to determine the validity of a warrant after a criminal defendant has made a ***prima facie showing that an **affidavit** submitted in support of the warrant contained material statements that were deliberately false or demonstrated reckless disregard for the truth. If the judge concludes such misconduct occurred, the offending material must be severed or stricken from the warrant application. If the information remaining after **severance** still establishes probable cause, then the warrant will be upheld. If, however, the information remaining in the affidavit after the offending data is set aside fails to establish probable cause, then "the search warrant must be voided and the fruits of the search excluded to the same extent as if probable cause was lacking on the face of the affidavit." 483 U.S. at 155–56.

Free Exercise Clause The provision in the First Amendment to the U.S. Constitution that provides that neither Congress nor a state legislature (by virtue of the Fourteenth Amendment) may enact any law that "prohibits the free exercise" of religion. This clause allows people to practice freely their religion so long as those practices do not conflict with otherwise valid laws.

fresh pursuit Immediate pursuit of a fleeing criminal with intent to apprehend him or her. Fresh pursuit generally refers to the situation in which a law enforcement officer attempts to make a valid arrest of a criminal within the officer's jurisdiction, and the criminal flees outside the jurisdiction to avoid arrest, with the officer immediately pursuing. An arrest made in fresh pursuit will be legal if the pursuit was started promptly and maintained continuously. Many states have adopted the Uniform Act on Fresh Pursuit to govern fresh pursuits that take an arresting officer into a neighboring state.

frisk A pat-down or limited search of a person's body and clothing for weapons conducted for the protection of the police officer when the officer has reasonable, articulable suspicion that he or she is dealing with an armed and dangerous individual.

fruit of the poisonous tree doctrine The doctrine that evidence is inadmissible in court if it was obtained indirectly by exploitation of some prior unconstitutional police activity (such as an illegal arrest or search or a coerced confession). The evidence indirectly obtained is sometimes called *derivative evidence*.

fundamental rights Those rights that are fundamental to U.S. notions of liberty and justice, such as the freedom of speech, the freedom of religion, the freedom to travel, the right to access the courts, and the right to vote. See **selective incorporation** and **standard of review**.

furtive gestures Secretive or evasive behaviors that contribute to a law enforcement officer's determination of reasonable, articulable suspicion to conduct a stop and/or frisk.

general warrant A warrant that fails to meet the Fourth Amendment's **particularity** requirement because it is too general.

Geneva Conventions A body of international law that has developed over the centuries to set rules for the treatment of civilians, the sick, and prisoners of war ("POW") captured on the battlefield in war time separate and distinct from the treatment of criminals.

Global Positioning System (GPS) device A satellite-based system consisting of a network of satellites orbiting the Earth that emit precise microwave signals such that a GPS enabled-receiver can determine the location, speed, direction, and time of a vehicle or container that is equipped with a GPS tracking device.

good-faith exception An exception to the **exclusionary rule** for illegal searches conducted in good faith. Under this exception, whenever a law enforcement officer acting with objective good faith has obtained a search warrant from a detached and neutral judge or magistrate and acted within its scope, evidence seized pursuant to the warrant will not be excluded, even though the warrant is later determined to be invalid. The good-faith

exception has been extended to protect police who acted in good-faith reliance upon a statute (subsequently found invalid) that authorized warrantless administrative searches.

grand jury A jury, usually composed of sixteen to twenty-three persons, selected according to law and sworn in, whose duty is to receive criminal complaints, hear the evidence put forth by the prosecution, and find indictments when it is satisfied that there is probable cause that an accused person has committed a crime and should be brought to trial. Grand juries may also investigate criminal activity generally and investigate the conduct of public agencies and officials. In many states, all felony charges must be considered by a grand jury before filing in the trial court. Unlike a trial jury, which hears a case in order to render a verdict of guilty or not guilty, a grand jury decides only whether there is sufficient evidence to cause a person to be brought to trial for a crime.

habeas corpus The name of a writ issued by a court and directed to a person detaining or confining another (usually the superintendent of a confinement facility) commanding him or her to bring the body of the person detained before a judicial officer and to show cause whether the detention is legal. Article I, Section 9, Clause 2, of the U.S. Constitution provides that "[t]he privilege of the Writ of Habeas Corpus shall not be suspended, unless when in Cases of Rebellion or Invasion the public safety may require it." The right of a person to the writ depends on the legality of the detention and not on the person's guilt or innocence.

harmless error doctrine The principle that an appellate court should not overturn a criminal conviction for minor errors that had little, if any, likelihood of having contributed to the ultimate result of the trial. In contrast, harmful errors—especially plain error—are those that likely contributed to a conviction and therefore require the overturning of a conviction in order to comport with the requirements of due process and the Sixth Amendment guarantee of a fair trial. See **appeal**.

hearsay evidence Evidence of a statement made other than by a witness testifying at a trial or hearing offered to prove the truth of the matter asserted. The statement may be oral or written, or may be nonverbal conduct intended as a substitute for words.

hearsay rule The hearsay rule, simply stated, is that **hearsay evidence** is inadmissible. The basis of the hearsay rule is that the credibility of the person making a statement is the most important factor in determining the truth of the statement. If a statement is made out of court, there is no opportunity to cross-examine the person making the statement or to observe the person's demeanor. Without these methods of determining the truth of the statement, the statement may not be admitted into evidence.

Many exceptions to the hearsay rule allow the admission of hearsay evidence for various reasons of trustworthiness of the evidence and practical necessity.

hot pursuit The immediate pursuit by a law enforcement officer of a person into a house or other constitutionally protected area in response to an emergency. Examples of emergencies that will justify a hot pursuit are escape of a fleeing felon or other dangerous person, avoidance of arrest by a person suspected of a crime, and prevention of the destruction or concealment of evidence. Once inside the house or other constitutionally protected area, officers may search the premises if necessary to alleviate the emergency; any items of evidence observed lying open to view may be legally seized under the plain view doctrine.

immunity Freedom or exemption from prosecution granted to a witness to compel answers to questions or the production of evidence, which the witness might otherwise refuse to do on the grounds of the Fifth Amendment privilege against self-incrimination. Two types of immunity that may be granted are transactional immunity and use immunity. Under *transactional immunity* a witness may be compelled to testify despite the privilege against self-incrimination, but the witness is protected from any prosecution for crimes to which his or her compelled testimony relates. Under *use immunity* a witness may be compelled to testify despite the privilege against self-incrimination, but the witness is protected from the use of the compelled testimony and any evidence derived from it. Use immunity would still permit prosecution for related offenses based upon evidence derived from independent sources. A witness's failure to answer questions or produce evidence within the subject of the investigation as ordered by the court constitutes contempt of court.

impound To take a vehicle, document, or other object into the custody of the law or of a court or law enforcement agency for safekeeping or examination.

incarceration Imprisonment in a correctional facility. A *jail* is typically a county-run detention center designed to hold inmates for short periods of time, typically up to a maximum of one year. A *prison* is a correctional facility designed to hold prisoners for long periods of time, typically for periods of at least one year and up to the time that a prisoner dies or is executed. See **correctional system/corrections**.

incommunicado interrogation The interrogation of a suspect cut off from the rest of the world in a police-dominated atmosphere. It often results in self-incriminating statements being made without full warnings of constitutional rights.

independent source An exception to the **fruit of the poisonous tree doctrine** that allows the admission of tainted evidence if that evidence was also obtained through a source wholly independent of the primary constitutional violation.

indeterminate sentencing See **sentence/sentencing**.

indictment A formal written accusation submitted by a grand jury to a court, alleging that a specified person has committed a specific offense. An indictment, like an **information**, is usually used to initiate a felony prosecution. In some jurisdictions, all felony accusations must be by indictment; but in others, felony trials will ordinarily be initiated by the filing of an information by a prosecutor.

inevitable discovery A variation of the **independent source** doctrine allowing the admission of tainted evidence if it would inevitably have been discovered in the normal course of events. Under this exception, the prosecution must establish by a preponderance of the evidence that, even though the evidence was actually discovered as the result of a constitutional violation, the evidence would ultimately or inevitably have been discovered by lawful means, for example, as the result of the predictable and routine behavior of a law enforcement agency, some other agency, or a private person.

inference A permissible conclusion or deduction that the trier-of-fact may reasonably make based on the facts which have been established by the evidence, but the trier-of-fact is not required to do so.

informant A person who gives information to the police regarding criminal activity.

information A formal, written accusation submitted to a court by a prosecutor, without the approval or intervention of a grand jury, alleging that a specified person has committed a specific offense. An information is similar in nature and content to an **indictment** and serves as an alternative to the indictment in some jurisdictions to initiate usually felony prosecutions. Some jurisdictions initiate felony prosecutions only through indictment; others allow use of the information only after the defendant has waived an indictment.

initial appearance The first appearance of an accused person in the first court having jurisdiction over his or her case. Its primary purpose is to ensure that an arrest was supported by probable cause.

instruction A direction or explanation given by a trial judge to a jury informing them of the law applicable to the case before them. Attorneys for both sides normally furnish the judge with suggested instructions.

intermediate sanctions A range of criminal sanctions that fall short of total incarceration but are more stringent than probation. Sanctions include house arrest; electronic monitoring; or required living in a community-based correctional facility such as a halfway house, a boot camp, a work furlough camp, etc. See **correctional system/corrections**.

intermediate scrutiny Asks if a governmental classification is substantially related to achieving an important governmental interest. Intermediate scrutiny is used to adjudicate Equal Protection Clause issues that involve **quasi-suspect classifications**. See **Standard of Review**.

interrogation The questioning (or its functional equivalent) of a person suspected of a crime with the intent of eliciting incriminating admissions from the person. Volunteered statements, questions directed at clarifying a suspect's statement, brief, routine questions, spontaneous questions, and questions necessary to protect the safety of the police and public are not considered interrogation for purposes of *Miranda*.

inventory search The routine practice of police departments of securing and recording the contents of a lawfully impounded vehicle. This is done to protect the vehicle owner's property while it remains in custody, and to protect the police from potential danger and from claims or disputes over lost or stolen property.

items subject to seizure Items for which a search warrant may be issued. Federal Rule of Criminal Procedure 41(c) specifies that "[a] warrant may be issued for any of the following: (1) evidence of a crime; (2) contraband, fruits of crime, or other items illegally possessed; (3) property designed for use, intended for use, or used in committing a crime; or (4) a person to be arrested or a person who is unlawfully restrained." Most states have similar rules.

judgment The final, authoritative determination or decision of a court upon a matter within its jurisdiction. Judgments include a court's decision of conviction or acquittal of a person charged with a crime, a final court order, the issuance of a writ, or the imposition of a criminal sentence.

judicial notice A process that excuses a party from having to introduce evidence in order to prove a fact because a court determines that the fact is commonly known in the community without the need for formal proof.

judicial review The power of courts to invalidate acts of the legislative or executive branches upon a judicial determination that such acts violate a provision of the U.S. Constitution.

jurisdiction 1. The territory, subject matter, or person over which lawful authority may be exercised by a court or other justice agency, as determined by statute or constitution. For example, criminal cases are not within the jurisdiction of the probate court. 2. The jurisdiction of a court, more specifically, is the lawful authority or power to hear or act upon a case or question and to pass and enforce judgment on it.

jury A body of persons, selected and sworn according to law, to inquire into certain matters of fact and to render a verdict or true answer based on evidence presented before it. Also referred to as a *petit jury*. See **grand jury**.

jury nullification The power of a jury to acquit regardless of the strength of the evidence against a defendant. Nullification usually occurs when the defendant is particularly sympathetic, or when the defendant is prosecuted for violating an unpopular law.

jury panel The prospective jurors for cases. See **venire**.

knock-and-announce rule Law enforcement officers must knock and announce their presence, authority, and purpose before entering premises to execute a search or arrest warrant, unless permission was granted to execute a **no-knock warrant**. This rule flows from the Fourth Amendment's requirement of reasonableness. As a result of the Supreme Court's decision in *Hudson v. Michigan*, evidence obtained following a knock-and-announce violation is no longer excluded from trial. (Note, however, that the police officer may be subject to a civil lawsuit or an internal disciplinary procedure for failure to comply with the knock-and-announce rule).

lineup A **confrontation** (definition 2) involving the presentation of several persons, which may or may not include the person suspected of committing a crime, to a victim or witness of the crime for the purpose of identifying the perpetrator.

magistrate A judicial officer of a court of limited jurisdiction, or with limited or delegated authority. A magistrate issues arrest warrants, search warrants, and summonses; sets bail; orders release on bail; and conducts arraignments and preliminary examinations of persons charged with serious crimes. A magistrate may also have limited authority to try minor cases or to dispose of cases on a guilty plea.

malleable characteristics Facially distinctive characteristics of a suspect that are easily changed by wearing a disguise or by altering hair style, hair color, the presence or absence of facial hair, the wearing of glasses, and so on.

memory The unconscious process of acquiring, storing, retaining, and recalling past experiences.

minimization requirements of Title III of the Omnibus Crime Control and Safe Streets Act of 1968 Requires authorized interceptions of electronic communication to be conducted in a manner that minimizes the interception of communications that are not specifically related to the purpose of the Title III intercept warrant. These efforts must be objectively reasonable under the circumstances.

misdemeanor In general, a crime of less serious nature than those designated as felonies. In jurisdictions that recognize the felony-misdemeanor distinction, a misdemeanor is any crime that is not a felony. Misdemeanors are usually punished by fine or by incarceration in a local confinement facility rather than a state prison or penitentiary. The maximum period of confinement that may be imposed for a misdemeanor is defined by statute and is usually less than one year.

motion An oral or written request made to a court at any time before, during, or after court proceedings, asking the court to make a specified finding, decision, or order. In criminal proceedings the prosecution, the defense, or the court itself can make a motion.

motion for judgment of acquittal A motion made by the defense in a criminal case arguing that no reasonable juror could possibly conclude that guilt was proven beyond a reasonable doubt. If the judge agrees and grants the motion, the trial ends and retrial is barred by **double jeopardy**.

no-knock warrant Warrants that specifically authorize law enforcement personnel to enter premises and execute the warrant without first knocking and announcing their authority and purpose. For such a warrant to issue, reasonable, articulable suspicion must exist for believing that compliance with the **knock-and-announce rule** would result in the destruction of evidence or in some harm to the executing officer or others.

nolo contendere From Latin, meaning "I do not wish to contest." A defendant's plea to a criminal charge in which the defendant states that he or she does not contest the charge, but neither admits guilt nor claims innocence. A plea of *nolo contendere* subjects the defendant to the same legal consequences as a guilty plea.

non-jury trial See **bench trial**.

obscenity Indecent or profane materials that are not protected by the First Amendment to the U.S. Constitution. When examined as a whole by an average person applying contemporary community standards, they appeal to the prurient interest by depicting sexual conduct in a patently offensive way and lack serious literary, artistic, political, or scientific value.

open fields The portions of a person's premises lying outside the **curtilage** of his or her home or business, and therefore not protected by the Fourth Amendment of the U.S. Constitution.

opening statement The part of a trial before the presentation of evidence in which the attorney for each party gives an outline of what that party intends to prove by the evidence it will present. The primary purpose of the opening statement is to acquaint the judge and jury in a general way with the nature of the case.

oral communication Any words spoken by a person, under the expectation that this communication will not be subject to interception. See **electronic communication**.

original jurisdiction Jurisdiction of a court or administrative agency to hear or act upon a case from its beginning, and to pass judgment on the law and the facts.

pardon A form of executive clemency in which a person convicted of a crime is legally "forgiven" and his or her sentence is commuted.

parole The conditional release of an incarcerated prisoner before his or her sentence term expires, and which requires the parolee to be supervised by a parole officer. See **correctional system/corrections; probation**.

particularity The constitutional mandate of the Fourth Amendment that warrants (and affidavits/applications for warrants) must describe very specifically "the place to be searched and the persons or things to be seized." Failure to comply with the level of specificity required to satisfy the particularity requirement can result in judicial denial for an application for a warrant. A warrant that was erroneously granted in the absence of particularity can later be invalidated, thereby jeopardizing the search(es) and/or seizure(s) conducted pursuant to the warrant. See **general warrant; good faith exception**.

pat-down See **frisk**.

perception The total mix of sensory signals received from one's basic senses and then processed by an individual at any one time.

pen register A device that records outgoing addressing information (such as numbers dialed from a particular, monitored telephone). Because such a device does not intercept a "communication" per se, **Title III of the Omnibus Crime Control and Safe Streets Act of 1968** does not apply to the use of pen registers.

petit jury See **jury**.

peremptory challenge A formal objection to a prospective juror for which no reason need be given. The judge will automatically dismiss a juror to whom a peremptory challenge is made so long as the peremptory challenge was not exercised in a discriminatory manner that violates the Equal Protection Clause of the Fourteenth Amendment to the U.S. Constitution. The number of peremptory challenges available to each party is limited by statute or court rule.

plain error See **appeal**.

plain feel doctrine Same as **plain touch doctrine**.

plain touch doctrine If police are lawfully in a position from which they can feel an object, and if its incriminating character is immediately apparent (e.g., police have probable cause to believe the item they are feeling is incriminating in character), and if the officers have a lawful right of access to the object, they may seize it without a warrant. If, however, the police lack probable cause to believe that the object felt is subject to seizure without conducting some further search of the object, its seizure is not justified. See **plain view doctrine**.

plain view doctrine "[I]f police are lawfully in a position from which they view an object, if its incriminating character is apparent (e.g., police have probable cause to believe the item they are viewing is incriminating in character), and if the officers have a lawful right of access to the object, they may seize it without a warrant." *Minnesota v. Dickerson*, 508 U.S. 366, 375 (1993).

plea A defendant's formal answer in court to the charge contained in a complaint, information, or indictment that he or she is guilty or not guilty of the offense charged, or does not contest the charge. The pleas in a criminal case in most U.S. jurisdictions include guilty, not guilty, *nolo contendere*, and not guilty by reason of insanity.

plea bargain The exchange of prosecutorial or judicial concessions, or both, in return for a guilty plea. Common concessions include a lesser charge, the dismissal of other pending charges, a recommendation by the prosecutor for a reduced sentence, or a combination of these. The guilty plea arrived at through the process of plea bargaining is sometimes called a *negotiated plea*.

post-event misinformation effect Subsequent exposure to incorrect information can affect the way in which memories are retained.

preliminary examination Same as **preliminary hearing**.

preliminary hearing The proceeding before a judicial officer in which three matters must be decided: whether a crime was committed; whether the crime occurred within the territorial jurisdiction of the court; and whether there is probable cause to believe that the defendant committed the crime. A chief purpose of the preliminary hearing is to protect the accused from an inadequately based prosecution in felony cases by making a judicial test of the existence of probable cause early in the proceedings.

presentence investigation and report Probation officers generally conduct *presentence investigations* into a convicted defendant's prior criminal background; financial condition; educational, military, employment, and social history; relationships with family and friends; use of alcohol and/or controlled substances; and circumstances affecting the defendant's behavior, such as their mental status, that may assist the court in imposing sentence. The results of this investigation are written up in a formal *presentence investigation report*, which typically includes a sentencing recommendation.

presumption A conclusion or deduction that the law requires the trier-of-fact to make in the absence of evidence to the contrary. The two presumptions that apply at the start of every criminal case are the *presumption of innocence* (i.e., that a criminal defendant is presumed innocent until proven guilty beyond a reasonable doubt), and the *presumption of sanity* (that a criminal defendant is presumed sane until the defendant proves that he or she was insane by the requisite **burden of persuasion**). See **inference**.

***prima facie* evidence/case** A case established by *prima facie* evidence, and which will prevail until contradicted and overcome by other sufficient evidence. *Prima facie* evidence is defined as evidence sufficient to establish a given fact and which, if not rebutted or contradicted, will remain sufficient.

principal challenges See **challenge for cause**.

privacy See **reasonable expectation of privacy**.

probable cause The fair probability that someone is involved in criminal activity, or that contraband or evidence of a crime will be found in a particular place. Probable cause is the level of proof required to justify: the issuance of an arrest warrant or search warrant; all arrests made without a warrant; and most searches made without a warrant. Probable cause exists when the facts and circumstances within a person's knowledge and of which he or she has reasonably trustworthy information are sufficient in themselves to justify a person of reasonable caution and prudence in believing that something is true. It means something less than certainty, but more than mere suspicion, speculation, or possibility. It has often been referred to as meaning "more likely than not."

probation The conditional freedom without imprisonment granted by a judicial officer to an alleged or adjudicated adult or juvenile offender, as long as the person meets certain conditions of behavior. See **correctional system/corrections; parole**.

probation revocation A formal process used to revoke an offender's probation and thereby subject the offender to a harsher criminal sentence, usually one involving some form of **incarceration**. This process involves a hearing in which the government must prove that a probationer has violated the terms of his or her probation. The burden of persuasion is typically preponderance of the evidence. Probation revocation proceedings are not technically part of the criminal prosecution process, so a probationer facing revocation has no constitutional right to be represented by court-appointed counsel at a revocation proceeding; state law, however, may grant such a right.

proportionality The principle that limits the criminal sanction by prohibiting punishment that is grossly excessive in relation to the crime committed. The Supreme Court has equivocated on whether the Eighth Amendment's **Cruel and Unusual Punishment Clause** includes, as part of its guarantee, any requirement of proportional punishment.

prospective search warrant See **anticipatory search warrant**.

protective sweep A doctrine that permits officers to conduct a quick and limited search of premises incident to an arrest to protect their own safety and the safety of others from potential accomplices linked to the arrestee. If officers believe evidence is about to be destroyed or removed as they make a home arrest, they may conduct a limited sweep of the premises to prevent this destruction or removal.

public safety exception An exception to *Miranda's* usual warning requirements, where the need for answers to questions in situations posing a threat to public safety outweighs the need to protect the Fifth Amendment's privilege against self-incrimination.

quasi-suspect classifications Laws that implicate the constitutional guarantee of equal protection of the laws by differentiating or drawing distinctions between classes of people based on sex/gender or illegitimacy.

rational basis test 1. In constitutional adjudication, the lowest standard of review (i.e., the most deferential) is *rational basis test*. It asks if the governmental classification at issue is rationally related to a legitimate governmental interest. It is used to adjudicate all Due Process Clause and Equal Protection Clause issues that do not involve a right or classification that gives rise to a higher, more deferential standard of review See **standard of review**.

reasonable, articulable suspicion The level of proof necessary to support a **stop and frisk**. Unlike *mere suspicion* (i.e., a hunch or intuitive feeling), it is the level of proof for which a person can articulate the reasons why he or she is suspicious, and thereby serve as the basis for suspicion being deemed objectively reasonable.

reasonable expectation of privacy An individual's honest expectation—and one that society would be willing to acknowledge as legitimate—that he or she would be entitled to be free from unreasonable governmental intrusion in a particular place or item Violations of a person's reasonable expectation of privacy constitute a **search** and/or **seizure** for Fourth Amendment purposes, thereby giving rise to various constitutional and statutory rights and procedures to persons with proper **standing**.

reasonable doubt In criminal cases or in juvenile delinquency cases, the accused is presumed innocent until proven guilty beyond a reasonable doubt. Proof beyond a reasonable doubt requires that all of the elements of a crime have been factually established to a reasonable, but not absolute or mathematical, certainty; a possibility or probability is not sufficient.

redaction In evaluating the constitutional sufficiency of a search warrant: the practice of invalidating clauses in the warrant that are constitutionally insufficient for lack of probable cause or **particularity**, while preserving clauses that satisfy the Fourth Amendment. Also referred to as the doctrine of severability.

redirect examination A reexamination of a witness by a prosecuting attorney in order to rehabilitate him or her after cross-examination.

reifying error A belief that events that were imagined were actually perceived.

roving wiretaps A special type of warrant that authorizes the wiretapping of a particular suspect's communications wherever they are made, thereby dispensing with the normal requirement that interceptions be limited to a fixed location. Roving taps on either landline or cellular phones do not violate the **particularity** requirement of the Fourth Amendment if the surveillance is limited to communications involving an identified speaker and relates to crimes in which the speaker is a suspected participant.

scientific jury selection The use of behavioral scientists from a variety of disciplines (e.g., sociology, psychology, marketing, communications, etc.) as jury consultants who assist in jury selection by attempting to compile and implement an "ideal" juror profile.

sealing/putting under seal The process of placing records in special protective custody so that they are not accessible to anyone without a special court order.

search 1. An examination or inspection of a location, vehicle, or person by a law enforcement officer for the purpose of locating objects believed to relate to criminal activities or wanted persons. 2. Any official intrusion into matters and activities as to which a person has exhibited **a reasonable expectation of privacy**. The general rule is that any search conducted without a search warrant is unreasonable. Courts, however, have fashioned several well-defined exceptions to this rule. A warrant is not required, therefore, for a **search incident to arrest**; a **consent search**; an observation of evidence falling under the **plain view doctrine**; search of a motor vehicle under the ***Carroll*** **doctrine**; searches conducted in the **open fields**; observations and seizures of **abandoned property**; and frisks conducted as a part of brief, limited, investigative detention (see **stop and frisk**).

search incident to arrest A recognized exception to the search warrant requirement that allows a law enforcement officer who legally arrests a person to conduct a warrantless search of that person contemporaneous with the arrest.

search warrant An order in writing, issued by a proper judicial officer, directing a law enforcement officer to search a specified person or premises for specified property and to bring it before the judicial authority named in the warrant. A search warrant may be issued for weapons, contraband, fruits of crime, instrumentalities of crime, and other evidence of crime (see **items subject to seizure**). The Fourth Amendment to the U.S. Constitution states that "no warrants shall issue, but upon probable cause, supported by oath or affirmation, and particularly describing the place to be searched and the persons or things to be seized." The judicial officer, before issuing the warrant, must determine whether there is probable cause to search based on information supplied in an affidavit by a law enforcement officer or other person.

seizable items Same as **items subject to seizure**.

seizure 1. Under the Fourth Amendment prohibition against unreasonable searches and seizures, a seizure of the *person* can be defined as follows: "[A] person has been 'seized' within the meaning of the Fourth Amendment only if, in view of all of the circumstances surrounding the incident, a reasonable person would have believed that he was not free to leave, ranging from a minimally intrusive **stop and frisk** to formal custodial arrests. 2. Under the Fourth Amendment's prohibition against unreasonable searches and seizures, a seizure of *property* "occurs when there is some meaningful interference with an individual's possessory interests in that property." *United States v. Jacobsen*, 466 U.S. 109, 113 (1984). Usually, a seizure involves the taking into custody by a law enforcement officer of an item of property believed to relate to criminal activity.

selective incorporation An approach to the interpretation of the Fourteenth Amendment's Due Process Clause positing that fundamental rights—those implicit in the concept ordered liberty—apply to the states as well as to the federal government. Under this approach, many, but not all, of the provisions of the **Bill of Rights** have been selectively incorporated by the Fourteenth Amendment. See **fundamental rights**.

selective prosecution A violation of the Constitution's guarantee of equal protection of the law in which similarly situated offenders are not prosecuted, but the defendant was prosecuted due to some unjustifiable standard such as race, religion, or other arbitrary classification.

sentence/sentencing The criminal penalties imposed by a court upon a person duly convicted of a crime within the relevant sentencing scheme. In *indeterminate sentencing* schemes, legislatures prescribed a range of permissible sentences, usually setting a minimum sentence, but leaving the maximum up to the discretion of the judge. In *determinate sentencing* schemes, legislatures

fix or predetermine the sentence for a given offense. *Minimum mandatory sentences* are a type of determinate sentence in which judges have no discretion whatsoever to vary from the statutorily defined punishment. In contrast, many determinate sentences allow a judge to make minor adjustments only if the specific facts of a case fall into some statutorily recognized reason for enhancing the sentence (called an *upward departure*) or diminishing the sentence (called a *downward departure*). A criminal sentence is usually imposed at a **sentencing hearing**.

sensory overload Incomplete sensory acquisition by a person overwhelmed with too much information in too short a period of time as a function of differential processing of stimuli.

sentencing hearing A **critical stage of a criminal prosecution** in which a judge reviews: *a presentence investigation report*; mitigating arguments made by the defendant, defense counsel, and, under some circumstances, defense witnesses; arguments made by the prosecution; and, in some jurisdictions, a **victim impact statement** made or submitted by the victim or the victim's family. After weighing all of this information, the judge imposes a formal criminal **sentence**.

severance The process of *severance* involves removing or redacting false portions of an affidavit in application for a warrant that were made either knowingly or with reckless disregard for the truth. See ***Franks* hearing**.

severability See **redaction**.

show of authority The combination of an officer's words and actions that would convey to a reasonable person that his or her freedom of movement is being restricted such that the person is not free to leave. If the person submits to the officer's authority, an arrest has been made. If the suspect does not submit to the officer's show of authority and attempts to flee, then no arrest occurs.

showup A **confrontation** (definition 2) involving the presentation of a single suspect to a victim or witness of a crime for the purpose of identifying the perpetrator of the crime.

sneak-and-peek warrants See **covert entry warrants**.

sneak-and-steal search See **covert entry warrants**.

special needs doctrine An exception to the warrant and probable cause requirements of the Fourth Amendment where special needs of the government "beyond the normal need for law enforcement, make the warrant and probable-cause requirement impracticable."

staleness Information on which probable cause was initially based is no longer valid because too much time has passed since the search warrant was issued (e.g., there may no longer be good reason to believe that property is still at the same location), thus rendering the warrant void. Staleness is an important factor in determining the validity of probable cause to search.

standard of review The strictness (or level of deference) with which an appellate court will review the actions of a lower court. See **rational basis test; intermediate scrutiny; strict scrutiny; clearly erroneous;** and **abuse of discretion**.

standing The legal right of a person to judicially challenge the conduct of another person or the government for an invasion of a **reasonable expectation of privacy**. In general, standing depends on whether the person seeking relief has a legally sufficient personal interest at stake to obtain judicial resolution of merits of the dispute.

statutory law Those laws duly enacted by a legislative body empowered to make such laws under the provisions of a constitution.

stop and frisk A shorthand term for the law enforcement practice involving the temporary investigative detention of a person and the pat-down search of the person's outer clothing for weapons.

strict scrutiny The most stringent standard of review, *strict scrutiny* examines whether a challenged law is narrowly tailored to achieve a compelling governmental interest. Strict scrutiny is used to adjudicate Equal Protection Clause issues that involve **suspect classifications**, and to adjudicate both Equal Protection Clause and Due Process Clause issues that infringe upon **fundamental rights**. See **standard of review**.

strikes for cause See **challenge for cause**.

subpoena A written order issued by a judicial officer requiring a specified person to appear in a designated court at a specified time in order to testify in a case under the jurisdiction of that court, or to bring a document, piece of evidence or other thing for use or inspection by the court. A subpoena to serve as a witness is called a subpoena *ad testificandum*. A subpoena to bring a document, piece of evidence, or other thing into court is called a subpoena *duces tecum*.

summons A written order issued by a judicial officer requiring a person accused of a criminal offense to appear in a designated court at a specified time to answer the charge or charges.

suspect classifications Laws that implicate the constitutional guarantee of equal protection of the laws by differentiating or drawing distinctions between classes of people based on race, religion, and national origin.

symbolic speech Conduct that expresses an idea or opinion, such as wearing buttons or clothing with political slogans, displaying a sign or a flag, or burning a flag, which is therefore protected by the First Amendment's guarantee of freedom of speech.

testimonial communication To be testimonial, a "communication must itself, explicitly or implicitly, relate a factual assertion or disclose information" that is "the expression of the contents of an individual's mind." *Doe v. United States*, 487 U.S. 201, 210 n.9 (1988). The Fifth Amendment protects a person against being incriminated by his or her own compelled testimonial communications. This protection is applicable to the states through the Fourteenth Amendment. The privilege against self-incrimination is not violated by compelling a person to appear in a lineup, to produce voice exemplars, to furnish handwriting samples, to be fingerprinted, to shave a beard or mustache, or to take a blood-alcohol or breathalyzer test.

time, place, and manner restrictions Restrictions by a governmental entity on free speech and expression that is protected by the First Amendment in content-neutral ways for the good of society. To be valid, a time, place, or manner regulation must further an important or substantial governmental interest; be unrelated to the suppression of free expression; be narrowly tailored to serve the government's interest such that the restriction on free speech is not greater than is necessary to achieve the governmental interest; and still leaves open ample, alternative means for people to communicate their message.

Title III of the Omnibus Crime Control and Safe Streets Act of 1968 A federal law governing *electronic surveillance* that applies to private searches and seizures of **wire communications, oral communications**, or **electronic communications**, as well as those involving governmental actors. The privacy protections under Title III are much greater than those provided under the Fourth Amendment. Title III has its own statutory exclusionary rule that applies only to wire or oral communications; it does not apply to illegally intercepted electronic communications, the remedies for which include criminal penalties and civil suits.

trap-and-trace device A device that records incoming addressing information to a phone line, such as caller ID information. Because such a device does not intercept a "communication" per se, **Title III of the Omnibus Crime Control and Safe Streets Act of 1968** does not apply to the use of these devices.

treason Actions that attempt or conspire to overthrow a government, or to help a foreign government overthrow, make war against, or seriously injure one's nation. Treason is the only crime to be defined in the U.S. Constitution (in Article III, Section 3).

trial *de novo* A new trial or retrial in which the whole case is gone into again as if no trial had been held before. In a trial *de novo*, matters of fact as well as law may be considered, witnesses may be heard, and new evidence may be presented, regardless of what happened at the first trial.

triggering condition A condition precedent (other than the passage of time) that will establish probable cause to conduct a search and/or seizure at some time in the future. See **anticipatory search warrant**.

unconscious transference A phenomenon in which different memory images may become combined or confused with one another.

venire The group of persons summoned to appear in court as potential jurors for a particular trial, or the persons selected from the group of potential jurors to sit in the jury box; from that second group those acceptable to the prosecution and the defense are finally chosen as the jury. Sometimes referred to as the *jury panel*.

venue The geographical area from which the jury is drawn and in which a court with jurisdiction may hear and determine a case—usually, the county or district in which the crime is alleged to have been committed.

verdict The decision made by a jury in a jury trial, or by a judicial officer in a non-jury trial, that a defendant is either guilty or not guilty of the offense for which he or she has been tried. In entering a judgment, a judicial officer has the power to reject a jury verdict of guilty, but must accept a jury verdict of not guilty. Thus, a jury verdict of not guilty results in a judgment of acquittal; but a verdict of guilty does not necessarily result in a judgment of conviction.

vindictive prosecution A due process violation that occurs when a prosecutor increases the number or severity of charges to penalize a defendant who exercises his or her constitutional or statutory rights.

voir dire French, meaning "to speak the truth." 1. An examination conducted by the court or by the attorneys of a prospective juror or witness to determine if he or she is competent or qualified for service. 2. During a trial, a hearing conducted by the court out of the presence of the jury on some issue upon which the court must make an initial determination as a matter of law.

waiver The voluntary and intentional relinquishment or abandonment of a known right or privilege.

warrant A written order or writ issued by a judicial officer or other authorized person commanding a law enforcement officer to perform some act incident to the administration of justice.

weapons effect A psychological phenomenon that occurs in crime situations in which a weapon is used, and witnesses spend more time and psychic energy focusing on the weapon rather than on other aspects of the event. The weapons effect results in incomplete or inaccurate information about the crime scene and the perpetrator. See *Yerkes–Dodson* law.

wire communication Any **aural transfer** made in whole or in part through the use of facilities for the interstate transmission of communications by the aid of wire or cable connections.

witness 1. A person who directly sees or perceives an event or thing or who has expert knowledge relevant to a case. 2. A person who testifies to what he or she has seen or perceived or what he or she knows. 3. A person who signs his or her name to a document to attest to its authenticity. Such a person is sometimes called an *attesting witness*.

writ of assistance A form of general warrant issued by the British Colonial courts against the American colonists in the mid-eighteenth century to enforce the Trade Acts. Writs of assistance authorized royal customs officers to search houses and ships at will in order to discover and seize smuggled goods or goods on which the required duties had not been paid. The reaction of the colonists against the writs of assistance was strong and was one of the major causes of the American Revolution.

writ of *certiorari* A discretionary writ issued from an appellate court for the purpose of obtaining from a lower court the record of its proceedings in a particular case. In the U.S. Supreme Court, and in some states, this writ is the mechanism for discretionary review. A request for review is made by petitioning for a writ of *certiorari*, and granting of review is indicated by issuance of the writ.

***Yerkes-Dodson* law** The optimal functioning of perception and memory as a function of an optimally moderate amount of stress. When stress levels are too low, people do not pay sufficient attention; and when stress levels are too high, the abilities to concentrate and perceive are negatively affected. See **weapons effect**.

Select Bibliography

Chapter 1. Individual Rights Under the United States Constitution

Baker, Sir John, *Human Rights and the Rule of Law in Renaissance England,* 2 NW. U. J. Int'l Hum. Rts. 3 (2004).

Berman, Harold J., *The Western Legal Tradition in a Millennial Perspective: Past and Future,* 60 La. L. Rev. 739 (2000).

Bradley, Craig, The Failure of the Criminal Procedure Revolution (1993).

Broussard, Sylvia, et al., *Undergraduate Students' Perceptions of Child Sexual Abuse: The Impact of Victim Sex, Perpetrator Sex, Respondent Sex, and Victim Response,* 6 J. Fam. Violence 267, 269-72 (1991).

Carr John A., *Free Speech in the Military Community: Striking a Balance Between Personal Rights and Military Necessity,* 45 A.F. L. Rev. 303 (1998).

Dollar, Katherine, et al., *Influence of Gender Roles on Perceptions of Teacher/Adolescent Student Sexual Relations,* 50 Sex Roles 91, 387 (2004).

Feld, Barry C., *Race, Politics, and Juvenile Justice: The Warren Court and the Conservative "Backlash,"* 87 Minn. L. Rev. 1447 (2003).

Friendly, Henry, *The Fifth Amendment Tomorrow: The Case for Constitutional Change,* 37 U. Cin. L. Rev. 671 (1968).

Gaubatz, Derek L., *RLUIPA at Four: Evaluating the Success and Constitutionality of RLUIPA'S Prisoner Provisions,* 28 Harv. J.L. & Pub. Pol'y 501 (2005).

Greene, David, *The Need for Expert Testimony to Prove Lack of Serious Artistic Value in Obscenity Cases,* 2005 Nexus 171.

Grossman, Steven, *Proportionality in Non-Capital Sentencing: The Supreme Court's Tortured Approach to Cruel and Unusual Punishment,* 84 Ky. L.J. 107, 167 (1995).

Johnson, Morgan F., *Heaven Help Us: The Religious Land Use and Institutionalized Persons Act's Prisoners Provisions in the Aftermath of the Supreme Court's Decision in* Cutter v. Wilkinson, 14 Am. U.J. Gender Soc. Pol'y & L. 585 (2006).

Kamisar, Yale, *Equal Justice in the Gatehouses and Mansions of American Criminal Procedure, in* A. E. Dick Howard, ed., *Criminal Justice in Our Time* 1, 14-19 (1965).

Lain, Corinna Barrett, *Countermajoritarian Hero or Zero? Rethinking the Warren Court's Role in the Criminal Procedure Revolution,* 152 U. Pa. L. Rev. 1361 (2004).

Levine, Kay L., *Women as Perpetrators of Crime: No Penis, No Problem,* 33 Fordham Urb. L.J. 357 (2006).

Monkkonen, Eric, *Police in Urban America, 1860-1920* (1981).

Neely, Richard, *The Warren Court and the Welcome Stranger Rule, in* Bernard Schwartz ed., *The Warren Court: A Retrospective* 185-86 (1996).

Palmer, John W. and Stephen E. Palmer, *Constitutional Rights of Prisoners* (Anderson Pub. Co., 6th ed 1999).

Quas, Jodi A., et al., *Effects of Victim, Defendant, and Juror Gender on Decisions in Child Sexual Assault Cases,* 32 J. Applied Soc. Psychol. 1993, 2011 (2002).

Riebli, Frank, *The Spectre of Star Chamber: the Role of an Ancient English Tribunal in the Supreme Court's Self-incrimination Jurisprudence,* 29 Hastings Const. L.Q. 807 (2002).

Shepherd, JoAnne Nelson, *Free Speech and the End of Dress Codes and Mandatory Uniforms in Mississippi Public Schools,* 24 Miss. C. L. Rev. 27 (2004).

Walker, Samuel, *Popular Justice* (Oxford University Press, 1980).

Chapter 2. Criminal Courts, Pretrial Processes, and Trials

Adler, Stephen J., *The Jury: Trial and Error in the American Courtroom* 243 (1994).

Allen, Francis A., *The Decline of the Rehabilitative Ideal* (Yale Univ. Press, 1981).

Barber, Jeremy W., *The Jury Is Still Out: The Role of Jury*

Science in the Modern American Courtroom, 31 Am. Crim. L. Rev. 1225 (1994).

Blackstone, William, *Commentaries* 24 (9th ed 1783).

Campbell, Curtis, Candace McCoy, and Chimezie Osigweh, *The Influence of Probation Recommendations on Sentencing Decisions and Their Predictive Accuracy,* 54 Fed. Probation 13-21 (1990).

Clear, Todd R., *Harm in American Penology: Offenders, Victims, and Their Communities* (SUNY Press, 1994).

Corinis, Jennifer W., Note: *A Reasoned Standard for Competency to Waive Counsel after* Godinez v. Moran, 80 B.U.L. Rev. 265, 280 (2000).

DeCicco, Fred Anthony, *Waiver of Jury Trials in Federal Criminal Cases: A Reassessment of The "Prosecutorial Veto,"* 51 Fordham L. Rev. 1091 (1983).

Felthous, Alan R., *The Right to Represent Oneself Incompetently: Competency to Waive Counsel and Conduct One's Own Defense Before and After* Godinez, 18 Mental & Physical Disability L. Rep. 105, 110 (1994).

Fuchs, Andrew J., *The Effect of* Apprendi v. New Jersey *on the Federal Sentencing Guidelines: Blurring the Distinction Between Sentencing Factors and Elements of a Crime,* 69 Fordham L. Rev. 1399, 1413 (2001).

Hale, Matthew, 1 *The History of the Pleas of the Crown* 34-35 (1736).

Johnstone, A. C., *Peremptory Pragmatism: Religion and the Administration of the* Batson *Rule,* 1998 U. Chi. Legal F. 441 (1998).

Jordan, Sandra D., *Have We Come Full Circle? Judicial Sentencing Discretion Revived in* Booker *and* Fanfan, 33 Pepp. L. Rev. 615 (2006).

Krug, Peter, *Prosecutorial Discretion and Its Limits,* 50 Am. J. Comp. L. 643 (2002).

Menninger, Karl, *The Crime of Punishment* (Penguin, 1968).

Meyers, Alaya B., *Supreme Court Review: Rejecting the Clear and Convincing Evidence Standard for Proof of Incompetence,* 87 J. Crim. L. & Criminology 1016 (1997).

Morris, Grant H., *Placed in Purgatory: Conditional Release of Insanity Acquittees,* 39 Ariz. L. Rev. 1061, 1063 (1997).

Mustard, David B., *Racial, Ethnic, and Gender Disparities in Sentencing: Evidence from the U.S. Federal Courts,* 44 J. Law & Econ. 285 (2001).

Norwood, Kimberly Jade, *Shopping for a Venue: The Need for More Limits on Choice,* 50 U. Miami L. Rev. 267, 270-74 (1995).

Olivares, Kathleen M., Velmer S. Burton, Jr., and Francis T. Cullen, *The Collateral Consequences of a Felony Conviction: A National Study of Legal Codes 10 Years Later,* 60 Fed. Probation 10, 13 (Sept. 1996).

Perlin, Michael L., *"The Borderline Which Separated You From Me": The Insanity Defense, the Authoritarian Spirit, the Fear of Faking, and the Culture of Punishment,* 82 Iowa L. Rev. 1375, 1380 (1997).

Reiman, Jeffrey, *The Rich Get Richer and the Poor Get Prison: Ideology, Class, and Justice* (Allyn & Bacon, 1995).

Rush, Christina and Jeremy Robertson, *Presentence Reports: The Utility of Information to the Sentencing Decision,* 11 L. Hum. Behav. 147-155 (1987).

Saunders, Kurt M., *Race and Representation in Jury Service Selection,* 36 Duq. L. Rev. 49, 64 (1997).

Shapiro, David L., *Ethical Dilemmas for the Mental Health Professional: Issues Raised by Recent Supreme Court Decisions,* 34 Cal. W. L. Rev. 177, 182 (1997).

Sommer, Robert, *The End of Imprisonment* (Oxford University Press, 1976).

Wang, Lu-in, *The Complexities of Hate,* 60 Ohio St. L.J. 799 (1999).

Winick, Bruce J., *Criminal Law: Reforming Incompetency to Stand Trial and Plead Guilty: A Restated Proposal and a Response to Professor Bonnie,* 85 J. Crim. L. & Criminology 571, 574 (1995).

Chapter 3. Basic Underlying Concepts: The Exclusionary Rule, Privacy, Probable Cause, and Reasonableness

Federal Torts Claim Act: 28 U.S.C.A. § 1346(b); 28 USCA § 2680(h).

Lynch, Timothy, *Reassessing the Exclusionary Rule,* 22-DEC Champion 12, 64 (1998).

Chapter 4. Criminal Investigatory Search Warrants

Adler, Andrew, *The Notice Problem, Unlawful Electronic Surveillance, and Civil Liability under the Foreign Intelligence Surveillance Act,* 61 U. Miami L. Rev. 393 (2007).

Duncan, Jr., Robert M., *Surreptitious Search Warrants and the USA PATRIOT Act: "Thinking Outside the Box but within the Constitution," or a Violation of Fourth Amendment Protections?* 7 N.Y. City L. Rev. 1 (2004).

Gilmore, Kelly A., *Preserving the Border Search Doctrine in a Digital World: Reproducing Electronic Evidence at the Border,* 72 Brook. L. Rev. 759 (2007).

Jekot, Wayne, *Computer Forensics, Search Strategies, and the Particularity Requirement,* 12 U. Pittsburgh J. Tech. L. & Pol'y 2 (2007).

Lichtblau, Eric and David Johnston, *Court to Oversee U.S. Wiretapping in Terror Cases,* N.Y. Times, Jan. 18, 2007, at A1.

Martin, Katherine Lee, *"Sacrificing the End to the Means": The Constitutionality of Suspicionless Subway Searches,* 15 Wm. & Mary Bill Rts. J. 1285 (2007).

Owen, Stephen S. and Tod W. Burke, *DNA Databases and Familial Searching,* 43(4) Criminal Law Bulletin 617 (2007).

Risen, James and Eric Lichtblau, *Bush Lets U.S. Spy on Callers Without Courts,* N.Y. Times, Dec. 16, 2005, at A1.

U.S. Dept. of Justice, *Searching and Seizing Computers and Obtaining Electronic Evidence in Criminal Investigations* pt. II.A (2002), *available at* http://www.cybercrime.gov/s&smanual2002.htm (last visited Nov. 27, 2007).

Chapter 5. Administrative Searches, Special Needs Searches, and Electronic Surveillance

Cronin, James M. and Joshua A. Ederheimer, *Conducted Energy Devices: Development of Standards for Consistency and Guidance* (U.S. Dep't. of Justice, 2006), *available at* http://www.policeforum.org/upload/CED-Guidelines_414547688_2152007092436.pdf (last visited Nov. 27, 2007).

Chapter 7. Stops and Frisks

108th Congress, 2d Session, S. 2131, "To prohibit racial profiling" (2004).

108th Congress, 2d Session, H.R. 3847, "To prohibit racial profiling" (2004).

Cole, David, *In Aid of Removal: Due Process Limits on Immigration Detention,* 51 Emory L.J. 1003, 1026 (2002).

Detention, Treatment, and Trial of Certain Non-Citizens in the War Against Terrorism, 3 C.F.R. § 918 (2002).

Executive Summary on 2006 Missouri Vehicle Stops, *available at* http://www.ago.mo.gov/racialprofiling/2006/racialprofiling2006.htm (last visited June 17, 2007).

Falk, 2007: 33-34.

Greenberg, Karen J. and Joshua L. Dratel, eds., *The Torture Papers: The Road to Abu Ghraib* (2005).

Hafetz, 2006.

Harris, 1997.

Harris, David A., *The Stories, the Statistics, and the Law: Why 'Driving While Black' Matters.* 84 Minn. L. Rev. 265 (1999).

Interim Report of State Police Review Team, 1994: 4.

Kowalski, Brian R. and Richard J. Lundman, *Vehicle Stops by Police for Driving While Black: Common Problems and Some Tentative Solutions,* 35 J. Crim. Just. 165 (2007).

Maryland State Conference of NAACP Branches v. Md.Dept. State Police, 72 F. Supp. 2d 560 (D. Md. 1999).

Parry, 2006: 772.

Parry, John T., *Terrorism and the New Criminal Process,* 15 Wm. & Mary Bill Rts. J. 765 (2007).

Schindler, Dietrich, and Jiri

Toman eds., *The Laws of Armed Conflicts* (4th ed 2004).

U.S. Dept. of Justice (2003). Civil Rights Div., Guidance

Regarding the Use of Race by Federal Law Enforcement Agencies (June 2003), *available at* http://www.usdoj.gov/crt/split/documents/guidance_on_race.htm (last visited Nov. 27, 2007).

U.S. Dept. of Justice (2005). Contacts between Police and the Public: 2005, Office of Justice Programs Special Report, *available at* http://www.ojp.usdoj.gov/bjs/pub/press/cpp05pr.htm (last visited Nov. 27, 2007).

U.S. Dept. of Justice, Contacts Between Police and the Public: 2005, Office of Justice Programs Special Report, at 5.

U.S. Dept. of Justice, Civil Rights Div., Guidance Regarding the Use of Race by Federal Law Enforcement Agencies, at 1 (2003).

Wolfowitz, Paul, Deputy Secretary for the Navy, to the Secretary of the Navy, Order Establishing Combatant Status Review Tribunal (July 7, 2004), *available at* http:// www.defenselink.mil/news/Jul2004/d20040707review.pdf.

Yin, Tung, *Procedural Due Process to Determine Enemy Combatant Status in the War Against Terror,* 73 Tenn. L. Rev. 351, 357 (2006).

Chapter 11. Search and Seizure of Vehicles and Containers

Whitebread and Slobogin, *Criminal Procedure: An Analysis of Cases and Concepts 199* (Foundation Press, 4th ed 2000).

Chapter 13. Interrogations, Admissions, and Confessions

Agar, James R. II, *The Admissibility of False Confession Expert Testimony,* 1999 Army Law. 26, 26 (1999).

Beyer, Marty, *Immaturity, Culpability and Competency in Juveniles: A Study of 17 Cases,* 15 Crim. Just. 26, 28 (2000).

Blackstone, William, *Commentaries on the Laws of England* *357 (1765).

Cassell, Paul G. and Bret S. Hayman, *Police Interrogation in the 1990s: An Empirical Study of the Effects of* Miranda, 43 UCLA L. Rev. 839 (1996).

Clymer, Steven D., *Are Police Free to Disregard* Miranda? 112 Yale L.J. 447 (2002).

Feld, Barry C., *Juveniles' Competence to Exercise Miranda Rights: An Empirical Study of Policy and Practice,* 91 Minn. L. Rev. 26 (2006).

Fulero, S. and C. Everington, *Assessing Competency to Waive Miranda Rights in Defendants with Mental Retardation,* 19 Law & Hum. Behav. 533-43 (1995).

Georgetown Annual Review of Criminal Procedure, *Custodial Interrogations,* 35 Geo. L.J. Ann. Rev. Crim. Proc. 162 (2006).

Godsey, Mark A. *Rethinking the Involuntary Confession*

Rule: Toward a Workable Test for Identifying Compelled Self-incrimination, 93 Cal. L. Rev. 465 (2005).

Gohara, Miriam S., *A Lie for a Lie: False Confessions and the Case for Reconsidering the Legality of Deceptive Interrogation Techniques,* 33 Fordham Urb. L.J. 791 (2006).

Grisso, Thomas, *Juveniles' Waiver of Rights: Legal and Psychological Competence* (1981).

Grisso, Thomas, *The Competence of Adolescents as Trial Defendants,* 3 Psychol. Pub. Pol. & L. 3, 11 (1997).

Hafetz, Jonathan, *Torture, Judicial Review, and the Regulation of Custodial Interrogations,* 62, N.Y.U. Ann. Surv. Am. L. 433 (2007).

Kahn, Rachel, Patricia A. Zapf, and Virginia G. Cooper, *Readability of* Miranda *Warnings and Waivers: Implications for Evaluating* Miranda *Comprehension,* 30 Law & Psychol. Rev. 119 (2006).

Kuller, Althea, Moran v. Burbine: *Supreme Court Tolerates Police Interference with the Attorney-Client Relationship,* 18 Loy. U. Chi. L.J. 251 (1986).

Larson, Kimberly, *Improving the "Kangaroo Courts": A Proposal for Reform in Evaluating Juveniles' Waiver of* Miranda, 48 Vill. L. Rev. 629 (2003).

Leo, Richard A., *The Impact of* Miranda *Revisited,* 86 J. Crim. L. & Criminology 621 (1996).

Marcus, Paul, *It's Not Just about* Miranda: *Determining the Voluntariness of Confessions in Criminal Prosecutions,* 40 Val. U. L. Rev. 601 (2006).

Meares, Tracey L. , and Bernard E. Harcourt, *Transparent Adjudication and Social Science Research in Constitutional Criminal Procedure,* 90 J. Crim. L. & Criminology 733 (2000).

Paulsen, Monrad G., *The Fourteenth Amendment and the Third Degree,* 6 Stan. L. Rev. 411 (1954).

Penney, Steven, *Theories of Confession Admissibility: A Historical View,* 25 Am. J. Crim. L. 309, 335-36 (1998).

Ruebner, Ralph, *Police Interrogation: The Privilege Against Self-incrimination, the Right to Counsel, and the Incomplete Metamorphosis of Justice White,* 48 U. Miami L. Rev. 511 (1994).

Skolnick, Jerome H. and James J. Fyfe, *Above the Law: Police and the Excessive Use of Force* 47-48 (1993).

Swift, Katherine M., *Drawing a Line Between* Terry *and* Miranda: *The Degree and Duration of Restraint,* 73 U. Chi. L. Rev. 1075 (2006).

Thomas III, George C. and Richard A. Leo, *The Effects of* Miranda v. Arizona: *"Embedded" in Our National Culture?* 29 Crime & Just. 203 (2002).

Wickersham Commission, National Commission on Law Observance and Enforcement, Pub. No. 11, Report on Lawlessness in Law Enforcement 158-60 (1931).

Wilson, Alexander J., *Defining Interrogation under the Confrontation Clause after* Crawford v. Washington, 39 Colum. J.L. & Soc. Probs. 257 (2005).

Chapter 14. Pretrial Visual Identification Procedures

Bartol, Curt R. and Anne M. Bartol, *Psychology and Law* 219 (2d ed., 1994).

Behrman, Bruce W. and Lance T. Vayder, *The Biasing Influence of a Police Showup: Does the Observation of a Single Suspect Taint Later Identification?* 79 Perceptual & Motor Skills, 1239 (1994).

Brigham, John C., Adina W. Wasserman, and Christian A. Meissner, *Disputed Eyewitness Identification Evidence: Important Legal and Scientific Issues,* 36 Ct. Rev. 12, 15 (1999).

Buckhout, Robert, *Psychology and Eyewitness Identification,* 2 Law & Psychol. Rev. 75, 76 (1976).

Chemay, Frederick E., *Unreliable Eyewitness Evidence: The Expert Psychologist and the Defense in Criminal Cases,* 45 La. L. Rev. 721, 724 (1985).

Clifford, *Eyewitness Testimony: The Bridging of a Credibility Gap,* in David P. Farrington, Keith Hawkins, Sally M. Lloyd-Bostock, eds., *Psychology, Law and Legal Processes* 167, 176-77 (1979).

Cohen, Peter J., *How Shall They Be Known?* Daubert v. Merrell Dow Pharmaceuticals *and Eyewitness Identification,* 16 Pace L. Rev. 237, 242 (1996).

Collins, Winn S., *Safeguards for Eyewitness Identification,* 77-Mar. Wis. Law. 8, 11 (2004).

Cowan, Nelson,*The Magical Number 4 in Short-Term Memory: A Reconsideration of Mental Storage Capacity,* 24 Behavioral & Brain Sciences 87 (2000).

Deffenbacher, Kenneth A., Brian H. Bornstein, Steven D. Penrod, and E. Kiernan McGorty, *A Meta-Analytic Review of the Effects of High Stress on Eyewitness Memory,* 28 Law & Hum. Behav. 687 (2004).

Doyle, James M., *Discounting the Error Costs: Cross-Racial False Alarms in the Culture of Contemporary Criminal Justice,* 7 Psychol., Pub. Pol'y & L. 253 (2001).

Ehlers, Scott, *Eyewitness Identification: State Law Reform,* 29 Apr. Champion 34 (2005).

Farmer, Jr., John J., New Jersey Attorney General, Letter to County Prosecutors et al. 1-2 (Apr. 18, 2001), *available at* http://www.state.nj.us/lps/dcj/agguide/photoid.pdf (last visited Nov. 27, 2007).

Forgas, Joseph P., Simon M. Laham, and Patrick T. Vargas, *Mood Effects on Eyewitness Memory: Affective Influ-ences on Susceptibility to Misinformation,* 41 J. Experimental Social Psychol. 574 (2005).

Friedland, Steven I., *On Common Sense and the Evaluation of Witness Credibility,* 40 Case W. Res. L. Rev. 165, 181 (1990).

Geiselman, R. Edward, David Haghighi, and Ronna Stown, *Unconscious Transference and Characteristics of Accurate and Inaccurate Eyewitnesses,* 2 Psychol., Crime & L. 197 (1996).

Giuliana, A. L., L. Mazzoni, Manila Vannucci, and Elizabeth F. Loftus, *Misremembering Story Material,* 4 Legal & Criminological Psychol. 93 (1999).

Golby, Alexandra J., John D. E. Gabrieli, Joan Y. Chiao, and Jennifer L. Eberhardt, *Differential Responses in the Fusiform Region to Same-Race and Other-Race Faces,* 4 Nature-Neuroscience 845 (2001).

Gross, William David, *The Unfortunate Faith: A Solution to the Unwarranted Reliance Upon Eyewitness Testimony,* 5 Tex. Wesleyan L. Rev. 307, 313 (1999).

Haber, Ralph N. and Lyn Haber, *Experiencing, Remembering and Reporting Events: The Cognitive Psychology of Eyewitness Testimony,* 6 Psychol, Pub. Pol'y & L. 1057 (2000).

Herrmann, Douglas J., Mary Crawford, and Michelle Holdsworth, *Gender-Linked Differences in Everyday Memory Performance,* 83 British J. Psychol. 221 (1992).

Hoffman, Jascha, *Suspect Memories,* Legal Affairs (Feb. 2005), at 42.

Huff, C. Ronald, Arye Rattner, and Edward Sagarin, *Convicted but Innocent: Wrongful Conviction and Public Policy* (Sage Publications 2003).

Judges, Donald P., *Two Cheers for the Department of Justice's Eyewitness Evidence: A Guide for Law Enforcement,* 53 Ark. L. Rev. 231, 254 (2000).

Kleider, Heather M., and Stephen D. Goldinger, *Stereotyping Ricochet: Complex Effects of Racial Distinctiveness on Identification Accuracy,* 25 Law & Hum. Behav. 605 (2001).

Klobuchar, Amy, Nancy K. Mehrkens Steblay, and Hilary Lindell Caligiuri, *Improving Eyewitness Identifications: Hennepin County's Blind Sequential Lineup Pilot Project,* 4 Cardozo Pub. L. Pol'y & Ethics J. 381 (2006).

Leippe, Michael R., Gary L. Wells, & Thomas M. Ostrom, *Crime Seriousness as a Determinant of Accuracy in Eyewitness Identification,* 63 J. Applied Psychol. 345-51 (1978).

Levi, Avaraham M., *Are Defendants Guilty If They Were Chosen in a Lineup?* 22 Law & Hum. Behav. 389 (1998).

Levi, Avraham M., and C. L. Lindsay, *Lineup and Photo Spread Procedures: Issues Concerning Policy Recommendations,* 7 Psych. Pub. Pol. & L. 776, 787 (2001).

Lindholm, Torun and Sven Ake Christianson, *Gender Effects in Eyewitness Accounts of a Violent Crime,* 4 Psychol., Crime & L. 323 (1998).

Loftus, Elizabeth F., *Ten Years in the Life of an Expert Witness,* 10 Law & Hum. Behav. 241, 254-55 (1986).

Loftus, Elizabeth F., Mahzarin R. Banaji, Jonathan W. Schooler, and Rachael A. Foster, *Who Remembers What? Gender Differences in Memory,* 26 Mich. Qtrly. Rev. 64 (1987).

MacLin, Otto H., M. Kimberly MacLin, and Roy S. Malpass, *Race, Arousal, Attention, Exposure and Delay: An Examination of Factors Moderating Face Recognition,* 7 Psychol., Pub. Pol'y & L. 134 (2001).

Medwed, Daniel S., *Anatomy of a Wrongful Conviction: Theoretical Implications and Practical Solutions,* 51 Vill. L. Rev. 337 (2006).

Memon, Amina and Fiona Gabbert, *Improving the Identification Accuracy of Senior Witnesses: Do Prelineup Questions and Sequential Testing Help?* 88 J. Applied Psychol. 341 (2003).

Memon, Amina, Lorraine Hope, and Ray Bull, *Exposure Duration: Effects on Eyewitness Accuracy and Confidence,* 94 British J. Psychol. 339 (2003).

Morgan, Charles A., et al., *Accuracy of Eyewitness Memory for Persons Encountered During Exposure to Highly Intense Stress,* 27 Int'l J. Psychiatry & L. 265 (2004).

National District Attorneys Association, *Task Force Recommendations on Eyewitness Identification,* 39 Apr. Prosecutor 16 (2005).

O'Toole, Timothy P. and Giovanna Shay, Manson v. Brathwaite *Revisited: Towards a New Rule of Decision for Due Process Challenges to Eyewitness Identification Procedures,* 41 Val. U. L. Rev. 109 (2006).

Patterson, Helen M. and Richard I. Kemp, *Co-witnesses Talk: A Survey of Eyewitness Discussion,* 12 Psychol., Crime & L. 181 (2006).

Penrod, Steven D. and Brian L. Cutler, *Witness Confidence and Witness Accuracy: Assessing Their Forensic Relation,* 1 Psychol. Pub. Pol'y & L. 817 (1995).

Perfect, Timothy J. and Lucy J. Harris, *Adult Age Differences in Unconscious Transference: Source Confusion or Identity Blending?* 31 Memory & Cognition 570 (2003).

Pickel, Kerri L., *The Influence of Context on the "Weapon Focus" Effect,* 23 Law & Hum. Behav. 299 (1999).

Plato, *Portrait of Socrates, Being the Apology, Crito, and Phaedo of Plato* 99, R. W. Livingstone, ed. (Oxford Univ. Press, 1938).

Pozzulo, Joanna D. and R. C. L. Lindsay, *Identification Accuracy of Children Versus Adults: A Meta-Analysis,* 22 Law & Hum. Behav. 549 (1998).

Rattner, Arye, *Convicted But Innocent: Wrongful Conviction and the Criminal Justice System,* 12 Law & Hum. Behav. 283, 287-91 (1988).

Ringel, William E., *Searches and Seizures, Arrests and Confessions* § 18:4 (2007).

Risinger, D. Michael, Michael J. Saks, William C. Thompson, and Robert Rosenthal, *The Daubert/Kumho Implications of Observer Effects in Forensic Science: Hidden Problems of Expectation and Suggestion,* 90 Calif. L. Rev. 1, 7 (2002).

Roberts, Andrew, *The Problem of Mistaken Identification: Some Observations on Process,* 8 Int'l J. Evid. & Proof 100 (2004).

Rosenberg, Benjamin E., *Rethinking the Right to Due Process in Connection with Pretrial Identification Procedures: An Analysis and a Proposal,* 79 Ky. L.J. 259, 292 (1991).

Sarno, Julie A. and Thomas R. Alley, *Attractiveness and the Memorability of Faces: Only a Matter of Distinctiveness?* 110 Am. J. Psychol. 81 (1997).

Scheck, Barry, Peter Neufeld, and Jim Dwyer, *Actual Innocence: Five Days to Execution, and Other Dispatches From the Wrongly Convicted* (2000).

Sikstrom, Sverker, *Forgetting Curves: Implications for Connectionist Models,* 45 Cognitive Psychol. 95 (2002).

Smith, Steven M., R. C. L. Lindsay, and Sean Pryke, *Postdictors of Eyewitness Errors: Can False Identifications Be Diagnosed?* 85 J. Applied Psychol. 542 (2000).

Sporer, Siegfried L., et al., *Psychological Issues in Eyewitness Identification,* 3 (1966).

Sporer, Siegfried Ludwig, *Recognizing Faces of Other Ethnic Groups: An Integration of Theories,* 7 Psychol., Pub. Pol'y & L. 36 (2001).

Steblay, Nancy Mehrkens, *A Meta-Analytic Review of the Weapon Focus Effect,* 16 Law & Hum. Behav. 413 (1992).

Steblay, Nancy Mehrkens, *Social Influence in Eyewitness Recall: A Meta-Analytic Review of Lineup Instruction Effects,* 21 Law & Hum. Behav. 283 (1997).

U.S. Dep't of Justice, Eyewitness Evidence: A Guide for Law Enforcement (Oct. 1999), *available at* http://www.ncjrs.org/pdffiles1/nij/178240.pdf (last visited Nov. 27, 2007).

Vrij, Aldert, *Psychological Factors in Eyewitness Testimony, in* Amina Memon, Aldert Vrij, & Ray Bull, eds., *Psychology and Law: Truthfulness, Accuracy, and Credibility* 105-19 (McGraw-Hill, 1998).

Weber, Nathan and Neil Brewer, *Positive Versus Negative Face Recognition Decisions: Confidence, Accuracy, and Response Latency,* 20 Applied Cognitive Psychol. 17 (2006).

Wells, Gary L. and Eric P. Seelau, *Eyewitness Identification: Psychological Research and Legal Policy on Lineups,* 1 Psychol., Pub. Pol'y & L. 765, 779 (1995).

Wells, Gary L., Mark Small, Steven D. Penrod, Roy S. Malpass, Solomon M. Fulero, and C. A. E. Brimacombe, *Eyewitness Identification Procedures: Recommendations for Lineups and Photospreads,* 22 Law & Hum. Behav. 603, 633 (1998).

Yarmey, A. Daniel, *The Elderly Witness,* in Siegfried Ludwig Sporer, Roy S. Malpass, & Guenter Koehnken, eds., *Psychological Issues in Eyewitness Identification* 259 (Lawrence Erlbaum Associates 1996).

Yarmey, A. Daniel, *Person Identification in Showups and Lineups,* in Charles P. Thompson & Douglas J. Herrmann eds., *Eyewitness Memory: Theoretical and Applied Perspectives* 131-54 (Lawrence Erlbaum 1998).

Case Index

Subject Index

TO THE OWNER OF THIS BOOK:

I hope that you have found *Criminal Procedure for the Criminal Justice Professional,* Tenth Edition, useful. So that this book can be improved in a future edition, would you take the time to complete this sheet and return it? Thank you.

School and address:_____

Department:_____

Instructor's name:_____

1. What I like most about this book is:_____

_____

_____

2. What I like least about this book is:

_____

_____

3. My general reaction to this book is:

_____

_____

4. The name of the course in which I used this book is:

_____

5. Were all of the chapters of the book assigned for you to read?_____

   If not, which ones weren't?_____

6. In the space below, or on a separate sheet of paper, please write specific suggestions for improving this book and anything else you'd care to share about your experience in using this book.

_____

_____

_____

_____

WADSWORTH
CENGAGE Learning

BUSINESS REPLY MAIL
FIRST-CLASS MAIL   PERMIT NO. 34   BELMONT CA

POSTAGE WILL BE PAID BY ADDRESSEE

Attn: Carolyn Henderson Meier, Criminal
Justice Editor

Wadsworth
10 Davis Dr
Belmont CA 94002-9801

OPTIONAL:

Your name:_____ Date: _____

May we quote you, either in promotion for *Criminal Procedure for the Criminal Justice Professional,* Tenth Edition, or in future publishing ventures?

Yes:_____   No: _____

Sincerely yours,

John Ferdico, Hank Fradella, and Chris Totten